D0417350

The
HIDDEN PLACES
of
ENGLAND

Edited by
Barbara Vesey

Published by:
Travel Publishing Ltd
7a Apollo House, Calleva Park
Aldermaston, Berks, RG7 8TN

ISBN 1-902-00743-3

© Travel Publishing Ltd

First Published: *1998*
Second Edition: *2000*

Regional Titles in the Hidden Places Series:

Cambridgeshire & Lincolnshire	Channel Islands
Cheshire	Chilterns
Cornwall	Derbyshire
Devon	Dorset, Hants & Isle of Wight
Essex	Gloucestershire & Wiltshire
Heart of England	Hereford, Worcs & Shropshire
Highlands & Islands	Kent
Lake District & Cumbria	Lancashire
Norfolk	Northeast Yorkshire
Northumberland & Durham	North Wales
Nottinghamshire	Potteries
Somerset	South Wales
Suffolk	Surrey
Sussex	Thames Valley
Warwickshire & W Midlands	Yorkshire Dales

National Titles in the Hidden Places Series:

England	Ireland
Scotland	Wales

Printing by: Ashford Press, Gosport
Maps by: © MAPS IN MINUTES ™ (2000)
Line Drawings: Sarah Bird
Editor: Barbara Vesey
Cover Design: Lines & Words, Aldermaston

Cover Photographs: Fishing Boats, Hastings, Sussex; Canterbury Cathedral, Kent
© Britain on View/Stockwave

Foreword

The Hidden Places series is a collection of easy to use travel guides taking you, in this instance, on a relaxed but informative tour of a country blessed with a wonderful range of inland and coastal landscapes, interesting local culture and an extraordinarily rich history.

The Hidden Places of England explores this diversity in a relaxed narrative style. It guides the reader to some of the established visitor attractions and focuses on the more secluded and less well-known places of interest as well as venues for food, drink and accommodation, many of which are easy to miss unless you know exactly where you are going.

We include hotels, b&b's and other types of accommodation, restaurants, pubs and bars, historic houses, museums, gardens and many other attractions throughout England, all of which are comprehensively indexed. Most places have an attractive line drawing and are cross-referenced to coloured maps found at the rear of the book. We do not award merit marks or rankings but concentrate on describing the more interesting, unusual or unique features of each place with the aim of making the reader's stay in the local area an enjoyable and stimulating experience.

Whether you are travelling around England for business or pleasure we do hope that you enjoy reading and using this book. We are always interested in what readers think of places covered (or not covered) in our guides so please do not hesitate to use the reader comment form provided to give us your considered views. We also welcome any general comments which will help us improve the guides themselves. Finally if you are planning to visit any other corner of the British Isles we would like to refer you to the list of other *Hidden Places* titles to be found at the rear of the book.

Travel Publishing Ltd

Contents

vi

1 Southeast England

INTRODUCTION

Rivers, woodlands and sea play an important role in forming the landscape and character of southeast England. Natural wonders, archaeological monuments and architectural gems seeming to crop up around every bend. The English can take a great sense of pride that Kent is the first county that most cross-Channel visitors encounter when visiting Great Britain. Few counties can combine its sense of regional identity, quintessentially English scenery and maritime history. A defining southeastern landscape can be found along the coast, from the busy seaside resorts to the stretches of the Romney Marsh in Kent, places of eerie beauty, a remote setting of flooded meadows, drainage ditches and wind-bent trees that were once the haunt of smugglers. Many of the countries most popular seacoast strips can be found in these counties. Hastings, together with Romney, Hythe, Dover and Sandwich joined in 1050 the institution known as the 'Cinque Ports'. The task of the Cinque Ports was to defend the Sussex and Kent coastlines from attack. At one point Hastings supplied 20 of the 57 ships which made up the Cinque Ports navy - the only English navy in existence until the 15th century. Great houses, as well as royal and Episcopal palaces, were built here from medieval times, and many villages have evidence of Saxon, Celtic, roman and even late Stone Ages settlements. Surrey's northern extremity contains the site of one of England's defining moments, the signing of the Magna Carta in 1215 at the riverside meadow of Runnymede.

East Sussex Coast is, of course, centred around the most famous date in English history: 1066. The Georgian and Victorian influence is also strong. The Weald remains one of the most consistently wooded areas of England and one that has preserved its traditions as well as its appearance. Lovely Weald villages throughout the region are set amid stretches of oak and beech woodlands that seem unchanged since medieval times or even earlier. Traditional Wealden buildings can be found throughout the region: timber-framed and hung with pantiles. The wooded slopes on the Surrey/Sussex border have led to the nickname "Little Switzerland". Indeed it is in that southern stretch of land, high up overlooking the Weald, that a sense of real remoteness - lost almost everywhere else in the southeast - can be felt.

The Surrey and Sussex Downs repay exploration with panoramic views and peaceful bucolic scenes. The South Downs Way, a nearly 100 mile long bridleway from Winchester and Buriton in the West to Beachy Head in the East, is characterised by expansive views right across the country. This fine chalk downland is peppered with beautiful rural hamlets and villages, with rolling hills, valleys, and spectacular natural beauty.

In the villages of the region, many no more than hamlets, visitors can appreciate just how even the earliest settlers scraped a living, and how later inhabitants developed crafts that exploited the rich natural surroundings. A mainstay of this part of the nation is its rich farming country alongside rolling hills. There is a story to be told - or heard - at every turn in this region, and it is not hard to understand how it has cast its spell on travellers for more than two millennia.

KENT

ROCHESTER

MAP 5 REF R19

10 miles N of London on the A2

Late Victorian terraces and a steady flow of traffic are the first impressions many people have of Rochester. But as so often, first impressions can be incomplete or even misleading, and with some care and scrutiny the discerning visitor can peel layer after layer of history from this Medway port. With associations ranging from Celtic warriors to Charles Dickens, Rochester keeps cropping up in history books and in literary tomes. The reason, of course, is location. Commanding a strategic situation by the mouth of the Medway - and therefore with easy links to the Continent via the Thames - Rochester was first settled more than two millennia ago. The first known inhabitants were Celts of the Belgic tribe. Then it was the turn of the Romans, whose Watling street crossed the Medway at this point. The Romans fortified their camp here, thereby creating a walled city of nearly 23 acres. Some five centuries later the settlement came under Saxon dominion, and at this time it acquired the name which would - with some alteration - become permanent: *Hrofesceaster*. Rochester later became linked with two famous kings. Alfred, determined to thwart Viking sea power, built a fleet of ships in Rochester and in doing so created England's first navy. The strategic importance of Rochester was not lost on a famous subsequent ruler, William the Conqueror who decreed that a castle be maintained there permanently. **Rochester Castle**, built by William's chief architect, Bishop Gundulph, stands as a testament to centuries of defence. Henry I ordered the massive keep to be raised and this huge edifice still stands as a symbol of Rochester. Towering 120 feet high and with walls up to 12 feet thick, it comprises four floors with many openings looking out. It was here, in 1215, that rebel barons were besieged by King John for seven weeks. The barons withstood a fusillade of stones thrown by huge siege engines but it was only after a tunnel was built beneath the keep, and its props burnt to cause a collapse, that the castle surrendered. Rochester Castle was severely damaged during the Civil War and much of today's structure is the result of extensive restoration in the last century.

Near the castle stands **Rochester Cathedral**, which was also built by Bishop Gundulph. It occupies the site of a Saxon church, which is significant because the Bishopric of Rochester is the second oldest in England, having been established in the 7th century. Like the castle it was badly damaged by Parliamentary troops during the Civil War and underwent a restorative treatment in the 19th century. Nevertheless there is still a great deal of original Norman, gothic and 15th century work still in evidence. Particularly noteworthy are the Norman west doorway, the 13th century transepts and the 13th century crypt which has heavy ribbed vaulting. The remains of former monastic buildings surround the Cathedral, and there are three ancient gates: **Priors Gate**, **Deanery Gate** and **Chertsey's Gate**, which leads on to the High Street. It is more popularly known as Jaspers Gate, the name under which it appeared in Dickens's last (unfinished) novel, *The Mystery of Edward Drood*.

Rochester Cathedral

Rochester makes the most of its Dickens connection, and it provides the setting for scenes in *Great Expectations*, *Pickwick Papers* and *The Uncommercial Traveller*. Each year there is a Dickens Festival, during which an assortment of Dickens characters wander the streets in Victorian costume. Eastgate House is the home of a popular and informative **Dickens Centre**, and in its garden is the chalet in which the great writer wrote in his last years. Many of the sights mentioned in his novels are linked along the **Charles Dickens Trail**. Following this walking tour is also a good way to appreciate some of the 17th and 18th century architecture along Rochester's High Street, and to spend some time in the docks which also feature in some works by Dickens.

COOLING
6 miles N of Rochester off the A228

Map 5 Ref S19

Cooling is an isolated village in the heart of the Hoo Peninsula, which juts out into the Thames Estuary north of Rochester. North of Cooling, but accessible only by footpath, lie the **Halstow Marshes**, which attract bird-watchers especially in the winter. The marshes and water meadows are nesting sites and feeding grounds for many water birds, including several species of duck and white-fronted geese. **Northward Hill Bird Reserve** is Britain's largest heronry, although access is very restricted and by permit only.

CHATHAM
1 mile E of Rochester on the A2

Map 5 Ref S19

Although a settlement existed here in Anglo-Saxon times, Chatham was a sleepy backwater until Henry VIII established a dockyard. The dockyard flourished and expanded under Elizabeth I and it continued to grow for the next four centuries. During that time many famous ships were built in Chatham, including Nelson's Victory, which was launched in 1765. A scale model of the famous ship can be seen in the Council Chamber of the **Town Hall**. The naval connection lay behind the steady growth of Chatham and its present commercial centre originally saw to the needs of naval personnel. Among these was one John Dickens, who was employed by the Navy Pay Office. His son Charles spent some of his boyhood years in Chatham. The house where he lived, **No 2 Ordnance Terrace** (now no 11), stands among a group of handsome 18th century houses. **Chatham Historic Dockyard**, located just north of the town centre, tells the story of Chatham's naval history. Visitors can trace the rise of the Royal Navy from the days of the squat Tudor ships to the sleek lines of today's nuclear submarines. Set strategically on a hill overlooking the docks is Fort Amherst, which was built in 1756 as part of the defensive structure of the Royal Naval Dockyards. There is an impressive gatehouse as well as storerooms, powder rooms and a labyrinth of tunnels burrowing inside the hill itself. Historical re-enactments take place on most Sunday evenings in the summer. To the south the urban feel of Chatham soon gives way to rolling, wooded countryside.

GILLINGHAM
MAP 5 REF S19
2 miles E of Rochester on the A2

The largest of the Medway Towns, Gillingham developed alongside its neighbour Chatham as a centre for servicing the naval dockyards and depot. Gillingham has much earlier traces, including evidence of prehistoric and Roman settlement. It became a manor under the Normans but only began to grow once the ship-building industry developed nearby. The parish **Church of St Mary** stands on The Green in the heart of the oldest part of town. Traces of its Norman origins are visible inside where the two pillars in the chancel are from the early 12th century. The font is - also dating from that period - an interesting feature, since it was built large enough for total immersion.

Gillingham is lucky to possess one of the most fascinating military attractions in the country, in the form of the **Royal Engineers Museum of Military Engineering**. The museum is a cornucopia of memorabilia, containing

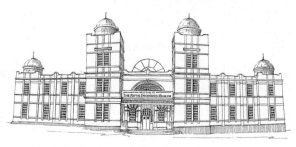

Royal Engineers Museum of Military Engineering

exciting displays of real equipment and many working models. The ingenuity displayed in many military engineering projects had beneficial knock-on effects for civilian life; early diving equipment and a 1915 smoke helmet are good examples.

TROTTISCLIFFE
MAP 5 REF R19
7 miles SW of Rochester off the A20

Trottiscliffe, as its written name implies (it is actually pronounced "Trosley"), occupies a hillside situation. It lies just to the south of **Trosley Country Park**, which can be reached by taking one of the many well-marked walks from the village. Trottiscliffe itself is a tidy, pretty little village with views over the Downs that lured the artist Graham Sutherland into living in the village. His house, in true Kentish weatherboard, is near the centre of the village. **Trottiscliffe parish church** occupies a magnificent setting, flush against the steep downland hillside. A series of paths and tracks leads from the church up to the plateau behind Trottiscliffe. Here, commanding a fine eastward view over the Medway Valley, are the **Coldrum Stones**, a magnificent archaeological site. Some 24 columns, each of a huge stone, once marked the perimeter of a circular long barrow some 50 feet in diameter. Only four of the original stones are still standing, and a huge burial mound inside the circle has disappeared, but what remains is evocative and mysterious. The columns measure up to 12 feet by 10 feet and are not of local stone. The Coldrum Stones have been maintained by the National Trust since 1926, some 16 years after it was excavated.

COBHAM   MAP 5 REF R19
3 miles W of Rochester off the A2

Cobham is a picturesque village which is famous for its half-timbered **Leather Bottle Inn**, which figures in *The Pickwick Papers*. It was here that Tracey Tupman was discovered by Mr Pickwick after having been jilted by Rachel Wardle. The village has a history that goes much further back than the Dickensian era, though, and there have been traces of the Roman occupation found around here. The parish church of **St Mary Magdalene** was built in the 13th century and enlarged in the 14th. On its floor are more than 18 brasses, which are reckoned to be the best in England. They commemorate members of the Cobham family and were produced over two centuries in the late Middle Ages. Behind the church are almshouses which incorporate a 14th century kitchen and hall. They were once part of the Old College, built by the 3rd Lord Cobham; he endowed them as living quarters for five priests who were to pray for the repose of his soul. In 1537, after the Dissolution of the Monasteries, the College was suppressed and it assumed its present use for almshouses in the 17th century.

Cobham Hall

Cobham Hall, one of the great houses of Kent, was built in the last two decades of the Elizabethan period. Its wings retain the features of late Tudor architecture but its great hall was rebuilt in the 17th century and substantially enlarged in the late 18th and early 19th centuries. It contains some excellent work by Inigo Jones and the Adam brothers. It is now a girls school and is sometimes open to the public.

GRAVESEND   MAP 5 REF R19
6 miles W of Rochester on the A226

Gravesend marks the point at which ships entering the Thames - some half a mile wide at this stage - take on a river pilot for the journey upstream. It is a busy maritime community, with cutters and tugs helping maintain a steady flow of river traffic. It is the river, with its bustle and atmosphere, that provides the attraction in Gravesend, partly because most of the old buildings were destroyed in the fire of 1727. Among the buildings lost to fire was the parish **Church of St George**, which was rebuilt in handsome Georgian fashion. The churchyard marks the final resting place of Pocahontas, the daughter of a Native American chieftain who reputedly saved the life of English settler John Smith in Virginia. Pocahontas was brought to England but died aboard ship on a journey back to Virginia. A life-sized statue marks her burial place in the churchyard.

CHISLEHURST
MAP 5 REF Q19

15 miles W of Rochester on the A208

Chislehurst developed as one of London's more select suburbs, tempting new residents with its mix of fresh air and a hint of the downland scenery further into Kent. It has managed to remain relatively unspoilt by further development, thanks in large part to the **common**, which remains an oasis of greenery despite being criss-crossed by a number of roads. The attraction that draws most visitors to Chislehurst, **The Chislehurst Caves**, are one of Britain's most interesting archaeological wonders, and visitors can join guided tours to explore them. The first stop is the Map Room, where it becomes clear that the system, which is entirely man-made, comprises three sections, each of which coincides with a historical era. The oldest, known as the Druids, dates back approximately 4,000 years. The largest section of the system, excavated some two millennia later, is the Romans. The smallest - and youngest - of the sections is the Saxons, excavated some 1,400 years ago. The caves are full of fascinating traces of these layers of history, as well as evidence of more recent events.

SEVENOAKS
MAP 5 REF R20

15 miles SW of Rochester off the A25

With its easy rail and road access to London and its leafy atmosphere Sevenoaks has come to epitomise the essence of the commuter belt in many people's eyes. This perception is not far from the truth but far enough away to reveal a genuine community with its own sense of history and identity. The leafiness is not that of a garden city creation, designed to soften the effect of wide-scale residential and commercial development. Instead it is a testament to the wooded countryside which formed the backdrop of this settlement some nine centuries ago. It is believed that there was a settlement on this site in ancient times but the first recorded mention came in AD 1114 when a record of local churches listed it as "Seovenaca". Local tradition has it that the name refers to a clump of seven oaks that once stood here, long gone but replaced - with much fanfare - by seven trees taken from **Knole Park** and ceremoniously planted on the common on the outskirts of town in 1955. These replacements gained national headline status in 1987, when they suffered badly during the Great Wind of October.

The rural feel of Sevenoaks - struggling against the odds - parallels the story of those trees. Despite the commuter tag which it must bear, Sevenoaks still has the appearance of a country market town, and it holds weekly cattle and produce markets not far from the station. A number of traditional Kentish tile-hung cottages, as well as a fine Regency pub and some grand houses, still line the main street before it assumes a more anonymous aspect.

Not far from the centre of Sevenoaks are further reminders of the town's heritage. The **Vine cricket ground** lies on a rise to the south of the town centre. It was given to the town in 1773 but the first recorded match at the Vine - between Kent and Sussex - took place in 1734. It witnessed a remarkable match in 1782 when the Duke of Dorset (one of the Sackvilles of Knole) and his estate-workers defeated a team representing All-England. The victory was particularly sweet because the Duke's team also won a bet of a thousand guineas.

The pride of Sevenoaks, and of Kent itself for many people, is of course **Knole House**, the huge manor house set in extensive parkland. It is one of the largest houses in England, with 365 rooms inside its foursquare structure. The present house stands on the site of a much smaller manor house which was bought by the Archbishop of Canterbury in 1456 and used as an ecclesiastical palace until 1532 when it was taken over by Henry VIII. Elizabeth I granted it to the Sackvilles, who still live there although the house is now owned by the National Trust. Impressive in its scale, Knole House also offers visitors the chance to wander past outstanding collections of tapestries, antique furniture and an extensive art collection which has master-

Knole House

pieces by Gainsborough and Reynolds. The great house is not without its sense of human involvement. The Sackvilles proved to have the flair for employing the best craftsmen to realise their creative architectural spirit. The writer Vita Sackville-West was born in Knole House in 1892; some five decades later Hitler intended to use it as his English headquarters. Surrounding Knole House is its majestic deer park, covering some 1000 acres of rolling countryside with dense beech woodlands giving way to hidden dells.

EYNSFORD
MAP 5 REF R19

6 miles N of Sevenoaks off the A225

The centre of Eynsford manages to preserve a sense of history, with a number of timber-framed houses and the church's tall shingled steeple rising above the busy A225. It is only by going down a side-street, however, that the visitor can appreciate the real charm of this village nestled cosily along the banks of the Darent. It is here that visitors come across the ford which gives its

Eynsford Ford

name to the village. The ford is passable by cars although a depth chart to the side indicates that water levels can rise as high as six feet when the river is swollen with floodwater. The Darent is also crossed by a hump-backed bridge, similar to that in Shoreham, and a brick-built viaduct that carries the Swanley to Sevenoaks railway line.

At the end of the lane is a modern building which nevertheless houses one of Kent's most important archaeological treasures: **Lullingstone Roman Villa**. The villa was only uncovered in

1949 although its existence was known since the 18th century when farm labourers uncovered fragments of mosaics which had been pierced when the labourers had driven fence posts into the ground. Not as large as some other Roman remains, Lullingstone is noteworthy in being extremely well preserved, allowing the visitor not only to trace the history of the building over four centuries but also the style of life adopted by wealthy country families in Roman Britain. A glass and timber pavilion protects the excavated villa from the elements and visitors can examine all the elements that made it a whole, including the main living rooms, the deep room, the original bath -house - with colourful mosaic flooring throughout. The deep room contains relics of pagan worship but the villa also has a Christian chapel - the only example of a chapel found within a private Roman villa in Britain.

DOWNE
MAP 5 REF Q19
8 miles NW of Sevenoaks off the A233

The village of Downe, which lies high up on the Downs near Biggin Hill, has a commanding setting with fine views, especially looking north towards London. Its appearance reflects its position at the cross-roads - in more ways than one. The central core of traditional Kentish flint cottages fights for survival against the rising tide of anonymous suburban housing spreading southwards from the capital. Even its natural setting, still evident in the outskirts of the village, is poised between the open uplands of the downs themselves and the more wooded areas of Kent such as the Weald further south. But more than any landscape Downe is associated with one man, and by extension to "Man" himself. It was here, in **Down House** that Charles Darwin lived for 40 years until his death in 1882. During that time the great naturalist analysed his findings from his voyages on the *Beagle*, wrestled with his Anglican conscience, and eventually produced the work that changed the way we looked at ourselves and our evolution - *On the Origin of Species*. The house, now owned by the Royal College of Surgeons and run as a Darwin museum, reflects much of its former owner's character. It has been painstakingly restored as it was in Darwin's time. Rambling though it might be, this is no comfortable country bolt-hole. In fact it would seem that the great scientist denied himself many of life's pleasures while attending to the matters of Life itself.

FRENCH STREET
MAP 5 REF Q20
7 miles SW of Sevenoaks off the B2042

A tiny hamlet, tucked in the folds of narrow wooded hills, French Street has the appearance of one of the most out of the way spots in Kent. In fact, many people arrive here by foot - and possibly by chance - as it suddenly appears round the bend of one of the footpaths that traverse the neighbouring woods. Rustic and unprepossessing French Street may be, but it is also on the doorstep of one of the county's most beloved attractions, **Chartwell**, the country home which Winston Churchill bought in 1924. When Churchill bought it, Chartwell was a modest house command-ing a splendid view across the Weald. He set about en-larging the house, helping it to match the magnifi-cence of its view. But the work was not designed to magnify Churchill's own sense of importance. In-stead the newly built wall and landscaped gardens enabled him to find pre-cious hours of diversion, occupying himself with the horticulture of the es-tate or in painting by its lake. The National Trust maintains Chartwell and

Chartwell

have successfully captured the spirit of the great statesman in the painstakingly preserved rooms. There is a real sense of his presence here, especially in the studio and in his library.

French Street is also a good starting point for visiting a more poignant sight, **Toys Hill**, which can be reached by following a footpath from the village through dense beechwoods. Toys Hill is also a National Trust property, comprising 200 acres of woodland which once surrounded a house known as Weardale Manor. The woodlands themselves were devastated by the hurricane-force winds of 16 October 1987, when south-eastern England felt the full force of the winds coming up from the Channel. Huge and ancient beech trees were felled or even snapped and the scene the next morning was one of almost total devastation. There has been an intensive replanting scheme in operation since the Great Storm, and new beeches are taking root on the brow of the hill. In the meantime there are marvellous views past where the great trees once stood.

WESTERHAM
5 miles W of Sevenoaks on the A25

MAP 5 REF Q20

Westerham is one of the westernmost communities in Kent, tucked against the Surrey border. The building of the M25, just a mile or so north of Westerham, eased the town's traffic congestion considerably and it now has a calmer aspect more in keeping with its former days as a coaching station. The town lies between two upland areas, with the North Downs to the north and Greensand Ridge - the source of the River Darent - just to the south. In the main street and around the tiny green of this small town are a number of old buildings, including two venerable coaching inns. The centre of the town, by the green, has statues of two British heroes with Westerham connections. General James Wolfe, victor of the decisive battle between the English and French at Quebec in 1759, was born in Westerham. The house where he grew up, built in the 17th century but renamed **Quebec House** in honour of his famous victory, stands to the east of town and is maintained by the National Trust. There are household items and other memorabilia relating to Wolfe on display, and in the stable block there is an exhibition about the Battle of Quebec.

Another mansion of the late 17th century, **Squerryes Court** also has Wolfe connections. Wolfe was a friend of the Warde family who owned this William and Mary house. It was here that Wolfe received his first commission in 1741 - at the age of 14. The house has a collection of paintings by the Dutch Old Masters, period furniture and tapestries, as well as a special room set aside for Wolfe exhibits. The Darent rises in Squerryes Park, which extends back from the house past formal gardens.

LIMPSFIELD AND LIMPSFIELD CHART
8 miles W of Sevenoaks off the A25

MAP 5 REF Q20

The churchyard at Limpsfield, just into Surrey, contains the grave of the composer, Frederick Delius, who despite having died in France, left instructions that he should be buried in an English country graveyard. **Detillens**, a rare 15th century "hall" house, is also located in Limpsfield. This striking building has an unusual "king-post" roof, and despite having been given a new facade in the 18th century, is a good example of a house belonging to a Surrey yeoman, a member of the class of small freeholders who cultivated their own land; inside, there is an interesting collection of period furniture, china and militaria. Limpsfield Chart, or simply **The Chart**, constitutes a hilltop common with some lovely views eastwards across Kent. Next to the common is a 17th century **Mill House**; the windmill itself was removed in 1925. Elsewhere in The Chart there are handsome groupings of stone-built houses, cottages, and farm buildings, best exemplified by the ensemble at Moorhouse Farm.

PLAXTOL
5 miles E of Sevenoaks off the A227

MAP 5 REF R20

A row of traditional Kentish weatherboard cottages flanks the side of the parish church of Plaxtol, a hilly village occupying a prominent location on the ridge near Ightham Mote. Just to the east of the village, and reached through a circuitous succession of narrow lanes, is **Old Soar Manor**, a manor house built in the 13th century. The house occupies the solar block of the original building, which served as a knight's dwelling. Of particular interest are the undercrofts below it, with graceful vaults curving upwards. The setting of Old Soar Manor is idyllic, with orchards and copses surrounding it. The woods grow more dense as they climb the ridge rising up from the orchards; at the top is one of southern England's largest forests, **Mereworth Woods**. Wild boar once roamed through its oaks and beeches, although today the wildlife is of a tamer variety.

Even closer to Plaxtol, but in the opposite direction from Old Soar Mansion, is **Ightham Mote**, one of England's finest Medieval manor houses. This gem of a building, owned by the National Trust, is set in a nar-

Ightam Mote

row wooded valley roughly halfway between Plaxtol and the even smaller village of **Ivy Hatch**. A moat surrounds the house, although the name "mote" probably refers instead to an Old English word meaning "meeting place". Ightham Mote was built in the 14th century, with its central courtyard retaining the meeting-place purpose. The outside walls, above the moat, are of soft ragstone, which catches the evening light with a warm glow. The construction inside utilised great amounts of local oak, with massive timbers still very much in evidence in the rafters and central hall (the solar), as well as in the main staircase, built in Jacobean times.

ROYAL TUNBRIDGE WELLS
MAP 5 REF R20
10 miles S of Sevenoaks on the A26

Unlike Canterbury and Rochester, Royal Tunbridge Wells can trace no Roman or ecclesiastical lineage. Sevenoaks to the north and Tenterden to the east can boast Medieval trading links but throughout the period during which these other towns were establishing their reputation Tunbridge Wells was nothing more than forest.

The secret of how this attractive town gained such prominence lies in the two words at the beginning and end of its name. First the "wells". Until 1606, when Lord North discovered the chalybeate springs, this was an unremarkable tract of forest land. North, however, realised the importance of his discovery and rushed back to the court. That is where the second word, "Royal", comes in. Soon members of the Royal Family and courtiers were taking the waters, and spreading the word of their health-restoring qualities. For three decades there were no buildings by the springs. In 1630 Queen Henrietta Maria, the wife of Charles I, came here to recuperate after giving birth to the future Charles II. She and her retinue simply camped on the grounds by the springs. By the end of that decade, though, enterprising local people began building the town around the springs. The town really came into its own in 1735 when Beau Nash, famous for his dominant role in Bath, arrived as Master of Ceremonies. With Nash at the helm, guiding and even dictating fashion, Tunbridge Wells went from strength to strength. Royalty was a constant factor in the following period, a fact that was officially recognised when Edward VII granted its "Royal" prefix in 1907.

Royal Tunbridge Wells is still a thriving town even if it no longer has the rakish atmosphere of the 18th century. With visitors - and money - pouring in for two centuries the town acquired a prosperous look, which it has managed to retain with great charm. Nowhere is this more evident than in the **Pantiles**, a lovely shaded walk which is lined with elegant shops and overhung in places with an 18th century "musick balcony". The Pantiles was originally grassed and known as The Walks. In 1699 Princess Anne visited Tunbridge Wells with her son, the Duke of Gloucester who slipped and hurt himself along The Walks. The irate Princess complained and the town authorities soon paved The Walk with square pantiles, and the name duly changed.

The Pantiles were the focal point of the hectic social life organised by Beau Nash, and there were concerts, balls and gambling houses throughout the Season. People such as Sarah Porter, the "Queen of the Touters", pestered strollers into entering the gambling halls. Only 15 of the original pantiles remain; these can be seen by the springs in Bath Square. The common extends down to the Pantiles, providing a sense of space and rural charm right in the heart of the town. It covers some 250 acres and is laced with gorse-lined footpaths along its grassy slopes. which also feature some curiously weathered rocks.

The Pantiles

With town and country so evenly balanced, a visitor's bracing ramble can quickly evolve into a stroll past a row of fine old houses. Some of the best Regency architecture can be found along the gracefully curving **Calverley Park Crescent**. White-painted iron pillars support a covered promenade over a handsome terrace. Near it is **Calverley Grounds**, with rose gardens, shrubs, tennis courts and a paddling pool for children. Other fine Regency houses add lustre to the Mount Sion district. The best place to learn about the history of Royal Tunbridge Wells is at the **Tunbridge Wells Museum and Art Gallery**, located in the Central Library in Mount Pleasant. It includes a fine selection of wooden souvenirs dating from the 17th century.

PENSHURST   MAP 5 REF R20
5 miles NW of Royal Tunbridge Wells off the B2027

One of the prettiest villages in Kent is Penshurst, which makes the most of its hilly wooded setting and its Tudor architecture. The houses at its core are all old - dating from two to four centuries ago, each with its own sense of charm and identity.

One of England's finest historic houses, **Penshurst Place** dominates the rural landscape of Penshurst and commands fine views over the Weald of Kent. The medieval house, renowned for its galleried Barons Hall, was built of local sandstone in 1341. Today it stands as an impressive - and remarkably well-preserved - example of a defended manor house. A fascinating collection of armour, tapestries, paintings and furniture fills the staterooms. Outside, there is the original ten-acre 16th century garden, the Toy Museum, a Venture Playground and extensive walking trails.

Penshurst Place

The heart of the village is the church of **Saint John the Baptist**, originally built in the 12th century and still containing elements from the 13th, 14th and 15th centuries. Of particular interest is the 15th century ornamental font. Almost as interesting as the church itself is the way it is reached - through an ancient lych-gate. The two-storey Tudor house which was built around the gate is now a test for geometry students, with its bulging walls and crooked beams hard-pressed to produce a right angle among them. Together with its neighbouring houses it makes up **Leicester Square**, although it would be hard to find a more tranquil counterpart to its namesake in the heart of the West End of London.

CHIDDINGSTONE

MAP 5 REF R20

6 miles NW of Royal Tunbridge Wells off the B2027

The village of Chiddingstone is maintained by the National Trust and it is not hard to see why the Trust should be so interested in this small village set in pleasant open woodland roughly midway between Hever Castle and Penshurst Place. Chiddingstone grew prosperous in the 16th and 17th centuries and half-timbered houses from that period line the village's single street. The Trust has done an excellent job in supporting the preservation of these houses. They comprise a remarkable time-capsule of how the increased wealth from the Wealden iron industry transformed itself into a handsome and harmonious row of houses. The church predates the houses, having been built in the 13th century. It has a fine Gothic tower and handsome Jacobean font and pulpit. At the head of the street, which in places is overhung by the upper storeys of the old houses, stands **Chiddingstone Castle**. This is a mock-Gothic reworking of a much older house, the home of the Streatfield family. It contains a collection of Stuart furnishings and paintings as well as Ancient Egyptian and Oriental exhibits.

Along a footpath behind the street is a block of sandstone known as the Chiding Stone. Legend has it that in the distant past miscreants, vagrants and assorted petty criminals were taken here for a public chastisement, or "chiding". One wonders whether the dozens of individuals whose initials are carved in the rock faced an on-the-spot chiding.

HEVER

MAP 5 REF R20

8 miles W of Royal Tunbridge Wells off the B2026

The tiny village of Hever, near Edenbridge, is set in delightfully unspoilt countryside, with orchards and woodlands surrounding it. Most visitors, impressed as they may be with this tidy settlement, make for the star attraction here, and the reason why Hever figures prominently on anyone's checklist of things to see in Kent. The village is the site of **Hever Castle**, which is redolent of history and more than a little tragedy. The castle achieved its present form in 1272 when Sir Stephen de Penchester received permission from Edward I to convert his house at Hever into a castle. The massive Gatehouse, the outer walls and the moat strengthened its position as a fortification. Two centuries later the Bullen (or Boleyn) family bought the castle and rebuilt much of it, adding a comfortable Tudor residence inside the walls. It was here that the ill-fated Anne Boleyn, mother of Elizabeth I, was courted by Henry VIII. The castle still contains many mementoes of her. In 1903

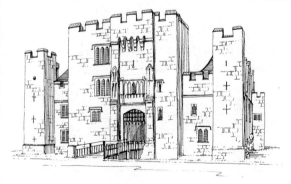

Hever Castle

Hever Castle was bought by American millionaire William Waldorf Astor, who restored the original buildings and set about building the "Tudor Village", gardens and lake.

TONBRIDGE
Map 5 Ref R20
4 miles N of Royal Tunbridge Wells on the A26

Tonbridge stands on the highest navigable point on the Medway and as such has been able to exploit this position over the centuries. There was an Anglo-Saxon settlement here and perhaps an earlier Roman community. Its most important historical landmark, on a rise in the centre of the town, is the ruined Norman castle, of which there are substantial remains. The walls date from the 12th century while the shell of the keep, as well as the massive gatehouse and drumtowers, were built in the early 14th century. Inside the wall is a mound which is thought to have been the site of an Anglo-Saxon fort. The parish **Church of Saints Peter and Paul** shows mainly evidence of the style of architecture known as Early English, in this case being built in the early 13th century. Subsequent restoration efforts and enlargements have altered the interior of the church, but it retains a sense of height and airiness that recalls the Middle Ages.

Tonbridge Castle

MARDEN
Map 5 Ref S20
7 miles E of Tonbridge off the A229/B2162

Tina and David Wickham, proprietors of the superb **West End Tavern** in Marden, are both trained chefs. They took over at this attractive and welcoming inn in January of 1998, and have made a real success of it. A Grade II listed building, the interior boasts a wonderful 17th-century inglenook fireplace, exposed beams and a central brick bar. A very friendly and inviting atmosphere awaits guests, popular with locals and visitors alike. There's an extensive lunch and evening menu as well as daily specials. Traditional home-made foods include specialities such as chicken Kiev, pies, curries, burgers and

West End Tavern, West End, Marden, Tonbridge, Kent TN12 9JB Tel: 01622 831956

steaks produced from locally-farmed meats, along with vegetarian dishes and lighter meals and snacks, using fresh local produce and available seven days a week (midday - 2 p.m. and 7 - 9.30 p.m.). Four real ales are on tap, including two local Kent ales, as well as a good selection of lagers, wines and spirits. Guests are welcome to enjoy these meals indoors or out in the large rear garden with its paved patio area and natural well.

CRANBROOK
Map 5 Ref S20

12 miles E of Royal Tunbridge Wells on the B2189

Cranbrook is an old town which sprang into prominence in the 15th century when it became a centre of the weaving industry. Several old buildings date back to this prosperous period and the winding streets, well away from any main road, are lined with weatherboarded shops and houses. The parish church, **St Dunstan's**, was built in the 15th century and is known locally as "the Cathedral of the Weald". Above the porch is a room known as "Baker's Jail", where "Bloody Baker" incarcerated the Protestants he had convicted before their execution. Dominating the town, however, is the **Union Mill**, a three-storey windmill built in 1816. Standing 72 feet high it is the second tallest in England. It is open to the public at certain times of the year.

MAIDSTONE
Map 5 Ref S20

15 miles NE of Royal Tunbridge Wells off the A26

Maidstone developed on the site of an important meeting place. The name means "the people's stone", and it is likely that a stone marked the site of the "moot". The River Medway is the ancient boundary which separated West and East Kent, and Maidstone was once the capital of the former. On the west of the river lived the "Kentish Men", while to the east lived the "Men of Kent". The distinction is still used proudly by many of the inhabitants of the county today. Although Maidstone has been extensively developed in recent years, there are several handsome Elizabethan and Georgian buildings to be found hidden away in the High Street and surrounding backstreets. Maidstone's **Museum and Art Gallery** is housed in the beautiful Chillington Manor House, a splendid Tudor residence which is in St Faith's Street. In the Museum is a chair from nearby **Allington Castle** which bears a fascinating inscription. Henry VIII is said to have first met Anne Boleyn at Allington, and the chair is a fitting testimony to this man who loved women. The motto reads: ".of this (chay)re iss entytled too one salute from everie ladie thott settes downe in itt - Castell Alynton 1530 - Hen. 8 Rex". Which, loosely translated, means that gallant Henry could demand a kiss from every woman fortunate (or possibly foolhardy) enough to sit on it!

For another unusual glimpse of the past, you should make your way to the Stables of the former **Archbishop's Palace** in Mill Street. Close to here you will find a wonderful exhibition of horse-drawn carriages, The **Tyrwhitt-Drake Museum**. This grand mixture of private and State carriages makes up one of the finest collections of its kind in England. Kent plays county cricket in **Mote Park**, to the east of the town, an extensive area of 450 acres of parkland with fishing and sailing on a lake formed by damming the River Len.

WEST MALLING
Map 5 Ref R20

5 miles W of Maidstone on the A20

A recent bypass has spared the centre of West Malling from the worst excesses of traffic problems. This enlightened move has left its wide high street - and the Georgian houses that line it - better able to present its handsome face to the outside world. There is a feeling of West Malling's being larger than a village and indeed it was once called Town Malling. It certainly has more history than most villages could absorb. An Anglican Abbey for nuns (in Swan Street) and a monastery in Water Street carry on traditions dating from the 11th century when William the Conqueror's bishop Gundulph founded the abbey. He also built **St Leonard's Tower**, the ruined keep of the house in which he lived. The tower stands by the entrance to **Manor Park Country Park**, which comprises 52 acres of parkland and an ornamental lake.

OFFHAM

MAP 5 REF R20

6 miles W of Maidstone on the A228

Offham, a lovely small village set in the orchards of the North Downs, was first settled by the Romans. Its main conversation piece today, however, is of slightly more recent vintage. In the middle of the attractive village green is a **quintain**, or tilting post. This aid for jousting practice consists of an upright with an arm that swivels when hit - particularly by a lance. The quintain comes into play each year during Offham's May Day celebrations.

LOOSE

MAP 5 REF R20

2 miles S of Maidstone off the B2010

Pronounced "Looze", this village has been fighting a partly losing battle to preserve its identity in the face of expansion from Maidstone. The older part of the village lies in a narrow little valley, where millponds once powered a flourishing woollen industry. When the wool trade declined the mills were converted to paper-making. This change signalled more contact with Maidstone, which has gradually absorbed the northern fringe of the village into its outskirts. **The Wool House**, located just off the A229, is a National Trust-owned property which traces the story of the wool trade in Loose.

LEEDS

MAP 5 REF S20

4 miles SE of Maidstone off the A2

The village of Leeds stands on the grounds of a former Abbey, which flourished until the Dissolution in the 16th century. Many of the older features of the village, such as its oast-houses, Norman church and surrounding farms, were part of the Abbey complex. The feature that dominates the village, however, is **Leeds Castle**, which stands on two islands in the middle of the River Len. This peaceful moat is the home of swans and ducks, and surrounding the castle are the extensive gardens laid out by Capability Brown in the 18th century. The present castle

Leeds Castle

structure, with its romantic turrets and stout walls, dates from the time of Edward I although there has been a defensive fortress on the site since the middle of the 9th century. It was Henry VIII who effected the transformation from a strategically sited fortress into a stately country residence. For 300 years it remained a royal residence, with additions, such as the main building, designed to blend harmoniously with the rest of the complex. Leeds also is the heart of a countryside district of hidden and attractive hamlets, some of which seem to be organic elements of the woodlands that still cover much of the area.

BOUGHTON MONCHELSEA

MAP 5 REF S20

4 miles S of Maidstone off the B2163

As the centre of Kentish ragstone quarrying it is not surprising that the centre of this pleasant village reflects the local building material. The **quarries**, on the edge of the village, have been worked almost continuously for seven centuries but archaeologists suggest that they were in use before both the Romans and the Saxons used the stone. Some of these stones were used in the building of Westminster Abbey and Henry III ordered a number of cannonballs to be made from the stone. The parish church, **St Peter's**, was built from ragstone in the Norman period. The lych-gate, erected in 1470, was built entirely without nails and is thought to be the oldest in England.

The manor house, **Boughton Monchelsea Place**, is another ragstone building. It was the home of Sir Thomas Wyatt who led the Men of Kent in revolt against Mary I and was executed in 1554. The present manor house dates from shortly after this but was extensively remodelled in the 18th century. The house and its extensive gardens are open to the public.

Boughton Monchelsea Place

LENHAM
Map 5 Ref S20

10 miles SE of Maidstone on the A2

Another lovely village straddling the border between the North Downs and the Weald of Kent, Lenham has a timeless feel to it. A group of handsome buildings, some more than six centuries old, front the village square. The countryside to the north and south differs dramatically. To the north, hamlets such as **Warren Street** cling to the uplands of the North Downs. To the south it is a different matter: **Lenham Heath** is set in rolling, open countryside, a lovely village that preserves its distinctive identity despite lying just north of the M20.

SHEERNESS
Map 5 Ref S19

17 miles NE of Maidstone on the A249

Sheerness is the point at which the River Medway meets the Thames. This was once the site of a naval dockyard, the first of which was surveyed in the 17th century by none other than Samuel Pepys, the famous diarist, who held the position of Secretary of the Admiralty during the reign of Charles II. It was here, too, that HMS *Victory* docked in 1805, bringing Nelson's body back home after the Battle of Trafalgar. In recent years, Sheerness has developed into a busy container and car-ferry port, and most of the Isle of Sheppey's prosperity is centred here. Most of the town itself is made up of drab Victorian housing for dockyard workers, and if it has a focal point at all it is the rather odd blue clock tower in the High Street.

MINSTER
Map 5 Ref S19

17 miles NE of Maidstone off the B2231

The unprepossessing seaside town of Minster is as unlikely a spot as you could imagine to find one of the oldest sites of Christianity in England. Nevertheless, it was here on the highest part of Sheppey that Sexburga, the widow of a Saxon king of Kent, founded a nunnery in the latter part of the 7th century. Sacked by the Danes in 855 AD, **Minster Abbey** was rebuilt around 1130 and re-established as a priory for Benedictine nuns; and in the 13th century, the parish church was built adjoining the old monastic church or "Nun's Chapel". And so it was that from the Middle Ages until the time of the Dissolution of the Monasteries, this ancient place served as a "double church", the church of St Mary and St Sexburga, with the nuns using the northern half of the building and the parishioners worshipping in the southern section. These two distinct parts were joined by an archway that was pierced in the south wall of the earlier Abbey church. To the west of the church is the 15th century abbey gatehouse, which now houses a museum with exhibits on Sheppey's history.

BURHAM

4 miles N of Maidstone off the A229

MAP 5 REF S19

Kits Coty House

Burham is set on slopes in the upper Medway Valley; above it the Downs reach one of their highest points at **Bluebell Hill**. However, Burham is noted for a man-made structure - a remarkable archaeological site known as **Kits Coty House**. Like Coldrum Long Barrow about 4 miles west across the Medway Valley, Kits Coty House represents the remains of a Neolithic burial chamber. It is smaller than Coldrum Long Barrow but is better preserved, its capstone still in place across the three huge upright stones. As is so often the case with Neolithic monuments it commands far-reaching views, looking out across the valley towards the Medway Gap.

TENTERDEN

15 miles SE of Maidstone on the A28

MAP 5 REF S20

Tenterden is known as the "Jewel of the Weald", although it occupies a site that is right in the border between the dense woodlands of the Weald and the flatter, farming country that leads eastwards into the Romney Marshes. Today's well-earned nickname is a far cry from its earliest days, when it was known as "Tenet-ware-den", or "pig-pasture of the men of Thanet"! Despite the fact that pigs flourished here, sheep inevitably became the more profitable animal to farm on these fertile lands, and the wool trade quickly took off. In 1331, the far-sighted Edward III prohibited the export of unwashed wool and encouraged weavers from Flanders to settle here and bring their dyeing and weaving techniques to the English. The town of Tenterden and some of its neighbouring villages were to become the most important centres for the manufacture of broadcloth. Once again, it was thanks to the earlier reclamation of the Romney Marsh that the area provided excellent grazing land, and brought about a profitable trade for the Wealden communities. Just outside Tenterden, Smallhythe and Reading Street provided access to the sea. These two small ports were founded as a means of transporting lumber from the Wealden forests, but by the 14th century, Smallhythe was firmly established as a boat-building centre.

The **Whistle Stop Cafe** takes its name from the working steam train situated a couple of hundred yards away. This popular tea room makes an ideal stop for a light meal. Proprietor Annie Oliver-Wanstall trained at catering college and has worked in a variety of hotels and pubs. The decor is bright and welcoming; knitted dolls festoon the two adjoining rooms with their delightful lace-covered tables and walls adorned with a delightful mix of plain and patterned ceramic plates. Seating for 40 is comfortable; the atmosphere intimate and cosy. There is also an outdoor patio. Annie offers all manner of home-made cakes to accompany the hot drinks; traditional cream teas

The Whistle Stop Cafe, 2 Coombe Lane, Tenterden, Kent TN30 6HD Tel: 01580 765450

with home-made scones are an afternoon favourite. In addition there is a chance to sample the all-day breakfast (egg, bacon, sausage, tomatoes, bean, mushrooms, tea and toast, to satisfy the hungriest of diners), or a lunch-time choice of soups, salads, jacket potatoes and excellent range of sandwiches made with fresh crusty bread, freshly baked baguettes or toast. The dessert menu includes mouth-watering treacle pudding, spotted dick, caramel apple flan, banana split or Movenpick Swiss ice cream.

The church of **St Mildred** can be found in the heart of Tenterden, and with its unusual twin doors at the western end, it is lovely. From the top of its 15th- entury tower - some 100 feet above the town - are far-reaching views across the Weald to the Channel Coast. Near the church is the **Town Hall** and the delightful Woolpack Inn, a proud reminder of the town's former days as a cloth trading centre. Another inn, the **William Caxton**, takes its name from the man who brought printing to England and who is said to have been born in Tenterden in 1422. The centre of Tenterden stretches along its broad High Street, lined with shops and houses, nearly all with their original facades dating from the 16th to 18th centuries. Most of them, however, were built in a busy period between 1720 and 1760, so there is something of a Georgian feel to the town as a whole.

Set back slightly from the traffic of the High Street but still very much in the heart of Tenterden, on the site of the former medieval house Pittlesden Manor, **Sparks Antiques** occupies pride of place amid a parade of shops built in the 1960s. This collection of 12 fascinating units trades in an astonishing range of antiques. Browsers and serious buyers from far and wide rub shoulders among the displays of antique English and Continental furniture from the 17th to 19th century, paintings, clocks, silver, militaria and collectibles. There are also decorative items on display, such as lamps, porcelain, early metal

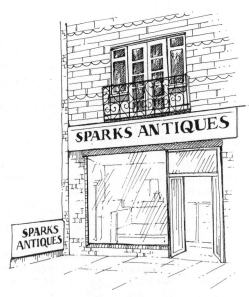

Sparks Antiques, 4 Manor Row, High Street, Tenterden, Kent TN30 6HP Tel: 01580 766696

work (including candlesticks), mirrors, rugs, tapestries and early textiles. Proprietor Roger Binning has been in the antiques trade since 1972 and his knowledge and enthusiasm are infectious. The shop gives the items for sale a real stage on which to perform. A lovely chandelier hangs over the elegant furniture and objets d'art, which can be viewed to full effect in this uncluttered setting.

SISSINGHURST
MAP 5 REF S20
6 miles NW of Tenterden on the A262

The long village of Sissinghurst has many of the old-fashioned white-painted weatherboard houses, giving it a feel of architectural unity. Many of the larger houses were built by prosperous weavers, who worked in the thriving industry introduced during Edward III's reign. Nothing of this former industry remains, apart from these testaments to the wealth the weaving created in the area. Sissinghurst, of course, is famous for the lovely gardens which were the creation of the writer Vita Sackville-West and her husband Harold Nicolson. The couple bought **Sissinghurst**

Sissinghurst Castle

Castle in 1930 and their purchase was in reality a wreck. Previously, during the Seven Years War, it had housed up to 3,000 French prisoners and the only part of the castle left standing after its role as a prison ended - and decades of neglect added their toll - was a workhouse. The pair restored what they could of the house and set about creating gardens in its grounds.

The garden is a wonder and a true testament to their creative spirit. Much of it is laid out in Elizabethan style; of particular interest is the White Garden planted entirely with silver-leafed white-flowering species, separated by box hedges. This garden, and the others, are set out as if they were "rooms", each with a different theme. Spring and summer brings a delightful scent of herbs, which are another speciality of the garden.

The Bull Inn is a Grade II listed building be-lieved to date back to the 1500s. The spacious bar area has beamed ceilings, a large wooden bar and comfortable bench seating in box pew style; there's a welcoming open fire in the colder months. The restaurant also has black-beamed ceilings and an open fire. It is large, airy and very comfortable, with a tasteful and very attractive decor. The inn's three qualified chefs are responsible for the superb menus, creating such made-to-order dishes as cod Mornay, lamb's liver and bacon, sirloin steak, beef Madras or lighter meals and

The Bull Inn, The Street, Sissinghurst, nr Cranbrook, Kent TN17 2JG
Tel: 01580 712821

snacks. Brothers Mukesh and Rajesh Sharma own and personally run this handsome establish-ment, which also offers guests three ensuite bedrooms (two double and one single), with all creature comforts and amenities. There is a lovely large garden with a natural pond, old oak tree, lawns, a covered pergola and lovely bedding plants, making it a welcoming haven day or night (when it is specially lit) for quiet relaxation.

BIDDENDEN
MAP 5 REF S19

4 miles N of Tenterden on the A262

Biddenden lies at the end of the A274 at the junction with the A262. Quite apart from the physical attractions of its architecture and picturesque High Street - crammed with pubs, restaurants and antique shops housed in fine half-timbered buildings - there is something else here that has assured the village of a permanent place in the history books. Way back around the beginning of the 12th century, two of its most famous residents were born. These were the "Biddenden Maids", Eliza and Mary Chulkhurst, who were Siamese twins joined at the hips. Rare enough today, the presence of Siamese twins in a medieval community was an occurrence of unheralded novelty. One of the finest of Biddenden's houses can be found just to the north of the village green. This is the **Old Cloth Hall**, a superb six-gabled building which was the centre of the local cloth trade in medieval and Tudor times, and housed the workshops of the weavers. As you enter the village, the road takes you past the beautifully maintained church. All Saints Church dates from Saxon times, the earliest parts remaining today are the nave, chancel and south aisle dating from the late 13th century.

EGERTON
MAP 5 REF S20

9 miles N of Tenterden off the A20

The George Inn in Egerton is a distinctive white clapboard inn serving traditional country ales and food. A hub of the community, this attractive and friendly public house dates back to 1576. The public bar has a large inglenook fireplace and memorabilia of the Canadian Air Force (stationed nearby during the war) - the chimney breast is covered with original signatures of the service personnel, and the annual reunion of the servicemen and -women is held here each October. The saloon bar is heavily beamed, with an open fire, and decorated with photographs of the village and villagers of old. The beamed dining room seats 32; the menu here boasts traditional favourites such as steak and Guinness pie, beef Wellington and

The George Inn, The Street, Egerton, Ashford, Kent TN27 9DB
Tel: 01233 756304

grilled lamb, as well as pasta and seafood dishes. The bar snacks are also delicious and filling. There are always five real ales on tap at this Free House, along with a range of lagers, cider, stout and good wines and spirits. The lovely garden to the rear has a barbecue, aviary - featuring 'Dave' the barn owl, quite an attraction in himself - picnic tables and lush lawns.

ASHFORD
MAP 5 REF T20

11 miles NW of Tenterden on the A28

Ashford still boasts some fine Georgian houses, and the earliest parts of the splendid parish church date back to the 15th century. The great central tower rises above the town, each of its four lofty pinnacles crowned by a golden weathervane shaped like an arrow. Ashford's central location makes it one of the most convenient touring centres in the county. It is a convenient spot altogether - you can get to Folkestone within 15 minutes with Hythe and New Romney just 20 minutes away. Leeds Castle is also near by, as are Chatham Historic Dockyards and Chilham Castle. Ashford is proud of the fact that it had the first volunteer Fire Service in the country. It was formed in 1826, and in 1836 purchased its first manual fire engine. It was here in 1925 that the first Leyland motor fire engine was put into service, all funds having been raised by public subscription. The original fire station has now sadly gone, in its place stands the Boots store.

An original 1916 British Mark IV tank, one of only three in existence, can be found standing proudly in **St George's Square**. It was presented to the people of Ashford in recognition of their splendid response to the war efforts in World Wars I and II. The tank is now designated as a listed building! The **Channel Tunnel Terminal** has in a relatively short period of time become a huge influence on the town, as Ashford is the only passenger boarding point between London and the continent. 10 to 15 services per day link Ashford to Lille, Paris or Brussels. The journey from Ashford to Paris takes about two hours.

SMALL HYTHE
MAP 5 REF S20

3 miles S of Tenterden on the B2082

It is hard to imagine that this little hamlet on the road between Tenterden and Hythe was once a flourishing port and ship-building centre. Yet during the Middle Ages the river Rother flowed past wide and deep enough to accommodate ships of the period. One of Henry VIII's warships was built here. Today there is little trace of this industry or indeed of the river, which is only a tiny stream even in the wettest weather. One clue, however, lies in the name of the Small Hythe bus stop, which is called the Ferry, a reminder of past times. The great actress Ellen Terry lived here and her home, Smallhythe Place, is now the **Ellen Terry Museum**. The museum offers a fascinating glimpse into her theatrical life but it would be worth visiting if only to examine the house, which was built in the late 15th century. It was originally the Port House and the home of a yeoman farmer. Much of the timber and the solid oak floors are original.

OLD ROMNEY
MAP 5 REF T21

11 miles SE of Tenterden on the A259

Romney Marsh

Old Romney, with its setting in the remote **Romney Marsh** which takes its name, has a forlorn feel that somehow calls to mind the tale of Ozymandias. It seems improbable, looking at today's quiet village with its small church, scattered cottages, and pub, that it was once a productive port. The Domesday Book records three fisheries, a mill and a wharf, indicating its waterfront setting. As the marsh gained more land from the sea, Romney's position - which had been as a busy island - became landlocked and trade became hampered considerably. It lost out to New Romney, which ironically also found itself a victim of the gradually accretion of land in the Marsh.

NEW ROMNEY
MAP 5 REF T21

14 miles SE of Tenterden on the A259

The peaceful little town of New Romney is known as the "capital" of the Marsh, one of the five original Cinque Ports, and headquarters of the **Romney, Hythe & Dymchurch Railway**. The station - roughly midway between the town and the seafront - contains workshops and the various engines in their sheds. Those keen on even smaller-scale models will also find the Romney Toy & Model Museum here. Vintage models, toys and photographs are on display, and there are two working model railways to enjoy.

A great storm in 1287 diverted the course of the River Rother and choked it with shingle, causing it to flow into the sea at Rye and leaving the port of Romney without a harbour. To see just how high the flood waters rose, you have only to visit the splendid Norman **church of St Nicholas**, where the floodmarks can be seen high up on the pillars inside. This disaster was a severe blow to the town's former days of glory as one of the most important of the Cinque Ports.

DYMCHURCH   MAP 5 REF T21
15 miles E of Tenterden on the A259

From Hythe heading along the A259 you can make your way down the coast towards Dymchurch. At various points along the road, you will notice those decidedly odd and not especially attractive buildings, the **Martello Towers**. Looking more like the truncated cooling towers of a modern power station than the pride of Britain's defence against Napoleon, there were at one time 74 of these massive "pepper pots" positioned along the coast. Their name derives from the fact that they were constructed along the lines of a tower at Cape Mortella in Corsica; an ironic choice of model bearing in mind that Napoleon himself was born on that particular island! At one time a quiet, secluded village, Dymchurch has now been transformed into a busy seaside resort. Amusement arcades, giftshops and cafes line the road, and you need to park the car and clamber over the formidable **Dymchurch Wall** before you can even catch a glimpse of the reason why everybody comes here! The sea-wall is the only thing that prevents the sea from flooding both town and marsh - Dymchurch lies about seven and a half feet below high-tide level - and a barrier of one sort or another has existed here since the Romans came to Kent.

BURMARSH   MAP 5 REF T20
17 miles E of Tenterden off the A259

Burmarsh lies at the northern end of the Romney Marsh, and for holidaymakers from the Channel Ports it provides the first glimpse of this remote corner of Kent. A narrow ditch crosses the sometimes flooded marshland meadows and leads to the parish church and the local inn, the Shepherd and Crook. It is in this sort of old-fashioned inn that patrons expect to hear tales of rum-runners, wreckers, owlers or marsh pilots - all of which were terms used to describe local smugglers.

Donkey Street, which twists its way either from Dymchurch and Burmarsh or from West Hythe and Botolph Bridge, leads past **Lathe Barn**, a rural hideaway featuring farmhouse teas, a children's farm and a gift shop. When Janet and Richard Andrew converted an old farm building into a house and tea room in 1979, some sceptics said that their out-of-the-way location took 'off the beaten track' just one stage too far. Of course, this seeming remoteness only adds to the charm, and the farm itself stands in 20 acres of grassland. The Tea Room offers old-fashioned light lunches, mouth-watering scones and cakes and a host of sundaes and ice-cream desserts. The grassland is home

**Lathe Barn, Donkey Street, Burmarsh, Romney Marsh,
Kent TN29 0JN Tel: 01303 873618**

to Fred the donkey and his companions, who include ponies, mature pot-bellied pigs, geese, goats, rabbits, chickens, a peacock, calves and owls. There is a play area for children and a putting green. Open Easter to September.

Dolly Plum Cottage is an idyllic cottage set in beautiful countryside surroundings. Owned by Kay Cowell, this delightful establishment enjoys a fine reputation for hospitality and service. Built at the turn of the century, it is a lovely building with leaded windows adorned with hanging baskets and window boxes. The lawned gardens are just the place to relax and the accommodation comprises three tasteful and comfortable ensuite bedrooms (all non-smoking; all with TV and tea/coffee-making facilities). Most rooms have views of the surrounding countryside and the gardens and orchard to the rear. Sheep graze in the orchard, which is full of apple and plum trees - hence the name Dolly Plum Cottage. The downstairs rear bedroom has views of the lovely water feature in the large pond - this room is also suitable for guests with disabilities. Every room is superbly decorated, each with a different colour theme which gives the room its name. This fine establishment has become known for its delicious breakfasts and warm welcome, with English and foreign visitors returning again and again. Most bookings are by recommendation, and the cottage is known locally as *the* place to stay.

Dolly Plum Cottage Guest House, Burmarsh Road, Burmarsh, Romney Marsh, Kent TN29 0JT Tel: 01303 874558

DOVER Map 5 Ref U20
27 miles E of Tenterden on the A20

The ancient town of Dover is Britain's major cross-Channel port. Known as the "Gateway to England" to those coming in, it is also one of the major routes to Europe for those going out. From here you can take a jetfoil, hovercraft or ferry to Calais, Boulogne, Zeebrugge or Ostend, and your choice of transport will soon be extended to include the new giant catamarans. Dating back to 1180, the massive **Dover Castle** sits astride a high hill above the clifftops, dominating the town from almost every angle. It was here on the site of an Iron Age fort that the Normans built this impressive stronghold during the last years of Henry II's reign at the then colossal cost of nearly £7,000, and today it ranks among the greatest fortresses in Western Europe. Apart from an impressive 19th century scale model of the

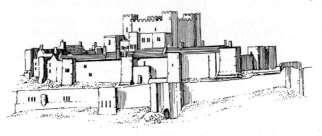

Dover Castle

Battle of Waterloo which is displayed in one of the first floor rooms, the chambers and passage-ways are relatively bare - yet the Castle exerts a forceful presence and it is not hard to visualise it as a busy working garrison, teeming with life.

Of course, Dover has many other attractions besides its castle. One of the most popular of these, **The Roman Painted House**, can be found in New Street in the centre of the town. The main feature of this Roman town house is a complex system of underfloor heating and the most beautifully preserved painted walls. First discovered in 1970, the house has won various awards for the way in which it has been preserved, and excavation is currently still in progress. One of the team, Wendy Williams, has put together a very special display using the features of those who once lived here. Working on the skulls excavated at the site, she has painstakingly built up their features to produce an uncanny group of extremely lifelike faces.

At first sight, the Victorian Town Hall in the High Street may not look as though it warrants any special attention, but if you step inside you will find that it incorporates the magnificent **Maison Dieu**, a hostel for Canterbury pilgrims which was originally founded in 1203. Beneath the building lie the cells of **Dover Old Town Gaol**, now open to the public throughout the year. Starting in the Court Room, your tour will take you back in time to the horrors of prison life during the Victorian era, including a visit to the exercise yard, washroom and cells. The prison-ers and gaolers themselves relate their stories to you, courtesy of 'hi-tech' talking heads and the very latest animation and audio-visual techniques.

FOLKESTONE   Map 5 Ref T20
7 miles W of Dover on the A20

Folkestone is the second busiest cross-Channel port on the south coast. What is most unusual about this particular seaside resort is that it does not have a recognisable seafront as such; instead, it has **The Leas**, a series of delightful clifftop lawns and flower gardens with a distinctly Mediterranean feel to them, which run for a mile and a half from the centre of town towards Sandgate to the west. A water-driven lift takes residents from the clifftop hotels to the beach below, and the warm south-facing aspect makes this a very pleasant area to explore.

Much of Folkestone's history is conveniently condensed into an area known as 'The Lan-terns' on the Sandgate Road. The attractions centred in this part of town are many and varied. **The Bayle** was once the site of an ancient fort, and the lovely 13th century **Church of St Mary and St Eanswythe** (the oldest building in Folkestone) stands nearby. The bones of the latter patron saint are buried here. **Church Street**, formerly called Mercery Lane, was home to the traders of silk and cloth, and William Harvey, one of England's most famous physicians, was born here in 1578. Perhaps Harvey's greatest gift to medicine was his discovery of the circula-tion of the blood; his statue can be seen near the centre of The Leas, appropriately clutching a human heart in his hand. It would seem, however, that all of Harvey's skills in the world of medicine came to naught when it came to his own fate, for he is reputed to have committed suicide in 1657 after discovering that he was going blind.

BARHAM   Map 5 Ref T20
7 miles NW of Dover on the A2

Barham is set in a delightful river valley near the point where the woodlands of the North Downs give way to the flatter agricultural land that leads northwards towards the Isle of Thanet. **Barham Downs** are mentioned in Arthurian legends as the site of a great battle and they were used as a military camp during the time when Britain expected a Napoleonic invasion.

The Old Coach House is a delightful bit of France nestling in the heart of Kent. This superb hotel and restaurant dates back in parts to 1640. Mentioned in one of the first travel guides ever written, in 1780, when it was known as Halfway House (being equidistant between Dover and Canterbury), there's an old Roman way to the rear of the building. Owned and personally run by Jean-Claude Rozard, a professional chef trained in France and Switzerland, this distinguished establishment offers a superb menu making best use of fresh local produce along with shellfish

and other ingredients imported from France to create delicious dishes such as steak au poivre, local game in season, langoustine, soupe de poissons and moules marinière. The 10 spacious ensuite guest bedrooms are decorated in traditional French country style with French furnishings and fabrics - very comfortable and welcoming. Guests are welcome to relax and enjoy the lush 2½-acre gardens.

The Old Coach House, Dover Road, Barham Down,
Kent CT4 6SA Tel: 01227 831218 Fax: 01227 831932

DEAL
8 miles NE of Dover on the A258

MAP 5 REF U20

The charming fishing town of Deal has altered very little in character since the 18th century. The fact that its beach is of shingle rather than sand meant that it escaped Victorian development into a full-blown seaside resort of the "bucket and spade" variety. The fishing trade has always played a major role along this coastline, and the roots of the industry are still very much in evidence today. The seafront is one of the most picturesque to be found anywhere on the Southeast coast, and with its quiet alleyways, traditional cottages and houses (many of them colour-washed), and shingle beach festooned with fishing boats, Deal is a delightful place to explore. The quiet waters just off the coast are known as **The Downs**, and they create a safe natural anchorage for shipping that may otherwise run aground on the treacherous Goodwin Sands. The Sands have been the setting for hundreds of tragic shipwrecks throughout the centuries, and the sad sight of 'drowned' ships with their masts poking above the water is still in evidence at low tide, serving as a permanent reminder of the darker side of the sea. The sands are mentioned in Shakespeare's *The Merchant of Venice* as a place where the eponymous merchant lost one of his ships. As many as 50,000 men may have perished on these Sands, and there are many tales of "ghost ships" having been sighted here.

A good way of learning more about these aspects of the town's past is to take the time to visit its various museums. In St George's Road, in stables once used to house army mules, is the **Maritime and Local History Museum**, where a large collection of models, pictures and other memorabilia relate the maritime history of the town. Also on display are a number of original boats constructed by local boat builders up until the turn of the century. **The Costume and Accessories Museum**, a personal collection of original costumes and accessories put together by Doris Salter, can be found in a private house at 18 Gladstone Road; while in the Town Hall is the **Victoriana Museum**, its displays of toys, dolls, china, ornaments and jewellery from the Victorian and Edwardian eras illustrating the growth of the 19th century souvenir trade.

You should also look out for the distinctive **Timeball Tower** near the (landward) end of the pier. Built in 1795 to give time signals to ships in the Channel, the four-storey tower had a curious device whereby a black copper ball was dropped down its central shaft to register 1.00pm Greenwich Mean Time each day - so sailors would always know when it was lunchtime! The original timeball was replaced by the modern radio time signal, but a replica ball now drops down the shaft on the hour. On the fourth floor of the building there is a museum devoted to time and telegraphy, including working models. Close to the Timeball Tower is **Deal Castle** with its distinctive "lily-pad" shape (you may have to take an aerial trip to fully appreciate this description!), which was built by Henry VIII during the early 1540's. The castle was actually designed to resemble a Tudor Rose, and was the largest in a chain of five coastal defences built along the south-east coast against possible French invasion. The ruins of another of these, **Sandown Castle**, can be seen at the northern end of town; its few remaining buttresses holding out valiantly against the encroaching sea. Deal Castle was built very

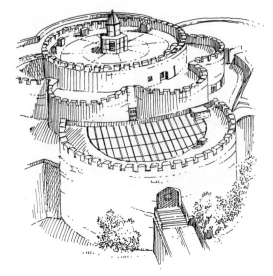

Deal Castle

specifically as a war bastion, and with 119 guns trained across the sea, it must have been a formidable sight. A permanent exhibition here describes Henry VIII's various castles and their defensive role throughout history.

SANDWICH   MAP 5 REF U20

12 miles N of Dover on the A256

Sandwich is one of the ancient Cinque Ports and is a town full of historical interest. It is not a big place, and one of the best ways of seeing it is to follow the **Sandwich Town Trail**. Your starting point is the **Guildhall**, built in 1579 and enlarged in 1912 and in 1973, when the New Hall and offices were added. It is the third Guildhall, the previous one being sited on what is now St Peter's churchyard, and the original having almost certainly stood between King Street and The Chain, in the area behind the Old Parsonage. It is well worth taking the time to seek out some of the fascinating historical pieces here in the Guildhall. One of these is the **Moot Horn**, which is brass and "of great antiquity", and has been used to summon the people of Sandwich to hear important announcements

The Barbican, Sandwich

from as far back as the 12th century. Today, it is still used to announce the death of a sovereign and the accession of the new. Then there is the **Hog Mace**, which, as the name implies, was used to round up straying animals after the Goose Bell had rung from St Peter's Church at 4.00am. All such animals, if not repossessed by their owners on payment of a fine, passed to the Brothers and Sisters of St John's Hospital. The evening curfew at 8.00pm is still rung every day, continuing a tradition going back some 800 years.

As you explore the narrow medieval streets, you will pass many buildings of historical importance; indeed, the entire town centre has been declared a conservation area. Guarding the northern entrance to the town is the **Barbican Gate**, a turreted 16th century gatehouse on the quayside. Sandwich is now almost two miles from the sea, and although its days as a major port have long since passed, it continues to be used as an inland berth by a colourful array of yachts and cruisers. Places that you should make a point of seeing include the Guildhall, the **Dutch House** in King Street, **Strand Street** with its fine timbered houses, Sandwich's three medieval churches, and **St Bartholomew's Hospital** at the far end of New Street, originally founded in the 12th century and consisting of a quadrangle of almshouses grouped around the old chapel.

John Montagu, the 4th Earl of Sandwich, was dissolute and corrupt, but his lasting claim to fame was to order a slice of beef between two pieces of bread as a substitute for a more conventional meal - a snack he could eat without having to leave the gambling table. Thus the Great British Sandwich was born!

CANTERBURY

Map 5 Ref T20

15 miles NW of Dover on the A2

Canterbury is one of the loveliest of England's Cathedral cities. Above the walled city soars the **Cathedral**. Its highlights include the central Bell Harry Tower designed by William Westall in the late15th century; Henry Yevele's lofty nave with its magnificent columns; the Trinity Chapel, which houses the splendid tomb of Edward the Black Prince on the south side, and the canopied tomb and alabaster effigies of Henry IV and his queen on the north side; the great north window; and the spectacular Crypt, the largest of any ecclesiastical building in the world. The

Canterbury Cathedral

Cathedral was founded just after AD 597 by St Augustine after his arrival from Rome. Before his death some seven years later, he had converted large numbers of the native Saxons to Christianity, and Canterbury became the seat of the Mother Church of the Anglicans. Today, the Archbishops of the Cathedral are the Primates of All England, attending all royal functions, and the present incumbent, Dr George Carey, is the 103rd Archbishop of Canterbury. Nothing now remains of the original, pre-conquest buildings; the present Cathedral having been constructed between 1071 and 1500.

This is the Cathedral that witnessed the treacherous murder of Archbishop Thomas Becket on its steps, slain by Henry II's knights. The simple stone marking the spot states that Becket "died here Tuesday 29th December 1170". Although the knights apparently "misinterpreted" the King's wishes, the horror has rung down the centuries, and as you walk through the hushed Cathedral this monstrous act is never far from your mind. A penitent Henry, full of remorse for the death of his former friend, came later as a pilgrim to Becket's shrine. Becket's magnificent tomb was destroyed during the Dissolution of the Monasteries in 1538, but visitors to the Cathedral can still see the Altar of the Swordpoint, commemorating the spot where the sword of one of his assassins shattered on the stone floor.

Canterbury is a compact city, and a short walk in any direction will bring you into contact with some part of its history. As for shopping, there are few cities in England that offer greater variety. Specialist shops of every kind stand side by side with all the familiar high street names (many of these can be found in the attractive covered Marlowe Arcade in St Margaret's Street), and surprisingly, neither look out of place in their medieval surroundings. However, if you can tear your gaze away from the shop windows every once in a while to look up above street level, you will find just as much to delight the eye there too; for although Canterbury's foremost architectural gems are well marked and easy to spot, many surprises crop up in unexpected places and, like the proverbial two-thirds of the iceberg, will elude the unobservant sightseer altogether. A good example of this is the glorious "chequer-board" effect above the entrance to the **Beaney Institute** at the end of the High Street, a splendidly ornate Victorian building which houses the public library, the **Royal Museum** and **Art Gallery**, and the **Buffs Regimental Museum**.

From the bridge you can see the ducking-stool once used to immerse all manner of miscreants - as the sign implicitly warns: "Unfaithful Wives beware; Butchers Bakers Brewers Apothecaries and all who give short measure". The bridge is now a favourite haunt for a motley collection of buskers, who go down well with passing tourists but are not quite so popular with the captive audience of local traders who have become intimately familiar with the repertoire! Opposite The Weavers' you can descend a flight of stone steps below street level to explore the vaults of the 12th century **Eastbridge Hospital**, founded in 1180 by Edward Fitzodbold as a hostel for poor pilgrims visiting St Thomas's tomb. The Poor Priests' Hospital in Stour Street dates back to the 14th century and was used as an almshouse for elderly clergy. It now houses the award-winning **Canterbury Heritage Museum**, which tells the story of the city from Roman times to the present day, making effective use of the latest computer, hologram and audio-visual technology. Highlights include an exciting video on the story of Thomas Becket, made by local celebrity and master-pupeteer Oliver Postgate, creator of many popular children's television programmes; an audio-visual presentation on Canterbury during the Blitz; and displays and memorabilia concerning Mary Tourtel, the creator of Rupert Bear, who was born at 52 Palace Street in 1874. Those who like their history to be liberally spiced with fun should also make a point of visiting **The Canterbury Tales**, which is housed in a medieval church in St Margaret's Street. Here you can enjoy superb re-creations of scenes from life in the Middle Ages, all based on Chaucer's famous stories.

Canterbury is also renowned as a centre for the arts, the main event being the annual **Canterbury Festival** in autumn, when a varied programme of music, drama, dance, film, exhibitions, walks, talks and community events takes place. Among the many places which play host to these events are the **Gulbenkian Theatre** at the University of Kent (reached by heading west from the city centre along St Dunstan's Street and London Road), and Canterbury's major theatrical venue, the **Marlowe Theatre**, re-located in recent years to The Friars, off St Peter's Street.

LITTLEBOURNE   Map 5 Ref T20
3 miles E of Canterbury off the A257

Littlebourne is an attractive village on the banks of the Little Stour, just to the east of Canterbury. It makes an excellent base from which to explore **Howletts Zoo Park**, set in the grounds of Howletts, an 18th century house with an excellent portico. Having built up a collection of animals from around the world John Aspinall opened the Zoo Park in 1975 with the twin aims of displaying exotic animals in well-maintained surroundings as well as breeding them. Today the parklands are the home of nearly 50 species, including the dhole (an Asiatic wild dog) and the Calamian deer from the Philippines.

HERNHILL
Map 5 Ref T19

6 miles W of Canterbury off the A2

Mount Ephraim Gardens

A lovely setting in smiling orchard country gives Hernhill a welcoming aspect, and it is just far enough off the A2 to have a sense of seclusion and tranquillity. In addition to the many commercial orchards in the surrounding countryside there is another horticultural attraction, **Mount Ephraim Gardens**, which comprises 8 acres of garden, including a Japanese rock garden, a small lake, a woodland area and a small walk.

OSPRINGE
Map 5 Ref T19

10 miles W of Canterbury on the A2

Maison Dieu, Ospringe

Ospringe straddles the A2 on the outskirts of Faverhsam but can claim a separate pedigree from its larger neighbour. Here, near the north coast of Kent, was a thriving Roman settlement and there have been numerous coins, medallions and household items unearthed to bear witness to its large population. In the centre of the village, on the corner of Water Lane, is a lovely half-timbered medieval building known as the **Maison Dieu**. It served as a combination hospital and hostel for pilgrims on their way to Canterbury. In parts dating from the 13th century it has stout beamed ceilings dating from the Tudor era. Inside lies a museum tracing the history of the area from Roman times, through the Saxon and Medieval period and including some fascinating information about the house itself.

RECULVER
Map 5 Ref T19

9 miles NE of Canterbury off the A299

From the promenade of Herne Bay, and from many other parts of the coast and certain stretches of the Thanet Way, your eyes will be drawn again and again to the distinctive silhouette of **Reculver Towers**, standing proud above the rocky beach at Reculver like a pair of giant binoculars. Reculver is the site of the Roman *Regulbium*, one of the forts built in the 3rd century AD to defend the shore from Saxon invasion. There are only the scantiest remains of this fortress left now, partly because of the incessant erosion and also because the site was taken over as a place of Christian worship. Typically the earlier structure provided the building materials. The Saxons built a church on the site in the 7th century and five centuries later it was expanded by the Normans. The Normans built the two huge Towers and the west front, which remain almost intact.

MINSTER-IN-THANET   Map 5 Ref U19
12 miles E of Canterbury off the A253

Minster-in-Thanet takes its name from the Isle of Thanet, the northeast corner of Kent which was once separated from the mainland by the Wanstum Channel. It is likely that there were settlements here before the Roman era, and it is generally accepted that the Isle of Thanet was the first landfall for invading Saxons. There are many old buildings in Minster, some of them dating from the Medieval period. **The Old House** was built in 1350 and the **Oak House**, located nearby, is probably almost as old.

One of England's first nunneries was established here in the 7th century, on land granted to Princess Ermenburga, who is usually better known by her religious name of Domneva. The land was granted by her uncle, King Egbert, in as *wergild* (compensation) for the murder of her two brothers by his thane Thunor. The princess demanded such land as could be encompassed by her pet hind at a single run. Thunor, alarmed by the amount of land being covered by the hind and attempting to halt it, fell with his horse into a ditch and was drowned - or so legend has it. In the end the hind completed a course that covered more than 1,000 acres. The story is illustrated in the windows of the parish **Church of St Mary**. The nunnery was later sacked by the Danes and later still came into the hands of the monks of St Augustine's Canterbury. They rebuilt it and added a grange, now called Minster Abbey. Much of the Norman work can still be seen in the cloisters and other parts of the ruins - the Abbey was one of the many victims of Henry VIII's Dissolution.

MARGATE   Map 5 Ref U19
16 miles E of Canterbury on the A28

Margate is a town that fulfils most people's expectations of the typical English seaside resort. Long sweeping stretches of golden sand, promenades, amusement arcades, candyfloss and fun fairs. In bygone days, the resort was a Mecca for the day-tripper from London (greatly assisted by excellent water-transport along the River Thames), and there are still those faithful patrons who come back year after year. The covered bathing machine was invented in Margate in 1753 by a Quaker and glovemaker called Benjamin Beale. **Tudor House**, in King Street, was built in the early 16th century during the reign of Henry VIII, and now contains an exhibition on the human occupation of Thanet from earliest times through to the end of the Tudor period. Half a mile inland on Nash Road is the medieval **Salmestone Grange**, originally a grange or farm of St Augustine's Abbey at Canterbury, and arguably the best-preserved example of a monastic grange in England. The chapel, crypt and kitchen are all open to the public.

Along St Peter's Footpath, off College Road, you can also visit **Drapers Windmill** on Sunday afternoons from late-May to mid-September and on Thursday evenings in July and August. This is a black smock windmill built sometime around 1840, now restored to full working order by the Drapers Windmill Trust. Margate also has two truly "hidden" treasures, to be found within a few hundred yards of each other at the eastern end of town. Firstly, there are the **Margate Caves** with their entrance in Northdown Road; enormous caverns which were cut from the chalk cliffs over 1,000 years ago. Used variously as a refuge, a medieval dungeon and church, and a hiding place for smugglers and their contraband, the Caves are open daily throughout the summer. Nearby, off Northdown Road on Grotto Hill, is the **Shell Grotto**. Do not be misled by the name, which may perhaps conjure up visions of a rather twee collection of shell-studded jewellery boxes, housed in somebody's cellar. In fact, the grotto is thought to have pagan origins, and the underground passages and chambers have been skilfully decorated with literally millions of seashells.

BROADSTAIRS
MAP 5 REF U19

18 miles E of Canterbury on the A255

Broadstairs is probably best known for its associations with Charles Dickens, and visitors who have come in search of Bleak House will find it high up on the cliffs at the northern end of town, overlooking the popular family beach at Viking Bay. The sands of the little harbour here (described by Dickens as "rare good sands") are partly protected by a small 16th century pier, a replacement for one built during the reign of Henry VIII. Other famous people associated with the town include Sir Edward Heath, who was born here in 1916, and another famous sailor, Sir Alec Rose, who lived here for many years. Frank Richards, the creator of "Billy Bunter", also lived in the town, as did John Buchan, whose popular spy thriller, The Thirty-Nine Steps, would become an even more popular film. He wrote the story at a house called St Cuby on Cliff Promenade, and the staircase that gave him his inspiration still stands opposite the house, its 78 steps halved by Buchan to make a better title. Another native of Broadstairs was the eminent Victorian railway engineer, Thomas Russell Crampton. Opposite the railway station you will find the **Crampton Tower**, a railway museum dedicated to his life and work, with exhibits of his blueprints, drawings and photographs. The Broadstairs Stagecoach is also on display, and there is a superb 00 gauge model railway for all you enthusiasts to enjoy.

RAMSGATE
MAP 5 REF U19

18 miles E of Canterbury on the A253

The ancient origins of Ramsgate were as a small fishing village, and this it continued to be until the harbour was built in 1749. In 1822 George IV landed here (the **obelisk** on the East Pier commemorates this historic event), and since that time it has adopted the title of "Royal Harbour". By the end of the 19th century, its fishing fleet had grown to become the largest of any port on the south coast of England, and even though the fishing industry fell into decline at the beginning of the First World War and the future of the harbour began to look uncertain, it was soon to enjoy a brief moment of glory that would earn it a permanent place in the history books. This was in 1940, when over 40,000 British troops evacuated from Dunkirk were landed here, snatched from the jaws of death by the brave armada of "Little Ships". The parish church of St George commemorates this important episode in Ramsgate's and England's history with a special stained glass window.

West of the harbour, in the old West Cliff Hall above the Sally Line ferry terminal, is the **Motor Museum**, where a fascinating range of veteran and vintage cars and motorcycles from Edwardian times to the 1950s are on display. Many famous marques are represented, and there are well over 100 exhibits to enjoy.

WEST SUSSEX

CHICHESTER
MAP 4 REF O21

28 miles E of Southampton off the A27

Chichester, the ancient county town of West Sussex, was founded by the Romans in the 1st century AD. Set on low-lying plains between the coast and the wooded South Downs, the city walls and four major thoroughfares - North, East, South and West Streets - follow the original Roman plan, criss-crossing at the spot where the fine 16th-century Butter Cross now stands. This ornate 50-foot octagonal edifice was built in 1500 by Bishop Edward Story to provide shelter for the many traders who came to ply their wares at the city's busy market. The invading Roman legions used Chichester as a base camp, christening it Noviomagus, the 'new city of the plain'. The city's modern name is derived from Cissa's ceaster (or castle) after the Saxon King Cissa, who ruled this part of Sussex around 500 AD. The city walls, constructed around 200 AD, originally consisted of raised earthwork embankments built in an irregular 11 sided polygon. Alterations and improvements proceeded over the next few centuries; today the city walls date back primarily to medieval times, as can be seen in the large sections that remain on the boundary of the old city. Modern Chichester is home to some first-rate examples of Georgian architecture and town planning. It is a charming and enjoyable place to explore.

Chichester has a long and colourful ecclesiastical history. Although St Wilfrid chose nearby Selsey as the site of the area's first cathedral in the 8th century, the conquering Normans decided to build a new cathedral in its present location at the end of the 11th century. Situated near the corner of West and South streets, the **Cathedral** rests on Roman foundations. Construction began in 1091; the new cathedral was finally consecrated in 1184. Three years later, however, it was almost totally destroyed by fire. The rebuilding programme was undertaken in the 13th century by Richard of Chichester, a venerated bishop who was canonised in 1262 and subsequently adopted as the town's patron saint. Chichester Cathedral is unique on two counts: it is the only medieval English cathedral which can be seen from the sea - rather than being secluded down its own close, as is more usual for cathedrals of this period - and has a detached belfry. This latter was built because it was feared the existing tower was insufficiently sturdy to hold the cathedral bells, and indeed in 1861 the spire blew down in a storm, demolishing a large section of the nave. The present 277 foot spire was designed by pre-eminent ar-

Chichester Cathedral

chitect Sir Gilbert Scott in keeping with the cathedral's original style, and can been seen for miles around in every direction. Inside, the cathedral contains some fine Norman arches, a double aisle, a set of 14th century choir stalls and some excellent modern works of art, including an altar tapestry by John Piper, a painting of Christ appearing to Mary Magdalene by Graham Sutherland, and a stained glass window by Marc Chagall. Other treasures include two of the most important Norman sculptures in Britain: *The Raising of Lazarus* and *Christ Arriving in Bethany*, on the south wall, near the altar, and a glass panel revealing a group of Roman mosaics uncovered during restoration in the late 1980s. Guided tours of the cathedral are possible. The **Prebendal School**, the cathedral choir school and the oldest school in Sussex, stands alongside the main building.

The 13th century **St Mary's Hospital** in St Martin's Square off Priory Road has some unique misericords in its chapel, and a pretty walled garden. This worthy establishment is still used to house 'the deserving elderly of the city'. The warden is pleased to show visitors around the chapel and certain parts of the residents' quarters. Other early buildings in Chichester include **St Olave's Church** in North Street, now a bookshop, and **The Bishop's Palace** (just south of the cathedral), which has delightful and pleasant gardens and a 12th century chapel containing a unique wall painting. (Permission to view this can be obtained from the bishop's office.)

In the post-Roman era, Chichester remained an important administrative centre and market town. Between the 14th and 18th centuries, it was a major trading and exporting centre for the Sussex wool industry, and many handsome merchants' houses remain, especially around St Martin's Square and the elegant Georgian enclave known as The Pallants. **Pallant House** is a fine example of an elegant redbrick town house built in 1713 by the local wine merchant Henry 'Lisbon' Peckham. The building is guarded by a wonderful pair of carved stone dodos and has an unusual observation tower where the owner would look out for his merchant vessels returning laden with goods from the Iberian Peninsula. The kitchen and furnishings of this fine house are Edwardian. Now restored and refurbished as a gallery, Pallant House is home to a collection of modern British art based around the impressive collection bequeathed to the city by the late Dean Hussey, an acknowledged patron of the arts. Exhibits include a lovely collection of Bow porcelain and some fine example of 20thcentury paintings by artists such as Paul Klee, Fernand Leger, Graham Sutherland and John Piper, as well as regular special exhibitions.

Chichester boasts a proud military history and is home to the **Royal Military Police**, or Redcaps, whose museum is open to the public. It can be found on Broyle Road. One of Chichester's most distinctive modern buildings can be found at Oaklands Park, just north of the city walls. Since the hexagonally shaped **Festival Theatre** was opened in 1962, it has built up an international reputation for staging the finest classical and contemporary drama, opera and ballet. The theatre is one of the focal points of the annual Chichester Festival, a two week programme of cultural events which takes place each July. Festivities include classical concerts in the cathedral and fireworks displays at Goodwood Racecourse. Along with Salisbury and Winchester, Chichester also plays its part in the summer Southern Cathedrals Festival. The acclaimed **Chichester District Museum** is located in the area of the city known as Little London. The museum's particularly good collection of Roman relics and artefacts is housed in the interesting former **Guildhall** in Priory Park, which began life as a Grey Friars church in medieval times.

The city is also a haven for all boat lovers and yachtsmen, with a bustling harbour from which you can set off on a boat trip, or alternatively spend some time strolling past some of the fabulous yachts moored in the marina, one of Europe's largest.

TREYFORD HILL MAP 4 REF O21
10 miles NW of Chichester off the B2141

On Treyford Hill a line of rounded mounds known as the **Devil's Jumps** can be seen. The name is derived from the superstitious habit of attributing unusual features in the landscape to the work of Satan. In fact, the five larger and two smaller mounds are bell-barrows - Bronze Age burial sites containing the remains of dead tribal leaders who, having been cremated, were then interred in pottery urns. Some two miles southeast of Treyford, just south of the crest of the South Downs escarpment, the B2146 road passes **Uppark**, a splendid late-17th century country mansion now owned by the National Trust. During the 1880s, H G Wells spent several years at Uppark where his mother was employed as a housekeeper The upper floors were almost completely destroyed by fire in 1989 (ironically just as a programme of restoration was nearing completion), the biggest restoration programme in the history of the National Trust saw it open again in 1995. Remarkably, most of the largely 18th century contents had been saved and put into safe storage. A testament to the restorers' skill, this fine house is always busy, and pre-booking is advisable. The gardens, landscaped in the early 19th century by Humphry Repton, feature a woodland walk and afford fine views towards the Solent.

WEST DEAN MAP 4 REF O21
5 miles N of Chichester off the A286

The beautiful 35 acre **West Dean Gardens** contain old rose species, a 100 yard pergola, wild garden, walled kitchen garden and a fine collection of rare trees, shrubs and stately mature conifers in St Roche's Arboretum and Park. Visitors can enjoy the two mile circular stroll taking in many of the Gardens' treasures. There is also an interesting exhibition of antique lawn mowers dating from 1850, including pony powered mowers and early mechanically driven garden machinery. A mile or so to the south of West Dean, the land rises towards the ancient hilltop site known as **The Trundle**, one of the four main Neolithic settlements in the county. The 12 acre site was later fortified during the Iron Age between 300 and 100 BC when massive circular earthwork ramparts and a dry ditch were constructed. The hill fort has two entrances, arranged in such a way as to expose attackers to defensive fire from above. Named after the Old English word for wheel, the Trundle enjoys fine views over Chichester, Singleton and nearby Goodwood Racecourse.

FISHBOURNE
MAP 4 REF O21
2 miles W of Chichester off the A27

Fishbourne marks the site of the largest non-military Roman building yet to be uncovered in Britain. **Fishbourne Roman Palace** was only rediscovered in 1960 when a new water main was being laid for a proposed housing scheme. The work revealed the remains of a grand and luxuriously fitted Roman villa set around a 250 foot square courtyard. This magnificent villa with its 100 odd rooms was occupied from the 1st to the 3rd centuries AD. It is believed to have been built between 75 and 100 AD for King Cogidubnus of the Atrebates, a leader of the ancient Britons who co-operated with the Romans and took on the role of Viceroy. His reward for collaborating was a palace containing an underfloor heating system, hot baths, a colonnade, an ornamental courtyard garden, and a series of elaborate floor mosaics, wall paintings and Purbeck marble carvings. The building is thought to have been largely destroyed by fire around 320 AD and then abandoned.

Present day visitors to Fishbourne can see the layout of the Roman Palace, including sections of the walls, plumbing and heating systems. They can also admire the remains of some 25 superb floor mosaics (the largest collection in Europe), the most outstanding of which is a 17 foot square panel with a central medallion depicting the winged Cupid sitting astride a dolphin. A recently constructed building protects the remains of the north wing allowing visitors to view the original rooms and corridors from above. There is also an interesting museum on the site describing the history of the palace and its role in the local economy of the day, along with a reconstruction of a 2nd century dining room, a garden laid out according to its 1st century plan, and an informative audio-visual presentation.

BOSHAM
MAP 4 REF O22
3 miles SW of Chichester off the A27

A couple of miles to the southwest of Fishbourne, the idyllic village of Bosham (pronounced Boz-am) stands beside Chichester Harbour on its own small peninsula. An important settlement since the days of the Romans, the Irish monk Dicul established a church here in the 7th century on the foundations of a Roman basilica, predating St Wilfrid's community at Selsey by several years. The village has strong associations with King Canute, whose youngest daughter is thought to have been buried here in the 11th century. (Indeed, a stone coffin containing a child's skeleton was discovered in the floor of the church in 1865).

Bosham's **Quay Meadow** may even have been the site of Canute's infamous confrontation with nature when the dauntless monarch, believing his power and influence to be absolute, ordered the incoming tide to roll back (predictably, he and his courtiers got very wet indeed). Quay Meadow features again a few decades later when King Harold embarked here in 1064 on his abortive journey to appease his rival for the English crown, William, Duke of Normandy. However, Harold's plans went awry when he was taken captive and made to swear to assist William in his claim to the throne, a promise which Harold failed to keep. This forced William into making a return visit and a couple of years later, he landed on the beaches near Hastings with decidedly more successful results. (Harold's Sussex estates were among the first to be seized by the conquering Normans.) Bosham's characteristic Saxon church spire, one of the finest of

Bosham Quay

its kind in the country, is featured alongside Harold's ship on the Bayeux Tapestry.

In more recent times, the painter Rex Whistler was a resident at the Old Ship in 1944, at which time it was an exclusive club. On one of the walls he painted his last work, just two days before meeting his death on the beaches of Normandy. The Bosham of today is a must for those keen on yachting, bird-watching or just relaxing in delightful surroundings. The streets are filled with elegant 17th and 18th century flint and red-brick shops, pubs and residential buildings, those on the sea front having short flights of steps to prevent the occasional invasion of the sea through the front door. An interesting place to visit is the Bosham Walk craft centre and art gallery in Bosham Lane - but be warned: visitors are often tempted to park beside the harbour side road, only to discover their car half-submerged when they return some hours later at high tide.

BOGNOR REGIS

MAP 4 REF P22

5 miles SE of Chichester off the A259

At the end of the 18th century, Bognor was transformed from a quiet fishing village by Sir Richard Hotham, a wealthy London milliner who had ambitions of creating a rival for Brighton, Eastbourne and Bournemouth. He set about constructing some imposing residences, including the Dome in Upper Bognor Road, and even planned to have his creation renamed Hothampton. However, the fashionable set of the day stayed away in droves, and Hotham's dream was never realised - at least not until 1929, when George V convalesced in the town following a serious illness. On the strength of this royal patronage, Bognor was granted the title Regis (of the King). Today, Bognor Regis is a pleasant south coast resort town with some elegant Regency features, traditional public gardens, a children's fun park, a lovely long, sandy beach, a pier and a 'sub-tropical waterworld' at Butlin's South Coast World. The resort hosts the annual Birdman Rally, usually held in August. This competition involves a variety of winged contestants launching themselves off the pier in an attempt to make the longest unpowered flight. There is also an informative local history museum at **Hotham Park Lodge** in the High Street.

LYMINSTER

MAP 4 REF P22

9 miles E of Chichester off the A284

Lyminster is an ancient settlement of flint-built cottages and protective walls which appears (as Lullyngminster) in Alfred the Great's will of 901. A marvellous view of Arundel Castle can be enjoyed from here, this time looking northwest across the water meadows of the lower Arun. Local legend has it that the deep pool known as the Knucker Hole, which lies 100 yards north-west of Lyminster church, was once inhabited by a savage sea dragon. This monster was said to have terrorised the local population to such an extent that the King of Wessex offered half his kingdom and his daughter's hand in marriage to the man who killed the beast. The dragon was finally done away with after a terrible fight, either by a gallant young farm boy known as Jim Pulk, or by a handsome knight, depending on which version of the legend you choose to read. Both versions agree, however, that the ancient tombstone in the north transept of the church is where the conquering hero was finally laid to rest - it is still known today as the Slayer's Stone.

FERRING
MAP 4 REF P22

15 miles E of Chichester off the A27

Ferring, and the nearby coastal communities of **East Preston, Angmering-on-Sea** and **Goring-by-Sea**, have a pleasant suburban air much loved by those in search of a peaceful retirement or holiday. The towns grew rapidly from small fishing villages following the arrival of the railways in the mid-19th century. An impressive avenue of mature ilex oaks connects Ferring with Goring-by-Sea, and the **English Martyrs Catholic Church** in Goring contains an astonishing replica of Michelangelo's Sistine Chapel ceiling, approximately two-thirds the size of the original, completed in 1992 by local craftsman, Gary Bevans. Other relics from the past include **St Mary's** church in East Preston, **St Andrew's** in Ferring, a neat little early English church full of tablets to the Henty and Olliver families, and a sprinkling of old cottages dating from pre-Victorian times. Modern Angmering-on-Sea has a couple of good restaurants and hotels, and East Preston a locally renowned eating place, the Old Forge Restaurant.

MIDHURST
MAP 4 REF O21

12 miles N of Chichester on the A286

Midhurst is a lovely, quiet and prosperous market town which stands on a sandstone rise just to the north of the South Downs, near the junction of the A272 and A286. Its origins lie in the early Middle Ages, and the town has a rich variety of buildings and streets of many types and ages. At St Ann's Hill there can be seen the remains of the once distinguished castle buildings and surrounding earthwork defences, commanding a view of the River Rother. Among the town's many noteworthy buildings are the tall timber-framed **Elizabeth House**, the 15th century **Spread Eagle** coaching inn, and the 19th century **cottage library** in Knockhundred Row. This delightfully named thoroughfare is believed to have been the focal point for the ancient custom of knocking for 100 militia men when there was a call to defend the town. Midhurst's renowned **Grammar School** was founded in 1672 in the16th century timber former Market Hall. Over two centuries later, it was attended by the young H G Wells when his mother was a housekeeper at nearby Uppark House. The town is the setting for several of Wells' short stories; in his autobiography Wells wrote, "Midhurst has always been a happy place for me. I suppose it rained there at times, but all my memories of Midhurst are in sunshine."

On the other side of the Rother in Midhurst stand the ruins of **Cowdray House**, the once magnificent courtyard mansion built of local sandstone in the early 16th century by the Earl of Southampton on the site of an earlier 13th century manor house. Henry VIII

Cowdray Park

stayed at Cowdray in 1538, and later in the century, Elizabeth I was a regular visitor. On one occasion the Queen and her entourage were said to have consumed three oxen and 140 geese during a week-long stay, no doubt making her departure something of a relief for her over-stretched host, Viscount Montague. In 1793, Cowdray House was gutted by fire and a week later, its owner, the last Lord Montague, was drowned while on a visit to Germany. This fulfilled a legendary curse placed on the owners of Cowdray House by a monk evicted from Battle Abbey by the first owner during Henry VIII's Dissolution of the Monasteries. Today, visitors can view the roofless remains of the east side of the quadrangle court, along with parts of the west side where the turreted three-storey gatehouse remains largely intact. The 17,000 acre **Cowdray Park** is one of the largest private estates in Sussex and is a well established venue for polo every weekend and some weekdays from the end of April until mid-July.

FERNHURST   Map 4 Ref O21
4 miles N of Midhurst off the A286

Fernhurst is blessed with a lovely village green surrounded by an assortment of tile-hung cottages. Just to the east, **Black Down** (or Blackdown Hill) rises abruptly from the Sussex Weald. The slopes of this 919 foot National Trust owned sandstone hill are covered in heather, gorse, silver birch and Scots pine, creating an ideal environment for a variety of upland birdlife. The summit of Black Down is the highest point in Sussex; from here there are spectacular views over the Weald and South Downs all the way to the English Channel. A particularly good viewpoint is the group of firs on the southern crest known as the **Temple of the Winds**. One of the paths leading to the top of Black Down is known as **Tennyson's Lane**, after the famous poet who lived for 20 years at Aldworth House on hill's the eastern slope. At one time a Royal Navy signal tower stood on **Tally Knob**, a prominent outcrop which lies to the southeast of the Temple of the Winds. As a development of their tried and tested system of fire beacons, in 1796 the Admiralty introduced the Shutter Telegraph as a more sophisticated means of passing messages between Portsmouth and London. Though ingenious, the system was found to be impractical and was soon abandoned.

STEDHAM   Map 4 Ref O21
1 miles W of Midhurst off the A272

Meadowhills is a small and comfortable country estate offering bed and breakfast accommodation. Attractive and welcoming, this true home from home is near many of the attractions and rural and urban sights of this part of Sussex, including Uppark, Goodwood, Fontwell, Petworth and Chichester. A walker's paradise, guests here also have access to fishing rights along the river. Secluded and peaceful, this lovely home makes for a wonderful place to relax and unwind. The gardens and 25 acres of grounds are filled with birdlife, and there are magnificent views over the South Downs. There are four fine rooms: three twin rooms and a family room. All are Victorian-style, with high ceilings and comfortable decor and furnishings. Two rooms

Meadowhills, Stedham, Midhurst, West Sussex GU29 0PT
Tel: 01730 812609

are en suite, while the other two have private baths. Owner Rosalie Reeves-Fisher is a warm and conscientious host, who makes every effort to ensure that guests have a pleasant stay at her rambling country home.

BEPTON

MAP 4 REF O21

3 miles SW of Midhurst off the A286

Park House is a distinguished and distinctive hotel set in the small downland village of Bepton. This peaceful and luxurious country retreat has been offering accommodation and a warm welcome to guests for over 50 years. Privately run by the O'Brien family, it is renowned for its relaxed atmosphere. This fully licensed hotel provides the perfect base from which to explore the outstanding surrounding natural beauty and all local attractions, including Goodwood, Cowdray Park, and Chichester. There are 10 lovely guest rooms in the main house, an annex with two double bedrooms and its own private sitting room, and the two-bedroomed Bay Tree Cottage. All rooms have private bath and all modern facilities. Within the secluded landscaped gardens guests are welcome to enjoy a range of activities.

Park House, Bepton, Midhurst, West Sussex GU29 0JB
Tel: 01730 812880 Fax: 01730 815643

There are two grass tennis courts, a nine-hole par three pitch and putt course, croquet and putting lawns, and a heated outdoor swimming pool. The adjacent old Sussex barn has been handsomely converted and refurbished to house the lovely Ione Gallery, displaying a range of artwork and sculpture by local artists.

SOUTH HARTING

MAP 4 REF O21

7 miles W of Midhurst off the B2141

South Harting, with its ancient thatched cottages, flint walls and unusually wide main street of fine Georgian houses and 17th century cottages, must be one of the most attractive villages in the South Downs. A twisting three mile journey from Habin Bridge, South Harting is the largest of the three settlements known collectively as the Hartings. Writer Anthony Trollope spent the last two years of his life here, during which time he created four novels. A pen and paper-knife belonging to the acclaimed 19th century novelist can be seen in the village **Church of St Mary and St Gabriel.** South Harting's famous church spire is faced with copper shingles, creating a bright verdigris hue which can be seen for miles. Memorials in the church include several to the former owners of the nearby downland estate, Uppark, including one to Sir Henry Fetherstonhaugh. The distinctive war memorial in the churchyard was carved in Portland stone by the renowned modern sculptor and typographer, Eric Gill. Near the entrance to the churchyard, an ancient set of parish stocks can also be found, along with a whipping post complete with three pairs of wrist irons.

South Harting stands at the foot of **Harting Down** beneath the steep scarp slope of the South Downs ridge. The ridge is traversed by the **South Downs Way**, the spectacular long-distance footpath which stretches for nearly 100 miles from Winchester and Buriton in the west to Beachy Head in the east. Here, the path skirts around **Beacon Hill**, which at 793 feet above sea level is one of the highest points in the Downs. A 2,500 year old rectangular Iron Age hill fort surrounds the summit; there are spectacular views from the surviving ramparts over the Weald to the north and as far as Chichester's harbour and Cathedral to the south. This very pretty village is also a good setting off point for scenic drives along the B2141 and B2146, and the South Downs footway through East Harting, Elsted and Cocking.

PETWORTH   MAP 4 REF P21
5 miles E of Midhurst off the A272

Five miles east of Midhurst off the A272, the historic town of Petworth stands on the crest of a sandstone ridge. Between the 14th and 16th centuries, Petworth was an important cloth-weaving centre; a number of fine merchants' and landowners' residences, including Daintrey House, North House and Tudor House, can be seen in its narrow streets. The cramped Market Place contains a fine late 18th century arcaded town hall and a striking bank building, the National Westminster, built in baroque style in 1901. Other noteworthy buildings include the Somerset Almshouses (or Upper Hospital), built in 1746 for 12 widows, each of whom received a princely pension of 10 pounds per year.

The most dominant feature of Petworth is the grand house and park which together make up the National Trust-owned **Petworth Estate**. Surrounded by a wall over 13 miles long, the 700-acre **Petworth Park** was landscaped by Lancelot 'Capability' Brown in the 1750s. The sweeping grounds contain many stately trees, a lake and deer park, and command views still recognisable as those celebrated by Turner. **Petworth House** was built between 1688 and 1696 on the site of a 13th century manor house, the present building incorporating the original medieval chapel and hall undercroft. The house, with its magnificent 320 foot west front, was built in French style on the instructions of Charles, Sixth Duke of Somerset. The design has been attributed to the Architect Daniel Marot, except for the south front which was added in 1869-72 to a design by Anthony Salvin. The magnificent galleries and state rooms of this splendid old house are filled with one of the finest art collections in the country, including works by Dutch old masters such as Rembrandt and Van Dyck, and 20 paintings by Turner, a frequent visitor in his day. Other work on show includes paintings by Holbein, Blake, Reynolds and Gainsborough. Additional treasures are the grand staircase with its elegant frescoes and some outstanding examples of the work of the master carver, Grinling Gibbons.

Returning to the A285 and crossing the River Rother at Coultershaw Bridge, one of the earliest pumped water systems was installed here in 1790 to pipe water the two mile distance to Petworth. The **Coultershaw Water Wheel and Beam Pump** is now a scheduled ancient monument which has been restored to working condition by the Sussex Industrial Archeology Society. The beam pump can still be seen in operation, and there is also an exhibition giving some interesting background information on water supply, pumps and local natural history.

BIGNOR   MAP 4 REF P21
5 miles S of Petworth off the A285

Bignor's central thoroughfares are arranged in an uneven square. The village contains some wonderful domestic buildings, including the photogenic 15th century Old Shop - a two-storey thatched house whose ramshackle timber-framed walls are infilled with brick, flint and plaster. Bignor is best known for having been the administrative centre of a large Roman agricultural estate, the focus of which was a sizable villa which was accidentally uncovered by a farmer's plough in 1811. Excavations revealed the foundations of **Bignor Roman Villa**, one of the largest villas discovered so far. A grand courtyard residence covering four and a half acres which was inhabited between the 1st and 4th centuries, the most striking feature of the building is its floor mosaics. These include depictions of gladiators, Diana, Venus, Ganymede and Medusa, and in the north corridor, there is an 82 foot mosaic pavement which is the longest of its type in the British Isles. Visitors can see excavations going on in summer. **Stane Street**, the remarkably straight Roman road which once connected the important administrative centre of Londinium with the port of Chichester, 57 miles away, now confined to just a path, cuts right across the beautiful downland nearby.

PULBOROUGH

Map 4 Ref P21

5 miles E of Petworth off the A29

The ancient settlement of Pulborough stands a mile or so from the confluence of the Rivers Arun and Rother. This scattered community was founded by the Romans as a staging post, or mansio, on Stane Street, the arterial road which once connected London with Chichester. Despite its strategically important location beside the Arun river crossing, Pulborough failed to grow like some of its rivals, and today it remains a sizable village which is perhaps best known for its excellent freshwater fishing. It also retains some fine early buildings; **Walberton House** (1803) was designed by Robert Smirke, the architect of the British Museum in London.

The magnificent **Parham Park**, probably the finest Elizabethan country house in Sussex, stands in the heart of a great deer park on an open plateau at the foot of the South Downs ridge. Designed in the classic 'E' shape, the mansion was built in the 1570s for Sir Thomas Palmer, a wealthy cloth merchant, on the site of a smaller monastic house which once belonged to Westminster Abbey. Parham contains one of the finest Elizabethan interiors in the country. The magnificent state rooms, including the 160 foot Long Gallery, Great Hall and Great Parlour, feature mullioned windows and wood panelled walls, and are furnished with an exceptional collection of period furniture, oriental carpets, rare needlework and fine paintings. The house is surrounded by seven acres of wooded parkland containing a statue garden, lake, picnic enclosure and a beautiful four acre walled garden with traditional herb beds. The diminutive church of St Peter stands close to the main house; rebuilt early in the 19th century, its interior features carved ceilings, an unusual lead font and a set of high box pews. The squire's pew had its own fireplace which he was reputed to stoke loudly when the vicar's sermon was becoming tiresome.

AMBERLEY

Map 4 Ref P21

6 miles S of Petworth off the B2139

The ancient settlement of Amberley consists of a delightful assortment of flint, brick, stone, timber and thatched cottages spread out below the steep scarp slope of the South Downs ridge. The village church of St Michael is thought to have been founded by St Wilfrid, the missionary who converted the South Saxons to Christianity. Rebuilt in the 12th century by Bishop Luffa of Chichester at around the same time as Chichester Cathedral, the church interior contains some strong Norman features. The murals to the right of the chancel arch date from the time of a further remodelling in the 13th century. The five bells in the tower, hung in 1742, are said to have the sweetest peal in the land. Nearby **Amberley Castle** began life in the 12th century as a fortified summer palace for the bishops of Chichester. More a manor house than a castle, alterations over the centuries have included the construction of a great curtain wall to enclose the entire manorial site. Charles II is believed to have stayed here en route to a safe haven in France following his defeat at the Battle of Worcester in 1651. The building now operates as a privately run hotel and restaurant. The series of water meadows to the north of the village are known as the **Amberley Wild Brooks**. Often flooded and inaccessible by car, this 30 acre conservation area and nature reserve is a haven for bird, animal and plantlife. Trains on the Arun Valley line cross the marshes along specially constructed embankments which were considered engineering marvels of their day when the line was opened in 1863. Amberley railway station lies a mile to the southwest of the village at Houghton Bridge, the point where the South Downs way crosses the River Arun.

Houghton Bridge is also the location of the renowned **Amberley Chalk Pits Museum**, a working museum of industrial history featuring a narrow gauge industrial railway, a collection of vintage motor buses, and a range of workshops which offer live demonstrations of traditional rural trades, including blacksmithing, pottery-making, printing, boat-building and ironmongery. This fascinating 36 acre open air museum is a must for all those with an interest in industrial archeology or transport history. During the 18th and 19th centuries, chalk was quarried at Amberley for shipping to the many lime kilns which could then be found throughout the lime-deficient farming areas of southern England. Later, large quantities of chalk were needed to supply a new industrial process which involved the high-temperature firing of chalk with small amounts of clay. The revolutionary product resulting from this process was named "Portland Cement", and the Amberley Chalk Pits Museum includes an exhibition on the background and history of this invaluable building material.

STEYNING
MAP 4 REF P21
15 miles SE of Petworth off the A283

Now a prosperous small country town, Steyning was founded in the 8th century by St Cuthman who, according to local legend, settled here as a boy after the cart in which he was pushing his invalid mother broke down on a journey from the West Country. St Cuthman went on to build a timber church in which Ethelwulf, father of King Alfred, is believed to have been buried. In the 12th century, the Saxon structure was replaced by the fine Romanesque church of St Andrew, which at one time was part of a larger monastic house belonging to the abbey at Fecamp in Normandy. Despite its unexceptional outward appearance, the building has a striking interior with towering Norman columns, a 12th century marble font and some impressive carved stonework.

By the late Saxon period, Steyning had grown to become an important port on the then navigable estuary of the River Adur, but around 1100, the silting up of the river forced the quay to close. However, the community had become sufficiently established by then to sustain itself as a small market town; many of the fine late medieval buildings which survive in High and Church Streets were constructed in a variety of styles and materials in the centuries which followed. Indeed, Steyning is filled with exceptional examples of early domestic buildings, and is home to 125 listed buildings. There are examples of several 14th- and 15th-century "hall" type houses, such as the **Post Office** and **Penfold Cottage**, and "Wealden" cottages, such as **Workhouse Cottage** in Mouse Lane. Another outstanding structure is Steyning's famous **Old Grammar School** which was founded in 1614 in a long timber-framed building in Church Street; this has a characteristic overhanging upper storey and a roof covered with thin slabs of Horsham stone, and is now used as a school library. A good place to discover more about the town's long and eventful history is the **Steyning Museum** in Church Street.

Steyning's close proximity to the South Downs Way and the Downs Link, the long-distance bridleway which follows the course of the old railway line to Christ's Hospital near Horsham and on to Guildford, makes this lovely village an excellent base for walking and riding holidays. The same can be said of Bramber, the former Norman administrative centre and garrison town which lies beside the Adur, one mile to the east.

BRAMBER
MAP 4 REF P21
5 miles SE of Petworth off the A283

Following the Norman Invasion, William the Conqueror granted the land at Bramber to his trusted lieutenant, William de Braose, who erected a wooden keep on top of a prominent chalky outcrop beside the river. Around 1070 the timber structure was replaced by stone fortifications which included a gatehouse and a number of domestic buildings surrounded by a curtain wall - **Bramber Castle** became an important stronghold which was visited by, among others, King John and Edward I; however, the town's subsequent decline and the effects of Parliamentarian cannon-fire reduced most of the castle to rubble except for the conspicuous 75 foot high section of the gatehouse keep which can be seen today. William de Braose was also responsible for building the chapel at the foot of the castle mound in 1075, now the parish church of St Nicholas.

Despite a number of major alterations throughout the centuries, the original nave and church tower remain.

In the 15th century the lands of the de Braose family were transferred to Magdalen College, Oxford, whose founder, William Wayneflete, the then Bishop of Winchester, constructed the striking medieval residence in Bramber known as **St Mary's** in 1470. This Grade I listed building, with its classic half-timbered Wealden facade, has a fine wood-panelled room with Elizabethan trompe l'oeil painting and medieval shuttered windows. Originally built as a monastic hospital to serve pilgrims en route along the South Downs Way to Canterbury, it was at one time inhabited by the monastic wardens of the adjacent bridge over the River Adur, a structure which until the 1470s had an unusual chapel at its centre. The King's Room is believed to have been Charles II's last sleeping-place on his flight from the Battle of Worcester before he embarked for the ship waiting to take him from Shoreham to safe exile in France. Recently restored, today's visitors to St Mary's can view the magnificent interior and exterior, including the topiary garden, before enjoying homemade refreshments in the music room.

Before the Reform Act of 1832 swept away the so called rotten boroughs, the tiny constituencies of Bramber, Steyning and Shoreham each returned two MPs to Westminster. This was in spite of the fact that at one time Bramber had only 32 eligible voters. One MP who benefited from the unreformed system was William Wilberforce, who was more or less 'awarded' one of the Bramber seats in recognition for his campaigning work against slavery and social injustice; he is said to have made only one fleeting visit to his constituency during the whole of his 12 year tenure.

ARUNDEL   Map 4 Ref P21
9 miles S of Petworth off the A27

A settlement since pre-Roman times, Arundel stands at the strategically important point where the major east-west land route through Sussex crosses the River Arun. One of William the Conqueror's most favoured knights, Roger de Montgomery, first built a **castle** on the high ground above the river. This was similar to the castle at Windsor in that it consisted of a motte and double bailey, a plan which, despite several alterations to the fabric of the building, remains largely unaltered to this day.

The period of stability the castle brought to the town in the late medieval period made Arundel into an important port and market town. It was during this era that the 14th century parish church of St Nicholas was built, a unique building in that it is now divided into separate Catholic and Anglican areas by a Sussex iron screen. The Fitzalan Chapel in the choir houses the tombs of the Catholic Earls of Arundel and Dukes of Norfolk, in whose family the castle has remained for the past 500 years; entry to this section can normally only be made through the castle grounds.

During the English Civil War, Parliamentarian forces bombarded the castle using cannons fired from the church tower. This bombardment led to the destruction of most of the Norman fortifications, the only parts to survive being the 12th cen-

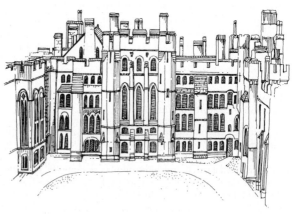

Arundel Castle

tury shell keep on the central mound and parts of the 13th century barbican and curtain wall. The rest of the structure remained in ruins until a programme of restoration during the 1790s made the castle habitable once again. (One of the finest rooms in Arundel Castle, the mahogany lined library, dates from this period.) A second restoration, amounting to a virtual rebuilding, was carried out about 100 years later by the 15th Duke, funded by profits from the family's ownership of the newly prosperous steel town of Sheffield. Most of the colossal structure which can be seen today is therefore a 19th century Gothic reproduction. However, the state apartments and main rooms contain some fine period furniture dating from the 16th century, a fine collection of tapestries, and paintings by such artists as Reynolds, Van Dyck, Gainsborough, Holbein and Constable. The nearby 1,000 acre Arundel Castle grounds are also open to the public.(Please note that the castle is closed during the winter months.)

Despite religious persecution, particularly during the 16th century, the Fitzalan family and the successive Dukes of Norfolk remained staunchly Roman Catholic. The 15th Duke, who was responsible for the 19th century rebuilding of the castle, also commissioned the substantial Catholic church of St Philip Neri which was designed in French Gothic style by J A Hansom and Son, the inventors of the Hansom cab, in 1870. In 1965, this impressive building became the seat of the Catholic bishopric of Brighton and Arundel, and was renamed the Cathedral of Our Lady and St Philip Howard. (St Philip Howard was the 13th Earl of Arundel who died in prison after being sentenced to death by Elizabeth I for his Catholic beliefs; his remains are now in the cathedral, along with an impressive memorial shrine.) Each June, the cathedral hosts the two-day Corpus Christi Festival during which the entire length of the aisle is laid out with a carpet of fresh flowers.

Other historic sites in Arundel include the **Maison Dieu**, a medieval hospital which can be found outside the Mill Road lodge of Arundel Castle. Founded in 1345 by Richard Fitzalan and dissolved by Henry VIII in 1546, this semi-monastic institution combined the roles of clinic, hotel and almshouse. The heart of the old town contains some fine Georgian and Victorian houses and inns, most notably in Maltravers and Tarrant Streets. The parish chuch dates from the 14th century. Arundel also contains a couple of interesting museums; the privately-owned **Arundel Toy and Military Museum** is located in a charming Georgian cottage in the High Street known as the Doll's House. Inside, visitors can see a unique collection of antique dolls, teddy bears, puppets, games, boats, tin toys and around 3,000 toy soldiers. Further along the High Street, the **Arundel Museum and Heritage Centre** gives an fascinating insight into the people and activities of the town through imaginative use of models, old photographs and historic artefacts.

Another good place to visit lies about two miles north of Arundel on the A284 road to Offham and South Stoke. The 60 acre woodland site run by the **Wildfowl and Wetlands Trust** contains a wide variety of ducks, geese, swans and other wildfowl from all over the world. Many of the birds can be viewed at close quarters, with Arundel Castle providing a dramatic backdrop. There is also an award-winning visitor centre with a viewing gallery, gift shop and restaurant.

HORSHAM
MAP 4 REF P20
14 miles NE of Petworth off the A24

The historic town of Horsham, which takes its name from a Saxon term meaning *horse pasture*, was founded in the mid 10th century. By the 13th century, Horsham had grown into a prosperous borough and market town which was considered sufficiently important to send two members to the new Parliament established in 1295. Between 1306 and 1830, Horsham took it in turns with Lewes and Chichester to hold the county assizes. During the weeks the court was in session, large numbers of outsiders were attracted into the town, which would take on something of a carnival atmosphere. Public executions were sometimes carried out on **Horsham Common** or at the Carfax (today a thriving pedestrianized shopping area), including one in 1735 of a man who refused to speak at his trial and was subjected to 'death by compression'. Three hundred weight of stones were placed on his chest for three days. When he still refused to speak the goaler added his own weight, killing the man outright. The last such execution of its kind in England took place in Horsham in 1844. During the 17th century, Horsham's county gaol was also used to accommodate members of the much persecuted Society of Friends. The old part of Horsham consists of a long wedge shaped former green, with the part-Norman 12th century **Church of St Mary** at one end. Stretching between the two is a unique walkway known as The Causeway; approached down a narrow passage called Pump Alley. Many of the town's finest buildings are located in the Causeway, including the town hall with its facade built by the Duke of Norfolk in 1812, the Manor House, headquarters of the RSPCA, and the 15th century King's Head Hotel. One of the finest examples of a timber-framed Sussex town house can be seen at **30 The Causeway**, whilst at No. 9, the Tudor built Causeway House is the location of the impressive **Horsham Museum**.

Horsham

HANDCROSS
MAP 4 REF Q21

4 miles E of Horsham off the A279

Handcross is home of the celebrated National Trust-owned **Nymans Garden**. Set around the ruins of a country mansion, this splendid 30 acre landscaped area is one of the great gardens of the Sussex Weald, with rare and beautiful plants collected from all corners of the world. The walled garden, with its fountain, the hidden sunken garden, old rose garden, topiary garden, laurel walk, pinetum and woodland walks make Nymans a delight all year round. Together, these contain a wonderful collection of specimen trees, shrubs and flowering plants, many of which are native to other continents. In 1997, a few rooms in Nymans house were opened to the public for the first time, affording insight into the family who first created this extraordinary garden. Another natural beauty in Handcross is **High Beeches Gardens Conservation Trust** - 20 acres of wonderful landscaped woodland and water gardens.

LOWER BEEDING
MAP 4 REF Q21

4 miles SE of Horsham off the A279

A distinctive hammer pond can be found just to the north of Lower Beeding on the southern fringe of **St Leonards Forest**. This 10,000 acre wooded heath is one of the few treed areas to survive the long-term ravages of the timber fuelled iron industry. Rising in places to around 500 feet, the forest lies on the undulating sandstone ridge bounded by Horsham, Crawley and Handcross. According to local folklore, St Leonards Forest is the home of a legendary nine foot dragon which roamed the heath and terrorised the surrounding villagers. Coincidentally, the bones of a prehistoric iguanodon have since been discovered in the Forest by the Sussex-based geologist, Dr Gideon Mantell.

HENFIELD
MAP 4 REF Q21

9 miles S of Horsham off the A281

Henfield was once an important staging post on the busy London to Brighton coaching route. The village contains a couple of good former coaching inns, a much restored church built on Saxon foundations, and an eccentric 16th century cottage known as the **Cat House** which is decorated with a collection of highly unusual iron cats. These were made by local joiner Bob Ward to scare off the vicar's cat after it had crept in and eaten his pet canary.

The **Henfield Village Museum** in the village hall contains an interesting collection of historic artefacts including agricultural tools, costumes, local paintings and photographs, illustrating life in a rural area from medieval times to the present day. The impressive headquarters of the **Sussex Wildlife Trust** are situated a mile to the south of Henfield at Woods Mill. Set within a 15 acre nature reserve, this three storey 18th century water mill contains a fascinating exhibition on the natural history of the locality.

POYNINGS
MAP 4 REF Q21

11 miles S of Horsham off the A23

At no other place are the Downs more dramatic than above the village of Poynings; this is the location of the famous local landmark, **Devil's Dyke**, a steep-sided dry ravine which, according to folklore, was dug by Satan in an unsuccessful attempt to flood the Christian churches of the Weald with the sea. At almost 700 feet above sea level, the 15 acre promontory above Devil's Dyke forms an easily defendable site on which the Iron Age people built a formidable hill fort. A high earthwork wall was built to defend the gently sloping southwestern approaches of the fortifications, the remains of which can still be seen today (indeed, the course of the present day road passes through the original fort entrance).

A little further along the South Downs Way, and inaccessible by road, lie two delightful areas of National Trust-owned downland which are worth making the effort to reach, **Fulking Escarpment** and **Newtimber Hill**.

CLAYTON
MAP 4 REF Q21

11 miles SE of Horsham off the A273

This unusual village has a parish church containing a series of 12th century wall murals which are thought to be by the same group of artists from the St Pancras Priory in Lewes who were responsible for those at Hardham and Coombes. Rediscovered in the 1890s, the murals depict some salutary scenes of eternal damnation from the Last Judgement. A unique pair of windmills known as **Jack and Jill** stand above the village on Clayton Hill. A couple of interesting country houses also lie within easy reach of Clayton: **Danny**, a characteristic E-shaped manor house with an impressive great hall, lies one mile to the northwest, and **Newtimber Place**, a moated flint and brick-built residence, lies on the western side of the A23 a couple of miles to the west.

ARDINGLY
MAP 4 REF Q21

10 miles E of Horsham off the B2028

The imposing redbrick edifice of **Ardingly College** (pronounced Arding-lye), the famous public school which, like Lancing College, was founded by the pioneering churchman Nathaniel Woodard, is roughly a mile and a half from the parish church in Ardingly village, which contains some fine monumental brasses of the Wakehurst and Culpeper families, the former owners of nearby Wakehurst Place. To the west of the village, a tributary of the River Ouse has been dammed to form **Ardingly Reservoir**, a 200 acre lake which offers some good fishing.

On a permanent site to the northwest, the three day South of England Show takes place each year in early June. As well as being the venue for the region's premier agricultural event, the showground hosts a range of other attractions, including showjumping competitions and antiques' fairs. Situated beside the B2028 a mile and a half north of Ardingly, the National Trust-owned **Wakehurst Place** is sometimes referred to as 'Kew in the Country'. This beautiful Elizabethan country mansion and estate was originally built for Sir Edward Culpeper in 1590 and is now managed by the Royal Botanic Gardens, Kew. The grounds contain an unrivalled collection of rare trees, flowering shrubs and plants which are laid out in a variety of imaginative settings; there is a rich diversity of formal gardens, natural woodland, wetland, fields and meadows. A picturesque water course links a series of ponds and lakes along a nature trail providing an important conservation resource for the plants and animals of the Sussex Weald.

WEST HOATHLY
MAP 4 REF Q20

10 miles E of Horsham off the B2028

West Hoathly (sometimes pronounced Hoath-lye, sometimes Hoath-lee) stands at an ancient road junction almost 600 feet up on a ridge of the High Weald. This historic settlement has some panoramic views of the South Downs. It also contains some outstanding old buildings: the Norman church was founded around 1090 and rebuilt in the 13th century, the Cat Inn was the haunt of smugglers in the 18th century, and the stone-built **Gravetye Manor** was constructed around 1627 for a local iron-master and is now a first-class country house hotel.

Perhaps most exceptional, however, is the **Priest House**, a delightful early 15th century Wealden hall-house, timber-framed and with a hefty Horsham 'slate' roof, set in a classic English country garden. The house was originally built with a large open hall, but was altered to its present layout in Elizabethan times; inside, there is a fine collection of 18th and 19th century furniture and a charming museum of village life. The building is owned by the Sussex Archeological Society and is open to the public.

COPTHORNE
MAP 4 REF Q20

12 miles NE of Horsham off the A264

Not far from London's Gatwick Airport yet peaceful and tranquil for all that, **"Linchens"** is a very pretty and comfortable house offering bed and breakfast accommodation. Owner Sally Smyth is a welcoming and attentive host, who makes every effort to ensure that all her guests have a relaxing and enjoyable stay. There are three delightful guest bedrooms in this unusually Y-shaped house, which sees the living area in the centre of the building. Set in three and a half acres of manicured lawns fringed by woodland to the rear, there is a lovely front garden and patio. The large and comfortable guests' sitting room boasts

"Linchens", Heron Close, New Domewood, Copthorne, West Sussex RH10 3HF Tel/Fax: 01342 713085 website: www.linchens.com

wonderful views from the large balcony. Each room is tastefully furnished and decorated to a high standard of comfort and quality. There's a special "collect and return" service to and from Gatwick or the railway or coach/bus stations. Guests can leave their car at the B&B, taking this special service to the airport.

EAST SUSSEX

BRIGHTON
MAP 4 REF Q21

27 miles E of Chichester on the A27

Before Dr Richard Russell of Lewes published his famous dissertation on "The Use Of Sea Water In Diseases Of The Glands" in 1753, Brighton was a small and unassuming fishing village which went under the name of Brighthelmstone. Dr Russell's ideas gradually gained favour amongst the rich and influential until, in 1783, the fashionable status of the town was affirmed when the Prince of Wales chose to sample the beneficial effects of the new resort for himself. The young prince, who was later to become Prince Regent and then George IV, was so taken with the place that he decided to build a permanent **Royal Pavilion** in the resort. Initially a small farmhouse, it was enlarged and added to over the years. In 1787, architect Henry Holland designed a classical style building with a dome and rotunda; in 1815, John Nash, the architect responsible for London's Regent's Park and the Mall, was asked to carry out a major renovation. Nash came up with a radical and exotic scheme based on an Indian maharajah's palace complete with minarets, onion shaped domes and pinnacles (not to everyone's liking, the upper part of the new building was once unkindly described as 'a large Norfolk turnip with four onions'). Inside, the flavour of the building moves from the Indian subcontinent to the Far East in what must be one of the finest examples of Regency chinoiserie in the world. The nearby **Dome** was once an arena for exercising the royal horses and is now a major concert venue; the Prince Regent's former tennis courts were converted into Brighton's acclaimed **Museum and Art Gallery**. Among its marvellous displays are art-nouveau and art-deco furniture and decorative art, musical instruments, fashion and costume, 18th and 19th century porcelain and pottery, and paintings by both English and European masters.

The Royal Pavilion

The town contains a number of other splendid Regency developments, most of which are dotted along the seafront on either side of the old medieval centre. Among the better known are Bedford Square, Regency Square, Russell Square, Kemp Town and, perhaps most famous of all, **Royal Crescent**. A hidden place which may be of interest to those keen on antique toys and model railways is situated in the arches underneath Brighton station.

The **Sussex Toy and Model Museum** includes collections of trains, aircraft, cars, soldiers, forts, teddy bears and dolls. One of Brighton's lesser known attractions is **Preston Manor**, a 13th century manor house which is set within beautiful landscaped grounds on the northern approaches to the town. The house was rebuilt in the 1730s and was left to the people of Brighton in 1932 on condition that it would remain an 'English country home'.

HOVE
MAP 4 REF Q21

1 mile W of Brighton off the A259

Genteel Hove is famous for its Regency squares - Brunswick and Palmeira to name but two - broad tree-lined avenues and sweeping lawns. Formerly a peaceful fishing village, major development occurred in the early 19th century when the seafront was built with its distinctive terraces painted in the colour known as Hove Regency Cream. **Hove Museum and Art Gallery**, located in a grand villa, features English paintings, pottery, glass, coins, medals, Victorian toys and an exhibition on the history of Hove. Outside, the Jaipur Gate is a large wooden pavilion transported from Rajashtan to London in 1886; it came to Hove in 1926. The **British Engineerium** is a museum containing exhibits of models, printing presses, hand tools and full size working steam traction engines, all housed in a former pumping station. As well as architectural treats, Hove is home to the lovely **Hove Park** and **St Ann's Well's Gardens**. A unique view of the Downs can be seen through a camera obscura at the **Foredown Tower Countryside Centre** on the outskirts of Hove.

DITCHLING
MAP 4 REF Q21

6 miles N of Brighton off the B2116

The lands around the historic village of Ditchling were once part of a royal estate belonging to King Alfred, who is also believed to have owned a small palace here. The parish church of St Margaret of Antioch has a shingled Sussex Cap spire and was rebuilt in Caen stone, flint and chalk in the 13th century (it was again much altered during the 1860s). Inside are rare chalk carvings and a Norman treasure chest. Opposite the church gate stands **Wings Place**, an unusual Tudor house built of flint, timbering and brickwork which is also referred to as **Anne of Cleves House**. This is because it is thought to have formed part of Henry VIII's divorce settlement with his fourth wife, although there is no evidence of her ever having stayed here. Old Ditchling is arranged around an ancient road junction; the area to the west of this contains some exceptional early buildings. **Cotterlings** dates from the Regency period and has a striking facade of redbrick window surrounds interspersed with black glazed tiles, **Pardons** has an unusual gazebo in the grounds, and **Court Farm** incorporates a village green and the foundations of an old tithe barn. The Five Mile Act of 1665 which banned Non-conformist worship within five miles of a town made Ditchling into something of a religious centre; the **Old Meeting House** in the Twitten is a handsome survivor from this period.

During the 1920s, Ditchling became home to a lively group of artists, printers and Bohemians whose number included Eric Gill, Sir Frank Brangwyn and Edward Johnston. The village is still inhabited by a thriving population of artists and craftspeople whose work can be seen in Ditchling's many studios, galleries and antique shops. Visitors wanting to discover more about the locality's long and interesting history should make a point of calling in at the superb **Ditchling Museum**, located in the Victorian former village school.

To the north of the village, Ditchling Common Country Park is a 188 acre nature reserve and beauty spot, with a lake, stream and nature trail. Nearby, the long-distance **Sussex Border Path** follows roughly the border between West and East Sussex. To the south of Ditchling, the land rises sharply onto the 813 foot summit of **Ditchling Beacon**, the third highest point in the South Downs. Once the site of a Neolithic hill fort and later, an Admiralty fire beacon, on a clear day this long established vantage point offers a 30 mile view northwards across the Weald to the North Downs.

LEWES
MAP 5 REF Q21

7 miles NE of Brighton on the A27

Lewes is the county town of East Sussex. This historic settlement stands at the strategically important point where the River Ouse is crossed by an ancient east-west land route. Because of the area's close proximity to Normandy, William the Conqueror divided his newly acquired

Sussex estates amongst some of his most trusted lieutenants. The lands around Lewes were granted to William de Warenne and his wife, Gundrada, who not only constructed the substantial double motte and bailey **Lewes Castle** on a hillside above the river, but also founded The **Priory of St Pancras** on the southern edge of the town. This once magnificent monastic house belonged to the abbey of Cluny in Burgundy and had a great church as large as Chichester Cathedral. The priory was the home of the renowned team of artists who painted the famous ecclesiastical murals at Hardham and Clayton during the 12th century. Following Henry VIII's Dissolution of the Monasteries in 1537, the building was forcibly demolished and its stone used for constructing residential dwellings in the town. The Sussex Archaeological Society's **Barbican House Museum** has fascinating exhibits on the history of Sussex; next door, the **Lewes Town Model** is a scale model of the town as it looked 100 years ago. A sound and light show illustrates Lewes' 1,000 year history. Like Ditchling, Lewes has an **Anne of Cleves House**, an early 16th century Wealden 'hall' house which formed part of Henry VIII's divorce settlement with his

fourth wife (also like Ditchling, the property was never lived in by the estranged queen). The structure has been much altered over the centuries and has evolved into an attractive concoction of buildings set around a reconstructed Tudor garden and known as The Museum of Local History, run by the Sussex Archaeological Society. Its rooms and galleries have been arranged to create an impression of domestic and working life in Lewes in the 17th and 18th centuries.

Lewes developed strong Protestant roots following the Reformation and the burning of 17 Protestant martyrs in the town during the Marian persecutions of 1555-1557 es-

Anne of Cleves House, Lewes

tablished an anti-Catholic fanaticism which can still be detected in the town's modern bonfire night festivities. In what must be the most extravagant 5th November celebrations in the country, rival bonfire societies march through the streets carrying flaming torches and specially made 'guys'.These are then carried to the edge of town and thrown onto huge bonfires - a spectacular annual custom.

GLYNDE   MAP 5 REF Q21
3 miles E of Lewes off the A27

The internationally renowned village of Glynde, although filled with well preserved traditional Sussex cottages, has a very untypical 18th century church, **St Mary the Virgin**, built in Palladian style. The churchyard contains the grave of one of Glynde's most noted sons, John Ellman, who was a pioneer of selective breeding and was responsible for producing the black-faced Southdown sheep, the breed on which most of the flocks in New Zealand and Australia are based. **Glynde Place**, the imposing brick and flint mansion near the church, was built in 1579 for William Morley. The house has an elegant wood panelled long gallery and contains some exceptional works of art, and the grounds are beautifully laid out and incorporate an aviary and a pottery. Glynde Place is owned by Viscount Hampden and is open to the public on a limited number of days each year (opening times displayed on site).

The distinctive local landmark known as **Mount Caburn** lies to the west of Glynde and can be reached along a footpath from the village. Many thousands of years ago, this steep sided chalk outcrop was separated from the rest of the Downs by the action of the River Glynde. This process created an artificial looking mound almost 500 feet in height whose natural defensive properties have long been exploited by man. The earthwork defences of an Iron Age hill-fort can still be made out near the summit, and evidence of an earlier Stone Age settlement has also been detected. The part Tudor, part Victorian country house lying one mile to the north of Glynde village is the home of the world famous **Glyndebourne Opera House**. This unique institution was founded by John and Audrey Christie in 1934, and since then it has built up an international reputation for presenting the finest opera in the most idyllic of English surroundings.

ALCISTON   MAP 5 REF R21
5 miles SE of Lewes off the A27

The original settlement of the 'forgotten village' of Alciston was abandoned following the Black Death; a new one was built some years later on the opposite side of the 13th century **Alciston Church**. To avoid the likelihood of flooding, this was built on the foundations of an earlier Saxon structure which stood at the top of a small hill. The remains of a substantial medieval dovecote can be seen nearby; during the late Middle Ages, large numbers of pigeons were kept here to provide a much prized supplement to the dreary winter diet. The fertile agricultural land around Alciston once belonged to the estates of Battle Abbey. At that time, the tenant farmers paid 'rent' to the abbot in the form of one-tenth of their annual farm output, and at harvest time each year, this was brought to Alciston and deposited in the abbey's huge medieval tithe barn. This magnificent structure is over 170 feet long and is one of the largest of its type in Sussex; it can be seen in a delightful farmyard setting on the southern side of the village, close to the point where the road into the hamlet narrows to a rough track. As well as being the focus of the estate, the adjacent farmhouse once served as a retirement home for the monks.

WILMINGTON   MAP 5 REF R21
7 miles SE of Lewes off the A27

The historic remains of **Wilmington Priory**, a once imposing Benedictine priory built between the 12th and 14th centuries, are rumoured to be inhabited by a number of legendary ghosts. Parts of the building, including the hall, gatehouse and courtyard, have now been restored by the Sussex Archaeological Society and the site includes an interesting museum of agricultural history. Originally part of the Priory buildings, the Church of St Mary and St Peter has in its North Chapel a remarkable stained-glass window depicting different species of butterflies and bees. There are marvellous views from the churchyard west to Firle Beacon. The mysterious figure of the **Long Man of Wilmington** can be seen from the Priory grounds. This remarkable 226 foot high 'geoglyph' of a man carrying a staff in each hand was carved into the chalky hillside of Windover Hill some time between pre-Roman times and 1779, the year it was first documented. Although his origins are thus uncertain, it is believed he is about 1,400 years old. Perhaps most astonishing is the fact that the design takes account of the slope of the hill, and so accurately maintains the proportions of a man even when viewed from below. To date, no one knows who was responsible for the carving or why it was done; various theories suggest that it is a figure of a pilgrim, a Saxon chieftain or even the 'Midsummer Man' of pagan folklore. In 1969, the carving was strengthened with over 700 concrete blocks. A quarter mile long footpath leads up to the site.

EXCEAT   MAP 5 REF R22
7 miles SE of Lewes off the A259

The small settlement of Exceat stands on the River Cuckmere at the northeastern corner of the Seaford Head Nature Reserve. Here, **The Living World** is a unique natural history centre which contains a fascinating collection of live butterflies, spiders, reptiles, stick insects and marine creatures, all of which can be viewed at close quarters and sometimes even handled. The centre is located in a group of converted farm buildings. Between the hamlet and the sea, the River Cuckmere makes a spectacular serpentine meander through the area known as Cuckmere Haven. This striking flood plain forms the western boundary of the **Seven Sisters Country Park**, a broad tract of County Council and National Trust-owned Heritage Coastline which incorporates the famous Seven Sisters chain of white chalk cliffs. The cliffs, which are now receding at around 3 feet per year, can also be accessed from the top of the Downs at Crowlink and from the east at the popular picnicking spot of Birling Gap. The downland above the Seven Sisters is strewn with evidence of early settlement, including a number of Neolithic bowl and round barrows.

UPPER DICKER
MAP 5 REF R21
8 miles E of Lewes off the A22

Upper Dicker is the site of one of the loveliest old monastic houses in Sussex, **Michelham Priory**. This surprisingly well-preserved Augustinian priory was founded in 1229 by Gilbert de Aquila, the Norman lord of Pevensey, and continued to flourish until Henry VIII's Dissolution of the Monasteries in 1537. It then became the focal point of a large agricultural estate which for nearly three centuries belonged to the Sackville family.

HALLAND
MAP 5 REF R21
6 miles NE of Lewes off the A22

The renowned **Bentley Wildfowl and Motor Museum** is located near Halland. The estate covers some 100 acres in the heart of beautiful Sussex countryside and has something to spark everyone's interest. The Wildfowl Reserve boasts more than 150 different species, 11 of which are listed as endangered. Keen and novice bird-watchers will find much to interest them here, whatever the season. Also on the estate, the Motor Museum is a must for motoring enthusiasts. Housing a magnificent collection of 50 cars and 25 motorbikes, ranging from veteran Edwardian and vintage motors to modern-day Lamborghinis. Many of the vintage models are regular participants in the London-to-Brighton run; some are very rare models indeed. These grounds are also home to Bentley House, an impressive Palladian-style masterpiece which began life as a Tudor farmhouse. It has since been extended and sympathetically altered to create the splendid building visitors see today. Particularly renowned for its Chinese room and the Philip Rickman gallery, which houses a grouping of over 150 of this Sussex artist's watercolours of wildfowl. The formal gardens are laid out as a series of rooms, leading to Glyndebourne Wood.

Bentley Wildfowl and Motor Museum, Halland,
nr Lewes, East Sussex BN8 5AF
Tel: 01825 840573 Fax: 01825 841322

PEVENSEY

18 miles E of Lewes off the A259

Map 5 Ref R21

The low lying land around Pevensey proved a good landing place for the invading Roman legions, and in order to protect their strategic anchorage, the Romans erected a massive fortification (they went on to build 10 such strongholds along the southern shores of Britain). Although **Pevensey Castle** now lies almost two miles inland, it once stood on the shoreline within a few yards of the Roman landing stages. The steady eastward drift of the shingle beach gradually isolated Pevensey from the English Channel, a process which was inadvertently accelerated by the draining of the Pevensey Levels during Tudor times. From its Roman origins to its involvement in the Second World War, Pevensey Castle has played an important role in history.

The village of Pevensey contains an unusual number of fine medieval buildings, including the **Mint House**, built in the 1340s on the site of a Norman mint, and the **Court House**, which served the borough as a combined courtroom and gaol; both buildings now house interesting museums of local history. There are also a number of excellent old inns in the village, and **Glyndley Manor**, on the edge of Pevensey, renowned for its mysterious atmosphere and celebrated colony of herons. In the days prior to the founding of the Royal Navy, Pevensey served as one of the nation's Cinque Ports - that is to say, it was granted certain privileges by the Crown in return for providing ships and men in defence of the Channel coast. Several centuries later, a series of **Martello Towers** was built along the coast to the east of Pevensey to defend the shore against a possible attack from the forces of Napoleon.

Inland lies the area of drained marshland known as the **Pevensey Levels**. At one time this was an area of tidal mud flats which were covered in shallow salt pans; since then, however, it has been reclaimed for agricultural use and is now covered in fertile arable fields.

HASTINGS

30 miles E of Lewes on the A259

Map 5 Ref S21

Long before William the Conqueror made his well publicised landing on the beaches of nearby Pevensey Bay, Hastings was the principal town of a small semi-independent Saxon province which straddled the Kent-Sussex border. Over the centuries, Hastings has been subjected to periodic attack from the sea, both from cross Channel raids, which on at least one occasion left the town a smouldering ruin, and from the waves themselves, which would regularly flood the streets during stormy conditions. The town's busy fishing harbour started to silt up during the Elizabethan era and now lies buried beneath a 20th century shopping development. Nevertheless, the fishing industry managed to survive and, today, fishing vessels continue to be hoisted onto the shingle beach by motor winch. One of Hastings' most characteristic features are the tall, narrow wooden huts which are used for for drying nets and storing fishing tackle; these date from the 17th century and are known as *net shops* or *deezes*. The old fishermen's church of St Nicholas now houses the **Fishermen's Museum**, an interesting exhibition which includes the full-sized sailing lugger, Enterprise. This was the last vessel to be built in Hastings before the shipyard closed in 1909; it was actively involved in the Dunkirk evacuation of 1940. The old part of Hastings consists of a network of narrow streets and alleyways, or *twittens*, which lie between Castle Hill and East Hill. The best way discover the many interesting old residential buildings, inns and churches is to take a walking tour along the High Street and All Saints Street.

Hastings Castle is forever linked with that most famous date in English history - 1066. The ruins of William the Conqueror's 900 year old castle stand on the West Hill cliff edge commanding panoramic views. It is also the home of 'The 1066 Story'. Here, from within a medieval siege tent, an audio-visual presentation transports visitors back in time, recounting the history of the castle. Hastings also contains a variety of attractions for the traditional seaside holidaymaker. The 600 foot long **Pier** was completed in 1872 and had to be repaired after the Second World War when it was deliberately holed in two places to prevent it being used as a landing stage by Hitler's forces. According to local legend, the Conqueror's Stone at the head of the pier was used by William the Conqueror as a dining table for his first meal on English soil in 1066. Eighty one events spanning 900 years of the town's history are remembered in the impressive **Hastings Embroidery** in the town hall. Inspired by the Bayeux Tapestry, this remarkable 240ft long embroidery was made by the Royal School of Needlework in 1966 to commemorate the ninth centenary of the Norman Invasion. Among the characters to be depicted is John Logie Baird, the Scottish pioneer of television who carried out his early experiments here in the 1920s.

The 600 acre **Hastings Country Park** to the east of the town offers some spectacular clifftop walking along two and a half miles of unspoilt coastline. Guided walks through this attractive area of woodland and heath are provided by the local ranger service throughout the summer.

BATTLE   Map 5 Ref S21
5 miles NW of Hastings off the A2100

The historic town of Battle is of course renowned as the location of the momentous battle on 14th October 1066 between the forces of Harold, the Saxon King of England, and William, Duke of Normandy. The **Battle of Hastings** actually took place on a hill which the Normans named Senlac, meaning lake of blood - even today, some believe in the myth that blood seeps from the battlefield after heavy rain (any discolouring of the water is, in fact, due to iron oxide in the subsoil). The High Street in Battle has plenty to occupy the passing tourist or local. Prior to 1066, the site of Battle was virtually uninhabited; however, one of William the Conqueror's first tasks on becoming King of England was to found a substantial Benedictine abbey on this exposed hillside in order to make amends for the loss of life in battle and so secure his future salvation. St Martin's Abbey was finally consecrated in 1094, the high altar in the great church being placed on the very spot where Harold was struck in the eye by an arrow from a Norman bow. Throughout the late Middle Ages, the abbey grew wealthy and powerful as it extended its influence over a wide area of East Sussex. This period of prosperity came to an abrupt end, however, following Henry VIII's Dissolution of the Monasteries in 1537. Several of the old monastic buildings are open to visitors, including the towering 13th century dormitory and the monks' common room with its magnificent vaulted ceiling. The mile long 'Battlefield Walk' guides visitors around the edge of Senlac Hill and describes the course of the battle with the help of information boards and audio tours, while the imposing 14th century gatehouse contains an exhibition which brings the history of the abbey to life.

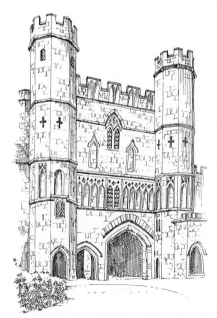

Under the custodial care of English Heritage, **Battle Abbey** has much to offer the visitor. The Prelude to Battle exhibition introduces visitors to the site and its history. This is followed by a 12-minute video on the Battle of Hastings. Other on-site attractions are a children's themed play and picnic area, an educational Discovery Centre and the recently rediscovered and consecrated Dunkirk Memorial, which was placed in the grounds in 1953 by the Men of the Trees organisation. Exciting events are held on a regular basis. Phone 01424 773792 for further details. Open daily 10 a.m.-4 p.m. October-March; 10 a.m.-6 p.m. April-September. Admission is charged.

**English Heritage, Battle Abbey, Battle,
East Sussex TN33 0AD
Tel: 01424 775705 Fax: 01424 775059**

The **Battle Museum of Local History** in Langton House contains a half-size reproduction of the Bayeux Tapestry, a facsimile of the Sussex volume of the Domesday Book, and an interesting collection of old maps, coins, toys and games. Just opposite Battle Abbey, in 600 year old Wealden Hall House, you will find **Buckleys Yesterday's World** - a collection of around 100,000 historic artefacts and items of memorabilia dating from Victorian and Edwardian times right up until 1950.

BODIAM
Map 5 Ref S21

10 miles N of Hastings off the A229

Bodiam is home to the impressive National Trust-owned **Bodiam Castle**. With its imposing stone walls, castellated turrets and lily-filled moat, this must be the epitome of a classic romantic castle. Bodiam was one of the last great medieval fortifications to be built in Britain; it was constructed in 1385 by Sir Edward Dalyngrigge to defend the upper Rother valley against possible attack from the French following the infamous cross-Channel raid on Rye eight years before. The castle was very well-appointed for its day, but never saw hostile fire until nearly three centuries later, when the Parliamentarian forces of General Waller reduced it to a shell to avoid it becoming a Royalist stronghold during the English Civil War. A long period of decay then followed until in 1829, plans to completely dismantle the castle were thwarted by 'Mad' Jack Fuller of Brightling. A programme of external restoration was begun by George Cubitt towards the end

Bodiam Castle

of the 19th century and completed by Lord Curzon, a former Viceroy of India, between 1917 and 1919. On his death in 1926, Curzon bequeathed Bodiam to the National Trust, who have carried on the process of restoration and conservation. Several floors in the towers have now been replaced, enabling visitors to climb to the top of the battlements. The castle hosts a number of events during the year, ranging from medieval archery and longbow competitions to family fun days.

NORTHIAM
Map 5 Ref S21

10 miles N of Hastings off the A28

Northiam is a large and picturesque village which is known for its characteristic white weatherboarded buildings. At the heart of the community is a sizable village green which is surrounded by a number of fine 17th and 18th century buildings. Perhaps the most impressive of these is a substantial three storey white-boarded house which stands on the edge of the green behind an unusual carved stone monument. **Great Dixter**, one of the finest examples of a late medieval hall-house, can be found three quarters of a mile to the northwest of Northiam. This superb building dates from around 1450.

RYE
Map 5 Ref S21

11 miles NE of Hastings off the A259

Along with its neighbour to the southwest, Rye was added to the five existing **Cinque Ports** of Hastings, Romney, Hythe, Dover and Sandwich in the 12th century. The town was also subjected to ferocious cross Channel raids - almost every non stone-built structure in the town was burnt to the ground in the notorious French raid of 1377. Later, the harbour suffered from the problems of a receding coastline, a dilemma which eventually required the building of a new port, Rye Harbour, closer to the repositioned mouth of the River Rother.

Rye's prominent hilltop site is partially ringed by the rivers Rother, Brede and Tillingham, a factor which has made it an easily defendable hill fort since early times. A substantial perimeter wall was built to defend the open northern approaches, and one of its four great gateways, the **Landgate**, still survives in the northeastern corner of the old town. This imposing 14th century structure once had oak gates, a drawbridge and a portcullis. The clock was added in 1863 in memory of Prince Albert, and was restored at the time of the Royal Wedding in 1981.

Rye grew prosperous in the late medieval period due to the activities of its fishing and merchant fleets, who brought in fish and cloth and sent out wool and processed iron to continental Europe. However, the silting up of the harbour gradually denied the town a means of earning a living and heralded a lengthy period of decline. This economic downturn halted the process of organic change in Rye and many of the buildings which would have been updated in more prosperous circumstances remained unchanged. As a result, present day Rye has inherited a superb legacy of late-medieval buildings, most of which have been restored in the years since the town was 'rediscovered' in the 19th century. **Mermaid Street** is one of the finest examples of an unspoilt medieval thoroughfare in Rye. This delightful cobbled lane is lined with early timbered buildings including the famous Mermaid Inn, a wonderful old hostelry which was rebuilt in 1420 following the devastating French raid of 43 years before. In the 18th century, the inn became the headquarters of the Hawkhurst Gang, one of the most infamous and powerful bands of smugglers on the south coast.

Set in peaceful surroundings yet still central for all of Rye's sights, shops and attractions,

Little Orchard House, West Street, Rye, East Sussex TN31 7ES Tel/Fax: 01797 223831

Little Orchard House is a charming and traditional guest house. Rebuilt in 1745, it has been lovingly and carefully renovated over the years. It retains many original features and its traditional character and ambience. Each of the three ensuite guest bedrooms is individually decorated in its own style and quality. This hidden place has a large walled garden with 18th-century Smugglers' Watchtower and secluded corners in which guests are welcome to relax and explore. In the peaceful panelled bookroom, books and games are provided for guests' use. There is also a cosy and comfortable guests' sitting room with open fire in winter, where visitors can browse through the newspaper or one of the many selected menus from Rye's excellent restaurants - proprietor Sara Brinkhurst is happy to advise and make bookings on your behalf. Named as a Hotel of the Year for 1999 by the *Which? Hotel Guide*, a feature of the generous country breakfasts are local organic, free-range and homemade produce. ETB 5 Diamonds Silver Award.

Church Square is Rye's wonderful centrepiece, which contains some of the town's finest late-medieval buildings. The parish church of **St Mary's** was severely damaged during the French raid of 1377, although not before its church bells were taken down and carried off to Normandy. However, a retaliatory raid the following year not only inflicted a similar fate on two French towns, but succeeded in recapturing the bells of St Mary. The church was sympathetically restored during the Victorian era and contains some fine features, including a 16th century turret clock with a spectacular 18 foot pendulum, some interesting 20th century stained-glass windows, and the original 'quarter boys' - 18th century cherubs which once stood above the clock face, but which have now been replaced by fibreglass replicas; these golden reproductions still come out to strike on the quarter hour (but not on the hour).

A little to the southwest is the **Ypres Tower and Museum**; one of the oldest surviving buildings in Rye, it was constructed around 1250 as a defensive fort. Two centuries later, it was acquired by John de Ypres as a private residence, then subsequently it became the town's court-house, gaol and mortuary. Today, it houses the award-winning Rye Museum and offers some magnificent views over the surrounding coastal plain. Tucked away in the streets below Ypres Tower, **The Ypres Inn** - known locally as The Wipers due to the English inability to pronounce French - is an attractive timber-clad building dating from the 17th century. The first landlord, in 1663, was a Mr Bourn; his 7th-generation grandson still uses the inn. Today, this well-known establishment is personally managed by Babs and Dick Pearce, a warm and friendly couple who serve a range of real ales, including a local micro-brewery ale, along with the usual beers, lagers and ciders. Visitors to the inn are also treated to a mouth-watering menu of traditional pub food and also Dick's speciality lamb dishes. All meals, from the sandwiches and ba-guettes to the splendid Sunday carvery, are freshly prepared and home-cooked. Everyone is welcome to take part in a game of darts, crib-bage or dominoes, while the more energetic may like to try their hand at the pub's most popular game,

The Ypres Inn, Gun Garden, Rye, East Sussex
TN31 7HH Tel: 01797 223248 Fax: 01797 227460

petanque, played in the garden opposite. However, it is as a blues pub that this fine place is particularly renowned. Live music (always blues) is played every Sunday evening, and the musicians who perform here have drawn keen music fans from near and far.

The nearly 1,800 acre **Rye Harbour Nature Reserve** spans much of the large tract of land bounded by the River Rother, the sea and the **Royal Military Canal**. A Site of Special Scientific Interest, the reserve has some of the finest coastal shingle vegetation anywhere in England.

Mountsfield is an elegant and gracious manor house offering accommodation in luxurious surroundings. Airy and spacious, it is furnished with antiques and tastefully decorated throughout. Owner Tia Romanoff is American-born, but has lived in England since 1979. Her

Mountsfield, Rye Hill, Rye, East Sussex TN31 7NH
Tel: 01797 227105 Fax: 01797 227106

husband Prince Rostislav's great-uncle was the last Czar of Russia. Memorabilia and photographs of the Romanoffs adorn this congenial manor. There are three charming guest bedrooms: The 'Wellington' has a four-poster bed and is tastefully furnished and decorated. There is a large shower room with power shower. The 'Nelson' is very large and luxurious, with a king-size four-poster and chaise/settee. It overlooks the grounds of this impressive stonebuilt home, and Rye Castle beyond. The 'York' is a twin room, again beautifully appointed and with all amenities. Breakfast is served in the elegant dining room. Guests are welcome to relax in the large walled garden with its lovely trees, shrubs, flowering plants and two fountains.

BECKLEY   MAP 5 REF S21
11 miles NE of Hastings on the A268

Jenny Farrant and her son Paul are in partnership running the superb **Farm World** in Beckley. Beginning as a children's farm in 1984, it now offers a range of interesting sights and experiences for children of all ages. It has become a popular attraction for locals and visitors alike, with a range of farm animals and offering an insight into traditional and modern farming methods. Located at Great Knelle Farm, set amid 600 acres of peaceful countryside, including

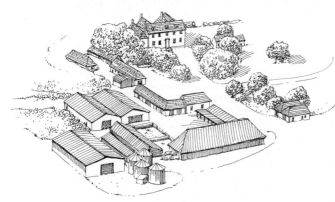

Farm World, Great Knelle Farm, Beckley, nr Rye,
East Sussex TN31 6UB Tel: 01797 260250/260321

woodland and a stretch of the River Rother, the farm makes a lovely day out for all the family. Other exciting and informative features include two miles of trails suitable for walkers of all levels, and fishing on the river. Also onsite is a charming letting cottage which sleeps four. The perfect rural retreat, with every amenity and where guests are ensured a friendly and hospitable welcome, Farm World is well worth a visit.

ICKLESHAM   Map 5 Ref S21
6 miles NE of Hastings off the A259

Oast House Inn is a welcoming Free House offering real ales, good food and accommodation. Built in 1535, when King Henry VIII occupied the throne, it was originally a hop farm with a brew house on site. It is from these origins that this welcoming establishment takes its name, as an oast house was a building used for drying out hops for breweries. Over its long and illustrious career it has seen careful alterations. During the 1960s and 1970s it was converted to a cottage and tea rooms, and then in 1983 into an hotel/ inn. The exposed black beams in the bar area, stone walls in the restaurant and other original features speak of its distinctive history. Comfortable and traditional throughout, there are

Oast House Inn, Main Road, Icklesham, East Sussex TN36 4AJ
Tel: 01424 814217

nine double ensuite bedrooms, refurbished, decorated and appointed to a high standard. One is said to be inhabited by a friendly ghost. The traditional English breakfast is hearty and filling. The restaurant serves an extensive range of home-cooked food; steaks and fresh local fish are specialities. In the bar, four hand pumps bring forth excellent real ales, including local Sussex ales. Bar snacks and lunches are also available. Outdoors there's a patio garden, just the place to relax on fine days.

HERSTMONCEUX   Map 5 Ref R21
8 miles W of Hastings off the A271

Herstmonceux (pronounced Herst-mon-soo) is of course famous for **Herstmonceux Castle** and **Observatory**. Built on the site of an earlier Norman manor house in 1440 by Sir Roger Fiennes, the castle was one of the first large-scale buildings in Britain to be constructed from red brick. Later, the castle passed into the hands of the Hare family, who presided over a long period of decline which culminated in its virtual dismantling in 1777. The structure then remained in a state of dilapidation for some 150 years until a major programme of restoration began in the 1930s. The careful and inspired work helped to restore the turrets and battlements to their former glory so that today the fully refurbished castle, which is now owned by Queen's University Canada and operates as an International Study Centre, stands in pristine condition at the centre of its highly photogenic moat.

The gardens and grounds of Herstmonceux Castle are open from 15th April to 29th October 2000 10 a.m. - 6 p.m. (last admission 5 p.m.; closing one hour earlier from October). In the grounds visitors will find the formal gardens including a walled garden, the Shakespeare garden, woodland sculptures, the Pyramid, the waterlily-filled moat and the Georgian-style folly.

Herstmonceux Castle, Hailsham, East Sussex BN27 1RN
Tel: 01323 833816 website: www.seetb.org.uk/herstmonceux

The woodland walks take the visitor to the remains of the 300-year-old sweet chestnut avenue and the rhododendron garden from the Lowther/Latham period. There is also a Nature Trail, Children's Play Area, Gift Shop and Tearoom. The castle is a working study centre and is not open to the public unless on a guided tour (extra charge and subject to availability) - please phone to confirm times.

TICEHURST

MAP 5 REF R21

16 miles N of Hastings on the B2099

Ticehurst is an ancient village filled with the attractive tile-hung and white weather-boarded buildings which are so characteristic of the settlements along the Kent-Sussex border. There are a number of noteworthy buildings here, including **Furze House**, a former workhouse, and **Whatman's**, an old carpenter's cottage with strangely curving exterior walls. The parish church of St Mary dates primarily from the 13th and 14th centuries, though it was restored in 1879. It contains a stained-glass window depicting scenes from the Last Judgment which is made up of fragments of medieval glass. The 16th century font cover is exceptionally fine. In 1975, the Southern Water Authority dammed the valley of the River Bewl to the north of Ticehurst to create **Bewl Bridge Reservoir**, the largest area of inland water in southeast England. A great many buildings were drowned in the process; however, one, the 15th century **Dunsters Mill**, was taken down brick by brick and moved to its present location above the new high water level. (A couple of timber-framed farm buildings found their way to the Weald and Downland Museum at Singleton in West Sussex.) The reservoir now offers a great many attractions for the visitor, including walking, picnicking, trout fishing and pleasure boat trips.

Bewl Water

Pashley Manor Gardens feature fine beds across the south front, a wide lawn and a moat leading to the manor itself. Numerous varieties of shrub roses, paeonies, hydrangea and many other plants bring fantastic colour and lushness to every corner. The 'Golden Garden' leads down to woodlands and a chain of ponds surrounded by rhododendrons, azaleas and climbing roses reflected in the still, dark waters.

ASHDOWN FOREST
MAP 5 REF Q20

20 miles N of Lewes off the B2188

This, the largest area of land in the southeast of England which has never been under the plough, is an extensive region of open heath and woodland on the high ridges of the Weald. The original meaning of the word 'forest' was 'Royal Hunting Area', and this is precisely what Ashdown Forest used to be. The earliest records (dating from 1268) indicate that the region's thriving population of deer made it a popular hunting ground for royalty and noblemen. Before the end of the 13th century, the forest was enclosed by a 'pale' - a ditch and bank topped by a wooden fence making it difficult for the deer to jump over. Keen royal huntsmen such as Henry VIII and James I visited Ashdown fairly often. In the chaos that was the English Civil War, the forest was neglected and, by 1657, no deer at all remained there. After many wrangles at the hands of competing would-be developers, the area was divided roughly into two: one went to speculator Alexander Staples, the other preserved for the people, to use for grazing and wood-cutting. In the 18th and 19th centuries many more claims were made on the land and resources, culminating in 1885 in an Act of Parliament affording public rights of access to specified areas of the forest for recreational purposes. In 1974, a new Act allowed public access (on foot) to wander the whole of the forest. Further information on what to do and see in the forest can be found at the **Ashdown Forest Centre**, one mile east of Wych Cross on the Coleman's Hatch road.

HARTFIELD
MAP 5 REF R20

20 miles N of Lewes off the B2110

Hartfield, an old hunting settlement which takes its name from the adult male red deer, or hart. The 13th century village church of St Mary's has a tower with a shingled broach spire and an unusual roofed churchyard gate. Close by stands an early 16th century timber-framed cottage with an overhanging upper storey which, appropriately, is known as the Lychgate. A A Milne, author of the much loved Winnie the Pooh stories, lived at Cotchford Farm, half a mile south of Hartfield. Along with the artist E H Shepard, he made the landscape of Ashdown Forest come alive to millions of young readers throughout the world. The timber bridge spanning the small tributary of the Medway where Milne's son, Christopher Robin, would meet with his fictitious friends to play 'Poohsticks', was restored in 1979 by Milne's publishers and East Sussex County Council.

Tucked away at the end of a winding, country track, **Bolebroke Water Mill**, Miller's Barn and Mill House nestle together in romantic seclusion, surrounded by woodland, mill streams and pasture. This idyllically unspoilt setting was chosen by Christoper Hampton for his film

Bolebroke Water Mill, Perry Hill, Edenbridge Road, Hartfield, East Sussex TN7 4JP Tel/Fax: 01892 770425 e-mail: b&b@bolebrokemill.demon.co.uk

Carrington, starring Emma Thompson and Jonathan Pryce (released 1995), and featured the beautifully natural grounds as well as several interiors. Bolebroke Mill was first recorded in the Domesday Book in AD 1086, and continued as a working corn-mill till 1948. Today corn is no longer ground, but all the internal machinery remains and the Mill has been sympathetically adapted to form charmingly unusual accommodation of great character which includes two quaint bedrooms with en suite bathrooms built into former corn storage bins, and a large lounge. Access to the adjoining Mill House is via a trap-door! Steep stairs in the Mill regrettably make it unsuitable for anyone with mobility difficulties and young children. There are no problems of access in the Elizabethan Miller's Barn, though all doors and some ceilings are low. The ground-floor "Burrow" with beamed walls and ceiling is available as either a twin or as a six-foot wide double. Upstairs are two honeymoon rooms, the "Honeymoon Hayloft" and the "Dovesnest", both with four-poster beds. The property is centrally heated throughout and rooms are equipped with all modern amenities. The final highlight of any stay here is the outstanding breakfast served in the Mill House, awarded "Best Breakfast in Britain" by the British Tourist Board magazine *In Britain*.

SHEFFIELD PARK   Map 5 Ref Q21
10 miles N of Lewes off the A275

Sheffield Park is situated in the northeast corner of the parish of Chailey. The village takes its name from its manor house, a Tudor building remodelled in 1775 by James Wyatt for the Earl of Sheffield, it is best known for the 100 acre National Trust-owned **Sheffield Park Gardens**. During the late 18th century, the grounds of Sheffield Park were laid out in a grand style, at first by 'Capability' Brown and then by Humphry Repton, on the instructions of John Baker Holroyd MP, the first Earl of Sheffield. At around the same time, he also commissioned James Wyatt to build **Sheffield Park House**, an impressive mansion which can be seen from a distance but is not open to the public. The third Earl of Sheffield was an enthusiastic cricketer who organised the first test tours of England by the Australians. He also established a tradition (which lasted only 20 years or so) where the Australian team would play the first match of their tour at Sheffield Park against an Earl of Sheffield's XI. The former cricket field, now studded with specimen trees and shrubs, can still be made out on a rise above the main lake.

Sheffield Park Station is the southern terminus of the famous **Bluebell Railway** (the entrance is almost opposite Sheffield Park Gardens). This privately-owned stretch of the former East Grinstead to Lewes line runs for five miles through a delightful wooded valley which, as the name suggests, is carpeted with bluebells in springtime. One of the first of the new generation of private steam railways, the line was acquired by the Bluebell Railway Preservation Company in 1961 and is largely staffed by a team of dedicated volunteers. Those travelling to the northern terminus at Horsted Keynes will find an interesting collection of railway carriages and an attractive picnic area.

Sheffield Park Gardens

SURREY

TWICKENHAM
MAP 4 REF P19
9 miles SW of London on the A310

Lying on the west side of the Thames just a few miles north of Hampton Court Palace, Twickenham is a thriving community that makes the most of its riverside setting. Perhaps more than anything else Twickenham is renowned as the headquarters of Rugby Union Football in Britain, a role it has played since 1907. The recently rebuilt stadium - "Twickers" to some of its dearest stalwarts - plays host to England home internationals as well as the annual Varsity match between Oxford and Cambridge. Admission to the **Museum of Rugby** allows visitors to savour the history and atmosphere of the sport. Running through the players tunnel is enough to get many people's blood rushing, and the museum provides a full account of Twickenham right up to its latest renovations. A number of fine old houses are dotted through the heart of Twickenham. Montpelier Row and Sion Row are wonderfully preserved terraces dating from the 18th century. Those eager to pursue other historical associations from that era can find the tomb of the poet Alexander Pope in the Twickenham churchyard. At **Strawberry Hill**, just to the south of Twickenham, is a Gothic Revival villa built between 1750 and 1776 for the author Horace Walpole. The motley assortment of architectural styles has led to its description as "part of a church, a castle, a monastery or a mansion". Strawberry Hill is now St Mary's University College, a teachers' training college, but it is open to the public. **Orleans House and Gallery**, which houses one of London's finest art collections outside of London's national collections, enjoys an enviable location in a woodland garden on the Riverside between Twickenham and Richmond. On the opposite riverbank is Ham House, with its extensive grounds, while next door is the Palladian villa of Marble Hill House.

RICHMOND
MAP 4 REF Q19
5 miles SW of London on the A307

Although a sizeable commercial centre with a wide range of high street chains and department stores, Richmond retains a distinct sense of its rich and varied history. Its twin blessings - a lovely riverside setting along a sweeping curve of the Thames and the extensive **Richmond Park** - act as counterpoints to the occasionally heavy traffic and the sound of planes approaching Heathrow Airport.

A good place to get acquainted with old Richmond is **Richmond Green**, a genuine village green that is hardly surpassed in all of Greater London. Handsome houses, built in the17th and 18th centuries, flank the southwest and southeast edges of the green. The southwest side has an older, and more royal, history. It was the site of Richmond Palace, built in the 12th century and passing into royal possession in 1125, when it was known as Shene Palace. The palace was destroyed by Richard II in 1394 but subsequent kings had it rebuilt in stages. The site, right by the green, made it an ideal spot for organising jousting tournaments. The rebuilding and extensions reached their peak under Henry VII, who renamed the palace after his Yorkshire earldom. Elizabeth I died in the palace in 1603. Sadly, very little of the palace survives as it was a victim of the turbulent Commonwealth upheavals in the 17th century. Look for the only surviving element - the brick gatehouse -

Richmond Theatre

beside the green. Just off the northeast flank of the green is the **Richmond Theatre**, an imposing Victorian building with an elaborate frontage facing the street. It is a showcase for excellent
theatrical productions. The combination of the repertoire and the lovely setting attracts a number
of renowned actors.

Richmond Riverside, a redevelopment scheme dating from the late 1980s, stretches along
the Thames. Pastiche Georgian buildings, complete with columns, cupolas and facades, house
offices and commercial premises. Among the modern buildings, however, there remain a few of
the original Georgian and Victorian houses, including the narrow, three-storey **Heron House**,
where Lady Hamilton and her daughter Horatia came to live soon after the Battle of Trafalgar.

Museum of Richmond

The riverside walk ends at **Richmond Bridge**, a handsome
five-arched structure built of Purbeck stone in 1777 and
widened in the 1930s. It is the oldest extant bridge spanning the Thames in London. Richmond's Old Town Hall,
set somewhat back from the new developments at Richmond Bridge, is the home of the **Museum of Richmond**, a
fascinating privately run museum which provides a unique
perspective on Richmond's history and special significance
in English life. The occasionally steep climb of **Richmond
Hill** leads southwards and upwards from the centre of Richmond. The view from the top, at Richmond Terrace, makes
the climb worth it. The Thames lies below, sweeping in
majestic curves to the west through wooded countryside.
Turner and Reynolds are among the many artists who have
tried to capture the essence of this scene, which takes in
six counties. A little further up the hill is the entrance to
Richmond Park, some 2,400 acres of open land where deer
roam. Set amidst this coppiced woodland are several landscaped plantations noted for their azaleas and
rhododendrons. The land achieved park status under
Charles I.

Occupying a tranquil location on the peaceful banks
of the Thames south of Richmond is **Ham House**, one of
the best examples of a Stuart stately home in the country.
Ham House was built in 1610 for one of James I's courtiers
and in 1626 it passed to William Murray, a close friend of Charles II and later made the first Earl
of Dysart. It was Murray, and to an even greater extent his daughter Elizabeth, who gave the
house its abiding character. The interior that captures the imagination with its imposing Great
Staircase leading the visitor into a world of exuberant Baroque furnishings and a wealth of fine
paintings and tapestries. The National Trust, which acquired Ham House in 1948, preserves this
architectural gem.

KEW AND KEW GARDENS   MAP 4 REF Q19
4 miles SW of London off the A310

Riverside Kew, lying just a couple of miles North of Richmond, came to prominence under the
early Hanoverian kings in the 18th century. High society followed royalty westward to the new
palace built on this pleasant stretch of the Thames just upstream from Chiswick and Hammersmith. The new village grew around triangular Kew Green, which is still surrounded by handsome
18th century houses.

Far more important than Kew's social history, however, are the **Royal Botanical Gardens**,
which are arguably the most famous gardens in the world. Princess Augusta, mother of George
III, laid out an 8 acre botanical garden on the grounds of Kew Palace in 1759. Tranquil and
spacious, these gardens now occupy 300 acres and also constitute one of the most important
botanical research centres in the world. More than 50,000 species are grown in plantations and

glasshouses, which themselves attract over a million visitors a year. The most famous - and oldest, built in 1848 - glasshouse is the **Palm House**, which houses most of the known palm species. Nearby is the Waterlily House, full of tropical vines and creepers overhanging its lily pond. The newest, however, is the Prince of Wales Conservatory, which opened in 1987. It houses plants from ten different climatic zones, from arid desert to tropical rainforest.

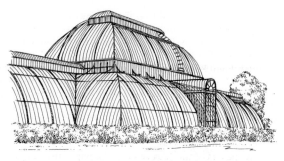

Kew Gardens Palm House

Several of the buildings constructed for Princess Augusta's amusement still stand in the grounds of the garden, but Kew also houses Britain's smallest royal residence. The three-storey **Kew Palace**, sometimes nicknamed the Dutch House because of its Flemish-bond brickwork, measures only 50 feet by 70 feet. The only king to have lived in this miniature palace was George III, confined here from1802 during his infamous madness. Behind the palace is a meticulously re-created 17th century garden, with helpful adages, such as "this cureth ill temper", added to the labels identifying the herbs.

Another Kew landmark is the **Chinese pagoda**, which was designed by Sir William Chambers who was responsible for much of the building in the gardens. The pagoda was purely for decoration, but it now serves as a practical purpose - as a navigational aid for visitors - since the ten storey octagonal structure stands 163 feet high. The bottom storey is 26 feet in diameter and 18 feet high. In each successive storey the diameter and height are reduced by one foot.

WIMBLEDON

MAP 4 REF Q19

5 miles SW of London on the A219

To most people Wimbledon is synonymous with the All-England Lawn Tennis Championships held each year at the end of June and in early July. However, the grounds of the All England Lawn Tennis and Croquet Club - the full name of the famous venue - are open throughout the year and there is still the chance for a buzz of excitement passing by the famous Centre Court stand in mid-winter. The Club also has the **Wimbledon Lawn Tennis Museum**, which offers the chance to peruse a range of exhibits stretching from the era of long flannel trousers to tie-breaks and disputed line calls.

There is more to Wimbledon than tennis. This suburb on the southern fringes of London is worth visiting throughout the year. In fact, the Championship fortnight is probably the best time to avoid Wimbledon, since the streets are thronged with would-be spectators and there are heavy traffic jams in and out of the town. The centre of Wimbledon, by its rail and Underground station, is a thriving commercial area, with stores lining the high street. Here, cheek by jowl with anonymous buildings dating from the 1960s, are a few gems. **Eagle House**, just west of the imposing National Westminster bank building, was built in 1613. It takes a bit of imagination today to see how this house would have towered over its neighbours, but its Jacobean appearance, with three large bay windows by its central entrance, still conveys an harmonious grandeur. Further on, and now occupying numbers 44-45, is an interesting L-shaped house dating from the late 17th century.

From Wimbledon itself, Wimbledon High Street then climbs steeply to the west towards **Wimbledon Village**, which has more of a boutique and bistro feel to it. Handsome residential streets lead off the High Street on its climb, and there are expansive views looking east across South London.

EPSOM
MAP 4 REF Q19

10 miles SW of London off the A240

The old market and spa town of Epsom is a prosperous residential centre which lies on the edge of London's southwestern suburbs. In the early 17th century, it was observed that cattle were refusing to drink from a spring on the common above the town and subsequent tests revealed the water to be high in magnesium sulphate, a mineral believed to have highly beneficial medicinal properties. As the fashion for "taking the waters" grew towards the end of the century, wealthy people from London came in increasing numbers to sample the benefits of Epsom salts and the settlement grew from a small village to a town with its own street market, a charter for which was granted in 1685.

By the end of the 18th century, the popularity of Epsom's spa was on the decline, but by this time, the town's pleasant rural location within easy reach of the City of London was already starting to attract well-to-do business people; a number of substantial residential homes were built in and around the town during this period, several of which survive to this day. A lively street market continues to be held every Saturday in Epsom High Street, a wide and impressive thoroughfare which contains some noteworthy old buildings, including a Victorian clock tower and the part 17th century **Waterloo House**, formerly the New Tavern.

Epsom's other main claim to fame is as a horse-racing centre. Each year in early June, the Downs to the southeast of the town take on a carnival atmosphere as tens of thousands of racing enthusiasts come to experience the annual Classic race meeting and the colourful funfair which accompanies it. Informal horse racing took place on **Epsom Downs** as long ago as 1683 when Charles II is said to have been in attendance. Racing was formalised in 1779 when a party of aristocratic sportsmen led by Lord Derby established a race for three year old fillies which was named after the Derbys' family home at Banstead, the Oaks; this was followed a year later by a race for all three year olds, the Derby, which was named after the founder himself, although only after he won a toss of a coin with the race's co-founder, Sir Charles Bunbury. (Had Lord Derby lost, the race would have become known as the Bunbury.) The Oaks and the Derby were a great success and soon achieved Classic status along with the St Leger at Doncaster, the earliest to be established in 1776, and the 1000 Guineas and 2000 Guineas at Newmarket, established in 1814 and 1809 respectively.

Hidden away in the conservation area of old Epsom, **Chalk Lane Hotel** is a delightful country house offering superior accommodation. Top-level service, quality cuisine and a professional, tranquil atmosphere are the bywords at this superb hotel/restaurant. Each of the luxurious, handsome and spacious en suite bedrooms has been recently refurbished and decorated to offer an impressive standard of quality and comfort. The restaurant (also open to

Chalk Lane Hotel, Chalk Lane, Epsom, Surrey KT18 7BB
Tel: 01372 721179 Fax: 01372 727878 email: chalklane@compuserve.com

non-residents) boasts a changing seasonal menu of delicious meals, which are traditional but with an innovative touch. All meals make use of mainly local suppliers to provide the freshest dishes, with over a dozen main courses from which to choose, including vegetarian options. Quietly situated at the base of the Downs, yet within walking distance of the town, this superb hotel, with its relaxing country house-style and efficient and welcoming staff, truly makes the perfect peaceful retreat.

WALTON ON THE HILL
MAP 4 REF Q20

3 miles S of Epsom off the A217

The "Hill" referred to in the name of this village is one of the many rolling hills that comprise the North Downs. Travellers heading south from London have a real sense of space by the time they reach Walton, and the upland farms strengthen this impression. Buildings - both residential and commercial - have the harmonious red-brick look so typical of this part of Surrey. They were built mainly in the Victorian era, but some of the earlier buildings were constructed from flint, hanging tile and weatherboarding.

Walton Manor is a good example of the tile-hung style and it was built in the 1890s. Its appearance shows the influence of the decorative Arts and Crafts movement, typified by architects such as Norman Shaw. Embedded in one end, however, are the walls of a stone-built manor house of the 14th century; a two storey hall and chapel protrude from the east of the house. The view south from the centre takes in the extent of the Downs, with the North Downs Way - the traditional Pilgrim's Way to Canterbury - running along the ridge on the other side of the broad valley. In the foreground are the rolling grounds of the championship golf course.

COULSDON
MAP 4 REF Q19

7 miles E of Epsom on the A23

Coulsdon is a pretty village that has managed to keep recent housing developments - notably Coulsdon Woods - discreetly removed from the traditional centre. There are pretty cottages in the heart of the village and some of the more substantial farmhouses nearby can be traced to the 15th century. **St John the Evangelist Church**, on the corner of the village green, was built in the late 13th century. The tower and spire were built more than 200 years later but the interior has some well-preserved elements from the original church. Most notable of these is the **sedilla**, with its circular piers and pointed arches. A sedilla was a seat for (usually three) priests and always located on the south side of the chancel.

The countryside around Coulsdon has more than its share of history. Traces of a 2nd century AD Romano-British settlement have been found on the ridge along Farthing Down, and 14 barrows on the ridge are the evidence of a 6th century Saxon burial ground. A number of iron knives, swords and other weapons have been dug from the site. **Coulsdon Common**, on the way to Caterham, is a tranquil and largely undeveloped spot. Since Saxon times it has been common land given over to grazing, its soil deemed too poor for cultivation.

CATERHAM
MAP 4 REF Q20

8 miles E of Epsom on the B2031

The sense of being high on the North Downs is pronounced in Caterham, which lies just north of the M25. The route into the town centre from the south passes close to Foster Down, a section of the North Downs Way which incorporates the impressive **Tupwood Viewpoint**; good views can also be enjoyed from the nearby 778 foot **Gravelly Hill**. Caterham itself is a modern and prosperous residential town which at first glance seems to have little to offer the casual visitor. On the other hand, the town is something of a time capsule. Until 1856 Caterham was a remote Downs village. The arrival of the railway in that year changed everything and the town developed around the new arrival and the barracks which were built in the 1870's. The railway was never extended, so Caterham is a terminus rather than a through station. As such, the 19th century town plan remains unchanged. Worthy of note, however, is the East Surrey

Museum in Stafford Road which offers an interesting insight into the natural history and archaeology of the surrounding area.

WARLINGHAM

MAP 4 REF Q19

8 miles E of Epsom on the B269

Successful enforcement of Green Belt policy since the Second World War has helped Warlingham retain much of its green and leafy look, and it is hard to imagine that it lies just a few miles south of bustling Croydon and its built-up suburbs. Warlingham's real fame stems from its church, **All Saints**, or more specifically two historic events that took place in it. The new English prayer-book, authorised by Edward VI, was first used in the parish church. Its compiler, Archbishop Cranmer, attended the service. Four centuries later Warlingham parish church was chosen to host Britain's first televised church service. The church itself was restored and enlarged in Victorian times but dates from the 13th century. It still contains many old elements, including a 15th century wall painting of Saint Christopher and a 15th century octagonal font. Modern housing has replaced most of the traditional cottages in the heart of Warlingham but there are a few survivors from past centuries. The **Atwood Almshouses**, a two-storey cottage flanked by single-storey cottages, were built in 1663. The vicarage, nearby, was built in the same year.

Dating back to the late 16th/early 17th century, **The White Bear** is a listed Grade II public house and restaurant with a traditional charm and ambience. This two-storey pristine whitewashed pub started life as cottages but was soon converted into a coaching inn. Outside, guests are greeted by a life-size white bear (thankfully, just a model). The original wooden model was stolen by Canadian soldiers during the Second World War. The interior of this wonderful

The White Bear, Fairchildes Lane, Warlingham, Surrey CR6 9PH
Tel: 01959 573166 Fax: 01959 541520

inn is made up of a series of separate rooms, each cosy and intimate, with comfortable seating and an attractive traditional decor. The open fire, exposed beams, flagstone floors and handsome wooden furniture add to the attractive yet homely atmosphere. There are said to be three resident ghosts who frequent the bar - the manager is happy to tell visitors of their history. Renowned locally and further afield for its real ales, this fine pub also serves food seven days a week - the Sunday roast is a speciality (booking advised).

WEYBRIDGE

MAP 4 REF P19

8 miles W of Epsom on the A317

Although in many people's minds the epitome of a comfortable and modern commuter belt settlement, Weybridge is a surprisingly long-established settlement. The town takes its name from the bridge over the River Wey on the highway to Chertsey, and there is evidence of such a bridge existing as early as 1235. Tradition also links Weybridge with Julius Caesar, and many historians believe he crossed the Thames near here in 55 BC.

The town once possessed a palace, Oatlands Park, in which Henry VIII married his fifth wife, Catherine Howard, in 1540; 110 years later, the building was demolished and the stone used in the construction of the **Wey Navigation**. Weybridge stands at the northern end of this historic inland waterway which was one of the first examples of its kind when it was completed in 1670. It extends for almost twenty miles southwards to Godalming and incorporates large sections of the main river. The middle of the 17th century, during the Interregnum, also saw a remarkable development in Weybridge. The Diggers, a radical left-wing group, attempted to build a commune on St George's Hill, although they were thwarted by angry commoners.

Elmbridge Museum, situated in the library in Church Street, is an excellent source of information about the history - and prehistory - of Weybridge. A wide range of exhibits takes in archaeological artefacts, old maps, photographs and paintings of the district. The costume collection is particularly interesting, as it consists of clothes worn by local residents from the late 18th century to the present day.

In 1907, the worlds first purpose-built motor racing track was constructed on the Brooklands estate, near Weybridge, and in the years which followed, this legendary banked circuit hosted competitions between some of the most formidable racing cars ever made. With the outbreak of World War I, however, racing came to an end; the track fell into disrepair and Brooklands was never again able to regain its once-pre-eminent position in British motor racing. For years, the only thing to interrupt the tranquillity of the empty track was the occasional eerie sound of screeching tyres and roaring engines, or the appearance of the goggled ghost of Percy Lambert, who tragically died after his car smashed into the end of the Railway Straight in 1913. In recent years, the circuit has undergone something of a revival with the opening of the **Brooklands Museum**, a fascinating establishment centred on the old Edwardian clubhouse which features a unique collection of historic racing cars, motorcycles and aircraft.

The Grotto Inn is a lively and popular inn, family run by Agnes and Eric Brookfield and their daughter Jill. There has been a pub on this site since at least 1869; it is said that before this the buildings were used as the laundry for the manor at nearby Oatlands Park. The spacious and attractive garden to the rear has a pond with Koi Carp, paved areas for sitting on fine days and a mass of flowers in hanging baskets and troughs. The interior is also impressive: intimate and cosy, it has low ceilings, a wealth of handsome wood and open log fire. This completely unspoilt traditional pub has a warm and friendly atmosphere. As a free house there is a good range of real ales, including seasonal ales, every conceivable lager and a good range of wines, ciders and spirits. The imaginative menu makes Thai dishes a speciality: East meets West at this wonderful inn, as there is also an excellent selection of modern English cui-

The Grotto Inn, Monument Hill, Weybridge, Surrey KT13 8RJ
Tel: 01932 842480

sine. Sundays are reserved for the delicious traditional Sunday roast. Food is available seven days a week for lunch (midday - 2.30), and Monday to Saturday evening (7-10).

CHERTSEY
2 miles NW of Weybridge on the A320

MAP 4 REF P19

Chertsey is an ancient riverside town which has altered almost beyond recognition over the centuries. The town once boasted a formidable abbey whose influence stretched over a wide

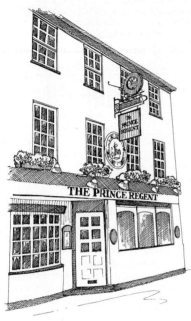

area of southern England; when it was demolished following the Dissolution of the Monasteries, its stone was used to build Hampton Court Palace and later, the River Wey Canal. One of the abbey bells now hangs in the parish church, St Peter; at one time it was used to sound the evening curfew and it is associated with a local romantic legend concerning Blanche Heriot, a young Chertsey woman who, on hearing that her lover was to be executed at the sound of the curfew bell, climbed into the tower and clung onto the tongue until his pardon arrived. This heroic action was commemorated in the ballad " The Curfew Must Not Ring Tonight" by the American poet Rose Hartwick Thorpe. Despite the upheavals that Chertsey has undergone, it still manages to preserve some lovely woodland scenery, with a number of green fields and commons including **Chertsey Mead**. A well-proportioned, seven arched bridge spans the Thames in the centre of the town.

The Prince Regent, 126 Guildford Street, Chertsey, Surrey KT16 9AH
Tel: 01932 562015

The Prince Regent public house in Chertsey has a distinguished history. Occupying a central High Street location, this welcoming pub dates back in parts to the 17th century, but came into its own, as The Regent Inn, circa 1812. This Grade II listed building houses a superior pub with a spacious and comfortable bar area and separate dining room. Original features include the exposed beamwork. There's a good range of beers, wines and spirits on offer, and a fine menu of traditional dishes from the all-day breakfast until evening meals. Snacks such as fresh filled baguettes and jacket potatoes are complemented by main course steaks, chops, pies, and changing daily specials. This popular and convivial establishment attracts a wide range of customers, and is just the place for a welcome break from sightseeing in the area.

HAMPTON COURT
4 miles NE of Weybridge on the A309

MAP 4 REF P19

The name of Henry VIII is forever linked with the magnificent palace and grounds occupying a stretch of the Thames some 13 miles southwest of London. Its stature and extensive gardens underpin its role as the most impressive of all royal residences, but Hampton Court was originally designed with a slightly different purpose in mind. It was the brainchild of Cardinal Wolsey, who had it built in 1516. Wolsey was an ambitious and powerful man, serving as Henry VIII's Lord Chancellor, so Hampton Court was never likely to remain simply an ecclesiastical abode. Banquets and balls were the order of the day, and Hampton Court gained such fame - or notoriety - that it prompted a certain amount of envy from the monarch. In 1525

Henry asked the Cardinal why he had built such a palace for himself and Wolsey, interpreting the potentially dangerous undercurrents, replied "to show how noble a palace a subject may offer to his sovereign". Even this huge gift was not enough to secure Wolsey's position. Four years later, after he had failed to secure a papal annulment for Henry's marriage to Catherine of Aragon, Wolsey found himself stripped of all his possessions, including the palace of Whitehall. He fell ill and died within a year. Hampton Court continued to grow under the ownership of Henry, who enlarged the kitchens, altered many rooms and rebuilt the chapel. It became the home of the last five of Henry's wives as well as a growing number of courtiers and assorted royal hangers-on.

The Great Hall, Hampton Court

Approached through **Trophy Gate**, Hampton Court gives a first impression of grandeur and scale. The courtyards and buildings to the left still contain a number of "grace and favour" apartments, where Crown officials and dependants of the Royal family live. Two side turrets contain terracotta roundels with the images of Roman emperors which date from Wolsey's time. Anne Boleyn's gateway, opposite Base Court, is carved with the initials H and A, for Henry and Anne. To the left of Clock Court, with its large astronomical clock, is the **Great Hall**, which Henry had completed in 1534, having forced the builders to work night and day. Mounted stag heads and fine tapestries line the walls beneath the intricate hammerbeam roof. The Great Hall was the scene of theatrical productions during the reigns of Elizabeth I and James I, and among the performing troupes was that of William Shakespeare. Under the Great Hall are the **Tudor Kitchens**, with their huge fireplaces and assortment of ancient cooking utensils.

The **Queen's Apartments** were built for Mary II, but were only completed after her death. They are reached by the grand Queen's Staircase which leads to the Queen's Guard Chamber. Life-sized marble guardsmen flank the main chimneypiece. The Queen's state rooms run along the east wing of Fountain Court, and include the Queen's Drawing Room and the Queen's Bedroom. The Queen's Gallery contains ornate marble fireplaces with mantelpieces decorated with images of doves and Venus. Gobelins tapestries, on the theme of Alexander the Great, hang from the walls. The King's Staircase also features Alexander the Great, although in this case it is really William III in the role of Alexander. The staircase leads to the **King's Apartments**, which comprise William's state rooms. A display of arms, numbering 3,000 pieces, is arranged in the King's Guard Chamber, set out as they would have been during William's time.

Outside are the **Palace Gardens**, Hampton Court's main attraction for many visitors and reflecting the influence of three kings: Henry VIII, Charles II and William III. William, with his Dutch background, was perhaps the most involved of these monarchs, and his influence is particularly evident in the Fountain Garden, fanning out from the east front and now mostly lawn, and the Privy Garden to the south of the Palace. The Privy Garden is being restored: shrubberies that were allowed to grow there in the 19th century have been removed to reveal traces of the formal beds and pathways that were William's legacy. A fully re-created 17th century formal garden will be the result of this horticultural archaeology. The **Broad Walk** runs from the Thames for half a mile past the east front and is lined with herbaceous borders. Just off the walk to the left and inside is the Tudor Tennis Court, a Real Tennis court built by Henry VIII, who was a keen player. To the north of the Palace is the famous **Maze**, planted in 1714 within

William III's "Wilderness" of evergreen trees. The Maze is extremely popular and, though a bit straggly in parts, can be surprisingly difficult to negotiate.

WHITELEY VILLAGE   MAP 4 REF P19
2 miles SE of Weybridge on the B365

A mile and a half to the southwest of Weybridge, and close to the St George's Hill residential area much-favoured by famous media personalities, lies the remarkable Whiteley Village. This unique 200 acre model village was founded on the instructions of the proprietor of a famous Bayswater department store who in 1907, left one million pounds in his will to house his retired staff. The community was designed to be self-contained with its own churches, hospital and shops, and was laid out in an octagonal pattern around a green containing a memorial to the project's benefactor. The site has been planted with a great many trees and flowering shrubs, and is best visited in late-spring and summer.

ESHER   MAP 4 REF P19
4 miles E of Weybridge off the A3

The part 16th century St George's church has an unusual three-tier pulpit and a marble monument to Princess Charlotte of Wales who died at nearby Claremont House in 1817. The part of Surrey nearest to London is well supplied with racecourses: as well as Kempton Park, near Sunbury, and the classic course at Epsom, regular meetings are held at **Sandown Park** on Esher's northern edge. Near here, and well worth a visit is the beautiful National Trust-owned **Claremont Landscape Garden** which lies on the southern side of the A307 Portsmouth road within a mile of the town centre. Having been laid out in the 1710s, this is believed to be one of the earliest surviving examples of an English landscape garden; later in the century, it was remodelled by William Kent whose work was continued by Capability Brown. The grounds have been designed to include a number of striking vistas and contain a grassed amphitheatre, grotto, lake, and an island with a pavilion. Nearby **Claremont House** operates as a school and is only occasionally open to visitors. It was designed in the 1700s by Vanbrugh and substantially remodelled in 1772 for Clive of India. One of the architects who undertook the renovation was Lancelot, or "Capability", Brown who not only remodelled the gardens but oversaw much of the work on the building itself.

WOKING   MAP 4 REF P20
5 miles SW of Weybridge on the A320

Woking is a commuter town which lies on the main railway line to Waterloo. In fact it was the railway that defined the present appearance - and location - of Woking. The original village was what is now called Old Woking, and when the railway arrived in 1838 the station was built two miles away in what was then open heathland. The town developed around this new arrival, and the original village centre dwindled as the population was drawn towards new employment. As a result, most of the heart of Woking dates from the middle of the 19th century. Among these Victorian-era buildings, however, is an unexpected "first". The first purpose-built mosque to be founded in Britain - **Shah Jehan Mosque** - can be found in Woking's Oriental Street. The construction of this unusual onion-domed structure was largely financed by the ruler of the Indian state of Bhopal who visited the town in 1889. **Old Woking** is a former market town which is now incorporated into the southeastern suburbs of its more modern neighbour. This is an old settlement, dating from the Saxon period and mentioned in the Domesday Book. Old Woking had the good fortune to be listed as a personal possession of the king and therefore it did not need to pay taxes. Its streets contain some noteworthy old buildings, including the 17th century old Manor House, and the part-Norman parish church of St Peter which has a late-medieval west tower.

There has always been a pub on the site of **The Plough**, a warm and welcoming inn built at the beginning of the last century. Part of the picturesque Horsell Common, it is spacious inside and out, with a large lawned garden to the rear and picnic tables out front. Inside, there's a warm and very comfortable main bar area with an open log fire. Here in the secluded wooded countryside, this traditional pub offers four real ales and a good range of lagers, ciders, wines and spirits. The home-cooked food is delicious and well worth staying for, and features a variety

The Plough, Cheapside, off South Road, Horsell, Woking, Surrey GU21 4JL Tel: 01483 714105

of tasty home-made pies, game dishes, fresh fish, lamb, curries and other popular favourites. Local produce is used whenever possible. Food is available every lunchtime and Tuesday to Saturday evenings. Owners Peter and Linda Adams are friendly and convivial hosts; together with their staff they offer a high standard of service.

RIPLEY   MAP 4 REF P20

2 miles E of Woking off the A3

Just a mile or so to the southwest of Wisley is the attractive village of Ripley, a former staging post on the old coaching route between London and Portsmouth. The main street contains a number of exceptional brick and half-timbered buildings, including the charming **Vintage Cottage** with its unusual crownpost roof. Most of the attractive houses lie on the gracefully curving High Street. Unusually, the long and wedge-shaped village green lies beside the street on the west side. The village seems to have grown away from the green rather than around as in most English villages. The distinguished and impressive **Talbot Hotel** in Ripley is an historic coaching inn dating back to 1453. Occupying quiet surroundings, it boasts a lovely private garden to the rear. This gracious and beautifully appointed hotel has an 18th century brick frontage concealing the much earlier timber framed structure. Comfortable and spacious, it is said that Lord Nelson and Lady Hamilton were once guests here. The bar and restaurant are picturesque and cosy; the service is always friendly, and the choice of cuisine is excellent, with a range of traditional and more innovative favourites,

The Talbot Hotel, High Street, Ripley, Surrey GU23 6BB Tel: 01483 225188 Fax: 01483 211332

all expertly prepared and presented. Each of the eight en suite guest bedrooms has its own unique character and is named for one of Lord Nelson's ships; they all share the highest standards of taste and comfort. The Honeymoon Suite boasts a beautiful four-poster bed. This oasis of peace combines a relaxed and welcoming ambience with luxury and style.

WISLEY
MAP 4 REF P20

3 miles E of Woking off the A3

The Royal Horticultural Society's internationally renowned **Wisley Garden** lies on the north side of the A3, one mile to the northwest of Ockham. As well as containing a wide variety of trees, flowering shrubs and ornamental plants, this magnificent 250 acre garden incorporates the Society's experimental beds where scientific trials are conducted into new and existing plant varieties. Wisley also acts as a centre for training horticultural students, and offers a wide range of plants, books, gifts and gardening advice at its first-class plant centre and shop.

SUTTON PLACE
MAP 4 REF P20

2 miles SE of Woking off the A3

Sutton Place was the creation of Sir Richard Weston, a protege of Henry VIII who was a Knight of the Bath, a Gentleman of the Privy Chamber and eventually Under-Treasurer of England. He had accompanied Henry to France for the famous meeting at the Field of the Cloth of Gold in 1520, so in every respect he had the right to expect to live in sumptuous surroundings that

Terracotta Panels, Sutton Place

reflected his high standing. The house he had built, after receiving the grant of the Sutton estate in 1521, is seen by many critics as one of the most important English houses to be built in the years after Hampton Court was completed. It was built to describe almost a perfect square, with sides measuring about 130-140 feet surrounding a central courtyard. The north side was demolished in the 18th century, so today's house appears to comprise a two-storey, red brick central building with two long projections. Symmetry is important in Sutton Place, as English architects were busy putting to use the elements of the Italian Renaissance in their buildings. Doorways and windows are balanced in each wing. The Italian influence is particularly evident in the terracotta ornamentation of the windows and even more dramatically in a series of terracotta panels depicting cherubs over the entrance. Terracotta had

been first used as an architectural feature, mainly as faience or majolica, in Hampton Court in 1521. Sutton Court was built probably no more than a decade later - records show that Henry VIII was a guest in 1533 - so it was obviously at the forefront of this style of ornamentation. It is the exterior, with its strict adherence to Renaissance tenets, that makes Sutton Place so fascinating. Inside there have been alterations and additions that make the effect less wholly linked to one period.

VIRGINIA WATER
MAP 4 REF P19

7 miles N of Woking on the A30

From Camberley, the A30 runs along the northeastern border of the county to Virginia Water, a surprising diversion which lies in the heart of the Surrey stockbroker belt. The "water" referred to is a mile and a half long artificial lake which is set within mature woodland at the southern end of **Windsor Great Park**; it was created by Paul and Thomas Sandby, two accomplished

Georgian landscapers who were also known for their painting. The picturesque ruins standing at the lakeside are genuine remains of a Roman temple which once stood at Leptis Magna in Libya. **The Valley Gardens** also contain an unusual 100 foot totem pole which was erected here in 1958 to mark the centenary of British Columbia.

A little further to the north, the **Savill Garden** is renowned as one of the finest woodland gardens in the country. The famous **Wentworth Golf Course** lies on the opposite side of the A30 on the southern edge of the genteel settlement which takes its name from the Sandbys' lake.

RUNNYMEDE MAP 4 REF P19
10 miles N of Woking on the A30

A meadow beside the River Thames to the north of Egham is where King John sealed the Magna Carta in 1215. The historic **Runnymede Site** and nearby **Cooper's Hill** are contained within a 300 acre tract of land which is now under the ownership of the National Trust. The area contains three separate memorials: a domed neoclassical temple which was erected by the American Bar Association to commemorate the sealing of the world's first bill of democratic rights, a memorial to John F Kennedy, and the Air Forces Memorial which was erected in memory of the World War II airmen who went missing in action. From the top of Cooper's Hill there are magnificent views across Windsor Great Park and the Thames Valley. The river below is populated by slow-moving motor cruisers and pleasure craft, and river trips to Windsor, Staines and Hampton Court can be taken from Runnymede, daily between May and October, and at weekends during winter.

LIGHTWATER MAP 4 REF P19
7 miles W of Woking off the M3

For many Londoners, Lightwater represents the first taste of countryside outside the metropolis. It has the advantage - from the visitor's point of view - of lying within easy reach of the M3. By turning south off the motorway, instead of north to Bagshot, drivers soon enter a countryside defined by heaths and scattered woodlands. **Bagshot Heath**, once a rough area peopled by highwaymen and duellists, begins at the western edge of Lightwater, and the bucolically named village of **Donkey Town** lies just to the south, its name providing some confirmation of the area's rural nature. Just on the western edge of Lightwater, between Bagshot Heath to the north and the Military training area to the south is **Lightwater and Heathland Visitor Centre**, a fascinating collection of exhibits about the history and natural history of this stretch of West Surrey countryside.

FRIMLEY MAP 4 REF O19
7 miles W of Woking off the M3

Frimley is an extremely old village on the Hampshire border and a site of several important prehistoric and Roman finds which are displayed at the Surrey Heath Museum in Camberley. Much of the more recent history, unfortunately, has been less well preserved and the old sense of the village's coaching significance has been erased with a series of housing developments over the last four decades. The area around **Frimley Green**, however, gives some indication of what Frimley - and even its larger neighbour Camberley - looked like in the late medieval period. **Cross Farmhouse** is one of the oldest surviving houses, its timber-frame and brick structure containing elements dating from the 15th century. The parish church of St Peter dates only from 1825 but its churchyard contains the graves of many famous people. Among them is Francis Bret Harte, the American novelist whose wanderings around the world led him to settle eventually in England.

Just south of Frimley, and also hugging the Hampshire border, is the village of **Mytchett**, which has also suffered from some unthinking urban planning. However, it does contain some-

Basingstoke Canal Visitors Centre

thing of an imaginatively designed one-storey primary school which was built in the 1960s. In itself functional and not an attraction as such, Mytchett Primary School displays how modern construction can be achieved without pastiche and with an awareness of the special surroundings.

The **Basingstoke Canal Visitors Centre**, which lies just east of **Farnborough** and only five minutes from the M3, offers a tranquil and relaxing way in which to discover the charming countryside. Visitors can take a leisurely trip on a narrowboat, gaining a fascinating insight into the points of interest from the informative guide. The Canal Exhibition provides an in-depth account of how barge skippers lived a century ago and how the Basingstoke Canal, and its wildlife habitats, have been conserved more recently.

FARNHAM

12 miles SW of Woking on the A31

MAP 4 REF O20

The most westerly town in Surrey is Farnham. This fine old settlement stands at the point where the old Pilgrims' Way from Winchester to Canterbury crosses the River Wey, and it has

Farnham Castle

long been an important staging post on the busy trading route between Southampton and London. The town first became a residence of the Bishops of Winchester during Saxon times, and following the Norman conquest, the new Norman bishop built himself a castle on a pleasant tree-covered rise above the centre of the town. This impressive structure underwent a number of alterations, most notably in the 15th century when the decorated brick-built tower was added, and it remained in the hands of the Bishops of Winchester until 1927. **Farnham Castle** has been visited on a number of occasions by the reigning English monarch and was besieged during the English Civil War. Today, it is approached along Castle Street, a delightful wide thoroughfare of Georgian and neo-Georgian buildings which was laid out to accommodate a traditional street market. The old Norman keep, now owned by English Heritage, is open daily, 10.00 to 18.00pm between 1 April and 30 September. The remainder of the castle, including the Great Hall, can be visited on Wednesdays only between 14.00 and 16.00 throughout the year. Farnham contains a number of other interesting historic buildings, including a row of 17th century gabled almshouses and Willmer House in West Street, a handsome Georgian-fronted structure which now houses the informative **Farnham Museum**. As well as some fine wood panelling, carvings and period furniture, the museum contains some interesting archaeological exhibits and a unique collection of 19th century glass paperweights.

WAVERLEY ABBEY

MAP 4 REF O20

2 miles E of Farnham on the B3001

Lying within easy striking distance of Farnham are the atmospheric ruins of **Waverley Abbey**. Dating from the 12th century, this was the first Cistercian abbey to be built in England. The first church was completed in 1160 and destroyed during the dissolution of the monasteries. Its monumental floor plan was only revealed after excavations this century. Although there is little in the way of architectural detail recognisable to the untrained eye, architectural historians have suggested that this early church might well have inspired the famous Gothic churches of Tintern, Fountains and Riveaulx abbeys, so the decline of

Waverley Abbey

Waverley takes on a sadder aspect. The Abbey remains are open during daylight hours and are said to have provided the inspiration for Sir Walter Scott's romantic novel, Waverley, published in 1814 during his stay at the nearby **Waverley Abbey House** whose imposing structure was built with stone taken from the abbey in 1723.

TILFORD

MAP 4 REF O20

3 miles E of Farnham off the B3001

A lovely two mile riverside walk from Waverley Abbey leads to Tilford, an attractive village which stands at the confluence of the two branches of the River Wey. The monks of Waverley are believed to have been responsible for rebuilding Tilford's two medieval bridges following the devastating floods of 1233 during which the abbey itself had to be evacuated. At the heart of Tilford stands a triangular village green which features a 900 year old oak tree with a 25 foot girth which is known as the King's or Novel's Oak; a pleasant early 18th century inn can be found nearby. Tilford's parish church of All Saints hosts a regular spring festival of early church music.

In Reeds Road to the southwest of Tilford is the **Rural Life Centre** and **Old Kiln Museum,** which contains an interesting display of historic agricultural equipment and rural memorabilia, along with working blacksmith's and wheelwright's workshops. The museum spreads over 10 acres of field, woodland, and barns and there is even a narrow gauge railway.

PUTTENHAM

MAP 4 REF O20

5 miles E of Farnham off the A31

The Hog's Back village of Puttenham lies stretched out along the route of the old Pilgrims' Way. An attractive mixture of building styles, the village contains a restored part-Norman church, several fine 15th and 16th century cottages, an 18th century farm with a number of period outbuildings and oast houses, and an impressive Palladian mansion, **Puttenham Priory**, which was completed in 1762. The mixture of building styles arose because of Puttenham's location, where chalk gives way to sandstone. Cottages use one or the other - or both - of these materials, and the effect is enlivened with brickwork usually dating from the 18th century.

THURSLEY
MAP 4 REF O20

6 miles SE of Farnham off the A3

Thursley is an exceptional village which takes its name from the Viking god Thor and the Saxon word for field, or lea. The settlement was once an important centre of the Wealden iron industry and a number of disused hammer ponds can still be seen to the east. These artificial lakes provided power to drive the mechanical hammers and bellows in the once-bustling iron forges. Today, the village is a tranquil place arranged around a green containing an acacia tree which was planted as a memorial to William Cobbett, the Georgian traveller and writer who is

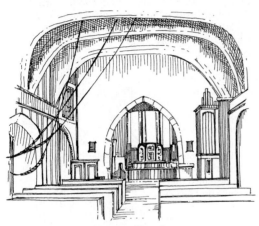

Thursley Church

best remembered for his book describing riding tours of England, "Rural Rides", which was published in 1830. Thursley is also the birthplace of the celebrated architect, Sir Edwin Lutyens, who at the age of only nineteen converted a row of local cottages into a single dwelling now known as the Corner. Thursley's two principal thoroughfares, the Lane and the Street, contain a wide variety of noteworthy domestic buildings. The latter leads to **St Michael's Church**, a part-Saxon structure which was heavily restored by the Victorians. The spire and belfry are 15th century and are supported by massive timber posts with tie-beams and arched braces, a good example of late-medieval engineering. The churchyard contains the grave of a sailor, who was murdered on Hindhead Heath in 1786 by three men he had gone to help. Although the villagers never discovered the victim's name, they gave him a full burial and erected an inscribed stone over his grave. Two interesting old buildings stand near the church, the half-timbered and tile-hung Old Parsonage and the part timber-framed Hill Farm, both of which date from the 16th century.

THE DEVIL'S PUNCH BOWL
MAP 4 REF O20

7 miles SE of Farnham off the A3

The Devil's Punch Bowl is a steep-sided natural sandstone amphitheatre through which the busy A3 Guildford to Petersfield road passes four miles to the southeast of **Frensham Great Pond**. As usual, Lucifer's name is invoked in the place name but the origins might have more to do with real events than with superstition. The deep valley provided excellent cover for thieves and highwaymen, and even in coaching days passengers would look on the natural wonder with a mixture of awe and apprehension.

HINDHEAD COMMON
MAP 4 REF O20

7 miles SE of Farnham off the A3

Lying just to the east of Hindhead itself is Hindhead Common, comprising a largely untamed collection of wild heathlands, pinewoods and steep valleys. The National Trust owns 1,400 acres of Hindhead Common, and maintains a series of trails and paths that takes visitors through evocatively named sites such as Polecat Copse, Golden Valley, Hurt Hill and Stoatley Green. On the summit of **Gibbet Hill** is a granite monument marking the spot where the gibbet stood. The glorious views across both the North and South Downs was the last earthly memory of the thieves and murderers who were executed here.

GUILDFORD

Map 4 Ref P20

10 miles E of Farnham off the A31

The route into Guildford from the northwest passes close to **Guildford Cathedral**, one of only two new Anglican cathedrals to have been built in this country since the Reformation (the other is Liverpool). This impressive redbrick building stands on top of Stag Hill, a prominent local landmark which enjoys panoramic views over the surrounding landscape. The building was designed by Sir Edward Maufe with a superb high-arched interior and was begun in 1936. However, work was halted during World War II and members of the local diocese had to wait until 1961 for the new cathedral to be finally consecrated. Guided tours and restaurant facilities are available all year round. In 1968, the **University of Surrey** relocated from London to a site on a hillside to the northwest of the cathedral. Pleasant and leafy, the campus contains a number of striking buildings including the university library and art gallery.

From the university, it is only a mile to the heart of Guildford, the ancient county town of Surrey. Guildford has been the capital of the region since pre-Norman times and in the 10th century, it even had its own mint. Henry II built a **Castle** here on high ground in the 12th century which later became the county gaol; today, the castle remains house a renowned brass-rubbing centre and the ruined keep provides a fascinating place from which to view the surrounding area. Those visiting the town for the first time should make straight for the old **High Street**, a wonderful cobbled thoroughfare of Georgian and older buildings which rises steeply from the River Wey.

Perhaps the most noteworthy of these is the **Guildhall**, a Tudor structure with an elaborately decorated 17th century frontage which incorporates a belltower, balcony and distinctive gilded clock. Abbot's Hospital, a little further along, is an imposing turreted almshouse which was built in 1619 by the Guildford-born Archbishop of Canterbury, George Abbot; at the top of the High Street, the **Royal Grammar School** dates from the early 1500s and was subsequently endowed by Edward VI. A number of interesting streets and alleyways run off Guildford High Street, including Quarry Street with its medieval St Mary's Church and old Castle

Guildhall, Guildford

Arch. The latter houses the **Guildford Museum**, an informative centre for local history and archaeology which also contains an exhibition devoted to Lewis Carroll, the creator of Alice In Wonderland who died in the town in 1898.

A charming bronze memorial to Lewis Carroll (real name Charles Lutwidge Dodgson) which is composed of a life-sized Alice chasing the White Rabbit into his hole can be found on the far bank of the River Wey, midway between the two footbridges. The famous **Yvonne Arnaud Theatre** stands in a delightful riverside setting at the foot of the castle mound on the town side of the river. As well as offering top quality productions, the theatre has an excellent bar, coffee lounge and restaurant which remains open throughout the day. In summer, rowing boats and guided pleasure boat trips are available at the nearby Guildford Boat House.

RYDES HILL

Map 4 Ref P20

5 miles W of Guildford off the A323

Gerry and Carol Pile, ably assisted by their daughter Julie and husband Mick, offer all guests a warm welcome to **The Cricketers** at Rydes Hill, a large and friendly public house. Built around the 1920s, the exterior boasts a very attractive lawned shrub garden to the rear and a large

The Cricketers, Rydes Hill, Aldershot Road (A323), Guildford, Surrey GU3 3AA Tel: 01483 575901

outdoor patio extending from the conservatory dining area. Hanging baskets and a safe children's play area complete the welcoming atmosphere outside. Indoors, guests will find two adjoining dining areas and a large lounge/bar area with welcoming open fire and comfortable, tasteful decor and seating. There's a good range of real ales on tap, including two changing guest ales (and always one from local breweries), together with lagers, wines and spirits. The home-cooked food merits attention: choices range from traditional snacks and meals to more innovative specials, including an excellent variety of fish dishes. The tempting puddings are well worth saving room for.

ALBURY
MAP 4 REF P20

4 miles E of Guildford on the A28

Albury dates largely from the last century and was constructed in fanciful neo-Gothic style as an estate village for nearby **Albury Park**. This large country mansion was built on the site of a Tudor manor house in the early 18th century and was much altered by Pugin in the 1840s. The most eccentric feature of the house is its collection of chimneys, 63 of them built for only 60 rooms in an amazing variety of shapes and sizes. Although the mansion has now been converted into flats, the estate gardens are open to visitors and are well worth a look. They were laid out by the diarist John Evelyn at the turn of the 18th century and feature a series of terraced orchards which rise above the house to the north. A number of smaller communities nestle around Albury.

CLANDON PARK
MAP 4 REF P20

5 miles E of Guildford on the A247

Set in the farming countryside east of Guildford and south of Woking is the National Trust-owned property, **Clandon Park**. This magnificent country mansion was designed in the 1730s by Giacomo Leoni, a Venetian architect who combined Palladian, Baroque and European styles to create one of the grandest 18th century houses in England. The interior is renowned for its magnificent two-storey marble hall, sumptuous decoration and fine Italian plasterwork depicting scenes from mythology. The Gubbay collection of furniture and porcelain is also housed here, along with the Ivo Forde collection of humorous Meissen figures. The surrounding parkland was landscaped by Capability Brown in characteristic style and includes a parterre, grotto and brightly painted New Zealand Maori house.

GOMSHALL
MAP 4 REF P20

5 miles E of Guildford on the A25

This once-industrialised community has a Victorian heart and was once an important centre of the tanning and leather-working industries. The old packhorse bridge over the River Tillingbourne dates from the 1500s and the manor house at the southern end of the village from the early 1700s. Gomshall is now known for its fine craft and antique shops, several of which are concentrated in an ancient and beautifully converted water mill, the **Gomshall Mill and Gallery**.

The **Compasses** pub on Station Road in Gomshall was built in 1830. Originally known as "God Encompasses", the name was so frequently mispronounced that "Goat and Compasses" became its name through overuse, and was finally known simply by its present name. The interior has everything guests could expect of a traditional English pub: exposed oak beams, horse brasses and a friendly atmosphere. Owner Nicky Whitworth is justly proud of this fine pub and restaurant and its enviable reputation for fresh home-cooked food and a range of well-kept real ales. Food is available lunch and evening seven days a

The Compasses Inn, Station Road, Gomshall, Surrey GU5 9LA Tel: 01483 202506

week. The picturesque Tillingbourne Stream runs between the pub and its popular beer garden - guests are advised to keep an eye out for the ghost that is said to skip along it. For those who wish to stay a bit longer in this charming part of Surrey, there are three tasteful and very comfortable en suite rooms offered as bed and breakfast accommodation.

SHALFORD
Map 4 Ref P20

3 miles S of Guildford on the A281

The residential community of Shalford contains a fascinating **Water Mill** which operated from the early 1700s right up to the First World War. Once powered by the waters of the Tillingbourne, this exceptional tile-hung structure retains most of its original machinery. During the 1930s, it was bought and restored by Ferguson's Gang, a secretive group of conservationists who hid their identities behind eccentric noms de plume and who eventually donated the building to the National Trust. Shalford stands near the northern entrance to the **Wey and Arun Junction Canal**, an ambitious inland waterway which was constructed in 1816 to connect the Thames with the English Channel. Conceived during the Napoleonic wars as a way of avoiding attacks on coastal shipping, unfortunately it opened too late to fulfil its function and was soon superseded by the railways. A towpath providing some delightful walks runs along almost two-thirds of the canal's 36 mile length, a significant proportion of which has now be restored by enthusiastic teams of volunteers. About a mile south of Shalford is **Great Tangley**, one of the finest 16th century half-timbered houses in Surrey. The exterior is made up of roughly square panels each with four curved diagonal braces. This combination creates a star shape for each panel, which is repeated across the sides of the house.

BLACKHEATH
Map 4 Ref P20

4 miles SE of Guildford off the A248

Set in the hills above Albury, this tidy Victorian hamlet gives the visitor a sense of remoteness despite being within easy striking distance of Guildford. Blackheath has some fine late-Victorian buildings. One of the most interesting is **Greyfriars**, a Franciscan monastery built in neo-Gothic style in 1895. The church and dormitories of this stone-built structure are contained under one roof. Another Victorian curiosity is the somewhat austere timbered residence, the Hallams.

Thought to date from the late 1800s, **The Villagers** pub in Blackheath is set apart from the town and surrounded by its own attractive patio and garden area which backs onto the heathland. Originally known as The Volunteer - a name that hearkens back to the days when Blackheath

was a prime recruitment area for Lord Kitchener during the First World War - the name later changed to reflect the pub's importance for the community of this remote countryside area. Ask to see the Visitors' Book - with entries dating back to the 1930s. Guests won't find any machines or live music at this traditional English inn. Comfortable, warm and cosy, it has lovely features such as the exposed beams, stone bar, flagstone floor and

The Villagers, Blackheath Lane, Blackheath, Surrey GU4 8RB
Tel: 01483 893152 Fax: 01483 894942

open log fire. There are always four real ales at this Free House, as well as a good range of lagers, wines and spirits. The restaurant specialises in fresh fish dishes, with a menu that changes weekly and features a superb variety of home-made dishes (lunch and evening daily except Monday nights). The accommodation consists of four comfortably furnished and decorated guest bedrooms (one family room, one double, one twin and one single), equipped with all the facilities today's guests have come to expect.

GODALMING   MAP 4 REF P20
5 miles S of Guildford on the A3100

The old market town of Godalming was once an important staging post between London and Portsmouth and a number of elegant 17th and 18th century shops and coaching inns can still be found in the High Street. A market was established here in 1300 and the town later became a centre for the local wool and textile industries. Perhaps the most interesting building in the old centre is the **Pepperpot**, the former town hall which was built at the western end of the High Street in 1814. Now surrounded on all sides by heavy traffic, this unusual arcaded building once contained an interesting **museum of local history** which has recently moved to new premises at 109a High Street. Godalming's part-Norman parish church of St Peter and St Paul is built of Bargate stone, a locally quarried hard brown sandstone that was much-loved by the Victorians. This material was also used extensively to build **Charterhouse School**, the famous public school which moved from London to a hillside site on the northern side of Godalming in 1872. Among its most striking features are the 150 foot Founder's Tower and the chapel designed by Giles Gilbert Scott as a memorial to those killed in the First World War. The timber-framed house once belonging to Gertrude Jekyll can be found in dense woodland on the opposite side of town; it was designed for her by Edwin Lutyens in characteristic rural vernacular style and partially constructed of Bargate stone.

Three miles along the B2130 to the southeast of Godalming lies the renowned **Winkworth Arboretum**, a 95 acre area of wooded hillside which was presented to the National Trust in 1952. The grounds contain two lakes and a magnificent collection of rare trees and shrubs, many of them native to other continents. **Hascombe**, one mile further on, is another characteristic Surrey village with great charm.

COMPTON   MAP 4 REF P20
2 miles N of Godalming off the B3000

The historic community of Compton was once an important stopping place on the old **Pilgrims' Way**. The village possesses an exceptional part-Saxon church, St Nicholas, with some remarkable internal features, including a series of 12th century murals which were only rediscovered in 1966, an ancient hermit's, or anchorite's, cell, and a unique two-storey Romanesque sanctuary which is thought to have once contained an early Christian relic. Compton is also renowned for being the home of the 19th century artist G F Watts, a chiefly self-taught painter and sculptor whose most famous work, Physical Energy, stands in London's Kensington Gardens. At the age of 47, Watts married the actress Ellen Terry, but the couple separated a year later; then at the age of 69, he successfully remarried, this time to Mary Fraser-Tytler, a painter and potter 33 years his junior who went on to design **Watts' Memorial Gallery**, which today contains over 200 pieces of the artist's work, along with the **Watts Mortuary Chapel**, an extraordinary building which was completed in 1904 and is decorated in exuberant Art Nouveau style. The Watts Gallery is a fascinating place to visit, housing a unique collection of his paintings, drawings and sculptures. The nearby memorial chapel is also worth visiting.

WITLEY   MAP 4 REF P20
4 miles S of Godalming on the A283

The historic village of Witley comprises an attractive collection of fine tile-hung and half-timbered buildings loosely arranged around the part-Saxon church of **All Saints**, a much-altered structure which contains some rare 12th century frescoes and a delicately carved 13th-century font, and incorporates a 17th century tower. The present village inn, the White Hart, was constructed in Elizabethan times to replace an even earlier hostelry. It is believed to be one of the oldest inns in the country and at one time stood adjacent to a marketplace which hosted a busy Friday market. Witley's **Old Manor** was visited by a number English monarchs, including Edward I and Richard II, and the village centre contains some delightful 15th and 16th century timber-framed houses, many of which are hung with characteristic fishtail tiles. These include the Old Cottage, Red Rose Cottage (so-called because the lease granted on Christmas Day 1580 called for an annual rent of one red rose), and Step Cottage, a former rectory which was once the home of Reverend Lawrence Stoughton who died aged 88 after serving the parish for 53 years and outliving four wives. At one time, Witley was a summer haven for artists and writers, the best known of which is perhaps George Eliot who wrote her last novel, Daniel Deronda, here between 1874 and 1876. Her home, the Heights, was designed by Sir Henry Cole, the architect of the Royal Albert Hall, and was visited by a series of eminent guests, including the novelist Henry James. Today, the building has been converted into a nursing home and is now known as **Roslyn Court**.

A large proportion of the common to the north of Thursley is a designated nature reserve which is known for its unusually large and varied population of dragonflies. The **Witley Common Information Centre** lies a few minutes' drive from Thursley Common on the eastern side of the A3. This purpose-built nature centre is managed by the National Trust and is set in woodlands at the edge of a substantial area of Trust-owned heathland. Inside, there is an audio-visual display and an exhibition outlining the history, geology and natural history of the area.

Tigbourne Court

Tigburne Court, which is regarded by many as Lutyens's finest work, is just over a mile south of Witley, standing right on the main Milford to Petworth road. It was built in 1899-1901 for Sir Edgar Horne. Lutyens was 30 years old when he designed Tigburne Court, and the house shows him at the height of his powers yet still full of youthful exuberance. He playfully mixed Tudor styles with 18th century classicism and mixed horizontal bands of tiles with the Bargate stone to create a powerful geometric effect. The gardens, like those of so many of the best Lutyens houses, are by Gertrude Jekyll.

HASLEMERE
9 miles SW of Godalming on the A286

MAP 4 REF O20

The genteel town of Haslemere lies in the southwestern corner of the county. Now a quiet and comfortable home for well-to-do commuters, it has central streets filled with handsome Georgian and Victorian buildings, most of which were constructed following the arrival of the railway in 1859. The building styles, including stucco, redbrick and tile-hung, combine to form an attractive and harmonious architectural mix. Some of Haslemere's finest pre-Victorian structures include the **Town Hall**, rebuilt in 1814, the **Tolle House Almshouses** in Petworth Road, Church Hill House, the Town House, and two noteworthy hotels, the Georgian and the White Horse. Towards the end of the last century, Haslemere became something of a centre for the arts. Alfred Lord Tennyson settled nearby, and a group known as the Haslemere Society of Artists was formed whose number included Birket Foster and the landscape painter, Helen Allingham. At the end of the First World War, the French-born musician and enthusiastic exponent of early music, Arnold Dolmetsch, founded what has become a world-famous **Musical Instrument Workshop** here. Present-day visitors can make an appointment to view the intricately handcrafted harpsichords, lutes and other authentic early instruments being made. Dolmetsch's family went on to establish the Haslemere Festival of Early Music in 1925 which is still held each year in July. Another of Haslemere's attractions is the **Educational Museum** in the High Street, an establishment which was founded in 1888 by local surgeon and Quaker, Sir James Hutchinson, and which now contains an imaginative series of displays on local birds, botany, zoology, geology and history.

EWHURST
8 miles SE of Godalming on the B2127

MAP 4 REF P20

Ewhurst is a long village containing a sandstone church, **St Peter and St Paul**, whose nave and south door are considered to be amongst the finest examples of Norman church architecture in the county. The rest of the structure would have been of a similar age had it not been for an unfortunate attempt to underpin the tower in the 1830s which resulted in the collapse, not only of the tower, but of the chancel and north transept as well. The structure was eventually rebuilt in "Norman style" with an unusual shingled broach spire. Inside, there is a carved 14th century font and a Jacobean pulpit, and outside, the churchyard contains a number of mature trees native to North America. The remainder of the village, part of which is set around a small square, contains some fine 18th and 19th century residential buildings, including the **Woolpit**, built for the Doulton family in the 1880s. The 843 foot **Pitch Hill** is situated a mile to the north and can be easily reached along a pleasant footpath from the village.

DORKING
MAP 4 REF P20
12 miles E of Guildford on the A25

Dorking is a long-established settlement which stands at the intersection of Stane Street, the Roman road which once connected London with Chichester, and the ancient Pilgrims' Way east-west ridgeway route which is roughly followed by the course of the modern North Downs Way. Despite evidence of Saxon and Viking occupation, present-day Dorking is a congested commuter town which owes most of its character to the Victorians. There are a small number of older buildings, most notably the part 15th century former coaching inn, the White Horse, and the shops and houses in North Street, West Street, and at the western end of the High Street; however, the town's two most distinctive architectural features are characteristically 19th century: the unexpectedly grand parish church of **St Martin** with its soaring spire, and the **Rose Hill** housing development, an assortment of Victorian villas arranged around a green and entered from South Street through an unusual neo-Gothic arch. St Paul's Church in Dorking is a fine piece of architecture, designed by Benjamin Ferray and constructed in 1857.

The evocatively-named **Old House at Home** combines the warmth and ambience of a traditional country pub while being at the heart of busy Dorking. Occupying a listed 16th century building, originally three cottages and later refurbished to become an inn, it is an inviting and comfortable place with original features such as the heavily beamed black oak work and open log fire. The bar area is large and welcoming; there's also a small dining area off the bar and a smaller, more intimate dining area in the former front room. Stephen and Penny Slogrove offer all their guests a friendly welcome. Real ales - including seasonal ales which change regularly - are a feature here, together with Stephen's excellent home-cooked food. A speciality is the home-made steak and kidney and "Crofters" (ham and chicken)

Old House at Home, 24 West Street, Dorking,
Surrey RH4 1BY Tel: 01306 889664

pies, but there's also an excellent variety of sandwiches, snacks and traditional pub fare. Food is available at lunch and in the evening every day except Sunday evenings.

Perhaps Dorking's most attractive feature is its close proximity to unspoilt countryside, a testimony to the success of the South East's Green Belt policy. As well as the open spaces in the downs to the north, **Holmwood Common**, 2 miles along the A24 to the south, is another tract of National Trust-owned land which offers some pleasant waymarked walks through mature oak and birch woodlands.

OCKHAM
MAP 4 REF P20
10 miles NW of Dorking on the B2039

Ockham once possessed a fine Jacobean mansion, Ockham Park. A serious fire in 1948 destroyed everything except for the orangery, stables, kitchen wing, and a solitary Italianate tower. The village church of **All Saints** still stands within the grounds of the estate; this largely 13th century building was constructed on the site of a pre-Norman structure and is known for its remarkable east window, a surprising combination of seven tall pointed lancets finished in marble with distinctive carved capitals. The window dates from around 1260 and is thought to have been brought here from nearby Newark Abbey following its dissolution in the 16th century. The church incorporates a brick chapel which contains a robed marble effigy of the first Lord King, the former owner of Ockham Park who died in 1734.

On **Chatley Heath**, 1 mile to the north of Ockham, there is a unique Semaphore Tower which was once part of the Royal Navy's signalling system for relaying messages between Portsmouth and the Admiralty in London. Although the semaphore mechanism soon fell into disuse, the structure has remained in good order and is open to the public at weekends. As well as offering outstanding views over the surrounding landscape, the **Chatley Heath Semaphore Tower** houses an interesting exhibition and model collection. It can be reached along a pleasant woodland pathway and is open on weekends and Bank Holidays.

LEATHERHEAD
MAP 4 REF P20
5 miles N of Dorking on the A24

Leatherhead is a pretty Mole Valley town which manages to retain some measure of tranquillity despite being crossed by a number of major trunk routes. Several buildings in the narrow streets of the old town are worthy of note, including the 16th century Running Horse Inn and the attractive part 12th century parish church of St Mary and St Nicholas. The grave of Anthony Hope (real name Sir Anthony Hawkins), the author of The Prisoner Of Zenda, can be found in the churchyard, and a short distance away in Church Street, the informative **Leatherhead Museum of Local History** is housed in a charming 17th century timber-framed cottage with its own small garden. Built in 1968 in the characteristic style of the period, Leatherhead's celebrated **Thorndike Theatre** offers a first-rate programme of drama, dance and music theatre; there is also a pleasant coffee shop and bar, and a small studio theatre, the Casson Room, offering a programme of more experimental work.

GREAT BOOKHAM
MAP 4 REF P20
4 miles N of Dorking on the A246

Although heavily built up since the Second World War, the residential area to the west of Leatherhead manages to retain something of its historic past. The earliest mention of a settlement in the area dates back to the 660's AD when a manor at Bocheham is recorded as belonging to Chertsey Abbey. Present-day Great Bookham contains an exceptional parish church, **St Nicholas**, which has an unusual flint tower with a shingled spire dating back to the Norman era in the 12th century. A substantial part of the building, including the chancel, is known to have been rebuilt in the 1340's by the Abbot of Chertsey, and the church was again remodelled by the Victorians. Inside, there is some fine 15th century stained glass and a number of noteworthy monumental brasses and memorials to the local lords of the manor. An early 18th century owner of the Bookham estate, Dr Hugh Shortrudge, left an endowment in his will to four local churches on condition that an annual sermon was preached on the subject of the martyrdom of Charles I. St Nicholas continues to uphold the tradition of the "Shortrudge sermon" which is preached each year on the final Sunday in January.

Nearby **Little Bookham** has a small single-roomed church with a wooden belfry which is believed to date from the 12th century. The adjacent 18th century manor house now operates as a school. **Bookham Common** and **Banks Common** to the northwest of Little Bookham provide some welcome relief from the commuter estates and offer some pleasant walking through relatively unspoilt open heathland. The commons are recorded in the Domesday Book as providing pannage, the right to graze pigs on acorns, for Chertsey Abbey. Now under the ownership of the National Trust, they are particularly known for their rich and varied birdlife. Another National Trust-owned property, **Polesden Lacey**, stands on high ground 2 miles to the

south of Great Bookham. The estate was once owned by the writer R B Sheridan who purchased it in 1797 with the intention of restoring its decaying 17th century manor house; however, a lack of funds prevented him from realising his ambitions, and following his death in 1816, the building was demolished and the estate sold. Then during the 1820s, the architect Thomas Cubitt built a substantial Regency villa in its place which was subsequently remodelled and enlarged by successive owners throughout the 19th century. In 1906, the estate was acquired by Captain Ronald Greville and his wife Margaret, the

Thatched Bridge, Polesden Lacey

daughter of a Scottish brewing magnate and a celebrated high society hostess. Over the following three decades, they invited a succession of rich and influential guests to Polesden Lacey whose number included Edward VII, and George VI and Queen Elizabeth (now the Queen Mother) who spent part of their honeymoon here in 1923. The Grevilles carried out a number of alterations of their own during this period and the extravagant "Edwardian-Louis XVI" internal decoration remains as a testimony to Margaret Greville's taste (or, some may say, the lack of it). Whatever the perspective, the house contains an undeniably fine collection of furniture, paintings, tapestries, porcelain and silver which the Grevilles accumulated over 40 years, and Margaret's personal collection of photographs provides a fascinating record of British high society at play during the early part of the century. The surrounding grounds amount to over 1,000 acres and incorporate a walled rose garden, open lawns, a YHA youth hostel and a large area of natural woodland; there is also a charming open-air theatre which holds an annual season of events in late-June and early-July.

The Polesden Lacey estate is bordered to the south by **Ranmore Common**, another area of National Trust-owned upland which is criss-crossed by scenic footpaths and bridleways. This scenic area of the North Downs provides some good walking, and also offers a couple of excellent places to restore oneself afterwards, including a superb tea room at Dunley Hill Farm.

ABINGER
4 miles SW of Dorking off the A25

Map 4 Ref P20

The parish of Abinger contains two villages, Abinger itself (or **Abinger Common**) which lies one mile west of Friday Street at the southern end of the parish, and **Abinger Hammer** which lies on the A25 Dorking to Guildford road to the north. Abinger claims to be one of the oldest settlements in the country, having been settled by Middle Stone Age people around 5000 BC. The remains of a Mesolithic pit-dwelling were discovered in a field near Abinger's old **Manor House** which, when excavated in 1950, revealed over 1,000 tools and artefacts which are now on display in an interesting little museum. Abinger's parish church of **St James** is an unlucky building. This part 12th century structure was largely destroyed by an enemy flying bomb during World War II. It was rebuilt, with great sensitivity, but was severely damaged in 1964 after being struck by lightning. In the churchyard there is a war memorial designed by Lutyens, and in the corner of the three-side village green, a set of old wooden stocks and a whipping post.

Abinger Common is a delightful hamlet that lies one and a half miles north of Leith Hill, the birthplace of the first Archbishop of Canterbury, Stephen Langton. Beautifully situated opposite the village church, **Abinger Hatch** is an attractive pub with a large old fig tree out front and an extensive lawned garden to the rear. The interior is heavily beamed and has flagstone floors. It is very comfortable and cosy throughout. In these warm and friendly surroundings, guests are welcome to roast their own chestnuts in front of the fire - and to enjoy the delicious home-cooked food, either in the main bar or in the separate restaurant. Run by brother-and-sister team Jan and Maria Walaszkowski, there's a welcoming atmosphere and fine service on offer at this superior pub. Jan does the cooking, preparing a good variety of filled rolls, ploughmans and soups as well as more hearty and traditional meals on an extensive menu - Jan's special nachos and other daily dishes are particularly popular. There's a good range of real ales, including Abinger Hatch Best, brewed at the local Weltons Brewery, together with a good complement of lagers, wines and spirits.

Abinger Hatch, Abinger Common, nr Dorking, Surrey RH5 6HZ Tel: 01306 730737

Abinger Hammer, just over a mile to the northwest, lies in the valley of the River Tillingbourne, a fast-flowing stream which in the 15th and 16th centuries was used to power the mechanical metal-working hammers from which the settlement takes its name. At one time, the village was known for the manufacture of cannon balls and a busy blacksmith's workshop can still be found here. Abinger Hammer's industrial past is reflected in the famous "Jack the Smith" hammer clock which was erected in 1909. This unique clock overhangs the road on the site of an old iron forge and is characterised by the figure of a blacksmith who strikes a bell with his hammer every half hour.

LEITH HILL

MAP 4 REF P20

5 miles SW of Dorking on the B2126

The 965 foot National Trust-owned Leith Hill is the highest point in the southeast of England. In 1766, a 64 foot tower was built on the tree-covered summit by Richard Hull, a local squire who lived at nearby Leith Hill Place; he now lies buried beneath his splendid creation. Present-day visitors climbing to the top on a clear day can enjoy a panorama which takes in several counties and reaches as far as the English Channel. The part 17th, part 18th century **Leith Hill Place** stands within beautiful rhododendron filled grounds which are open to public on a limited number of days each year. In its time, the house has been owned by the Wedgwood and Vaughan Williams families, and inside, there is a fine collection of Wedgwood pottery and paintings by such artists as Reynolds and Stubbs. An Edwardian country house designed by Sir Edwin Lutyens can be found on the northern slopes of Leith Hill; Goddards on Abinger Common stands within attractive grounds laid out by Gertrude Jekyll and was first opened to visitors in the spring of 1992.

COLDHARBOUR
Map 4 Ref P20

5 miles S of Dorking off the A29

A remote hamlet set 700 feet up in the Surrey Hills, Coldharbour has an atmosphere that is light-years away from most people's preconception of surrey as a county of cosy suburbs and smiling farmland. Sturdy, stone-built houses cling to the hilltop, from which there are magnificent views sweeping south over the Weald. Just to the north of Coldharbour is **Anstiebury Camp**, an Iron Age fort that was probably built in the 1st or 2nd century BC. The fort is oval in plan, covering more than 11 acres and is defended by triple banks with double ditches to the north and northeast.

OCKLEY
Map 4 Ref P20

8 miles S of Dorking on the A29

At Ockley there is a village green which, at over 500 feet in diameter, is one of the largest in Surrey. In summer, village cricket is played in this classic English setting which is enhanced by a number of handsome period houses and cottages. Ockley has had a long and eventful history: the village once stood on **Stane Street**, the old Roman road between Chichester and London which is now partially followed by the route of the A29, and in the mid 9th century, a momentous battle between the forces of King Ethelwulf of the West Saxons and the marauding Vikings reputedly took place near here. Following the Norman invasion, the surrounding woodlands were designated a royal hunting forest and in the 12th century, the Normans built a fortification half-a-mile to the north of the present village green which has long since disappeared. However, the nearby part 14th century church of St Margaret remains, although this was extensively remodelled by the Victorians during the 1870s. Among the many other noteworthy buildings in Ockley are the 18th century **Ockley Court**, which stands opposite the church, and the groups of cottages surrounding the green which are built in a variety of styles and materials, including brick, tiling and weatherboarding. An interesting private sculpture and ceramics gallery, the **Hannah Peschar Gallery-Garden**, which incorporates a delightful water garden can be found in Standon Lane.

CHARLWOOD
Map 4 Ref Q20

8 miles SE of Dorking off the A24

A charming period village on the Sussex border, Charlwood is all the more admirable in that it is so near Crawley and Gatwick Airport and yet preserves so much of its own rural identity. Although it lacks the sense of remoteness which it must once have possessed - and which only rarely survives in villages such as Coldharbour - Charlwood still has many 18th century cottages and a sprinkling of earlier, slightly larger yeomen's houses such as the 15th century **Charlwood House** to the southeast of the village centre.

The parish **Church of St Nicholas** was built in the 11th century and underwent a series of alterations, extensions and renovations beginning in the 13th century. The impression, surprisingly, is one of an organic building that has evolved with the centuries. One of its prized possessions is the late medieval screen, one of the most intricately carved pieces of ecclesiastical woodwork in Surrey.

REIGATE
Map 4 Ref Q20

6 miles E of Dorking on the A25

Reigate is a prosperous residential town whose expansion at the hands of postwar developers has done much to conceal its long and distinguished history. The settlement was once an important outpost of the de Warenne family, the assertive Norman rulers whose sphere of influence stretched from the Channel coast to the North Downs. As at Lewes, they built a castle on a rise above the village streets of which nothing remains today except for an arch which was reconstructed in the 1770s from material recovered from the original castle walls. Today, this striking neo-Gothic reproduction stands at the heart of a pleasant public park.

A steep path leads down from the castle mound to the attractive mixture of Victorian, Georgian and older buildings which line Reigate's High Street. The **Old Town Hall**, a handsome redbrick building constructed in 1729, stands at its eastern end, and a short distance away to the north, the entrance to a disused road tunnel can be seen which was built beneath the castle mound in 1824 to ease the through-flow of traffic on the busy London to Brighton coaching route. Other noteworthy buildings in this part of town include the timber-framed and tile-fronted **"La Trobes"** in the High Street, and the 400 year old **Old Sweep's House** in the charmingly named Slipshoe Street.

As well as being effective administrators, the de Warennes were known for their devout religious beliefs, and again as at Lewes, they founded a priory in the town some distance from the centre. After the Dissolution, this became the home of Lord Howard of Effingham, the commander-in-chief of the English navy at the time of the Spanish Armada. The building has been remodelled on a number of occasions since then, in particular during the Georgian era, and now operates as a school. The interior contains some fine period features and an interesting museum. Also set away from the town centre, and probably standing on the site of pre-Norman Reigate, is the pale stone-built church of **St Mary Magdalene**. This contains a number of striking memorials, including one carved by Joseph Rose the Elder around 1730.

NUTFIELD   Map 4 Ref P20
2 miles E of Reigate off the A25

A warm and friendly welcome awaits guests at **Hillside Cottage**, a farmhouse bed and breakfast here in the heart of the Surrey countryside. There are three lovely guest bedrooms, all double rooms though also let as singles. Each has a large and comfortable bed, tasteful decor and furnishings, and excellent views over the spacious garden and surrounding countryside. All

rooms are non-smoking. Roomy, peaceful and truly delightful, this charming establishment makes for a welcome haven of tranquillity. In the attractive and comfortable lounge and dining room there are original features such as the exposed beams and open fires. The farmhouse is particularly impressive for the high standards of cleanliness and the quality of the generous breakfast, which includes boiled eggs,

**Hillside Cottage, Coopers Hill Road, Nutfield,
Surrey RH1 4HX Tel/Fax: 01737 822916**

ham and cheese, home made preserves and freshly brewed coffee or traditional English teas. Owner Jürgen and his partner Gunda are conscientious and friendly hosts who offer all their guests a high standard of service.

SOUTH NUTFIELD
MAP 4 REF Q20

2 miles SE of Reigate off the A25

The Station Hotel is a large and friendly public house dating from the 1880s. Outside there is a large garden with sweeping lawns, benches and safe children's play area. Inside, the warm and attractive interior features a wealth of railway memorabilia, with photos and models of trains. Handsome old leather travelling cases and hat boxes hang suspended from the ceilings. The open fires add to the intimate and welcoming atmosphere. Popular with locals and visitors alike, this pub is renowned for its great real ales, draught ciders and good range of lagers, wines and spirits. The tradi-

The Station Hotel, The Avenue, South Nutfield, Surrey RH1 5RY Tel: 01737 823223

tional pub fare on offer includes a variety of delicious snacks and meals, as well as daily specials. Food is available at lunch and in the evenings every day (except Sunday evening). The Sunday roast is particularly popular. Owners Mike and Diana Rees and their capable, friendly staff help to make this terrific pub well worth seeking out.

GODSTONE
MAP 4 REF Q20

6 miles E of Reigate off the A22

Although Godstone is now thankfully bypassed by the A22, the A25 east-west route still passes through its heart, making a sharp change in direction as it does so. Fortunately, the village manages to endure the periodic onslaught of traffic and indeed, its Tudor and Elizabethan character has survived relatively intact. Godstone's most distinguished building, the White Hart Inn in the High Street, claims to have been visited by Richard II, Elizabeth I, Queen Victoria, and even the Tsar of Russia who broke his journey here in 1815. A series of attractive lanes and alleyways connects the High Street to the village green, a broad open space with a cricket pitch which is surrounded by a wonderful collection of 16th and 17th century buildings, including the Tudor-built Hare and Hounds Inn.

Godstone's parish church of **St Nicholas** is situated half a mile east of the centre and can be reached from the White Hart along an old thoroughfare known as Bay Path. Although Norman in origin, the building was virtually rebuilt in the 1870s by Sir George Gilbert Scott, a local resident at the time. Inside, there is a marble memorial to a cousin of John Evelyn, the famous 17th century diarist. The area around the church contains some fine old buildings, including a row of 19th century almshouses and the 16th century timber-framed **Old Pack House**, which lies a short distance away to the south. Bay Path also leads to a former hammer pond, **Bay Pond**, which is now a designated nature reserve. At one time, its water would have been used to power the mechanical hammers in a nearby iron foundry, an indication of Godstone's lost industrial past which also included the manufacture of gunpowder and leatherware.

OUTWOOD
Map 4 Ref Q20

5 miles SE of Reigate off the M23

Although Outwood is accessible from the M23 a more pleasant approach leads southwards from Bletchingley along a country road across the Weald. **Outwood Common**, the area of high ground to the east of village, is best known for being the location of one of the most interesting

The Post Mill

windmills in the country. **The Post Mill** is acknowledged as the oldest working windmill in England. It was built in 1665 and it is said that from the top of the mill, some 39 feet up, the Great Fire of London was visible 27 miles away. Unlike other ancient buildings in England, the Post Mill's early history is not shrouded in mystery and conjecture: it was built by Thomas Budgen, a miller of Nutfield, and the original deeds are still in existence. The term "post mill" describes the structure and mechanism of this remarkable building. The whole body of the mill, including its sails and machinery, balances on a huge central post. This post is made from oak which, it is said, was drawn seven miles by oxcart from Crabbet Park, near Crawley, where it was felled. It is supported by four diagonal quarter bars and two crosstrees; these in turn rest on four brick piers. The purpose of this post system is to allow the mill to be turned to face the breeze; it is so finely balanced that a single person can turn the sails into the wind. Another special design feature incorporated around 100 years later allows the angle of the sails to be adjusted to suit different wind conditions using a system of elliptical springs. For over a century a second "smock" windmill stood nearby, and the pair were known as the Cat and Fiddle; sadly, the Fiddle blew down in a storm in the early 1960s. Visitors can tour the various floors of the mill and the surrounding common land and National Trust woodland.

BURSTOW
Map 4 Ref Q20

8 miles SE of Reigate off the B2037

The lanes to the south of Outwood lead through Smallfield to Burstow, a well-kept village whose church, **St Bartholomew's**, has a surprisingly well preserved late medieval timber-framed tower. This hefty 15th century structure supports a peal of six bells, the largest of which weighs over half a ton. The church itself is an attractive mixture of Norman, Perpendicular, and Victorian influences; the chancel contains the remains of John Flamsteed, a former rector and the first Astronomer Royal, who is best remembered for his maps of the night skies which were compiled in the late 17th century as an aid to marine navigation. About one mile north of Burstow is **Smallfield Place**, regarded by many as the best example of a stone-built country home in Surrey. Its almost forbidding appearance is at odds with the mellow brick or aged timber exteriors of so many Surrey manor houses. The house was built at the beginning of the 17th century and presents a long, largely unadorned two-storey Wealden stone face to the curious public.

LINGFIELD   MAP 4 REF Q20
12 miles SE of Reigate off the A22

Lingfield is a large village which is set within delightful wooded countryside in the southeast-ern corner of the county. Almost large enough to be called a town, "leafy Lingfield" is perhaps best known to the world at large for its **racecourse**. However, the settlement has long been an important agricultural centre whose largely Perpendicular church of **St Peter and St Paul** has been enlarged over the centuries to create what has become known as the "Westminster Abbey of Surrey". As well as having a rare double nave and an exceptional collection of monumental brasses, the church also contains a surprising number of memorials to members of the Cobham family, the medieval lords of the manor who lived at the now demolished Starborough Castle, a mile and a half to the east. Each of the first four barons has a sizeable tomb showing an effigy of its occupant; these date between 1361 and 1471 and are particularly fascinating to those with an interest in the development of late-medieval armour over this period.

The broad thoroughfare leading down from the church is lined with characteristic weatherboarded and tile-fronted buildings, including Pollard Cottage, with its unusual 15th century shop front, the 16th century Old Town Stores, and the Star Inn Cottages, built around 1700. The country library on the opposite side of the church is a former farmhouse which was built in the 17th century on the site of a Carthusian college founded in the 1400's by Sir Reginald Cobham. Elsewhere in Lingfield, a couple of interesting features can be found near the pond in Plaistow Street: the 15th century village cross and the old lock-up, a small local gaol which was built in 1772 and in use until 1882.

Greathed Manor, to the southeast of Lingfield, is a substantial Victorian manor house built in 1868 for the Spender Clay family. Haxted Mill, 2 miles to the northeast of Lingfield, is a working late 17th century water mill which also contains an informative mill museum; exhib-its include machinery, equipment and artefacts relating to the history of water-power.

2 The South of England

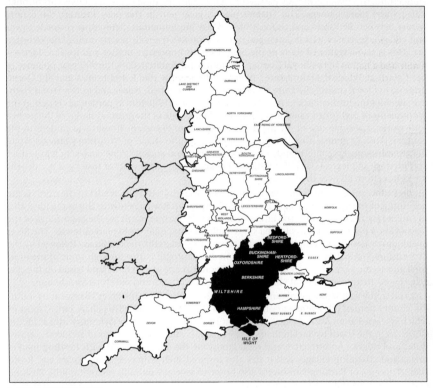

INTRODUCTION

From the southernmost tip of the Isle of Wight to the northern tip of Bedfordshire, this is a region of contrasts. From the North Downs of northeastern Hampshire - honouring the perverse tradition of English place-names, the Downs are actually uplands, softly-rolling, wooded hills in whose folds lie scores of picturesque villages - to the Chilterns, the region has some of the nation's prettiest scenery. The charming Isle of Wight has adopted a motto which declares: "All this beauty is of God". Most of the island's 125,000 residents live in the northeast quadrant of the island, with its main resort towns of Sandown and Shanklin strung along the east coast. The rest of Wight is wonderfully peaceful with a quiet, unassertive charm all of its own.

Hampshire's coastal crescent stretches from Southampton through Fareham and Portsmouth to Havant. Like most major ports, Southampton and Portsmouth have something of a cosmopolitan air about them, making an intriguing contrast with the rural charms of the inland villages. Some of Hampshire's grandest scenery lies in the part of the county where the North

Downs roll westwards towards Salisbury Plain. Hampshire's New Forest is the largest wild area in lowland Britain, and contains ideal walking country with vast tracts virtually unpopulated but criss-crossed by a cat's cradle of footpaths and bridle-ways.

Berkshire contains the ancient Ridgeway path, England's oldest road, which follows the county border with Oxfordshire. The Kennet and Avon Canal, completed in 1810, crosses southern England from Bristol to join the River Thames at Reading. Entering the county at Hungerford, this major waterway passes through a charming rural landscape as it winds through villages and market towns. The Thames plays a great part in this area, forming the county border between Berkshire and Oxfordshire.. There are numerous picturesque riverside towns and villages, several of which developed into fashionable riverside resorts during the Victorian era. This is also a region of some of the nation's most impressive houses and royal residences. The western region of the Royal County of Berkshire is dominated by the 900 year presence of the Crown at Windsor. Oxfordshire's Blenheim Palace, the thank you from a grateful Queen Anne to her loyal subject the Duke of Marlborough, is a superb palace and now a World Heritage site. Moving further back in history, the region — and Wiltshire in particular - is rich in the monuments of prehistoric man, including Stonehenge, one of the great mysteries of the prehistoric world; it also has one of the highest concentrations of historic houses and gardens in the country. And, of course, the area has its surprises in the shape of Wiltshire's famous white horses, intriguing crop circles and, above all, the great and ancient stone circles, rich in history and mystery and legend. Part of traditional England, with 6,000 years of history, it is a delight for visitors from all over the world.

In Oxfordshire can be found the beginnings of the Chiltern Hills, whilst to the north is the beginning of the flat Oxford Plain. A rural landscape with few large towns, this is the ideal area to explore for those who love the English countryside. Further north are the beginnings of the Cotswolds, a place of honey coloured stone buildings and quaint old market towns. The River Evenlode divides this region, into two and along this stretch the riverbanks are followed by the Oxfordshire Way. Some 65 miles long, this marked footpath passes through some of the most rural and scenic parts of the county. Even further north one of rich farm land based on the clay soil. There are numerous rural villages, with ancient cottages and old stone farmhouses.

And so the visitor moves to southern Buckinghamshire, with the River Thames as its southern county border, lying almost entirely within the Chiltern Hills. This chalk range, most of which is classed as an Area of Outstanding Natural Beauty. The Vale of Aylesbury runs from the Chilterns in the south to Buckingham in the north, It offers visitors miles of secluded country walks and ridges. An attractive and rural landscape the area is littered with bustling market towns and charming villages and it has also inspired such writers as Shakespeare and Roald Dahl. This area of Buckinghamshire is also home to several windmills including Brill, Pitstone and Ford End. Naturally, the rich have found this an excellent place in which to settle and there are many fine houses including: Ascott House, a former Rothschild mansion; Stowe, which is now a school but the gardens of which are magnificent and open to the public; and Winslow Hall, designed by Sir Christopher Wren. However, perhaps the most famous house in the area, but not necessarily the grandest, is Claydon House, the home of the Verney family and where Florence Nightingale was a frequent visitor particularly in the last years of her life.

Southern Bedfordshire has Royal connections with the Tudors. The central region would, at first, appear to be essentially a rural community, an area of ancient settlements and rich diversity of places of interest. The region's waterways have played a part in history. There are several interesting old houses in the area and perhaps the most famous is Houghton House at Houghton Conquest. There is also a wealth of fine gardens. Northern Bedfordshire is a contrast from the southern part of the county as the influence of the capital has lessened greatly. An attractive, rural region of pretty country villages, this is a gentle undiscovered countryside that has changed little over the years.

Though Hertfordshire borders London, it remained essentially rural until the building of the Grand Union Canal. There are peaceful walks along the towpath of the Grand Union Canal which flows through a gap in the Chiltern Hills on its journey to the Midlands. A place of old market towns and farming communities, southeast Hertfordshire certainly does not lack for historical interest. The northern part of the county lies furthest away from the capital and has therefore received considerably less influence that the rest of Hertfordshire. Chiefly a rural landscape, this is a region of attractive country villages with old timber framed cottages and old market towns that were made wealthy with the produce of the surrounding area. This part of Hertfordshire has also been occupied for many centuries and as well as the Roman Baths at Welwyn, there is Knebworth House, home of the Lytton family since the 15th century, James I's hunting lodge at Royston, and the Physic Garden at Hitchin to discover.

HAMPSHIRE

BASINGSTOKE   Map 4 ref N20
30 miles NE of Southampton off the A30

It comes as something of a surprise to discover that this busy, prosperous town with its soaring multi-storey buildings can boast no fewer than 25 parks and open spaces. A useful leaflet available from the Tourist Information Centre gives details of them all, ranging from the 16-hectare **War Memorial Park**, an 18th century park complete with bandstand, aviary and sports facilities, to **Southview Cemetery**, a site with a fascinating history. Some 800 years ago, during the reign of King John, England languished under an Interdict pronounced by the Pope. Throughout the six years from 1208 to 1214, any baby christened, or dead person buried, lacked the official blessing of Mother Church. At Basingstoke during those years, the deceased were interred in the graveyard known as **The Liten** and when the Interdict was finall lifted, the ground was consecrated and a chapel built, the **Chapel of the Holy Ghost**. Today, it's a striking ruin surrounded by a well-managed site which provides a peaceful refuge from the bustling town. As befits such a thriving place, Basingstoke offers visitors a wide choice of attractions: theatre, cinema, a vast Leisure Park, and an "Old Town" area which is a lively cosmopolitan mix of bars, theme pubs and restaurants. Here too is the excellent **Willis Museum** (free) which charts the town's history with lively displays featuring characters such as "Fred", a Roman skeleton, and "Pickaxe", a 19th century farm worker "forced to scrape a living from the streets of Basingstoke as a scavenger".

Just to the east of Basingstoke, **Basing House** was once one of the grandest residences in the realm. Built during the reign of Henry VIII, it rivalled even the king's extravagant mansions. Less than a hundred years later, during the Civil War, Cromwell's troops besieged the house for an incredible three years, one of them reporting that the mansion was 'as large as the Tower of London'. When Basing House was finally captured the victorious New Army burnt it to the ground, but a magnificent 16th century barn survived, its timber roof a marvel of the carpenter's craft.

The Vyne, Nr Basingstoke

The Vyne (National Trust), 4 miles north of Basingstoke, has enjoyed a much happier history. Built in the early 1500s for Lord Sandys, Lord Chamberlain to Henry VIII, the house enjoys an idyllic setting with lawns sweeping down to a shimmering lake. A classical portico was added in 1654, the first of its kind in England. The Vyne's treasures include a fascinating Tudor chapel with Renaissance glass, a Palladian staircase, and a wealth of old panelling and fine furniture.

ALDERSHOT
15 miles E of Basingstoke on the A331

MAP 4 REF O20

Back in 1854, Aldershot was a village of some 800 inhabitants. Then the Army decided to build a major camp here and the population has grown steadily ever since to its present tally of around 55,000. The story of how Aldershot became the home of the British Army is vividly recounted at the **Aldershot Military Museum** which stands in the middle of the camp and is a must for anyone with an interest in military history. Housed in the last two surviving Victorian barrack blocks, its tiny appearance from the outside belies the wealth of fascinating information contained inside. For example, there's a detailed cutaway model of a cavalry barracks showing how the soldiers' rooms were placed above the stables, an economic form of central heating described as "warm, but aromatic". It was the army at Aldershot who became the first aviators in Britain, using Farnborough Common for their flying, and building their aircraft sheds where the Royal Aircraft Establishment stands today. The **Airborne Forces Museum** has many interesting exhibits illustrating the part these pioneers played during the early days of the 20th century and during two World Wars. In memory of those who lost their lives in these conflicts, **The Heroes Shrine** in Manor Park, commemorates the dead of World War I, while the nearby walled and sunken garden, shaded by a huge deodar tree, honours the fallen of World War II. Another celebrated military figure, the Duke of Wellington, is celebrated by an imposing bronze statue on Round Hill. It originally stood in London on top of the Triumphal Arch at Hyde Park Corner and was removed to Aldershot in 1885.

PHOENIX GREEN
7 miles E of Basingstoke off the A30

MAP 4 REF O20

The **Stilton Dish Restaurant** is a charming and distinguished eatery set in an attractive and well-maintained Tudor-style building. The restaurant enjoys a faithful local clientele, though guests come from much further afield, attracted to this fine establishment and its reputation for excellent food. The dining room is very pleasant and nicely appointed. In the small pre-meal bar there is a well-chosen wine list and a good compliment of beers and spirits. Owners Jesus and Carol Conde have been undertaking this labour of love since 1986; they have over 30 years' experience in catering. The restaurant is cosy and intimate. The menu is first class and will satisfy the most discerning of tastes. There is an accent on Mediterranean specialities among the variety of superb traditional

Stilton Dish Restaurant, Phoenix Green, Hartley Wintney, Hampshire RG27 8RT Tel: 01252 842107

favourites which include game, seafood, fish, poultry, beef, pork and vegetarian dishes. All meals are expertly prepared and presented. Open: lunchtime Tuesday to Friday; evenings Monday to Saturday.

HARTLEY WINTNEY

MAP 4 REF O20

9 miles NE of Basingstoke on the A30

Riding through Hartley Wintney in 1821, William Cobbett, the author of *Rural Rides* and a conservationist long before anyone had thought of such a creature, was delighted to see young oaks being planted on the large village green. They were the gift of Hartley Wintney's lady of the manor, Lady Mildmay, whose far-sighted benevolence now provides the village centre with a uniquely sylvan setting of majestic oak trees. The magnificent gardens of **West Green House** are about a mile to the west of Hartley Wintney. Owned by the National Trust, the pretty early-18th century house is surrounded by lovely gardens planted with a dazzling variety of trees, shrubs and plants. One of its interesting features is a stone column surmounted by an elaborate finial which was erected in 1976. It bears a Latin inscription which declares that a large sum of money was needed to put the column in place, money "which would otherwise have fallen, sooner or later, into the hands of the Inland Revenue".

The Lamb Hotel is a lively local pub with excellent food, ales and accommodation. Situated in Hartley Wintney's High Street, it offers a high standard of comfort and quality. As befits

a pub with a long and distinguished history, there is a wealth of exposed woodwork. The main bar is a convivial yet relaxing place in which to enjoy a pint or glass from the fine range of beers, wines and spirits available, or to sample some of the freshly prepared and delicious items from the menu or specials board, which includes a good selection of traditional favourites served in hearty portions. The seven en suite guest bedrooms

The Lamb Hotel, High Street, Hartley Wintney, Hampshire RG27 8NW Tel: 01252 842006

are well appointed and offer guests every modern amenity together with a real taste of a more gracious and age. Tasteful and restrained, they are supremely comfortable. There is also a cosy and welcoming guests' lounge.

SILCHESTER

MAP 4 REF N19

5 miles N of Basingstoke off the A340

Romans Country House Hotel is an impressive and stylish hotel build in the style of Lutyens. Sympathetically converted and refurbished, it offers guests the best in modern facilities while retaining the gracious atmosphere and period detail of an Edwardian country residence. The character of an original country manor house pervades the 25 well appointed en suite guest bedrooms, each of which has been individually styled to provide all modern comforts. The hotel boasts a four-poster suite and a sumptuous suite with Jacuzzi bath. Guests can book treatment from a reflexologist, beautician or masseuse. The hotel's mature and colourful gardens are wonderfully for enjoying a relaxing stroll, before enjoying a pre-dinner drink (perhaps sampling from

Romans Country House Hotel, Little London Road, Silchester, Hampshire RG7 2PN
Tel: 0118 970 0421 Fax: 0118 970 0691

among the hotel's extensive range of speciality whiskies) and a meal at the distinguished restaurant. The hotel takes justifiable pride in providing the highest standard of service and cuisine, using only the best available ingredients. The menu offers a range of innovative and tempting dishes.

WHITCHURCH

MAP 4 REF N20

10 miles W of Basingstoke off the A34

Whitchurch is a very pleasant village with many buildings dating from the 15th century, a truly delightful and charming place to spend some time. The **White Hart Hotel** in Whitchurch is a popular yet relaxed and quiet hotel and restaurant. This charming hotel in the heart of the village has during its long and distinguished career served as an important coaching inn. It remains an esteemed establishment, highly regarded by locals and the many visitors who come from all points on the globe. Full of character, the hotel boasts a wealth of exposed beams and other original features. There are 20 guest bedrooms, each supremely comfortable, well furnished and hand-

The White Hart Hotel, The Square, Newbury Street, Whitchurch, Hampshire RG28 7DN Tel: 01256 892900

somely decorated. In the small and cosy bar, there's a good choice of beers, wines and spirits. The Lord Denning Restaurant offers a superb menu of freshly prepared dishes. The decor in the restaurant is also worthy of note, with some truly interesting plasterwork that is most original and carefully looked after. Owner Maureen Kavanagh and her able, helpful and friendly staff ensure that every guest has an enjoyable and relaxing stay.

ALTON
MAP 4 REF O20

13 miles S of Basingstoke off the A31

Surrounded by hop-fields and some of Hampshire's loveliest countryside, Alton is an appealing market town with a history stretching back far beyond Roman times. (The name actually means "Old Town"). Alton boasts a large number of old coaching inns, and the impressive, partly-Norman **St. Lawrence's Church** which was the setting for a dramatic episode during the Civil War. A large force of Roundheads drove some eighty Royalists into the church where 60 of them were killed. The Royalist commander, Colonel Boles, made a last stand from the splendid Jacobean pulpit, firing repeatedly at his attackers before succumbing to their bullets. The church door and several of the Norman pillars are still pock-marked with bullet holes fired off during this close-combat conflict. More cheerful are the comical carvings on these pillars of animals and birds, amongst them a wolf gnawing a bone and two donkeys kicking their heels in the air.

Nearby is the old cemetery and the well-tended Grave of Fanny Adams. The expression "Sweet Fanny Adams" arose from the revolting murder in 1867 of a young girl in the town who was hacked into pieces by her assassin. With macabre humour, sailors used the phrase "Sweet Fanny Adams" to describe the recently-issued tinned mutton for which they had a certain mistrust. Over the years, the saying became accepted as a contemptuous description for anything considered valueless. A poor memorial for an innocent girl.

Well worth a visit while you are in Alton is the **Allen Gallery** in Church Street (free), home to an outstanding collection of English, Continental and Far Eastern pottery, porcelain and tiles. Housed in a group of attractive 16th and 18th century buildings the Gallery's other attractions include the unique Elizabethan Tichborne Spoons, delightful watercolours and oil paintings by local artist William Herbert Allen and a comfortable Coffee Lounge.

A good time to visit the town is mid-July when the **Alton Show** takes place. Established in 1840, this is one of southern England's most important agricultural gatherings with a wide range of events featuring such attractions as Heavy Horses, llamas, beagles, gun dogs and birds of prey.

BENTWORTH
MAP 4 REF O20

3 miles W of Alton off the A339

The Sun Inn in Bentworth is a traditional 17th century Free House set here in this quintessential unspoilt village. It retains a relaxed, tranquil and country-style feel and atmosphere not often found anymore these days. This truly special pub boasts traditional features such as ex-

posed beamwork, low ceilings, log fire and a small and intimate bar bristling with olde worlde charm. Lively and popular, its reputation attracts visitors from near and far. The various agricultural implements which adorn the pub are interesting and attractive, and serve as a reminder of the village's agricultural heritage. All the food served is home cooked and home prepared. The Sunday

The Sun Inn, Bentworth, nr Alton, Hampshire GU34 5JT
Tel: 01420 562338

lunch is a real feast, renowned locally. A menu of changing daily specials complement the choice of hearty and delicious favourites. As a Free House, there is a wonderful variety of real ales, lagers, wines and spirits on offer.

CHAWTON
MAP 4 REF O20

2 miles S of Alton off the A31

From the outside, the home in which Jane Austen spent the last eight years of her life, **Chawton House**, and where she wrote three of her most popular novels (*Mansfield Park*, *Emma* and *Persuasion*), is a disappointingly dull, blank-faced building. Sadly, once you step inside, the interior is equally dispiriting. You can see the sitting-room in which she penned those cleverly-crafted novels, the bedroom to which she retired, but the house is curiously empty, as elusive as the author herself. Unless you are a really dedicated Jane-ite, this is a literary shrine which radiates only a minimum charge of magic.

Chawton House

The Wakes, the home of Gilbert White in **Selborne**, about 3 miles south of Chawton, is quite different. A humble curate of the parish from 1784 until his death in 1793, Gilbert spent his spare hours meticulously recording observations on the weather, wild-life and geology of the area. Astonishingly, a percipient publisher to whom Gilbert submitted his notes recognised the appeal of his humdrum, day-to-day accounts of life in what was then a remote corner of England. *The Natural History and Antiquities of Selborne* was first published in 1788, has never been out of print, and still provides what is perhaps the most entertaining and direct access to late-18th century life, seen through the eyes of an intelligent, sceptical mind.

The Wakes, Selborne

ALRESFORD
MAP 4 REF N20

10 miles SW of Alton off the A31

Pronounced Allsford, Alresford was created around 1200 by a Bishop of Winchester, Geoffrey de Lucy, as part of his grand plan to build a waterway from Winchester to Southampton. Where the river Arle flows into the Itchen, he constructed a huge reservoir covering 200 acres, its waters controlled to keep the Itchen navigable at all seasons. The **Bishop's Reservoir** is now reduced to some 60 acres but it's still home to countless wildfowl and many otters. Known today as Old Alresford Pond, it's one of the most charming features of this dignified Georgian town. Alresford can also boast one of the county's most beautiful streets, historic **Broad Street**, lined with elegant, colour-washed Georgian houses interspersed with specialist shops and inviting hostelries.

Alresford's most famous son was Admiral Lord Rodney, a contemporary of Lord Nelson, who built the grand Manor House near the parish church, but the town can also boast two famous daughters. One was Mary Sumner, wife of the Rector of Alresford, who founded the Mother's Union here in 1876. The other was Mary Russell Mitford, author of the fascinating collection of sketches of 18th century life, *Our Village*, published in 5 volumes between 1824-1832. Mary's prolific literary output was partly spurred on by the need to repay the debts of her spendthrift father. Dr Mitford managed to dissipate his own inherited fortune of many thousands of pounds; his wife's lavish dowry which almost doubled that income disappeared equally quickly, and when Mary at the age of ten won the huge sum of £20,000 in a lottery, the good doctor squandered that as well. Mary's classic book tells the story

One of Alresford's attractions that should not be missed is the **Watercress Line**, Hampshire's only preserved steam railway, so named because it was once used to transport watercress from the beds around Alresford to London and beyond. The line runs through 10 miles of beautiful countryside to Alton where it links up with main line services to London. Vintage steam locomotives make the 35-minute journey up to 8 times a day, and there are regular dining trains as well as frequent special events throughout the year. More details on 01962 733810.

PETERSFIELD   MAP 4 REF O21
12 miles S of Alton on the A3

An appealing market town, Petersfield is dominated by the bulk of **Butser Hill**, 900ft high and the highest point of the South Downs offering grand panoramic views over the town and even, on a clear day, to the spire of Salisbury Cathedral, some 40 miles distant. In the 1660s, Samuel Pepys noted his stay in Petersfield, at a hotel in which Charles II had slept before him. Another king is commemorated in the Square where William III sits on horseback, incongruously dressed in Roman costume. Unusually, the statue is made of lead. Most of the elegant buildings around the Square are Georgian, but the **Church of St Peter** is much older, dating back to Norman times and with a fine north aisle to prove it. Just off the Square, the **Flora Twort Gallery** was once the home and studio of the accomplished artist of that name who moved to Petersfield at the end of World War I. Her delightful paintings and drawings capture life in the town over some 40 years - "reminders of some of the things we have lost" as she put it shortly before her death at the age of 91 in 1985. From the Gallery, a short walk along Sheep Street, (which has some striking timber-framed 16th century houses and Georgian cottages), brings you to **The Spain**, a pleasant green surrounded by some of the town's oldest houses. It apparently acquired its rather unusual name because dealers in Spanish wool used to hold markets there.

ANDOVER   MAP 4 REF M20
20 miles W of Basingstoke off the A303

Andover has expanded greatly since the 1960s when it was selected as a "spillover" town to relieve the pressure on London's crowded population. But the core of this ancient town, which was already important in Saxon times, retains much of interest. One outstanding landmark is St Mary's Church, completely rebuilt in the 1840s at the expense of a former headmaster of Winchester College. The interior is said to have been modelled on Salisbury Cathedral and if it doesn't quite match up to that sublime building, St Mary's is still well worth a visit. Equally striking is the **Guildhall** of 1825, built in classical style, which stands alone in the Market Place where markets are still held every Tuesday and Saturday. Andover has also managed to retain half a dozen of the 16 coaching inns that serviced 18th century travellers at a time when the fastest stage coaches took a mere 9 hours to travel here from London. As many as 50 coaches a day stopped at these inns to change horses and allow the passengers to take refreshments.

For a fascinating insight into the town's long history, do pay a visit to the **Andover Museum** (free) in Church Close. There are actually two museums here, both of them housed in buildings which began life as an elegant Georgian town house in 1750 and were later extended to serve as Andover's Grammar School from the 1840s to 1925. The Andover Museum traces the story of the town from Saxon times to the present day with a range of colourful exhibits. Another good way of getting to know the town is to join one of the guided tours along the **Andover Heritage Trail**. Scheduled tours, lasting about 90 minutes, take place on Tuesday and Saturday afternoons but can also be arranged for groups at other times.

HIGHCLERE

MAP 4 REF N20

14 miles N of Andover on the A343

About 5 miles east of Faccombe, **Highclere Castle** is an example of Victorian neo-Gothic architecture at its most exuberant. If the central tower reminds you of another well-known building, that may be because the Castle was designed by Sir Charles Barry, architect of the Houses of Parliament. It stands on the site of a former Palace of the Bishops of Winchester, overlooking an incomparably lovely park, one of Capability' Brown's greatest creations. The ornate architecture and furnishings of the Castle interior delights many, others feel somewhat queasy at its unrelenting richness. Highclere is the family home of the 7th Earl and Countess of Carnavon and it was the present Earl's grandfather who in 1922 was with Howard Carter at the opening of Tutankhamun's tomb. A small museum in the basement of the Castle recalls that breath-taking moment. Another display reflects the family's interest in horse racing. For more than a century, Earls of Carnavon have owned, bred and raced horses, and the present Earl is racing manager to the Queen. In addition to the superb parkland, there's also a Walled Garden, planted entirely with white blooms, a gift shop, restaurant and tea rooms.

A couple of miles northeast of Highclere Castle, at Burghclere, the Sandham Memorial Chapel (National Trust) is, from the outside, a rather unappealing construction, erected in 1926 by Mr and Mrs J.L. Behrend in memory of a relation who died in World War I. Their building may be uninspired but the Behrends can't be faulted on their choice of artist to cover the walls with a series of 19 murals. Stanley Spencer had served during the war as a hospital orderly and 18 of his murals represent the day-to-day life of a British Tommy in wartime. The 19th, covering the east wall of the Chapel, depicts the Day of Resurrection with the fallen men and their horses rising up. The foreground is dominated by a pile of white wooden crosses the soldiers have cast aside. The whole series is enormously moving, undoubtedly one of the masterpieces of 20th century British art.

NETHER WALLOP

MAP 4 REF M20

8 miles SW of Andover on minor road off the A343

The names of the three Wallops, (Over, Middle and Nether), have provided a good deal of amusement to visitors over the centuries, so it's slightly disappointing to discover that Wallop is just a corruption of the Old English word *waell-hop*, meaning a valley with a stream. At Nether Wallop the stream is picturesquely lined with willow trees, while the village itself is equally attractive with many thatched or timbered houses. The most notable building in Nether Wallop, though, is **St Andrew's Church**, partly because of its Norman features and handsome West Tower of 1704, but also because of its striking medieval wall paintings which provide an interesting contrast with Stanley Spencer's at Burghclere. Some 500 years old, these lay hidden for generations under layers of plaster and were only rediscovered in the 1950s. The most impressive of them shows St George slaying the dragon. Outside St Andrew's stands an item of great interest for collectors of churchyard oddities. It's a dark grey stone pyramid, 15ft high, with red stone flames rising from its tip. This daunting monument was erected at his own expense and in memory of himself by Francis Douce, 'Doctor of Physick', who died in 1760. Dr

Douce also left an endowment to build a village school on condition that the parishioners would properly maintain the pyramid.

MIDDLE WALLOP
MAP 4 REF M20

7 miles SW of Andover on the A343

A mile or so to the northwest, the village of Middle Wallop became famous during the Battle of Britain when the nearby airfield was the base for squadrons of Spitfires and Hurricanes. Many of the old buildings have been incorporated into the **Museum of Army Flying** which traces the development of Army Flying from the balloons and kites of pre-World War I years, through various imaginative dioramas, to a helicopter flight simulator in which visitors can test their own skills of 'hand and eye' co-ordination. Other attractions include a Museum Shop, licensed café & restaurant, and a grassed picnic area.

The George Inn Restaurant & Bar, in Middle Wallop presents a charming Tudor-style exterior to the world, with black-and-white timbers to the upper storey and a pristine lawn and carpark area to the front, and a spacious garden with safe children's play area and adjacent large patio area to the rear. The interior is no less impressive: warm and welcoming, with a superb range of wines, beers and spirits on offer. The restaurant's innovative and exciting menu offers an extensive selection of light bites and main courses, with a main menu offering everything from the inn's own "melts" (avocado and brie, chicken and stilton and mushroom and cheddar) to "Half-Shoulder of Lamb roasted with honey mustard & rosemary"

The George Inn, The Crossroads, Middle Wallop, nr Stockbridge, Hampshire SO20 8EG Tel: 01264 781224 Fax: 01264 782830

or "Breast of Chicken filled with Prawn & Mango in a tikka cream sauce". There are three additional "Specials" blackboards and a "Desserts" board. All food is freshly prepared and cooked to order by Chef/proprietors Michael & Joanne Abraham. Quality accommodation is offered with two double-bedded en suite rooms, furnished in pine. Both are non-smoking and carry a 4 Diamond Tourist Board rating. Open: Monday to Saturday 11 - 3 and 6 - 11 (food served until 2pm and 10pm); Sundays 12 noon - 3 and 7 - 10.30 (food served until 2pm and 9.30pm).

About 3 miles east of Middle Wallop, **Danebury Ring** is Hampshire's largest Iron Age hill fort. Intensively occupied from about 550 BC until the arrival of the Romans, the site has been meticulously excavated over the last 30 years and the finds are now displayed at the Museum of the Iron Age in Andover. Visitors can wander the 13 acre site and with the help of explanatory boards, reconstruct the once-bustling community with its clearly defined roads, shops, houses and what were probably temples.

WINCHESTER
MAP 4 REF N21

14 miles SE of Andover off the A33

One of the country's most historic cities, Winchester was adopted by King Alfred as the capital of his kingdom of Wessex, a realm which then included most of southern England. There had been a settlement here since the Iron Age and in Roman times, as Venta Belgarum, it became an important military base. **The Brooks Experience**, located within the modern Brooks Shopping Centre, has displays based on excavated Roman remains with its star exhibit a reconstructed room from an early-4th century town-house.

When the Imperial Legions returned to Rome, the town declined until it was refounded by Alfred in the late 800s. His street plan still provides the basic outline of the city centre. A Saxon cathedral had been built in the 7th century but the present magnificent **Cathedral**, easily the most imposing and interesting building in Hampshire, dates back to 1079. It's impossible in a few words to do justice to this glorious building and its countless treasures such as the famous Winchester Bible. Winchester Cathedral boasts the longest nave in Europe, a dazzling 14th century masterpiece in the Perpendicular style, a wealth of fine wooden carvings, and gems within a gem such as the richly decorated Bishop Waynflete's Chantry of 1486.

Sumptuous medieval monuments, like the effigy of William of Wykeham, founder of Winchester College, provide a striking contrast to the simple black stone floorslabs which separately mark the graves of Izaak Walton and Jane Austen. Just south of the Cathedral, on College Street, are two other buildings of outstanding interest. No. 8, College Street, a rather austere Georgian house with a first-floor bay window, is **Jane Austen's House** in which she spent the last six weeks of her life in 1817. The house is private but a slate plaque above the front door records her residence here. Right next door stands **Winchester College**, the oldest school in England, founded in 1382 by Bishop William of Wykeham to provide education for seventy 'poor and needy scholars'. Substantial parts of the 14th century buildings still stand, including the beautiful Chapel. The Chapel is always open to visitors and there are guided tours around the other parts of the College from April to September. If you can time your visit during the school holidays, more of the College is available to view.

The city's other attractions are so numerous one can only mention a few of

Winchester Cathedral

the most important. **The Great Hall**, (free), off the High Street, is the only surviving part of the medieval Castle rebuilt by Henry III between 1222 and 1236. Nikolaus Pevsner considered it "the finest medieval hall in England after Westminster Hall". Other buildings of interest include the early-14th century Pilgrim Hall (free), part of the **Pilgrim School**, and originally used as lodgings for pilgrims to the shrine of St Swithun, and **Wolvesey Castle** (English Heritage), the residence of the Bishops of Winchester since 963. The present palace is a gracious, classical building erected in the 1680s, flanked by the imposing ruins of its 14th century predecessor which was one of the grandest buildings in medieval England. Also well worth a visit is the 15th century **Hospital of St Cross**, England's oldest almshouse. Founded in 1132 by Henri du Blois, grandson of William the Conqueror, it was extended in 1446 by Cardinal Beaufort, son of John of Gaunt. It is still home to 25 Brothers and maintains its long tradition of hospitality by dispensing the traditional Wayfarer's Dole to any traveller who requests it.

SPARSHOLT
MAP 4 REF N20

2½ miles W of Winchester off the B3049

Elegant, refined and peaceful, **Lainston House Hotel and Restaurant** occupies splendid grounds encompassing the surrounding 63 acres, and retains all its architecturally graceful 17th century style. When Charles II commissioned Christopher Wren to build a new palace in Winchester, Lainston would have been within the Great Park planned to go with it. There are 38 opulent guest bedrooms, each with individual charm, all offering warmth, comfort and privacy. The past and present are fused in the superb exposed beams, four-poster beds and other period details combined with every modern amenity. The reception rooms also elegantly reflect the charm and serenity of this

Lainston House Hotel and Restaurant, Sparsholt, Winchester, Hampshire SO21 2LT Tel: 01962 863588 Fax: 01962 776672
e-mail: enquiries@lainstonhouse.com
website: www.lainstonhouse.com

William and Mary period house. The Restaurant commands views of the spectacular avenue of English Lim trees. Expertly prepared and presented dishes offer the ideal blend of traditional cooking with simplicity, freshness and purity. The hotel also has rods on the River Trent, and guests are welcome to take part in other country pursuits within the grounds.

ROMSEY
MAP 4 REF M21

10 miles SE of Winchester on the A27/A3090

"Music in stone", and "the second finest Norman building in England" are just two responses to **Romsey Abbey**, a majestic building containing some of the best 12th and 13th century architecture to have survived. Built between 1120 and 1230, the Abbey is remarkably complete. Unlike so many monastic buildings which were destroyed or fell into ruin after the Dissolution, the Abbey was fortunate in being bought by the town in 1544 for £100. Subsequent generations of townspeople have carefully maintained their bargain purchase. The Abbey's most spectacular feature is the soaring Nave which rises more than 70ft and extends for more than 76ft. Amongst the Abbey's many treasures is the Romsey Rood which shows Christ on the cross with the hand of God descending from the clouds. Just across from the Abbey, in Church Court, stands the town's oldest dwelling, King John's House, built around 1240

Romsey Abbey

for a merchant. It has served as a royal residence but not, curiously, for King John who died some 14 years before it was built. He may though have had a hunting lodge on the site. The house is now a museum and centre for cultural activities. In addition to its Abbey, Romsey also boasts one

Broadlands, Nr Romsey

of the finest stately homes in the county, **Broadlands**, a gracious Palladian mansion built by Lord Palmerston's father in the mid-1700s. The architect was Henry Holland, the landscape was modelled by the ubiquitous 'Capability' Brown. The important collections of furniture, porcelain and sculpture were acquired by the 2nd Viscount Palmerston. The house passed to the Mountbatten family and it was Lord Louis Mountbatten who first opened Broadlands to the public shortly before he was killed in 1979. The present owner, Lord Romsey, has established the Mountbatten Exhibition in tribute to his grandfather's remarkable career as naval commander, diplomat, and last Viceroy of India. An audio-visual film provides an overall picture of the Earl's life and exhibits include his dazzling uniforms, the numerous decorations he was awarded, and an astonishing collection of the trophies, mementoes and gifts he received in his many rôles.

SOUTHAMPTON

MAP 4 REF N21

5 miles S of Romsey on the A33

From this historic port, Henry V set sail for Agincourt in 1415, the Pilgrim Fathers embarked on their perilous journey to the New World in 1620, and, on April 10th, 1912, the *Titanic* set off on its maiden voyage, steaming majestically into the Solent. The city's sea-faring heritage is vividly recalled at the excellent **Maritime Museum** (free), housed in the 14th century **Wool House**. The museum tells the story of the port from the age of sail to the heyday of the great ocean liners.

As a major sea-port, Southampton was a prime target for air raids during World War II and suffered grievously. But the city can still boast a surprising number of ancient buildings. Substantial stretches of the medieval Town Walls have miraculously survived, its ramparts interspersed with fortifications such as the oddly-named 15th century **Catchcold Tower** and **God's House Gate and Tower**, which now houses the city's archaeological museum. Perhaps the most impressive feature of the walls is **Bargate**, one of the finest medieval city gates in the country. From its construction around 1200 until the 1930s, Bargate remained the principal entrance to the city. Its narrow archway is so low that South-

Bargate, Southampton

ampton Corporation's trams had to be specially modified for them to pass through. Inside the arch stands a statue of George III, cross-dressing as a Roman Emperor. Bargate now stands in its own pedestrianised area, its upper floor, the former Guildhall, now a Museum of local history and folklore.

Another remarkable survivor is the **Medieval Merchant's House** in French Street which has been expertly restored and authentically furnished, now appearing just as it was when it was built around 1290. One of the most popular visitor attractions in Southampton is the

Tudor House Museum, Southampton

Tudor House Museum & Garden, a lovely 15th century house with an award-winning Tudor Garden complete with fountain, bee skeps and 16th century herbs and flowers. There's so much history to savour in the city, but Southampton has also proclaimed itself "A City for the New Millennium". West Quay, one of the largest City Centre developments in Europe, is scheduled to open in 2000; a £3.4m injection from the Heritage Lottery Fund will enhance Southampton's already highly acclaimed central parks; the £27m Leisure World offers a wide range of leisure activities; and the new, state-of-the-art Swimming & Diving Complex incorporates separate championship, diving and fun pools.

Another major development is **Ocean Village**, an imaginatively conceived waterfront complex with its own 450-berth marina, undercover shopping, excellent restaurants and a multi-screen cinema. As you'd expect in a city with such a glorious maritime heritage, there's a huge choice of boat excursions, whether along the River Hamble, around the Solent, or over to the Isle of Wight. Blue Funnel Cruises operate from Ocean Village; Solent Cruises from Town Quay. The city also occupies an important place in aviation history. A short step from Ocean Village, the **Hall of Aviation** presents the story of aviation in the Solent and incorporates the **R.J. Mitchell Memorial Museum**. Mitchell lived and worked in Southampton in the 1930s and not only designed the Spitfire but also the S6 Seaplane which won the coveted Scheider Trophy. The centrepiece of the Hall of Aviation is the spectacular Sandringham Flying Boat which you can board and sample the luxury of air travel in the past - very different from the Cattle Class standards of today's mass travel. Tel: 01703 635830.

HAMBLE Map 4 ref N21
5 miles SE of Southampton on the B3397

Famous throughout the world as a yachting centre, Hamble takes its name from the river, a mere 10 miles long, that flows past the village into **Southampton Water**. Some 3,000 vessels have berths in the **Hamble Estuary**, so there's an incredible variety of boats thronging the river during the season, anything from vintage barges to the sleekest of modern craft.

Anyone interested in England's industrial heritage should travel a couple of miles north from Hamble to **Bursledon**. Ships have been built here since medieval times, the most famous being the *Elephant*, Nelson's flagship at the Battle of Copenhagen. The yard where it was built, now renamed the Elephant Boatyard is still in business. On a rise to the north of the village stands **Bursledon Windmill**, the only working windmill in Hampshire. Built in 1814 at a cost of £800, its vanes ground to a halt during the great agricultural depression of the 1880s. Happily, all the machinery remained intact and after a lengthy restoration between 1976 and 1991, the sails are revolving once again whenever a good northerly or southerly wind is blowing, producing stoneground flour for sale. The windmill is open to visitors at weekends, or whenever the sails are turning! The village can boast yet another unique industrial site. When **Bursledon Brickworks** was established in 1897 the machinery installed was at the very forefront of brickmaking technology. The works closed in 1974 but a Charitable Trust has now restored its gargantuan machines, thus preserving the last surviving example of a steam-driven brickworks in the country.

Heritage of a different kind can be found a couple of miles northwest of Hamble, at ruined **Netley Abbey** (English Heritage), a wonderfully serene spot surrounded by noble trees. "These are not the ruins of Netley" declared Horace Walpole in the mid-1700s, "but of Paradise". Jane Austen was equally entranced by the Abbey's romantic charm and she made many visits. Dating back to 1300, the exten-

Burlesdon Windmill

sive ruins provide a spectacular backdrop for open air theatre performances during the summer.

PORTSMOUTH
15 miles SE of Southampton off the A27

MAP 4 REF N22

Currently, any brochure promoting Portsmouth always adds the words "Flagship City". With good reason, since the port is home to the most famous flagship in naval history, **_HMS Victory_**. From the outside it's a majestic, three-masted ship: inside it's creepily claustrophobic, except for the Admiral's and Captain's spacious, mahogany- panelled quarters. Visitors can pace the very same deck from which Nelson master-minded the decisive encounter with the French navy off Cape Trafalgar in 1805. Standing on this deck, ostentatiously arrayed in the gorgeous uniform of a British Admiral of the Fleet, Nelson presented a clear target to a sharp-sighted French sniper. The precise spot where Nelson fell and the place on the sheltered orlop (lowest) deck where he died are both marked by plaques.

The death of Nelson was a tragedy softened by a halo of victory: the loss of the _Mary Rose_, some 260 years earlier was an unmitigated disaster. Henry VIII had ordered the ship, the second largest in his fleet, to be built.

HMS Victory, Portsmouth

He was standing on Southsea Common above Portsmouth in 1545, watching the _Mary Rose_ manoeuvre, when it suddenly heeled over and sank. All seven hundred men on board drowned. "And the King he screeched right out like any maid, 'Oh, my gentlemen! Oh, my gallant men!'" More than four centuries later, in

1982, the hulk of the *Mary Rose* was carefully raised from the seabed where it had lain for so long. Some seventeen years after that recovery, its oak frame is still drying out, the impressive remains now housed in the timber-clad **Mary Rose Museum** and open to visitors.

Like Southampton, Portsmouth suffered badly during World War II, losing most of its 17th and 18th century buildings. **St George's Church**, a handsome Georgian building of 1754 with large galleries, was damaged by a bomb but has been fully restored, and just to the north of the church, the barn-like **Beneficial Boy's School**, built in 1784, is another survivor. One of the most interesting buildings is to be found in **Southsea**, the city's resort area. **Southsea Castle** was built in 1544 as one of Henry VIII's series of forts protecting the south coast from French attacks. It has been modified several times since then but the original Keep is still intact and there are good views across the Solent from the gun platforms.

Portsmouth also offers visitors a wealth of varied museums, three of which deserve special mention. **The Royal Armouries**, housed in the huge Victorian Fort Nelson, claims to be 'Britain's Loudest Museum', with live firings every day; the **Charles Dickens Birthplace Museum** at 393, Old Commercial Road, has been restored and furnished to show how the house looked when the great novelist was born here in 1812; and the **D-Day Museum** in Southsea commemorating the Allied invasion of Europe in 1944 and most notable for the 83 metre long Overlord Tapestry, a 20th century equivalent of the Bayeux Tapestry which is well worth seeing.

Standing at the head of Portsmouth Harbour, **Portchester Castle** is not only the grandest medieval castle in the county but also stands within the best-preserved site of a Roman fort in northern Europe. Sometime around 280 AD, the Romans enclosed 8 acres of this strategic headland and used it as a base for their ships clearing the Channel of pirates. The original walls of the fort were 20ft high and 10ft thick, their depth much reduced by local people pillaging the stone for their own buildings. The medieval castle dates back to 1120 although the most substantial ruins are those of the royal palace built for Richard II between 1396 and 1399. Richard was murdered in 1399 and never saw his magnificent castle. Also within the walls of the Roman enclosure is **Portchester Church**, a superb Norman construction built between 1133 and 1150 as part of an Augustinian Priory. For some reason, the Priors moved inland to Southwick, and the church remained disused for more than five and a half centuries until Queen Anne personally donated £400 for its restoration. Apart from the east end, the church is entirely Norman and, remarkably, its 12th century font of wondrously carved Caen stone has also survived the centuries.

NEW FOREST   MAP 4 REF M21
9 miles W of Southampton off the A31

The New Forest, as is the way with English place-names, is neither New nor a Forest, although much of it is attractively wooded. Some historians believe that 'Forest' is a corruption of an

ancient British word, *gores* or *gorest*, meaning waste or open ground. 'Gorse' comes from the same root word. The term New Forest came into use after William the Conqueror proclaimed the area a royal hunting ground, seized some 15,000 acres that Saxon farmers had laboriously reclaimed from the heathland, and began a programme of planting thousands of trees. To preserve wildlife for his sport, (the deer especially), William adopted all the rigorous venery laws of his Saxon royal predecessors and added some harsh measures of his own. Anyone who killed a deer would himself be killed. If he shot at the beast and missed, his hands

New Forest Ponies

were cut off. And, perhaps most ruthless of all, anyone who disturbed a deer during the breeding season had his eyes put out. There are still plenty of wild deer roaming the 145 square miles of the Forest Park, confined within its boundaries by cattle grids, (known to Americans as Texas Gates). You are much more likely though to see the famous New Forest ponies, free-wandering creatures which nevertheless are all privately owned. They are also something of a hazard for drivers, so do take care, especially at night.

The largest wild area in lowland Britain, the Forest is ideal walking country with vast tracts virtually unpopulated but criss-crossed by a cat's cradle of footpaths and bridle-ways. The Forestry Commission has also established a network of waymarked cycle routes which make the most of the scenic attractions and are also designed to help protect the special nature of the Forest. A map detailing the cycle network is available, along with a vast amount of other information about the area, from the **New Forest Museum and Visitor Centre** in Lyndhurst. Visitors can watch an audio visual show, see life-sized models of Forest characters, make use of its Resource Centre and Library, and explore a gift shop specialising in locally made Forest crafts. The only town of any size within the New Forest, Lyndhurst is generally regarded as its 'capital', a good place then to begin a tour of the area.

LYNDHURST
8 miles SW of Southampton on the A35/A337

MAP 4 REF M21

The most striking building in this compact little town is the **Church of St Michael**, rebuilt in mid-Victorian times in what John Betjeman described as 'the most fanciful, fantastic Gothic style that I ever have seen'. The rebuilding co-incided with the heyday of the Pre-Raphaelite movement so the church contains some fine stained glass by Burne-Jones, produced by the firm of William Morris, as well as a splendidly lush painting by Lord Leighton of *The Wise and Foolish Virgins*. In St Michael's churchyard is the Grave of Alice Liddell who, as a young girl, was the inspiration for Lewis Carroll's Alice in Wonderland. As Mrs Reginald Hargreaves, Alice lived all her married life in Lyndhurst and was very active in local affairs.

Next to the church is the **Queen's House** which rather confusingly is re-named the King's House whenever the reigning sovereign is male. Originally built as a royal hunting lodge, its medieval and Tudor elements are still visible. Many Kings and Queens have lodged here and the last monarch to stay, George III, graciously allowed loyal villagers to watch through the window as he ate dinner. The House is now the headquarters of the Forestry Commission and is also home to the Verderer's Court, an institution dating back to Norman times which still deals with matters concerning the forest's ancient commoning rights. This little town is noted for its variety of small shops where you can find "anything from fresh food to Ferraris!" Many are located in the High Street, an attractive thoroughfare of mostly Edwardian buildings, which gently slopes down the hill to Bolton's Bench, a tree-crowned knoll where grazing ponies can usually be found and there are excellent views over Lyndhurst and the surrounding forest. At the other end of the town, **Swan Green**, surrounded by picturesque thatched cottages, provides a much-photographed setting where cricket matches are held in summer.

BEAULIEU
7 miles SE of Lyndhurst on the B3056

MAP 4 REF M22

The ruins of a 13th century Cistercian Abbey, a stately home which grew up around the Abbey's imposing gatehouse, and the **National Motor Museum** sited in its grounds are three good reasons why the village of Beaulieu has become one of the county's major visitor attractions. When Lord Montagu of Beaulieu first opened his family home to the public in the 1950s, he organised a display of a few vintage motor vehicles in homage to his father who had been a pioneer of motoring in Britain. That modest clutch of cars has now expanded to include some 250 of the oldest, newest, slowest and fastest motor-cars and bikes in British motoring history, plus some rare oddities. The motoring theme is continued in fun features such as Go Karts, Miniature Motors, and 'Fast Trax', described as the 'best in virtual racing simulators'.

National Motor Museum, Beaulieu

It was an ancestor of Lord Montagu, the 2nd Duke of Montagu, who created the picturesque riverside village of **Buckler's Hard** in the early 1700s. It was designed as an inland port to receive and refine sugar from the Duke's West Indian estates and His Grace planned his model village on a grand scale: the streets, for example, were to be 80ft wide. Unfortunately, the enterprise failed and only a single street was built. That 18th century street remains intact and unspoiled, and one of its buildings has been converted into a **Maritime Museum** reflecting the subsequent history of the village when it became a ship-building centre. More than 50 naval ships were built at Buckler's Hard, amongst them one of Nelson's favourite ships, the *Agamemnon*.

Just across the Beaulieu River from Buckler's Hard, as the crow flies, is **Exbury Gardens**. By road, that's about a 10-mile detour but one which is definitely worth making. One visitor described the Exbury Gardens as "Heaven with the gates open". Created by Lionel de Rothschild in the 1920s, Exbury is still run by his descendants, Mr & Mrs Edmund de Rothschild. They welcome visitors to share their own appreciation of these spectacular gardens where you can wander through some 200 acres of breathtakingly landscaped displays of noble trees, shrubs and botanical rarities. Tel: 01703 891203.

RINGWOOD   Map 3 ref M21
10 miles W of Lyndhurst on the A31/A338

Wednesday morning is a good time to visit Ringwood, since that is when its market square is filled with a notable variety of colourful stalls. The town has expanded greatly in recent years but its centre still boasts a large number of elegant Georgian houses, both large and small. **Ringwood Meeting House**, built in 1727 and now a Museum, is an outstanding example of an early Nonconformist chapel, complete with the original, rather austere, fittings. **Monmouth House** is of about the same period and stands on the site of an earlier house in which the luckless Duke of Monmouth was confined after his unsuccessful uprising against James II. The Duke had been discovered hiding in a ditch just outside the town and despite his abject pleas to the King to spare his life he was beheaded at Tower Hill a few days later.

Five miles west of the town stretch the great expanses of **Ringwood Forest**, which includes the **Moors Valley Country Park**. Since this area lies across the River Avon and is therefore in East Dorset, it really belongs in the next chapter but its landscape makes it clearly part of the New Forest. One of the most popular attractions in the Moors Valley Country Park is the **Moors Valley Railway**, a delightful narrow gauge steam railway with rails just 7¼ inches apart. The railway has eleven locomotives, all in different liveries, and 33 passenger vehicles. At busy periods, there may be up to six trains on the track so signalling is taken seriously and strictly controlled in accordance with British Rail procedures. The signal box at Kingsmere, the main station, was purpose-built but all the equipment inside comes from old redundant signal boxes - the main signal lever frame for example came from the Becton Gas Works in East London. At Kingsmere Station, in addition to the Ticket Office and the Engine and Carriage Sheds, there's also a Railway Shop, Buffet and Model Railway Shop. The route southwards runs alongside the Moors Lake, a manmade feature which also serves as a flood diversion area when the River

Moors, notorious for causing flooding in the area, is running high. The southern terminus of the railway is at Lakeside Station where there's a Visitor Centre, Information Point, Tearoom and Country Shop.

A mile or so south-east of Ringwood, in the hamlet of **Crow**, the **New Forest Owl Sanctuary** is home to the largest collection of owls in Europe, housed in more than 100 aviaries. There are flying displays, both inside and out,

Moors Valley Railway, nr Ringwood

daily lectures to entertain visitors of all ages, a café and shop. In the hospital units Bruce Berry, founder of the sanctuary, and his dedicated staff have prepared hundreds of birds for release back into the world. The Sanctuary is open daily from March to November and weekends only during the winter. Tel: 01425 476487.

MILFORD-ON-SEA   MAP 4 REF M22
9 miles S of Lyndhurst on the B3058

This sizeable coastal village is most notable for its grand views across The Solent to the Isle of Wight, and the odd-looking construction called **Hurst Castle**. At the centre of Hurst Castle is a squat fort built by Henry VIII to guard the Solent entrance against incursions by the French. Its tower is flanked by two long low wings added in the 1860s for gun emplacements, the square openings making them look rather like shopping arcades. The Castle was used as a garrison right up until World War II but is now in the care of English Heritage which has an on-site exhibition explaining its history. Hurst Castle stands at the tip of a long gravel spit which stretches out across the Solent to within three quarters of a

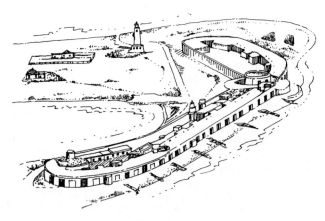

Hurst Castle

mile of the Isle of Wight coast. It can only be reached by a mile and a half walk along the shingle beach, or by ferries operated by Hurst Castle Ferry & Cruises at Keyhaven Quay, one mile east of Milford on Sea.

THE ISLE OF WIGHT

The Isle of Wight has adopted a motto which declares: "All this beauty is of God". It echoes the poet John Keats' "A thing of beauty is a joy for ever", the first line of his poem *Endymion* which he wrote while staying on the island in the hope that its crisp country air would improve his health. Other distinguished visitors have described Wight as "The Garden Isle", and "England's Madeira" but it was quite late in the day before the island became popular as a resort. This was partly because for centuries, right up until the 1600s, the island was a first port of call for pestiferous French raiders who made the islanders' lives a misery with their constant incursions. The turning point came in the 1840s when Queen Victoria and Prince Albert bought an estate near East Cowes, demolished an existing house, and Albert designed and built an Italianate mansion he named Osborne House. A few years later, the Poet Laureate, Alfred, Lord Tennyson, bought Farringford on the eastern side of the island. Socially, the Isle of Wight had arrived.

NEWPORT
MAP 4 REF N22
5 miles S of Cowes on the A3020

Set around the River Medina, Newport has a history going back to Roman times. Excavations in 1926 uncovered the well-preserved remains of a **Roman Villa**, a 3rd century farmhouse in which one side of the building was given over entirely to baths. A Roman style garden has been re-created in the grounds and provides an interesting insight into the wealth of new plants the Romans introduced into Britain. Some striking buildings have survived, amongst them **God's Providence House**, built in 1701 and now a tea room; John Nash's elegant Town Hall of 1816; an 18th century brewers warehouse near the harbour which now houses the **Quay Arts Centre**, incorporating a theatre, two galleries, a craft shop, café and bar; and a charming **Tudor Old Grammar School**.

CARISBROOKE
MAP 4 REF N22
1 mile SW of Newport on the B3323/B3401

Another quote from John Keats: "I do not think I shall ever see a ruin to surpass Carisbrooke Castle". The **castle** is set dramatically on a sweeping ridge and it's quite a steep climb up from the picturesque village to the massive Gatehouse. This was built in 1598 but the oldest parts of the castle date back to Norman times, most notably the mighty Keep which, apart from Windsor, is the most perfect specimen of Norman architecture in Britain. Archaeologists believe that the Castle stands on the site a Roman fort built some thousand years earlier.

Carisbrooke Castle

During the season costumed guides, or storytellers as English Heritage prefers to call them, conduct visitors around the noble ruins. The most poignant of their stories concern Charles I and his youngest daughter, Elizabeth. Charles was imprisoned here in the months before his trial and the guides will point out the mullioned window through which he unsuccessfully attempted to escape. After the King's execution, Cromwell's Council of State ordered that his daughter Elizabeth, 'for her own safety', should also be incarcerated at Carisbrooke. The 14 year old implored them not to send her to her father's former prison, but they were adamant. Elizabeth was a sickly child and less than a week after her arrival at the Castle she 'was stricken by fever and passed away, a broken-hearted child of fourteen'. The story touched the heart of Queen Victoria who set up a monument in Newport church where the Princess was buried. The effigy, in pure white Carrara marble, bears an inscription stating that it had been erected "as a token of respect for her virtues, and of sympathy for her misfortunes by Victoria R 1856". More cheerful aspects of a visit to the Castle include the Donkey Centre. Donkeys walking a treadmill were once used to turn the huge 16th century wheel in the Wellhouse to draw water from a well 161ft deep. A light at the bottom of the well gives some idea of its depth. Before donkeys were trained to raise the water, the task was performed by prisoners and nowadays visitors are invited to have a go at walking the treadmill themselves. Also within the Castle grounds are a **Coach House Exhibition** and **Victorian Island Exhibition**, the **Isle of Wight Museum** and a tea room.

COWES   Map 4 ref N22
5 miles N of Newport on the A3020

Cowes' origins as the most famous yachting resort in the world go back to the early 1800s. It was then a rather shabby port whose main business was shipbuilding. In 1811, the Duke of Gloucester came to stay and as part of the rather limited entertainment on offer watched sailing matches between local fishermen. The Duke's patronage led to amateur gentlemen running their own race and founding a club. The Prince Regent joined in 1817 and on his accession as George IV it was first re-christened the **Royal Yacht Club**, and then the **Royal Yacht Squadron**. Nowadays, **Cowes Week** has become the premier yachting event of the year and also a fixture in the aristocratic social calendar. Across the River Medina, **East Cowes** is most famous for **Osborne House**, a clean-cut, Italianate mansion designed and built by Prince Albert in 1846. Queen Victoria loved "dear beautiful Osborne" and so did her young children. They had

their very own house in its grounds, a full-size Swiss Cottage, where they played at house-keeping, cooking meals for their parents, and tending its vegetable gardens using scaled-down gardening tools. In the main house itself, visitors can wander through both the State and private apartments which are crammed with paintings, furniture, ornaments, statuary and the random bric-à-brac that provided such an essential element in the decor of any upper-class Victorian home. Osborne House possessed a special place in the Queen's affections. It had been built by the husband she adored with an almost adolescent infatuation: together they had spent many happy family days here. After Albert's premature death from typhoid in 1861, she often returned to Osborne, her staff instructed to lay out the Prince's clothes in his dressing-room each night, and the Queen herself retiring to bed with his nightshirt clasped in her arms. In 1901 she returned to Osborne for the last time, dying here in

Osborne House, East Cowes

her 83rd year, her death co-incidentally signalling the beginning of the slow decline of the British Empire over which she had presided as Queen-Empress.

BEMBRIDGE MAP 4 REF N22
9 miles E of Newport on the B3350

The most easterly point of the island, Bembridge was itself an island until the reclamation of the huge inland harbour of Brading Haven in the 1880s. The story of that major work is one of many aspects of the town's history featured in the **Bembridge Maritime Museum** which also displays ship models, artefacts from shipwrecks, and diving equipment, as well as action videos of underwater footage and lifeboat rescues. A fascinating exhibition of life in Bembridge, past and present, is portrayed in photographs and artefacts at the **Bembridge Roy Baker Heritage Centre** in Church Road. Also well worth a visit is the **Bembridge Windmill** (National Trust). Dating from around 1700, it is the only windmill to have survived on the island, with much of its wooden machinery still intact.

BRADING MAP 4 REF N22
7 miles E of Newport on the A3055

For what is little more than a large village, Brading is remarkably well-stocked with visitor attractions, amongst them a diminutive **Town Hall** with whipping post and stocks outside, and a fine church housing some striking tombs of the Oglander family. The most ancient of the village's sights is the **Brading Roman Villa** which in the 3rd century was the centre of a rich and prosperous farming estate. It covers some 300 square feet and has fine mosaic floors with a representation of that master-musician, Orpheus, charming wild animals with his lyre.

On the edge of the village stands **Morton Manor**, a lovely old house, dating back to 1249, largely rebuilt in 1680, set amidst one of the finest gardens in England. The landscaped grounds feature rose and Elizabethan sunken gardens, ponds and cascades, and many mature specimen trees including the largest London Plane you're ever likely to see. Other attractions include the Stable Shop, licensed tearooms, a safe children's Play Area with a traditional Elizabethan Turf Maze, and even a Vineyard. In fact, Brading has two vineyards. The other is the well-known Adgestone Vineyard, planted in 1968 and the oldest on the island. Entry is free, as is the wine tasting. There are pony trap rides around the vineyard during the season, a gift shop and café.

A mile or so northwest of the village, **Nunwell House & Gardens** should definitely not be missed. The picturesque house has been a family home since 1522 and is of great historic and architectural interest. It was here that Sir John Oglander, an ancestor of the present owner, was host to Charles I on his last night of freedom and modern day visitors can still see the Parlour Chamber in which they met. The house is beautifully furnished, there are exhibits recalling the family's military connections, and Nunwell is surrounded by 5 acres of tranquil gardens enjoying views across the Solent.

Some of the grandest views on the island can be enjoyed from **Brading Down**, just west of the village on the minor road that leads to Downend.

SANDOWN MAP 4 REF N22
6 miles SE of Newport on the A3055

"A village by a sandy shore" was how a guide-book described Sandown in the 1870s. Since then, its superb position on sweeping Sandown Bay has transformed that village into the island's premier resort. Now a lively town, Sandown offers its visitors every kind of seaside attraction. There are miles of flat, safe sands where a Kidzone safety scheme operates during the season, a traditional Pier complete with theatre, colourful gardens, a Sunday market, abundant sporting facilities, and even pleasure flights from the nearby airfield. On the edge of the town, the **Isle of Wight Zoological Gardens** specialises in breeding severely endangered exotic species and is home to the UK's largest variety of Royal Bengal, Siberian and Chinese tigers. The Zoo is also a

World Health Organisation centre for venomous snakes, their venom extracted for use in antidotes for snake bites. You may well see TV "Snake Man" Jack Corney handling these lethal reptiles and children who are photographed with a small harmless snake are presented with a handling certificate to prove it! There are all-weather snake and parrot shows, a kiddies' play area and Pets' Corner, a seafront pub and café, the Zoofari Gift Shop, and a snack bar. A Road-Runner Train operates frequent services between the Zoo and the town centre. In Sandown's High Street, the **Museum of Isle of Wight Geology** is especially popular with children who love its life-sized dinosaurs - the Isle of Wight is renowned for the number and quality of the dinosaur remains that have been discovered here.

SHANKLIN
Map 4 ref N22

12 miles SE of Newport on the A3055

Like Sandown, Shanklin was just a small village a century or so ago. The old village has survived intact, a charming little complex of thatched houses standing at the head of the **Shanklin Chine**. The famous Chine is a spectacular ravine some 300ft deep, 180ft wide, noted for its waterfalls and rare flora. There's a Nature Trail to follow or you can join a guided tour. **The Heritage Centre** includes an interesting exhibit on PLUTO (the PipeLine Under The Ocean) secretively constructed during World War II to transport fuel from the island to the Continent during the D-Day landings. There's also a memorial to the soldiers of 40 Commando who trained in this area for the disastrous assault on Dieppe in 1942.

VENTNOR
Map 4 ref N22

11 miles S of Newport on the A3055

Along the south-eastern corner of the island stretches a 6-mile length of ragged cliffs known as Undercliffe. Clinging to the slopes at its eastern end, Ventnor has been described as "an alpinist's town" and as "a steeply raked auditorium with the sea as the stage". Promoted as a spa town in the 1830s, its distinguished visitors have included a young Winston Churchill and an elderly Karl Marx. **Ventnor Heritage Museum** houses a fascinating collection of old prints, photographs and working models relating to the town's history, while **Ventnor Botanical Gardens** shelters some 10,000 plants in 22 acres of grounds, amongst them many rare and exotic trees, shrubs, alpines, perennials, succulents and conifers. There's a picnic area and children's playground, and during August the Gardens host open-air performances of Shakespeare plays. Above the town, **St Boniface Down** (National Trust), at 785ft the highest point on the island, provides some dizzying views across coast and countryside.

SHORWELL
Map 4 ref N22

7 miles SW of Newport on the B3323

Pronounced 'Shorell' by Caulkheads, as Isle of Wight natives are known, the village of Shorwell has no fewer than three venerable manor houses within its boundaries. **West Court, Wolverton**, and **North Court** were built respectively during the reigns of Henry VIII, Elizabeth I, and James I. They possess all the charm you would expect from that glorious age of English architecture but sadly none of them is open to the public. However, you can visit St Peter's Church to gaze on its mesmerisingly beautiful 15th century wall-painting and admire its 500-year-old stone pulpit covered by an elaborate wooden canopy of 1620. This small village has yet another attraction. **Yafford Mill** is an 18th century water mill in full working order. It's surrounded by ponds and streams where you'll find Sophie, the resident seal, and within the grounds there are paddocks which are home to rare cattle, sheep and pigs, a collection of antique farm machinery, a steam engine and narrow-gauge railway. There are also waymarked nature walks, a playground, picnic area, gift shop, tea gardens and licensed bar.

Located in an area of outstanding natural beauty on the Shepherd's Trail, **Bucks Farm** is home to the Jones family, who have lived here since 1994. An ex-riding instructor, Carol Jones now divides her time between running several lovely holiday cottages, providing superior bed

**Bucks Farm Holidays, Shorwell, Newport,
Isle of Wight PO30 3LP Tel: 01983 551206**

and breakfast accommodation, and horse-riding. Her husband Edwin oversees the farm itself, breeding cattle and taking visitors on farm trips. Three sides of the island can be seen from one of the farm's fields. The holiday cottages are wonderfully converted barns. Stonebuilt with traditional slate roofing, many boast rooms with exposed beams and other traditional features, and offer marvellous views of this beautiful location. The cottages offer guests every amenity they need to ensure a comfortable and very pleasant stay. Bed and breakfast or self-catering accommodation is available, and evening meals can be arranged with some advance notice. Some of the cottages are equipped for people with disabilities. Child-minding, maid and laundry services are also available. For a truly enjoyable and memorable short break or holiday, look no further.

FRESHWATER   Map 4 ref M22
11 miles W of Newport on the A3055

Freshwater and the surrounding area are inextricably linked with the memory of Alfred, Lord Tennyson. In 1850, he succeeded Wordsworth as Poet Laureate, married Emily Sellwood, and shortly afterwards moved to **Farringford**, just outside Freshwater. Tennyson was an indefatiga-

The Needles

ble walker and, however foul the weather, would pace along nearby High Down dramatically arrayed in a billowing cloak and a black, broad-brimmed sombrero. After his death, the area was re-named Tennyson Down and a cross erected high on the cliffs in his memory.

About a mile south of the town, Freshwater Bay was once an inaccessible inlet, much favoured by smugglers. From the Bay there are regular cruises around the island's most spectacular natural feature, the dreaded **Needles**. The boat trip takes you through the swirling waters around the lighthouse, and past the line of jagged slabs of gleaming chalk towering some 200ft high. The sea has gouged deep caves out of the cliffs. Two of them are known as Lord Holmes' Parlour and Kitchen, named after a 17th century Governor of the Island who once entertained his guests in the "Parlour" and kept his wines cool in the "Kitchen". The Needles are undoubtedly at their most impressive when viewed from the sea, but they are still a grand sight from the land. There are some particularly striking vistas from the **Needles Old Battery** (National Trust), a Victorian coastal fort standing 250ft above the sea. Visitors pass through a 200ft long tunnel and emerge onto a platform with panoramic views. Alternatively, **The Needles Pleasure Park** at Alum Bay also has good views and offers a wide range of family entertainments, a chairlift from the clifftop to the beach, boat trips to the lighthouse, a glass-making studio and many other attractions.

YARMOUTH
MAP 4 REF M22

10 miles W of Newport, on the A3054

A regular ferry links this picturesque little port to Lymington on the mainland. It was once the principal port on the island which was why Henry VIII ordered the building of **Yarmouth Castle** (English Heritage) in the 1540s. It was garrisoned until 1885 but is now disused, though much remains. The town also boasts a quaint old **Town Hall**, a working Pier, and a 13th century church rather unhappily restored in 1831. It's worth going inside to see the incongruous statue on the tomb of Sir Robert Holmes, Governor of the Island in the mid-17th century. During one of the endless conflicts with the French, Sir Robert had captured a ship on board which was a French sculptor with an unfinished statue of Louis XIV. He was travelling to Versailles to model the King's head from life. Sir Robert decided that the elaborate statue of the King (in full French armour) would do nicely for his own tomb. The sculptor was ordered to replace the Royal head with Sir Robert's. No doubt deliberately, the artist made a poor fist of the job and the head is decidedly inferior to the rest of the statue.

WILTSHIRE

SWINDON
MAP 3 REF M19

32 miles N of Andover on the A420

Think Swindon, think the Great Western Railway. Think GWR, think Isambard Kingdom Brunel. The largest town in Wiltshire, lying in the northeast corner between the Cotswolds and the Marlborough Downs, was an insignificant agricultural community before the railway line between London and Bristol was completed in 1835. Swindon Station opened in that year, but it was some time later, in 1843, that Brunel, the GWR's principal engineer, decided that Swindon was the place to build his locomotive works. Within a few years it had grown to be one of the largest in the world, with as many as 12,000 on a 320-acre site that incorporated the Railway Village; this was a model development of 300 workmen's houses built of limestone extracted from the construction of Box Tunnel. This unique example of early-

Great Western Railway Museum, Swindon

Victorian town planning is open to the public as the **Railway Village Museum**. **The Great Western Railway Museum** moved from the same site in Faringdon Road in the autumn of 1999 to a new home in the former GWR works, with a new name, a great deal more space and a host of new interactive exhibits. **STEAM** will keep the collection of locomotives (6000 *King George V* is the star), nameplates, signalling equipment and an exhibition of the life and achievements of Brunel; it will also focus on the human aspect of a hard industry, telling the story of the men and women who built and repaired the locomotives and carriages of God's Wonderful Railway for seven generations. There's lots more to Swindon than the legacy of the GWR: it's a bustling and successful commercial town with excellent shopping and leisure facilities and plenty of open spaces. One such is **Coate Water Country Park** on the Marlborough road.

CRICKLADE   MAP 3 REF L18
6 miles N of Swindon off the A419

The only Wiltshire town on the Thames was an important post on the Roman Ermin Street and had its own mint in Saxon times. There are many buildings of interest, notably the Church of St Sampson, with its cathedral-like four-spired tower, where a festival of music takes place each September; the famous school founded by the London goldsmith Robert Jenner in 1651; and the fancy Victorian clock tower. Nearby **North Meadow** is a National Nature Reserve where the rare snakeshead fritillary grows. Cricklade is the centre of the Cricklade Corridor Trust set up to secure the maximum economic, heritage, leisure and environmental benefits from a number of projects between Swindon and Cricklade and beyond. These include railway and canal restoration, nature conservation and the development of a branch of the National Cycle Network. Tel: 01249 706111.

WROUGHTON   MAP 3 REF M19
3 miles S of Swindon on the A4361

Wroughton Airfield, with its historic Second World War hangars, is home to the **National Museum of Science and Industry's** collection of large aircraft, and the road transport and agricultural collection. The museum is open on event days at the airfield.

Nearby **Clouts Wood Nature Reserve** is a lovely place for a ramble, and a short drive south, by the Ridgeway, is the site of **Barbury Castle**, one of the most spectacular Iron Age forts in southern England. The open hillside was the scene of a bloody battle between the Britons and the Saxons in the 6th century; the Britons lost and the Saxon kingdom of Wessex was established under King Cealwin. The area around the castle is a country park.

LYDIARD TREGOZE   MAP 3 REF L18
2 miles W of Swindon off the A3102

On the western outskirts of Swindon, **Lydiard Park** is the ancestral home of the Viscounts Bolingbroke. The park is a delightful place to explore, and the house, one of Wiltshire's smaller stately homes, is a real gem, described by Sir Hugh Casson as "a gentle Georgian house, sunning itself as serenely as an old grey cat". Chief attractions inside include the little blue Dressing Room devoted to the 18th century society artist Lady Diana Spencer, who became the 2nd Viscountess Bolingbroke. St Mary's Church, next to the house, contains many monuments to the St John family, who lived here from Elizabethan times. The most striking is the **Golden Cavalier**, a life-size gilded effigy of Edward St John in full battledress (he was killed at the 2nd Battle of Newbury in 1645).

MALMESBURY   MAP 3 REF L18
14 miles W of Swindon on the A429

England's oldest borough and one of its most attractive. The hilltop town is dominated by the impressive remains of the **Benedictine Malmesbury Abbey**, founded in the 7th century by St

Aldhelm. In the 10th century, King Athelstan, Alfred's grandson and the first Saxon king to unite England, granted 500 acres of land to the townspeople in gratitude for their help in resisting a Norse invasion. Those acres are still known as King's Heath and are owned by 200 residents who are descended from those far-off heroes. Athelstan made Malmesbury his capital and is buried in the abbey, where several centuries later a monument was put up in his honour. The abbey tower was the scene of an early attempt at human-powered flight when in the early part of the 11th century Brother Elmer strapped a pair of wings to his arms, flew for about 200 yards and crashed to earth, breaking both legs and becoming a cripple for the rest of his long life. The flight of this intrepid cleric, who reputedly forecast the Norman invasion following a sighting of Halley's Comet, is commemorated in a stained glass window. The octagonal **Market Cross**

Market Cross, Malmesbury

in the town square is one of many interesting buildings that also include the Old Stone House with its colonnade and gargoyles, and the arched Tolsey Gate, whose two cells once served as the town jail. In the **Athelstan Museum** are displays of lace-making, costume, rural life, coins, early bicycles and tricycles, a manually-operated fire engine, photographs and maps. Personalities include a local notable, the philosopher Thomas Hobbes. A more recent piece of history concerns the **Tamworth Two**, the pigs who made the headlines with their dash for freedom. Their trail is one of many that can be followed in and around the town.

The **Abbey House Gardens** offer five acres of horticulture and history, planted for continuous spring to autumn colour. Adjacent to the Abbey and developed round a late-Tudor house, it has been described as one of the best gardens in the country. The Abbey House dates from about 1545 and was built on the remains of a 13th-century Abbey building. Owners Ian and Barbara Pollard and their family came to live here in 1994. Together their passion for gardening has led to a superb planting scheme with formal areas, yew hedges, orchard, herb garden, herbaceous borders, laburnum tunnel, stew pond and loggia. A massive planting scheme complete for the new millennium features 2,000 different roses, 2,000 herbs and an expanding collection of trees and shrubs. Lovely walks take the visitor past the river, many rare plants, woodland, fruit and foliage plants and local wildlife. This is a garden that is worth visiting again and

The Abbey House Gardens, Market Cross, Malmesbury, Wiltshire SN16 9AS Tel: 01666 822212

again, a truly superb example of the art of gardening. Open daily 1st March - 31st October, 11 a.m.-6 p.m. Light refreshments are available and there are plants for sale.

CASTLE COMBE
MAP 3 REF K19

8 miles SW of Malmesbury on the B4039

The loveliest village in the region, and for some the loveliest in the country, Castle Combe was once a centre of the prosperous wool trade, famed for its red and white cloth, and many of the present-day buildings date from the 15th and 16th centuries, including the Perpendicular Church of St Andrew, the covered market cross and the manor house, which was built with stones from the Norman castle that gave the village its name. One of the Lords of the Manor in the 14th century was Sir John Fastolf, who was reputedly the inspiration for Shakespeare's Falstaff. A small museum dealing with the village's history is open on summer Sunday afternoons.

CHIPPENHAM
MAP 3 REF L19

10 miles S of Malmesbury on the A429

This historic settlement on the banks of the Avon was founded around 600 by the Saxon king Cyppa. It became an important administrative centre in King Alfred's time and later gained further prominence from the wool trade. It was a major stop on the London-Bristol coaching run and is served by the railway between the same two cities. Buildings of note include the Church of St Andrew (mainly 15th century) and the half-timbered Hall, once used by the burgesses and bailiffs of the Chippenham Hundred and latterly a museum (as we went to press the museum was due to move into a Heritage Centre in the market place). At Hardenhuish Hall on the edge of town, John Wood the Younger of Bath fame built the Church of St Nicholas; completed in 1779, it is notable for its domed steeple and elegant Venetian windows. In the flood plain to the east of Chippenham stands the 4½ mile footpath known as **Maud Heath's Causeway**. This remarkable and ingenious walkway consisting of 64 brick and stone arches was built at the end of the 15th century at the bequest of Maud Heath, who spent most of her life as a poor pedlar trudging her often muddy way between her village of Bremhill and Chippenham. She died a relatively wealthy woman, and the land and property she left in her will provided sufficient funds for the upkeep of the causeway, which is best seen near the hamlet of Kellaways. A statue of Maud, basket in hand, stands overlooking the flood plain at Wick Hill.

CALNE
MAP 3 REF L19

5 miles E of Chippenham on the A4

A former weaving centre in the valley of the River Marden; the prominent wool church reflects the prosperity of earlier times. One of the memorials in the church is to Dr Ingenhousz, who is widely credited with creating a smallpox vaccination before Jenner. A short distance from Calne, to the west, stands **Bowood House**, built in 1625 and now a treasury of Shelborne family heirlooms, paintings, books and furniture. In the Bowood Laboratory Dr Joseph Priestley, tutor to the 1st Marquess of Lansdowne's son, conducted experiments that resulted in the identification of oxygen. The house is set in lovely Capability Brown grounds with a lake and terraced garden. The mausoleum was commissioned in 1761 by the Dowager Countess of Shelborne as a memorial to her husband and was Robert Adam's first work for them. A separate woodland garden of 60 acres, with azaleas and rhododendrons, is open from late April to early June. The **Atwell Motor Museum**, on the A4 east of Calne, has a collection of over 70 vintage and classic cars and motorcycles from the years 1924 to 1983.

LACOCK
MAP 3 REF L19

4 miles S of Chippenham on the A350

The National Trust village of Lacock is one of the country's real treasures. The quadrangle of streets - East, High, West and Church - holds a delightful assortment of mellow stone buildings, and the period look (no intrusive power cables or other modern-day eyesores) keeps it in great demand as a film location. Every building is a well-restored, well-preserved gem, and overlooking everything is **Lacock Abbey**, founded in 1232 by Ela, Countess of Salisbury in memory of her husband William Longsword, stepbrother to Richard the Lionheart. In common with all monastic houses Lacock was dissolved by Henry VIII, but the original cloisters, chapter houses, sacristy and kitchens survive. Much of the remainder of what we see today dates from the mid 16th century, when the abbey was acquired by Sir William Sharington. He

Lacock Village Street

added an impressive country house and the elegant octagonal tower that overlooks the Avon. The estate next passed into the hands of the Talbot family, who held it for 370 years before ceding it to the National Trust in 1944.

The most distinguished member of the Talbot family was the pioneering photographer William Henry Fox Talbot, who carried out his experiments in the 1830s. The **Fox Talbot Museum** commemorates the life and achievements of a man who was not just a photographer but a mathematician, physicist, classicist, philologist and transcriber of Syrian and Chaldean cuneiform. He also remodelled the south elevation of the abbey and added three new oriel windows. One of the world's earliest photographs shows a detail of a latticed oriel window of the abbey; made in 1835 and the size of a postage stamp, it is the earliest known example of a photographic negative.

BRADFORD-ON-AVON
9 miles SW of Chippenham on the A363

Map 3 ref K19

An historic market town at a bridging point on the Avon, which it spans with a superb nine-arched bridge with a lock-up at one end. The town's oldest building is the **Church of St Lawrence**, believed to have been founded by St Aldhelm around 700. It 'disappeared' for over 1,000 years, when it was used variously as a school, a charnel house for storing the bones of the dead, and a residential dwelling. It was re-discovered by a keen-eyed clergyman who looked down from a hill and noticed the cruciform shape of a church. The surrounding buildings were gradually removed to reveal the little masterpiece we see today. Bradford's Norman church, restored in the 19th century, has an interesting memorial to Lieutenant-General Henry Shrapnel, the army officer who, in 1785, invented the shrapnel shell. Another of the town's outstanding buildings is the mighty **Tithe Barn**, once used to store the grain from local farms for Shaftesbury Abbey, now housing a collection of antique farm implements and agricultural machinery. The centrepiece of the museum in Bridge Street is a pharmacy which has stood in the town for 120 years before being removed lock, stock and medicine bottles to its new site.

Leigh House is a 16th-century farmhouse, said to be one of four chief farms of the tithing granted to Elizabeth I's 'favourite', Robert Dudley, in 1574. Set amid six acres of land, it commands further views across fields and paddocks. Every room is a pleasure, from the lovely guests' lounge with its magnificent inglenook fireplace to the beamed dining room with its flagstone floor, handsome chestnut table and rustic country furniture. All the guest bedrooms

Leigh House, Leigh Road West, Bradford on Avon, Wiltshire BA15 2RB Tel: 01225 867835

are ensuite, and furnished and decorated to the highest standards of taste and quality. Some offer views to the walled garden, others across to the Westbury hills and Westbury White Horse, set below the outline of Bratton Castle, an Iron Age hill fort.

The beautifully decor continues throughout this wonderful manor house, both in decor, furnishings and touches like the lush drapes in the bedrooms. Breakfasts is delicious and filling; evening meals by arrangement. The Bakehouse, adjacent to the main farmhouse, is as its name indicates a converted 16th-century bakehouse, available for bed and breakfast or as self-catering accommodation for up to seven people. It retains many original features such as the open hearth fireplace, bread and smoking ovens and exposed beams. It has views into the main courtyard and its own private entrance to the walled garden. For a taste of Tudor elegance combined with every modern comfort, look no further.

Off the A363 on the northern edge of town, **Barton Farm Country Park** offers delightful walks in lovely countryside by the River Avon and the Kennet & Avon Canal. It was once a

Kennet & Avon Canal, Bradford-on-Avon

medieval farm serving Shaftesbury Abbey. Barton Bridge is the original packhorse bridge built to assist the transportation of grain from the farm to the tithe barn. Half a mile south of town by the River Frome is the Italian-style **Peto Garden** at **Iford Manor**. Famous for its romantic, tranquil beauty, its steps and terraces, statues, colonnades and ponds, the garden was laid out by the architect and landscape gardener Harold Ainsworth Peto between 1899 and 1933. He was inspired by the works of Lutyens and Jekyll to turn a difficult hillside site into "a haunt of ancient peace".

MARLBOROUGH
MAP 3 REF M19

19 miles E of Chippenham on the A4

Famous for its public school and its wide high street, Marlborough is situated in the rural eastern part of Wiltshire in the upland valley of the Kennet, which flows through the town. It was once an important staging post on the coaching run from London to Bath and Bristol, and the presence of the A4 means that it still has easy links both east and west. Its main street, one of the finest in the country, is dignified by many Tudor houses and handsome Georgian colon-naded shops, behind which are back alleys waiting to be explored. St Mary's Church, austere behind a 15th century frontage, stands in **Patten Alley**, so named because pedestrians had to wear pattens (an overshoe with a metal sole) to negotiate the mud on rainy days. The porch of the church has a ledge where churchgoers would leave their pattens before entering. Other buildings of interest include those clustered round The Green (originally a Saxon village and the working-class quarter in the 18th and 19th centuries); the turn-of-the-century Town Hall looking down the broad High Street; and the ornate 17th century Merchant's House, now restored as a museum. **Marlborough College** was founded in 1843 primarily for sons of the clergy. The Seymour family built a mansion near the site of the Norman castle. This mansion was replaced in the early 18th century by a building which became the Castle Inn and is now C House, the oldest part of the College.

SAVERNAKE FOREST   Map 3 ref M19
2 miles E of Marlborough off the A346

The ancient woodland of **Savernake Forest** is a magnificent expanse of unbroken woodland, open glades and bridle paths. King Henry Vlll hunted wild deer here and married Jane Seymour, whose family home was nearby. Designated an SSSI (Site of Special Scientific Interest), the forest is home to abundant wildlife, including a small herd of deer and 25 species of butterfly.

WEST OVERTON   Map 3 ref M19
3 miles W of Marlborough off the A4

The area between Marlborough and Avebury sees the biggest concentration of prehistoric re-mains in the country. The scattered community of West Overton stands at the foot of **Overton Hill**, the site of an early Bronze Age monument called **The Sanctuary**. These giant standing stones are at the southeastern end of West Kennet Avenue, an ancient pathway which once connected them to the main megalithic circles at Avebury (see below). Overton Hill is also the start point of the Ridgeway long-distance path, which runs for 80 miles to the Chilterns. Just off this path is **Fyfield Down**, now a nature reserve, where quarries once provided many of the great stones that are such a feature of the area. **Devil's Den** long barrow lies within the reserve. The local legend that Satan sometimes appears here at midnight attempting to pull down the stones with a team of white oxen has not in recent times been corroborated.

EAST AND WEST KENNET   Map 3 ref M19
4 miles W of Marlborough on the A4

West Kennet Long Barrow, one of Britain's largest neolithic burial tombs, is situated a gentle stroll away from the twin villages. The tomb is of impressive proportions - 330' long, 80' wide and 10' high - and is reached by squeezing past some massive stones in the semicircular fore-court.

SILBURY HILL   Map 3 ref L19
5 miles W of Marlborough on the A4

The largest man-made prehistoric mound in Europe, built around 2800BC, standing 130' high and covering five acres. Excavation in the late 1960s revealed some details of how it was constructed but shed little light on its purpose. Theories include a burial place for King Sil and his horse and a hiding place

Silbury Hill

for a large gold statue built by the Devil on his way to Devizes. Scholarship generally favours the first.

AVEBURY   MAP 3 REF L19
6 miles W of Marlborough on the A4361

A 28-acre World Heritage Site is the centre of the **Avebury Stone Circles**, the most remarkable ritual megalithic monuments in Europe. A massive bank and ditch enclose an outer circle and

two inner circles of stones. The outer circle of almost 100 sarsen stones (sand and silica) enclose two rings with about 40 stones still standing. Archaeologists working on the site have recently found the remains of a long-vanished avenue of stones leading south towards Beckahmpton. This discovery seems to vindicate the theory of the 18th century antiquary William Stukeley, who made drawings of the stone circles with this avenue marked. The stones in

Avebury Stones

the avenue had disappeared so completely (perhaps destroyed out of some superstition in the Middle Ages) that few believed Stukeley. The research team from Southampton, Leicester and Newport Universities uncovered a series of subterranean features which appear to be buried stones and the sockets in which they were set. Two large stones, known as Adam and Eve, had always been known about on this route, but there were no further traces until the team's discoveries in 1999. The **Avebury Stones** bear testimony to the enormous human effort that went into their construction: some of the individual stones weigh 40 tons and all had to dragged from Marlborough Downs. The Avebury stones are in two basic shapes, which have been equated

with male and female and have led to the theory that the site was used for the observance of fertility rites. Many of the archaeological finds from the site are displayed in Avebury's **Alexander Keiller Museum**, which also describes the reconstruction of the site by Keiller in the 1930s. Avebury has a gem from Elizabethan times in **Avebury Manor**, which stands on the site of a 12th century priory. The

Avebury Manor

house and its four-acre walled garden, which features a wishing well, topiary, a rose graden and an Italian walk, are owned by the National Trust. Open daily except Monday and Thursday.

COLLINGBOURNE KINGSTON   MAP 3 REF M20
10 miles SE of Marlborough on the A338

The Old School House, built in 1845 and still visited by former pupils, is now top of the class in the local dining-out stakes. Livio and Lynda Guglielmino came here in 1987 and turned the former assembly hall of the school - which was at that time a tea shop - into a restaurant of real quality that has acquired an ever-growing band of enthusiastic regulars. The decor is superb throughout, and in complete sympathy with the original high-pitched ceilings and beams. The walls are adorned with details of the school's history and photographs of pupils down the years. Livio's menu makes appetising reading, and the results on the plate fully live up to the anticipation. Classics include pepper steak, steak Diane, veal Marsala and pollo verbena (chicken breast

The Old School House, Collingbourne Kingston,
nr Marlborough, Wiltshire SN8 3SD Tel: 01264 850799

topped with cheese, tomato, asparagus and white sauce). School dinners were never like this! The Old School House also offers high-quality overnight accommodation in four bedrooms with en suite facilities and TVs.

PEWSEY   MAP 3 REF M19
7 miles S of Marlborough on the A345

In the heart of the beautiful valley that bears its name, this is a charming village of half-timbered houses and thatched cottages. It was once the personal property of Alfred the Great, and a statue of the king stands at the crossroads in the centre. The parish church, built on a foundation of sarsen stones, has an unusual altar rail made from timbers taken from the *San Josef*, a ship captured by Nelson in 1797. Attractions for the visitor include the old wharf area and the **Heritage Centre**. In an 1870 foundry building it contains an interesting collection of old and unusual machine tools and farm machinery. The original **Pewsey White Horse**, south of the village on Pewsey Down, was cut in 1785, apparently including a rider, but was redesigned by a Mr George Marples and cut by the Pewsey Fire Brigade to celebrate the coronation of King George VI. **Pewsey Carnival** takes place each September, and the annual Devizes to Westminster canoe race passes through **Pewsey Wharf**.

ENFORD   MAP 3 REF M20
12 miles S of Marlborough off the A345

This peaceful village is on the River Avon south of Upavon. Visitors from all walks of life endorse **The Swan at Enford**, where Bob and Phil Bone are the hands-on proprietors. The brick and flint building dates from the 17th century, and has a thatched roof, beautiful gardens front and back, and oak beams in the lounge bar and restaurant. The latter is a non-smoking area with seats for 18 and a menu to set the tastebuds tingling. In addition to classic pub fare -

**The Swan at Enford, Long Street, Enford, nr Pewsey,
Wiltshire SN9 6DD Tel: 01980 670338 Fax: 01980 671318
e-mail: theswanatenford@easynet.co.uk**

ploughman's, basket meals, chicken Kiev, steak and kidney pie, and steaks - there are always some interesting specials including trout (the River Avon runs 60 yards from the front of the pub) and seasonal game, the basis for delicious dishes such as warm salad of pigeon breast or stuffed venison fillet served on a bed of pickled cabbage with a port wine sauce. There's a particularly good choice for vegetarians, including dishes such as a lentil-based moussaka or apricot and quorn pie. Real ales and a worldwide selection of wines accompany the fine food. Tuesday night is quiz night - always a popular occasion - and four times a year a jazz group or blues band performs.

DEVIZES   MAP 3 REF L19

14 miles SW of Marlborough on the A361

At the western edge of the Vale of Pewsey, Devizes is the central market town of Wiltshire. The town was founded in 1080 by Bishop Osmund, nephew of William the Conqueror. The bishop was responsible for building a timber castle between the lands of two powerful manors, and this act brought about the town's name, which is derived from the Latin ad divisas, or 'at the boundaries'. After the wooden structure burnt down, Roger, Bishop of Sarum, built a stone castle in 1138 that survived until the end of the Civil War, when it was demolished. Bishop Roger also built two fine churches in Devizes. Long Street is lined with elegant Georgian houses and also contains the Wiltshire Archaeological and Natural History Society's **Devizes Museum**, which has a splendid collection of artefacts from the area, and a gallery with a John Piper window and regularly changing exhibitions.

Market Cross, Devizes

The newly opened **Devizes Visitor Centre** offers a unique insight into the town. The Centre is based on a 12th century castle and takes visitors back to medieval times, when Devizes was home to the finest castle in Europe and the scene of anarchy and unrest during the struggles between Empress Matilda and King Stephen. An interactive exhibition shows how the town came to be at the centre of the 12th century Civil War and thrived as a medieval town, many traces of which remain today, and on into the present. Many more of the town's finest buildings are situated in and around the old market place, including the Town Hall and the Corn Exchange. Also here is an unusual **market cross** inscribed with the story of Ruth Pierce, a market stall-holder who stood accused, in 1753, of swindling her customers. When an ugly crowd gathered round her, she stood and pleaded her innocence, adding "May I be struck dead if I am lying". A rash move, as she fell to the ground and died forthwith. Devizes stands at a key point on the Kennet & Avon Canal, and the **Kennet & Avon Canal Museum** tells the complete story of the canal in fascinating detail. Many visitors combine a trip to the museum with a walk along the towpath, which is a public footpath. Each July the Canalfest, a weekend of family fun designed to raise funds for the upkeep of the canal, is held at the Wharf, which is also the start point, on Good Friday, of the annual Devizes-Westminster canoe race.

WESTBURY   Map 3 ref L20
13 miles SW of Devizes on the A350

Westbury, at the western edge of the chalk downlands of **Salisbury Plain**, was a major player in the medieval cloth and wool trades, and still retains many fine buildings from the days of great prosperity, including some cloth works and mills, Westbury was formerly a 'rotten borough' and returned two MPs until 1832. Scandal and corruption were rife, and the **Old Town Hall** in the market place is evidence of such goings-on, a gift from a grateful victorious candidate in 1815. This was Sir Manasseh Massey Lopes, a Portuguese financier and slave-trader who 'bought' the borough to advance his political career. Just west of Westbury, at **Brokerswood**, is **Woodland Park and Heritage Centre**, 80 acres of ancient broadleaf woodland with a wide range of trees, plants and animals, nature trails, a lake with fishing, a picnic and barbecue area, a tea room and gift shop, a museum, a play area and a narrow-gauge railway. By far the best-known Westbury feature is the famous **Westbury White Horse**, a chalk carving measuring 182' in length and 108' in height. The present steed dates from 1778, replacing an earlier one carved to celebrate King Alfred's victory over the Danes at nearby Ethandun (Edington) in 878. The white horse is well looked after, the last major grooming being in 1996. Above the horse's head are the ruins of Bratton Castle, an Iron Age hill fort covering 25 acres.

CODFORD ST PETER & CODFORD ST MARY   Map 3 ref L20
8 miles SE of Westbury on the A36

Sister villages beneath the prehistoric remains of **Codford Circle**, an ancient hilltop meeting place which stands 617' up on Salisbury Plain. The church in Codford St Peter has one of Wiltshire's finest treasures in an exceptional 9th century Saxon stone carving of a man holding a branch and dancing. East of Malmpit Hill and visible from the A36 is a rising sun emblem carved by Australian soldiers during World War l. In the military cemetery at Codford St Mary are the graves of Anzac troops who were in camp here. Anzac graves may also be seen at nearby Baverstock.

A stonebuilt late-Georgian house with later additions and set in 2½ acres of beautiful grounds, **Little Ashton** is a gracious and distinguished bed and

Little Ashton, High Street, Codford St Peter, Warminster, Wiltshire BA12 0NH Tel/Fax: 01985 850923

breakfast that retains a real home-from-home ambience. Beautifully decorated throughout and adorned with many objets d'art, it boasts two attractive guest bedrooms - a double with private bath, and a suite with double bedroom and adjoining bedroom/sitting room and large ensuite bath. All modern facilities are included. The large and comfortable drawing room is open to guests, and is stocked with books, magazines, local information and other gentle diversions for guests' enjoyment. Breakfast offers free-range eggs raised on the grounds - as can be seen from the geese, guinea fowl, chickens and ducks roaming free. For evening meals there are some excellent local pubs and restaurants nearby. The superb original features, open fireplaces and other accoutrements make for a wonderful atmosphere. A warm welcome is guaranteed at this superior establishment.

WYLYE
Map 3 ref L20

10 miles SE of Westbury off the A36/A303

Peace arrived in Wylye in 1977, when a bypass diverted traffic from the busy main roads. It had long been an important junction and staging post on the London-Exeter coaching route. A statue near the bridge over the River Wylye (from which the village, Wilton and indeed Wiltshire get their names) commemorates a brave postboy who drowned here after rescuing several passengers from a stagecoach which had overturned during a flood.

The Bell Inn at Wylye is a traditional coaching inn that dates back to 1373. The interior retains many period features, including its large inglenook fireplace and wealth of exposed timber. There are always at least four real ales on tap, as well as a range of lagers, ciders, stouts, wines from the world over as well as from the local Wylye Valley Vineyard, and spirits. The first-class menu includes salmon, sirloin steaks, smoked Wiltshire ham and vegetable crumble, as well as a choice of daily specials - fresh local game is a speciality. The three charming letting rooms comprise two ensuite and one with separate private bathroom and toilet. Each of the rooms is decorated and furnished in traditional style, Proprietors Keith and Linda Bidwell have been at The Bell since June of 1999, and have already made a great impact on increasing the reputation and renown of this distinguished establishment. They have been in the trade for over 30 years.

The Bell Inn at Wylye, High Street, Wylye, Warminster, Wiltshire BA12 0QP Tel: 01985 248338 Fax: 01985 248389

Keith trained at the Grosvenor Hotel in Park Lane; here at The Bell he is chef, benefiting from his experience working in many Michelin restaurants. Both are very keen on course fishing and fly fishing - the latter a local speciality, as the River Wylye runs right through this very pretty village - and are happy to advise guests on this most relaxing of pursuits.

Above the village is the little-known **Yarnbury Castle**, an Iron Age hill fort surrounded by two banks and an outer bank. To the west is a triangular enclosure from Roman times which could have held cattle or sheep. From the 18th century to World War l Yarnbury was the venue of an annual sheep fair.

WARMINSTER

Map 3 ref L20

4 miles S of Westbury on the A350

The largest centre of population is a historic wool, corn-trading and coaching town with many distinguished buildings, including a famous school with a door designed by Wren. In addition to the 18th and 19th century buildings, Warminster has a number of interesting monuments: the Obelisk with its feeding troughs and pineapple top erected in 1783 to mark the enclosure of the parish; the Morgan Memorial Fountain in the Lake Pleasure Grounds; and *Beyond Harvest*, a statue in bronze by Colin Lambert of a girl sitting on sacks of corn. Warminster's finest building is the Church of St Denys, mainly 14th century but almost completely rebuilt in the 1880s to the design of Arthur Blomfield. The **Dewey Museum**, in the public library, displays a wide range of local history and geology. To the west of town is the 800' **Cley Hill**, an Iron Age hill fort with two Bronze Age barrows. Formerly owned by the Marquess of Bath, the Hill was given to the National Trust in the 1950s and is a renowned sighting place for UFOs. (The region is also noted for the appearance of crop circles and some have linked the two phenomena.) On the northern edge of Warminster **Arn Hill Nature Reserve** along public footpaths forms a circular walk of two miles through woodland and open downland.

LONGLEAT

Map 3 ref K20

6 miles SW of Westbury off the A362

1999 saw the 50th anniversary of the opening of **Longleat House** to the public. The magnificent home of the Marquess of Bath was built by an ancestor, Sir John Thynne, in a largely symmetrical style, in the 1570s. The inside is a treasure house of old masters, Flemish tapestries, beautiful furniture, rare books.....and Lord Bath's murals. The superb grounds of Longleat House were landscaped by Capability Brown and now contain one of the country's best known venues for a marvellous day out. In the famous **safari park** the Lions of Longleat, first introduced in 1966, have been followed by a veritable Noah's Ark of exotic creatures, including elephants, rhinos, zebras and white tigers. The park also features safari boat rides, a narrow-gauge railway, children's amusement area, garden centre and the largest hedge maze in the world.

STOURTON

Map 3 ref K20

9 miles SW of Westbury off the B3092

The beautiful National Trust village of Stourton lies at the bottom of a steep wooded valley and is a particularly glorious sight in the daffodil season. The main attraction is, of course, **Stourhead**, one of the most famous examples of the early 18th century English landscape movement. The lakes, the trees, the temples, a grotto and a classical bridge make the grounds a paradise in the finest 18th century tradition, and the gardens are renowned for their striking vistas and woodland walks as well as a stunning selection of rare trees and specimen shrubs, including tulip trees, azaleas and rhododendrons. The house itself, a classical masterpiece built in the 1720s in Palladian style for a Bristol banker, contains a wealth of Grand Tour paintings and works of art, including furniture by Chippendale the Younger and wood carvings by Grinling Gibbons. On the very edge of the estate, some three miles by road from the house, the imposing King Alfred's Tower stands at the top of the 790' Kingsettle Hill.

Stourhead Gardens

This 160' triangular redbrick folly was built in 1772 to commemorate the king, who reputedly raised his standard here against the Danes in 878.

SALISBURY

MAP 3 REF M21

24 miles S of Devizes on the A360

The glorious medieval city of Salisbury stands at the confluence of four rivers, the Avon, Wylye, Bourne and Nadder. Originally called New Sarum, it grew around the present Cathedral, which was built between 1220 and 1258 in a sheltered position two miles south of the site of its windswept Norman predecessor at Old Sarum. Over the years the townspeople followed the clergy into the new settlement, creating a flourishing religious and market centre whose two main aspects flourish to this day.

One of the most beautiful buildings in the world, **Salisbury Cathedral** is the only medieval cathedral in England to be built in the same Early English style - apart from the spire, the tallest in England which was added some years later and rises to an awesome 404 feet. The Chapter House opens out of the cloisters and contains, among other treasures, one of the four surviving originals of Magna Carta.

Six hundred thousand visitors a year come to marvel at this and other priceless treasures, including a number of magnificent tombs. The oldest working clock in Britain and possibly in the world is situated in the fan-vaulted north transept; it was built in 1386 to strike the hour and has no clock face. The Cathedral is said to contain a door for each month, a window for each day and a column for each hour of the year. A small statue inside the west door is of Salisbury's 17th century **Boy Bishop**. It was a custom for choristers to elect one of their number to be bishop for a period lasting from St Nicholas Day to Holy Innocents Day (6-28 December). One year the boy bishop was apparently literally tickled to death by the other choristers; since he died in office, his statue shows him in full bishop's regalia.

The Close, the precinct of the ecclesiastical community serving the cathedral, is the largest in England and contains a number of museums and houses open to the public. **Salisbury Museum**, in the 17th century King's House, is home of the Stonehenge Gallery and the winner of many awards for excellence. Displays include Early Man, Romans and Saxons, the Pitt Rivers collection (see under Tollard Royal), Old Sarum, ceramics, costume, lace, embroidery and Turner watercolours. A few doors away is **The Royal Gloucestershire, Berkshire and Wiltshire Museum** housed in a 13th century building called the Wardrobe, which was originally used to store the bishop's clothes and documents. The museum tells the story

Salisbury Cathedral Spire

of the county regiments since 1743 and the exhibits include Bobbie the Dog, the hero of Maiwand, and many artefacts from foreign campaigns. The house has a riverside garden with views of the famous water meadows. The historic **Medieval Hall** is the atmospheric setting for a 30-minute history of Salisbury in sound and pictures. **Mompesson House**, a National Trust property, is a perfect example of Queen Anne architecture notable for its plasterwork, an elegant carved oak staircase, fine period furniture and the important Turnbull collection of 18th century drinking glasses. In the Market Place is the **John Creasey Museum and the Creasey Collection of Contemporary Art**, a permanent collection of books, manuscripts, objects and art. Also in the Market Place, in the library, is the Edwin Young Collection of 19th and early 20th century oil paintings of Salisbury and its surrounding landscape. There are many other areas of Salisbury to explore on foot and a short drive takes visitors to the ruins of **Old Sarum**, abandoned when the bishopric moved into the city. Traces of the original cathedral and palace are visible on the huge uninhabited mound, which dates back to the Iron Age. Old Sarum became the most notorious of the 'rotten boroughs', returning two Members of Parliament, despite having no voters, until the 1832 Reform Act stopped the cheating. A plaque on the site commemorates Old Sarum's most illustrious MP William Pitt the Elder.

Down a quiet lane and overlooking Salisbury's Victoria Park, **Stratford Lodge** is a spacious and welcoming hotel dating back to 1870. Adorned with hanging baskets and surrounded by paved areas and beautiful secluded gardens, with lawns, shrubs, rose beds and many fruit trees, it is a charming oasis of peace and relaxation. Tastefully furnished and decorated throughout, this superb establishment boasts eight ensuite guest bedrooms - each decorated in pastel colours with matching fabrics and fittings - guests' sitting room and main lounge with log fire. One of the upper-storey rooms has its own charming verandah/fenced balcony area. Breakfast is served in the very attractive conservatory - with its pitched roof and whitewashed walls it is bright and airy. All meals use local produce and fresh herbs, vegetables and fruit. At breakfast there are dishes such as kedgeree, mushrooms on toast, scrambled eggs and the traditional English breakfast, as well as fresh fruit, muesli, fruit compote and local Wiltshire honey. In the evening, candlelit dinners are served in the lovely restaurant.

Stratford Lodge, 4 Park Lane, Castle Road, Salisbury, Wiltshire SP1 3NP Tel/Fax: 01722 325177

WILTON   MAP 3 REF L21
3 miles W of Salisbury on the A30

The third oldest borough in England, once the capital of Saxon Wessex. It is best known for its carpets, and the **Wilton Carpet Factory** on the River Wylye continues to produce top-quality Wilton and Axminster carpets. Visitors can tour the carpet-making exhibition in the historic courtyard then go into the modern factory to see the carpets made on up-to-date machinery using traditional skills and techniques. Alongside the factory is the Wilton Shopping Village offering high-quality factory shopping in a traditional rural setting. **Wilton House** is the stately home of the Earls of Pembroke.

When the original house was destroyed by fire in 1647, Inigo Jones was commissioned to build its replacement. He designed both the exterior and the interior, including the amazing Double Cube Room, and the house was further remodelled by James Wyatt. The art collection is one of the very finest, with works by Rembrandt, Van Dyke, Rubens and Tintoretto; the furniture includes pieces by Chippendale and Kent. There's plenty to keep children busy and happy, notably the Wareham Bears (a collection of 200 miniature costumed teddy bears), a

treasure hunt quiz and a huge adventure playground. There's a Tudor kitchen, a Victorian laundry and 21 acres of landscaped grounds with parkland, cedar trees, water and rose gardens and an elegant Palladian bridge. During World War ll the house was used as an

Wilton House

operations centre for Southern Command and it is believed that the Normandy landings were planned here. Open daily late March-end October.

STAPLEFORD   Map 3 ref L20
6 miles NW of Salisbury

One of a number of delightful unspoilt villages including the three Langfords and **Berwick St James**, where the grid of the medieval board game Nine Men's Morris can be seen on a stone bench in the church porch. At Stapleford there was once a castle belonging to Waleran, chief huntsman of William the Conqueror.

'Free House, Restaurant and Accommodation' - **The Pelican Inn**, on the A36 Warminster-Salisbury road, is a fine old inn of many attractions, not least of which is a large garden with a frontage on the River Till. Maion and Chris Pitcher have a friendly greeting for one and all; families are very welcome, and there's a special children's menu and a play area. Chris is in charge of the kitchen,

producing a fine range of dishes for both bar and restaurant menus; daily specials and traditional favourites make excellent use of local ingredients. A peaceful and very comfortable overnight stay is provided in five superbly equipped double bedrooms of the highest quality, with ensuite shower and toilet, TV, radio, hairdryer, trouser press and iron and well-

The Pelican Inn, Warminster Road, Stapleford, Salisbury, Wiltshire SP3 4LT Tel: 01722 790241

stocked fridge. All the rooms are on the ground floor and two are suitable for family occupation. No smoking and no pets in the rooms. The inn's name commemorates the ship (later called the Golden Hind) in which Sir Francis Drake set sail in 1575 on a round-the-world voyage. A painting and a model of the ship can be seen in the bar.

AMESBURY

Map 3 ref M20

8 miles N of Salisbury on the A345

Queen Elfrida founded an abbey here in 979 in atonement for her part in the murder of her son-in-law, Edward the Martyr, at Corfe Castle. Henry ll rebuilt the abbey's great Church of St Mary and St Melor, whose tall central tower is the only structure to survive from the pre-Norman monastery. A mile to the north of Amesbury, the A345 passes along the eastern side of **Woodhenge**, a ceremonial monument even older than Stonehenge. It was the first major prehistoric site to be discovered by aerial photography, its six concentric rings of post holes having been spotted as cropmarks by Squadron Leader Insall in 1925. Like Stonehenge, it seems to have been used as an astronomical calendar. When major excavation was carried out in the 1920s, a number of neolithic tools and other artefacts were found, along with the skeleton of a three-year-old child whose fractured skull suggested some kind of ritual sacrifice.

Two miles west of Amesbury at the junction of the A303 and A344/A360 stands **Stonehenge** itself, perhaps the greatest mystery of the prehistoric world, one of

Stonehenge

the wonders of the world, and a monument of unique importance. The World Heritage Site is surrounded by the remains of ceremonial and domestic structures, many of them accessible by road or public footpath. The great stone blocks of the main ring are truly massive, and it seems certain that the stones in the outer rings - rare bluestones from the Preseli Hills of west Wales - had to be transported over 200 miles. Stonehenge's orientation on the rising and setting sun has always been one of its most remarkable features, leading to theories that the builders were from a sun-worshipping culture or that the whole structure is part of a huge astronomical calendar ...or both. The mystery remains, and will probably remain for ever.

CHOLDERTON

Map 3 ref M20

9 miles NE of Salisbury on the A338

The Red House Hotel and conference centre is a family-run concern not far from Stonehenge. A large and impressive establishment, it was used as an officers' mess during the Second World War. Offering superb business or family accommodation, the hotel boasts 30 high-standard ensuite rooms, each with tea and coffee making facilities, remote-control TV, direct dial telephone with Internet access, king-size beds and power showers. With a challenging 18-short hole golf course and a gour-

The Red House Hotel, Parkhouse Corner, Cholderton, Salisbury, Wiltshire SP4 0EG Tel: 01980 629542
Fax: 01980 629481 website: www.redhousehotel.co.uk

met Bistro restaurant, with a reputation to exceed expectation this hotel delivers the kind of accommodation only an independent hotel can - outstanding value and sumptuous dining in super surroundings. The Red House Bistro with its country farmhouse atmosphere and top-quality fresh foods offers an attractively priced menu of dishes that include noisettes of lamb, medallions of pork, sesame-crusted chicken, pan-fried trout and beef stroganoff. A fine selection of well-chosen wines complement the gourmet dining.

BERKSHIRE

LAMBOURN   Map 4 ref M19
9 miles SE of Swindon on the B4000

Lying up on the Berkshire Downs, in the extreme west of the county, this village, which has the feel of a small town, is well known for the race horses that are trained here. Once known as Chipping - which means market - Lambourn, the village once had not only a weekly market but also three annual fairs. Whether a horse racing fan or not, Lambourn has plenty to amuse and occupy the visitor. Its medieval **Church of St Michael** is one of the finest parish churches in Berkshire. Originally Norman and constructed on the cruciform plan, over the years the church has been greatly altered and extended though the west end still has its Norman doorway, complete with zigzag ornamentation. Close to the church can be found the pleasing **Isbury Almshouses**, built around a quadrangle, that were founded in 1502 though the present houses date from 1852.

To the north of the village are **Lambourn Seven Barrows**, one of the most impressive Bronze Age burial sites in the country. However, the name is somewhat misleading as there are no fewer than 32 barrows up here but arguably the best group consists of six bowl barrows, two double bowl barrows, two saucer barrows, and a single disc barrow.

EAST ILSLEY   Map 4 ref N19
10 miles E of Lambourn off the A34

This attractive downland village has managed to retain several interesting features and, in particular, by the village pond can be seen the winding mechanism of the now long disused village well. However, it is on sheep that the village prospered and from the beginning of the 17th century East Ilsley held fortnightly sheep fairs that were second only in size to Smithfield, London. At their peak in the 19th century, permanent pens were erected in the main street to contain the animals and, on one day, it was recorded that 80,000 sheep were penned. There is an old jingle about the village which goes: "Far famed for sheep and wool, though not for spinners, for sportsmen, doctors, publicans, and sinners." Naturally, whilst the sheep fairs were flourishing, the publicans were also making good money but after the last fair, in 1934, the number of inns fell from as many as 26, at one time, to just three. Today, along with its neighbour, West Ilsley, the village is associated with race horses which use the gallops on the downs as their training grounds. Though not as large as Lambourn, there are still successful stables in the area.

HAMPSTEAD NORREYS   Map 4 ref N19
12 miles E of Lambourn on the B4009

Just to the north of the village lies **Wyld Court Rainforest**, a fascinating conservation centre that is owned by the World Land Trust. The Trust, a charitable organisation founded in 1989, not only purchases and protects areas of tropical forests all over the world but also concerns itself with education. Here, at the indoor rainforest, where the temperature never falls below 70°C, visitors have the opportunity to walk through the humid and shadowy jungles of the

Lowland Tropical Forests, the cool, orchid-festooned and ferny Cloudforests, and the Amazon with its amazing flowers and wonderful bromeliads. There is also a unique collection of spectacular and rare plants, tranquil pools, the sounds of the topics, and rainforest animals including a pair of time marmosets, tree frogs, iguanas, and Courtney, the dwarf crocodile.

NEWBURY   MAP 4 REF N19
18 miles SE of Swindon on the A4

This crossroads town has, for many years, dominated the rural area of West Berkshire. Prospering during the Middle Ages, and afterwards, on the importance of the woollen industry, the town became famous as **The Cloth Town**. Among the various characters who made their money out of the weaving of the wool the best known is Jack of Newbury (John Smallwood or Winchcombe), who died in 1519. Asked to raise two horsemen and two footmen for Henry VIII's campaign against the Scots, Jack raised 50 of each and led them himself. However, they only got as far as Stony Stratford in Buckinghamshire before news of the victory of Flodden reached them and they turned for home.

Found in quiet surroundings close to the Kennet Canal, **Beaumont House** is a delightful guest house that is also well placed for the centre of Newbury and its station. Owned and personally run by Mrs Beaumont, a charming Frenchwoman who has lived in the UK since the late 1970s, the accommodation in this comfortable house is excellent. There are five guest rooms, each with its own bathroom, and, like the rest of the house, possessing a distinctly Gallic atmosphere and style. Guests take their breakfast in the large conservatory, surrounded by orange trees and exotic plants, and overlooking the beautifully maintained large town

Beaumont House, 4 St Johns Road, Newbury, Berkshire RG14 7LX Tel/Fax: 01635 47858

garden. Well decorated and furnished, there is plenty of interesting and unusual curios dotted around the house - guests should look out for the veteran rocking horse in the hallway.

During the Civil War there were two battles fought nearby, in 1643 and 1644, and following the war, the town's clothing industry declined. However, the 18th century saw the construction of turnpike roads and Newbury became a busy coaching stop on the road from London to Bath. The town further opened up to travellers and the needs of carriers with the completion of the **Kennet and Avon Canal** in 1810. **Newbury Lock**, built in 1796, was the first lock to be built along the canal and it is also the only one to have lever-operated ground paddles (the sluices that let in the water) which are known as 'Jack Cloughs'. Back in the centre of the town, in the Market Square is the **Newbury Museum**, housed in the 17th-century cloth hall and the adjacent 18th-century granary, a store used by traders travelling the canal. As well as the archaeological section, the history of the town is fully explained, including the two battles of Newbury during the Civil War. Though much of the town centre dates from the

Victorian age, there are some other interesting older buildings to be found. Just to the north of the town lies **Shaw House**, a splendid example of Elizabethan architecture and the finest in Berkshire, that dates from 1581. Built by a wealthy clothing merchant, Thomas Dolman, he chose to put his money into this elaborate house rather than his business, much to the displeasure of his workers. Though not open to the public, glimpses of the house can be seen from the road. Those arriving in Newbury from the south will pass the Victorian **Falkland Memorial**, which should not be confused with the 1980s conflict in the South Atlantic. It is, in fact, a memorial to Lord Falkland who was killed at the first battle of Newbury in 1643. Finally, to the east of the town lies the first class **Newbury Racecourse** which offers both flat and National Hunt racing throughout the year.

DONNINGTON
1 mile N of Newbury on the B4494
Map 4 ref N19

Despite being so close to the town of Newbury, Donnington has managed to retain its village identity and atmosphere. To the west of the village, and visible from the road, is Donnington

Donnington Castle

Grove House. Built in 1759 and designed by the architect John Chute, this was the home, in the late 18th century, of the Brummell family and Beau Brummell, the instigator of the Bath Society, lived here as a child. However, most visitors to the village come to see the **Donnington Castle**, a late 14th-century defence that was built by Sir Richard Abberbury. Once a magnificent structure, only the twin towered gatehouse survives amidst the impressive earthworks. Owned by English Heritage, the castle had its most eventful period during the Civil War when it was the scene of one of the longest sieges of the conflict. Charles I's troops were held here for 20 months and this was the time when most of the castle was destroyed. During the second of the two battles of Newbury, Charles I stayed at nearby Shaw House, whilst Sir John Boys defended the castle.

THATCHAM
2 miles E of Newbury on the A4
Map 4 ref N19

Believed to be the oldest village in Britain, it is hard to imagine that this now large suburb of Newbury was once a small place. **Thatcham Moor** is one of the largest areas of inland freshwater reed beds in the country and, as well as the reeds which can grow up to six feet in height, the area supports numerous species of marshland and aquatic plants. Birds too abound here and it is an important breeding ground for reed and sedge warblers.

BURGHCLERE
4 miles S of Newbury off A34
Map 4 ref N19

The village is home to the **Sandham Memorial Chapel**, which was built in the 1920s to remember the dead of World War I. What, however, makes this chapel so interesting are the internal murals which entirely cover the walls that are considered by many to be Stanley Spencer's greatest achievement. An extraordinary project, the murals illustrate the artist's experiences as a medical orderly during the war and he celebrates the everyday routine of a soldier's life. The pictures reach a climax with the huge *Resurrection of the Soldiers* which completely fills the east wall. This modern chapel is found amidst beautiful and tranquil scenery with views across **Watership Down**.

With a large and attractive garden overlooking Watership Down country, **The Carpenters Arms** is the ideal place to stop for some refreshment whilst visiting the area and families, particularly, are welcome. Built in 1820, the pub building has retained many of its original features and the open log fire in the lounge bar certainly adds to the warm and cosy feel of this typical country inn. With over 25 year experience in the trade, landlord and lady, Christopher and Audrey Ayling, with the help of their daughter Fiona, are very well placed to provide all customers, both locals and visitors, with a friendly welcome and some superb hospitality. With a good range of real ales and a fine selection of wines available, the high standard of the drinks served here is matched by the tasty and delicious menu of bar snacks and restaurant meals that are also served. The intimate conservatory restaurant area is not only a pleasant place for a quiet and relaxing din-

**The Carpenters Arms, Harts Lane, Burghclere,
Berkshire RG20 9JY Tel: 01635 278251**

ner but it is also popular on Sundays when the traditional roast lunch, a house speciality, is served. The summer sees many of the pub's patrons moving from the cosy interior out into the flower-filled garden and patio areas where the regular barbecues prove to be another popular feature of this excellent establishment. Finally, one further attraction is the Stanley Spencer Memorial Chapel, with its collection of paintings, that lies just 100 yards or so from the pub.

HUNGERFORD
8 miles W of Hungerford on the A4

MAP 4 REF M19

Although not mentioned in the Domesday Book, by the Middle Ages this old market town was well established and the manor of Hungerford had some distinguished lords including Simon de Montford and John of Gaunt. A quiet and peaceful place, Hungerford's heyday came in the 18th century when the turnpike road from London to Bath, which passes through the town, was built. By 1840, the town had eight coaching inns serving the needs of travellers and the prosperity continued with the opening of the **Kennet and Avon Canal** but the building of the railway took much of the trade away and the town reverted back, once more, to its early, gentle lifestyle. However, several of the old coaching inns have survived and, in particular, The Bear Hotel. Although it has an impressive Georgian frontage , the building actually dates back to 1494, making it one of the oldest in the town. It was here, in 1688, that a meeting took place between William of Orange and representatives of James II which culminated in the end of the House of Stuart and the flight of James II to France.

As well as still holding a weekly market, the town also continues the ancient tradition known as the Hocktide Festival or Tutti Day (tutti meaning a bunch of flowers). Held every year on the second Tuesday after Easter, the festival was originally used as a means of collecting an early form of council tax. During the colourful event, two men carrying a six foot pole decorated with ribbons and flowers go around each household collecting the tax. To ease the burden of their visit, the men share a drink with the man of the house, give him an orange, and kiss his wife before collecting their penny payment. Today, however, though the visits are made no money is collected.

INKPEN   MAP 4 REF M19
7 miles SW of Newbury off the A338

The village lies below the steep chalk ridge which separates the Thames basin from Hampshire. **Inkpen Common**, to the east of the village, is a Site of Special Scientific Interest where there is, amongst the heath and woodland, a wet valley bog and pond created from an old clay pit. As well as the unusual collection of plants, this is a popular breeding site for many birds and there is also an abundance of butterflies. Found in the heart of the countryside, **The Swan Inn** is a charming 17th-century inn that is certainly more than it would first appear to be. The Swan Inn was purchased by Mary and Bernard Harris in 1996 and, during the past three years, they have turned the inn and adjacent buildings into a real haven for both visitors and locals. Open

seven days a week, the menu covers everything from bar snacks to full à la carte in the organic restaurant. As well as ensuring that all the dishes are prepared from the very best ingredients, there is also a wide range of vegetarian options. There are four excellent real ales and The Swan Inn features in the CAMRA Good Beer Guide. Popular with locals, The Swan Inn is a well known stopping

**The Swan Inn, Lower Green, Inkpen, Hungerford,
Berkshire RG17 9DX Tel: 01488 668326
website: www.theswaninn-organics.co.uk
e-mail: enquiries@theswaninn-organics.co.uk**

place for walkers and all those travelling in the area, whether on foot, cycling, or in a car will be glad to hear that comfortable accommodation is also available here. The inn has 10 charming en-suite guest rooms. Finally, adjoining the pub, but with a separate entrance, is a shop that will be of great use to walkers and those new to the area. As well as stocking organic produce, maps, and guide books, there is a range of craft items and paintings by local artists on sale.

READING   MAP 4 REF O19
17 miles E of Newbury on the A4

This thriving commuter town is a delightful combination of over a thousand years of history and a vibrant and modern city. There are Victorian brick buildings nestling beside beautiful medieval churches, famous coaching inns opposite high tech offices and some of the best shopping in the area. However, Reading began as a Saxon settlement between the Rivers Thames and Kennet. A defensible site, it was used by the Danes as a base for their attack on Wessex in the 9th century. The town grew up around the **Abbey**, which was founded in 1121 by Henry I, the youngest son of William the Conqueror, and it was consecrated by Thomas à Becket in 1164. The abbey went on to become one of the most important religious houses - its relics include a piece of Jesus' shoe, the tooth of St Luke, and a slice of Moses' rod - and parliament were known to meet here on occasions. As Henry I is also buried here, Reading is one of only a handful of towns where Kings of England have been laid to rest. Today, the abbey ruins can be found in **Forbury Gardens** on the banks of the River Kennet. Fortunately, some of the abbey's wonderful architecture can still be seen and, in particular, there is St Laurence's Church and the abbey Gatehouse. The Gatehouse was, after the Reformation, turned into a school and, in 1785, Jane Austen was a pupil here. The gardens are also home to the **Maiwand Lion**, which commemorates the men of the Berkshire Regiment who died in the Afghan Campaign of 1879.

Another originally Norman building in the town is **St Mary's Church**, the south arcade of which dates from around 1200. The most attractive feature here is the church tower: erected in 1550 it is of a high distinguished chequerboard pattern which uses stone blocks and flint panels. Adjacent to the abbey ruins is another of Reading's famous buildings - **Reading Prison**. Hardly a tourist attraction, it was here that Oscar Wilde was imprisoned and where he wrote *De Profundis*. His confinement here also inspired the writer to compose the epic *Ballad of Reading Gaol* whilst staying in Paris in 1898.

Though the town developed during the Middle Ages as a result of a flourishing woollen industry, it was during the 18th century with the coming of both the turnpike roads and the opening of the **Kennet and Avon Canal** which saw the town boom. By the 19th century, Reading was known for its three Bs: beer, bulbs, and biscuits. As the trade of the canal and River Thames increased, the movement of corn and malt explains the growth of the brewing trade here whilst bulbs is a reference to Sutton Seeds who were founded here in 1806. The world renowned biscuit-making firm of Huntley and Palmer began life here in 1826, when Joseph Huntley founded the firm, to be joined, in 1841, by George Palmer, inventor of the stamping machine. **The Story of Reading**, a permanent exhibition at the **Reading Museum**, is the ideal place to gain a full understanding of the history of the town, from the earliest times to the present day. Here, too, can be seen the world's only full size replica of the Bayeux Tapestry, made in the 19th century and which features Edward the Confessor, once Lord of the Royal Manor in Reading, as a central figure. As a contrast to the museum's displays depicting the life of the town in the 20th century, The Silchester Gallery is devoted to the describing day to day life at Calleva Atrebatum, the Roman town of Silchester, using Roman artefacts unearthed there during early excavations.

Situated on the banks of the River Kennet and housed in a range of canal buildings, **Blake's Lock Museum** describes the life of the town in the 19th and early 20th centuries. Originally part of a pumping station built at Blake's Weir in the 1870s, the buildings themselves are also of interest and are

Blake's Lock Museum, Reading

superb examples of Victorian industrial architecture combined with decorative Reading brickwork. As well as covering the town's close links with its waterways and the part they played in Reading's prosperity, visitors can wander around the reconstructed shops and workshops.

SWALLOWFIELD
5 miles S of Reading off the A33

MAP 4 REF O19

This ancient settlement has been inhabited since prehistoric times and, by 1071, the manor was held by Roger de Breteuil, the originator of the Domesday Survey. Since then, the manor house, **Swallowfield Park**, has been associated with both royalty and notable personalities. The present house (unfortunately now all but a shell) was built in 1678 by Wren's assistant William Talman, for the 2nd Earl of Clarendon who acquired the estate upon marrying the heiress. In 1719, the park was purchased by Thomas Pitt, a former Governor of Madras, who used the proceeds of the sale of a large diamond he bought whilst out in India. The diamond can now be seen in the Louvre Museum, Paris, and Pitt's story was the basis of the novel, *The Moonstone*, by the author Wilkie Collins, who visited the house in 1860. The Italian Doorway, by Talman, is probably the house's most outstanding remaining feature and it marks the entrance to the walled garden. Here can be found a dog's graveyard where one of Charles Dickens' dogs, was bequeathed to his friend and owner of the house, Sir Charles Russell, by the novelist.

Set in beautiful gardens beside the River Loddon, **The Mill House Restaurant and Hotel** is a superb family run establishment where guests can relax in the glorious surroundings. A splendid Georgian house, built in 1823 as part of the 1st Duke of Wellington's Stratfield estate, Mill House has been restored to its original grandeur and in many ways still has the atmosphere of a grand country home. Personally managed by owners Mark and Kim Pybus, the restaurant here is magnificent and, whether it is lunch or dinner, visitors are sure to enjoy the excellent menus that are prepared and served by the hotel's resident chef. Well known locally and highly regarded, The Mill House Restaurant has gained an enviable reputation for delicious and interesting dishes that would certainly not be out of place in any London establishment. Those lucky enough to be staying at the hotel can not only take full advantage of the dining facilities but the splendour of the hotel's well proportion rooms. Each of the ten en-suite guest rooms is fully equipped with the extras to-

The Mill House Restaurant and Hotel, Swallowfield, nr Reading, Berks RG7 1PY
Tel: 0118 988 3124 Fax: 0118 988 5550

day's modern traveller expects but they also have a charm and character that is often lacking elsewhere. Surrounding the hotel is the delightful garden, a mixture of formal and informal, that is floodlit at night. The Mill House Hotel is also licensed for wedding ceremonies and, with much experience in holding receptions, this makes it an ideal location for such an important day.

MORTIMER
6½ miles SW of Reading off the A33

MAP 4 REF O19

Although, at first glance, this village looks and seems to date from the 19th century, it has a long history and it takes its name from Ralf Mortimer who held the manor here in 1086. However, in the churchyard of **St Mary's Church**, can be found a rare Saxon tombstone, marking the burial place of Aegalward, the son of the lord of the manor, that was erected by Toki, an important and wealthy courtier to King Canute in the early 11th century. The present day church was built in 1866 under the patronage of John Benyon, the then Lord of the Manor. This though is probably the fifth church on the site and some Norman fragments from the original building, such as the stained glass window behind the organ, can still be seen. Also in the village is one of the few remaining examples of Brunel's original station design (Mortimer Station) and the War Memorial that commemorates the 56 men of Mortimer who died during World War I. Close by lies **Windmill Common**, which was so named in the 18th century when the Rev James Morgan arranged for a windmill and cottage to be built here. Following the Enclosure Act of 1804, the land passed back into the hands of the lord of the manor who went on to plant the common with Scots pine. By 1832, the trees were causing the miller great problems and he wrote: "It lays under the necessity to remove because the fir plantation has overgrown and keep the wind off the mill." Though the mill has now gone, the pine trees are still standing on the common.

Found on the main road through the village, **The Turners Arms** is a traditional village pub that started life as three cottages and became a pub in the 1860s. Though situated on the road, to the rear of the building is a delightful, secluded, and enclosed beer garden which can only add to the charm of the inn. Run by Belinda Routledge, with the help of her two grown up daughters, this is a popular place with both locals and visitors alike. Appealing to all ages, the interior of the pub contains plenty of comfortable seating so that patrons can enjoy their drinks in a lei-surely manner and the walls are decorated with gleaming brasses, dried wild flowers, and numerous prints and photographs. As well as serving drinks, it is

The Turners Arms, Mortimer, Reading, Berks RG7 3TW
Tel: 0118 933 2961 Fax: 0118 933 1521

well worth taking the time to enjoy a meal from the pub's ever-changing menu. Seafood is certainly a speciality of the inn and, along with the daily specials, there is sure to be something to tempted everyone here.

ALDERMASTON   Map 4 ref N19
9 miles SW of Reading on the A340

It was in this tranquil village, in 1840, that the William pear was first propagated by John Staid, the then village schoolmaster. First known as the Aldermaston pear, a cutting of the plant is believed to have been taken to Australia where is it now called the Bartlett pear. Still retaining much of its original 12th-century structure and with a splendid Norman door, the lovely **St Mary's Church** provides the setting for the York Mystery Cycle, nativity plays dating from the 14th century which are performed here each year. Using beautiful period costumes and con-temporary music, including a piece written by William Byrd, the cycle lasts a week and the plays attract visitors from far and wide. Another old custom still continued in the village is the auctioning of the grazing rights of Church Acres every three years. Using the ancient method of a candle auction, a pin, in this case a horseshoe nail, is inserted into the tallow of a candle one inch from the wick. The candle is lit while bidding takes place and the grazing rights go to the highest bidder as the pin drops out of the candle. Outside under a yew tree in the church-yard lies the grave of Maria Hale, formerly known as the Aldermaston witch. She was said to turn herself into a large brown hare and although the hare was never caught or killed, at one time a local keeper wounded it in the leg and from then on it was noticed that Maria Hale was lame!

Close to the village there is a delightful walk along the Kennet and Avon Canal to **Aldermaston Wharf**. A Grade II listed structure of beautifully restored 18th-century scalloped brickwork, the wharf is home to the **Kennet and Avon Canal Visitor Centre**, where the canalman's cottage houses an exhibition on the canal with information on its leisure facilities. More recent history has seen the famous protest marches of the1950s outside the Atomic Research Establishment, which though situated in the grounds of Aldermaston Court, rather mysteriously, does not feature on Ordnance Survey Maps.

WOOLHAMPTON
MAP 4 REF N19

10 miles SW of Reading on the A4

This tranquil village on the banks of the **Kennet and Avon Canal**, has had a watermill since the time of the Domesday Survey in 1086 and it was again mentioned in 1351, when the manor and mill was owned by the Knights Hospitallers. The present mill, which today has been converted into offices, was built in 1820 and further extended in 1875. Powered by a brook which runs into the Kennet, the mill was last used in 1930.

Built in 1714 and with the addition of a striking Dutch roof in the 1930s, **The Falmouth Arms** is a distinctive building in this quiet village that is hard to miss. Managed since 1996 by Mary and Christopher Scott, this attractive and popular inn is also a lively meeting place for residents of the village and those who live locally. Light and airy inside, the open plan bar, with

a large fireplace at either end, is an excellent place to come to for a relaxing drink and to while away a couple of hours catching up on the local news. The numerous pictures and photographs on display, of the pub and the village through this century, are also a major talking point. Food too is very much on the menu here and customers can enjoy a

The Falmouth Arms, Bath Road, Woolhampton, Berkshire RG7 5RT Tel: 0118 971 3202

wide range of tasty bar snacks and meals that are served throughout the day. As well as the monthly theme evenings, Christopher and Mary also provide their customers with lively entertainment in the form of music at the weekends and quiz nights. Finally, The Falmouth Arms, in the true tradition of an inn, has nine en-suite guest rooms that not only provide the overnight visitor with comfortable accommodation but they are also fitted with all the latest amenities.

BASILDON
MAP 4 REF N19

8 miles NW of Reading on the A417

This small village is the last resting place of the inventor and agricultural engineer, Jethro Tull, and his grave can be seen in the churchyard. Here too is a monument which commemorates the tragic drowning of two brothers. Outside the churchyard is a further memorial, a classic pavilion built in memory of his parents by the late Mr Childe-Beale which is, today, the focal point of **Beale Park**. Covering some 300 acres of ancient water meadow, the park is home to a wide range of birds and animals. There are carefully tendered small herds of unusual farm animals, including rare breeds of sheep and goats, Highland cattle, deer, and South American llama, over 120 species of birds living in their natural habitat, and a pets' corner for smaller children. However, the park's work is not confined to the keeping of animals and, as well as planting a **Community Woodland**, an ancient reed bed has been restored.

However, the village's main feature is the National Trust owned **Basildon Park**, an elegant, classical house designed in the 18th century by Carr of York, which is undoubtedly Berkshire's foremost mansion. Built between 1776 and 1783 for Francis Sykes, an official of the East India Company, the house is almost text book in style though it does have the unusual addition of an Anglo-Indian room. The interior, finished by JB Papworth and restored to its original splendour after World War II, is rich in fine plaster work, pictures, and furniture and the rooms open to the public include the Octagon Room and a decorative Shell Room. If the name Basildon seems familiar it is probably as a result of the notepaper: the head of the papermaking firm of Dickinson visited the house and decided to use the name for the high quality paper.

ALDWORTH
MAP 4 REF N19

11 miles NW of Reading on the B4009

The parish Church of St Mary is famous for housing the **Aldworth Giants** - the larger than life effigies of the de la Beche family which date back to the 14th century. The head of the family, Sir Philip, who lies here with eight other members of his family, was the Sheriff of Berkshire and valet to Edward II. Though now somewhat defaced the effigies were so legendary that the church was visited by Elizabeth I. Outside, in the churchyard, are the remains of a once magnificent 1000 year old yew tree that was sadly damaged in a storm.

WINDSOR
MAP 4 REF P19

15 miles E of Reading on the A308

This old town grew up beneath the walls of the castle in a compact group of streets leading from the main entrance. Charming and full of character, this is a place of delightful timber-framed and Georgian houses and shop fronts, with riverside walks beside the Thames, and a wonderful racecourse. The elegant **Guildhall**, partly built by Wren in the 17th century, has an open ground floor for market stalls whilst the council chambers are on the first floor. Concerned that they might fall through the floor onto the stalls below the council members requested that Wren put in supporting pillars in the middle of the market hall. As his reassurances that the building was sound fell on deaf ears, Wren complied with their wishes but the pillars he built did not quite meet the ceiling - there by proving his point! The grand central station, in the heart of the town, was built in 1897 to commemorate Queen Victoria's Diamond Jubilee and it is now home to a fascinating exhibition, **Royalty and Empire**, which charts the life and times of the country's longest reigning monarch. Close by, in the High Street, is another exhibition well worth visiting, **The Town and Crown Exhibition.** Here the development of the town and the influences of the Crown are explained in an imaginative and visual manner.

Meanwhile a trip to **The Dungeons of Windsor** provides a step back in time and an investigation of the town's history with a special regard for stories of crime and punishment from the early days of 13th-century lawlessness through to the harsh Victorian era. The Household Cavalry also have their home in Windsor, at Combermere Barracks, and here there is the superb **Household Cavalry Museum**, which displays collections of their uniforms, weapons, and armour from 1600 through to the present day. In a perfect setting beside the River Thames, **Royal Windsor Racecourse** is one of the most attractive in the country. Though less grand than neighbouring Ascot, the summer evening meetings here are particularly enjoyable.

However, it is **Windsor Castle**, situated on Castle Hill, which draws thousands of tourists annually to this small town. The largest castle in the country and a royal residence for over 900 years, the castle was begun in the late 11th century by William the Conqueror as one in a chain of such defences which stood on the approaches to London. Over the years various monarchs have added to the original typical Norman castle , the most notable additions being made by Henry VIII, Charles II, and George IV.Various aspects of the castle are open to the public, in particular the sixteen state apartments which hold a remarkable collection of furniture, porcelain, and armour. Carvings by Grinling Gibbons are to be seen everywhere and the walls are adorned with a plethora of masterpieces, including paintings by Van Dyck and Rembrandt. On a somewhat smaller scale, but nonetheless impressive, is **Queen Mary's Dolls' House**. Designed by Sir Edwin Lutyens for Queen Mary, this is a perfect miniature palace, complete with working lifts and lights and also running water. Taking over three years to build, 1500 tradesmen were employed to ensure that every last detail was correct and the house was presented to the queen in 1924. In November 1992, a massive fire swept through the northeast corner of the castle and no-one in the country at the time will forget the incredible pictures of the great tower alight. After much restoration, the affected rooms, including the massive St George's Hall, the scene of many state banquets, have all been completed and are once again open to the public. Windsor Castle is not just a defensive structure but it was also an ecclesiastical centre and, within its walls, is the magnificent **St George's Chapel**. Started by Edward IV in 1478, and taking some 50 years to finish, the chapel is not only one of the country's greatest religious buildings but also a wonderful example of the Perpendicular Gothic style. As well as being the

Frogmore House, Windsor

last resting place of several monarchs, it is also the Chapel of the Most Noble Order of the Garter, Britain's highest order of chivalry.

Frogmore House, a modest manor house from the early 18th century, stands in Home Park, and over the years it has acted as a second, more relaxed royal residence than nearby Windsor Castle. During Queen Victoria's reign it was the home of her mother, the Duchess of Kent and now, famously, it is also home to the magnificent **Royal Mausoleum** dedicated to Prince Albert and also where Queen Victoria herself is buried beside her beloved husband. Only open to the public on two days in May, the mausoleum, in the delightful gardens laid out in the 1790s, remains a sombre yet restful place.

To the south of the town lies **Windsor Great Park**, a remnant of the once extensive Royal Hunting Forest, and a unique area of open parkland, woodland, and impressive views. The **Long Walk** stretches from the castle to Snow Hill, some three miles away, on top of which stands a huge bronze of George III on horseback put there in 1831. Queen Anne added the three mile ride to nearby Ascot race course. On the park's southern side lies **Smith's Lawn**, where polo matches are played most summer weekends. Windsor Great Park is also the setting for the Cartier International competition, polo's highlight event held every July, and the National Driving Championships.

ETON   MAP 4 REF P19
1 mile N of Windsor on the A355

Found just across the River Thames from Windsor, this town has grown up around **Eton College**, the famous public school that was founded in 1440 by Henry VI. Originally intended for 70 poor and worthy scholars and to educate students for the newly created King's College, at Cambridge University, the college has been added to greatly over the years. Of the original school buildings, only the College Hall and the kitchen have survived; the great gatehouse and Lupton's Tower were added in the 16th century and the Upper School dates from around 1690. However, the school has kept many ancient traditions over the years including the black tail mourning coats that were originally worn on the death of George III in 1820 and which are still worn today. For centuries the college has educated the great and the good, including 19 prime ministers, artists, poets, and authors including William Pitt the Elder, Harold Macmillan, Thomas Gray (author of *Elegy Written in a Country Churchyard*), Henry Fielding, Shelley, George Orwell, and Ian Fleming. Eton has also been famous in the past for its strict discipline, personified in 1832 by a master who told the pupils when they rebelled: "Boys, you must be pure of heart, for if not, I will thrash you until you are."

Eton College, Eton

ASCOT
MAP 4 REF P19

6 miles SW of Windsor on the A329

A small village until 1711 when Queen Anne moved the Windsor race meeting to here and founded the world famous **Ascot Racecourse**. Its future secured when the Duke of Cumberland established a stud at Windsor in the 1750s, by the end of the century the meetings were being attended by Royalty on a regular basis. Today, Royal Ascot, held every June, is an international occasion of fashion and style with pageantry and tradition that is followed by racing enthusiasts world wide.

SANDHURST
MAP 4 REF O19

11 miles SW of Windsor on the A3095

The town is famous as being the home of the **Royal Military Academy**, the training place for army officers since it was established in 1907. The academy's **Staff College Museum** tells the history of officer training from its inception to the present day. Long before the academy was founded, in Saxon times, this settlement, in the valley of the River Blackwater, was part of the Parish of Sonning. Close by is **Trilakes**, a picturesque country park set in 18 acres and, naturally, there are lakes here. This is a wonderful place to visit with children as there are a wide assortment of pets and farm animals which they can get to know, including miniature horses, pygmy goats, donkeys, aviary birds, pot-bellied pigs and Soay sheep.

BRACKNELL
MAP 4 REF O19

7 miles SW of Windsor on the A329

Designated a new town in 1948, Bracknell has developed quickly from a small place in poor sandy heathland into a large modern town with one of the first purpose built shopping centres in the country - opened in the 1960s. As well as being home to a number of high tech companies, Bracknell is also the home of the Meteorological Office. However, the first mention of Bracknell has been traced back to a 10th-century Saxon document where, spelt as *Braccan Heal*, the name is thought to mean a piece of land belonging to Bracca. The community developed here at the junction of two major routes through Windsor Forest. Seen from many parts of the town and a very prominent landmark is the centrally located **Bill Hill**. At the top of the hill can be found a circular mound of earth, hollowed out at the centre, which is all that remains of a Bronze Age round barrow. Used through out that period, these burial mounds, which may cover either individuals or groups, are the most common prehistoric monuments in the country even if this location, in the heart of a modern town, seems a little curious.

Eastern Gateway to Caeser's Camp, Bracknell

What remains of the great royal hunting ground, **Windsor Forest** (also called **Bracknell Forest**) lies to the south of the town and this vast area has over 30 parks and nature reserves and some 45 miles of footpaths and bridleways. Of particular interest in the area is The **Lookout Discovery Park**, an interactive science centre that brings to life the mysteries of both science and nature. Throughout the woodland surrounding the centre there are nature trails and walks to points of interest as well as the inappropriately named **Caesar's Camp**. Not a Roman fort, this camp is an Iron Age hill fort built over 2000 years ago but, close by, lies the Roman link road between London and Silchester. Locally known as the **Devil's Highway**, it is said to have acquired the name as the local inhabitants, after the Romans had left, thought that only the Devil could undertake such a feat of engineering.

WARGRAVE

10 miles W of Windsor on the A321

MAP 4 REF O19

This charming village developed as a settlement in the 10th century at the confluence of the Rivers Thames and Loddon on an area of flat land in a wooded valley. Mentioned in the Domesday Book, when it was referred to as Weregrave, in 1218, the Bishop of Winchester was granted the rights to hold a market here by Henry III. However, this was obviously not a great success as there is no record of a market taking place after the 13th century. Now an attractive riverside village, the peace was disturbed here in 1914 when suffragettes burnt down the church in protest at the vicar's refusal to remove the word 'obey' from the marriage service. In the churchyard however, undisturbed by the riot, lies the **Hannen Mausoleum**, a splendid monument that was designed for the family by Sir Edwin Lutyens in 1906.

Another interesting sight here can be found on the outskirts of the village, at Park Place. In 1788, the estate was owned by General Henry Conway, Governor of Jersey and, in recognition of his services, the people of the island gave the general a complete **Druids' Temple**. The massive stones were transported from St Helier to the estate and erected in a 25 foot circle in the gardens of his mansion. In 1870, Park Place was destroyed by fire and the estate broken up but today the temple stands in the garden of **Temple Combe**, close to a house designed by the famed American architect, Frank Lloyd Wright. The only house of his in this country, it was built, in 1958, on an elaborate U-shaped design and has suede panelled walls inside.

COOKHAM

6 miles NW of Windsor on the A4094

MAP 4 REF O18

This pretty, small town, on the banks of the River Thames, was made famous by the artists Sir Stanley Spencer, who used Cookham as the setting for many of his paintings. Born here towards the end of the 19th century, the town's tribute to its most renowned resident is the **Stanley Spencer Gallery**, a permanent exhibition of his work which is housed in the converted Victorian chapel Stanley visited as a child.

DORNEY   MAP 4 REF P19
2 miles NW of Windsor off the A308

One of the finest Tudor manor houses in England, **Dorney Court**, just a short walk from the River Thames, has been the home of the Palmer family since 1530. Built in around 1440, it is an enchanting building which also houses some real treasures including early 15th and 16th century oak furniture, beautiful 17th century lacquer furniture, and 400 years of family portraits. It is also here that the first pineapple in England was grown in 1665. However, it is one owner who is perhaps remembered above all the others: Sir Roger Palmer was the husband of Charles II's most notorious mistress, Barbara, an intelligent and beautiful woman, Roger was given the title Earl of Castlemaine for his compliance with the affair.

OXFORDSHIRE

HENLEY-ON-THAMES   MAP 4 REF O19
8 miles NE of Reading on the A4155

Reputed to be the oldest settlement in Oxfordshire, this attractive riverside market town has over 300 listed buildings covering several periods. But it is the fine Georgian and Victorian houses and villas fronting on to the River Thames which epitomises the style of Henley-on-Thames. A quiet and gentle town in 1829 the first inter-varisty boat race, between Oxford and Cambridge, took place here on the river and, within a decade, the event was enjoying royal patronage. Today, Henley's **Regatta**, held every year in the first week of July, is a marvellous and colourful event with teams competing on the mile long course from all over the world. It is also a stylish occasion and is still seen as very much part of the season.

Set in the heart of Henley-on-Thames, **Daisy's** is a fascinating shop that sells a wealth of crafted goods, mostly by local people. Excellent gift ideas include native american Dream Catchers, china dolls and silver jewellery as well as traditional English toiletries. With one of the largest collections of Beanie Babies in Oxfordshire, Daisy's appeals to all ages. After browsing through this exciting store, relax in Cafe Nikki which serves mouthwatering food and refreshments. Whilst taking breakfast, lunch or tea travel plans can be discussed with the fully bonded (ABTA,IATA) resident travel agent, Gloria Wright.

Opened in 1998, the **River and Rowing Museum** is a fascinating place to visit which traces the rowing heritage of Henley, the river's changing role in the town's history, and there is even the opportunity to 'walk' the length of the River Thames, from source to sea, taking in all the locks.

Daisy's, 45-47 Duke Street, Henley-on-Thames, Oxfordshire RG9 1UR Tel: 01491 410770

Housed in a spacious, purpose-built building by the award-winning architect, David Chipperfield, visitors can also see the boat in which the British duo, Redgrave and Pinsent, won their gold medal at the 1996 Olympics. Also situated on the riverbank, beside the town's famous 18th-century bridge, which is appropriately decorated with the faces of Father Thames and the goddess Isis, is the Leander Club, the headquarters of the equally famous rowing club. Whilst on the opposite bank is the attractive Church of St Mary which also acts as a local landmark. Apart from the boating, which is available throughout the summer, and the pleasant walks along the riverbanks, there are lots of interesting shops, inns, and teashops in the town. Most of the inns are old coaching houses with yards that were once the scene of bull and bear fights. Just down river from the town centre lies **Fawley Court**, a wonderful private house that was designed by Christopher Wren and built in 1684 for Col W Freeman. Now owned by the Marian Fathers, the **Museum** it contains includes a library, documents relating to the Polish Kings, and memorabilia of the Polish army. The house, gardens, and museum are open to the public from March to October.

To the northwest of Henley lies another interesting house, **Greys Court**, which was rebuilt in the 16th century though it has been added to since. However, it does stand within the walls of the original 14th-century manor house and various of the old outbuildings can still be seen. The property of the National Trust, the gardens of the court contain the **Archbishop's Maze**, which was inspired, in 1980, by Archbishop Runcie's enthronement speech.

EWELME
9 miles NW of Henley-on-Thames off the B4009

MAP 4 REF N18

At the centre of this pretty village is a magnificent group of medieval buildings, including the Church, almshouse, and school which were all founded in the 1430s by Alice Chaucer, granddaughter of the poet Geoffrey, and her husband, the Duke of Suffolk. There is a wonderfully elegant alabaster carving of Alice inside the church and under this effigy is another rather macabre carving of a shrivelled cadaver. In the churchyard is the grave of Jerome K Jerome, author of *Three Men in a Boat*, who moved to the village following the success of his book. Founded in 1437, the **Almshouses** were built to house 13 poor men and two chaplains were provided to take care of them. They are one of the earliest examples of almshouses built around a quadrangle and they are also one of the earliest brick buildings in the county. The **School** was founded in the same year and it too is of brick though it was extensively altered in Georgian times

Shepherd's Hut, The Street, Ewelme,
Oxfordshire OX10 6HQ Tel: 01491 835661

The **Shepherd's Hut** in Ewelme is owned and personally run by Di Campbell-White, a personable and accommodating host who makes all her guests at this charming country pub feel welcome. Though new to the licensing trade, she has brought a wealth of enthusiasm and good ideas to making this lovely pub a success. Popular and lively, this excellent inn is well worth seeking out. The menu boasts a selection of snacks and meals, freshly prepared and expertly presented.

WOODCOTE

Map 4 ref N19

7 miles W of Henley-on-Thames off the A4074

To the east of Goring lies the pretty village of Woodcote. Very much at the centre of village life in Woodcote, **The Red Lion** is a dream come true for Londoner Dennis Smith who, after 20 years in football administration, has always wanted to run a pub in a village with a green. He and his wife, Jean, have been here since 1996 and, in that time, they have certainly made their mark here and in the local community. Appealing to all ages, The Red Lion is very popular with the people of Woodcote as well as being a favourite for walkers and cyclists discovering the local countryside. Built at the turn of the century, the pub has a comfortable and welcoming atmosphere enhanced by the high quality, modern furniture and fittings, the main L-shaped bar is complemented by the non-smoking restaurant extension that will open towards the end of March 2000. As well as being a delightful place for a quiet drink, The Red Lion has a

The Red Lion, Goring Road, Woodcote, near Reading, Oxfordshire RG8 0SD Tel: 01491 680483

comprehensive range of menus that take the customer from lunchtime snacks through to full evening meals and there is also a special Sunday lunch menu. Very much a part of the village, not only does the pub have a cricket and a football team but numerous pub games are played here and each Sunday evening Jean and Dennis host a quiz night.

CHECKENDON

Map 4 ref O19

6 miles W of Henley-on-Thames off the A4074

Situated high in the Chiltern Hills, this small village of timber-framed cottages around a green is many people's idea of the typical English village. To complete the perfect picture, the village church is Norman and, as well as overlooking the green, the interior contains several wall paintings and brasses.

Found deep in rural England, **The Black Horse** has been run by the same family for nearly 100 years and today the pub is managed by Margaret Morgan. A popular place with people from the local area, the pub is also a favourite stopping off point for cyclists and walkers who are taking advan-

The Black Horse, Checkendon, nr Reading, Oxfordshire RG8 0TE Tel: 01491 680418

tage of the nearby Oxford Cycleway and the Ridgway Walk. Dating back to the 16th century, this wonderful old coaching inn is, as many village pubs were, part of a farm and this is run by Margaret's husband, Martin. Still maintaining a family theme, Margaret's daughter also has a horse livery business running from the farm buildings. In this idyllic setting, visitors to The Black Horse can enjoy warm and friendly hospitality in the quaint old surroundings of this ancient building. The pub comprises three small rooms, end-to-end, and with low ceilings and exposed beams, the place is very cosy indeed, particularly in winter when the fires are lit. As well as serving customers a superb range of real ales and the usual drinks, Margaret also offers a variety of filled rolls that are all prepared here. For a real country pub that has lost none of its charm over the years, visitors should look no further than The Black Horse.

GORING-ON-THAMES

MAP 4 REF N19

9½ miles W of Henley-on-Thames on the B4009

This ancient village lies across the River Thames from its equally ancient neighbour, Streatley, and, whilst today they are in different counties, they were once in different kingdoms. This is a particularly peaceful stretch of the river, with the bustle of Pangbourne and Henley-on-Thames lying down stream and it is some distance to the towns of Abingdon and Oxford further up stream. However, this has not always been the case as, at one time, the two settlements were often in conflict with each other and excavations in the area have found numerous weapons which date back as far as the Bronze Age. In the 19th century, after Isambard Kingdom Brunel had laid the tracks for the Great Western Railway through Goring Gap, the village began to grow as it was now accessible to the Thames-loving Victorians. Though there are many Victorian and Edwardian villas and houses here, the original older buildings have survived and they add an air of antiquity to this attractive place.

Found in an idyllic situation, **Goring Mill Gallery** is housed in one of the village's oldest buildings. This picturesque and historic watermill dates from the 17th century although it stands on the site of another mill that was recorded in the Domesday Book. The subject of a painting by Turner in 1805, which also takes in the adjacent Norman church, it is fitting that the building should now be such a splendid gallery. Owned and personally run by Diana Davies and Ron Bridle, the gallery's policy is to exhibit only the work of the very best regional artists and craftsmen in the country. Also in keeping with the age and setting of the building, the works here are generally representational pieces rather than modern or abstract in style.

On display here are over 500 paintings, ceramics and sculptures that represent the work of some 50 professional artists and craftspeople. Not surprisingly, the gallery also specialises in landscapes and riverside paintings and, whilst all the works are original pieces, the price range is within the reach of most pockets. In addition to the exceptional display of paintings and craftwork, Goring Mill Gallery also offers customers a wide range of services including commission work, from portraits through to architectural subjects and a framing service. For anyone who

**Goring Mill Gallery, Lock Approach,
Goring-on-Thames, Oxfordshire RG8 9AD
Tel: 01491 875030 Fax: 01491 872519**

enjoys the English countryside at its best, a visit to Goring Mill Gallery is a must and they will also have an opportunity to take home a unique souvenir of their time by the River Thames.

ABINGDON
25 miles NW of Reading off the A34

MAP 4 REF N18

This is an attractive town and it is also one of the country's oldest as it grew up around a 7th-century Benedictine **Abbey** that was founded here in 675. Sacked twice for its gold and silver when the town was attacked by Danes, the abbey was practically derelict by the 10th century but, under the guidance of Abbot Ethwold, the architect of the great Benedictine reform, it once again prospered and was, in its heyday, larger than Westminster Abbey. Unfortunately little remains today of this great religious house, but the **Gatehouse**, built in the late 15th century, is a splendid reminder. Built on to the abbey gateway is the **Church of St Nicholas**, a much altered building but one which also has managed to retain some of its original Norman features.

The largest town in the Vale of the White Horse, Abingdon was also the county town of Berkshire between 1556 and 1869, in deed, at one time the Abbot here was the second largest landowner in Berkshire after the Crown. This prosperity and importance has given the town an interesting history which can be discovered at the **Abingdon Museum**. Housed in the old County Hall, which was originally built as the County Assize Court and Market Hall in 1678, there is plenty to see inside as well as out.

Helensbourne is an historic house set in lovely surroundings. Situated on one of Abingdon's most prestigious streets, which boasts a wealth of plaques noting the great and good who have made their homes here over the centuries, this lovely property is within a stone's throw of the River Thames. The house (originally three separate homes) dates back to late 13th century, and is believed at one time to have been a chantry house for the Fraternity of the Holy Cross, a brotherhood of chaplains undertaking charitable works. The beautifully proportioned rooms retain their original character and are decorated with great taste and style. The garden forms an attractive viewpoint. The two bedrooms are spacious and very comfortable, equipped with every modern amen-

Helensbourne, 34 East St Helena Street, Abingdon,
Oxfordshire OX14 5EB Tel: 01235 530200

ity while remaining cosy and traditional in style and ambience. Breakfast is hearty and delicious, while there are of course a wealth of fine eateries nearby for evening meals.

FYFIELD
MAP 4 REF N18

5 miles W of Abingdon on the A420

The White Hart at Fyfield is a 15th-century chantry house with an interesting history. It was built by the executors of Sir John Golafre, lord of the manor of Fyfield, who died in 1442, leaving money for the establishment of a charity to be known as the House or Hospital of St John the Baptist. The existing building was erected to include a hall and kitchen, with accom-

modation for a priest in the two-storey western wing. The priest's lower room is now the dining room; the former kitchen is now the public bar. In 1548 all the chantries in England were abolished. This 'chantry house' was put up for sale, becoming in 1580 the property of St John's College, Oxford. The college leased it to tenants, and it saw many refurbishments until in the 1960s it was returned to something of its original character and proportions, with exposed 15th-century

The White Hart, Fyfield, Oxfordshire OX13 5LN
Tel: 01865 390585

arch-braced roof. This unique and characterful Free House offers a fine range of beers, wines and spirits, while the restaurant has an extensive menu of traditional and more innovative meals, expertly prepared and presented. Open: Monday to Saturday 11 - 2.30 and 6 - 11; Sundays midday-3 and 7-10.30. Food is available daily from midday - 2 and 7-10.

DIDCOT
MAP 4 REF N18

4½ miles S of Abingdon on the A4130

The giant cooling towers of Didcot's power station dominate the skyline for miles around and there is little left to be found of the old town. However, the saving grace is the **Didcot Railway Centre**, a shrine to the days of the steam engine and the Great Western Railway. Isambard Kingdom Brunel designed the Great Western Railway and its route through Didcot, from London to Bristol, was completed in 1841. Until 1892 its trains ran on their unique broad gauge tracks and the GWR retained its independence until the nationalisation of the railways in 1948. Based around the engine shed, where visitors can inspect the collection of steam locomotives, members of the Great Western Society have recreated the golden age of the railway at the centre which also includes a beautiful recreation of a country station, complete with level crossing. Steam days are held through out the year when locomotives once again take to the broad gauge track and visitors can also take in the Victorian signalling system and the centre's Relics Display.

WANTAGE
MAP 4 REF N18

7 miles SW of Abingdon on the A338

This thriving market town was, in 849, the birthplace of Alfred the Great and Wantage remained a Royal Manor until end of the 12th century. In the central market place, around which there are some fine Georgian and Victorian buildings, is a huge statue of the King of the

West Saxons, who spent much of his life (he died in 899) defending his kingdom from the Danes in the north before becoming the overlord of England. An educated man for his time, as a boy Alfred had visited Rome, he not only codified the laws of his kingdom bur also revived learning.

Unfortunately, only the **Church of St Peter and St Paul** has survived from medieval times and, though much restored in 1857 by GE Street, there are various features that have remained from the original 13th-century structure and visitors can also see a brass commemorating the life of Sir Ivo Fitzwarren, the father of Dick Whittington's wife, Alice.

Opposite the church is the **Vale and Downland Museum Centre**, which is found in another of the town's old buildings - a house dating from the 16th century - and a reconstructed barn. Dedicated to the geology, history, and archaeology of Wantage and the Vale of the White Horse, the displays cover the centuries from prehistoric times to the present day. Built as the home of the Wantage Sisterhood, an Anglican Order, in the 19th century, three architects were involved in the construction of **St Mary's Convent**: GE Street; William Butterfield, architect of Keble College, Oxford; and John Pearson, architect of Truro Cathedral.

KINGSTON BAGPUIZE
8 miles N of Wantage off the A415

MAP 4 REF N18

This straddling village's intriguing name dates back to Norman times when Ralf de Bachepuise, a contemporary of William the Conqueror, was given land in the area. The village grew to serve the estate of Kingston Bagpuize House and many of the buildings, including the church and village school date from the 18th century.

Kingston Bagpuize House is the home of Francis and Virginia Grant and their two young children, Elizabeth and Alexander. Though the manor of Kingston was in existence before the Norman Conquest, much of the documentary evidence regarding the origins of the manor house were lost before World War II. However, it is known that a 16th-century moated farmhouse was still standing when the present house was built in the 1660s though both the exterior and the interior were extensively remodelled in the early 1700s. Visitors to the house, which remains very much a family home, will see, among the treasures, the magnificent cantilevered staircase and gallery, the elegant drawing room with its twin 18th-century fireplaces, and the panelled library and dining room.

However, it is the gardens which bring many visitors to the house. Showing traces of much earlier gardens, the grounds contain a large collection of trees, shrubs, and perennials, including some rare and unusual species. Some of the yews are over 300 years old and there are handsome Wellingtonias planted in the last century. The greatest influence on the present garden was Miss Marlie Raphael, Great Aunt of Francis Grant, and owner of the house from 1939 until her death in 1976. In the 1950s and 1960s she planted extensively including the creation of her woodland garden with the aim of giving colour and interest throughout the year. She was advised by Sir Harold Hillier from whose nurseries the majority of her plants came. Along with

**Kingston Bagpuize House and Gardens,
Kingston Bagpuize, near Abingdon, Oxfordshire
OX13 5AX Tel: 01865 820259 Fax: 01865 821659**

restoring the gardens to their former glory, Virginia and Francis have also spent time in identifying many of the plants found here and their garden map is sure to add to visitors' enjoyment.

On all open days teas with a selection of home-made cakes, scones, and biscuits are available in the tea room which is in the original basement kitchen of the house. For pre-booked group visits morning coffee and light lunches are also available. The house and gardens are open on specific days from March to October and, at all other times for group visits by written appointment.

ARDINGTON   Map 4 ref N18
2 miles E of Wantage off the A417

Just to the east of the town lies **Ardington House**, a beautifully symmetrical, early 18th-century building that is the home of the Baring family. Occasionally open to the public, the best feature here is the Imperial Staircase - where two flights come into one - of which this is a particularly fine example.

The Boar's Head in Ardington is a large and welcoming pub/restaurant located next to the pretty village church. This charming establishment sets a high standard of service and quality. Owner Mark Stott's great interest is wine, and this is evident in the superb wine list. Mark seeks

the best vintages from many sources to offer guests a great selection. The interior, too, is adorned with maps of wine regions as well as lovely prints and paintings. It is a relaxing and welcoming place with informal yet professional service. The dining areas are set in an extension to the main building. The first-rate chef prepares a menu of fresh fish and seafood, partridge, duck and lamb dishes, as well as an excellent range of cheeses and puddings, which may be accompanied

The Boar's Head, Church Lane, Ardington, nr Wantage, Oxfordshire OX12 8QA Tel: 01235 833254

by one of the superb wines. Anyone looking for a higher standard of imaginative food and a very good selection of wines will find it here.

EAST HANNEY   Map 4 ref N18
3 miles NE of Wantage off the A338

La Fontana restaurant brings a little bit of Italy to rural Oxfordshire. This charming and well-presented restaurant boasts a lovely ambience. Owners Mattia and Cristina Merola offer all guests a genuine and hospitable welcome. The dining areas include the old 17th-century part of the building complete with original oak beams and wonderful open fireplace. Decorated in a rose/terracotta colour, the restaurant has a warm and inviting feel. Pride of place, of course, has to go to the superb menu. The choice is extensive, with a range of northern and southern Italian specialities such as pasta dishes (cannelloni alla Neopolitana, tagliatelle alla arrabbiata), veal (scaloppine al limone), chicken (pollo alla cacciatora), fish (including Dover sole and monkfish) and seafood (king prawns, mussels) dishes, to name just a brief selection from the varied menu, all expertly prepared and presented. The restaurant is open Monday to

La Fontana, Oxford Road, East Hanney, nr Wantage, Oxfordshire OX12 0HP
Tel: 01235 868287 Fax: 01235 868019

Saturday midday - 2 p.m. and 6 - 10 p.m. Closed Sunday. Accommodation is also available, with seven pristine and comfortable en suite guest bedrooms which are furnished and decorated to a high standard of quality and comfort.

LETCOMBE BASSETT
MAP 4 REF M18

2 miles SW of Wantage off the B4001

This tiny village has a notable place in literary history: it is called Cresscombe in *Jude the Obscure*, which Thomas Hardy wrote whilst staying here. Earlier, Jonathan Swift spent the summer of 1714 at the village's rectory where he was visited by the poet Alexander Pope. Just to the east of the village lies **Segsbury Camp**, which is sometimes also referred to as **Letcombe Castle**. Set on the edge of the Berkshire Downs, this massive Iron Age hill fort encloses some 26 acres of land.

KINGSTON LISLE
MAP 4 REF M18

4½ miles W of Wantage off the B4507

Just to the southwest of the attractive Norman Church of St John lies the **Blowing Stone** (or **Sarsen Stone**), a piece of glacial debris that is perforated with holes. When blown, the stone emits a fog-horn like sound and tradition has it that the stone was blown by King Alfred.

UFFINGTON
MAP 4 REF M18

5½ miles W of Wantage off the B4507

This large village was, in 1822, the birthplace of Thomas Hughes, the son of the vicar. The author of *Tom Brown's Schooldays*, Hughes incorporates many local landmarks, including the White Horse and Uffington Castle, in his well known work. The **Tom Brown's School Museum** tells the story of Hughes' life and works. However, the village is perhaps best known for the **Uffington White Horse**, where on the hillside a mysteriously abstract and very beautiful figure of a horse, some 400 feet long, has been created by removing the turf to expose the gleaming white chalk beneath. It is a startling sight which can be seen from far and wide, and many a tantalising glimpse of it has been caught through the window of a train travelling through the valley below. Popular tradition links it with the victory of King Alfred over the Danes at the battle of Ashdown, which was fought somewhere on these downs in 871, but modern thinking now considers that it dates from about 100 BC. Above the White Horse is the Iron Age camp known as **Uffington Castle**, and to one side is a knoll known as **Dragon's Hill** where legend has it that St George killed the dragon.

WITNEY   MAP 4 REF M18
4 miles NW of Abingdon off the A420

Situated at the bottom of the valley of the River Windrush, this old town's name is derived from
Witta's Island and it was once of importance as the Wittan, the Council of the Saxon Kings, met
here. Developed as a planned town in the early Middle Ages, under the guidance of the Bishop
of Winchester, the site of the Bishop's Palace lies alongside **St Mary's Church**. With an attractive exterior, though the interior does not live up to the promise, the church provides a dramatic
focus to the town's market place. By 1278, Witney had a weekly market and two annual fairs
and in the centre of the market place still stands the Buttercross. Originally a shrine, the cross
has a steep roof with rustic-looking stone columns and it was probably built in 1600. Wool was
the economic base of life here and Witney developed weaving and, in particular, the making of
blankets. The Witney Blanket Company was incorporated in 1710 but before that there were
over 150 looms here working in the blanket trade employing over 3000 people. The **Blanket
Hall**, in the High Street, has on it the arms of the Witney Company of Weavers and it was built
for the weighing and measuring of blankets in an age before rigid standardisation. The trade
began in the 16th century and, even though there has been a great decline in the industry since
World War I, there are sill a couple of blanket factories here.

Just outside the town is the **Cogges Manor Farm Museum**, which stands on the site of a
now deserted medieval village of which only the church, priory, and manor house remain. A
museum of farming and country life, the displays tell the story of the lives of those who have
worked the surrounding land over the centuries.

When Ian Pout first came to Witney in 1977, little did he know that his antiques shop
would grow to become the world-famous **Teddy Bears of Witney**. Some eight years after opening this shop near the centre of town, with teddy bear-collecting still in its infancy, his was the
first establishment to specialise in selling new and old teddy bears. Today the success story

continues. The shop is packed with
over a thousand bears, each carefully
selected from the world's best manufacturers and artists. The teddies are
beautifully displayed amidst the antique furniture and other collectibles
in the shop, enhancing the cosy and
charming atmosphere. From the traditional Steiff and Merrythought
bears to contemporary bears designed by craftsmen from all over the
world, there is surely something to
suit every taste. By no means an ordinary teddy bear shop, this
emporium is also a labour of love.
Ian is a keen collector himself, and
on display in the shop are two of the
world's most famous bears. The first
is Aloysius - star attraction, for many,
of the television adaptation of
Evelyn Waugh's *Brideshead Revisited*,

**Teddy Bears of Witney, 99 High Street, Witney,
Oxfordshire OX8 6LY Tel: 01993 702616**

where he featured as the constant
companion of Sebastian Flyte. Ian
was able to purchase the bear for a

record price - many will be surprised to learn that the bear had spent 60 years of its lifetime
sitting in a delicatessen in Maine. An exclusive limited edition of the bear, nicknamed 'Deli',
has been created for Ian's shop. The second of Ian's famous bears is Alfonzo, the red mohair
bear first given to Princess Xenia by her father the Grand Duke George of Russia in 1908. The

famous manufacturer Steiff has produced a limited edition of this bear, dressed in a traditional Cossack tunic and trousers. For all teddy bear lovers, and children of all ages, a trip to this fine shop is a must.

CHURCH HANBOROUGH
5 miles NE of Witney off the A4095

MAP 4 REF N17

Visitors come from near and far to **The Hand & Shears** in Church Hanborough, attracted by its fine reputation for great food, drink and service. This "destination pub" is more appropriately termed a bar/restaurant, for it boasts an excellent restaurant and is well-presented and impressive. Informal and pristine, it has an attractive decor and is furnished with an eye towards comfort and style. The young, friendly staff are efficient and helpful. Manager Grant Middleton has brought a wealth of experience of working in several other successful country inns. A stylish simplicity also informs the superb menu, which boasts a range of traditional and innovative dishes such as king prawn thermidor, grilled pork and leek sausages, slow-roasted lamb, and fresh penne pasta with sautéed chicken breast.

The Hand & Shears Inn, Church Hanborough, Oxfordshire OX8 8AB
Tel: 01993 883337/883575 Fax: 01993 883337

All meals and snacks make use of the freshest local ingredients. And guests should be sure to leave room for one of the delightful desserts! This wonderful inn is well worth seeking out.

EYNSHAM
5 miles E of Witney on the A40

MAP 4 REF N18

This ancient market town probably began as a Roman settlement and it was first referred to as a town in documents dating from as early as AD 571 when the name was spelt *Egonesham*. The site of an important Benedictine Abbey, founded in 1005, the town's early markets were controlled by the religious house. The town prospered and expanded in the early Middle Ages and, after the Black Death, a grant allowing two weekly markets was made in 1440. Elements of the town's original medieval plan can still be seen, particularly around the market place, where there are some fine 16th- and 17th-century buildings that were constructed using materials from the abbey which was dismantled at the time of the Dissolution.

BARNARD GATE
5 miles E of Witney off the A40

MAP 4 REF N18

The Boot is a popular and lively pub and restaurant which attracts a great mix of locals and visitors, brought by its reputation for marvellous food and a superb wine list. The menu of traditional meals with a Continental flair to them boasts a range of fresh fish, beef, chicken,

The Boot Inn, Barnard Gate, nr Eynsham, Oxfordshire
OX8 6XE Tel: 01865 881231/880762 Fax: 01865 882119

and vegetarian dishes, all expertly prepared and beautifully presented. The staff are friendly and conscientious hosts who ensure guests a wonderful time in this quaint country setting. One unique feature of this upmarket pub helped put it on the map: "The Boot Collection" of famous names. Celebrities such as Jeremy Irons, Stan Smith, George Best, Gary Lineker, David Gower, The Bee Gees, Rick Stein and many more have all donated an item of their footwear, along with amusing letter and photograph, in return for which the proprietor donated £200 to their favourite charity. This fascinating collection is displayed proudly throughout the pub.

OXFORD   Map 4 ref N18
8 miles N of Abingdon off the A34

The skyline of this wonderful city can be seen from many of the hilltops which surround it and the view is best described by the 19th-century poet, Matthew Arnold: "that sweet City with her dreaming spires." However, Oxford is not all beautiful, ancient buildings but a town of commerce and industry and, around the academic centre, there are suburbs and factories. A city which has been the centre of the country's intellectual, political, and architectural life for over 800 years, it is still an academic stronghold amidst fine architecture. A walled town in Saxon times, which grew on a ford where the River Thames meets the River Cherwell, the first students came here in the 12th century when they were forced out of Europe's leading academic centre, Paris. Intellectual pursuits, then, were chiefly religious, and the town already had an Augustinian Abbey and, in a short space of time, Oxford became the country's seat of theological thinking. However, there was much tension between the townsfolk and the intellectuals and, in the 14th century, in a bid to protect their students, the university began to build colleges - enclosed quadrangles with large, sturdy front doors. The first colleges, Merton, Balliol, and University, where soon joined by others which still maintain their own individual style whilst also coming under the administration of the university.

Merton College was founded in 1264 by Walter de Merton, Lord Chancellor of England, as a small community of scholars from the income of his Surrey estates. Though the present buildings mostly date from the 15th to 17th centuries, Mob Quad is the university's oldest. The key feature of the college is its splendid medieval library where the ancient books are still chained to the desks. Once considered the poor relation to other, wealthier colleges, **Balliol College** was founded in 1263 as an act of penance by John Balliol and for many years it was reserved for only the poor students. Most of the college buildings now date from the 19th century when the college was instrumental in spearheading a move towards higher academic standards. Thought by some to have been founded by Alfred the Great, **University College** was endowed in 1249 although the present college buildings are mostly 17th century. The poet Shelley was the college's most famous scholar though he was expelled in 1811 for writing a pamphlet on atheism. Whilst in Italy, at the age of 30, Shelley drowned and his memorial can be seen in the Front Quad.

One of the most beautiful colleges in the city, **Christ Church College**, was founded in 1525 as Cardinal College by Thomas Wolsey and then refounded as Christ Church in 1546 by Henry VIII after Wolsey had fallen from royal favour. The main gateway into the college leads through the bottom of Tom Tower (designed by Christopher Wren and home of the Great Tom bell) and into Tom Quad, the largest of the city's quadrangles. From here there is access to the rest of the college and also to the college's chapel. The only college chapel in the world to be designated a cathedral, Christ Church Cathedral is also England's smallest: it was founded in 1546 on the remains of a 12th-century building.

Another splendid college well worth a visit is **Magdalen College** (pronounced "Maudlin" for reasons best known to itself), which has the most extensive grounds that include a riverside walk, a deer park, three quadrangles, and a series of glorious well manicured lawns. Founded in 1458 by William Waynflete, Bishop of Winchester, the colleges 15th-century bell tower is one of the city's most famous landmarks. During the 17th century, the college was at the centre of a revolt against James II's pro-Catholic policies and, a century later, academic standards here had slipped so far that Edward Gibbon, author of *The Decline and Fall of the Roman Empire*, called his time here as "the most idle and unprofitable" of his whole life.

As well as the college buildings, Oxford has many interesting and magnificent places to explore. At the city's central crossroads, unusually named **Carfax** and probably derived from the Latin for four-forked, is a tower, **Carfax Tower**, which is all that remains of the 14th-century Church of St Martin. A climb to the top of the tower offers magnificent views across the city. One of the most interesting buildings, the **Radcliffe Camera**, was built between 1737 and 1749 to a design by James Gibb. Eng-

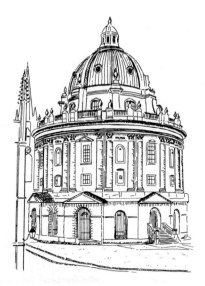

land's earliest example of a round reading room (camera is a medieval word for room), this splendid building still serves this purpose for the **Bodleian Library**. Named after Sir Thomas Bodley, a diplomat and a fellow of Merton College, Sir Thomas refounded the University Library in 1602 on the site of an earlier building. With over 5½ million books it is one of the world's greatest libraries and one of only six entitled to a copy of every book published in Great Britain. The collection of early printed books and manuscripts is second only to the British Library in London and, though members of the University can request to see any book here, this is not a lending library and they must be read and studied on the premises.

Close by is the **Clarendon Building**, the former home of the Oxford University Press and now part of the Bodleian. Designed by Nicholas Hawksmoor, a pupil of Christopher Wren, and constructed in the early 18th century, two of the original nine lead muses on the roof have had to be replaced by fibre-

Radcliffe Camera

glass replicas. Also in this part of the city is the **Bridge of Sighs**, part of Hertford College and a 19th-century copy of the original bridge which can be found in Venice. Here the bridge crosses a street rather than a canal.

However, Oxford's most famous building is the magnificent **Sheldonian Theatre** which was designed and built in the style of a Roman theatre by Christopher Wren between 1664 and 1668 whilst he was Professor of Astronomy at the University. It is still used today for its intended purpose, as a place for University occasions including metriculation, degree ceremonies,

Bridge of Sighs, Hertford College

and the annual Encaenia, when honorary degrees are conferred on distinguished people. As well as the superb wooden interior, the ceiling has 32 canvas panels, depicting Truth descending on the Arts, which are the work of Robert Streeter, court painter to Charles II.

Naturally, the city has several museums and the best place to start is at the innovative **Oxford Story**, which presents a lively review of the last 800 years of university life, from the Middle Ages to the present day. First opened in 1683 and the oldest museum in the country, the **Ashmolean Museum** was originally established to house the collection of the John Tradescants, father and son. On display in this internationally renowned museum are archaeological collections from Britain, Europe, Egypt, and the Middle East; Italian, Dutch, Flemish, French, and English old masters; far eastern art, ceramics, and lacquer work; and Chinese bronzes. Found in a splendid high Victorian building, near the University Science Area, is the **University Museum** where the remains of a dodo, extinct since around 1680, and a mass of fossilised dinosaur remains are on display. Another place worthy of a visit and a particularly peaceful haven in the city are **the Botanic Gardens**, down by the river. Founded in 1621, when plants were the only source of medicines, this was a teaching garden where the plants grown here were studied for their medicinal and scientific use. The rose garden here commemorates the work of Oxford's scientists in the discovery and use of penicillin. Oxford is also the place where the River Thames changes its name to the poetic Isis and, at **Folly Bridge**, not only are there punts for hire but river trips can be taken, both up and down stream, throughout the day and evening.

BERRICK SALOME   Map 4 ref N18
8 miles SE of Oxford of the A329

This tranquil and lovely village boasts a 1,000-year-old church. **The Chequers Inn** in Berrick Salome is owned and personally run by "Quinnie" - she has a wealth of experience in catering

The Chequers Inn, Berrick Salome, Oxford, Oxfordshire OX10 6JN Tel: 01865 891279

with the RAF in Germany, and has a friendly and welcoming manner with all her guests. This classic country pub has a cosy atmosphere, enhanced by the understated decor and the open log fires when the weather is cold. For those fine days there are large and attractive gardens with children's play area. In what was once the granary, the oak-beamed "Hillbilly's" restaurant is a delightful place to enjoy a delicious meal or snack.

Timber rafters and beams soar up to the roof. The extensive menu includes starters such as home-made Stilton and walnut paté, main courses like huntsman's grill, calf's liver, steak, Dover sole, and rack of lamb, and tempting desserts such as baked Alaska and treacle sponge. All make use of the freshest local produce. Quinnie also hosts occasional gourmet evenings, which have proved very popular. Please phone for details.

TIDDINGTON
MAP 4 REF N18

7 miles E of Oxford on the A418

Just to the west of the village lies **Rycote Chapel**, a private chapel that is found amongst the trees. Built in 1449 and still with some of its original seating, the real treat here is are the glorious 17th-century fittings which include two magnificent domes and canopies pews. One may have been used by Elizabeth I, who is known to have stayed at the long since vanished mansion here, whilst the other was installed for Charles I.

Found on the main road through the village, **The Fox** is a charming old coaching inn that has lost none of its character over the years. Still on a major route, the pub continues to offer travellers excellent food and drink whilst they take a break in their journey. The inn too is also a central point of the village and, as well as providing a local meeting place, there are several teams based here including darts and the local game of Aunt Sally. Managed by Martin Blackburn, Gavin Smith and their wives since 1998, these two well travelled friends have created a warm and friendly pub that is an ideal place to bring the whole family. The interior reflects the age of the building and the olde worlde feel is enhanced by the mass of gleaming brass and copper ware that is on display throughout. As well as serving an excellent pint of real ale, there is always

The Fox, Oxford Road, Tiddington, Oxfordshire OX9 2LH
Tel: 01844 339245 Fax: 01844 338556

a choice of four, The Fox has an enviable reputation for the delicious meals that are prepared here under Gavin's watchful eye. Not only do the menus include many favourites there are also some interesting and unusual dishes that must have been influenced by the friends' trips abroad. Finally, for warm summer days there are beer gardens to the front and rear of the pub, ideal for enjoying the sunshine as well as the hospitality, and the pub has ample car parking.

THAME
MAP 4 REF O18

11 miles E of Oxford on the A418

Founded in 635 as an administrative centre for the Bishop of Dorchester, Thame first became a market town in the 13th century and its importance as a commercial centre is evident by the wide main street it still has today. Lined with old inns and houses, some of which go back to the 15th century, this is a delightful place to visit. The imposing **Church of St Mary**, tucked away at one end of the High Street, was built in the 13th century though the aisles were widened in the 14th century and the tower was heightened in the 15th century. In the centre of the chancel is a monument to Lord John Williams, and his wife, who was notorious for having helped burn Archbishop Thomas Cranmer in the 16th century. To the west of the church lies the **Prebendal House** which, in its oldest parts, dates from the 13th century. A prebend was an income granted to a priest by a Cathedral or Collegiate Church and, at Thame, the prebend was established in around 1140 by Lincoln Cathedral. A special residence for the holders of the office was first mentioned in 1234.

The town also has a famous **Grammar School**, housed in a Tudor building in Church Lane. The schoolmaster's house faces the road and over the doorway are the arms of Lord Williams, who founded the school in 1558. John Hampden, one of the Parliamentary leaders during the Civil War, was at school here and he also died at Thame. An MP from 1621, Hampden sat in Parliament whenever it had not been dissolved by the King. He denied the right of the King to raise taxes without the sanction of Parliament and in 1636 refused to pay the 'ship tax' the King was demanding. As a result he was successfully prosecuted and, at the same time, became a popular leader in the country. When the Civil War broke out he raised a regiment of infantry for the Parliamentary Army and fought with great bravery at Edgehill and Reading. However, he was wounded at the battle of Chalgrove Field in June 1643 and was carried back to Thame, where he died some days later in an inn which stood on the High Street.

Munch 'n' Judy, 57 North Street, Thame, Oxfordshire OX9 3BH Tel: 01844 213007

Situated in the centre of the town is the striking **Munch 'n' Judy**, a charming tea room that is owned and personally run by Alison Phillips. The single-fronted, black and white, 16th-century shop opens into a delightful, intimate room, with a lovely olde worlde fireplace and then into a similar room to the rear. Warm and cosy, both of the café's rooms have a mass of pictures hanging from the walls and knick-knacks lying around which give the place a truly homely feel. Open every day except Mondays, Munch 'n' Judy is a popular place with the people of Thame and particularly with those who enjoy a traditional English tea room. Alison does all the cooking herself and, whilst admitting to being a highly strung chef, she has a warm personality and great sense of humour that is sure to endear her to all customers. As well as the menu, which covers everything from breakfast to afternoon tea, there is always a mouthwatering list of daily specials that, as with everything else, are prepared by Alison. Certainly a place not to be missed, Munch 'n' Judy is well worth seeking out.

A little to the south of the town is **Thame Park**, a house built on the site of a Cistercian Abbey founded in 1138 and which, after the Dissolution, became the home of Lord Williams. The present, privately owned house incorporates some of the former monastic buildings to which has been added a gracious Georgian house.

GARSINGTON
Map 4 ref N18

4 miles SE of Oxford off the B480

The main reason for visiting this village, which is surprisingly rural considering it's so close to Oxford, is the 16th-century **Garsington Manor**. Between 1915 and 1927, this was the home of the socialite Lady Ottoline Morrell who, along with her husband Philip, were unflaggingly hospitable to a whole generation of writers, artists, and intellectuals including Katherine Mansfield, Lytton Strachey, Clive Bell, Siegfried Sassoon, DH Lawrence, TS Eliot, Rupert Brooke, Bertrand Russell, and Aldous Huxley. Huxley based an account of a country house party in his novel *Crome Yellow* on his experiences at Garsington, thereby causing a rift with his hostess. She found his description all too apt, and felt betrayed. Huxley insisted that he had not meant any harm, but she remained hurt and they were estranged for some time. It seems that Lady Ottoline was not very lucky in the artists on whom she lavished her attention and hospitality. DH Lawrence also quarrelled with her after drawing a less than flattering, but clearly recognisable, portrait of life at her house in *Women in Love*.

WOODSTOCK   MAP 4 REF N17
7 miles NW of Oxford on the A34

Situated in the Glyme Valley, in an area of land that was originally part of the Wychwood Forest, the name of this elegant Georgian market town means a 'place in the woods'. To the north of the River Glyme is the old Saxon settlement whilst, on the opposite bank, lies the new town which was developed by Henry II in the 13th century to serve the Royal Park of Woodstock. There had been hunting lodges for the Kings of England here long before the Norman Invasion and it was Henry I who established the deer park around the manor of Woodstock. It was whilst at his palace here that Henry II first seduced Rosamund, who he is said to have housed in a bower in the park. One story tells how Henry's wife, Queen Eleanor, managed to uncover the couple by following an unravelled ball of silk that had become attached to her husband's spur. Rosamund, the daughter of a local nobleman, became a nun at the infamous Godstow Nunnery where she also bore him several children. This long since disappeared medieval palace was also the birthplace of the Black Prince in 1330 and Princess Elizabeth was held prisoner here in 1558 during the reign of her sister, Queen Mary. On ascending the throne, a grateful Elizabeth I granted the town a second weekly market and two fairs for its loyalty. The palace was damaged during the Civil War, when it served as a Royalist garrison and the last remains were demolished in 1710.

Woodstock

Whilst the new town became an important coaching centre, many of the old inns survive to this day, and prospered as a result of the construction of the Oxford Canal and, later the railway, in 1886. The old town's trade was glovemaking and traditionally a pair of new gloves are presented to a visiting monarch. Today's visitors can look round both the factory and showroom of **Woodstock Gloves**. The town is also home to the **Oxfordshire County Museum**, which is housed in the wonderful and imposing 16th-century **Fletcher's House**. As well as the permanent displays on the life of the county through the centuries, the museum has a peaceful garden open to the public and, at the entrance, can be seen the town's old stocks.

One of the 'Potato Pubs', **The Kings Head**, in the centre of this historic town, is an attractive old building dating from around 1700. A typical old local, but with a high standard of decoration and furnishing, this is a wonderful place to stop at for some excellent food, drink,

The Kings Head, 11 Park Lane, Woodstock, Oxfordshire OX20 1UD
Tel: 01993 812164 Fax: 01993 811092

and company. The traditional atmosphere found here is enhanced by the roaring log fire in winter, the old prints on the walls, and the mass of brass and copper ware that is found everywhere. In keeping with the common philosophy of the other pubs in the group, The Kings Head offers customers good value food and drink in comfortable surroundings and one glance at the menu will confirm that this is certainly achieved. As well as featuring a range of filled jacket potatoes, there are many favourites and, though this is a popular place for meals, the pub also plays hosts to several darts teams and has an Aunt Sally pitch.

However, it is the magnificent **Blenheim Palace**, one of only four sites in the country to be included on the World Heritage List, which brings most people to Woodstock. The estate and cost of building the palace was a gift from a grateful Queen Anne to the heroic John Churchill, 1st Duke of Marlborough, for his victory at the Battle of Blenheim during the Spanish War of Succession. However, the Queen's gratitude ran out before the building work was complete and the duke had to pay the remainder of the costs himself. As his architect, Marlborough chose Sir John Vanbrugh whose life was even more colourful than that of his patron. He was at the same time both an architect (although at the time of his commission he was relatively unknown) and a playwright, and he also had the distinction of having been imprisoned in the Bastille, Paris. The result of his work was the Italianate palace (built between 1705 and 1722), which is now seen sitting in a very English park that was later landscaped by Capability Brown. Unfortunately, once completed, the new house did not meet with universal approval: it was ridiculed by Jonathan Swift and Alexander Pope whilst Marlborough's wife, Sarah, who seems to have held the family purse strings, delayed paying Vanbrugh as long as possible. A marvellous, grand place with a mass of splendid paintings, furniture, porcelain, and silver on show, visitors will also be interested in the more intimate memorabilia of Sir Winston Churchill. Born here in 1874, Churchill was a cousin of the 9th Duke and the family name remains Churchill. First grown by George Kempster, a tailor from Old Woodstock, the Blenheim Orange apple took its name from the palace. Though the exact date of the first apple is unknown, Kempster himself died in 1773 and the original tree blew down in 1853. So famous did the spot where the tree stood become that it is said London-bound coaches and horses used to slow down so that passengers might gaze upon it.

WOOTTON

MAP 4 REF N17

2 miles N of Woodstock on the B4027

A quiet and pleasant village, with a bridge over the River Glyme, the 13th-century **Church of St Mary** saw the wedding, in 1879, of the diarist, Francis Kilvert and Elizabeth Anne Rowland. Unfortunately, Kilvert died of peritonitis just over a month later.

Built in 1637 by Thomas Killingworth, the **Killingworth Castle Inn**, on the edge of the village of Wootton, once served as a coaching halt on the London to Worcester road. Run by the Killingworth family for several generations, this attractive and picturesque inn is now owned and managed by Maureen and Paul Barrow. Retaining much of its original character and charm, the interior of the Killingworth Castle is a cosy and comfortable mix of the building's original features, such as the beamed ceiling and large stone fireplaces, with more recent additions like the pine scrubtop tables in the bar and the small games room. As

Killingworth Castle Inn, Glympton Road, Wootton, Woodstock, Oxfordshire OX20 1EJ Tel & Fax: 01993 811401 e-mail: kil.cast@btinternet.com

one of the first pubs in the country to be awarded the new Cask Marque accreditation, a system to ensure the quality of real ales, visitors can be sure that all of the cask conditioned ales at the Killingworth Castle Inn will be in tip top condition. In addition, there is a selection of lagers, keg beers, and spirits, an important feature being a sizeable selection of malt whiskies. For those preferring wine the full list of reasonably priced quality wines is offered by the glass as well as by the bottle. An extensive menu of à la carte dishes, ranging from snacks to three course meals, is served every day, at lunch times and evenings. Live music is an important feature at the Killingworth Castle. Folk music, every Friday evening, has been a continuous event for the past 20 years or so. More recently, Maureen and Paul have added live jazz, presenting national and international performers on the first and third Wednesdays of the month. As well as having a beautiful and well maintained garden, which includes the traditional Oxfordshire game of Aunt Sally, the Killingworth Castle Inn also offers superb bed and breakfast accommodation in a recently converted stable area. Each of the four rooms is spacious and well decorated, with full en-suite facilities and the latest amenities, and, as they are separate from the pub, access is easily obtained outside of the licensing hours.

CHARLBURY
MAP 4 REF M17
5 miles NW of Woodstock on the B4026

Now very much a dormitory town for Oxford, Charlbury was once famous for its glovemaking as well as being a centre of the Quaker Movement - the simple Friends' Meeting House dates from 1779 and there is also a Friends' cemetery. **Charlbury Museum**, close to the Meeting House, has displays on the traditional crafts and industries of the town and the town's charters given by Henry III and King Stephen can also be seen. Well known for its olde worlde **Railway Station**, built by Isambard Kingdom Brunel, complete with its fishpond and hanging baskets, the town has two interesting great houses. On the other bank of the River Evenlode from the main town lies **Cornbury Park**, a large estate that was given to Robert Dudley by Elizabeth I. Although most of the house now dates from the 17th century, this was originally a hunting lodge in Wychwood Forest that has been used since the days of Henry I. Glimpses of the house can be seen from the walk around the estate.

BURFORD
MAP 4 REF M17
20 miles W of Oxford off the A40

Often referred to as The Gateway to the Cotswolds, Burford is an attractive old market town of honey coloured Cotswold stone found on the banks of the River Windrush. The site of a battle between the armies of Wessex and Mercia in 752, after the Norman Conquest, Burford was given to William I's brother, Bishop Odo of Bayeux. Lying on important trade routes, both north-south and east-west, the town prospered and its first market charter was granted in 1087. By the 16th century, the town was an important centre of the woollen trade and it was used as the setting for *The Woolpack*, in which the author, Celia Harknett, describes the medieval wool trade in Europe. After the decline in the wool, Burford became an important coaching centre and many of the old inns can still be seen today.

The **Church of St John the Baptist** was built on the wealth of the wool trade and this grand building has the atmosphere of a small cathedral. Originally Norman, the church has been added to over the centuries and there are several interesting monuments and plaques to be found. In the south wall of the tower stair is a caring, which shows the goddess Epona, with two male supporters whilst, the monument erected to Edmund Harman, the barber-surgeon to Henry VIII, shows North American natives - possibly the first representation of Red Indians in the country. Finally, in the south porch, is a small plaque which commemorates three Levellers who were shot in the churchyard in 1649. The Levellers were troops from Cromwell's army who mutinied against what they saw as the drift towards the authoritarian rule they had been fighting against. While they were encamped at Burford, the Levellers were taken by surprise by Cromwell's forces. After a brief fight, some 340 prisoners were taken and placed under guard in the church. The next day there was a court martial and three of the rebels were shot as an example to the rest, who were made to watch the executions. The town's old court house, built in the 16th century with an open ground floor and a half-timbered first floor, is now home to the **Tolsey Museum**. An interesting building in its own right, the collection on display here covers the history of the town and the surrounding area. Other buildings worth seeking out also include the 16th-century **Falkland Hall**, the home of Edmund Sylvester a local wool and cloth merchant, and **Symon Wysdom's Cottages**, which were built in 1572 by another of the town's important merchants.

CHASTLETON
MAP 4 REF M17
10½ miles N of Burford off the A44

Chastleton is home to one of the best examples of Jacobean architecture in the country. In 1602, Robert Castesby, one of the Gunpowder Plot conspirators, sold his estate here to a prosperous wool merchant from Witney, Walter Jones. A couple of years later, Jones pulled the house down and built **Chastleton House**, a splendid Jacobean manor house with a dramatic five-gabled front. Though the style suggests that the house was designed by Robert Smythson, the most famous architect of his day, there is no absolute proof of this. Inside, the house has a wonderful collection of original panelling, furniture, tapestries, and embroideries. Of the rooms themselves, the Long Gallery, which runs the entire length of the top floor at the back of the house, is particularly impressive. This has a wonderful barrel-vaulted ceiling plastered in intricate patterns of interlacing ribbons and flowers.

MINSTER LOVELL
MAP 4 REF M18
4½ miles E of Burford off the B4047

One of the prettiest villages along the banks of the River Windrush, Minster Lovell is home to the ruins of a once impressive 15th-century manor house. **Minster Lovell Hall** was built about 1431-42 and was, in its day, one of the great aristocratic houses of Oxfordshire, the home of the Lovell family. However, one of the family was a prominent Yorkist during the Wars of the Roses and, after the defeat of Richard III at Bosworth Field, he lost his lands to the Crown. The house was purchased by the Coke family in 1602, but around the middle of the 18th century the hall was dismantled by Thomas Coke, Earl of Leicester, and the ruins became lowly farm buildings. They were rescued from complete disintegration by the Ministry of Works in the 1930s and are now in the care of English Heritage. What is left of the house is extremely picturesque, and it is hard to imagine a better setting than here, beside the River Windrush. One fascinating feature of the manor house which has survived is the medieval dovecote, complete with nesting boxes, which provided pigeons for the table in a way reminiscent of modern battery hen houses.

SHIPTON-UNDER-WYCHWOOD
MAP 4 REF M18

4 miles NE of Burford on the A361

The suffix 'under-Wychwood' derives from the ancient royal hunting forest, **Wychwood Forest**, the remains of which lie to the east of the village. The name has nothing to do with witches - wych refers to the Hwicce, a Celtic tribe of whose territory the forest originally formed a part in the 7th century. Though cleared during the Middle Ages, it was still used as a royal hunting forest until the mid-17th century. By the late 18th century there was little good wood left and the clearing of the forest was rapid to provide arable land. The forest was one of the alleged haunts of Matthew Arnold's scholar gypsy and, in the poem, published in 1853, Arnold tells the legend of the brilliant but poor Oxford scholar who, despairing of ever making his way in the world, went to live with the gypsies to learn from their way of life.

CHIPPING NORTON
MAP 4 REF M17

10 miles NE of Burford on the A44

The highest town in Oxfordshire, at 650 feet above sea level, Chipping Norton was once an important centre of the wool trade and King John granted the town a charter to hold a fair to sell wool. Later changed to a **Mop Fair**, the tradition continues to this day when the fair is held every September. The town's medieval prosperity can be seen in the fine and spacious **Church of St Mary** which was built in 1485 with money given by John Ashfield, a wool merchant. The splendid east window came from the Abbey of Bruern, a few miles to the southwest, which was demolished in 1535 during the Dissolution.

As with many buildings in the town, there has been substantial 19th-century remodelling and the present church tower dates from 1823. However, in 1549, the minister here, the Rev Henry Joyce, was charged with high treason and hanged from the then tower because he refused to use the new prayer book introduced by Edward VI. Still very much a market town today - the market is held on Wednesdays - Chipping Norton has been little affected by the influx of visitors who come to see this charming place. The **Chipping Norton Museum** is an excellent place to start any exploration and the permanent displays here cover local history from prehistoric and Roman times through to the present day.

Found just to the west of the town centre is **Bliss Tweed Mill**, an extraordinary sight in this area as it was designed by a Lancashire architect, George Woodhouse, in 1872 in the Versailles style. With a decorated parapet and a tall chimney which acts as a local landmark, this very northern looking mill only ceased operation in the 1980s.

Located on the original old road between London and Stratford, and equidistant between Oxford and Stratford, the **Chequers Inn** is a delightful

**Chequers Inn, Goddards Lane, Chipping Norton, Oxfordshire OX7 5NP
Tel: 01608 644717 Fax: 01608 646237
website: www.chequers-pub.co.uk**

public house dating back to the 16th century. Deceptively small from the outside, this charming establishment is close to the well-known Chipping Norton Theatre and a row of very interesting and attractive alsmhouses. This attractive stonebuilt inn has retained many original features inside, including the exposed beams, stone-flagged floor, real log fires and cosy nooks and crannies. Old photographs and prints of the town adorn the walls. Owners Kay and Josh Reid came to the pub in 1991; they have built up its reputation so that today it is very much a part of life in Chipping Norton. The range of beers, wines and spirits is excellent. Food is served every day; fresh fish dishes are a speciality. Kay has spent time in Thailand at several cookery schools - the menu reflects her interest in Thai cuisine. Customers can try these wonderful, fragrant dishes along with the more traditional English meals, in the delightful surroundings of the Conservatory restaurant, created from the old coaching inn courtyard. Well worth seeking out, this welcoming pub has a relaxed and friendly atmosphere.

OVER NORTON
Map 4 ref M17

11 miles N of Burford off the A3400

To the northwest of the village lies the **Rollright Stones** - one of the most fascinating Bronze Age monuments in the country. These great gnarled slabs of stone stand on a ridge which offers fine views of the surrounding countryside. They also all have nicknames: the **King's Men** form a circle; the **King Stone** is to the north of the circle; and, a quarter of a miles to the west, stand the **Whispering Knights**, which are, in fact, the remnants of a megalithic tomb. Naturally, there are many local legends connected with the stones and some say that they are the petrified figures of a forgotten king and his men that were turned to stone by a witch.

Rollright Stones, Nr Over Norton

BICESTER
Map 4 ref N17

12 miles N of Oxford on the A43

Though the name (which is pronounced Bister) suggests that this was a Roman settlement, the town was not, in fact, established until Saxon times and the Roman name comes as a result of the nearby and long since vanished Roman town of **Alchester**. By the time of the 12th century, the town was the home of both an Augustinian priory and also a Benedictine nunnery. Growing up around these religious houses and its market, the town suffered a disastrous fire in the early 18th century and most of the buildings seen here today date from that time onwards. Hunting and horse-racing played as much a part of the prosperity of Bicester as agriculture though industrialisation has been sporadic. The founding here of the Army's ordnance depot in 1941 has brought much new development which continued until the 1960s.

KIRTLINGTON
Map 4 ref N17

5 miles SW of Bicester on the A4095

Set in five acres of gardens and paddocks adjacent to an 18-hole golf course and driving range, **Vicarage Farm** is an oasis of peace and tranquillity. Owner Judith Hunter is a welcoming and accommodating host. This impressive stonebuilt farmhouse has three pleasant and airy rooms

(two double and one twin room, with separate bathroom, shower room and toilet), which are comfortable, well-furnished and equipped with all modern facilities. Each room affords beautiful views over the surrounding countryside. Guests can arrange to have a round of golf on the nearby course. The delicious breakfast of traditional favourites plus fresh fruit in season makes use of the freshest local produce, expertly prepared and

Vicarage Farm, Kirtlington, Oxfordshire OX5 3JY
Tel/Fax: 01869 350254

presented, and sets guests up for exploring nearby Blenheim Palace, Woodstock, the Cotswolds, Warwick Castle, Oxford and Stratford. There are several very good hostelries locally for evening meals. No smoking. No pets or children. ETB 3 Diamonds.

BANBURY   MAP 7 REF N16

25 miles N of Oxford on the A423

Famous for its cross, cakes, and the nursery rhyme, this historic and thriving market town has managed to hang on to many of its old buildings as well as become home to Europe's largest livestock market. The famous **Banbury Cross** can be found in Horsefair where it was erected, in 1859, and replaced the previous one which had been demolished by the Parliamentarians during the Civil War. Built to commemorate the marriage of Queen Victoria's oldest daughter to the Prussian Crown Prince, the figures around the bottom of the cross, of Queen Victoria, Edward VII, and George V, were added in 1914. This, obviously, is not the cross referred to in the old nursery rhyme and that cross's whereabouts is now unknown. The town's other legendary claim to fame is its cakes, made of spicy fruit pastry, which can still be bought. Banbury was also, at one time, famous for its cheeses, which were only about an inch thick. This gave rise to the expression 'thin as a Banbury cheese'.

On the east side of the Horsefair stands **St Mary's Church**, a classical building of warm-coloured stone and hefty pillars which are pleasantly eccentric touches. The original architect was SP Cockerell, though the tower and portico were completed between 1818 and 1822 by his son, CR Cockerell. The style reflects the strong influence on English architecture of Piranesi's Views of Rome, using massive shapes and giving stone the deliberately roughened appearance which comes from the technique known as rustication. The **Banbury Museum** also lies nearby and here can be found the story of the town's development, from the days when it came under the influence of the bishops of Lincoln, through the woollen trade of the 16th century, to the present day. The affects of the Civil War on the town were also great; the Royalists held Banbury Castle and there were two sieges here. The completion of the Coventry to Oxford Canal in 1778, the coming of the railway in 1850, and the opening of the M40 in 1991, have all played their part in making Banbury a large and successful commercial town.

Tucked away in the pedestrian precinct in the centre of Banbury, **Banesberie** is a wonderful award-winning licensed café that is well worth seeking out. The name Banesberie is thought to be the original Anglo-Saxon name for the town, and it can be found mentioned in the Domes-

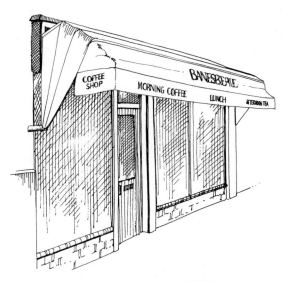

**Banesberie, 10 Butchers Row, Banbury,
Oxfordshire OX16 8JH Tel: 01295 269066**

day Book. Owned and personally run by Tony Carney, this marvellous place is ideal for anyone who appreciates good food. Housed in a turn-of-the-century shop, with patio seating outside and a traditional double front, the café is well decorated and comfortably furnished. With local-interest prints and photographs mingling with the Art Deco prints on the walls, the style of this excellent place matches the interesting and Continental flavour of the menu. From the traditional and famous Banbury Cakes - made and sold by the proprietor to the original genuine recipe which, they say, can be traced back 400 years - to the mouthwatering hot French- and Italian-style sandwiches, there is sure to be something to suit everyone here. All home-cooked and with a menu that follows the seasons, it is easy to see why Banesberie has been awarded so many accolades.

MIDDLETON CHENEY
2½ miles E of Banbury on the A422

Map 7 ref N16

This large village, which saw one of the many conflicts in this area during the Civil War, is home to a church, restored in 1865 by Sir George Gilbert Scott, which contains some splendid stained glass by Morris and Burne-Jones. Built in the 17th century as a turnpike inn, **The New Inn** is a charming old building situated close to the road through the village. Purchased in 1998 by Tim and Jenny Kinchin, the couple have completely refurbished this wonderful old place and returned it to its former glory. With a stone flagged floor, low ceilings, and the now reinstated old brick fireplace, this is an attractive pub inside as well as outside. One unusual decorative feature are the family horse racing colours framed and mounted on the wall. Very much a family place, children will enjoy the

**The New Inn, 45 Main Road, Middleton Cheney,
Oxfordshire OX17 2ND Tel: 01295 710399**

pet's in the garden, which include rabbits and bantam chickens, whilst they also have a play tree all to themselves. As well as serving an excellent pint of real ale, The New Inn has a fine reputation for the delicious menu of homecooked dishes that are all freshly prepared to order. Served at both lunchtime and in the evening (except Mondays and Sunday evenings), a meal here is a treat well worth taking the time to enjoy. However, this is not all this superb family pub has to offer as, most weekends, there is live music - no juke boxes here.

BARFORD ST MICHAEL
4 miles SW of Banbury off the A361

MAP 7 REF N17

Jo and Andrew Baker-Holmes extend a warm welcome to all guests at **The George Inn**, a charming 17th-century country pub with a thatched roof and other original features such as the exposed beams and open fireplaces. Extensively renovated in 1999, it nevertheless retains a traditional and cosy ambience.
There's a great atmos-
phere at this marvellous
pub. Jo's brother Steve is
the chef at this family-
run business. Away
from it all in this small
and appealing village,
tucked away off the
main road, the pub
boasts a huge garden -
perfect for enjoying a relaxing drink on fine
days. Meals are available
every lunchtime (mid-
day - 2.30) and Tuesday
- Sunday evenings (7 -
9), and can be taken in
the main bar or in the
new private dining
room. The menu offers
a variety of traditional

The George Inn, Barford St Michael, nr Bloxham,
Oxfordshire OX15 0RH Tel: 01869 338226 Fax: 01869 337804
website: www.banburycross.co.uk/georgeinn

fare such as home-made steak and ale pie or lamb stew, along with more modern dishes such as chili or nachos. There is also a tempting range of daily specials. The wine list is extensive.

SWERFORD
7 miles SW of Banbury off the A361

MAP 7 REF M17

Lying deep in the valley of the River Swere, the village is home to the **St Mary's Church** which has architectural features from the 13th, 14th, and 15th centuries as well as some fascinating exterior gargoyles. Behind the church can be found, in the mounds and earthworks, evidence of an old castle.

With stunning views over the Swere Valley, **The Masons Arms** is a delightful country inn that is owned and personally run by Linda and Trevon. With a philosophy of *"set out of town, but still in the High Street"*, this charming place is a happy mix of relaxed style with excellent service. Dating back over approximately 200 years, this charming old building has been well looked after over the years and today it is a comfortable place with a warm and welcoming decor. As Trevon has been a family butcher, it is not surprising to see a set of butchers weights and scales on display in the pub. From the bar a range of well kept traditional ales from an award winning local brewery are served. Food, too, is very important here and an excellent menu of delicious homemade meals are prepared by the pub's chef. Served in the cosy and

separate restaurant, a meal here is a treat well worth trying. Those looking for less formal dining may like to try the more traditional menu of pub meals served in the bar area. As this is a true inn, accommodation in the form of three en-suite guest rooms is available, which all come up to the same high standard

The Masons Arms, Swerford, near Chipping Norton, Oxfordshire OX7 4AP Tel: 01608 683212 Fax: 01608 683105

as the rest of this superb inn. Easy to reach and well located for the attractions of north Oxfordshire, The Masons Arms is an ideal place for all the family and the children, particularly, will enjoy their purpose built play area as well as watching the birds in the aviary. The Masons Arms has been modernised in the last few years and has excellent disabled facilities. Groups are already using the pub on tour for day excursions.

NORTH NEWINGTON   MAP 7 REF N17
2 miles SW of Banbury off the A422/B4035

Patti Ritter and Michael Canning have owned and personally run the fine **La Madonette Country Guest House** since 1989. This former miller's house bordered by a lovely mill stream was built in the 17th century with additions over the intervening centuries. Just a short journey from the busy market town of Banbury, this peacefully situated guest house is stonebuilt with attractive mullioned windows. The interior is tasteful and subdued, adding to the peace and tranquillity of the ambience. The country house feel is enhanced by the charming furnishings and decor. The inviting reception area doubles as a place for a quiet drink. Intriguing and beautiful tapestries adorn the walls. There are five comfortable and spacious bedrooms with en suite or private facilities. One boasts a romantic four-poster bed. All offer superb open views over the surrounding Cotswold countryside. There are also three delightful cottages available for self-catering

La Madonette Country Guest House, North Newington, Banbury, Oxfordshire OX15 6AA Tel: 01295 730212 Fax: 01295 730363 email: lamadonett@aol.com

accommodation, set in the gardens of the guest house. Each two-storey cottage consists of one double bedroom (extra "Z" beds are available), lounge/dining area and fully fitted kitchen. Facilities such as a laundry service and small conference facilities make this ideal for the business traveller as well as for tourists. The emphasis at this charming country retreat is on warm hospitality and comfort. The heated outdoor swimming pool (not open in the winter months) is another feature of this excellent guest house, which successfully combines a traditional rural idyll with all modern amenities.

SWALCLIFFE
Map 7 ref M17

5 miles W of Banbury on the B4035

The village is dominated by the large **Church of St Peter and St Paul** which towers over all the other buildings here. Founded in Saxon times, the bulk of the building dates from the 12th, 13th, and 14th centuries and it is the tracery in the east window which makes the church noteworthy. However, by far the most impressive building in Swalcliffe is the **Barn**, which has been acknowledged as one of the finest 15th-century half-cruck barns in the country. Built as the manorial barn by New College, Oxford, in 1400-1409, it was used to store produce from the manor and never to store tithes. Today, it is home to a collection of agricultural and trade vehicles. To the northeast of the village, on **Madmarston Hill**, are the remains of an Iron Age hill fort which was occupied from the 2nd century BC to the 1st century AD.

BUCKINGHAMSHIRE

CHALFONT ST GILES
Map 4 ref P18

10 miles N of Windsor off the A413

This excellent example of a typical English village dates from Roman times and there was a reference to Stonewells Farm in the Domesday Book. Of the various ancient buildings of interest here there is an Elizabethan mansion, The Vache, that was the home of friends of Captain Cook and, in the grounds, is a monument to the famous seafarer. Madame Tussaud, famous for her fascinating exhibitions in London, started her waxworks here in the village. However, by far the most famous building in Chalfont St Giles, with an equally famous resident, is **Milton's Cottage**. A grade I listed building, dating from the 16th century, John Milton moved to this cottage, found for him by fellow Quaker and former pupil Thomas Ellwood, in 1665 to escape the plague in London. Though the blind poet moved back to London in 1666, Milton wrote *Paradise Lost* and began work on its sequel, *Paradise Regained*, whilst taking refuge in the village. The only house lived in by the poet to have survived, the cottage and its garden have been preserved as they were at the time Milton was resident. The building is now home to a museum which includes collections of important first editions of Milton's works and a portrait of the poet by Sir Godfrey Kneller.

Another fascinating and unusual place to visit in the village is the **Chiltern Open Air Museum** which rescues buildings of historic or architectural importance from across the Chilterns region and re-erects them on its 45 acre site. Though offers of buildings come from many sources, the museum will only accept one that is to be demolished. Once the decision to move a building has been taken the painstaking task of dismantling the structure, piece by piece, is undertaken, followed, finally, by its reconstruction at the museum site. The buildings rescued by the museum are then used to house and display artefacts and implements that are appropriate to the building's original use and history. Also on the museum site are a series of fields farmed using medieval methods where, amongst the historic crops, organic woad is grow from which indigo dye is extracted for use in dyeing demonstrations.

A little to the northwest lies Chalfont St Peter, dating back to the 7th century and, as its name means 'the spring where the calves come to drink', there is a long history here of raising cattle in the surrounding lush meadows. First mentioned in 1133, the parish Church of St Peter was all but destroyed when its steeple collapsed in 1708. The building seen today dates from that time as it was rebuilt immediately after the disaster. Housed in a barn at Skippings Farm is the **Hawk and Owl Trust's National Education and Exhibition Centre**. Dedicated to conserving wild birds of prey in their natural habitats, the Trust concerns itself with practical research, creative conservation and imaginative educational programmes.

BEACONSFIELD MAP 4 REF P18
3 miles SW of Chalfont St Giles on the A40

This is very much a town in two parts: the old town, dating back to medieval times and, to the north, the new town which grew up following the construction of the Metropolitan line into central London and consisting chiefly of between the wars housing. The old town, home to the Church of St Mary and All Saints which is considered by many to be one of the finest in the Chilterns, is best known for its literary connections. The poet Edmund Waller, born in the village of Coleshill, just to the north, was a resident. After getting involved in a Royalist plot in 1643, he was banished from Parliament and spent some time in exile before returning to Beaconsfield to concentrate on writing. Somewhat more wise than in his youth, Waller took care to write poems in favour of Cromwell and, after his restoration to the throne, the King. Beaconsfield was also the home of GK Chesterton, author of the popular Father Brown crime stories, poet Robert Frost and the much loved children's author Enid Blyton. For a unique step back in time to the 1930s, visitors should seek out the charm of **Bekonscot**, a rural model village. The oldest model village in the world, Bekonscot was begun in the 1920s by Roland Callingham, a London accountant, who started by building models in his garden. As the number of buildings and models grew, Callingham purchased more land and, with the aid of a friend from Ascot who added a model railway, created the village seen today. When the village first opened, people started throwing coins into bucket for charity and, even today, all surplus profits go to charity.

CHENIES MAP 4 REF P18
3 miles NE of Chalfont St Giles off the A404

This picturesque village, with a pretty green surrounded by an old school, a chapel and a 15th-century parish church, is also home to **Chenies Manor**, a fascinating 15th-century manor house. Originally the home of the Earls (later Dukes) of Bedford, before they moved to Woburn, this attractive buildings has stepped gables and elaborately patterned high brick chimneys. Built by the architect who enlarged Hampton Court for Henry VIII, the house has played host not only to the king but also his daughter Elizabeth I. Naturally, there is a ghost here, that of Henry VIII, whose footsteps can be heard as he drags his ulcerated leg around the manor house in an attempt to catch Catherine Howard in the act of adultery with one of his entourage. Whilst the house has much to offer, not just from the exterior but also inside where there are tapestries, furniture and a collection of antique dolls, the gardens should not be overlooked. Among the delights are a Tudor style sunken garden and a physick garden with a variety of herbs that were used for both medicinal and culinary purposes.

HIGH WYCOMBE MAP 4 REF O18
6 miles W of Chalfont St Giles on the A40

The largest town in Buckinghamshire, High Wycombe is traditionally known for the manufacture of chairs and, in particular, the famous Windsor design. It is still a centre of furniture manufacture today as well as being a pleasant town in which to live for those commuting to London. Originally an old Chilterns gap market town, High Wycombe is still home to several old buildings of note. The **Little Market House** was designed by Robert Adams in 1761 and is of a rather curious octagonal shape, while the 18th-century Guildhall is the annual venue for a traditional ceremony showing a healthy scepticism for politicians when the mayor and councillors are publicly weighed - to see if they have become fat at the expense of the citizens.

Found in an 18th-century house, with a flint facade, the **Wycombe Local History and Chair Museum** has displays which give the visitor an excellent idea of the work and crafts of the local people over the years. There is, of course, a superb collection of chairs and other furniture here which are more suited to the houses

Little Market House, High Wycombe

of ordinary people rather than those of the wealthy. In the grounds of the museum is a medieval motte which would normally indicate that a castle once stood here but, in this case, the structure was probably little more than a wooden tower..

WEST WYCOMBE
Map 4 ref O18
2 miles NW of High Wycombe on the A40

This charming estate village, where many of the houses are owned by the National Trust, has a main street displaying architecture from the 15th through to the 19th century. Close by is **West Wycombe Park**, the home of the local landowners, the Dashwood family until the 1930s and now a National Trust property. Of the various members of the family, it was Sir Francis Dashwood who had most influence on both the house and the village. West Wycombe house was originally built in the early 18th century but Sir Francis boldly remodelled it several years later as well as having the grounds and park landscaped by Thomas Cook, a pupil of Capability Brown. Very much a classical landscape, the grounds contain temples and an artificial lake shaped like a swan whilst the house has a good collection of tapestries, furniture and paintings. Hewn out of a nearby hillside are **West Wycombe Caves**, that were created, possibly from some existing caverns, by Sir Francis as part of a programme of public works. After a series of failed harvests, which created great poverty and distress amongst the estate workers and tenant farmers, Sir Francis employed the men to extract chalk from the hillside to be used in the construction of the new road between the village and High Wycombe.

The village **Church of St Lawrence** is yet another example of Sir Francis' enthusiasm for remodelling old buildings. Situated on the remnants of an Iron Age fort, the church was originally constructed in the 13th century. Its isolated position, however, was not intentional as the church was originally the church of the village of Haveringdon which has long since disappeared. Dashwood remodelled the interior in the 18th century in the style of an Egyptian hall and also heightened the tower, adding a great golden ball to the top. There is room in the ball for six people and it was here that Sir Francis entertained his notorious friends. Apart from this building, Sir Francis had a racier side to his character and, as well as being remembered as a great traveller and a successful politician, he was the founder of the Hell Fire Club. This groups of rakes, who were also known as the Brotherhood of Sir Francis or Dashwood's Apostles, met a couple of times a years to engage in highly colourful activities. Though their exploits were legendary and probably loosely based on fact, they no doubt consumed large quantities of alcohol and enjoyed the company of women. Traditionally, the group meetings were held in the caves, or possibly the church tower, though between 1750 and 1774, their meeting place was nearby Medmenham Abbey.

The George & Dragon Hotel is approached through a cobbled archway on West Wycombe High Street. This charming and traditional coaching inn was built in the early 18th century. Liked the village itself, the hotel is steeped in history and it too is linked with the local Dashwood family and the infamous Hell Fire Club. Today the hotel, which is owned and personally run by

Cass Todd, offers all its guests the very best in hospitality as well as the opportunity to step back in time to enter a more gracious age. The most striking feature inside this glorious old inn is the magnificent oak staircase. The main bar, too, has many original features such as the vast beams and large open fire. Behind the bar there is a good range of beers and ales on offer, as well as a fine selection of malt whiskies. Serving the

George & Dragon Hotel, High Street, West Wycombe, High Wycombe, Buckinghamshire HP14 3AB Tel: 01494 464414

needs of guests comes high on the list of priorities here; the superb bar menu includes not only many favourites but also more innovative dishes. The comfortable accommodation comprises eight en suite guest bedrooms, two with four-poster beds. Beautifully decorated and furnished, they offer a high standard of comfort and quality.

HUGHENDEN
2 miles N of High Wycombe off the A4128

Map 4 ref O18

This village is famous for being the home of the great Victorian Prime Minister Benjamin Disraeli, from 1847 to his death in 1881, and he is buried in the estate church. The son of a writer and literary critic, Isaac D'Israeli, who lived for a time in the village of Bradenham on the other side of High Wycombe, Disraeli was also a novelist. He bought **Hughenden Manor** shortly after the publication of his novel *Tancred*. Though not a wealthy man, Disraeli felt that a leading Conservative politician should have a stately home of his own and, in order to finance the purchase, his supporters lent him the money so that he could have this essential characteristic of an English gentleman. The house seen today, which, along with the grounds, is now in the hands of the National Trust and open to the public, is a remodelled 18th-century house refaced with various coloured bricks. The interior is less controversial and is an excellent example of the Victorian Gothic style. Here can be found an interesting collection of memorabilia of Disraeli's life as well as his library and much of his furniture. A great friend of Queen Victoria, she is said to have preferred Disraeli to the other great statesman of her reign, William Gladstone.

IVINGHOE
7 miles E of Aylesbury on the B488

Map 4 ref P17

As the large village church would suggest, Ivinghoe was once a market town of some importance in the surrounding area. In this now quiet village can be found **Ford End Watermill**, a listed building that, though probably much older, was first recorded in 1767. The only working watermill, with its original machinery, left in Buckinghamshire, the farm in which it is set has also managed to retain the atmosphere of an 18th-century farm. To the east lies **Ivinghoe**

Beacon, owned by the National Trust, that is a wonderful viewpoint on the edge of the Chiltern Hills. The site of an Iron Age hill fort, the beacon was also the inspiration for Sir Walter Scott's Ivanhoe.

PITSTONE
MAP 4 REF P17

7 miles E of Aylesbury off the B489

Though the exact age of **Pitstone Windmill**, owned by the National Trust, is not known, it is certainly one of the oldest post mills in Britain. The earliest documentary reference to its existence was made in 1624. It is open to the public on a limited basis. Also in the village is a **Farm Museum**, where all manner of farm and barn machinery, along with domestic bygones, are on display.

GREAT KIMBLE
MAP 4 REF O18

5 miles S of Aylesbury on the A4010

Though the village is home to a church with an interesting series of 14th-century wall paintings, its real claim to fame is the nearby 16th-century mansion, **Chequers**, the country residence of the British Prime Minister. Originally built by William Hawtrey in 1565, but much altered and enlarged in the 18th and 19th centuries, the house was restored to its original form by Arthur Lee in 1912. Later, in 1920, as Lord Lee of Fareham, he gave the house and estate to the nation to be used as the prime minister's country home. The first Prime Minister to make use of Chequers was Lloyd George and many who have known the house have since moved, or stayed, in the area: Ramsay MacDonald's daughter lived at nearby Speen; Harold Wilson bought a house in Great Missenden; and Nye Bevan owned a farm in the Chilterns.

WADDESDON
MAP 4 REF O17

4 miles NW of Aylesbury on the A41

The village is home to another of the county's magnificent country houses, in this case **Waddesdon Manor**. Built between 1874 and 1889 for Baron Ferdinand de Rothschild, in the style of a French Renaissance chateau, the house is set in rolling English countryside and makes a lasting impression. The Baron came from the Austrian branch of the great banking family, but he made his home in Britain from the age of 21. In 1874 he bought the Waddesdon and Winchenden estates from the Duke of Marlborough and set about creating his fantastic country house. The manor's construction was an immense operation and a steam railway was specially built to move the materials. After 15 years of work what had been a bare hill was topped with a superb building which borrows elements from several different French chateaux, surrounded by formal gardens and landscaped grounds.

Waddesdon Manor

The French influence even extended to the carthorses used on the site - powerful Percheron mares that were imported from Normandy. Now in the hands of the National Trust, the house is home to one of the best collections of 18th-century French decorative arts in the world, including Sèvres porcelain, Beauvais tapestries and fine furniture. There are also paintings by Gainsborough, Reynolds and 17th-century Dutch and Flemish masters on display.

CHESHAM
MAP 4 REF P18
9 miles SE of Aylesbury on the A416

This pleasant town, situated among wooded hills, has traditionally been a rival to Amersham and, in 1454, the Bishop of Lincoln allowed the parishioners here to process around their Church of St Mary at Whitsun to avoid the fighting associated with their processions at St Mary's Church in Amersham. Standing on a prehistoric holy site, as indicated by the great pudding stone foundations, the parish Church of St Mary was begun in the mid 12th century and has a sanctuary bell that was cast in 1458.

A successful combination of a commuter town, industrial centre and country community, Chesham's growth from a sleepy market town was due to its Metropolitan underground railway link with central London. The Metropolitan Railway Company began operating the first urban underground railway in the world in 1863, running trains from Paddington to Farringdon Street, but was never content with being just an urban or suburban railway. So the company pursued its main line ambitions through a policy of acquiring other lines to link into its system as well as building its own. At its high point the company ran trains as far into Buckinghamshire as Aylesbury and Quainton Road. Today, Chesham still retains its Metropolitan links with central London.

Whilst the town has seen itself expand at the hands of the railway, it has also had some interesting inhabitants. Chesham was the birthplace of Arthur Liberty, the son of a haberdasher and draper, who went on to found the world famous Liberty's department store in London's Regent Street in 1875. Another resident was Roger Crabbe who, having suffered head injuries during the Civil War, was sentenced to death by Cromwell. After receiving a pardon, Crabbe opened a hat shop in the town where he is reputed to have worn sack-cloth, eaten turnip tops and given his income to the poor. Not surprisingly, Crabbe was used by Lewis Carroll as the model for the Mad Hatter in *Alice in Wonderland*.

HAWRIDGE COMMON
MAP 4 REF P18
4 miles N of Chesham off the A41

The Full Moon is a classic old coaching inn dating back over 300 years. This Grade II listed building has been a welcoming and characterful alehouse since 1693. Boasting many traditional features including exposed beams and stone floors, it is located here in the glorious

Chiltern Hills in the centre of Hawridge Common surrounded by beautiful wooded areas with extensive walks and bridlepaths. This popular retreat offers a view of a lovely restored windmill (now a private house) from the back garden. The inn also boasts its own paddock and hitching rails for those guests arriving on horseback! The garden is a wonderful place to sit and enjoy a quiet drink or meal on fine days. The beams of the large and pristine interior are adorned with a superb collection of hanging jugs and brasses; the pub also has an

The Full Moon, Hawridge Common, nr Chesham, Buckinghamshire HP5 2VH Tel: 01494 758959

attractive collection of pottery and china. There are two restaurant areas (one non-smoking) as well as dining areas in the main bar itself. Winner of Regional Pub of the Year two years running, an excellent range of snacks and three-course meals is available at lunch and dinner. The selection of wines, beer and spirits is very good.

GREAT MISSENDEN   MAP 4 REF O18
3 miles W of Chesham off the A413

Home to the only other court house in the Chiltern Hundreds (the other is at Long Crendon), Great Missenden's **Old Court House** dates from the early 1400s. Also in this attractive village is an attractive flint and stone church and Missenden Abbey, which was founded in 1133 by the Augustinian order. A daughter community of St Nicholas's Abbey in Normandy, the abbey has long since gone and in its place stands a fashionable Gothic mansion dating from 1810. The village too has had its fair share of famous visitors and amongst them is Robert Louis Stevenson, the author of *Treasure Island* and the anti-slavery campaigner, William Wilberforce. However, Great Missenden is probably best known as being the home of the late Roald Dahl, the internationally recognised author of, particularly, children's books. He lived here for 30 years and the gardens of his home are open the public once a year.

WENDOVER   MAP 4 REF O18
6 miles NW of Chesham on the A413

This delightful old market town, situated in a gap in the Chiltern Hills, has an attractive main street of half timbered, thatched houses and cottages of which the best examples are **Anne Boleyn's Cottages**. A picturesque place, often seen as the gateway to the Chilterns, Wendover also has a fine selection of antique shops, tea rooms and bookshops. Whilst it is a great place for visitors today, in the past there have been several famous guests here including Oliver Cromwell and Robert Louis Stevenson who both stayed at the Red Lion. The town also offers visitors an opportunity of seeing the glorious countryside as, situated on the edge of the Chiltern escarpment, lies **Wendover Woods**. Created for recreational pursuits as well as for conservation and timber production, these Forestry Commission owned woods offer visitors numerous trails through the coniferous and broadleaved woodland.

BUCKINGHAM   MAP 7 REF O17
17 miles N of Aylesbury on the A413

This pleasant town, the centre of which is contained in a loop of the River Ouse, dates back to Saxon times and was once granted a charter by Alfred the Great. Although it became the county town in AD 888, when King Alfred divided the shires, from an early date many of the functions of a county town were performed by the more centrally located Aylesbury. According to the Saxon Chronicle, it was Edward the Elder who fortified the town in AD 918 when he brought his army here during his advance on the Danish invaders. The stronghold he built, on which later stood a Norman castle, is now the site of the parish Church of St Peter and St Paul. A prosperous medieval market town there have been several notable visitors to Buckingham including Catherine of Aragon, who stayed at Castle House in 1514, Edward VI, who founded the Latin School, and Elizabeth I, who dined at

Old Gaol Museum, Buckingham

the manor house whilst on a journey to Bicester. Unfortunately few buildings remain from those times as, in 1725, there was a disastrous fire which destroyed much of the town. Many buildings were replaced and, particularly in Castle Street, there are some fine Georgian houses of which Castle House (which is actually in West Street) is the best example. The town's old gaol, is another fine building which dates from the mid 18th century though it has been extensively restored. Today it houses the **Old Gaol Museum**, which not only reflects the building's history but also has displays on the town's past and the county's military exploits. One building that did survive the devastating fire in the 18th century is the **Buckingham Chantry Chapel**. Now owned by the National Trust, the chapel was constructed in 1475 on the site of a Norman building whose doorway has been retained. Well worth a visit, the chapel was restored by George Gilbert Scott in 1875.

MIDDLE CLAYDON
MAP 7 REF O17

5 miles S of Buckingham off the A413

The village is home to **Claydon House**, an historic building that dates from the 17th century but has 19th century additions. The home of the Verney family and now owned by the National Trust, the house contains a number of state rooms with magnificent carved wood and plaster decorations. Particularly delightful are the Chinese rooms which reflect the 18th century enthusiasm for all things Oriental. However, what makes the house particularly interesting is its associations with Florence Nightingale. Florence's sister married into the Verney family and the pioneer of modern hospital care spent long periods at the house, especially during her old age. Her bedroom in the house and a museum of her life and experiences during the Crimean War can be seen here. Now that nursing has become one of the most respected professions, it is difficult to imagine the strength of character needed by a young Victorian woman of a good family to go abroad to train as a nurse, which Florence did in 1851. At that time nursing had a poor reputation and was thought to be a menial job done by women who had no other means of supporting themselves. Florence died in 1910 after a long career which embraced concerns of public health as well as the training of nurses and she was the first woman to be awarded the Order of Merit.

DADFORD
MAP 7 REF O17

3 miles N of Buckingham off the A422

Just to the south of the village lies **Stowe School**, a leading public school which occupies an 18th-century mansion that was once the home of the Dukes of Buckingham. Worked upon by two wealthy owners who both had a great sense of vision, the magnificent mansion house, which was finally completed in 1774, is open to the public during school holidays. Between 1715 and 1749, the owner, Viscount Cobham hired various well known landscape designers to lay out the fantastic gardens that can still be seen around the house. Taking over the house in 1750, Earl Temple, along with his nephew, expanded the grounds and today they remain one of the most original and finest landscape gardens in Europe. Worked on by the best designers of the day, the gardens at Stowe contain temples, alcoves and rotundas

Stowe Landscape Gardens

scattered around the landscape that were placed to evoke in the onlooker a romantic and poetic frame of mind. It is one of the more intriguing quirks of fate that Lancelot Brown, always known as Capability Brown supposedly because he told his clients that their parks had capabilities, was head gardener at Stowe for 10 years. He arrived here in 1741 and began to work out his own style, a more natural style of landscape gardening which was to take over where gardens like the ones at Stowe left off. Brown's concept was to ensure that the landscape element of the garden, the tree planting, lakes and lawns, should look as natural as possible. **Stowe Landscape Gardens** are now in the hands of the National Trust and are open to the public.

THORNBOROUGH
MAP 7 REF O17

3 miles E of Buckingham off the A422

This lively and attractive village is home to Buckinghamshire's only surviving medieval bridge. Built in the 14th century, the six-arched structure spans Claydon Brook. Close by are two large mounds which were opened in 1839 and revealed a wealth of Roman objects. Though it was known that there was a Roman temple here its location has not been found.

The **Lone Tree** in Thornborough is an award-winning Free House dating back to the 17th century. With its unique name among public houses, this fine establishment offers rare cask ales, cider, lager and unusual wines not normally found elsewhere. Built from local stone, the adjoining thatched barn has rafters made from tree branches and a traditional pebble floor. Renovations undertaken in 1997 uncovered the old exposed beamwork. The pub boasts a comfortable and relaxing ambience and is the ideal stop-off point for good food and fine drink. The traditional and hearty English fare is complemented by

The Lone Tree, Bletchley Road, Thornborough,
Buckinghamshire MK18 2DZ Tel: 01280 812334

delicious daily specials and vegetarian options. Booking is recommended. Almost 1,000 guest ales have been served up here, and the pub is fast gaining an enviable reputation for showcasing the brews of several small and micro breweries throughout the land.

MILTON KEYNES
MAP 7 REF O16

12 miles E of Buckingham off the A5

Most people's perception of this modern town is of a concrete jungle but the reality of Milton Keynes could not be more different. The development corporation that was charged, in 1967, with organising the new town has provided a place of tree-lined boulevards, uncongested roads, spacious surroundings, and acres of parkland. It is too, of course, a modern town, with new housing, high-tech industries, modern leisure facilities, and a large covered shopping centre. One of the town's most notable buildings is **Christ Church**, built in the style of Christopher Wren. The first purpose-built ecumenical city church in Britain it was opened in March 1992 by HM the Queen. However, whilst Milton Keynes is certain a place of the late 20th century it has not altogether forgotten the rural past of the villages which are now incorporated into the suburbs of the town. The **Museum of Industry and Rural Life**, with its large collection of industrial, domestic, and agricultural bygones, is devoted to the lives of the people who lived in the area in the 200 years leading up to the creation of the new town. Meanwhile, exhibitions on art, crafts, local history, and social life can be seen at the **Exhibition Gallery**, next to the town's library.

BLETCHLEY
MAP 7 REF O17

2 miles S of Milton Keynes on the A421

Now more a suburb of Milton Keynes, Bletchley is famous for **Bletchley Park**, the Victorian mansion which housed the wartime codebreakers. During World War II, 12,000 men and women worked here and in outstations, unable to tell family and friends what they were employed doing, but their work is thought have helped end the war two years early and to have saved countless lives. The park is now opened to the public where, in the **Cryptology Museum**, the famous and now rebuilt Colossus, the world's first electronic valve computer which helped to break Hitler's messages to his generals, can be seen.

OLNEY
MAP 7 REF O16

8 miles N of Milton Keynes on the A509

This pretty town on the banks of the River Ouse is famous for its association with William Cowper, who came to the town to be under the ministry of the Rev. John Newton, curate of Olney. Newton was a reformed slave-trader as well as a fiery preacher However there is more here to discover than the rather sad life of the poet Cowper. The earliest recorded evidence of the town dates back to a Saxon Charter of AD 979 although archaeological finds in the area have been dated at 1600 BC. The parish Church of St Peter and St Paul, where Newton was curate, is a spacious building dating from the mid 14th century and its spire rises some 185 feet to dominate the skyline of Olney. For over 300 years, this was a centre of hand lace making using wooden or bone bobbins. At its most expensive, in the 1700s, only the well-to-do could afford the lace but the rise in machine made lace from Nottingham saw a sharp decline in Olney lace. A revival of the trade was tried by Harry Armstrong when, in 1928, he opened the Lace Factory but, although handmade lace is still produced locally, the factory only lasted until Armstrong's death in 1943.

The house in which Cowper lived from 1768 to 1786 is now the **Cowper and Newton Museum**, an interesting place that not only concentrates on Cowper's life and work but also has some exhibits and collections concerned with times in which he lived and the life of Olney. Each of the rooms of the large early 18th-century town house have been specially themed and there are numerous displays of Cowper's work, including the "Olney Hymns". Cowper wrote 67 of these and the remaining 281 were written by his friend Rev. John Newton whose most famous hymn is probably "Amazing Grace". William Cowper was also a keen gardener and the summer house, where he wrote many of his poems, can still be seen out in the rear garden where he also chose to experiment with plants that were new to 18th-century England. Also at the Museum is the nationally important Lace Collection which reflects the fact that Olney was at the centre of the bobbin lace making for over 300 years. Other displays include the finds from local archaeological digs which have unearthed dinosaur bones, Roman coins, and medieval fishing weights, Civil War relics, and items particular to the shoe making industry which was another busy local trade in the 19th and early 20th century.

The town's present day claim to fame is its annual Pancake Race held every Shrove Tuesday. Legend has it that the first 'race' was run in the 15th century when a local housewife heard the Shriving Service bell ringing and she ran to church complete with her frying pan and pancake. Today's re-enactment is open to any lady of Olney over 18 years and she must wear a skirt, an apron, and a scarf as well as carry a frying pan and pancake.

Nearby **Emberton Country Park**, found on the site of former gravel pits, is an ideal place to relax. Not only are there four lakes and a stretch of the River Ouse within the park's boundaries but facilities here include fishing, sailing, and nature trails.

CHICHELEY
MAP 7 REF O16

5 miles NE of Milton Keynes on the A422

This attractive village is home of **Chicheley Hall**, a beautiful baroque house that was built in the early 18th century for Sir John Chester and which remains today one of the finest such houses in the country. However, over the years the hall's history has been somewhat uncertain and, whilst it has been used by the military and as a school, in 1952 it was bought by the 2nd Earl Beatty who restored it to its former glory. The Earl's father, the 1st Earl, was a particularly courageous naval commander and, as well as receiving the DSO at the age of just 25, he was also a commander in the decisive battle of Jutland in 1916. Mementoes of the 1st Earl's illustrious career at sea can be seen in the study when the hall is occasionally open to the public.

GREAT LINFORD
MAP 7 REF O16

2 miles N of Milton Keynes on the A422

Situated on the banks of the Grand Union Canal, this village , which is now more a suburb of Milton Keynes, has a 13th-century church, a 17th-century manor house, and a **Stone Circle**,

Stone Circle, Great Linford

one of only a few such prehistoric monuments in the county. Despite the encroachment of its much larger neighbour, the village has retained a distinctive air that is all its own.

WILLEN
MAP 7 REF O16

1 mile N of Milton Keynes on the A509

Whilst the village Church of St Mary Magdalene, built in the late 17th century, is an elegant building in the style of Sir Christopher Wren, Willen is also home to the **Peace Pagoda and Buddhist Temple**, opened in 1980. It was built by the monks and nuns of the Nipponsan Myohoji, and it was the first peace pagoda in the western hemisphere. A place of great tranquillity and beauty, a thousand cherry trees and cedars, donated by the ancient Japanese town of Yoshino, have been planted on the hill surrounding the pagoda, in memory of the victims of all wars.

BEDFORDSHIRE

LUTON
MAP 7 REF P17

15 miles SE of Milton Keynes off the A6

The largest town in Bedfordshire and perhaps best known for Luton Airport and Vauxhall cars, Luton first began to prosper in the 17th century on the strength of its straw plaiting and straw hat making industries. However, excavations around the town have unearthed Bronze Age urns and Iron Age pottery which certainly suggests that there has been a settlement here for some considerable time. At the centre of this essentially modern town is **Wardown Park**, a traditional town park with all the usual amenities, and, housed within the Victorian mansion, is **Luton Museum and Art Gallery**. There can be few towns that possess a more picturesque setting for their museum. This charming house, built in 1875, and its surroundings are particularly splendid. In 1903, the town council was offered the fine brick and red Mansfield stone house and land but they hesitated and it was two members of the board who purchased the property. Fortunately, Edwin Oakley and Asher Hucklesby were philanthropic and, having seen the value to Luton, sold the house and grounds to the town without profit.

However, though the park was opened to the public shortly afterwards, the house was became first a restaurant and then, during World War I, an officers' hospital. It was not until 1931 that the town's museum and art gallery, originally housed in the library, moved here. As well as having a re-creation of a Victorian shop and pub, the museum is also home to a range of collections covering the hat trade, costume, local history, archaeology, and childhood. As lace making was one of the two main cottages industries in Bedfordshire, visitors will not be surprised to learn that the museum also has the largest collection of lace anywhere in the country except London. The Lace Gallery illustrates the traditions and methods of the East Midlands lace makers who, since the end of the 16th century, have produced fine lace in competition with such continental lace making areas as Brussels and Lille. Although Luton has expanded rapidly from a market town in the early 19th century to a major industrial centre by the mid 20th century, visitors can also take a step back in time by seeking out **Stockwood Craft Museum and Gardens**. Housed in a Georgian stable blook, the was once part of the main house, the museum has a collection of Bedfordshire craft and rural items. The walled garden to the original house is equally impressive and the period garden includes knot, medieval, Victorian, cottage, and Italian gardens. Also here can be found the **Mossman Collection** of over 60 horse drawn vehicles dating from the 18th, 19th, and 20th centuries. Replicas of some of the vehicles on display here have found their way into films such as *Ben Hur* and *Out of Africa*.

Just to the south of the town is the magnificent house **Luton Hoo**, originally designed by Robert Adams. It is set in 1500 acres of parkland landscaped by Capability Brown, who began work in 1764. Construction of the house began in 1767, though it was extensively remodelled in 1827 and again in 1903, when the interior was given a French style for Sir Julius Wernher. Now home to his art collection, there are superb examples of jewellery by Faberge, porcelain and china, furniture, tapestries, and paintings, including the work of Rembrandt and Titian, to be seen. One unexpected touch is an exhibition of robes worn at the court of the Tsars before the Russian revolution and other mementoes of the Imperial family. The gardens include a restored Edwardian rose garden and formal gardens laid out at the turn of the century with wonderfully colourful herbaceous borders.

WHIPSNADE
MAP 7 REF P17

5 miles SW of Luton off B489

This small village with a charming, simple church is surrounded by common land on which stands a **Tree Cathedral** which is now in the hands of the National Trust. After World War I, a local landowner, Edmund Kell Blyth, planted, over some 20 acres, trees in the shape of a cathedral, with a nave, transepts, a chancel, and cloisters. A curiously moving place, particularly as the trees have matured, services are held here during the summer. To the south of the village can be seen the white silhouette of a lion cut into the green hillside, which is reminiscent of the much older White Horse at Uffington. A magnificent landmark, the lion also advertises the whereabouts of **Whipsnade Wild Animal Park**, the country home of the Zoological Society of London. Set within the 600 acres of parkland, Whipsnade is one of Europe's largest wildlife conservation centres and it specialises in the breeding of endangered species such as cheetahs, rhinos, and the scimitar-horned oryx.

LEIGHTON BUZZARD
MAP 7 REF O17

9 miles W of Luton on A505

The town's interesting name tells a lot about its history: Leighton is Old English and refers to a centre for market gardening whilst the Buzzard is a reference to a local clergyman, Theobald de Busar the town's first Prebendary, and not the bird of prey. The town's past prosperity as a market place is reflected in the grandeur of its fine Market Cross, a pentagonal 15th-century structure with an open base and statues under vaulted openings all topped off by pinnacles. The market is still held here every Tuesday and Saturday.

The spire of **All Saints' Church** is over 190 feet high and it is a local landmark. This big ironstone church dates from 1277 and inside there are a number of endearing features in the form of graffiti left by the medieval stone masons: one is a sketch of a traceried window whilst another shows a man and woman quarrelling over whether to boil or bake a simnel cake. Seriously damaged by fire in 1985, the church has been carefully restored to its medieval glory and the painstaking work included regilding the roof, which is particularly fine with carved figures of angels.

Leighton Buzzard and its neighbour Linslade are on the Grand Union Canal and visitors can now take leisurely boat trips along this once busy waterway on the *Leighton Lady*. Historic forms of transport seem to be the thing in the town as visitors can also take a steam train journey on the **Leighton Buzzard Railway**. The railway was built in 1919 as an industrial line to carry sand from the local quarries. Now run by volunteers, the railway has over 50 steam engines, which have come from all over the world, including India, Africa, and Britain, as well as a unique heritage collection of industrial diesel locomotives. For life at an even more leisurely pace than steam trains, the town lies at one end of the **Greensand Ridge Walk** which extends across Bedfordshire to finish some 40 miles away at Gamlingay, Cambridgeshire. The name Greensand comes from the geology of the area, a belt of greensand which stretches from Leighton Buzzard up to Sandy and beyond.

AMPTHILL
MAP 7 REF P17

12 miles N of Luton on the A5120

This historic town, situated on a rise and with fine views over the surrounding countryside, was a great favourite with Henry VIII and it was here that Catherine of Aragon stayed during her divorce. At that time there was also a castle here, built by Sir John Cornwall for his bride, the sister of Henry IV. This is where she would have lived and on its site now stands Catherine's Cross, erected in 1773, and bearing the arms of Castile and Aragon. On land given to his family by Charles II, the 1st Lord Ashburnham built the castle's replacement, Ampthill Park, in 1694. The house was enlarged a century later and the 300 acre park was landscaped by Capability Brown. Now the **Ampthill Deer Park** is open to the public, it is famous for its old oak trees and visitors can also take in part of the Greensand Ridge Walk which runs through the grounds.

SILSOE
MAP 7 REF P17

3 miles SE of Ampthill off A6

Although the manor of Wrest has been held by the de Grey family since the late 13th century, the house standing today dates from the 1830s. Built for the 1st Earl de Grey from the designs

Wrest Park, Silsoe

of a French architect, it follows faithfully the style of a French chateau of the previous century. However it is a much more restrained and classical building than Waddesdon Manor. Parts of **Wrest Park** are open to the public but the real glory are the gardens. They are a living history of English gardening from 1700-1850 and they include work by Capability Brown. In spite of his influence, the layout remains basically formal, with a full range of garden furniture in the grand manner - there is a Chinese bridge, an artificial lake, a classical temple, and a rustic ruin. Two buildings of particular interest are the Baroque Banqueting House, designed by Thomas Archers, which forms a focus of the view from the house across the lake, and the Bowling Green House, dating from about 1740 and said to have been designed by Batty Langley. If this is so it is indeed a rarity for Langley was mostly known as a writer of architectural books for country builders and built little himself. Immediately beside the house is an intricate French-style garden, with flower beds, statues, and fountains.

TODDINGTON   Map 7 ref P17
5 miles S of Ampthill on A5120

Situated on a hill above the River Flitt, this village is often overlooked, particularly by those travelling the nearby M1 who think only of the service station of the same name. However, the village is an attractive place, with cottages and elegant houses grouped around the village green. Unfortunately all that remains of **Toddington Manor** house is a small oblong building with a hipped roof which is believed to be the Elizabethan kitchen of the large quadrangular house that was built here in around 1570. Toddington is a place which makes much of its folklore and there are Morris dancers in the summer and mummers who tour the village giving the traditional entertainments at Christmas. Local legend also has it that a witch lives under Conger Hill - which is actually a motte that would, at one time, have had a castle on top - and, on Shrove Tuesday, the children put their ears to the ground to listen to her frying their pancakes.

To the south of Toddington is **Chalgrave Church**, which survives surrounded by chestnut trees though the village has long since disappeared. Inside is an exceptional collection of wall paintings, dating from about 1310, which have recently been restored as well as a monument to Sir Nigel Loring. A hero of the Hundred Years War between England and France, Sir Nigel was also a founder member of the Order of the Garter, traditionally founded in 1348 by Edward III.

WOBURN   Map 7 ref P17
6 miles W of Ampthill on A4012

First recorded as a Saxon hamlet in the 10th century, and again mentioned in the Domesday Book, Woburn grew into a small market town after the founding of the Cistercian Abbey here in 1145. All but destroyed by fire in 1720, this pretty village has retained many of the pleasant Georgian houses that were built subsequently and the attractive shop fronts give the place a cheerful air. Situated at a major crossroads, between London and the north and Cambridge and Oxford, Woburn also saw prosperity during the stagecoach era and, by 1851, there were 32 inns here.

The abbey from which **Woburn Abbey** takes its name was a daughter community of the Cistercian Abbey at Fountains in Yorkshire. After the Dissolution of the Monasteries under Henry VIII it was granted, in 1547, to the 1st Earl of Bedford. Elements of the present house go back to about 1630, but the stately home seen today is almost entirely 18th century. The Dukes of Bedford have lived here for over 400 years, and today it is the home of the Marquess of Tavistock and his family. Within the house is one of the world's most impressive art collections still in private hands and among the famous works by Van Dyck, Gainsborough, and Reynolds, are 21 views of Venice by Canaletto. Also to be seen on a tour of the mansion is a magnificent Sèvres dinner service presented to the 4th Duke by Louis XV of France and some fine 18th-century French and English furniture.

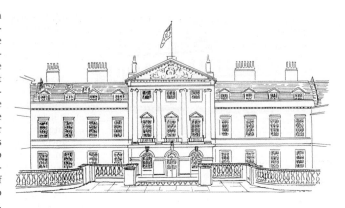

Woburn Abbey

However, Woburn Abbey caters for a wide range of tastes and, as well as tours of the superb house, there are antiques shops, a gift shop, and a garden centre. Finally, there is also the 3000 acre deer park, landscaped by Sir Humphrey Repton, that is also now home to the **Wild Animal Kingdom and Leisure Park**. The famous deer park not only has nine species of deer but one, the Père David, was saved from extinction by Woburn and they now have the largest breeding herd. The animal kingdom has a vast range of animals and includes eland, zebra, hipps, rhinos, lions, tigers, elephants, and sea lions.

BEDFORD
MAP 7 REF P16

7 miles N of Ampthill on the A6

This bustling town, in a splendid riverside location, was already a thriving market place before the Norman Conquest and the Church of St Peter de Merton, built in the 10th century, has some substantial Norman additions. The fine Norman south doorway, though, was not actually intended for this building but was brought here from the Church of St Peter in Dunstable. However, St Peter's is not Bedford's main church, this is St Paul's Church, found in the centre of the market place. A mainly 14th and 15th-century building, with a recently restored roof and furnishings, there are some interesting monuments and brasses inside. Beside the River Great Ouse and running through the heart of the town are the **Bedford Embankment Gardens** which provide an all year round display of plants. Close by is also the **Priory Country Park**, an area with a diversity of habitat which represents the flood meadows, reed beds and woodland that once surrounded the town. With such a variety of plant life, the park is able to support a wide diversity of animals, insects and birds as well as providing recreational opportunities for local people and visitors. For a greater insight into the history of the town and surrounding area the **Bedford Museum** is well worth a visit. Among the many interesting displays is a piece of wall which shows the construction of the wattle walls that were an essential building technique in the 14th century. Housed within the unlikely combination of a Victorian mansion and an adjoining modern gallery, the **Cecil Higgins Art Gallery** was started by a wealthy Bedford brewery family. Visitors can not only see the internationally renowned collection of watercolours, prints, and drawings but also some fine glass, ceramics, and furniture.

No mention of Bedford would be complete without including something of the life and work of the town's most famous son. Born just south of the town, in Elstow, John Bunyan lived and was imprisoned here in the 1660s and 1670s. The son of a tinsmith, a repairer of metal utensils, Bunyan followed the same trade as his father and so was able to travel the countryside more than most people of that time. During the Civil War he was drafted, at the age of 16, into the Parliamentarian Army and was very much affected by the ferment of religious ideals that were a characteristic of those times. In the 1650s, Bunyan met John Gifford, the then pastor of the Independent Congregation which held its meetings at St John's Church. It was their lengthy discussions that led to Bunyan's conversion and he was baptised shortly afterwards by Gifford in a backwater that leads off the Great Ouse. St John's Rectory is now occupied by the St John Ambulance but one room has been set aside for Bunyan memorabilia and it is open to the public by arrangement.

It was whilst preaching in the villages of Bedfordshire that Bunyan came into conflict with the authorities. He was arrested in 1660, near Ampthill, and placed in prison for the first of his two such confinements. Though Bedford had a Town Gaol, which was, during the 17th century, part of the main structure of the bridge across the river, it seems likely that Bunyan served his two terms in the County Gaol. However, some still believe that he served his second sentence, in 1676, in the Town Gaol. The County Gaol was demolished in 1801 and it was during his first imprisonment, between 1660 and 1672, that he wrote many of his works including his most famous, *Pilgrim's Progress*. Following his release from prison in 1672, Bunyan was elected as pastor of the Independent Congregation. One of his first tasks was to find a permanent meeting place and he promptly bought a barn to act as a temporary measure which was used until 1707 when the meeting house was finally built. The church seen today was constructed in 1849 and the magnificent bronze doors, with illustrations from *Pilgrim's Progress* were given to the church by the Duke of Bedford. Within the church is also the **Bunyan Museum**, which tell graphically the story of the man as well as the times through which he lived. Among the many displays are the jug in which his daughter Mary brought him soup whilst in prison, his chair, his tinker's anvil, and his violin and flute which he made in prison.

One final tribute to Bunyan to be found in the town is **Bunyan's Statue** which was presented to the town in 1874 by the Duke of Bedford. Made of bronze, the statue is the work of Sir J E Boehm and around the pedestal of the nine foot high figure are three bronze panels depicting scenes from *Pilgrim's Progress*.

OLD WARDEN
MAP 7 REF P16
4 miles SE of Bedford off B658

This enchanting village of thatched cottages along a single street has developed its unique character as a result of the influence of two local families. In the early 18th century, Sir Samuel Ongley, a London merchant, shipowner, and former director of the South Sea Company, bought this country seat for himself and his family, who stayed here for over 200 years. Elevated to the peerage in 1776 when Robert Henley Ongley was awarded an Irish title for his services to Parliament, it was his grandson, also called Robert, who created Old Warden as it is seen today.

Taking the original estate cottages, and also building new ones, Sir Robert developed this rustic village which still has a distinctly Swiss air. He also embellished the local 12th-century church with some interesting Belgian woodwork. However, Sir Robert's most famous piece of work is the **Swiss Garden**, laid out in the early 19th century. A romantic fantasy, with a tiny thatched Swiss style cottage, iron work bridges, and arches of creepers, the garden is well worth taking the time to explore.

Unfortunately, this extensive building and remodelling programme left Sir Robert in severe financial difficulty and, in 1872, he sold the estate to Joseph Shuttleworth. A partner in a firm of iron founders, it was Joseph who lead the way to the development of the steam traction engine and also built the Jacobean style mansion house that can still be seen today. Here, on the estate, can also be found Old Warden's other great attraction, the Shuttleworth Collection of historic aircraft. The origin of this magnificent collection is, however, born in tragedy. Already a keen motor racing driver and collector of motor cars, in 1932, the 23 year old Richard Ormande Shuttleworth inherited the estate and also purchased a de Havilland Moth plane. From here his interests turned towards aviation and he

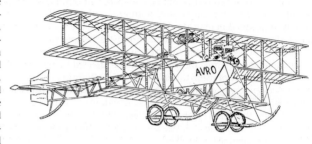

Shuttleworth Collection, Old Warden (Avro Triplane IV, 1910)

began the foundations of the collection when, in 1935, he bought a 1909 Bleriot and a 1920 Deperdussin. At the outbreak of World War II, Richard joined, naturally, the RAF and he was killed in a flying accident in 1940. After the war, Richard's mother founded a trust which had among its objectives the promotion of education and training in the science, practice, and history of aviation and automotive transport. The famous collection, which includes a Spitfire in flying condition, opened to the public in the 1960s and, along with the various vintages planes, there are also vintage cars and horse drawn vehicles.

HOUGHTON CONQUEST   MAP 7 REF P16
3 miles S of Bedford off B530

That this village is home to Bedfordshire's largest parish church seems fitting as Houghton Conquest also has links with the county's most famous son, John Bunyan. Just to the south of the village, standing on a hill, lies **Houghton House**, which is reputedly the inspiration for the House Beautiful in *Pilgrim's Progress*.

Built in 1615 for Mary, Countess of Pembroke, the house would have been a relatively new addition to the landscape in the time of Bunyan and records show that he visited here during his days as a tinker. The property came into the hands of the Dukes

Houghton House, Houghton Conquest

of Bedford, one of whom had the house partially demolished in 1794, and the ruins today are owned by English Heritage.

STEVINGTON   MAP 7 REF P16
4 miles NW of Bedford off A428

This is a typical English village with a church that was certainly here at the time of the Domesday survey, a village **Cross** decorated with capitals and a large finial, and a holy well that attracted visitors in the Middle Ages. However, the most important building in the village is its

Post Mill, the only one of the county's 12 remaining windmills that still retains its sails. Dating from the 1770s, the mill continued to operate until 1936, having been rebuilt in 1921. Extensively restored in the 1950s, it is in full working order today. Though milling was an important part of village life here for many years, lace making too was a thriving industry and mat makers also settled here, taking advantage of the rushes growing on the banks of the nearby River Ouse.

BROMHAM
Map 7 ref P16
2 miles W of Bedford off A428

This quiet residential village has a splendid 26 arch, 13th-century bridge spanning the River Ouse. Close to the river is a watermill that dates back to the 17th century. Now fully restored and in working order, **Bromham Mill** is also home to displays of natural history, crafts and other special exhibitions. Charles I is known to have stayed at Bromham Hall, the home of Royalist Sir Lewis Dyve, who made his escape from the house during the Civil War by swimming the river.

HERTFORDSHIRE

HEMEL HEMPSTEAD
Map 4 ref P18
9 miles SW of Luton off the A41

This is a place with two distinct identities: the charming old town centred around the ancient Church of St Mary and tranquil Gadebridge Park; and the new town, one of the first to be built following World War II. Built as integrated series of communities, each with their own individual centre, the new town was built to expend and extend the old. **Gadebridge Park** is an extensive expanse of open parkland through which runs the River Gade. The park's attractive walled garden adjoins the High Street of the old town alongside the grounds of **St Mary's Church**. This large 12th century church, said to be one of the finest in the country, has a 200 foot timber spire that was added in the 14th century. Though there are also some 15th-century additions, this is essentially an exceptional Norman building. Evidence of a settlement here long before the Norman Conquest can be found surprisingly close to the town's industrial area. Protected by a fenced enclosure and visible from the road lies the mound of a Bronze Age barrow. By the time of the compilation of the Domesday Book, Hemel Hempstead was an attractive market town with several mills along the banks of the River Gade. The **Charter Tower**, just inside one of Gadebridge Park's entrances, is reputed to be the tower from the upper window of which Henry VIII handed down Hemel Hempstead's royal charter. However, this is not quite accurate as the tower is all that remains of a mansion house called The Bury. Though Henry was certainly a visitor to the house, The Bury was rebuilt several times, each in a different location, and the tower dates from the second mansion house, built long after the charter was given.

FLAUNDEN
Map 4 ref P18
5 miles SW of Hemel Hempstead off A404

This attractive, scattered village lies on a wooded hillside close to the county border with Buckinghamshire. Here can be found a medieval chapel that was built following the plan of a Greek cross: it has four equal arms. Left to decay since 1838, when a new village church was built, all that remains of the chapel and the adjoining curate's house are overgrown ruins.

The **Bricklayers Arms**, in the heart of the village, is an attractive 300-year-old building which began life as a row of cottages though, at one time, it was also a filling station. As attractive inside as it is from the exterior, the pub can certainly be called a traditional English country inn. There are low ceilings, oak beams, an open log fire and a mass of gleaming brassware decorating the walls. However, what the inn does not have is television, music or machines - just welcome peace and quiet. The ideal place for real ale lovers, there are always seven on tap, with guest ales changing weekly, and the pub supports many small and micro breweries. Food, too, is a very important aspect of life at the

Bricklayers Arms, Hog Pits Bottom, Flaunden, Hertfordshire HP3 0PH Tel: 01442 833322

inn. The wonderful menu of freshly prepared dishes is served at both lunchtime and in the evening. With a large garden and a substantial covered patio area there is plenty of opportunity to eat outside and, every Sunday during the summer, there are lunchtime barbecues.

BEDMOND   MAP 4 REF P18
3 miles SE of Hemel Hempstead off A4147

This delightful village was the birthplace of Nicholas Breakspear, the only British pope, who was crowned Adrian IV in 1154. Built in 1635, **The Bell Inn** is a small, unspoilt, traditional country inn. According to local folk lore it has always been an inn though at one time it was called The Blue Bell Inn after the nearby woods. Owned and run by Vince Horsley, a keen Formula 3 racing driver, and his wife, Janet, this is a well known pub in the area that is popular with the locals as well as those exploring the surrounding countryside. With many of the building's original features still intact, the interior has a cosy, olde worlde atmosphere

The Bell Inn, 18 High Street, Bedmond, Hertfordshire WD5 0QR Tel: 01923 262910

that is enhanced by the display of gleaming horse brasses hanging from the black ceiling beams. Another striking feature is the large brick inglenook fireplace, at one end of the bar, which has, on the mantelpiece, an array of golfing and motor racing trophies. Just in case there is any doubt as to Vince's love of motor sports, pictures of his accomplishments at the wheel hang from the walls and the couple's dog is called Brabham. Very much a traditional pub, not only is there an excellent range of real ales served from the bar but at lunchtimes, from Monday to Saturday, a tasty menu of bar food and snacks are on offer to hungry customers.

TRING
MAP 4 REF P17
8 miles NW of Hemel Hempstead off the A41

Situated on the edge of the Chiltern Hills and on the banks of the Grand Union Canal, Tring is a bustling little market town whose character has been greatly influenced by the Rothschild family. However, this rich and famous family are not the only people of note to be associated with the town and, in **St Mary's Church**, can be found the grave of the grandfather of the first US president, George Washington, whilst the 17th-century **Mansion House**, designed by Sir Christopher Wren, was reputedly used by Nell Gwynne. The town's narrow winding High Street, off which lead little alleyways and courtyards, is home to many late Victorian buildings, all designed by local architect William Huckvale. In particular there is the **Market House**, built by public subscription in 1900 to commemorate Queen Victoria's Diamond Jubilee. A fine example of the arts and crafts style, so popular at the turn of the century, the building was later converted into a fire station and today it is home to the town council chamber. Just off the High Street, on Frogmore Street, was the house where Lawrence Washington, grandfather to the US president and his fam-

Market House, Tring

ily lived between 1630 and 1650. Unfortunately the house is no longer standing.

Tring's main focal point is **The Square**, remodelled in 1991 and which features an ingenious **Pavement Maze** in the form of a zebra's head - a tribute to the work of Walter Rothschild. The town's war memorial, unveiled in 1919, stands in The Square as does the flint and Totternhoe stone Church of St Peter and St Paul. Dating chiefly from the 15th century, this parish church contains some fine medieval carvings as well as 18th-century memorials. The old **Silk Mill**, first opened in 1824, once employed over 600 people, including Gerald Massey, the Chartist poet and the prototype of Felix Holt in George Eliot's novel, who was sent to work here at the age of eight. Towards the end of the 19th century the silk trade fell into decline and Lord Rothschild ran the mill at a loss to protect his employees rather than see them destitute. Unable to carry on in this fashion, the mill closed to the silk trade and, after reducing its height, the building was converted into a generating station. From 1872 to the 1940s, the Rothschild family lived at Tring Park and from here they exercised their influence over the town. Perhaps, however, their greatest lasting feature is the **Walter Rothschild Zoological Museum** which first opened in 1892 and, on Walter's death in 1937, became part of the British Museum (Natural History). An eccentric man with an interest in natural history, Walter collected over 4000 rare and extinct species of animals, birds and reptiles with the help and encouragement of Mr Minall.

MARSWORTH
MAP 4 REF O17
2 miles N of Tring off B489

Mentioned in the Domesday Book and situated on the banks of the Grand Union Canal, Marsworth was known as Mavvers to the canal people. The village is also home to the **Tring Reservoirs National Nature Reserve**. The four reservoirs were built between 1802 and 1839 to store water for the then Grand Junction (now Grand Union) Canal which reached its summit close by. Declared a nature reserve in 1955, this is a popular place for birdwatchers though there is also a nature trail and trees and marshland flora can be studied here.

NORTHCHURCH
MAP 4 REF P18
3 miles SE of Tring on A4251

Not surprisingly Northchurch does have an ancient place of worship though it is hard to believe that **St Mary's Church** dates back to Saxon times. In fact, the original pre-Norman church is now the nave of the present building which dates from the 13th century though the north aisle, vestries and porch are late Victorian. On the south wall is a memorial plaque to Peter the Wild Boy who is buried close to the porch. Found living wild in a wood near Hanover, Germany in 1725, he was brought to this country by the royal family and entrusted to the care of a farmer in this parish. He died in 1785 at an estimated age of 75. Though the full length of the **Grand Union Canal** towpath, in Hertfordshire, can be walked, the section of canal from Northchurch to Tring has been developed particularly with recreational use in mind. As well as the attractive canalside walk there are numerous maintenance and conservation projects to preserve this magnificent waterway and the wealth of wildlife and plant life found along its banks.

HATFIELD
MAP 4 REF Q18
9 miles E of Hemel Hempstead off the A414

This historic town grew up around the gateway to the palace of the abbots and Bishop of Ely. Beside the palace gatehouse is the parish church which is dedicated to St Ethedreda, the East Anglian princess and first abbess of Ely in the 7th century. Today, all that remains of the **Royal Palace of Hatfield**, where Elizabeth I spent her early life and held her first council in 1558, is a single wing. This can be seen in the delightful gardens of the impressive Jacobean mansion, **Hatfield House**, which now stands on the site. Built between 1607 and 1611 by Robert Cecil, the 1st Earl of Salisbury, who was the Chief Minister to King James I, the elaborate architecture of the building is equalled by the exquisite interior. Famous throughout the world for its collection of beautiful tapestries and paintings,

Hatfield House

there is also some fine furniture from the 16th, 17th, and 18th centuries which complement the interior decoration that was the work of English, Dutch, and French craftsmen. The magnificent banqueting hall still hosts regular Elizabethan banquets throughout the year, and the intricately carved Grand Staircase is one of the finest examples of its kind in existence. The beautiful gardens are open daily except Good Friday, and visitors can wander at their leisure following nature trials through the woodlands and by the lake. Designed by the celebrated plant hunter, John Tradescant the Elder, they were laid out in 1611 after the house had been completed. Though much of his work fell to the great landscape garden movement of the 18th century, the present Marchioness of Salisbury is continuing the work of restoring and redeveloping these ancient formal gardens.

Back in the town lies the **Eight Bells pub** which was frequented by Charles Dickens when, as a newspaper reporter for the *Morning Chronicle*, he visited Hatfield to report on the fire which not only destroyed a substantial part of Hatfield House but also resulted in the death of the Dowager Lady Salisbury. The pub also features in Dickens' novel, *Oliver Twist*, as following the murder of Nancy, Bill Sykes makes for Hatfield and, in the tap room of the Eight Bells, a fellow drinker sees the blood on Sykes' hat. The idea of Hatfield New Town was nothing new in post World War II Britain as, in 1848, proposals for such a new town were advertised to coincide with the completion of the railway line in 1850. Though some development did take place it was not until the 1950s that the rapid expansion began. However, the two areas remain separate, on either side of the railway line and, fortunately, much of the older part of the town has survived.

WELWYN GARDEN CITY   Map 4 ref Q17
2 miles N of Hatfield on A1000

As the name of this town would suggest it is indeed a Garden City, one of two in Hertfordshire that followed the ideas and plans of Ebenezer Howard. After seeing the squalor in which people lived in the cities, particularly London, Howard conceived the idea of provided working class people with an opportunity to live in well spaced out housing with access to the clean air of the countryside and the industrial areas close by. The land for Welwyn Garden City was first acquired in 1919 and the building began a year later with the present station completed in 1926. Howard's idea are still perhaps best seen here as the railway line also acts as the demarcation line for the two areas of the town: industry to the east; the shopping and commercial areas to the west; and the residential areas, with extensive planting and many open spaces beyond.

Just to the south of the town lies **Mill Green Museum**, in the tiny hamlet of Mill Green. Housed in the workers' cottages for the adjoining watermill, this was, between 1911 and 1973, a private residence. There are two permanent galleries here where local items from Roman times to the present day are on display, including pottery, craft tools, underwear, and school certificates. A further gallery is used for temporary exhibitions.

The adjoining **Mill Green Mill** is a wonderful watermill that has been fully restored to full working order. Standing on the site of one of the four such mills in Hertfordshire that featured in the Domesday Book, Mill Green Mill was originally in the possession of the Bishops of Ely. Reconstructed and altered many times the mill finally ceased to grind corn at the beginning of the 20th century when the Miller, Sidney Christmas Lawrance, emigrated to Australia in 1911. Milling recommenced in 1986, after much careful restoration work by the Mill Green Water Mill Restoration Trust, and now only can it be seen working but freshly ground flour is also on sale.

ST ALBANS   Map 4 ref P18
5 miles E of Hemel Hempstead off the A414

This historic cathedral city, whose skyline is dominated by the magnificent Norman abbey, is a wonderful blend of the old and new. One of the major Roman cities in Britain, the remains of **Verulamium** were only excavated this century - there was already a settlement here before

Julius Caesar's invasion in 54 BC. Attacked and ruined by Boadicae in the 1st
century, the city was rebuilt and today the
remains of the walls, the only Roman
theatre in Britain, and a hyopcaust can
still be seen in **Verulamium Park**. Also
in the park is the **Verulamium Museum**,
where the story of everyday life in a Roman city is told. This is a fascinating
insight into those times and among the
displays are ceramics, mosaic floors, personal possessions, and room recreations.
The cathedral, **St Albans Abbey**, was built
on the site where Alban, the first British
martyr, was beheaded in the 4th century.
Dating from the 11th century and built
from flint and bricks taken from the Roman remains, the cathedral has been
added to and altered in every century
since. Among the many features inside
the cathedral, the medieval paintings, said
to be unique in Britain, are the most interesting. The abbey was designated as a
cathedral in 1887.

Clock Tower, St Albans

Found in the town's central market
place is the **Clock Tower**, the only medieval town belfry in England that was built
between 1403 and 1412. Originally con-
structed as a political statement by the town, it asserted the St Albans' freedom and wealth in
the face of the powerful abbey as the town was allowed to sound its own hours and curfew. The
original 15th century bell, Gabriel, is still in place. Open at weekends and bank holidays, there
are fine views over the town and surrounding countryside from the top. Close to the peaceful
and tranquil Verulamium Park, on the banks of the River Ver, is **Kingsbury Watermill**, a wonderful 16th-century mill that is built on the site of an earlier mill that was mentioned in the
Domesday Book. Beautifully restored, the waterwheel is still turned by the river and visitors
can not only enjoy this idyllic setting but also see the milling machinery in action and a collection of agricultural implements.

Two other museums in the town are very well worth a visit. The **Museum of St Albans**
relates the fascinating history of the town, from Roman times through to the present day.
Among the exhibits on show is the famous Salaman collection of trade and craft tools that is
considered to be the finest in the country. Meanwhile, the **St Albans Organ Museum** is,
obviously, a more select place altogether. Certainly not just for the musically inclined, visitors
can enjoy the stirring sounds of an amazing collection of working mechanical musical instruments which include two theatre organs, musical boxes, and reproducing pianos, all of which
have been lovingly restored.

Just to the north, in the tiny hamlet of **Redbournbury**, lies **Redbournbury Mill**, an 18th-
century watermill that stands on the site of a mill that featured in the Domesday Book. Once
belonging to the abbey at St Albans, the mill was seized by the crown following the Dissolution
of the Monasteries. First coming into private hands in 1652 when it was sold to an ancestor of
the present Earl of Verulam, it stayed in the family until 1931 when it once again became
Crown property. Now back in private hands, this splendid mill, on the banks of the River Ver,
has been restored to its former glory and now in full working order it is powered by a large 1935
Crossley oil engine. Open to the public on Sundays from March to October, and on other days
for special events, the mill also sells its own stoneground flour and bread.

HARPENDEN
MAP 4 REF P17
4 miles N of St Albans on A1081

The whole of the town centre is now a conservation area and, in particular, the High Street is lined with many listed 17th and 18th-century buildings. The **Harpenden Local History Centre** is an ideal place to find out more about this charming old agricultural community and, as well as the small permanent collection there are regularly changing themed exhibitions. Meanwhile the **Harpenden Railway Museum,** a small private collection that was begun in 1963 by a husband and wife, contains several thousand items of railway memorabilia, many of which originate from the county.

SHENLEY
MAP 4 REF P18
4 miles S of St Albans on B5378

A traditional country village with, at its centre, two inns, a pond, the site of a former pound for stray animals, and the village lock-up. One of several in Hertfordshire, this **Lock-up** is a brick built beehive-shaped construction where the village's drunks and petty criminals were locked up overnight before being put before the magistrate the next day. On either side of the door is the warning sign: "Be sober, do well, fear not, be vigilant."

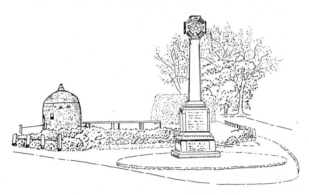

Lock-up and War Memorial, Shenley

Just north of the village lies the impressive **Salisbury Hall,** surrounded by a moat, that was built by the Treasurer of Henry VIII and modernised in the 17th century. A prototype of the de Havilland Mosquito aircraft was built here in secret.

CHISWELL GREEN
MAP 4 REF P18
3 miles SW of St Albans on A414

This village is home to probably one of the biggest attractions in Hertfordshire, the **Gardens of the Rose,** a 20 acre site run as a charitable trust that contains one of the most important rose collections in the world. It is not necessary to be a horticultural enthusiast to appreciate the sheer natural beauty of beautiful displays such as The President's Walk or The Queen Mother Rose Garden, named after the Garden's patron, which contains some of the oldest varieties of rose. With the model gardens, the miniature roses, and the breathtaking Pergola, it would be impossible to list the endless beauty of this place which really has to be visited to be appreciated.

WARE
MAP 4 REF Q17
10 miles E of Hatfield off the A10

Situated at the point where Ermine Street crosses the River Lea, Ware was the scene of a famous encounter between King Alfred and the Danes in 895 and, during the Middle Ages, it became a trading rival to Hertford. The construction of a viaduct in the 1970s, to carry the A10 across the valley, has removed much of the traffic from the town and, despite development over the years,

Ware still retains many of its original buildings. Behind the east end of the High Street, there is access to Blue Coat Yard where, on the right, stands **Place House**, possibly one of Ware's two Domesday manor houses, which was rebuilt during the 13th century as a splendid aisled hall and in the 1680s was purchased by the governors of Christ's Hospital for use as a school for boys being fostered in Ware. Most of this building still remains and on the opposite side of the yard stand the cottages which were built in 1698 and provided accommodation for a foster mother and up to 14 boys!

The High Street crosses the River Lea at Bridgefoot, and here can still be seen some unique 18th-century gazebos, many of which has been restored to their former glory. The riverside path leads on into an attractive public garden behind what was once a Franciscan **Priory**, of which only a few traces remain. Founded in 1338 as a friary, the priory became a private house in 1568 and remained so until earlier this century. In 1920, the owner, Mrs Page-Croft, gave the house and gardens to the town and, fully restored in 1994, the building is surrounded by seven acres of parkland.

No trip to Ware would be complete with out a visit to **Scott's Grotto**, built by the poet John Scott in the late 18th century. The son of a wealthy Quaker family, Scott devised this elaborate series of passageways and artificial caves during the 1760s and they are decorated with flints, minerals, and shells. A popular garden feature that was fashionable during the 18th century, Scott's Grotto is one of the finest examples in England. Finally, the fascinating history of Ware and its major role in the malting industry is explained at **Ware Museum**, which is found at Priory Lodge.

HERTFORD
MAP 4 REF Q17
2 miles SW of Ware on A414

Dating back to Saxon times, the town was founded at a ford across the River Lea, the then boundary between Saxon and Viking England. A once important waterway linking Hertford with London, the River Lea, which became the Lea Navigation at Hertford, was used to transport flour and grain but today its traffic is leisure cruises. The **Hertford Nature Walk** is situated in the meadows between the Rivers Lea and Beane, and takes in the canal basin, known by the interesting name of The Folly. With the growth of Hertford restricted by surrounding cornfields until the mid 19th century, expansion was upwards rather than outwards, with extra storeys added to the building which has created the town's familiar uneven skyline. Hertford is very much a mix of the old and new. Among the interesting buildings is the particularly beautiful Norman **Church of St Leonard, Bengeo** and the **Quaker meeting house**. Said to be the oldest purpose built meeting house in the world that has been in constant use as a place of worship, the building dates from 1669 and stands behind a walled courtyard. The meeting house has one further claim to fame in that is has a unique four-tiered platform for the ministers that is screened from the entrance.

Hertford Castle

Found in a 17th-century town house, that is complemented by a reconstructed Jacobean garden, is the **Hertford Museum**. The collections here were initially started in the 1890s, and they cover a wide variety of subjects that relate to the town and surrounding area. Unfortunately little remains of the original **Hertford Castle** that was constructed by King Alfred's son Prince Edward to protect London from the Danes. However, the 15th-century gatehouse is still standing and, now modernized, it is used as administrative offices for the borough council. The site of the castle is now a public park and evidence of the castle's original motte and bailey can still be seen in the lie of the land. There is also a short length of the massive Norman flint wall, complete with a 14th-century postern gate, preserved in the park. To the south of the town lies **Cole Green Way**, a delightful nature trail that follows the route of the now disused Hertford and Welwyn Junction Railway. Passing through attractive meadowland, the trail runs from Hertford to Cole Green, where the former station provides a pleasant picnic spot.

MUCH HADHAM   Map 5 ref Q17
3 miles W of Bishop's Stortford on B1004

This large unspoilt village, which still retains many old timber framed houses and cottages, the oldest of which dates back to the 15th century, became the home of Henry Moore. Following bomb damage to his London studio in 1941, the famous sculptor moved to the peace and tranquillity of the village and he remained here for many years. The **Forge Museum and Victorian Cottage Garden** not only tells the story of the work of the blacksmith over the years but is also home to a delightful cottage garden. As well as displaying and growing plants that would have been familiar to a 19th-century country gardener, the garden houses an unusual 19th-century bee shelter.

HITCHIN   Map 7 ref P17
8 miles NE of Luton on the A505

Situated on the banks of the River Hiz, this old town was, during medieval times, a vast market area where straw was purchased for the local cottage industry of straw plaiting and where the completed plaits were sold. As the trade in straw declined so the market at Hitchin reduced in size but there is still a small market place today, west of the parish church. However, many of the town's older buildings have survived, if now surrounded by newer developments. The oldest parts of **St Mary's Church** date from the 12th century though there was a minster church here at the time of the Domesday Survey. The low 12th-century tower is the only part of the original building which survived an earthquake of 1298. Rebuilt in the 14th century, the grandeur of the church reflects the prosperity which Hitchin once enjoyed. Standing on the site of a Gilbertine

St Mary's Church, Hitchin

Priory is **The Biggin**, constructed in the early 17th century. For a while it was a private residence, then a school, before becoming, in 1723, an almshouse for "poore auncient or middle aged women', a function which, in modern times, it still performs today.

Another building worthy of a mention is **The Priory**, which takes in fragments of a Carmelite Priory founded in the 14th century. Built in 1770 by Robert Adams as the private residence of the Radcliffe family, it was extensively renovated in the 1980s after being disused for many years. The Priory is said to be haunted by the ghost of Goring, a Royalist, who was killed in front of his fiancée by Roundheads at nearby High Down House. Supposedly, each year on the anniversary of his death, June 15th, his headless ghost is seen riding to its hiding place in the priory grounds.

Finally, **Hitchin Museum**, home to the county's largest collection of period costumes, is an excellent place to visit. Housed with the **Museum of the Hertfordshire Imperial Yeomanry** - mustered to fight Napoleon's threatened invasion - as well as the numerous displays of local social history, part of the museum includes the **Victorian Chemist Shop** and **Physic Garden**. This recreation of a chemist's shop uses many of the stock and fittings from Perks and Llewellyn who ceased trading as a pharmacy in 1961 and the original cabinets still contain the lavender toiletries for which the firm was world famous. To carry the connection further between the town and pharmacy, the medical pioneer, Lord Lister, had family ties with Hitchin and began his education here. The Physic Garden reflects the historical and modern importance of plants that are a source of medicine.

LETCHWORTH
MAP 7 REF Q17
2 miles NE of Hitchin on A505

This attractive country town is proud to be the first garden city where the ideals of Ebenezer Howard were put into practice. Howard's aim was to create a comfortable and attractive living environment where residential, industrial, and commercial areas of the town would be within easy reach and where the residents would have countryside and clean air virtually on their doorsteps. The site for Letchworth was purchased in 1903 and Barry Parker and Raymond Unwin were appointed architects. The residential cottages were designed and built by different architects for the 1905 Cheap Cottages Exhibition and, with none costing more than £150, they each demonstrated new techniques and styles of building and living accommodation. The Parker and Unwin office is now home to the **First Garden City Heritage Museum**, a unique place which traces the history and development of this special town. Among the many displays are the original plans and drawings of Letchworth. Meanwhile, the **Letchworth Museum and Art Gallery** is home to displays of local natural history and archaeology including finds of late Iron Age and Roman origin that were discovered at Baldock.

ROYSTON
MAP 7 REF Q16
12 miles NE of Stevenage on A10

This light industrial town grew up at the intersection of the Ickneild Way and Ermine street and it is named after the wayside cross erected by Lady Roysia. A favourite hunting base for royalty, **James I's Hunting Lodge** can still be seen though the only original features which remain are the two large chimneys. Discovered in 1742 below the junction of the two ancient thoroughfares is the man-made **Royston Cave**. Bottle-shaped and cut out of the chalk, the cave is 28 feet deep and 17 feet across though the purpose of its construction is unknown. Inside the chamber there are a series of crude carvings on the walls, including St Christopher and the Crucifixion, but the age of the cave and artwork has not been determined.

The **Royston Museum**, in the former Congregational Schoolroom building, houses the Royston and District Local History Society collections which relate to the history of this late medieval town and surrounding area. There is also a substantial collection of late 19th-century ceramics and glass.

KNEBWORTH
Map 7 ref Q17
2 miles S of Stevenage off A602

The town is best known, today, for the open air rock concerts held in the grounds of **Knebworth House**, however, both old and new Knebworth, which are just a mile apart, both pre-date the electic guitar by many years. The home of the Lytton family since 1490, the present magnificent Gothic mansion house was built during the 19th century by the Victorian statesman and novelist, Edward Bulwer-Lytton.

However, fragments of the original Tudor house (built in 1492) remain and these include the Jacobean great hall and the superb panelling in the hall which date from the 17th century. Other members of the Lytton family of note include Constance Lytton, the suffragette and Robert Lytton, Viceroy of India. In deed, there is a fascinating exhibition at the house which brings to life the story of Lord Lytton's viceroyship and the Great Delhi Durbar of 1877. The house has also played host to several famous visitors such as Elizabeth I, Benjamin Disraeli, Sir Winston Churchill, and Charles Dickens, who is said to have taken part in amateur theatrical performances here. A close friend of Sir Edward Lytton, the success of the performances prompted the two gentlemen to embark on the financing of a charity to establish a Guild of Literature and Arts by such amateur theatricals. The aim being to provide housing for poor and aged actors and artists.

The grounds of Knebworth House are also well worth visiting and as well as the beautiful formal gardens laid out by Lutyens there is the wonderful herb garden established by Gertrude Jekyll, a lovely Victorian wilderness area, and acres of grassland that are home to herds of red and sika deer. Children, however, will enjoy the adventure playground where they will find Fort Knebworth, a monorail suspension slide, and a bouncy castle among the amusements.

WELWYN
Map 7 ref Q17
5 miles S of Stevenage on A1(M)

This historic town has grown up along the route of the Great North Road, which became the High Street, but, since the construction of the A1(M) took the route away from the town centre, Welwyn is now relatively traffic-free. During the excavations for the new motorway, the famous **Welwyn Roman Baths** were uncovered. Part of a 3rd-century villa or farm that was occupied for over 150 years, the revealed bath house is preserved in a steel vault within the motorway embankment. On the north side of The Wellington public house stands **Ivy Cottage** which dates back to around 1450 and was, during the 1870s, Miss Applegarth's School. During this time Ann Van Gogh was the French mistress here and stayed at Rose Cottage in Church Street, where her famous artist brother is believed to have visited her.

Welwyn Roman Baths

3 Southwest England

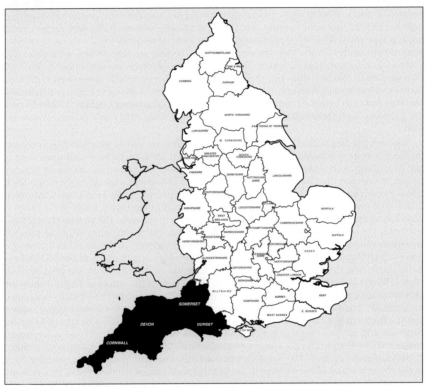

INTRODUCTION

The first choice of a summer holiday for many Britons and those travelling from abroad, even the names of England's southwestern counties of Dorset, Somerset, Devon and Cornwall conjure up images of superb coastal resorts, delightful fishing villages and acres and acres of rural farmland. Within a comparatively small area, East Dorset provides an extraordinary variety of attractions, with wonderful beaches and charming coastal and inland villages. Corfe Castle, set on a high hill above the charming village of the same name, is one of the grandest sights in southwest England and should not be missed. This region of Dorset also boasts two of the most spectacular natural features in the county: the enchanting Lulworth Cove and the soaring limestone arch carved by the sea known as Durdle Door. Largely agricultural, north Dorset represents rural England at its most appealing. It's a peaceful, unspoilt area embracing half a dozen small market towns and many attractive villages. Running along the northwestern border of the district, Blackmoor Vale is still much as Thomas Hardy described it in Tess of the d'Urbervilles. The landscape here is on an intimate scale, tiny fields bordered by ancient hedgerows which have escaped the wholesale uprooting inflicted by agribusiness elsewhere.

Somerset, too, has its share of natural and manmade beauties, as well as attractive big towns such as Bath and Bristol. The wilds of Exmoor and the ranges of spectacular hills such as the Quantocks and Mendips add to this county's allure. In the far northwest corner of the county, and straddling the border with Devon, can be found the smallest national park in the country - Exmoor. With dramatic coastal cliffs, rolling heather moorland and secluded wooded valleys, this was once wild hunting country. Its abundance of prehistoric sites, ancient pack-horse bridges and wild deer and ponies easily makes it one of the more romantic and mysterious parts of the country. As the Mendips are limestone, the hills are full of holes, with caves and potholes and streams that disappear underground. The Mendips are also home to the well known caves at Wookey Hole and spectacular Cheddar Gorge, which carves a path through them as well as lending its name to the cheese. The city of Wells, below the hills, is a charming old town and from here the county's plain stretches out to Glastonbury and on to Taunton near the boundary with Devon. Somerset also has a long coastline with many popular seaside resorts.

Devon's "Heritage Coast" boasts acres of rich farmland watered by the rivers Axe, Otter and Madford, and narrow, winding lanes lead to villages that are as picturesque and interesting as any in England. Steep-sided hills rise towards the coastline where a string of elegant Regency resorts. Home, too, to "The English Riviera" there's a Mediterranean character to the town house gardens which have become a symbol of the area's identity. The South Hams have been called "The frutefullest part of all Devonshire' ; this tract of land lying south of Dartmoor is bounded by the River Dart to the east and the River Erme to the west. The climate is exceptionally mild, the soil fertile and the pastures well watered. The South Hams coastline presents enormous variety with some of the most spectacular cliff scenery in Devon running from the Erme to Start Point. To the north and west, the puckered green hills of North Devon roll away to the coast; here can also be found the wildest stretches of Dartmoor with the great peaks of High Willhays and Yes Tor rising to more than 2,000 feet. In the whole of England there are only three areas which the Council for the Protection of Rural England has officially designated as "tranquil", and one of them is North Devon. This is the heartland of Lorna Doone Country and the homeland of Tarka the Otter who has given his name to a 180-mile trail of footpath, cycle-way and rail link that winds its way around this wonderfully unspoilt region. The captivating scenery, the picturesque villages and the relaxed lifestyle help to explain why so many visitors fall under its spell. The North Devon coast offers some of the grandest coastal scenery in the country. Many of the settlements are genuinely villages, or hamlets, linked by a network of country lanes meandering around rolling hills, while the twin villages of Lynton and Lynmouth exert an irresistible allure with their romantic setting and almost Mediterranean charm. We begin our survey of this unique corner of the county at Ilfracombe.

And so on to Cornwall, westernmost county of England, with the English Channel to the south and the Atlantic Ocean to the north. Separated from the rest of mainland Britain by the River Tamar, which rises just behind the north coast to the northeast of Bude, and forms the boundary with Devon, northeast Cornwall, like the rest, is plentiful in small villages of granite houses and narrow, winding lanes. The natural barrier of the Tamar has, over the centuries, preserved Cornwall's Celtic heritage - still very much in evidence today. The northeastern area of Cornwall is dominated by the bleak expanse of Bodmin Moor, which covers some 80 square miles.

Where the north of Cornwall is dominated by high cliffs, the south is a series of secluded rocky coves and bays. Here, innumerable cloistered and scenic villages and small seaside towns are redolent with the legacy of their long history as fishing, privateering and smuggling centres. The inescapable romance of the landscape, which has inspired writers, artists, natives and visitors for centuries, is complemented by gentle Gulf Stream breezes, assuring mild weather throughout spring, summer and autumn.

Mid-Cornwall boasts historic towns and picturesque coves and villages along the coast; further inland, this region of Cornwall is a treasure trove of quiet bays, lively and popular resorts, and fabulous walks along the renowned Camel Trail, which follows the winding path of the Camel Estuary. Rugged coastlines and stunning gardens are also a feature here. The most southwesterly area of mainland Britain juts out into the Atlantic and, as a result, experiences a mild climate with the help of the warm flowing waters of the Gulf stream. The southern coast, the Cornish Riviera, is characterised by small fishing harbours built in quiet natural coves and the strange village names of Marazion, Mousehole and Lamorna. Perhaps more than in any other region of Cornwall, legends and myths of exotic sea creatures, shipwrecks and smugglers abound. The northern coast is the most rugged, wild and spectacular in the county. Here, bracken-covered and boulder-strewn moorland tumbles dramatically into the sea in a series of sharp headlands and rocky coves. And what of Land's End, westernmost point of mainland Britain? Here, the granite backbone of West Penwith succumbs to the Atlantic in a series of savage cliffs, reefs and sheer-sided islets, encompassing some awe-inspiring cliff scenery. Lying some 28 miles southwest, the Avalon of legend, where King Arthur is said to rest eternal: the Isles of Scilly, a granite archipelago of over 100 islands, of which only five are inhabited.

DORSET

BOURNEMOUTH
30 miles SW of Southampton on the A338

MAP 3 REF L22

In 1998, no less a magazine than Harpers & Queen predicted that Bournemouth was on its way to becoming the "next coolest city on the planet", and another dubbed the town "Britain's Baywatch", a reference to the comely young lifeguards who patrol the six miles of golden beaches. This cosmopolitan town has been voted the greenest and cleanest resort in the UK. (Even the town centre streets are washed and scrubbed every morning). Two hundred years ago, the tiny village of Bourne was a mere satellite of the bustling port of Poole a few miles to the west. The empty coastline was ideal for smugglers, and Revenue men were posted to patrol the area. One of them, Louis Tregonwell, was enchanted by Bourne's glorious setting at the head of three deep valleys, or chines. He and his wife bought land here, built themselves a house and planted the valleys with the pines that give the present-day town its distinctive appearance. Throughout Victorian times, Bournemouth, as it became known, grew steadily and the prosperous new residents beautified their adopted town with wide boulevards, grand parks and public buildings, creating a Garden City by the Sea.

They also built a splendid **Pier** (1855) and, around the same time, **St Peter's Church** which is much visited for its superb carved alabaster by Thomas Earp, and tomb in which Mary Shelley, the author of Frankenstein, is buried along with the heart of her poet-husband, Percy Bysshe Shelley. The **Casa Magni Shelley Museum**, in Shelley House where the poet's son lived from 1849 to 1889, is the only one in the world devoted entirely to Shelley's life and works. Other museums include the **Russell-Cotes Art Gallery & Museum**, based on the collection of the globe-trotting Sir Merton Russell-Cotes; the **Rothesay Museum** which follows a mainly nautical theme but also has a display of more than 300 vintage typewriters; the **Teddy Bear Museum** in the Expocentre; and, north of the town, the **Aviation Heritage Museum** at Bournemouth International Airport, home to a collection of vintage jet aircraft which are flown on a regular basis.

As you might expect in such a popular resort, every conceivable kind of sport and recreation facility is available: anything from surfboarding to paragliding, from classical, pop and jazz concerts to international golf tournaments. And if you're looking for a novel experience, and a really spectacular aerial view of the town and coastline, **Vistarama**, in the Lower Gardens near the Pier, offers day or night ascents in a tethered balloon which rises up to 650 feet.

POOLE
MAP 3 REF L22
5 miles W of Bournemouth off the A35/A350

Once the largest settlement in Dorset, Poole is now a pleasant, bustling port. Its huge natural harbour, actually a drowned river valley, is the most extensive anchorage in Europe with a history going back well beyond Roman times. A 33-foot long Logboat, hollowed from a giant oak tree and dating back to around 295 BC, has been found off **Brownsea Island**, the largest of several islands dotting the harbour.

The Quay is a great place to relax with a drink and watch people "just messing about in boats". Nearby is the **Waterfront Museum**, which celebrates 2,000 years of maritime heritage, and the internationally famed Poole Pottery which has been producing high-quality pottery for more than 125 years. Here visitors can watch a 12-minute video summarising two millennia of ceramic production, watch the age-old processes under way, and children can "have a go" themselves at this tricky craft. **The Pottery Shop** offers factory-direct prices and special savings on seconds, there are superb displays of the Pottery's distinctively designed creations, and a brasserie and bar overlooking the harbour.

Close by, The Aquarium Complex brings you eyeball to eyeball with sharks, piranhas and crocodiles, although anyone with a horror of rattlesnakes, monster pythons, tarantulas or toads might be well-advised to have a stiff drink before paying a visit. Model train enthusiasts, on the other hand, will be delighted with the 3,000 feet of track of the **Great Scenic Model Railway**. From the Quay there are regular ferries to **Brownsea Island** (National Trust), where there are quiet beaches with safe bathing and visitors can wander through 500 acres of heath and woodland which provide one of the few refuges for Britain's native red squirrel. Here, in 1907, General Robert Baden-Powell carried out an experiment to test his idea of teaching boys from all social classes the scouting skills he had refined during the Boer Wars. Just 20 boys attended that first camp: in its heyday during the 1930s, the world-wide Scouting Movement numbered some 16 million members in more than 120 countries.

CORFE CASTLE
MAP 3 REF L22
10 miles SW of Bournemouth off the A351

One of the grandest sights in the country is the impressive ruin of **Corfe Castle** (National Trust), standing high on a hill and dominating the attractive grey stone village below. Once the most impregnable fortress in the land, Corfe dates back to the days of William the Conqueror, with later additions by King John and Edward I. The dastardly John threw 22 French knights into the castle dungeons and left them to starve to death. Later, Edward II was imprisoned here before being sent to Berkeley Castle and his horrible murder. Corfe remained important right up until the days of the Civil War, when it successfully withstood two sieges before it fell into Parliamentary hands through treachery. A month later, Parliament ordered the castle to be "slighted" - rendered militarily useless. Although Corfe now stands in splendid ruin,

Corfe Castle and Swanage Railway

you can see a smaller, intact version at the **Model Village** in West Street. This superbly accurate replica is built from the same Purbeck stone as the real thing and the details of the miniature medieval folk going about their daily business are wonderful. Surrounded by lovely gardens, this intriguing display is well worth a visit.

WAREHAM
Map 3 ref L22

8 miles SW of Bournemouth off the A351/A352/A35

Situated between the rivers Frome and Piddle, Wareham is an enchanting little town lying within the earthworks of a 10th century encircling wall. Standing close to an inlet of Poole Harbour, Wareham was an important port until the River Frome clogged its approaches with silt. Then, in 1726, a devastating fire consumed the town's timber buildings, a disaster which produced the happy result of a rebuilt town centre rich in handsome Georgian stone-built houses.

Wareham's history goes back much further than those days. It was Roman conquerors who laid out its street plan: a stern grid of roads which faithfully follows the points of the compass. Saxons and Normans helped build the **Church of St Mary**, medieval artists covered its walls with devotional paintings of remarkable quality. It was in the grounds surrounding the church that King Edward was buried in 879 AD after his stepmother, Queen Elfrida, contrived his murder at Corfe Castle. Elfrida added insult to injury by having the late King buried outside the churchyard, in unhallowed ground.

WEST HOLME
Map 3 ref L22

12 miles SW of Bournemouth off the A352

Luckford Lake Farm inWest Holme is a charming and relaxing guest house set in a farmhouse amid 43½ acres of a working horse-breeding farm. Partners Sinead Kenney and Tom Smith have been running this guest house since 1991. Built in the early 1930s as a farmhouse, in the surrounding acres Tom and Sinead, both keen horseriders themselves, breed Irish draught and

sports horses for eventing. The spacious and well-proportioned rooms bring to mind a much older farmhouse, and the tasteful decor and antique furnishings throughout ensure a comfortable and relaxing stay. The airy family room overlooks the sprawling fields and horses, and offers one double and two single beds and private bathroom. There is also a large ensuite single room with double bed, and

Luckford Lake Farm, West Holme, Wareham, Dorset BH20 6AQ Tel: 01929 551254

another ensuite double. The guests' lounge is warm and welcoming, the tranquil garden and patio are also for guests' use. The traditional English breakfast, with the addition of a selection of fresh fruits, is home-prepared and hearty; any special requests are also catered for.

WINFRITH NEWBURGH
Map 3 ref K22

17 miles SW of Bournemouth off the A352

This charming little village stands on a minor road that leads to one of the county's best-known beauty spots, **Lulworth Cove**. An almost perfectly circular bay, the Cove is surrounded by towering 440-foot cliffs. Over the centuries, the sea has gnawed away at a weak point in the limestone here, inadvertently creating a breathtakingly beautiful scene. Best to visit out of season, however, as parking places nearby are limited. About a mile to the west of Lulworth Cove stands another remarkable natural feature which has been sculpted by the sea. **Durdle Door** is a magnificent archway carved from the coastal limestone. There' s no road to the coast at this point, but you can reach it easily by following the **South West Coast Path** from Lulworth Cove. Along the way, you will also see another strange outcrop, a forest of tree-stumps which have become fossilised over the centuries.

A couple of miles inland, **Lulworth Castle** (English Heritage) looks enormously impressive from a distance: close-up, you can see how a disastrous fire in 1929 destroyed most of it. Amongst the remains, though, is a curious circular building dating from 1786: the first Roman Catholic church to be established in Britain since Henry VIII' s defiance of the Pope

Durdle Door, Lulworth Bay

in 1534. Sir Thomas Weld was given permission to build this unique church by George III. The King cautiously added the proviso that Sir Thomas' new place of worship should not offend Anglican sensibilities by looking like a church. It doesn't, and that's a great part of its appeal.

TOLPUDDLE
20 miles W of Bournemouth off the A35

MAP 3 REF K22

The small village of Tolpuddle sits quietly just off the main road. In the early 19th century, Tolpuddle was a far sleepier place than it is now. Not the kind of place one would expect to foment a social revolution, but it was here that six ill-paid agricultural labourers helped to lay the foundations of the British Trade Union Movement. In 1833, they formed a "confederation"

in an attempt to have their subsistence wages improved. The full rigour of the landowner-friendly law of the time was immediately invoked. Even the judge in their case was forced to say that it was not for anything they had done, or intended to do, that he passed the sentence of transportation to Australia, but "as an example to others".

The Martyrs Inn in Tolpuddle is run by Steve Riddiford-Smith, who brings over 20 years' experience in Dorset hotels

The Martyrs Inn, 49 Main Road, Tolpuddle, Dorchester, Dorset DT2 7ES Tel: 01305 848249 Fax: 01305 848977

and pubs to managing this pub, which he took over in May of 1999, having lived in the village since 1994. He is friendly and hospitable, and spends part of his days driving a team of traditional Shire horses for the local Hall and Woodhouse brewery. Local people, walkers, cyclists and those interested in the history of the famous Tolpuddle martyrs find a warm welcome here at this large and attractive pub. Built in the 1950s on the site of a much older inn known as The Crown, it of course takes its name from the six farm labourers transported to Australia in 1834 for forming a trade union. After a nationwide outcry they were pardoned in 1836, and returned to England. All but one later migrated to Canada.

The interior boasts a vast amount of memorabilia, photographs and framed articles about the martyrs, whose names are inscribed on the beam over the attractive brick fireplace. Outside, the lovely frontage is festooned with hanging baskets, troughs and outdoor seating. There's a lawned garden to the rear with several handsome trees and shrubs - the perfect place to relax on fine days. Open seven days a week, real ales served here include Hall and Woodhouse, Tanglefoot and Dorset Best, together with a good range of lagers, cider, stout and spirits. The wine list is excellent. The menu offers fresh local produce and meats such as farm-supplied eggs, pork, venison and pheasant. There is also a variety of tempting daily specials. All snacks and meals are home-cooked and home-prepared to order. Booking is advised, particularly for the popular Sunday roast.

The Martyrs' Museum at Tolpuddle tell an inspiring story, but it's depressing to realise that the 7-shilling (35p) weekly payment to those farmworkers were protesting against actually had more buying power in the 1830s than the 1998 legally enforced minimum wage.

Tolpuddle Hall is a gracious and distinctive country house offering superior bed and breakfast accommodation. Owner Paul Wright is a retired headmaster and teacher of English as a second language, son of a Shropshire clergyman, who is a keen gardener and ornithologist. He moved to Tolpuddle in 1993, starting up this thriving concern at the same time. Nearly all the guests are return bookings, attesting to the quality and comfort of this country retreat. Its location makes it a popular base for walkers, horseriders and people in pursuit of the great outdoors; being not far from the coast it also has a fair share of clientele from abroad, including visitors from Australia and Canada interested in the history of the Tolpuddle Martyrs. Built during the Georgian era with Victorian additions, it is an impressive brickbuilt manor with tall casement windows, elegant and gracious inside and out. Lovingly restored over the past six

Tolpuddle Hall, Main Road, Tolpuddle, Dorchester, Dorset DT2 7EW Tel: 01305 848986

years, it offers four distinctive guest bedrooms, one a large and airy family room. All rooms are very comfortable, combining traditional comforts with modern amenities. They boast open fireplaces, attractive decor and cosy furnishings. Flowering plants from the garden complete the homely ambience. The residents' lounge and dining room are very large and impressive, yet losing none of their comfort or cosiness. Guests are welcome to roam the lush and extensive landscaped garden. The traditional full English breakfast makes use of the freshest local produce in a home-cooked and home-prepared repast that sets guests up for the day. Paul is a conscientious and amiable host, who takes pride in providing all his guests with a memorable and relaxing stay.

CHARLTON MARSHALL
MAP 3 REF L22
15 miles NW of Bournemouth on the A350

Built in 1860, **Poppy Cottage** is a charming little flint-and-brick house with a slate roof and a fenced garden that's a safe haven for children and pets. Trees and bushes provide shade, and patio furniture invites guests to while away the odd hour in the mature garden. There's an inviting home-from-home feel the moment guests staying at this self-catering accommodation go through the porch into a cosy lounge with its traditional furnishings and open fireplace. From the well-equipped kitchen, steep stairs lead up to the two bedrooms, (one double, one single). A Z-bed or bed settee are available for extra accommodation, and a cot can be provided free of charge - children of all ages are welcome. The cottage is situated on the edge of Charlton Marshall, which stands in the beautiful Stour Valley by the A350 on the road from Blandford Forum to Poole. It's part of a small community (Charlton on the Hill) of about a dozen properties and is very rural and peaceful, with no passing traffic. The cottage, which stands up a narrow unmade road, is run by June and John Dunn who made the break from

Poppy Cottage, "Fountains", 19 River Lane, Charlton Marshall, Dorset DT11 9NZ
Tel: 01258 452013

the London area in 1994, having enjoyed the cottage for themselves as a weekend retreat. Walking and fishing are favourite pastimes at this most delightful and relaxing spot.

MORETON
MAP 3 REF K22
20 miles W of Bournemouth off the B3390

Thomas Hardy may be Dorset's most famous author, but in this small village it is another distinguished writer (also a scholar, archaeologist and military hero) who is remembered. In 1935 T.E. Lawrence, "Lawrence of Arabia", left the RAF where he was known simply as Aircraftsman T.E. Shaw and retired to a spartan cottage he had bought ten years earlier. It stands alone on the heath outside Moreton village and here Lawrence lived as a virtual recluse, without cooking facilities and with a sleeping bag as his bed. He was to enjoy this peaceful, if comfortless, retreat for only a few weeks. Lawrence loved speeding along the Dorset lanes on his motor-cycle and one lovely spring day his adventurous driving led to a fatal collision with a young cyclist. The King of Iraq attended the hero's burial in the graveyard at Moreton, and the home Lawrence occupied for such a short time, **Cloud' s Hill** (National Trust), is now open to the public.

BLANDFORD FORUM

MAP 3 REF L21

17 miles NW of Bournemouth on the A350

Blandford Forum, the administrative centre of North Dorset, is beautifully situated along the wooded valley of the River Stour. It's a handsome town, thanks mainly to suffering the trauma of a great fire in 1731. The gracious Georgian buildings erected after that conflagration, most of them designed by local architects John and William Bastard, provide the town with a quite unique and soothing sense of architectural harmony. Three important ancient buildings escaped the fire of 1731: the **Ryves Almshouses** of 1682, the **Corn Exchange**, and the splendid 15th century **Old House in The Close**. The old parish church did not survive the fire, but its 18th century replacement, crowned by an unusual cupola, now dominates the market-place. It's well worth stepping inside the church to see the massive columns of Portland stone, and the elegant pulpit, designed by Sir Christopher Wren, removed here from St Antholin's Church in the City of London.

CASHMOOR

MAP 3 REF L21

10 miles NE of Blandford Forum off the A354

Cashmoor House, built in the 17th to 19th centuries, is an attractively decorated and furnished traditional country house offering bed and breakfast accommodation. Owners Mary and Spencer Jones offer all their guests a warm and friendly welcome. The five ensuite bedrooms are charming and comfortable, with hand-embroidered quilts, pictures and soft furnishings adding to the homely farmhouse ambience and ensuring a very comfortable stay. An ancient wisteria and miles of rolling countryside surrounding the house add to the rural charm. A hearty Aga-cooked breakfast awaits guests every morning in the oak-beamed breakfast room, with open log fire in winter. Ideally situated in the heart of Cranborne

**Cashmoor House, Cashmoor, nr Blandford, Dorset DT11 8DN
Tel: 01725 552339**

Chase, the surrounding area offers a wealth of good walking, bird-watching, touring and cycling opportunities, and the coast, golfing and several National Trust properties are just a short drive away. There are also several good pub and restaurants within walking distance or just a short drive away. Open all year. No credit cards.

SHAFTESBURY

MAP 3 REF L21

12 miles N of Blandford Forum, on the A350/A30

Set on the side of a hill 700ft high, Shaftesbury was officially founded in 880 AD by King Alfred who fortified the town and also built an Abbey of which his daughter was first Prioress. A hundred years later, the King Edward who had been murdered by his step-mother at Corfe

Castle was buried here and the Abbey became a major centre of pilgrimage. Very little of Shaftesbury Abbey remains but the associated Museum contains many interesting artefacts excavated from the site. Shaftesbury is a pleasant town to explore on foot. In fact, you *have* to walk if you want to see its most famous sight, **Gold Hill**, a steep, cobbled street, stepped in places and lined with 18th century cottages. Already well-known for its picturesque setting and grand views across the Vale of Blackmoor, Gold Hill became

Gold Hill, Shaftesbury

even more famous when it was featured in the classic television commercial for Hovis bread. Also located on Gold Hill is the Shaftesbury Local History Museum which vividly evokes the story of this ancient market town.

BUCKLAND NEWTON
Map 3 ref K21

15 miles W of Blandford Forum off the B3143

Buckland Newton is a peaceful village in the heart of Hardy's Dorset, surrounded by rolling hills and many good walks, with the Wessex Ridgeway running close by. It is well situated for exploring the glorious countryside and coastline, with the historic towns of Sherborne and Dorchester both approximately 10 miles away, and the coast only half an hour's drive away. **Holyleas House**, opposite the village cricket pitch, is a gracious and welcoming country house set in half an acre of lovely walled gardens. Dating back to the Victorian period, it is a delightful, spacious family home offering bed and breakfast accommodation. There are three pretty guest rooms: one double, one twin and a single commanding views over unspoilt countryside, all with private or ensuite facilities. The guests' sitting room is relaxed and comfortable, with a blazing log fire in winter and a selec-tion of books and

Holyleas House, Buckland Newton, Dorset DT2 7DP
Tel: 01300 345214 Fax: 01305 264488

other relaxing diversions. The full English breakfast is served in the elegant dining room, and consists of free-range eggs, home-made marmalade and jams or a choice of continental or vegetarian breakfast, with fresh orange juice, fresh or dried fruits, cereals and organic yoghurts. Proprietors Tia and Julian Bunkall are friendly and conscientious hosts.

SHERBORNE
16 miles NW of Blandford Forum off the A352

MAP 3 REF K21

One of the most beautiful towns in England, Sherborne beguiles the visitor with its serene atmosphere of a "Cathedral City", although it is not a city and its lovely **Abbey** no longer enjoys the status of a cathedral. Back in AD 705 though, when it was founded by St Aldhelm, the Abbey was the Mother Cathedral for the whole of southwest England. Of that original

Saxon church only minimal traces remain: most of the present building dates back to the mid-1400s which, by happy chance, was the most glorious period in the history of English ecclesiastical architecture. The intricate tracery of the fan vaulting above the nave of the Abbey looks like the supreme culmination of a long-practised art: in fact, it is one of the earliest examples in England. There is much else to admire in this majestic church: 15th century misericords in the choir stalls which range from the sublime (Christ sitting in majesty on

Sherborne Abbey

a rainbow) to the scandalous, (wives beating their husbands); a wealth of elaborate tombs amongst which is a lofty six-poster from Tudor times, a floridly baroque late-17th century memorial to the 3rd Earl of Bristol, and another embellished with horses' heads in a punning tribute to Sir John Horsey who lies below alongside his son. As well as founding the Abbey, St Aldhelm is also credited with establishing **Sherborne School**, which numbered amongst its earliest pupils the two elder brothers of King Alfred, (and possibly Alfred himself), and in later times the Poet Laureate Cecil Day-Lewis and the writer David Cornwell, better known as John le Carré, author of The Spy Who Came in from the Cold and many other thrillers.

Perhaps the best-known resident of Sherborne, however, remains Sir Walter Raleigh. At a time when he enjoyed the indulgent favour of Elizabeth I he asked for, and was granted, the house and estate of **Sherborne Old Castle** (English Heritage). Sir Walter soon realised that the medieval pile with its starkly basic amenities was quite unsuitable for a courtier of his sophistication and ambition. He built a new castle alongside it, **Sherborne New Castle**, a strange three-storeyed, hexagonal structure which must rate, from the outside, as one of the most badly-

designed, most unlikeable mansions to be erected in an age when other Elizabethan architects were creating some of the loveliest buildings in England. Inside Sir Walter's new castle, it is quite a different story: gracious rooms with elaborately-patterned ceilings, portraits of the man who single-handedly began the

Sherborne Castle

creation of the British Empire, and huge windows which at the time Sir Walter ordered them proclaimed a clear message that its owner had the wealth to pay the enormous cost of glazing such vast expanses. After Sir Walter's execution, the castle was purchased in 1617 by Sir James Digby and it has remained with his descendants ever since. They added exquisite gardens designed by "Capability" Brown and in the late 1800s re-decorated the interior in Jacobean style. Amongst the castle's greatest treasures is the famous painting by Robert Peake depicting Elizabeth I on procession, being carried on a litter and surrounded by a sumptuously dressed retinue. The old cellar of the castle is now a museum housing an eclectic display of items, most gruesome of which is the skull of a Royalist soldier killed in the siege of 1645 with a bullet still lodged in his eye socket. Sherborne New Castle, incidentally, is one of several locations claiming to be the genuine setting for the old story of Sir Walter enjoying a pipe of tobacco and being doused with a bucket of water by a servant who believed his master was on fire.

MILBORNE PORT   MAP 3 REF K21
3 miles NE of Sherborne, on the A30

Surrounded by mature gardens and 3½ acres of grounds, **The Old Vicarage** at Milborne Port is a gracious, listed Victorian house, originally built in 1870. It's now owned by Jörgen Kunath and Anthony Ma, formerly of the highly acclaimed "Noughts & Crosses Restaurant" in West London. At The Old Vicarage they offer bed and breakfast throughout the week, and also special weekend breaks which include an outstanding 4-course dinner on the Friday and Saturday evenings. Served in the (non-smoking) conservatory overlooking the garden Anthony's menus (changed daily) provide a unique blend of traditional and innovative cuisine, making good use of fresh local produce and Dorset specialities such as vinney cheese or air dried Dorset ham. The Old Vicarage is able to offer visitors a choice of accommodation. In the main house, there

The Old Vicarage, Sherborne Road, Milborne Port,
Dorset DT9 5AT Tel: 01963 251117 Fax: 01963 251515

are 3 large en suite bedrooms, all decorated with style and panache, and all enjoying delightful views of open country or the gardens. The Coach House, with its rustic charm has 4 smaller en suite bedrooms with a sun terrace overlooking the garden. All guests are welcome to make themselves at home in the spacious lounge which is tastefully decorated with a wealth of interesting antiques.

BRADFORD ABBAS   MAP 3 REF K21
2 miles SW of Sherborne off the A30

This picturesque village of thatched cottages is famous for the Bradford Abbas fossil bed. Built approximately 400 years ago as a resting place for monks en route from Sherborne to Glastonbury, **Rose & Crown** is a friendly and welcoming public house with a long stonebuilt frontage festooned with hanging baskets and pots. Located alongside the village church, this is a family business run by Mary and Tom Sugrue since 1991. Their son, Philip, is the qualified chef. Large and spacious, the attractive central bar has a thatched canopy. The bar area is very comfortable, with an interesting collection of agricultural tools on the walls. There are two (non-smoking)

dining areas furnished in shiny pine, with low beamed ceilings, photographs of bygone villagers on the walls and a large inglenook fireplace. This lovely country pub offers real ales including Bass, Popes and Hardy Country. All food is home-cooked and prepared by Philip, who creates a menu that includes fresh fish, steaks and a variety of specials at lunch and evening seven days a week. In the garden to the side of the pub can be found a children's area and a skittle alley.

Rose & Crown, Church Road, Bradford Abbas, nr Sherborne, Dorset DT9 6RF Tel/Fax: 01935 474506

DORCHESTER
MAP 3 REF K22
26 miles W of Bournemouth off the A35

One of England's most appealing county towns, Dorchester's known history goes back to AD 74 when the Romans established a settlement called Durnovaria at a respectful distance from the River Frome. At that time the river was much broader than it is now and prone to flooding. The town's Roman origins are clearly displayed in its street plan, in the beautiful tree-lined avenues known as **The Walks** which follow the course of the old Roman walls, at **Maumbury Rings**, an ancient stone circle which the Romans converted into an amphitheatre, and in the well-preserved **Roman Town House** behind County Hall in Colliton Park. As the town's most famous citizen put it, Dorchester "announced old Rome in every street, alley and precinct. It looked Roman, bespoke the art of Rome, concealed dead men of Rome". Thomas Hardy was in fact describing "Casterbridge" in his novel The Mayor of Casterbridge, but his fictional town is immediately recognisable as Dorchester. One place he describes in great detail is **Mayor Trenchard's House**, easily identified as what is now Barclays Bank in South Street which bears a plaque to that effect. Hardy made his home in Dorchester in 1883 and two years later moved in to Max Gate (National Trust) on the outskirts of the town, a strikingly unlovely "two up and two down" Victorian villa designed by Hardy himself and built by his brother at a total cost of £450. Here he would entertain a roll-call of great names - Robert Louis Stevenson, G.B. Shaw, Rudyard Kipling and H.G. Wells among many others - to tea at 4 o' clock.

For many visitors, the most accessible introduction to the town and the county will be found at the excellent **Dorset County Museum** in High Street West. Designated Best Social History Museum in the 1998 Museum of the Year Awards, the museum houses a comprehensive range of exhibits spanning the centuries, from a Roman sword to a 19th century cheese press, from dinosaur footprints to a stuffed Great Bustard which used to roam the chalk uplands of north Dorset but has been extinct in this country since 1810. Founded in 1846, the museum moved to its present site in 1883, into purpose-built galleries with lofty arches of fine cast ironwork inspired by the Great Exhibition of 1851 at the Crystal Palace. The building was designed by G. R. Crickmay, the architect for whom Thomas Hardy worked in 1870, and the great poet and novelist is celebrated in a major exhibit which includes a fascinating reconstruction of his study at Max Gate, his Dorchester home. The room includes the original furnishings, books, pictures and fireplace. In the right-hand corner are his musical instruments, and the very pens with which he wrote Tess of the d'Urbervilles, Jude the Obscure, and his epic poem, the Dynasts are also here. More of his possessions are displayed in the Gallery outside - furniture, his watch, music books, and some of his notebooks. Also honoured in the Writers Gallery is William Barnes, the Dorset dialect poet, scholar and priest, who was also the first secretary of the Dorset Natural History and Archaeological Society which owns and runs the museum. Other galleries display the rich and varied environment of Dorset in the past and present. There's a fossil tree, around 135 million years old, from Portland, skeletons of Iron Age warriors from Maiden Castle cemetery, part of a Roman mosaic from Dorchester, a 12th century ivory carving of a King found near Milborne St Andrew, a 19th century Dorset bow waggon, and much, much more. The museum also stages regularly changing temporary exhibitions on topics as varied as whales to sculpture, Dorset in wartime to abstract art.

Just outside the museum stands the Statue of William Barnes and, at the junction of High Street West and The Grove, is the Statue of Thomas Hardy. Opposite the Museum, the Antelope Hotel and the 17th century half-timbered building beside it (now a tea-room) were where Judge Jeffreys (1648-89)

The Dorset County Museum

tried 340 Dorset men for their part in Monmouth's Rebellion of 1685. As a result of this "Bloody Assize", 74 men suffered death by being hanged, drawn and quartered, and a further 175 were transported for life. Jeffreys' ferociousness has been attributed to the agony he suffered from gallstones for which doctors of the time could provide no relief. Ironically, when his patron James II was deposed, Jeffreys himself ended up in the Tower of London where he died. A century and a half after the "Bloody Assizes", another infamous trial took place in the Old Crown Court and Cells nearby. Here, 6 farm labourers who later became known as the Tolpuddle Martyrs were condemned to transportation for their part in organising a "Friendly Society" - the first agricultural trade union. The **Court and Cells** are now open to the public where they are invited to "stand in the dock and sit in the dimly-lit cells ... and experience four centuries of gruesome crime and punishment". Also in High Street West is the **Tutankhamun Exhibition**, an impressive reconstruction of the young Pharaoh's tomb and treasures, including his famous golden mask, with "sight, sound and smell combining to re-create the world's greatest discovery of ancient treasure". Close by, at the **Teddy Bear House**, visitors join Mr Edward Bear and his family of human-size bears as they relax around the house or busy themselves making teddies in the **Old Dorset Teddy Bear Factory**. Hundreds of the cuddly creatures are on sale in the exhibition's period shop. The **Dinosaur Museum** was declared Dorset's Best Family Attraction in 1997. Actual fossils, skeletons and life-size reconstructions combine with audio-visual and hands-on displays to inform and entertain. Somewhat surprisingly, this is the only museum in Britain dedicated exclusively to these fascinating creatures. The museum is open daily throughout the year. Also well worth a visit is **The Keep Military Museum** housed in an interesting, renovated Grade II listed building. Audio technology and interactive computerised displays tell the remarkable story of those who have served in the regiments of Dorset and Devon. An additional bonus is the spectacular view from the battlements across the town and surrounding countryside.

There can be few churches in the country with such a bizarre history as that of **Our Lady, Queen of Martyrs & St Michael**. It was first erected in Wareham, in 1888, by a Roman Catholic sect who called themselves the Passionists, a name derived from their obsession with Christ's passion and death. When they found that few people in Wareham shared their fixation, they had the church moved in 1907, stone by stone to Dorchester where it was re-assembled and then served the Catholic community for almost 70 years. By the mid-1970s the transplanted church had become too small for its burgeoning congregation. The Passionists moved out, ironically taking over an Anglican church whose communicants had become too few to sustain it. A decade later, their abandoned church was acquired by an organisation called World Heritage which has transformed its interior into a reconstruction of the tomb of Tutankhamun.With the help of a running commentary, visitors can follow the footsteps of the archaeologist Howard Carter who discovered the real tomb in 1922, a tour which ends beside a life-size facsimile of the youthful Pharoah's mummy constructed from a genuine skeleton covered with organic-substitute flesh and animal skin.

Just a mile or so northeast of the town, **Kingston Maurward Gardens** are of such historical importance that they are listed on the English Heritage register of Gardens. The 35 acres of classical 18th century parkland and lawns sweep majestically down to the lake from the stately Georgian house. The Edwardian Gardens include a croquet lawn, rose garden, herbaceous borders and a large display of tender perennials, including the National Collection of Penstemons and Salvias. There's also an Animal Park with an interesting collection of unusual breeds, nature trails, plant sales and the Old Coach House Restaurant serving morning coffee, lunches and teas. Of even greater historical significance is **Maiden Castle**, a couple of miles southwest of Dorchester and one of the most impressive prehistoric sites in the country. This vast Iron Age fortification covering nearly 50 acres dates back some 4,000 years. Its steep earth ramparts, between 60 and 90 feet high, are nearly 2 miles round and, together with the inner walls, make a total of 5 miles of defences. The settlement flourished for 2,000 years until AD 44 when its people were defeated by a Roman army under Vespasian. Excavations here in 1937 unearthed a war cemetery containing some 40 bodies, one of which still had a Roman arrowhead embedded in its spine. The Romans occupied the site for some 30 years before moving closer to the River Frome and founding Durnovaria, modern Dorchester. Maiden Castle was never settled again and it is a rather forbidding, treeless place but the extensive views along the Winterborne valley by contrast are delightful.

MINTERNE MAGNA   Map 3 ref K21
8 miles N of Dorchester off the A352

A couple of miles south of this village is the famous **Cerne Abbas Giant** (National Trust), a colossal 180-foot high figure cut into the chalk hillside. He stands brandishing a club, naked and full-frontal, and there can be absolutely no doubt about his gender. An ancient tradition asserts that any woman wishing to become pregnant should sit, or preferably sleep the night, on the Giant's huge erect penis. The age of this extraordinary carving is hotly disputed, but a consensus is emerging that it was originally created by ancient Britons as a fertility symbol and that the Giant's club was added by the Romans. (There are clear similarities between the Giant and the representation of Hercules on a Roman pavement of AD 191, preserved at Sherborne Castle.) As with all hill-carvings, the best view is from a distance, in this case from a layby on the A352. A curious puzzle remains: The Giant's outlines in the chalk need a regular scouring to remove grass and weeds. Should this be neglected, he would soon fade into the hillside. In medieval centuries, such a non-essential task of conservation could only have been authorised by the locally all-powerful Abbots of Cerne. What possible reason did those Christian advocates of chastity have for carefully preserving such a powerful pagan image of virility?

Minterne Magna itself is notable for its parish church, crowded with memorials to Napiers, Churchills and Digbys, the families who once owned the great house here and most of the Minterne valley. The House itself, rebuilt in the Arts & Crafts style around 1900, is not open - but its splendid **Minterne Gardens** are. The gardens are laid out in a horseshoe below the house and landscaped in the 18th century style of Capability Brown. They contain an important collection of Himalayan rhododendrons and azaleas, along with Cherries, Maples and many other fine and rare trees. The gardens are open daily from late March to early November.

CATTISTOCK
MAP 3 REF K22

12 miles NW of Dorchester off the A37

Midway between Dorchester and Yeovil and Dorset, this pretty rural village boasts a traditional shop/post office and village pub, The Fox and Hounds. The surrounding countryside is typical of West Dorset, with rolling hills, wooded valleys and streams. The famous Chesil Bank is about 12 miles' distance; from Eggardon Hill, a 10-minute drive away, there are wonderful views of the White Cliffs.

Michael and Vanessa Roca purchased **Sandhills Cottage** in Cattistock in October of 1998. Michael was previously an independent wine importer. Vanessa is a passionate gardener and is slowly landscaping and planting part of the five acres of grounds and paddocks. Their other interests include classic cars. Dating back to the 1600s, this restful retreat offers bed and breakfast accommodation in three ensuite bedrooms (two twin, one double). All rooms are bright and cheerful, with tasteful furnishings and decor. The blue-and-white breakfast room is cosy and comfortable, just the place to relax and enjoy Vanessa's superb breakfasts. In the grounds adjacent to the main house, the former stable, now called 'Potash Cottage', has been renovated to a very high standard so that it is a light and airy self-catering cottage. There are four bedrooms and two bathrooms; the

Sandhills Cottage, Sandhills, Cattistock, Dorchester, Dorset DT2 0HQ Tel: 01300 321146

kitchen, dining and living area form an open-plan L-shaped room with stable door leading to a private garden with wooden table and chairs. ETB 4 Diamonds.

ABBOTSBURY
MAP 3 REF J22

8 miles SW of Dorchester off the B3157

Surrounded by hills, picturesque Abbotsbury is one of the county's most popular tourist spots and by any standards one of the loveliest villages in England. Its most striking feature as you approach is the 14th century **St Catherine's Chapel**, perched on the hill-top. Only 45 feet by 15 feet, it is solidly built to withstand the Channel gales with walls more than 4 foot thick. St Catherine was believed to be particularly helpful in finding husbands for the unmarried, and in medieval times spinsters would climb the hill to her chapel chanting a dialect jingle which concludes with the words "Arn-a-one's better than Narn-a-one" - anyone is better than never a one. Abbotsbury takes its name from the important **Benedictine Abbey** that once stood here but was comprehensively cannibalised after the Reformation, its stones used to build the attractive cottages that line the village streets. What has survived however is the magnificent **Great Abbey Barn**, 247 feet long and 31 feet wide, which was built in the 1300s to store the Abbey's tithes of wool, grain and other produce. With its thatched roof, stone walls and a mightily impressive entrance it is one of the largest and best-preserved barns in the country. It now houses a Terracotta Warriors exhibition and is surrounded by a Children's Farm where youngsters can feed the animals. The Barn is open all year round.

About a mile south of the village is the famous **Abbotsbury Swannery**, established in Saxon times to provide food for the Abbey during the winter months. More than 600 free-flying swans have made their home here and visitor figures rocket from the end of May to the end of June - the baby swans' hatching season. There's also a children's Ugly Duckling Trail and the oldest known duck decoy still working. Just to the west of the village, **Abbotsbury Sub-Tropical Gardens** enjoy a particularly well-sheltered position and the 20 acres of grounds contain a huge variety of rare and exotic plants and trees. Other attractions include an 18th century walled garden, beautiful lily ponds and a children's play area.

WEYMOUTH
8 miles S of Dorchester off the A354

MAP 3 REF K22

No wonder the good citizens of Weymouth erected a statue of George III to mark the 50th year of his reign in 1810. The troubled king had brought great kudos and prosperity to their little seaside resort by coming here to bathe in the sea water. George had been advised that sea-bathing would help cure his "nervous disorder" so, between 1789 and 1805, he and his royal retinue spent a total of 14 holidays in Weymouth. Fashionable society naturally followed in his wake. The imposing statue is unusual in being painted. Not far away, at the head of King Street, his grand-daughter Victoria's own 50th year as Queen is commemorated by a colourful Jubilee Clock erected in 1887. Nearby, the picturesque **Harbour** is always busy - fishing boats, paddle steamers, pleasure boats, catamarans servicing the Channel Islands and St Malo in France, and if you're lucky you may even see a Tall Ship or two. One of the town's premier tourist venues is **Brewers Quay**, an imaginatively redeveloped Victorian brewery offering an enormous diversity of visitor attractions amidst a labyrinth of paved courtyards and cobbled streets. There are no fewer than 22 different establishments within the complex, ranging from craft shops and restaurants through a fully automated Ten Pin bowling alley to the "Timewalk Journey" which promises visitors that they will "See, Hear and Smell over 600 years of Weymouth's spectacular history."

From Brewers Quay, a path leads through Nothe Gardens to **Nothe Fort**, built between 1860 and 1872 as part of the defences of the new naval base being established on Portland. Ten huge guns face out to sea; two smaller ones are directed inland. The fort's 70 rooms on three levels now house the **Museum of Coastal Defence**, which has many interesting displays illustrating past service life in the fort, history as seen from the Nothe headland, and the part played by the people of Weymouth in the Second World War. Nothe Fort is owned and operated by the Weymouth Civic Society, which also takes care of **Tudor**

Tall Ship, Weymouth

House, just north of Brewers Quay. One of the town's few remaining Tudor buildings, the house originally stood on the edge of an inlet from the harbour and is thought to have been a merchant's house. It's now furnished in the style of an early-17th century middle class home.

ISLE OF PORTLAND
MAP 3 REF K23

3 miles S of Weymouth off the A354

Portland is not really an island at all, but a 4½-mile long peninsula, well known to devotees of shipping forecasts and even more famous for the stone from its quarries. Numerous buildings in London are constructed of Portland stone, among them St. Paul's Cathedral and Buckingham Palace, and the stone was also favoured by sculptors such as Henry Moore. There are good cliff-top walks with grand views of **Chesil Beach**, a vast bank of pebbles worn smooth by the sea which stretches for some 10 miles to Abbotsbury. Inexplicably, the pebbles are graded in size from west to east. Fishermen reckon they can judge whereabouts on the beach they are landing by the size of the pebbles. In the west they are as small as peas; at Portland they have grown to the size of cooking apples! The area of water trapped behind the beach is known as **The Fleet**.

LYME REGIS
MAP 3 REF J22

22 miles W of Dorchester on the A3052

Known as "The Pearl of Dorset", this captivating little town enjoys a setting unrivalled in the county, an area of outstanding natural beauty where the rolling countryside of Dorset plunges to the sea. The town itself is a maze of narrow streets with many charming Georgian and Regency houses, and the picturesque harbour will be familiar to anyone who has seen the film The French Lieutenant's Woman, based on the novel by Lyme resident, John Fowles. The scene of a lone woman standing on the wave-lashed Cobb has become one of the cinema's most enduring images. **The Cobb**, which protects the harbour and the sandy beach with its clear bathing water from south-westerly storms, was first recorded in 1294 but the town itself goes back at least another 500 years to Saxon times when there was a salt works here. A charter granted by Edward I allowed Lyme to add "Regis" to its name but during the Civil War the town was staunchly anti-royalist, routing the forces of Prince Maurice and killing more than 2,000 of them. Some 40 years later, James, Duke of Monmouth, chose Lyme as his landing place to start the ill-fated rebellion that would end with ferocious reprisals being meted out to the insurgents by Judge Jeffreys. Happier days arrived in the 18th century when Lyme became a fashionable resort, famed for its fresh, clean air. Jane Austen and her family visited in 1803 and part of her novel Persuasion is set in the town. A few years later, a 12-year-old girl called Mary Anning was wandering along the shore when she noticed bones protruding from the cliffs. She had discovered the first ichthyosaur to be found in England. Later, as one of the first professional fossil collectors, she also unearthed locally a plesiosaur and a pterodactyl. The 6-mile stretch of coastline on either side of Lyme is world famous for its fossils and some fine specimens of local discoveries can be seen at the **Philpot Museum** in Bridge Street and at **Dinosaurland** in Coombe Street, which also runs guided "fossil walks" along the beach.

Just around the corner from Dinosaurland, in Mill Lane, you'll find one of the town's most interesting buildings. It was in January 1991 that a group of Lyme Regis residents got together in an effort to save the old **Town Mill** from destruction. There has been a mill on the River Lym in the centre of the town for many centuries, but most of the present buildings date back to the mid-17th century when the mill was rebuilt after being burned down during the Civil War siege of Lyme in 1644. Visitors to the Town Mill who enjoy walking will find a delightful riverside walk leading either to the inland village of Uplyme or back through the town to the harbour. The **South West Coast Path** also passes through Lyme: if you follow it eastwards for about 5 miles it will bring you to **Golden Cap**, the highest point on the south coast with spectacular views from every vantage point. Or you can take a pleasant stroll along **Marine Parade**, a traffic-free promenade stretching for about a mile from The Cobb.

WHITCHURCH CANONICORUM

MAP 3 REF J22

3 miles NE of Lyme Regis off the A35

Clinging to the steep hillside above the valley of the River Char, Whitchurch Canonicorum is notable for its enchanting setting and for its **Church of St Candida and Holy Cross**. This noble building with its Norman arches and an imposing tower built around 1400 is remarkable for being one of only two churches in England still possessing a shrine to a Saint. (The other is that of Edward the Confessor in Westminster Abbey). St Candida was a Saxon woman named Wite - the Anglo-Saxon word for White, which in Latin is Candida. She lived as a hermit but was murdered by a Viking raiding party in AD 831. During the Middle Ages a major cult grew up around her memory. A large shrine was built of golden Purbeck stone, its lower level pierced by three large ovals into which the sick and maimed thrust their limbs, their head or even their whole body, in the hope of being cured. The cult of St Wite thrived until the Reformation when all such "monuments of feigned miracles" were swept away. That might have been the end of the story of St Wite but during the winter of 1899-1900 the foundations of the church settled and cracked open a 13th century tomb chest. Inside was a lead casket with a Latin inscription stating that "Here rest the relics of St Wite," and inside the casket the bones of a small woman about 40 years old. The shrine still attracts pilgrims today, the donations they leave in the openings beneath the tomb now being devoted to causes which aid health and healing.

BRIDPORT

MAP 3 REF J22

9 miles E of Lyme Regis off the A35

With its broad streets, (inherited from the days when they were used for making ropes), Bridport is an appealing little town surrounded by green hills and with a goodly number of 17th and 18th century buildings. Most notable amongst these are the medieval **Prior's House**, the stately Georgian **Town Hall**, and the pleasing collection of 17th century houses in the street running south from the Town Hall. If you visit the town on a Wednesday or Saturday you'll find its three main streets chock-a-block with dozens of stalls participating in the regular **Street Market**. The Town Council actively encourages local people who produce goods at home and not as part of their regular livelihood to join in. So there's an extraordinary range of artefacts on offer, anything from silk flowers to socks, fossils to fishing tackle. Another popular attraction is **Palmers Brewery** in West Bay Road. Established in 1794, part of the brewery is still thatched. During the season, visitors are welcomed on Tuesdays and Wednesdays for a tour of the historic brewery, the charge for which includes a commemorative Certificate and also a glass or two of beer. (More details on 01308 427500).

    Bridport Museum is good on local history and family records and also has an interesting collection of dolls. You can also learn about two distinguished visitors to the town. One was Joan of Navarre, who landed at Bridport in 1403 on her way to marry Henry IV; the other, Charles II, who arrived in the town after his defeat at the Battle of Worcester. He was fleeing to France, pretending to be the groom in a runaway marriage. As he attended to his horses in the yard of an inn, an ostler approached him saying "Surely I know you, friend?" The quick-thinking king-to-be asked where the ostler had been working before. When he replied "In Exeter", Charles responded "Aye, that is where we must have met,"excused himself and made a speedy departure from the town. If the ostler's memory for faces had been better, he could have claimed the £1,000 bounty for Charles' capture, and subsequent English history would have followed a very different course.

EYPE

MAP 3 REF J22

8 miles E of Lyme Regis off the A35

This charming village just a mile from Bridport is home to an abundance of wildlife, including foxes and badgers, and is a truly peaceful retreat. Built at the turn of the century as two villas and converted to a hotel in the 1930s, **Eype's Mouth Country Hotel** was fashioned into a

French-style hotel by a former owner. It is spacious, airy and welcoming. To the front there is a large patio area commanding views of the sea. It is secluded yet just a five-minute walk from the beach. The hotel has 18 ensuite rooms, equipped with all modern facilities, two rooms having four-poster beds, and others offering views to the sea and the rolling Dorset hills. Adjoining the patio there is the 'Smugglers' Bar', intimate and heavily beamed, with a wonderful old-fashioned ambience. Real ales on tap come from the

Eype's Mouth Country Hotel, Eype, nr Bridport, Dorset DT6 6AL Tel: 01308 423300 Fax: 01308 420033 e-mail: Eypehotel@aol.com

local Palmers Brewery in Bridport. Bar snacks are served lunchtime and evening. The restaurant boasts a menu offering fresh local fish specialities and a range of classic dishes, all home-cooked and home-prepared. The restaurant is open seven days a week for lunch and evening meals. Hotel open all year round.

BEAMINSTER   MAP 3 REF J22
14 miles NE of Lyme Regis off the A3066

In Hardy's novel, when Tess Durbeyville arrives in Beaminster ("Emminster" in the novel), she finds a delightful little market town. Outwardly, nothing much has changed: the 17th century almshouse, the majestic church tower in gold-tinted Hamstone, and the charming **Market Square** with its stone roofed market cross are all much the same as they were then. What have disappeared are the many small industries that thrived in those days - rope and sailcloth, embroidered buttons, shoes, wrought ironwork and clockmaking were just some of the artefacts produced here. Visitors to Beaminster's imposing 15th century church tend to be overwhelmed by the grandiose, over-lifesize sculptures of the Strode family, who lived at Parnham House, a gem of Tudor architecture about a mile south of the town. The splendidly restored manor house has extensive gardens where visitors can picnic and play croquet. There's also a tea room and craft shop. About as far west as you can get in Dorset, **Forde Abbey** enjoys a lovely setting beside the River Axe. Founded as a Cistercian monastery more than 800 years ago, it is now the home of the Roper family. The Abbey church has gone but the monks of those days would still recognise the chapter house, dormitories, kitchen and refectories. The Upper Refectory is particularly striking with its fine timbered roof and carved panelling. The gardens, extending to 30 acres with origins in the early 1700s, are landscaped around this enchanting house - a fitting place to bring this tour of the county to an end.

Beaminster Market Cross

SOMERSET

BATH
MAP 3 REF K19

12 miles SE of Bristol on the A4

Bath is one of the most remarkable cities in Britain. It is a glorious concoction of architectural set-pieces which have been constructed around the only hot thermal springs in the country since the time of the ancient Romans. Best explored on foot, magnificent examples of the city's Roman, medieval or Georgian heritage lie around almost every corner. Since time immemorial, over half a million gallons of water a day at a constant temperature of 46 degrees Celcius have bubbled to the surface at this point. The ancient Celts believed the mysterious steaming spring was the domain of the goddess Sulis, and it is likely they were aware of its healing properties long before the arrival of the Roman legions in 43 AD. However, the Romans were the first to enclose the spring, and within a few short years of their arrival they had created the spectacular health resort known as Aquae Sulis, a name coined as a gesture to the Celtic population they now controlled. Indeed, they even dedicated the temple adjoining the baths to the joint goddess, Sulis-Minerva, to embody both the Celtic and Roman ideologies. By the 3rd century, Bath had become so renowned that high-ranking soldiers and officials were coming here from all over the Roman world. Public buildings, such as a temple and forum, were added, and the whole city enclosed behind a stone wall. However, by the year 410 the Empire was crumbling and the last remaining legions were forced to return home. Aquae Sulis was abandoned, and within a few decades the drainage systems failed and the marsh returned.

Bath Abbey and Roman Baths

With the possible exception of Hadrian's Wall, the Roman remains at Bath are the most outstanding to survive in Britain. The main reason for their exceptional state of preservation is that for over a thousand years they remained buried under several feet of dense alluvial mud. Ironically, the ancient baths remained hidden throughout the entire period of Bath's 18th century renaissance as a spa town and were only rediscovered in the late 19th century; indeed, they were not fully excavated until the 1920s. The restored remains which can be seen today are centred around the **Great Bath**, a rectangular lead-lined pool which is surrounded by steps and the truncated remains of a colonnaded quadrangle. Five separate phases were constructed over a 200-year period which began in the middle of the 1st century. The result is a superb complex of buildings incorporating swimming pools, mineral baths and a series of chambers heated by underfloor air ducts which would have functioned as saunas and Turkish baths. Open daily throughout the year, a visit to the Roman Baths includes admission to a fascinating museum of Roman coins, artefacts, jewellery and, perhaps the finest exhibit of all, a bronze head of the goddess Sulis Minerva.

The population of Bath fell away during the Dark Ages, and it wasn't until the 8th century that the Saxons founded a nunnery here which put the settlement back on the map. This was later elevated to monastic status when King Edgar of Wessex chose to be crowned "King of all England" here in 973. The present great church was begun in 1499 after its Norman predecessor had been destroyed by fire; however in 1539, Henry VIII's Dissolution of the Monasteries brought work to a halt. The church then had to remain without a roof for three quarters of a century, and indeed, the structure wasn't fully completed until 1901. With its soaring buttresses, spiky ramparts and vast windows of clear glass, **Bath Abbey** is now considered the ultimate example of English Perpendicular church architecture. Its delicate stone fan-vaulting hangs 70 feet above the nave, and its curious castellated tower is rectangular rather than square because it was built using the pillar-foundations of the earlier building. Inside, there is an unusual 18th century portable oak font and a surprising number of monuments and tablets, more than in any church outside Westminster Abbey. Some were erected in memory of the many wealthy invalids who flocked here in the 18th and early 19th centuries and were never well enough to return home.One tablet in the abbey stands as a memorial to Richard "Beau" Nash, a legendary Bath figure who was one of the three people generally considered responsible for turning Bath into a fashionable Georgian spa town. Prior to Nash's arrival in the first decade of the 1700s, Bath had been a squalid community of around 2,000 inhabitants whose former prosperity as a medieval wool town had all but disappeared. Historical accounts tell of farm animals roaming freely within the confines of the old Roman town, and sewage running down the streets. Notwithstanding, small numbers of the rich and aristocratic continued to be attracted to Bath for its curative hot spring, and in the mid 17th century the authorities finally took action to improve sanitary conditions, an initiative which was rewarded in 1702 by a visit from Queen Anne.

A good place to begin a walk around central Bath is at the **Roman Baths**, whose adjoining **Pump Room** looks much as it did when it was completed in 1796. Now an elegant tearoom, a restorative cup of tea, coffee or spa water can be enjoyed here, often to the accompaniment of live chamber music. Items on show include two sedan chairs, one of which was used as a public taxi by the idle or infirm. The abbey is situated almost adjacent the Pump Room, and a short distance away, the magnificent **Pulteney Bridge** spans the River Avon. The only example of the work of Robert Adam in Bath, it was inspired by Florence's Ponte Vecchio and is the only bridge in Britain to incorporate a terrace of buildings. The nearby weir, with its graceful curving steps, is a superb example of Georgian refinement.

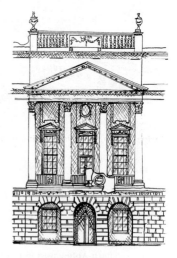

Set in beautiful gardens at the end of Great Pulteney Street only 10 minutes' walk from Pulteney Bridge and the centre of the city, the **Holburne Museum** is a jewel in Bath City's crown and one of the finest examples of its elegant Georgian architecture. Originally a spa hotel, the building was adapted for the purposes of a museum by Sir Reginald Blomfield early in the 20th century to house the nucleus of the decorative and fine art collections of Sir William Holburne (1793-1874). On show can be seen superb examples of English and continental silver and porcelain, Italian maiolica and bronzes, together with glass, furniture, miniatures and paintings by such leading English and continental old masters as Gainsborough, Turner, Ramsay, Raeburn and Zoffany. The museum's collection has been added to over the years, with the emphasis remaining on work from the 17th and 18th centuries.

Holburne Museum

The **Crafts Study Centre** was founded at the Holburne Museum in 1977. This unique establishment incorporates an historic archive of reference books, working notes, documents and photographs relating to leading 20th century artist-craftspeople, along with a permanent exhibition of their work. Items on display include woven and printed textiles, furniture, exquisite calligraphy and ceramics by such artist-potters as Bernard Leach, and also an important collection of work on long-term loan from the Crafts Council. The museum organises a lively programme of events throughout the year, including lectures, concerts and special presentations. In addition, it mounts a series of temporary art and craft exhibitions on a variety of themes, including shows of work by leading contemporary artists and craftspeople. There is also an ongoing education programme, with study facilities being made available for individuals and groups by prior appointment, including access to the extensive library of archive material.

Moving to the north of the area once enclosed by Bath's Roman walls, Gay Street leads through Queen Square to **The Circus**, a striking example of neoclassical unity of design which is divided into three evenly-proportioned blocks of 11 houses. The street to the northeast leads to the National Trust-owned **Assembly Rooms**, one of the places polite 18th century society used to congregate to dance, play cards or just be seen. The building was severely damaged during the Second World War, and wasn't reopened until 1963. It is now leased to the Bath and North Somerset Council and incorporates an interesting Museum of Costume. The street leading west from the Circus leads to **Royal Crescent**, a superb architectural set piece which is popularly regarded as the climax of Palladian achievement in this most classical of English

cities. Built between 1767 and 1774 on a site which then overlooked unspoilt countryside, its huge sweep comprises 30 houses, each of which is divided by a giant Ionic half column. No. 1 Royal Crescent has been meticulously restored to its original Georgian splendour by the Bath Preservation Trust and is now designated a World Heritage Building. Although the facades of Bath's Geor-

Royal Crescent, Bath

gian houses were strictly controlled, the internal structure was left to the discretion of their individual owners, many of whom had very different ideas. The result is a fascinating jumble of contrasting masonry, narrow alleys, tradespeople's entrances and eccentric guttering - a half-hidden world which is well worth an inspection. Bath contains an exceptional number of fine art galleries and specialist museums. The **Victoria Art Gallery** near Pulteney Bridge is the city's principal venue for major touring exhibitions. It also has a permanent collection of classical paintings and a smaller gallery displaying work from the area. The **British Folk Art Collection** (formerly the Museum of English Naive Art) in the Paragon is an absorbing anthology of 18th and 19th century paintings which are characterised by their "direct simplicity". On the same site is the **Bath Museum**, a fascinating collection of models, drawings and illustrations which chronicle the city's unique architectural evolution.

The first recorded mailing of a Penny Black postage stamp was made in 1840 at No. 8 Broad Street, now the site of the **Bath Postal Museum**; exhibits include a reconstruction of a Victorian sorting office and a children's activity room. **Sally Lunn's House** in North Parade Passage is thought to be the oldest house in Bath. Its cellar museum contains the kitchen used by the celebrated 17th century cook who is attributed with inventing the Bath bun. The **Bath Indus-**

trial Heritage Centre in Julian Road is a re-creation of an aerated water manufactory which provides an insight into one of the city's traditional industries.

Close to Weston on the northern edge of Bath, the ground rises onto Lansdown, a spur of downland which is the site of one the most remarkable follies in Britain. **Beckford's Tower** was built in the 1820s by the wealthy and eccentric scholar, William Beckford, to house his extensive art collection. Crowned by a lantern based on the Lysicrates monument in Athens, the pavilion and bell tower are a wonderful combination of Tuscan, Roman, Greek and Byzantine influences. Visitors climbing the 156 steps to the belvedere are rewarded with a magnificent view stretching from Wiltshire Downs in one direction to the Black Mountains of Wales in the other. There is also a small museum charting Beckford's extraordinary life in pictures, prints and models.

Another of Bath's follies, **Sham Castle**, was constructed on a hill to the east of the city by the quarry-owner Ralph Allen. Built to be seen from his town house, as its name suggests it is merely a romantic facade which is made even more picturesque by night-time illumination. Later in his career, Allen moved out to **Prior Park**, an ostentatious country mansion on the southeastern edge of Bath which now houses a co-educational school. Designed in classic Palladian style by John Wood the Elder, the house stands within impressive landscaped grounds whose ornamental lakes and superb neoclassical bridge were created under the guidance of "Capability" Brown and the poet Alexander Pope. The garden, which has undergone major restoration, enjoys magnificent views of the city. The National Trust owns 560 acres of countryside and woodland which together form the magnificent **Bath Skyline Walk**. Described in a leaflet obtainable from the National Trust shop in the abbey churchyard, the eight-mile footpath offers some spectacular views of Bath's Georgian outline. The route starts above Bathwick to the east of the city and also takes in an Iron Age field system.

CLAVERTON
MAP 3 REF K19
2 miles E of Bath off the A36

The ostentatious tomb of Ralph Allen, the quarry-owning co-founder of 18th century Bath, lies in the churchyard at Claverton. The church itself is an unremarkable Victorian reconstruction whose most notable feature is a panel of 14th century stained glass in the north transept. Six years before his death in 1764, Allen bought **Claverton Manor**, a 16th century country mansion which was later demolished leaving only a series of overgrown terraces with impressive stonework balustrades. Some of the stone from the ruined house was used to construct the present manor on the hill above the village. The building was designed in elegant neoclassical style by Sir Jeffrey Wyatville, whose work is much in evidence at Windsor Castle, and is set in superb landscaped grounds.

Sir Winston Churchill is reputed to have made his first political speech at Claverton Manor in 1897; however, it is as a **Museum of American History** that the building is now best known. This absorbing museum was founded in 1961 by Americans Dallas Pratt and John Judkyn and is the only es-

American Museum

tablishment of its kind outside the United States. The rooms have been furnished to show the gradual changes in American living styles, from the arrival of the Pilgrim Fathers in 17th century New England to the Philadelphia and New York of the 18th and 19th centuries. The New Orleans room is like a set from Gone With the Wind, and there are scenes from the days of the Mississippi steamboats and the early Spanish colonisers of New Mexico. There is also a large section devoted to the history of the North American Indian and a display dedicated to the religious sect, the Shakers.

The narrow river valley between Bath and Bradford-on-Avon is shared by the A36, the main railway line and the Kennet and Avon Canal. For around two centuries, water has been mechanically transferred to the canal from the River Avon at the impressive **Claverton Pumping Station**. A mile further south, the canal makes a spectacular diversion over both river and railway by way of the **Dundas Aqueduct**, an impressive Bath-stone structure which is finished in characteristic neoclassical style. Designed by the great engineer, John Rennie, the **Kennet and Avon Canal** was constructed between 1794 and 1810 to link the Thames with the Bristol Avon via Newbury and Devizes. A costly and ambitious project, much of its 75 mile length had to be cut through permeable rock which had to be lined with clay. The enterprise nevertheless succeeded in paying its investors a small dividend before the Great Western Railway arrived in 1841 to poach all its business.

In recent years, the Kennet and Avon Canal Trust has done much to restore this historic waterway, and it is now fully navigable between Bath and Caen Hill near Devizes. For those interested in joining a guided canal trip, narrowboats set out at regular intervals from Sydney Wharf and Bath's Top Lock. Alternatively, small electrically-powered self-drive boats are available from a variety of places including the Dundas Aqueduct.

BRISTOL
MAP 3 REF K19
115 miles W of London on the A4

With a population of over 400,000 and a history dating back to the time of the Saxons, Bristol is a diverse regional capital which takes time to get to know. A good place for the visitor to begin is **Brandon Hill**, an area of open ground near the city centre which can be found to the west of the Park Street shopping area. Here, visitors can climb to the top of the **Cabot Tower**, a 100-foot monument standing near the site of a chapel dedicated to St Brendan the Navigator which was erected in memory of another maritime pioneer, John Cabot. The first non-Scandinavian European to set foot on Newfoundland, Cabot's expedition of 1497 was financed by local merchants. For centuries Bristol was a major commercial seaport, and the magnificent view from the top of the tower reveals a complex series of docks and wharves along a curving stretch of water known as the **Floating Harbour**. This semi-artificial waterway was created

when the course of the River Avon was diverted to the south early in the 19th century. A massive feat of civil engineering, the work took over five years to complete and was largely carried out by Napoleonic prisoners using only picks and shovels. Today, the main docks have moved downstream to Avonmouth and the Floating Harbour has become home to a wide assortment of recreational and smaller working craft.

Bristol was founded during Saxon times at the point

Bristol Harbour

where the curving River Frome joined the River Avon. This strategically-important bridging point at the head of the Avon gorge soon became a major port and market centre, and by the early 11th century, the town had its own mint and was trading with other ports throughout western England, Wales and Ireland. In 1067, the Normans began to build a massive stone keep on a site between the present-day Floating Harbour and Newgate, a place which is still known as **Castle Park** despite the almost total demolition of the structure at the end of the English Civil War. The heart of the old city lies to the west of here, around the point where Corn, Broad, Wine and High Streets converge.

Half a mile further west, **Bristol Cathedral** stands at the foot of Park Street on College Green. Founded in the 12th century as the great church of an Augustinian abbey, several original Norman features remain, including the southeast transept walls, chapter house, gatehouse and east side of the abbey cloisters. Elsewhere there is some good 14th century stained glass and a series of striking roof bosses in the north transept. Following the Dissolution of the Monasteries in 1539, Henry VIII took the unusual step of elevating the church to the status of cathedral, and soon after, the richly-carved choir stalls were added. This was followed over a century later by Grinling Gibbons' superbly carved organ case. The structure wasn't fully completed until the 19th century when a new nave was built in sympathetic style to the existing choir. This now contains some exceptional monuments and tombs, along with a pair of unusual candlesticks which were donated in 1712 by the rescuers of Alexander Selkirk, the actual castaway on whom Daniel Defoe's character Robinson Crusoe was modelled.

During the Middle Ages, Bristol expanded enormously as a trading centre and at one time it was second only to London as a seaport. This medieval trade was built on the export of raw wool and woollen cloth from the Mendip and Cotswold hills and the import of wines from Spain and southwest France. The city's first major wharf development was carried out at this time - the diverting of the River Frome from its original course into the wide artificial channel now known as **St Augustine's Reach**. A remarkable achievement for its day, the excavation created over 500 yards of new berthing and was crucial for Bristol's developing economy. The city's increasingly wealthy merchants founded one of the most impressive parish churches in the west of England during this period. Originally set in a suburb to the east of the main channel, the church of St Mary Redcliffe is a wonderful arrangement of pinnacles, flying buttresses and sweeping stained-glass windows. Its soaring 290-foot spire is a 19th century addition to the original 13thcentury tower, and its ornately decorated north porch was built to an unusual hexagonal design which is reputed to have been influenced by the architecture of China. An unusual roof boss in the shape of a circular maze can be seen in the north aisle. A giant replica of this, complete with water channels and raised walkways, can be seen in **Victoria Park**, half a mile away to the south. The sandstone beneath St Mary Redcliffe is riddled with underground passages known as the **Redcliffe Caves**.

A stroll around Bristol city centre reveals an unusual number of interesting historic buildings. Queen Square, to the northwest of Redcliffe Bridge, is lined with handsome early 18th-century buildings, although two sides had to be rebuilt following their destruction in a riot in 1831. The **Theatre Royal** in King Street is the home of the acclaimed Bristol Old Vic theatre company. One of the oldest theatres in the country still in regular use, it was built in the 1760s with a semicircular auditorium, a rare feature for the time. Also in King Street, a striking timber-framed merchant's house of 1669 known as **Llandoger Trow** can be seen at its eastern end. The main **City Museum and Art Gallery** in Queen's Road occupies an imposing building at the top Park Street. Among its many fine exhibits is an exceptional collection of Chinese glass. Also worth seeing are **John Cabot's House** in Deanery Road and the **Trinity Almshouses** in Old Market Street to the east of the city centre. Much of Bristol's waterfront has been redeveloped for recreational use. Two impressive attractions lie across the swing bridge to the south of the Arnolfini Gallery: the **Lifeboat Museum** and **Bristol Industrial Museum**. The latter houses a fascinating record of the achievements of the city's industrial pioneers, including those with such household names as Harvey (wines and sherries), Fry (chocolate), Wills (tobacco) and McAdam (road building). Visitors can find out about Bristol's history as a port, view the aircraft and aero engines made in the city since 1910, and inspect some of the many famous motor vehicles which have borne the Bristol name since Victorian times. During the summer, the museum offers interesting working demonstrations of some of its more spectacular exhibits. These a giant crane, steam railway, printing workshop and a variety of motor vessels.

An excellent museum dedicated to the pioneering Victorian engineer Isambard Kingdom Brunel is located in the Great Train Shed at old Temple Meads station. The nearby **Exploratory** is a hands-on educational facility designed to put fun into everyday science. Situated in Gasferry Road on the southern side of the Floating Harbour, the **Maritime Heritage Centre** is an impressive visitor attraction which is dedicated to the history of Bristol shipbuilding. Brunel was responsible for designing the **Clifton Suspension Bridge**, one of Bristol's most graceful landmarks which spans the Avon gorge a mile and a half to the west of the city centre. Opened five years after his death in 1864, it continues to carry an important route into the city. The bridge is suspended more than 200 feet above the river and offers drivers and pedestrians a magnificent view over the city and surrounding landscape.

Goldney Grotto

The National Trust-owned **Avon Gorge Nature Reserve** on the western side of the bridge offers some delightful walking through Leigh Woods to the summit of an Iron Age hill fort. A former snuff mill on the eastern side has been converted into an observatory whose attractions include a rare working example of a camera obscura. A nearby passage leads to the Giant's Cave, a subterranean chamber which opens onto a ledge high above the Avon.

Modern Clifton is home to **Goldney Grotto**, which dates from the 1730s. A fantastic labyrinth filled with spectacular rock formations, foaming cascades and a marble statue of Neptune, its walls are covered with thousands of seashells and "Bristol diamonds" - fragments of a rare quartz found in nearby Avon Gorge. The renowned **Bristol Zoo Gardens** are located on the northwestern edge of Clifton in Clifton Down.

WESTON-SUPER-MARE
Map 3 ref J19
12 miles SW of Bristol off the A370

Weston-Super-Mare is a popular seaside resort which in recent years has developed as a centre of light industry. The town developed relatively belatedly as a seaside resort. In 1811, it was still a fishing hamlet with only 170 inhabitants; however, within the next 100 years it had grown to become the second largest town in Somerset and it now has a population of well over 50,000. Despite its relatively modern character, the locality has been inhabited since prehistoric times. The wooded promontory at the northern end of Weston Bay was the site of a sizable Iron Age hill settlement known as **Worlebury Camp**. In the 1st century AD, this was reputedly attacked and captured by the ancient Romans with great loss of life, an event confirmed by recent excavations which revealed a number of skeletons showing the effects of sword damage. A pleasant walk from the town now leads up through attractive woodland to the ancient hilltop site from where there is a magnificent view across the mouth of the Severn to Wales. Another spectacular view can be had from the clifftop site of the semi-ruined church at Uphill, a part-Norman structure which is situated at the southern end of Weston Bay, a couple of miles to the south.

Weston's early tourist development took place in the 1830s around the Knightstone, an islet joined to the shore at the northern end of Weston Bay onto which was eventually built a large theatre and swimming baths. Following the arrival of the railway in 1841, the town began its most rapid period of development and in 1867, a pier was built on the headland below Worlebury Camp which connected offshore Birnbeck Island with the mainland. Intended mainly as a berth for steamer traffic, it was found to be slightly off the tourist track and in due course, a more impressive pier was built nearer the town centre which, prior to serious fires in the 1930s and the Second World War, was approximately twice its present length. Now, as then, the Grand Pier stands at the centre of an area crammed with souvenir shops, ice cream parlours, cafes and assorted attractions which are designed to appeal to the holidaymaker. The **Woodspring Museum** in Burlington Street contains a series of fascinating displays on the social and natural history of the area, including the Victorian seaside holiday, royal potteries, early bicycles and period costume. It also incorporates an art gallery which offers a constantly changing programme of exhibitions. Situated adjacent to the museum, Clara's Cottage is a typical Victorian dwelling furnished in the style of 1900.

Woodspring Museum

The narrow coast road to the north of Weston-Super-Mare passes along the beach at Sand Bay before terminating at Middle Hope, a high ridge jutting out into the Severn Channel whose western end, Sand Point, provides another fine viewpoint. The ridge overlooks a lonely salt marsh which is home to a wide variety of wading birds, including shelduck and oystercatchers. To the east, a path leads down to the Landmark Trust-owned **Woodspring Priory**, a surprisingly-intact medieval monastery which was founded around 1220 by a grandson of one of Thomas à Becket's murderers, William de Courtenay. The priory fell into disrepair following the Dissolution of the Monasteries of 1539 and its buildings were given over to agricultural use for many years. However, the church, tower, refectory and tithe barn have all survived, and the outline of the cloister can also be made out.

CLEVEDON   Map 3 ref J19
8 miles W of Bristol off the B3130

The impressive National Trust-owned **Clevedon Court** lies near junction 20 on the M5, five miles to the northeast of Woodspring Priory. One of the earliest surviving country houses in Britain, the main part dates from the early 14th century, and the tower and great hall are even older, dating from the 12th and 13th centuries respectively. Once partly fortified, this imposing manor house has been the home of the Elton family since 1709. Long-standing patrons of the arts, during the early 19th century they invited some of the finest poets and writers of their day to Clevedon Court, including Coleridge, Thackeray and Tennyson. Clevedon Court is set within a delightful terraced garden which is known for its rare plants and shrubs. An attractive footpath leads up from here through nearby Clevedon Court Woods onto a ridge overlooking the Gordano valley.

Clevedon Pier is a remarkably slim and elegant structure which was built in the 1860s from iron rails which were intended for Brunel's ill-considered South Wales railway. When part of the pier collapsed in the 1970s, its long-term future was placed in jeopardy. During the 1980s, however, a major programme of restoration was begun which took around 10 years to complete. Now open to the public once more, throughout the summer the pier is used as a landing stage by large pleasure steamers such as the Balmoral and the Waverley, the only surviving seagoing paddle steamers in the world.

Among Clevedon's many fine old buildings is the **Market Hall** of 1869 which was built to provide a place for local market gardeners to sell their produce. The Poet's Walk, a flower-lined footpath said to be popular with Victorian bards, begins at Clevedon promenade and leads up around Church and Wain's hills. The latter is topped by the remains of an Iron Age coastal fort and offers some magnificent views over the Severn estuary, the Levels, and the town itself.

FROME

MAP 3 REF K20

10 miles S of Bath off the A36

Standing beside the river from which it takes its name, the ancient settlement of Frome is the largest centre of population in northeast Somerset. The parish church of St John the Baptist was founded as a Saxon monastic house by St Aldhelm in the 7th century, and by the time of the Norman invasion, Frome was already a sizable market town which extended from the river to the church on the hill above. The Frome valley became an important centre of the wool industry during the late Middle Ages when a series of weirs was constructed to regulate the flow of water to the many water-powered weaving and fulling mills which lined the riverbank. (Fulling was a process which softened and increased the volume of woven cloth by immersing it in water and feeding it through a series of mechanically-driven rollers.) However, the industry largely collapsed in the 18th century when textile production transferred to the industrial North, although one mill, A H Tucker's, continued in production right up until the 1960s.

The prolonged decline of the textile industry meant that little of central Frome was redeveloped during the 19th and early 20th centuries, and as a result, many of its narrow medieval streets and alleyways have survived intact. Some have wonderful names like Pudding Bag Lane and Twattle Alley, and others, such as Gentle Street, the steeply-sloping Catherine Hill, and Cheap Street with its water course running down the centre, are highly impressive in their own right. The bridge over the River Frome incorporates an 18th-century lockup gaol, near to which can be seen the famous Bluecoat School and the restored **Blue House**, an elegant almshouse dating from 1726. Best explored on foot, the centre of Frome is an attractive conservation area which contains an unusual number of interesting shops, cafes and residential buildings. Lively markets continue to be held in the town every Wednesday and Saturday, and for those interested in local history, there is an excellent museum. There is also an interesting arts and crafts complex, the **Black Swan Centre**, situated in Bridge Street.

FARLEIGH HUNGERFORD

MAP 3 REF K20

6 miles NE of Frome off the A3666

The old fortified settlement of Farleigh Hungerford is worth visiting for the impressive remains of **Farleigh Castle** (English Heritage), a medieval fortification which stands on a rise above the River Frome to the northeast of the centre. The structure was built by Sir Thomas Hungerford, the first Speaker of the House of Commons, on the site of an old manor house which he acquired in the late 14th century. According to local lore, Sir Thomas failed to obtain proper permission from the Crown for his fortifications, an oversight which almost led to his downfall. However, the Hungerfords were a powerful family who owned land throughout Wiltshire, and so he was able to pacify the situation and survive the king's displeasure. A century and a half later, another member of the Hungerford family was less successful in avoiding royal disfavour. After having imprisoned his wife in one of the castle towers for four years, he was eventually executed by Henry VII for "treason and unnatural vice". The castle then changed hands in the early 18th century; however, the new owners saw the structure more as a stone quarry than a place to live and proceeded to remove most of its walls to build a new Gothic-style mansion on the opposite side of the village. Nevertheless, an impressive shell of towers and perimeter walls has survived intact, along with the castle **Chapel of St Leonard's**. This contains a striking 15th century mural of St George, some fine stained glass and a number of interesting monuments, including the tomb of Sir Thomas Hungerford himself.

MELLS
MAP 3 REF K20
3 miles NW of Frome off the A362

Mells must be one of the loveliest villages in northeast Somerset. Once the easternmost limit of the lands belonging to the mighty Glastonbury Abbey, Abbot Selwood drew up plans to rebuild the village in the shape of a St Anthony's cross (a cross with four arms of equal length) in the 15th century. Only one, **New Street**, was completed and this architectural gem can be seen to the south of St Andrew's parish church. The church itself is a magnificent example of Somerset Perpendicular, with a soaring 104-foot tower and spectacular pinnacled south porch. The interior contains a remarkable collection of monuments designed by some of the 20th century's most acclaimed artists, including Lutyens, Gill, Munnings and Burne-Jones. A memorial to the pacifist and antiwar poet Siegfried Sassoon can be seen in the churchyard. According to legend, the Abbot of Glastonbury, in an attempt to stave off Henry VIII's Dissolution of the Monasteries, dispatched his steward, John Horner, to London with a gift for the King consisting of a pie into which was baked the title deeds of twelve ecclesiastical manor houses. Far from persuading Henry, however, Horner returned to Somerset the rightful owner of three of the manors himself - Mells, Nunney and Leigh-upon-Mendip - for which he paid of total of £2,000. This remarkable act of disloyalty is commemorated in the nursery rhyme Little Jack Horner which describes how Jack "put in his thumb and pulled out a plum", - that is, the deeds to the property.

Hidden in the lanes to the northwest of Mells, the 18th-century country mansion, **Babington House**, stands at the end of a striking avenue of beech trees a mile from the A362 Frome to Radstock road. Dating from around 1700, with a wing of 1790, the house and nearby church of St Margaret form an elegant composition. The church, with its original timber panelling and box pews, is a rarity in Somerset having been left virtually unchanged since it was constructed in 1750. These two buildings are the only evidence of the medieval hamlet of Babington, a settlement which suffered as a result the 18th century fashion for "emparking" - that is, removing the dwellings of the local inhabitants in order to create an uninterrupted view of the landscaped grounds from the big house.

GREAT ELM
MAP 3 REF K20
2 miles W of Frome off the A362

Jackdaws Educational Trust is a centre for musical excellence founded in 1993 by former international mezzo-soprano and current Artistic Director Maureen Lehane with the support of Jackdaws Patron Dame Joan Sutherland. The Trust grew out of the successful Great Elm Music

Jackdaws Educational Trust, Bridge House, Great Elm, Frome, Somerset BA11 3NY
Tel: 01373 812383 Fax: 01373 812083 e-mail: music@jackdaws.org
website: www.jackdaws.org

Festival (1987-98). Its mission is to provide an opportunity for people to discover that the deepest pleasure in and appreciation for music comes from understanding and hard work. Set in a converted stable block by a millpond in the picturesque Vallis Vale, Jackdaws holds an all year round programme of weekend courses and workshops for amateur musicians and young professionals on piano music, chamber music, Italian opera and many other disciplines. There is also a distinguished concert series of top-class classical music performances. These superb concerts, and the residential music courses, benefit from the tranquillity and beauty of Jackdaws' rural setting and a superior standard of musical instruction and accomplishment.

TRUDOXHILL
5 miles SW of Frome off the A361

Map 3 ref K20

The White Hart is a traditional old coaching inn dating back to the early 1600s. This charming and atmospheric pub/restaurant is one of the oldest inns in Somerset, with many features worth

boasting about. The old smithy next door was refurbished over 10 years ago to become a brewery, producing the superb Ash Vine real ales. Although no longer brewed on the premises, the bar still stocks a range of Ash Vine and other quality real ales, together with a good variety of lagers, wines and spirits. The pub's "take out real ale" service has also proved very popular. The open plan L-shaped bar has exposed timber beams, stone walls and a welcoming open fire with its original baulk timber lintel. The atmosphere is convivial and marvellous. In the Stable Restaurant the menu offers a range of freshly prepared á la carte dishes. Available in the bar are snacks and meals such as traditional favourites like steaks pork chops, roast chicken and leg of lamb, along with vegetarian dishes, lasagne and Korma dishes. The pub is warm and welcoming and serves as a good base for exploring this part of Somerset.

The White Hart, Trudoxhill, Frome, Somerset BA11 5DP
Tel: 01373 836324 Fax: 01373 836566

DOULTING
10 miles SW of Frome off the A361

Map 3 ref K20

The village of Doulting is unusual in Somerset in that its church has a tall spire, rather than a tower. An imposing part 12th century building with a handsome exterior, it also has a splendid two-storey porch which incorporates a curious carving of the green man into its vaulting. The village dates back to the 8th century when King Ine of Wessex gave the local estate to Glastonbury Abbey after his nephew, St Aldhelm, the Abbot of Malmesbury and first Bishop of Sherborne, died here in 709. The saint's body was carried back to Malmesbury along a circuitous route which was marked for posterity by a series of tall stone crosses. The church, a statue, and the spring in the former vicarage garden are all dedicated to St Aldhelm. The spring was later incorporated into a holy well which became a place of pilgrimage during the Middle Ages.

The 15th century **Tithe Barn** at the southern end of the village is a relic of Doulting's monastic past. This great building was constructed to store tithes, one-tenth of the local tenant farmers' crops which they paid annually to their ecclesiastical landlords. Another important source of revenue came from the great quarry which lay to the north of the village. The fine cream-coloured stone from here was used in the construction of Wells cathedral and for later additions to Glastonbury abbey.

GLASTONBURY

MAP 3 REF J20

21 miles W of Frome on the A361

The ancient ecclesiastical centre of Glastonbury, a small town with an immense history, is a mecca for those encompassing such diverse beliefs as paganism, Christianity, Arthurian legend and the existence of UFOs. Before the surrounding Somerset Levels were drained in the 18th century, the dramatic form of **Glastonbury Tor** stood out above a great expanse of mist-covered marshland. Known throughout the region as the Isle of Avalon, one of the first outsiders to sail up the River Brue and land at this distinctive conical hill was the early Christian trader, Joseph of Arimathea, who arrived from the Holy Land around 60 AD. According to local legend, Joseph was walking one day on nearby Wearyall Hill when he plunged his staff into the ground. Miraculously, the stick took root

Glastonbury Tor

and burst into leaf, and this he took as a sign he should found a church. A wattle and daub structure was duly erected at the spot which later became the site of the great **Glastonbury Abbey**. Joseph's staff is reputed to have grown into the celebrated Christmas-flowering Glastonbury hawthorn, and although the original is believed to have been felled during Cromwellian times by an overzealous Puritan (he was blinded by a flying shard of wood in the process, no doubt as a gesture of retribution), one of its windswept ancestors can still be seen on the crest of Wearyall Hill. In an extended version of the legend, Joseph was accompanied on one of his visits to Glastonbury by his nephew, the young Jesus Christ, an occurrence which is reputed to have provided William Blake with the inspiration for his hymn, Jerusalem. Glastonbury Tor remains a landmark which can be seen from miles around, although curiously, it is often less conspicuous when viewed from close by. The 520-foot hill has been inhabited since prehistoric times, and excavations on the site have uncovered evidence of Celtic, Roman and pre-Saxon occupation. Because of its unusually regular shape, it has long been associated with myth and legend. For example, in its time it has been identified as the Land of the Dead, the Celtic Otherworld, a Druid's temple, magic mountain, Arthurian hill-fort, ley line intersection, and rendezvous point for passing UFOs. Along with mystical energy, the tor offers a magnificent panorama across Somerset to Wells, the Mendips, the Quantocks and the Bristol Channel.

The view from the top is most breathtaking on a misty day when the tor is surrounded by a sea of silver cloud. The striking tower at the summit is all that remains of the 15th century Church of St Michael, an offshoot of Glastonbury Abbey which fell into disrepair following the Dissolution of the Monasteries in 1539. In that turbulent year, the tor became a place of execution when the last abbot of Glastonbury, Richard Whiting, and two of his monks were hanged near the summit for opposing the will of Henry VIII.

The wooded rise standing between Glastonbury Tor and the town centre is known as **Chalice Hill**. During one of his visits in the 1st century AD, Joseph of Arimathea is supposed to have buried the Holy Grail (the cup used by Christ at the Last Supper) beneath a spring which emerges from the foot of the hill's southern slope. The spring forms a natural well which was partially enclosed within a masonry structure during medieval times. This is now situated in an attractive garden maintained by the Chalice Well Trust.

The dramatic remains of **Glastonbury Abbey** can be found to the northwest of Chalice Hill in the heart of old Glastonbury. If the legend of Joseph of Arimathea is to be believed, this is the site of the earliest Christian foundation in the British Isles. The abbey is thought to have been founded by King Ine around 700 AD, and under St Dunstan, the 10th century abbot who went on to become the Archbishop of Canterbury, it grew in influence so that by the time of the Norman invasion, it owned estates covering an eighth of the county of Somerset. The abbey continued to grow under the guidance of the Benedictines until a disastrous fire destroyed most of the abbey buildings in 1184. When the foundations of the replacement great church were being excavated seven years later, a wooden sarcophagus was discovered 16 feet down between the shafts of two ancient crosses. Inside were found the bones of a large man and a slender woman, and one story tells of how the woman's long golden hair seemed in a perfect state of preservation until a monk touched it, transforming it to dust. A lead cross found nearby convinced the abbot that he had discovered the remains of King Arthur and Queen Guinevere,

although it was known at the time that this was the burial place of at least three kings from the later, Saxon period.

The abbot's discovery could well be described as timely, given his pressing need for funds to pay for the abbey's reconstruction. Notwithstanding, Glastonbury soon became an important place of pilgrimage, and when the main part of the abbey had been completed in 1278, King Edward himself arrived to witness the final re-interring of Arthur's bones in a magnificent new tomb in the choir. The regenerated great church was a massive 560 feet in length, with a splendid central bell-tower, twin west towers, a

Glastonbury Abbey

unique clock, and a series of shrines to the great and the good. The abbey continued to wield considerable power until Henry VIII's Dissolution of the Monasteries of 1539 forced it to close. The building was abandoned and soon fell into disrepair: its walls were plundered for building stone and Arthur's tomb was destroyed. A number of impressive remains have nevertheless survived, the best-preserved being **St Mary's Chapel**, the shell of the great church, and the 14th century **Abbot's Kitchen**. The last named is a charming structure with a vaulted roof and a fireplace in each corner which has survived almost intact.

The abbey's principal **Tithe Barn** stands on its own to the southeast of the main monastic buildings. Although it is relatively small for such a great estate, it incorporates some fine sculptured detail, notably the carved heads on the corner buttresses and emblems of the four Evangelists on the gables. The barn is now the home of the **Somerset Rural Life Museum**, an imaginatively-presented exhibition dedicated to the era of pre-mechanised farming. As well as a collection of historic farm implements, there are special displays devoted to cider making, willow shoot (or withy) cutting, peat digging and thatching.

Another historic place of interest can be found to the northwest of Glastonbury town centre in a field beside the road to Godney. This was the site of a prehistoric **Lake Village** which was discovered in 1892 when it was noticed that a section of an otherwise level site was studded with irregular mounds. Thought to date from around 150 BC, the dwellings were built on a series of tall platforms which raised them above the surrounding marshland. An interesting collection of artefacts recovered from the site can be seen in the town museum. One of the greatest mysteries of the locality, indeed one which may possess something of a credibility gap, is difficult to observe except from the air. Much loved and eagerly propounded by those with an interest in astrology, the **Glastonbury Zodiac** was brought to light in 1935 by Katherine Maltwood when she was researching a book on the Holy Grail. According to Maltwood, the 12 signs of the zodiac appear in their correct order as recognisable features of the landscape, their outlines being delineated by streams, tracks, ridges and ancient boundaries. The entire formation lies within a circle with a seven-mile radius whose centre lies three miles to the south of Glastonbury near the village of Butleigh. Its origins remain a subject of speculation.

BURROW BRIDGE
Map 3 ref J21
10 miles SW of Glastonbury off the A361

An interesting pumping station can be seen beside the River Parrett at Burrow Bridge. It also contains a fine collection of Victorian pump engines and is open to the public on certain days each year.

Set in 15 acres of pastureland, **Saltmoor House** is a listed Georgian brickbuilt property in the heart of the Somerset Levels and Moors. The front of the house overlooks the River Parrett, and there is an abundance of wildlife including deer and a badger set within view of the house, as well as traditional farm buildings. All-round views of unspoilt countryside make this a peaceful retreat and a nature-lover's paradise. Elegant and comfortable throughout, there are three charming and homely guest bedrooms, one a twin-bed room with en suite shower room, and two further bedrooms each with private bathroom. Flagstone floors, open fires and furnishings of simple elegance are the hallmarks of this gracious and welcoming guest house. Guests are served breakfast in the garden room overlooking the old walled lawns and terrace. The guests' sitting room is warm and inviting. Dinner is available by prior arrangement, served in the candlelit dining room. Owner Elizabeth Deacon is a friendly and conscientious host, who prepares all the delicious meals herself.

Saltmoor House, Saltmoor, Burrowbridge, Bridgwater, Somerset TA7 0RL Tel: 01823 698092

The conspicuous conical hill which can be seen nearby is known as **Burrow Mump**. This isolated knoll is reputed to be the site of an ancient fort belonging to King Alfred, the 9th century King of Wessex, who is thought to have retreated to this lonely spot to escape a Viking incursion. In many ways reminiscent of Glastonbury Tor, Burrow Mump is crowned by the picturesque remains of a medieval church which can be seen from miles around. Burrow Mump is situated in the heart of the low-lying area known as the King's Sedge Moor, an attractive part of the Somerset Levels which is drained by the rivers Cary (here renamed the King's Sedgemoor Drain) and Parrett. This rich area of wetland is known for its characteristic pollarded willows whose straight shoots, or withies, have been cultivated on a substantial scale ever since the taste for wicker developed during the Victorian era. The traditional craft of basket-making, one of Somerset's oldest commercial activities, once employed thousands of people. Though now very much scaled down, the industry is still alive and well and is even enjoying something of a revival.

WELLS   MAP 3 REF J20
6 miles NE of Glastonbury off the A39

The ancient ecclesiastical centre of Wells, with a population of under 10,000, is the smallest city in England, and were it not for its cathedral and neighbouring bishop's palace it would be unlikely to be more than an attractive small market town. However, the magnificent **Cathedral of St Andrew**, the first entirely Gothic structure of its kind in Britain, and its adjacent cathedral close undoubtedly make this one of the gems of north Somerset. Deriving its name from a line of springs which rises from the base of the Mendips, King Ine of the West Saxons is believed to have founded the first church at Wells around 700 AD. After a diocesan tussle with Bath, the present cathedral was begun in the 12th century and took over three centuries to complete. As a consequence, it demonstrates the three main styles of Gothic architecture - Early English, Decorated and Perpendicular. Its 13th century west front is generally considered to be its crowning glory: although defaced during the English Civil War, it incorporates over 100 larger-than-life-size statues of saints, angels and prophets who gaze down silently onto the cathedral lawn. The building's twin west towers were added a couple of centuries later; curious squat structures, they look as if they would benefit from the addition of spires. The cathedral's many superb internal features include the beautiful and ingenious scissor arches which support the central tower, the great 14th century stained-glass window over the high altar, the sweeping chapter house staircase with its elegant branching steps, and the great 14th-century astronomical clock, one of the oldest working timepieces in the world. This shows the minutes, hours and phases of the moon on separate inner and outer dials, and marks the quarter hours with a lively mechanised knights' tournament.

The Vicars' Close, one of the oldest planned streets in Europe, lies on the northern side of the cathedral green. This remarkable cobbled thoroughfare was built in the mid 14th century, although the ornate chimneys were added a century later. Originally intended for cathedral choristers, it is still

Vicars' Close

occupied by officers of the cathedral. The close is connected to the cathedral by a bridge which leads directly from the Vicars' Hall to the chapter house stairs. Known as the Chain Gate, it was built so that the innocent cathedral clergymen could avoid having to run the gauntlet of temptation by having to cross one of the town streets. (In a similar vein, the name of a thoroughfare in the town's former red light district was changed by the easily-affronted Victorians from Grope Lane to Union Street. The 52-acre cathedral close is a tranquil city within a city. Indeed for many centuries, Wells functioned as two distinct entities: the ecclesiastical city and civic city. At that time, the parishioners were not welcomed into the cathedral and instead had to listen to the choir through strategically-placed holes in the cathedral walls. Similarly, the clergymen who died in the Black Death were buried under the cathedral green rather than in the town graveyard. The green itself is surrounded by a high wall which is breached at only three castellated entrance points. One of these sturdy gateways stands in the corner of the Market Place; known as **Penniless Porch**, it is where the bishop allowed the poor of the city to beg for alms from visitors entering the cathedral.

The fortified **Bishop's Palace** is situated in an adjoining site to the south of the cathedral cloisters. This remarkable medieval building is surrounded by a moat which is fed by the springs which give the city its name. The palace is enclosed within a high stone wall, and in order to gain access from the Market Place, it is necessary to pass under a 13th century arch known as the **Bishop's Eye** and then cross a drawbridge which was last raised for defensive purposes in 1831. Although still the official residence of the Bishop of Bath and Wells, several parts are open to visitors, including the bishop's chapel and Jocelin's hall. The wide palace moat is home to a family of swans which are renowned for their ability to ask for food by ringing a bell on the wall below the gatehouse window. The impressive **Bishop's Tithe Barn** is situated to the south of the Bishop's Palace; in its day, it has served as a billet for Cromwell's troops and it is now used for private functions. For those keen to find out more about the history of the locality, **Wells Museum**, near the west front of the cathedral, contains an interesting collection of locally-found artefacts. The splendid Cathedral Library possesses a number of rare books and manuscripts, a selection of which are on open display. The Market Place still hosts a lively street market on Wednesdays and Saturdays, or for those wanting a view of the city from a distance, an attractive footpath starts from Moat Walk and leads up onto the summit of Tor Hill.

WOOKEY HOLE

MAP 3 REF J20

7 miles NE of Glastonbury off the A371

The minor roads to the northeast of the A371 Wells to Cheddar road ascend into the Mendip Hills, an area of rolling limestone upland which is popular with walkers, cavers and motorised sightseers. Wookey Hole, one of the best known visitor attractions in this Area of Outstanding Natural Beauty, lies on its southeastern edge, two miles to the northwest of Wells. Throughout the centuries, the carboniferous limestone core of the hills has been gradually dissolved by the small amount of carbonic acid in rainwater, an effect which has turned cracks into fissures, fissures into underground rivers and, on rare occasions, underground rivers into immense subterranean caverns such as these. During the Palaeolithic and subsequent eras, Wookey Hole was lived in by wild animals such as lions, bears and woolly mammoths. Evidence of their occupation is supported by the large cache of prehistoric mammals' bones which was discovered in a recess known as the **Hyena's Den**, many of them showing the animals' teeth marks. There is also evidence of human occupation during the Iron Age. In total, there are over 25 caverns, although only the largest half dozen are open to visitors. The **Great Cave** contains a rock formation known as the Witch of Wookey which casts a ghostly shadow and is associated with gruesome legends of child-eating. The river emerging from Wookey Hole, the Axe, has been harnessed to provide power for industrial use since the 16th century. Originally constructed in the mid-1800s as a paper mill, the present building on the site was acquired in 1973 by **Madame Tussaud's** who have installed a number of popular visitor attractions. These include an exhibition on the history of waxworks, a museum of Victorian fairground equipment, and a workshop where paper continues to be produced by hand.

CHEDDAR
MAP 3 REF J20

10 miles NW of Glastonbury off hte A371

A spectacular ravine, the Cheddar Gorge carries the B3371 southwestwards towards the Somerset Levels. One of the most famous and often-visited natural attractions in Britain, it is characterised by towering cliffs of weathered limestone and precariously-rooted bands of undergrowth. As well as being known for its gorge, the sprawling village of Cheddar is internationally-renowned for its caves and, of course, its cheese.

Although much embellished by modern tourist paraphernalia, its two main show caverns, **Gough's Cave** and **Cox's Cave**, are worth seeing for their sheer scale and spectacular calcite formations. An almost complete skeleton dubbed "Cheddar Man" was discovered in Gough's Cave in 1903. This can now be seen in a nearby museum along with further evidence of human occupation of the caves, including flint and bone tools dating from the last Ice Age and artefacts from the Iron Age and the Romano-British period.Starting from a little lower down the hill, the 322 steps of **Jacob's Ladder** lead up the side of the gorge to the site of Pavey's Lookout Tower, a novel vantage point which offers a spectacular view of the surrounding landscape. An unusual market cross stands at the centre of the old part of Cheddar village. Really two crosses in one, a hexagonal superstructure was added to the original 15th century preaching cross around a century later.

The term Cheddar cheese refers to a recipe which was developed in the mid 19th century by Joseph Harding, a farmer and pioneer food scientist from near Bath who made the first scientific investigation into cheese-making. As the name refers to a recipe and not the place, the cheese can be made anywhere in the world; however, North Somerset is dotted with cheese manufacturers of various sizes, from single farmhouses to large-scale dairies.

YEOVIL
MAP 3 REF J21

14 miles S of Glastonbury on the A37

With its 28,000 inhabitants and strategic position at the junction of several main routes, Yeovil is the largest centre of population in south Somerset. A modern light industrial and market town whose best-known employer is Westland Helicopters, it offers a comprehensive range of shopping and recreational facilities. Despite its up-to-date character, Yeovil's origins go back to the time of the ancient Romans. During the Middle Ages, a lively livestock and produce market was established in the town which continues to be held here every Friday. Yeovil's parish **Church of St John the Baptist** is the only significant medieval structure to survive, most of its other early buildings having been destroyed in a series of town fires in the 17th century. A substantial Ham-stone structure dating from the second half of the 14th century, the church has surprisingly austere exterior given its exceptional number of windows. (Indeed, it has so many that it is sometimes referred to as the "lantern of the West".) Perhaps its finest internal feature is the plain brass lectern which is believed to date from around 1450. One of only five still in existence, it is the only one to be found in a parish church.

During the 18th century, Yeovil developed into a flourishing coaching and industrial centre whose output included gloves, leather, sailcloth and cheese. This rapid expansion was enhanced by the arrival of the railway in the mid 19th century, then in the 1890s, James Petter, a local ironmonger and pioneer of the internal combustion engine, founded a business which went on to become one of the largest manufacturers of diesel engines in Britain. Although production was eventually transferred to the Midlands, a subsidiary set up to produce aircraft during the First World War has since evolved into the present-day helicopter plant. A fascinating museum documenting the social and industrial history of the area from prehistoric and Roman times through to the agricultural and industrial revolutions can be found near the Octagon Theatre in the centre of Yeovil. Situated in Wyndham House in Hendford, the **Museum of South Somerset** uses a series of imaginative settings to recapture the atmosphere of the times.

Right in the centre of Yeovil, **Mulberry's Bistro** is a friendly and welcoming restaurant. The conservatory, patio, profusion of plants and touches like the musical instruments and other adornments lend a homely and festive air to this charming eatery. Spacious, airy and light, there are tables indoors and out where guests can enjoy a drink, snack or full meal. The cuisine on offer is international, boasting a range of a la carte and bistro fare, fine wines, morning coffee and more. Relaxing and pleasant, this makes a perfect place to enjoy a quiet meal or just a break from sightseeing around Yeovil. The menu features steaks, scampi, salmon, lamb and other traditional favourites, superbly prepared and

Mulberry's Bistro, 9 Union Street, Yeovil, Somerset BA20 1PQ Tel/Fax: 01935 434188 email: mulbistro@aol.com website: www.yeoviltown.com

beautifully presented. A selection of pasta, chilli, vegetarian and curry dishes add to the many choices faced by diners. This charming restaurant is open Monday to Saturday 10 a.m.-2.30 p.m. lunch and 7-closing (last orders 2.30 p.m. and 10.30 p.m. respectively).

LITTLE NORTON
7 miles W of Yeovil off the A303

MAP 3 REF J21

This peaceful hamlet nestles beneath Ham Hill in a particularly idyllic part of south Somerset. Set in six acres of superb gardens and grounds, **Little Norton Mill** is a rural haven offering all the peace, tranquillity and comfort guests could ask for. The grounds include a fully restored 18th-century water mill and mill pond, stocked with pet aylesbury ducks and visiting wild ducks. Here in this marvellous setting, guests will find eight comfortable self-catering cottages and apartments. All properties are furnished and decorated to a high standard of comfort and quality, and all boast fully equipped kitchens and other amenities. Four of the cottages have two bedrooms, spacious open-plan living/dining rooms and superb views of the mill pond and/ or garden. Two cottages have bedrooms with lovely four-poster beds. The original mill barn has been tastefully converted to form four cosy one-bedroom apartments, each of which sleep two. Two are on the ground floor. There are many opportunities for excellent walking and cycling in the area, and guests are also welcome to use the tennis court nearby by arrangement.

Little Norton Mill, Little Norton, Norton Sub Hamdon, Somerset TA14 6TE Tel/Fax: 01935 881337

DOWLISH WAKE

13 miles W of Yeovil off the B3168

MAP 3 REF J21

Those with an interest in traditional cider making should make a point of finding **Perry's Cider**

Perry's Cider Mills

Mills at Dowlish Wake, a pleasant community which lies hidden in the lanes to the southeast of Ilminster. The village contains some attractive honey-coloured Ham-stone cottages and an imposing parish church which stands on a steep rise a little way from the centre. Inside can be seen the tomb of John Hanning Speke, an intrepid Victorian explorer who journeyed for over 2500 miles through some of the harshest terrain in Africa to confirm Lake Victoria as the source of the River Nile.

Speke returned to England a hero, but tragically, on the very morning he was due to report his findings to the British Geographical Association, he accidentally shot himself while out partridge shooting.

EAST COKER

3 miles S of Yeovil off the A30/A37

MAP 3 REF J21

East Coker is one of Somerset's most beautiful villages, with a wealth of thatched cottages, impressive Manor house and St Michael's parish church, set on a hill overlooking the village and traditional Almshouses. The famed explorer William Dampier was born here, as was T S

The Helyar Arms, East Coker, Somerset BA22 9JR
Tel: 01935 862332

Eliot, the "American" poet (his family emigrated to Missouri when he was very young) who later returned to Britain and mentions the village in his poems.

The Helyar Arms occupies a Grade II listed building built around 1460. The original Welsh slate and stone are still standing in this attractive pub, restaurant and hotel. The bar is large and welcoming, with plenty of room for diners and those wishing only to "slake their thirst" with the pub's range of hand-drawn ales and ciders, or good selection of wines and spirits. The Apple Restaurant is charming and refined, with a full menu that uses the very best of local produce to produce a range of dishes from local specialities to a broad selection of international favourites, all expertly prepared and presented. The six en suite guest bedrooms offer fabulous views, and are furnished and fitted to the highest standards of taste and comfort. Open-plan throughout, the pub is adorned with hundreds of local scenes in prints and photographs. The simple lighting and period furniture add to this fine establishment's superb comfort and homeliness. Each room is individually themed, named and decorated. All boast all modern amenities.

SPARKFORD
MAP 3 REF K21

8 miles NE of Yeovil off the A303

Another interesting museum can be found on the northeastern edge of Sparkford. Situated beside the A359 near its junction with the A303, the **Haynes Motor Museum** is a unique collection of over 200 veteran, vintage and classic cars and motorbikes which is though to be the largest of its kind in the UK. Nearly every "exhibit" is driven at least once every six months around a specially-constructed 1-kilometre demonstration track. Special displays include Jaguars, Minis, Chevrolet Corvettes and red-painted sports cars.

Handy for the A303, the **Sparkford Inn** is a homely and welcoming old coaching inn with en suite accommodation. A rambling series of beamed bars and carvery restaurant, all with a mix of antique furniture and interesting old prints and photographs. No pool table, juke box or darts. There is a log fire in the lounge bar and restaurant. The inn has a large carpark, beer garden and children's adventure play area. Open every day - Monday to Saturday 11 a.m. to 11 p.m.; carvery lunch and snack menus midday to 2 p.m. On Sundays the inn opens from midday to 11

Sparkford Inn, High Street, Sparkford, nr Yeovil, Somerset
BA22 7JD Tel: 01963 440218 Fax: 01963 440358

p.m. At the Sunday luncheon with speciality choice of roasts, the two-course carvery is very reasonably priced. There is also a specials board in the bars. Every evening including Sundays there are a la carte and chalkboard specialities. Evening meals are served from 7 to 10 p.m. The puddings are wonderful. The pub is a Free House and there are always five real ales available. There are no-smoking areas. Children are welcome in the restaurant and some areas in the bars.

SOMERTON
MAP 3 REF J21

10 miles NW of Yeovil off the B3153

This fine old town which was the capital of Somerset for a time under the West Saxons. The settlement grew up around an important crossroads to the northwest of the church. However,

Somerton Market Cross

an expansion towards the end of the 13th century altered the original layout and created the present open market place with its distinctive **Market Cross** and town hall, both later additions. Between 1278 and 1371, Somerton became the location of the county gaol and meeting place of the shire courts. It also continued to develop as a market town, a role which is reflected in such delightfully down-to-earth street names as Cow Square and Pig Street (now Broad Street). Present-day Somerton is filled with handsome old shops, inns and houses, the majority of which are constructed of local bluish lias limestone. The general atmosphere of mature prosperity is enhanced by the presence of a number of striking early buildings. These include the 17th century **Hext Almshouses** and the part 13th century church with its magnificent 15th century tie-beam roof and unusual transeptal south tower.

MUCHELNEY
10 miles NW of Yeovil off the A372

MAP 3 REF J21

Muchelney is the location of an impressive part-ruined Benedictine monastery which was founded in Saxon times (around 950). During the medieval period, **Muchelney Abbey** grew to emulate its great rival at Glastonbury; however, after the Dissolution of the Monasteries in 1539, the building gradually fell into disrepair and much of its stone was removed to provide building material for the surrounding village. In spite of this, a substantial part of the original structure remains, including the south cloister and abbot's lodge. Now under the custodianship of English Heritage, the abbey is open daily between 1st April and 30th September, 10 a.m. to 6 p.m. Muchelney's parish church is worth seeing for its remarkable early 17th-century illuminations on the ceiling of the nave. Opposite stands the **Priest's House**, a late-medieval hall house with large Gothic windows which was originally a residence for priests serving at the church across the road. Refurbished by the National Trust, it is open Sundays and Mondays only between late March and late September from 2.30 to 5.30 p.m.

Muchelney Pottery, Muchelney, Langport, Somerset TA10 0DW Tel: 01458 250324

Just a mile south of the village and its fine Abbey, **Muchelney Pottery** showcases the work of John Leach, who makes hand-thrown stoneware pottery which is sold in the adjoining shop. Often featured in displays at Muchelney Abbey itself, the pottery includes a range of kitchen pots and oven-to-tableware. At the workshops, visitors can watch the throwing and handling of pots. Leach is a third-generation potter who produces a range of stoneware pots based on the simple strength of English country pottery. The range includes more than 50 designs of everyday tableware, from jugs, casseroles, bowls and plates to storage jars, bread crocks, chicken bricks and pasta pods. Their pleasing rounded shapes, glazed interiors and warmly 'toasted finish', combined with expert craftsmanship, have made them popular with kitchen and craft shops nationwide. The pottery is open Monday to Friday to Saturday 9.00 to 1.00 and 2.00 to 5.00. Just along the road from the pottery, visitors can walk down a typically green and lovely Somerset drove to John's award-winning wildlife pond.

CADBURY CASTLE   MAP 3 REF K21
8 miles E of Somerton off the A303

Cadbury Castle is a massive Iron Age hill fort which is also reckoned by some to be the location of King Arthur's legendary Camelot. This ancient hilltop site was occupied for some 5,000 years from the middle to the Neolithic period right up to the 13th century. Heavily fortified throughout the Iron Age, the Romans are reputed to have carried out a massacre here around 70 AD to put down a revolt by the ancient Britons. A major archaeological excavation in the 1960s uncovered a wealth of Roman and pre-Roman remains on the site. It also confirmed the existence of a substantial fortification dating from around 500 AD, the time when King Arthur would have been spearheading the Celtic-British resistance against the advancing Saxons. If Cadbury Castle had indeed been Arthur's Camelot, it is likely that it would have been a timber fortification and not the turreted stone structure mythologised by the storybooks.

The easily-defended hilltop site was again refortified during the reign of Ethelred the Unready, this time against the Danes. The poorly-advised king also established a mint here around 1000 AD, most of the coinage from which was used to buy off the Norse invaders in an act of appeasement which led to the term Danegeld. As a consequence, most of the surviving coins from the Cadbury mint are now to be found in the museums of Scandinavia.

BRIDGWATER   MAP 3 REF I20
14 miles W of Glastonbury on the A38

The ancient inland port and industrial town of Bridgwater stands at the lowest medieval bridging point on the River Parrett. Despite having been fortified since before the Norman invasion, the settlement remained little more than a village until an international trade in wool, wheat and other agricultural produce began to develop in the late Middle Ages. During this period, Bridgwater grew to become the most important town on the coast between Bristol and Barnstaple, and the fifth-busiest port in Britain. The largely 14th century parish **Church of St Mary**, with its disproportionately large spire, is the only building to survive from this medieval era of prosperity, the castle having been dismantled after the English Civil War, and the 13th-century Franciscan friary and St John's hospital having long since disappeared. The oldest and most interesting part of the town lies between King Street and the West Quay, an area whose layout is medieval, but whose buildings are amongst the finest examples of Georgian domestic architecture in Somerset. Prior to the construction of a canal dock a short distance downstream early in the 19th century, ships used to tie up on both riverbanks below Bridgwater's medieval three-arched bridge. The last remnant of the castle, **The Water Gate**, can still be seen here on the West Quay, along with a number of fine Georgian residences, the most notable of which, the Lions, was built in 1725.

DODINGTON   MAP 3 REF I20
6 miles W of Bridgwater off the A39

Castle of Comfort in Dodington near Nether Stowey is a gracious country house hotel dating back to at least the 16th century. This Grade II listed building is an impressive stonebuilt structure which has in its day been a coaching inn, coffee house and cider house. The poets Coleridge and Wordsworth lived nearby; Dorothy Wordsworth is known to have visited the Castle of

Comfort in 1789. Set in four acres of grounds in the Quantock Hills, this charming establishment boasts six attractive and supremely comfortable en suite rooms, two with four-poster bed. The hills offer opportunities for walking, riding and other country pursuits. The stables to the rear can accommodate guests' horses. Superb quality marks out this fine establishment. Each room is individually styled, furnished and decorated. The swimming pool is just another touch of luxury in this gracious and distinctive hotel/restaurant. The menu offers a range of delicious two- and three-course meals. The regular gourmet evenings are very popular - please phone for details. No smoking.

Castle of Comfort, Dodington, Nether Stowey, Somerset TA5 1LE
Tel: 01278 741264 Fax: 01278 741144 Mobile: 07050 642002
email: castle.comfort@virgin.net
website: www.castle-of-comfort.co.uk

TAUNTON

MAP 3 REF I21

10 miles S of Bridgwater on the A38

Taunton, the county town of Somerset, has only been its sole centre of administration since 1936, previous county towns having been Ilchester and Somerton. The settlement was founded as a military camp by the Saxon King Ine in the 8th century, and by Norman times it had grown to have its own Augustinian monastery, minster and castle. An extensive structure whose purpose has always been more administrative than military, the castle was nevertheless the focus of two important sieges during the English Civil War. A few years later, over 150 followers of the Duke of Monmouth were sentenced to death here by the infamous Judge Jeffreys during the Bloody Autumn Assizes which followed the Pitchfork Rebellion of 1685. Even now, the judge's ghost is said to haunt the castle grounds on September nights. Today the much-altered castle houses the **Somerset County Museum**, an informative local museum containing a large collection of exhibits on the archaeology and natural history of the county. There is also a special display chronicling the colourful history of the Somerset Light Infantry. Somerset's famous County Cricket Ground occupies part of the old priory grounds which once stretched down to the river. A section of

Somerset County Cricket Museum

the old monastic gatehouse known as the Priory Barn can still be seen beside the cricket ground. Now restored, this medieval stone building now houses the fascinating **Somerset County Cricket Museum**.

In common with many other towns and villages in the West Country, Taunton was a thriving wool, cloth-making, and later silk, centre during the late Middle Ages. The profits earned by the medieval clothiers went to build not one, but two huge churches: St James' and St Mary's. Both have soaring Perpendicular towers, which have since been rebuilt, and imposing interiors; the former contains a striking carved stone font and the latter an elegant painted roof adorned with angels. The town centre is scattered with other fine buildings, most notably the timber-framed Tudor House in Fore Street and the 17th century almshouses. Present-day Taunton continues to be an important commercial centre with a lively weekly market. Other visitor attractions include **Vivary Park** with its ponds, gardens and jogging trail, and the impressive **Brewhouse Theatre and Arts Centre**.

A pleasant walk follows the towpath of the **Bridgwater and Taunton Canal**, a 14-mile inland waterway which was constructed in the 1820s and fully reopened in the summer of 1994 following decades of neglect and a 20 year programme of restoration. A relative latecomer when it first opened in 1827, the canal was constructed as part of an ambitious scheme to create a freight route between Exeter and Bristol which avoided the treacherous journey around the Cornish peninsula. For many years, the canal was the principal means of importing coal and iron from South Wales to the towns of inland Somerset, and of exporting wool and agricultural produce to the urban centres of Britain. The towpath winds its way through some of the most attractive countryside in the Somerset Levels, and the restored locks, swing bridges, engine houses and rare paddle-gearing equipment add interest to the walk. The canal also offers a variety of recreational facilities, including boating, fishing, canoeing and bird watching, and passes close to some attractive villages. At the canal's southern end, boats have access to the River Tone via **Firepool Lock** in the heart of Taunton.

WELLINGTON MONUMENT   MAP 3 REF I21
7 miles SW of Taunton off the A38

A good place to begin a tour of South Somerset is from the **Wellington Monument**, the conspicuous 170-foot obelisk which stands on a spur of the Blackdown hills overlooking the Vale of Taunton Deane. This striking landmark was constructed in honour of the Duke of Wellington on the estate bought for him by the nation following his victory at the Battle of Waterloo. (Despite his adopted title, the Duke had no connections with the locality and is known to have visited the estate only once in 30 years.) The monument's foundation stone was laid in 1817 following a wave of enthusiastic public support. However, the necessary funds to complete the project did not materialise and a number of radical economies had to be introduced. These included the redesigning of the structure to give it three sides instead of four and the cancelling of an ostentatious cast iron statue of the Duke which had been proposed for the top. As it was, the modified triangular pinnacle remained unfinished until 1854, two years after Wellington's death. Visitors can still make the formidable 235-step climb to the top where they are rewarded with spectacular views across lowland Somerset to Exmoor and the Mendips. Travelling eastwards, the B3170 to the south of Taunton skirts Taunton Racecourse, then a little further on, a lane to the west leads to **Poundisford Park**, a small H-shaped Tudor mansion standing within a delightful wooded deer park which once belonged to the bishops of Winchester. The house is renowned for its fine plasterwork ceilings and the grounds incorporate a formal garden laid out in the Tudor style.

WATCHET   MAP 3 REF I20
15 miles NE of Taunton off the A39

Watchet, a small town on the coast to the north of Taunton, has been a port since Saxon times. In the 6th century, St Decuman is reputed to have landed here from Wales, bringing with him a cow to provide sustenance, and in the 9th and 10th centuries, the settlement was important enough to have been sacked by the Vikings on at least three occasions. By the 17th century, Watchet had become an important paper manufacturing centre, and by the mid 19th, around 30,000 tons of iron ore from the Brendon hills were being exported each year through its docks. Coleridge's imaginary crew set sail from here in "The Rime Of The Ancient Mariner", the epic poem which was written when the author was residing at nearby Nether Stowey. Unlike many similar-sized ports which fell into disuse following the arrival of the railways, Watchet docks has somehow managed to survive.

Despite the total decline in the iron ore trade, sizable cargo vessels continue to tie up here to be loaded with goods bound for the Iberian peninsula and elsewhere. The scale of Watchet's parish church reflects the town's long-standing importance. Set well away from the centre, it contains several fine tombs to members of the Wyndham family, the local lords of the manor who did much to develop the economic potential of the locality. One 16th-century family member, Florence Wyndham, had to be buried twice: the day after her first funeral, the church sexton went down to the vaults to surreptitiously remove a ring from her finger and the old woman suddenly woke up. In recent years, Watchet has also developed as something of a coastal resort whose attractions include an interesting small museum dedicated to local maritime history.

ROADWATER
16 miles NE of Taunton off the A396

MAP 2 REF H20

Anyone who loves the peace and beauty of the countryside will find a welcome haven at **Stamborough Farm** in Roadwater. Situated in the BrendonHills and near to the Quantock Hills in the Exmoor National Park, it is surrounded by rolling countryside and tranquil wooded

areas, while still being just a short distance from Minehead and Dunster. This handsome Georgian farmhouse is set in 17 acres of farmland. The adjacent Tudor barn is a listed building. There are three supremely comfortable and spacious guest bedrooms, all en suite with full sized bathrooms, furnished and decorated to the highest standard of taste and quality. Guests have their own large and attractive sitting room, where a welcoming fire awaits them on chilly evenings. The traditional farmhouse breakfast is served in the elegant dining room. Candlelit dinners are lovingly prepared by owner Sue Riley by arrangement; she uses the freshest ingredients to create delicious dishes. There is also a games room for guests' use, complete with full-size pool table. A relaxed and friendly atmosphere pervades this welcoming and homely establishment.

**Stamborough Farm, Roadwater, Watchet, Somerset
TA23 0RW Tel: 01984 640258 Fax: 01984 641051
email: rileystamco@compuserve.com
website: www.westcountry.net**

DUNSTER   MAP 2 REF H20

20 miles NE of Taunton off the A396

The ancient fortified settlement of Dunster has an almost fairy-tale appearance when approached from the southeast. With its huge turreted castle rising above the trees and distinctive ruined folly on nearby Conygar hill, it is a place well-worth visiting, particularly out of season. **Dunster Castle** was founded by William de Mohun on a natural promontory above the River Avill a few years before the Domesday Book was compiled in 1086. In 1404, it passed to the Luttrells for the then colossal sum of 5,000 marks, about £3,300, in whose family it remained until Lt. Col. G W F Luttrell presented the property to the National Trust in 1975. Dunster Castle is surrounded by an attractive 28-acre park containing an 18th century flour mill which was built on the site of a Norman predecessor. Restored to working order in 1979, **Dunster Working Water Mill** continues to produce flour and other cereals for wholesale and retail sale.

The old feudal settlement of Dunster has a wide main street which is dominated by the castle. At the northern end stands the former **Yarn Market**, a small octagonal building erected by the Luttrells around 1600 when the village was a centre of the cloth trade. Indeed, such was its importance that at one time, Dunster gave its name to a type of woollen cloth which was renowned for its quality and strength. The nearby **Luttrell Arms** is over a century older; a private residence which was converted to an inn around 1650, it has a fine 15th century porch and a room lined with carved oak panelling. It once belonged to Cleeve Abbey, as did the 14th century nunnery in Church Street. Dunster's principal medieval monastic house, **Dunster Priory**, was an outpost of Bath Abbey. Now largely demolished, the only parts to survive are its splendid priory church and unusual 12th century dovecote. This can be seen in a nearby garden and still contains the revolving ladder which was used to reach the roosting birds.

Dunster's former priory church is now one of the finest parish churches in Somerset. Rebuilt of rose pink sandstone by the monks after 1100, its 100-foot tower was added in the 15th century at a cost of 13s 4d per foot, with an extra 20s for the pinnacles. The building's most outstanding internal feature is its fan vaulted rood screen which extends across the nave and aisles, one of the widest and most impressive of its kind in the country. There are also some fine 15th and 16th century fittings, an unusual painting of the Brazen Serpent thought to be by Thornhill, and several monuments to members of the Luttrell family. On the southern edge of the village, the River Avill is spanned by the ancient **Gallox Bridge**, a medieval packhorse bridge which is now under the care of English Heritage.

Set on the edge of Exmoor and surrounded by 30 acres of rural splendour, **Periton Park Court** offers excellent self-catering accommodation and a range of leisure facilities. A high standard of comfort and quality is maintained throughout the four self-catering apartments. "The Coach House" , a semi-detached cottage, sleeps five to seven people and is spacious and attractive. "The Studio" sleeps two to three people and offers its own private patio area. "The Stables" sleeps four and is a ground-floor cottage-style apartment. "The Bunk House" is a Cedar wood chalet in a garden setting, which sleeps four. All have hand-crafted antique pine kitchens with every modern amenity. The large outdoor heated swimming pool and

Periton Park Court and Riding Stables, Periton Road, nr Minehead, Somerset TA24 8SN Tel: 01643 705970

barbecue facilities are exclusively for residents' use. The riding stables within the grounds accommodate all standards of rider, from beginner to very accomplished. Rides and treks can be arranged when required. And at just a mile and a half from Minehead, visitors are in close proximity to the many attractions of Exmoor and the west Somerset/Devon coast.

EXMOOR NATIONAL PARK
NW of Taunton

Map 2 ref H20

The characteristic heartland of the Exmoor National Park, 70 per cent of which lies within Somerset, is a high treeless plateau of hard-wearing Devonian shale which has been carved into a series of steep-sided valleys by the prolonged action of the moor's many fast-flowing streams. Whereas the upland vegetation is mostly heather, gorse and bracken, the more sheltered valleys are carpeted with grassy meadows and pockets of woodland. The deep wooded combes also provide shelter for herds of shy red deer which roam at will, but are seldom seen. Easier to spot are the hardy Exmoor ponies, now almost all cross-breeds, which often congregate at roadside parking areas where there can be rich pickings from holidaymakers. Exmoor is criss-crossed by a network of paths and bridleways which provide some superb opportunities for walking and pony-trekking. Many follow the routes of the ancient ridgeways across the high moor and pass close to the numerous hut circles, standing stones, barrows and other Bronze and Iron Age remains which litter the landscape. Among the finest examples are the stone circle on Porlock Hill, **Alderman's Barrow** north of Exford, and the delightfully-named **Cow Castle** near Simonsbath. The remarkable medieval packhorse bridge known as **Tarr Steps** lies to the north of the village of Hawkridge, near Dulverton. A superb example of a West Country clapper bridge, it is composed of massive flat stones placed across solidly-built dry stone uprights. The Roman relic known as the **Caractacus Stone** can be seen a couple of miles to the east of here near Spire Cross.

SOUTH DEVON

HONITON
15 miles S of Taunton off the A30

Map 3 ref I22

Honiton is the "capital" of east Devon, a delightful little town in the valley of the River Otter and the "gateway to the far southwest". It was once a major stopping place on the Fosse Way, the great Roman road that struck diagonally across England from Lincoln to Exeter. Honiton's position on the main traffic artery to Devon and Cornwall brought it considerable prosperity, and its broad, ribbon-like High Street, almost two miles long, testifies to the town's busy past.

Although Honiton was the first town in Devon to manufacture serge cloth, the town is much better known for a more delicate material, Honiton lace. Lace-making was introduced to east Devon by Flemish immigrants who arrived here during the reign of Elizabeth I. By the end of the 17th century some 5,000 people were engaged in the industry, most of them working from their own homes making fine "bone" lace by hand. Children as young as five were sent to "lace schools"where they received a rudimentary education in the three Rs, and a far more intense instruction in the intricacies of lace-making. Almost wiped out by the arrival of machine-made lace in the late 1700s, the industry was given a new lease of life when Queen Victoria insisted upon Honiton lace for her wedding dress and created a new fashion for lace that persisted throughout the century. The traditional material is still made on a small scale in the town and can be found on sale in local shops, and on display in **Allhallows Museum**. This part 15th century building served as a school for some 300 years but is now an interesting local museum housing a unique collection of traditional lace and also, during the season, offers daily demonstrations of lacemaking. Allhallows Schoolroom was one of the few old buildings to survive a series of devastating fires in the mid-1700s. However, that wholesale destruction had the fortunate result that the new buildings were gracious Georgian residences and Honiton still retains the pleasant, unhurried atmosphere of a prosperous 18th century coaching town. Another building which escaped the flames unscathed was **Marwood House** in the High Street. It was built in 1619 by the second son of Thomas Marwood, one of Queen Elizabeth's many physicians. Thomas achieved great celebrity when he managed to cure the Earl of Essex after all others had failed. (He received his Devonshire estate as a reward.) Thomas was equally successful in preserving his own health, living to the extraordinary age of 105. **St Margaret's Hospital**, to the west of town, was founded in the middle ages as a refuge for lepers who were denied entry to the town itself. Later, in the 16th century, this attractive thatched building was reconstructed as an almshouse. To the east of Honiton, an early 19th century toll house known as **Copper Castle** can be seen. The castellated building still retains its original iron toll gates. And just a little further east, on Honiton Hill, stands the massive folly of the **Bishop's Tower**, erected in 1842 and once part of Bishop Edward Copplestone's house.

Unlike the rolling hills which characterise much of the rest of Devon, to the north of Honiton the landscape is a high, flat-topped plateau which is sliced into long fingers by a series of south-flowing rivers. On the northern edge of Honiton lies the National Trust-owned **Dumpdon Hill**, an 850-foot high steep-sided outcrop which is crowned by a sizeable late-Iron Age fort. Both the walk to the summit and the views over the Otter Valley are breathtaking.

CULMSTOCK
9 miles N of Honiton off the B3391

MAP 3 REF I21

Lovers of R D Blackmore's novel Lorna Doone will be interested in Culmstock, for it was here that the author lived as a boy during the years that his father was the vicar. One of his playmates in the village was Frederick Temple, another bright boy, and the two friends both went on to Blundell's School at Tiverton, where they shared lodgings. Blackmore was to become one of the most successful novelists of his time; Temple entered the church and after several years as Headmaster of Rugby School reached the pinnacle of his profession as Archbishop of Canterbury. Culmstock's parish church has a famous **yew tree** growing from the top of the tower. The tree has been growing there for more than 200 years and, despite the fact that its only nourishment is the lime content of the mortar in which it is set, the trunk has now achieved a girth of 18 inches. It's believed that the seed was probably carried up in the mortar used to repair the tower when its spire was demolished in 1776. The church's more traditional kind of treasures are a magnificently embroidered cope of the late 1400s, now preserved in a glass case; a remarkable 14th century tomb rediscovered during restoration in the 19th century; and a richly-coloured memorial window designed by Burne-Jones.

AXMINSTER
10 miles E of Honiton off the A35/A358

MAP 3 REF I22

This little town grew up around the junction of two important Roman roads, the Fosse and the Icknield, and was important in medieval times for its Minster beside the River Axe. Its name has entered the language as the synonym for a very superior kind of floor-covering which first appeared in the early 1750s. Wandering around London's Cheapside market, an Axminster weaver named Thomas Whitty was astonished to see a huge Turkish carpet, 12 yards long and 8 yards wide. Returning to the sleepy little market town where he was born, Thomas spent months puzzling over the mechanics of producing such a seamless piece of work. By 1755 he had solved the problem, and on Midsummer's Day that year the first of these luxurious carpets was revealed to the world. The time and labour involved was so prodigious that the completion of each carpet was celebrated by a procession to St Mary's Church and a ringing peal of bells. Ironically, one distinguished purchaser of an Axminster carpet was the Sultan of Turkey, who in 1800 paid the colossal sum of £1,000 for a particularly fine specimen. But the inordinately high labour costs involved in producing such exquisite hand-tufted carpets crippled Whitty's company. In 1835 their looms were sold to a factory at Wilton. That was the end of Axminster's pre-eminence in the market for top-quality carpets, but echoes of those glorious years still reverberate. **St Mary's Church** must be the only house of worship in Christendom whose floor is covered with a richly-woven carpet, and a new factory in Woodmead Road (visitors welcome) is now busy making 20th century Axminster carpets.

MEMBURY
6 miles E of Honiton off the A30/A35

Map 3 ref I22

Here in the midst of rural Devon, near both the Dorset and Somerset borders, **Lea Hill Hotel** is an enchanting 14th-century country hotel set on a hilltop and commanding stunning views. An abundance of wildlife make their home in the 8 acres of formal gardens, woodland and pastureland in which this fine hotel is set. The main building is a wonderful example of a thatched Devon Long House. Its history and provenance have been the subject of the BBC's House Detectives series, as the farm has in its time been owned by leading Quakers of the 17th

century. John Smith, a leader of the Quaker movement, lived here from 1650 and was sentenced to death in 1685 for supporting the Duke of Monmouth's attempts to seize the crown. Successfully combining medieval charm with 21st century standards, this superb family-run hotel offers the perfect retreat. There are 11 en suite bedrooms, each individually furnished

Lea Hill Hotel, Membury, nr Axminster, Devon EX13 7AQ
Tel: 01404 881881 Fax: 01404 881890

with fine fabrics. Many rooms boast their own private garden area. There are two spacious suites and one room with luxurious four-poster bed. A wealth of original features such as exposed beams and flagstone floors grace this charming establishment. The grounds include a six-hole par three golf course. In the attractive split-level dining room guests are treated to an innovative yet classic menu of English and Pacific Rim cuisine. The comfortable and welcoming residents' study is a quiet haven lined with books. In the cosy bar, guests can enjoy a relaxing drink.

SEATON
11 miles SE of Honiton off the B3172

Map 3 ref I22

Set around the mouth of the River Axe, with red cliffs on one side and white cliffs on the other, Seaton was once a quite significant port. By the 16th century, however, the estuary had filled up with stones and pebbles, and it wasn't until moneyed Victorians came and built their villas (and one of the first concrete bridges in the world, in 1877) that Seaton was accorded a new lease of life. The self-confident architecture of those times gives the little town an attractive appearance which is enhanced by its well-maintained public parks and gardens. From Seaton, an attractive way of travelling along the valley of the River Axe is on the **Seaton Tramway**, whose colourful open-topped tramcars trundle through an area famous for its bird life to the villages of Colyford and Colyton. Really dedicated tram fans, after a short lesson, are even permitted to take over the driver's seat.

COLYTON
9 miles SE of Honiton off the A3052

MAP 3 REF I22

Those alighting from the Seaton Tram at Colyton will find an ancient and very appealing small town of narrow winding streets and interesting stone houses. Throughout its long history Colyton has been an important agricultural and commercial centre with its own corn mill, tannery, sawmill and iron foundry. Many of the older buildings are grouped around the part-Norman **Church of St Andrew**, a striking build-

ing with an unusual 15th century lantern tower and a Saxon cross brilliantly reconstructed after its broken fragments were retrieved from the tower, where they had been used as building material. Nearby is the vicarage (1529) and the Old Church House, a part-medieval building enlarged in 1612 and used as a grammar school until 1928. Look out also for the **Great House** which was built on the road to Colyford by a wealthy Elizabethan merchant.

The **Kingfisher** is a relaxing and friendly family-run public house in the heart of Colyton, a peaceful town just a short distance from the coast. A warm and hospitable welcome is guaranteed from owners Graeme and Cherry and their son Iain. Father and son run 'front of house', while Cherry oversees the excellent food. This cheerful one-time coaching inn dates back to 1642. Inside, traditional features such as low-beamed ceilings and exposed stone walls add to the cosy and welcoming ambience. The room to the rear is the site of the dining area. The menu boasts a wealth of op-

The Kingfisher, Dolphin Street, Colyton, Devon EX24 6NA Tel: 01297 552476

tions from sandwiches and salads to steaks, chicken, seafood and a range of daily specials. Food is served daily from midday to 1.45 p.m. and 7 to 9.30 p.m. There are always four real ales from local brewers, as well as a good selection of wines and spirits.

Half a mile to the north of Colyton, **Colcombe Castle** contains some exceptional 16th and 17th century remains, including an impressive kitchen hearth.

OTTERY ST MARY
5 miles SW of Honiton off the B3177

MAP 3 REF I22

The glory of Ottery St Mary is its magnificent 14th century **Church of St Mary**. From the outside, St Mary's looks part mini-Cathedral, part Oxford college. Both impressions are justified since, when Bishop Grandisson commissioned the building in 1337, he stipulated that it should be modelled on his own cathedral at Exeter. He also wanted it to be "a sanctuary for piety and learning", so accommodation for 40 scholars was provided. The interior is just as striking. The church's medieval treasures include a brilliantly-coloured altar screen, canopied tombs, and a 14th century astronomical clock showing the moon and the planets which still functions with its original machinery. Ottery's vicar during the mid-18th century was the Reverend John Coleridge, whose 13th child grew up to become the celebrated poet, Samuel Taylor Coleridge. The family home near the church has since been demolished, but in one of his poems Samuel recalls:

> *"my sweet birth-place, and the old church-tower*
> *Whose bells, the poor man's only music, rang*
> *From morn to evening, all the hot Fair-day."*

A bronze plaque in the churchyard wall honours Ottery's most famous son. It shows his profile, menaced by the albatross that features in his best-known poem, The Ancient Mariner.It's a delight to wander around the narrow, twisting lanes that lead up from the River Otter, admiring the fine Georgian buildings among which is an old wool manufactory by the riverside, a dignified example of early industrial architecture. An especially interesting time to visit Ottery is on the Saturday closest to November 5th. The little town's Guy Fawkes celebrations include a time-honoured, and rather alarming, tradition of rolling barrels of flaming tar through the narrow streets.

Just a mile outside the town, to the northwest, is one of the few remaining Tudor mansions in the county. **Cadhay Manor** is a charming Elizabethan building constructed around a quadrangle known as the "Court of the Kings", its four entrances guarded by statues of Henry VIII and his three children, Edward VI, Mary Tudor, and Elizabeth I. The house has a grand Long Gallery, extending some 60 feet, a Great Hall even older than the Tudor building itself, and medieval fish ponds in the garden.

SIDMOUTH

MAP 3 REF I22

8 miles S of Honiton off the A3052

Sidmouth's success, like that of many other English resorts, had much to do with Napoleon Bonaparte. Barred from the Continent by the Emperor's conquest of Europe (and their favoured resorts), the leisured classes were forced to find diversion and entertainment within their own

island fortress. At the same time, sea bathing had suddenly become fashionable, so these years were a boom time for the south coast - even as far west as Sidmouth which until then had been a poverty-stricken village dependent on fishing.

Situated in Sidmouth town centre, **The Tudor Rose** bar and restaurant is a charming and welcoming eatery. Owner Mark Thompson has been personally running this fine establishment since 1997. Dating back to the 18th century, it boasts a traditional and comfortable ambience. A short passageway leads guests to the large reception and bar area (well-behaved dogs welcome) and on to the large non-smoking restaurant and attractive courtyard to the rear. The bar/restaurant boasts an Art Deco style, with bright light oak tables and half-panelled walls, decorated in attractive pastel shades. The rear courtyard is a natural suntrap, though totally enclosed to make it comfortable whatever the weather. The accent, of course, is on the food, which is superb. The changing menu and daily specials offer a range of traditional and more innovative dishes, from light meals and snacks to full a la carte choices. All

The Tudor Rose, 30 High Street, Sidmouth, Devon EX10 8EL Tel: 01395 514720

dishes make use of the freshest local produce and are expertly prepared and presented. Beef, chicken, lamb and seafood dishes are complemented by a fine range of vegetarian meals. Add to this the friendly atmosphere and superior choice of beer, wine and spirits, and you have the perfect place to pass an enjoyable few hours of fine dining and good company.

Sidmouth's spectacular position at the mouth of the River Sid, flanked by dramatic red cliffs soaring to over 500 feet and with a broad pebbly beach, assured the village's popularity with the newcomers. A grand Esplanade was constructed, lined with handsome Georgian houses, and between 1800 and 1820 Sidmouth's population doubled as the aristocratic and well-to-do built substantial "cottages" in and around the town. A stroll around the town reveals a wealth of attractive Georgian and early-Victorian buildings; in all, Sidmouth can boast nearly 500 listed buildings. Curiously, the Victorians seemed incapable of creating architecturally interesting churches and Sidmouth's two 19th century churches are no exception. But it's worth seeking out the curious structure known as the **Old Chancel**, a glorious hotch-potch of styles using bits and pieces salvaged from the old parish church and elsewhere, among them a priceless window of medieval stained glass. **Sidmouth Museum**, near the sea-front, provides a vivid presentation of the Victorian resort along with such curiosities as an albatross' swollen foot once used as a tobacco pouch. There's an interesting collection of local prints, a costume gallery and a display of fine lace. One of the most striking exhibits in the museum is the "Long Picture" by Hubert Cornish, which is some 8 foot long and depicts the whole of Sidmouth seafront as it was around 1814.

BUDLEIGH SALTERTON
Map 3 ref I22
12 miles SW of Honiton off the B3178

With its trim Victorian villas, broad promenade and a spotlessly clean beach flanked by 500 foot high red sandstone cliffs, Budleigh Salterton retains the 19th century atmosphere of a genteel resort. Victorian tourists "of the better sort" noted with approval that the two mile long beach was of pink shingle rather than sand. (Sand attracted the rowdier kind of holiday-maker, so it was thought.) The steeply-shelving beach was another deterrent, and the sea here is still a place for paddling rather than swimming. One famous Victorian visitor was the celebrated artist Sir John Everett Millais, who stayed during the summer of 1870 in the curiously-shaped house called **The Octagon**. It was beside the beach here that he painted his most famous picture The Boyhood of Raleigh, using his two sons and a local ferryman as his models.

The name Budleigh Salterton derives from the salt pans at the mouth of the River Otter which brought great prosperity to the town during the Middle Ages. The little port was then busy with ships loading salt and wool, but by 1450 the estuary had silted up and the salt pans flooded. The Domesday Book records a mill on the River Otter here, almost certainly on the site of the present **Otterton Mill**. This handsome, part-medieval building was restored to working order in the 1970s; visitors can now buy packs of flour ground by the same methods that were in use long before the compilers of the Domesday Book passed through the village. The site also includes a craft centre, shop and restaurant.

EXETER
Map 2 ref H22
15 miles W of Honiton off the A30

A lively and thriving city with a majestic Norman cathedral, many fine old buildings, and a wealth of excellent museums, Exeter's history stretches back for more than two millennia. Its present High Street was already in place some two centuries or more before the Romans arrived, part of an ancient ridgeway striking across the West Country. The inhabitants then were the Celtish tribe of the Dumnonii and it was they who named the river Eisca, 'a river abounding in fish'. The Romans made Isca their south-western stronghold, surrounding it with a massive defensive wall. Most of that has disappeared, but a spectacular caldarium, or **Roman Bath House** was uncovered in the Cathedral Close in 1971.

In the Dark Ages following the Roman withdrawal, the city was a major ecclesiastical centre and in 670 AD King Cenwealh founded an abbey on the site of the present cathedral. That, along with the rest of Exeter, was ransacked by the Vikings in the 9th century. They occupied the city twice before King Alfred finally saw them off. The Normans were next on the scene, although it wasn't until twenty years after the Battle of Hastings that William the Conqueror finally took possession of the city after a siege that lasted eighteen days. He ordered the construction of **Rougemont Castle**, the gatehouse and tower of which still stand at the top of Castle Street.

During the following century, the Normans began building **St Peter's Cathedral**, a work not completed until 1206. Half a century later, however, everything except the two sturdy towers was demolished and the present cathedral took shape. These years saw the development of the Decorated style, and Exeter is a sublime example of this appealing form of church architecture. In the 300ft long nave, stone piers like a forest rise 60ft and then fan out into sweeping arches. Equally impressive is the west front, a staggering display of more than sixty sculptures, carved between 1327 and 1369. They depict a curious mix of Biblical characters, soldiers, priests and a royal flush of Saxon and Norman kings.

St Peter's Cathedral, Exeter

Other treasures include an intricately-carved choir screen from about 1320, an astronomical clock built in 1376 which is one of the oldest timepieces in the world, a minstrels' gallery with a wonderful band of heavenly musicians, a monumental organ, and a colossal throne with a canopy 59ft high, carved in wood for Bishop Stapledon in 1316. Such is the grandeur of the Cathedral that other ecclesiastical buildings in Exeter tend to get overlooked. But it's well worth seeking out **St Nicholas' Priory**, an exceptional example of a small Norman priory. It is now an interesting museum where visitors can view the original Prior's cell, the 15th century kitchens, and the imposing central hall with a vaulted ceiling and chunky Norman pillars. The **Church of St Mary Steps** also repays a visit just to see its beautifully-preserved Norman font, and its ancient 'Matthew the Miller' tower clock, named after a medieval miller noted for his undeviating punctuality. The church stands in Stepcote Hill, a narrow cobbled and stepped thoroughfare which until as late as 1778 was the main road into Exeter from the west. The remarkable **Guildhall** in the High Street has been in use as a Town Hall ever since it was built in 1330, making it one of the oldest municipal buildings in the country. Its great hall was remodelled around 1450, and the Elizabethans added a striking, if rather fussy, portico, but the interior is still redolent of the Middle Ages. Another interesting medieval building is **The Tucker's Hall** in Fore Street, built in 1471 for the Company of Weavers, Fullers and Shearmen. Inside there is some exceptional carved panelling, a collection of rare silver, and a huge pair of fulling shears weighing over 25lbs and almost 4ft long. Nearby Parliament Street claims to be the world's narrowest street.

Exeter's one-time importance as a port is reflected in the dignified **Custom House**, built in 1681, and now the centrepiece of **Exeter Historic Quayside**, a fascinating complex of old warehouses, craft shops, cafes, and the **Seahorse Nature Aquarium** which is specially dedicated to these beautiful and enigmatic creatures. There are riverside walks, river trips, Canadian canoes and cycles for hire, and a passenger ferry across the river to the **Piazza Terracina** which explores five centuries of Exeter's trading connections around the world. The museum contains an extraordinary collection of boats, amongst them an Arab dhow, a reed boat from Lake Titicaca in South America, and a vintage steam launch. A special attraction of the museum is that visitors are positively encouraged to step aboard and explore in detail the many craft on show. Other excellent museums in the city include the **Royal Albert Memorial Museum** in Queen Street, (local history, archaeology and paintings); the **Devonshire Regiment Museum** (regimental history); and the **Rougemont House Museum** near the castle which has a copious collection of costumes and lace.

One of the city's most unusual attractions lies beneath its streets: the maze of **Underground Passages** constructed in the 14th and 15th centuries to bring water from springs beyond the city walls. A guided tour of the stone-vaulted caverns is an experience to remember.

EXMOUTH
Map 2 ref H22
10 miles SE of Exeter, on the A376

With its glorious coastal scenery and splendid beach, Exmouth was one of the earliest seaside resorts to be developed in Devon, *'the Bath of the West, the resort of the tip-top of the gentry of the Kingdom'*. Lady Byron and Lady Nelson came to stay and found lodgings in The Beacon, an elegant Georgian terrace overlooking the Madeira Walk and Esplanade. This early success suffered a setback when Brunel routed his Great Western line along the other side of the estuary, (incidentally creating one of the most scenic railway journeys still possible in England), and it wasn't until a branch line reached Exmouth in 1861 that business picked up again. The town isn't just a popular resort. Exmouth Docks are still busy with coasters and in summer a passenger ferry crosses the Exe to Starcross.

While in Exmouth, you should make a point of visiting what has been described as *'the most unusual house in Britain'*. **A La Ronde** is a fairy-tale thatched house built in 1765 by the sisters Jane and Mary Parminter who modelled it on the church of San Vitale in Ravenna. Despite its name, the house is not in fact circular but has 16 sides with 20 rooms set around a 45ft high octagon. The sisters lived here in magnificent feminist seclusion, forbidding the presence of any male in their house or its fifteen acres of grounds.

TOPSHAM
Map 2 ref H22
3 miles S of Exeter, on minor road off the A376 or A379

It's not surprising to find that the whole of the old town of Topsham has been declared a conservation area. Its narrow streets are lined with fine examples of 17th and 18th century merchants' houses, many built in the Dutch style with curved gable ends, there's a wealth of specialist and antique shops, and some stunning views over the Exe estuary.

TIVERTON
Map 2 ref H21
14 miles N of Exeter on the A396

Running due north from Exeter, the Exe Valley runs through the heart of what is known as 'Red Devon'. The soil here has a distinctive colour derived from the red Permian rocks that underlie it. Unlike most Devon land, this is prime agricultural land, fertile, easily-worked and, for some reason, particularly favourable to growing swedes to which it gives a much sought-after flavour.

The only town of any size in the valley is Tiverton, originally Twyfyrde, or two fords, for here the Exe is joined by the River Lowman. The town developed around what is now its oldest building, **Tiverton Castle**, built at the command of Henry I in 1106. Unfortunately, the castle found itself on the wrong side during the Civil War. General Fairfax himself was in charge of the successful onslaught in 1645. A few years later Parliament decreed that it should be 'slighted', destroyed beyond any use as a fortification. Cromwell's troops observed the letter of their in-

Duke diverted some of the profits from his copper mines to build the imposing Guildhall, Tavistock Guildhall and several other civic buildings. He also remodelled the Bedford Hotel, and constructed a model estate of artisans' cottages on the western side of the town. One of the legacies of the Abbey is the annual three-day fair, granted in 1105, which has now evolved into **Goose Fair**, a wonderful traditional street fair held on the second Wednesday in October. Tavistock was also permitted to hold a weekly market which, almost 900 years later, takes place every Friday in the Pannier Market, so named because country folk used to arrive carrying their produce in pannier bags.

PLYMOUTH   MAP 2 REF F23
48 miles SW of Exeter on the A38

Although Plymouth is one of the most celebrated names in British maritime history, it was surprisingly late in the day before its potential as one of the finest deep-water harbours in Europe was recognised. Only towards the end of the 13th century were the first quays erected and it wasn't until Elizabethan times that it became the main base for the English fleet guarding the western Channel against an attack from Spain. Perhaps the best way of getting to know this historic city is to approach **Plymouth Hoe** on foot from the main shopping area, along the now-pedestrianised Armada Way. It was on the Hoe on Friday, July 19th, 1588, that one of the most iconic moments in English history took place. Commander of the Fleet and erstwhile pirate Sir Francis Drake was playing bowls here when he was informed of the approach of the Spanish Armada. With true British phlegm, Sir Francis completed his game before boarding The Golden Hind and sailing off to harass the Spanish fleet. A statue of Sir Francis, striking a splendidly belligerent pose and looking proudly to the horizon, stands on the Hoe which is still an open space, combining the functions of promenade, public park and parade ground. Just offshore, the striking shape of **Drake's Island** rises like Alcatraz from the deep swirling waters at the mouth of the River Tamar. In its time, this stark fortified islet has been used as a gunpowder repository (it is said to be riddled with underground tunnels where the powder was stored), a prison and a youth adventure centre.

Two miles from the Hoe, Plymouth's remarkable **Breakwater** protects the Sound from the destructive effects of the prevailing south-westerly winds. Built between 1812 and 1840, this massive mile-long construction required around four million tons of limestone. The surface was finished with enormous dove-tailed blocks of stone, and the structure rounded off with a lighthouse at one end. On a clear day it's possible to see the famous **Eddystone Lighthouse**, 12 miles out in the Channel. The present lighthouse is the fourth to be built here. The first, made of timber, was swept away in a huge storm in 1703 taking with it the man who had built the lighthouse, the ship-owner Winstanley. In 1759, a much more substantial structure of dove-tailed granite blacks was built by John Smeaton. It stood for 120 years and even then it was not the lighthouse but the rocks on which it stood which began to collapse. The lighthouse was dismantled and re-erected on the Hoe where, as **Smeaton's Tower**, it is one of the city's most popular tourist attractions. From the top, there are good views of **Millbay Docks**, Plymouth's busy commercial port which was once busy with transatlantic passenger liners. Today, the docks handle a variety of merchant shipping, including the continental ferry services to Brittany and northern Spain. To the east, the view is dominated by **The Citadel**, a massive fortification built by Charles II, ostensibly as a defence against seaborne attack. Perhaps bearing in mind that Plymouth had resisted a four-year siege by his father's troops during the Civil War, Charles' Citadel has a number of gun ports bearing directly on the city. The Citadel is still a military base, but there are guided tours every afternoon from May to September. Near to the Citadel is Plymouth's oldest quarter, the **Barbican**. Now a lively entertainment area filled with restaurants, pubs and an innovative small theatre, it was once the main trading centre for merchants exporting wool and importing wine.

Close by are the **Mayflower Steps** where the Pilgrim Fathers boarded ship for their historic voyage to Massachusetts. The names of the Mayflower's company are listed on a board on nearby Island House, now the tourist information office. Many other emigrants were to follow in the Pilgrim Fathers' wake, with the result that there are now more than 40 communities named Plymouth scattered across the English-speaking world.

A number of interesting old buildings around the Barbican have survived the ravages of time and the terrible pasting the city received during the Second World War. **Prysten House**, behind St Andrew's Church, is a 15th century priest\rquote s house; the **Elizabethan House** in New Street has a rich display of Elizabethan furniture and furnishings, and the **Merchant's House** in St Andrew's Street is generally regarded as Devon's finest Jacobean building. A fascinating exhibit in the Merchant's House is the **Park Pharmacy**, a genuine Victorian pharmacy complete with its 1864 fittings and stocked with such preparations as Ipecacuanha Wine (one to two tablespoonfuls as an emetic) and Tincture of Myrrh and Borax, "for the teeth and gums".

Locally, the Tamar estuary is known as the Hamoaze (pronounced ham-oys), and it's well worth taking one of the boat trips that leave from the Mayflower Steps. This is certainly the best way to see Devonport Dockyard, while the ferry to Cremyll on the Cornish bank of the Tamar drops off passengers close to **Mount Edgcumbe Country Park** and the old smuggling village of **Cawsand**. The blackest date in Plymouth's history is undoubtedly March 21st, 1941. On that night the entire centre of the city was razed to the ground by the combined effects of high-explosive and incendiary bombs. More than a thousand people were killed; another 5,000 injured. After the war, the renowned town planner Sir Patrick Abercrombie was commissioned to design a completely new town centre. Much of the rebuilding was carried out in the 1950s, which was not British architecture's Golden Age, but almost half a century later the scheme has acquired something of a period charm. The new city has some excellent facilities, including a first-rate **Museum and Art Gallery**, near Drake Circus, the **Theatre Royal** with its two auditoria in Royal Parade, the Arts Centre in Looe Street, and the **Pavilions** complex of concert hall, leisure pool and skating rink at the foot of Western Approach.

On the southern edge of the city stands one of Devon's grandest mansions, **Saltram House** (National Trust). Built during the reign of George II for the Parker family, this sumptuous house occupies a splendid site overlooking the Plym estuary. In the 1760s Robert Adam was called in, at enormous expense, to decorate the dining room and "double cube" saloon, which he accomplished with his usual panache. There are portraits of the Parkers by the locally born artist Sir Joshua Reynolds, and among the fine furniture, a magnificent four-poster bed by Thomas Chippendale. Other attractions include the great kitchen with its fascinating assortment of period kitchenware, an orangery in the gardens, and the former chapel, now a gallery displaying the work of West Country artists.

SALCOMBE

MAP 2 REF G24

18 miles SE of Plymouth off the A381

Standing at the mouth of the Kingsbridge "Estuary", Salcombe enjoys one of the most beautiful natural settings in the country. Sheltered from the prevailing west winds by steep hills, it also basks in one of the mildest micro-climates in England. It's not unusual to see mimosa, palms and even orange trees in the terraced gardens rising from the water's edge. The peaceful gardens at **Overbecks** (National Trust), overlooking Salcombe Bar, have an almost Mediterranean character. Like other small South Devon ports, Salcombe developed its own special area of trading. While Dartmouth specialised in French and Spanish wine, at Salcombe high-sailed clippers arrived carrying the first fruits of the pineapple harvest from the West Indies, and oranges from the Azores. That traffic has ceased, but pleasure craft throng the harbour and a small fishing fleet still operates from **Batson Creek**, a picturesque location where the fish quay is piled high with lobster creels. The town's sea-faring history is interestingly evoked in the **Salcombe Maritime & Local History Museum** in the old Customs House on the quay.

The coastline to the south and west of Salcombe, among the most magnificent in Britain, is now largely owned by the National Trust. Great slanting slabs of gneiss and schist tower above the sea, making the clifftop walk here both literally and metaphorically breathtaking. At **Bolt Head**, the rock forms a jagged promontory protruding onto the western approaches to the

Kingsbridge estuary, and further west, the spectacular cliffs between Bolt Head and **Bolt Tail** are interrupted by a steep descent at **Soar Mill Cove**. After rounding Bolt Tail, the footpath drops down to the sheltered sandy beach of Hope Cove.

DARTMOUTH
MAP 2 REF H23

22 miles E of Plymouth off the A3122

For centuries this entrancing little town clinging to the sides of a precipitous hill was one of England's principal ports. During the 1100s, Crusaders on both the Second and Third Crusades mustered here, and from here they set sail. In its sheltered harbour, Elizabeth's men o' war lay in wait to pick off the stragglers from the Spanish Armada. Millions of casks of French and Spanish wine have been offloaded onto its narrow quays. And in 1620, the Mayflower put in here for a few days for repairs before hoisting sail for Plymouth in August and then on to the New World, where it arrived three months later. The quay from which the Pilgrims embarked later became the major location for the BBC-TV series The Onedin Line, and was also seen in the feature film Sense and Sensibility starring Emma Thompson and Hugh Grant.

Geoffrey Chaucer visited the town in 1373 in his capacity as Inspector of Customs and is believed to have modelled the Shipman in his Canterbury Tales on the character of the then-Mayor of Dartmouth, John Hawley. Hawley was an enterprising merchant and seafarer who was also responsible for building **Dartmouth Castle** (English Heritage). Dramatically sited, it guards the entrance to the Dart estuary and was one of the first castles specifically designed to make effective use of artillery. In case the Castle should prove to be an inadequate deterrent, in times of danger a heavy chain was strung across the harbour to Kingswear Castle on the opposite bank. (Kingswear Castle is privately owned and not open to the public.) There'a striking monumental brass to John Hawley and his two wives in the **Church of St Saviour's**, a part 14th century building against whose wall ships used to tie up before the New Quay was constructed in the late 1500s. Nearby is the Custom House, a handsome building of 1739 which has some fine internal plasterwork ceilings. Also worth seeking out are **The Butterwalk**, a delightful timber-framed arcade dating from 1640 in which the **Dartmouth Museum** occupies the ground floor, and the working steam pumping engine built to a revolutionary design by Thomas Newcomen, the celebrated inventor, who was born in Dartmouth in 1663.

Dartmouth's oldest building, and many would say its loveliest, is **The Cherub Inn**. It was built in 1380 for a wealthy wool merchant and during the course of its long history has managed to escape both a great fire in 1864 which destroyed much of Higher Street, and a German bomb in 1943 which flattened the house across the road. The Cherub's name doesn't have any heavenly connotations but comes from a type of boat, constructed locally, which was specifically designed for carrying wool. Appropriately enough, when the house was restored in the 1950s its ancient beams were found to be ship's timbers.

BRIXHAM
MAP 2 REF H23

23 miles E of Plymouth off the A3022

In the 18th century, Brixham was the most profitable fishing port in Britain. Fishing is still the most important activity in this engaging little town, although the trawlers now have to pick their way between flotillas of yachts and tour boats. On the quay there are stalls selling freshly caught seafood and around the harbour a maze of narrow streets harbour a host of small shops, tea rooms and galleries.

TOTNES
MAP 2 REF H23

20 miles E of Plymouth off the A385

This captivating little town claims to have been founded by an Ancient Trojan named Brutus in the 1200 BC. The grandfather of Aeneas, the hero of Virgil's epic poem The Aeneid, Brutus sailed up the River Dart, gazed at the fair prospect around him and decided to found the first town in this new country which would take its name, Britain, from his own. The **Brutus Stone**, set in the pavement of the main shopping street (Fore Street) commemorates this stirring incident when both the town and a nation were born. Well, it could be true. The first recorded evidence of this town, set on a hill above the highest navigable point on the River Dart, doesn't appear until the mid 10th century when King Edgar established a mint here. The Saxons already had a castle of sorts here, but the impressive remains of **Totnes Castle** are Norman, built between the 1100s and early 1300s. Towering over the town, it is generally reckoned to be the best-preserved motte and bailey castle in Devon. A substantial section of Totnes' medieval town wall has also survived. The superb **East Gate**, which straddles the steep main street is part of that wall, and although grievously damaged by fire in 1990 has been meticulously restored. Just a little way down the hill from East Gate is the charming **Guildhall** of 1553, a remarkable little building with a granite colonnade. It houses both the Council Chamber (which is still in use) and the underground Town Gaol (which is not). Almost opposite the Guildhall is another magnificent Elizabethan building, currently occupied by Barclays Bank. It was built in 1585 for Nicholas Ball who had made his fortune from the local pilchard fishery. When he died, his wife Anne

Totnes Museum

married Sir Thomas Bodley and it was the profit from pilchards that funded the world-famous Bodleian Library at Oxford University.

The town's Elizabethan heritage really comes alive if you are visiting on a Tuesday in summer. You will find yourself stepping into a pageant of Elizabethan colour, for this is when the people of Totnes array themselves in crisp, white ruffs and velvet gowns for a charity market which has raised thousands of pounds for good causes.

The parish church of Totnes is **St Mary's**. It was entirely rebuilt in the 15th century when the town's cloth industry was booming, - second in importance only to Exeter. The church's most glorious possession is a stone rood-screen delicately carved in stone from the quarry at Beer. Close by at 70 Fore Street is the **Totnes Museum**, housed in an attractive half-timbered Elizabethan building whose upper floors overhang the street. One of the fascinating exhibits here honours a distinguished son of Totnes, Charles Babbage (1791-1871) whose "analytical Machine" is universally acknowledged as the forerunner of the electronic computer. The Museum display records his doomed struggle to perfect such a calculator using only mechanical parts. A little further up the hill, in High Street, the **Butterwalk** and **Poultry-walk** are two ancient covered shopping arcades whose upper storeys rest on pillars of granite, timber or cast iron.

PAIGNTON
Map 2 ref H23
22 miles W of Plymouth off the A379

Today, Torquay merges imperceptibly into Paignton, but in early Victorian times Paignton was just a small farming village, about half a mile inland, noted for its cider and its "very large and sweet flatpole cabbages". The town's two superb sandy beaches, ideal for families with young children, were to change all that. A pier and promenade add to the town's appeal, and throughout the summer season there's a packed programme of specials events, including a Children's Festival in August, funfairs and various firework displays.

The most interesting building in Paignton is undoubtedly **Oldway Mansion**, built in 1874 for Isaac Singer, the millionaire sewing-machine manufacturer. Isaac died the following year and it was his son, Paris, who gave the great mansion its present exuberant form. Paris added a south side mimicking a music pavilion in the grounds of Versailles, a hallway modelled on the Versailles Hall of Mirrors, and a sumptuous ballroom where his mistress Isadora Duncan would display the new, fluid kind of dance she had created based on classical mythology. Paris Singer sold the mansion to Paignton Borough Council in 1946 and it is now used as a Civic Centre, but many of the splendid rooms (and the extensive gardens) are open to the public free of charge and guided tours are available.

An experience not to be missed in Paignton is a trip on the **Paignton and Dartmouth Steam Railway**, a seven-mile journey along the lovely Torbay coast and through the wooded slopes bordering the Dart estuary to Kingswear where travellers board a ferry for the 10-minute crossing to Dartmouth. The locomotives and rolling stock all bear the proud chocolate and gold livery of the Great Western Railway, and on certain services you can wine and dine in Pullman style luxury in the "Riviera Belle Dining Train". During the peak season, trains leave every 45 minutes or so.

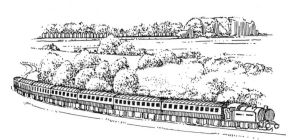

Paignton and Dartmouth Steam Railway

The town's other major attraction is **Paignton Zoo**, set in 75 acres of attractive botanical gardens, home to some 300 species of world animals. A registered charity dedicated to protecting the global wildlife heritage, the Zoo is particularly concerned with endangered species such as the Asiatic lions and Sumatran tigers which are now provided with their own forest habitat area, and orang utans and gorillas who roam freely on large outdoor islands, free from cages. The route of the Jungle Express miniature railway provides good views of these and many other animals.

TORQUAY
MAP 2 REF H23
23 miles E of Plymouth off the A3022

In Victorian times, Torquay liked to be known as "The English Naples", a genteel resort of shimmering white villas set amongst dark green trees and spread, like Rome, across seven hills. It was indisputably the West of England's premier resort with imposing hotels like the Imperial and the Grand catering for "people of condition" from across Europe. At one time, the town could boast more royal visitors to the square mile than any other resort in the world. Edward VII came here on the royal yacht Britannia and anchored in the bay. Each evening he would be discreetly ferried across to a bay beneath the Imperial Hotel and then conducted to the first floor suite where his mistress, Lily Langtry, was waiting.

The town's oldest building is **Torre Abbey**, founded in 1195 but largely remodelled as a Georgian mansion by the Cary family between 1700 and 1750. The Abbey was sold to Torbay Council in 1930 and, together with its extensive gardens, has been open to the public ever since. One of its most popular attractions is the **Agatha Christie Memorial Room** in the Abbot's Tower, containing fascinating memorabilia loaned by her daughter. Dame Agatha was born in Torquay in 1890 and the town has created an **Agatha Christie Mile** which guides visitors to places of interest that she knew as a girl and young woman growing up in the town. **Torquay Museum** also has an interesting exhibition of photographs recording her life, as well as a pictorial record of Torquay over the last 150 years, and displays chronicling the social and natural history of the area. Amongst the Museu's other treasures are many items discovered at **Kents Cavern**, an astonishing complex of caves regarded as "one of the most important archaeological sites in Britain". Excavations in the 1820s revealed an remarkable collection of animal bones - the remains of mammoths, sabre-toothed tigers, grizzly bears, bison, and cave lions. These bones proved to be the dining-room debris of cave dwellers who lived here some 30,000 years ago, the oldest-known residents of Europe.

Kents Cavern

The caves are open daily, all year, offering guided tours, a sound and light show, a gift shop and refreshment room. Just a mile or so from the town centre is **Cockington Village**, a phenomenally picturesque rural oasis of thatched cottages, a working forge, and the Drum Inn designed by Sir Edward Lutyens and completed in 1930. From the village there's a pleasant walk through the park to Cockington Court, now a Craft Centre and Gallery. Partly Tudor, this stately old manor was for almost three centuries the home of the Mallock family. In the 1930s they formed a trust to preserve "entire and unchanged the ancient amenities and character of the place,

Cockington Village

and in developing its surroundings to do nothing which may not rather enhance than diminish its attractiveness". The Trust has been spectacularly successful in carrying out their wishes.

TEIGNMOUTH
Map 2 ref H23

23 miles E of Plymouth off the A381/A379

Teignmouth has something of a double personality. On the coastal side is the popular holiday resort with its 2 miles of sandy beaches, a splendid promenade almost as long, and a pier. There's also a 25 foot high lighthouse which serves no apparent purpose apart from looking rather fetching. The residential area contains much fine Regency and Georgian building. Particularly noteworthy are the **Church of St James** with its striking octagonal tower of 1820, and the former **Assembly Rooms**, a dignified colonnaded building which now houses the Riviera Cinema. Teignmouth's Georgian past is recalled on Wednesdays during the season when local people dress up in 18th century costume. On the river side of the town is the working port, approached by the narrowest of channels. The currents here are so fast and powerful that no ship enters the harbour without a Trinity House pilot on board. The Quay was built in 1821 when there was great demand for granite from the quarries on Haytor Down. Amongst the many buildings constructed in this durable stone were London Bridge (the one now in the US) and the British Museum. The main export today is potter's clay from pits beside the River Teign, but boat building continues on a small scale. Teignmouth itself is an interesting town to explore with a number of attractive thoroughfares dating from the Regency and early Victorian periods such as Regent Street and Northumberland Place. Den Crescent is a grandiose development set back from the seafront and incorporates the Assembly Rooms of 1826. The sea front naturally is a major attraction with its wide promenade, sandy beach, safe bathing, and Grand Pier offering all the traditional entertainments as well as newer ones such as King Neptune's Seabed Band.

DAWLISH   Map 2 ref H23
25 miles E of Plymouth off the A379

This pretty seaside resort, with one of the safest beaches in England, has the unusual feature of a main railway line separating the town from its seafront. The result is, in fact, much more appealing than it sounds. For one thing, the railway keeps motor traffic away from the beachside, and for another, the low granite viaduct which carries the track has weathered attractively in the century and a half since it was built. The arches under which beach-goers pass create a kind of formal entrance to the beach and the Victorian station has become a visitor attraction in its own right.

By the time Brunel's railway arrived here in 1846, Dawlish was already well-known as a fashionable resort. The architect John Nash had designed several ornate "cottages"; John Keats, with his convalescent brother, Tom, visited the town in 1818. The great poet was inspired to pen the less-than-immortal lines:

> Over the hill and over the Dale
> And over the bourne to Dawlish
> Where Gingerbread wives have a scanty sale
> And gingerbread nuts are smallish.

At the time of his visit, the town was being transformed with scores of new villas springing up along the Strand. Earlier improvers had already "beautified" the River Daw, which flows right through the town, by landscaping the stream into a series of shallow waterfalls and surrounding it with attractive gardens like The Lawn. Until Regency times, The Lawn had been a swamp populated by herons, kingfishers and otters. Then in 1808, the developer John Manning filled in the marshy land with earth removed during the construction of Queen Street. Today, both The Lawn and Queen Street still retain the elegance of those early-19th century days.

NORTH DEVON

ILFRACOMBE   Map 2 ref G20
50 miles N of Exeter on the A361

With a population of around 11,000, Ilfracombe is the largest seaside resort on the North Devon coast. Up until 1800, however, it was a small fishing and market town relying entirely on the sea both for its living and as its principal means of communication. The boundaries of the old town are marked by a sheltered natural harbour to the north, and a part-Norman parish church half-a-mile away to the south. The entrance to the harbour is guarded by **Lantern Hill**, a steep-sided conical rock which is crowned by the restored medieval **Chapel of St Nicholas**. For centuries, this highly-conspicuous former fishermen's chapel doubled as a lighthouse, the light being placed in a lantern at the west end of the building. Today, Lantern Hill provides a spectacular view of Ilfracombe's old street plan, busy harbour and craggy coastline. Like so many west country resorts, Ilfracombe developed in response to the

Ilfracombe Harbour

early 19th century craze for sea bathing. **The Tunnel Baths**, with an extravagant Doric facade, were opened in Bath Place in 1836, by which time a number of elegant residential terraces had been built on the hillside to the south of the old town. The arrival of the railway in 1874 brought a huge influx of visitors and around the same time the harbour was enlarged to cope with the paddle steamers bringing in tourists from Bristol and South Wales. Much of the town's architecture, which could best be described as decorated Victorian vernacular, dates from this period, the new streets spreading inland in steeply undulating rows. For walkers, the coastal path provides some spectacular scenery, whether going west to Capstone Point, or east to Hillsborough Hill.

LYNTON

MAP 2 REF G20

17 miles E of Ilfracombe off the A39

Lynton and Lynmouth, though often mentioned in the same breath, are very different in character. Lynton is the younger of the two settlements and sits atop a great cliff 600 feet high; Lynmouth, far below, clusters around the junction of the East and West Lyn rivers just before they reach the sea. Lynton is a bright and breezy village, its houses and terraces mostly Victorian. **Exmoor Museum**, housed in a restored 16th century house, has an interesting collection of the tools and products of bygone local craftsmen and other exhibits recounting local history.

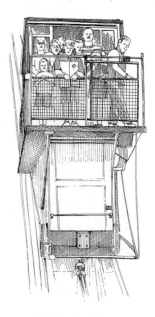

To the west of Lynton, about a mile or so along a minor road mile, is one of the most remarkable natural features in Devon, the **Valley of the Rocks**. When the poet Robert Southey visited the area in 1800, he was most impressed by this natural gorge "covered with huge stones ... the very bones and skeletons of the earth; rock reeling upon rock, stone piled upon stone, a huge terrific mass". In Lorna Doone, the author R D Blackmore transforms the site into the "Devil's Cheesering" where Jan Ridd visits Mother Meldrun who is sheltering under "eaves of lichened rock". Lynton is connected to its sister-village Lynmouth by an ingenious **Cliff Railway** which, when it opened on Easter Monday, 1890, was the first of its kind in Britain. A gift from Sir George Newnes, the publisher and newspaper tycoon, the railway is powered by water, or rather by two 700 gallon water tanks, one at each end of the 450 foot track. When the tank at the top is filled, and the one at the bottom emptied, the brakes are released and the two passenger carriages change place.

Lynton Cliff Railway

LYNMOUTH

MAP 2 REF G20

18 miles E of Ilfracombe off the A39

One of the most picturesque villages in Devon (do seek out Mars Hill, an eye-ravishing row of thatched cottages), Lynmouth has a tiny harbour surrounded by lofty wooded hills and a curious Rhenish Tower on the pier. For centuries the people of Lynmouth subsisted on agriculture and fishing, especially herring fishing and curing. By good fortune, just as the herring shoals were moving away to new waters, the North Devon coast benefited from the two new enthusiasms for "Romantic" scenery and sea bathing. Coleridge and Wordsworth arrived here on a walking tour in the 1790s, Shelley wrote fondly of his visit in 1812, and it was Robert Southey, later Poet Laureate, who first used the designation "the English Switzerland" to describe the dramatic scenery of the area. the painter Gainsborough had already described it as "the most delightful place for a landscape painter this country can boast."

Lynmouth's setting beside its twin rivers is undeniably beautiful, but it has also proved to be tragically vulnerable. On the night of August 16th, 1952, a cloudburst over Exmoor deposited 9 inches of rain onto an already saturated moor. In the darkness, the normally placid East and West Lyn rivers became raging cataracts and burst their banks. Sweeping tree trunks and boulders along with it, the torrent smashed its way through the village, destroying dozens of houses and leaving 31 people dead. That night had seen many freak storms across southern England, but none had matched the ferocity of the deluge that engulfed this pretty little village.

BARNSTAPLE

MAP 2 REF G20

10 miles S of Ilfracombe on the A361

Barnstaple enjoys a superb location at the head of the Taw estuary, at the furthest point downstream where it was possible to ford the river. The first bridge across the Taw was built in the late 1200s, but the present impressive structure that stands here now, 700 foot long with 16 arches, dates from about 1450 although it has been altered and widened many times. Barnstaple is the administrative and commercial capital of the region, a pre-eminence it already enjoyed when the Domesday Book recorded it as one of only four boroughs in the county, with its own Mint and regular market. There are still produce markets on Tuesdays and Fridays, but the **Pannier Market** is open every weekday. This huge glass-roofed building covering some 45,000 square feet was built in 1855 and resembles nothing more than a major railway station. Each day of the week has a different emphasis: crafts on Monday and Thursday, for example, antiques on Wednesday. The Market takes it name from the pannier baskets in which country people would carry their produce to the town. Just across from the Pannier Market is **Butchers Row**, a quaint line of booth-like Victorian shops built mostly of wood and with a brightly painted wooden canopy. Back in 1855, they were occupied exclusively by butchers, but now visitors find a variety of goods on sale, seaweed among them. Each week in season 300 lbs of it are sold, most of which apparently ends up as a breakfast dish, served with bacon and an egg on top.

In the High Street stands the rather austere **Guildhall**, built in

Barnstaple

the Grecian style in 1826 and housing some interesting civic memorabilia: portraits, regalia and silverware. The **Church of St Peter and St Paul** dates back to the early 1300s but, after having its spire twisted by a lightning strike in 1810, suffered even more badly under the heavy hand of the Victorian restorer Sir Gilbert Scott. Much more appealing are the charming 17th century **Horwood's Almshouses** and the 15th century **St Anne's Chapel**, which served for many years as the town's Grammar School. It is now a museum with a schoolroom re-created as it might have been in the late 17th century when John Gay, author of The Beggar's Opera, numbered among its pupils. Another interesting museum has the unusual distinction of being housed in a former signal box. The **Lynton and Barnstaple Railway Museum** records the history of the narrow-guage railway that ran between Barnstaple and Lynton from 1898 to 1935. **Queen Anne's Walk** is a colonnaded arcade with some lavish ornamentation and sur-mounted by a large statue of the Queen herself. Opened in 1708, it was used by the Barnstaple wool merchants. The building stands on the old town quay from which, in 1588, five ships set sail to join Drake's fleet against the Armada. One of Barnstaple's most enduring industries has been pottery, made here continuously since the 13th century. In Litchdon Street, the **Royal Barum Pottery** welcomes visitors to its workshop, museum, and well-stocked shop.

Walkers along the **Tarka Trail** will know Barnstaple well as the cross-over point in this figure-of-eight long-distance footpath. Inspired by Henry Williamson's celebrated story of Tarka the Otter, the 180-mile trail wanders through a delightful variety of Devon scenery - tranquil countryside, wooded river valleys, rugged moorland, and a stretch of the North Devon coast, with part of the route taking in the **Tarka Line Railway**. A guide book is available covering the whole trail; and there are pamphlets detailing individual sections.

MUDDIFORD
MAP 2 REF G20

4 miles N of Barnstaple off the B3230

Despite its rather unappealing name, Muddiford is a very attractive little village. (The village really did get its name from the "muddy ford" that once crossed the river here.) At **Hewish**, three former farm buildings barns have been imaginatively transformed, with glass frontages to take advantage of the lovely views of the strikingly beautiful surrounding countryside. Just eight miles from Woolacombe's long sandy beach, the first of these three establishments is called "The Wheelhouse". Set at the end of a private road, this 300-year-old converted barn sleeps eight and benefits from its own large south-facing garden. Spacious and comfortable, it has a large living room with French doors opening on to the patio area. The dining room is warm and comfortable, the farmhouse-style kitchen well equipped with every modern amen-

ity. "Woodland View" sleeps four, "Valley View" sleeps six. These, too, like The Wheel-house, are beautifully appointed and boast a tumble dryer, micro-wave oven, dishwasher, fridge/freezer, large gar-den with patio and furniture, and barbecue. All the bedrooms in the three cottages are en suite. Every effort has been made to ensure

Hewish, Muddiford, nr Barnstaple, Devon EX31 4HH
Tel: 01271 850513 Fax: 01271 850368

that the cottages meet the highest standards of comfort and quality. They are homely and welcoming, relaxing and tranquil. Whether exploring the beautiful beaches nearby, walking and riding at Exmoor National Park or visiting the sights of Arlington Court, Marwood Gardens and the many other attractions of the region, Hewish makes the perfect base.

Less than 2 miles to the east of Muddiford, **Marwood Hill Gardens** offers visitors some 18 acres of trees and shrubs, many of them rare and unusual. The collection was started more than half a century ago and now includes an enormous number and variety of plants. The three lakes, linked by the largest Bog Garden in the West Country, are busy with ducks and multi-coloured carp. From spring, when camellias and magnolias are in bloom, through to the brilliant hues of Autumn, the gardens provide a continuous spectacle of colour.

MIDDLE MARWOOD
MAP 2 REF G20

5 miles NW of Barnstaple off the A39/A361

Surrounded by three acres of gardens, **Westcott Barton** is a distinguished guest house, set in its own valley. There is an atmosphere of undisturbed peace and tranquillity as befits a home which dates from the time of the Domesday Book. Owner Ann Burnham is a charming and

welcoming host. There are four en suite double bedrooms, each individually decorated. All rooms are very spacious and beautifully furnished. The "Pink- Room" has a four-poster bed. The "Cider House" has a double room upstairs and a twin room on the ground floor with wheelchair access. The "Wood Shed" is the honeymoon cottage, with bathroom downstairs and bedroom upstairs with a door out onto the gardens. All rooms have a welcome tray and television. The big sitting room has an open log fire on chilly eve-

Westcott Barton, Middle Marwood, Barnstaple, Devon EX31 4EF Tel: 01271 814825

nings. All the produce used to make breakfast and evening meals is fresh, including local meats and fish, fruit and vegetables. There is a small lake in the grounds available for coarse fishing. For a truly relaxing break away from the hustle and bustle, look no further.

BIDEFORD
MAP 2 REF F21

8 miles W of Barnstaple off the A39

Named the "Little White Town" by Charles Kingsley, this attractive town set beside the River Torridge was once the third busiest port in Britain. The first bridge across the shallow neck of the Torridge estuary was builtaround 1300 to link Bideford with its aptly-named satellite village, East-the-Water. That bridge must have been very impressive for its time. It was 670 foot long, and built of massive oak lintels of varying length which created a series of irregular archesbetween 12 and 25 feet apart. These erratic dimensions were preserved when the bridge was rebuilt in stone around 1460 (the old bridge was used as scaffolding), and despite widening during the 1920s they persist to this day. Unusually, Bideford Bridge is managed by an ancient corporation of trustees, known as feoffees, whose income, derived from property in the town, not only pays for the upkeep of the bridge but also supports local charities and good causes.

Bideford received its Market Charter from Henry III in 1272. Markets still take place every Tuesday and Saturday. Since 1883 they have been held in the splendid **Pannier Market** building, reckoned to be one of the best surviving examples of a Victorian covered market. Along with local produce, there's a huge selection of gifts, crafts, and hand-made goods on offer. Evidence of Bideford's golden age can still be seen in the opulent merchants' residences in Bridgeland Street, and most strikingly in the **Royal Hotel** in East-the-Water, a former merchant's house of 1688 with a pair of little-seen plasterwork ceilings which are perhaps the finest and most extravagant examples of their kind in Devon. It was while he was staying at the Royal Hotel that Charles Kingsley penned most of Westward Ho! A quarter of a million words long, the novel was completed in just seven months. There's a statue of Kingsley, looking suitably literary, on **Bideford Quay**. Broad and tree-lined, the Quay stands at the foot of the narrow maze of lanes which formed the old seaport, a pleasant reminder of the town's maritime past. Just round the corner from the Quay, on the edge of Victoria Park, is the **Burton Museum & Art Gallery**, opened in 1994.

Lundy Island Lighthouse

One excursion from Bideford that should not be missed is the day trip to **Lundy Island**. Lundy is a huge lump of granite rock, 3 miles long and half a mile wide, with sheer cliffs rising 500 feet above the shore. Its name derives from the Norse for "puffin island", and these attractive birds with their multi-coloured beaks are still in residence, along with many other species. More than 400 different birds have been spotted on Lundy. The island has a ruined castle, a church, a pub, and a shop selling souvenirs and the famous stamps. There's even a hotel, but if you hope to stay overnight you must book well ahead.

YARNSCOMBE

MAP 2 REF G21

6 miles SE of Bideford off the B3232

Set in four acres of formal and informal gardens, surrounded on three sides by a a tranquil wooded glade, **Netherne** is a haven of peace and tranquillity offering bed and breakfast accommodation. Owners Janet and Christopher Brice are warm and welcoming hosts, who work hard to ensure that all their guests have an enjoyable and relaxing stay. There are three comfortable guest bedrooms (two doubles, one twin), furnished and decorated to a high standard of taste and quality. The original conservatory runs the total width of the house, filling it with sunlight and making it even more charming and pleasant, as well as affording superb views across Dartmoor. The residents' lounge is supremely attractive, with a roaring wood fire in chilly

Netherne, Clogshill Cross, Yarnscombe, Barnstaple, Devon EX31 3LY Tel: 01271 858297

weather and a cosy ambience whatever the season. With some of Britain's finest sandy beaches no more than half an hour away by car, the historic town of Great Torrington just a short distance away, and many other interesting and lovely sights in the region, it makes an ideal base.

WESTWARD HO! MAP 2 REF F21
2 miles N of Bideford, on the B3236

Is there any other place in the world that has been named after a novel? Following the huge success in 1855 of Charles Kingsley's tale of Elizabethan derring-do, a company was formed to develop this spectacular site with its rocky cliffs and 2 miles of sandy beach. Today Westward Ho! is a busy holiday resort well worth visiting for its beach and the nearby **Northam Burrows Country Park** - 670 acres of grazed burrows rich in flora, fauna and migratory birds, and offering tremendous views across Bideford Bay.

CLOVELLY MAP 2 REF F21
12 miles W of Bideford off the A39

Even if you've never been to Devon, you may well have heard of this unbelievably quaint and picturesque village that tumbles down a steep hillside in terraced levels. Almost every flower-strewn cottage is worthy of its own picture postcard and from the sheltered little harbour there is an enchanting view of this unique place. The only access to the beach is on foot or by donkey, although there is a Land Rover service from the Red Lion Hotel for those who can't face the climb back up the hill. The only other forms of transport are the sledges which are used to deliver weekly supplies. During the summer months there are regular boat trips around the bay, and daily excursions to Lundy Island.

HARTLAND MAP 2 REF F21
15 miles W of Bideford, on the B3248

From the village, follow the signs to **Hartland Abbey**. Founded in 1157, the Abbey was closed down in 1539 by Henry VIII who gave the building and its wide estates to William Abbott, Sergeant of the Royal wine cellars. His descendants still live here. The house was partly rebuilt in the mid 18th century in the style known as Strawberry Hill Gothic, and in the 1850s the

architect George Gilbert Scott added a front hall and entrance. The Abbey's owner at that time, Sir George Stucley, had recently visited the Alhambra Palace in Spain, which he much admired. He asked Scott to design something in that style and the result is the elegant Alhambra Corridor with a blue

Hartland Abbey

vaulted ceiling with white stencilled patterns. The Abbey has a choice collection of pictures, porcelain and furniture acquired over many generations and, in the former Servants' Hall, a unique exhibition of documents dating from 1160. There's also a fascinating Victorian and Edwardian photographic exhibition which includes many early photographs.

CORNWALL

LAUNCESTON
MAP 2 REF F22
23 miles N of Plymouth off the A30

Launceston (the local pronunciation is Lawson) is one of the most pleasant inland towns in Cornwall. For centuries it was an important regional capital which guarded the main overland route into the county. Shortly after the Norman invasion, William the Conqueror's half-brother, Robert of Mortain, built a massive Castle here on an elevated site above the River Kensey. From this castle fort, subsequent Earls of Cornwall tried to govern the fiercely independent Cornish people. A fine example of a motte and bailey castle, the outer bailey is now a public park; there is also a round double keep, the outer walls of which are 12 foot thick in places. Also in its time used as a gaol, where prisoners were kept in appalling conditions in this decaying fortress, its inmates included founder of the Quakers, George Fox.

Launceston boasts a number of fine old buildings and churches. In medieval times a settlement grew up around an Augustinian priory on the northern side of the River Kensey. It is here that the original parish **Church of St Stephen** stands. Nearby there is a Byzantine-style Roman Catholic church, built early in the 20th century. The oldest surviving ecclesiastical building in the town is the 12th century **Church of St Thomas**, near the southern end of the medieval footbridge that crosses the river - surprisingly, within this tiny building stands the largest Norman font in Cornwall. Some of the most impressive stonework in the area is used in the **Church of St Mary Magdelene**, a 16th century granite structure built by a local landowner after the tragic death of his wife and son. He assembled the finest stonemasons in Cornwall to create, in their memory, a remarkable cornucopia of ornamental carving which covers nearly every surface of the building. Elsewhere in Launceston, the streets around the castle are filled with handsome buildings dating

Launceston Steam Railway

from Georgian times and earlier, including the National Trust-owned **Lawrence House** in Castle Street. Housing an interesting town museum, this was built in 1753 and contains some fine plasterwork ceilings. The art gallery near the medieval South Gate, the only remaining vestige of Launceston's town walls, is also worth a visit. To the west of the town, a **Steam Railway** runs along the Kensey valley. Other nearby attractions include **Tamar Otter Park** and **Trethorne Leisure Farm**.

BODMIN MOOR
MAP 2 REF E23
SW of Launceston

The bleak expanse of Bodmin Moor stretches either side of the A30. This 80 square-mile area of granite upland is characterised by saturated moorland and weather-beaten tors. The exposed

Bodmin Moor

area to the north of the main road supports the 1,377-foot hill known as **Brown Willy**, the highest point in Cornwall. Almost as high, and standing on National Trust-owned land a bit to the northwest, is **Rough Tor**, a magnificent viewpoint which is also the site of a memorial to the men of the Wessex Regiment killed in the Second World War. This dramatic area of the moor is best approached from the northwest along the lane leading up from the A39 at Camelford. Like Dartmoor, Bodmin Moor is covered in prehistoric remains. Typical of many are the scattered Bronze Age hut circles and field enclosures which can be seen on the side of Rough Tor. Slightly south of this lies the **Fernacre Stone Circle**. Also Bronze Age, it contains more than 30 standing stones and is the largest of this kind of structure on the Moor. Evidence of even earlier occupation can be found between the A30 and **Hawks Tor**, the site of a Neolithic henge monument known as the **Stripple Stones**.

BUDE
MAP 2 REF E21

15 miles N of Launceston off the A39

Bude, with its sweeping expanse of sand and Atlantic breakers rolling in from the west, seems to change its character with every change in the weather - a winter gale can make it seem like a remote outpost clinging to the edge of the world, while a warm summer breeze transforms it into a genial holiday town with some excellent facilities for beach-lovers, surfers and coastal walkers. It enjoys its status as a prime north coast resort with find sandy beaches, rock pools, and tidal swimming pool. Bude's late-Victorian and Edwardian centre is sheltered from the worst Atlantic extremes by a low cliff which separates the shallow valley of the River Neet from the ocean. The town stood at the northern end of the now-disused **Bude Canal**, an ambitious early-19th century inland waterway which was intended to connect the Atlantic with the English Channel by way of the River Tamar. The only stretch to be completed, that between Bude and Launceston, was largely used for transporting seaweed, sand and other fertilisers to inland farms. Abandoned when the railway arrived in the 1890's, the two mile long section at the northern end has now been restored for use as a recreational amenity. The small fort guarding the northern entrance to the canal was built in the 1840's as an eccentric private residence, and the old forge on the canalside has been converted into an interesting **Museum** exploring Bude's maritime heritage. The **Bude-Stratton Historical Folk Exhibition**, also on the canal, and the **World of Nature** in the town centre, are two more fascinating places to visit. Bude is also host to an Annual Jazz Festival every summer.

BOSCASTLE
MAP 2 REF E22

12 miles SW of Bude off the B3263

Lying on a delightful, unspoilt stretch of the north Cornwall coastline, this was a thriving seaport up to the 19th century and is now used by local inshore fishermen and visitors. The National Trust own and protect the harbour area as well as a considerable amount of the land and coastline in north Corwall. This ancient and picturesque fishing community stands in a combe at the head of a remarkable S-shaped inlet from the Atlantic. The village grew up around, and takes its name from, the now demolished Bottreaux castle which was built by the de Botterell family in Norman times. Its unique natural harbour was formed by the rivers Valency and Jordan having to carve their way through a high slate cliff to the sea.

St Christopher's Hotel is a lovely part-stonebuilt Georgian house offering excellent accommodation. Set in the older, upper part of the village of Boscastle, it was once the home of a wealthy merchant and his family, and has also in its lifetime been the site of the village store. This charming family-run hotel boasts nine en suite guest rooms (five doubles, two twins, two singles). Each room is decorated and furnished to a high standard of comfort and quality, with antique furnishings and a charming country-style decor. Some rooms offer sea views. The guests' lounge is the perfect place to relax before a roaring fire on cold days, and just as cosy and peaceful on fine ones. The garden is an idyllic spot, lush and sunny. This licensed hotel enjoys a growing reputation for fine food. A range of traditional favourites is served at breakfast and dinner. Boscastle also boasts several historic watering holes serving good real ales.

Boscastle harbour's inner jetty was built by the renowned Elizabethan seafarer, Sir Richard Grenville, when the village was prospering as a fishing, grain and slate port. The outer jetty was added 350 years later when Boscastle was being developed as a seaport for the manganese and iron ore mines near Launceston. This latter structure was accidentally blown up by a stray mine during the Second World War, and had to be repaired by the National Trust at considerable expense.

St Christopher's Hotel, High Street, Boscastle, Cornwall PL35 0BD
Tel: 01840 250412
email: stchristophers@hotnail.com

The Trust owns the harbour and much of the coastline around Boscastle. The spectacular slate headlands on either side of the community provide some excellent - if demanding - walking. The village itself is set around a steep broad thoroughfare lined with attractive houses, inns and shops, most of which cater for the holiday-maker. A tourist information centre is located in the old forge by the harbour; there is also an interesting **Witchcraft Museum** which contains some sinister relics of the ancient black arts. The esteemed author Thomas Hardy was a regular visitor to Boscastle when he worked as an architect on the restoration of the church at St Juliot, two miles southeast. The village appears as "Castle Boterel" in Hardy's early novel, A Pair of Blue Eyes. Other attractions in the village include the **Cave Holography & Illusion Exhibition** and **Lye Rock**, a great place for puffin-spotting.

TINTAGEL   Map 2 ref E22
16 miles SW of Bude off the B3263

The romantic remains of **Tintagel Castle** stand on top of **Tintagel Head**. Prior to a series of rock falls in the 19th century, this formidable headland was connected to the mainland by a natural stone bridge; now only a narrow isthmus remains. Many like to believe that this was the birthplace of the legendary King Arthur, or even that it was the site of Camelot, the mythical headquarters of the Knights of the Round Table (other possibilities are Caerleon in Wales and South Cadbury in Somerset). Fragments of a Celtic monastic house dating from the 6th century have been uncovered on the headland; their origins coincide with the activities of the Welsh military leader on which the Arthurian legends are thought to be based; however, the fortification we see today was founded by Reginald Earl of Cornwall, the illegitimate son of Henry I, in

Tintagel Castle

the 12th century, over 600 years after Arthur would have died. Whatever the true heritage of Tintagel castle, the scramble down towards the sea and back up to its clifftop site 250 feet above the Atlantic is a breathtaking experience. Tintagel, of course, owes much of its popularity to the Arthurian connection. One of its most noteworthy attractions is "King Arthur's Halls"; these were built in the 1930s by devotees of the legends and include the'Hall of Chivalry", a room with over 70 stained-glass windows depicting the coats of arms of the Knights of the Round Table. Elsewhere, Arthurian eating places and souvenir shops abound.

Perhaps the finest building in Tintagel is the **Old Post Office**, a small 14th century slate-built manor house which in the 19th century found new life as a letter-receiving station. Now owned by the National Trust, this charming and strangely organic-looking structure has been carefully restored to its Victorian livery. A good sandy beach can be found a couple of miles to the south of Tintagel at **Trebarwith Strand**, one of the few breaks in the wild craggy cliffscape.

Established in1980, **Tregeath Cottage** in Tregeath Lane on the outskirts of Tintagel, is a peaceful and relaxing place providing self-catering accommodation. Connected to a working 50-acre farm and set in a quite parish lane, it is popular with those wishing to explore the scenic delights of the region, and with anyone seeking a truly tranquil break away from it all. This picturesque cottage overlooks the North Cornish coast. Sleeping up to five people in comfort, this traditional farmworker's cottage is built of stone and slate. It boasts two double bedrooms on the first floor and a single bedroom on the ground floor. The double bedrooms have 4-foot and 4-foot-six beds. The range of modern amenities includes the superbly equipped galley-style

kitchen, TV, video and payphone. The open-plan sitting/dining room has exposed beams and a lovely open fireplace. The private garden is stocked with garden furniture, making it a welcome retreat for enjoying sunny days and quiet evenings. Shops and the post office are close to hand. With the attractions of Tintagel and the natural beauty of Bossiney, Benoath, Trebarwith Strand and other coastal communities just a couple of miles away, this makes the ideal base for exploring this rich and impressive part of the county. Parking available to the side of the cottage.

Davina, Trevillett, Tintagel, Cornwall PL34 0HL
Tel/Fax: 01840 770217

PORT ISAAC
Map 2 ref E22

8 miles SW of Tintagel off the B3314

This lovely old fishing community of stone and slate houses is divided by narrow alleyways, or drangs (one goes by the charming name of "Squeeze-Belly Alley"), and has a lovely small beach. At one time, huge quantities of herring were landed here. After the arrival of the railway, these were gutted and packed in the village's many fish cellars before being despatched by train to Britain's inland centres of population by train. One of these old cellars is now an inshore lifeboat station, while others are used at boathouses or retail outlets.

PADSTOW
Map 2 ref D23

16 miles SW of Tintagel on the A389

For many centuries, Padstow's sheltered position on the western side of the Camel estuary has made it a welcome haven for vessels seeking shelter from the perils of the north Cornish coast. However, the silting of the river in the 19th century created a new hazard for shipping, the evocatively named Doom Bar, which restricted entry to the estuary mouth and effectively spelled the end for the ancient settlement as a major port. Once the ecclesiastical capital of Cornwall, the town's name is derived from St Petroc, the Irish missionary saint who landed here from Wales in the 6th century. The parish church is dedicated to him, although the present building dates from the 13th and 14th centuries; inside there is a striking Elizabethan pulpit and some comical bench ends, one of which depicts a fox preaching to a gaggle of geese. St Petroc also founded a monastery here, but in the 10th century it was moved to Bodmin to protect its occupants from Viking raids.

Virtually in the centre of the harbour at Padstow, **The Golden Lion** is a 400-year-old public house offering a range of traditional ales and tempting bar snacks. This appealing and homely pub has three main bars - the front two are open plan in design; all have a wealth of exposed beams, dressed stone walls, low ceilings and adorned with old prints of the harbourside and old-fashioned bric-a-brac. Fine refreshments can be taken in front of a roaring fire from the original stone fireplace, or outdoors in the attractive beer garden. Lunchtime offers quite a range of snacks and light meals, including salads, grills, fish and hot and cold sandwiches. In the evening, the menu is made up of traditional favourites such as Dover sole, fresh crab, steaks and

**The Golden Lion Inn, Lanadwell Street, Padstow,
Cornwall PL28 8AN Tel: 01841 532797**

jacket potatoes. The pub's quiet village location near the sea is tranquil and relaxing. Owners Lorraine and Alex Rickard are the convivial and attentive hosts. The Golden Lion also offers accommodation in three spacious and welcoming guest bedrooms.

Today, Padstow's harbour and nearby shopping streets throng with visitors throughout the summer, some of whom arrive along the beautiful **Camel cycle path** which follows the course of the old railway line from Wadebridge; the long curved bridge which crosses the mouth of Little Petherick creek is one of its highlights. The **Padstow Shipwreck Museum** is also well worth a visit. Padstow's original monastery is believed to have stood on the site of the present-day Prideaux Place, a handsome Elizabethan mansion at the top of the town which was built in the 1580s by the Prideaux family. Still occupied by descendants of the original owners, the house is set in extensive grounds incorporating a 20 acre deer park and formal Italianate garden. Highlights of the interior include the library, drawing room and great chamber with its fine plasterwork ceiling. Several monuments to the Prideaux family can be seen in the parish church. With its narrow alleyways and tightly packed slate-hung buildings, Padstow's old quarter retains much of its medieval character. The harbour still supports a sizable fishing fleet and is enhanced by the addition of floodgates which retain the sea water at low tide. The area around the old port contains a number of interesting old buildings, including the 15th century **Merchants' Guild House** on the north quay, and the 16th century **Court House** of Sir Walter Raleigh on the south quay; the latter was used by Sir Walter's agents for collecting Stannary taxes.

One of Padstow's great traditions is the festival of the "ObbyOss", a boisterous street celebration with origins going back to pagan times whose modern observance still makes little concession to outsiders. (The Obby Oss is a ferocious figure with a primitive mask, tall conical hat, flat circular body and sailcloth skirt.) Throughout the day on May 1, rival Osses are led on a wild dance through the narrow thoroughfares of Padstow by a staff-wielding "Teaser" to the accompaniment of traditional music and singing. This ancient ritual, with its strong undertones of pagan fertility rites, is believed to be one of the oldest celebrations of its kind in Europe. Among the fine beaches in Padstow are those at **St George's Well** and **Trevone Bay**. The Camel Trail makes for excellent walking, and follows a former railway line.

WADEBRIDGE

Map 2 ref E23

7 miles SE of Padstow off the A39

This ancient port and busy market town stands at the historic lowest bridging point on the Camel (a bypass to the north now carries the A39 over the river). At 320 feet, the town's medieval 14 arched road bridge is one of the longest in Cornwall. Originally composed of 17 arches, it was built in the 15th century by the local priest to convey his flock across the river in safety. It is still known by its traditional name, the **"Bridge on Wool"**, for reasons that are unclear: either it was paid from by wealthy local wool merchants, or its foundations were laid on bales of raw wool, an absorbent material which solidifies when soaked and compressed. Once a thriving river port and railway town, Wadebridge is now a tranquil place with a good selection of shops. Each June, the **Royal Cornwall Show** is held in the county showground, a mile west of the centre. Wadebridge is also home to the **John Betjeman Centre**, a tribute to the man and his works, and hosts an annual folk festival. To the west of Wadebridge, the A39 leads up onto the **St Breock Downs**, the site of such striking Bronze Age remains as the ancient St Breock Longstone and Nine Maidens stone row.

BODMIN

Map 2 ref E23

8 miles SE of Padstow off the A389

Bustling by day, yet quiet by night, the historic former county town of Bodmin lies midway between Cornwall's north and south coasts at the junction of two ancient cross-country trading routes. For many centuries, traders between Wales, Ireland and northern France preferred the overland route between the Camel and Fowey estuaries to the hazardous sea journey around Land's End. **Castle Canyke** to the southeast of the town was built during the Iron Age to defend this important trade route, and a few centuries later the Romans erected a fort on a site above the River Camel to the west of the town, one of a string they built in the Southwest to defend strategic river crossings; the remains of a quadrilateral earthwork can still be made out today. The ancient cross-country route is now a waymarked footpath known as the Saints' Way.

Bodmin's most famous early visitor was perhaps St Petroc, one of the most influential of the early Welsh missionary saints who landed in Cornwall in the 6th century. The monastery he founded near Padstow was moved to Bodmin in the 10th century to protect it from seaborne Viking raids; although it survived until the Dissolution of the Monasteries in 1539, little of it remains today. Bodmin's parish church, perhaps the most impressive and definitely the largest in Cornwall, is dedicated to St Petroc. Rebuilt in the 15th century and renovated in the 19th, it contains a magnificent Norman font whose immense bowl is supported on five finely carved columns, and a priceless ivory casket in which the remains of the saint were placed in 1177, after they have been recovered from a light-fingered Augustinian monk.

Bodmin is also renowned for its holy wells - 11 in all. Some, such as **Eye Water Well**, are known for their restorative properties, and some, such as **St Guron's Well** opposite the church, for being ancient places of baptism. Bodmin was the only market town in Cornwall to be mentioned in the Domesday Book, and at one time it boasted its own mint and, later, the county assizes. However, the 19th century rise of Truro as Cornwall's cathedral city stripped Bodmin of its county town status. A number of impressive relics of its former glory neverthe-less remain, including the Tudor guildhall, the former court buildings, and the **Turret Clock** where former mayor, Nicholas Boyer, was hanged for his part in the Prayer Book Rebellion on 1549. Public executions were also held at Bodmin Gaol in Berrycombe Road, a once-feared place which now operates as an hotel and features a fascinating exhibition that takes in the former dungeons.

Bodmin also contains two first-rate museums: The **Town Museum**, and the **Regimental Museum** (also known as the Duke of Cornwall' Light Infantry Museum), which is housed in the Duke of Cornwall's old headquarters. Turf Street leads up past **Mount Folly** to the **Beacon**, a scenic picnic area with a 140 foot obelisk at its summit which was built to commemorate the Victorian general, Sir Walter Raleigh Gilbert. One of Britain's earliest railways was opened in 1830 to link Bodmin with the Camel estuary at Wadebridge. In recent years the track has been reopened as a public cyclepath and walkway, **The Camel Trail**, which runs all the way from Boscarne Junction to Padstow.

ST ERVAN
MAP 1 REF D23
7 miles SW of Padstow off the B3276

Carnewas Tea Rooms and Garden is run by Norma Archer, who has been here since 1983. She is the driving force behind this impressive and charming establishment. Popular with locals, visitors, walkers and the celebrities and politicians whom Norma includes among her circle of friends, the tea rooms have been featured in the BBC Good Food Book for the high standard of the atmosphere, decor and, most importantly, the menu. Situated at the top of the world-famous Bedruthan Steps, this one-story stonebuilt building commands fantastic views over the surrounding landscape. Originally the stables for the horses employed at the iron ore mine that

Carnewas Tea Rooms and Garden, nr Bedruthan Steps, St Ervan, Wadebridge,
Cornwall PL27 7UW Tel: 01637 860701

once stood on these grounds, it was converted into tea rooms in 1932. The comprehensive menu offers everything from tea cakes and other confectionery - all of it home-made - to delicious sandwiches and tempting snacks, accompanied by speciality teas and coffees. Open February to November daily; December to January at weekends.

ST COLUMB MAJOR
Map 1 ref D23

12 miles S of Padstow off the A39

Thankfully bypassed by the main road, the small town of St Columb Major was once considered as the location for Cornwall's cathedral (it lost out to Truro). The parish **Church of St Columba** is unusually large, with a four-tiered tower and a wide through-arch; inside there are some fine 16th and 17th century monumental brasses to the Arundell family. The church is adjoined to the south and east by handsome old residential buildings, creating something of the atmosphere of a cathedral close. The town is home to an annual music festival.

The Red Lion in Fore Street is renowned for its former landlord, James Polkinghorne, a famous exponent of Cornish wrestling who is depicted in action on a plaque on an external wall. Another of St Columb Major's inns, the Silver Ball Hotel, marks the town's other great sporting tradition, "hurling the silver ball". This rowdy medieval game is played twice a year - on Shrove Tuesday and on the Saturday 11 days later - and involved two teams of several hundred people (the 'townsmen' and the 'countrymen') who endeavour to carry a silver-painted ball made of apple wood through goals set two miles apart. Once a common pastime throughout the county, this ancient Cornish game is now only practised here and, in a less rumbustious form, at St Ives. Such is the passion for the St Columb event that windows of houses and shops in the locality have to be boarded up for the occasion.

Two miles southeast of St Columb Major, the land rises to 700 feet above sea level on Castle Downs, site of the massive Iron Age hill fort known as **Castle-an-Dinas**, whose three earthwork ramparts enclose an area of over six acres. The climb to the gorse-covered summit is rewarded with panoramic views over the leafy Vale of Lanherne to the northwest, and towards the unearthly landscape of the china clap spoil heaps to the south.

LISKEARD
Map 2 ref F23

16 miles W of Plymouth on the A38

Standing on an undulating site between the valleys of the East Looe and Seaton rivers, Liskeard is a pleasant old market town which was one of Cornwall's five medieval Stannary towns (the others being Bodmin, Lostwithiel, Truro and Helston). The name comes from the Latin word for tin, stannum, and these five towns were the only ones licensed to weigh and stamp the metal. The town has a long history as a centre for mineral extraction: for centuries, the medieval Cornish tinners brought their smelted tin down from Bodmin Moor for weighing, stamping and taxing, then in the early 19th century, great quantities of copper ore from the nearby **Caradon mines** and granite from the **Cheesewring quarries** were loaded onto barges here and despatched to the coast along the newly-constructed Looe canal. In the 1850s, the canal was replaced by the Looe valley branch of the Great Western Railway, a scenic stretch of line which still operates today although its industrial cargoes have long been replaced by passenger holiday traffic. Perhaps Liskeard's most unusual feature can be found in Well Lane, where an arched grotto marks the site of **Pipe Well**, a medieval spring which is reputed to have curative powers.

ST KEYNE
Map 2 ref F23

2½ miles S of Liskeard off the B3254

This small village is home to the fascinating **Paul Corin's Mechanical Music Centre**, a unique museum of mechanical instruments housed in a lovely old mill which stands near the bridge over the East Looe River, half a mile east of the centre of the village. Exhibits include street, cafe and fairground organs, all of which are kept in working order and played on a regular basis.

One of the more unusual episodes in St Keyne's history took place during the reign of the Catholic Mary Tudor, when the local rector and his wife (who had married during the reign of the Protestant Edward VI) were dragged from their bed in the middle of the night and placed on the village stocks. A famous holy well known as **St Keyne Well**, lies a mile south of the village beneath a great tree which is said to bear the leaves of four different species. According to local legend, the first member of a newly-married couple to drink from the spring will be the one who wears the trousers, a notion which captured the imagination of Victorian newlyweds and brought them here in their thousands.

Penbugle Farm offers some wonderful bed and breakfast accommodation in three spacious and comfortable rooms. Relaxed and welcoming, the atmosphere at this superb establishment ensures that guests have a pleasant and peaceful break away from it all. The farm is a 283-acre working beef and sheep farm, part of the Duchy of Cornwall estate. With many scenic countryside and coastal walks within easy reach, guests can take the opportunity while here to indulge in their love of fishing, riding, golf, or visiting one of the many National Trust properties in the area. There are two en suite family rooms and one double room with adjacent private bath. They are furnished and decorated to a high standard of taste and comfort. The guests' lounge is warm and welcoming. The hearty

Penbugle Farm, St Keyne, Liskeard, Cornwall PL14 4RS
Tel/Fax: 01579 320288

breakfast is the perfect recipe for an enjoyable day's sightseeing or relaxing. Host Brenda Light has lived here all her life, and is happy to provide guests with information about the surrounding area.

LOOE

9 miles S of Liskeard on the A387

MAP 2 REF F23

At the mouth of the East and West Looe rivers stands the bustling coastal resort and fishing port of Looe. Originally two separate towns facing each other across the estuary, **East** and **West Looe** were first connected by a bridge in the early 15th century, and were officially incorporated in 1883. The present seven-arched bridge dates from the 19th century and is wide enough to carry the A387 Polperro road. In common with many other Cornish coastal settlements which have had to scratch a living by whatever means available, Looe has always been something of a jack-of-all-trades. As well as having a long-established pilchard fishing fleet, it has also served the mineral extractors of Bodmin Moor as a port for exporting tin - and later, copper - ore.

As early as 1800, a bathing machine was constructed at the top of Looe's sandy beach, and when visitors began to arrive in numbers with the coming of the railway in 1859, the town began to develop as a resort. More recently, Looe has established itself as Britain's premier shark-fishing centre, regularly hosting an International Sea Angling Festival. Over the years, Looe has evolved into a small seaside resort which has managed to retain a good deal of its original character, despite the annual invasion of holiday-makers. The old quarters on either side of the river are mazes of narrow lanes lined with old stone fisherman's cottages and inns, some of which are partially constructed from old ships' timbers. The 16th century **Guildhall** in East Looe is now an impressive local museum. The **Living from the Sea Museum** and **Southeast Cornwall Discovery Centre** also merit a visit.

In summer, pleasure boats depart from the quay for trips along the coast to Polperro and Fowey, and boat trips can also be taken to **St George's Island** half a mile offshore. Now a privately-run bird sanctuary, this was once the refuge of the notorious pirate and smuggler, Black Joan, who along with her brother Fyn terrorised the population of this lonely stretch of coast. The **Looe Valley Line** runs from Liskeard to Looe, taking in Coombe, St Keyne and many breathtaking local sights, with walks available from each station.

POLPERRO
MAP 2 REF E23
3½ miles SW of Looe off the A387

This lovely old fishing community is many people's idea of the archetypal Cornish village. It stands at the point where a steep-sided wooded combe converges with a narrow tidal inlet from the sea. Its steep narrow streets and alleyways are piled high with white-painted fishermen's cottages, many of which have now been converted into art galleries and specialist shops. All routes seem to lead down to Polperro's highly photogenic double harbour, a working fishing

Polperro Harbour

port which normally contains an assortment of attractive inshore fishing vessels. The mouth of the inner harbour was fitted with movable timber gates after a southeasterly storm destroyed over 20 boats which were sheltering there in the early 19th century (they have now been replaced by a modern tidal floodgate). Polperro has had a long association with smuggling: the practice was so rife in the 18th century that many of the village's inhabitants were involved in shipping, storing or transporting contraband goods. To combat the problem, H M Customs and Excise established the first "preventive station" in Cornwall here in the early 1800s. The atmosphere and events of those days are brought to life in a fascinating **Smugglers' Museum** which can be found near the inner harbour.Another attraction is a model village of old Polperro, which is set within pleasant flower-filled gardens. Houses of interest include **Couch's House** (1595), **House on Props**, and the **Old Watch House**. A cliffpath leads to bays and beaches. Modern Polperro has had to succumb to the holiday industry - in summer, cars are banned from the narrow streets.

LOSTWITHIEL
MAP 2 REF E23
12 miles W of Liskeard on the A390

This attractive small market town stands at the head of the Fowey estuary at the historic lowest bridging point on the river. One of Cornwall's medieval Stannary towns, tin and other raw metals were brought here for assaying and onward shipping until upstream mining activity caused the anchorage to silt up, forcing the port to move down-river to the estuary mouth. Present-day Lostwithiel is an atmospheric touring and angling centre whose long history has left it with a legacy of interesting old buildings, many of which are set in characteristic narrow alleyways, or opes. The remains of the 13th century great hall which served as the treasury and stannary offices can be seen in Quay Street, and in Fore Street there is a fine example of an early 18th century arcaded Guildhall which now serves as the civic museum. The nearby municipal offices date from later in the century, as does the old grammar school in Queen Street, and elsewhere in the town there are some fine Georgian residences and shop fronts. The old malt house is worth finding for its unusual plaque, declaring ''Walter Kendal founded this house and hath a lease for 3,000 years beginning 29 September 1652.''

Lostwithiel's 14th century parish **Church of St Bartholomew** has a rare octagonal spire; one of only six in the county, its style is reminiscent of the church architecture of northern France. Another unusual feature is the row of upper windows in the aisle, or clerestory, which is one of only four in Cornwall. The early 14th century font is unusually large and richly carved. During the Civil War, the Parliamentarians made this the focus for their anti-Royalist feeling when they brought a horse into the church and provocatively christened it Charles 'in contempt of his sacred Majesty''.

The spectacular National Trust-owned property, **Lanhydrock House**, lies midway between the A38 and B3269 north of Lostwithiel. Prior to the Dissolution of the Monasteries, the 400 acre estate belonged to Bodmin's Augustinian priory of St Petroc, then in 1620 it was acquired by the Robartes family, in whose possession it remained until it passed to the National Trust in 1953. The house is set in a superb position in the valley of the River Fowey and is approached along an avenue of sycamore and

beech trees, some of which were originally planted over three centuries ago. Visitors pass through an imposing 17th century gatehouse which, along with the north wing, is one of the few parts of the original structure to have escaped the fire which tore through the building in 1881. Thankfully, the magnificent first floor gallery in the north wing survived; over 115 feet long, it is illuminated by broad mullioned windows and contains a remarkable plasterwork ceiling showing scenes from the Old Testament which is believed to be the work of the Abbott family, master plasterers of North Devon.

Lanhydrock House

Because of the fire, most of Lanhydrock House is a Victorian reconstruction built in the 1880s to the original 17th century design. The updated interior contains a maze of comfortably appointed rooms, over 40 of which are now open to the public. Highlights include the estate offices, servants' quarters, buttery and nursery, which together create a unique picture of life in an opulent Victorian country mansion. The grounds contain an attractive woodland shrubbery, and a much-photographed formal garden and parterre which is overlooked by the small estate church of St Hyderoc.

A mile and a half downstream, the imposing Norman keep of **Restormel Castle** stands on a promontory overlooking the wooded valley of the River Fowey. The fortress was built in the early 12th century by Edmund, Earl of Cornwall, and is remarkably well preserved for its age. The walls of the massive circular shell are 30 feet high in places, and the whole structure is surrounded by a deep dry moat which is lined with flowers in spring. The castle was in use until the 16th century, and was reoccupied for a time by Parliamentarian forces during the English Civil War. Now under the care of English Heritage, visitors can climb a series of walkways onto the ramparts. The road to the south passes close to the site of a disused mine which was once the largest source of iron ore in Cornwall. Material was transported from here by tramway to Lostwithiel, and then by barge to Fowey for loading onto seagoing vessels. Bradock Down, to the east, was the site of a famous Royalist victory.

FOWEY
MAP 2 REF E23

5 miles S of Lostwithiel off the B3269

The lovely old port and historic seafaring town of Fowey (pronounced Foy) guards the western entrance to the river from which it takes its name. The narrow lanes and alleyways of the old town rise abruptly from the water's edge in a pleasant mixture of architectural styles from Elizabethan to Edwardian. The deep water harbour has been used as an anchorage for seagoing vessels since the time of the ancient Romans, and china clay continues to be exported from the whitened jetties which lie half a mile or so upstream. The town's long history is closely linked with its maritime traditions. During the Hundred Years War, local mariners recruited to fight the French became known as the 'Fowey Gallants'; some refused to disband, and instead formed a notorious gang of pirates who would attack any vessel straying too close to this stretch of coast. Following a devastating French raid in 1457, a chain was stretched across the estuary mouth at night to deter hostile ships from entering the harbour.

Present-day Fowey is a peaceful community which is connected by vehicle ferry to Bodinnick on the eastern bank, and by passenger ferry to Polruan. The harbour is filled with pleasure craft from all over Britain and continental Europe, and there a number of fine old buildings which are worth closer inspection, for example the **Noah's Ark Museum**, housed in one of the oldest structures in Fowey, the medieval town hall in Trafalgar Square, which is occupied by another interesting local museum, and the Ship Inn, a part-15t -century building with a Victorian facade which was once the town house of the Rashleigh family.

The Rashleigh family seat, **Menabilly**, lies to the southeast of the town and was subsequently the home of Daphne du Maurier, who used the setting - rechristened 'Manderley' - in her famous novel, Rebecca. Another of Fowey's literary residents was the Cornish novelist Sir Arthur Quiller-Couch, who lived for over 50 years at the Haven on the Esplanade. There are some excellent beaches nearby.

NEWQUAY
MAP 1 REF D23

20 miles W of Bodmin on the A392

A settlement since ancient times, evidence of an Iron Age coastal fort can be seen among the cliffs and caves of **Porth Island**, a detached outcrop which is connected to the mainland by an elegant suspended footbridge and which lies to the northeast of the centre of this popular

seaside and surfing resort. In common with many Cornish coastal communities, Newquay was an important pilchard fishing centre in the centuries leading up to the industry's decline early in the 20th century. An original 'huer's' hut can still be seen on the headland to the west of the harbour; this was where a local man would keep a look-out for shoals of red pilchards and alert the fishing crews when one was sighted close to shore by calling 'hevva' through a long loud-hailer. He would then guide the seine boats towards their quarry with

Newquay Beach

semaphore-style signals using a pair of bats known as 'bushes'. The town takes its name from the new harbour which was built in the 1830's by Joseph Treffry of Fowey for exporting china clay, a trade which continued for several decades until the purpose-built port facility was completed on the south coast at Par. The decline of Newquay as a port was tempered by the arrival of the railway in 1875, and before long train-loads of visitors were arriving to enjoy the town's extensive sandy beaches, scenic position and mild climate. Today Newquay is one of Cornwall's most popular and liveliest resorts. Over the years, a number of popular attractions have been constructed to satisfy tourist demand, including **Trenance Leisure Park** with its boating lake and miniature railway. **Newquay Zoo** is also in the park, and features a range of environments and habitats for the resident wildlife, including an African Plains enclosure and Tropical House. The **Sea Life Centre** is another of the town's interesting attractions, and **Tunnels Through Time** brings to life stories of bygone days in Cornwall's past, with over 70 life-size figures. **Towan Beach** is one of a succession of fine beaches overlooked by the town, a good sheltered beach with a tidal paddling pool which is ideal for children, which can be found at the base of Porth Island. In recent decades Newquay has also acquired a reputation as one of the finest surfing centres in the British Isles. Throughout the year, thousands of keen surfers arrive in camper vans and the like to catch the waves of **Fistral Beach**, or to watch the increasing number of national and international surfing competitions held here each season. Another colourful summer attraction involves Newquay's fleet of traditional pilot gigs, 30 foot rowing boats which race each other over a six-mile course in the bay.

ST AGNES   MAP 1 REF D23
11 miles SW of Newquay on the B3277

Once known as the source of the finest tin in Cornwall, the old mining community of St Agnes lies at the head of a steep valley. Despite being subjected to 200 years of mineral extraction, and almost 100 years of tourism, it still manages to retain its original character, especially around the narrow-spired parish church and nearby terrace of stepped miners' cottages which are known locally as the "Stippy-Stappy". The village is also renowned as the birthplace of the Georgian society painter, John Opie, and is known to thousands of readers of Winston Graham's Poldark novels as "St Ann". A good local museum can be found near the church, and there is also a popular leisure park to the south of the village which features a model of Cornwall in miniature and a number of themed areas, all set in seven acres of attractive landscaped grounds.

Trevaunance Cove near St Agnes is one of the best surfing beaches in Cornwall. A quay constructed here in the 18th century for loading tin ore survived here until it was washed away in a storm during the 1930s; its four predecessors having suffered a similar fate. The surrounding landscape is littered with abandoned pump houses and mine shafts (walkers should keep to the paths): many of the mines, such as Wheal Kitty and Wheal Ellen, were named after female members of the mine-owning families, or, in the case of Wheal Freedom and Wheal Friendly, were given other romantic associations. One of the most photogenic of Cornwall's derelict pump houses stands on a narrow cliff platform 200 feet above **Chapel Porth**, a mile and a half west of St Agnes. Now under the ownership of the National Trust, Wheal Coates was in operation for 30 years between 1860 and 1890. A good circular walk from the car park at Chapel Porth also takes in St Agnes Head and St Agnes Beacon, a 628 foot peak which offers outstanding views across Cornwall to Bodmin Moor in the east and St Ives in the west; it is said that over 30 church towers can be seen from here on a clear day.

ST AUSTELL   MAP 1 REF E23
16 miles SE of Newquay on the A3058

This sprawling former market and mining town was transformed in the second half of the 18th century when William Cookworthy discovered large deposits of china clay, or kaolin, here in 1755. Over the years, waste material from the clay pits has been piled into great conical spoil heaps which dominate the landscape to the north and west of the town. These bare bleached uplands are sometimes referred to as the 'Cornish Alps', although in recent years steps have been taken to landscape their surface and seed them with grass. The narrow streets of old St Austell create an atmosphere more befitting a market town than a mining community. The central thoroughfares radiate from the parish church of the **Holy Trinity**, an imposing structure with a tall 15th century tower which is decorated on all four sides with carved figures and topped by impressive pinnacles and crenelations. The granite facing stones were brought from the famous Pentewan quarries three miles to the south. The church interior has a fine wagon roof and some interesting early features, including a rare pillar piscina and a Norman font carved with a curious assortment of human heads and mythical creatures. Elsewhere in the town centre there are some notable old buildings, including the **Town Hall**, **Quaker Meeting House** and White Hart Hotel, as well as a good modern shopping precinct. Nearby, there's the **Mid-Cornwall Craft Centre** (at Biscovey), and the **Automobilia Motor Museum** at St Stephen.

MEVAGISSEY   MAP 1 REF E24
5 miles S of St Austell on the B3273

Once aptly known as Porthilly, Mevagissey was renamed in late medieval times after the Welsh and Irish saints Meva and Itha. The village is a renowned fishing port which was once an important centre of the pilchard industry. Each year during the 18th and 19th centuries, thousands of tons of this oily fish were landed here for salting, packing or processing into lamp oil. Some pilchards were exported to southern Europe, or supplied to the Royal Navy - to whose sailors they became known as ''Mevagissey Ducks''. The need to process the catch within easy reach of the harbour created a labyrinth of buildings separated by steeply sloping alleyways,

some of which were so narrow that the baskets of fish sometimes had to be carried on poles between people walking one behind the other. At one time up to 100 fishing luggers could be seen jostling for a berth in Mevagissey's picturesque harbour. Today, all but a handful of inshore fishing craft have gone and, in common with most of Cornwall's coastal communities, the local economy relies heavily on visitors, an annual influx which has given rise to a proliferation of cafes and gift shops, but

Mevagissey Harbour

which thankfully has failed to diminish the port's essential character. It remains the largest working fishing port in St Austell Bay. The part-13th century Pentewan-stone **Church of St Peter** is worth a look for its Norman font and amusingly inscribed monument to Otwell Hill, an early in-comer who died here in 1617. Elsewhere, there are a number of more modern indoor attractions, including a **World of Model Railways**, **Aquarium**, and a **Folk Museum** containing an interesting assortment of fishing and agricultural equipment.

TRURO   MAP 1 REF D24
14 miles SW of St Austell on the A390

This elegant small city has grown to become the administrative capital of Cornwall. Its site at the head of a branch of the Fal estuary has been occupied for thousands of years, but it wasn't until large-scale mineral extraction began in medieval times that the settlement took on any significance. One of the first Cornish towns to be granted rites of Stannary, huge quantities of smelted tin or and other metals were brought here for weighing, taxing and shipping until the industry went into decline in the 17th century. By this time the estuary had also begun to silt up, allowing Falmouth to take over as the area's principal seaport. A number of picturesque alleyways or opes (pronounced opps) have survived from Truro's heyday as a port, many of which have colourful names such as Tippet's Backlet, Burton's Ope and Squeezeguts Alley. An increase in metal prices during the 18th century led to a revival in Truro's fortunes; wealthy merchants and banks moved in, and the town became a centre for fashionable society with a reputation to rival Bath. This Georgian renaissance has left a distinctive mark on the town's architecture, particularly around **Pydar Street**, with its handsome Assembly Room and Theatre, Walsingham Place, and **Lemon Street**, one of the finest complete Georgian streets in the country. Also worth seeing are the indoor Pannier Market and the city hall in Boscawen Street.

TRESILLIAN   Map 1 ref D24
3 miles E of Truro off the A390

Owners Carlton and Gillian Jackson are professional caterers who have brought their wealth of experience to make **Manor Cottage** a success. Combining a thriving bed and breakfast establishment with a superb restaurant, this distinguished and charming Georgian house, built about 1820, provides guest with a wonderful base from which to explore Truro and all of Cornwall.

The five guest bedrooms - one family room, two doubles, one twin and one single - are tastefully and comfortably furnished and decorated, with old pine and oak furniture and country-style patchwork quilts. The cosy and well-appointed residents' lounge is a relaxing place to enjoy a quite pre-dinner drink. The conservatory-style licensed restaurant has a marvellous and imaginative menu which changes with the seasons and makes best use of the freshest local ingredients. All dishes -

Manor Cottage, Tresillian, Truro, Cornwall TR2 4BN
Tel: 01872 520212

including such delights as grilled spring chicken, fillet of brill and best end of lamb - are home-cooked and home-prepared. Open Thursdays to Saturdays, reservations are essential.

BISSOE   Map 1 ref D24
5 miles SW of Truro off the A39

Amid scenes of truly exceptional rural beauty, near a large duck pond, waterfall, flowing streams and rolling countryside, **The Old Mill** is the setting for three superb holiday cottages converted from a delightful stonebuilt 17th-century corn mill and its adjacent converted stables. Restored by local craftspeople, every effort has been made to retain the character of the original buildings, complete with working water wheels. The Mill sleeps four to six people, with two double bedrooms, spacious and tasteful sitting room with attractive exposed beamwork, and kitchen/dining area with all modern amenities. The Mill Cottage sleeps four to five people in one twin

The Old Mill, Hicks Mill, Bissoe, Truro, Cornwall TR4 8RB
Tel/Fax: 01872 865480

and one double room. Charming and cosy, it, like The Mill accommodation, is furnished and decorated to a superb standard of taste and comfort. The Stables sleeps four persons - particularly suitable for families, it boasts one double room and a room equipped with bunk beds. There is also a communal laundry room complete with washing machine and tumble dryer. The gardens are lush and welcoming; a gas barbecue can be made available at no additional cost. Handy for the sights and attractions of the surrounding region, including the cycle trail that runs from here to Portreath, these cottages make an ideal base for the holiday-maker or anyone wanting a peaceful and relaxing break. With over two and a half acres of walks amid rural scenes, with a wealth of wildlife and fascinating plantings (including tropical palms), every 10 paces reveals something interesting and different to the visitor.

RUAN LANIHORNE   MAP 1 REF D24
7 miles SE of Truro off the A3078

The King's Head is a welcoming and friendly public house, opposite the churchyard, in the heart of this charming creekside village. Russell and Katherine Weightman own this excellent Free House. Russell is a talented chef who has worked throughout the country. Both have brought a wealth of enthusiasm and flair to running this former coaching inn. There are three main bar

The King's Head, Ruan Lanihorne, Truro,
Cornwall TR2 5RX Tel: 01872 501263

areas set end to end. Open fires, beamed ceilings, panelled walls and copper brasses add to the traditional and cosy ambience. The decor features hundreds of framed cigarette cards and historical memorabilia. One room is devoted to a fine restaurant, with a menu of freshly prepared home-cooked cuisine such as corn-fed chicken breast, beef and horseradish sausages, fresh fish of the day and other dishes that are a happy blend of tradition and innovation. Real ales on tap include Sharps (a local brew) and a changing guest ale. Beer garden and families are welcome.

FALMOUTH
10 miles S of Truro on the A39

Map 1 ref D24

Falmouth stands in a magnificent position at the entrance to the **Carrick Roads**, a spectacular deep-water anchorage which is formed by the merging of seven river estuaries. Although a settlement has existed here for many hundreds of years, it wasn't until the 17th century that the port was properly developed as a mail packet station which subsequently became the communications hub for the British Empire. During its heyday in the early 19th century, Falmouth was the base for almost 40 sailing ships which carried documents, personal effects and cargo to almost every corner of the globe. A few decades later, however, the introduction of steam-powered vessels heralded the end for Falmouth, and by the 1850's the packet service had moved to Southampton.

Three centuries before, Henry VIII built a pair of fortresses on either side of the estuary mouth to protect the strategically important deep-water anchorage from attack by forces loyal to the Catholic faith. (The Pope's disapproval of Henry's marital and religious extravagance was well known.) **Pendennis Castle** on the western side is superbly sited on a 200 foot promontory overlooking the entrance to Carrick Roads. Its low circular keep has immensely thick walls and stands within a 16 sided enclosure; the outer curtain wall was added during Elizabethan times in response to the threat of a second Spanish Armada. One of the last Royalist strongholds to fall during the English Civil War, Pendennis only succumbed to the Parliamentarians following a grim siege lasting five months. The castle remained in use as a coastal defence station until the end of the Second World War and is now under the ownership of English Heritage. The spectacular viewpoint of **Pendennis Point** is also the location of the Maritime Rescue Centre, the operational headquarters which was opened in 1981 to coordinate all search and rescue operations around the British coastline.

That Falmouth was developed as a port at all was due to Sir Walter Raleigh, a man whose early vision was later realised by the influential local buccaneering family, the Killgrews. A monument to the family erected in 1737 can be seen in Grove Place, a short distance from the remains of their once-splendid Tudor mansion, **Arwenack House**. Falmouth's Royalist sympathies are demonstrated in the 17th century parish church which is dedicated to ''King Charles the Martyr''; much altered, it retains its curious rectangular tower and arcades with Ionic plaster capitals. Elsewhere in the town there are some handsome early 19th century buildings, including the **Falmouth Arts Centre** in Church Street, which began life as a Quaker institute 'to promote the useful arts', the synagogue in Vernon Place, and the Custom House with its fine colonnaded facade. A curious chimney near the Custom House was used for burning contraband tobacco and is still referred to as the ''King's Pipe''. The area around Custom House Quay has been made into a conservation area, the centrepiece of which is the tall-funnelled steam tug, the St Denys. This fascinating little ship forms part of the **Cornwall Maritime Museum**.

Modern Falmouth has a dual role as a commercial port and holiday centre. The docks continue to be used by merchant shipping, and there is still an indigenous ship-repairing yard. However, these traditional activities are perhaps overshadowed by the town's increasing popularity as a yachting and tourist destination. Throughout the year, visitors arrive by land and sea to enjoy the mild climate, pleasant atmosphere and excellent facilities. For those keen to explore the upper reaches of the Carrick Roads by boat, a variety of pleasure trips depart from the Prince of Wales pier, as do the cross-estuary passenger ferries to St Mawes and Flushing. The tree-lined square known as the ''Moor'' can be found a short distance inland from the pier; on one side stands the town hall and art gallery, and on the other a steep flight of 111 steps known as Jacob's Ladder leads up to a Wesleyan chapel. An attractive sight throughout the summer months are the periodic races between Falmouth's old gaff-rigged working boats. These colourful competitions evolved from the traditional practice of racing out to newly-arrived sailing ships to tender for work. A number of these handsome working vessels, some of the last examples in the country still to operate under sail, are used for dredging oysters from the Helford estuary.

Waving palm trees herald guests' entrance to **Cotswold House Hotel**, a striking dark blue hotel located on the edge of the town, to the west of town on a main road to the coast (just half a mile away). This spacious and charming establishment has 10 attractive and very comfortable en suite guest bedrooms. All rooms are individually styled with superb co-ordinates, furnishings and fittings. Some enjoy marvellous sea and

Cotswold House Hotel, 49 Melvill Road, Falmouth, Cornwall TR11 4DF Tel: 01326 312077 Fax: 01326 319181

river views. The superb dining room boasts an excellent wine list. A four course dinner offers our guests a selection of freshly prepared Continental and English cuisine using the finest local produce and cooked and presented to the highest standard. The service is always friendly and helpful. Visitors can take advantage of Falmouth's four main beaches, thought by many to be second to none.

FLUSHING
3 miles N of Falmouth off the B3292

MAP 1 REF D24

Flushing is another attractive yachting centre, built by settlers from the Low Countries in the 17th century - it owes its name to seamen from Vlissingen, Holland - and still retains a distinctive Dutch/Flemish appearance. The narrow streets have several fine Queen Anne houses, many of these the former homes of Packet captains. It is served by the ferry from Falmouth.

The passenger ferry arrives virtually at the door of **Flushing Quay Restaurant**, a charming and welcoming eatery located within yards of the water's edge at the picturesque marina. Popular with discerning diners from far and wide, this tasteful and intimate restaurant has a relaxed

Flushing Quay Restaurant, Flushing, Falmouth, Cornwall TR11 5TY Tel/Fax: 01326 374303

ambience that goes well with the stylish yet understated decor. Built from Cornish granite, it has open-plan seating - individual tables grouped in the centre, as well as cosy-nook style compartmental seating down one side of the restaurant. Seating 40 people altogether, the superb menus at this classic restaurant change with the seasons, but always offer an extensive range of freshly prepared and tempting dishes making best use of the finest local ingredients. A typical selection would include fresh seasonal fish and seafood - including locally caught sole, scallops, prawns and lobster - succulent 8-ounce steaks, breast of Maigret duck, whole rack of lamb and vegetarian dishes. There is also a daily specials board offering guests even more choice. Imaginative and expertly cooked and presented, these delightful dishes are sure to suit every palate. Owner Maggie Clynick and her capable and friendly staff offer excellent service, making any meal here a real treat. Open: Easter to September Monday to Saturday. October to Easter weekends and evenings only. Please ring to confirm opening times.

HELSTON   Map 1 ref C24

10 miles W of Falmouth on the A394

Helston is the westernmost of Cornwall's five medieval Stannary towns. During the early Middle Ages, streamed tin was brought here for assaying and taxing before being despatched throughout southern Britain and continental Europe. Although difficult to imagine today, this was a very busy port up until the 13th century, when a shingle bar formed across the mouth of the River Cober, preventing access to the sea. Goods were then transported to a new quay at Gweek, until further silting and a decline in tin extraction brought an end to the trade.

Helston's long and colourful history has left it with a legacy of interesting old buildings. The **Blue Anchor Inn**, a hostel for monks in the 15th century, can be found at the lower end of the main Coinagehall Street; further up, the part-16th century Angel Hotel is the former town house of the Godolphin family. In the 1750's, the Earl of Godolphin was responsible for re-building the parish **Church of St Michael** at the back of the town. It features an imposing exterior, fine plaster ceiling in the chancel, and impressive internal gallery on three sides of the nave. The church tower dates from the 1830's, its predecessor having been destroyed in a lightning storm almost a century earlier. The churchyard contains a memorial to Henry Trengrouse, the Helston man responsible for inventing the rocket-propelled safety line which saved so many lives around the British coast. Trengrouse devoted himself to developing the device after the frigate Anson ran aground on nearby **Loe Bar** in 1807, resulting in the unnecessary loss of 100 lives. An exhibit devoted to his life's work can be found in Helston's **Folk Museum**, a fascinating collection of historical artefacts which is housed in the old Butter Market.

Helston is perhaps best known, however, for its **"Furry Fair"**, which takes place each year on 8th May. This ancient pagan celebration takes its name from the Cornish word fer, meaning ''feast day'', although in the 18th century it was renamed after the Roman goddess, Flora. According to local legend, what is now often referred to as the Floral Dance is performed in commemoration of St Michael's victory over the Devil, who tried to claim possession of the town. (The final boulder thrown by Satan, so they say, missed its target and ended up in the garden of the Angel Hotel, where it stayed until 1783.) Every 8th May the town is closed to traffic and formally-dressed couples and pairs of children dance through the streets, and in and out of people's houses, to the strains of traditional folk melodies.

When the shingle bar formed across the mouth of the River Cober in the 13th century, the dammed river created the largest natural freshwater lake in the county. Lying a couple of miles southwest of Helston and once forming part of an estate belonging to the Rogers family, **Loe Pool** is now under the ownership of the National Trust. A delightful six-mile walk leads around the wooded fringes of the lake, although those less inclined to walk the full distance can take a shorter stroll through the woods on the western side. This tranquil body of water is a haven for sea-birds and waterfowl, and is a paradise for ornithologists and picnickers. A Cornish folk tale links Loe Pool with the Arthurian legend of the Lady of the Lake: like Bodmin Moor's Dozmary Pool, a hand is said to have risen from the depths to catch the dying King Arthur's sword, Excalibur. Another story connects Loe Bar with the legendary rogue Jan Tregeagle, who was set the task of weaving a rope from its sand as a punishment. A second monument to Henry Trengrouse, the inventor of the rocket-propelled safety line, can be seen on the cliff to the southeast of Loe Bar.

LIZARD PENINSULA
S of Helston

MAP 1 REF D25

The landscape changes dramatically to the south of Helford, from the luxuriance of the Helford River to the rugged splendour of the Lizard Peninsula. Here the land rises onto Goonhilly Downs, an area of windswept granite and serpentine heathland which is littered with Bronze Age remains and some rather more up-to-the-minute human creations - the huge saucer aerials and satellite dishes of British Telecom's **Goonhilly Downs Earth Station**. Chosen for its location on solid bedrock near the most southerly point on the UK mainland, this important international telecommunications link can be seen beside the B3293 midway between Helston and the coast. A guided tour of the station can be taken during the summer months which incorporates an informative audiovisual presentation on the development of modern satellite communications. The peninsula's moorland and cliffs are home to a number of rare wild plants, including the pink-flowering "Cornish Heath", and a nature reserve has been established on **Predannack Downs** to preserve this valuable natural habitat. The rugged and undulating stretch of the **South West Coast Path** around the Lizard is among the most spectacular in Cornwall.

Lizard Point is the southernmost point on mainland Britain. Once the location of a coastal beacon, it was from here that the alarm was raised when the Spanish Armada was first sighted entering the western English Channel in 1588. The jagged fingers of serpentine and granite which project into the sea have long been a hazard for shipping, and as long ago as 1620, a lighthouse was erected on the headland to alert passing vessels of the danger. The original coal-fired warning light was erected by the notorious Killigrew family of Falmouth who were subsequently accused of trying to prevent shipwrecks on the Lizard so that vessels might founder nearer the Carrick Roads, where they held the appropriate rights of salvage. A more dependable lighthouse was established here in 1752, which was then taken over by **Trinity House** in 1790. Converted from coal to oil in 1815 and then to steam-driven electric power in 1878, it now has a tremendously powerful beam which can sometimes be seen from over 50 miles out at sea.

REDRUTH
10 miles NW of Falmouth on the A30

MAP 1 REF D24

The southern approach to Redruth is dominated by the dramatic form of **Carn Brea** (pronounced Bray), a 738 foot granite prominence which is the site of the earliest known Neolithic settlement in southern Britain. The legendary home of a Cornish giant, many of the hill's features are dubbed with such names as Giant's hand, Giant's cradle, Giant's head, and even Giant's cups and saucers. (The last-named are natural rain-eroded hollows which over-imaginative Victorians thought had been made by bloodthirsty Druids.) The summit is crowned by an unprepossessing 90 foot monument dedicated to Francis Basset de Dunstanville, a benevolent Georgian mine- and landowner who did much to improve the lot of poor labourers. Much more attractive is the small castle on the lower eastern summit, a part-medieval building which in its time has been used as a hunting lodge and is now a restaurant. More easily approached from the south, the whole site is strewn with fascinating industrial and archeological remains.

Once the bustling centre of the Cornish mining industry, Redruth and the neighbouring **Camborne** have administratively combined to form the largest urban centre of population in the county. In the mid-19th century, the surrounding area was the most intensely mined in the world, and the district is still littered with evidence of this lost era. In the 1850's, Cornwall had well over 300 mines, which together produced two-thirds of the world's copper and employed around 50,000 workers. However, most had to close in the first few decades of the 20th century, when the discovery of extensive mineral deposits in the Americas, South Africa and Australia rendered the local industry no longer economically viable. The National Trust's **Norris Collec-**

tion of minerals can be seen here in the geological museum of the old Camborne School of Mines Museum and Art Gallery. Still one of the foremost institutes of mining technology, the School moved to these new premises in Redruth in the 1970's.

The home of Scots inventor William Murdock, who settled in the area at **Cross Street**, is open to the public. Murdock was responsible for such innovations as coal-gas lighting and the vacuum-powered tubes which were once a common feature in most department stores. Redruth also contains pockets of Victorian, Georgian and earlier buildings, particularly in **Churchtown** where there are some attractive old cottages, a Georgian church with a 15th century tower, and a lychgate whose unusually long coffin-rest was built to deal with the aftermath of mining disasters. The B3300 to the northwest of Redruth leads past the **Tolgus Tin Mill**, an 18th century streaming mill where tin deposits were extracted from the river bed by a process of sifting and stamping. Nearby, at Treskillard, there is an interesting shire horse centre.

CAMBORNE
MAP 1 REF C24

1½ miles SW of Redruth off the A30

Along with Redruth, Camborne has much to offer those with an interest in industrial archeology. The home of pioneer Cornish engineer Richard Trevithick can be seen at **Penponds** on the southwestern outskirts of Camborne. This little-known inventor was responsible for developing the high-pressure steam engine, the screw propeller, and an early locomotive which predated Stephenson's Rocket by 12 years, yet he died penniless and was buried in an unmarked grave in Dartford, Kent. Known locally as the Cornish Giant, a statue of this underrated genius and accomplished amateur wrestler can be seen outside Camborne Library; he is also commemorated in the colourful Trevithick Day procession which is held in the last week of April. The **Mineral Tramways Discovery Centre** is also here.

POOL
MAP 1 REF D24

1 mile SW of Redruth off the A30

Midway between Redruth and Camborne, Pool is home to a pair of National Trust-owned massive old high-pressure **beam engines**, one of which has a cylinder over 7 feet in diameter. One was built by Holmans of Camborne in 1887 as a winding engine for raising ore and delivering workers into the mine; the other was built by Harveys of Hayle in 1892 for pumping water from depths of up to 1,700 feet.

ST IVES
MAP 1 REF C24

12 miles W of Redruth on the A3074

With its five sandy beaches, maze of narrow streets and picturesque harbour and headland, the attractive fishing and former mining centre of St Ives manages to retain a special atmosphere, despite being deluged with visitors throughout the summer. The settlement takes its name from the 6th century missionary saint, St Ia, who is said to have landed here having sailed across from Ireland on an ivy leaf. The 15th century parish church near the harbour's shorter west pier bears her name. An impressive building with a soaring pinnacled tower, it contains an unusual granite font carved with stylised angels and lions. Another striking ecclesiastical building, a mariner's chapel, stands on **St Ives Head**, the promontory to the north of the harbour which is known locally as the"`Island". The headland is also the location of a "huer's" hut, the viewpoint from which a local man would keep a look-out for shoals of pilchards in the bay. When one was sighted, he would alert the crews of the seine boats (open rowing boats) by calling 'hevva' through a long loud-hailer, before guiding the fishermen towards their goal with semaphore-type signals using a pair of oval bats known as "bushes".

St Ives was one of Cornwall's most important pilchard fishing centres until the industry went into decline early in the 20th century. The town holds a record dating back to 1868 for the greatest number of fish caught in a single seine net. Once the pilchards were brought ashore, they were compressed to release fish oil before being salted and packed into barrels for despatch to southern Europe, where the Catholic stricture regarding not eating meat on Fridays guaranteed a steady demand. On catch days the streets of St Ives would stream with the oily residue of these plentiful fish, and the air would be filled with an appalling smell which would drive away all but the most determined outsiders. A local speciality, ''heavy'', or hevva cake, was traditionally made for the seiners on their return with their catch. As well as providing shelter for the fishing fleet, St Ives' harbour was built for exporting locally-mined metal ores. The sturdy main pier was built by John Smeaton, the 18th century marine architect who was responsible for designing the famous Eddystone lighthouse which now stands on Plymouth Hoe.

Like many parts of western Cornwall, the surrounding valley was once rich in veins of tin, copper and other minerals, and indeed the building which now houses **St Ives Museum** began life as Wheal Dream copper mine. The town's labyrinth of narrow streets was once divided into two communities: ''Downalong'', where the fishing families lived, and ''Upalong'', which was inhabited by the mining community. There was much tension between the two, and fights would often break out between gangs of young rivals, a practice which ended with the closing of the mines and the steady reduction in the fishing fleet.

Tregenna Castle Hotel stands within its own impressive estate overlooking St Ives. Within the grounds there are meandering footpaths, tennis courts and a heated outdoor swimming pool. A wealth of leisure facilities await the guest here: from a billiard room to badminton court, squash court, gymnasium with sauna and solarium, beauty salon and children's play areas. The accommodation ranges from spacious executive and family suites to intimate rooms with four-poster beds. All rooms are ensuite and have all amenities; most offer wonderful sea views. In the splendid restaurant the menu makes use of the freshest local ingredients, includ-

Tregenna Castle Hotel, Golf and Country Club, St Ives, Cornwall TR26 2DE
Tel: 01736 795254 Fax: 01736 796066

ing fresh fish and seafood. Guests will find it difficult to choose from among the many delicious and exciting dishes. There is an excellent range of wines to accompany the meal. In the Squire Stephens cocktail bar guests can enjoy a pre-dinner drink or a snack any time of day. The 18-hole golf course is 3,250 yards and a par 60. Nearby is the Golf Shop, stocked with a range of everything needed for the novice or experienced golfer, and the attractive and welcoming Fairways Restaurant. With something for everyone - including conference facilities, self-catering cottages and apartments and a superb venues for weddings and other celebrations, this superb hotel maintains its reputation for quality and service.

One of St Ives' most colourful inhabitants was John Knill, the 18th century mayor who was responsible for constructing the unusual steeple to the south of the town, supposedly as a mausoleum. Despite being a customs officer by profession, Knill was also widely rumoured to be an energetic smuggler who built the tall monument for the purpose of guiding vessels filled with contraband to the shore (it still serves as a mariners' daymark). He was actually buried in London, but bequeathed a sum to the citizens of St Ives for holding a curious ceremony which continues to be held in the town at five yearly intervals. On 25 July in the first and sixth years of the decade, a procession led by a fiddler, two widows and ten young women sets out from the centre to dance around the steeple and sing the old 100th Psalm.

St Ives' decline as a mining and fishing centre has been offset by its rise as an artists' colony. The painter William Turner visited the town towards the end of his life, and both Whistler and Sickert are known to have been attracted here by the special quality of the light in west Cornwall. In the first half of the 20th century, Barbara Hepworth, Ben Nicholson and others began to convert the disused pilchard cellars and sail lofts around the harbour into artists' studios, and a ''St Ives School'' was established which gained an international reputation. The town's artistic standing was also boosted by the arrival in the 1920's of the potter Bernard Leach, who established a workshop at **Higher Stennack** (beside the B3306) which is still in operation.

One of the highlights of any stay in St Ives is a visit to the **Barbara Hepworth Sculpture Garden** and Museum in Barnoon Hill. After she died in a fire on the premises in 1975, the sculptor's living quarters, studio and garden were turned into a museum and gallery dedicated to her life and work. The garden is packed with a remarkable concentration of her work, and two particularly poignant features are the little summerhouse where she used to rest in the afternoons, and the workshop which has been left entirely untouched since her death. Barbara Hepworth's studio is now administered by the **Tate Gallery**, the London-based institution which has also opened a large-scale annexe in the town which is dedicated to the work of the St Ives School. An imposing white-painted building which uses Porthmeor Beach as a stunning backdrop, its architecture is thought by some to dwarf the quality of the work inside. The narrow thoroughfares of St Ives contain an unusual number of museums and galleries. **Penwith Galleries** in Back Street West is a good place to see the work of the St Ives Society of Artists, a group founded by Sir Alfred Munnings. The St Ives Museum in Wheal Dream contains a

Tate Gallery

unique collection of artefacts illustrating the natural, industrial and maritime history of the district, and includes a special feature on the exploits of John Knill. As a child, the writer Virginia Woolf spent most of her summers at Talland House overlooking St Ives Bay, from where it is possible to see the Godrevy lighthouse - the setting which provided the inspiration for her evocative and wonderful novel, To the Lighthouse.

A good way to travel to St Ives, especially in high summer when traffic congestion and parking can be a headache, is to park in **St Erth** or **Leland** and take the local train. The railway skirts St Ives Bay, with its five-mile long stretch of unbroken sand, and is widely regarded to be one of the loveliest coastal branch lines in Britain. The train also passes close to **Lelant Saltings**, a 500 acre tidal area at the mouth of the Hayle estuary which is now a RSPB bird sanctuary. The eastern side of St Ives Bay is lined with one of the finest sandy beaches in Cornwall. A popular centre for windsurfing, various competitive events are staged here throughout the season, including breathtaking demonstrations of wave jumping.

PENZANCE   MAP 1 REF C24
18 miles W of Redruth on the A30

Penzance is the principal town of West Penwith, lying in the northwestern corner of **Mount's Bay**. For centuries, this was a remote market town which made its living from fishing, mining and smuggling. Along with nearby Newlyn and Mousehole, it was sacked by the Spanish in 1595, then at the end of the English Civil War it suffered a similar fate for being such a staunch supporter of the Royalist cause. However, the fortunes of the town were transformed by the arrival of the railway in 1859, a development which permitted the direct despatch of early flowers, vegetables and locally-caught fish to the urban centres of Britain, and which also allowed increasing numbers of holidaymakers to make the journey here easily. Today it is a bustling town and harbour, with Cornwall's only promenade. The main, broad thoroughfare of Penzance, **Market Jew Street**, takes its name from the Cornish term for "Thursday market"; it has a high stepped pavement on one side, and at its southwestern end there is a domed neoclassical **Market House** that was built in 1837. In front of this stands the statue of Penzance-born Humphry Davy, the 19th century scientists who is remembered for inventing the miners' safety lamp.

A number of interesting buildings are located in Chapel Street, a narrow thoroughfare which winds southwards from the Market House to the quay. The most unexpected of these is the **Egyptian House**, with its exotic 1830s facade, which has been restored by the Landmark Trust; the National Trust occupy the ground-floor shop.

The Union Hotel opposite has an impressive Elizabethan interior which is concealed behind a Georgian frontage; the first mainland announcement of victory at Trafalgar and the death of Nelson was made from a minstrel's gallery in its main assembly room. At the rear stands the shell of one of the earliest theatres in the country, where performances were first held in 1787.

Further down Chapel Street there are two quaint old hostelries, the 13th century Turk's Head, and the Admiral Benbow Inn with its famous figure of a smuggler on the roof. Almost facing the latter, the **Maritime Museum** contains a unique collection of artefacts recovered from shipwrecks around the Cornish coast. Marie Branwell, the mother of the Bronte sisters, was brought up at No 25 Chapel Street, and at its lower end the early 19th century St Mary's Church stands on a ledge above the harbour and Customs House, a reassuring landmark for returning sailors. Elsewhere in Penzance there is an interesting **Geological Museum** in Alverton Street, a good local history museum and an exhibition of paintings by the Newlyn School in **Penlee House Museum and Art Gallery**, and a striking collection of subtropical trees and flowers in **Morrab Gardens**. The **Aquarium and National Lighthouse Centre**, on the Quay, are also worth a look. The town is also a good stepping-off point for the ferry or helicopter to the Isles of Scilly.

MARAZION   MAP 1 REF C24
3 miles E of Penzance off the A394

It's well worth diverting off the A30 to visit Marazion, the ancient trading point on the mainland opposite St Michael's Mount. Cornwall's oldest charter town, Marazion was a port as long ago as the Bronze Age, and for many centuries this was the most important settlement on Mount's Bay. Its long history has left a legacy of fine old inns and residential buildings, and there is also a long sandy beach to the west which offers magnificent views of the Mount. **Marazion Marsh**, on the inland side of the main road, is a protected breeding ground for many rare species of waterfowl. The town features a good stretch of sands, and a windsurfing centre.

The hotel closest to St Michael's Mount, **The Marazion** is a listed building dating back to the early 1700s. Set just 50 yards from one of the safest bathing beaches in Cornwall, this charming family-run hotel offers a relaxed and friendly atmosphere. Fully licensed and open throughout the year, it boasts 10 en suite bedrooms, each individually decorated, comfortably furnished and equipped with every modern facility guests have come to expect. Renowned for the quality and value of its food, there are two attractive and welcoming restaurant/dining areas. Fresh fish and local produce are brought together to create innovative and traditional dishes. Everything from light snacks to full a la carte meals is available. On display is memorabilia from the *HMS Warspite* (including the captain's bunk), which sank off Marazion in 1946. A regular bus service stopping just outside the hotel travels to Penzance, Helston and The Lizard peninsula.

The Marazion Hotel and Cutty Sark Bar and Restaurant, The Square, Marazion, Cornwall TR17 0AP
Tel: 01736 710334

ST MICHAEL'S MOUNT

MAP 1 REF C24

½ mile E of Penzance off the A30

A third of a mile offshore, and connected by a cobbled causeway which is exposed at low tide, St Michael's Mount is a remarkable granite outcrop which rises dramatically from the waters of Mount's Bay. The steep-sided islet has been inhabited by human beings since prehistoric times, and it has been a place of religious pilgrimage since a party of fisherman saw a vision of St Michael on the seaward side of the rock in the 8th century. Three centuries later, Edward the Confessor founded a priory here which was granted to the Benedictine monks of Mont St Michel in Normandy, the island's even more spectacular cousin across the Channel. The monastery was fortified after the Dissolution in 1539, and later passed to the St Aubyn family who incorporated the old monastic buildings into a series of 18th and 19th century improvements to form the striking multi-layered structure we can see today. A direct descendant of the family, Lord St Levan, donated the 21 acre site to the National Trust in 1954. The present-day structure contains some impressive medieval remains, most notably in the Chevy Chase room, the old chapel, and the central tower which soars to a height of over 250 feet above Mount's Bay. One

St Michael's Mount

of the relatively more recent additions is the southeast wing, which was designed in the 19th century by Piers St Aubyn, a cousin of the first Lord St Levan. The interior contains some fine period furniture, silver and paintings, including a number by St Agnes-born John Opie.

LAND'S END
MAP 1 REF B24

10 miles W of Penzance on the A30

Land's End is a curious mixture of natural spectacle and manmade indulgence. Here, the granite backbone of West Penwith succumbs to the Atlantic in a series of savage cliffs, reefs and sheer-sided islets, encompassing some awe-inspiring cliff scenery. On a clear day it is possible to see beyond the **Longships** (a mile and a half offshore) and the **Wolf Rock** (7 miles offshore) lighthouses to the Isles of Scilly, over 25 miles away to the southwest. The Land's End site, mainland Britain's most westerly point, has long been in private hands and, over the years, various attempts have been made to create a visitor attraction worthy of this illustrious setting. The **"Land's End Experience"** heritage centre offers a range of impressive audio-visual presentations on the natural and maritime history of the area, which since Roman times has been known as the 'Seat of Storms'. There is also a hotel with magnificent sea views, and a number of children's attractions. The Land's End airport is situated beside the B3306 to the northeast of Whitesand Bay; as well as a regular service to the Isles of Scilly, short flights can be taken which offer visitors a spectacular bird's-eye view of the surrounding coastline.

ST JUST
MAP 1 REF B24

4 miles NE of Land's End off the B3306

St Just stands at the southwestern margin of one of the most remarkable areas of industrial archeology in the country. An austere community of low granite houses and inns, this was once an important tin- and copper-mining centre. Despite the demise of the industry, the streets still have a solemn working air: there are two Methodist chapels, one with a neoclassical facade and room for almost 100 worshippers, and a solid 15th century church which contains some fascinating early relics, including two medieval wall paintings, now restored, and a 5th or 6th century headstone carved with a faint inscription from the dawn of British Christianity. A shallow grassy amphitheatre can be found near the clock tower in the centre of town; known as **"Plen-an-Gwary"**, it was once used for performing medieval miracle plays and is now a venue for an annual carnival. There is a convenient Skybus from here to the Isles of Scilly.

ISLES OF SCILLY

Lying approximately 28 miles southwest of Land's End, the Scillies are a granite archipelago of over 100 islands, of which only five are inhabited: St Mary's, Tresco, St Martin's, St Agnes and Bryher. Legend has it that this was Lyonesse, or the last remnant remaining above the waves, as well as Avalon, to which the bier of King Arthur was sorrowfully transported. The islanders' traditional occupations of fishing, boat building and smuggling have given them a fierce sense of independence from both Cornwall and the rest of Britain. However, in recent decades the economy has grown more and more dependent on the income from visitors as increasing numbers fly in from Penzance, Newquay and St Just, or arrive aboard the ferry from Penzance.

Most come to escape from the pressures of modern living (there are very few cars on the islands, and only 9 miles of drivable road), to visit some of the 100 or so Bronze Age sites, to observe migrating birds, or simply to enjoy the unique flora which thrive in this exceptionally mild climate. A good time to visit is during the flower harvest in early spring, a busy season which culminates in an annual flower show in March. The origin of the Scillies' flower industry is believed to go back to 1867, when a local farmer sent some early blooms to Covent Garden in his aunt's hat box. The industry was later encouraged by Augustus Smith, the benevolent landlord who administered the islands in the mid-19th century.

ST MARY'S

MAP 1 REF A25

SW of Lands End

St Mary's, the main island, is the first port of call for most visitors. Most arrive at the small air terminal at Old Town, or step ashore in the harbour in Hugh Town, the main centre of population which stands on a narrow isthmus between the 'mainland' and the Garrison peninsula on the island's southwestern corner. A pleasant walk around the peninsula takes in a number of gun emplacements dating from the time the island was fortified against possible Spanish aggression in the 1590s. **Star Castle** was built during this era in the shape of an eight-pointed star (it is now a hotel), and the Garrison, with its imposing gateway, was completed 150 years later. The peninsula is an excellent place from which to view the other islands and the sun setting over the Atlantic.

TRESCO

MAP 1 REF A25

SW of Lands End

The inter-island ferry departs from St Mary's quay at regular intervals throughout the day. A crossing to Tresco provides an opportunity to observe some of the island's abundant wildlife, including puffins and Atlantic grey seals. Tresco's internationally renowned **Abbey Botanical Gardens** were planted in the 1830s by Augustus Smith in the grounds of a ruined 10th century Benedictine priory. Begun as a small collection of plants from Kew, specimens from all over the world have gradually been added to create one of the finest subtropical gardens in the world. Augustus Smith also established the **Valhalla Figurehead Museum** within the grounds of the Abbey Gardens, a unique collection of figureheads and other artefacts salvaged from ships wrecked off the Scillies.

ST MARTIN'S

MAP 1 REF A25

SW of Lands End

St Martin's island, the third largest of the Scillies, is peaceful, picturesque and renowned for its beautiful white sandy beaches, which are safe for bathing. Sailing and diving tuition are available on the island. Birdwatching walks are a regular popular event, as are boat trips to view the local wildlife. Pleasure launches leave daily for the other Isles of Scilly; fishing trips can also bearranged. Two evenings a week there's the opportunity to follow the inter-island gig-boat racing. The islands Village Hall (known as the Reading Room) has indoor games facilities, for which temporary membership is available. St Martin's also features an outdoor tennis court and a local cricket team, happy to take on a ''visitors eleven'' every week in summer.

ST AGNES

MAP 1 REF A25

SW of Lands End

The whitewashed lighthouse on St Agnes is one of the earliest examples of its kind in the British Isles; now disused, it still serves as an effective mariners' daymark. Elsewhere on St Agnes, and on the other two inhabited islands, St Martin's and Bryher, there are fine sandy beaches and some interesting prehistoric remains. The western island of Annet is a sanctuary for seabirds - landing is not permitted during the breeding season.

4 East Anglia

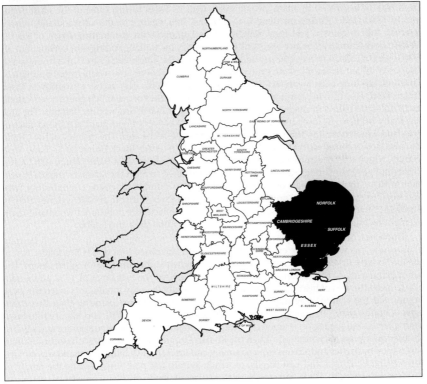

INTRODUCTION

East Anglia includes the easternmost counties of England - Suffolk and Norfolk - as well as Essex (much more than just a glorified suburb of London) and the Fens of Cambridgeshire.

Northeast Essex has the true feel of East Anglia, particularly around the outstanding villages of the Stour Valley - which has come to be known as Constable Country, shared with its near neighbour Suffolk. The inland villages and small towns here are notably historic and picturesque, offering very good touring and walking opportunities. A plethora of half-timbered medieval buildings, farms and churches mark this region out as of particular historical interest. Southern Essex is redolent with distinguished history and a strong maritime heritage, as exemplified in towns like Harwich, Manningtree and Mistley. Further examples are the fine Martello Towers - circular brick edifices built to provide a coastal defence against Napoleon's armies. The Tendring Coast contains an interesting mix of extensive tidal inlets, sandy beaches and low cliffs. The Stour Estuary, Hamford Water and Colne Estuary are all renowned for seabirds and other wildlife. Many areas are protected nature reserves. This is of course also the part of the county known as 'the sunshine holiday coast'. Northwest Essex is home to a wealth of picturesque villages boasting weatherboarded houses and pargetting. The quiet country lanes are perfect for walking, cycling or just exploring. This area also retains three beautiful and historic windmills. Some 600 years ago this region would have been covered in the purple haze of the saffron crocus, highly valued for its healing properties, as a dye and in cooking. It was this humble plant that first brought prosperity to the northwest corner of the county. Southwestern Essex may be associated by many people solely with its larger towns, some of the most populous in Essex, but focusing on these is to overlook this region's wealth of woodland, nature reserves, superb gardens and rural delights. With Epping Forest dominating much of the far western corner there are many excellent opportunities for walking, riding and cycling, but all of this part of Essex is rich in countryside, forests and parks. Southwest Essex is also home to the famous Waltham Abbey. Bordering the north bank of the Thames, the southeastern borough of Thurrock has long been a gateway to London but also affords easy access to southwest Essex and to Kent. This thriving borough encompasses huge swathes of green belt country, and along its 18 miles of Thames frontage there are many important marshland wildlife habitats. The area has many bridleways, footpaths and country parks. The river's flood plain is a broad tract of grassland which is an important feature of the landscape of the area. The defence of the capital was also closely linked with Thurrock. Henry VIII built riverside Block Houses at East and West Tilbury, which later became Coalhouse Fort and Tilbury Fort. It was at West Tilbury that Queen Elizabeth I gave her famous speech to her troops, gathered to meet the Spanish Armada threat. Here at the extreme southeast of the county, there are a number of seaside communities large and small to explore. Further north, but still in eastern Essex, the countryside is dominated by hundreds of acres of ancient woodland, much of it coppiced, the traditional woodland management technique which encourages a vast array of natural flora and fauna.

Northwest Suffolk encompasses picturesque villages, bustling market towns, rich farming countryside, the fens, and the expanse of sandy heath and pine forest that is Breckland. Before the forests were developed the area was sometimes known as the Great East Anglian Desert. The forest is the work of the Forestry Commission, who planted the first pines in 1922 and gradually reduced the area of heathland. Rabbits were practically the only inhabitants when the work began, and the Commission had to destroy 83,000 of them before planting their first 6,000 acres. Country parks, nature reserves and heritage centres bring wildlife and history into fascinating focus, and the region is among the most abundant in the land in antiquities and signs of thousands of years of civilisation. When the Roman Empire collapsed in the 5th century Britain was settled by Angles and Saxons from Germany and Jutes from Denmark. England was divided into several kingdoms and East Anglia, of which Suffolk was part, was ruled by the family of Wuffinga. The wealth, trade and culture of those times is gradually being unearthed, mainly in Suffolk. Many of the remains of the Anglo-Saxon period are on display, notably, at West Stow and in Bury St Edmunds, and in museums in Ipswich and Woodbridge. The area south and west of Bury towards the Essex border contains some of Suffolk's most attractive and peaceful countryside. The beauty is largely unspoilt and the motorist will come upon a succession of picturesque villages, historic churches, stately homes, heritage centres and nature reserves. There are some 500 medieval churches in Suffolk, each reflecting the life of its community and the changes effected by wars, invasions and religious upheavals. The heart of Suffolk is the place in the county to get away from it all, lying between the heathland and the coast. Many of the villages are little changed from olden days. The Rivers Deben and Gipping run through much of the region, which naturally has its fair share of churches, museums, fayres and festivals. Also in this part of Suffolk, some of the best-preserved windmills and watermills are to be found. While inland Suffolk has few peers in terms of picturesque countryside and villages, Suffolk is also very much a maritime county, with over 50 miles of coastline. All those miles have been constantly bombarded by the North Sea, and out at sea the sandbanks have often proved disastrous to shipping; at one time as many wrecks were recorded here as anywhere around Britain's shores. The estuaries of the Waveney, Blyth, Alde, Deben, Orwell and Stour have somewhat minimised the erosion, and the whole stretch is a marvellous mixture of estuaries, beaches, marshes, reedland, heath and pasture. In 1993 the Suffolk Coast and Heath Project was created to protect and conserve this area of outstanding natural beauty, which is home to an amazing variety of flora and fauna. The whole coast is a conservation area, which the 50-mile Suffolk Coastal Path makes walkable throughout. Like Essex, Suffolk has its share of Martello Towers. They are generally around 30 feet in height, with immensely thick walls on the seaward side, and surrounded by a moat. Entry was usually by bridge or ladder on the land side. They were never needed for their original purpose, and now stand as a picturesque oddity along the shore. The marshes by the coast have traditionally been a source of reeds, the raw material for the thatch that is such a pretty sight on so many Suffolk buildings. Reed cutting happens between December and February, the beds being drained in preparation and reflooded after the crop has been gathered. Thatching itself is a highly skilled craft, but 10 weeks of work can give a thatched roof 50 years of life. Organised walks of the reed beds take place from time to time - waterproof footwear essential. The Orwell and the Stour rivers mark the boundaries of Suffolk's Shotley Peninsula. The countryside here is largely unspoilt, with wide-open spaces between scattered villages. The relative flatness of Suffolk gives every encouragement for motorists to leave their machines, and the peninsula, still relatively peaceful, is ideal for a spot of walking or cycling or boating. "Constable Country" on the Suffolk/Essex border denotes England's greatest land-scape painter, who remained at heart a Suffolk man throughout his life. The six large paintings which became his best known works are all set on a short stretch of the Stour.

Strange to say, Norfolk is actually an island, surrounded by sea to the north and east, iso-lated from Cambridgeshire by the River Great Ouse, and from Suffolk by the Little Ouse River and the River Waveney, bulging out into the North Sea. It is a predominantly agricultural county with some 700 villages scattered across its 70-mile length and 40-mile breadth. Despite its ranking as the 4th largest of the English counties, Norfolk is listed 23rd in terms of population, a happy imbalance which results in great tracts of sparsely populated land, especially in the southwestern corner of the county. And of all English counties, Norfolk is most notable for its endowment of a wealth of historic buildings: some 750 medieval churches, the ruins of 50 monasteries, hundreds of prehistoric and Roman remains, half a dozen of the stateliest homes in England, as well as thousands of interesting houses, cottages, barns and other buildings. The architectural historian Nikolaus Pevsner, compiling his monumental *Buildings of England* series, found it necessary to devote two books to this county rather than the usual single volume, and in Arthur Mee's comprehensive survey of *The King's England*, his book on Norfolk is the fattest of all the county tomes. Norfolk owes this rich heritage to its prosperity during the Middle Ages when intensive agriculture and a thriving woollen trade greatly enriched its land-owning citi-zens. They in turn expressed their gratitude to the Divine Providence which had made them so wealthy by expending a moiety of their profits in funding the building of churches. Happily, these were the years when English ecclesiastical architecture was at its most inventive and ambitious: the medieval masons constructed buildings that were both sublime in scale and delicate in detail. It's not at all clear how the huge sea-bite of The Wash earned its name: perhaps one should settle for the simple explanation that for centuries it has been trying to wash away as much of the Norfolk and, especially, the Lincolnshire coast as it can. In good weather, The Wash is a placid lake, but when a north, or north-easterly gale blows in, its shal-low waters boil up into a spume-flecked, destructive force. It's a mariner's nightmare, feared because of its ever-shifting sandbanks designated by such respectful names as Thief, Bull Dog, Roaring Middle and Pandora. Inland, the central part of the county is effectively a plateau, where the gentle contours never rise or fall more than a few metres. It's far from dull, though. The valleys of the Rivers Nar and Wensum display some of the most enchanting scenery in the county, and the area boasts two of the finest Gothic parish churches in England, at Cawston and Salle. In pre-historic times, this was the most wooded part of Norfolk, and a good number of medieval natural woods still remain, a feature which adds another visual attraction to this pastoral area of the country. Norfolk has more than a hundred miles of coastline. The whole of the North Norfolk coast is of course a birdwatcher's paradise, with an extraordinary number of different species of birds to be spotted. An admirable way to experience the area to the full is to walk all or part of the Coastal Footpath which begins at Holme next the Sea and follows the coastline for some 36 miles eastwards to Cromer, for most of its route well away from any roads. The eastern part of the county approaches the Highlands of Norfolk - the Cromer Ridge which attains the not very dizzying height of 330 feet above sea level. The coast undergoes a great deal of contrast here, with marshy wetlands giving way to low cliffs. Substantial stretches of the coast are, happily, in the care of the National Trust, but anyone in search of a beach holiday will be much more interested in the coastline east of Sheringham. From this decorous resort, a broad strip of excellent sands runs almost uninterruptedly past Cromer and southwards to Great Yarmouth and that unique area of the country which is in serious danger of being loved to death, the Norfolk Broads. The Broads are an area of outstanding natural beauty, but a beauty that is desperately fragile. In 1988, the Norfolk Broads Authority was invested with the kind of powers enjoyed by National Parks to resist any further degradation of the area. The Authority's declared ambition is that by around the year 2050 they will have restored these lovely water-ways to their erstwhile purity, an undertaking which it readily admits is "a marathon, not a sprint".

And so to Cambridgeshire. The southern part of the county covers some 350 square miles around the city of Cambridge and is rich in history, with a host of archaeological sites and monuments to visit, as well as many important museums. The area is fairly flat, so it makes for great walking and cycling tours, and offers a surprising variety of landscapes. The Romans planted vines here and to this day the region is among the main producers of British wine. At the heart of it all is Cambridge itself, one of the leading academic centres in the world and a city which deserves plenty of time to explore - on foot, by bicycle or by the gentler, romantic option of a punt. Further north, and far removed from the hustle and bustle of modern life, the Fens are like a breath of fresh air. Extending over much of Cambridgeshire from the Wash, these flat, fenland fields contain some of the richest soil in England and the villages such as Soham and small towns like Ely rise out of the landscape on low hills. Before the Fens were drained this was a land of mist, marshes and bogs; of small islands, inhabited by independent folk, their liveli-hood the fish and waterfowl of this eerie, watery place. The region is full of legends of web-footed people, ghosts and witchcraft.

ESSEX

WALTHAM ABBEY
12 miles N of London on the A121

MAP 5 REF Q18

The town of Waltham began as a small Roman settlement on the site of the present-day Market Square. The early Saxon kings maintained a hunting lodge here; a town formed round this, and the first church was built in the 6th century. By the 8th, during the reign of Cnut, the town had a stone minster church with a great stone crucifix that had been brought from Somerset, were it had been found buried in land owned by Tovi, a trusted servant of the king. This cross became the focus of pilgrims seeking healing. One of those cured of a serious illness, Harold Godwinsson, built a new church, the third on the site, which was dedicated in 1060 - and it was this self-same Harold who became king and was killed in the battle of Hastings six years on. Harold's body was brought back to Waltham to be buried in his church. The church that exists today was built in the first quarter of the 12th century. It was once three times its present length, and incorpo-rated an Augustinian Abbey, built in 1177 by Henry II. The town became known for the Abbey, which was one of the largest in the country and the last to be the victim of Henry VIII's disso-lution of the monasteries, in 1540.

The Abbey's **Crypt Centre** houses an interesting exhibition explaining the history of both the Abbey and the town, highlighting the religious significance of the site. Some visible re-mains of the Augustinian Abbey include the chapter house and precinct walls, cloister entry and gateway in the surrounding Abbey Gardens. The Abbey Gardens are also host to a Sensory

Trail exploring the highlights of hundreds of years of the site's history; there's also a delightful Rose Garden. Along the Cornhill Stream, crossed by the impressive stone bridge, the town's **Dragonfly Sanctuary** is home to over half the native British species of dragonflies and damselflies. It is noted as the best single site for seeing these species in Greater London, Essex and Hertfordshire.

A Tudor timber-framed house forms part of the **Epping Forest District Museum** in Sun Street. The museum has several hands-on displays which help to bring history to life, and features special events and adult workshops throughout the year. Sun Street is the town's main thoroughfare, and it is pedestrianised. It contains many buildings from the 16th century onwards. The Greenwich Meridian (0 degrees longitude) runs through the street, marked out on the pavement and through the Abbey Gardens. In spite of its proximity to London and more recent development, the town retains a peaceful, traditional character, with its timber-framed buildings and small traditional market which has been held here since the early 12th century (now every Tuesday and Saturday). The whole of the town centre has been designated a conservation area. The Market Square boasts many fine and interesting buildings such as the Lych-gate and The Welsh Harp, dating from the 17th and 16th centuries respectively. The **Town Hall** offers a fine example of Art Nouveau design, and houses the Waltham Abbey Information Office.

To the west of town, the **Lee Navigation Canal** offers opportunities for anglers, walkers, birdwatching and pleasure craft. Once used for transporting corn and other commercial goods to the growing City of London, and having associations with the town's important gunpowder industry for centuries, the canal remains a vital part of town life.

Gunpowder production became established in Waltham as early as the 1660s; by the 19th century the **Royal Gunpowder Mills** employed 500 workers, and production did not cease until 1943, after which time the factory became a research facility. In the spring of 2000, however, all this is set to change, and the site will be opened to the public for the first time. Of the 175 acres the site occupies, approximately 80 have been designated a Site of Special Scientific Interest, and the ecology of the site will offer a rare opportunity for study. With two-thirds of the site a Scheduled Ancient Monument, there are some 21 listed buildings to be found here, some of which date from the Napoleonic Wars. The site also contains some of the finest examples of industrial archaeology in the world. Up until 2000 there are free site tours being held on special National Heritage Open Days, giving visitors the opportunity to experience the Royal Gunpowder Mills prior to its development as a nationally recognised Heritage attraction.

Lee Valley Regional Park is a leisure area stretching for 23 miles along the River Lea (sometimes also spelled Lee) from East London to Herfordshire. The Lee Valley is an important area of high biodiversity, sustaining a large range of wildlife and birds. Two hundred species of birds, including internationally important populations of Gadwall and Shoveler ducks, can be seen each year on the wetlands and water bodies along the Lea. The Information Centre in the Abbey Gardens provides displays and information on a range of countryside pursuits and interests, sport, leisure and heritage facilities and special events. Of national importance for overwintering waterbirds including rare species of bittern and smew, this fine park makes an ideal place for a picnic. Guided tours by appointment.At the southern end of Lee Valley Park, **The House Mill**, one of two tidal mills still standing at this site, has been restored by the River Lea Tidal Mill Trust. It was built in 1776 in the Dutch style, and was used to grind grain for gin distilling.

Lee Valley Park Farms, along Stubbins Hall Lane, boasts two farms on site: Hayes Hill Farm, where visitors can interact with the animals and enjoy a picnic or the children's adventure playground. This traditional farm also boasts old-fashioned tools and equipment, an exhibition in the medieval barn and occasional craft demonstrations. The entry fee to Hayes Hill Farm also covers a visit to Holyfield Hall Farm, a working farm and dairy where visitors can see milking and learn about modern farming methods. Seasonal events such as sheep-shearing and harvesting are held, and there's an attractive farm tea room and a toy shop. Recently a farm trail has been added to this site's attractions, offering wonderful views of the Lee Valley, an expanse of open countryside dotted with lakes and wildflower meadows, attracting a wide range of wildlife including otters, bats, dragonfly, kingfisher, great crested grebe and little ringed plover. The area is ideal for walking or fishing and the bird hides are open to all at weekends; permits available for daily access. Guided tours by arrangement.

HARLOW
Map 5 ref Q18

8 miles NE of Waltham Abbey on the A414

The 'New Town' of Harlow sometimes gets short shrift, but it is in fact a lively and vibrant town with a great deal more than excellent shopping facilities. There are some very good museums and several sites of historic interest. **The Gibberd Collection** in Harlow Town Hall in The High offers a delightful collection of British water-colours, featuring works by Blackadder, Sutherland, Frink, Nash and Sir Frederick Gibberd, Harlow's master planner and the founder of the collection. **Harlow Museum** in Passmores House, Third Avenue, occupies a Georgian manor house set in picturesque gardens which includes a lovely pond and is home to several species of butterfly. The museum has extensive and important Roman, post-medieval and early 20th century collections, as well as a full programme of temporary exhibitions. **Mark Hall Cycle Museum and Gardens** in Muskham Road offers a unique collection of cycles and cycling accessories illustrating the history of the bicycle from 1818 to the present day, including one made of plastic, one that folds, and one where the seat tips forward and throws its rider over the handlebars if the brakes are applied too hard. The museum is housed in a converted stable block within Mark Hall manor. Adjacent to the museum are three period walled gardens.

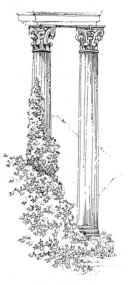

Gibberd Gardens

Gibberd Gardens, on the eastern outskirts of Harlow in Marsh Lane, Gilden Way, is worth a visit, reflecting as it does the taste of Sir Frederick Gibberd, the famous architect. This 7-acre garden was designed this century by Sir Frederick on the side of a small valley, with terraces, wild garden, landscaped vistas, pools and streams and some 80 sculptures. **Harlow Study and Visitors Centre** in Netteswellbury Farm is set in a medieval tithe barn and 13th century church. The site has displays outlining the story of Harlow New Town.**Parndon Wood Nature Reserve**, Parndon Wood Road, is an ancient woodland with a fine variety of birds, mammals, and insects. Facilities include two nature trails with hides for observing wildlife, and a study centre.

INGATESTONE
Map 5 ref R18

12 miles SE of Harlow off the B1002

Ingatestone Hall on Hall Lane is a 16th century mansion set in 11 acres of grounds. It was built by Sir William Petre, Secretary of State to four Monarchs, whose family continue to reside here. The Hall contains family portraits, furniture and memorabilia accumulated over the centuries. Guided tours by prior arrangement.

SAFFRON WALDEN
Map 5 ref R16

17 miles N of Harlow on the B184

The town was named after the Saffron crocus, which was grown in the area to make dyestuffs and fulfil a variety of other uses in the Middle Ages. A great deal of the street plan of the town from those times survives, as do hundreds of fine buildings, many timbered with overhanging upper floors and decorative plastering (also known as pargetting). Gog and Magog (or in some versions folk-hero Tom Hickathrift and the Wisbech Giant) battle forever in plaster on the gable of the **Old Sun Inn**, where, legend has it, Oliver Cromwell and General Fairfax both lodged during the Civil War. A typical market town, Saffron Walden's centrepiece is its magnificent church.

At the **Saffron Walden Museum**, as well as the gloves worn by Mary Queen of Scots on the day she died, is a piece of human skin which once coated the church door at Hadstock. The museum first opened to the public at its present location in 1835, and was founded 'to gratify the inclination of all who value natural history'. It remains faithful to this credo, while widening the museum's scope. The museum has won numerous awards, including joint winner of the Museum of the Year Award for best museum of Industrial or Social History in 1997. At this friendly, family-sized museum visitors can try their hand at corn grinding with a Romano-British quern, see how a medieval timber house would have been built, admire the displays of Native American and West African embroidery and come face to face with Wallace the Lion, the museum's faithful guardian. Over two floors, exhibits focus

Saffron Walden

on town and country (with a wealth of wooden plough and other agricultural artefacts), furniture and woodwork, costumes, ancient Egyptian and Roman artefacts, geology and ceramics and glass. In the 'ages of man' gallery, the history of northwest Essex is traced from the Ice Age to the Middle Ages. The ruins of historic Walden Castle are also on-site. This truly distinguished museum merits a closer look.

On the local **Common**, once Castle Green, is the largest surviving **Turf Maze** in England. Only eight ancient turf mazes survive in England: though there were many more in the Middle Ages, if they are not looked after they soon become overgrown and are lost. This one is believed to be some 800 years old. Though many miles from the sea, Henry Winstanley, inventor, engineer and engraver, and designer of the first Eddystone Lighthouse at Plymouth, was born here in 1644. He is said to have held 'lighthouse trials' with a wooden lantern in the lavishly decorated 15th to 16th century church. The Lighthouse, and Winstanley with it, were swept away in a fierce storm in 1703. The town was also famous for its resident Cockatrice, which was hatched from a cock's egg by a toad or serpent and could, it was said, kill its victims with a glance. The Cockatrice was blamed for any inexplicable disaster in the town. Like Perseus and Medusa the Gorgon, a Cockatrice could be destroyed by making it see its own reflection, thereby turning it to stone. The Saffron Walden Cockatrice's slayer was said to be a knight in a coat of 'cristal glass'.

To the north of the town is **Bridge End Gardens**, a wonderfully preserved example of an early Victorian garden, complete with the unique Hedge Maze, which is open only by appointment (which can be made at the TIC). Next to the gardens is the **Fry Art Gallery**, which has a unique collection of work by artists who have lived in and around the town. It also exhibits work by many notable 20th century artists who lived and worked in the area before and after the Second World War, as well as contemporary artists working in Essex today. Close to Bridge

End is the Anglo-American War Memorial dedicated by Field Marshal the Viscount Montgomery of Alamein in 1953 to the memory of all the American flyers of the 65th Fighter Wing who lost their lives in the Second World War.

Audley End House was, at one time, home of the first Earl of Suffolk. The original 17th century house, with its two large courtyards, had a magnificence claimed to match that of Hampton Court. Unfortunately the subsequent earls lacked their forebear's financial acumen, and much of the house was demolished as it fell into disrepair. Nevertheless it remains today one of England's most impressive Jacobean mansions; its distinguished stone facade set off perfectly by Capability Brown's lake. The remaining state rooms retain their palatial magnificence and the exquisite state bed in the Neville Room is hung with the original embroidered drapes. This jewel also has beautiful gardens landscaped by Capability Brown, and the Audley End Miniature Railway is 1.5 miles long and takes visitors through the beautiful private woods of the house. Within the rolling parkland of the grounds there are several elegant outbuildings, some of which were designed by Robert Adam. Among these are an icehouse, a circular temple and a Springwood Column.

SEWARDS END   Map 8 ref R16
2 miles E of Saffron Walden off the B1053

In the attractive village of Sewards End, half a mile from the B1053, Redgates Lane leads out into lovely open countryside. At **Redgates Farmhouse**, guests can enjoy all the comforts of home in a peaceful and very relaxing setting. Owner Alison Colbert offers bed and breakfast accommodation within this lovely property, parts of which date back to the 16th century. This smallholding is set in 10 acres of grassland, commanding lovely views in every direction. There

are two comfortable guest bedrooms, delightfully furnished and decorated with taste and a truly homely feel. In these peaceful surroundings guests can enjoy country walks after starting the day with one of Alison's outstanding breakfasts (she is, after all, a former Cordon Bleu chef!). Delicious evening meals are also available by prior arrangement. The decor and ambience of this attractive B&B are very traditional, from the handsome hall-way and charming

Redgates Farmhouse, Redgates Lane, Sewards End, Saffron Walden, Essex CB10 2LP Tel: 01799 516166

breakfast room to the lovely, intimate and friendly guests' sitting room with its open log fire. Other amenities offered guests include a taxi service to and from local airports and, for those seeking a riding holiday, facilities for guests bringing their own horses. Alison offers the very best in hospitality and service to all her guests. This delightful establishment is open all year round.

RADWINTER   Map 8 ref R16
4 miles E of Saffron Walden off the B1053

Radwinter boasts a fine church, which was largely renovated and rebuilt in the 19th century by architect Eden Nesfield and has a fine 14th-century porch. The village also has Nesfield-designed cottages and almshouses. At the crossroads of the B1053 and B1054 in the pretty village

The Plough Inn at Radwinter, Sampford Road, Radwinter, Saffron Walden, Essex CB10 2TL Tel: 01799 599222 Fax: 01799 599161

of Radwinter, **The Plough Inn at Radwinter** is a welcoming pub and restaurant, which also offers accommodation. It is set in a handsome 17th-century building. Owner Tony Burdfield arrived in late 1998, and has been busy maintaining the pub's reputation for quality and service. This part-thatched free house boasts traditional comforts. Open every session, and all day on Saturdays and Sundays from May-September, it provides delicious meals lunchtimes and evenings from either the extensive menu or blackboard specials of the day. The fine real ales on hand include Greene King IPA, with the locally brewed Golden Gate proving particularly popular. Booking advised for Friday and Saturday evenings and Sunday lunch. The three ensuite letting rooms on the ground-floor annexe (one twin, one double) are very attractive and comfortable. To the rear of this welcoming establishment there's a lovely secluded patio and gardens overlooking views of the surrounding countryside.

WICKEN BONHUNT
4 miles SW of Saffron Walden off the B1038

MAP 8 REF R17

This tiny village (population approximately 25), though not far from the M11, is a haven of rural peace and tranquillity, with some lovely 16th-century buildings. **The Coach & Horses** is a welcoming public house in Wicken Bonhunt. This handsome pub dates back to the 16th century, and started life as a forge before it became an inn. The thatched roof, flagstone floors and open fires in both bars speak of its historical origins. The atmosphere is cosy and friendly, as this is a very popular pub with both locals and visitors alike, a favourite spot for ramblers, walkers, local farmers and 'City' folk - co-owner Nicky Freeman gave up her life as a City stockbroker for the peace and tranquillity of the Essex countryside. Her hus-

The Coach and Horses, Wicken Road, Wicken Bonhunt, Nr Saffron Walden, Essex CB11 3UG Tel: 01799 540516

band Mike has many years experience in the pub trade, and together they are charming and gregarious hosts. The walls are decorated with caricatures of locals drawn by Gill Potter of *Yellow Submarine* fame. There is a range of beers, wines and spirits on offer, and the home-cooked bar snacks and evening meals make good use of delicious fresh ingredients; with fresh fish delivered twice a week, fish and chips proves very popular with visitors and locals alike.

THAXTED
MAP 8 REF R17
6 miles SE of Saffron Walden off the B184

This small country town has a recorded history which dates back to before the Domesday book. Originally a Saxon settlement, it developed around a Roman road. Yet, although the town is full of beautiful old buildings, it has a special character all its own. To its credit Thaxted has no need of artificial tourist attractions and is today what is has been for the last ten centuries: a thriving and beautiful town. Thaxted has numerous attractively pargetted and timber-framed houses, and a magnificent **Guildhall**, built as a meeting-place for cutlers around 1390. The demise of the cutlery industry in this part of Essex in the 1500s led it to becoming the admin-

istrative centre of the town. Restored in Georgian times it became the town's Grammar School, as well as remaining a centre of administration. Once more restored in 1975, today the Parish council still meet here. The town's famous **Tower Windmill** was built in 1804 by John Webb. In working order until 1907, it fell into disuse and disrepair but has now been returned to full working order. Close to the wind-mill are the town's **Almshouses**, which provided homes for the elderly even 250 years after they were built for that very purpose.

Thaxted Tower Windmill

    Thaxted Church stands on a hill and soars ca-thedral-like over the town's streets. It has been described as the finest Parish church in the country and, though many towns may protest long and loud at this claim, it certainly is magnificent. It was also the somewhat unlikely setting for a pitched battle in 1921. The rather colourful vicar and secretary of the Church Socialist League, one Conrad Noel, hoisted the red flag of communism and the Sinn Fein flag in the church. Incensed Cambridge students tore them down and put up the Union Jack; Noel in turn ripped that down and, with his friends, slashed the tyres of the students' cars and motorbikes. A fine bronze in the church celebrates this adventurous man of the cloth. Conrad Noel's wife is remembered for encouraging Morris dancing in the town. Today, the famous **Morris Ring** is held annually (usually on the Spring Bank Holiday), attracting over 300 dancers from all over the country who dance through the streets. Dancing can also be seen around the town on most Bank Holiday Mondays, usually in the vicinity of a pub! Gustav Holst, composer of, amongst other pieces, the renowned 'Planets' Suite, lived in Thaxted from 1914-1925, and often played the church organ. To celebrate his connection with the town, there is a month-long music festival in late June/early July which attracts performers of international repute.

BROXTED
MAP 8 REF R17
3 miles SW of Thaxted off the B1051

The paris church of St Mary the Virgin here in the handsome village of Broxted has two remark-ably lovely stained glass windows commemorating the captivity and release of John McCarthy and the other Beirut hostages, dedicated in January 1993. Though just a few minutes' drive from Stansted Airport off the M11, it is a welcoming haven of rural tranquillity.

Peter and Sandy Russell have owned and personally run **The Old Post Office Guest House** in Broxted since 1996. Peter is a former civil airline pilot, Sandy a former flight director. They did not have to look far to find this gem: Just three miles from Stansted Airport, it makes an excellent touring base. As its name suggests this was originally the village post office, and dates

back to 1821. An extension and conversion of the post office in 1987 saw the adjoining cottage become part of the property. Accommodation at this charming guest house comprises six bedrooms (doubles and singles), three

The Old Post Office Guest House, Church End, Broxted, Essex CM6 2BU Tel/Fax: 01279 850050

of which have ensuite facilities. Furnished with lovely pine and decorated to a high standard of taste and comfort, they are cosy and welcoming. There is also a pleasant front garden for guests to enjoy. The full English breakfast makes a hearty start to the day; for evening meals there is a wide selection of local country pubs. No smoking. Children welcome. ETB 2 Star Commended.

GREAT DUNMOW
MAP 8 REF R17

12 miles SE of Saffron Walden off the A120

Great Dunmow

The town is famous for the *"Flitch of Bacon"*, an ancient ceremony which dates back as far as the early 12th century. A prize of a flitch, or side, of bacon was awarded to the local man who, in the words of then-Lord Mayor Robert Fitzwalter, *'does not repent of his marriage nor quarrel, differ or dispute with his wife within a year and a day after the marriage'*. Amidst great ceremony the couple would be seated and presented with their prize. The custom lapsed on the dissolution of the monasteries, was briefly revived in the 18th century and became established again after 1885. 'Trials' to test the truth are all in good fun, and carried out every leap year. The successful couple are carried through the streets on chairs and then presented with the Flitch. The 'bacon chair' can be seen in Little Dunmow parish church.

NORTHEND
MAP 8 REF R17

2 miles SE of Great Dunmow off the A130

Here in the attractive village of Northend, **The Butchers Arms** is a distinguished and traditional public house. This comfortable, welcoming pub began life in the 16th century, as evidenced by the wealth of original features in the pub. Tenants Chris and Maxine Durham have been here since 1997, Chris having been in the trade most of his working life. They are friendly and hospitable hosts. The pub comes well recommended by and is popular with locals and visitors alike for its excellent food, served either in the bar areas or in the cosy and intimate 26-cover restaurant (booking advised). Guests choose from the array of dishes on the chalkboard, which changes regularly and includes such tempting morsels as 'the Butcher's Breakfast' - a mammoth

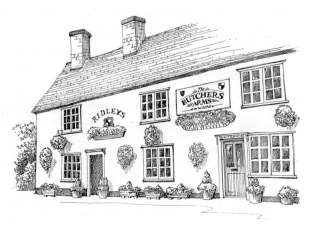

The Butchers Arms, Dunmow Road, Northend, Nr Great Dunmow, Essex CM6 3PJ Tel: 01245 237481

English breakfast served throughout the day - as well as excellent sandwiches and Essex 'Huffers'. Fresh ingredients, including fresh fish when available, are made use of. To wash down your meal there's a fine selection of well-kept Ridley's ales, including Ridley's Champion Mild. There is an extremely attractive and award-winning garden with picnic tables, barbecue area, lawn and central flower display in the former aviary, as well as a secure, large children's play area. This excellent pub is open lunch and evenings daily (no food Monday evenings).

FELSTED   MAP 8 REF R17
3 miles SE of Great Dunmow off the A130

The major part of **Pot Ash Farmhouse** was built in 1490, as the wealth of exposed beams and other original features attests. The house is half-surrounded by a moat, and there are two acres of lovely well-kept gardens, a croquet lawn, badminton/clock golf course and 40 acres of arable farmland with public

footpaths, all available to guests. Bed and breakfast accommodation comprises two twin rooms and one double, all tastefully furnished. One of the twin rooms overlooks the moat, while the other has exposed beamwork and is said to be visited by a friendly ghost - a girl with kind and gentle features and long hair. The double room is spacious and airy. The guests' lounge, also

Pot Ash Farmhouse, Causeway End Road, Cobblers Green, Felsted, Great Dunmow, Essex CM6 3LX
Tel: 01371 820510 email: rgs.potash@compuserve.com

extremely comfortable, has a television and a variety of books and magazines to browse through. The dining room is heavily beamed and decorated with an abundance of shining brasswork. The large brick fireplace is complemented by the antique furnishings. The hearty full English breakfast includes home-made jams and marmalades. Continental or vegetarian breakfast also available. No children or pets, due to the proximity of the outside moat. ETB 4 Diamonds Highly Commended.

CHELMSFORD

Map 5 ref R18

15 miles E of Harlow off the A12

Roman workmen cutting their great road linking London with Colchester built a fort at what is today called Chelmsford. Then called *Caesaromagus*, it stands at the confluence of the Rivers Chelmer and Can. The town has always been an important market centre and is now the bustling county town of Essex. It is also directly descended from a new town planned by the Bishop of London in 1199. At its centre are the principal inn, the **Royal Saracen's Head**, and the elegant **Shire Hall** of 1791. Three plaques situated high up on the eastern face of the Hall overlooking the High Street represent Wisdom, Justice and Mercy. The building now houses the town magistrates court. Christianity came to Essex with the Romans and again, later, by St Cedd (AD 654); in 1914 the diocese of Chelmsford was created.

Chelmsford Cathedral in New Street dates from the 15th century and is built on the site of a church constructed 800 years ago. The cathedral is noted for the harmony and unity of its perpendicular architecture. It was John Johnson, the distinguished local architect who designed both the Shire Hall and the 18th century **Stone Bridge** over the River Can, who also rebuilt the Parish Church of St Mary when most of its 15th century tower fell down. The church became a cathedral when the new diocese of Chelmsford was created. Since then it has been enlarged and re-organised inside. The cathedral boasts memorial windows dedicated to the USAAF airmen who were based in Essex from 1942-5. The Marconi Company, pioneers in the manufacture of wireless equipment, set up the first radio company in the world here in Chelmsford in 1899. Exhibits of those pioneering days of wireless can be seen in the **Chelmsford and Essex Museum** in Oaklands Park, as can interesting displays of Roman remains and local history. The **Essex Regiment Museum** is also situated in Oaklands Park. Together these two fine museums exhibit temporary and permanent displays exploring local and social history from prehistoric times up until the present. The history of the distinguished Essex Regiment, a wealth of fine and decorative arts (including costume, ceramics and glass), coins, natural history displays recounting the geology and wildlife of the region (including a live beehive) and changing special exhibitions add to the interest and informative power of these two Chelmsford landmarks.

Also in the town, at Parkway, is **Moulsham Mill**, an early 18th century water mill that has been renovated and now houses a variety of craft workshops and businesses. Crafts featured include jewellery, pottery, flowers, lace-making, dolls houses and bears, and decoupage work. There is a charming picnic area nearby, and a good café.

MALDON

Map 5 ref S18

8 miles E of Chelmsford off the A414

The steep winding streets of Maldon are full of intriguing shops and welcoming inns. The town's High Street, of which the **Moot Hall** is a distinctive feature, runs right down to the River Blackwater estuary. Filled with craft of all shapes and sizes, the quayside is overlooked by the Queen's Head pub, which organises an annual mud race across the river at low tide. Part of the old Moot Hall is used to display the arresting and ambitious tapestry commemorating the 1,000th anniversary of the crucial Battle of Maldon. The rest of the hall can only be seen by prior arrangement. Built in the 15th century for the D'Arcy family, the original spiral brick staircase and 18th century court room are of particular interest.

Just outside the town lies the spot where this decisive battle of England's early history took place. At the Battle of Maldon in 991, the English leader, Byrrhnoth, was killed by the invading Danes after a fierce three-day battle. As a result of this defeat the English king, Ethelred the Unready, was obliged to pay an annual tribute to his conquerors. The Danes soon tired of this arrangement, however, and overthrew Ethelred, putting Cnut on the throne. Maldon is also famous for its sea salt, produced for generations in the traditional manner of letting sea water evaporate naturally, leaving just the mineral-rich salt behind. Maldon's **Millenium Gardens** are also named in commemoration of the Battle of Maldon, and re-create what a garden would have looked like at the time of this famed event.

Maldon District Museum at 47 Mill Road is a handsome and traditional museum with a range of changing exhibits showcasing a selection of objects associated with the area and the people

Hythe Quay, Maldon

of the Maldon District. The museum stands adjacent to **Promenade Park**, stretching into nearby Hythe Quay. This Edwardian park boasts magnificent river walks and views. The park comprises a marine lake, amusement centre, mini-golf, boat hire and numerous year-round events. There's also an interesting museum.

At the top of this waterside town, a narrow staircase in the church tower leads to the wonderful **Plume Library**, which is still much as it was when the founder, Dr Plume, died in 1704. He built it as a home for the 6,000 books he had collected and then gave it to the town. The Maldon Public Library is below. Above the town stand the ruins of **St Giles the Leper Hospital**, founded by King Henry II in the 12th century. As with all monastic buildings, it fell into disuse after Henry VIII's dissolution of the monasteries, though it retained its roof and was used as a barn until the late 19th century. The lively boat and barge quay at **Heybridge Basin** just outside the town offers visitors the best chance to see one of the classic Thames barges with their oxblood sails in action.

COLCHESTER

Map 8 ref S17

24 miles NE of Chelmsford off the A12

This ancient market town and garrison stands in the midst of rolling East Anglian countryside. England's oldest recorded town, it has over 2,000 years of history to discover. First established during the 7th century BC, west of town there are the remains of the massive earthworks built to protect Colchester in pre-Roman times. During the 1st century, its prime location made it an obvious target for invading Romans. The Roman Emperor Claudius took the surrender of 11 British Kings in Colchester. In AD 60 Queen Boudica helped to establish her place in history by taking revenge on the Romans and burning the town to the ground, before going on to destroy London and St Albans. Here in this town that was once capital of Roman Britain, Roman walls - the oldest in Britain - still surround the oldest part of town. Balkerne Gate, west gate of the original Roman town, is the largest surviving Roman gateway in the country and remains magnificent to this day. Today the town is presided over by its lofty town hall and enormous Victorian water tower, nicknamed 'Jumbo' after London Zoo's first African elephant, controversially sold to P T Barnum in 1882. The tower has four massive pillars of one and a quarter million bricks, 369 tons of stone and 142 tons of iron, which work to support the 230,000 gallon tank. Colchester (a name given the town by the Saxons) was an important borough. The Normans built their **castle** on the foundations of the Roman temple of Claudius. Having used many of the

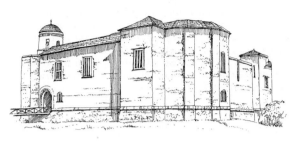

Colchester Castle

Roman bricks in its construction, it boasts the largest Norman keep ever built in Europe - the only part still left standing. The keep houses the **Castle Museum**, one of the most exciting hands-on historical attractions in the country. Among its fascinating collection of Iron Age, Roman and medieval relics there are tombstones carved in intricate detail and exquisite examples of Roman glass and jewellery. Visitors can try on Roman togas and helmets, touch some of the 2,000-year-old pottery unearthed nearby, and experience the town's murkier past by visiting the Castle prisons, where witches were interrogated by the notorious Witchfinder General Matthew Hopkins.

Hollytrees Museum in the High Street is located in a fine Georgian home dating back to 1718. This museum on the edge of Castle Park houses a wonderful collection of toys, costumes, curios and antiquities from the last two centuries. Purchased for the town by Viscount Cowdray it first opened as a museum in 1920. Also nearby, housed in the former All Saints' Church, is the **Natural History Museum**, with exhibits and many hands-on displays illustrating the natural history of Essex from the Ice Age right up to the present day. Around the corner on Trinity Street, another former church, Holy Trinity - the only Saxon building left in Colchester - is home to the Museum of Social History, containing displays of rural crafts and country life. An arch opposite this museum leads to **Tymperleys Clock Museum**, 15th century timber-framed home of William Gilberd, who entertained Elizabeth I with experiments in electricity. Today this fine example of architectural splendour houses a magnificent collection of 18th and 19th century Colchester-made clocks. The **Colchester Arts Centre**, not far from Balkerne Gate, features a regular programme of visual arts, drama, music, poetry and dance; the **Mercury Theatre** is the town's premiere site for stage dramas, comedies and musical theatre.

At, the **Posthouse Colchester**, part of the distinguished chain of Forte hotels, guests can be assured of a high standard of comfort and quality of service. The wide range of facilities and friendly, efficient service offered to guests ensure that guests will feel completely at home and will have a pleasurable and relaxing stay. Centrally located near good road and rail links, making this a good base from which to explore Colchester and the surrounding area, accommodation at this superior hotel comprises 110 ensuite rooms (including 30 family rooms), with a diversity of amenities tailor-made to suit guests' every need. Smoking and non-smoking rooms are available, all equipped with the facilities discerning guests have come to expect. This large and

Posthouse Colchester, Abbotts Lane, Eight Ash Green, Colchester, Essex CO6 3QL
Tel: 0870 400 9020 Fax: 01206 766577 email: gm1064@forte-hotel.com

beautifully appointed hotel has a charming and informal Traders restaurant and bar serving morning, afternoon and evening repasts, with a menu that incorporates the best of traditional and more innovative British favourites and international dishes. Twenty-four hour room service is also provided, and light snacks can be taken in the sumptuous hotel lounge. The bar is a relaxing place to enjoy a quiet drink, or to indulge in watching a favourite sport on the dedicated satellite sport channel. The hotel's health and fitness club boasts an indoor heated swimming pool, spa pool, gym, sauna, solarium and treatment rooms, so that guests can invigorate (or pamper) themselves to their hearts' delight. The facilities for guests with disabilities are excellent, and include three fully adapted bedrooms. For families, there is a baby-listening service and a play room for children available at weekends. For the business traveller, this hotel lives up to Forte's reputation for providing communications equipment and conference facilities to suit the large or small business.

Dutch Protestants arrived in Colchester in the 16th century, fleeing Spanish rule in the Netherlands, and revitalised the local cloth industry. The houses of these Flemish weavers in the **Dutch Quarter** to the west of the castle, and the Civil War scars on the walls of Siege House in East Street, bear testimony to their place in the town's history. The Dutch Quarter west of the castle remains a charming and relatively quiet corner of this bustling town. Close to the railway station are the ruins of **St Botolph's Priory**, the oldest Augustinian priory in the country. Victim of the long siege of Colchester during the Civil War, when the Royalists, who held out for 11 weeks, were finally starved into submission, its remains are a potent reminder of the bitterness of those times. On Bourne Road, south of the town centre just off the B1025, there's a striking stepped and curved gabled building known as **Bourne Mill**. Built in 1591 from stone taken from the nearby St John's Abbeygate, this delightful restored building near a lovely mill-pond was originally a fishing lodge, later converted (in the 19th century) into a mill - and still in working order.

Colchester Zoo, just off the A12 outside the town, stands in the 40-acre park of Stanway Hall, with its 16th century mansion and church dating from the 14th century. Founded in 1963, the zoo has a wide and exciting variety of attractions. The zoo has gained a well-deserved reputation as one of the best in Europe. Its award-winning enclosures allow visitors closer to the animals and provide naturalistic environments for the 170 species. There are 15 unique daily displays including opportunities to feed an African elephant, bear, chimp or alligator, stroke a snake and watch a penguin parade. Colchester has been famous in its time for both oysters and roses. This legacy is remembered in the annual **Oyster Feast** and **Colchester Rose Show**. Colchester oysters are still cultivated on beds in the lower reaches of the River Colne, which skirts the northern edge of town. A visit to the **Oyster Fisheries** is a fascinating experience, and the tour includes complimentary fresh oysters and glass of wine.

LAYER MARNEY
6 miles SW of Colchester off the B1022

Map 8 ref S17

The mansion, which was planned to rival Hampton Court, was never completed, but its massive 8-storey Tudor gatehouse, known as **Layer Marney Tower**, is very impressive. Built between 1515 and 1525, it is one of the most striking examples of 16th century architecture in Britain. Its magnificent four red brick towers, covered in 16th century Italianate design, were built by Lord Marney, Henry VIII's Lord Privy Seal. As well as spectacular views from the top of the towers, they are surrounded by formal gardens designed at the turn of the century, with lovely roses, yew hedges and herbaceous borders. There is also on site a rare breeds farm, farm shop and tea room.

BRAINTREE
13 miles W of Colchester off the A120

Map 8 ref S17

This town, along with its close neighbour Bocking, are sited at the crossing of two Roman roads and were brought together by the cloth industry in the 16th century. Flemish weavers settled here, followed by many Huguenots. One, Samuel Courtauld, set up a silk mill in 1816 and, by 1866, employed over 3,000 Essex inhabitants. The **Working Silk Museum** on South Street features demonstrations of silk production - from start to finish - in a former mill building that has been faithfully restored. The original hand looms, some over 150 years old, are still used to weave silk fabrics for many of the royal houses throughout the world. The magnificent former Town Hall is another of the many Courtauld legacies. It was built in 1928 with oak-panelled walls, murals by Grieffenhagen showing stirring scenes of local history, and a grand central tower with a five-belled striking clock. A smaller but no less fascinating reminder of Courtauld's generosity is the 1930s bronze fountain, with bay, shell and fish, at the centre of Braintree. Huguenot names such as Courtauld are connected with international enterprises to this day. Their reason for coming to Britain is a fascinating and poignant tale. Formed in France in 1559 as an organised Protestant group taking direction from Calvin and the Calvinistic Reformation in Geneva, the Huguenots were at first allowed to live and worship freely. However, as political and religious rivalries grew in France, the Catholic majority started to persecute them; a century of war, massacre and bloodshed followed. Finally in 1685 all their rights were stripped. In the chaos that ensued, many died and thousands fled. It was to turn out to be France's loss, for the Huguenots were among the most industrious and economically advanced elements in French society. Others gained at France's expense; Huguenots poured into England, and especially East Anglia, where their skills soon made them welcome and valued members of the community.

The **Braintree District Museum** on Manor Street tells the story of Braintree's diverse industrial heritage and traditions. The Town Hall Centre is a Grade II listed building housing the Tourist Information Centre and the Art Gallery, which boasts a continuous changing programme of exhibitions and works.

STRATFORD ST MARY
MAP 8 REF T17

7 miles NE of Colchester off the A12

Stratford St Mary's parish church is a fine building dating back to the 13th century. It features some ancient glass in the west window of the north aisle, historic brass memorials and inscriptions on the exterior walls. The church produces a guide for visitors outlining the church's history and attributes. Stratford St Mary was a stopping-off point for travellers on the old coaching route from London to Norfolk. The village is home to a post office/shop, a garage, and several handsome houses and places to stay. It is within easy walking distance of Dedham, the home of artist Sir Alfred Munnings, and Flatford Mill, where another famous artist, John Constable, grew up.

The **Black Horse** is a 15th-century public house located near the River Stour, which meanders through this peaceful rural village. There are numerous scenic walks and cycle paths in the area, fishing from the riverbanks and boating nearby. A popular venue for locals, visitors, campers and caravanners - the

The Black Horse, Lower Street, Stratford St Mary, Essex CO7 6JS
Tel: 01206 323112

adjacent meadow can accommodate up to 10 caravans - the pub is open seven days a week and has a wide selection of real ales, lagers and spirits. Owner Elaine Pulford is a friendly and welcoming host. Meals can be taken in the bar or in the restaurant, or outdoors in the large and attractive garden: lunch is served from noon - 2.30 pm, while the evening meal is served from 6 - 9 pm. The menu covers a full range of home-made traditional British fare, together with daily specials from around the world. In summer, the barbecue heats up and paella - made with rice brought in from Barcelona - is served from a gaily-painted yellow and red static boat in the garden.

HALSTEAD
MAP 8 REF S17

10 miles NW of Colchester off the A1124

The name 'Halstead' comes from the Anglo-Saxon for Healthy Place. Like Braintree and Coggeshall, Halstead was an important weaving centre. **Townsford Mill** is certainly the most picturesque reminder of Halstead's industrial heritage. Built in the 1700s, it remains one of the most handsome buildings in town. This white, weatherboarded three-storey mill across the River Colne at the Causeway was once a landmark site for the Courtauld empire, producing both the famous funerary crepe and rayon. Today the Mill is an antiques centre. Though it may now seem somewhat improbable, Halstead's most famous product was once mechanical elephants. Life-sized and weighing half a ton, they were built by one W Hunwicks. Each one consisted of 9,000 parts and could carry a load of eight adults and four children at speeds of up to 12 miles per hour. Rather less unusual but certainly better remembered is the Tortoise Foundry Company for its warm 'tortoise stoves'.

GREAT YELDHAM
MAP 8 REF S17

4½ miles NW of Halstead off the A1017

Great Yeldham repays visitors with lovely views of the River Colne and the surrounding countryside. Adjacent to the A1017 at Great Yeldham, **The Waggon & Horses** is an attractive and welcoming public house and restaurant that also offers accommodation. First built in the 16th century as three separate cottages, this impressive establishment is adorned with an eye-catching historic wooden wagon on the forecourt. The bar and beer garden of this stylish free house are open all day; the restaurant is open for meals and bar snacks every day from 12-2 pm and 7-9 pm. Owner Mike Shiffner has owned the place since 1994, though he has been in the trade a good deal longer. He and his staff provide the best in hospitality and service. Ales on offer include Greene King IPA and Abbot ale, plus two guest ales, one of which will be a local brew. Great Yeldham makes an excellent base from which to explore the many places of interest nearby, and this pub boasts six comfortable guest rooms (three twin, two doubles and one single).

The Waggon & Horses, High Street, Great Yeldham,
Essex CO9 4EX Tel: 01787 237936

CASTLE HEDINGHAM
2 miles NW of Halstead off the B1058

MAP 8 REF S17

This town is named for its Norman **Castle**, which dominates the town. One of England's strongest fortresses in the 11th century, even now it is impossible not to sense its power and strength. The impressive stone keep is one of the tallest in Europe, with four floors and rising over 100 feet, with 12-ft thick walls. The banqueting hall and minstrels' gallery can still be seen. It was owned by the Earls of Oxford, the powerful de Veres family, one of whom was among the barons who forced King John to accept the Magna Carta. Amongst those entertained at the castle were Henry VII and Elizabeth I.

Castle Hedingham

The village itself is a maze of narrow streets radiating from Falcon Square, named after the half-timbered Falcon Inn. Attractive buildings include many the Georgian and 15th century houses comfortably vying for space, and the **Church of St Nicholas**, built by the de Veres, which avoided Victorian 'restoration' and is virtually completely Norman, with grand masonry and interestingly carved choir seats. There is a working pottery in St James' Street. At the **Colne Valley Railway and Museum**, a mile of the Colne Valley and Halstead line between Castle Hedingham and Great Yeldham has been restored and now runs steam trains operated by enthusiasts. The lovingly restored Victorian railway buildings feature a collection of vintage engines and carriages; short steam train trips are available.

GESTINGTHORP
5 miles N of Halstead off the A131

MAP 8 REF S17

The Pheasant is an attractive and welcoming public house located here in the lovely village of Gestingthorp, on a quiet country lane near the church of St Mary the Virgin. This evocative pub features exposed oak beams, brasses, open log fires and a large, pleasant garden. There is a range of real ales (the pub is mentioned in the CAMRA Guide) on offer, and a good wine list. In the restaurant, chef Paul Drury brings his experience of working in the West End of London to bear on preparing dishes from the extensive a la carte menu - all freshly prepared and well worth the wait. Owners Mr and Mrs Sullivan make every effort to meet guests' every requirement, in comfortable and relaxing surroundings.

The Pheasant, Audley End, Gestingthorp, Halstead, Essex CO9 3AX Tel: 01787 461196

WALTON-ON-THE-NAZE

MAP 8 REF T17

18 miles E of Colchester on the B1034

Walton is all the fun of the fair. It is a traditional, singular and cheerful resort which focuses on the pier and all its attractions, including a ten-pin bowling alley. The gardens at the seafront are colourful and the beach has good sand. The Backwaters to the rear of Walton are made up of a series of small harbours and saltings, which lead into Harwich harbour. Walton has an outstanding sandy beach. The town's seafront was developed in the 1825 and provides a fine insight into the character of an early Victorian seaside resort. The charming narrow streets of the town contain numerous shops, restaurants and pubs overlooking the second longest pier in the country. **Marine Parade**, originally called The Crescent, was built in 1832. The Pier, first built in 1830, was originally constructed of wood and measured 330 feet long. It was extended to its present lenght of 2,610 feet in 1898, at the same time as the electric train service began.

The wind-blown expanse of **The Naze** just north of Walton is an extensive coastal recreation and picnic area, pleasant for walking, especially out of season when the visitor is likely to have all 150 acres virtually to him- or herself, with great views out over the water. The shape of the Naze is constantly changing, eroded by wind, water and tide. The year 1796 saw the demise of the medieval church, and somewhere beyond the 800-foot pier lies medieval Walton. The sandstone cliffs are internationally important for their shell fossil deposits. Inhabitants have been enjoying the bracing sea air at Walton since before Neolithic times: flint-shaping instruments have been found here, and the fossil teeth and the ears of sharks and whales have been discovered in the the Naze's red crag cliffs. **The Naze Tower** is brickbuilt and octagonal in shape, originally built as a beacon in 1720 to warn seamen of the West Rocks off shore. A nature trail has been created nearby and the Essex Skipper butterfly and Emperor moth can be seen here. The **Old Lifeboat House Museum** at East Terrace, in a building over 100 years old, houses an interpretive museum of local history and development, rural and maritime, covering Walton, Frinton and the Sokens.

HARWICH

MAP 8 REF T17

19 miles E of Colchester on the A120

Harwich's name probably originates from the time of King Alfred, when 'here' meant army, and 'wic' a camp. This attractive old town was built in the 13th century by the Earls of Norfolk to exploit its strategic position on the Stour and Orwell estuary; the town has an important and fascinating maritime history , the legacy of which continues into the present. During the 14th and 15th century French campaigns it was an important naval base.

Harwich remains popular as a vantage point for watching incoming and outgoing shipping in the harbour and across the waters to Felixstowe. Nowadays, lightships, buoys and miles of strong chain are stored along the front, and passengers arriving on North Sea ferries at Parkeston Quay see the 90 foot high, nine-sided **High Lighthouse** as the first landmark. Now housing the **National Vintage Wireless and Television Museum**, it was built in 1818 along with the **Low Lighthouse**. When the two lighthouses were in line they could indicate a safe shipping channel into the harbour. Each had replaced earlier wooden structures, and were themselves replaced by cast iron structures (one of which still stands on the front in nearby Dovercourt) in 1863 when the shifting sandbanks

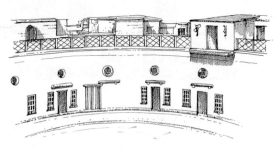

The Redoubt, Harwich

altered the channel. Shipping now relies on light buoys to find its way. The Low lighthouse is now the town's **Maritime Museum**, with specialist displays on the Royal Navy and commercial shipping.

Two other worthwhile museums in the town are the Lighthouse Museum off Wellington Road, which contains the last Clacton offshore 34 foot lifeboat and a history of the lifeboat service in Harwich, and the **Ha'penny Pier Visitor Centre** on the Quay, with information on everything in Harwich and a small heritage exhibition.

The **Treadwell Crane** now stands on Harwich Green, but for over 250 years it was sited in the Naval Shipyard. It is worked by two people walking in two 16 foot diameter wheels, and is the only known example of its kind. Amazingly it was operational up until the 1920s. Another fascinating piece of the town's history is the **Electric Palace Cinema**, built in 1911 and now the oldest unaltered purpose-built cinema in Britain. It was restored by a trust and re-opened in 1981. The importance of Harwich's port during the 19th century is confirmed by **The Redoubt**, a huge grey fort built between 1808 and 1810. Its design is an enlarged version of the Martello towers which dotted the English coast awaiting a Napoleonic invasion which never came (some of these towers of course still exist). Today the Harwich Society has largely restored it and opened it as a museum. The old town also contains many ancient buildings, including the **Guildhall**, which was rebuilt in 1769 and is located in Church Street. The Council chamber, Mayor's Parlour and other rooms may be viewed. The former gaol contains unique graffiti of ships, probably carved by prisoners, and is well worth putting aside an afternoon to explore. Interesting documents on show include those detailing the connection of Harwich with Pepys, the Pilgrim Fathers, and the Virginia settlement.

GREAT BROMLEY
MAP 8 REF T17
9 miles SW of Harwich off the A120

This handsome rural village has some lovely walks that pass Badley Halley and a series of working farms, leading to the neighbouring village of Little Bromley. Both hamlets have lovely country churches. Brenda and Richard Perry took over at **The Cross Inn** early in 1999. This pristine and welcoming country pub is popular with locals and visiting walkers, cyclists and tourers alike, as it makes an eminently charming place to relax and enjoy great food and drink. The pub is renowned for its good pint, with a range of choice including real ales from Greene King and a changing local brew, an excellent wine list and a good selection of lagers and spirits. Food is available every day but Tuesday; Brenda home-prepares and home-cooks all the fare on offer, using fresh home-gown or locally produced vegetables and ingredients. Meals can be enjoyed in the large main bar area - handsomely appointed with large open brick fireplace and wood-burning stove - in the separate, very comfortable non-smoking dining area, or in the spacious and secure garden. Guests can choose from the extensive a la carte or specials menu. There

The Cross Inn, Ardleigh Road, Great Bromley,
Essex CO7 7TL Tel/Fax: 01206 230282

are also two ensuite twin rooms available for bed and breakfast accommodation, fitted out with every amenity to make a stay here comfortable and memorable.

BRIGHTLINGSEA
MAP 8 REF T17

12 miles SW of Harwich off the A133

Brightlingsea enjoys a long tradition of shipbuilding and seafaring. In 1347, 51 men and five ships were sent to the siege of Calais. Among the crew members of Sir Francis Drake's fleet which vanquished the Spanish Armada was one 'William of Brightlingsea'. Brightlingsea has the distinction of being the only limb of the Cinque Ports outside Kent and Sussex. The 13th century **Jacobes Hall** in the town centre is one of the oldest occupied buildings in Essex. It is timber-framed with an undulating tile roof and an external staircase. Used as a meeting hall during the reign of Henry III, its name originates from its first owner, Edmund Vicar of Brightlingsea, who was known locally as Jacob le Clerk. **All Saints Church**, which occupies the highest point of the town on a hill about a mile from the centre, is mainly 13th century. Here are to be found some Roman brickwork and a frieze of ceramic tiles commemorating local residents whose lives were lost at sea. Its 97 foot tower can be seen from 17 miles out to sea. A light was once placed in the tower to guide the town's fishermen home. The **Town Hard** is where you can see all the waterfront comings and goings, including the activities of the Colne Smack Preservation Society, which maintains a seagoing link with the past.

Brightlingsea Museum in Duke Street offers an insight into the lives, customs and traditions of the area, housing a collection of exhibits relating to the town's maritime connections and the oyster industry. There are plenty of superb walks along Brightlingsea Creek and the River Colne, which offer a chance to watch the birdlife on the saltings and the plethora of boats on the water. Today the town is a haven for the yachting fraternity and is the home of national and international sailing championships, with one of the best stretches of sailing on the East Coast.

MERSEA ISLAND
MAP 8 REF T17

2 miles SW of Brightlingsea off the B1025

Much of this island is a National Nature Reserve, home to its teeming shorelife. The island is linked to the mainland by a narrow causeway which is covered over at high tide. The towns of both East and West Mersea have excellent facilities for sailing enthusiasts. East Mersea is also a mecca for birdwatchers. **The Dog & Pheasant** is a handsome brickbuilt and thatched public house located in East Mersea. The atmosphere and amenities are unbeatable in this characterful pub, run by Inge and Charlie Sheath - and their friendly and popular dogs Toby, Dusty and Oscar, three cats and three ducks. The original pub, now the restaurant area, was built in 1750,

The Dog & Pheasant, East Road, East Mersea, Essex CO5 8TP
Tel: 01206 383206

with additions made in the early 20th century. One unusual feature of the pub is the mystery of the mini-farmyard collection. Beginning with a single plastic sheep found in the main bar after closing time one night, soon more and more tiny animals, miniature farm machinery and even figures bearing the names of the pub's regulars joined the collection, which now adorns a shelf over the bar. So far all possible suspects have come up with cast-iron alibies. It's a puzzle to ponder while choosing from the delights on the menu, which changes weekly and features such favourites as all-day breakfast, banger of the week, vegetarian meals and a good selection of puddings. The fine choice of real ales includes Greene King IPA and a guest ale every week.

MANNINGTREE
MAP 8 REF T17

9 miles W of Harwich off the B1352

The Walls, on the approach to Manningtree along the B1352, offer unrivalled views of the Stour estuary and the Suffolk coast, and the swans for which the area is famous. Lying on the River Stour amid beautiful rolling countryside, it has often been depicted by artists over the centuries. Back in Tudor times, Manningtree was the centre of the cloth trade, and later a port filled with barges carrying their varied cargoes along the coast to London. Water still dominates today and the town is a centre of leisure sailing.

Manningtree has been a market town since 1238, and is still a busy shopping centre. It is the smallest town in Britain, and a stroll through the streets reveals the variety of its past. There are still traditional (and mainly Georgian) restaurants, pubs and shops, as well as handcraft and specialist outlets. The views over the river are well known to birdspotters, sailors and ramblers. The town has an intriguing past - as a river crossing, market, smugglers' haven and home of Matthew Hopkins, the reviled and self-styled Witchfinder General who struck terror into the local community during the 17th century. Some of his victims were hanged on Manningtree's small village green. It is believed that the reference in Shakespeare's *Henry IV* to Falstaff as 'that roasted Manningtree ox' relates to the practice of roasting an entire ox at the town's medieval annual fair.

Dating back to the 16th century, **The Crown Hotel** is one of Manningtree's oldest and most distinguished pubs. Winner of the prestigious Cask Marque Award for excellence in the serving of cask ales in 1998, this attractive and comfortable former coaching inn overlooks the tidal River Stour to the rear. In 1998 the pub was regional winner (for the London, Essex, Hertfordshire and Berkshire region) of Pub Caterer of the Year Award. Open every day, food is available 12-3 pm and 7-9.15 pm. Booking is advised. The extensive menu includes steaks, chicken, fish and vegetarian dishes, all expertly prepared and presented. Specialities include a good range of curries and Yorkshire puddings. Bar meals and snacks are also available, as well as a choice of daily specials. Among the excellent ales on offer are Greene King IPA, Abbot or mild, as well as a good selection of other beers, wines and spirits. This popular pub is adorned with memorabilia donated by local customers, reflecting the life and times of Manningtree and the River Stour. There are also two self-catering flats available for short or long stays.

The Crown Hotel, 51 High Street, Manningtree, Essex CO11 1AH Tel: 01206 396333

SUFFOLK

NEWMARKET

Map 8 ref R16

16 miles N of Saffron Walden off the A14

On the western edge of Suffolk, Newmarket is home to some 16,000 human and 3,000 equine inhabitants. The historic centre of British racing lives and breathes horses, with 60 training establishments, 50 stud farms, the top annual thoroughbred sales and two racecourses (the only two in Suffolk). Thousands of the population are involved in the trade, and racing art and artefacts fill the shops, galleries and museums; one of the oldest established saddlers even has a preserved horse on display - *"Robert the Devil"*, runner-up in the 1880 Derby. History records that Queen Boadicea of the Iceni, to whom the six-mile Devil's Dyke stands as a memorial, thundered around these parts in her lethal chariot behind her shaggy-haired horses and she is said to have established the first stud here. In medieval times the chalk heathland was a popular arena for riders to display their skills and in 1605 James I paused on a journey north to enjoy a spot of hare coursing. He enjoyed the place and said he would be back; in moving the royal court to his Newmarket headquarters he began the royal patronage which has remained strong down the years. Charles I maintained the royal connection but it was Charles II who really put the place on the map when he, too, moved the Royal court in the spring and autumn of each year. He initiated the Town Plate, a race which he himself won twice as a rider and which, in a modified form, still exists.

One of the racecourses, the **Rowley Mile**, takes its name from Old Rowley, a favourite horse of the Merry Monarch. Here the first two classics of the season, the 1,000 and 2,000 Guineas, are run, together with important autumn events including the Cambridgeshire and the Cesarewich. The visitor to Newmarket can learn almost all there is to know about flat racing and racehorses by making the grand tour of the several establishments which are open to the public (sometimes by appointment only). **The Jockey Club**, which was the first governing body of the sport and until recently the ultimate authority, was formed in the middle of the 18th century and occupies an imposing building which was restored and rebuilt in Georgian style in the 1930s. Originally a social club for rich gentlemen with an interest in the turf, it soon became the all-powerful regulator of British racing, owning all the racing and training land. When holding an enquiry the stewards sit round a horseshoe table and the jockey or trainer under scrutiny faces them on a strip of carpet by the door - hence the expression "on the mat". Next to the Jockey Club in the High Street is the **National Horseracing Museum**. The chief treasures among the art collection are equine paintings by Alfred Munnings, while the most famous item is probably the skeleton of the mighty Eclipse, whose superiority over his contemporaries gave rise to the saying *"Eclipse first, the rest nowhere"*.

A few steps away is **Palace House**, which contains the remains of Charles II's palace and which, as funds allow, is being restored for use as a visitor centre and museum. In the same street, and still standing, is **Nell Gwynn's house**, which some say was connected beneath the street to the palace. The diarist John Evelyn spent a night in (or on?) the town during a royal visit and declared the occasion to be "more resembling a luxurious and abandoned rout than a Christian court". The palace is the new location for the Newmarket Tourist Information Centre. Other must-sees on the racing enthusiast's tour are **Tattersalls**, where leading thoroughbred sales take place from April to December; the **British Racing School**, where top jockeys are taught the ropes; the **National Stud**, open from March till August plus race days in September and October (booking essential); and the **Animal Health Trust** based at Lanwades Hall, where a Visitor Centre has recently opened. The National Stud at one time housed no fewer than three Derby winners - Blakeney, Mill Reef and Grundy.

Newmarket has things to offer the tourist outside the equine world, including the churches of **St Mary and All Saints**, and **St Agnes**, and a landmark at each end of the High Street - a Memorial Fountain in honour of Sir Daniel Cooper and the Jubilee Clock Tower commemorating Queen Victoria's Golden Jubilee.

MILDENHALL

MAP 8 REF R15

8 miles NE of Newmarket off the A11

On the edge of the Fens and Breckland, Mildenhall is a town which has many links with the past. It was once a port for the hinterland of West Suffolk, though the River Lark has long ceased to be a trade route. Most of the town's heritage is recorded in the excellent **Mildenhall & District Museum** in King Street. Here will be found exhibits of local history (including the distinguished RAF and USAAF base), crafts and domestic skills, the natural history of the Fens and Breckland and, perhaps most famously, the 'Mildenhall Treasure'. This was a cache of 34 pieces of 4th century Roman silverware - dishes, goblets and spoons - found by a ploughman in 1946 at Thistley Green and now on display in the British Museum. There is evidence of much earlier occupation than the Roman era, with flint tools and other artefacts being unearthed in 1988 on the site of an ancient lake. The parish of Mildenhall is the largest in Suffolk so it is perhaps fitting that it should boast so magnificent a parish church as **St Mary's**, built of Barnack stone; it dominates the heart of the town and indeed its west tower commands the flat surrounding countryside. Above the splendid north porch (the largest in Suffolk) are the arms of Edward the Confessor and of St Edmund. The chancel, dating back to the 13th century, is a marvellous work of architecture, but pride of place goes to the east window, divided into seven vertical lights. Off the south aisle is the Chapel of St Margaret, whose altar, itself modern, contains a medieval altar stone. At the west end, the font, dating from the 15th century, bears the arms of Sir Henry Barton, who was twice Lord Mayor of London and whose tomb is located on the south side of the tower. Above the nave and aisles is a particularly fine hammerbeam roof whose outstanding feature is the carved angels. Efforts of the Puritans to destroy the angels failed, but traces of buckshot and arrowheads have

Market Cross, Mildenhall

been found embedded in the woodwork. Sir Henry North built a manor house on the north side of the church in the 17th century and his successors included a dynasty of the Bunbury family who were Lords of the Manor from 1747 to 1933. Sir Henry Edward Bunbury was the man chosen to let Napoleon Bonaparte know of his exile to St Helena, but the best known member of the family is Sir Thomas, who in 1780 tossed a coin with Lord Derby to see whose name should be borne by a race to be inaugurated at Epsom. Lord Derby won, but Sir Thomas had the satisfaction of winning the first running of the race with his colt Diomed. The other focal point in Mildenhall is the **Market Place**, with its 16th century timbered cross.

BRANDON

MAP 8 REF S15

9 miles NE of Mildenhall on the A1065

On the edge of **Thetford Forest** by the Little Ouse, Brandon was long ago a thriving port, but flint is what really put it on the map. The town itself is built mainly of flint, and flint was mined from early Neolithic times to make arrowheads and other implements and weapons of war. The gun flint industry brought substantial wealth, and a good flint-knapper could produce up to 300 gun flints in an hour. The invention of the percussion cap killed off much of their work so they turned to shaping flints for church building and ornamental purposes. **The Heritage Cen-**

tre, in a former fire station in George Street, provides visitors with a splendid insight into this industry, while for an even more tangible feel a visit to **Grimes Graves**, just over the Norfolk border, reveals an amazing site covering 35 acres and 300 pits (one of the shafts is open for visits). With the close proximity of numerous warrens and their rabbit population, the fur trade also flourished here, and that, too, along with forestry, is brought to life in the Heritage Centre.

The whole of this north west corner of Suffolk, know as **Breckland**, offers almost unlimited opportunities for touring by car, cycling or walking. A mile south of town on the B1106 is **Brandon Country Park**, a 30-acre landscaped site with a tree trail, forest walks, a walled garden and a visitor centre. There's also an orienteering route leading on into Thetford Forest, Britain's largest lowland pine forest. **The High Lodge Forest Centre**, by Santon Downham (off the B1107), also attracts with walks, cycle trails and adventure facilities.

ELVEDEN
Map 8 ref S15

5 miles S of Brandon on the A11

The road from Brandon leads south through the forest to a historic estate village with some unusual architectural features. Where the three parishes of Elveden, Eriswell and Icklingham meet a tall war memorial in the form of a Corinthian column is a landmark. **Elveden Hall** became more remarkable than its builders intended when Prince Duleep Singh, heir to the throne of the Punjab, a noted sportsman and shot, and the man who handed over the Koh-I-Noor diamond to Queen Victoria, arrived on the scene. Exiled to England with a handsome pension, he bought the Georgian house in 1863 and commissioned John Norton to transform it into a palace modelled on those in Lahore and Delhi. Although it is stated that in private Duleep Singh referred to Queen Victoria as "Mrs Fagin......receiver of stolen goods" (the diamond), he kept close contact with the royal household and the Queen became his son's godmother. The Guinness family (Lord Iveagh) later took it over and joined in the fun, adding even more exotic adornments including a replica Taj Mahal, while at the same time creating the largest arable farm in the whole of the country. Elveden and its purlieus, like so much of Suffolk, abounds in Neolithic and Iron Age sites, one of which was honoured with a visit by no less a person than Sir Arthur Evans, the British archaeologist who excavated the ruins of Knossos in Crete.

BURY ST EDMUNDS
Map 8 ref S16

13 miles E of Newmarket off the A14

A gem among Suffolk towns, rich in archaeological treasures and places of religious and historical interest. The town takes its name from St Edmund, who was born in Nuremberg in 841 and came here as a teenager to become the last king of East Anglia. He was a staunch Christian, and his refusal to deny his faith caused him to be tortured and killed by the Danes in 870. Legend has it that although his body was recovered, his head (cut off by the Danes) could not be found. His men searched for it for 40 days, then heard his voice directing them to it from the depths of a wood, where they discovered it lying protected between the paws of a wolf. The head and the body were seamlessly united and, to commemorate the wolf's deed, the crest of the town's armorial bearings depicts a wolf with a man's head. Edmund was possibly buried first at Hoxne, the site of his murder, but when he was canonised in about 910 his remains were moved to the monastery at Beodricsworth, which changed its name to St Edmundsbury. A shrine was built in his honour, later incorporated into the Norman Abbey Church after the monastery was granted abbey status by King Canute in 1032. The town soon became a place of pilgrimage and for many years St Edmund was the patron saint of England, until replaced by St George. Growing rapidly around the great abbey, which became one of the largest and most influential in the land, Bury prospered as a centre of trade and commerce, thanks notably to the cloth industry. The next historical landmark was reached in 1214, when on St Edmund's Feast Day the Archbishop of Canterbury, Simon Langton, met with the Barons of England at the high altar of the

Norman Tower, Bury St Edmunds
Abbey

Abbey and swore that they would force King John to honour the proposals of the Magna Carta. The twin elements of Edmund's canonisation and the resolution of the Barons explain the motto on the town's crest: "sacrarium regis, cunabula legis" - "shrine of a king, cradle of the law".

Rebuilt in the 15th century, the Abbey was largely dismantled after its dissolution by Henry VIII, but imposing ruins remain in the colourful Abbey Gardens beyond the splendid Abbey Gate and Norman Tower. **St Edmundsbury Cathedral** was originally the Church of St James, built in the 15th/16th century and accorded cathedral status (alone in Suffolk) in 1914. The original building has been much extended down the years (notably when being adapted for its role as a cathedral) and outstanding features include a magnificent hammerbeam roof, whose 38 beams are decorated with angels bearing the emblems of St James, St Edmund and St George. The monumental Bishop's throne depicts wolves guarding the crowned head of St Edmund, and there's a fascinating collection of 1,000 embroidered kneelers. Millennium funds granted in 1997 should guarantee that the tower which the cathedral lacks is finally built.

The Abbey Visitor Centre, open daily from Easter to the end of October, is situated in Samson's Tower, part of the west front of the Abbey. The centre has displays and hands-on activities concerning the Abbey's history. **The Abbey Gardens**, which were laid out in 1831, have as their central feature a great circle of flower beds following the pattern of the Royal Botanical Gardens in Brussels. Some of the original ornamental trees can still be seen, and other - later - features include an Old English rose garden, a water garden and a garden for the blind where fragrance counts for all. Ducks and geese live by the little River Lark, and there are tennis courts, putting and bowls greens and children's play equipment. Bury is full of fine non-ecclesiastical buildings, many with Georgian frontages concealing medieval interiors. Among the most interesting are the handsome **Manor House Museum** with its collection of clocks, paintings, furniture, costumes and objets d'art; the **Victorian Corn Exchange** with its imposing colonnade; the Athenaeum, hub of social life since Regency times and scene of Charles Dickens's public readings; **Cupola House**, where Daniel Defoe once stayed; the **Angel Hotel**, where Dickens and his marvellous creation Mr Pickwick stayed; and the **Nutshell**, owned by Greene King Brewery and probably the smallest pub in the country. (Tours of the town's Greene King Brewery can be booked by calling 01284 763222.) The Theatre Royal, now in the care of the National Trust, was built in 1819 by William Wilkins, who was also responsible for

Bury St Edmunds Art Gallery

the National Gallery. It once staged the premiere of Charley's Aunt and still operates as a working theatre. **The Bury St Edmunds Art Gallery** is housed in one of Bury's noblest buildings, built to a Robert Adam design in 1774. It filled many roles down the years, and was rescued from decline in the 1960s to be restored to Adam's original plans. It is now one of the county's premier art galleries, with eight exhibitions each year and a thriving craft shop. Perhaps the most fascinating building of all is **Moyses Hall** at one end of the Buttermarket. Built of flint and limestone about 1180, it has claims to being the oldest stone domestic building in England. Originally a rich man's residence, it later saw service as a prison, a workhouse, a police station and a railway office, and for the past 100 years it has been a museum. It houses some 10,000 items, from a Bronze Age hoard, Roman pottery and Anglo-Saxon jewellery to a 19th century doll's house and some grisly relics of the notorious Red Barn murder.

Steeped though it is in history, Bury also moves with the times, and its sporting and leisure facilities are impressive. A mile and a half outside town on the A14 (just off the East Exit) is **Nowton Park**, 172 acres of countryside landscaped in Victorian style and supporting a wealth of flora and fauna; the avenue of limes, carpeted with daffodils in the spring, is a particular delight. There's also a play area and a ranger centre.

HENGRAVE
Map 8 ref S15
3 miles NW of Bury St Edmunds on the A1101

A captivating old-world village of flint and thatch. Excavations and aerial photography indicate that a settlement has been here since Neolithic times, and the parts of the village of archaeological interest are now protected. The chief attraction is **Hengrave Hall**, a rambling Tudor mansion built partly of Northamptonshire limestone and partly of yellow brick between 1525 and 1538 by Sir Thomas Kytson, a wool merchant. A notable visitor in the early days was Elizabeth I, who brought her court here in 1578. Several generations of the Gage family were later the owners and one of them, with a particular interest in horticulture, imported various kinds of plum tree from France. Most of the bundles were properly labelled with their names but one had lost its label. When it produced its first crop of luscious green fruit someone had the bright idea of calling it the green Gage. The name stuck, and the descendants of the trees, planted in 1724, are still at the Hall, which may be visited by appointment (Tel: 01284 701561). In the grounds stands a lovely little church with a round Saxon tower and a wealth of interesting monuments. The church was for some time a family mausoleum; restored by Sir John Wood, it became a private chapel and it now hosts services of various denominations.

THE BRADFIELDS
Map 8 ref S16
7 miles SE of Bury St Edmunds off the A134

The Bradfields - St George, St Clare and Combust - and Cockfield thread their way through a delightful part of the countryside and are well worth a little exploration, not only to see the picturesque villages themselves but for a stroll in the historic **Bradfield Woods**. These woods stand on the eastern edge of the parish of Bradfield St George and have been turned into an outstanding nature reserve, tended and coppiced in the same way for more than 700 years and home to a wide variety of flora and fauna. They once belonged to the Abbey of St Edmundsbury and part of them is still today called Monk's Park Wood. Coppicing involves cutting a tree back down to the ground every ten years or so. Woodlands were managed in this way to provide an annual crop of timber for local use, and the regrowth after coppicing is very fast as the root is already strongly established. Willow and hazel are the trees most commonly coppiced. Willow is often pollarded, a less drastic form of coppicing where the trees are cut far enough from the ground to stop grazing animals having a free lunch.

Bradfield St Clare, the central of the three Bradfields, has a rival claim to that of Hoxne as the site of the martyrdom of St Edmund. The St Clare family arrived with the Normans and added their name to the village, and the church, originally All Saints, was rededicated to St

Clare; it is the only church in England dedicated to her. Bradfield Combust, where the pretty River Lark rises, probably takes it curious name from the fact that the local hall was burnt to the ground during the 14th century riots against the Abbot of St Edmundsbury's crippling tax demands. Arthur Young (1741-1820), noted writer on social, economic and agricultural subjects, is buried in the village churchyard.

COCKFIELD   MAP 8 REF S16
8 miles SE of Bury St Edmunds off the A1141

Cockfield is perhaps the most widely spread village in all Suffolk, its little thatched cottages scattered around and between no fewer than nine greens. Great Green is the largest, with two football pitches and other recreation areas, and Parsonage Green has a literary connection: the **Old Rectory** was once home to a Dr Babbington, whose nephew Robert Louis Stephenson was a frequent visitor and who is said to have written Treasure Island while staying there. Cockfield also shelters one of the last windmills to have been built in Suffolk (1891). Its working life was very short but the tower still stands, now in use as a private residence.

HAWSTEAD   MAP 8 REF S16
1 miles S of Bury St Edmunds off the A134

Ruth and Robert Fryer took over at **The Metcalfe Arms** early in 1999. They are amiable and welcoming hosts, and have continued the tradition of service and quality at this marvellous pub. A traditional country pub in all the best ways, it has two separate bars. The games room

boasts a large brick open fire and a collection of carpentry tools from bygone days adorning the walls, as well as old photographs of village life and a list of previous landlords, going back to 1840. The lounge bar also has an open fire, and is cosy and comfortable. Real ales on hand include Greene King IPA, Abbot and a changing guest ale. There's also a good range of lagers, wines and spirits. The menu changes regularly, but always makes use of the freshest locally-grown ingredients in a wide variety of

**The Metcalfe Arms, Lawshall Road, Hawstead,
Suffolk IP29 5NR Tel: 01284 386321**

traditional home-cooked dishes. The cream teas available daily are a particular treat. Drinks and meals can be enjoyed indoors or outside in the large and well-kept garden. The atmosphere throughout this friendly pub is relaxing and peaceful.

KETTLEBASTON

MAP 8 REF S16

10 miles S of Bury St Edmunds off the A1141

Anne of Cleves lived in the manor house at Kettlebaston after her divorce from Henry VIII. There are many thatched cottages and houses in this peaceful rural hamlet making it weel worth the visit. In addition **Box Tree Farm** is owned by Mike and June Carpenter, who have lived in the hamlet for eight years and have been offering bed and breakfast accommodation at their spacious and comfortable home since 1995. Originally a wattle and daub house, modern additions have been made

over the years. June is a keen gardener, as reflected in the two acres of beauti-fully tended and well-loved lawn, gardens, magnificent trees and or-chard to the rear of the house. She and Mike are hospitable and conscien-tious hosts, who make every effort to ensure that all their guests have a re-laxing and enjoyable stay. Each of the two guest bed-

Box Tree Farm, Kettlebaston, Suffolk IP7 7PZ
Tel: 01449 741318

rooms (one double, one twin) has its own private bathroom, and is furnished to a high standard of taste and quality, with pine furniture and fine views overlooking the garden and the sur-rounding fields. The guests' lounge has an open fire (when required), plush seating and tasteful decor. The attractive dining room boasts a painting of four naval warships, a nod to Mike's days as a naval officer.

LONG MELFORD

MAP 8 REF S16

13 miles S of Bury St Edmunds off the A134

The heart of this atmospheric wool town is a very long and, in stretches, fairly broad main street, set on an ancient Roman site in a particularly beautiful part of south Suffolk. In Roman times the Stour was a navigable river and trade flourished. Various Roman finds have been unearthed, notably a blue glass vase which is now on display in the British Museum. The street is filled with antique shops, book shops and art galleries and is a favourite place for collectors and browsers. Some of the houses are washed in the characteristic Suffolk pink, which might originally have been achieved by mixing ox blood or sloe juice into the plaster. **Holy Trinity Church**, on a 14-acre green at the north end of Hall Street, is a typical exuberant manifestation of the wealth of the wool and textile trade. It's big enough to be a cathedral, but served (and still serves) comparatively few parishioners. John Clopton, grown rich in the woollen business, was largely responsible for this magnificent Perpendicular-style edifice, which has a 180-foot nave and chancel and half timbers, flint flashwork of the highest quality and 100 large windows to give a marvellous sense of light and space. Medieval glass in the north aisle depicts religious scenes and the womenfolk of the Clopton family. John Clopton's largesse is recorded rather modestly in inscriptions on the roof parapets. His tower was struck by lightning in the early 18th century and the present brick construction dates from around 1900. The detail of this great church is of endless fascination, but it's the overall impression that stays in the memory, and the sight of the building floodlit at night is truly spectacular. The distinguished 20th cen-tury poet Edmund Blunden spent his last years in Long Melford and is buried in the churchyard. The inscription on his gravestone reads "I live still to love still things quiet and unconcerned".

Melford Hall, east of town beyond an imposing 16th gateway, was built around 1570 by Sir William Cordell on the site of an earlier hall that served as a country retreat, before the Disso-

museum; the mill building exists to this day, supplying animal feed. This is marvellous walking country, and **Knettishall Heath Country Park**, on 400 acres of prime Breckland terrain, is the official starting place of the Peddars Way National Trail and of a path that stretches 77 miles to Great Yarmouth by way of the Little Ouse and Waveney valleys.

WALSHAM-LE-WILLOWS
9 miles NE of Bury St Edmunds off the A143

MAP 8 REF S15

A pretty name for a pretty village, with weatherboarded and timber-framed cottages along the willow-banked river which flows throughout its length. **St Mary's Church** is no less pleasing to the eye, with its sturdy western tower and handsome windows in the Perpendicular style. Of particular interest inside is the superb tie and hammerbeam roof of the nave, and (unique in Suffolk and very rare elsewhere) a tiny circular medallion which hangs suspended from the nave wall, known as a 'Maiden's Garland' or 'Virgin's Crant'. These marked the pew seats of unmarried girls who had passed away, and the old custom was for the young men of the village to hang garlands of flowers from them on the anniversary of the girl's death. This particular example celebrates the virginity of one Mary Boyce, who died (so the inscription says) of a broken heart in 1685, just 20 years old. There is also a carving on the rood screen which looks rather like the face of a wolf: this may well be a reference to the benevolent creature that plays such an important role in the legend of St Edmund. A museum by the church has changing exhibitions of local history.

The Six Bells Inn is a 16th-century part-thatched and timber-framed house offering drink

and accommodation here in picturesque Walsham-le-Willows. Occupying a corner location opposite the large village Church of St Mary, this pub takes its name from the six bells of the church. The large and attractive curved oak bar is adjacent to a brick fireplace. Other original features include the exposed beamed ceilings. Peaceful and welcoming, this charming pub of-

The Six Bells Inn, Summer Road, Walsham-le-Willows, Suffolk IP31 3AH Tel: 01359 259726

fers Greene King real ales as well as seasonal guest beers. The guest bedrooms (one twin, two double and one family room) are cosy and comfortable - and no one leaves hungry after the full and hearty English breakfast!

WOOLPIT
6 miles E of Bury St Edmunds on the A14

MAP 8 REF S16

The Church of St Mary the Virgin is Woolpit's crowning glory, with a marvellous porch and one of the most magnificent double hammerbeam roofs. The village was long famous for its brick industry, and the majority of the old buildings are faced with 'Woolpit Whites'. The yellowish-white brick looked very much like more expensive stone and for several centuries was widely exported. Some was used in the building of the Senate wing of the Capitol in Washington DC. Red bricks were also produced, and the **Bygones Museum** (open weekends in summer, Tel: 01359 240822) has a brick-making display and also tells the story of the evolution of the village. Nearby is a moated site known as **Lady's Well**, a place of pilgrimage in the Middle Ages. The water from the spring was reputed to have healing properties, most efficacious in curing eye troubles. A favourite Woolpit legend concerns the Green Children, a brother and sister with green complexions who appeared one day in a field, apparently attracted by church bells. Though hungry, they would eat nothing until some green beans were produced. Given shelter by the lord of the manor, they learned to speak English and said that they came from a place called St Martin. The boy survived for only a short time, but the girl thrived, lost her green colour, was baptised and married a man from

Village Pump, Woolpit

King's Lynn – no doubt leaving many a Suffolk man green with envy!

RATTLESDEN
Map 8 ref S16
6 miles E of Bury St Edmunds off the A45/B1115

Rattlesden is a small and pretty village - population approximately 700 - with a handsome village church, the Church St Nicholas. Built in the 1700s, **The Five Bells** in Rattlesden is a place away from it all for those seeking refreshment and a welcoming ambience. Located close to the village church, this small pub is popular and busy, a free house with a good variety of beers including Bartrams, Furkin IPA, Ind Coope dark mild, Guinness and more - the choice changes regularly. The interior boasts black-beamed ceilings in the main bar, and an attractive wooden ceiling in the extended games area, which overlooks the terraced and grassed garden with its barbecue and petanque pitch. The brick bar is most attractive, and in winter the open fire is the ideal place to enjoy a quiet drink. One interesting and unusual feature of this superior pub is the aviary in the garden, home to a pair of barn owls and a Turkermanian eagle who answers to the

The Five Bells, High Street, Rattlesden, Suffolk IP30 0RA
Tel: 01449 737373

name 'Maud'. Proprietor Debbie Caley is a gregarious and warm host to all her guests.

ELMSWELL
MAP 8 REF S16

7 miles E of Bury St Edmunds off the A14

Clearly visible from the A14, the impressive Church of St John the Baptist with its massive flint tower stands at the entrance to the village facing Woolpit across the valley. **Elmswell Hall** at Elmswell is a delight-

ful establishment offering bed and breakfast accommodation. Owner Kate Over was born at the Hall. She is a charming and hospitable host, and has been running this bed and breakfast since 1994. Her husband Peter farms the 500 acres of arable land which is the site of this Grade II listed establishment. There are two large and airy rooms, capable of accommodating up to six guests. This Geor-

Elmswell Hall, Elmswell, Nr Bury St Edmunds, Suffolk IP30 9EN Tel/Fax: 01359 240215

gian farmhouse dates back in parts to the 16th century, but incorporates every modern feature guests have come to expect. The former home of the Abbot of Bury, it includes a beautifully well-kept garden and a heated outdoor swimming pool for guests' use. It is set amid quiet and relaxing surroundings, overlooking the Suffolk countryside and Elmswell Church. Tastefully decorated throughout, the guests have access to a comfortable sitting room with open inglenook fireplace and the large dining room. Kate, an accomplished cook, provides a hearty English or Continental breakfast.

A short drive north of Elmswell lies **Great Ashfield**, an unspoilt village whose now-disused airfield played key roles in both World Wars. In the churchyard of the 13th century All Saints is a memorial to the Americans who died during the Second World War; inside there is a commemorative altar. Some accounts say that Edmund was buried here in 903 after dying at the hands of the Danes; a cross was put up in his memory. The cross was replaced in the 19th century and now stands in the garden of Ashfield House.

STOWMARKET
MAP 8 REF T16

16 miles E of Bury St Edmunds off the A14

The largest town in the heart of Suffolk, Stowmarket enjoyed a period of rapid growth when the River Gipping was still navigable to Ipswich and when the railway arrived. Much of the town's history and legacy are brought vividly to life in the splendid **Museum of East Anglian Life**, which is situated in the centre of town to the west of the market place, in a 70-acre meadowland site on the old Abbot's Hall Estate (the aisled original barn dates from the 13th century). Part of the open-air section features several historic buildings which have been moved from elsewhere in the region and carefully re-erected on site. These include an engineering workshop from the 1870s, part of a 14th century farmhouse, a watermill from Alton and a wind pump which was rescued in a collapsed state at Minsmere in 1977. There's also a collection of working steam engines, farm animals and year-round demonstrations of all manner of local arts and crafts, from coopering to candle-making, from sheep shearing to saddlery. Stowmarket's Church of St Peter and St Mary acquired a new spire in 1994, replacing the 1715 version (itself a replacement) which was dismantled on safety grounds in 1975. The town certainly merits a major stroll, while for a peaceful picnic the riverbank beckons. Serious scenic walkers should make for the **Gipping Valley River Park** walk, which runs all the way to Ipswich.

SAXTEAD   MAP 8 REF T16
14 miles E of Stowmarket off the A1120

One of the prettiest sights in Suffolk is the white 18th century mill that stands on the marshy green. This is a wonderful example of a post mill, perhaps the best in the world, dating back to 1796 and renovated first in the 19th century. She worked until 1947 and has since been kept in working order, with the sails turning though the mill no longer grinds. You can climb into the buck (body) of the elegant weatherboarded construction and explore the machinery. It's open for visits in the summer. The **Ivy Farm** Bed and Breakfast occupies a 19th-century farmhouse on Saxtead Green. It overlooks the post mill, with arresting views of the surrounding 400-acre family farmland. This friendly family-run establishment is owned by Sara and Dennis Higgins; the accommodation available comprises one double and one twin room, both ensuite and equipped with all the amenities guests have come to expect. Both are furnished and decorated to a high standard of comfort and good

Ivy Farm, The Green, Saxtead, nr Woodbridge,
Suffolk IP13 9QG Tel/Fax: 01728 685621
mobile: 07957 690544 email: sarahiggins@skynow.net

taste. Guests are also welcome to make use of the lounge/breakfast room. The farmhouse breakfast is a hearty affair with free range eggs and locally made preserves. Sara and Dennis have a wealth of knowledge of the locality and are only too pleased to advise on local places of interest and good restaurants and pubs in the area. Interesting farm walks are available, with the option of hiring a bicycle. There's also an attractive garden in which to relax. No smoking.

FRAMLINGHAM   MAP 8 REF U16
15 miles E of Stowmarket off the A1120

The marvellous **castle**, brooding on a hilltop, dominates this agreeable market town, as it has since Roger Bigod, 2nd Earl of Norfolk, built it in the 12th century (his grandfather built the first a century earlier but this wooden construction was soon demolished). The Earls and Dukes of Norfolk, the Howards, were here for many generations before moving to Arundel in 1635. The castle is in remarkably good condition, partly because it was rarely attacked – though King John put it under siege in 1215. Its most famous occupant was Mary Tudor, who was in residence when proclaimed Queen in 1553. In the reign of Elizabeth I it was used as a prison for defiant priests and in the 17th century, after being bequeathed to Pembroke College, Cambridge, it saw service as a home and school for local paupers. Nine of the castle's 13 towers are accessible and the climb up the spiral staircase and walk round the battlements are well worth the effort. On one side the view is of the meres, which is a bird sanctuary. In the north wing is the Lanman Museum, devoted to farm and craft tools and domestic bygones. The castle brought considerable prestige and prosperity to Framlingham, evidence of which can be found in the splendid **Church of St Michael**, which has two wonderful works of art. One is the tomb of Henry Fitzroy, bastard son of Henry VIII, beautifully adorned with scenes from Genesis and Exodus and in a superb state of repair. The other is the tomb of the 3rd Duke with carvings of the apostles in shell niches. Also of note is the Carolean organ of 1674, a gift of Sir Robert Hitcham, to whom the Howards sold the estate. Cromwell and the Puritans were anti-organ so this instrument was lucky to escape the mass destruction of organs at the time of the Commonwealth. Sir Robert is also buried in the church. On a humbler level, the people of Framlingham are very proud of their two Victorian post boxes, which were installed in 1856.

OTLEY   MAP 8 REF T16
7 miles SE of Stowmarket on the B1079

The 15th century **moated hall** is open to the public at certain times (Tel: 01473 890264). Standing in ten acres of gardens that include a canal, a nuttery and a knot garden, the hall was long associated with the Gosnold family, whose coat of arms is also that of the village. The best-known member of that family is Bartholomew Gosnold, who sailed to the New World, named Martha's Vineyard, discovered Cape Cod and founded the settlement of Jamestown, Virginia. The 13th century Church of St Mary has a remarkable baptistry font measuring 6 feet in length and 2 feet 8 inches in depth. Though filled with water, the font is not used and was only discovered in 1950 when the vestry floor was raised. Perhaps it was used for adult baptisms.

WORTHAM   MAP 8 REF T15
10 miles N of Stowmarket off the A143

The Olde Tea Shoppe - Wortham occupies an Elizabethan hay barn adjoining the village Post Office stores. The extensive menu offers breakfasts, lunch, afternoon teas, all-day snacks and meals. Open every day in summer from 9 am to 7 pm, winter 9 to 6 (closed Sundays and Tuesday afternoons in January and February), it makes a charming place to relax and enjoy pots of tea and coffee, sandwiches, home-made cakes and cream teas with scones and toasted tea cakes, savouries, jacket potatoes, salads, home-made steak and kidney and cottage pies, fish dishes and more. This licensed establishment is set back from the main road in a picturesque commonland. There is an attractive tea garden in which to relax and enjoy the fine refreshments on offer. Proprietors Alison and Leslie Dumbell are friendly and conscientious hosts. Accommodation is also available, in the Old Tea Shoppe Apartment, a modern conversion which retains much of the original character and traditional appeal of this historic structure. This comfortable and spacious apartment comprises three bedrooms, bathroom and lounge/kitchen/dining area.

**Olde Tea Shoppe, Bury Road, Wortham, Nr Diss,
Norfolk IP22 1PP Tel: 01379 783210**

FRESSINGFIELD
18 miles NE of Stowmarket on the B116

Map 8 ref T15

The Fox and Goose restaurant is one of the best in Suffolk, but the spiritual centre is the Church of St Peter and St Paul. It has a superb hammerbeam roof and a lovely stone bell tower that was built in the 14th century. On one of the pews the initials AP are carved. These are believed to be the work of Alice de la Pole, Duchess of Norfolk and grand-daughter of Geoffrey Chaucer. Was this a work of art or a bout of vandalism brought on by a dull sermon? At nearby **Ufford Hall** lived the Sancroft family, one of whom became Archbishop of Canterbury. He led the revolt of the bishops against James II and was imprisoned in the Tower of London. Released by William IV and sacked for refusing to swear the oath of allegiance, he returned home and is entombed by the south porch of the church. The village sign is a pilgrim and a donkey, recording that Fressingfield was a stopping place on the pilgrim route from Dunwich to Bury St Edmunds.

Chippenhall Hall is a listed Tudor building, with origins dating back to Saxon times. It is referred to in the Domesday Book as Cybenhalla. Secluded at the end of a long, leafy drive, the hall enjoys a wonderful setting of rural tranquillity amid seven acres of lawns, trees, ponds and gardens. A superb candlelit dinner is available every evening, prepared by Barbara and served in convivial surroundings. This excellent four-course occasion can make use of game and local fresh fish, available together with the freshest vegetables from the Hall's kitchen garden. Proprietor Barbara Sargent prides herself on the fine choice of wines from the cellar to complement the excellent meals.

The Shallow End bar room has a copper-canopied inglenook fire and is an ideal place to relax and enjoy a pre-dinner drink, and stocks a choice selection of beers, wines and spirits. Original features such as exposed beams throughout the house add to the period feel, while each of the five ensuite bedrooms is named after a significant historical event. There is a heated outdoor swimming pool set in the rose-covered courtyard - the perfect place to wile away the hours of a lazy summer afternoon. Winner of the Johansens 1998 Country Houses and Small Hotels Award in all Great Britain and Ireland, ETB Highly Commended and AA Premier Selected, this former family home has a charm and informality that will appeal to all guests. The bedrooms are spacious and sumptuously furnished; while maintaining their original character, they also boast every modern amenity. All bedrooms are double- or twin-bed rooms with ensuite shower or bath. Continental or English breakfast or, if preferred, Lowestoft kippers on request for breakfast. Afternoon tea can be taken at the swimming pool or on the croquet lawn. No smoking in bedrooms or dining room. No children under 16.

Chippenhall Hall, Fressingfield, Eye, Suffolk IP21 5TD
Tel: 01379 588180/586733 Fax: 01379 586272
website: www.hotelnet.co.uk/cgi-.../
OpenThreads.dbm&HotelID=3481&Lang=E&User_ID=

LOWESTOFT MAP 8 REF U14
52 miles E of Bury St Edmunds on the A146

The most easterly town in Britain had its heyday as a major fishing port during the late 19th and early 20th centuries, when it was a mighty rival to Great Yarmouth in the herring fishing industry. That industry has been in major decline since the First World War but Lowestoft is still a fishing port, and the trawlers still chug into the harbour in the early morning with the catches of the night. Guided tours of the **fish market** and the **harbour** are available. Tel: 01502 523000/730514.

Lowestoft is also a popular holiday resort, the star attraction being the lovely South Beach with its golden sands, safe swimming, two piers and all the expected seaside amusement and entertainment. Claremont Pier, over 600 feet in length, was built in 1902, ready to receive day trippers on the famous Belle steamers. The buildings in this part of town were developed in mid-Victorian times by the company of Sir Samuel Morton Peto, also responsible for Nelson's Column, the statues in the Houses of Parliament, the Reform Club and Somerleyton Hall.

Flying Fifteens, named after a class of racing boat designed by Uffa Fox, overlooks the beach and the sea, which inspires the tasteful decor and china. Diana and Peter Knight have created a high-quality tea room and gift shop where the excellent waitress service, quality of tea (over 20 varieties) and cleanliness have ensured continued membership in the National Tea Council's Guild of Tea Shops. A 1999 winner of the Tea Council's Award of Excellence, at this quality tea shop visitors can relax indoors or sit in the colourful lawned garden watching the world go by. Diana bakes a variety of cakes and scones, among which Adnams Suffolk Ale boozy fruit cake and strawberry scones are particularly popular. The menu includes home-made soups, sandwiches, baguettes and omelettes. Beers and wine are also available. Peter's gift shop is home to the work of local craftspeople, hand-crafted ceramics, unusual pieces and colourful items from around the world. Open 10.30-5 (excluding Mondays) from June to September, and some weekends out of season. High chairs available. No smoking indoors.

Flying Fifteens, 19a The Esplanade,
Lowestoft, Suffolk NR33 0QG
Tel: 01502 581188 Fax: 01502 586991

At the heart of the town is the old harbour, home to the **Royal Norfolk & Suffolk Yacht Club** and the **lifeboat station**. Further upriver is the commercial part of the port, used chiefly by ships carrying grain and timber. The history of Lowestoft is naturally tied up with the sea, and much of that history is recorded in fascinating detail in the **Lowestoft & East Suffolk Maritime Museum** with model boats, fishing gear, a lifeboat cockpit, paintings and shipwrights' tools. The setting is a flint-built fisherman's cottage in Sparrow's Nest Gardens. The **Royal Naval Patrol Museum** nearby remembers the minesweeping service in models, photographs, documents and uniforms. Lowestoft had England's first lighthouse, installed in 1609. The present one dates from 1874. Also in

Sparrow's Nest Gardens is the **War Memorial Museum**, dedicated to those who served in the Second World War. There's a photographic collection of the bombing of the town, aircraft models and a chapel of remembrance . St Margaret's Church, notable for its decorated ceiling and copper-covered spire, is a memorial to seafarers, and the north aisle has panels recording the names of fishermen lost at sea from 1865 to 1923. Lowestoft has some interesting literary and musical connections. The Elizabethan playwright, poet and pamphleteer, Thomas Nash(e), was born here in 1567. His last work, Lenten Stuffe, was a eulogy to the herring trade and specifically Great Yarmouth. Joseph Conrad (Jozef Teodor Konrad Korzeniowski), working as a deckhand on a British freighter bound for Constantinople, jumped ship here in 1878, speaking only a few words of the language in which he was to become one of the modern masters. Benjamin Britten, the greatest English composer of the 20th century, is associated with several places in Suffolk, but Lowestoft has the earliest claim, for it is here that he was born in 1913.

Oulton Broad, on the western edge of Lowestoft, is a major centre of amusement afloat, with boats for hire and cruises on the Waveney. It also attracts visitors to Nicholas Everitt Park to look around **Lowestoft Museum**, housed in historic Broad House. Opened by The Queen and Prince Philip in 1985, the museum displays archaeological finds from local sites, some now lost to the sea, costumes, toys, domestic bygones, and a fine collection of Lowestoft porcelain. (The porcelain industry lasted from about 1760 to 1800, using clay from the nearby Gunton Hall Estate. The soft-paste ware, resembling Bow porcelain, was usually decorated in white and blue.) Another museum, the **ISCA Maritime Museum**, has a unique collection of ethnic working boats, including coracles, gondolas, junks, dhows, sampans and proas.

BUNGAY
13 miles W of Lowestoft off the A144

MAP 8 REF U15

An ancient fortress town on the River Waveney. The river played an important part in the town's fortunes until well into the 18th century, with barges laden with coal, corn, malt and timber plying the route to the coast. The river is no longer navigable above Geldeston but is a great attraction for anglers and yachtsmen. Bungay is best known for its castle, built in its original form by Hugh Bigod, 1st Earl of Norfolk, as a rival to Henry II's castle at Orford. In 1173 Hugh took the side of the rebellious sons of Henry, but this insurrection ended with the surrender of the castle to the king. Hugh was killed not long after this episode while on the Third Crusade; his son Roger inherited the title and the castle, but it was another Roger Bigod who came to Bungay in 1294 and built the round tower and mighty outer walls which stand today.

To the north of the castle are Bungay's two surviving churches of note (the Domesday Book recorded five). The Saxon round tower of Holy Trinity Church is the oldest complete structure in the town, and a brass plate on the door commemorates the church's narrow escape from the fire of 1688 that destroyed much of the town (similar disasters overtook many other towns with close-set timber-and-thatch buildings). The Church of St Mary – now redundant – was not so lucky, being more or less completely gutted. The tower survives to dominate the townscape, and points of interest in the church itself include a woodcarving of the Resurrection presented by Rider Haggard, and a monument to General Robert Kelso, who fought in the American War of Independence. A century before the fire the church received a visit, during a storm, from the devilish Black Shuck, a retriever-like hound who, hot from causing severe damage at Blythburgh, raced down the

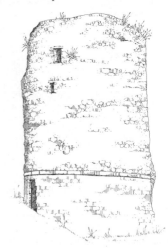

Bigod Castle, Bungay

nave and killed two worshippers. A weather vane in the market place puts the legend into verse:

"*All down the church in midst of fire*
The Hellish Monster Flew
And Passing onwards to the Quire
He many people slew."

Nearby is the famous octagonal **Butter Cross**, rebuilt after the Great Fire and topped by Justice with her scales and sword. This building was once used as a prison, with a dungeon below.

Opened in May 1999, **Castles Bar & Restaurant** is run by business partners Ian Hillyard and Mike Wilkinson. Visitors to Bungay Castle - Ian and Mike are keyholders to the castle - and locals alike frequent this welcoming establishment, which is earning a growing reputation for its excellent food and friendly ambience. Built in the 16th century on the site of the outer bailey of the castle, this former coaching inn is tastefully furnished with comfortable seating and adornments such as horse brasses on the walls. As guests enter, to the right and left are the

separate dining areas (non-smoking and smoking, respectively); directly ahead is the central bar. Real ales at this Free House include Greene King and guest ales. There is also a back bar, known as Bigods Bar after Hugh Bigod, who built five castles including Bungay's. Each of the four comfortable ensuite letting rooms - three doubles and one twin, including a room with a luxurious four-poster bed - is named after one of Bigod's castles; the bar represents the fifth. All food on the varied menu - featuring delights such as Cajun chicken, steak and kidney pudding, and sirloin steak among its many meat, fish and vegetarian dishes - is home-cooked and home-prepared. The wine list is extensive. Booking is advised for the three-course Sunday lunch.

Castles, 35 Earsham Street, Bungay, Suffolk NR35 1AF
Tel: 01986 892283

SOMERLEYTON

MAP 8 REF U14

5 miles NW of Lowestoft on the B1074

Somerleyton Hall, one of the grandest and most distinctive of stately homes, is a splendid Victorian mansion built in Anglo-Italian style by Samuel Morton Peto. Its lavish architectural features are complemented by fine state rooms, magnificent wood carvings (some by Grinling Gibbons) and notable paintings. The grounds include a renowned yew-hedge maze, where people have been going round in circles since 1846, walled and sunken gardens and a 300-foot pergola. There's also a sweet little miniature railway, and **Fritton Lake Countryworld**, part of the Somerleyton Estate, is a 10-minute drive away. The Hall is open to the public on most days in summer.

Samuel Morton Peto learned his skills as a civil engineer and businessman from his uncle and was still a young man when he put the Reform Club and Nelson's Column into his cv. The Somerleyton Hall he bought in 1843 was a Tudor and Jacobean mansion. He and his architect virtually rebuilt the place, and also built Somerleyton village, a cluster of thatched redbrick cottages. Nor was this the limit of Peto's achievements, for he ran a company which laid railways all over the world and was a Liberal MP, first for Norwich, then for Finsbury and finally for Bristol. His company foundered in 1863 and Somerleyton Hall was sold to Sir Francis Crossley, one of three brothers who made a fortune in mass-producing carpets. Crossley's son became Baron Somerleyton in 1916, and the Baron's grandson is the present Lord Somerleyton.

HERRINGFLEET
Map 8 ref U14
5 miles NW of Lowestoft on the B1074

Standing above the River Waveney, the parish Church of St Margaret is a charming sight with its Saxon round tower, thatched roof and lovely glass. **Herringfleet Windmill** is a beautiful black-tarred smock mill in working order, the last survivor of the Broadland wind pump, whose job was to assist in draining the marshes. This example was built in 1820 and worked regularly until the 1950s. It contains a fireplace and a wooden bench, providing a modicum of comfort for a millman on a cold night shift. To arrange a visit call 01473 583352.

SOUTHWOLD
Map 8 ref U15
14 miles S of Lowestoft on the A1095

A town full of character, and full of interest for the holidaymaker and for the historian. Though one of the most popular resorts on the east coast, Southwold has very little of the kiss-me-quick commercialism that spoils so many seaside towns. It's practically an island, bounded by creeks and marshes, the River Blyth and the North Sea, and has managed to retain the atmosphere of the last century. There are some attractive buildings, from pink-washed cottages to elegant Georgian town houses, many of them ranged around a series of greens which were left undeveloped to act as firebreaks after much of the town was lost in the great fire of 1659.

In a seaside town whose buildings present a wide variety of styles, shapes and sizes, William Denny's **Buckenham House** is among the most elegant and interesting. On the face of it a classic Georgian town house, it's actually much older, dating probably from the middle of the 16th century. Richard Buckenham, a wealthy Tudor merchant, was the man who had it built and it was truly impressive in size, as can be deduced from the dimensions of the cellar (now the Coffee House). Many fine features survive, including moulded cornices, carefully restored sash windows, Tudor brickwork and heavy timbers in the ceilings.

The town, which was granted its charter by Henry VII in 1489, once prospered, like many of its neighbours, through herring fishing, and the few remaining fishermen share the harbour on the River Blyth with pleasure craft. Also adding to the period atmosphere is the pier, though as a result of storm damage this is

Buckenham House

much shorter than in the days when steamers from London called in on their way up the east coast. Southwold first became favoured as an elegant, civilised holiday resort in Victorian times. There are bathing huts and a brilliant white lighthouse that's approaching its 100th birthday. It stands 100 feet tall and its light can be seen 17 miles out to sea. Beneath the lighthouse stands a little Victorian pub, the Sole Bay Inn, whose name recalls a battle fought off Southwold in 1672 between the British and French fleets and the Dutch. This was an episode in the Third Anglo-Dutch War, but why Sole Bay? Because the Duke of York, Lord High Admiral of England and later to be crowned James II, had taken Sutherland House in Southwold as his headquarters and it was from there that his fleet (along with the French) set sail. A distinguished victim of the battle was Edward Montagu, 1st Earl of Sandwich, great-grandfather of the man whose gambling mania did not allow him time for a formal meal. By inserting slices of meat between slices of bread, the 4th Earl ensured that his name would live on. Southwold's maritime past is recorded in the **museum** set in a Dutch-style cottage in Victoria Street. Open daily in the summer, it records the famous battle and also local archaeology, geology and natural history, and the history of the Southwold railway. The Southwold Sailors' Reading Room contains pictures, ship models and other items, and at Gun Hill the Lifeboat Museum has a small collection of RNLI-related material with particular reference to Southwold. The main attraction at Gun Hill is a set of six 18-pounder guns, captured in 1746 at the Battle of Culloden and presented to the town (hitherto more or less undefended) by the Duke of Cumberland.

No visitor to Southwold should leave without spending some time in the splendid **Church of St Edmund King and Martyr**, which emerged relatively unscathed from the ravages of the Commonwealth. The lovely painted roof and wide screen are the chief glories, but the slim-stemmed 15th century pulpit and the Elizabethan Holy Table must also be seen. Outside the church, a splendid Jack o'the Clock – a little wooden man in War of the Roses armour – strikes his bell on the hour.

BROADWAY

MAP 8 REF U15

8 miles E of Southwold on the A144

The Triple Plea public house in Broadway takes its name from an old aphorism about a man's last hours, when he is surrounded by three supplicants: the doctor wants his body, the lawyer his money, and the parson his soul. Behind them all is the Devil, knowing that whatever the result he will put forward his own claim and find a use for his pitchfork! Family run by father-and-daughter Philip and Monique Townshend, this charming Free House presents a pristine and welcoming exterior to the world, festooned with hanging baskets. Inside there's a friendly yet tranquil atmosphere. The exposed beams and wooden bar add to the cosy ambience. In the separate dining room, guests partake of the excellent dishes on the menu, which include a fantastic beef pie, locally oak-smoked ham, king prawns in filo pastry and sirloin steak, to name just four. All snacks and meals are home cooked and home prepared. Real ales served at this traditional village pub include Adnams and a changing range of guest ales.

The Triple Plea, Broadway, Halesworth, Suffolk IP19 8QW
Tel: 01986 874750

HALESWORTH
8 miles E of Southwold off the A144

MAP 8 REF U15

Granted a market in 1222, Halesworth reached the peak of its trading importance when the River Blyth was made navigable as far as the town in 1756. A stroll around the streets reveals several buildings of architectural interest. The Market Place has a handsome Elizabethan timber-framed house, but the chief attraction for the visitor is the **Halesworth and District Museum** at Steeple End, a conversion of a row of 17th century almshouses. Local geology and archaeology are the main interests, with various fossils and flints on display, and there's a fascinating account of the Halesworth witchcraft trials of 1645. An art gallery is in the same building. Among Halesworth's distinguished inhabitants were Sir William Jackson Hooker and his son Sir Joseph Dalton Hooker, renowned botanists who were the first two directors of the Royal Botanical Gardens at Kew. They lived at Brewery House, which still stands, though its gardens have not survived.

The **Angel Hotel**, located in the historic pedestrianised Thoroughfare in the heart of Halesworth, dates back to the 1500s and is a distinctive and impressive traditional coaching inn. Steeped in history, it retains its character and many graceful features such as the Georgian doorways and fireplaces, and the Tavern clock, made in 1780 by Halesworth clocksmith

The Angel Hotel, Thoroughfare, Halesworth, Suffolk
IP19 8AH Tel: 01986 873365 Fax: 01986 874891

George Suggate, in the covered courtyard at the centre of the old inn, a light, airy room with a high glass roof. The atmosphere is always welcoming and friendly, offering guests a relaxing and comfortable home from home. The seven ensuite bedrooms are well furnished and appointed. The Back Bar is a quiet and relaxing place to enjoy a drink, while the Front Bar is a superior Georgian room where guests can enjoy a freshly cooked bar meal along with their drink. Cleone's Italian Restaurant is well established and extremely popular with locals as well as hotel residents, for its warm ambience and excellent menu.

DUNWICH
4 miles SW of Southwold off the B1105

MAP 8 REF U15

Surely the Hidden Place of all Hidden Places! Dunwich was once the capital of East Anglia, founded by the Burgundian Christian missionary St Felix and for several centuries a major trading port (wool and grain out; wine, timber and cloth in) and a centre of fishing and shipbuilding. The records show that in 1241 no fewer than 80 ships were built for the king. By the middle of the next century the best days were over as the sea attacked from the east and a vast bank of sand and shingle silted up the harbour. The course of the river was diverted, the town was cut off from the sea and the town's trade was effectively dead. For the next 700 years, the relentless forces of nature continued to take their toll, and all that remains now of ancient

Dunwich are the ruins of a Norman leper hospital, the archways of a medieval friary and a buttress of one of the nine churches which once served the community.

Today's village comprises a 19th century church and a row of Victorian cottages, one of which houses the **Dunwich museum**. Local residents set up the museum in 1972 to tell the Dunwich story; the historical section has displays and exhibits from Roman, Saxon and medieval times, the centrepiece being a large model of the town at its 12th century peak. There are also sections for natural history, social history and the arts. Experts have calculated that the main part of old Dunwich extended up to seven miles beyond its present boundaries, and the vengeance of the sea has thrown up inevitable stories of drama and mystery. The locals say that when a storm is threatening, the sound of submerged church bells can still be heard tolling under the waves as they shift in the current. Other tales tell of strange lights in the ruined priory and the eerie chanting of long-gone monks.

Dunwich Priory

Dunwich Forest, immediately inland from the village, is one of three – the others are further south at Tunstall and Rendlesham – named by the Forestry Commission as Aldewood Forest. Work started on these in 1920 with the planting of Scots pine, Corsican pine and some Douglas fir; oak and poplar were tried but did not thrive in the sandy soil.

The three forests, which between them cover nearly 9,000 acres, were almost completely devastated in the hurricane of October 1987, Rendlesham alone losing more than a million trees, and the replanting will take many years to restore them.

South of the village lies **Dunwich Heath**, one of Suffolk's most important conservation areas, comprising the beach, splendid heather, a field study centre, a public hide, and an information centre and restaurant in converted coastguard cottages. 1998 marks the 30th anniversary of the heath being in the care of the National Trust.

Around Dunwich Heath are the attractive villages of Westleton, Middleton, Theberton and Eastbridge. In **Westleton**, the 14th century thatched Church of St Peter, built by the monks of Sibton Abbey, has twice seen the collapse of its tower. The first fell down in a hurricane in 1776 and its smaller wooden replacement collapsed when a bomb fell in the Second World War. The village is the main route of access to the RSPB-managed **Minsmere Bird Sanctuary**, the most important sanctuary for wading birds in eastern England. The marshland was flooded during the Second World War, and nature and this wartime emergency measure created the perfect habitat for innumerable birds. More than 100 species nest here, and a similar number visit. It's a birdwatcher's paradise, with many hides, and the **Suffolk Coastal Path** runs along the foreshore. A little way inland from Westleton lies **Darsham**, where another nature reserve is home to many varieties of birds and flowers.

THORPENESS
MAP 8 REF U16
13 miles SW of Southwold on the B1353

A unique holiday village with mock-Tudor houses and the general look of a series of eccentric film sets. Buying a considerable pocket of land called the Sizewell estate in 1910, the architect, barrister and playwright Glencairn Stuart Ogilvie created what he hoped would be a fashionable resort with cottages, some larger houses and a shallow boating and pleasure lake called the Meare. The 85' water tower, built to aid in the lake's construction, looked out of place, so Ogilvie disguised it as a house, known ever since as the **House in the Clouds**, and now available for rent as a holiday home. The neighbouring mill, moved lock, stock and millstones from Aldringham, stopped pumping in 1940 but has been restored and now houses a visitor centre. Every August, in the week following the Aldeburgh Carnival, a regatta is held on the Meare, culminating in a splendid fireworks show. Thorpeness is very much a one-off, not at all typical Suffolk, but with a droll charm that is all its own.

ALDEBURGH   Map 8 ref U16
15 miles SW of Southwold on the A1094

And so down the coast road to Aldeburgh, another of those coastal towns that once prospered as a port with major fishing and shipbuilding industries. Drake's *Greyhound* and *Pelican* were built at Slaughden, now taken by the sea, and during the 16th century some 1,500 people were engaged in fishing. Both industries declined as shipbuilding moved elsewhere and the fishing boats became too large to be hauled up the shingle. Suffolk's best-known poet, George Crabbe, was born at Slaughden in 1754 and lived in the poor times. Crabbe it was who created the character of the solitary fisherman Peter Grimes, later the subject of an opera composed by another Aldeburgh resident, Benjamin Britten.

Aldeburgh's role gradually changed into that of a holiday resort, and the Marquess of Salisbury, visiting early in the 19th century, was one of the first to be attracted by the idea of sea-bathing without the crowds. By the middle of the century the grand houses that had sprung up were joined by smaller residences, the railway arrived, a handsome water tower was put up (1860) and Aldeburgh prospered once more. There were even plans for a pier, and construction started in 1878, but the project proved too difficult or too expensive and was halted, the rusting girders being removed some time later. One of the town's major benefactors was Newson Garrett, a wealthy businessman who was the first mayor under the charter of the Local Government Act of 1875. This colourful character also developed the **Maltings at Snape**, but is perhaps best remembered through his remarkable daughter Elizabeth, who was the first woman doctor in England (having qualified in Paris at a time when women could not qualify here) and the first woman mayor (of Aldeburgh, in 1908). This lady married the shipowner James Skelton Anderson, who established the golf club in 1884. As for the arts, there is, of course, the **Aldeburgh Festival**, started in 1948 by Britten and others; the festival's main venue is Snape Maltings, but many performances take place in Aldeburgh itself.

The maritime connection remains very strong. There has been a lifeboat here since 1851 and down the years many acts of great heroism are recorded. The very modern lifeboat station is one of the town's chief attractions for visitors, and there are regular practice launches from the shingle beach. A handful of fishermen still put out to sea from the beach, selling their catch from their little wooden huts, while down at Slaughden a thriving yacht club is the base for sailing on the Orde and sometimes on the sea. At the very southern tip of the town the Martello tower serves as a reminder of the power of the sea: old pictures show it standing well back from the waves, but now the seaward side of the moat has disappeared and the shingle is constantly being shored up to protect it. Beyond it a long strip of marsh and shingle stretches right down to the mouth of the river at Shingle Street.

Back in town, there are several interesting buildings, notably the **Moot Hall** and the parish **Church of St Peter and St Paul**. Moot Hall is a 16th century timber-framed building that once apparently stood in the centre of town. It hasn't moved, but the sea long ago took away several houses and streets. Inside the hall is a museum of town history and finds from the nearby Snape burial ship. Britten set the first scene of Peter Grimes in the Moot Hall. A sundial on the south face of the hall proclaims, in Latin, that it only tells the time when the sun shines.

SNAPE   MAP 8 REF U16
18 miles SW of Southwold on the A1094

The "boggy place" has a long and interesting history, and in 1862 an Anglo-Saxon ship was discovered. Since that time regular finds have been made, with some remarkable cases of almost perfect preservation. Snape, like Aldeburgh, benefited from the philanthropy of the Garrett family, one of whose members built the primary school and set up the **Maltings**, centre of the **Aldeburgh Music Festival**. The last 30 years have seen the development of the **Snape Maltings Riverside Centre**, a group of shops and galleries that offers a unique shopping experience. The site is a complex of restored Victorian granaries and malthouses that is also the setting for the renowned Aldeburgh festival. The Maltings began their designated task in the 1840s and continued thus until 1965, when the pressure of modern techniques brought them to a halt. There was a real risk of the buildings being demolished but George Gooderham, a local farmer, bought the site to expand his animal feeds business and soon saw the potential of the redundant buildings (his son Jonathan is the current owner of the site, Julia Pipe the Director of Retailing). The concert hall came first, in 1967, and in 1971 the Craft Shop was established as the first conversion of the old buildings for retailing. Conversion

The Snape Maltings Riverside Centre

and expansion continue to this day, and in the numerous stylish outlets visitors can buy anything from fudge to country-style clothing, from herbs to household furniture, from silver buttons to top hats. Plants and garden accessories are also sold, and art galleries feature the work of local painters, potters and sculptors. The centre hosts regular painting, craft and decorative art courses, and the latest expansion saw the creation of an impressive country-style department store.

A short distance west of Snape, off the B1069, lies Blaxhall, slightly famous for its growing stone. **The Blaxhall Stone**, which lies in the yard of Stone Farm, is reputed to have grown to its present size (5 tons) from a comparative pebble, the size of a football, when it first came to local attention 100 years ago. Blaxhall getting mixed up with 'Blarney'?

CAMPSEA ASHE   MAP 8 REF U16
10 miles SW of Southwold on the B1078

Campsea Ashe, in the parish of Campsey Ashe, has the 14th century Church of St John the Baptist with an interesting brass showing a 14th century rector in full priestly garb. **The Old Rectory**, a spacious Georgian house next to the village church, offers one of Suffolk's most agreeable experiences of fine dining and civilised country-house living. Four acres of gardens afford tranquillity and splendid views, and shrubs and rhododendrons screen the house from the road. Stewart Bassett is a genial character who greets guests with an eccentric charm and proposes a no-choice three-course meal in consultation with diners. His cooking is exceptional, relying on the best, freshest produce, and a meal here has the feel of a high-class dinner party.

The old-style dining rooms with log fires are used in winter, while the wicker-furnished conservatory comes into is own in summer.

A distinguished wine list complements the splendid cooking, and Stewart does the rounds of the tables towards the end of dinner. Up the handsome staircase are eight beautifully furnished bedrooms, each with its own style and character. They include

The Old Rectory, Campsea Ashe, nr Woodbridge, Suffolk IP13 0PU Tel: 01728 746524

two four-posters, a Victorian room and an Attic room. No smoking in the dining rooms or bedrooms. No dinner on Sundays.

WOODBRIDGE

MAP 8 REF T16

25 miles SW of Southwold on the A12

Udebyge, Wiebryge, Wodebryge, Wudebrige ... just some of the ways of spelling this splendid old market town since first recorded in 970. As to what it means, it could simply be 'wooden bridge' or 'bridge by the wood', but the most likely and most interesting explanation is that it is derived from Anglo-Saxon words meaning 'Woden's (or Odin's) town'. Standing at the head of the Deben estuary, it is a place of considerable charm, with a wealth of handsome, often historic buildings and a considerable sense of history, as both a market town and a port. The shipbuilding and allied industries flourished here as at most towns on the Suffolk coast, and it is recorded that both Edward III, in the 14th century, and Drake in the 16th sailed in Woodbridge ships. There's still plenty of activity on and by the river, though nowadays it is all leisure-oriented. The town's greatest benefactor was Thomas Seckford, who rebuilt the abbey, paid for the chapel in the north aisle of St Mary's Church and founded the original almshouses in Seckford Street. In 1575 he gave the town the splendid Shire Hall on Market Hill. Originally used as a corn exchange, it now houses the **Suffolk Horse Museum**, which is an exhibition devoted to the Suffolk Punch breed of heavy working horse, the oldest such breed in the world. The history of the breed and its rescue from near-extinction in the 1960s is covered in fascinating detail, and

Suffolk Punch Horses

there's a section dealing with the other famous Suffolk breeds – the Red Poll cattle, the Suffolk sheep and the Large Black pigs. Opposite the Shire Hall is **Woodbridge Museum**, a treasure trove of information on the history of the town and its more notable residents, and from here it is a short stroll down the cobbled alleyway to the magnificent parish Church of St Mary, where Seckford was buried in 1587. Seckford naturally features prominently in the museum, along with the painter Thomas Churchyard, the map-maker Isaac Johnson and the poet Edward Fitzgerald. 'Old Fitz' was something of an eccentric and, for the most part, fairly reclusive. He loved Woodbridge and particularly the River Deben, where he often sailed in his little boat *Scandal*.

The Tide Mill and Quay

Woodbridge is lucky enough to have two marvellous mills, both in working order, and both great attractions for the visitor. **The Tide Mill**, on the quayside close to the town centre, dates from the late 18th century (though the site was mentioned 600 years previously) and worked by the power of the tide until 1957. It has been meticulously restored and the waterwheel still turns, fed by a recently created pond which replaced the original huge mill pond when it was turned into a marina. **Buttrum's Mill**, named after the last miller, is a tower mill standing just off the A12 by-pass a mile west of the town centre. She is a marvellous sight, and her six storeys make her the tallest surviving tower mill in Suffolk. There is a ground-floor display of the history and workings of the mill. Many of the town's streets are traffic-free, so shopping is a real pleasure. If you should catch the Fitzgerald mood and feel like 'a jug of wine and a loaf of bread', Woodbridge can oblige with a good variety of pubs and restaurants.

ORFORD

Map 8 ref U16

12 miles E of Woodbridge at the end of the B1084

Without doubt one of the most charming and interesting of all the places in Suffolk, with something to please everyone. The ruins of one of the most important castles in medieval England are a most impressive sight, even though the keep is all that remains of the original building commissioned by Henry II in 1165. The walls of the keep are 10 feet deep, and behind them are many rooms and passages in a remarkable state of preservation. A climb up the spiral staircase to the top provides splendid views.

St Bartholomew's Church was built at the same time, though the present church dates from the 14th century. A wonderful sight at night when floodlit, the church is regularly used for the performance of concerts and recitals, and many of Benjamin Britten's works were first heard here. At the east end lie the still-splendid Norman remains, all that is left of the original chancel. These two grand buildings indicate that Orford was a very important town at one time. Indeed it was once a thriving port, but the steadily growing shingle bank of **Orford Ness** gradually cut it off from the sea, and down the years its appeal has changed. The sea may have gone, but the river is still there, and in summer the quayside is alive with yachts and pleasure craft. On the other side of the river is Orford Ness, the largest vegetated shingle spit in England which is home to a variety of rare flora and fauna. The lighthouse marks the most easterly point in Britain (jointly with Lowestoft). Access to the spit, which is in the hands of the National Trust, is by ferry from Orford quay only. For many years the ness was out of bounds to the public, being used for various military purposes, including pre-war radar research under Sir

Robert Watson-Watt. Boat trips also leave Orford quay for the RSPB reserve of **Havergate Island**, haunt of avocet and tern (the former returned in 1947 after being long absent).

As its name suggests, **The Old Warehouse** began life as a storehouse for coal before being converted, first to a chandler's (candle-making studio) and then a restaurant, in 1993. There are two spacious and airy dining areas, seating 30 and 25 respectively (both non-smoking). The exterior patio dining area overlooking the quay seats 25. The speciality here is fresh fish and seafood, supplied daily by the restaurant's own fishing boats, which land their catches at Orford Quay. Dishes include prawns, plaice, skate, scampi, mussels and fresh local cod caught by the owner himself, William Pinney. In addition there is a daily specials board and an excellent variety of home-made cakes, scones and other desserts. To accompany the superb food there is a good selection of wines. For those wishing to spend more time in this charming part of Suffolk, there is also a holiday flat available above the restaurant which sleeps five and is equipped with every modern convenience.

The Old Warehouse, The Quay, Orford, Suffolk IP12 2NU Tel: 01394 450210

IPSWICH
MAP 8 REF T16

8 miles SW of Woodbridge off the A12

History highlights Ipswich as the birthplace of Cardinal Wolsey, but the story of Suffolk's county town starts very much earlier. It has been a port since the time of the Roman occupation and by the 7th century the Anglo-Saxons had expanded it into the largest port in the country. King John granted a civic charter in 1200, confirming the townspeople's right to their own laws and administration, and for several centuries the town prospered as a port exporting wool, textiles and agricultural products.

Thomas Wolsey arrived on the scene in 1475, the son of a wealthy butcher and grazier. Educated at Magdalen College, Oxford, he was ordained a priest in 1498 and rose quickly in influence, becoming chaplain to Henry VII and then Archbishop of York, a cardinal and Lord Chancellor under Henry VIII. He was quite indispensable to the king and had charge of foreign policy as well as powerful sway over judicial institutions. He also managed to amass enormous wealth, enabling him to found a grammar school in Ipswich and Cardinal's College (later Christ Church) in Oxford. Wolsey had long been hated by certain nobles for his low birth and arrogance, and they were easily able to turn Henry against him when his attempts to secure an annulment from the Pope of the king's marriage to Catherine of Aragon met with failure. Stripped of most of his offices following a charge of overstepping his authority as a legate, he was later charged with treason but died while travelling from York to London to face the king. His death put an end to his plans for the grammar school, and all that remains now is a red-brick gateway.

When the cloth market fell into decline in the 17th century a respite followed in the following century, when the town was a food distribution port during the Napoleonic Wars. At the beginning of the 19th century the risk from silting was becoming acute at a time when trade was improving and industries were springing up. The Wet Dock, constructed in 1842, solved the silting problem and, with the railway arriving shortly after, Ipswich could once more look forward to a safe future. The Victorians were responsible for considerable development and symbols of their civic pride include the handsome **Old Custom House** by the Wet Dock, the Town Hall and the splendid **Tolly Cobbold brewery**, rebuilt at the end of the 19th century, 150 years after brewing started on the site. Guided tours take visitors through the whole brewing process. In Grimwade Street stands **Peter's Ice Cream Factory**, built 100 years ago. Guided tours take place several times a day, and there's a museum, restaurant and shop. Victorian enterprise depleted the older buildings, but a number survive, notably the Tudor houses where Wolsey was born, the Ancient House with its wonderful pargeting, and a dozen medieval churches. St Margaret's is the finest of these, boasting some very splendid flintwork and a double

Corn Hill, Ipswich

hammerbeam roof. **Christchurch Mansion** is a beautiful Tudor home standing in a 65-acre park. Furnished as an English country house, it contains a major collection of works by Constable and Gainsborough and many other paintings, prints and sculptures by Suffolk artists from the 17th century onwards.

The town's main **museum** is in a Victorian building in the High Street. Displays include a natural history gallery, a wildlife gallery complete with a model of a mammoth, a reconstruction of a Roman villa and replicas of Sutton Hoo treasures. A recent addition is a display of elaborately carved timbers from the homes of wealthy 17th century merchants. In a former trolleybus depot on Cobham Road is the **Ipswich Transport Museum**, a fascinating collection of vehicles, from prams to fire engines, all made or used around Ipswich.

On the outskirts of town, signposted from Nacton Road, is **Orwell Country Park**, a 150-acre site of wood, heath and reedbeds by the Orwell estuary. At this point the river is crossed by the imposing Orwell Bridge, a

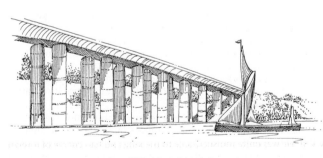

Orwell Bridge, Ipswich

graceful construction in pre-stressed concrete that was completed in 1982 and is not far short of a mile in length.

BILDESTON
Map 8 ref S16

14 miles W of Ipswich on the B1115

Fine old buildings abound here, incluidng timber-framed cottages with overhanging upper floors. The Church of St Mary has a superb carved door and a splendid hammerbeam roof. A tablet inside the church commemorates Captain Edward Rotherham, Commander of the *Royal Sovereign* at the Battle of Trafalgar. He died in Bidleston while staying with a friend, and is buried in the churchyard.

Christmas Hall is a large imposing Georgian house with great charm and character, overlooking the village square in the old wool village of Bildeston. It is run by artist Christina Hawkins and her family. The accommodation is comfortable with an atmosphere which is both friendly and relaxed. Christmas Hall has a wealth of Georgian features and the decor is of the period with splashes of artistic interpretation. There are six guest bedrooms, 3 of which are en suite, including a four-poster room. Comfy beds, white cotton sheets and fluffy towels ensure the guests comfort. Breakfast offers a choice of full English, Continental, smoked fish, fresh fruit, juices, yogurts and/or cereals; special diets are

Christmas Hall, Market Square, Bildeston, Suffolk IP7 7EN
Tel: 01449 741428

happily catered for. There are several excellent local pubs and restaurants nearby for guests' midday and evening meals. Pets welcome. ETB 4 Diamonds Highly Recommended.

LAVENHAM   Map 8 ref S16
18 miles W of Ipswich on the A1141

An absolute gem of a town, the most complete and original of the medieval 'wool towns', with crooked timbered and whitewashed buildings lining the narrow streets. From the 14th to the 16th centuries, Lavenham flourished as one of the leading wool and cloth-making centres in the land, but with the decline of that industry the prosperous times soon came to an end. It is largely due to the fact that Lavenham found no replacement industry that so much of the medieval character remains: there was simply not enough money for the rebuilding and development programmes that changed many towns, often for the worse. The medieval street pattern still exists, complete with market place and market cross.

More than 300 buildings are officially listed as being of architectural and historical interest, and none of them is finer than the **Guildhall**. This superb 16th century timbered building was originally the meeting place of the Guild of Corpus Christi, an organisation that regulated the production of wool. It now houses exhibitions of local history and the wool trade, and its walled garden has a special area devoted to dye plants. **Little Hall** is hardly less remarkable, a 15th century hall house with a superb crown post roof. It was restored by the Gayer Anderson brothers, and has a fine collection of their furniture. The Church of St Peter and St Paul dominates the town from its elevated position. It's a building of great distinction, perhaps the greatest of all the 'wool churches' and declared by the 19th century architect August Pugin to be the finest example of Late Perpendicular style in the world. It was built, with generous help from wealthy local families (notably the Spryngs and the de Veres) in the late 15th and early 16th centuries to celebrate the end of the Wars of the Roses. Its flint tower is a mighty 140 feet in

Lavenham Guildhall

height and it's possible to climb to the top to take in the glorious views over Lavenham and the surrounding countryside. Richly carved screens and fine (Victorian) stained glass are eye-catching features within. **The Priory** originated in the 13th century as a home for Benedictine monks and the beautiful timber-framed house on the site dates from about 1600. In the original hall, at the centre of the building, is an important collection of paintings and stained glass. The extensive grounds include a kitchen garden, a herb garden and a pond. John Constable went to school in Lavenham, where one of his friends was Jane Taylor, who wrote "Twinkle Twinkle Little Star".

EAST BERGHOLT

MAP 8 REF T17

8 miles SW of Ipswich off the A12

England's greatest landscape painter was born at East Bergholt in 1776 and remained at heart a Suffolk man throughout his life. His father, Golding Constable, was a wealthy man who owned both Flatford Mill and Dedham Mill, the latter on the Essex side of the Stour. The river was a major source of inspiration to the young John Constable, and his constant involvement in country matters gave him an expert knowledge of the elements and a keen eye for the details of nature. He was later to declare "I associate my careless boyhood with all that lies on the banks of the Stour. Those scenes made me a painter and I am grateful." That interest in painting developed early and was fostered by his friendship with John Dunthorne, a local plumber and amateur artist. He became a probationer at the Royal Academy Schools in 1799 and over the following years developed the technical skills to match his powers of observation. He painted the occasional portrait and even attempted a couple of religious works, but he concentrated almost entirely on the scenes that he knew and loved as a boy.

Narrow lanes lead to this picturesque and much visited little village. The **Constable Country Trail** starts here, where the painter was born, and passes through Flatford Mill and on to

The Stour at Flatford

Dedham in Essex. The actual house where he was born no longer stands, but the site is marked by a plaque on the fence of its successor, a private house called Constables. A little further along Church Street is Moss Cottage, which Constable once used as his studio. St Mary's Church is one of the many grand churches built with the wealth brought by the wool trade. This one should have been even grander, with a tower to rival that of Dedham across the river. The story goes that Cardinal Wolsey pledged the money to build the tower but fell from grace before the funds were forthcoming. The tower got no further than did his college in Ips-

Flatford Mill

wich, but a bellcage constructed in the churchyard as a temporary house for the bells became their permanent home, which it remains to this day. In this unique timber-framed structure the massive bells hang upside down and are rung by hand by pulling on the wooden shoulder stocks; an arduous task, as the five bells are among the heaviest in England.

The church is naturally something of a shrine to Constable, his family and his friends. There are memorial windows to the artist and to his beloved wife Maria Bicknell, who bore him seven children and whose early death was an enormous blow to him. His parents, to whom he was clearly devoted, and his old friend Willy Lott, whose cottage is featured famously in The Hay Wain, are buried in the churchyard. East Bergholt has an interesting mix of houses, some dating back as far as the 14th century. One of the grandest is **Stour House**, once the home of Randolph Churchill. Its gardens are open to the public, as is **East Berholt Place Garden** on the B1070. The Suffolk tradition of painting continues to this day, with many artists drawn particularly to Walberswick and the beautiful Constable country. That beauty is not always easy to appreciate when crowds throng through the Stour valley at summer weekends, but at other times the peace and beauty are much as they were in Constable's day.

A leafy lane leads south from the village to the Stour, where two of Constable's favourite subjects, **Flatford Mill** and **Willy Lott's cottage**, both looking much as they did when he painted them, are to be found. Neither is open to the public, and the brick watermill is run as a residential field study centre. Nearby Bridge Cottage at Flatford is a restored 16th century building housing a Constable display, a tea room and a shop. There's also a restored dry dock, and the whole area is a delight for walkers; it is easy to see how Constable drew constant inspiration from the wonderful riverside setting.

NORFOLK

Of all English counties, Norfolk is most notable for its endowment of a wealth of historic buildings: some 750 medieval churches, the ruins of 50 monasteries, hundreds of prehistoric and Roman remains, half a dozen of the stateliest homes in England, as well as thousands of interesting houses, cottages, barns and other buildings. The architectural historian Nikolaus Pevsner, compiling his monumental *Buildings of England* series, found it necessary to devote two books to this county rather than the usual single volume, and in Arthur Mee's comprehensive survey of *The King's England*, his book on Norfolk is the fattest of all the county tomes.

Norfolk is actually an island, surrounded by sea to the north and east, isolated from Cambridgeshire by the River Great Ouse, and from Suffolk by the Little Ouse River and the River Waveney. Bulging out into the North Sea, the county is by-passed far away by the Great North Road, the A1, and there is still not a single mile of classified motorway within its boundaries. High-speed road travel in Norfolk is not an available option. That's a good thing in the opinion of many who believe that this is a county not to be rushed through, but to be savoured slowly, mile by mile.

NORWICH
45 miles NE of Bury St Edmunds off the A11

MAP 8 REF T14

"Norwich has the most Dickensian atmosphere of any city I know" declared J.B. Priestley in his English Journey of 1933. "What a grand, higgledy-piggledy, sensible old place Norwich is!" More than half-a-century later, in a European Commission study of "most habitable" cities, Norwich topped the list of British contenders, well ahead of more favoured candidates such as Bath and York. The political, social and cultural capital of Norfolk, Norwich has an individual charm which is difficult to define, a beguiling atmosphere created in part by its prodigal wealth of sublime buildings, partly by its intriguing dual personality as both an old-fashioned Cathedral town and a vibrant, modern metropolis.

Back in prehistoric times, there were several settlements around the confluence of the Rivers Wensum and Yare and, by the late fourth century, one of them was important enough to have its own mint. This was Northwic and by the time of the Domesday Book, 700 years later, Northwic/Norwich, had become the third most populous city in England, only outnumbered by London and York. To the Norman conquerors such a major centre of population (about 5,500 residents) needed a **Castle** to make sure its Saxon inhabitants were kept in order. The first structure, in wood, was replaced in the late 1100s by a mighty fortress in stone which, unlike most blank-walled castles of the period, is decorated with a rich facade of blind arcades and ornamental pilasters. The great fort never saw any military action and as early as the 13th century it was being used as the county gaol, a role it continued to fill until 1889. From its walls, in December 1549, the leader of the rebellion against land enclosures, Robert Kett, was hung in chains and left to starve to death. The Castle is now a lively **Museum** where the old dungeons house a forbidding display of instruments of torture, along with the death masks of some of the prisoners who were executed here. Amongst the countless other fascinating exhibits are the *Bulwer and Miller* collection of more than 2,600 English china teapots; the Langton collection of around 100 cats, fashioned in porcelain, ivory, bronze, glass, and wood, and originating from anywhere between Derbyshire and China; and Margaret Elizabeth Fountaine's mind-boggling accumulation of 22,000 butterflies which she had personally netted during her travels around the world. Pride of place must go however to the Museum's incomparable collection of paintings by the celebrated Norwich artist, John Sell Cotman (1782-1842), and others in the group known as the Norwich School. Their subjects were mostly landscape scenes, such as John Crome's The Poringland Oak, and quite apart from the artistic quality of their works, they have left a fascinating pictorial record of early 19th century Norfolk.

Norwich Castle

The Castle's function has changed over the years, but the **Cathedral** is still the focus of ecclesiastical life in the county. It's even older than the castle, its service of consecration taking place almost 900 years ago, in 1101. This peerless building, its flint walls clad in creamy-white stone from Caen is, after Durham, the most completely Norman cathedral in England, its appeal enhanced by later Gothic features such as the flying buttresses. The Norman cloisters are the largest in the country and notable for the 400 coloured and gilded bosses depicting scenes from medieval life. Another 1,600 of these wondrous carvings decorate the glorious vaulted roof of the nave.

Outside, beneath the slender 315-foot high spire soaring heavenwards, the **Cathedral Close** is timeless in its sense of peace. There are some 80 houses inside the Close, some medieval, many Georgian, their residents enjoying an idyllic refuge free from cars. At peace here lie the remains of Nurse Edith Cavell. A daughter of the rector of Swardeston, a few miles south of Norwich, Nurse Cavell worked at a Red Cross hospital in occupied Brussels during World War I. She helped some 200 Allied soldiers to escape to neutral Holland before being detected and court-martialled by the Germans. As she faced execution by firing squad on 12 October 1915, she spoke her own resonant epitaph: "Standing as I do, in the view of God and eternity, I realize that patriotism is not enough. I must have no hatred or bitterness towards anyone".

Norwich Cathedral

A stroll around the Close will take you to **Pull's Ferry** with its picturesque flint gateway fronting the River Wensum. In medieval times, a canal ran inland from here so that provisions, goods, and in the earliest days, building materials, could be moved direct to the Cathedral. A short stroll along the riverside walk will bring you to **Cow Tower**, built around 1378, and the most massive of the old city towers. And at the western end of the Cathedral Close is the magnificent **Erpingham Gate**, presented to the city in 1420 by a hero of the Battle of Agincourt, Sir Thomas Erpingham.

Beyond this gate, in Tombland, (originally Toom- or waste-land), is **Samson and Hercules House**, its entrance flanked by two 1674 carvings of the giants, and, diagonally opposite, the 15th century Maid's Head Hotel. About 400 yards to the west is the great open space of the Market Square where every weekday a colourful jumble of traders' stalls offer just about every conceivable item for sale. Dominating the western side of the market square is , modelled on Stockholm City Hall and opened by George VI in 1938. Opinions differ about its architectural merits, but there are no such doubts about its predecessor as Civic Centre, the nearby Guildhall, a fine example of 15th century flintwork which now houses the Tourist Information Centre and a small museum.

The **Bridewell Museum** in Bridewell Alley is a late 14th century merchant's house now dedicated to Norfolk's crafts and industries. And right next door a museum/shop celebrates the county's great contribution to world cuisine, mustard. Back in the early 1800s, Jeremiah Colman perfected his blend of mustard flours and spice to produce a condiment that was smooth in texture and tart in flavour. Together with his nephew James he founded J & J Colman in 1823 and, a century and a half later, **The Mustard Shop** was established to commemorate the company's history. It also serves as a showcase for the range of Colman products which nowadays includes a va-

Cow Tower

riety of drinks and foods. The shop has an appropriately Victorian atmosphere with lots of mahogany and marble, and a fascinating display of vintage containers and advertisements, amongst them a series of cod detective stories featuring such characters as Lord Bacon of Cookham and Miss Di Gester, written by no less distinguished a writer than Dorothy L. Sayers. A very appetising exhibition.

There are still 32 churches in Norwich, all worth attention, although many are now used for purposes other than worship. Outstanding among them are **St Peter Mancroft**, a masterpiece of Gothic architecture built between 1430-55, and St Peter Hungate, a handsome 15th century church which, since 1933, has been a museum illustrating all aspects of the arts and crafts involved in ecclesiastical decoration and ritual. St Peter Hungate stands at the top of **Elm Hill**, a narrow, unbelievably picturesque lane where in medieval times the city's wool merchants built their homes, close to their warehouses beside the River Wensum.

To the south of Norwich are the remains of **Venta Icenorum**, the Roman town established here after Boadicea's rebellion in AD 61. Unusually, this extensive site has not been disturbed by later developments, so archaeologists have been able to identify the full scale of the original settlement. Sadly, very little remains above ground, although in dry summers the grid pattern of the streets show up as brown lines in the grass. Most of the finds discovered during excavations in 1920s and 30s are now in Norwich Castle Museum, but the riverside site is still worth visiting, especially if you have a vivid imagination.

SHOTESHAM ALL SAINTS

MAP 8 REF T14

6 miles S of Norwich off the A140

Built as an alehouse in 1687, **The Globe** in Shotesham All Saints has a distinguished past and a bright future. This small but very welcoming public house boasts half an acre to the rear with a children's play area and a grassed goat compound. The attractive frontage is dotted with out-

door seating. The picnic area opposite the pub runs alongside the Beck and overlooks Shotesham Common. The interior boasts a wealth of exposed beams and a warm and friendly atmosphere. There is a bar area and separate restaurant. Real ales from the cask include Greene King varieties and guest ales changed regularly. The home-cooked dishes on offer include fa-

The Globe, The Common, Shotesham All Saints, Norfolk NR15 1YG Tel: 01508 550475

vourites such as salmon steak, Norfolk chicken and sirloin steaks, as well as a variety of daily specials and vegetarian meals. The wine cellar is excellent, and the selection and quality of bar snacks on offer are truly superb. Fortnightly there are theme nights in the restaurant, when dishes from Mexico, China, Greece and a selection of the best offered by different counties of England can be sampled. Advance bookings are recommended for the full Sunday roast.

WYMONDHAM   MAP 8 REF T14
9 miles SW of Norwich, off the A11

The exterior of **Wymondham Abbey** presents one of the oddest ecclesiastical buildings in the county; the interior reveals one of the most glorious. The Abbey was founded in 1107 by the Benedictines, or Black Friars, as they were known from the colour of their habits. The richest and most aristocratic of the monastic orders, the Black Friars apparently experienced some difficulty in respecting their solemn vows of poverty and humility. Especially the latter. The monks were constantly in conflict with the people of Wymondham. In 1249, the dissension between them was so bitter that Pope Innocent IV himself attempted to reconcile their differences. When his efforts failed, a wall was then built across the interior of the Abbey, dividing it into an area for the monks and another for the parishioners. Even that drastic measure failed to bring peace. Both parties wanted to ring their own bells, so each built a tower. The villagers erected a stately rectangular tower at the west end; the monks an octagonal one over the crossing, thus creating the Abbey's curious exterior appearance. Step inside however and you find a magnificent Norman nave, 112ft long. (It was originally twice as long, but the eastern end, along with most of the Abbey buildings, was demolished after the Dissolution of the Monasteries).

The superb hammerbeam roof is supported by 76 beautifully carved angels; there's an interesting 16th century tomb, of the last Abbot, in delicate terracotta work; and a striking modern memorial, a gilded and coloured reredos and tester, commemorating the local men who lost their lives in World War I. The rectangular western tower of the Abbey was the setting for one of the last acts in the ill-fated Kett's Rebellion of 1549. From its walls, William Kett was hung in chains and left to die: his brother, Robert, the leading figure in the uprising, suffered the same fate at Norwich Castle.

Although many of Wymondham's oldest houses were lost in the fire of 1615 when some 300 dwellings were destroyed, there are still some attractive Elizabethan buildings in the heart of the town. **The Market Place** is given dignity by the picturesque octagonal Market Cross, rebuilt two years after the fire. Crowned by a pyramid roof, this appealing timber-framed building is open on all sides on the ground floor, and its upper floor is reached by an outside stairway. Also of interest is **Becket's Chapel**, founded in 1174 and restored in 1559. In its long history it has served as a pilgrim's chapel, grammar school, and coal store. Currently, it houses the town library. **The Bridewell**, or House of Correction, in Bridewell Street, was built as a model prison in 1785 along lines recommended by the prison reformer, John Howard, who had condemned the earlier gaol on the site as "one of the vilest in the country". Wymondham's Bridewell is said to have served as a model for the penitentiaries established in the United States. Now owned by the town's Heritage Society, Bridewell is home to several community projects, including the **Wymondham Heritage Museum**. Railway buffs will also want to visit the historic **Railway Station**, built in 1845 on the Great Eastern's Norwich-Ely line. At its peak, the station and its section employed over 100 people. Still providing a rail link to Norwich, London and the Midlands, the station has been restored, and its buildings house a railway museum, restaurant and tea room, and a piano showroom.

THETFORD   MAP 8 REF S15
30 miles SW of Norwich off the A11

Some 2000 years ago, Thetford may well have been the site of **Boadicea's Palace**. In the 1980s, excavations for building development at Gallows Hill, north of the town, revealed an Iron Age enclosure. It is so extensive it may well have been the capital of the Iceni tribe which gave the Romans so much trouble. Certainly, the town's strategic location at the meeting of the Rivers Thet and Little Ouse made it an important settlement for centuries. At the time of the Domesday Book, 1086, Thetford was the sixth largest town in the country and the seat of the Bishop of East Anglia, with its own castle, mint and pottery. Of the **Castle**, only the 80-foot motte remains, but it's worth climbing to the top of this mighty mound for the views across the town.

Thetford Priory

An early Victorian traveller described Thetford as "An ancient and princely little town....one of the most charming country towns in England". Despite major development all around, the heart of the town still fits that description, with a goodly number of medieval and Georgian houses presenting an attractive medley of flint and half-timbered buildings. Perhaps the most striking is the **Ancient House Museum** in White Hart Street, a magnificent 15th century timber-framed house with superb carved oak ceilings. It houses the Tourist Information Centre and a museum where some of the most interesting exhibits are replicas of the Thetford Treasure, a 4th century hoard of gold and silver jewellery discovered as recently as 1979 by an amateur archaeologist with a metal detector. The originals of these sumptuous artefacts are housed in the British Museum. Admission to the museum is free, except during July and August when a small charge is made.

Even older than the Ancient House is the 12th century **Cluniac Priory** (English Heritage), now mostly in ruins but with an impressive 14th century gatehouse still standing. During the Middle Ages, Thetford could boast 24 churches, today only three remain.

Thetford's industrial heritage is vividly displayed in the **Burrell Steam Museum**, in Minstergate, which has full-size steam engines regularly "in steam", re-created workshops and many examples of vintage agricultural machinery. The Museum tells the story of the Burrell Steam Company which formed the backbone of the town's industry from the late 18th to the early 20th centuries, their sturdy machines famous around the world.

In King Street, the Thomas Paine Statue commemorates the town's most famous son, born here in 1737. The revolutionary philosopher, and author of "The Rights of Man", emigrated to America in 1774 where he helped formulate the American Bill of Rights. Paine's democratic views were so detested in England that even ten years after his death in New York State, the authorities refused permission for his admirer, William Cobbett, to have the remains buried in his home country. And it wasn't until the 1950s that Thetford finally got around to erecting a statue in his honour. Ironically for such a robust democrat, his statue stands in King Street and opposite **The King's House**, named after James I who was a frequent visitor here between 1608 and 1618. At the Thomas Paine Hotel in White Hart Street, the room in which it is believed that Paine was born is now the Honeymoon Suite, complete with four-poster bed.

To the west of the town stretch the 90 square miles of **Thetford Forest**, the most extensive lowland forest in Britain. The Forestry Commission began planting in 1922 and although the woodland is largely given over to conifers, with Scots and Corsican Pine and Douglas Fir predominating, oak, sycamore and beech can also be seen throughout. There is a particularly varied trail leading from the Forestry Commission Information Centre which has detailed information about this and other walks through the area. On the edge of the forest, about 2 miles west of Thetford, are the ruins of **Thetford Warren Lodge**, built around 1400. At that time a huge area here was preserved for farming rabbits, a major element of the medieval diet. The vast warren was owned by the Abbot of Thetford Priory and it was he who built the Lodge for his gamekeeper. Still in the forest, reached by a footpath from the village of Santon Downham, are **Grimes Graves** (English Heritage), the earliest major industrial site to be discovered in Europe. At these unique Neolithic flint mines, Stone Age labourers extracted the materials for their sharp-edged axes and knives. It's a strange experience entering these 4000 year old shafts which descend some 30 feet to an underground chamber. (The experience is even better if you bring your own high-powered torch).

EAST WRETHAM   MAP 8 REF S15
4 miles NE of Thetford off the A11/A1075

It's possible to see how Breckland used to look by visiting the **East Wretham Heath Nature Reserve**. There are nature trails here, hides for watching the birds and deer, and an abundance of wild flowers. Admission is free. Landlord Brian Ashman took over at East Wretham's **Dog & Partridge** in July of 1998. A local born and bred, Brian combines his landlord duties with being gamekeeper on a local estate and the village postmaster (there's a post office inside the pub!). This characterful establishment also offers bed and breakfast accommodation in six attractive and comfortable guest bedrooms - two double, three twin and one family room. Built in the 1800s, this extensive pub began life as three distinct cottages. The large garden has swings for the children and a lovely patio area. The long

Dog & Partridge, Watton Road, East Wretham, Thetford,
Norfolk IP24 1QS Tel/Fax: 01953 498245

central bar is simple and comfortable, the lounge cosy, the bar area with leather settees and a pool table. Army memorabilia such as badges, plaques and shoulder flashes adorns the walls. A friendly and hospitable atmosphere pervades this traditional public house. Real ales on offer include Adnams and Tetleys, along with a good range of ciders, lagers, wines and spirits. Food is available seven days a week, and ranges from excellent bar snacks and meals to freshly prepared Sunday roast.

THOMPSON   MAP 8 REF S14
10 miles NE of Thetford on minor road off the A1075

This is a quiet village with a marshy man-made lake, **Thompson Water**, and a wild common. **The Peddars Way** long-distance footpath passes about a mile to the west and, about the same distance to the north-east, the Church is a splendid early-14th century building notable for its fine carved screen and choice 17th century fittings. **The Chequers Inn** at Thompson takes its name from the medieval method of counting money paid for rent and other expenses onto a chequered cloth. This 16th-century inn presents the kind of picture that used to appear on chocolate box covers, with its thatched roof, white-painted walls and multitude of colourful hanging baskets. The interior is equally charming, with exposed timber beams (possibly 14th century), low ceilings and an abundance of gleaming brasses and other vintage agricultural bygones. Heather and Richard McDowall arrived early in 1998 and have added an excellent choice of wholesome, carefully prepared and presented food. Richard is the chef and his varied

menu ranges from light meals, bar snacks to a la carte menu. Appetising starters such as chicken liver pate through vegetarian selections and a children's menu to a wonderfully indulgent choice of desserts. The specials board offers a wide variety of fresh fish dishes and local meats and seasonal dishes. In addition to the extensive bar area and cosy snug (which seats four) there is a dedicated

The Chequers Inn, Griston Road, Thompson, Thetford, Norfolk IP24 1PX Tel/Fax: 01953 483360

dining area, adorned with traditional carpentry memorabilia, which seats 30 in the no-smoking section and an additional 20 in the smoking section. A choice of four real ales, a beer garden and a safe, secluded children's play area all confirm one's feeling that at The Chequers one has found the ideal English pub. The adjacent barn will be converted by the Spring of 2000 to luxury accommodation.

ATTLEBOROUGH

15 miles NE of Thetford off the A11

MAP 8 REF T14

The greatest glory of this pleasant market town is to be found in its **Church of St Mary**. Here, a remarkable 15th century chancel screen stretches the width of the church and is beautifully embellished with the arms of the 24 bishoprics into which England was divided at that time. The screen is generally reckoned to be one of the most outstanding in the country, a remarkable survivor of the Reformation purging of such beautiful creations from churches across the land. Collectors of curiosities will be interested in a strange memorial in the churchyard. It takes the form of a pyramid, about 6ft high, and was erected in 1929 to mark the grave of a local solicitor with the rather splendid name of Melancthon William Henry Brooke, or "Lawyer" Brooke as he was more familiarly known. Melancthon was an amateur Egyptologist who became convinced by his studies of the Pharoahs' tombs that the only way to ensure an agreeable after-life was to be buried beneath a pyramid, precisely placed, and of the correct physical dimensions. Several years before his death, he gave the most punctilious instructions as to how this assurance of his immortal existence should be constructed and located. A couple of miles west of Attleborough, the **Tropical Butterfly Gardens and Bird Park** is set in 2400 square feet of landscaped tropical gardens and provides a congenial home for hundreds of exotic tropical butterflies. There's also a Falconry Centre with flying displays twice daily; 1½ miles of paths and a waterside walk; a 2-acre Garden Centre with more than 2000 plant varieties on offer; a gift shop; coffee shop and tea gardens.

DISS

19 miles E of Thetford on the A1066/A140

MAP 8 REF T15

The late Poet Laureate, John Betjeman, voted Diss his favourite Norfolk town, and it's easy to understand his enthusiasm. The River Waveney running alongside forms the boundary between Norfolk and Suffolk, but this attractive old market town keeps itself firmly on the north-ern bank of the river. The town is a pleasing mixture of Tudor, Georgian and Victorian houses grouped around **The Mere** which gives the town its name, derived from the Anglo-Saxon word for "standing water". The old town grew up on the hill above The Mere perhaps because, as an 18th century resident observed, "all the filth of the town centering in the Mere, beside the many conveniences that are placed over it, make the water very bad and altogether useless;...it stinks exceedingly, and sometimes the fish rise in great numbers, so thick that they are easily taken; they are chiefly roach and eels". A proper sewerage system was finally installed in 1851. There's a public park beside the 6-acre Mere and from it a narrow street leads to the small **Market Place**. This former poultry market is dominated by the somewhat over-restored **St Mary's Church**. The oldest parts date back some 700 years and the St Nicholas Chapel is par-ticularly enjoyable with its wonderful corbels, angels in the roof, and gargoyles. In the early 1500s, the Rector here was John Skelton, Court poet and tutor to Prince Henry, later Henry VIII. A bitter, quarrelsome man, Skelton was appointed Poet Laureate through the patronage of Car-dinal Wolsey despite the fact that most of Skelton's output has been described as "breathless doggerel". Appointed Rector of Diss in 1502, he appears to have been suspended nine years later for having a concubine. Not far from his church is the delightful **Victorian Shambles** with a cast-iron veranda and a small Museum inside.

KING'S LYNN
MAP 8 REF R13
30 miles N of Thetford off the A47

In the opinion of James Lee-Milne, the National Trust's architectural authority, "The finest old streets anywhere in England" are to be found at King's Lynn. Tudor, Jacobean and Flemish houses mingle harmoniously with grand medieval churches and stately civic buildings. It's not surprising that BBC Television chose the town to represent early-19th century London in their production of *Martin Chuzzlewit*. It seems, though, that word of this ancient sea-port's many treasures has not yet been widely broadcast, so most visitors to the area tend to stay on the King's Lynn by-pass, making their way to the better-known attractions of the north Norfolk coast. They are missing a lot.

The best place to start an exploration of the town is at the beautiful **Church of St Margaret**, founded in 1101 and with a remarkable leaning arch of that original building still intact. The architecture is im-pressive but the church is especially famous for its two outstanding 14th century brasses, generally reck-oned to be the two largest and most monumental in the kingdom. Alongside the north wall of St Margaret's is the **Saturday Market Place**, one of the town's two market places, and a few steps further is one of the most striking sights in the town, the **Guildhall of the Holy Trinity** with a distinctive chequerboard design of black flint and white stone. The Guildhall was built in 1421, extended in Elizabethan times, and its Great Hall is still used today for wedding ceremo-nies and various civic events. Next door to the Guildhall is the Town Hall of 1895, which in a good-neighbourly way is constructed in the same flint and stone pattern. The Town Hall also houses the **Museum of Lynn Life** where along with displays telling the story of the town's 900 years you can also admire the municipal regalia. The greatest treasure in this collec-tion is King John's Cup, a dazzling piece of medieval workmanship with coloured enamel scenes set in gold.

Custom House

The Cup was supposed to be part of King John's treasure which had been lost in 1215 when his overburdened baggage train was crossing the Nene Estuary and sank into the treacherous quicksands. This venerable legend is sadly undermined by the fact that the Cup was not made until 1340, more than a century after John was dead.

A short distance from the Town Hall, standing proudly by itself on the banks of the River Purfleet, is the handsome **Custom House** of 1683, designed by the celebrated local architect, Henry Bell. There's not enough space here to list all of the town's many other important buildings, but mention must be made of the **Hanseatic Warehouse** (1428), the **South Gate** (1440), the **Greenland Fishery Building** (1605), and the **Guildhall of St George**, built around 1406 and reputedly the oldest civic hall in England. The Hall was from time to time also used a theatre and it's known that Shakespeare's travelling company played here. It's considered highly likely that the Bard himself trod the boards. If true, his appearance would be very appropriate since the Guildhall is now home to the **King's Lynn Arts Centre** which is active all year round with events and exhibitions, and since 1951 has arranged an annual Arts Festival in July with concerts, theatre, and a composer in residence. Some of the concerts are held in **St Nicholas' Chapel**, a medieval building whose acoustics outmatch many a contemporary high-tech Concert Hall. And for an insight into the life of King's Lynn's old fishing community, a visit to **True's Yard** is highly recommended. Two tiny cottages are all that is left of the North End which was once a busy little place with its own boatbuilders, chandlers, sailmakers, pubs, bakehouses and school. Everything else was swept away during the slum clearances of the 1930s. One of the cottages is furnished in the style of the 1850s, the other in that of the 1920s, and they are both stocked with a wealth of memorabilia from the days of fishing under sail.

WALPOLE CROSS KEYS
Map 8 ref R13
8 miles W of King's Lynn off the A17/A47

The Woolpack Inn in Walpole Cross Keys is the first public house in Norfolk to greet visitors arriving from the west. This whitewashed stuccoed pub dates back in parts to the 18th century. To the front there is a lawned garden with picnic benches; to the rear additional gardens and

lawned area with an attractive children's play area. There is ample car parking space at both front and rear. The cosy bar area has an intimate snug and attractive furnishings, and lovely features such as a wood-burning stove. To the rear there is a large pool and darts room. Adnams real ales are on offer here, as well as a good mix of ales, lagers, excellent house wines and vintages from France, Australia, South Africa and California.. The pub boasts a

The Woolpack Inn, Sutton Road, Walpole Cross Keys, Kings Lynn, Norfolk P34 4HD Tel: 01553 828327

separate dining area with black timbered pitched ceiling. Seating 24, this non-smoking area is pristine and comfortable. Food ranges from the excellent good-value bar meals to a full menu of steaks, chicken, fish and salad dishes. The service is friendly and efficient at all times.

DOWNHAM MARKET
Map 8 ref R14
10 miles S of King's Lynn off the A10/A1122

Once the site for a major horse fair, this compact little market town stands at the very edge of the Fens, with the River Great Ouse and the New Bedford Drain running side by side at its western edge. Many of its houses are built in the distinctive brick and carrstone style of the area. One of the finest examples of this traditional use of local materials can be seen at Dial House in Railway Road, (now a guest house), which was built in the late 1600s. The parish church has managed to find a small hill on which to perch. It's an unassuming building with a rather incongruously splendid glass chandelier from the 1730s. Another feature of the town, much loved by postcard manufacturers, is the elegant, riotously decorated cast-iron **Clock Tower** in the market place. This was erected in 1878 at a cost of £450 and "was worth every penny of it!" The tower's backdrop of attractive cottages provides a charming setting for a holiday snap.

It's well worth making the short excursion a couple of miles or so north of Downham Market to **Holy Trinity Church** at **Stow Bardolph** to see one of the oddest memorials in the country. Before her death in 1744, Sarah Hare, youngest daughter of the Lord of the Manor, Sir Thomas Hare, arranged for a life-sized effigy of herself to be made in wax. It was said to be an exceptionally good likeness: if so, Sarah appears to have been a rather uncomely maiden, and afflicted with boils to boot. Her death was attributed to blood poisoning after she had pricked her finger with a needle, an act of Divine retribution apparently for her sin of sewing on a Sunday. Sarah was attired in a dress she had chosen herself, placed in a windowed mahogany cabinet, and the monument set up in the Hare family's chapel, a grandiose structure which is larger than the chancel of the church itself.

To the southwest of Downham Market, **Denver Sluice** was originally built in 1651 by the Dutch engineer, Cornelius Vermuyden, as part of a scheme to drain 20,000 acres of land owned by the Duke of Bedford. Various modifications were made to the system over the years, but the principle remains the same, and the oldest surviving sluice, built in 1834, is still in use today. Running parallel with it, is the modern **Great Denver Sluice**, opened in 1964: together these two sluices control the flow of a large complex of rivers and drainage channels, and are able to divert floodwaters into the Flood Relief Channel that runs alongside the Great Ouse. The two great drainage cuts constructed by Vermuyden are known as the Old and New Bedford rivers, and the strip of land between them, never more than 1000yds wide, is called the Ouse Washes. This is deliberately allowed to flood during the winter months so that the fields on either side remain dry. The drains run side by side for more than 13 miles, to Earith in Cambridgeshire, and this has become a favourite route for walkers, with a rich variety of bird, animal and insect life to be seen along the way.

OXBOROUGH   Map 8 ref S14
10 miles E of Downham Market on minor road off the A134

How many hamlets in the country, one wonders, can boast three such different buildings of note as those to be seen at Oxborough. Firstly, there's the **Church of St John the Evangelist**, remarkable for its rare brass eagle lectern of 1498, and its glorious Bedingfeld Chapel of 1525, sheltering twin monuments to Sir Edmund Bedingfeld and his wife fashioned in the then newly popular material of terracotta.

It was Sir Edmund who built **Oxburgh Hall** (National Trust), a breathtakingly lovely moated house built of pale-rose brick and white stone. Sir Edmund's descendants still live in what a later architect, Pugin, described as "one of the noblest specimens of domestic architecture of the 15th century". Henry VII and his Queen, Elizabeth of York, visited in 1497 and lodged in the splendid State Apartments which form a bridge between the lofty gatehouse towers, and which ever since have been known as the King's Room and the Queen's Room. On display here is the original Charter of 1482, affixed with Edward IV's Great Seal of England, granting Sir Edmund permission to build with "stone, lime and sand", and to fortify the building with battlements. These rooms also house some magnificent period furniture, a collection of royal letters to the Bedingfelds, and the huge Sheldon Tapestry Map of 1647 showing Oxfordshire and Berkshire. Another, more poignant, tapestry, known as the Marian Needlework, was the joint handiwork of Elizabeth, Countess of Shrewsbury, and Mary, Queen of Scots, during the latter's captivity here in 1570. The Bedingfelds seemed always to draw the short straw when the Tudors needed someone to discharge an unpleasant or difficult task. It was an earlier Sir Edmund

Oxburgh Hall

who was charged with the care of Henry VIII's discarded wife, Catherine of Aragon, and his son, Sir Henry, was given the even more onerous task of looking after the King's official bastard, the Princess Elizabeth. After Elizabeth's accession as Queen, Sir Henry presented himself at Court, no doubt with some misgivings. Elizabeth received him civilly but, as he was leaving, tartly observed that "if we have any prisoner whom we would have hardlie and strictly kept, we will send him to you". As staunch Catholics, the Bedingfelds were, for the next two and a half centuries, consigned to the margins of English political life. Their estates dwindled as portions were sold to meet the punitive taxes imposed on adherents of the Old Faith. By the middle of the 20th century, the Bedingfelds long tenure of Oxburgh was drawing to a close. In 1951, the 9th Baronet, another Sir Edmund, sold Oxburgh to a builder who promptly announced his intention of demolishing the house. Sir Edmund's mother, the Dowager Lady Sybil, was shocked by such vandalism and used her considerable powers of persuasion to raise sufficient funds to buy back the house. She then conveyed it into the safe keeping of the National Trust. The grounds at Oxburgh provide the perfect foil for the mellow old building, reflected in its broad moat. There's a wonderfully formal, and colourful, French Garden; a walled Kitchen Garden; and woodland walks. The Hall and Gardens are open from late March to early November: for further details, telephone 01366 318258.

CASTLE RISING
Map 8 ref R13

5 miles NE of King's Lynn on minor road off the A149

As the bells ring for Sunday morning service at **Castle Rising**, a group of elderly ladies leave the mellow red brick Bede House and walk in procession to the church. They are all dressed in long scarlet cloaks, emblazoned on the left breast with a badge of the Howard family arms. Once a year, on Founder's Day, they add to their regular Sunday costume a tall-crowned hat typical of the Jacobean period, just like those worn in stereotypical pictures of broomstick-flying witches. These ladies are the residents of the almshouses founded by Henry Howard, Earl of Northampton, in 1614, and their regular Sunday attendance at church was one of the conditions he imposed on the 11 needy spinsters who were to enjoy his beneficence. Howard also required that each inmate of his "Hospital of the Holy and Undivided Trinity" must also "be able to read, if such a one may be had, single, 56 at least, no common beggar, harlot, scold, drunkard, haunter of taverns, inns or alehouses". The weekly tableau vivant of the procession of these blameless virgins to the church seems completely in keeping with this picturesque village which rates high on any "must-not-miss" list of places to visit in Norfolk. The church to which the ladies are making their way, St Lawrence's, although much of it has been reconstructed, is an outstanding example of Norman and Early English work. But overshadowing everything else in this pretty village is the massive **Castle Keep** (English Heritage), its well-preserved walls rising 50ft high, and pierced by a single entrance. The Keep's towering presence is made even more formidable by the huge earthworks on which it stands. The Castle was built in 1150, guarding what was then the sea approach to the River Ouse. (The marshy shore is now some 3 miles distant and still retreating).

Despite its fortress-like appearance, Castle Rising was much more of a residential building than a defensive one. In 1331, when Edward III found it necessary to banish his ferocious

French-born mother, Isabella, to some reasonably comfortable place of safety, he chose this far-from-London castle. She was to spend some 27 years here before her death in 1358, never seeing her son again during that time. How could Edward treat his own mother in such a way? Her crime, in his view, was that the '"he-Wolf of France", as

Castle Rising

all her enemies and many of her friends called Isabella, had joined forces with her lover Mortimer against her homosexual husband Edward II, (young Edward's father), and later colluded in the king's grisly murder at Berkeley Castle. A red-hot poker, inserted anally, was the instrument of his death. For three years after that loathsome assassination, Isabella and Mortimer ruled England as Regents. The moment Edward III achieved his majority, he had Mortimer hung, drawn and quartered. His mother he despatched to a lonely retirement at Castle Rising. Six and a half centuries later, the spacious grounds around the castle provide an appropriate backdrop for an annual display by members of the White Society. Caparisoned in colourful medieval garments and armed with more-or-less authentic replicas of swords and halberds, these modern White Knights stage a battle for control of the castle.

A couple of miles north of Castle Rising is the entrance to **Sandringham Country Park** and **Sandringham House**, the royal family's country retreat where, since 1989, the Queen has chosen to spend every Christmas. Unlike the State Rooms at Windsor Castle and Buckingham Palace where visitors marvel at the awesome trappings of majesty, at Sandringham they savour the atmosphere of a family home. The rooms the visitor sees at Sandringham are those used by the Royal Family when in residence, complete with family portraits and photographs, and comfy armchairs. Successive royal owners have furnished the house with an intriguing medley of the grand, the domestic, and the unusual. Entering the principal reception room, The Saloon, for example, you pass a weighing-machine with a leather-covered seat, a common amenity apparently in great houses of the 19th century. In the same room, with its attractively carved Minstrels' Gallery, hangs a fine family portrait by one of Queen Victoria's favourite artists, Heinrich von Angeli. It shows the Prince of Wales (later Edward VII), his wife Alexandra and two of their children, with Sandringham in the background.

Sandringham House

The Prince first saw Sandringham on 4th February 1862. At Victoria's instigation, the 20-year-old heir to the throne had been searching for some time for a country property, a refuge of the kind his parents already enjoyed at Balmoral and Osborne. A courtier accompanying the Prince reported back that although the outside of house was ugly, it was pleasant and convenient within, and set in pretty grounds. The surrounding countryside was plain, he went on, but the property was in excellent order and the opportunity of securing it should not be missed. Within days, the purchase was completed. Most of the "ugly" house disappeared a few years later when the Prince rebuilt the main residence; the "pretty grounds" have matured into one of the most beautiful landscaped areas in the country. And the "plain" countryside around, - open heath and grassland overrun by rabbits, has been transformed into a wooded country park, part of the coastal Area of Outstanding Natural Beauty.

One of the additions the Prince made to the house in 1883 was a Ballroom, much to the relief of Princess Alexandra. "It is beautiful I think & a great success", she wrote, "& avoids pulling the hall to pieces each time there is a ball or anything". This attractive room is now used for cinema shows and the estate workers Christmas party. Displayed on the walls is a remarkable collection of Indian weapons, presented to the Prince during his state visit in 1875-6, and hidden away in a recess, are the two flags planted at the South Pole by the Shackleton expedition. Just across from the house, the old coach-houses and stables have been converted into a fascinating museum. There are some truly splendid royal vehicles here, including the first car bought by a member of the royal family, - a 1900 Daimler, and an evocative series of old photographs depicting the life of the royal family at Sandringham from 1862 until Christmas 1951. Other attractions at Sandringham include a Visitor Centre; Adventure Playground; Nature Walks; Souvenir Shop; Restaurant and Tearoom.

SNETTISHAM   MAP 8 REF R13
11 miles N of King's Lynn off the A149

Snettisham is best known nowadays for its spacious, sandy beaches and the **RSPB Bird Sanctuary**, both about two miles west of the village itself. But for centuries Snettisham was much more famous as a prime quarry for carrstone, an attractive soft-white building-block that provided the "light relief" for the walls of thousands of Georgian houses around the country, and for nearby Sandringham House. The carrstone quarry is still working, its product now destined mainly for "goldfish ponds and the entrance-banks of the more pretentious types of bungalow". Unfortunately, one has to go the British Museum in London to see Snettisham's greatest gift to the national heritage: an opulent collection of gold and silver ornaments from the 1st century AD, the largest hoard of treasure trove ever found in Britain, discovered here in 1991. On the edge of the village, **Park Farm** is a 320-acre working farm which offers visitors a good insight into such farming operations as lambing, shearing, and red deer calving. Children can help feed lambs, kid goats and piglets; take a tractor-drawn safari to see the red deer herd, have a horse or pony ride, try their skills as a potter, or walk a farm trail. There's an Adventure Playground, Craft; Leather and Gift Shops; and a tea room serving home-made refreshments. Open daily throughout the year; for more information call 01485 542425.

About two miles north of Snettisham is the famous **Norfolk Lavender**, the largest lavender-growing and distilling operation in the country. Established in 1932, it is also the oldest. The information point at the western entrance is sited in an attractive listed building which has become something of a Norfolk landmark.

SWAFFHAM   MAP 8 REF S14
15 miles SE of King's Lynn on the A47/A1065

Swaffham's one-time claim to be the "Montpellier of England" was justified by the abundance of handsome Georgian houses that used to surround the large, wedge-shaped market place. A good number still survive, along with the **Assembly Room** of 1817 where the quality would foregather for concerts, balls and soirees. The central focus of the market square is the elegant **Butter Cross** presented to the town by the Earl of Orford in 1783. It's not a cross at all but a classical lead-covered dome standing on eight columns and surmounted by a life-size statue of Ceres, the Roman goddess of agriculture, an appropriate symbol for this busy market town from which ten roads radiate out across the county.

From the market place an avenue of limes leads to the quite outstanding **Church of St Peter & St Paul**, a 15th century masterpiece with one of the very best double hammerbeam roofs in the county, strikingly embellished with a host of angels, their wings widespread. The unknown mason who devised the church's harmonious proportions made it 51ft wide, 51ft high and 102ft long. Carved on a bench-end here is a man in medieval dress accompanied by a dog on a chain. The same two figures are incorporated in the town's coat of arms, and also appear in the elegantly designed town sign just beyond the market place. The man is the "Pedlar of Swaffham", a certain John Chapman who according to legend dreamed that if he made his way to London Bridge he would meet a stranger who would make him rich. The pedlar and his dog set off for London and on the bridge he was eventually accosted by a stranger who asked him what he was doing there. John recounted his dream. Scoffingly, the stranger said "If I were a dreamer, I should go to Swaffham. Recently I dreamt that

Butter Cross, Swaffham

in Swaffham lived a man named Chapman, and in his garden, buried under a tree, lay a treasure". John hastily returned home, uprooted the only tree in his garden, and unearthed two jugs full of gold coins.

John Chapman may be Swaffham's best known character locally, but internationally the name of Howard Carter, the discoverer of Tutankhamen's tomb, is much better known. Carter was born at Swaffham in 1874 and his death in 1939 was attributed by the popular press to the "Curse of Tutankhamen". If so, it must have been an extremely sluggish curse. Some 17 years had elapsed since Carter had knelt by a dark, underground opening, swivelled his torch, and found himself the first human being in centuries to gaze on the astonishing treasures buried in the tomb of the teenage Pharaoh.

Move on some 1400 years from the death of Tutankhamen to Norfolk in the 1st century AD. Before a battle, members of the Iceni tribe, led by Boadicea, would squeeze the blue sap of the woad plant onto their faces in the hope of affrighting the Roman invaders, (or any other of their many enemies). At **Cockley Cley Iceni Village and Museums**, three miles southwest of Swaffham, archaeologists have reconstructed a village of Boadicea's time, complete with wooden huts, moat, drawbridge and palisades. Reconstruction though it is, the village is remarkably effective in evoking a sense of what daily life for our ancestors entailed more than 1900 years ago. A recent addition to Swaffham's attractions is the **EcoTech Discovery Centre**, opened in 1998. Through intriguing interactive displays, and hands-on demonstrations, visitors can discover what startling innovations current, and possible, technology may have in store for us during the next millennium.

CASTLE ACRE   MAP 8 REF S14
4 miles N of Swaffham off the A1065

Set on a hill surrounded by water meadows, Castle Acre seems still to linger in the Middle Ages. William de Warenne, William the Conqueror's son-in-law, came here very soon after the Conquest and built a Castle that was one of the first, and largest, in the country to be built by the Normans. Of that vast fortress, little remains apart from the gargantuan earthworks and a squat 13th century, gateway. Much more has survived of **Castle Acre Priory**, founded in 1090 and set in fields beside the River Nar. Its glorious West Front gives a powerful indication of how majestic a triumph of late Norman architecture the complete Priory must have been. With five apses and twin towers, the ground plan was modelled on the Cluniac mother church in Burgundy where William de Warenne had stayed while making a pilgrimage to Rome. Despite the Priory's great size, it appears that perhaps as few as 25 monks lived here during the Middle Ages. And in

Castle Acre

some comfort, to judge from the well-preserved Prior's House which has its own bath and built-in wash-basin. The Priory lay on the main route to the famous Shrine at Walsingham with which it tried to compete by offering pilgrims a rival attraction in the form of an arm of St Philip. Today the noble ruins of the Priory are powerfully atmospheric, a brooding scene skillfully exploited by Roger Corman when he filmed here for his screen version of Edgar Allan Poe's ghostly story, "The Tomb of Ligeia". Castle Acre village is extremely picturesque, the first place in Norfolk to be designated a Conservation Area, in 1971. Most of the village, including the 15th century parish church, is built in traditional flint with a few later houses of brick blending in remarkably happily.

The Old Red Lion in Castle Acre has a long tradition of serving travellers who seek refreshment and repose. Centrally located, near shops, the post office, pubs, restaurant, tea rooms and other local amenities, this bright red-painted and friendly inn offers both private rooms and dormitories which can accommodate up to 20 people. There are three separate areas for reading and meeting other guests. The delicious and exclusively wholefood/vegetarian meals are served communally (special diets can also be catered for). There is also a fully-equipped self-catering unit, and self-service breakfasts are available from midnight until noon. This welcoming establishment makes for a very relaxing and peaceful retreat. No smoking.

The Old Red Lion, Bailey Street, Castle Acre, Norfolk PE32 2AG
Tel: 01760 755557

DEREHAM

MAP 8 REF S14

16 miles W of Norwich on the A47

One of the most ancient towns in the county, East Dereham has a recorded history stretching back to 654AD when St Withburga founded a Nunnery here. Her name lives on at **St Withburga's**

Well, just to the west of the church. This is where she was laid to rest but, some 300 years later, the Abbot and monks of Ely robbed her grave and ensconced the precious, fund-raising relic in their own Cathedral. In the saint's desecrated grave a spring suddenly bubbled forth, its waters possessed of miraculous healing properties, and St Withburga's shrine attracted even more pilgrims than before. Some still come. In the Church of St Nicholas, the second largest in Norfolk, there are features from every century from the 12th to the 16th: a magnificent lantern tower, a lofty Bell Tower, painted roofs, and a Seven Sacrament Font. This is the largest of these notable fonts of which only 30 have survived, 28 of them in Norfolk and Suffolk. In the northeast transept is buried a poet some of whose lines have become embedded in the language:

"Variety's the very spice of life, the monarch of all I survey
God made the country and man made the town".

They all came from the pen of William Cowper who, despite being the author of such cheery poems as "John Gilpin", suffered grievously from depression, a condition not improved by his association with John Newton, a former slave trader who had repented and become "a man of gloomy piety". The two men collaborated on a book of hymns which included such perennial favourites as "Oh! for a closer walk with God", "Hark, my soul, it is the Lord", and "God moves in a mysterious way". Cowper spent the last four years of his life at East Dereham, veering in and out of madness. In a late-flowering romance, he had married the widow Mary Unwin but the strain of caring for the deranged poet drove her in turn to insanity and death. She too is buried in the church.

William died four years after Mary, in 1800. Three years later another celebrated writer was born at the quaintly named hamlet of **Dumpling Green** on the edge of the town. George Borrow was to become one of the great English travel writers, producing books full of character and colour such as "Wild Wales" and "The Bible in Spain". In his autobiographical novel "Lavengro" he begins with a warm recollection of the town where he was born: "I love to think on thee, pretty, quiet D[ereham], thou pattern of an English market town, with thy clean but narrow streets branching out from thy modest market place, with thine old-fashioned houses, with here and there a roof of venerable thatch". The house in which George Borrow was born, Borrow's Hall, still stands in Dumpling Green.

A much less attractive character connected with East Dereham is Bishop Bonner, the enthusiastic arsonist of Protestant "heretics" during the unhappy reign of Mary Tudor. He was rector of the town before being appointed Bishop of London and he lived in the exquisite thatched terrace now called **Bishop Bonner's Cottages**. The exterior is ornamented with delightful pargetting, a frieze of flower and fruit designs below the eaves, a form of decoration which is very unusual in Norfolk. The cottages now house a small Museum.

Three miles northwest of Dereham, off the B1146 road at **Gressenhall**, is the **Norfolk Rural Life Museum**. It's housed in a former workhouse which, like so many of those detested institutions, is an extremely imposing late 18th-century building, this one built in rose-red brick. Gressenhall Workhouse was designed to accommodate some 700 unfortunates, so it was built on a very grand scale indeed. There's ample room for the many exhibits illuminating the working and domestic life of Norfolk people over the last 150 years. The surrounding 50 acres of countryside, Union Farm, is run as a typical 1920s farm, with rare breeds of sheep, pigs, cattle and poultry, and demonstrations of the real nature of bygone agricultural labour. The museum hosts numerous special events during the season, ranging from Steam Days to an international folk dance festival with more than 200 dancers taking part. For more details, telephone 01362 860563.

A mile or so south of Gressenhall, the tiny community of **Dillington** has great difficulty in getting itself noticed on even the most large-scale of maps. This very Hidden Place is worth seeking out for **Norfolk Herbs at Blackberry Farm**, a specialist herb farm located in a beautiful wooded valley. Visitors are invited to browse through a vast collection of aromatic, culinary and medicinal herb plants, and to learn all about growing and using herbs. Admission is free. For more details (and directions) phone 01362 860812.

AYLSHAM   MAP 8 REF T13
14 miles N of Norwich, on the A140

From Hevingham, the A140 leads due north to the attractive little town of Aylsham, set beside the River Bure, the northern terminus of the **Bure Valley Railway**. It has an unspoilt **Market Place**, surrounded by late 17th and early-18th century houses, reflecting the prosperity the town enjoyed in those years from the cloth trade, and a 14th/15th century church, St Michael's, said to have been built by John O'Gaunt. In the churchyard is the tomb of one of the greatest of the 18th century landscape gardeners, Humphrey Repton, the creator of some 200 parks and gardens around the country.

One of Repton's many commissions was to landscape the grounds of **Blickling Hall** (National Trust), a "dream of architectural beauty", which stands a mile or so outside Aylsham. Many visitors have marvelled at their first sight of the great Hall built for Sir Henry Hobart in the 1620s. "No-one is prepared on coming downhill past the church into the village, to find the main front of this finest of Jacobean mansions, actually looking upon the road, unobstructedly, from behind its velvet lawns" enthused Charles Harper in 1904. "No theatrical manager cunning in all the artful accessories of the stage could devise anything more dramatic". From the outside, Sir Henry's house fully satisfied the current architectural vogue for perfect symmetry. Four towers topped with lead-covered turret-caps rise at each corner, there are lines of matching Dutch gables and mullioned windows, and even the chimneys were placed in corresponding groups of twos, threes or fours. Inside, the most spectacular feature is the Long Gallery which

extends for 135ft and originally provided space for indoor exercise in bad weather. Its glory is the plaster ceiling, an intricately patterned expanse of heraldic panels bearing the Hobart arms, along with others displaying bizarre and inscrutable emblems such as a naked lady riding a two-legged dragon. Other treasures at Blickling include a dramatic double-flight carved oak staircase, the Chinese Bedroom lined with 18th century hand-painted

May Day at Blickling Hall

wallpaper, and the dazzling Peter the Great Room. A descendant of Sir Henry Hobart, the 2nd Earl of Buckinghamshire, was appointed Ambassador to Russia in 1746, and he returned from that posting with a magnificent tapestry, the gift of Empress Catherine the Great. This room was re-designed so as to display the Earl's sumptuous souvenir to its full effect, and portraits of himself and his Countess by Gainsborough were added later. The Earl was a martyr to gout and his death in 1793 at the age of 50 occurred when, finding the pain unbearable, he thrust his bloated foot into a bucket of icy water, and suffered a heart attack. He was buried beneath the idiosyncratic Egyptian Pyramid in the grounds, a 45ft high structure designed by Ignatius Bonomi who combined Egyptian and classical elements to create a mausoleum which, if nothing else, is certainly distinctive. Blickling also offers its visitors miles of footpaths through lovely grounds, a Plant Centre, Picnic Area, Restaurant and Shop.

Within a few miles of Blickling Hall are two other stately homes, both the properties of Lord and Lady Walpole. Neither of the houses, **Mannington Hall** and **Wolterton Park**, is normally open to the public but their gardens and grounds are. At Mannington there are country walks and trails, a Heritage Rose Garden featuring thousands of roses set in small gardens reflecting their period of origin, a Garden Shop, and tea room. Wolterton Park, the stately 18th century Hall built for Horatio Walpole, brother of Sir Robert, England's first Prime Minister stands in grounds landscaped by Humphrey Repton. Here there are miles of waymarked walks and trails, orienteering, an Adventure Playground and various special events are held throughout the year. For more information on either property, call 01263 761214

Just north of Mannington Hall stands the village of **Little Barningham** where St Mary's Church is a magnet for collectors of ecclesiastical curiosities. Inside, perched on the corner of an ancient box pew, stands a remarkable wood-carved skeletal figure of the Grim Reaper. Its fleshless skull stares hollow-eyed at visitors with a defiant, mirthless grin: a scythe gripped in one clutch of bones, and an hour-glass in the other, symbolise the inescapable fate that awaits us all. This gruesomely powerful memento mori was donated to the church in 1640 by one Stephen Crosbie who, for good measure, added the inscription: "As you are now, even so was I, Remember death for ye must dye". Those words were a conventional enough adjuration at that time, but what is one supposed to make of Stephen's postscript inscribed on the back of the pew: "For couples joined in wedlock this seat I did intend"?

HUNSTANTON
16 miles N of Kings Lynn on the A149

Map 8 ref R13

Hunstanton town is a comparative newcomer, developed in the 1860s by Mr Hamon L'Estrange of nearby Hunstanton Hall to take advantage of the arrival of the railway here, and to exploit the natural appeal of its broad, sandy beaches. The centre is well-planned with mock-Tudor houses grouped around a green that falls away to the shore. Hunstanton's social standing was assured after the Prince of Wales, later Edward VII, came here to recover from typhoid fever. He stayed at the Sandringham Hotel which, sadly, has since been demolished, along with the grand Victorian pier, and the railway. But Hunston, as locals call the town, still has a distinct 19th century charm about

The Cliffs at Hunstanton

it and plenty to entertain visitors. The huge stretches of sandy beach, framed by those multi-coloured cliffs, are just heaven for children who will also be fascinated by the **Kingdom of the Sea**, on the South Promenade, where an underwater glass tunnel provides a fascinating opportunity to watch the varied and often weird forms of marine life that inhabit Britain's waters. A popular excursion from Hunstanton is the boat trip to **Seal Island**, a sandbank in The Wash where seals can indeed often be seen sunbathing at low tide.

THORNHAM
4 miles NE of Hunstanton off the A149

Map 8 ref R13

Set opposite the local village church, **The Kings Head** occupies the immediate centre of Thornham. This distinguished pub dates back to the mid-1600s. Originally two cottages, it was established as a pub by the early 1800s. The interior retains many traditional features, including exposed oak beams. There is a bar area with narrow wood tongue and grooved floor, wood bar with unusual bar stools, and a large open fire with a wonderful oak lintel marked with hot poker marks of days gone by. The small lounge bar features an open fire, low beamed ceiling, pew benches and other comfortable seating. The beer garden to the rear boasts a children's play

The Kings Head, High Street, Thornham, Hunstanton, Norfolk PE36 6LY Tel: 01485 512213 Fax: 01485 512424

area, two petanque pistes and barbecue. Four real ales including two Greene King brews and two changing guest beers are on tap. The restaurant menu includes a good selection of imaginative and tried-and-true dishes to tempt every palate. Owners Ann and Michael John offer all guests a warm and hospitable welcome. Three comfortable guest rooms are available for anyone wishing to stay and explore this lush region of Norfolk.

DOCKING
MAP 8 REF S13
9 miles SE of Hunstanton on the B1454 & B1153

One of the larger inland villages, Docking was at one time called Dry Docking because, perched on a hilltop 300ft above sea level, it had no water supply of its own. The nearest permanent stream was at Fring, almost 3 miles away, so in 1760 the villagers began boring for a well. They had to dig some 230ft down before they finally struck water which was then sold at a farthing (0.6p) per bucket. A pump was installed in 1928 but a mains supply didn't reach Docking until the 1930s.

On the edge of the village is **The Pilgrim's Reach Restaurant**, owned and run by James Lee and Sally Mash, who in a short time have made this fine restaurant a 'must-visit' for anyone in the area. Housed in a traditional Norfolk building of stone, chalk and flint, parts of which are believed to date back to the 1500s, the interior is decorated with some fascinating local memorabilia: old hand tools, eel picks, the tools of the shepherd's trade, old implements used by marshmen and thatchers, all relating to a bygone Norfolk. A collection of old photographs of wherries and punts on the Norfolk Broads, and sailing vessels and lifeboats on the Norfolk coast enhance the strong 'local flavour'. Flavours of a different kind are evoked by the quite outstanding menu in which fish dishes have pride of place - grilled Lowestoft cod fillet with pesto, pine nuts and prawns, for example, or escalopes of local Grey Mullet topped with pan-fried citrus prawns and cockles. Winter specialities include mussels, which are harvested just a few hours before being served. The distinct mussels menu features Brancaster mussels prepared in six different styles, from steamed in white wine to Thai-style with sherry herbs and spices. In summer crabs are the theme, with dishes such as crab

The Pilgrim's Reach Restaurant, High Street, Docking, Norfolk PE31 8NH Tel: 01485 518383

salad and crab and prawns cooked with Calvados, covered with cream and breadcrumbs, and baked. If your preference is for meat, poultry or vegetarian dishes, you'll also find a good selection to choose from, including prime local steaks and smoked duck breasts in the restaurant, or grilled bacon steaks and home-roast ham available in the bar, and a blackboard menu of daily specials such as Brancaster Samphire (in season) or steamed sea bass and sea trout. Baguettes are available every day except Sunday for lunch. Grants of St James-supplied cask-conditioned ales and wines complete the culinary experience awaiting visitors to this superb establishment.

WELLS-NEXT-THE-SEA
MAP 8 REF S13
17 miles E of Hunstanton on the A149

It's difficult to decide whether Wells is a small town or a large village, but there's no doubt about the appeal of its picturesque quayside, narrow streets and ancient houses. Wells has been a working port since at least the 13th century but over the years the town's full name of Wells-next-the-Sea has become increasingly inapt, - its harbour now stands more than a mile from the sea. In 1859, to prevent the harbour silting up altogether, Lord Leicester of Holkham Hall built an Embankment cutting off some 600 acres of marshland. This now provides a pleasant walk down to the sea. The Embankment gave no protection however against the great floods of 1953 and 1978. On the 11th January, 1978, the sea rose 16ft 1in above high tide, a few inches less than the 16ft 10in recorded on the 31st January, 1953 when the flood-waters lifted a ship on to the quay. A silo on the harbour is marked with these abnormal levels. Running alongside the Embankment is the **Harbour Railway**, which trundles from the small Museum on the quay to the lifeboat station by the beach. This narrow-gauge railway is operated by the same company as the **Wells & Walsingham Light Railway** which carries passengers on a particularly lovely ride along the route of the former Great Eastern Railway to Little Walsingham. The 4-mile journey takes about 25 minutes with stops at Warham St Mary and Wighton. Both the WWLR and the Harbour Railway services are seasonal. In a curious change of function, the former GER station at Wells is now home to the well-known Burnham Pottery, the former signal box is now the station, while the old station at Walsingham is now a church! In addition to being the largest of North Norfolk's ports, Wells is also a popular resort with one of the best beaches in England bordered by the curiously named **Holkham Meals**, a plantation of pines established here in the 1860s to stabilise the dunes.

The **Old Police House** in Wells-next-the-Sea was once, as its name suggests, the local police sergeant's house. Built in 1962, this non-smoking bed and breakfast establishment is close to the town centre and quayside, here in the heart of Norfolk's heritage coast. The custom-built ground floor accommodation annexe was erected in 1988. It has a separate entrance and offers three spacious ensuite twin-bedded rooms fitted with every modern convenience. The rooms are light, airy and comfortably furnished. The large lawned garden to the rear has a small summer house and can

**The Old Police House, Polka Road, Wells-next-the-Sea,
Norfolk NR23 1ED Tel: 01328 710630**

be used as a relaxing retreat by guests. The breakfasts are hearty and healthy, just the thing to start off a day of walking or sightseeing in this part of Norfolk. ETB Three Diamonds.

FAKENHAM
MAP 8 REF S13
20 miles E of Kings Lynn on the A148

Fakenham is a busy and prosperous-looking market town, famous for its National Hunt Racecourse, antique & bric-a-brac markets and auctions, and as a major agricultural centre for the region. Straddling the River Wensum, this attractive country town has a number of fine late-18th and early-19th century brick buildings in and around the Market Place. And it must surely be one of the few towns in England whose the former gasworks (still intact) has been turned into a **Museum of Gas & Local History**, housing an impressive historical display of domestic gas appliances of every kind. Fakenham Church also has an unusual feature, a powder room, - although the room over the large porch, built in 1497, was used for storing gunpowder rather than cosmetics. Even older than the church is the 700 year-old hunting lodge, built for the Duchy of Lancaster, which is now part of the Crown Hotel. As an antidote to the idea that Norfolk is unremittingly flat, take the B1105 north out of Fakenham and after about half a mile take the first minor road to the left. This quiet road loops over and around the rolling hills, a ten-mile drive of wonderfully soothing countryside that only ends at Wells-next-the-Sea. Southeast of Fakenham, off the A1067, **Pensthorpe Waterfowl Park** is home to Europe's best collection of endangered and exotic waterbirds. Over 120 species of waterfowl can be seen here in their natural surroundings. There are good facilities for the disabled and children, a Wildlife Brass Rubbing Centre, nature trails through 200 acres of the Wensum Valley countryside, a restaurant, and shop.

SCULTHORPE
MAP 8 REF S13
2 miles W of Fakenham off the A148

As its name tells us, **Sculthorpe Mill** was once a working watermill. This charming and impressive stonebuilt 18th-century listed building now offers ensuite accommodation, an a la carte restaurant and a wide variety of bar food and real ales. Set in a tranquil location yet central to the main tourist localities of north Norfolk, the mill straddles the banks of the River Wensum and is set within six acres of watermeadow; adjacent is an attractive unbridged ford. The building has been renovated to provide a high standard of comfort and convenience to all guests. The oak-beamed restaurant overlooks the river, while the which combines the best of

Sculthorpe Mill, Lynn Road, Sculthorpe, Norfolk NR21 9QG
Tel: 01328 856161 Fax: 01328 856651

traditional favourites with more innovative dishes. A relaxed atmosphere is guaranteed at this superior establishment.

GREAT SNORING
Map 8 ref S13
5 miles NE of Fakenham on minor road off the A148

The names of the twin villages, Great and Little Snoring, are such a perennial source of amusement to visitors it seems almost churlish to explain that they are derived from a Saxon family called Snear. About three miles northeast of Great Snoring stands what is perhaps the most unusual museum in Norfolk, **The Thursford Collection**. George Cushing began this extraordinary collection of steam-powered traction engines, fairground organs and carousels back in 1946 when "one ton of tractor cost £1". Perhaps the most astonishing exhibit is a 1931 Wurlitzer organ whose 1,339 pipes can produce an amazing repertoire of sounds, - horses' hooves, fire engine sirens, claps of thunder, waves crashing on sand, and the toot-toot of an old railway engine are just some of the Wurlitzer's marvellous effects. There are regular live music shows when the Wurlitzer displays its virtuosity and other attractions include a steam-powered Venetian Gondola ride; shops selling a wide variety of goods, many of them locally made; and a tearoom. The museum is open daily from Easter to October, afternoons only: A mile or so north of the Thursford museum, in the village of Hindringham, **Mill Farm Rare Breeds** is home to dozens of cattle, sheep, pigs, goats, ponies, poultry and waterfowl which were once commonplace but are now very rare. These intriguing creatures have some 30 acres of lovely countryside to roam around. Children are encouraged to feed the animals and there's also an Adventure Playground, crazy golf course, craft & gift shop, picnic area and tearoom.

LITTLE WALSINGHAM
Map 8 ref S13
5 miles N of Fakenham on the B1105

Every year, some half a million pilgrims make their way to this little village of just over 500 souls to worship at the **Shrine of Our Lady of Walsingham**. In 1061 the Lady of the Manor of Walsingham, Lady Richeldis de Faverches, had a vision of the Holy Virgin in which she was instructed to build a replica of the Holy House in Nazareth, the house in which the Archangel Gabriel had told Mary that she would be the mother of Christ. Archaeologists have located the original house erected by Lady Richeldis. It was just 13ft by 23ft and made of wood, later to be enclosed in stone.

These were the years of the Crusades, and the **Holy House** at Walsingham soon became a major centre of pilgrimage, because it was regarded by the pious as an authentic piece of the Holy Land. Around 1153, an **Augustinian Priory** was established to protect the shrine, now encrusted with jewels, gold and silver, and to provide accommodation for the pilgrims. The Priory is in ruins now but the largest surviving part, a stately Gatehouse on the east side of the High Street is very impressive.

Little Walsingham is an exceptionally attractive village, set in the midst of parks and woodlands, and

Clink in Common Place

with fine medieval and Georgian houses lining its streets. Also of interest are the 16th century octagonal **Clink in Common Place**, used in medieval times as a lock-up for petty offenders; the scanty ruins of Walsingham's Franciscan Friary of 1347; and the former Shire Hall which is now a museum. For almost 500 years, Walsingham prospered. Erasmus of Rotterdam visited in 1511 and was critical of the rampant commercialisation of the Shrine with its plethora of bogus relics and religious souvenirs for sale. He was shown a gigantic bone, "the finger-joint of St Peter" no less, and in return for a small piece of translation was presented with a highly aromatic fragment of wood - a sliver of a bench on which the Virgin had once seated herself.

St David's House is an attractive brickbuilt guest house offering bed and breakfast accommodation. The large bright blue Georgian door welcome visitors to this comfortable establishment, orignally built in the mid-1500s. Originally the residence of the Bishop of Northampton, it comprises three storeys and is a Grade II listed building. There are five spacious and airy guest rooms: one double, one twin, two triples, one family room and one single. All are quiet, well-furnished and with charming accoutrements like the hand-made colourful bed quilts. The ground floor boasts the cosy and homely guest sitting room with inglenook fireplace and dining room. Proprietors Jennifer and Charles Renshaw moved to Little Walsingham and this guest house in 1993, and have worked hard to maintain the highest standards of taste, quality of service and comfort here. Their work has paid off: a happy and relaxed atmosphere pervades this charming establishment, and it makes a wonderful base from which to explore this part of Norfolk.

St David's House, Friday Market, Little Walsingham, Norfolk
NR22 6BY Tel: 01328 820633

EAST BARSHAM
3 miles NW of Fakenham off the B1105

MAP 8 REF S13

In the same year that Erasmus visited Little Walsingham, Henry VIII made the pilgrimage that all his royal predecessors since Richard I had undertaken. He stayed overnight at the enchanting early-Tudor mansion, **East Barsham Hall**, a glorious medley of mullioned windows, towers, turrets, and a group of 10 chimneys, each one individually carved with an amazing variety of styles. Since the King's visit, the Hall has had a succession of owners over the years, amongst them a Hapsburg Duke who entertained his neighbours in truly Imperial style before disappearing leaving behind some truly Imperial debts, and the pop group, the "Bee Gees". The Hall is today owned by a London businessman and not open to the public, but it stands for all to see as you enter the village.

After his overnight stay at East Barsham Hall, Henry VIII, like most other pilgrims, went first to the **Slipper Chapel**, a beautiful 14th century building about a mile away in Houghton St Giles. Here he removed his shoes and completed the last stretch on foot. Despite this show of piety, some 25 years later Henry had no hesitation in closing the Priory along with all the other monastic institutions in his realm, seizing its treasures and endowments, and having its image of the Virgin publicly burnt at Chelsea.

Custom-built as a guest house in 1993, bed and breakfast accommodation at the superior **Fieldview Guest House** combines the best features of a modern farmhouse with traditional standards of comfort and quality. Proprietors of Simon Batty and Christine Parker have a keen interest in astronomy, and will share this with interested guests. There are two double- and three twin-bedded rooms which share three well-appointed bathrooms. In addition, the ensuite Astronomer Royal room on the top floor has velux windows which allow for spectacular all-round views of the night sky. Extra beds are available upon prior request, so the house can sleep up to 16 people in comfort. Seven reflecting telescopes are on hand for guests to use, along with free training and advice. North Norfolk

Fieldview Guest House, West Barsham Road, East Barsham, Norfolk NR21 0AR Tel: 01328 820083 email: fieldview@csi.com website: www.ourworld.compuserve.com/homepages/fieldview

is the driest area of the UK, with a greater than average number of clear nights. Almost 100 miles from the nearest industrial area, the skies suffer from little or no light pollution and no industrial pollution.

The adjacent *Earth and Sky* bookshop is probably the largest specialising in astronomy in the UK. But guests certainly do not have to be astronomers to appreciate a break at Fieldview. Anyone wanting a relaxing break in one of the last unspoilt areas of England will enjoy a stay here. The large back garden is bordered by seemingly endless views of the countryside. The coast is designated an area of outstanding natural beauty and offers vast sandy beaches, saltmarsh, coastal woodland and miles of footpath to explore. Cycles are available for hire by residents (the National Cycle route passes close by the door) and Birdwatching and General Natural History Tours of the area are offered by the proprietors, conducted by expert Dr Ian Burrows. These tours take in some of the best birdwatching areas in the UK, as well as special secluded sites known only to a privileged few. Not suitable for children under six years of age. No smoking.

NEW HOUGHTON
7 miles W of Fakenham off the A148

Map 8 ref S13

About seven miles west of Fakenham stands **Houghton Hall**, home of the Marquess of Cholmondely and one of Norfolk's most magnificent buildings. This glorious demi-palace was built in the Palladian style during the 1720s by Sir Robert Walpole, England's first Prime Minister. The Walpoles had been gentlemen of substance here since the 14th century. With his family revenues augmented by the considerable profits Sir Robert extracted from his political office, he was in a position to spend lavishly and ostentatiously on his new house. The first step was to completely destroy the village of Houghton, (it spoilt the view), and re-house the villagers a mile away at New Houghton.

Although Sir Robert deliberately cultivated the manner of a bluff, down-to-earth Norfolk squire, the personal decisions he made regarding the design and furnishings of the house reveal a man of deep culture and refined taste. It was he who insisted that the Hall could not be built in homely Norfolk brick, but in the whole of the county there is virtually no stone suitable for construction on this scale. The expensive decision was taken to use the exceptionally durable stone quarried at Aislaby in North Yorkshire, transporting it by sea from Whitby to King's Lynn.

16th century was a farmhouse. The old farm buildings have been splendidly renovated and converted to tell the story of village life and Cambridgeshire farming up to modern times. **Anglesey Abbey** dates from 1600 and was built on the site of an Augustinian priory, but the house and the 100-acre garden came together as a unit thanks to the vision of the 1st Lord Fairhaven. The garden, created in its present form from the 1930s, is a wonderful place for a stroll, with wide grassy walks, open lawns, a riverside walk, a working water mill and one of the finest collections of garden statuary in the country. There's also a plant centre, shop and restaurant. At nearby **Cottenham**, on the B1049, All Saints Church has an unusual tower of yellow and pink Jacobean brick topped with four pinnacles that look like pineapples. The original tower fell down in a gale and this replacement was partially funded by former US President Calvin Coolidge, one of whose ancestors had been living in the village when the tower fell down.

SWAFFHAM
MAP 8 REF R16

8 miles NE of Cambridge on the B1102

Swaffham Prior gives double value to the visitor, with two churches in the same churchyard and two fine old windmills. The Churches of St Mary and St Cyriac stand side by side, a remarkable and dramatic sight in the steeply rising churchyard. One of the mills, a restored 1850s tower mill, still produces flour and can be visited by appointment. At **Swaffham Bulbeck**, a little way to the south, stands another Church of St Mary, with a 13th century tower and 14th century arcades and chancel. Look for the fascinating carvings on the wooden benches and a 15th century cedarwood chest decorated with biblical scenes.

LINTON
MAP 8 REF R16

10 miles SE of Cambridge on the B1052

The village is best known for its zoo, but visitors will also find many handsome old buildings and the Church of St Mary the Virgin, built mainly in Early English style. A world of wildlife set in 16 acres of spectacular gardens; **Linton Zoo** is a major wildlife breeding centre and part of the inter-zoo breeding programme for endangered species. Collections include wild cats, birds, snakes and insects. For children there is a play area and, in summer, pony rides and a bouncy castle. **Chilford Hall vineyard**, on the B1052 between Linton and Balsham, comprises 18 acres of vines, with tours and tastings available.Some two miles further off the A604, **Bartlow Hills** are the site of the largest Roman burial site to be unearthed in Europe.

SHEPRETH
MAP 7 REF Q16

8 miles S of Cambridge off A10

A paradise for lovers of nature and gardens and a great starting point for country walks. **Shepreth L Moor Nature Reserve** is an L-shaped area of wet meadowland - now a rarity - that is home to birds and many rare plants. The nearby **Willers Mill Wildlife Park & Fish Farm** is a haven in natural surroundings to a wide variety of animals, which visitors can touch and feed. Around 18th century **Docwra's Manor** is a series of enclosed gardens with multifarious plants that is worth a visit at any time of year. Fowlmere, on the other side of the A10, is another important nature reserve, with hides and trails for the serious watcher.

DUXFORD
MAP 8 REF R16

8 miles S of Cambridge off A505, by J10 of the M11

Part of the Imperial War Museum, **Duxford Aviation Museum** is probably the leader in its field in Europe, with an outstanding collection of over 150 historic aircraft from biplanes through Spitfires to supersonic jets. The American Air Museum, where aircraft are suspended as if in flight, is part of this terrific place, which was built on a former Raf and US fighter base. Major air shows take place several times a year, and among the permanent features are a reconstructed wartime operations room, a hands-on exhibition for children and a dramatic land warfare hall with tanks, military vehicles and artillery. Everyone should take time to see this marvellous show - and it should be much more than a flying visit! At nearby **Hinxton** is another mill: a 17th century water mill that is grinding once more.

ARRINGTON
Map 7 ref Q16

8 miles SW of Cambridge off the A603

18th century **Wimpole Hall**, owned by the National Trust, is probably the most spectacular country mansion in the whole county. The lovely interiors are the work of several celebrated architects, and there's a fine collection of furniture and pictures. The magnificent formally laid-out grounds include a Victorian parterre, a rose garden and a walled garden. Landscaped **Wimpole Park**, with hills, woodland, lakes and a Chinese bridge, provides miles of wonderful walking and is perfect for anything from a gentle stroll to a strenuous hike. A brilliant attraction for all the family is **Wimpole Home Farm**, a working farm that is the largest rare breeds centre in East Anglia. The animals include Bagot goats, Tamworth pigs, Soay sheep and Longhorn cattle, and there's also a pets corner and horse-drawn wagon ride. Children can spend hours with the animals or in the adventure playground.

ELY
Map 8 ref R15

13 miles NE of Cambridge off the A10

Ely is the jewel in the crown of the Fens, in whose history the majestic **Cathedral** and the Fens themselves have played major roles. The Fens' influence is apparent even in the name: Ely was once known as Elge or Elig (eel island) because of the large number of eels which lived in the surrounding fenland. Ely owes its existence to St Etheldreda, Queen of Northumbria, who in 673AD founded a monastery on the 'Isle of Ely', where she remained as abbess until her death in 679. It was not until 1081 that work started on the present Cathedral, and in 1189 this remarkable example of Romanesque architecture was completed. The most outstanding feature in terms of both scale and beauty is the Octagon, built to replace the original Norman tower, which collapsed in 1322. Alan of Walsingham was the inspired architect of this massive work, which took 30 years to complete and whose framework weighs an estimated 400 tons. Many other notable components include the 14th century Lady Chapel, the largest in England, the Prior's Door, the painted nave ceiling and St Ovin's cross, the only piece of Saxon stonework in the building. The Cathedral is set within the walls of the monastery, and many of the ancient buildings still stand as a tribute to the incredible skill and craftsmanship of their designers and builders. Particularly worth visiting among these are the monastic buildings in the College, the Great Hall and Queens Hall. Just beside the Cathedral is the Almonry, in whose 12th century vaulted undercroft visitors can take coffee, lunch or tea - outside in the garden if the weather permits. Two other attractions which should not be

Ely Cathedral and Market Square

missed are the **Brass Rubbing Centre**, where visitors can make their own rubbings from replica brasses, and the **Museum of Stained Glass**. The latter, housed in the south Triforium of the Cathedral, is the only museum of stained glass in the country and contains over 100 original panels from every period, tracing the complete history of stained glass.

Just a five-minute walk from Ely's famous Cathedral, **The West End House** pub is a convenient spot for a quiet drink amid traditional comforts. Owner Vincenzo Teti is originally from Rome, Italy; he has run this distinguished pub since 1998. He is a friendly and hospitable host, helping to make the pub popular with locals and visitors alike. Formerly three separate cottages dating back to around the 15th century, the buildings were converted into one extensive pub in 1913. The exterior is a striking white with red and green trimming (mirroring the

colours of the Italian flag), while the interior is warm, friendly and inviting. This completely unspoilt traditional pub has a central brick and black-beamed bar. The main bar area is open-plan in design, incorporating separate 'rooms' and intimate areas. There is a large open fire, attractive carpeting, comfortable seating and decorative touches on the walls, including a collection

The West End House, 16 West End Road, Ely, Cambridgeshire CB6 3AY Tel: 01353 662907

of shining brassware and war-time Air Force memorabilia. In one part of the bar area there is a small snug with upholstered bench seating and attractive exposed brick walls. The drink on offer has earned this pub a well-deserved place in the *Good Beer Guide*, and include Courage Directors, Marston's Pedigree, Boddington's, Wadworth 6X and Webster's Yorkshire Bitter. This wet bar has these and many other excellent well-kept beers, as well as a choice selection of wines, spirits, lagers and non-alcoholic beverages. Vincenzo also stocks some fine beers from his native Italy, including Birra Peroni and Nastro Azzuro. The choice and welcoming ambience in this fine establishment make it well worth a visit.

Ely's **Tourist Information Centre** is itself a tourist attraction, since it is housed in a pretty black and white timbered building that was once the home of Oliver Cromwell. It is the only remaining house, apart from Hampton Court, where Oliver Cromwell and his family are known to have lived; parts of it trace back to the 13th century, and its varied history includes periods as a public house and, more recently, a vicarage. The Old Gaol, in Market Street, houses **Ely Museum**, with nine galleries telling the Ely story from the Ice Age to modern times. The tableaux of the condemned and debtors' cells are particularly fascinating and poignant. Ely is not just the past, and the fine architecture and sense of history blend well with the bustle of the streets and the shops and the riverside. That bustle is at its most bustling on Thursday, when the largest general market in the area is held.

HADDENHAM

MAP 8 REF R15

5 miles SW of Ely on the A1123

More industrial splendour: **Haddenham Great Mill**, built in 1803 for a certain Daniel Cockle, is a glorious sight, and one definitely not to be missed. It has four sails and three sets of grinding stones, one of which is working. The mill last worked commercially in 1946 and was restored between 1992 and 1998. Open on the first Sunday of each month and by appointment. Tel: 01353 740798. The Church of St Andrew stands on a hillside. Look for the stained-glass window depicting two souls entering Heaven, and the memorial (perhaps the work of Grinling Gibbons) to Christopher Wren's sister Anne Brunsell.

STRETHAM   MAP 8 REF R15

5 miles S of Ely off A10/A1123

The **Stretham Old Engine**, a fine example of a land drainage steam engine, is housed in a restored, tall-chimneyed brick engine house. Dating from 1831, it is one of 90 steam pumping engines installed throughout the Fens to replace 800 windmills. It is the last to survive, having worked until 1925 and still under restoration. During the great floods of 1919 it really earned its keep by working non-stop for 47 days and nights.

WICKEN   MAP 8 REF R15

9 miles S of Ely off the A1123

Owned by the National Trust, **Wicken Fen** is the oldest nature reserve in the country, 600 acres of undrained fenland, famous for its rich plant, insect and bird life and a delight for both naturalists and ramblers. Features include boardwalk and nature trails, hides and watchtowers, a cottage with 1930s furnishings, a working windpump (the oldest in the country), a visitor centre and a shop. Open daily dawn to dusk. St Lawrence's Church is well worth a visit, small and secluded among trees. In the churchyard are buried Oliver Cromwell and several members of his family. One of Cromwell's many nicknames was Lord of the Fens: he defended the rights of the Fenmen against those who wanted to drain the land without providing adequate compensation.

SOHAM   MAP 8 REF R15

6 miles SE of Ely on the A142 bypass

Do not sail past Soham without stopping to look at (or visit if it is a Sunday or Bank Holiday) **Downfield Windmill**. Built in 1726 as a smock mill, it was destroyed by gales and rebuilt in 1890 as an octagonal tower mill. It still grinds corn and produces a range of flours and breads for sale. St Andrew's Church is a fine example of the Perpendicular style of English Gothic architecture. Very grand and elaborate, it was built on the site of a 7th century cathedral founded by St Felix of Burgundy. The 15th century west tower has an ornate parapet and two medieval porches. Note, too, the chancel with its panelling and stained glass. A plaque in Soham commemorates engine driver Ben Gimbert and fireman James Nightall, who were taking an ammunition train through the town when a wagon caught fire. They uncoupled it and began to haul it into open country. The wagon exploded, killing the fireman and a signalman.

HUNTINGDON   MAP 7 REF Q15

18 miles W of Ely on the A141

The former county town of Huntingdonshire is an ancient town first settled to any extent by the Romans. It boasts many grand Georgian buildings, including the handsome three-storeyed Town Hall, and the Church of All Saints displays many architectural styles, from medieval to Victorian. Oliver Cromwell was born in Huntingdon in 1599 and attended Huntingdon Grammar School, where Samuel Pepys was also a pupil. Cromwell was MP for Huntingdon in the Parliament of 1629, was made a JP in 1630 and moved to St Ives in the following year. Rising to power as an extremely able military commander in the Civil War, he raised troops from the region and made his headquarters in the Falcon Inn. Appointed Lord Protector in 1653, Cromwell was never proclaimed King, though he ran the country until his death in 1658. The school he attended is now the **Cromwell Museum**, housing the only public collection relating specifically to him. The museum's exhibits include portraits and personal objects, among them a hat and a seal. Open Tuesday-Sunday.

GRAFHAM
MAP 7 REF P15
5 miles SW of Huntingdon on the B661

Created in the mid-1960s as a reservoir, **Grafham Water** offers a wide range of outdoor activities for visitors of all ages, with 1,500 acres of beautiful countryside, including the lake itself. A ten-mile perimeter track is great for jogging or cycling, and there's excellent sailing, windsurfing and fly fishing. The area is a Site of Special Scientific Interest, and an ample nature reserve at the western edge is run jointly by Anglian Water and the Wildlife Trust. There are nature trails, information boards, a wildlife garden and a dragonfly pond. Many species of waterfowl stay here at various times of the year, and bird-watchers have the use of six hides, three of them accessible by wheelchair. An exhibition centre has displays and video presentations of the reservoir's history, a gift shop and a café.

ST NEOTS
MAP 7 REF P16
10 miles SW of Huntingdon off the A1

Founded in the 10th century by Benedictine monks, St Neots repays a visit on foot, since there are many interesting old buildings tucked away. The Church of St Mary is a very fine edifice, a good example of Late Medieval Architecture. **St Neots Museum** - opened in 1995 - tells the story of the town and the surrounding area. Housed in the former magistrates court and police station, it still has the original cells. Open Wednesday to Saturday. Three miles north of St Neots at **Little Paxton** is **Paxton Pits Nature Reserve**, where there are bird hides, nature trails and a visitor centre. It has thousands of visiting waterfowl, including one of the largest colonies of cormorants. Just north again is the Saxon Minster at Great Paxton.

HOUGHTON
MAP 7 REF Q15
4 miles E of Huntingdon on the A1123

Houghton Mill is a popular tourist attraction, signposted from the A1123 and enjoying a quiet island location. An impressive watermill built in the 17th century, the mill is owned by the National Trust and is open most afternoons in the summer. Milling takes place on Sundays and Bank Holiday Mondays, and the site also contains an art gallery, miniature millstones to turn by hand, and a tea room. **Houghton Meadows** is a Site of Special Scientific Interest with an abundance of hay meadow species. One of the most popular walks in the whole area links Houghton with St Ives.

ST IVES
MAP 7 REF Q15
5 miles E of Huntingdon off the A1123

"As I was going to St Ives I met a man with seven wives.
Each wife had seven sacks, each sack had seven cats, each cat had seven kits.
Kits, cats, sacks and wives, how many were going to St Ives?"
None, of course, but let's hope they had a good time while they were there. St Ives, named after St Ivo - a Persian bishop who came here in the Dark Ages to spread a little light, is an ancient town which once held a huge annual fair . In the Middle Ages, kings bought cloth for their households at great wool fairs and markets, and a market is still held every Monday. The Bank Holiday Monday markets are particularly lively affairs, and the Michaelmas fair fills the town centre for three days. Seagoing barges once navigated up to the famous six-arched bridge that was built in the 15th century and has a most unusual two-storey chapel in its middle. Oliver Cromwell lived in St Ives in the 1630s and the statue of him on Market Hill, with its splendid hat, is one of the most familiar landmarks. It was made in bronze, with a Portland stone base,

and was erected in 1901. It was originally designed for Huntingdon, but they wouldn't accept it! Clive Sinclair developed his tiny TVs and pocket calculators in the town, and a famous son of St Ives was the great Victorian rower John Goldie, whose name is remembered each year by the second Cambridge boat in the Boat Race.

The **Norris Museum**, in a delightful setting by the river, tells the story of Huntingdonshire for the past 60 million years or so, with anything from fossils, mammoth tusks and models of the great historic reptiles through flint tools, Roman artefacts and Civil War armour to lace-making and ice-skating displays, and contemporary works of art. A truly fascinating place that is open throughout the year, admission free.

Just outside St Ives are **Wilthorn Meadow**, a Site of Natural History Interest where Canada geese are often to be seen, and **Holt Island Nature Reserve**, where high-quality willow is being grown to re-introduce the traditional craft of basket-making. Spot the butterflies, dragonflies and kingfishers.

EARITH   Map 7 ref Q15
9 miles E of Huntingdon on the A1123

The **Ouse Washes**, a special protection area, run north-east from the village to Earith Pits, a well-known habitat for birds and crawling creatures; some of the pits are used for fishing. The Washes are a wetland of major international importance supporting such birds as ruffs, Bewick and Whooper swans, and hen harriers. The average bird population is around 20,000. Some of the meadows flood in winter, and ice-skating is popular when the temperature really drops. There's a great tradition of ice skating in the Fens, and the Fenmen were the national champions until the 1930s.

PETERBOROUGH   Map 7 ref P14
20 miles N of Huntingdon off the A15

The second city of Cambridgeshire has a long and interesting history that traces back to the Bronze Age, as can be seen in the archaeological site at Flag Fen. Although a cathedral city, it is also a New Town (designated in 1967), so modern development and expansion have vastly increased its facilities while retaining the quality of its historic heart. Its crowning glory is, of course, the Romanesque **Cathedral**, built in the 12th and 13th centuries on a site that had seen Christian worship since 655AD. Henry VIII made the church a cathedral, and his first queen, Catharine of Aragon, is buried here, as for a while was Mary Queen of Scots after her execution at Fotheringay. Features to note are the huge (85') arches of the West Front, the unique painted wooden nave ceiling, some exquisite late-15th century fan vaulting, and the tomb of Catharine. Though the best known of the city's landmarks, the Cathedral is by no means the only one. The **Peterborough Museum and Art Gallery** covers all aspects of the history of Peterborough from the Jurassic period to Victorian times.

There are twin attractions for railway enthusiasts in the shape of **Railworld**, a hands-on exhibition dealing with modern rail travel, and

Peterborough Cathedral

the wonderful **Nene Valley Railway**, which operates 15-mile steam-hauled trips between Peterborough and its HQ and museum at Wansford. Thomas the Tank Engine, which used to work at a local sugar beet factory, is the children's favourite, but there are many other locomotives from the British Railways days, including 'Brittania' (away in 1999 for a major refit) and a Bulleid Battle of Britain Pacific. A feature on the main railway line at Peterborough is the historic Iron Bridge, part of the old Great Northern Railway and still virtually as when built by Lewis Cubitt in 1852.

Just outside the city, by the river Nene, is **Thorpe Meadows Sculpture Park**, one of several open spaces in and around the city with absorbing collections of modern sculpture.

THORNEY   MAP 7 REF Q14
8 miles E of Peterborough on the A47

Thorney Abbey, the church of St Mary and St Botolph, is the dominating presence even though what now stands is but a small part of what was once one of the greatest of the Benedictine Abbeys. Gravestones in the churchyard are evidence of a Huguenot colony settling here after fleeing from France in the wake of the St Bartholomew's Day massacre of 1572. The **Thorney Heritage Museum** is a small, independently run museum of great fascination, describing the development of the village from a Saxon monastery, via Benedictine Abbey to a model village built in the 19th century by the Dukes of Bedford. The main innovation was a 10,000 gallon water tank that supplied the whole village; other villages had to use unfiltered river water.

MARCH   MAP 7 REF Q14
15 miles E of Peterborough off the A141

March once occupied the second largest 'island' in the great level of Fens, and as the land was drained the town grew as a trading and religious centre, and in more recent times as a market town and major railway hub. **March and District Museum**, in the High Street, tells the story of the people and the history of March and the surrounding area, and includes a working forge and a reconstruction of a turn-of-the-century home. St Wendreda's uniquely dedicated church, at Town End, is notable for its magnificent timber roof, a double hammerbeam with 120 carved angels, a fine font and some impressive gargoyles. John Betjeman declared the church to be 'worth cycling 40 miles into a headwind to see'.

The **Nene-Ouse Navigation Link** runs through the town, affording many attractive riverside walks, and just outside the town, off the B1099, is **Dunhams Wood**, four acres of woodland set among the fens. The site contains an enormous variety of trees, along with sculptures and a miniature railway. Also on the outskirts, signposted from the A141 and B1101, is **Stagsholt Farm Park and Stud**, home to many horses (including the superb Suffolk Punch) and housing a fascinating array of farming and rural bygones.

WISBECH   MAP 8 REF R14
21 miles E of Peterborough off the A47

One of the largest of the Fenland towns, a port in medieval times and still enjoying shipping trade with Europe. Somewhere along the navigable channel to the sea King John lost his jewels. Wisbech is at the centre of a thriving agricultural region and the 18th century in particular saw the building of rows of handsome houses, notably in North Brink and South Brink, which face each other across the river. The finest of all the properties is undoubtedly **Peckover House**, built in 1722 and bought at the end of the 18th century by Jonathan Peckover, a member of the Quaker banking family. The family gave the building to the National Trust in 1948. Behind its elegant facade are splendid panelled rooms, Georgian fireplaces with richly carved overmantels, and ornate plaster decorations. At the back of the house is a beautiful walled garden with summerhouses and an orangery. No 1 South Brink is the birthplace of Octavia Hill (1838-1912), co-founder of the National Trust and a tireless worker for the cause of the poor, particularly in the sphere of housing. The house is now the **Octavia Hill Museum** with displays and exhibits commemorating her work. More Georgian splendour is evident in the area where the Norman castle stood. The castle was replaced by a bishop's palace in 1478 and in the 17th century by a mansion built

Peckover House

for Cromwell's Secretary of State John Thurloe. Local builder Joseph Medworth built the present Regency villa in 1816, and of the Thurloe mansion only the gate piers remain. The **Wisbech and Fenland Museum** is one of the oldest purpose-built museums in the country, and in charming Victorian surroundings visitors can view displays of porcelain, coins, rare rocks, Egyptian tomb treasures and several items of national importance, including the manuscript of Charles Dickens' *Great Expectations*, Napoleon's Sèvres breakfast set captured at Waterloo, and an ivory chess set that belonged to Louis XIV.

Wisbech is the stage for East Anglia's premier church **flower festival**, with flowers in four churches, strawberry teas, crafts, bric-a-brac, plants and a parade of floats. The event takes place at the beginning of July. The most important of the churches is the Church of St Peter and St Paul, with two naves under one roof, and an independent tower with a peal of ten bells. Note the royal arms of James I and the 17th century wall monuments in the chancel. Other sights to see in Wisbech include Elgoods Brewery on North Brink and the impressive 68' limestone memorial to Thomas Clarkson, one of the earliest leaders of the movement to abolish slavery. The monument was designed by Sir Giles Gilbert Scott in Gothic style.

5 Heart of England

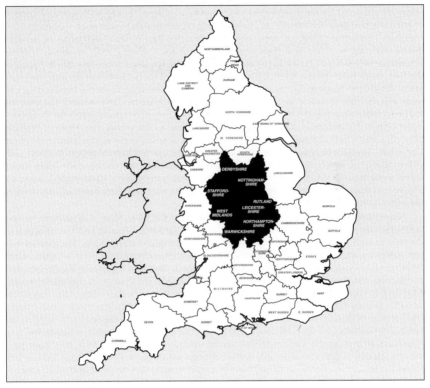

INTRODUCTION

The Heart of England region denotes the green and pleasant centre of the nation, represented by the counties of Warwickshire and the West Midlands, Northamptonshire (known as the Rose of the Shires), tiny Rutland, Leicestershire, Staffordshire, Derbyshire and Nottinghamshire. It is a region rich in history, natural beauty and a proud industrial heritage.

The extreme northwest of Warwickshire, dominated by the major West Midlands cities of Birmingham and Coventry, often gets overlooked by visitors but repays a closer look. It boasts a wealth of beautiful gardens, some excellent museums and historic buildings, and a long and distinguished industrial and cultural heritage. For northeastern Warwickshire, Rugby - home of the famous public school which introduced the game of rugby football to the world - is the largest town, which is predominated by smaller and very picturesque villages and hamlets. This part of the county is also home to some outstanding country parks, woodland and waterways. The Oxford and Union Canals run through it, as do the Rivers Leam, Avon, Itchen and Swift, all affording a wealth of boating and watersports facilities as well as some very peaceful and attractive walks along the towpath and riverbanks. This part of the county is also rich in its own history, having seen the hatching and foiling of the Gunpowder Plot in 1605, and some of the greatest battles of the English Civil War. The region also boasts many fine museums.

A rich vein of medieval and Tudor history runs through the heart of Warwickshire. The romantic ruins of Kenilworth Castle, the grandeur of Warwick Castle, and the elegance of Leamington Spa set the tone for this most delightful part of the county. While Stratford will be the obvious focal point for most visitors to southern Warwickshire, the region boasts any number of attractive and peaceful villages and hamlets well off the beaten tourist track. Southern Warwickshire's waterways form an important and extensive part of the 2,000 miles of Britain's inland network, boasting as it does long stretches of the Oxford Canal, as well as restored lengths of the Stratford Canal and the upper Avon. This part of the county was also the scene of the first major battle of the English Civil War - at Edgehill in 1645. As will be seen, there are many delights to treasure in this part of Warwickshire, quite apart from the outstanding cultural and historic treasures in Stratford-upon-Avon itself, particularly around the extreme southern edge of the county, which skirts the Cotswold Scarp and is dotted with the distinctive ochre-coloured ironstone cottages indigenous to this part of the world. The 'Heart of England Way' runs south from the remains of the historic Forest of Arden to the northeastern edge of the Cotswolds. As might be expected, this part of Warwickshire is rich in rural delights. Village after village along the Rivers Avon, Arrow or Alne, many relatively untouched since Tudor times, reflect some of the best traditional architecture and scenery to be found in the region. There are also several impressive hilltop views to be had along the way, revealing breathtaking views of the surrounding countryside.

Northamptonshire is shaped like a laurel leaf, with the River Nene a distinctive feature. Wherever one journeys across the county one is never far from its banks and the reflection of the trees in high summer on its shimmering waters can be quite breathtaking. The alluvial soils and gravel terraces of the Nene Valley have been continuously farmed since Neolithic times and there are remains of many Anglo-Saxon settlements. Bones of horses, woolly rhinoceroses and mammoths have been unearthed, giving some hint as to the kind of animal life Paleolithic man used to contend with. Polished stone axes indicate that their basic way of life was mixed farming. During the Roman occupation, the Nene Valley lay within the most densely populated region of Britain. Forts were built a day's march apart round the Fens and towards the Trent and Humber. One such fortress, some 30 acres in size, was discovered at Lonthorpe near Peterborough and, as the legionnaires advanced towards the north and west, they built their famous straight roads. The most impressive sections are those of Watling Street (A5), which enters the county at Old Stratford and runs in a rigid straight line for eight and a half miles to Towcester. And whatever your taste in scenery, there is something for everyone from rolling meadows to a spectacular view over seven counties. The main centres of population all have their own delightful corners, but the county is perhaps even better known for the many picturesque villages which dot the landscape.

Rutland has emerged once again as a county in its own right, after over 20 years of being forced into marriage with Leicestershire. Rutland has villages of thatch and ironstone, clustered around their churches and the countryside is rich in pasture where once deer were hunted. Its central feature is Rutland Water, its 3,100 acres making it one of the largest man-made lakes in northern Europe. Started in 1971 to supply water of the East Midlands towns, it was created by damming the valley near Empingham. The result is an attractively landscaped lake, around five miles long which also serves as a popular recreational and leisure centre where sailing, water skiing and windsurfing are pursued. And among its lovely villages are the larger towns such as Uppingham and Oakham, offering their own diversions, sights and sounds for the visitor.

Leicestershire is generally dismissed by those who have merely driven through it as flat and pretty well covered with red brick towns and villages. Its most attractive features are shy and quiet and have to be sought out but they amply reward the explorer. The county is divided into two almost equal parts by the River Soar, which flows northward into the Trent. It separates the east and west by a broad valley, flowing like a silver ribbon through historic Leicester in the very heart of the county. This capital town was thriving in Roman days and is one of the oldest towns in England. It has managed to retain outstanding monuments of almost every age of English history. Nearly half of the county live in Leicester, the rest are in over 200 villages. Agriculture and industry grew hand in hand; the long hair of the sheep is famous for producing fine woollens, and the end of the 17th century saw the beginning of the now world-wide hosiery trade. Loughborough has been famous for making bells for more than 100 years, their product pealing from many of England's church towers. At Melton Mowbray, wondrous pies have been made on a commercial scale since 1830. Red Leicester cheese was made in the southern part of the county in the 1700s, but now the only genuine product is made at Melton Mowbray, which also makes Stilton and of course the superlative pork pies. And every schoolchild knows the name of Bosworth Field, one of the momentous battles which changed the course of English history. All who know Leicestershire know Swithland Wood; the experience of walking through the dense carpet of bluebells in early summer is without parallel. Charnwood Forest has an area of 60 square miles, but the little mountain region has lost much of its woodland. Even so it remains an area of outstanding natural beauty, rich in flora and fauna of all kinds.

The Staffordshire Moorland region, bordering the Peak District National Park, is an attractive area often overlooked for its better known neighbour. The undulating pastures of the moorlands, along with the fresh air and ancient weather-worn crags, make this the ideal place to walk, cycle or trek. It is also an area full of character with charming villages and a wealth of history. An ancient countryside, with many of the farms going back hundreds and hundreds of years, the Industrial Revolution has also left its marks upon the landscape. The two great reservoirs of Rudyard and Tittesworth, built to provide a water supply to the growing industry and population of the Midlands, offer peaceful havens for a wide variety of plants, animals and birds as well as recreational facilities such as fishing and boating. The area around Stoke-on-Trent is famous the world over for its pottery industry. Originally centred on the five towns of Stoke, Tunstall, Burslem, Hanley and Longton, The Potteries were at the heart of the Industrial Revolution. Both coal and clay were found locally, though imported clay from Cornwall was later used, which gave rise to the start of the industry but it was the foresight and ingenuity of men such as Joshua Wedgwood and James Minton, that really turned the cottage industry into production on a much larger scale. To support the industry in and around the centre, a network of canals, and later railways, was begun. The Trent and Mersey Canal, built by James Brindley with the support of Wedgwood and his friend the Duke of Bridgewater, was finally completed in 1777 and made possible navigation from coast to coast, between the busy ports of Liverpool and Hull. Together, the Trent and Mersey Canal, the Staffordshire and Worcester Canal, begun in the same year, the Shropshire Union Canal to the west and the Middlewich branch of the Llangollen Canal, form a wonderful four counties ring that can be undertaken wholly or partly by boat. Southwest Staffordshire encompasses many changing landscapes, from the busy, industrial towns of Stafford and Burton upon Trent to the peace and quiet of Cannock Chase. In the 18th century, to serve these two major towns, and in grander schemes that joined the Midlands to such ports as Liverpool and Bristol, the area's rivers were supplemented by a series of canals. The Trent and Mersey Canal and the Shropshire and Worcester Canal, which join together to the west of Stafford, are now the preserve of pleasure boats. The towpaths, which can be joined at many points, make for easy walking but in this relatively flat landscape, cycling offers a quicker means of changing the horizon. Lying between Stafford and Burton upon Trent is the ancient hunting ground of Cannock Chase. Along with the Hednesford Hills, the Chase provides a wonderful open area of woodland and moorland that is one of the county's great recreational centres. Southeast Staffordshire, meanwhile, also has a lot to offer. Both Lichfield, a cathedral city, and Tamworth have roots which date back well beyond the Industrial Revolution and, behind the modern city offices, medieval buildings can still be found.

Derbyshire's northwestern region has come to be synonymous with The Peak District. The first of Britain's National Parks, The Peak District covers an area of 540 square miles. Its situation, close to the large industrial conurbations of Manchester, Sheffield, Derby, Nottingham and Staffordshire, have meant that this region of high, windswept moorland and charming river valleys has always been popular. From the time of the first railways into the area, in the mid 19th century, the Peak District has been a mecca for walkers and those wishing to discover its many secrets. The National Park is scattered with the remains of ancient settlements. The origin of the word 'peak' probably comes from the Pecsaetans, or hill people, a primitive tribe who are thought to have settled here in around the 7th century. At most of the crossings into the Park there are millstones standing on stone plinths at the side of the road. These are used as boundary markers by the Park Authority, which has also adopted the millstone symbol as its logo. The high moors of this northern part of the Peak District National Park are ripe for exploring on foot, and a walk from the Kinder Reservoir will lead to the western edge of Kinder Scout. This whole area is really a series of plateaus, rather than mountains and valleys, with the highest point on Kinder Scout some 2,088 feet above sea level. In this remote and wild area the walker can feel a real sense of freedom - however, it is worth remembering that the moors, with their treacherous peat bogs and unpredictable mists which can rise quickly even in summer, should not be dismissed as places for a casual ramble. To the eastern side of this region are the three reservoirs created by flooding of the upper valley of the River Derwent. Howden, Derwent, and Ladybower provide water for the East Midlands but their remote location, along with the many recreational activities found there, make them popular places to visit. The Derwent dam is particularly famous as the site of practice exercises for the Dambusters of the Second World War. The Derbyshire Dales, sometimes also known as the Central Peaks and occupying the central area of the Peak District National Park, are less wild and isolated than the remote High Peak area. The two main rivers, the Wye and the Derwent, which both have their source further north, are, in this region, at a more gentle stage of their course. The southern section of the Peak District is probably best known for the beautiful Dovedale, yet it is not the only dale worth exploring. The River Manifold offers some equally wonderful scenery and, in particular, there is Ilam. A beautifully preserved estate village, with a well established youth hostel, this is also a popular starting point from which to explore the Manifold Valley. The ancient custom of well-dressing is almost exclusively confined to the limestone areas of the county. The porous rock, through which rainfall seeped leaving the surface completely dry just a few hours after heavy rainfall, meant that, for the people of these closeknit communities, the well or spring was of utmost importance. If this dried up, the lives of the whole community were at risk. In the last 50 years or so, many villages who had not dressed a well for centuries, if ever, are now joining in the colourful tradition. Northeast Derbyshire and the District of Bolsover, with the Peak District to the west, South Yorkshire to the north and Nottinghamshire to the east, centres around Chesterfield. This was the heart of the county's coal-mining area, and many of the towns and villages reflect the prosperity the mines brought in Victorian times. Sadly, the vast majority of the collieries are now closed; there was for a while a period of decline, but visitors today will be surprised at the wealth of history and fine architecture to be seen throughout the region. Sometimes overlooked, this part of Derbyshire is well worth exploring, and there are many new and interesting sights and attractions to discover. The ancient custom of well-dressing is just as popular and well-executed here as elsewhere in the county, plus there are curiosities such as a "castle that isn't a castle despite its battlements, a church clock that has 63 minutes in an hour and an Italian-style garden in the grounds owned by a famous English family", according to the North East Derbyshire District Council. Derbyshire's Amber Valley and Erewash regions cover the eastern and southeastern parts of Derbyshire respectively. The Rivers Amber, Derwent and Trent run through this part of the county. Though the scenery is perhaps less dramatic than the popular Peak District, in which most of north Derbyshire lies, there are ample opportunities to enjoy pleasant walks in the extensive grounds of many of the estates. The southeast area of Derbyshire has been heavily influenced by the two towns of Derby and Nottingham. Originally, small farming communities many of the villages grew at the time of the Industrial Revolution and they can, in many cases, be characterised by rows of workers' cottages. However, notwithstanding this there are some interesting and unique buildings to be found in this corner of Derbyshire.

Finally, in the valley of the River Trent which runs through the southern part of the county can be found many splendid stately homes. The scenery affords ample opportunities to enjoy pleasant walks. Derbyshire was at the forefront of modern thinking at the beginning of the Industrial Revolution. The chief inheritor of this legacy was Derby, and this city is still a busy industrial centre and home to the Industrial Museum. There are plenty of other places to visit in Derby, which is not, as is often supposed, the county town (that honour goes to Matlock). Truly an area of hidden places, there are many picturesque villages to be found here.

The county of Nottinghamshire, in the north Midlands, lies mainly on the low ground basin of the River Trent between the peaks of Derbyshire and South Yorkshire and the lowlands of Lincolnshire. It is a county of contrasts: Nottinghamshire has plenty of industry but it has also retained much of its rural heritage as well as the remains of the famous Forest of Sherwood. The county town, Nottingham, lies in the southwestern corner of Nottinghamshire and is, by far, the largest town. A lively mix of the old and new, Nottingham has a colourful history which spans the ages - from Anglo-Saxon times when it was founded by a tribal chief called Snot to the industrial expansion of the 19th century. Today, this blend of ancient and modern makes Nottingham a place worthy of exploration. The southeastern area of the county, south of the great Roman road, Fosse Way (now known as the A46), is a mass of small rural villages and hamlets. In the south, bordering the county of Leicestershire, these ancient settlements overlook the Vale of Belvoir and it was here that Thomas Cranmer, in the village of Aslockton, spent his early years. The region that could be termed "Industrial Nottinghamshire" lies close to the border with Derbyshire, and was once dominated by the coal mining industry. Once part of the great Forest of Sherwood, coal has been mined here for centuries though, until the late 18th century, this was always on a small scale. As Nottingham and the surrounding towns and villages became an important centre for the textile industry, chiefly hosiery but later there were some cotton mills, the need for reliable energy sources grew. Rural market towns expanded into industrial towns and their whole character changed as quick and cheap terraced housing was built for the influx of workers coming to jobs in the mills and the mines. The landscape also changed; though the forest and other land was cleared to make way for buildings and mines. During this time many agricultural communities were lost forever as the labourers moved to the more lucrative factories. Transportation was also important and the Erewash Canal was started in 1777 to take coal from the fields to the River Trent. Once a hive of activity, the canal fell into disrepair in the 1920s but it is now, once again, bustling though this time with pleasure craft.

Sherwood Forest is known to old and young alike, all over the world, thanks to the tales of Robin Hood and the various stories, films, and, television series made about this legendary hero of the people. Sherwood, the shire wood of Nottinghamshire, was once part of a great mass of forest land which covered much of central England; stretching from Nottingham in the south to Worksop in the north and from the Peak District to the Trent Valley in the east.

The area of Nottinghamshire through which the River Trent flows is a maze of country lanes and ancient villages. Only the southern area was ever part of the Royal Hunting Forest of Sherwood, and this flat and fertile land has been farmed for centuries. From the quiet and, basically, rural area of northern Nottinghamshire can be traced the origins of the United States of America. During the late 16th century, in the villages of north Nottinghamshire, those opposed to Elizabeth I's policy of Church government began to form themselves into the Pilgrim movement, held together in their firm belief in the freedom from State control of religious matters. The members of the Separatists group increased and they held their meetings in secret to escape persecution. By 1608, their persecution by James I became so great that the Pilgrim Fathers, as they were later to be called, fled to Holland. Some years later, in 1620, they sailed from Plymouth to America on board the *Mayflower*, landing at Cape Cod. From there they sent out an expedition to find a suitable settlement and, at a place now known as Forefathers Rock, in Plymouth, Massachusetts, the New World was established.

WARWICKSHIRE AND THE WEST MIDLANDS

BIRMINGHAM
MAP 6 REF L15
105 miles NW of London on the A45

Birmingham is perceived by many who don't know it well as a maze of glass-and-steel buildings and other modern monstrosities. It rewards a visit many times over, however, in its wealth of museums, marvellous public spaces, historic buildings and wealth of sights, sounds and attractions. It is a city with a rich and varied industrial history taking in everything from the first steam engine to button, buckles, clocks and chocolate.

In Birmingham's parish **Church of St Martin** there are memorials to the two Lords of the Manor, the de Berminghams. The Birmingham Symphony Orchestra, recognised as one of the finest in the world, perform a regular season in the classical Roman-inspired **Town Hall**, built by Joseph Hansom, of hansom cab fame , and E Welch. Mendelssohn gave several organ recitals here.

There are no fewer than 6,000 acres of parkland and open space in Birmingham. **Cannon Hill Park** in Edgbaston is one particular highlight. It has 80 acres of flower and ornamental gardens. Also in Edgbaston, on Westbourne Road, the **Botanical Gardens** comprise 15 acres and boast a Tropical House with lily pond, banana and cocoa trees, the Palm House, Orangery, National Bonsai Collection, Cactus House and the gardens themselves, filled with rhododendrons, azaleas and a good collection of trees. **Birmingham Nature Centre**, not far away on Pershore Road, has British and European wildlife - including wallaby, fallow deer, otters and reptiles - in indoor and outdoor enclosures resembling as closely as possible the creatures' native habitats. At **Edgbaston Reservoir** there is every kind of water recreation visitors could wish for.

The focus for shopping is New Street, Corporation Street, and the Bull Ring Shopping Centre; coming away from these areas there are some very attractive Victorian arcades which house the smaller speciality shops. Birmingham is tradition-

Botanical Gardens

ally a centre of jewellery - indeed there is an 18th-century church in St Paul's Square known simply as The Jewellers Church. The **Jewellery Quarter Discovery Centre** is a good place to start if you'd like to learn more about times past and present in the Birmingham jewellery trade. It is located on Vyse Street, centred round the preserved workshops of Smith & Pepper, still much as they were at the turn of the century. You will find jewellers still abound, especially in the Hockley area. Gunsmiths are also to be found here, another craft for which Birmingham is renowned.

The **Museum and Art Gallery** in Chamberlain Square represents the 17th, 18th, and 19th centuries, including the world's finest examples of works by the Pre-Raphaelites. The contemporary art of sculpture is also well represented. Costume, silver, textiles and ceramics as well as works of ethnography from around the world, among which is a large and rare copper Buddha from Sultangani. Public works of art include the murals in Colmore Circus. One of these depicts a Civil War battle, another the Industrial Revolution. **Holloway Circus** has an enormous mural measuring 85 feet by 14 feet and showing The Horse Fair of 1908. The **Barber Institute** at Birmingham University houses an excellent collection of paintings and sculptures. There is a wealth of Impressionist pieces, as well as the work of European masters.

Birmingham's newest museum is **Soho House**, a handsome Georgian building which has been carefully restored to its original elegance. Former home of the pioneering industrialist Matthew Boulton, James Watt's business partner and founder of the Soho Mint, who lived here from 1766 to 1809, it contains some of his original furnishings. Displays relate the story of the man and his times, and offer a chance to see some of the fruits of Boulton's nearby factory - buttons and buckles, ormolu clocks and vases, silver and Sheffield plate tableware - where he and Watt developed the steam engine.

There are some 2,000 listed buildings in Birmingham, dating from the Elizabethan, Jacobean, Georgian and Victorian periods. The 1879 neo-Renaissance **Council House** is an impressive testament to the city's success and achievements. The Curzon Street **Goods Station** is a colonnaded building dating from 1838. Built by Philip Hardwick, its Ionic portico celebrates the wonder of the then-new railway industry.

Let it not be forgotten that Birmingham is a city of canals. **Gas Street Basin** in the centre of Birmingham marks the hub of a 2,000 mile canal network. Canals run from here to Liverpool, Nottingham, London and Gloucester. The Basin also has quiet towpaths made for quiet strolling. The Tourist Information Centre has a great deal of information on pleasant walks that can be taken along Birmingham's extensive network of waterways, taking in many historic buildings, locks, factories and cottages along the way, as well as the plants and wildlife who make their home here.

Gas Street Basin

Sarehole Mill in Cole Bank Road in Hall Green is Birmingham's only working water mill. The former childhood haunt of J R R Tolkein (author of *The Hobbit* and *Lord of the Rings*), it was used as a flour mill and also to roll and smooth metal needed during the Industrial Revolution. The present buildings are mainly Georgian, having been rebuilt in the 1760s, were in use, commercially, right up to 1919.

Another nearby attraction well worth a visit is **Castle Bromwich Hall Gardens**, on Chester Road, about four miles east of the city centre. This boasts a collection of plants grown here in the 18th century, including historic herbs and vegetable species, shrubs and border plants, in a classic formal layout popular in the 1700s. Guided tours available.

KINGSBURY
7 miles NE of Birmingham off the A4097

MAP 6 REF M14

Kingsbury Water Park boasts over 600 acres of country park, with loads to see and do, including birdwatching, picnic sites, nature trails, fishing and good information centre. There is also a cosy cafe and special unit housing the park's shop and exhibition hall. Also with the park, **Broomey Croft Children's Farm** makes for an enjoyable and educational day out for all the family, with a wealth of animals housed in renovated early 19th-century farm buildings.

ASTON

Map 6 ref L14

2 miles N of Birmingham off the A34

Aston Hall was one of the last great Jacobean country houses to be built in England. Like Hatfield House and Blickling Hall, it has a highly intricate plan and a dramatic skyline of turrets, gables and chimneys. It is also administered by Birmingham Museum and Art Gallery, who have done much to make it a memorable place to visit. The house was built between 1618 and 1635 by Sir Thomas Holte, and remained the seat of the Holte family until it was sold off in 1817. King Charles I came to Aston Hall in 1642, at the beginning of the Civil War, and it was later be-

Aston Hall

sieged and sacked by Parliamentarian soldiers. Much Jacobean decorative work of high quality still survives, especially the moulded plasterwork. The house has a most wonderful staircase and Long Gallery.

BOURNVILLE

Map 6 ref L15

4 miles S of Birmingham off the A4040

This planned village built by the Cadbury family, which moved its factory from the city centre in 1879, is a testament to good labour relations. **Cadbury World** is located in the heart of the famous Bournville factory. Here visitors can follow the story of chocolate, from tropical rainforests to 16th century Spain and on to Georgian London and, finally, Victorian Birmingham. Of course, a highlight of any tour here is the chance to sample the modern day product! In the heart of Cadbury Village, **Selly Manor** comprises two carefully restored and maintained timber-framed Tudor houses, furnished in keeping

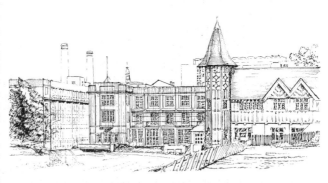

Cadbury's Bournville Plant

with the period and surrounded by abundant gardens. Chocolate magnate George Cadbury saved the Manor from demolition in the late 1800s; his son Lawrence carried on the restoration work by combing Europe in search of accurate furnishings, some of which date back to 1500.

YARDLEY
Map 6 ref M15
2 miles E of Birmingham off the A45/A4040

Blakesley Hall is Birmingham's finest Elizabethan building. Built in 1590, it is an extremely attractive timber-framed farmhouse which has been carefully restored. Owned by Birmingham Museum and Art Gallery, its rich, decorative framing and jettied first and second floors reflect the wealth of its Elizabethan owner and builder, Richard Smallbroke, one of the leading merchants of the time. A diminutive and rare Long Gallery survives, whilst in Smallbroke's bedroom the original wall paintings were uncovered in 1950. Some of the 12 rooms are furnished to look as they did in 1684, when an inventory of the house's contents was drawn up. Old Yardley village is one of Birmingham's outstanding conservation areas. Within walking distance of Blakesley Hall, it is truly remarkable for its medieval church and Trust School. Of particular note are the pretty Georgian cottages.

COVENTRY
Map 7 ref M15
15 miles E of Birmimgham off the A45

Although on the fringe of the West Midlands conurbation, Coventry is surrounded by some of the finest scenery and places of historic interest in the country. It claims among many of its famous native sons and daughters the novelist George Eliot, who attended boarding school in Warwick Row and lived with her father here between 1841 and 1849 in Floeshill Road, and poet Philip Larkin, born in the city in 1922.

The three spires of Coventry's **Christchurch**, **Holy Trinity** and **St Michael's** dominate the city skyline. During the terrible bombing inflicted on the city during the Second World War, St Michael's suffered direct hits. Its spire and ruined windows are all that remains, evoking both the horror and the spirit of reconciliation that arose from those times. Standing in the ruins of these 14th century remains can be a strange and moving experience. The altar is made of broken stones gathered from the night of 15th November 1940. It is surmounted by a cross of charred roof beams and a cross of medieval nails, behind which are inscribed the words from Calvary, 'Father Forgive.' The new **Cathedral**, designed by Basil Spence, stands by its side, and

together they symbolise sacrifice and resurrection. Yet unashamedly modern, its vast and striking interior conveys a powerful sense of the past.

This modern city has many ancient treasures: **Bond's Hospital** in Hill Street is a beautiful 16th century Tudor almshouse, now a home for the elderly. The exterior and courtyard are open to the public. **Ford's Hospital** in Greyfriar's Lane is another half-timbered Tudor almshouse founded in 1509

Ford's Hospital

by Coventry merchant William Ford. Another half-timbered building, **Cheylesmore Manor House** in New Union Street, was once owned by the Black Prince when he was Lord of the Manor. This attractive half-timbered building is now used as the Register Office, and as such is the oldest in Britain, dating back to 1250. Nearby, in Whitefriars Gate, is the **Toy Museum**, which houses a collection dating from the 18th century. In London Road stands **Whitefriars**, a renovated Carmelite friary dating from 1342 which plays host to art exhibitions, theatre productions and concerts. Near the cathedral is the **Herbert Art Gallery and Museum**, which includes the story of Coventry and reconstructed rooms showing weaving and other skills that have been associated with the city over the years.

In Bayley Lane is **St Mary's Guildhall**, where Kings and Queens have been entertained and Mayors appointed to their office since the 14th century. Its tower once imprisoned Mary, Queen of Scots, and it has a restored 600 year-old crypt. The **Museum of British Road Transport** in St Agnes Lane, Hales Street, examines the enormous contribution made by the city to the transport industry, spanning over 100 years, from the first cycles to the very latest advances in technology. Over 400 magnificent cars, motorcycles, cycles and commercial vehicles are on display. A few minutes' walk from the city centre, **Coventry Canal Basin** has a distinguished history. It opened to boat traffic in September 1769, and the warehouses on Leicester Row span the late 18th to early 20th centuries. These warehouses, originally built for unloading and storing bulk goods, have been restored and are now home to artists' studios, boat-builders and specialist craft workshops.

Coventry also boasts some outstanding parkland and public spaces. **Lady Herbert's Garden** in Hales Street lies near two of the town's ancient gates. It is a beautiful secluded garden which incorporates part of the old city wall. **Greyfriars Green** in Greyfriars Road is a conservation area with attractive open land and two distinct terraces of fine buildings. The **War Memorial Park** in Kenilworth Road is Coventry's premier park, with beautiful tree-lined walkways, a Peace Garden and Cenotaph. **Coombe Country Park**, a few miles east of the city centre off the B4027, comprises almost 400 acres of beautiful historic parkland with formal gardens, woodland and lakeside walks which make up the grounds of Coombe Abbey, landscaped by 'Capability' Brown. It has taken 10 centuries and the vision of many people for this magnificent country park to reach its present splendour. Home to Warwickshire's largest heronry, it also boasts bird hides, picnic area, and informative Visitors' Centre, as well as a restaurant, bar and gift shop.

BAGINTON
MAP 7 REF M15

5 miles S of Coventry off the A444

The **Midland Air Museum** at Coventry Airport in Baginton houses a unique collection of aircraft, engines and exhibits telling the story of the jet engine. In this hands-on museum visitors can sit in the cockpit of a Vulcan Bomber or Meteor, and with over 35 aircraft on display there is something to interest everyone. This very relaxed and informal museum features local aviation history, with a 'Wings Over Coventry' gallery and a wealth of Coventry-produced aircraft and other exhibits, dominated by the giant Armstrong Whitworth Argosy freighter of 1959. The museum guides are happy to offer information and make all visitors feel welcome.

RUGBY
MAP 7 REF M15

9 miles E of Coventry off the A45

The only town of any great size in northeastern Warwickshire, Rugby's Market Place is surrounded by handsome buildings which act as reminders of the town's origins during the reign of Henry III. The **Church of St Andrew** was built by the Rokeby family after their castle had been destroyed by Henry II. The old tower dates from the 1400s. With its fireplace and 3 foot-thick walls, it looks more like a fortress and was, indeed, a place of refuge. The nave and second tower were the work of William Butterfield. Rugby, however, is probably most famous for **Rugby School**, founded in 1567. Having originally been situated near the Clock Tower in the town, it moved to its present site in 1750. Their are many fine buildings, splendid examples of their period, the highlight being the school chapel, designed by William Butterfield. These buildings house treasures such as stained glass believed to be the work of Albrecht Durer, the 15th century German artist and engraver. There are few places in the world where you can gaze with any certainty over the birthplace of a sport that gives pleasure to millions. The game of Rugby originated here at the school when William Webb Ellis broke the rules during a football match in 1823 by picking up and running with the ball. The school has not always been the calm and peaceful seat of learning that it is today. In November 1797, the Riot Act was read to a group of rebellious pupils, who had made a bonfire of books, pictures and other school property before retreating to the moated island in the school grounds. They were eventually captured by a large force of soldiers, schoolmasters and volunteers from the town, who waded through the water to the island.

Rugby School Museum is an award-winner, featuring displays and exhibits highlighted with sound and music which bring to life the school's history, its place in the history of rugby football and the lives of its more notable pupils, such as the poets Matthew Arnold and Rupert Brooke, and mathematician and writer Charles Lutwidge Dodgson (Lewis Carroll), and Thomas Hughes, whose Tom Brown's Schooldays was based on his life at Rugby. Visitors will learn a great deal about the remarkable events in a history dating back to 1567. Guided tours leave from the School Museum Tuesday-Saturday 2.30 throughout the year, except over the Christmas period.

Rugby Town Trail is a two-hour walk that brings to life the history of this attractive market town from its Saxon beginnings to the present day. The walk begins and ends at the Clock Tower in Market Place. This edifice was intended to commemorate the Golden Jubilee of Queen Victoria in 1887, yet it was not completed until 1889 because over-indulgent citizens had dipped too deep into the Tower funds to feast and drink at the Jubilee. You will see many of the town's main tourist attractions, including the house where Rupert Brooke was born, and his statue in Regent Place. Information and maps of the trail are available from Rugby Library, the Town Hall or the town's museums. Rugby is also the home of the **James Gilbert Rugby Museum**, housed in the original building where, since 1842, the Gilberts have been making their world-famous rugby footballs. This Museum is crammed with memorabilia of the game and its development.

Caldecott Park in the centre of town has beautiful floral displays, trees and a herb garden. Picnicking areas and a play area are two more of the highlights of this lovely park, and there are also facilities for bowls, putting, tennis and boules. Rugby is bounded by two of the greatest Roman roads, Fosse Way and Watling Street, which meet just northwest of Rugby, at High Cross. This is one of the landmarks of the area. The town is as far inland as it is possible to get in the British Isles, yet Rugby is an excellent centre for all kinds of water sports and aquatic activities. The Oxford Canal winds its way through the borough, and the Rivers Avon, Leam and Swift provide good angling, pleasant walks and places to picnic. **Cock Robin Wood** is a nature reserve on Dunchurch Road, near the junction with Ashlawn Road. Here the visitor will find extensive areas of oak, ash, rowan, cherry and field maples, as well as grassy areas and a central pond, a haven for insects, frogs and butterflies. The **Great Central Walk** is a four-mile ramble through Rugby. Along the way visitors will encounter an abundance of wildlife, plants and shrubs, as well as conservation areas and picnic sites.

DUNCHURCH   Map 7 ref N15
1½ miles S of Rugby off the A426

'The gunpowder plot village': on November 5th, 1605, the Gunpowder Plot conspirators met at the Red Lion Inn, Dunchurch, to await the news of Guy Fawkes' success in blowing up the English Houses of Parliament. The Red Lion still exists today, as a private residence known as Guy Fawkes House. This attractive village with its rows of thatched cottages has a 14th-century church built by the monks of Pipewell Abbey, with one of the oldest parish registers in England.

THURLASTON   Map 7 ref N15
5 miles SW of Rugby off the A45/M45

Whitefields Hotel, Golf and Country Club in Thurlaston is a modern hotel with excellent facilities. There are 50 ensuite rooms, all decorated and furnished with style and comfort in mind. One bedroom has been adapted for guests with disabilities. The guests' lounge is just the place for a relaxing pre-dinner drink while perusing the menu for the a la carte garden restaurant. There is a good selection of real ales and an excellent range of wines available, as well as a

**Whitefields Hotel, Golf and Country Club, Coventry Road, Thurlaston, nr Rugby, Warwickshire CV23 9JR
Tel: 01788 521800 Fax: 01788 521695**

good complement of lagers, ciders, stout and spirits. The extensive menu features traditional favourites and more innovative choices, all freshly prepared and using the freshest ingredients. Alternatively, residents and non-residents alike can enjoy a drink at the bar, where good value bar snacks are available all day. The hotel's 18-hole golf course overlooks the beautiful Draycote Water Country Park. It is a challenging 6,443-yard par 71 course, and is open all year round. At the golf shop there is a wide range of equipment, along with professional advice for every golfer, from the novice to the expert. Warm-up practice can be taken at the 16-bay illuminated driving range. Throughout this superior hotel the decor is very pleasant. Other features include the large conservatories and outside patio gardens. For business clients there is a handsome conference centre and boardroom.

PRINCETHORPE
MAP 7 REF N15
6 miles NE of Leamington Spa off the A453/B4453

Originally hailing from Maryland in the US, owner Elizabeth Best has lived in the UK since 1976. She has brought a fresh and innovative style of decor to **Stretton Lodge**, her handsome Georgian home, and to the converted barns adjacent to the house to offer self-catering accommodation. Popular as a touring base for the many delights of this part of Warwickshire and further afield, it has, in a short time, built up such an excellent reputation for quality that it is

**Stretton Lodge, Oxford Road, Princethorpe, Warwickshire
CV23 9QD Tel: 01926 632351 e-mail: c.best@btinternet.com**

advisable to book well in advance. The barn conversions accommodate up to eight people. Set in 50 acres of pastureland and 400 yards off the main road, this graceful establishment offers a peaceful and relaxing environment. All amenities are available, and guests' every need catered for. The decor and furnishings are tasteful and very comfortable, creating a real home-from-home atmosphere.

FRANKTON

MAP 7 REF N15

5 miles SW of Rugby off the A423/A45

Here in the picturesque village of Frankton, **The Friendly Inn** lives up to its name with a growing reputation for genuine warmth and hospitality. Originally the home of Richard Fosterd, founder of Fosterd's Bridge Charity in the mid-16th century, the property was rented out after his death to raise money for the charity, to be used in building and maintaining many of the local bridges and roads. By 1903 the property had become a public house. Well recommended for its good food, ales and atmosphere, the menu at this wonderful inn boasts a range of tempting meals including traditional English favourites. All are home-made and

The Friendly Inn, Main Street, Frankton, nr Rugby, Warwickshire CV23 9NY Tel: 01926 632430

make use of fresh local produce wherever possible. There are also very good daily specials. The real ales available change regularly; some come from local breweries. Proprietor Nick Rushbrooke has owned the pub since 1997; he and his amiable staff maintain the pub's success and renown for its high quality of service.

STOCKTON

MAP 7 REF N16

6 Miles SW of Rugby off the A426

The Crown Inn in Stockton is a family-run pub with a warm and welcoming atmosphere. Owner Pat O'Flynn took over in 1998, bringing a wealth of experience in the trade. Popular with locals and visitors alike, some of whom come from Coventry and further afield to sample the good-value food and drink, this traditional public house is well worth a visit. Dating back to the 18th century, the old barn building to the rear is now the headquarters of the British Petanque (Boule) Society. The selection of real ales is excellent, including Tetleys, Ansells and guest beers. There is a classic range of malt whiskies, as well as lagers, cider, stout, wines and spirits. In

The Crown Inn, High Street, Stockton, nr Southam, Warwickshire CV23 8JZ Tel: 01926 812255

the spacious restaurant diners can partake of a range of traditional favourites, such as steaks, home-made pies, bar snacks and sandwiches, as well as vegetarian and pasta dishes and daily specials.

RYTON-ON-DUNSMORE
6 miles W of Rugby off the A45

MAP 7 REF N15

This village is home to the Henry Doubleday Research Association at **Ryton Gardens**. This organic farming and gardening organisation leads the way in research and advances in horticulture. The grounds are landscaped with thousands of plants and trees, all organically grown. There is also on site a herb garden, rose garden, garden for the blind, shrub borders and free-range animals. Special events are held throughout the year.

Ryton Pools Country Park is a 100 acre country park opened in 1996. The 10 acre Ryton Pool is home to Greatcrested Grebes, Swans, Moorhen and Canada Geese. There is also an attractive meadow area for strolling or picnicking, Visitor Centre, shop and exhibition area. Pagets Pool near the northeastern end of the park is one of the most important sites in Warwickshire for dragonflies, with 17 species including the Common Blue, Emperor Dragonfly and Black-tailed Skimmer. Other highlights include guided walks and a model railway run by Coventry Model Engineering Society.

LONG LAWFORD
1½ miles W of Rugby off the A428

MAP 7 REF N15

Long Lawford is a beautiful village along the banks of the River Avon. Just a mile and a half from the centre of Rugby, **Lodge Farm** in Long Lawford is a camping and caravan site occupying a five-acre smallholding. Owned and run by Alec and Jane Brown, and set in lovely countryside, this excellent site has facilities for up to 35 campers, caravans or tents. Featuring soft standings on level grass, all with electric hook-ups, there is also a new toilet and showers block. Also on-site are two lovely self-catering cottages, barn conversions of the highest order, with full facilities and ideal to use as a base for exploring this beautiful part of

Lodge Farm, Bilton Lane, Long Lawford, Rugby, Warwickshire CV23 9DU Tel: 01788 560193 Fax: 01788 550603 e-mail: alec@lodgefrm.demon.co.uk

the county. Each cottage sleeps two and is equipped with every modern convenience. There are also four new self-catering studio apartments underway, which will be finished early in the year 2000. The local pub, the Sheaf and Sickle, is just half a mile away.

Half a mile further on from the farm, Alec and Jane also provide bed and breakfast accommodation in a lovely and comfortable house with five double rooms. Whatever your choice of accommodation, Lodge Farm can provide it. Campsite open Easter to end-October. Self-catering and B&B available all year round.

CHURCH LAWFORD
MAP 7 REF N15

2 miles W of Rugby off the A428

The **Old Smithy** in Church Lawford is a pristine and welcoming public house full of traditional character. The interior features highly polish bars and woodwork. Proprietors Kathy and John O'Neill have created an atmosphere which is truly inviting, with warming open fires in winter and an extended conservatory area for finer weather. There are seven traditional ales to choose from at this superb Free House - the new Frankton Braby Brewery is onsite, offering fine 'new'

ales. The menu offers an extensive choice of starters and main courses including royal dim sum, sizzling garlic prawns, succulent steaks, rack of lamb, chicken fajitas, fresh fish, curries, vegetarian options and more - a choice

The Old Smithy, Green Lane, Church Lawford, nr Rugby, Warwickshire CV23 9EF Tel: 02476 542333

of around 50 dishes in all. There is also a mouthwatering selection of puddings, a special children's menu, and an impressive list of wines to accompany the meal. Booking is advised. On Sundays, a traditional three-course lunch is also served. In addition to its fine ale, good food and welcoming atmosphere, within the lifetime of this book there will also be six guest rooms available.

NUNEATON
MAP 7 REF M15

8 miles N of Coventry on the A444

Originally a Saxon town known as *Etone*, Nuneaton is mentioned in the Domesday Book of 1086. The 'Nun' was added when a wealthy Benedictine priory was founded here in 1290. The **Priory ruins** left standing are adjacent to the church of **St Nicholas**, a Victorian edifice occupying a Norman site which has a beautiful carved ceiling dating back to 1485. The town has a history as a centre for coal-mining, which began in Nuneaton as early as the 14th century. Other industries for which the town has been famous include brick and tile manufacture and ribbon-making on hand looms. As the textile and hatting industries boomed, the town began to prosper. Today's Nuneaton is a centre of precision engineering, printing, car components and other important trades. Nuneaton's vivid **Riversley Park** boasts a large recreation area and children's playground, a sports centre and boating facilities as well as lush conservatories and fascinating aviaries.

  Nuneaton Museum and Art Gallery, located in Riversley Park, features displays of archaeological interest ranging from prehistoric to medieval times, and items from the local earthenware industry. There is also a permanent exhibition of the town's most illustrious daughter, the novelist and thinker George Eliot. Born to a prosperous land agent at Arbury Hall in 1819, Eliot (whose real name was Mary Ann Evans) was an intellectual giant and free thinker. She left Warwickshire for London in adulthood, and met George Henry Lewes, a writer and actor who was to become her lifelong companion. Lewes, married with three children, left his family so that he and Eliot, very bravely for the time, could set up house together. Eliot's novels return again and again to the scenes and social conventions of her youth, and are among the greatest works of English - in particular her masterpiece, Middlemarch.

A series of walkways extends around the Nuneaton area, linking public footpaths, bridleways, areas of open space, disused railway lines and canal towpaths. This system is known as the **Green Track**. Information and 'Walks Around...' leaflets, available from Nuneaton or Bedworth library and Nuneaton Town Hall and Council House, identify the various routes and points of interest along the way.

MONKS KIRBY
MAP 7 REF N15

9 miles SE of Nuneaton off the A427

This very old settlement dates back to about the time of the Bronze Age. Indeed, it is thought that the mound on which the parish church now stands was originally built by these primitive people as a meeting place for pagan worship and social gatherings. Following these ancient tribes came the Celts, Romans and Saxons. The Saxons were the first people to build a church on the site, probably a wooden structure originally, being replaced by a stone building later. The Danes arrived about 864 AD as part of their conquest of this part of the country. The field at the rear of the church is still known as the Denmark Field.

After the Norman Conquest, a Benedictine Priory was established and a church rebuilt on the old site. Most of the present building dates from the 14th century. The tall spire, built above the tower in the 15th century, could be seen by travellers for many miles around until it was blown down by a great storm on Christmas night in 1701. From its earliest days Monks Kirby grew in size and importance, eventually taking on the full status of a market town. Pilgrims and merchants were accommodated in the Priory's guest house, which probably stood on the site of the current Denbigh Arms public house. This rural, quiet village, dominated by the ancient church, also boasts many pretty cottages along its main streets.

ARBURY HALL
MAP 7 REF M15

3 miles SW of Nuneaton off the B4102

A visit to **Arbury Hall** fits another piece in the jigsaw of George Eliot's life and times. Still the ancestral seat of the Viscount and Viscountess Daventry, and home to the Newdigate family for over 400 years, it is built on the ruins of an Augustinian monastery and is now one of the best examples of 18th century Gothic Revival architecture in the country. Largely the creation of Sir Roger Newdigate, who began the work in 1748, it stands amid rolling lawns and is surrounded by acres of beautiful parkland. This lovely Elizabethan mansion house was refurbished and renovated by Sir Roger during the second half of the 18th century, and boasts soaring fan vaulting, plunging pendants and delicate filigree tracing in most rooms. Before Sir Roger's day, in the 1670s his forebear Sir Richard Newdigate built the impressive stable

Arbury Hall

block - designed partly by Christoper Wren. There are a few works by Christopher Wren in the former stables, which now house a collection of vintage cycles. Arbury contains important collections of paintings, furniture, glass and china collected through the centuies by successive generations of the family. George Eliot was born on the estate, where her father was land agent; in *Mr Gifgil's Love Story* she portrays Arbury as Cheverel Manor, and gives detailed descriptions of many of the rooms in the house, including the Saloon and the Dining Room - comparing the latter, unsurprisingly given its grandeur, to a cathedral.

ANSLEY
MAP 7 REF M15
5 miles W of Nuneaton off the B4112

Ansley is best known for adjacent **Hoar Park**, which dates back to the 1430s. The existing house and buildings date from 1730, and now form the centrepiece of the 143 acre Park, which contains a handsome Craft Village. The Park, as well as being a craft, antique and garden centre, is still a working farm.

HARTSHILL
MAP 7 REF M14
3 miles NW of Nuneaton off the A5

Hartshill Hayes Country Park is an ideal place for exploring the developing rural attractions of this part of Warwickshire. Although surrounded by a network of roads, here visitors find only woodland trails and walks, and magnificent views. The park boasts 136 acres of woodland, meadow and open hilltop. Winner of the Forestry Authority's 'Centre of Excellence Award' in 1996, the park boasts three self-guided walks, an informative Visitors' Centre and truly wonderful views. Hartshill itself was the birthplace of the poet Michael Drayton (1563-1631).

CALDECOTE
MAP 7 REF M14
3 miles NW of Nuneaton off the B4111

For the past five years Jane Cox has been offering superb bed and breakfast accommodation from **Hill House**. Overlooking the Anchor Valley to the north, the views of uninterrupted countryside range for miles in every direction, it is also convenient for Birmingham along the A5 or M42. The oldest part of this extensive and charming home was built in 1720. In its day it has been used by the then-Prince of Wales, later Edward VII, to visit one of his mistresses. The 11 brickbuilt coaching arches set into the garden are impressive and eye-catching. Occupying some 20 acres, this is a true rural idyll. The four spacious ensuite guest bedrooms are tastefully and comfortably furnished. Two rooms have balconies. One of the upstairs bedrooms also has its own lovely sitting room. Guests are welcome to use the spacious and airy conservatory; breakfast is served in the tasteful dining room. There are open fires in many rooms. Every morning Jane serves up a full English breakfast or a choice of smoked haddock, kippers, vegetarian choices or a simple repast of croissants, all accompanied by freshly brewed coffee, a range of teas or fresh juice. Evening meals by arrangement. All meals are cooked on Jane's AGA and use only fresh free-range and organic produce. In summer guests can enjoy the summer house and garden games. When the weather isn't fine, there is a

Hill House, off Mancetter Road, Caldecote, Nuneaton, Warwickshire CV10 0RS Tel: 02476 396685

full-sized billiards table in the attractive games room. No smoking. ETB 4 Diamonds Highly Recommended.

NEWTON REGIS
Map 7 ref M14

10 miles NW of Nuneaton off the B5453

One of the most unspoilt villages in Warwickshire, Newton Regis has been voted Best Kept Small Village on numerous occasions. Near the Staffordshire border and between the M42 and B5453, this lovely village is built around an attractive duck pond which was once a quarry pit. The village's name is thought to derive from its former royal ownership, having once been the property of King Henry II. It has in its day also been known as King's Newton and Newton-in-the-Thistles - the latter perhaps referring to the abundance of thistles or specially grown teasels which were used in the carding of flax fibre. Linen looms were worked in the house which is now the Queens Head Inn.

ALVECOTE
Map 7 ref M14

10 miles NW of Nuneaton off the M42

Alvecote Priory, just on the border with Staffordshire, was formed by William Burnett in 1159, who built it as a penance after having (mistakenly) believed that his wife had been unfaithful during his pilgrimage to the Holy Land. This small Benedictine Priory was founded as a Cell to the Great Malvern Priory in Worcestershire. As with many others it was dissolved in 1536, when the buildings were converted into a house, which was pulled down in about 1700 when another house was constructed using some of the old materials. The 14th century remains include a fine moulded doorway and dovecote. Alvecote Priory Picnic Area boasts canalside picnic spots and a nearby nature reserve. There is also an interesting circular walk that takes in lakes, wildlife, many unusual plants, the old North Warwicks Colliery tip, and handsome canal bridges.

KENILWORTH
Map 6 ref M15

6 miles SW of Coventry on the A452

Although the town was here before the Domesday Book was compiled, Kenilworth's name is invariably linked with its castle. Today the remains of this castle stand as England's finest and most extensive castle ruins, dramatically ensconced at the western edge of the town. **Kenilworth Castle's** red sandstone towers, keep and wall glow with an impressive richness in the sun, particularly at sunrise and sunset. Here you can learn about the great building's links with Henry V (who retired to Kenilworth after the Battle of Agincourt), King John, Edward II and John of Gaunt. The tales of this great fortress, immortalised (if enhanced) in Sir Walter Scott's novel *Kenilworth,* written in 1821, are many and varied. An audio tour guides you on a revealing journey around the Castle, recounting stories of Kenilworth's turbulent past. There are fine views from the top of Saintlowe Tower, and lovely grounds for exploring and picnicking, as well as beautifully reconstructed Tudor gardens. Special events

Kenilworth Castle

throughout the year include a festival of Tudor Music, Saxon and Viking exhibitions, medieval pageantry, various re-enactments, plays and operas in the grounds and much more. The remains of Kenilworth's abbey can be seen in the churchyard of the Norman parish church of **St Nicholas** in the High Street. Much of interest was discovered during excavations and there are many relics on display in the church, including a pig made of lead. It is said that this formed part of the roof at the time of the Dissolution, but was then melted down and stamped by the Commissioners of Henry VIII.

WARWICK   MAP 6 REF M16
9 miles SW of Coventry off the A46

Over the past ten centuries **Warwick Castle** has witnessed some of the most turbulent times in English history. From the era of William the Conqueror to the grand reign of Queen Victoria, the Castle has left us a fascinating legacy to enjoy today. Dominating the town, it is surely everyone's ideal of a medieval building, one of the country's most splendid castles and certainly one of the most visited. It still serves as a home as well as retaining the greater part of its original masonry. A tour of this palatial mansion takes you from the grim austerity of the

original dungeons with their gruesome torture chambers to the gloomy but sumptuous opulence of rooms later adapted for comfortable living. The castle's magnificent State Rooms, once used to entertain the highest members of the nobility, house some superb art treasures including works by Holbein, Rubens and Velasquez. As the castle is owned by Madame Tussaud's, striking waxworks take their part in the displays. In the castle's Ghost Tower, visitors can learn of the dark and sinister secrets

Warwick Castle

surrounding the fatal stabbing of Sir Fulke Greville, said to haunt the premises to this day. In the Great Hall visitors come face to face with Oliver Cromwell's death mask. And the armoury houses one of the best private collections in the country. The castle exterior is best viewed from Castle Bridge, where the 14th century walls can be seen reflected in the waters of the River Avon. There is a walk along the ramparts, and much to explore within 60 acres of grounds, including a re-created Victorian formal rose garden, the Peacock Gardens and an expanse of open parkland designed by Capability Brown. Events throughout the year include Medieval Tournaments, open-air firework concerts and special entertainment days.

The centre of Warwick was rebuilt after a fire in 1694. Though many older buildings survived, the centre is dominated by elegant Queen Anne rebuilding. A walk around High Street and Northgate Street takes in some of the finest buildings, including Court House and Landor House. Court House on Jury Street houses the **Warwickshire Yeomanry Museum**, with displays of uniforms, arms, swords, sabres and selected silver, and **Warwick Town Museum**, which features changing exhibitions. Some of the town's oldest structures can be found around **Mill Street**, an attractive place for a stroll, with several antique shops along the way. **Warwickshire Museum** in Market Place occupies a 17th century market hall housing collections that illustrate the geology, wildlife and history of the county. Notable exhibits include giant fossils, live bees, ancient jewellery and the historic Sheldon Tapestry map of Warwickshire. Changing programmes in the ground floor galleries offer exciting exhibitions of acclaimed local and national artists' work. History of a different kind can be seen at picturesque **Oken's House**, an ancient building once owned by Thomas Oken, a self-made businessman who died childless in 1573 and left his fortune to found almshouses for the poor. Today his home houses **The Doll Museum**, just 100 yards from the castle in Castle Street. This carefully restored Elizabethan house is home to hundreds of dolls, teddies and toys from days gone by. Visitors can have a go at hopscotch or spinning tops, or hunt for Teddy's friends, while video bring the exhibits to life, demonstrating how all the mechanical toys on display work.

One of the most important buildings in Warwick is **St John's House**, dating from 1666 and considered a very good example of the period. Today the building houses a museum where visitors can find out how people lived in the past. The displays include a gallery of costume, a kitchen full of drawers to open and cupboards to explore, a parlour, and a schoolroom just waiting for Victorian children. Upstairs there is the Museum of the Royal Warwickshire Regiment.

Two of Warwick's medieval town gateways survive, complete with chapels. Of these, Westgate Chapel forms part of **Lord Leycester's Hospital**, a spectacularly tottering and beautiful collection of 15th century half-timbered buildings enclosing a pretty galleried courtyard. Inside, the main interest is provided by the Queen's Own Hussars regimental museum. This 600-

Lord Leycester's Hospital

year-old medieval treasure has a unique chantry Chapel, magnificent Great Hall and Guildhall together with other timber-framed buildings, first established by the Earl of Leicester as an old soldiers' home in 1571. The candlelit chapel dates from 1123, and the Regimental Museum of the Queen's Own Hussars is another site of interest in this medieval masterpiece. The historic Master's Garden, featuring a Norman arch and 2,000 year-old vase from the Nile, is a spectacular summer attraction.

Halfway between Warwick and Leamington Spa on the A445, **The Simple Simon** public house derives its name from the local pie factory. This traditional pub is owned by Eddie and Melanie Sykes-Blythe, friendly and welcoming hosts. Eddie is ex-Royal Navy; born in Leamington Spa, he and Melanie purchased the pub in 1998 and have made extensive alterations, to bring it in keeping with their (and their guests') vision of what a welcoming and comfortable pub should be. The pub has been revitalised and is very popular with locals and visitors to Warwick alike. Attractive inside and out, it dates back to the late 1800s. Located very close to the canal, among its clientele are canal-boat holiday makers who stop in for supper and the range of excellent real ales including Wadsworth 6X, Flowers IPA and changing guest ales. Fresh home-cooked food on offer is served in generous portions, beautifully presented and good value

The Simple Simon, 105 Emscote Road, Warwick, Warwickshire CV34 5QY Tel: 01926 774078

for money, and includes a full selection of imaginative grills, vegetarian dishes and sensational puddings. Booking for meals is recommended at weekends; no food served Mondays.

ROWINGTON
2 miles NW of Warwick off the A41

MAP 6 REF M15

High House is a secluded Grade II listed farmhouse surrounded by rolling countryside. Built in 1690, this charming guest house has beamed rooms, antique furniture and four-posters in two of the three spacious ensuite guest bedrooms. Each room is individually furnished with taste and style, offering a comfortable home from home ambience. Owners John and Beryl Penn have been offering excellent bed and breakfast accommodation since 1996. The lovely grounds are secluded and peaceful, with a collection of rare breed chickens who provide the eggs for the

High House, Old Warwick Rd, Rowington, Warwickshire CV35 7AA
Tel: 01926 843270 Fax: 01926 843689 Mobile: 0797 962 8609

hearty and filling breakfasts. Nominated by the AA for the Best Breakfast award, this repast comprises home-made bread (baked by John), smoked salmon, kedgeree and eggs or the traditional English breakfast. Beryl also provides her own home-made jams and preserves. Guests are welcome to use the delightful and cosy sitting room and dining room. Evening meals can be arranged at one of the many excellent local pubs. ETB 4 Diamonds Highly Recommended.

WESTON-UNDER-WETHERLY
5 miles NE of Warwick off the B4453

MAP 7 REF N15

Home cooking is the speciality at the superb **Bull Inn**. With over 13 years' experience in the trade, owners Mark and Carol Jones and their efficient and courteous staff offer guests a real treat. Converted from cottages to a public house in the late 19th century, this traditional establishment has a cosy bar and separate restaurant. The freshest produce is used to create dishes such as pan-fried pork, sirloin steak, lamb cutlets, Mexican chicken, seafood catch of the day and vegetarian lasagne, to name just a few from the extensive menu. There are also delicious daily specials and a choice of home-made

The Bull Inn, Rugby Road, Weston-under-Wetherley,
Leamington Spa, Warwickshire CV33 9BP Tel: 01926 632392

puddings. Lunch is served daily, while evening meals are available Tuesday to Sunday (closed Mondays except for Bank Holidays). To accompany the meal there are cask-conditioned real ales including Greene King Abbot, as well as Marstons Pedigree, Guinness and a good selection of lagers, cider and spirits. The wine list is impressive, offering up a selection of three house wines, six white varieties, five red and two sparkling wines.

BARFORD

MAP 6 REF M16

3 miles S of Warwick off the A429

Barford is a pretty village one mile south of the M40 junction 15. The River Avon flows through on its way to Stratford. **The Joseph Arch Inn** is a friendly and convivial public house. Rob and Krys Rourke have recently taken over here; as locals of Barford they have a wealth of knowledge about the lovely village of

Barford. Popular with locals and tourists for its traditional English pub atmosphere, this three-storeyed house was built in the 1700s and became a pub some 200 years ago. Recently redecorated, the interior has two peaceful bars, with traditional decor and fittings and plenty of space in which to relax. Photographs of old Barford and memorabilia of the life and times of Joseph Arch - a farm labourer who in 1872 founded the National Farmers' Union and became the first MP to represent farming interests - adorn the walls. Krys prepares the food, using fresh local produce wherever

The Joseph Arch Inn, 7 Bridge Street, Barford, nr Warwick, Warwickshire CV35 8EH Tel: 01926 624365

possible. The imaginative menu includes fish and chicken dishes, lasagne and vegetarian choices, plus four daily specials and a good range of excellent puddings. Real ales include Theakstons, Marstons IPA and Flowers, as well as a good choice of lagers and stout, wines, malt whiskies and other spirits. Lunch and evening meals served daily (except Sunday evening).

ROYAL LEAMINGTON SPA

MAP 7 REF M15

2 miles NW of Warwick on the A445

This attractive town boasts a handsome mixture of smart shops and Regency buildings. **The Parade** is undoubtedly one of the most handsome street in Warwickshire. It starts at the railway bridge, dives between a double row of shops and comes up again at the place marked with a small stone temple announcing 'The Original Spring Recorded by Camden in 1586''. In 1801 very few people knew of the existence of Leamington, but by 1838 all this had changed. By this time the famous waters were cascading expensively over the many 'patients' and the increasingly fashionable spa was given the title 'Royal' by permission of the new Queen, Victoria. The Pump Rooms were opened in 1814 by Henry Jephson, a local doctor who was largely responsible for promoting the Spa's medicinal properties. This elegant spa resort was soon popularised by the rich, who came to take the waters in the 18th and 19th centuries. Immediately opposite the Spa itself are Jephson's Gardens containing a Corinthian temple which houses a statue of him. The town's supply of saline waters is inexhaustible, and a wide range of 'cures' are available, under supervision, to this day. **Warwick District Council Art Gallery and Museum** in

Avenue Road boasts collections of pottery, ceramics and glass, as well as some excellent Flemish, Dutch and British paintings from the 1500s to the present.

New owners Susan Buckley and Jonathan Felles have completely refurbished and renovated the impressive public house **The Cricketers** since taking over in 1998. In a short time they have gained an enviable reputation for outstanding food, great ales and warm hospitality. Located in the centre of Leamington Spa adjacent to the internationally famous Bowling Greens alongside the River Leam, the open spaces of Victoria Park and Jefferson Gardens are just a short walk

away. Popular with locals and visitors alike, this handsome Georgian inn has a light and airy interior, with walls painted a warm terracotta and stylish and comfortable sofas, chairs and high-backed chairs. Meals can be taken at any table in the large front room or rear snug. The bar area is open-plan, with gleaming brass work. Cricket memorabilia adorns the walls - for many years the pub was the site of the changing rooms for the local cricketing and rugby teams. There is a full selection of delicious bar

The Cricketers, 19 Archery Road, Leamington Spa, Warwickshire CV31 3PT Tel: 01926 881293

snacks, while the menu boasts a wonderful range of home-made traditional English favourites, served from midday to 8.30 p.m. daily. There are always at least four cask-conditioned real ales on offer, including a local Warwickshire brew.

HARBURY
6 miles SE of Warwick off the B4452

MAP 7 REF N16

The history of this area goes back many years; dinosaur fossils have been found in the local quarries and the Fosse Way, a major Roman road, passes close by. Just outside the village lies **Chesterton Windmill**. This unusual mill was built in 1632 and was the work of Inigo Jones.

Occupying the rolling hills above the Vale of Avon, **The Old New Inn** is a traditional stonebuilt inn dating back to the 1700s. It began life as a bakehouse, and is constructed from local Hanbury stone. The interior has its original beams and flagstone floors, and has a wealth of cosy corners and relaxing log fires. Adorned with golf memorabilia and horseracing prints,

The Old New Inn, Farm Street, Harbury, nr Warwick, Warwickshire CV33 9LS Tel: 01926 614023 here guests can enjoy a range of real ales as well as some excellent house wines and malt whiskies, lagers and spirits. Home-cooked bar snacks, fresh sandwiches and grills are available every day, and the traditional Sunday roast has proved very popular (booking advised). Owner Brian Moffitt has been here since 1993, and offers a warm welcome and quality service to all his customers. Trout fishing on the Avon at the nearby Twaites Estate can be arranged for visitors.

STRATFORD-UPON-AVON
9 miles SW of Warwick on the A439

Map 6 ref M16

After London, for many visitors to England Stratford-upon-Avon is the next place on their itinerary, and all because of one man. William Shakespeare was born here in 1564 , found fame in London and then retired here, dying in 1616. Each of the houses associated with the Bard has its own fascinating story to tell. Staff at the houses are happy to guide visitors on a journey encompassing what life might have been in Stratford-upon-Avon during Shakespeare's day.

Some 500,000 people each year visit **Shakespeare's birthplace** alone, located in the very centre of the town, in Henley Street. Further along, on Chapel Street, stands **Nash's House**. This half-timbered building was inherited by Shakespeare's grand-daughter, Elizabeth Hall, from her first husband, Thomas Nash. It now contains an exceptional collection of Elizabethan furniture and tapestries, as well as displays, upstairs, on the history of Stratford. Next door, in **New Place**, Shakespeare bought a house where he spent his retirement years, from 1611 to 1616. Today all that can be seen are the gardens and foundations of where the house once stood. An exhibit in Nash's House explains why this, Shakespeare's final home in Stratford, was destroyed in the 18th century. Opposite New Place is the **Guild Chapel**, and beyond this is the **Grammar School**, where it is believed that Shakespeare was educated.

Hall's Croft in Old Town is one of the best examples of a half-timbered gabled house in Stratford. It stands near **Holy Trinity Church**, an inspiration for many poets and artists because of its beautiful setting beside the River Avon. It is here that Shakespeare is buried. Dating partly from the 13th century, it is approached down an attractive avenue of limes. The north door has a sanctuary knocker, used in the past to ensure any fugitive who reached it 37 days' grace. Shakespeare's wife Anne Hathaway and their daughter Susanna and her husband John Hall are also buried here. The tomb of the great man himself carries a sobering inscription:

> *Good friend, for Jesus sake, forbeare*
> *To digg the dust enclosed heare;*
> *Blese be ye man yt spares these stones*
> *And curst be he yt moves my bones.*

Shakespeare is not the only illustrious name to have associations with the town. **Harvard House** in the High Street, dating from 1596, was the childhood home of Katherine Rogers. Her son, John Harvard, went to the American Colonies in the early 1600s and founded the famous university named after him in 1636. In 1909 Harvard House was restored and presented to Harvard University. It boasts

Harvard House

the most ornately carved timbered frontage in the town. Cared for by the Shakespeare Birthplace Trust, it houses the nationally important Neish Collection of Pewter.

There are many fascinating old buildings in Stratford. The old market site in Rother Street has a history dating from 1196, when a weekly market was granted by King John. In the square is an ornate fountain-cum-clock tower, a gift from G W Childs of Philadelphia in the jubilee year of Queen Victoria. It was unveiled by the famous actor Henry Irving, who when knighted in 1895 became the first ever 'Sir of the Stage'.

A tour of the **Royal Shakespeare Theatre** gives visitors the opportunity to discover what goes on behind the scenes. The itinerary for tours varies according to rehearsal schedules and the technical work underway on stage, but they are very informative and fun, and usually include both the Royal Shakespeare and Swan Theatres, as well as the RSC Collection - with over a thousand items on view, including costumes, props, pictures and sound recordings depicting changes in staging from medieval times to the present. The displays compare and contrast theatrical productions past and present, giving an insight into the many interpretations adopted and styles used in the presentation of great works of classical drama over the years.

A short walk from the centre of town are the Bancroft Gardens, near the 14-arch Clopton Bridge. This delightful leisure area contains the great **Shakespeare Memorial**, designed by Lord Ronald Gower and built in Paris. The work took 12 years to complete and was finally presented to the town in 1888. Only a few yards away is a preserved industrial tram, employed on the horse-drawn tramway connecting wharfs in Stratford with those in Shipston-on-Stour and Moreton-in-the-Marsh in Gloucestershire. The canal was completed in 1816.

The Ragdoll Shop on Chapel Street was created by the founder of Ragdoll Productions, which produce the charming and popular children's television series Rosie and Jim. On sale there's a wealth of books, videos and other merchandise which can be purchased, including guides to water safety produced by British Waterways, which runs the two-centuries-old network of canals and inland waterways in England, Scotland and Wales, conserving the canalside historic buildings and structures, and protecting the wildlife and plantlife along the water's edge. Stratford's **Teddy Bear Museum** occupies an original Elizabethan setting on Greenhill Street. The collection comprises hundreds of wonderful teddy bears from around the world - including some of the oldest, most valuable and most unusual to be found. The Royal Shakespeare Theatre Summer House on Avonbank Gardens is home to the **Stratford Brass Rubbing Centre**, which contains a large collection of exact replicas of brasses of knights and ladies, scholars, merchants and priests of the past. Admission is free; a small charge is made for the special paper and wax required.

Just a short walk from Shakespeare's home and the centre of Stratford, in a lovely and quiet street, **The Marlyn Hotel** offers bed and breakfast accommodation of the highest standard. This family hotel has been welcoming visitors for over 100 years. Perfect for quiet weekend or short breaks, it has eight charming guest bedrooms (four ensuite) which are cosy and comfortable, comprising two ensuite double/family rooms, two ensuite twins, an additional double and a single room. All rooms are equipped with modern facilities while retaining their period Victorian charm. Proprietors Andrew and Rosie Evans are convivial and friendly hosts. Tours of the Cotswolds or local area can be arranged to suit guests' requirements. Aromatherapy and reflexology treatments are also readily available. Breakfast is light or full English, whichever guests prefer. Evening meals are available upon request. For the last

The Marlyn Hotel, 3 Chestnut Walk, Stratford-upon-Avon, Warwickshire CV37 6HG Tel/Fax: 01789 293752

word in rest and relaxation, look no further. Children and well-behaved pets are welcome. ETB 4 Diamonds Commended.

SHOTTERY
MAP 6 REF M16
1 mile W of Stratford off the A422

This was the birthplace of Anne Hathaway, Shakespeare's wife. Here visitors will find the Elizabethan farmhouse now known as **Anne Hathaway's Cottage**, and can retrace the steps which the courting couple, who married in 1582, might have taken. The epitome of the traditional thatched cottage, this delightful spot has been home to Hathaways since the 15th century, up until some 70 years ago when the Shakespeare Birthplace Trust decided it was time to open up the home to the public. The Hathaway bed, settle and other pieces of furniture owned by the family remain, and there is a traditional English cottage garden and orchard - plants and herbs grown by the Shakespeare Trusts' gardeners can be purchased. Other attractions of this handsome village are the Shakespeare Tree Garden, the tranquil Shottery Brook, and well-laid-out Jubilee Walks.

WILMCOTE
MAP 6 REF M16
3 miles NW of Stratford off the A34

Another notable house connected with the poet is that of his mother, situated here in the village of Wilmcote, slightly off the well-beaten tourist track. **Mary Arden's House** is a striking Tudor farmhouse. Guided tours are available and the house boasts the Shakespeare Countryside Museum of farming and rural life. Note in particular the bread oven doors, which are made of bog oak, which never burns, and are seen only very rarely now in England. Best of all, however, is the dovecote of the house. Robert Arden, who was lord of the manor, was in this capacity the only villager allowed to have one. It has over 600 pigeon holes and, at nesting time, would house about 3,000 birds. Wilmcote is also one of the few small villages left which retains its Victorian Gothic railway station. The Stratford Canal runs alongside the railway. After many years of neglect, the Canal was taken over by British Waterways and now carries many holiday cruisers on their way to join the Avon.

CHARLECOTE
MAP 6 REF M16
3 miles E of Stratford off the B4086

The National Trust's **Charlecote Park** is a magnificent stately home occupying extensive grounds overlooking the River Avon. A treasure-trove of historic works of sculpture and painting, no visitor can fail to be impressed by the house's sheer magnitude, grace and beauty. The park was landscaped by 'Capability' Brown and reflects his use of natural and man-made features complementing each other. The park supports herds of Red and Fallow deer (in about 1583 the young William Shakespeare is alleged to have been caught poaching Sir Thomas' deer; years later he is said to have taken his revenge by using Sir Thomas as his inspiration for the fussy Justice Shallow in The Merry Wives of Windsor), as well as a flock of Jacobs sheep first introduced here in 1756. Special events are held throughout the year; at any time a visit to this national treasure is an assured lovely and informative day out.

Charlecote Park

roses. The rest of the garden, covering 24 acres, consists of shrubs and trees interspersed with spacious lawns providing vistas across the 400 acre park. The lake, created in 1625, is now used for fishing, sailing, swimming and water skiing; there is also a lakeside picnic area. The cricket pitch is in regular use. A country trail of about two miles wends its way through the park and the woods, to end at a very popular adventure playground.

EXHALL
MAP 6 REF L16
16 miles S of Solihull off the A46/B4085

South of the A46, where there is a marked trail through the woods at Oversley, visitors will come to Exhall, recorded in the Domesday Book though its history probably dates back to Roman times. Roman coins have been found in one of the village gardens. The architecture in this handsome village is varied, reflecting the history and development from Elizabethan to modern times. The village is also home to some interesting black-and-white half-timbered buildings and a farmhouse dating back to the 16th century. Most of the houses stand on steep banks on each side of the road, and this adds much to the picturesque quality of the village. The pretty parish **Church of St Giles** has a fine Norman door; the views from the churchyard are beautiful.

Glebe Farm is a working farm offering both bed and breakfast accommodation, within the brickbuilt farmhouse, and eight self-catering cottages. The pretty farmhouse dates back to the 11th-13th centuries and has a lovely garden. It was once the village vicarage (Glebe is an old

word used for a church) where the local clergyman cultivated the land and preached in the tiny church next door. The four lovely B&B rooms are cosy and comfortable, with exposed beams, open fireplaces and other original features. There is a sitting room for guests and a separate dining room. The breakfast is hearty and delicious. Surrounding the old farmyard close to the farmhouse are the eight self-catering cottages, which have been skilfully and imaginatively converted from redundant farm buildings. Timber framed, some thatched,

Glebe Farm, Exhall, nr Alcester, Warwickshire B49 6EA
Tel: 01789 772202

these charming cottages feature a living room with fitted kitchen units, pine furnishings, carpets, and bath with shower. They sleep between two and six; one is suitable for visitors with disabilities. There is a shop and laundry facilities on site. Guests using the cottages out of season can take breakfast in the farmhouse, where they can experience for themselves the warm hospitality of owners John and Margaret Canning..

LONG MARSTON
MAP 6 REF M16
5 miles SW of Stratford off the B4632

Charles I stayed at a house here in Long Marston after his flight from the Battle of Worcester. The village's 14th-century church has a half-timbered turret and porch. From Long Marston there's access to **The Greenway**, a converted railway line ideal for cycling or walking. This open public greensward boasts two and a half miles of surfaced paths amid beautiful scenery, with picnic areas and a tranquil atmosphere of rural calm.

ILMINGTON   MAP 6 REF M16
7 miles S of Stratford off the B4632

Along the northeastern Cotswolds, at the foot of the Wilmington Downs, you'll come to the village of Ilmington. This eye-catching place has several lovely old houses. The village's name means 'the elm grown hill'. It was made famous on Christmas Day 1934, when the first radio broadcast by George V was introduced by Walton Handy, the village shepherd, and relayed to the world from **Ilmington Manor**, the fine Elizabethan house once owned by the De Montfort family. The nearby **Ilmington Downs** are, at 850 feet, the highest point in the county, commanding fine views of the surrounding country.

NORTHAMPTONSHIRE

BRACKLEY   MAP 7 REF N17
28 miles SE of Stratford off the A43

The origin of Brackley is to be found in a cluster of farms two and a half miles to the north. Here was the centre of the old Saxon parish of **Halse**, with a church mentioned in Domesday Book. This medieval seignorial borough grew to be quite prosperous in the early Middle Ages and then rather faded away. The Saxon old town is distinguished by its huddle of houses round a tangle of streets. The prosperity brought by the marketing of wool in the broad High Street in the 13th century enabled the church of St Peter's to be rebuilt with its fine early English west tower and south aisle. Magdalen College School, founded in 1548 by William of Waynflete, incorporates the chapel of a Hospital of St John and St James, and the **Town Hall**, with its fine clock tower built in 1706, stands in High Street. The Duke of Bridgewater was responsible for the latter; its open arched windows on the ground floor used to be an open market place. The outsize station built in the 19th century is called Brackley Central, though in fact it is on the northern edge of town.

SULGRAVE   MAP 7 REF N16
6 miles N of Brackley off the B4525

There would seem to be little connection between an Elizabethan manor house and the US as we know it today. Yet it was from Sulgrave that George Washington's ancestors emigrated to a new life in the New World. **Sulgrave Manor** today is faithfully preserved and open to the public as a Washington Museum. The house was sold to Laurence Washington, George's great grandfather, in 1539. He was a distingiuished wool merchant and twice

Sulgrave Manor

Mayor of Northampton. The walls and ceilings have been stripped of their plaster and the panels of their coats of paint. The massive oak beams and the planks of the floors now gleam with a deep golden lustre as they must have done when Elizabeth I paid a visit. The seven feet wide fireplaces are fitted with medieval implements, and there is a captivating miniature dresser with a child's play set of cups, plates and pots all made of shining pewter. Georges black coat has pride of place and there is a fragment of Martha Washington's wedding dress on display. Outside the porch bears the family coat of arms, sometimes regarded as the origin of the "stars and stripes". The village church, **St James the Less**, contains a memorial brass to Laurence Washington and his wife, as well as the 17th century Washington family pew. It has also been enriched over the years by gifts from American pilgrims, one of which is a light oak tower screen with tracery picked out in scarlet and blue where the flags of England and the US hang side by side. Another gift is the organ donated by the colonial Dames of America. On the village green are the old stocks which actually pre-date the founding of the United States.

TOWCESTER
Map 7 ref O16
11 miles NE of Brackley off the A43

Britons, Romans, Saxons and Normans have all had a hand in shaping Towcester, although little remains to testify to this. During Romans times it was a walled town called *Lactodorum*. During the Civil War, it was the only Royalist stronghold in the area and later, during the heyday of coaches, it was an important staging post between Holyhead and London. The Towcester **Church of St Lawrence** contains the work of many centuries; the crypt, reached by a doorway from the sanctuary, dates back to the 13th century, while the arcades with their lofty piers originate from the 13th and 14th centuries. On the arch of the south chapel is a carved jester's head, probably 600 years old. The massive 90 foot tower with carved angels and font are about 500 years old. To the east you'll come to the **Grand Union Canal**, constructed between 1793 and 1805, winding its way and taking its place in tranquil scenes until its waters are raised by seven locks and vanish into the Blisworth Tunnel, which is nearly two miles long.

ROADE
Map 7 ref O16
5 miles E of Towcester off the A508

Chapter House in Roade is a magnificent listed building dating back to the 17th century. Steeped in history, it stands back from the High Street in its own grounds. Formerly a Baptist chapel (where it is thought John Bunyan once preached), owners Mr and Mrs Morgan have

personally managed this fine guest house since 1995; they have lovingly restored and renovated the old chapel into a delightful nine-bedroomed home, of which three are let. There are three lounges to relax in, each peaceful and well appointed, as well as a handsome dining room. The guest bedrooms are spacious and very comfortable. The bedrooms lead onto a galleried area overlooking the im-

Chapter House, High Street, Roade, Northamptonshire NN7 2NW Tel: 01604 862523 Fax: 01604 864117

pressive main hall. The breakfasts are hearty and filling - just the thing to set one up for a day's sightseeing in the area. This beautiful and tranquil guest house offers superior accommodation in a lush rural setting, yet near Northampton and Silverstone, and within walking distance from a restaurant and two pubs.

FOSTERS BOOTH
Map 7 ref O16
5 miles SE of Towcester off the A5

An ideal stopping-off point for travellers en route north or south along the A5, **The Red Lion** is a warm and welcoming pub that dates back to the 17th century, when it began life as a traditional coaching inn. The lounge bar is tastefully furnished and boasts low beamed ceilings, an open fireplace and other cosy and homely original features. The food and drink on offer are superior: there's a wide selection of sandwiches, snacks and traditional favourites such as sausage and mash, steaks, chops, grills and chicken dishes, along with home-made daily specials, all in generous portions and at good-value prices. Ales on tap include Boddington's and John Smith's, together with

The Red Lion, Watling Street, Fosters Booth, nr Towcester Northamptonshire NN12 8LB Tel: 01327 830259

a very good choice of house wines, lagers and spirits. This attractive pub is open lunchtimes Wednesday - Friday and all day weekends, evenings seven days a week. Althorp House, Canons Ashby (National Trust), Towcester, the Grand Union Canal and the racecourse at Silverstone are all just a short distance away. Caravans are welcome on site by prior arrangement.

DAVENTRY
Map 7 ref N16
10 miles NW of Towcester off the A45

Daventry's streets of dignified Georgian houses follow the lines of the medieval thoroughfare. In the High Street can be found many fine old buildings, and in the **Market Place** stands the **Moot Hall**, built in 1769 of ironstone, and home to **Daventry Museum** and the tourist information centre. Built as a private house, the building became Daventry's Town (or Moot) Hall in 1806 following demolition of the original. The museum has a permanent exhibition illustrating the story of Borough Hill, the local trades, rural life and the development of Daventry. As one of the town's main education and cultural centres, the museum also has a programme of temporary exhibitions that are changed regularly and range from village life in Ghana to the work of professional artists on the ever popular theme of cats.

HELLIDON
Map 7 ref N16
12 miles NW of Towcester off the A361

Hellidon is a picturesque conservation village; many of the properties are built of locally quarried stone. It also boasts a tennis, croquet and fishing club, which residents at **The Red Lion** have complimentary use of. This traditional country inn has open fires and a wood burning stove; the walls are adorned with interesting country prints. The ambience is warm and wel-

Croyland Abbey, with dormer windows in the 500 year old roof. Near to it, in public grounds, stands an old tithe barn, stone walled and thatched, 70 feet long and 22 feet wide. It was built in the 15th century and has two great doorways at either side, one of which is 13 feet high. All these buildings escaped a great fire which razed most of the town in fours hours in 1738. The handsome 13th century tower and spire of the parish church of All Hallows rises amongst the trees in the centre of town. The great tower seen from across the Nene is that of St Mary's, a modern church built between1906 and 1930.

KETTERING   Map 7 ref O15
12 miles NE of Northampton off the A43

The second biggest town in the north of the county, Kettering stands above the River Ise. Its name is familiar far and wide, for its produces clothing and shoes. It is here that the missionary William Carey and the famous preacher Andrew Fuller founded the Baptist Missionary Society, which gave a new impetus to the cause of foreign missions all over the world. Kettering's great parish church, built of Barnack stone, is one of the most impressive in the country. The tower and spire, rising 178 feet, are a landmark for miles around. Much of the old town has disappeared in its rapid growth, but a few old houses linger in narrow lanes. Hands-on heritage is on offer at the **Kettering Heritage Quarter** and well worth investigating. Explore the local history at the **Manor House Museum**, where both permanent and temporary exhibitions are held. Many regular activities take place and visitors of all ages will find plenty to interest them.

CRANFORD ST ANDREW   Map 7 ref P15
5 miles E of Kettering off the A14

The Old Dairy Farm in Cranford St Andrew makes an ideal base for touring in the area. There are four comfortable and gracious guest bedrooms, including a ground-floor self-contained mews flat suitable for people with disabilities. Within the main house itself there are two double rooms and one twin. Dating back to Jacobean times, and first built in 1610, this characterful

stonebuilt establishment has a thatched roof and mullioned lattice windows, and overlooks meadows and parkland. There's a delightful garden and summerhouse where guests can take afternoon tea. The guests' sitting room is cosy and welcoming, with its lovely inglenook fireplace and comfortable furnishings. Fresh fruit and home-made jams and marmalade are features of the delicious breakfasts. Evening meals are also available on request. These

The Old Dairy Farm, St Andrew's Lane, Cranford St Andrew, Kettering, Northamptonshire NN14 4AQ Tel: 01536 330273

tempting repasts make use of the freshest local produce. There are many opportunities for walks and cycling, as well, of course, as the sightseeing available in the area.

ROTHWELL
MAP 7 REF O15

4 miles NW of Kettering off the A605

A couple of miles north of Rothwell, at the **Rushton Triangular Lodge**, the visitor will find a fascinating piece of pious eccentricity built by Sir Thomas Tresham. He owned Rushton Hall, and he built a folly in 1593 to symbolise the Holy Trinity. Everything about the Lodge relates to the number three or multiples thereof - it has three sides, three stories and is 27 feet high. Each side has three windows and three gables, and the theme is continued in the triangular decoration. It even has a three-sided chimney. It is difficult to understand the full meaning of Sir Thomas's personal philosophy, but the building is nevertheless quite beautiful. In a way it still partly fulfils his original idea, for it certainly provokes the visitor to think about this strange embodiment of religious fervour. Nearby Rushton Hall was Tresham's home, now a school of the Royal Institute for the Blind.

BRIGSTOCK
MAP 7 REF P15

8 miles NE of Kettering off the A6116

On the banks of a tributary of the Nene called Harpers Brook is the Saxon village of Brigstock in the Rockingham Forest. The **Church of St Andrew** has a substantial Saxon tower built and its bell used to be tolled three times a day as a guide for travellers through the forest. The forest itself was once the hunting grounds of Norman aristocracy, but evidence has been unearthed to show that Brigstock had been settled during the Iron Age and during Roman occupation. The village has delightful old stone cottages and a 16th century manor house. By the little tree-covered green, a quaint Elizabethan cross stands on four steps and is carved on four sides. On the top stands a ball weather-vane. About a mile away is **Fermyn Woods Hall**, a house which has grown through the centuries from the 14th to the 19th. It was a forest hunting lodge 600 years ago, its gateway was brought from the house known as the Old Building (or Bield) at Lyveden and bears the coat of arms of Sir Lewis Tresham, second son of Sir Thomas the Builder. His New and Old Buildings at Lyveden are about two miles from Brigstock; one a farmhouse, the other a ruin, bearing witness to the erratic devotion and architectural interest of their creator.

   The Olde Three Cocks in Brigstock is a handsome limestone-fronted traditional coaching inn right on the village's main street. This charming and relaxing pub and restaurant has a large and welcoming lounge area with large open fireplace and a wealth of comfortable seating. Open every day for breakfast (7-9.30 a.m.), lunch (midday-3 p.m.; until 4 p.m. Sundays) and evening meals (6-10 p.m.), the excellent restaurant offers a superb choice of snacks and main courses, together with morning coffee and afternoon tea. Just a sample of what's on the menu would include Brigstock rack of lamb, sirloin steak,

The Olde Three Cocks Inn, 14 High Street, Brigstock,
nr Kettering, Northamptonshire NN14 3HA
Tel: 01536 373214 Fax: 01536 373767

fettucini with smoked salmon, duck St Clement's and fresh local trout. There's always a choice of vegetarian dishes and daily specials. All are expertly prepared and well-presented. The friendly staff are conscientious and helpful. The range of real ales includes John Smiths and changing guest ales, along with a good choice of stout, lagers, wines and spirits.

RUTLAND

OAKHAM
Map 7 ref O14
20 miles N of Kettering on the A606

Oakham, the county town of Rutland, is where visitors will see some of the beauty of the place and learn something of the county's history. The infamous Titus Oates was born here in 1649. His ability to create malignant fantasy in order to set the Catholics and the Protestants against each other became well-known, as he invented the idea of a Popish Plot against Charles II. A street market is still held twice weekly in the **Market Place** which contains an historic **Buttercross** and a set of stocks. Just off the market place is **Oakham Castle**. This romantic Norman castle has a sense of history epitomised by the 12th century **Great Hall**. The pillars supporting its magnificent arcades have carved capitals so much like the ones in the chancel of Canterbury Cathedral that it must have been the same craftsman who were responsible for both. There is a lot to take in but what is especially memorable is the amazing collection of horseshoes. It is a longstanding tradition apparently that any peer of the realm coming to Oakham for the first time must present the castle with a horseshoe. You can see them hanging all around the walls of the hall. They are all shapes and sizes, large and small, some wooden some rusty and in amongst them you will see one presented by Queen Elizabeth I and one by Queen Elizabeth II

It is no distance from the castle to **All Saints church** with its 14th century tower, a fine parish church and standing watchfully over the town. **The Rutland County Museum**, on Catmos Street, is dedicated to Rutland life and includes agricultural equipment, implements and wagons. There are local craft tools, 19th and early 20th century domestic items and a whole range of archeological finds. The Museum is housed in a splendid 18th century former riding school of the Rutland Fencibles, a volunteer cavalry regiment. Rutland, like the counties that surround it, has villages of thatch and ironstone clustered around their churches and is rich in pasture where once deer were hunted. Its central feature is **Rutland Water**, just a few miles east of Oakham. Its 3,100 acres makes it one of the largest manmade lakes in northern Europe. Started in 1971, it was created by damming the valley near Empingham. The result is an attractively landscaped lake, around five miles long which also serves as a popular recreational and leisure centre where sailing, water skiing and windsurfing are pursued.

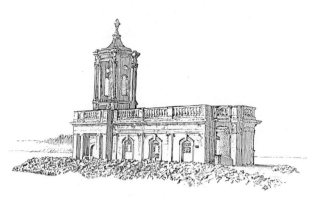

Normanton Tower, Rutland Water

EXTON
Map 7 ref O14

4 miles NE of Oakham off the A606

Exton is situated in one of the largest ironstone extraction areas in the country. It is a charming village and the **Old Hall**, now ruined, is thought to have been built during the reign of Elizabeth I. It was burned down in 1810 and was replaced by a **New Hall** in the middle of that century.

GREETHAM
Map 7 ref O14

5 miles NE of Oakham off the A606/B668

Since 1990, Richard and Ann Haworth have built up the reputation for service and quality at **The Wheatsheaf Inn** in Greetham. This characterful pub has a good local following and is also popular with walkers taking the Viking Way - which passes through the village on the way to Oakham - and other visitors. This 300-year-old inn is a Grade II listed building, and has always been a pub and a centre of village life. There is a lovely garden area with a stream running through it - just the place to relax on fine days. The excellent choice of beers includes Tetleys

**The Wheatsheaf Inn, Stretton Road, Greetham,
Rutland LE15 7NP Tel: 01572 812325**

and Boddingtons, as well as a good range of lagers, cider, stout, wines and spirits. Home-cooked food available makes a feature of traditional English favourites, such as steak and Guinness pie and mixed grills, together with vegetarian dishes and a selection of bar snacks. The Sunday lunch is justly popular. This fine inn also boasts three guest bedrooms - one family, one twin and a single - which are homely and attractive, offering guests comfort in a relaxed and informal atmosphere. Pets welcome by prior arrangement.

CLIPSHAM
Map 7 ref P14

8 miles NE of Oakham off the A606

The most precious possession of the little hamlet of Clipsham is the heraldic glass in the north chapel. As you look at it, remember that it was shattered during the Wars of the Roses and brought here; when you see the sun glisten on it, it gives one an eerie feeling to think that the same sun was lighting the glass in the war that drove the Plantagenets off the throne and put the Tudors in their place. It was from the ancient church at Pickworth, by the Lincolnshire border, that this glass came.

EMPINGHAM
MAP 7 REF P14

4 miles E of Oakham off the A606

Following the south shore of Rutland Water takes the visitor Empingham, which is dominated by the attractive tower and spire of **St Peter's Church**. It is a well proportioned building with an eye catching west front. Its interior features include fragments of ancient glass.

RYHALL
MAP 7 REF P14

7 miles E of Oakham off the A1/A6121

One of the most beautiful sights in the county has to be the 13th century tower and spire of the church at Ryhall, which stands just beyond **Tolethorpe Hall**, which boasts some lovely pannelling. There is a nice little legend about the village, which bestrides a little river. In the church, St Tibba, niece of King Penda of Mercia, is said to held up by two flying horses and surmounted by a helmet and eagle crest, the whole being supported by cherubs.

UPPINGHAM
MAP 7 REF O14

6 miles S of Oakham off the A47

Uppingham, standing by the A6003 and near the A47, is a very lovely town where **Uppingham School** was founded in 1587 to become one of the leading public schools under the headship of DR Edward Tring during the 19th century. Adjacent to the church in Market Square in Uppingham, **The Vaults** is a 400-year-old public house with great character and atmosphere.

Owned by John Pearson, a former county cricketer for 34 years, the pub is a friendly hub for both locals and visitors alike, and is adorned with cricketing memorabilia and photographs of benefit matches John has taken part in. This family-run Free House serves Pedigree, Marstons and Tetleys ales, together with a range of lagers, ciders, stout, wines and spirits. Bar meals and a full a la carte menu offer a selection of delicious traditional dishes; there are also tempting daily specials. For those who wish to stay in this de-

The Vaults, Market Square, Uppingham, Rutland LE15 9QH Tel: 01572 823259

lightful part of the county, handy for Leicester, Peterborough, Melton Mowbray and Rutland Water, accommodation is available in the shape of three twin rooms and one family room, in cottages to the rear of the pub. A full English breakfast is also provided.

BARROWDEN
MAP 7 REF P14

8 miles SE of Oakham off the A47

A warm welcome awaits visitors to **Ashleigh House**, a comfortable and charming house offering superior bed and breakfast accommodation. This attractive stonebuilt house is set on the edge of the picturesque and peaceful village of Barrowden, with marvellous views over the

Welland valley to Wakerley woods. Angus and Jayne Kennedy have made this their home since 1987. There are three lovely guest bedrooms, which are well-furnished and cosy. A real home-from-home atmosphere fills this relaxed and informal establishment. Guests are invited to make use of the spacious and well-appointed sitting room. Home-made preserves and the freshest local ingredients to into preparing the hearty and delicious breakfasts. The house is within easy

Ashleigh House, 2 Wakerley Road, Barrowden, nr Uppingham, Rutland LE15 8EP Tel: 01572 747398 Fax: 01572 747117 email: ashleighhouse@cwcom.net

walking distance of the excellent local inn on the village green, for evening meals. within about three miles of Rutland Water and six miles of Stamford and Kirby Hall, it makes an excellent base from which to explore these and the many other attractions of the region.

LEICESTERSHIRE

MARKET HARBOROUGH
11 miles NW of Kettering off the A6

Map 7 ref O15

One of the most attractive features of the picturesque small town is its wide main square. Its most notable building is the former grammar school, built in 1614. It stands above the street on carved wooden pillars; pedestrians can walk underneath it. The space below the school used to be a butter market but sadly no more. The parish **Church of St Dionysius**, built circa 1200, is topped by a steeple which is a landmark for miles around. The interior of the church has galleries added since 1683 to accommodate an overflow in the congregation. The town was a trading centre as early as 1203, and markets are still held every Tuesday and Saturday. Industrial development has not destroyed the town's wealth of fine Georgian buildings. The inn sign that swings outside **The Three Swans**

Old Grammar School

is a worthy example of 18th century ironwork. Charles I made his headquarters in the town before the Battle of Naseby, and when he was defeated Cromwell occupied Market Harborough and from here wrote to Parliament telling them of his victory.

SWINFORD
MAP 7 REF N15
8 miles SW of Market Harborough off the M1/A427

Stanford Hall, just a mile and a half from Swinford, is with the village part of the ancient parish of Stanford. Some years after it was given to the Benedictine Abbey of Selby by a Norman companion of the Conqueror in 1069, another grant of Stanford land was made in 1140 to the Abbey by King Stephen. When the Dissolution of the Monasteries took place, Sir Thomas Cave purchased the original manor from Henry VIII in 1540. The present building dates from the reign of William and Mary, around 1690, and has a majestic facade that adds to the its pleasing design. Inside, the rooms contain interesting collections of Stuart and Jacobite paintings, costumes and furniture. The stables house a motor museum and a replica of an 1898 flying machine.

NEVILL HOLT
MAP 7 REF O15
5 miles NE of Market Harborough off the B664

Since 1989 Sally Beaty has been offering wonderful bed and breakfast accommodation at **Medbourne Grange**, an impressive 150-year-old farmhouse set amid marvellous rural scenery two miles from the centre of Medbourne. This handsome ivy-covered farmhouse commands

magnificent views to the Welland Valley. A working farm, Sally's husband David has farmed here for the past 37 years. A popular base for the Shires and Rutland, it makes an ideal place for short break holidays. There are four charming guest rooms - one double room, one twin and two single - comfortably and attractively furnished with tasteful furnishing and decor. Guests are welcome to enjoy

Medbourne Grange, Nevill Holt, Market Harborough, Leicestershire LE16 8EF Tel: 01858 565249 Fax: 01858 565257

the lovely sitting room, garden and outdoor heated swimming pool (when the weather permits in summer). The full English breakfast includes farm-fresh eggs and is served in the large and attractive dining room. With Rutland Water and Eyebrook Reservoir nearby, it is a peaceful retreat with some fine walks and birdwatching opportunities. Open all year round.

GLOOSTON
MAP 7 REF O14
5 miles N of Market Harborough off the A6/A47

Glooston, a village in a hollow, was occupied during Roman times. The site of a Roman villa was discovered in 1946 on the east bank of the stream, and the Roman Gartree Road runs just south of here. The lovely Church of St Peter dates back to the 13th century. **The Old Barn Inn** is an excellent public house with an accent on upholding the long-standing traditions of a welcoming and quality inn. Owner Andrew Price is a qualified chef with a wealth of experience of working in hotels in Lancashire. He bought the pub in

The Old Barn Inn, Andrews Lane, Glooston, nr Market Harborough, Leicestershire LE16 7ST Tel: 01858 545215

1998, and together with his wife Joanne and their two daughters offers all guests a warm welcome and genuine hospitality. Here in this charming hamlet, visitors come from far and wide to sample the delights of the menu and cellars. The interior of this 16th-century Free House boasts real log fires and other original features. A superb choice of real ales, malt whiskies, lagers, wines and other spirits await the visitor. In the handsome restaurant the imaginative menu offers up a range of wonderful dishes and changing specials, freshly prepared and expertly presented. Winner of the Leicestershire Dining Award in 1999, and voted by *Wine Magazine '99* as having award-winning wines, this fine establishment is well worth seeking out.

HALLATON
MAP 7 REF O14

6 miles N of Market Harborough off the A6/A47

Mentioned in the Domesday Book as Alctone, this village lies in rich grazing lands of the Welland Valley. Every Easter Monday the villagers of Hallaton turn out in force to challenge neighbouring Medbourne in a boisterous "bottle kicking" contest, steeped in pagan ritual. First a huge hare pie is cut into portions and distributed by the rector. Some is left over to be scattered on Hare Pie Bank. The T-shaped house at the eastern end of the village reveals, behind its 17th century facade, a remarkable 13th century dwelling. The old hall, southeast of the church, is an H-plan house built in 1650. Near the church is a medieval bridge of three arches, and the church itself is surrounded by sycamore, oak and beech trees. It is notable for the great beauty of an aisle in the south transept which has a 20-foot window flooding it with light. In the tower arch the huge clock pendulum can be seen swinging.

LEICESTER
MAP 7 REF N14

15 miles NW of Market Harborough off the A6

The historic centre still retains much of interest from Roman times to the 20th century. There is a great open air market held in the square near **Gallow Tree Gate**. It has been here on the same site since at least 1200 and probably long before. There is something going on here every weekday; but the most interesting days are Wednesday, Friday and Saturday, and there are many bargains to be had or you can just soak up a wonderful atmosphere. Leicester was founded just before the Roman conquest and they called it *Ratae Coritanorum* (capital or Coritani); it is also mentioned in Domesday Book under the name of Ledecestre. If you enjoy ancient ruins, **The Jewry Wall Museum and Site** in St Nicholas Circle is to be recommended, being devoted to archaeology up to 1500 AD. It is a modern building adjacent to the Roman bath site and houses some extremely important exhibits. The Bronze Age Welby Hoard and the Roman Milestone from Thurmaston are here. There are several important Romano-British mosaics, Roman wall plaster and items from Anglo-Saxon burials. **St Nicholas Church**, close to the Jewry Wall, is one of the best known Anglo-Saxon churches in England. It stands on the site of the Roman basilica and was built with materials from the Roman ruins. In the walls can be seen stones from four different periods - namely Roman, Saxon, Norman and Medieval English. Courses of herringbone masonry formed by Roman tiles are round the massive central tower built by the Normans and enriched with arcading. There is Saxon masonry in the west wall and two deeply splayed windows, their round heads formed by double rows of Roman tiles.

The **Guildhall** in Guildhall Lane has been described as one of the most remarkable civic buildings in England. The Great Hall was built of timber in 1390 as a meeting place for members of the Corpus Christi Guild and later used by the Mayor and his brethren. The hall was used as the town hall until the new municipal building 1876 was erected. The Mayor's Parlour, adjoining the Great Hall, was built early in the reign of Henry VII, and has a wonderful oak panelled chimney-piece. Set in the leaded panes of the windows is black and gold painted glass showing the Tudor Rose, the Prince of Wales feathers, a chalice and some of the seasons.

Wygston's House is an important medieval building at 12, Applegate, St Nicholas Circle. It houses a fantastic display of 18th-20th century costume. The materials and colours are superb and looking at some of the fantastic gowns you can almost hear the swish of silk skirts as the ladies moved round a room. In addition to the costumes there is also a reconstruction of a draper's and shoe shop of the 1920s. From here it is just a short walk to the **Castle**. The 12th century Great Hall is now concealed within 18th century brickwork as it is used as the Crown Court. It has a charming setting, however, with the riverside gardens on one side and the spacious green on the other. The remains of the original Norman motte (or central mound) can still be seen. In a wonderful setting on the edge of the castle green above the River Soar is the **Church of St Mary de Castro**. It was founded in 1107 by the first Earl Leicester as a collegiate chapel, and was extended several times during the next 300 years. Near the altar are five stone *sedilia*, or seats for the clergy, which date from 1180 and are regarded as the finest of their kind in England. Its spire, rebuilt in 1783, makes a dramatic impact - acrobats were once wont to slide down a rope from the top to the castle green below.

A visit to **Newarke Houses Museum** offers an introduction to the history of Leicestershire. It is a social history collection from 1500 to the present day. There are displays showing 17th century panelled rooms and a 19th century street scene among others. An amazing array of clocks is laid out in one room, musical instruments in another, and sports and pastimes have not been forgotten either. Even the garden has been kept in period with the right flowers and a marvellous herb garden. **The Museum of the Royal Leicestershire Regiment** provides a complete picture of the history of the Royal Leicestershire Regiment (17th Foot) including momentous battle trophies and relics. The city is a good transport centre with seven great roads radiating from it. There are also three railway stations and the Grand Union Canal linking it with the Trent and the Thames. It was from Leicester that Thomas Cook organised his first excursion, to Loughborough of all places, and of course, never looked back. **Leicestershire Museum and Art Gallery**, in New Walk is considered to be a major regional art gallery, for its European art collection travels from the 15th century to include German Expressionism and French Impressionism. The art collection is by no means the only treasure in this fine building. There are displays of natural history including the Rutland Dinosaur.

Several 18th century buildings survive in Leicester, among them **Belgrave Hall** in Church Road, built during the Queen Anne period in 1709 and two miles north of the city centre. With great care the Hall has been kept in its original state. The rooms are all delightfully furnished with items of the era. In the stable block there are well preserved coaches, the harness room has tack still hanging on the walls and there are agricultural implements that would have been in use at that time. The gardens are a sheer pleasure, some period, some botanical, including a rock and water garden and greenhouses with over 6,500 species of plants.

KIRKBY MALLORY
MAP 7 REF N14

5 miles SW of Leicester off the A47

Set in a peaceful location half a mile from the pretty village of Kirkby Mallory, **The Oaks** is a secluded farmhouse with 2½ acres of land, including woodland and ponds. Visitors to Mallory Park for the motor-racing, Market Bosworth, Shackstone Steam Railway, Bradgate Park and Leicester itself find this a convenient and relaxing retreat. Graham and Vicki Penney have been offering bed and breakfast accommodation at this lovely farmhouse since 1989. Built in 1916 after the design of the keeper's cottage of the Mallory Park estate, it has been carefully restored and extended by the Penneys to incorporate every modern comfort. The pleasant gardens, patio and woodland are perfect places in which to

**The Oaks, Stapleton Lane, Kirkby Mallory,
Leicestershire LE9 7QJ Tel: 01455 848125**

relax or wander. There's an abundance of wildlife nearby. The two guest bedrooms are cosy and comfortable. The lovely breakfast room has charming features such as its original oak floor and country style dressers and tables. The full English breakfast boasts fresh eggs from the Penneys' own chickens.

MARKET BOSWORTH
MAP 7 REF N14

10 miles W of Leicester off the A447

Market Bosworth is just a couple of miles north of nearby Sutton Cheney and it is from this small 700 year old market town that the Battle of Bosworth took its name. It is a village of no great size but its former grammar school had a high reputation in the Midlands. Originally founded in early Tudor times, in 1601, it was given a new lease of life by Sir Wolstan Dixie. It was to this school that Samuel Johnson came to teach after leaving university. He hated it so much that even Boswell failed to induce him to talk about his time here. At Ambion Hill, near Market Bosworth, is **Bosworth Battlefield Visitor Centre and Country Park**. It was here, on 22nd August 1485, that the armies of Richard III and Henry Tudor faced eachother. The battle that followed put a new king on the throne and changed the course of history. Here, visitors have the opportunity to visit one of Britain's best interpreted Battlefields. Exciting exhibitions bring thse events of the 15th century to life. A medieval street has been recreated, and the collections of arms, armour and heraldry of the period are extensive. Across the park there is a unique Battle Trail with a series of imaginatively illustrated Trail Boards.

ELMESTHORPE
MAP 7 REF N14

10 miles SW of Leicester off the B581

The atmosphere at **Badgers Mount** is relaxed and informal. Set in lovely countryside, this large and impressive hotel has an eye-catching exterior with gabled windows, pitched roof, spacious

patio area, gardens and heated outdoor swimming pool (for summer use). Inside all is reminiscent of traditional country style and comfort. The six ensuite guest bedrooms are charming and comfortable. The full English or Continental breakfast is served in the warm and welcoming dining room. Evening meals can also be taken on request. There is also a guests' bar overlooking the patio, where a fine

**Badgers Mount, 6 Station Road, Elmesthorpe,
Leicestershire LE9 7SG Tel: 01455 848161**

selection of beers, wines and spirits is served. All creature comforts are satisfied here, in a tranquil and relaxing ambience. Owners Ivor and Jill, who have lived here since 1988, have created a truly friendly and comfortable guest house that is an ideal base for exploring the natural and man-made beauties of the region. ETB 4 Diamonds Highly Commended.

TILTON-ON-THE-HILL
10 miles E of Leicester off the B6074

Map 7 ref O14

Not far from the village of Tilton-on-the-Hill, the delectable rolling park of **Launde Abbey** lies close to the Rutland frontier. Nestling in its own world of lonely lanes and ancient woodlands, from all directions the drives lead to the house, an H-Shaped Elizabethan and 17th century manor with gabled wings and dormers. The chancel of the Augustinian priory church stands behind the north wing, still in use for worship.

BURROUGH-ON-THE-HILL
12 miles NE of Leicester off the B6074

Map 7 ref O14

Burrough-on-the-Hill stands nearly 600 feet above sea level on the marlstone escarpment. The great earthwork of **Burrough Hill** is the grandest Iron Age hill fort in the county. Some of the ancient mounds are still 20 feet high; the countryside is seen in a vast panorama all around this 82 acre site.

LOUGHBOROUGH
9 miles N of Leicester on the A6

Map 7 ref N13

Loughborough, known for its bells, which have rung around the world since 1858 when the bell foundry of John Taylor moved to the town from Oxford. The tower of the parish **Church of All Saints** has a peal of 10 bells, and contains a memorial to the bell-founding Taylor family. Much of the building dates from the 14th century despite its 19th century appearance, and the aisles have windows dating from about 1300. The oak roof of the nave is carried on beams which spring from carved musician angels resting one stone supports and the west wall is decorated with 15th century brasses.

In **Queen's Park** stands the impressive Loughborough War Memorial Tower and Carillon. The tower was "erected in Grateful Memory of the Men of Loughborough who gave their lives for freedom in the Great War". It is an impressive sight which is enhanced by the rather special carillon contained within. This carillon consists of 47 bells and, because the playing of such sets of bells is such an art, it is necessary to appoint a Borough Carilloner. Recitals are performed throughout the summer months by both the resident carilloner and guest players.

In Steeple Row, behind the Parish Church, you will find the **Old Rectory Museum**. This historic building is a rare survival of a 13th century stone built manor house. It was members of the Loughborough and District Archaeological Society who discovered that parts of the original medieval building were hidden behind later alterations. Their work created national interest, and saved the Rectory from being demolished. For those interested in steam trains, go to the Central Station and there you will see Loughborough's links with the steam age preserved. The **Main Line Steam Trust** runs locomotives from here to Quorn and Birstall, a distance of about 10 miles which includes the Swithland Reservoir viaduct.

On the edge of Loughborough, just five minutes' walk from the town centre, on the main A6 and close to the Great Central Steam Trust, the **De Montfort Hotel** is a homely and welcoming establishment owned and personally run by Rachel Howard. Rachel is an attentive and friendly host. The hotel is named after Simon De Montfort, the 13th

De Montfort Hotel, 88 Leicester Road, Loughborough, Leicestershire LE11 2AQ
Tel: 01509 216061 Fax: 01509 233667

century Earl of Leicester and "Father of Parliament". A hotel since 1947, this charming Victorian house is spacious and comfortable. Furnished and decorated in traditional Victorian style, there are nine lovely guest bedrooms, including three family rooms. Each is tastefully decorated and offers guests every modern amenity. The guests' sitting room is warm, cosy and relaxing; there is also a bar area where guests can enjoy a quiet drink. The traditional English breakfast is expertly prepared, hearty and filling. Home-cooked evening meals are available by arrangement, and served in the attractive restaurant. A true home-from-home atmosphere can be found at this informal and charming hotel.

ROTHLEY
MAP 7 REF N14
5 miles SE of Loughborough off the A6

One of Rothley's two greens - Town Green - incorporates some of the finest timber framed houses in the county. One or two are cruck-built, in which curved tree trunks are joined to form the framework of the house. Slightly more "modern"are the Tudor box-frame houses also in evidence here. Town Green lies on the edge of **Rothley Park**, site of Rothley Temple which was built in the 13th century by the Knights Templars. The temple was later incorporated into an Elizabethan house which was added to over the succeeding centuries and finally converted in 1960 into the Rothley Court Hotel. From about 1550 it was the seat of the Babington family. William Wilberforce, a family friend, drafted his bill for the abolition of slavery at the house while on a visit in 1791. A small monument records the occasion.

In 1800, the historian Thomas Babington Macaulay, later Lord Macaulay of Rothley, was born here, and the hotel maintains the room as it was on the day he was born. The original

Templar chapel is still used for occasional services and the parish church of St Mary the Virgin has some fine memorials and a carved Norman font. In the churchyard is a Saxon cross of the 8th or 9th century. Rothley Station, which was built for the Central Railway in the 1890s, is restored to its original condition, complete with nostalgic advertising where you can catch the restored steam train from Loughborough.

APPLEBY MAGNA
10 miles SW of Loughborough off the A444

Map 7 ref M14

Appleby Magna has a 14th century church and a moated manor house which unfortunately is not open to the public. Set amid acres of farmland, **Elms Farm** is a charming and lovely bed and breakfast. Run since 1989 by proprietor Elizabeth Frisby, it is a welcoming base for explor-

ing the many sights and places of historical and cultural interest in the area, and enjoying the excellent walking locally. Elizabeth and her family are convivial hosts who ensure that all their guests have an enjoyable break in their home. The original house dates back to the 18th century, with modern additions. There are three tastefully furnished and spacious guest bedrooms, with all the amenities guests have come to expect. The conservatory is also open to guests' use, and is a fine place to relax and enjoy the surrounding scenery. On fine days guests are also welcome to explore the appealing garden, which includes the old stabling block at one end. A hearty breakfast is served in the attractive dining room. Dogs welcome by prior arrangement. ETC 3 Diamonds.

Elms Farm, Atherstone Road, Appleby Magna, Leicestershire DE12 7AP Tel: 01530 270450

ASHBY-DE-LA-ZOUCH
12 miles W of Loughborough off the A50

Map 7 ref M14

Sir Walter Scott's romantic novel *Ivanhoe* sets the scene well for the northwest region of Leicestershire. The superbly named Ashby-de-la-Zouch was noted for the noble sport of jousting, where no doubt many a maiden's honour was upheld by knights in shining armour. Such tournaments took place near **Ashby Castle**, which was later attacked by Cromwell's Roundheads and consequently ruined. Much of the region's attraction and beauty dates back still further; to the east is the edge of the **Charnwood Forest**, whose exposed volcanic rocks and granites are over two thousand million years old. Although the Leicestershire coalfield is not far away, Ashby remains a pleasant little town and there is much to see. Market Street takes its name from the weekly market granted in 1219, and there were also no fewer than four annual fairs. Visually the most rewarding part of the town is the west end of Market Street where the **Spa quarter** is situated. Old, half-timbered buildings blend with modern architecture to make an attractive town with good shopping facilities, a number of impressive churches, parks and an imposing castle ruin. **The Bull's Head** is thought to be the oldest building. Cromwell reputedly had a drink here when the 15th century castellated manor was taken by Parliament after a years siege in the Civil War. In the former upper courtyard of the castle stands the 19th century **Manor House**, now a school. Also of interest is the elegant 70 foot high monument to the Countess of Loudoun, erected in 1874 and inscribed with a tribute to her from Disraeli. The castle ruin has a massive keep and many of the rooms are easily identifiable.

Dolce Café is a bright and cheerful place in Market Street of Ashby. Owner Filippo Vazzana is the genuine article, hailing from Cefalu, an historic fishing port in northern Sicily. He brings a bit of the Mediterranean to the menu and decor of this popular and lively café. Frescos on the walls depict traditional Sicilian scenes, while Italian music adds to the ambience of this lovely place. Superb Italian dishes on the menu include bruschette, panini (Italian bread), five pasta dishes, at least three daily specials and an excellent range of snacks, baguettes and main courses such as aubergine pie (*melanzane alla parmigiana*). There is also a wonderful selection of coffees on offer, including, of course, cappuccino and espresso. The delights of Sicily and southern Italy are here in this excellent range of classic dishes and lighter snacks. Pieces from the collection of Sicilian pottery on display in the window are for sale. Open Monday to Saturday from 9 a.m. to 6 p.m.

Dolce Café, 36 Market Street, Ashby de la Zouch, Leicestershire LE65 1AN Tel: 01530 563385

KEGWORTH

Map 7 ref N13

6 miles NW of Loughborough off the M1/A453

Kegworth is a large village with several interesting examples of what is now called "vernacular architecture" - native building including much dating from the days when it was a manufacturing village full of framework-knitters. It possesses an almost faultless late decorated church, which is largely 14th century, with some stained glass and a splendid Royal Arms dated 1684.

Owners Jane and Kevin Evley have refurbished **The Anchor Inn** so that the new front lounge area now has a boating theme, in keeping with the nautical name of this friendly and welcoming pub. Popular with locals, walkers, canal boaters and other visitors, this attractive late Victorian pub sits just 50 yards from the Soar Valley River, half a mile east of Kegworth on the edge of the village, along the road to Radcliffe-on-Soar. Visiting birdwatchers can enjoy the herons and kingfishers that make their home by the river,

The Anchor Inn, 139 Station Road, Kegworth, Leicestershire DE74 2FR Tel: 01509 672722

and keen anglers can get day or season tickets for fishing at the pub. Comfortably furnished throughout, in the Boaters' Bar a woodburning stove adds to the cosy ambience, while there's a comfortable back room and an open fire in the locals' bar. The menu offers a range of plain and simple home cooking - hearty, delicious and using the freshest ingredients. Among the traditional real ales on tap are Bass, Marstons and Theakstons; there are also good ciders, lagers, spirits and house wines.

SHEPSHED

Map 7 ref N14

4 miles W of Loughborough off the A6

Located in the centre of the charming village of Shepshed, just two miles from Junction 23 of the M1, **Croft Guest House** is a spacious, light and airy establishment with a warm family atmosphere. This attractive and traditional town house has been stylishly decorated and fur-

Croft Guest House, 21 Hall Croft, Shepshed, Loughborough, Leicestershire LE12 9AN Tel: 01509 505657 Fax: 08700 522266 Mobile: 07970 594825 e-mail: enquiries@croftguesthouse.demon.co.uk

nished by proprietors Jeremy, Ray and Denise Savage, who have been running this wonderful bed and breakfast since 1998. Ray and Jeremy are firemen by trade, and Denise a paramedic. A comfortable home from home, the guest house offers 10 lovely guest bedrooms, five ensuite. In the cosy and smart guests sitting room visitor can relax amid very pleasant surroundings. Breakfast is served in the charming dining room, and consists of a delicious and hearty full English breakfast - special dietary requirements can be accommodated by prior arrangement. Convenient for East Midland Aiport (just six miles away), Loughborough,

Leicester, Nottingham, Derby and further afield, there are several very good pubs and restaurants nearby for evening meals. The guest house offers easy access for visitors with disabilities. Children under five stay free. ETB 3 Diamonds.

MELTON MOWBRAY

Map 7 ref O14

15 miles NE of Leicester on the A607

Crossing an elegant bridge built in 1832 across the Eye (a tributary of the Wreake) and the canal, visitors will find themselves in the ancient market town of Melton Mowbray. The town's market days were recorded as a profitable concern in 1077 and certainly date from Saxon times. The Old English settled here as early as the 5th century; one of their pagan cemeteries has been discovered on the outskirts of town. Melton takes the second part of its name from the great Norman family of Mowbray, who owned the manor by 1125. Bright and cheerful with many fine 18th and 19th century houses, Melton boasts several notable buildings. The **Anne of Cleves house**, though now used as a restaurant, is primarily 15th century and was either a Chantry House belonging to the church or perhaps the dwelling house of one of the rich woolmerchants, who must have subscribed to the magnificent enlargement of the once Norman **Church of St Mary** in the late 15th century. Opposite the church is the **Maison Dieu**, founded as an almshouse in 1640. In the market place, the former **Swan Inn** retains a fine porch over the pavement.

Melton became the hunting metropolis of England; the meeting place of the Quorn, Cottesmore and Belvoir hunts, and was frequented by the nobility and gentry from all parts of the country. As late as 1939 it was said that, at the beginning of the season, a thousand fine hunters were stabled in the town. Many of the stables

Nottingham Street, Melton Mowbray

have now been converted into flats, but a number of the larger houses belonging to the wealthy are still to be seen. A very pleasant way to explore Melton Mowbray is to follow the **Jubilee Way** - a fifteen and a half mile waymarked walk mostly on field and woodland paths between Melton and Woolsthorpe, just across the Lincolnshire border. It will take you through the Vale of Belvoir via Scalford, Belvoir Woods and Belvoir Castle, eventually linking up with the Viking Way at Woolsthorpe. A gentler meander is the **Egerton Park Riverside Walk** in Melton which ends up in the **Melton Carnegie Museum** at Thorpe End. It has good coverage of the history and the environment of the Borough of Melton.

AB KETTLEBY

MAP 7 REF O13

3 miles N of Melton Mowbray off the A606

The renowned racehorse Desert Orchid is the most famous local celebrity of Ab Kettleby, born and bred at a nearby manor house in the village. Just 20 minutes from Belvoir Castle and near the centres of Rutland Water, Lincoln and Newark, **White Lodge Farm** in Ab Kettleby is a welcoming retreat offering bed and breakfast accommodation in three lovely guest rooms taste-

White Lodge Farm, Nottingham Road, Ab Kettleby, nr Melton Mowbray, Leicestershire LE14 3JB Tel: 01664 822286 or 823729

fully converted from farm buildings adjacent to the main farmhouse. This working mixed farm occupies rolling Leicestershire countryside on the edge of the picturesque Vale of Belvoir. The three self-contained ensuite rooms overlook the pretty garden, in which guests are welcome to relax on fine days. All rooms have colour TV and tea- and coffee-making facilities. The traditional English breakfast is served in the farmhouse dining room. Owner Margaret Spencer is a friendly host who offers quality of service at very reasonable prices. This charming home from home is just the place for a peaceful break, and makes a good base for exploring the area. Adjacent to the farm there's also the farm shop, selling locally-produced honey, free-range eggs and other wholesome produce.

OLD DALBY   Map 7 ref O13
6 miles NW of Melton Mowbray off the A46/A606

In a cul-de-sac in the middle of this charming village, **The Crown** is a superior public house with a warm and friendly ambience. Originally a farmhouse, it was built in 1519. The decor calls to mind a country cottage, with four separate rooms and many cosy snugs. Owners Lynn Busby and Graham Richards offer genuine hospitality to all their guests. Chef Amy worked for Anthony Worrall Thompson before joining the team at the pub. Her menus offer home-made traditional and more innovative dishes such as roast lamb, sesame roast duck, fillet tournedos and wild mushroom stroganoff. All dishes are prepared to order using the freshest ingredients.

**The Crown, Debdale Hill, Old Dalby, Melton Mowbray, Leicestershire LE14 3LF
Tel: 01664 823134**

The bar menu and range of puddings also offer a variety of tempting options. The excellent choice of real ales includes Ruddles and Wadworth 6X. There's also a superb wine list. This excellent pub is well worth seeking out. Open: Monday-Saturday noon-3, 6-11; Sunday noon-3, 7-10.30. Bar food Monday-Friday noon-2, 7-10; Sunday noon-2. Restaurant Tuesday 7-10; Wednesday-Saturday noon-2, 7-10; Sunday noon-2.

SALTBY   Map 7 ref O13
10 miles NE of Melton Mowbray off the A607

Saltby, high up towards the Lincolnshire border, has a little 700 year old church, one of its farms has a windmill and under its surface a Roman pavement has been found. Not far away, on Saltby Heath, are the mysterious earthworks known as **King Lud's Entrenchments**, a long mound of earth with a tumulus at each end. Lud was the sky god worshipped by the ancient Britons; tradition has it that King Lud was buried at one end during the Dark Ages. There was certainly a King of Mercia call Ludeca, who was killed in battle in 827, but it is more likely that the mounds were the boundary between two ancient Kingdoms. The Welsh name for London was Caer Ludd (Lud's town); Ludgate Hill preserves the name.

Five miles northeast is **Belvoir Castle**, well worth a visit. It was built in the closing decade of the 11th century by Robert de Todeni, one of William the Conqueror's standard bearers. The name is first recorded in 1130 as Belveder and in 1145 as Bello Videre - beautiful view. The castle suffered great damage in the Civil War and the 8th Earl built a mansion on the site in 1654, but in 1816 it suffered again in a great fire. The castle was finally completed in 1830 and today is one of the showplaces of the Midlands. There are some wonderful paintings including work by Van Dyck, Reynolds, Hogarth, and one of the finest of the Holbein portraits of Henry VIII. The gardens are particularly beautiful. On the side of the hill, the Duchess' Garden is full of terraces and stone statues; the Duke's Walk is an entire valley filled with flowerbeds and trees, and the Water Garden in summer is filled with azaleas and rhododendrons, a marvellous spectacle. A dovecote in the grounds stands on the site of Belvoir Priory, founded in 1076 and suppressed in 1539. Only four monks ever lived there.

STAFFORDSHIRE

LEEK

MAP 6 REF L12

9 miles NE of Stoke-on-Trent on the A53

Known as the 'Capital of the Moorlands', this is an attractive textile centre which lies on the banks of the River Churnet. It was here that French Huguenots settled, after fleeing from religious oppression, and established the silk industry that thrived due to the abundance of soft water coming off the nearby moorland. Until the 19th century, this was a domestic industry with the workshops being located on the top storey of the houses; many examples of these 'top shops' have survived to this day. Leek also became an important dyeing town, particularly after the death of Prince Albert, when 'Raven Black' was popularised by Queen Victoria who remained in mourning for her beloved husband for many years. William Morris, founder of the Arts and Crafts movement, lived and worked in Leek for many months between 1875 and 1878. Much of his time here was spent investigating new techniques of dyeing but he also revived the use of traditional dyes. His influence cannot only be seen in the art here but also in the architecture.

Leek is by no means a recent town that grew up in the shadow of the Industrial Revolution. An ancient borough, granted its charter in 1214, Leek was a thriving market centre rivalling Macclesfield and Congleton. The **Butter Cross**, which now stands in the Market Place, was originally erected near the junction of Sheep Market and Stanley Street by the Joliffe family in 1671. Every road coming into the town seems to converge on the old cobbled Market Place and the road to the west leads down to the Parish Church. Dedicated to Edward the Confessor (the full name is **St Edward's and All Saints' Church**), the original Church was burnt down in 1297 and rebuilt some 20 years later though the building is now largely 17th century. The timber roof of the nave is well worth a second look and is the Church's pride and joy. It is boasted that each of the cross beams was hewn from a separate oak tree and, in the west part of the nave, an enormous 18th century gallery rises up, tier on tier, giving the impression of a theatre's dress circle! Very much a focal point for Leek, a one time vicar, Rev PDS Blake, wrote a guide book about the Church in which he managed to express, with biblical comparisons, the approaches to Leek: "Coming down over Ladderedge, the sight of Leek on its hill in its valley, reminds one of coming over the Mount of Olives and seeing Jerusalem standing on Mount Zion."

Although much has been altered inside the Church, most notably in 1865 when GE Street rebuilt the chancel, reredos, sanctuary, pulpit and stalls, there still remains a rather unusual wooden chair. Traditionally this is believed to have been a ducking stool for scolds that was used in the nearby River Churnet. Outside, in the churchyard, can be found a rather curious inscription on a gravestone: "James Robinson interred February the 28th 1788 Aged 438"! To the north side of the Church is an area still known locally as 'Petty France', which holds the graves of many Napoleonic prisoners of war who lived nearby. Another building worthy of a second glance is the imposing **Nicholson Institute**, with its copper dome. Completed in 1884 and funded by the local industrialist Joshua Nicholson, the Institute offered the people of Leek an opportunity to learn and also expand their cultural horizons. Many of the great Victorian literary giants, including George Bernard Shaw and Mark Twain, came here to admire the building. The town's War Memorial, built in Portland stone and with a clock tower, has a dedication to the youngest Nicholson son who was killed in the First World War. Next door to the Institute is **Greystones**, now a tea shop, that is one of the oldest buildings in the town.

The **River Churnet**, though little known outside Staffordshire, has a wealth of scenery and industrial archaeology and, being easily accessible to the walker, its valley deserves better recognition. The River rises to the west of Leek, in rugged gritstone country but for most of its length it flows through softer red sandstone countryside in a valley that was carved out during the Ice Age. Though there are few footpaths directly adjacent to the riverbank, using a combination of canal towpaths and former railway tracks, most of the valley can be walked close to the River.

Four miles to the north of Leek on the A53 rise the dark, jagged gritstone outcrops of **The Roaches**, **Ramshaw Rocks** and **Hen Cloud**. Roaches is a corruption of the French word 'roches' or rocks and was reputedly given by Napoleonic prisoners: 'cloud' is a local word used for high hills. Just below The Roaches there is another delightful stretch of water, **Tittesworth Reservoir**, which is extremely popular with trout fishermen. It has some super trails, a visitors centre and a pretty picnic place.

BIDDULPH
MAP 6 REF L12
6 miles NW of Leek on the A527

John Wesley was a frequent visitor to this isolated moorland town but the history of Biddulph goes back to long before the days of Methodism. After the Norman Conquest the manor of Biddulph was granted by William the Conqueror to Robert the Forester, an overlord of what

was then the extensively forested area of Lyme. The Biddulphs, a staunchly Catholic family, took control of the area. John Biddulph fought under the Royal flag during the Civil War and was killed at the Battle of Hopton Heath. His son entrusted the defence of Biddulph Hall to Lord Brereton, who withstood a determined siege until 1644, when he was finally subjected to heavy artillery. The Hall was then demolished to prevent its regarrisoning.

Chinese Garden, Biddulph

Biddulph Grange belonged to the Cistercian monks of the Abbey at Hulton until the Dissolution and its gardens, created between 1842 and 1862, are opened to the public. Situated just below Biddulph Moor, these exceptional gardens contain many species of trees, shrubs, and other plants from all over the world. The gardens are owned by the National Trust.

RUDYARD
Map 6 ref L12

2 miles NW of Leek off the A52

In fond memory of the place where they first met in 1863, Mr and Mrs Kipling named their famous son, born in 1865, after this village. The nearby two mile long **Rudyard Reservoir** was built in 1831 by John Rennie to feed the Caldon Canal. With steeply wooded banks the lake is now a leisure centre where there are facilities for picnicking, walking, fishing and sailing. The west shore of the Reservoir is also a section of the **Staffordshire Way**, the long distance footpath which runs from Mow Cop to Kinver Edge. Back in Victorian days, Rudyard was a popular lakeside resort which developed after the construction of the North Staffordshire Railway in 1845. Its popularity became so great that, on one particular day in 1877, over 20,000 people came here to see the famous Captain Webb swim in the Reservoir.

CHEDDLETON
Map 6 ref L12

3 miles S of Leek on the A520

The restored **Cheddleton Flint Mill**, in the rural surroundings of the Churnet valley, makes an interesting visit. The water powered machinery was used to crush flint that had been brought in by canal and then transported, again by water, to Stoke where it was used in the hardening of pottery. The small museum includes a rare 18th century 'haystack' boiler and a Robey steam engine and there are also collections of exhibits which relate to the preparation of raw materials for the pottery industry. Trips by narrow boats along the **Caldon Canal** can be taken from the mill. The village of Cheddleton itself seems to perch dangerously on the side of a hill which is why it has such spectacular views. The **Parish Church of St Edward** stands in open country and has some wonderful Morris windows as well as a lot of interesting Victorian decoration, the result of the restoration by George Gilbert Scott in the 1860s and a sight well worth seeing. The village station is home to the **Churnet Valley Railway and Museum** which will give great delight to all railway enthusiasts. The Museum has a fine collection of beautifully preserved locomotives and other railway memorabilia which is sure to bring back many memories. Open to the public at weekends in the summer. To the west of Cheddleton is **Deep Hayes Country Park**

Cheddleton Flint Mill

which lies in a secluded valley by the Caldon Canal and Staffordshire Way. From the ridge there are breathtaking views but, for the less energetic, there is a very pleasant walk around two pools which has many offshoots into lovely countryside.

CONSALL
Map 6 ref L12

4 miles S of Leek off the A520

This is a beautiful spot hidden in a particularly deep section of the Churnet Valley downstream from Cheddleton. The little cottages keep in close company with the small bridges over the Caldon Canal. Originally known as **Consall Forge**, the hamlet took its name from an old iron forge that existed here in the first Elizabethan Age. As iron making became uneconomic here, the forge altered its operation and became one of the major lime making centres after the completion of the Caldon Canal. Equally well hidden and reached only through Consall village is **Consall Nature Park**, an RSPB reserve that is a quiet and peaceful haven with much to delight the avid birdwatcher. Only accessible on foot or by canal, the village is very popular with walkers and boaters and has a pub to provide the necessary refreshment.

OAKAMOOR
MAP 6 REF L13
9 miles S of Leek on the B5417

This village was once the home of the Thomas Bolton & Sons copper works that produced some 20,000 miles of copper wire for the first transatlantic cable in 1856. Little now remains of the works, which were demolished in the 1960s, but the site of the mill has been turned into an attractive picnic site complete with the very large mill pond. At Moneystone Quarry the red sandstone that is extracted becomes, after chemical treatment, pure white sand which is used in the glass industry. Now transported by road, the sand was, until recently, moved down by river and then taken by rail. Nearby **Hawksmoor Nature Reserve** and bird sanctuary covers some 300 acres of the Churnet Valley and is managed by a local committee. The trail through the Reserve includes glorious landscapes, abundant natural history and industrial architecture and it even goes over farmland to a riverside Victorian farm. A section of the 90 mile long **Staffordshire Way** passes through the Reserve.

UTTOXETER
MAP 6 REF L13
16 miles SE of Leek on the A518

Today, the town is perhaps best known for its **Race Course**, a National Hunt track which lies to the southeast. The venue for the Midlands Grand National, a gruelling steeplechase, the spectator facilities have recently undergone an extensive refurbishment which makes this a very comfortable and increasingly popular sporting venue. A traditional, rural market town, a busy livestock and street market is still held here on Wednesdays. There are several pleasant, old, timbered buildings in Uttoxeter but, unfortunately, disastrous fires in 1596 and 1672 destroyed most the town's architectural heritage. As well as a visit to the **Heritage Centre**, housed in some old timber-framed cottages in Carter Street, **St Mary's Church** should also appear on sightseers itinerary's as it has a typical 'preaching box' dating from 1828. The 13 miles extension of the Caldon Canal, from Froghall to Uttoxeter, was finally opened in 1811 but its life was short lived as, in 1847, it made way for the Churnet Valley branch railway.

KINGSTONE
MAP 6 REF L13
4 miles SW of Uttoxeter off the A518

The Blythe Inn is a secluded and tranquil country inn located along the River Blythe, a tributary of the River Trent which flows right past this charming pub, just three miles south of the Blithfield Reservoir. The atmosphere is friendly and welcoming and the inn enjoys a fine repu-

The Blythe Inn, nr Kingstone, Uttoxeter, Staffordshire
Tel: 01889 500487 Fax: 01889 500436

tation for its great food and drink. Built in the early 17th century, it is an attractive cottage-style inn that is spacious and tastefully decorated and furnished. The separate restaurant area seats 80 and specialises in a variety of traditional favourites alongside more innovative dishes, including fresh Scottish fish daily, pheasant casserole, local game and a full range of a la carte choices. There are three cask ales including local brews from Shardlow Brewery and Bass Brewery. The wine list is very good. Proprietors Barry and Lynda Edwards offer genuine hospitality to all their guests. Open all day every day. Children welcome - there's a large play area for their enjoyment.

STOKE-ON-TRENT
40 miles N of Birmingham off the A34

MAP 6 REF L12

The city was established as late as 1910 when Fenton joined the five towns (Tunstall, Burslem, Hanley, Longton and Stoke) immortalized by the novels of Arnold Bennett. Once fiercely independent, the towns became progressively involved with each other as improvements in roads, water supplies and other amenities forced them towards amalgamation. The new city's crest, of an ancient Egyptian potter at his wheel in one quarter, sums up the fortune on which the wealth of the area was created. Each of the old towns is also represented in the crest and the joint motto translates to "Strength is stronger for unity".

It was the presence of the essential raw materials for the manufacture and decoration of ceramics, in particular marl clay, coal and water, that led to the concentration of pottery manufacture in this area. Though production started in the 17th century it was the entrepreneurial skills of Josiah Wedgwood and Thomas Minton, who brought the individual potters together in factory-style workplaces, that caused the massive leap forward in production that took place in the 18th century. Their factories were large but there were also hundreds of small establishments producing a whole range of more utilitarian chinaware. Production in The Potteries reached its height towards the end of the 19th century and it was at this time that the area was described as being the most unhealthy in the country.

The **Trent and Mersey Canal**, flowing right through the city, is home to the industry that has made the fortune of the area. The Royal Doulton factory lines both banks and from here the Stoke flight of locks lifts the Canal some 50 feet into Etruria. For those interested in industrial and Victorian architecture, Stoke-on-Trent is a wonderful place to visit, with many museums and factories opening to the public to tell the story of the wealth of the city. For many though, Stoke-on-Trent will always be remembered for its football team, Stoke City, and the local hero, Sir Stanley Matthews.

HANLEY
Central district of Stoke-on-Trent

MAP 6 REF L12

One of the five towns of The Potteries and now part of the Stoke-on-Trent conurbation, Hanley was the birthplace of Arnold Bennett, Sir Stanley Matthews and John Smith (the captain of the ill-fated Titanic). As well as being home to the **Potteries Museum**, which houses Britain's finest collection of pottery and porcelain, there is lush green space of **Hanley Forest Park** to be found amid the Victorian and more modern buildings.

The Potteries shopping centre, situated in the heart of Hanley, is every shopper's dream with a fantastic range of famous shops all brought together in a beautiful environment. Natural daylight cascades through the Centre's many glazed roofs and plants, trees and water features create an outdoor feel.

Situated on the **Caldon Canal**, this remains an industrial area and bottle kilns can still be seen. Today, there is still some commercial traffic along the canal as the pottery manufacturers rediscover that they can move their goods with fewer breakages by boat! There is also an interesting bridge here; with a counterbalance used to raise the hinged portion of the roadway.

KIDSGROVE
MAP 6 REF K12
5 miles N of Stoke-on-Trent on the A50

Now chiefly a residential town, Kidsgrove is well worth a visit for anyone interested in canals. The two **Harecastle Tunnels** were major engineering feats of their time and they carry the **Trent and Mersey Canal** from Cheshire into The Potteries. It was Josiah Wedgwood who first dreamt of building a canal to link the area with the major Trent and Mersey navigation and thus create a waterway link right across the country from Liverpool to Hull. He fought long and hard to get the necessary Bill passed through Parliament, undaunted by the fact that a 3,000 yard long tunnel would needed to go through Harecastle Hill. The Bill was passed and, though many scoffed at his plans, Wedgwood's canal and required tunnel, both built by James Brindley, were constructed over an 11 year period. Those who had their doubts at Wedgwood's grand plan nearly had the last laugh when, some years later, there was almost a catastrophe when Harecastle started to subside. Fortunately, Thomas Telford was on hand to come to the rescue and another tunnel was built, alongside the first, thus averting disaster. The two tunnels can still be seen today and make a very impressive sight: although Josiah's original tunnel is not in use, the Telford tunnel has been restored.

ETRURIA
MAP 6 REF L12
District of Stoke-on-Trent to the E of the city centre

Now just another suburb of the city, Etruria was created by Josiah Wedgwood in 1769 as a village for the workers at the pottery factory he built in this once rural valley. Though the factory has gone (it moved to Barlaston in the 1940s and the land on which the factory stood had been greatly affected by mining subsidence), **Etruria Hall**, Wedgwood's home, is still standing in what is now the National Garden Festival site. The pottery industry dominated the village, as did Wedgwood, and the **Etruria Industrial Museum** here displays a steam powered potters' mill as well as other exhibits connected with the industry. Situated on the Trent and Mersey Canal, Etruria was also the point at which the Caldon Canal branches off to Froghall and Leek.

NEWCASTLE-UNDER-LYME
MAP 6 REF K13
2 miles W of Stoke-on-Trent on the A53

This ancient borough, which received its first charter from Henry II in 1173, was, for several centuries, the largest town in north Staffordshire. Today, the town maintains its individuality from its close neighbour, Stoke-on-Trent, and its centre is designated a conservation area. One of the best ways of exploring the delights of Newcastle-under-Lyme is to follow either, or both, of the town trails which take in many of the town's most notable buildings. Both begin in Nelson Place and the first takes in not only the early 19th century Church of St George and Mayer House, the former home of a famous veterinary family, but also some fine Georgian houses and, in Marsh Parade, the vast 19th century building which once housed the town's first silk mill. The second of the two trails takes in the particularly eye-catching Merrial Street before moving on to **St Giles's Church**, where the base of the tower dates from the 13th century. The original medieval Church was replaced by a brick building in 1720 and, in 1870, it was again rebuilt, this time by George Gilbert Scott, who managed to capture much of the beauty of medieval times. One of Newcastle-under-Lyme's oldest buildings also features on the route; The Guildhall, built in 1713 to replace an earlier timber building, stands beside the base of a medieval cross. Details of the town trails can be found at the Tourist Information Centre.

MADELEY
MAP 6 REF K13
7 miles W of Stoke-on-Trent on the A525

Situated on an ancient packhorse route from Newcastle-under-Lyme, this village's name comes from the Anglo-Saxon 'maden lieg', which means 'clearing in the woods'. The focal point of the centre of this enchanting place, which has been designated a conservation area, is The Pool. It was formed by damming the River Lea to provide water power for the corn mill that still stands at its northern end. However, Madeley's grandest building is the **Old Hall**, an excellent example of a 15th century squire's

Old Hall, Madeley

timber framed residence. This beautifully preserved building, with its magnificent brick chimney, is now two star listed and it still dominates the heart of the village. Still possessing many of the original motifs, the Old Hall's most striking feature must be the inscription carved into the main beam on the west front facing the road: "Walke knave what lookest at 47 I.S.B." The statement is thought to have been directed at local Roundheads so they would not suspect the owners of being sympathetic to the Royalist cause. The village's large sandstone church can be seen through the trees from the mill pond. Standing in a raised churchyard, with ancient yew trees, All Saints Parish Church is originally Norman but was extensively enlarged in the 15th century and the Chapel was rebuilt in 1872. An interesting building it has a noteworthy Pre-Raphaelite window and the early 16th century alabaster tombs of Ralph Egerton and his wife.

ONNELEY
Map 6 ref K13
8 miles W of Stoke-on-Trent on the A525

Built in 1769 as a coaching inn along the fast western route from Wales to Stoke-on-Trent, **The Wheatsheaf Inn** in Onneley is a large and impressive pub, hotel and restaurant. The bar has a welcoming ambience, with numerous alcoves and snugs, and log fires adding to the cosiness of the place. There is always a good range of real ales on offer, together with a fine complement of lagers, stout, ciders, wines and spirits. There are six comfortable and attractive en suite guest bedrooms, each tastefully furnished to a high standard. The menu changes with the seasons; each dish is freshly prepared. The cuisine succeeds in being both imaginative and inspiring, offering a distinctive yet relaxed dining experience. As part of Pernickety chain of inns dotted across England,

The Wheatsheaf Inn, Barhill Road, Onneley,
Staffordshire CW3 9QF Tel: 01782 751581 Fax: 01782 751499

the staff take justified pride in upholding a tradition for a high standard of conscientiousness and friendly service.

WHITMORE MAP 6 REF K13
7 miles SW of Stoke-on-Trent on the A53

Whitmore Hall is a splendid 17th century country mansion built in rich red brickwork with stone dressings and a stone balustrade at the top. Though not immediately obvious, the Hall is actually of four stories, constructed around an older timber-framed house. Whitmore has been the home of the Mainwaring family since Norman times and, strolling through the vast and ornately decorated rooms, visitors can trace the family's history from the portraits that have made the Hall famous. Set in an elegantly landscaped park, the original drive from the estate village to the Hall forms an avenue and passes by the medieval **Church of St Mary and All Saints**. Largely 12th century, the Church was extensively restored in the 1880s and is worth a visit just to see its unusual timber-framed clock tower: the only example in North Staffordshire of this form of construction.

BARLASTON MAP 6 REF L13
5 miles S of Stoke-on-Trent off the A34

A visit to The Potteries would not be complete without a visit to the **Wedgwood Museum and Visitor Centre** just outside Barlaston. Few places in this area of Staffordshire have escaped from the influence of Josiah Wedgwood and, in particular, there is Etruria, where he built his first factory, and the Caldon Canal, which he fought so hard to have constructed. The Museum has faithfully recreated the 18th century workshops, complete with a reconstructed bottle kiln and an original engine turning lathe, which went into disuse after the 1940s.

The display vividly brings to life the working conditions of early days in the industry and also tell the fascinating story of over two centuries of the company's history. In rooms designed to recapture the style of specific periods there are hundreds of Wedgwood pieces from those eras. George Stubbs and Joshua Reynolds both painted portraits of the Wedgwood family and they are hanging in the art gallery. In the craft centre potters and decorators can be watched as they use traditional skills to create today's Wedgwood products.

HANCHURCH MAP 6 REF L13
5 miles S of Stoke-on-Trent on the A5182

This tiny hamlet itself is unlikely to ring any bells with visitors as they pass by but the nearby gardens are world famous. The earliest reference to Trentham relates to a nunnery which was established by St Werburgh, daughter of the Anglo Saxon King of Mercia in AD 680, and later by the daughter of Alfred the Great in around 907. Ownership then passed, via Edward the Confessor and William the Conqueror, to William Rufus. After the Dissolution of the Monasteries, the estate was bought by James Leveson, a wealthy wool merchant who founded the dynasty of the Dukes of Sutherland, owners of the estate for over 300 years.

Trentham Gardens were landscaped by Capability Brown and given a more formal style by Sir Charles Barry, whose work can be observed in the lovely Italian gardens. Although the Hall was sadly demolished in 1911, this style can still be recognised in such buildings as the orangery and sculpture gallery which remain today and form a framework for the outstanding conference, exhibition and banqueting centre that is Trentham.

There is, normally, unrestricted access to 800 acres of woodland, lake and gardens, with opportunities for woodland walks, boating and jet skiing. There are first class facilities for trout and coarse fishing and clay pigeon shooting. Tuition in fishing and shooting is available for the individual or for parties. The vast grounds and lake create a huge natural amphitheatre in which many sporting and other outdoor events take place in idyllic setting under a backdrop which is breathtakingly beautiful in all seasons.

STONE
MAP 6 REF L13

9 miles S of Stoke-on-Trent on the A34

Augustinian monks founded a priory here in the 12th century, of which only one arch and some cloisters now remain, and, in 1251, Henry II granted the monks a charter to hold a market here, thus making it a mecca for the surrounding hamlets. In its heyday as a trading town, some 38 coaches pulled up at the bow-windowed Crown Hotel, still one of the most attractive buildings along the High Street. Built during this period of prosperity, the early Gothic Revival Parish Church of St Michael contains several interesting monuments including a bust of Admiral John Jervis, Earl St Vincent, the hero of the great naval victory off Cape St Vincent in 1797. Also worth a second glance is the brass erected in memory of Thomas Crompton who died in 1619. Situated outside, at the rear of the Church, is the impressive Jervis Mausoleum.

ECCLESHALL
MAP 6 REF K13

5 miles SW of Stone on the A519

For over a thousand years **Eccleshall Castle** was the palace of the bishops of Lichfield but, at the beginning of this century, it became a family home when the Carter family moved from Yorkshire. The present simple sandstone house is typical of the best architecture of the William and Mary period and it incorporates part of the earlier 14th century castle. The interior of the house has been augmented by successive members of the family, one of whom added a magnificent Victorian staircase and dome. Perhaps to remind them of the county from which they came, the Carters have collected a very interesting number of 19th century paintings by Yorkshire artists. The library is full of superb books, amongst them many first additions, including a complete set of the works of Charles Dickens. The gardens have been created around the ruins of the old castle and have a great deal of romanticism. The old walls give wonderful support to the espaliered pear trees as well as sheltering the rose garden.

The George Inn is an attractive family-run hotel owned by Moyra and Gerard Slater, who with the help of their daughter Vicky and son Andrew have made it a popular and welcoming retreat. Dating back to the 17th century when it was a distinguished coaching inn, it is located in the centre of this charming market town, within easy reach of many local sights and attractions. The handsome oak bar has features such as exposed oak beams and an inglenook fireplace. Traditional ales on tap include the Slaters' own beer, brewed on the premises, as this fine hotel boasts its own micro-brewery, regional winner of "Brewer of the Year" in 1996. Four different ales are brewed on-site, for guests' enjoyment in the bar. The superb restaurant offers a range of delicious evening meals. At lunch there are

The George Inn, Castle Street, Eccleshall, Staffordshire
ST21 6DF Tel: 01785 850300 Fax: 01785 851452

snacks and 10 weekly specials to be enjoyed. All dishes make use of the freshest local produce. The accommodation comprises nine beautiful guest rooms. Spacious and welcoming, they offer guests a chance to relax in comfort.

The Badger Inn is owned by Tina and Martin King. They are friendly and welcoming hosts, who have over 10 years experience in the licensing trade. They came to this popular pub on the outskirts of the village of Eccleshall in 1998. Tina is an accomplished cook who has brought her

own recipes and flair to the excellent menu of traditional home-cooked English fare. Originally built to be the village railway station, it became a country inn in the 1800s. The airy and attractive conservatory extension was added in 1991. The award-winning gardens are the perfect place to enjoy a relaxing drink or meal on fine days. There are three real ales on tap along with a

The Badger Inn, Green Lane, Eccleshall, nr Stafford, Staffordshire ST21 6BA Tel: 01785 850564

good selection of lagers, stout, wines and spirits. The accommodation comprises four handsome and comfortable en suite guest bedrooms. They are pristine and homely, furnished and decorated in traditional country style.

SANDON
Map 6 ref L13

4 miles SE of Stone on the B5066

Near the village of Sandon stands the ancestral home of the Earl of Harrowby, Sandon Hall. Rebuilt in 1850 after an earlier house had been damaged by fire, the Hall is surrounded by 400 acres of parkland which include a notable arboretum. The Hall is steeped in history and, along with the impressive interior, it makes an interesting and informative visit. The family, too, has led a fascinating life, with no fewer than seven generations in Parliament and three successive members of the family holding office in the Cabinet. The museum tells of their lives and also includes costumes, toys and the 0duelling pistols of William Pitt the Younger. The Hall is open throughout the year, with many special events such as antiques fairs and exhibitions.

STAFFORD
Map 6 ref L13

14 miles S of Stoke-on-Trent on the A34

The county town of Staffordshire is Saxon in origin though little of its early history is visible except the extensive earthworks close to the Castle and the foundations of a tiny Saxon Chapel in the grounds of St Mary's Church. Like many old towns around Britain, Stafford originally had a medieval town wall and evidence of it can still be seen today in the names of the town's main streets. However, it is only **East Gate** that remains of the structure. This was where Elizabeth I met with the town councillors on her visit here in 1575 and the Gate can be found at the top of the appropriately named Queensgate.

Stafford lies on the banks of the River Sow and **Green Bridge** marks the site of the ancient ford across the river. There has been a bridge on this spot since the late 13th century but the gate in the town's medieval walls that was also at this point was demolished in 1777. Just to the east of the Bridge is Victoria Park, opened in 1908 and later extended to incorporate land reclaimed from the River Sow. There are many pleasant walks through the Park, which includes a mill pond and a weir, and, in particular, to the **Windmill** at Broad Eye. Built in 1796 by John Wright, the mill moved over to steam power in 1847 and continue to be used until 1880. There is also some, but only circumstantial, evidence that this was the site of a castle built by William the Conqueror.

Like many town's today, Stafford has its busy shopping streets and also an impressive shopping centre. However, many picturesque cobbled lanes still remain and provide the visitor with a quiet and relaxing contrast to the hurly burly of the late 20th century. In particular are Church Lane, with its timbered buildings, and Mill Street with a varied array of shops, restaurants and pubs.

A place well worth visiting during any stay in Stafford is **The Ancient High House**, a beautiful Elizabethan house built in 1595 that is in fact the largest timber-framed town house in England. Through painstaking efforts over several years, Stafford Borough Council have restored this amazing piece of architecture to its former glory and, today, the building houses the **Museum of the**

Church Lane, Stafford

Staffordshire Yeomanry and the Tourist Information Centre. The Ancient High House's varied history can be followed through the permanent displays in the period room settings taking the visitor through the 17th, 18th and 19th centuries and telling the life stories of people who came to know this House so intimately. Not surprisingly, the House has Royal connections with both King Charles I and Prince Rupert having stayed here in 1642. The House also has a small heritage shop selling a variety of interesting and locally crafted gifts for those seeking a memento of their visit.

Close to the High House is the **Collegiate Church of St Mary**, an unusual building which dates, in part, from the late 12th century, but has received additions in the early English, Gothic and Victorian styles. The huge tower arches in the nave seem to divide the building into two, which is, in fact, exactly what they were intended to do, as St Mary's is two churches under one roof. The nave was the Parish Church of Stafford with its own altar whilst the chancel beyond was used by the Deans of the College of St Mary, whose duty it was to pray for deceased members of the Royal family. Although the College was abolished in 1548, the screens which divided the Church remained until 1841 and today the Church is still referred to as the Collegiate. Sir Izaak Walton was baptized here on 21st September 1593 and his bust can be seen on the north wall of the

Collegiate Church of St Mary, Stafford

nave. Each year, at a civic service, a wreath is placed around the bust to commemorate his supposed birthday (9th August). Those interested in ecclesiastical architecture will, however, prefer to visit the little Norman and medieval Church of St Chad.

Situated high up above the town, one Stafford landmark that is viewed by countless travellers along the M6 are the impressive earthworks of the **Norman Castle** which can be reached via the A518 Newport Road, about a mile and a half from the town centre. Set within 20 acres, the remains of this splendid fortress are open to the public and visitors who can follow an illustrated trail which leads from the outer bailey and onto the site of a medieval settlement. There is also a modern Visitor Centre where a video and detailed model reconstructions bring the past vividly to life. The Castle grounds are often used for historical re-enactments by such groups as the Napoleonic Society and are often the site for Sealed Knot battles as well as other outdoor entertainment which provides an added attraction for those who happen to visit at the right time. A call to the local Tourist Information Centre will provide details of such events.

Best known today for his work *The Compleat Angler*, throughout his lifetime, Sir Izaak Walton was famous as a writer of biographies. However, the story of his own life is somewhat obscure: it is certain that he was born in Stafford in 1593, though the date is less certain. From humble origins, Walton became accepted in the intellectual and ecclesiastical circles of the day and, during the Civil War, he remained a staunch Royalist and stayed in the Stafford area. As might be expected Walton is associated with several buildings in the town though the house of his birth, in Eastgate Street, was demolished in 1888 and the site is now occupied by the Stafford Police Station. Also in Eastgate Street, is the **William Salt Library**, which houses a sizable collection of interesting local history documents, including several relating to Sir Izaak.

In Staffordshire, as in many rural areas in the days before the first Divorce Court was established in 1857, the practice of selling a wife was the usual manner in which an unhappy marriage was ended. The practice followed a rigid pattern: the husband would go, with his wife, to town where he would pay a toll which gave him the right to sell merchandise, then he would parade his wife around the town extolling her virtues. An auction then followed and once a bid had been accepted, the husband would hand over the toll ticket as proof of ownership and the trio would retire to an inn to seal the deal. As inhuman as the practice may seem today, in fact all parties tended to accept the arrangement with, in some cases, the husband agreeing a price with his wife's lover before the auction. Prices ranged from a few pence to as much as £1 and here, in 1800, it was recorded that a chimney-sweep named Cupid Hodson sold his wife for 5 shillings and 6 pence.

WESTON-UNDER-LIZARD
11 miles SW of Stafford on the A5

MAP 6 REF K14

Situated on the site of a medieval manor house, **Weston Park** has been the home of the Earls of Bradford for 300 years. Disraeli was a frequent visitor here and, at one time, presented the house with a grotesque stuffed parrot. The parrot became famous when the present Earl, after leaving Cambridge, published a book entitled *My Private Parts and the Stuffed Parrot.*

Weston Park, Weston-under-Lizard

The stuffed parrot still enjoys the hospitality of Weston Park. The parkland at Weston has matured over several hundred years into a masterpiece of unspoilt landscape. Many have left their mark, yet each successive generation has taken note of its predecessors. Disraeli loved the Park and, in one of his letters to Selina, 3rd Countess of Bradford, he refers to the "stately woods of Weston".

There are some wonderful architectural features in the Park including the Roman Bridge and the Temple of Diana, both designed and built by James Paine for Sir Henry Bridgeman in about 1760. Fallow deer and rare breeds of sheep roam the vast parklands and there are plenty of other interesting attractions for visitors of all ages including nature trails, a miniature railway and a **Museum of Country Bygones**.

TONG   MAP 6 REF K14
11 miles SW of Stafford off the A5

Near the village, just over the county border in Shropshire, lies **Boscobel House**, a timber-framed building that is famous as a hiding place of Charles II. The story goes that, after being defeated at the Battle of Worcester in 1651, the King fled and found shelter at the House overnight. The following morning, fearing that the House would be searched by Cromwell's men, Charles II hid in the top most branches of an oak tree. At night fall, he then began his journey to France and nine years of exile. Visitors to Boscobel House, which is owned by English Heritage, can still see the secret room in which the King spent the night and the Royal Oak which has grown from an acorn taken from the tree in which he also hid.

FEATHERSTONE   MAP 6 REF L14
12½ miles S of Stafford off the A449

Just to the south of the village is **Moseley Old Hall**, which once stood in a remote part of Staffordshire and was surrounded by its own agricultural estate. Today, that remoteness no longer exists for the outskirts of Wolverhampton reach to within a mile of the house and motorway access is clearly signposted from Junction 1 of the M54. At first sight, visitors to the Hall can be forgiven for thinking that the house belongs to the 19th century, but it dates from the first Elizabethan Age and, inside, much of the original panelling and timber framing is still visible. Though of no great architectural merit, the Hall once sheltered King Charles II for a short time following the Battle of Worcester in 1651 and it is for this that the house is best remembered. Under cover of darkness the defeated King, disguised as a woodcutter, was escorted into the house by Thomas Whitgreave, the owner, and his chaplain, John Huddlestone. He rested here for two days and even evaded capture when Parliamentarians visited the house in search of the monarch before leaving, again in disguise, and fleeing to France. In 1940, the house was acquired by the Wiggin family and, in 1962, it became the property of the National Trust.

GREAT HAYWOOD   MAP 6 REF L13
5 miles E of Stafford on the A51

This ancient village is famous for having the longest packhorse bridge in England. Built in the 16th century, the **Essex Bridge** (named after the famous Elizabethan Earl who used nearby Shugborough Hall when hunting in the area) still has 14 of its original 40 arches spanning the River Trent. Here, too, is the interesting Roman Catholic Church of St John the Baptist. Built in 1828, in 1845 the whole church was moved from its original site at Tixall to Great Haywood by the local Roman Catholic community. With an ornate west front and Perpendicular windows, it is the richness of the west gallery that is the highlight of the building.

Most visitors to the village however, pass swiftly through it on their way to one of the most impressive attractions in the county, **Shugborough Hall**, the 17th century seat of the Earls of Lichfield. This magnificent 900 acre estate includes Shugborough Park Farm, a Georgian farmstead built in 1805 for Thomas, Viscount Anson, and now home to rare breed animals and to demonstrations of traditional farming methods such as hand milking, butter and cheese making and shire horses at work. The former servants' quarters have been restored to the days of the 19th century and offer an insight into life below stairs. The mansion itself is a splendid piece of architecture, altered several times over its 300 years, but always retaining its distinct grandeur. The vast rooms, with

Shugborough Hall, Great Haywood

their ornate plasterwork and cornicing, contain an impressive collection of paintings, ceramics and silverware as well as a wealth of elegant French furniture. Outside, in the beautiful parkland can be found an outstanding collection of neoclassical monuments dotted around and the Lady Walk leads along the banks of the River Sow to the delightful terraced lawns and rose garden.

RUGELEY
Map 6 ref L14
7½ miles SE of Stafford on the A51

On first arriving in the town, visitors can be mistaken for thinking that Rugeley is all modern but, at its heart, there are some fine 17th and 18th century buildings that have survived the years of industrialisation. Market Street has long been the main street of the town and here is the former coaching inn, the Shrewbury Arms. Between 1860 and 1967, the cattle market was held behind the inn and a market bell was rung from the steps of the Shrewbury Arms to summon the farmers back from their lunch. Rugeley's original parish church, the **Old Chancel**, was founded in the 12th century though it is only the tower, chancel and north chapel that remain from those early days and are dated from the 13th and 14th centuries. The nave was demolished in 1823 to help pay for the building of the imposing new church which, too, is well worth a visit.

Next to the Old Chancel is **Church Croft**, a fine Georgian house and the birthplace of William Palmer. Later in life, as Dr William Palmer, he brought unhappy notoriety to the town in Victorian times as he poisoned his hapless victims after insuring them. The Tudor House, rented by the evil Dr Palmer, can still be seen and, eventually, he was caught, found guilty of murder and publically hanged in Stafford in 1856.

CANNOCK CHASE
Map 6 ref L14
5 miles SE of Stafford on the A34

Though near to areas of dense population, Cannock Chase is a surprisingly wild place of heath and woodland that has been designated an Area of Outstanding Natural Beauty. Covering some 20,000 acres, the Chase was once the hunting ground of Norman kings and, later, the Bishops of Lichfield and deer are still plentiful. **Sherbrook Valley** is a good starting point from which to find these timid creatures. Now chiefly planted with conifers it is still possible to find the remains of the ancient oak forest and, in the less well walked marshy grounds, many rare species survive. A popular place for leisurely strolls, the Chase is also ideal for more strenuous walking and other outdoor recreational activities. Excellent view points can be found at **Coppice Hill** and **Brereton Spurs** whilst **Castle Ring**, an impressive Iron Age hillfort, is well worth the effort to find. Amid all this natural beauty, there are also reminders of the 20th century and, in particular, the unique military cemeteries near **Broadhurst Green**, where some 5,000 German soldiers from the Great War lie buried. Cannock Chase was used as a training ground during the First World War and was the last billet for many thousands of soldiers before they left for France. The remnants of the training area can still be seen as can the prisoner of war camp. The use of the Chase as a training ground was not a new idea, in 1873, there were extensive manoeuvres here with one army base at Etching Hill and the other army at Hednesford Hills, where the battle took place.

The **Museum of Cannock Chase** at the Valley Heritage Centre is only one of the many wonderful parts of Cannock Chase. The Council have encouraged visitors by helping in the conservation of areas of beauty. Opened in May 1989, the Centre is a new concept in the world of museums, arts and crafts and its galleries provide different exhibitions, with rooms dedicated to the natural history of the Hednesford Hills and Castle Ring hillfort. Subjects covered in these galleries change every six months to deal with as many aspects of the area's history as possible.

HEDNESFORD
MAP 6 REF L14
8 miles SE of Stafford on the A460

This former mining town lies on the edge of Cannock Chase and its oldest building, The Cross Keys Inn, is a splendid hostelry built around 1746 which survives at the town's centre. The Anglesey Hotel, built in 1831 by Edmund Peel of Fazeley, was originally designed as a form of summerhouse in a Tudor style with stepped gables and this too lies on the heart of Hednesford. Nearby the **Hazel Slade Reserve** represents the adaptability of nature which has produced an old fashioned countryside of small fields, hedges, streams, marshes and woodland. Thirty five years ago the old broadleaved wood here was felled for timber and hedges were planted and cattle grazed the cleared fields. However, a small area of the wood managed to recover and grew from the stumps and seeds that remained in the ground. Then, five years later, a pool and marsh started to form as the land began to subside as a result of the local mining activity. Now well established, the Reserve is a popular place for fishermen as well as those interested in natural history. Rising over 700 feet above sea level, the **Hednesford Hills** are a prominent local landmark which bring the countryside of Cannock Chase into the heart of Hednesford. Originally covered in oak and birch, these 300 acres of heathland have been the scene of varied activities over the years. They have been quarried for sand and gravel, mined for coal and used for military training. The land is now a registered common and the Hills are a tract of wild landscape with a plethora of heathland plants, abundant wildlife and the opportunity for recreation for the people who live nearby.

TUTBURY
MAP 6 REF M13
4 miles N of Burton upon Trent on the A50

For the people of this small market town, 1989 was a very special year as they celebrated the 900th anniversary of the foundation of **St Mary's Priory Church**. Established by Henry de Ferrers, the splendid Norman architecture makes the Priory one of the most impressive relics of that time. Tutbury owes its existence, and its name, to the naturally defensive outcrop of rock on which, not surprisingly, a castle has stood for centuries. From 1086 to 1265, **Tutbury Castle** belonged to the Ferrers family, who had connections here and in Derbyshire, and for a time it belonged to the Duchy of Lancaster. Today, the Castle is in ruins but it remains an attraction particularly for those interested in Mary, Queen of Scots as she was imprisoned here for a while. During the Civil War, Tutbury Castle, once again, became a focus of attention as it remained loyal to the Crown whilst the town was under the control of Parliament. After a three week long siege, the Castle surrendered and the following year, in 1647, Parliament ordered its destruction.

Situated on the crest of a hill and commanding lovely views over farmland to Tutbury

Castle and the Dove Valley, **Woodhouse Farm** dates back to the 11th century, with Georgian additions. Proprietor Maria Guest and her family are friendly and convivial hosts who work hard to ensure that all their guests have a relaxing and enjoyable stay. There are four gracious and lovely ensuite guest bedrooms, including the spacious rooftop room perfect for families. Beams made of old ships' timbers abound, and other traditional features add to the homely and welcoming ambience. Each room is individually styled and furnished to a high standard of comfort and taste. The full farmhouse breakfast includes locally-produced sausages and fresh farm eggs. Convenient not just for Tutbury, half a mile away, but also for Sudbury Hall, the Royal Crown Derby museum, Alton Towers and Castle Donington, this makes an excellent touring base with some wonderful walking locally. Dogs by arrangement. Stabling available. Barbecue facilities available. ETC 3 Diamonds.

Woodhouse Farm, Tutbury, Burton-on-Trent, Staffordshire DE13 9HR Tel: 01283 814046/812185 Fax: 01283 815743 email: enquiries@tutbury.co.uk website: www.tutbury.co.uk/woodhouse

ABBOTS BROMLEY
10 miles W of Burton upon Trent on the B5234

MAP 6 REF L13

This delightful 13th century village, in the Vale of Trent, continues the tradition of the annual Horn Dance, held on the first Monday after the first Sunday in September. An ancient fertility dance, it is performed by 'deermen' and other interesting characters who, in the early morning, tour the local farms before congregating in the main street. Then there is dancing and even mock battles with deer heads and reindeer antlers. On reaching the picturesque conservation village of Abbots Bromley, visitors would be wise to make for **The Crown Inn**, a late 17th-century former coaching inn right in the village square. The exterior is very pretty, with a half-timbered frontage. Owner Frank Bromley has revitalised this charming place,

The Crown Inn, Market Place, Abbots Bromley, nr Rugeley, Staffordshire WS15 3BS Tel/Fax: 01283 840227

so that in 1997 it was winner of Best Regional Pub of the Year. This successful and welcoming inn has six very comfortable and handsomely decorated and furnished guest bedrooms in a variety of sizes. Imaginative and delicious daily specials complement the set menus, which feature such traditional favourites as home-made soups, fresh sandwiches, fresh fish and steaks. This Free House offers a range of cask ales and guest real ales including Brakespear, Abbot ale and Morlands Old Speckled Hen. There is also a good range of malt whiskies and a fine wine list. Other facilities include a Long Skittle Alley and function room, cosy lounge bar and lively locals bar.

LICHFIELD

MAP 6 REF M14

15 miles SE of Stafford on the A51

During the 18th century Lichfield was a prominent city but it failed to compete with other towns in extensive rebuilding programmes and consequently it still retains its medieval grid pattern streets with elegant Georgian houses and, mixed in amongst them, black and white Tudor cottages. Little alleyways, such as Tudor Row, invite shoppers to visit specialist boutiques and a 16th century café-so different from the usual high streets found in today's cities and towns. First settled by the Celts and also close to the crossroads of the two great Roman roadways, Ryknild Street (the A38) and Watling Street (the A5), Lichfield was one of the most important towns of that time. So much so that the King of Mercia offered St Chad the seat of Lichfield and, on his death, the town became a place of pilgrimage and so began its importance as an ecclesiastical centre.

The first cathedral was built here in 669 but no traces of this building, or the later Norman structure, remain. The **Lichfield Cathedral** seen today dates from the 12th century and is particularly famous for its magnificent three spires which dominate the City skyline. Inside there are many treasures including the beautiful 8th century illuminated manuscript The Lichfield Gospels and Sir Francis Chantrey's famous sculpture The Sleeping Children. The surrounding Cathedral Close, regarded as the most unspoilt in the country, is particularly fine and, as the Close is separated from the rest of the city by Stowe and Minster Pools, it is also a peaceful haven of calm. The Minster Pool is particularly beautiful, it was landscaped in the late 18th century by Anna Seward and is now a haven for wildfowl.

At the very heart of Lichfield is the **Lichfield Heritage Exhibition and Treasury**, part of St Mary's Centre in the Market Place. A church has stood on this site since the 12th century and the present building, the third, dates from 1868. As with many ecclesiastical buildings, the decline in the church-going population made St Mary's redundant and, to save it from being demolished altogether, the Centre was formed. A stroll round here will enthral all the family and, for the energetic, there are superb views across the city from the viewing platform on the spire. There are exhibitions on the history and every day life of the city as seen through the eyes of its inhabitants over the centuries and it also includes the story of the siege of Lichfield Cathedral during the Civil War.

The City has been a place of pilgrims and travellers for centuries and, in 1135, **St John's Hospital** opened to offer shelter to those passing through Lichfield. One of the finest Tudor brick buildings in the country, the Hospital is now a home for the elderly. The Hospital Chapel, with its magnificent stained glass window by the designer of the celebrated east window at Coventry Cathedral, John Piper, is open daily. The **Guildhall**, the meeting place of the city governors for over 600 years, has, at various times, also been the courthouse, a police station and a prison. Behind its Victorian façade, lie the remains of the city jail, complete with stocks and cells and the **City Dungeons** can be visited on Saturdays throughout the summer.

Lichfield's most famous son is Dr Samuel Johnson, the poet, novelist and author of the first comprehensive English dictionary. The son of a bookseller, Johnson was born in 1709, in Breadmarket Street, and the house is now home to the **Samuel Johnson Birthplace Museum**. Open every day except Sundays, the Museum, as well as exhibiting artefacts relating to his life and works, also has a series of tableaux showing how the house looked in the early 18th century. Apart from the historic pleasure that Lichfield gives there is also plenty of parkland to enjoy and, in particular, the **Beacon Park and Museum Gardens**. The 75 acre Park encloses playing fields and a small boating lake and, in the Museum Gardens, can be found a statue of Commander John Smith, captain of the ill-fated Titanic, that was sculpted by Lady Katherine Scott, widow of Scott of the Antarctic.

Owned by Tamworth and Lichfield College since 1993, **The Swan Hotel** is a distinguished establishment that has been restored to its former stature as a premier coaching inn. Located in

the centre of Lichfield, visitors staying here can stroll to the famous Cathedral and its beautiful close, just 200 yards from the hotel. The first recorded reference to the hotel appears in 1535. Throughout its history it has played host to many famous (and some infamous!) guests, including George Eliot and Lichfield's own Samuel Johnson. Throughout 1994 work was carried out to produce a sympathetic restoration resulting in a building which retains all its historic charm while at the same time boasts every modern convenience. Throughout the year, residential courses are available here in subjects ranging from languages and French cuisine to textiles and catering, offering students work experience in the hotel while upholding its venerable tradition of playing a central role in the life of the city. There are 19 beautiful ensuite rooms, both traditional and modern; some are suitable for people with disabilities. The bar and restaurant are tastefully decorated in period style and adorned with prints of local scenes and, at times, with the work of the College's art students. Cream teas can be taken in the terrace garden, offering splendid views of the Cathedral. The menus for morning coffee, light lunches, business lunches and evening meals, as well as traditional Sunday fare, are superb. The bar boasts an excellent choice of ales, wines, lagers and spirits.

The Swan, Bird Street, Lichfield, Staffordshire WS13 6PT Tel: 01543 414777 Fax: 01543 411277

BURNTWOOD

Map 6 ref L14

4 miles W of Lichfield on the A5190

The 700 acres of land and water known as **Chasewater** is an unexpected find in this otherwise urban setting. On the fringes of the village, Chasewater offers a true wilderness experience with a combination of heath and woodland environments. Crisscrossed by paths and bridleways, the collection of plants and animals found here is so rare that a large area of Chasewater has been designated a Site of Special Scientific Interest. **The Chasewater Light Railway** runs from Burntwood round the north and west edges of the lake and out of the county. A remnant of the ancient forest of Cank, old buildings from the industrious days of coal mining which took place here can still be seen as can the remains of the time when this was an inland waterside resort.

YOXALL
6 miles N of Lichfield on the A515

MAP 6 REF M14

The centre of this charming village has been designated a conservation area and it is here that the visitor will find some distinguished houses as well as the attractive Norman and medieval village church. Legend has it that Robin Hood was the lord of the manor here and that he married Maid Marion at nearby Tutbury.

Thimble Hall is a welcoming and lovely cottage dating back to the 16th century. Since 1973 this has been Jo and Duncan Smith's home; they have been providing superior bed and breakfast accommodation since 1996. This truly relaxing and peaceful retreat boasts five large, comfortable and attractive guest bedrooms - three in the main cottage and two new rooms in the converted stables. The cottage has been completely restored to incorporate every modern amenity while retaining the charm and traditional feel of its origins. Overlooking the village green, this wonderful establishment boasts large gardens to the rear, well-stocked with mature shrubs, flowering plants and fruit trees. Separate stairs to the guest bedrooms ensure guests' privacy and freedom to come and go as they please. The

Thimble Hall, School Green on Hadley Street, Yoxall, nr Burton on Trent, Staffordshire DE13 8NB Tel: 01543 472226

Smiths have an interesting collection of antiques and family memorabilia. Breakfast is made with fresh local produce, and includes home-baked bread and home-made preserves.

ALREWAS
5 miles NE of Lichfield on the A38

MAP 6 REF M14

The main street of this enchanting village is lined with delightful black and white thatched cottages, some of which date back to the 15th century. The village Church of All Saints is equally beautiful, its doorways are all that remain of the original Norman church and the chancel was built in the 13th century. The **National Memorial Arboretum**, nearby, is the first large arboretum and wildlife reserve to be created in Britain for 200 years. With a theme of wartime remembrance and reconciliation, the central feature will be the Millennium Avenue created from cuttings from a 2,000 year old lime tree.

BARTON-UNDER-NEEDWOOD
7 miles NE of Lichfield on the B5016

MAP 6 REF M14

This lively village, in the pleasant open countryside of the Trent Valley, has six pubs and an interesting church. The Needwood under which the village sits is a long, straight escarpment with woodland and meadow. Right in the centre of the village, **The Shoulder of Mutton** public house is renowned for its excellent real ales and hospitality. Bob and June Spurrier have been running this handsome and friendly pub since 1994, and offer all guests a warm and sincere

welcome. Located opposite the village church, it is a black and white 17th-century establishment with two cosy bar lounges and a locals' bar. There is a changing selection of guest ales on offer at this CAMRA member, in addition to Pedigree Bass and Worthington real ales, a good range of house wines and no fewer than 14 malt whiskies.

The Shoulder of Mutton, Main Street, Barton under Needwood, Staffordshire DE13 8AA Tel: 01283 712568

The freshly-prepared bar snacks include daily specials, vegetarian dishes, fish, home-made steak and kidney pudding, and tempting casseroles. In 2000 there will be a new bistro-style restaurant and, above the pub, five comfortable and well-appointed ensuite letting rooms, making this an excellent base for exploring Staffordshire and the Peak District.

TAMWORTH   Map 6 ref M14
7 miles SE of Lichfield on the A51

A modern, busy town, Tamworth is actually much older than it first appears. Straddling the famous Roman Watling Street (now the A5), it has a fascinating and turbulent past. The first reference to the town dates back to the 8th century when it was the capital of the Kingdom of Mercia and the King, Offa, built his palace here. Raiding Danes managed to destroy the town twice and it was later invaded by the Scandinavians who left evidence of their visit in some of the street names such as Gungate.

Alfred's daughter, Ethelfleda was busy here too and excavations in the town centre have revealed Saxon fortifications. Dominating Tamworth today is the fine Norman motte and bailey **Castle** set in the Pleasure Grounds which have truly magnificent floral terraces. The sandstone Castle, with its superb herringbone wall, dates originally from the 1180s, having replaced a wooden tower on the present artificial mound constructed shortly after the Norman Conquest.

A Saxon nun, Editha, is said to haunt Tamworth Castle. The story goes that when de Marmion took posses-

Tamworth Castle

sion of his lands he expelled the nuns from a nearby convent. The order had been founded by Editha in the 9th century and the expelled nuns summoned her from her grave. Editha attacked de Marmion in his bedroom and, as a result of her severe beating, he restored the nuns to their home. The Parish **Church of St Editha**, founded in 963, is vast and was rebuilt after the Norman Conquest; then, again, after the Great Fire of Tamworth in 1345. The splendid 15th century tower at the west end contains a most remarkable double staircase. The mixture of Victorian and modern stained glass found inside is surprisingly harmonious.

Daniel Defoe called Tamworth "a small but very handsome market town". Since then much has disappeared but in Market Street and Lady Bank there are still some fine 18th century buildings. The **Town Hall**, built in 1701, is charming with open arches and Tuscan columns below. The building was paid for by Thomas Guy, the local Member of Parliament, who is probably more famous as the founder of the London hospital which bears his name. Thomas Guy also gave the town its 14 almshouses in Lower Gungate, which were rebuilt in 1913. Tamworth's other famous son was Sir Robert Peel, Prime Minister under both William IV and Queen Victoria, and, in front of the Town Hall, there is a fine bronze statue of the great man.

HARLASTON
Map 6 ref M14

3 miles N of Tamworth off the A513/M42/A38

Lying on the left bank of the River Mease, Harlaston is a small and pretty village that was mentioned in the Domesday Book. Today's population numbers about 350 inhabitants. Voted Best Kept Small Village in Staffordshire for 1995 and 1999, it was here that soldiers on the way to the Battle of Bosworth 1485 stopped for the night. St Matthew's Church stands in the middle of the village. Although its exact date of origin is unknown, parts are Saxon, dating back to the 9th century. The village manor house dates back to 1540 and, after many years of neglect, has been restored as a Grade II listed building of historical interest.

The **Harlaston Post Office** has been a focal point of this charming village for years, serving as post office and village store and open seven days a week. Joyce Rowe has been providing excellent bed and breakfast accommodation since 1996. Together with her partner Tony she has refurbished and redecorated all six ensuite rooms to a high standard of comfort and quality. One of the rooms occupies the ground floor, and is therefore suitable for guests with disabilities. Tasteful and cosy throughout, this is a true home from home. Joyce and Tony are friendly and helpful hosts. There is a lovely private garden to the rear for guests' use. The full English breakfast makes use of fresh local produce from the shop, free-range farm eggs, fresh rolls and orange juice, freshly brewed coffee and a selection of teas. Many tourists and overseas visitors return again and again to this welcoming establishment.

Harlaston Post Office, Main Road, Harlaston, Tamworth, Staffordshire B79 9JU Tel: 01827 383324

The White Lion public house in Harlaston is popular with locals and visitors alike. It offers a warm and friendly atmosphere and some superb food and drink. Owners Bill and Moira Yates have been here since 1986; their hard work and enthusiasm has made this family-run pub a real treat to wile away time in, enjoying the great range of ales, wines, lagers and spirits. There are always at least two real ales, including a changing guest ale each week. Moira is a qualified chef; her speciality is Chicken Supreme, a delicious dish but just one on the extensive menu, which features all home-cooked traditional English fare such as steaks, fish, Cumberland sausage and great pies. Daily

The White Lion, Main Street, Harlaston, nr Tamworth, Staffordshire B79 9HT Tel: 01827 383691

specials can include mussels, lobster tails and more. This 300-year-old coaching inn retains many original features and enhances the homely and cosy ambience of this fine pub. Open for lunch and evening meals, booking is advised at dinner.

DERBYSHIRE

BUXTON
Map 6 ref L12

20 miles NE of Stoke-on-Trent off the A6

Referred to as the heart of the Peak District, Buxton, England's highest market town at 1,000 feet above sea level, provides a wealth of things to do. The current popularity of the town can be attributed to the 5th Duke of Devonshire, however it was the Romans who first discovered the waters here and named the place *Aquae Arnemetiae* - The Spa of the Goddess of the Grove. With waters maintained at a constant temperature of 82 degrees F (28 degrees C), Buxton soon became a place of pilgrimage, particularly for sufferers of rheumatism. Among the pilgrims from all over Britain was Mary Queen of Scots, held at Chatsworth for many years. **St Anne's Well** still provides water and many people coming to the town make a point of trying the tepid waters. The people of Buxton also say that it makes the best cup of tea possible, and collect bottles of it to take home.

In the 18th century, the 5th Duke of Devonshire, with the intention that Buxton would rival Bath as a spa town, commissioned the building of **The Crescent** to ensure that visitors would flock here. Designed by John Carr of York, the building is similar to the architecture found in Bath and, after suffering from neglect, underwent a huge restoration programme. As with many places, the coming of the railway to Buxton in 1863 marked the height of popularity of the town. Nothing, however, could be done to alter the harsh climate, and the incessant rainfall meant that the Duke's dream of making Buxton the 'Bath of the North', was never truly realised.

Among the other notable architectural features of the town are **The Colonnade** and the **Devonshire Royal Hospital**. They were originally built as stables for hotel patrons of The Crescent and, after their conversion by the 6th Duke in 1858, the largest unsupported dome in the world was built to enclose the courtyard in 1880. Originally built in 1905, the attractive **Opera House** was restored, in 1979, to its grand Edwardian style. After being used as a cinema for many years, it is once again the host of live performances and, as well as offering a comprehensive and popular programme throughout the year, also has one of the largest stages in England.

The attractive **Pavilion Gardens** have a conservatory and octagon within the grounds - antique markets and arts shows are often held here, and it is a very pleasant place to walk any time of year. Laid out in 1871 by Edward Milner, with money donated by the Dukes of Devonshire, the 23 acres include formal gardens, serpentine walks and decorative iron bridges across the River Wye. The conservatory was reopened in 1982 following extensive renovation; there is also a swimming pool filled with warm spa water.

The White Lion public house is a distinguished establishment located in a traffic-free precinct in Buxton town centre, close to all of the town's amenities, including the Opera House. Occupying a listed building dating back in parts to 1661, which has always been a coaching inn, there are three bars, including one with pool tables and a football table. The Tap Room has a traditional feel. Furnished with an eye towards comfort, it is a relaxing place where guests can enjoy Marstons Pedigree and bitter, a selection of lagers and a good variety of wines and spirits. Owner Ann Smith has

The White Lion, Spring Gardens, Buxton, Derbyshire SK17 6BZ Tel: 01298 23099

run the pub for over 20 years - she brings a wealth of experience to the task and offers every visitor a genuinely warm welcome.

St John the Baptist church was built in Italian style in 1811 by Sir Jeffrey Wyatville. That same year Wyatville laid out The Slopes, the area below the Market Place in Upper Buxton. The grand **Town Hall** was built 1887—1889 and dominates the Market Place. Further down Terrace Road is the **Buxton Museum**, which reveals the long and varied history of the town and its surrounding area. As well as housing an important local archaeology collection, the Museum also has a fine collection of Ashford Marble, Blue John ornaments, paintings, prints, pottery and glassware.

It is not known for certain whether well-dressing took place in Buxton before 1840, though there are stories that Henry VIII put a stop to the practice, but it has certainly been a part of Buxton's cultural calendar since the Duke of Devonshire provided the townsfolk with their first public water supply at Market Place Fountain. From then on, High Buxton Well (as the fountain came to be called) and St Anne's Well were decorated sporadically. In 1923, the Town Council set about organising a well-dressing festival and carnival that continues to this day. Every year on the second Wednesday in July, this delightful tradition is enacted.

Buxton is surrounded by some of the most glorious of the Peak District countryside. These moorlands also provide one of the town's specialities - heather honey. Several varieties of heather grow on the moors: there is *ling*, or common heather which turns the land purple in late summer; there is bell-heather which grows on dry rocky slopes; and there is cross-leaved heather which can be found on wet, boggy ground.

The town is also the starting point for both the **Brindley Trail** and the **Monsal Trail**. Covering some 61 miles, the Brindley Trail, which takes its name from the famous canal engineer, leads southwest to Stoke-on-Trent, while the Monsal Trail, beginning just outside Buxton at Blackwell Mill Junction, finishes as Coombs Viaduct near Bakewell, some 8 miles away.

To the west of the town lies **Axe Edge**, the highest point of which rises to 1,807 feet above sea level. From this spot on a clear day (and the weather here is notoriously changeable) the panoramic views of Derbyshire are overwhelming. Just beyond, at 1,690 feet above sea level, the **Cat and Fiddle Inn** is the second highest pub in England. Axe Edge Moor, which receives an average annual rainfall of over 4 feet, is strictly for hardened walkers. It should come as no surprise that this Moor is the source of several rivers which play important roles in the life of the Peak District. The **River Dove** and the **River Manifold**, which join at Ilam, rise not far from one another; the **River Wye** rises above Buxton to join the Derwent further south; the **River Goyt**, a major source of the Mersey, rises to the west of Axe Edge.

The entire length of the River Goyt can be walked, from its source to its confluence with the River Etherow to the north and just outside the boundaries of the National Park. Once marking the boundary between Derbyshire and Cheshire (which now lies just to the west), a walk along the Goyt takes in sections of the riverbank as well as the Errwood and Fernilee reservoirs before leaving Derbyshire just north of New Mills. Although the two reservoirs look well established and very much part of the landscape, they are relatively recent additions: the Fernilee was opened in 1938 while the Errwood was flooded in 1967.

Those who venture to **Errwood Reservoir** will be surprised to see rhododendrons growing near the banks of a man-made lake. They once stood in the grounds of Errwood Hall, which was built in the 1830s for the Grimshawe family. The house was demolished before the Reservoir was flooded, but the gardens were left to grow wild. Not far away can be seen the strange-looking Spanish Shrine. Built by the Grimshawes in memory of their Spanish governess, it is a small stone building with an unusual beehive roof.

Poole's Cavern, Buxton

The highest point in this area is **Shining Tor**, overlooking Errwood Reservoir and standing some 1,834 feet above sea level. To the north is Pym Chair, the point at which an old packhorse road running east to west crosses this gritstone ridge. An old salters' route, it was used for transporting salt from the Cheshire plains across the Peak District moorlands to the industrial and well-populated areas of south and west Yorkshire.

During the 19th century, the Goyt valley with its natural resources of both coal and water developed rapidly into one of the nation's major textile production centres. In order to service this growth, the valley also developed an intense system of transport including canals and railways. The rugged terrain that had to be negotiated has made for some spectacular solutions to major engineering difficulties.

Also to the west of town, **Poole's Cavern** on Green Lane is a natural limestone cave which was used by tribes from the Neolithic period onwards. Visited by Mary, Queen of Scots (the 'chair' she used is still in evidence, and pointed out during the regular tours of the cave on offer) evidence of prehistoric remains have been found near the cave entrance. Above the cavern and about 20 minutes' walk away is **Grin Low Country Park** and the prominent folly and scenic viewpoint, built in 1896, known as **Solomon's Temple**.

COMBS   MAP 6 REF L11
3 miles N of Buxton off the A6

Combs Reservoir southwest of Chapel-en-le-Frith is crossed at one end by Dickie's Bridge. 'Dickie' is said to have resided at a farm in Tunstead where he was known as Ned Dixon. Apparently murdered by his cousin, he nevertheless continued his 'working life' as a sort of guard-skull, alerting the household whenever strangers drew near. Various strange occurrences are said to have ensued when attempts were made to move the skull. The new road from Combs to Chapel was created because the railway bridge would not stand over the Dane Hey Road on account of 'Dickie's Skull', or more likely because of soft foundations. The Bridge was completed, but one night it collapsed, burying the workmen's tools. Local superstition has it that it was because Dickie was annoyed at the railway crossing Tunstead land.

Samuel Bagshaw's *Directory for Derbyshire* mentions that there were two beer houses and one public house in the village of Combs. One beer house was kept by John Lake at Dove Cottages, on the old road to Chapel which was then called Dove Lane. A second beer house was kept by Isaac Lomas. It is said that this latter was once called the Robin Hood, while the one at Dove Cottages was known as the Little John.

The Beehive Inn public house began life in the 1860s - purportedly from profits made from the construction of the railway and the then 'new' road to Chapel - from stone out of Spire Holllin's Quarry, near the village. The cottage at the side of the Beehive was part of the old inn, and was enlarged with stone from the Combs Mill in about 1914. The landlord at the time, W Newlands, had his portrait painted by the famous artist Dugdale, who was then living in the cottage adjacent to the inn. This portrait was exhibited at the Royal Academy. Present owners Graham and Beth Peddie

The Beehive Inn, Combs, nr Chapel-en-le-Frith, Derbyshire SK23 9UT Tel: 01298 812758

took over in 1998. The pub offers a comfortable and very pleasant ambience in which to enjoy a range of home-made and home-prepared dishes - Beth is a fully-trained chef - all making use of fresh local produce. There is a full lunch-time and evening menu. For drinking, there are cask-conditioned ales and good-quality wines, as well as a full complement of spirits.

On Castleton Road just a few miles northeast of the town, the **Chestnut Centre** is a fascinating wildlife conservation centre, popular with children and adults alike. It is famed for its otters, with award-winning otter and owl enclosures set along an extensive circular nature trail which meanders through some historic wooded parkland.

LYME PARK   MAP 6 REF L11
8 miles NE of Buxton off the A6

Lyme Park is an ancient estate, now in the hands of the National Trust, was given to Sir Thomas Danyers in 1346 by a grateful King Edward III after a battle at Caen. Danyers then passed the estate to his son-in-law, Sir Piers Legh, in 1388. It remained in the family until 1946, when it was given to the Trust. Not much remains of the original Elizabethan manor house; today's visitors are instead treated to the sight of a fantastic Palladian mansion, the work of Venetial architect Giacomo Leoni. Not daunted by the bleak landscape and climate of the surrounding Peak District, Leoni built a corner of Italy here in this much harsher countryside. Inside the mansion there is a mixture of styles: the elegant Leoni-designed rooms with rich rococo ceilings, the panelled Tudor drawing room, and two surviving Elizabethan rooms. Much of the three-dimensional internal carving is attributed to Grinling Gibbons, though a lot of the work was also undertaken by local craftsmen.

As well as the fantastic splendour of the mansion, the estate includes a late 19th-century formal garden and a medieval deer park. The grounds now form a country park administered by the local Borough Council. Though close to the Manchester suburb of Stockport, the estate lies wholly within the Peak District National Park.

HAYFIELD

Map 6 ref L11

9½ miles N of Buxton off the A624

This small town below the exposed moorland of **Kinder Scout** is a popular centre for exploring the area and offers many amenities for hillwalkers. Like its neighbour New Mills, Hayfield grew up around the textile industry, in this case wool weaving and calico printing. Many of the houses seen today were originally weavers' cottages. A curious building can be found in **Market Street** on the left of a small square known as **Dungeon Brow**. Built in 1799, this was the town's lock-up and was referred to as the New Prison. However, the stocks in front of the building appear to be somewhat newer than the prison itself. At the other end of the Sett Valley Trail, the old station site has been turned into a picnic area and information centre.

Three miles northeast of the town is **Kinder Downfall**, the highest waterfall in the county, found where the River Kinder flows off the edge of Kinder Scout. In low temperatures the fall freezes solid - a sight to be seen. It is also renowned for its blow-back effect: when the wind blows, the fall's water is forced back against the rock and the water appears to run uphill! There are not many natural waterfalls in Derbyshire, so Kinder Downfall appears on most visitors' itineraries. Not far from the bottom of the fall is a small lake known as **Mermaid's Pool**. Legend has it that those who go to the pool at midnight on the night before Easter Sunday will see a mermaid swimming in the dark waters.

GLOSSOP

Map 6 ref L11

13 miles N of Buxton off the A624

At the foot of the Snake Pass, Glossop is an interesting mix of styles: the industrial town of the 19th century with its towering Victorian mills and the 17th-century village with its charming old cottages standing in the cobble streets. Further back in time, the Romans came here and established a fort now known as **Melandra Castle**, but probably then called Zerdotalia (or Ardotalia). Built to guard the entrance to Longdendale, little survives today but the stone foundations. The settlement developed further, as part of the monastic estates of Basingwerk Abbey in north Wales and the village received its market charter in 1290 but, subsequently, there was a decline in its importance. Little remains of Old Glossop except the medieval parish Church of All Saints.

Old Glossop

Planned as a new town in the 19th century by the Duke of Norfolk, the original village stood on the banks of the Glossop Brook at the crossing point of three turnpike roads. The brook had already been harnessed to provide power for the cotton mills, as this was one of the most easterly towns of the booming Lancashire cotton industry. Many still refer to the older Glossop as Old Glossop and the Victorian settlement as Howard Town, named after the Duke, Bernard Edward Howard. From Glossop, the A57 East is an exhilarating stretch of road, with hair-pin bends, known as the **Snake Pass**. The road is frequently made impassable by landslides, heavy mist and massive snowfalls in winter but, weather permitting, it is an experience not to be missed. For much of the length of the turnpike road that Thomas Telford built across Snake Pass in 1821, the route follows the line of an ancient Roman road, known as **Doctor's Gate**, which ran between Glossop and a fort at Brough. The route was so named after it was rediscovered, in the 16th century, by Dr Talbot, a vicar from Glossop. The illegitimate son of the Earl of Shrewsbury, Talbot used the road with great frequency as he travelled from Glossop to his father's castle at Sheffield.

HADFIELD
Map 6 ref L11

14 miles N of Buxton off the A624

The small village of Hadfield is the terminus of the **Longdendale Trail**, a route following the line of a former railway line and part of the Trans-Pennine Trail. **Old Hall** in The Square is the oldest building in the village, built in 1646. The Roman Catholic church of St Charles was built in 1868 by Baron Howard of Glossop; members of the Howard family are buried here. The Longdendale Trail continues eastward from here. Longdendale itself is the valley of the River Etherow, and is a favourite place for day-trippers. Along the footpath through this wild and desolate valley there ae many reminders of the past, including **Woodhead Chapel**, the grave-yard of which has numerous memorials to the navvies, and their families, who died in an outbreak of cholera in 1849 while working on the Sheffield to Manchester railway line.

PEAK FOREST
Map 6 ref L11

5 miles NE of Buxton off the A623

High on the White Peak plateau, Peak Forest takes its name from the fact that it once stood at the centre of the Royal Forest of the Peak. The parish **Church of King Charles the Martyr** speaks of the fierce independence of the village inhabitants. It was built in 1657 by the wife of the 2nd Earl of Devonshire, during a time when there was a ban on building churches. The church that stands today on the site of the former chapel was built in 1878. A quirk of ecclesiastical law ensured - up until early in the 19th century - that the village was outside the jurisdiction of the bishop. Thus is was not subject to the laws regarding posting the banns before marriage; hence it became known as 'the Gretna Green of the Peak'. If one or other of the couple has lived in the village for 15 days prior to the ceremony, to this day they can still be married in the church without banns being read.

At Chamber Farm, rebuilt in the 18th century, the Forest courts were held, attended by some 20 foresters whose job it was to maintain the special laws of the area. The **Peak Forest Canal**, completed in 1800, followed the valley of the River Goyt and had its terminal basin at Buxworth. At this time the whole area around the River Goyt was in the grip of the booming textile industry and, in 1831, the **Peak Forest Tramway** was built to join up with the canal. Within walking distance of Peak Forest is the 'bottomless' pit of **Eldon Hole**. Once thought to be the Devil's own entrance to Hell, stories abound in which various people were lowered down on increasingly longer pieces of rope. They all returned, in differing states of mental anguish, but none ever reached the bottom! However, seasoned pot-holers, who view the hole as no more than a practice run, maintain that it is, in fact, 'only' 180 feet deep.

EDALE
Map 6 ref M11

8 miles NE of Buxton off the A625

In the valley of the River Noe, Edale marks the start of the **Pennine Way**. Opened in 1965, this long-distance footpath follows the line of the backbone of Britain for some 270 miles from here to Kirk Yetholm, just over the Scottish border. Though the footpath begins in the lush meadows of this secluded valley, it is not long before walkers find themselves crossing the wild and bleak moorland of featherbed Moss before heading further north to Bleaklow. Many travellers have spoken of Derbyshire as a county of contrasts, and nowhere is this more apparent than at Edale. Not only does the landscape change dramatically within a short distance from the heart of the village, but the weather - as all serious walkers will know - can alter from brilliant sunshine to snowstorms in the space of a couple of hours. The village, in the heart of dairy-farming and stock-rearing country, began as a series of scattered settlements that had grown around the shepherds' shelters or bothies. The true name of the village is actually Grindsbrook Booth, but it is commonly known by the name of the valley. Tourism first came to Edale with the completion of the Manchester to Sheffield railway in 1894, though at that time there was little in the way of hospitality for visitors. Today there are several hotels, camping sites, a large Youth Hostel and adventure and walking centres. Not far from the village is the famous **Jacob's Ladder**, overlooking the River Noe. Nearby is the tumbledown remain of a hill farmer's cottage; this was the home of Jacob Marshall, who some 200 years ago cut the steps into the hillside leading up to Edale Cross.

CASTLETON   Map 6 ref M11
8 miles NE of Buxton off the A625

Situated at the head of the Hope Valley, Castleton is sheltered by the Norman ruin of **Peveril Castle** (built by Henry II in the 1170s) and is overlooked by Mam Tor. Approaching Castleton from the west along the A625, the road runs through the **Winnats Pass**, a narrow limestone gorge. Thought to have been formed under the sea, from currents eroding the seabed, the gorge has been used as a road for centuries and is still the only direct route to the village from the west. Originally laid out as a planned town below its castle, the shape of the village has changed little over the years and it has become a popular tourist centre. The mainly 17th-century church of St Edmund was heavily restored in 1837, but retains its box pews and a fine Norman arch, as well as a Breechers Bible dated 1611.

The hills to the west of Castleton are famous for their caves. The **Blue John Mine and Caverns**, which have been in the hands of the Ollerenshaw family for many years, are probably one of Derbyshire's most popular attractions. Amazing trips down into the caves themselves can be made. During these trips, as well as seeing the incredible natural beauty of the caverns and the unique rock formations, there are collections of original 19th-century mining tools. Above ground, in the gift shops various items can be bought made with the distinctive Blue John fluorspar with its attractive purplish veining. The village's **Ollerenshaw Collection** of huge vases and urns made with the same unique stone is open to the public. Once prized by the Romans, it is said that Petronius paid the equivalent of around £40,000 for a wonderfully ornate vase carved from the stone. It is said that in a fit of petty-mindedness he preferred to smash the vase rather than relinquish it to the Emperor Nero.

At the bottom of Winnats Pass lies **Speedwell Cavern**, a former lead mine which used boats on an underground canal to ferry the miners and iron ore to and from the rockface. Visitors can follow the same boat journey underground in the company of a guide. The mine had a short life: it started up in 1771 and, following an investment of £14,000, closed in 1790 after only £3,000 worth of iron ore had been extracted.

Peak Cavern, reached by a delightful riverside walk, has the widest opening of any cave in Europe. Up until the 17th century, little cottages used to stand within the entrance. The ropemakers who lived in these tiny dwellings used the cave entrance, dry in all weathers, for making rope: the ropewalk, which dates back some 400 years, can still be seen. Guides re-enact the process of making rope, and one ropemaker's cottage is still extant. Recently the cave was used by the BBC, who filmed an episode of *The Chronicles of Narnia* series here. Over the years successive Kings and Queens would entertain deep within the belly of the cave, which would be festooned with candles and other open flames - visitors can see the ledge on which the Royal musicians would perch. Peak Cavern was originally known as The Devil's Arse, though the

Victorians - ever fastidious - felt this was 'inappropriate' and changed it to the name it carries today.

Above Peak Cavern is **Peveril Castle** with its spectacular views over Castleton and the surrounding countryside. The Castle, originally called Castle of the Peak, was built as a wooden stockade in 1080 by William Peveril, illegitimate son of William the Conqueror. Later rebuilt in stone, the keep was added by Henry II. It remains the only surviving example of a Norman castle in Derbyshire, and is among the best preserved and most complete ruins in Britain.

Peveril Castle, Castleton

No description of Castleton would be complete without a mention of **Mam Tor**. The name means 'Mother Hill', and locally the Tor is referred to as Shivering Mountain, because the immense cliff face near the summit is constantly on the move owing to water seepage. A climb to the top of the ridge is well worth while, as the views are splendid - in particular of the two diverse rock formations which can be made out and white separate the White (limestone) Peak from the northern Dark (gritstone) Peak.

HOPE
Map 6 ref M11
9 miles NE of Buxton off the A625

Hope gets its first mention in 926 as the site of a battle won by King Athelstan. By the time of the Domesday survey of 1086, the parish of Hope had extended to embrace much of the High Peak area and included places such as Buxton, Chapel-en-le-Frith and Tideswell. It remained one of the largest parishes in the country until the 19th century, though a market charter was not granted it until 1715. Hope lies at the point where the River Noe meets Peakshole Water; the stream rises in **Peak's Hole** (better known as Peak Cavern), hence its name.

The parish church of St Peter was built at the beginning of the 13th century; the only part remaining from the original church is the Norman font. The Latin inscription on a chair in the north aisle reads (in translation) 'You cannot make a scholar out of a block of wood' and is said to have been carved for Thomas Bocking, the vicar and schoolmaster here during the 17th century. His name also appears on the fine pulpit; his Breechers Bible is displayed nearby. From the outside, the squat 14th-century spire gives the church a rather curious shape; in the churchyard can be found the shaft of a Saxon cross. The **Hope Agricultural Show** is held every year on August Bank Holiday Monday.

BRADWELL
Map 6 ref M11
9 m NE of Buxton off the B6049

Usually abbreviated in the unique Peak District way to 'Bradder' - is a charming little limestone village sheltered by Bradwell Edge. At one time this former lead-mining community was famous as the place where miners' hardhats - hard, black, brimmed hats in which candles were stuck to light the way underground - were made; thus these hardhats came to be known as Bradder Beavers. It owes its fortune to the lead mining industry of the 18th and 19th centuries, though among other items manufactured in Bradwell include coarse cotton goods, telescopes and opera glasses. It was also the birthplace of Samuel Fox, the 17th-century inventor of the folding-frame umbrella. Legend has it that Bradwell was also once a Roman slave camp, to serve the lead mines. Today it is more famous for producing delicious ice cream.

During the period of struggle that followed the Romans' departure, the mysterious fortification to the north of the village, known as **Grey Ditch**, was built. It may have been constructed to defend Bradford Dale and the village against the Hope Valley. A different local legend speaks of Bradwell as the scene of the hanging of the Saxon King Edwin. The local name 'Eden Tree' is said to stem from this. A key attraction here is the massive **Bagshawe Cavern**, a cave reached by a descending flight of 98 steps through an old lead mine. Along the half-mile walk to the main show cave there are wonderful rock formations and other interesting sights. For the more adventurous there are caving trips available.

A mile south of the village is the mid-16th-century **Hazelbadge Hall**. One of several manors of the Vernon family, whose main seat was at Haddon Hall, their coat of arms can be seen above the upper mullioned windows. It house dates from 1549 and was part of Dorothy Vernon's dowry to her new husband, John Manners.

On the Saturday before the first Monday in August, four wells are dressed in the village. Although wells were dressed even at the turn of the 20th century, the present custom dates back only to 1949, when the Bowling Green Well was dressed during Small Dale Wakes. The village has its own particular method for making the colourful screens, section by section, so that the clay does not dry out.

BAMFORD
MAP 6 REF M11
11 miles NE of Buxton off the A6013

This charming village situated between the Hope Valley and Ladybower Reservoir, stands at the heart of the Dark Peak below Bamford Edge and close to the Upper Derwent Valley Dams. When the Derwent and Howden Dams were built in the early years of the 20th century, the valley of the Upper Derwent was flooded, submerging many farms under the rising waters. The 1,000 or so navvies and their families were housed at Birchinlee, a temporary village which came to be known locally as 'Tin Town', for its plethora of corrugated iron shacks. During the Second World War the third and largest reservoir, the **Ladybower**, was built. This involved the inundating two villages — Derwent and Ashopton. The dead from Derwent's church were re-interred in the churchyard of St John the Baptist in Bamford. The living were rehoused in Yorkshire Bridge, a purpose-built hamlet located below the embankment of the Ladybower Dam. There is a Visitor Centre at **Fairholmes** (in the Upper Derwent Valley) which tells the story of these 'drowned villages'.

The **Derwent Dam**, built in 1935, was the practice site for the Dambusters, who tested dropping their bouncing bombs here. Along the A57 towards Sheffield, the road dips and crosses the gory-sounding **Cutthroat Bridge**. The present bridge dates back to 1830, but its name comes from the late 16th century, when the body of a man with his throat cut was discovered under the bridge which then stood here.

HATHERSAGE
MAP 6 REF M11
12 miles NE of Buxton off the A625

The name Hathersage comes from the Old English for 'Haefer's ridge' - probably a reference to the moorland slopes of Stanage Edge above the town. Once a centre for needle-making, it is difficult to know whether to classify Hathersage as a large village or a small town. In either event, it is a pleasant place with interesting literary connections. Charlotte Bronte stayed at Hathersage vicarage, and the village itself appears as 'Morton' in her novel *Jane Eyre*. The name Eyre was probably gleaned from the monuments to the prominent local landowners with this surname, as can be seen in the village church of St Michael and its churchyard.

The Eyre family has been associated with this area for over 800 years. The 15th-century head of the family, Robert Eyre, lived at Highlow Hall. Within sight of this Hall he built seven houses, one for each of his seven sons. **North Lees** was one, and the grounds of this Elizabethan tower house are open to the public. Another was **Moorseats**, where Charlotte Bronte stayed on holiday and used as the inspiration for Moor House in *Jane Eyre*.

In Hathersage churchyard lie the reputed remains of Little John, Robin Hood's renowned companion. Whether or not the legend is to be believed, it is worth mentioning that when the grave was opened in the 1780s, a 32-inch thighbone was discovered. This would certainly indicate that the owner was well over seven feet tall.

Hathersage also boasts a superb outdoor swimming pool, open to the public at certain times throughout the summer holidays.

CROWDECOTE
6 miles SE of Buxton off the B5053

MAP 6 REF L12

Crowdecote is situated in the deep limestone valley of the River Dove, just on the border with Staffordshire. The limestone reef knolls of the upper part of the valley can be clearly seen from vantage points near the village. Seen as hills, such as **Chrome Hill** and **Parkhouse Hill**, they are as close to peaks as they get in the Peak District. These knolls are actually the remnants of coral reefs - hard to believe, but perhaps not so puzzling when one remembers that much of this landscape has been formed by the action of water.

Here in the heart of upper Dovedale, in the Dove Valley, the renowned **Packhorse Inn** is one of the most picturesque hostelries in the Peak District, a lovely limestone public house/ restaurant dating back to the 16th-century. Once a coaching inn used by traders passing through on their way to Leek and Buxton, below the inn there once stood a wooden bridge, replaced by a stone one in 1709, which stands to this day. This marked one of four crossing points for the river. The inn has seen 27 landlords come and go; present proprietors Jim and Lynn Milburn offer their guests a genu- inely warm welcome. In sight of Crome Hill and Park House Peaks, with stunning views in all directions, this su- perior establishment also provides bed and breakfast accommoda- tion. The decor and

Packhorse Inn, Crowdecot, Nr Buxton, Derbyshire SK17 0DB
Tel: 01298 83618

furnishings are cosy and comfortable. The restaurant menu focuses on traditional English cook- ing, with all produce locally produced and fresh daily - some of it from Jim and Lynn's own garden! The flowers for the hanging baskets that festoon the inn are grown in their own green- houses. The three guest bedrooms overlook the River Dove, and offer every comfort and convenience. The Milburns are native to this part of Derbyshire, and have extensive knowledge of the locality which they are happy to share with their guests. The attractive beer gardens are home to their friendly Shetland ponies.

LONGNOR
6 miles S of Buxton off the B5053

MAP 6 REF L12

Over the county line into Staffordshire yet in the heart of the Peak District, on a gentle slope between the River Manifold and the River Dove, Longnor was once the meeting-point of sev- eral packhorse routes. Then an important market town and the centre of a prosperous farming community, its **Market Hall** was built in 1873 - outside the hall there is a posting of the market charges of the time. The town's prosperity declined with the onset of the agricultural depression, and there was an accompanying fall in the population. However, this decline has in recent years been reverses. Longnor is now a conservation area and has attracted a good many craftspeople. The Market Square is one of the oldest in England, dating back to medieval times. The village also has some fascinating narrow flagged passages which seem to go nowhere but suddenly emerge into the most beautiful scenery.

Though the late 18th-century church of St Bartholomew is rather plain, the churchyard has a most interesting gravestone. The epitaph tells the tale of the life of William Billinge, born in 1679, died in 1791 - which made him 112 years old at the time of his death! As a soldier Billinge served under Rooke at Gibraltar and Marlborough at Ramilles; after being sent home wounded he recovered to take part in defending the King in the rebellions of 1715 and 1745.

Opposite the village square stands **The Crewe and Harpur Arms Hotel**, an imposing brickbuilt structure which takes its name from the local estate to which it once belonged. Despite its impressive exterior, the building required a considerable amount of refurbishment when proprietors Pam and Alan Naden took over in 1993. Through sheer hard work they have created a very comfortable inn which is ideally situated as a holiday or touring base. The seven guest rooms (five of which are ensuite) are attractive and comfortable. The bar is open every day, all day Saturday and Sunday, serving Marston ales and lunch and evening meals. In the dining room there's an extensive menu which includes traditional English, Indian and Chinese dishes such as mixed grill, chicken korma and peppered pork, as well as a range of salads, sandwiches and snacks (booking advised for Sunday lunch). The Nadens also have three lovely holiday cottages available for weekly lets in season and long weekend breaks out of season.

The Crewe & Harpur Arms Hotel, Longnor, nr Buxton
Derbyshire SK17 0NS Tel: 01928 83205

BAKEWELL

Map 6 ref M12

10 miles SE of Buxton on the A6

The only true town in the Peak District National Park, Bakewell attracts many day-trippers, walkers and campers as well as locals who come to take advantage of its many amenities. The beautiful medieval five-arched bridge spanning the River Wye is still in use today as the main crossing point for traffic. A stonebuilt town set along the banks of the River Wye, Bakewell enjoys a picturesque setting among well-wooded hills. With only 4,000 inhabitants it is nevertheless generally acknowledged as the capital of the Peak District National Park.

However, for most people it is a dessert that has made the name of Bakewell so famous, but please remember it is referred to locally as a *pudding* and most definitely not as a tart! Its invention is said to have been an accident when what was supposed to have been a strawberry tart turned into something altogether different. The cooking mishap took place in the kitchens of the Rutland Arms Hotel, which was built in 1804 on the site of a coaching inn. One of the hotel's more famous guests was the novelist Jane Austen, who stayed there in 1811. The Rutland Arms featured in her book *Pride and Prejudice*, while Bakewell itself appears as the town of Lambton. Bakewell's situation has always made it the ideal place for a settlement and, as well as being home to the Romans, an Iron Age fort has been discovered close by. Another reason for the popularity of the town was the existence of 12 fresh water springs and they also gave the town its name - Bad kwell means bath spring. This Old English name means "Badeca's spring" or "well", and is a reference to the warm, iron-bearing springs which rise in and around the town.

The large parish church of All Saints was founded in Saxon times, as the ancient preaching crosses and stonework. Its graceful spire, with its octagonal tower, can be seen for miles around. One of the few places in Derbyshire in the Domesday book to record two priests and a church, the churchyard and church itself contain a wonderful variety of headstones and coffin slabs and, near the porch, a most unusual cross. Behind the church is the lovely **Old House Museum**, housed in a building on Cunningham Place which dates back to 1534. It is thought to be the oldest house in Bakewell. This beautiful building escaped demolition and has been lovingly restored by the Bakewell Historical Society and now displays its original wattle and daub interior walls. It was extended during the early 17th century and, at one time, the building was converted into tenements by the industrialist Richard Arkwright for his mill-workers. Now established as a folk museum, it houses a fascinating collection of rural bygones.

The town is full of delightful, mellow stone buildings, many of which date from the early 17th century and are still in use today. The **Old Town Hall**, famous as the scene of the Bakewell riots, is now the Tourist Information Centre of the Peak District. Few buildings remain from the days when Bakewell was a minor spa town, but the **Bath House**, on Bath Street, is one such building. Built in 1697 for the Duke of Rutland, it contained a large bath which was filled with the spa water and kept at a constant temperature of 59 degrees Fahrenheit. At the nearby Bath Gardens a Roman bath was discovered near the British Legion's Garden of Remembrance.

Traditionally well-dressing flourished in the town in the 18th century, when Bakewell had aspirations to become a fashionable spa. However, the recent revival dates back only to the 1970s, when the British Legion - with the help of the well-dressers of Ashford in the Water - dressed the warm well at Bath House. Today, all five wells - all in the same room - are dressed on the last Saturday in June.

Only a mile to the south of Bakewell down the Matlock Road, on a bluff overlooking the Wye, the romantic **Haddon Hall** stands hidden from the road by a beech hedge. The Hall is thought by many to have been the first fortified house in the country, although the turrets and battlements were actually put on purely for show. The home of the Dukes of Rutland for over 800 years, the Hall has enjoyed a fairly peaceful existence, in part no doubt because it stood empty and neglected for neary 300 years after 1640, when the family chose Belvoir Castle in Leicestershire as their main home. Examples of work from every century from the 12th to the 17th are here in this treasure trove. As with all good ancestral homes, it has a family legend. In this case the story dates from the 16th century when Lady Dorothy Vernon eloped with Sir John Manners. Although there is no historical evidence to back the claim that Dorothy Vernon eloped with John Manners during a ball - many feel this

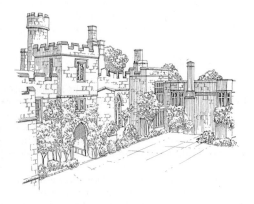

Haddon Hall, Bakewell

legend was invented by the Victorians, in part because neither the steps nor the pretty little packhorse bridge across the Wye, over which Dorothy is supposed to have escaped, existed during her time - a small museum by the gatehouse tells of their romantic journey, as well as the history of the Hall. Little construction work has been carried out on the Hall since the days of Henry VIII and it remains one of the best examples of a medieval and Tudor manor house. The 16th-century terraced gardens are one of the chief delights of the Hall and are thought by many to be the most romantic in England. The Hall's splendour and charm have led it to be used as a backdrop to television and film productions including *Jane Eyre*, *Moll Flanders* and *The Prince and the Pauper*. Nikolaus Pevsner described the Hall as "The English castle par excellence, not the forbidding fortress on an unassailable crag, but the large, rambling, safe, grey, loveable house of knights and their ladies, the unreasonable dream-castle of those who think of the Middle Ages as a time of chivalry and valour and noble feelings. None other in England is so complete and convincing." The Hall's chapel is adorned with medieval wall paintings; the kitchens are the oldest extant part of the house, and feature time-worn oak tables and dole cupboards. The oak-panelled Long Gallery features boars' heads (to represent Vernon) and peacocks (Manners) in the panelling.

ASHFORD IN THE WATER   Map 6 ref M12
1½ miles NW of Bakewell off the A6

Not exactly in the water, but certainly on the River Wye, Ashford is another candidate for Derbyshire's prettiest village. Developed around a ford that spanned the river and was once an important crossing place on the ancient Portway. The medieval **Sheepwash Bridge** crosses the

Wye, with overhanging willows framing its low arches. It is one of three bridges in the village, and a favourite with artists. There is a small enclosure to one side that provides a clue to its name, as this is still occasionally used for its original purpose - crowds gather to witness sheep being washed in the river to clean their fleece before they are shorn. Mill Bridge dates back to 1664.

So-called Black Marble, actually a highly polished grey limestone from quarries and mines near the village, was mined nearby for some con-

Sheepwash Bridge, Ashford-in-the-Water

siderable time, and particularly during the Victorian era when it was fashionable to have decorative items and fire surrounds made from the stone. It was also exported all over the world. Once a thriving cottage industry, Ashford Marble, as it was known, was inlaid with coloured marbles, shells and glass.

The great limestone parish **Church of the Holy Trinity**, largely rebuilt in 1871 but retaining the base of a 13th-century tower, has a fine Ashford marble table on show as well as a tablet to the memory of Henry Watson, the founder of the marble works who was also an authority on the geology of the area. Several of the pillars within the church are made of the rare Duke's Red marble, which is only found in the mine at Lathkill Dale owned by the Duke of Devonshire. The church also boasts a Norman tympanum, complete with Tree of Life, lion and hog, over the south door. Hanging from the roof of Ashford's church are the remains of four "virgin's crants" - paper garlands carried at the funerals of unmarried village girls.

Churchdale Hall, near the village, dates from the 18th century and is part of the vast Chatsworth estate. It was also the home of the 10th Duke of Devonshire, who never resided at Chatsworth, until his death in 1950. To the south of Ashford is another manor House, **Ashford Hall**. Again owned by the Dukes of Devonshire, it was built in 1780 and for a time was occupied by the family, until it was sold in the early 1950s.

Ashford is perhaps most famous for its six beautifully executed well-dressings, which are held annually in early June. After a break of many years the custom of well-dressing was briefly revived at Sheepwash Well in 1930, though this revival petered out until the arrival in the village of an enthusiastic vicar in the 1950s that the well dressings became an annual custom once more. Rather than adhering strictly to the custom of depicting scenes from the Bible, the well-dressers of Ashford have pictured such unusual themes as a willow pattern to celebrate the Chinese Year of the Dog, and have also paid tribute to the Land Girls of the First World War. The village also has a pleasant range of mainly 18th-century cottages, and a former tithe barn which now serves as an art gallery.

Enjoying a most delightful setting beside the River Wye, **Riverside House** at Ashford-in-the-Water provides an idyllic base for a relaxing break away from it all. Just a glimpse of the graceful Georgian exterior tells guests that that have made a real find. This traditional country house is set in its own lovely gardens. The hotel was purchased in 1998 by Penelope Thornton (of the famous chocolates family). Together with her general manger Sonia Banks, Penelope has overseen a tasteful refurbishment programme to create this elegant yet still delightfully informal retreat. Guests want for nothing at this stylish and superb establishment. With just 15 bedrooms, the ambience is always low key, warm and friendly in this charming and dis-

Riverside House, Ashford-in-the-Water, Bakewell, Derbyshire DE45 1QF Tel: 01629 814275 Fax: 01629 812873 e-mail: riversidehouse@enta.net

tinctive establishment. These individually appointed ensuite guest rooms are enhanced by beautiful antique furniture and rich country house fabrics. The handsome guests' lounge has an inglenook fireplace and fine oak panelling. In the elegant restaurant, dishes worthy of the most discerning palate are created by the imaginative chef (winner of 2 AA rosettes for the restaurant), drawing on fresh local produce to offer simple modern English dishes where delicate fish, succulent meats and rich game are to the fore, as in choices such as Organic Derbyshire-reared lamb, roasted squab pigeon and seared turbot. The restaurant is open daily to non-residents and residents alike for luncheon and dinner. The service is always professional and friendly in this elegant yet informal ambience.

GRINDLEFORD

MAP 6 REF M11

6 miles N of Bakewell off the B6521/B6001

This is one of the smallest Peak District villages and from here, each year in July, there is a pilgrimage to **Padley Chapel** to commemorate two Catholic martyrs of 1588. The ruins of ancient Padley Manor House, found alongside the track bed of the old railway line, are all that remain of the home of two devout Roman Catholic families. It was from here that two priests, Robert Ludlam and Nicholas Garlick were taken, in the 16th century, and sentenced to death, in Derby, by hanging, drawing and quartering. The then owner of the house, Thomas Fitzherbert, died in the Tower of London three years later whilst his brother died at Fleet Prison in 1598. In 1933, the charming chapel seen today was converted from the still standing farm buildings.

To the northwest of the village is the **Longshaw Country Park**, some 1,500 acres of open moorland, woodland and the impressive Padley Gorge. Originally the Longshaw estate of the Dukes of Rutland, the land was acquired by the National Trust by the 1970s. At the heart of the country park, is the Duke's former shooting lodge.

EYAM   Map 6 ref M11
5 miles N of Bakewell off the B6521

Pronounced "Eem", this village will forever be known as the **Plague Village**. In 1666, a local tailor received a bundle of plague-infected clothing from London. Within a short time the infection had spread and the terrified inhabitants prepared to flee the village. However, the local rector, William Mompesson, persuaded the villagers to stay put and, thanks to his inter-

vention, most neighbouring villages escaped the disease. Eyam was quarantined for over a year, relying on outside help for supplies of food which were left on the village boundary. Out of a total of 350 inhabitants, only 83 survived.

An open-air service is held each August at Cucklet Delf to commemorate the villagers' brave self-sacrifice, and the well-dressings are also a thanksgiving for the pureness of the water. Taking place on the last Sunday in August, known as Plague Sunday, this also commemo-

Plague Cottages, Eyam

rates the climax of the plague and the death of the rector's wife, Catherine Mompesson. The village itself is quite large and self-contained, and typical of a mining and quarrying settlement. An interesting place to stroll around, there are many information plaques documenting events where they took place. The **Church of St Lawrence** houses an excellent exhibition of Eyam's history. Also inside the Church are two ancient coffin lids; the top of one of the lids is known as St Helen's Cross.

Born in Derbyshire, St Helen was the daughter of a Romano-British chief and the mother of Emperor Constantine. She is said to have found a fragment of the cross on which Jesus was crucified. In the churchyard is the best preserved Saxon cross to be found in the Peak District, along with an unusual sundial which dates from 1775.

The home of the Wright family for over 300 years, **Eyam Hall** is a wonderful, unspoilt 17th-century manor house that is now open to the public. As well as touring the house and seeing the impressive stone-flagged hall, tapestry room and the magnificent tester bed, there is also a cafe and gift shop. The Eyam Hall Crafts Centre, housed in the farm building, contains several individual units which specialise in a variety of unusual and skilfully-fashioned crafts.

MILLER'S DALE
MAP 6 REF M11
7 miles NW of Bakewell off the B6049

This tiny settlement, situated in the narrow valley of the River Wye, began life as late as the 1860s when it was built to provide housing for the workers building the London to Manchester railway. All this has now gone but the dramatic Monsal Dale Viaduct (built in the 1860s to carry the railway line) remains and is now crossed by walkers taking the **Monsal Trail**. The hamlet takes its name from one of several charming and compact dales that lie along the River Wye and provide excellent walking. The nearby nature reserve occupies land that was originally a limestone quarry which was blown up in 1971.

FLAGG
MAP 6 REF M12
5 miles W of Bakewell off the A515

The characteristic ridges and furrows of the medieval open fields, enclosed by stone walls in the 17th and 18th century, have been preserved in the farmland around Flagg. During the period of enclosure, hundreds of miles of stone walls were built, dividing the land into geometric patterns. Most of this can still be seen today, all over the Peak District, and is one of the particular features of the area. Elizabethan **Flagg Hall**, set back off the main road, is well worth seeing.

The **Plough Inn** in Flagg is a truly top of the range, hidden gem surrounded by scenic countryside here in the heart of the Peak National Park. There's something to appeal to everyone here, locals and visitors alike, with excellent food, ale and accommodation on offer. Owned and personally run by Peter and Julie since 1997, this Free House dates back to the early 19th century, when it was known as The Star. They are friendly and welcoming hosts, who care about quality and service. Open for both sessions weekdays in summer and all day Saturday and Sunday, closed Monday lunch (except for Bank Holidays) and Tuesday and Wednesday lunch-

The Plough Inn, Flagg, nr Buxton, Derbyshire SK17 9QR
Tel: 01298 85557

time in winter. The well-kept ales on tap include Mansfield Bitter and Dark Smooth, plus a different guest ale weekly. There's also Guinness, Carling and Storford Press Cider, as well as a good range of wines and spirits. Food is available daily (except for Monday nights). The dining room is attractive and comfortable, with traditional dark oak tables and beamed ceilings, tastefully decorated throughout. Meals can also be taken in the family room and the bar, or in the lovely beer garden which contains animals for children to view and pet, including various breeds of poultry and "Sid", a delightful pot-bellied pig. Booking is advised for the dining room at weekends. The menu boasts a range of traditional English favourites; there's also a selection of daily specials. Wednesday night is always fish and chips night (to eat in or take away), and there are regular themed nights - please ring for details. This superb establishment also has two cosy and pretty ensuite rooms, situated adjacent to the inn with their own separate entrance and occupying the former (refurbished) stables. And in a nearby field there's room for up to seven touring caravans or campers. This secluded and scenic location is available all year round, and the site has showers, running water and waste disposal facilities.

EDENSOR   Map 6 ref M12
2 miles E of Bakewell off the B6012

This model village (the name is pronouced Ensor) was built by the 6th Duke of Devonshire between 1838 and 1842 after the original village had been demolished because it spoilt the view from Chatsworth House. Unable to decide on a specific design for the buildings, as suggested by his architect Paxton, the Duke had the cottages and houses in the new village built in a fascinating variety of styles. The village church was built by Sir George Gilbert Scott; in the churchyard is buried the late President Kennedy's sister Kathleen, who had married into the Cavendish family. Both she and her husband, the eldest son of the 10th Duke, were killed during the Second World War. The original village of Edensor lay nearer to the gates of Chatsworth House; only Park Cottage remains there now.

The home of the Dukes of Devonshire, **Chatsworth House**, known as the "Palace of the Peak", is without doubt one of the finest of the great houses in Britain. The origins of the House as a great showpiece must be attributable to the redoubtable Bess of Hardwick, whose marriage into the Cavendish family helped to secure the future of the palace. Bess' husband, Sir William Cavendish, bought the estate for £600 in 1549. It was Bess who completed the new House after his death. Over the years, the Cavendish fortune continued to pour into Chatsworth, making it an almost unparalleled showcase for art treasures. Every aspect of the fine arts is here, ranging from old masterpieces, furniture, tapestries, porcelain and some magnificent alabaster carvings. The gardens of this stately home also have some marvellous features, including the Emperor Fountain, which dominates the Canal Pond and is said to reach a height of 290 feet. There is a maze and a Laburnum Tunnel and, behind the house, the famous Cascades. The overall appearance of the park as it is seen today is chiefly due to the talents of "Capability" Brown, who was first consulted in 1761. However, the name perhaps most strongly associated with Chatsworth is Joseph Paxton. His experiments in glasshouse design led him eventually to his masterpiece, the Crystal Palace, built to house the Great Exhibition of 1851.

MATLOCK   Map 6 ref M12
7 miles SE of Bakewell on the A6

Much of the southeastern Peakland area around Matlock lies outside the boundaries of the National Park, but the towns, villages and much of the surrounding countryside has plenty of the typical Peak District characteristics. Matlock and its various satellite settlements provide the focus and, after a period of decline, this essentially Victorian town is, once again, a busy and bustling place with plenty to offer the visitor as well as some fine views over the Lower Derwent Valley from its well planned vantage points.

As the northern, gritstone landscape of the Peak District is often referred to as the Dark Peak, the southern, limestone plateaux have gained the equally obvious name of White Peak. Though the hilltops are often windswept and bleak, the numerous dales, cut deep into the limestone, provide a lush and green haven for all manner of wild and plant life. Several of the rivers are famous for their trout, particularly the Lathkill, which was greatly favoured by the keen angler and writer Sir Izaak Walton.

Matlock is a bustling town nestling in the lower valley of the River Derwent, and is the administrative centre of Derbyshire as well as being a busy tourist centre bordering the Peak District National Park. There are actually eight Matlocks which make up the town, along with several other hamlets. Most have simply been engulfed and have lost their identity as the town grew, but **Matlock Bath**, the site of the spa, still maintains some individuality.Matlock itself is famed as, at one time, having the steepest-gradient (a 1-in-5½) tramway in the world; it was also the only tram system in the Peak District. Opened in 1893, the tramcars ran until 1927 and the Depot can still be seen at the top of Bank Street. The old Ticket Office and Waiting Room at Matlock station have been taken over by the Peak Rail Society and here can be found not only their shop, but also exhibitions explaining the history and aims of the society. The Peak Rail has its southernmost terminus just a few minutes' walk from the mainline station.

Peak Rail is a rebuilt, refurbished and now preserved railway running between Matlock Riverside station (just a five-minute walk from the mainline station at Matlock) through the charming rural station of Darley Dale to the terminus Rowsley South. Run entirely by volunteers, a restaurant car is fitted for every journey. The full journey (one way) takes just 20 minutes, and passengers can alight to enjoy the picnic area at the entrance to Rowsley South Station, or the exhibition coach at Darley Dale platform. Inside Matlock's **Church of St Giles** can be seen the faded and preserved funeral garlands or "virgin crants" that were once common all over Derbyshire. Bell-shaped, decorated with rosettes and ribbons and usually containing a personal item, the garlands were made in memory of a deceased young girl of the parish. At her funeral the garland was carried by the dead girl's friends and, after the service, it would be suspended from the church rafters above the pew she had normally occupied.

High up on the hill behind the town is the brooding ruin of **Riber Castle**. The castle was built between 1862 and 1868 and is often linked with the McCaig folly which overlooks Oban on the west coast of Scotland. The castle's creator, John Smedley, a local hosiery manufacturer who became interested in the hydropathic qualities of Matlock, drew up the designs for the building himself. Lavishly decorated inside, Smedley constructed his own gas-producing plant to provide lighting for the Castle and it even had its own well. Following the death of first Smedley and then his wife, the castle was sold and for a number of years it was boys' school. During the Second World War, the school having closed, the castle was used as a food store before it was left to become a ruined shell. Today the building and surrounding grounds are home to a sanctuary for rare breeds and endangered species; the Wildlife Park has been particularly successful at breeding lynx, and boasts the world's largest collection of this magnificent animal. To the west of Matlock, down a no-through road, can be found one of Derbyshire's few Grade I listed buildings, the secluded and well-hidden **Snitterton Hall**. Little is known of the history of this fine Elizabethan manor house, though it is believed to have been built by John Milward in 1631, around the same time that he purchased half the manor of Snitterton.

ASHOVER   MAP 7 REF M12
4 miles NE of Matlock off the B6036

Viewed from the southern rocky ridge known as **The Fabric** (apparently because it provided the "fabric" for much of the local building stone) and with the monolith of **Cocking Tor** in the foreground, Ashover can be seen as a scattered village filling the pleasantly wooded valley of the River Amber. The name of this village means "ash tree slope" and though there are, indeed, many ash trees in the area, many other varieties including oak and birch also flourish. Ashover lies just outside the boundary of the Peak District National Park but it still captures the typical character of a Peak village. At the heart of the largest parish in northeast Derbyshire, the village is chiefly constructed from limestone and gritstone which were both quarried locally. The ruined shell of **Eastwood Hall**, once a large fortified Elizabethan manor house, also lies in the village. Owned, over the years, by several prominent Derbyshire families, including the Willoughbys, the house was blown up by the Roundheads dur-

Ashover

ing the Civil War. The Crispin Inn, next to the interesting parish **Church of All Saints**, claims to date from the time of Agincourt, 1415. However, it is far more likely that, like many other buildings in the parish, it dates from the 17th century. The inn's name reflects one of Ashover's traditional trades: St Crispin is the patron saint of shoemakers and cobblers. The church, with its 15th-century tower, houses the alabaster tomb of Thomas Babington and his wife, said by many to be the best in Derbyshire. There are also some handsome brasses. What is surprising is the lead-lined Norman font, described by Pevsner as "the most important Norman font in the country", the only lead-lined font in this area that is so well known for its mining.

DARLEY DALE Map 6 ref M12
2½ miles NW of Matlock off the A6

One of the most unassuming heroines of this part of Derbyshire must be Lady Mary Louisa Whitworth. She was the second wife of Sir Joseph Whitworth, the famous Victorian engineer whose name is associated with the Great Exhibition of 1851 and who also invented the screw thread. Sir Joseph made a fortune manufacturing, amongst other items, machine tools, munitions and nuts and bolts. Following his death in 1887, Lady Mary undertook to bring sweeping changes to the lifestyle of the local poor and needy. She allowed the grounds of her home, Stancliffe Hall, to be used for school outings and events. In 1889, the Whitworth Cottage Hospital was opened under her auspices. The **Whitworth Institute** was opened in 1890, bringing to the community a wide range of facilities including a swimming pool, an assembly hall, a natural history museum and a library. At a time when a woman was required to take a secondary role in society, Lady Mary was determined to credit her late husband with these changes, which so benefited Darley Dale. Lady Whitworth died in France in 1896, and is buried next to her husband at the parish Church of St Helen, in the hamlet of Churchtown. The churchyard is also home to the

Darley Yew, one of the oldest living trees in Britain which has a girth of some 33 feet. The yew predates the Norman origins of the Church and may be older than the Saxon fragments found here earlier this century. Much of the stone used for building in the village came from nearby Stancliffe Quarry, which also supplied stone for the Thames Embankment and Hyde Park Corner in London and the Walker Art Gallery in Liverpool. To the north of the 15th-century Darley Bridge, which carries the road to Winster over the River Derwent, are the remains of **Mill Close Mine**. This was the largest and most productive lead mine in Derbyshire until 1938, when flooding caused it to be abandoned. Darley Dale has an extensive park which is very pretty in all seasons. Another of this small village's attractions is **Red House Stables**, a working carriage museum featuring some fine examples of traditional horse-drawn vehicles and equipment.

STANTON IN PEAK Map 6 ref M12
5 miles NW of Matlock off the B5056

This is a typical Peak District village, with numerous alleyways and courtyards off its main street. A quick glance at the village cottages and the visitor will soon notice the initials WPT that appear above most of the doorways. The initials are those of William Paul Thornhill, the owner of Stanton Hall, which stands near the church and is still home to his descendants. The village pub, The Flying Childers, is named after one of the 4th Duke of Devonshire's most successful racehorses.

The gritstone landscape of **Stanton Moor**, which rises to some 1,096 feet and overlooks the village, is encircled by footpaths and is a popular walking area. There are also several interesting features on the moorland. The folly, Earl Grey's Tower, was built in 1832 to commemorate the reform of Parliament. There is also an ancient stone circle dating from the Bronze Age and with over 70 burial mounds. Known as the **Nine Ladies**, the stone circle has a solitary boulder nearby called the King's Stone. Legend has it that one Sunday nine women and a fiddler came up onto the moor to dance and, for their act of sacrilege, they were turned to stone.

The nearby **Rowtor Rocks** contain caves which were carved out at some stage in the 17th century. Not only was the living space made from the rock but tables, chairs and alcoves were also made to create a cosy retreat for the local vicar, Rev Thomas Eyre. Prior to these home improvements, the caves were reputedly used by the Druids, who did not believe in such creature comforts. Also in the area is the site of an Iron Age hillfort known as **Castle Ring**.

ROWSLEY
4 miles NW of Matlock off the A6

MAP 6 REF M12

On the banks of the River Wye lies **Caudwell's Mill**, a unique Grade II listed historic roller flour mill. A mill has stood on this site for at least 400 years; the present mill was built in 1874, powered by water from the River Wye, and was run as a family business for over a century up until 1978. Since then the Mill has undergone extensive restoration by a group of dedicated volunteers and, using machinery that was installed at the beginning of this century, the Mill is once again producing wholemeal flour. Other mill buildings on the site have been converted to house a variety of craft workshops, shops and a restaurant. On Chatsworth Road near the terminus of the Peak Rail line, **Peak Village** is an extensive factory outlet shopping centre offering a range of ladies' and men's fashion, sports and outdoor wear, home furnishings, jewellery, toys and books, and eateries. Also on-site is the charming **Wind in the Willows** attraction, created by an award-winning team of craftsmen and designers to bring the adventures of Ratty, Mole, Badger and Mr Toad to life.

Set in 10 acres of picturesque Derbyshire countryside, near Matlock and the Peak Rail steam train line at Rowsley South station, **East Lodge** takes its name from the fact that was once the east lodge to Haddon Hall, Derbyshire seat of the Duke of Rutland. This superior hotel has a reputation for comfort, tranquillity, style and a relaxed and friendly atmosphere. Each of the 15 ensuite bedrooms is individually furnished and decorated - and equipped with every modern convenience to enhance guests' comfort and enjoyment. In addition there is an elegant period lounge and fully licensed bar on the premises. The award-winning restaurant is open for lunch and dinner every day. The chef and his devoted and tal-

East Lodge Country House Hotel & Restaurant, Rowsley, Matlock, Derbyshire DE4 2EF
Tel: 01629 734474 Fax: 01629 733949
e-mail: info@eastlodge.com

ented staff provide a range of appealing menus, serving up such delicacies as rack of spring lamb, baked turbot, port and asparagus wellington and many, many more innovative and tempting dishes. Elegance and charm are assured in this delightful period setting, where guests will find the perfect blend of tradition and comfort.

YOULGREAVE
6½ miles NW of Matlock off the B5056

MAP 6 REF M12

This straggling village, known locally as Pommey, lies in Bradford Dale. The village **Church of All Saints** contains some parts of the original Saxon building though its ancient font is, unfortunately, upturned and used as a sundial. Inside, the working font is Norman and still retains its stoop for holding the Holy Water. It is well worth taking the time to have a look at, as it is the only such font in England. The Church also contains a small tomb with an equally small alabaster effigy; dated 1488, it is a memorial to Thomas Cockayne, who was killed in a brawl when only in his teens.

Further up the village's main street is **Thimble Hall**, the smallest market hall in the Peak District and still used for selling goods today. Typical of the White Peak area of Derbyshire the Hall dates from 1656 and there are also some rather grand Georgian houses to be found in the village. Standing opposite the old shop built in 1887 for the local Co-operative Society (now a youth hostel) is the **Conduit Head**, a gritstone water tank that has the unofficial name of The Fountain. Built by the village's own water company in 1826, it supplied fresh soft water to all those who paid an annual fee of sixpence. In celebration of their new, clean water supply, the villagers held their first well-dressing in 1829. Today, Youlgreave dresses its wells for the Saturday nearest to St John the Baptist's Day (24th June). Such is the standard of the work that the villagers, all amateurs, are in great demand for advice and help.

WINSTER
MAP 6 REF M12
4 miles W of Matlock off the B5056

This attractive gritstone village was once a lead-mining centre and market town. Today, it is a pleasant place with antique shops in the high street and some fine late 18th-century houses. Less splendid than the surrounding houses, but no less interesting, are the ginnels - little alleyways - which run off the main street. The most impressive building here, however, must be the Market House, owned by the National Trust and found at the top of the main street. The Trust's first purchase in Derbyshire, the rugged, two-storey   dates from the 17th and early 18th century and is an excellent reminder of Winster's past importance as a market town. Built from an attractive combination of brickwork and stone, the House is open to the public and acts as an information centre and shop for the Trust.

Winster Hall, built in 1628 by Francis Moore, has, like all good manor houses, its own ghost which haunts the grounds. The ghost is said to be that of a daughter of the Hall who fell in love with one of the coachmen. Her parents were horrified at her choice of husband and vowed to find a more suitable partner. However, before such a match could be made the girl and her lover climbed to the top of the Hall and jumped, together, to their deaths.

MATLOCK BATH
MAP 6 REF M12
1 mile S of Matlock off the A6

It is not known whether the Romans discovered the hot springs here, but by the late 17th century the waters were being used for medicinal purposes and the Old Bath Hotel was built. Like many other spa towns up and down the country, it was not until the Regency period that Matlock Bath reached its peak. As well as offering cures for many of the ills of the day, Matlock Bath and the surrounding area had much to offer the visitor and, by 1818, it was being described as a favourite summer resort. The spa town was compared to Switzerland by Byron and it has also been much admired by the Scottish philosopher, Dr Thomas Chalmers, and Ruskin, who stayed at the New Bath Hotel in 1829. Many famous people have visited the town, including the young Victoria before she succeeded to the throne. The coming of the railways, in 1849, brought Matlock Bath within easy reach, at small cost, to many more people and it became a popular destination for day excursions. Rather than being a town for the gentility, it became a place for the genteel. Today, it is still essentially a holiday resort and manages to possesses an air of Victorian charm left over from the days when the puritanical Victorians descended on the town looking for a "cure".

One of the great attractions of the town is **The Aquarium**, which occupies what was once the old **Matlock Bath Hydro** that was established in 1833. The original splendour of the Bath Hydro can still be seen, in the fine stone staircase and also in the thermal large pool which now is without its roof. The pool, maintained at a constant temperature of 68 degrees Fahrenheit, was where the rheumatic patients came to immerse themselves in the waters and relieve their symptoms. Today, the pool is home to a large collection of Large Mirror, Common and Koi Carp whilst the upstairs consulting rooms now house tanks full of native, tropical and marine fish. Visitors are welcome to feed the fish with food obtainable from the Aquarium. Also at The Aquarium is the **Hologram Gallery** a mind-boggling exhibition of three dimensional pictures made using the latest laser technology, the **Petrifying Well** - where visitors can see the petrifying process taking place as the famous Matlock Bath thermal water is sprayed onto objects, gradually turning them to stone - and the beautiful **Gemstone and Fossil Collection**. The Aquarium is open daily from Easter to the endof October.

Down by the riverbank and housed in the old Pavilion can be found the **Peak District Mining Museum and Temple Mine**, the only one of its kind in the world. Opened in 1978 and run by the Peak District Mines Historical Society, the Museum tells the story of lead mining in the surrounding area from as far back as Roman times to the 20th century. As well as the more usual displays of artefacts and implements used by the miners over the years, one of the Museum's most popular features are the climbing shafts and tunnels which allow the whole family to get a real feel for the life of a working lead miner. The Museum also houses a huge engine, dating from 1819, which was recovered from a mine near Winster. A unique survivor in Britain, the engine used water instead of steam to provide it with pressure. Adjacent to the Museum can be found the restored workings of Temple Mine.

For spectacular views of Matlock Bath, nothing beats a walk on **High Tor Grounds**. There are 60 acres of nature trails to wander around, while some 400 feet below the River Derwent appears like a silver thread through the gorge. A popular viewing point for Victorian visitors to the town, today rock climbers practise their skills climbing the precipitous crags of the Tor. For the less energetic, the walk to the top is rewarded by the views and the chance of a cup of tea and slice of home-made cake from the summit cafe.

On the opposite side of the valley are the beautiful wooded slopes of Masson Hill, the southern face of which has become known as the **Heights of Abraham**; this particular name was chosen after the inhabitants of Matlock had shown great enthusiasm for General Wolfe's victory in Quebec, this part of the Derwent valley being seen to resemble the gorge of the St Lawrence River and the original Heights of Abraham lying a mile north of Quebec. Today it is a well-known viewing point, reached on foot or, more easily, by cable car. The Heights of Abraham have a long history. For many years the slope was mined for lead but, in 1780, it was first developed as a Pleasure Garden and since then trees and shrubs have been planted to make it a pleasing attraction for those visiting the town to take the waters.

In 1812, the **Great Rutland Show Cavern**, on the slope, was opened to the public, a new experience for tourists of the time, and it was visited by many including the Grand Duke Michael of Russia and Princess Victoria. Following this success, in 1844, the Great Masson Cavern was opened and construction of the Victoria Prospect Tower was begun. Built by redundant lead miners, the Tower became a new landmark for the area and today still provides a bird's eye view over Derbyshire. The Heights of Abraham are today as popular as ever and provide all the amenities of a good country park.

CROMFORD
MAP 6 REF M12
2 miles S of Matlock off the A5012

Cromford is a model village known the world over, which was developed by Richard Arkwright into one of the first industrial towns. In addition to housing, he also provided his workers with a market place and a village Lock-Up. Born in Lancashire in 1732, Arkwright was the inventor of the waterframe, a machine for spinning cotton that was powered by water. He built his first mill at Cromford in 1771, the project taking a further 20 years to complete. It was the world's first successful water-powered cotton spinning mill. The area he had chosen proved to be perfect: the River Derwent, described by Daniel Defoe as "a fury of a river", provided an ample power supply; there was an unorganised but very willing workforce, as the lead-mining industry was experiencing a decline, and probably most importantly, Cromford was away from the prying eyes of Arkwright's competitors. In 1792, Arkwright commissioned the building of the village church, where he now lies. The Mill proved to be a great success and became the model for others both in Britain and abroad, earning Arkwright the accolade "Father of the Factory System". His pioneering work and contributions to the great Industrial Age resulted in a knighthood in 1786, and one year later he became High Sheriff of Derbyshire. **Cromford Mill** and the associated buildings are now an International World Heritage site. Tours of the mill and Cromford village are available throughout the year. Continuing refurbishment and conservation by The Arkwright Society, who bought the site in 1979, ensures that future visitors will be able follow the fascinating history behind this pioneering establishment. It is sponsored by Derbyshire County Council and the Derbyshire Dales District Council. Within the complex of the mill site there are a range of craft workshops and also the Mill Restaurant with its excellent home-cooked refreshment including a wide selection of wholefood dishes.

Cromford has a rather odd 15th-century bridge, which has rounded arches on one side and pointed arches on the other. It was from this bridge, in 1697, so local folklore has it, that a horse and rider took a flying leap from the parapet, plunged into the river 20 feet below and lived to tell the tale. For lovers of waterways, there is an opportunity at **Cromford Canal** to potter along the five-mile stretch of towpath to Ambergate, or better still, to take a peaceful canal boat ride. The Cromford Canal Society, which organises the boat trips along the canal, also maintains the **Cromford Wharf Steam Museum**. Its exhibits include the 1902 Robey horizontal engine donated by Friden Brickworks from nearby Hartington. The Museum is open by arrangement for private steamings and working demonstrations. The old **Leawood Pumping Station**, which transferred water from the River Derwent to the Cromford Canal, has been fully restored. Inside the engine house is a preserved Cornish-type beam engine which is occasionally steamed up. Close by the Pump House is the **Wigwell aqueduct**, which carries the Canal high over the River Derwent.

The **High Peak Trail**, which stretches some 17 miles up to Dowlow near Buxton, starts at Cromford and follows the trackbed of the Cromford and High Peak Railway. First opened in 1880, the railway was built to connect the Cromford Canal with the Peak Forest Canal and is somewhat reminiscent of a canal as it has long level sections interspersed with sharp inclines (instead of locks) and many of the stations are known as wharfs. After walking the trail it is not surprising to learn that its chief engineer was really a canal builder! The railway was finally closed in 1967; the old stations are now car parks and picnic areas; there is an information office in the former Hartington station signal box. Surfaced with clinker rather than limestone, the trail is suitable for walkers, cyclists and horses.

WIRKSWORTH

Map 6 ref M12

4 miles S of Matlock off the B5023

Carsington Water just outside Wirksworth is one of Britain's newest reservoirs. This 741-acre expanse of water is a beauty spot that has attracted over a million visitors a year since it was opened by Queen Elizabeth in 1992. It can be reached on foot from Wirksworth along a series

Carsington Water, Wirksworth

of footpaths. Sailing, windsurfing, fishing and canoeing can be enjoyed here, as well as just quiet strolls or bike rides. The Visitor Centre on the west bank offers visitors the opportunity to learn about Severn Trent Water and all aspects of water supply.

LEA

Map 6 ref M12

4 miles SE of Matlock off the A615

The charming village is famous for its associations with Florence Nightingale, who spent many happy summers as a girl in nearby Holloway. The building now home to **The Jug & Glass** public house in Lea was once a hospital for the employees of the Nightingale family, who resided at nearby Lea Hurst; it was perhaps here that Florence Nightingale discovered her vocation for tending the sick.

The edifice dates back to 1782, though is older in some parts. Proprietors Roy and Gill have owned this delightful pub since 1983. In the ensuing years they have totally refurbished it, restoring it to its original character. It is open every session for quality ales and food. Both Roy and Gill cook, and everything on the lunchtime and dinner

The Jug & Glass, Lea, Matlock, Derbyshire DE4 5GJ
Tel/Fax: 01629 534232

menus is home-made. Choices include carvery meals, steaks, sausage and apple mash, Stilton mushroom lasagne and other traditional and more innovative dishes. The good selection of ales includes Marstons Pedigree. Sunday nights are folk evenings from 8.30 p.m. Bed and breakfast accommodation is also available here, in addition to the two charming self-catering cottages adjacent to the pub.

Owned and personally run by Barbara and Alan Hobson, **The Coach House** is a perfect holiday retreat for all the family. As its name suggests, it began life as stables and harness rooms, which have now been carefully and tastefully converted into a licensed restaurant, tea rooms, ice cream parlour and farm, craft and giftshop. The Harness Room Restaurant, set within

the old groom's quarters, is warm and welcoming. Morning coffee, hot and cold lunches, an extensive range of tempting evening meals and scrumptious sweets make this a very popular venue - bookings are recommended. In the ice cream parlour, visitors are again spoiled for choice: 15 different flavours of delicious home-

The Coach House, Lea, Nr Matlock, Derbyshire DE4 5GJ
Tel/Fax: 01629 534346

made Jersey ice cream are on offer. The farm/craft shop sells home-made cakes, pies, patés and soft cheese, along with fresh eggs, crafts and gifts - some of which are produced by local craftspeople. Three characterful bedrooms are available for bed and breakfast or full-board accommodation, and two delightful two-bedroomed self-catering apartments with all amenities for four people and a cosy "Pad" for two, have been created from the loft areas of the old farm buildings, and overlook the courtyards and surrounding countryside.

SOUTH WINGFIELD
MAP 7 REF M12

6 miles SE of Matlock off the A6

Above the village, on the rise of a hill, stand the graceful ruins of the 15th-century **Wingfield Manor**. Built by Ralph Lord Cromwell, the manor house was used as Mary Queen of Scots' prison on two separate occasions in 1569 and 1584 when she was held under the care of the Earl of Shrewsbury. The local squire, Anthony Babington, attempted to rescue the Queen and lead her to safety but the plot failed and, instead, lead to them both being beheaded.

CRICH
MAP 7 REF M12

6 miles SE of Matlock off the A6

This large village, with its hilltop church and market cross, is probably most famous as the home of the **National Tramway Museum**. Referring to itself intriguingly as "the museum that's a mile long", it offers a wonderful opportunity to enjoy a tram ride along a Victorian Street scene. The signposts, stone flags and gas lamps are all original and come from such diverse places as Liverpool, Oldham and Leeds. Today, in many towns and cities, trams are making a come back, but here the Museum gives visitors the opportunity to view the real thing.

ASHBOURNE
MAP 6 REF M13

12 miles SW of Matlock on the A515

Featuring as "Esseburn" (ash tree stream) in the Domesday Book, Ashbourne was originally a small settlement lying in the northern bank of Henmore Brook, which already had a church. It was a 13th-century lord of the manor who laid out the new town to the east around its unusual shaped market place. Many of the town's traders, in order to continue to enjoy the benefits without paying the town's tolls, built themselves houses on the south side of the Brook. The area became known as Compton and it was slowly absorbed into the town. When writing *Adam Bede*, George Eliot based "Oakbourne" in "Stonyshire" on the town.

Often called The Gateway to the North, today this is one of Derbyshire's finest old towns, with a wealth of wonderful Georgian architecture. It is a pleasure to visit, with plenty of shop-filled streets to potter up and down. The triangular cobbled **Market Square**, in the heart of Ashbourne, was part of the new development begun in the 13th century that shifted the town to the east, away from the Church. Weekly markets have been held in the square since 1296, and now take place every Saturday. It was from this market place, that used to be lined with ale houses, that Bonnie Prince Charlie proclaimed his father to be King James III, and so started the Jacobite Rebellions. Though the old bull ring no longer exists, the town boasts many fine examples of 18th-century architecture as well as some older buildings, notably the Gingerbread Shop which is timber framed and probably dates from the 15th century. Traditional Ashbourne gingerbread is said to be made from a recipe that was acquired from French prisoners of war who were kept in the town during the Napoleonic Wars.

Also worthy of a second glance is the **Green Man and Black's Head Royal Hotel**. The inn sign stretches over the St John's Street and was put up when the Blackamoor Inn joined with the Green Man in 1825. Though the Blackamoor is no more, the sign remains and it claims to be the longest hotel name in the country. Of Georgian origin, the amalgamated Hotel has played host to James Boswell, Dr Johnson and the young Princess Victoria. Ashbourne was, in fact, one of Dr Johnson's favourite places; he came to the town on several occasions between

1737 and 1784. He also visited the hotel so often that he had his own chair with his name on it! The chair can still be seen at the Green Man.

A stroll down Church Street, described by Pevsner as one of the finest streets in Derbyshire, takes the walker past many interesting Georgian houses - including the Grey House which stands next to the **Grammar School**. Founded by by Sir Thomas Cockayne on behalf of Elizabeth I in 1585, the school was visited on its 400th anniversary by the present Queen. Almost opposite the Grey House is **The Mansion**, the late 17th-century home of the Reverend Dr John Taylor, oldest friend of Dr Johnson. In 1764, a domed, octagonal drawing room was added to the house, and a new brick facade built facing the street. Next to The Mansion are two of the many almshouses established in Ashbourne during the 17th and 18th centuries.

Ashbourne also retains many of its narrow alleyways and, in particular, there is Lovatt's Yard where the town lock-up can be seen.

In **St Oswald's Parish Church** Ashbourne has one of the most impressive and elegant churches in the country, described by George Eliot as "the finest mere parish church in England". James Boswell said that the church was "one of the largest and most luminous that I have seen in any town of the same size". St Oswald's stands on the site of a minster church mentioned in the Domesday Book, though most of what stands today dates from rebuilding work in the 13th century. There is a dedication brass in the south transept dated 1241. The south doorway, with its dog-toothed decoration and ribbed moulding, reflects the church's classic Early English style. St Oswald's has chapels to its transepts, adding to the spacious feeling that is more reminiscent of a small cathedral than a parish church.

Ashbourne is home, too, to the famous Shrovetide football game played on Shrove Tuesday and Ash Wednesday. The two teams, the "Up'ards" (those born north of the Henmore Brook) and the "Down'ards" (those born south of it) begin their match at 2 p.m. behind the Green Man Hotel. The game continues until well into the evening. The two goals are situated three miles apart, along the Brook, on the site of the old mills at Clifton and Sturston. It is rare for more than one goal to be scored in this slow-moving game.

YELDERSLEY
3 miles SE of Ashbourne off the A52

Map 6 ref M13

Yeldersley has long been the home of gentlemen farmers and those who love the countryside. This picturesque village offers many scenic delights including **Yeldersley Hall**, a spacious country house which was built in 1760. There are four superb self-catering apartments at this gracious Georgian house, in the former stable block and in the beautiful East Wing of the Hall. All have been converted into attractive and well-appointed flats, furnished and decorated to a high

Yeldersley Hall, Yeldersley, Ashbourne, Derbyshire DE6 1LS
Tel: 01335 343432

standard of taste and comfort. Pride of place goes to the East Wing apartment, an outstanding holiday apartment for four persons which has earned the ETB's highest rating of 5 Keys De Luxe. Occupying the entire first floor of the east wing, it is furnished with some genuine antiques and commands views over the gardens and countryside beyond. The other three apartments are for two persons. The Stable apartment is also top of the range, having been awarded the ETB 5 Keys De Luxe rating. The Archway and Yew Tree apartments also rate highly, with 4 Keys Commended and Highly Commended respectively. Surrounded by 12 acres of wonderful gardens, woodland and other scenic delights, these lavish apartments are designed with comfort in mind, with some original features and fittings. The marvellous gardens contain a Victorian greenhouse and orangery, and the grounds also boast a first-rate tennis court, available for guests' use.

WATERHOUSES   Map 6 ref L12
6½ miles NW of Ashbourne off the A523

Between here and Hulme End, the Leek and Manifold Valley Light Railway, a picturesque narrow-gauge line, used to follow the valleys of the Manifold and the Hamps, crisscrossing the latter on little bridges. Sadly trains no longer run but its track bed has been made into the **Hamps-Manifold Track**, a marvellous walk which is ideal for small children and people in wheelchairs, since its surface is level and tarred throughout its eight miles. The Track can be reached from car parks at Hulme End, Waterhouses, Weags Bridge near Grindon, and Wetton. The **River Hamps** is similar to the River Manifold and, indeed, other rivers which pass over limestone plateaux, in that it too for some of its course disappears underground: in the case of the Hamps, at Waterhouses; it then reappears again near Ilam before it merges with the River Manifold.

THORPE   Map 6 ref M12
3 miles N of Ashbourne off the A515

Thorpe lies at the confluence of the Rivers Manifold and Dove, and is dominated by the conical hill of **Thorpe Cloud**, which guards the entrance to **Dovedale**. Although the Dale becomes over-crowded at times, there is always plenty of open space to explore on the hill as well as excellent walking. For much of its 45-mile course from Axe Edge to its confluence with the River Trent, the **River Dove** is a walker's river as it is mostly inaccessible by car. The steep sides to its valley, the fast-flowing water and the magnificent white rock formations all give Dovedale a special charm. Dovedale, however, is only a short section of the valley; above Viator Bridge it becomes **Mill Dale** and further upstream again are **Wolfscote Dale** and **Beresford Dale**.

The **Stepping Stones**, a delight for children, are the first point of interest, though for those who do not want to cross the river at this point there is a foot bridge closer to the carpark just below Thorpe Cloud. Further up the Dale is the limestone crag known as **Dovedale Castle** and, on the opposite bank, the higher hill known as Lover's Leap after a failed lover's suicide. Other interesting natural features with romantic names found along the way include the Twelve Apostles and the Tissington Spires.

SANDYBROOK   Map 6 ref M12
1½ miles N of Ashbourne off the A515

Sandybrook is a peaceful community not far from Ashbourne yet retaining an unspoilt, tranquil atmosphere. **Hurtswood** is a family-run bed and breakfast located in Sandybrook just a short drive from Ashbourne town centre. The property was built in 1908 for artist Louis Hurt, and sits amid 1.6 acres of lovely gardens. Mike and Betty Hadley have lived here since 1997; during this time the property has been extended to include a conference centre run by their son-in-law and daughter, Gary and Sue Loveridge. There are seven lovely guest rooms available all year round. All are ensuite and furnished and decorated with great taste and an eye for comfort. Two single rooms occupy the ground floor, while the rest are doubles/ twins or family rooms. The attractive guests' lounge is comfortable and fitted with a log fire. There is a choice of breakfasts - the healthy eating special featuring a choice of cereals, yoghurts, cheeses, bread rolls and more, and a cooked breakfast available for a small extra

Hurtswood, Sandybrook, Ashbourne, Derbyshire DE6 2AQ
Tel/Fax: 01335 342031
e-mail: hurtswoodbandb@netscapeonline.co.uk
website: www.hurtswood.co.uk

charge. Within easy reach of many local attractions and facilities, it makes an excellent base. Children welcome. No smoking.

PARWICH
5 miles N of Ashbourne off the A515

Map 6 ref M12

This typical Peak District village is delightful, with stone houses and an 1870s church around the village green. Conspicuous amongst the stonebuilt houses is Parwich Hall, constructed of brick and finished in 1747. The wonderful gardens at the Hall were created at the turn of the 20th century and it remains today a family home though, over the years, it has changed hands on several occasions. **Parwich Moor**, above the village, is home to many mysterious Bronze Age circles, which vary in size. Though their function is unknown, it is unlikely that they were used as burial chambers. Close to Parwich is Roystone Grange, an important archaeological site where, to the north of the farmhouse, the remains of a Roman farmhouse have been excavated and, to the south, are an old engine house and the remains of the old medieval monastic grange. Both Roystone Grange and Parwich lie on an interesting and informative **Roystone Grange Archaeological Trail** which starts at Minniglow car park. Some 11 miles long, the circular trail follows, in part, the old railway line that was built to connect the Cromford and the Peak Forest Canals in the 1820s before taking in some of the Tissington Trail.

ARBOR LOW
13 miles N of Ashbourne off the A515

Map 6 ref M12

This remote **stone circle** is often referred to as the "Stonehenge of the Peaks", and although many of the stones now lie on the ground it is still an impressive sight. There are several stone circles in the Peak District but none offer the same atmosphere as Arbor Low, nor the same splendid views. Built around 4,000 years ago by the early Bronze Age people, there are a total of 40 stones each weighing no less than 8 tonnes. Probably used as an observatory and also a festival site, it is likely that the stones, which have been placed in pairs, never actually stood up. The circular mound to the south of the stone circle, which originally rose some 20 feet above the ditch, offers some protection against the weather and this is from which Arbor Low got its name - "sheltered heap".

BRASSINGTON
7 miles NE of Ashbourne off the B5056

Map 6 ref M12

This grey stone village has its past firmly entrenched in the lead-mining and quarrying traditions of this part of Derbyshire. The hollows and bumps in the green meadows tell of 200 years of underground industry in pursuit of lead, and now lead-tolerant flowers such as mountain pansy, sandwort and orchids flourish here. Protected from the wind by the limestone plateau that soars some 1,000 feet above sea level, the village sits by strange shaped rocks, the result of weather erosion, with names like **Rainster Rocks** and **Harborough Rocks**. Stone Age man found snugs amongst these formations and there is evidence that animals like the sabre-toothed tiger, brown bear, wolf and hyena also found comfort here in the caves. As late as the 18th century families were living in the caves.

Once standing on the main London to Manchester road, this was once a prosperous village and many of the 17th- and 18th-century cottages survive from those days. Today's post office used to be the tollhouse on the Loughborough to Brassington road, which became a turnpike in 1738; the Gate Inn stood next to the turnpike gate.

Brassington's oldest "resident" is a relief carving depicting a man with one hand over his heart, which can be seen inside the Norman tower of the parish church of St James. It may date back to Saxon times, but most of the rest of the church is Norman, heavily restored by the Victorians. Nearby is the Wesleyan Reform Chapel, one of the so-called "Smedley Chapels" built by local millowner, Mr Smedley, in 1852. Smedley was a keen Revivalist and his two other chapels in the village are now the village hall and a private house respectively.

BRADBOURNE

MAP 6 REF M12

4 miles NE of Ashbourne off the A5056

For more than 300 years the monks at Dunstable Priory grazed their sheep on the land round Bradbourne, and also supplied vicars to the parish **Church of All Saints**. Essentially Norman, but with some fragments of Saxon work - especially on the north side of the nave where typical long-and-short work is visible - the church is surrounded by its hilltop churchyard which contains not only the remains of a Saxon cross but also the grave of Nat Gould. Nat worked on his uncle's farm opposite the Church and by the time of his death in 1919 he had written 130 horse racing novels. The church's large, unbuttressed west tower is Norman and has an elegantly decorated south door. Most of the rest of this appealing little church dates from the 14th century, but there are some fine modern furnishing which owe much to William Morris' Arts and Crafts movement. Some of the wall paintings date from the 17th and 18th centuries.

This is an ancient village and, even at the time of the recording of the Domesday Book its name, Bradeburne (meaning broad stream) was well established. Whilst in the village it is also worth taking a look at the fine grey stone Elizabethen manor house Bradbourne Hall (private), with its three gables and beautiful terraced gardens. The Old Parsonage, which has a rather peculiar appearance as it was built in three completely different styles and materials, is also worthy of note.

HOGNASTON

MAP 6 REF M12

4 miles NE of Ashbourne off the B5035

This hillside village, with its extraordinary Norman carvings over the church doorway, lies close to Carsington Water, Britain's newest reservoir, owned by Severn Trent Water. There is plenty to do here besides the more usual water sports such as canoeing, sailing and fishing. Opened by the Queen in 1992, the reservoir has already blended well with the local countryside. Unlike many of the Peak District reservoirs, which draw their water from the acid moorland, Carsington is different and the lake and surrounding area is able to support a whole host of wildlife. One controversial resident is the American ruddy duck. Once unknown outside wildlife reserves, the duck escaped and, in little over 50 years, the breed has become widespread throughout Europe.

The Visitor Centre, always a good place to start, not only has a well-stocked gift and souvenir shop but also has an excellent all-day restaurant and an exhibition. Through a series of interesting and imaginative displays the journey of water, from the reservoir to the tap, is told. Outside, just to show how versatile water really is, there is the Kugel Stone, a one-tonne granite ball held up by a thin film of water! It is also easy to escape from the crowds and follow one of the many footpaths, or cycle routes, around the reservoir and adjoining countryside. The Wild-life Centre allows visitors to take a closer look at the birds and animals they might come across, and there are a series of hides for keen birdwatchers.

CHESTERFIELD   MAP 7 REF M12
9 miles NE of MAtlock on the A61

This friendly, bustling town on the edge of the **Peak District National Park** grew up around its open-air market which was established over 800 years ago and claims to be England's largest. As the town lies at the crossroads of England, the hub of trade routes from all points of the com-pass, the town's claim seems easily justified. Life in Chesterfield has revolved around this market since the town's earliest days. Escaping the prospect of redevelopment in the 1970s, the mar-kets are as popular as ever and are held every Monday, Friday and Saturday, with a flea market each Thursday.

The town centre has been conserved for future generations by a far-sighted council, and many buildings have been saved, including the Victorian **Market Hall** built in 1857. The tradi-tional cobbled paving was restored in the Market Place, and New Square was given a complete facelift. Though there are several Tudor buildings in the heart of Chesterfield, most notably the former Peacock inn which is now home to the **Peacock Heritage Centre** and the tourist infor-mation office - built in 1500 for the wealth Revell family, who later moved ot Carnfield Hall near Alfreton - the black-and-white timbering in Knifesmithgate was built only in the 1930s, to resemble the famous rows in Chester.

Visitors to the town are drawn to a peculiarly graceful spire reaching high into the skyline; twisting and leaning, it is totally confusing to the eye. Recognised as one of Chesterfield's landmarks, the **Crooked Spire** of **St Mary & All Saints' Church** has dominated the skyline for so long that local folk have ceased to notice its unusual shape. Superstition surrounds it, and sadly the real story to its unusual appearance has been lost over the years. The truth probably lies in the wake of the Black Death during the 14th century, when the people of Chesterfield were building their beautiful new church and awe-inspiring steeple. Many must have fallen to the plague and, among them, skilled craftsmen who knew how to season wood. The survivors built the spire out of green timber which, over the years, has distorted under the heavy lead covering. However, some stories say it was the Devil, who, pausing for a rest during one of his flights, clung to the spire for a moment or two. Incense from the Church drifted upwards and the Devil sneezed, causing the spire to twist out of shape.

This magnificent spire rises to 228 feet and leans 9 feet 4 inches from its true centrepoint. It is eight-sided, but the herringbone pattern of the lead slates trick the eye into seeing 16 sides from the ground. The Crooked Spire is open most Bank Holidays and at advertised times; the church is open all year, Monday to Saturday 9 a.m. to 5 p.m. (9 a.m. to 3 p.m. January and Febru-ary), and Sundays at service times only.

Opposite the Church is **Chesterfield Museum and Art Gallery**, home to exhibitions depicting the story of the town, from the arrival of the Romans to the first days of the market town, the industry of the 18th cen-tury and the coming of the "Father of the Railways", George Stephenson. The Art Gallery displays paintings by local artists such as Joseph Syddall (who lived at nearby Whittington).

St Mary & All Saints' Church

WHITTINGTON

MAP 7 REF M11

3 miles NE of Chesterfield off the B6052/A61

During the 17th century, **Revolution House** was part of an alehouse called the Cock and Pynot ("pynot" being the local dialect word for magpie). It was here that three local noblemen - the Earl of Devonshire, the Earl of Danby and John D'Arcy - met to begin planning their part in the events which led to the overthrow of James II in favour of his daughter Mary and her husband, William of Orange. The Glorious Revolution took place later in the same year, November 1688, and it was in the year of its 250th anniversary that this modest house was turned into a museum.

BARLBOROUGH

MAP 7 REF N11

7 miles NE of Chesterfield off the A619

Lying close to the county borders with both Nottinghamshire and Yorkshire, this village still retains its manor house. Lying just north of the village centre, **Barlborough Hall** (private) was built in 1584 by Lord Justice Francis Rodes to plans drawn up by the designer of Hardwick Hall, Robert Smythson. Those who visit both houses will notice the strong resemblance. As well as building houses, Rodes was also one of the judges at the trial of Mary, Queen of Scots. Barlborough Hall should not be confused with **Barlborough Old Hall**: this is an easy mistake to make as Barlborough Old Hall is actually the younger of the two! Built in 1618, as the date stone over the front door states, the Old Hall is of a large H-plan design and has mullioned windows.

The village also boasts some fine old stone houses with pantile roofs, though there is also a lot of new development, particularly around Barlborough Links. The village **Church of St James** dates from the beginning of the 13th century, though it was heavily restored in 1899. Among the medieval work extant is the four-bay north arcade. The church contains the effigy of a grieving woman. This is said to be Lady Furnival, who died in 1395. The monument was probably brought here from Worksop, where she is buried.

CRESWELL

MAP 7 REF N12

9 miles E of Chesterfield off the A616

Once a sleepy hamlet nestling amid peaceful farming country, the character of Creswell was irreversibly changed at the end of the 19th century. It was then that Creswell Colliery was opened, and now the village is one of the biggest in the county. There is also a village within a village here as, between 1896 and 1900 a model village of houses and cottages was built. Lying close to the Derbyshire-Nottinghamshire border, the limestone gorge of the **Creswell Crags** are well worth seeing. Formed thousands of years ago by the erosion of a river which cut through the limestone, this rock, which is porous and subject to erosion underground as well as on the surface, contributes by its very nature to the forming of natural chambers. The subterranean movement of water created a vast network of caves, which were subsequently exposed. Used by Neanderthal man as shelters while out hunting, tours can be taken from the visitor centre, where there is also a display of artefacts found in the area. Not far from the village and close to the county border with Nottinghamshire is **Steetley Chapel**, thought by many to be the most perfect specimen of Norman architecture in Europe.

BOLSOVER

MAP 7 REF N12

7 miles E of Chesterfield off the A632

The approach to Bolsover from the north and east is dominated by the splendid, sandstone structure of **Bolsover Castle**, which sits high on a limestone ridge. A castle has stood here since the 12th century, though the present building is a fairytale "folly" built for Sir Charles Cavendish during the early 1600s on the site of a ruined castle. Pevsner remarked that not many large houses in England occupy such an impressive position as Bolsover Castle, as it stands on the brow of a hill overlooking the valley of the River Rother and Doe Lea. Now owned by English

Heritage, visitors can explore the Little Castle, or Keep, which is decorated in an elaborate Jacobean celebration with wonderful fireplaces, panelling and wall paintings. The series of remarkable rooms includes the Vaulted Hall, the Pillar Room, the Star Chamber, the Elysium and the Heaven Room.

Bolsover Castle

HEATH

Map 7 ref N12

5 miles SE of Chesterfield off the A617

To the north of Heath, overlooking the M1, are the ruins of what was one of the grandest mansions in Derbyshire, **Sutton Scarsdale**. Built in 1724 for the 4th Earl of Scarsdale, to the designs of Francis Smith, the stonework of the previous Tudor manor house was completely hidden behind the Baroque splendour of the new hall. The magnificent Italian plasterwork can now be seen at the Philadelphia Museum, in Pennsylvania, and demolition of the back of the house has revealed some Tudor brickwork. At the beginning of the 20th century Sutton Scarsdale was owned by a descendent of Sir Richard Arkwright, the famous industrialist. Also close to Heath is the National Trust-owned **Stainsby Mill**. With its machinery now restored to illustrate the workings of a 19th-century water-powered corn mill, Stainsby is well worth a visit.

Stainsby Mill

AULT HUCKNALL

Map 7 ref N12

6 miles SE of Chesterfield off the A617

The strange name of this village probably means 'Hucca's high nook of land', and this pleasant place, standing on a ridge close to the Nottinghamshire border, is home to the magnificent Tudor house, **Hardwick Hall**. "More glass than wall", it is one of Derbyshire's Big Three stately homes alongside Chatsworth and Haddon, all three glorious monuments to the great landowning families who played so great a role in shaping the history of the county. Set in rolling parkland, the house, with its glittering tiers of windows and crowned turrets, offers quite a spellbinding sight. Inside, the silence of the chambers strewn with rush matting, combined with the simplicity of the white-washed walls, gives a feeling of almost overwhelming peace. The letters E S can be seen carved in stone on the outside of the house: E S, or Elizabeth of Shrewsbury, was perhaps better known as Bess of Hardwick. The Gallery at Hardwick Hall, with its gorgeous lavender-hued tapestries, has, in pride of place, a portrait of this formidable woman. The portrait depicts a personage who could be mistaken for Elizabeth R, and it seems only right to compare the two. First the "Virgin" Queen who commanded so forcibly the men around her yet never married, and then Bess, who married and survived four husbands.

As well as viewing the Hall, there are some wonderful grounds to explore. To the south are the formal gardens, laid out in the 19th century and separated by long walks lined with yew. One area has been planted as a Tudor herb garden and is stocked with both culinary and medicinal plants used at that time. The parkland, which overlooks the valley of the Doe Lea and the M1, is home to an impressive herd of Longhorn cattle among the stag-headed oaks. The ruins of Hardwick Old Hall (English Heritage) also stand in the grounds, and are the interesting remains of Bess' former Tudor mansion.

The village church of **St John the Baptist**, situated on a back lane, is one of the finest in Derbyshire. Overlooking Hardwick Hall's beautiful parklands, the battlemented church exterior does not prepare visitors for its dark, mysterious interior, which reveals the church's much earlier origins. There are many Norman features, including the north arcade, nave and the narrow arches holding up the rare crossing tower. There is more Norman work in the plain capitals of the north arcade.

PILSLEY   Map 7 ref N12
5 miles S of Chesterfield off the B6039

The Herb Garden in Pilsley is one of the foremost gardens in the country. Consisting of four display gardens, the largest is the Mixed Herb Garden, boasting an impressive established parterre. The remaining three gardens are the Physic, the Lavender and the Pot Pourri, each with its own special theme and housing many rare and unusual species. Areas of native flowers and wild spring bulbs can be enjoyed from March to September. On the grounds there is also a lovely tea room serving such delicacies as lavender cake, rosemary fruit slice and cheese and herb scones.

BARLOW   Map 7 ref M11
3 miles NW of Chesterfield off the B6051

Barlow is mentioned in the Domesday Book, and was the home of Robert Barlow, the first of Bess of Hardwick's four husbands. Although situated outside the limestone area, Barlow has been dressing its main well for longer than most. It is not known for certain when the custom began in the village, though it *is* known that, like Tissington, the well here provided water throughout the drought of 1615; this may have marked the start of this colourful practice. Another theory suggests that the tradition in Barlow could date back to the days of Elizabeth I's reign, as the church register of 1572 states that the festival of St Lawrence was celebrated. Whatever the origins of the well-dressings in the village, it is known that they have continued, unbroken even through two World Wars, throughout living memory. The wells are dressed during the second week of August every year.

West of the village, **Barlow Woodseats** are not as uncomfortable as they sound for this is the name of an irregular gabled 16th-century house, also called Woodseats Hall (private), which has a cruck barn in its grounds. Home to the Mower family - Arthur Mower was the agent to the Barlow family in the 16th century, and kept a truly remarkable diary from 1555 to 1610. All 52 volumes are now kept in the British Museum. He records the death of Bess of Hardwick in 1608, recalling her as "a great purchaser and getter together of much goods" and notes that she "builded Chattesworth, Hardwick and Owlcotes".

ALFRETON   Map 7 ref N12
10 miles S of Chesterfiled on the A61

This historic town dates back to Saxon times and, despite obvious appearances, Alfred the Great was not immortalised in the naming of the place. This attractive former coal-mining town stands on a hill close to the Nottinghamshire border. Along the charming High Street can be found the George Hotel, a fine Georgian building that looks down the length of the High Street. There are also a number of other 18th-century stonebuilt houses.

Among the many splendid old buildings in Alfreton, the most impressive is **Alfreton Hall** (private), the centrepiece of an attractive public park. In soft mellow stone, the Hall was built around 1730, with 19th-century additions. Owned until fairly recently by the Palmer Morewood family, owners of the local coal mines, it is now used as an Arts and Adult Education Centre. The park is quite extensive, boasting its own cricket ground and a horse-riding track around its perimeters. In **King Street** there is a house of confinement, or Lock-up, which was built to house lawbreakers and catered mainly for the local drunkards. The close confines of the prison with its two cells, minute windows and thick outer walls must have been a very effective deterrent.

TIBSHELF   MAP 7 REF N12
6 miles N of Alfreton off the B6014

Stretching from here north, to Grassmoor, the **Five Pits Trail** is a scenic route which passes the old collieries at Tibshelf, Pilsley, Alameda, Williamthorpe and Grassmoor. At first the idea of exploring these old coal workings may not appeal, but since their reclamation by Derbyshire County Council this is now an interesting and entertaining seven-mile walk. Suitable for walkers, cyclists and horse riders, the Trail is quite lovely, and offers some splendid views.

BELPER   MAP 7 REF M12
6 miles SW of Alfreton on the A6

Famous for its cotton mills, the town is situated alongside the **River Derwent** on the floor of the valley. In 1776, Jedediah Strutt, the wheelwright son of a South Normanton famer, set up one of the earliest water-powered cotton mills here to harness the natural powers of the river to run his mills. With the river providing the power and fuel coming from the nearby South Derbyshire coalfield, the valley has a good claim to be one of the cradles of the Industrial Revolution. To discover more about the cotton industry, the influence of the Strutt family on the town and of Samuel Slater, Strutt's apprentice who emigrated to America in 1789, built a mill there and went on to become "the Father of American manufacturers", a visit to the **Derwent Valley Visitor Centre** is a must.

The oldest mill still surviving is the two-storey **North Mill** at Bridgefoot, near the magnificent crescent-shaped weir in the Derwent and the town's main bridge. Built in 1876, the mill has cast-iron columns and beams, and hollow tile floors which provided a warm-air central heating system. It is now the visitor centre. The massive, neighbouring redbrick **East Mill** was constructed in 1912, but now is largely empty. A Jubilee Tower in terracotta was erected on the mill site in 1897 to mark Queen Victoria's 60th anniversary on the throne.

Train travellers through Belper are among those treated to a glimpse of George Stephenson's mile-long cutting, walled in gritstone throughout and spanned by no fewer than 10 bridges. When completed in 1840 it was considered an engineering wonder of its day. In addition to all industrial history the town goes back to well before the Industrial Revolu-

Derwent Valley, Belper

tion. Not only was it mentioned in the Domesday Book (as *Beau Repaire* - the beautiful retreat), but in 1964 the remains of a Roman kiln were found here.

There are also some lovely waterside walks in this bustling little town. Among the town's other interesting buildings are the **Christ Church**, a lofty, spacious house of worship built in 1849, the parish church of St Peter with its pinnacled west tower (1824) and Chapel of St John the Baptist in The Butts, dating from 1683. A monument to George Brettle can be seen in St Peter's Church - **George Brettle's Warehouse**, in Chapel Street, is a distinctive and elegant building created in 1834. **The River Gardens** were established in 1905 and today they are a pleasant place for a stroll among the beautifully tended gardens. Rowing boats can be hired for a trip along the Derwent. The Gardens are a favourite with the film industry, having been used in Ken Russell's *Women in Love*, as well as television's *Sounding Brass* and *In the Shadow of the Noose*. The riverside walk through the meadows is particularly rich in bird life.

SHOTTLE   MAP 7 REF M12
2 miles W of Belper off the A517

Dannah Farm Country House and Restaurant is well known both far and wide. Featuring in many travel guides, it has earned several awards for its facilities and quality of service. On the outskirts of the tiny village of Shottle, it is a true hidden place - a tenanted farm which is part of the Chatsworth estate, set within its own 128 acres. It is a working mixed farm. The accommodation and restaurant are housed within the lovely main 18th-century farmhouse and old farm buildings, which have been lovingly restored and refurbished by owners Joan and Martin Slack. The Slacks came here in 1985, and have continued to develop and improve the facilities from that time right up until the present. Beautifully furnished throughout, with its own tranquil atmosphere and character, there are now eight superb ensuite guest rooms, all with excellent amenities. Some of these are extra special rooms with traditional four-poster beds. The clientele includes many return visitors, who come again and again for the unique brand of hospitality and luxury available at this superior establishment. There are two sitting rooms exclusively for guests' use, and large and peaceful gardens. The restaurant, housed in what were once the old mixing buildings of the farm, is fittingly known as The Mixing Place. It is open on Saturday evenings to non-residents, and every evening to residents. Seating 30, bookings are required at

all times. These licensed premises have won many awards. Joan runs the kitchen with flair and expertise, producing, with the help of her staff, a range of mouth-watering dishes making use of the freshest ingredients, such as breast of Derbyshire chicken, fresh Scottish salmon and fillet steak, along with a variety of home-made puddings. All this and the Peak District on the doorstep makes this wonderful country house and restaurant well worth a visit.

**Dannah Farm, Bowmans Lane, Shottle, Belper, Derbyshire
DE56 2DR Tel: 01773 550273 Fax: 01773 550590
e-mail: reservations@dannah.demon.co.uk**

HEANOR

MAP 7 REF N13

5 miles E of Belper off the A608

The hub of this busy town centres on the market place, where the annual fair is held, as well as the twice weekly market (Fridays and Saturdays). Away from the bustle of the market are the **Memorial Gardens**. This peaceful setting always promises a magnificent spread of floral arrangements, herbaceous borders and shrubberies.

To the south of Heanor is the **Shipley Country Park**, on the estate of the now demolished Shipley Hall. In addition to its magnificent lake, the Country Park boasts over 600 acres of beautiful countryside which should keep even the most enthusiastic walker busy.

Shipley Country Park, Heanor

DERBY

MAP 7 REF M13

7 miles S of Belper off the A38

Essentially a commercial and industrial city, Derby's position, historically and geographically, has ensured that is has remained one of the most important and interesting cities in the area and, consequently, there is much for the visitor to see, whether from an architectural or historical point of view. There are, however, two things almost everyone, whether they have been to the city before or not, know of Derby: Rolls-Royce engines and Royal Crown Derby porcelain. When in 1906 Sir Henry Royce and the Hon C S Rolls joined forces and built the first Rolls-Royce (a Silver Ghost) at Derby, they built much more than just a motor car. Considered by many to be the best cars in the world, it is often said that the noisiest moving part in any Rolls-Royce is the dashboard clock!

The home of **Royal Crown Derby**, any visit to the city would not be complete without a trip to the factory and its museum and shop. The guided tours offer an intriguing insight into the high level of skill required to create the delicate flower petals, hand gild the plates and hand paint the Derby Dwarves.

The city's **Cathedral of All Saints** possesses a fine 16th-century tower, the second highest perpendicular tower in England. The airy building was actually built in the 1720s by James Gibbs. Inside is a beautiful wrought-iron screen by Robert Bakewell and, among the splendid monuments, lies the tomb of Bess of Hardwick Hall. Originally Derby's Parish Church, it was given cathedral status in 1927. In the late 1960s the building was extended eastwards and the retrochoir, baldacchino and sacristy were added along with the screen.

One of Derby's most interesting museums is **Pickford House**, situated on the city's finest Georgian street at number 41. It is a Grade

Derby Cathedral

I listed building, erected in 1770 by the architect Joseph Pickford as a combined family home and place of work. Pickford House differs from the majority of grand stately homes; unlike most it does not have a wealth of priceless furniture and works or art. Instead, visitors are able to gain an insight into everyday middle-class life during the 1830s. Pickford House is the epitome of a late Georgian professional man's residence. Just a short walk from Pickford House is the **Industrial Museum**. What better place to house a museum devoted to the preservation of Derby's industrial heritage than the beautiful old **Silk Mill**; a building which stands on one of the most interesting sites in the country and which preceded Richard Arkwright's first cotton mill by over 50 years. The **City Museum and Art Gallery** is also well worth visiting. Opened in 1879, it is the oldest of Derby's museums and the displays include natural history, archaeology and social history exhibits. The **Derby Heritage Centre** has local history displays, tea room and souvenir shop housed in one of the city's oldest buildings. Another of the city's treats is the **Derbyshire Constabulary Memorabilia Museum**, which has a display of uniforms and weapons dating from the mid-17th century to the present day.

DALE ABBEY
4 miles NE of Derby off the A6096

Map 7 ref N13

The village takes its name from the now ruined abbey that was founded here by Augustinian monks in the 13th century. Beginning life in a very humble manner, local legend has it that a Derbyshire baker came to the area in 1130, carved himself a niche in the sandstone and devoted himself to the way of the hermit. The owner of the land, Ralph FitzGeremunde, discovered the baker and was so impressed by the man's devotion that he bestowed on him the land and tithe rights to his mill in Borrowash. The sandstone cave, known as, and the romantic ruined 40-foot high windown archway (all that now remains of the original abbey) are popular attractions locally and a walk around the village is both an interesting and pleasurable experience. Nearby **Hermit's Wood** is an ancient area of woodland with beech, ash, oak and lime trees. It is wonderful at any time of year, but particularly in the spring when the woodland floor is covered with a sea of bluebells. To the north of the village is the **Cat and Fiddle Windmill**, built in the 18th century and a fine example of the oldest type of mill. The stone roundhouse is capped with a box-like wooden structure which houses the machinery and which is fitted onto an upright post round which it can rotate to catch the wind.

OCKBROOK
4 miles E of Derby off the A52

Map 7 ref N13

This quiet village, close to but hidden from the busy main road between Derby and Nottingham, is quite a place and well worth a visit. The village is also unusual in that, in the mid-18th century, a **Moravian Settlement** was founded here when a congregation of the Moravian Church was formed. The Settlement has several fine buildings, including The Manse, built in 1822, and the Moravian Chapel. Within the Settlement there is also a girls' boarding school.

Historical research has discovered that Ockbrook may have been a Pagan religious site well before **All Saints' Church** was built. It became the parish church in the mid-1500s and its most interesting features include a Saxon font, the 12th-century tower, some fine windows and the oak chancel screen dating from around 1520. This is farming country and many of the ancient hedgerows remain, sustaining all manner of wildlife that has disappeared from many other areas. Several old farm buildings also remain, including an impressive 17th-century timber-framed building at Church Farm. Little but the ground floor, however remains of **Ockbrook Windmill**, one of only 10 windmill sites extant in Derbyshire.

ELVASTON
5 miles SE of Derby off the B5010

Map 7 ref N13

Elvaston is gathered around the edge of the **Elvaston Castle** estate, home of the Earls of Harrington. The magnificent Gothic castle seen today replaced a 17th-century brick and gabled manor house; part of the original structure can be seen on the end of the south front. Designed by James Wyatt, the castle was finished in the early 19th century but, unfortunately, the 3rd Earl died in 1829 and had little time to enjoy his new home.

It is, perhaps, the grounds which make Elvaston Castle famous today. They were originally laid out and designed for the 4th Earl by William Barron. Barron, who was born in Berwickshire in 1805, started work in 1830 on what, at first, appeared to be an impossible task. The 4th Earl wanted a garden 'second to none', but the land available, which had never been landscaped, was flat, water-logged and uninspiring with just two avenues of trees and a walled kitchen garden (but no greenhouses or hot houses). First draining the land, Barron then planted trees to offer shelter to more tender plants. From there the project grew. In order to stock the gardens, Barron began a programme of propagation of rarer tree species and, along with the tree-planting methods he developed specially to deal with Elvaston's problems, his fame spread. The gardens became a showcase of rare and interesting trees, many to be found nowhere else in Britain. Barron contined to work for the 5th Earl, but resigned in 1865 to live in nearby Barrowash and set up his own nursery. Now owned by Derby County Council, the gardens, after years of neglect, have been completely restored and the delights of the formal gardens, with their fine topiary, the avenues and the kitchen garden can be enjoyed by all visitors to the grounds, which are now a Country Park. As well as fine formal gardens and the walled kitchen garden, there are gentle woodland walks and, of course, the man-made lake. However, no visit to Elvaston would be complete without a walk down to the **Golden Gates**. Erected in 1819 at the southern end of the formal gardens, the gates were brought from the Palace of Versailles by the 3rd Earl of Harrington. Little is known of the Gates' history, but they remain a fine monument and are the symbol of Elvaston. Around the courtyard of the castle can be found a restarant as well as an information centre and well-stocked gift shop. All manner of activities take place from the castle; details can be found there.

SHARDLOW
MAP 7 REF N13
7 miles SE of Derby off the A6

After 1777, when the **Trent and Mersey Canal** was opened, Shardlow became a canal port, one of only a few in the country. With Liverpool, Hull and Bristol now linked by water, the warehouses here were quickly filled with heavy goods of all descriptions that could be carried at half of cost of road transport and with greater safety. Many of the homes of the canal carriers and their warehouses survive to this day and the port is now a modern marina, linked to the River Trent, and filled with all manner of pleasure barges.

REPTON
MAP 7 REF M13
7 miles SW of Derby off the B5008

This village, by the tranquil waters of the River Trent, is steeped in history. The first mention of Repton came in the 7th century when it was established as the capital of the Saxon kingdom of Mercia. A monastery, housing both monks and nuns, was founded here sometime after 653 but the building was sacked by the Danes in 874. A battleaxe, now on display in the school museum, was excavated a little distance from the church. It had apparently lain undisturbed for well over 1,000 years. The ancient **Cross**, still at the central crossroads in the village, has been the focal point of life here for centuries and it has also stood at the heart of the Wednesday market. Right up until the late 19th century a Statutes Fair, for the hiring of farm labourers and domestics, was also held here at Michaelmas. Parts of an Augustinian priory, founded in 1170, are incorporated in the buildings of **Repton College**, itself founded in 1557. Two of its headmasters, Dr Temple and Dr Fisher, went on to become Archbishops of Canterbury. Film buffs will recognise the 14th-century gatehouse and causeway, as they featured in both film versions of the popular story *Goodbye, Mr Chips*. Just to the west of the village is **Foremark Hall**, built by Robert Adam in the 1762 for the Burdett family. It is now a preparatory school for Repton College.

CALKE
MAP 7 REF M13
9 miles S of Derby off the B587

Calke Abbey

In 1985 the National Trust bought **Calke Abbey**, a large Baroque-style mansion built in 1701 on the site of an Augustinian priory founded in 1133. However, it was not until 1989 that the Trust were able to open the house to the public, for this was no ordinary house at all. Dubbed "the house that time forgot" since the death of the owner, Sir Vauncy Harpur-Crewe in 1924 nothing had been altered in the mansion! In fact, the seclusion of the house and also the rather bizarre lifestyle of its inhabitants had left many rooms and objects untouched for over 100 years. There was even a spectacular 18th-century Chinese silk state bed that had never been unpacked.

SWARKESTONE
MAP 7 REF M13
6 miles S of Derby off the A5132

Excavations in the village of Swarkestone, at Lowes Farm, led to the discovery that the district was occupied in the Bronze Age and also in Saxon times. This small village has also been, quite literally, a turning point in history. The **Swarkestone Bridge**, with its seven arches and three-quarter-mile long causeway, crosses the River Trent. In 1745, during the second Jacobite Rebellion, the advance guard of Bonnie Prince Charlie reached the Bridge and, had they managed to cross the River at this point, they would have faced no other natural barriers on their 120-mile march to London. As it transpired, the army retreated and fled north, Bonnie Prince Charlie managed to escape and the Jacobite Rebellion was no more.

MELBOURNE
MAP 7 REF M13
7 miles S of Derby off the B587

This small town, which lent its name to the rather better-known city in Australia, is a successful market garden centre. A famous son of Melbourne, who started his working life in one of the market gardens, was Thomas Cook, who was born here in 1808. He went on to pioneer personally-conducted tours and gave his name to the famous worldwide travel company.

The birthplace of the 19th-century statesman Lord Melbourne, and also the home of Lady Caroline Lamb, **Melbourne Hall** is another fine building in this area of Derbyshire. A modest building, the Hall is surrounded by beautiful gardens, the most notable feature of which is a beautiful wrought-iron birdcage pergola built in the early 1700s by Robert Bakewell, a local blacksmith from Derby. Unfortunately the house is only open to the public in August, but the splendid and famous formal gardens are open throughout the summer season and are well worth a visit.

CHURCH GRESLEY
MAP 7 REF M14
14 miles S of Derby off the A444

This former mining village has a distinguished history dating back to the time of the Augustinian monks who settled here in the 12th century and founded a priory here. The village's name, like that of nearby Castle Gresley, recalls the great Gresley family, said to have been the only Derbyshire family to have retained their lands from the time of the Domesday Book up until the 20th century. The village church retains some links with the past. The priory and chancel buildings were pulled down during the Tudor age, and the church remained in a sad state of disrepair up until the early 19th century. A new chancel was built in 1872. Remains of the priory have been found, including fragments of painted glass, stone coffins and medieval tiles. What remains of the old church are the sturdy 15th-century tower and two 14th-century arches that lead to the church's north aisle. An impressive alabaster monument depicts **Sir Thomas Gresley**, surrounded by arms showing the marriages of his ancestors dating back to the time of William the Conqueror. The church's treasure, though, are the 10 large and wonderfully carved stalls.

OAKTHORPE

MAP 7 REF M13

15 miles S of Derby on the B586 off the main A42

The Holly Bush Inn is surrounded by acres of scenic countryside. Owners Marisa and Billy took over at this charming traditional country inn in March of 1998, and have a real success on their hands. The low beamed ceilings and exposed brickwork add to the ambience of this homely and welcoming inn.
The eye-catching interior has been refurbished with loving care by the owners; they have also added on a new restaurant wing. Marisa rules the kitchen - she is an excellent cook who formerly ran her own restaurant in Germany for many years. Meals can be taken in the bar, lounge or restaurant. The extensive menu offers a great deal of variety and choice,

Holly Bush Inn, Main Street, Oakthorpe, Swadlincote, Derbyshire DE12 7RB Tel: 01530 270943

in dishes such as Wiener schnitzel, chicken Cordon Bleu, mixed grill, lemon sole, gnocci pomodoro and other Continental favourites. All starters, main courses and the selection of tempting desserts are home-cooked to order. The ales on offer include Pedigree, Worthington and a changing guest ale. On-site there is also a small caravan park, available for up to five tourers, for those who wish to prolong their stay in this lovely part of the county.

SUDBURY

MAP 6 REF M13

12 miles W of Derby off the A50

This is the estate village to **Sudbury Hall**, the late 17th-century mansion and home of a branch of the Vernon family who lived at Haddon Hall. The house is intriguing, the garden restful. Gifted to the National Trust in 1967, the Hall is an unexpected mixture of architectural styles. A splendid example of a house of Charles II's time, inside Sudbury Hall contains elaborate plasterwork and murals throughout, wood carvings by Grinling Gibbons, and some fine examples of mythological paintings by Laguerre. Of particular interest is the **Museum of Childhood** which is situated in the servants' wing and provides a fascinating insight into the lives of children down the ages. Fascinating displays range from a wealthy family's nursery and an Edwardian schoolroom to a "chimney climb" and coal tunnel for the adventurous. The formal gardens and meadows lead to the tree-fringed lake. Wildlife abounds, including Kestrels, Grey Herons, Grass Snakes, dragonflies, newts, frogs, toads, Little and Tawny Owls and woodpeckers. Special events are held throughout the year.

LONG LANE
MAP 7 REF M14

8 miles NW of Derby off the A52

Long Lane village is truly a hidden place, not found on most maps. It is south off the A52, and can be reached by heading for the village of Lees and then following the sign for Long Lane. It is well worth finding, for it offers wonderful views of bucolic bliss. **The Three Horseshoes** in Long Lane is a quality traditional English pub. The extensive building dates back to 1750, when

it was a grain store where ale was brewed for the adjacent black-smith's. Unusually, the property is owned by the village itself. Robin Wigham has been running this distinguished pub since early in 1999, ably assisted by his mother Jo. Open lunchtime and eve-nings Monday to Saturday and all day Sundays, there's excel-lent food on offer midday until 3 p.m. and from 6 - 8 p.m. (Sundays from midday

The Three Horseshoes, Long Lane, Long Lane Village, Derbyshire DE6 5BJ Tel: 01332 824481

through to 4 p.m.). Robin is a superb chef; guests will find it hard to choose from among the delicious meals on the comprehensive and varied menu or from the daily specials. There are always at least five daily main courses to choose from. Bookings are requested for larger parties. Ales include Pedigree and a range of guest ales, as well as a good complement of lagers, stout, cider, wines and spirits. From the lovely frontage with its wealth of flowers and shrubs to the picturesque garden, every inch of this pub says 'class'. The handsome and relaxing interior features a large open fire with brick fire surround, exposed beamwork, quarry tiled floor and other attractive and welcoming features. The lounge area is cosy and comfortable lounge, while the intimate dining area overlooks the picturesque garden. Proud holder of a children's certifi-cate, this superior pub boasts an outstanding and safe children's area in the large beer garden to the rear.

NOTTINGHAMSHIRE

NOTTINGHAM
MAP 7 REF N13

15 miles E of Derby on the A52

Nottingham, the self-proclaimed Queen of the Midlands, is justifiably said to be one of Eng-land's finest cities. It is ripe for exploration but visitors are regaled with the Robin Hood theme wherever they go. However, there is much more to this fascinating city than the legend of the people's outlaw: an interesting and ancient history, fine architecture, and many unusual attractions make this an ideal start to anyone's discovery of the county.

The settlement of Nottingham was founded by the unfortunately named Snot, chief of a 6th-century Anglo-Saxon tribe. He and his people carved out dwellings in the soft local sandstone and the settlement thrived to become Snottingaham - home of the followers of Snot. The name changed into its currently more acceptable form at some stage in Nottingham's ancient history but when that was has never been established.

Commanding an imposing position, high above the city centre and situated on a rocky outcrop, **Nottingham Castle** is an excellent place from which to begin any tour of the city. The original castle was built after the Battle of Hastings by William the Conqueror and William Peveril as part of the king's general fortification of many strategically important sites. Its elevated position, overlooking the city and the River Trent, made Nottingham Castle one of the foremost castles in Norman England and it played host to many important visitors. Notting-

ham Castle's heyday came in the 14th and 15th centuries however, when, not only was King David II of Scotland held prisoner here for a while in around 1346 but, in the mid-15th century, Edward IV proclaimed himself king from Nottingham Castle and, later, his brother, Richard III, built new state apartments and lived at the castle for most of his reign. Thereafter, though, the castle gradually fell into disrepair until Charles I came to Nottingham in 1642 and raised his standard at the castle at the start of the Civil War. Unfortunately, the king found little support for his cause in the city and he moved on to Shrews-

Nottingham Castle Gatehouse

bury, leaving the castle in the hands of the Parliamentarians. Over the course of the war, the Royalists made several attempts to recapture the castle but Cromwell's supporters held out. After the fighting was over the castle building was rendered uninhabitable and it was finally demolished in 1674 by the Duke of Newcastle, who went on to build his palace on the site. Today, the duke's palace, rebuilt after it was ramsacked by supporters of the Reform Bill in 1831, is home to the **Castle Museum**. However, visitors here are still able to see some of the remains of the original castle. The 13th-century gatehouse, though much restored, is still standing and parts of the moat and outer bailey can be seen. The museum, when it was opened by the Prince of Wales in 1878, was also the first municipal art gallery in the country outside London and, today, the collection is particularly noted for its fine selection of Victorian paintings.

At the base of Castle Rock lies the famous **Trip to Jerusalem Inn** where the crusaders are said to have stopped for a pint to fortify themselves before their long journey to the Holy Land. Dating back to around 1189, it is said to be the oldest pub in England. Also at the base of Castle Rock and housed in a terrace of four 17th-century cottages is the **Brewhouse Yard Museum**. Depicting the life of the people of the city up to the present, the museum has accurately furnished rooms as well as a series of shops: from a Victorian kitchen to shop window displays from the 1920s. Opposite the Trip to Jerusalem Inn is a charming medieval building that is home the **Lace Centre**. As well as holding lace making demonstrations, there is also a vast selection of high quality lace available for purchase. A fine example of a timber framed house of around 1450, the building itself was moved from its original site on Middle Pavement in 1968. Not far away and set in the heart of Nottingham's historic Lace Market is the **Lace Hall**, housed in a restored chapel. Continuing with the theme of textiles, the **Museum of Costume and Textiles**, in Castle Gate, contains a fine collection of costumes from 1790 to the mid-20th century, all displayed in period rooms. There are also many other exhibits on show including tapestries; knitted, woven, and printed textiles; and fashion accessories through the ages. The museum is housed in a terrace of brick houses that was constructed in 1788 by Cornelius Launder, a former High Sheriff. Castle Gate is an interesting street in itself and well worth a second look. Further down Castle Gate is **Newdigate House** built in a refined fashion in 1680 though its wrought iron screen and gates date from the early 18th century. The house now forms part of the United Services Club and it was, between 1705 and 1711, the home of Marshall Tallard, commander of the defeated French army at the Battle of Blenheim in 1704. The present red brick building of **St Nicholas' Church** replaces the medieval church which stood here until 1643 and the days of the Civil War. It was from this church's tower that Royalists fired upon the

Caves of Nottingham

castle in an attempt to regain control and, after the attack, the Parliamentarian governor of the castle ordered the church's destruction so no further attacks could take place. Rebuilding the church was completed in 1682 and, inside, at the east end of the south aisle, there is a tombstone to Lawrence Collin, the master gunner of the castle during the Civil War. Beneath Broad Marsh Centre, one of the city's major shopping precincts, lie the **Caves of Nottingham**. The city is built on sandstone and throughout Nottingham's history the rock has been tunnelled to provide first shelter and then hiding places. Now, thanks to local voluntary groups, these man-made caves have been saved for future generations. Nearby is the city's **Galleries of Justice** and the unusual and interesting attraction of justice 19th-century style.

Found near the bottom of High Pavement is Nottingham's largest parish church: **St Mary's Church** is also, probably, the city's oldest as it appears to have been founded in Saxon times. However, today's church dates from the 15th century though there are some 19th- and early 20th-century additions which include windows by a series of renowned stained glass makers. Also inside is a Bishop's Throne carved in 1890, when it was thought that the church would become the cathedral for the diocese of Southwell. Though no market has been held here since the 1920s, the vast expanse of the **Old Market Square** is still at the centre of the life of Nottingham. Nottingham is particularly famous for its **Goose Fair** which gained this name from the large flocks of geese that were sold here around Michaelmas. Mentioned in a charter dated 1284, the Goose Fair is still held today on the first Thursday in October.

Nottingham's links with the legend and tales of Robin Hood are well known and, for those interested in the story, a visit to **The Tales of Robin Hood** is well worth while. The life of the outlaw is told through a series of historically accurate displays, from his imprisonment by the Sheriff of Nottingham to feasting in Sherwood Forest.

As in many other industrial towns, the late 18th century saw the building of canals to serve the expanding populations and aid the transportation of goods. Nottingham was no exception and, in 1796, the **Nottingham Canal** was completed, thus linking the town with many of the country's more well-known waterways. Almost 15 miles in length and rising, by a series of 20 locks, some 130 feet, the canal ran from the River Trent, through the centre of Nottingham, to the Cromford Canal at Langley Mill, in neighbouring Derbyshire. Along the Nottingham Canal, and still with its own basin found under an arch for easy loading and unloading, is the **Canal Museum**. Dating from the mid-19th century, this four storey building was the warehouse for one of the largest firms of canal carriers. The firm went into liquidation in 1948 and this magnificent building has been restored and refurbished to house many displays and models which illustrate the history of the Trent Valley.

Frampton's hotel and restaurant in Nottingham's St James's Terrace occupies a Grade II listed building dating back to the 1700s. The quietly elegant exterior welcomes the visitor into the intimate and comfortable bar and, upstairs, a cosy restaurant. Chef Paul Hanley was once head chef at the British Embassy in Berlin, working on both sides of the wall! He brings a wealth of expertise and creativity to the excellent menu, which includes both traditional and innovative Modern English dishes such as rack of lamb with fresh rosemary jus, and sweet potato fritters with red Thai sauce. The third floor comprises six attractive and

Frampton's, St James's Terrace, Nottingham, Nottinghamshire   Tel: 0115 941 1997

well-appointed en suite guest bedrooms. The informal atmosphere and wonderful standard of service make Frampton's a cut above the rest. This unique establishment, within the city walls and just a minute's walk from the castle, makes the perfect base from which to explore Nottingham and the surrounding area.

HOLME PIERREPONT
3 miles E of Nottingham off A52

Map 7 ref N13

Although Holme has been in the hands of the Pierrepont family since 1284, the present **Holme Pierrepont Hall** only dates from the early 16th century but it remains one of the best examples of a brick built house in the county. Open to the public on a restricted timetable, the hall is well worth a visit as, not only have some of the ground floor rooms been restored to their original state and furnished in the style of the early 17th century, but also, the ceiling of one of the first floor bedrooms has been removed to reveal the impressive roof construction. However, these days, Holme Pierrepont is more widely known as the home of the **National Watersports Centre**. Built to Olympic standards, there is a full size rowing course and a wild water slalom course, all man-made from the pasture and quarries which once dominated the area. The planting of trees and shrubs to landscape the whole site has ensured that there is plenty on and off the water for those not quite up to world class competition.

WOLLATON
2 miles W of Nottingham on A609

Map 7 ref N13

Built in the 1580s to the designs of Robert Smythson, who is famous for designing Harwick Hall in Derbyshire, **Wollaton Hall** was the home of the Willoughby family. Francis Willoughby, head of the family at that time, had made his money from his ownership of the local coal mines and he wanted to construct a grand and lavish house. However, the grandiose building plans coupled with losses incurred by some of his other business interests nearly bankrupted the family. Fortunately, the extravagant front façade of classical columns, busts of philosophers and mythological characters, and flamboyant gables remains. The hall now houses many

Wollaton Hall

items of interest though only three rooms have been restored to their former grandeur: the great hall, the entrance hall, and a beautiful salon. The building is also home to the **Natural History Museum** which is based on the collection of Francis Willoughby who was a noted naturalist of the mid-17th century and a friend of John Ray. Meanwhile, the hall's outbuildings have been transformed into the **Nottingham Industrial Museum** and the city's major industries are all represented. There are bicycles, from boneshakers and penny-farthings through to Raleigh and Humber models, and the progression to the motorcycle is given space in the form of the Brough machines of the 1920s and 1930s. It was whilst riding a Brough motorcycle that TE Lawrence had his fatal crash in 1935. Textiles, and particularly stocking frames and knitting machines, can be found here as can machinery from the pharmaceutical industry. Finally, the local coal mines are also represented and there is a particularly fine example of a horse winding gin from 1844 on display in the courtyard. **Martin's Pond**, thought to be the first nature reserve opened in a city, was probably a medieval fishpond belonging to Wollaton Hall and, in the surrounding land, over 150 species of flowering plants and 70 species of birds have been recorded. Nearby **Harrison's Plantation**, which is also managed by the Nottinghamshire Wildlife Trust, is an area of mixed woodland which dates back to the 18th century.

STAPLEFORD
Map 7 ref N13

4 miles W of Nottingham off A52

In Stapleford churchyard can be found the best preserved Saxon carving in the county in the form of a 10 foot high cross shaft. Dating from the late 11th century, the intricate carving depicts an eagle standing on a serpent, which is said to be the symbol for St Luke. The church, which dates mainly from the 13th and 14th centuries, has many war memorials to its lost heroes. The village was once a thriving centre for framework knitting and terraced cottages built specifically for the workers can still be seen in Nottingham Road.

One other feature of Stapleford which is worthy of a look in **The Hemlockstone**, a massive redstone boulder standing 30 feet high and situated opposite Bramcote Park. It has come to be associated with the Devil, who apparently threw the rock at Lenton Priory whilst in a bad mood and missed. Despite the inaccuracy of aim, the rock was probably deposited here by glacial action, whilst wind erosion has contributed to its brooding appearance. Its geological make up consists of sandstone cemented by the mineral barite, which is found in large quantities throughout the Stapleford and Bramcote Hills. The origins of its name are Celtic and it simply means the stone in the border enclosure.

THRUMPTON
Map 7 ref N13

5 miles SW of Nottingham off A453

This quiet village lies right on the border with Derbyshire and, though it has seen many changes, including the building of new houses for those who wish to work in nearby Nottingham and

Derby, there is still a village spirit here. Originally called Turmodeston, the small settlement once lay inside the present park of **Thrumpton Hall**. In the 17th century, John Emerton enclosed the park and new cottages were built for the villagers around the church where some can still be seen today. The H-shaped hall, with Flemish gables, has inside such wonders as a balustrade carved with acanthus scrolls, richly carved doors, and some fine wall panelling dating back to the days of Charles II. The 8th Lord Byron inherited the house through marriage and some relics of the poet Byron are displayed here. During the 19th century, Lucy, Lady Byron, lived at the hall and it was thanks to her that the village choir was much in demand. She insisted that all her staff have good voices and the choir often sang at Southwell Minster. Lady Byron was also responsible for the restoration of the village church though the old font can now be seen in the churchyard.

RUDDINGTON
Map 7 ref N13

6 miles S of Nottinham on the A60

This historic village, whose name is derived from the Saxon word Rudda - meaning headman - was once the home of many hosiery workers and several of their cottages still remain here. In 1829, a factory and frameworkers cottages were built around a courtyard in Chapel Street. This group of buildings now houses the **Framework Knitters' Museum** and shows the living and working conditions for the workers of the trade. Of the 25 hand frames seen here today, most are fully operational and there is an opportunity to buy samples made at the museum. The industry reached its height in 1880, with the staggering number of 20,000 frames operating in Nottingham, Derbyshire, and Lincolnshire. As well as the knitting frames on show, the museum also has other machinery of specific importance to the village and the hosiery industry and regular demonstrations are given using the working exhibits. Not far away is the **Ruddington Village Museum**, housed in the old village school building of 1852. Concentrating on the everyday life of the villagers there are reconstructions of several shops and craftsmen's workshops including an Edwardian fish and chip shop. As well as having one of the school rooms restored to look as it once did, there is also a room devoted to a collection of farming implements.

BUNNY
Map 7 ref N13

8 miles S of Nottingham on A60

This pretty village has a wealth of lovely architecture and owes much of its charm to the eccentricities of its former 18th-century squire, Sir Thomas Parkyns. A man obsessed with the sport of wrestling, he employed two full time professionals to spar with him at Bunny Hall. He also organised an annual tournament in the village to promote local wrestling talent and this event continued nearly 70 years after its originator's death. In St Mary's Church, which was designed by Sir Thomas, his memorial graphically illustrates his commitment to the sport. It depicts the squire standing victorious over his defeated opponent on a wrestling mat, while Old Father Time stands by, perhaps as referee. The village has some ancient woodland, **Bunny Wood**, which was mentioned in the Domesday Book. Consisting mainly of elm, oak and ash, the woodland is also home to over 30 species of birds. It is managed by the Nottinghamshire Wildlife Trust.

CAR COLSTON
Map 7 ref O13

9 miles E of Nottingham off the A46

Now a conservation area, this village is fortunate in that it has remained unspoilt by modern development. Of particular interest here are the village's two greens which both date from the reign of Elizabeth I. At that time individual strips of land were cultivated by the villagers and the typical ridge and furrow appearance can still be made out. In 1598, the parish was enclosed, the land being turned into the fenced fields that are now common today, but the land in the middle of the village was left open so that the villagers could graze their cattle. The Large

Green, at 16½ acres, is the largest in the county and, at the other end of the village lies Little Green (a mere 5½ acres).

REDMILE
MAP 7 REF O13

15 miles E of Nottingham off the A52

Situated in the beautiful Vale of Belvoir, **The Peacock at Redmile** occupies a 280 year old farmhouse tastefully modernised, where guests enjoy old fashioned hospitality combined with truly professional service. Views of Belvoir Castle and the surrounding countryside can be had from most of the 10 superior en suite guest bedrooms. Each room is comfortable and handsomely decorated and furnished. At the impressive beamed restaurant the menu offers Modern English and Continental dishes, all expertly prepared and presented. Non-residents are welcome to dine here, or have a drink at the fully licensed bar, where there's a good range of beers, wines and spirits. The atmosphere throughout this wonderful inn is relaxed and informal. The surrounding countryside offers many opportunities for golfing, shooting and fishing, all available locally. As part of Pernickety chain of inns dotted throughout the country, the staff take justified pride in upholding a tradition for a high standard of conscientiousness and friendly service.

The Peacock at Redmile, Church Corner, Main Street, Redmile, Nottinghamshire NG13 0GA Tel: 01949 842554 Fax: 01949 843746 e-mail: peacock@pernickety.co.uk

CALVERTON
MAP 7 REF N13

6 miles NE of Nottingham off the B6386

The charming cottages in this industrial village date back to the early 19th century and they were the homes of framework knitters. Carefully restored by the Nottinghamshire Building Preservation Trust, the cottages originally formed three sides of a rectangle, though one side is now missing. Unusually, the large windows which provided the light for the knitters are found on the ground floor where, elsewhere, they are usually on an upper storey. Framework knitting was the main industry of the village, and of many others, at that time. The stocking knitting frame was invented in nearby Woodborough by William Lee in 1589. Born in Calverton, Lee's wooden frame so revolutionised the stocking industry that he attempted to seek patronage from Elizabeth I. Unfortunately, the wind was taken out of his sails as she refused to grant a patent for something that would mean great job losses for her loyal subjects! Little is known of William Lee, though there is no doubt of him having invented the knitting frame. There is also no information which supports romantic suggestions that Lee wanted to impress his wife or to outdo a woman knitter. After being refused a patent by Elizabeth I, Lee travelled to France and gained the promise of support from Henry of Navarre. Unfortunately, Henry was assassinated before any promises were made good and it is believed that Lee died in Paris in 1610. Lee's brother, James, brought the frame back to London where the hosiery industry first developed before it settled in the Midlands later in the 17th century. The **Calverton Folk Museum** (open by appointment) houses many items particular to the hosiery industry as well as some period furnishings. Also at Calverton is **Painters' Paradise**, a series of gardens that have been designed with the artist in mind. Covering some 38 acres, the gardens, which have elements based on Monet's garden at Giverny, include woodlands, meadows, butterfly gardens, and a special disabled garden with raised flower beds. Old farming implements are used as props and there are several gazebos so that people can paint in comfort.

SOUTHWELL
MAP 7 REF O12

12 miles NE of Nottingham on the A612

An elegant market town, Southwell also boasts a fine **Cathedral**, which may sound implausible to the uninitiated, but the lovely 12th-century **Minster** was elevated to the status of cathedral in 1884, when the new Diocese of Southwell was created. This has given rise to the building often being referred to as the village cathedral. The two west towers, with their pyramidal roofs, make a striking landmark as they stand proud, dominating the cathedral green. Inside, the choir screen is quite stunning, bearing no less than 200 human carvings, and the eagle lectern, which stands in the choir, was salvaged from the lake at Newstead Abbey in 1750. It had been thrown there by the monks to protect it from the looting that occurred during the Dissolution and was presented to the minster in 1805. The chapter house also has some beautiful carvings which date from the 13th century. To the south of the minster can be found the ruins of the palace of the archbishops of York which dated from the 14th and 15th centuries. Parts of the old palace, closest to the minster's south doorway, have been incorporated into the present **Bishop's Palace**. Southwell itself has many fine buildings and a wealth of fascinating places to discover. Among these are the Prebendal houses where the secular canons resided, sequestered alleyways, and charming coaching inns like the **Saracen's Head** where Charles I spent his last hours of freedom before his final surrender. At the time of the king's final visit the inn was called the King's Head but the name of this wonderful 16th-century inn was changed after Charles's execution.

The now disused railway line from Southwell to Mansfield, which was first opened to trains in 1871, is now an attractive and comfortable footpath known as the **Farnsfield to Southwell Trail**. As well as the varied plant and wildlife that can be found along the 4 ½ mile walk, there is also plenty of industrial archaeological interest including the **Farnsfield Waterworks** of 1910, a late 18th-century cotton mill, and **Greet Lily Mill**, a corn mill on the banks of the River Greet. **Norwood Park** is the only one of the four original parks around Southwell which remains today. The property of the Archbishops of York, the park remained in the possession of the Church until 1778 and, though a house was built here in Cromwell's day, the present building dates from 1763. Open to visitors during the summer months, the house has a very lived in feel and, as well as many 17th- and 18th-century family portraits, there is also a fine collection of china.

NEWARK-ON-TRENT
MAP 7 REF O12

17 miles NE of Nottingham off the A1

Historically, Newark-on-Trent has always been a strategic point: it lies close to the Roman road, Fosse Way, and also guards the first upstream crossing of the River Trent. Though there is no evidence of a Roman settlement here, the remains of pottery and coins found in the vicinity of the castle suggest that there was possibly a fort here at one time. The Saxons certainly settled here and part of their defences for the town have been excavated. It was, however, the Danes who began the formation of Newark-on-Trent as it is known today. The evidence of their occupation is particularly obvious in the use of gate (from the Danish gata meaning street) in the names of the many roads - Castle Gate, Balderton Gate, and Barnby Gate. By the time of the

Newark Castle

Domesday Survey, the name Newark, a corruption of New Work, was being used. This name was either used to refer to the rebuilding of the town following the Danish invasion or it could have been a reference to the new town defences that were constructed around that time. Occupying a strong defensive position beside the River Trent, **Newark Castle** did not serve a particular military service. Built in the 12th century, it is not known for certain which parts of the castle are the oldest and there may have been a former wooden structure on this site prior to the great stone building still seen today. However, it is known that the castle was founded by Alexander, Bishop of Lincoln. Over the next 300 years, the castle saw extensive improvements made to its original construction and, in 1483, it was taken from the bishops of Lincoln by Henry VII, who leased it to a succession of noblemen until the time of the Civil War. In order to ensure that Newark had suitable defences to withstand attack, two small forts were built to guard this strategic crossing over the River Trent. (The only other crossing, at Nottingham, was held by the Parliamentarians.) The King's Sconce, to the northeast, has since disappeared but its twin, **Queen's Sconce**, still lies to the southeast. Named after Queen Henrietta Maria, who brought supplies into the town after the first siege in 1643, this square earthwork had a bastion in each corner and a hollow in the middle.

There are other reminders of the Civil War in Newark-on-Trent and, in the middle of the town, on Kirk Gate, are **Henrietta Maria's Lodgings**, where, legend has it, the queen stayed on her visit to the town in 1643. Travelling from Bridlington to the king's headquarters at Oxford, the queen was carrying with her men and arms from the continent which she had paid for by selling some of the Crown Jewels. Close by can be found **The Governor's House**; the place where the governors of Newark lived during the Civil War and also the place where Charles I quarrelled with Prince Rupert after the prince had lost Bristol to Parliament. This wonderful timber framed building was restored in the late 19th century and during the work a medieval wall and some beam paintings were revealed along with some graffiti dating from 1757.

Also found in the heart of Newark-on-Trent is Nottinghamshire's finest parish church; its fine spire dominating the town and acting as a local landmark. The **Church of St Mary Magdalen** dates back to the early 12th century though all that survives of that structure is the crypt which now houses the treasury. Much of the building seen today dates from the 14th, 15th, and 16th centuries and its exterior is a fascinating blend of carvings and tracery. With such a wealth of history inside its boundaries, Newark-on-Trent also has its fair share of museums. **Newark Museum** is housed in a former school which dates back to 1529 and the history of the town is traced from its early beginnings, with exhibitions of prehistoric artefacts and Roman finds, through to the desperate days of the Civil War. A large Anglo-Saxon cemetery, discovered in Millgate, is also on display. At the town hall, the town's fine collection of silverware, including some 99 siege pieces, can be seen in the **Newark Civic Plate Collection**. Planned by the town council, the **Civil War Trail** is a 23 mile walking and driving route which takes in many of the villages and towns between Newark-on-Trent and Nottingham that have links with either side in the bloody dispute. Details of the trail from the tourist information centre.

KELHAM

15 miles NE of Nottingham on the A617

MAP 7 REF O12

Situated beside the River Trent the village grew up around the crossing which was probably upstream of the present bridge. An old farming community, it seems fitting that the estate village of Kelham should be used to develop the growing of sugar beet in this country when it was introduced during World War I. The experiment was successful and, in 1921, the Kelham sugar beet processing factory was opened. Now called the Newark factory, it is one of the largest and most up to date in Europe. The present **Kelham Hall** is the third manor house to be built on the site and this monument to all that is best in Victorian architectural splendour was designed by architect, Sir George Gilbert Scott. Today, the hall is home to the Newark and Sherwood District Council but, in 1903, it was the home of the a group of monks led by Father Herbert Kelly. Becoming known as the Kelham Fathers, Kelly not only trained monks for missionary work but also was responsible for the planting of what has now become a fine collection of trees.

The gracious and impressive **Red House County Manor** hotel and restaurant in Kelham is a substantial brickbuilt house built in the Dutch style in 1903. Amid 8 beautiful acres of grounds, it is an oasis of peace and comfort. From the lovely reception hall to the six distinctive en suite guest bedrooms - each simple and comfortable, decorated in pastel shades and with comfortable furnishings - quality and attention to detail are the by-words here. The delightful restaurant has a menu which combines tradition with innovation in dishes such as sirloin coated with mustard and cracked black peppercorns, or quail stuffed with rice and apricots. This fine establishment also serves delicious and hearty breakfasts and tempting lunchtime repasts. The wine list is excellent; there's also a good range of beers and spirits. Tasteful and welcoming throughout, this fine hotel makes a relaxing and supremely comfortable base from which to explore the many sights and attractions of the area.

**Red House Country Manor, Main Street, Kelham, Newark,
Nottinghamshire NG23 5QP Tel/Fax: 01636 705266
e-mail: theredhousehotel@aol.com**

EASTWOOD

10 miles NW of Nottingham on the A610

MAP 7 REF N13

This town is very much an industrial town, dominated by the coal mining industry. A close knit community, the town is best known as the birthplace, in 1885, of David Herbert Lawrence. The Lawrence family home, a two up, two down, terrace house in Victoria Street is now the **DH Lawrence Birthplace Museum** and it has been furnished in a late 19th-century style with which the Lawrence family would have been familiar. There are also some household items on display which belonged to the family and anyone visiting the museum will see that the house's front window is larger than others in the same street. This is where Mrs Lawrence displayed the children's cloths and other linen items which she made and sold to supplement the fluctuating wages brought home by her miner husband.

In 1887, the Lawrence family moved to a larger, end of terrace house in Eastwood which today is known as the **Sons and Lovers Cottage** as it featured as the Morels' house, The Bottoms, in Lawrence's novel. This house too is open to the public, though by appointment only, and is also laid out with furnishings and artefacts which are appropriate to the times. Lawrence's father was a miner at the nearby Brinsley Pit and though the family moved house in Eastwood several times, the Lawrences remained short of money. First attending the local school, Lawrence was the first Eastwood boy to gain a scholarship to Nottingham High School, where he was a pupil until 1901. Lawrence started his working life as a clerk before undertaking a teacher training course and moving to Croydon to begin life as a teacher.

The **Erewash Canal**, completed in 1779, runs close to Eastwood and it provided an efficient form of transport for the coal away from the numerous pits in this area. At Shipley Lock, in the town, an aqueduct carries the canal over the River Erewash and it was constructed by first building the aqueduct and then diverting the river to run underneath. In the 1980s, following years of neglect, the canal was cleared and made suitable for use by pleasure craft whilst the towpath was resurfaced and it is now a pleasant and interesting walk.

BESTWOOD
5 miles N of Nottingham off the B683

MAP 7 REF N13

Once part of the Royal hunting park of Bestwood, it was whilst staying at **Bestwood Lodge** that Richard III heard of Henry Tudor's invasion of Wales in 1485. The king left his lodge and was killed defending his crown at the Battle of Bosworth Field. The village's royal connections did not, however, die with King Richard. Bestwood was also a favourite hunting ground of Charles II and he enjoyed staying here with Nell Gwynne. One local story tells of a wager the king struck with Nell, saying she could have all the land she could ride around before breakfast. Nell, not known for being an early riser, made an exception and, the next morning, she rose at dawn and rode through the countryside surrounding the village dropping handkerchiefs along the way. Arriving back before breakfast, Nell is said to have won the wager and Charles kept his side of the bargain. Whether or not the story is true, Nell certain was given substantial quantities of land in the area and her son, by the king, became the 1st Duke of St Albans. The present Bestwood Lodge was built by the 10th Duke of St Albans on a low hill. Begun in 1862, the lodge is a grand house with flying buttresses, gables, and chimneys, and it best feature is undoubtedly the loft entrance tower with its high pyramidal roof.

By the 18th century, the lands of the royal hunting grounds were being broken up into farms and only a small area was left forested. Two mills were built taking power from the River Leen and, in 1872, the 10th Duke of St Albans leased some land to John Lancaster who sank a mine shaft. The village expanded to accommodate the new workers and their families arriving to work in the mills and the mine. The first colliery houses were built in 1876 and soon the Bestwood Coal and Iron Village was established with all those living there dependent on the company. Although the colliery closed down in 1967 the spoil heap can still be seen though now it is grassed over and is a true haven for wildlife. Now called the **Bestwood Country Park**, the land also includes areas of the old royal hunting park and the 450 acres offer many differing landscapes. One of the best views of the **Bestwood Winding House** can be found in the country park. A listed building, the winding house, along with the headstocks, still stand even following the closure of the colliery. Unique in that it has a steam driven vertical winding engine, the house lies to the north of the colliery's old spoil heap. Also at Bestwood can be found the **Model Aviation Centre**, a museum which specialises in accurate models of aircraft of up to half the scale of the original machine. As well as seeing the finished models, visitors can watch them fly and also see models in various stages of construction.

NEWSTEAD
9 miles N of Nottingham off the A608

MAP 7 REF N12

The village of Newstead, often overlooked for the famous abbey which lies close by, is another example of a colliery village. The terrace houses were built for the miners and their families working at the nearby pits belonging to the Byron family.

The grand mansion house, **Newstead Abbey**, lies just to the east of the village and this was, famously, the home of the poet, Lord Byron and his ancestors for many years. Originally, Newstead was a true place of worship when, in the late 12th century an Augustinian priory was founded here by Henry II in atonement for his part in the death of Thomas à Becket. However, most of the medieval remains that can still be seen date from building work which was carried out some 100 years after the abbey's foundation. The abbey was bought, in 1539, by Sir John Byron, who converted the monastic buildings for his own private use. Despite destroying much of the building somewhat surprisingly a statue of Christ still stands above the main entrance hall and there is also a statue of the Virgin and Child in the gable.

Though the Byron family have lived here since the mid-16th century and added a whole new wing, the family was beset by money troubles due, in some part, to their own extrava-gances. One of the more colourful characters within the family, the 5th Lord Byron, known as Devil Byron, not only enjoyed playing with a warship on the lake but was involved in the killing of one of his neighbours during a drunken brawl in a London tavern: though the lord was acquitted of murder. By the time the 5th Lord Byron died the scullery was the only room in this huge mansion that did not have a leaking roof and this was were his body was found. The poet Lord Byron, the 5th lord's great nephew, then succeeded to the title and began, with some success, to make some of the rooms habitable but he too ran out of money and was forced, in 1817, to sell the house.

The magnificent Newstead Abbey owes as much to the priors and the Byrons as it does to its subsequent owner Colonel Wildman who carried out some much needed renovation work. In 1931, the house was given to the City of Nottingham. Though the abbey welcomes many visitors throughout the year the grounds still contain a wealth of hidden places. There is a secret garden, a beautifully carved fountain decorated with fantastic animals, the elaborate memorial to Byron's dog Boatswain, and the large lake where the 5th lord re-enacted naval battles. The house, home to the **Byron Museum**, too is well worth a visit and a tour around the many rooms reveals a whole host of splendid treasures.

Although Newstead Abbey has had many interesting occupants it is still best known as the home of the poet and many of his relics can be seen inside. Born in 1788 and baptised George Gordon, the poet's mother, Catherine Gordon, was abandoned by her husband Captain Mad Jack Byron before George's birth and the child was brought up in Aberdeen in relative poverty as his father had spent Catherine's fortune before his premature death in 1791. Following the death of the 5th lord, George succeeded to the title at the age of 10 and such was the state of Newstead Abbey that he lived elsewhere in the county. Educated at Harrow and Cambridge, Byron did not forget the poverty he had seen at first hand during his childhood and, for his maiden speech in the House of Lords, he took up the framework knitters' cause.

UPTON
13 miles N of Nottingham on the A612

MAP 7 REF O12

Upton boasts a couple of very good pubs and its nine-pinnacled church is worthy of a visit too. As a point of interest, a famous son of the village was James Tenant, the man who cut the world renowned Koh-I-Noor diamond. But, perhaps, the most impressive building here is **Upton Hall**, a stylish Grecian villa with a central dome and elegant colonnade, built in the early 19th century. The hall is now the headquarters of the **British Horological Institute** and, inside, visitors can see the **National Exhibition of Time** - a fascinating display of clocks, watches, and other horological pieces.

MANSFIELD
MAP 7 REF N12
14 miles N of Nottingham of the A60

Lying close to the Robin Hood country and near to Lord Byron's splendid ancestral home, this old market town has plenty to offer the visitor. In the heart of the town, a plaque and new tree mark the historic centre of Sherwood Forest and the famous place where Robin Hood first encountered Friar Tuck lies just outside the town at Rainworth Water. Of the stories and songs that have been told over the years about the mysterious forest one ballad tells the story of a miller and a king. Whilst out hunting in Sherwood Forest Henry II found himself lost and fortunately found a miller, John Cockle, who failed to recognise him. Being a hospitable man, Cockle offered the king some venison pie but asked him not to let on that they made free with the royal deer. So amused was Henry II with the miller's simple country ways that he made Cockle a forest overseer, gave him £300 a year, and made him a knight. Further along Westgate is **Cromwell House**, named after Dr Samuel Cromwell who lived here for some 40 years in the late 17th and early 18th centuries and the house may have been built for him as it dates from around the 1680s.

Bentinck Monument, Mansfield

The old market place, which still holds markets on Mondays, Thursdays, Fridays, and Saturdays, is also the centre of Mansfield and around the square can be seen some of the town's more interesting buildings. Pride of place, however, goes to the impressive Gothic **Bentinck Monument** erected in 1848 in memory of Lord George Bentinck. The younger son of the Duke of Portland, Bentinck was a long serving Member of Parliament and a great friend of Disraeli. Funds for the memorial were raised by public subscription but they unfortunately ran out before the finishing touch, a statue of Bentinck himself, could be placed in the central space. The original market cross, dating from the 16th or 17th century, lies in Westgate. As well as the Moot Hall, built in 1752 by Lady Oxford, Waverley House, which lies close by and dates from the same period, is an interesting mixture of architectural styles. During the 17th century, Mansfield was noted for its nonconformist leanings and, in Stockwell Gate, is the **Old Meeting House** and parsonage, which date from the early 18th century. Much altered over the years and with some splendid William Morris stained glass added, this is one of the oldest chapels still in use in the county. There has been a place of worship on the site of the present parish **Church of St Peter and St Paul** since the time of the Domesday Book. The church standing today was built over many years and some of its stones are thought to have come from a Saxon building.

Found just to the northwest of the market place, **Mansfield Museum** concentrates its collections largely on local interest, including a model of a Roman villa that once stood at nearby Mansfield Woodhouse. The collection spans the centuries from that early occupation right up to more recent times, with pictures and artefacts relating to the industry of the town and surrounding villages. The adjoining art gallery also carries a local theme and features works by artists of the area including the watercolourist AS Buxton, who is well known for his works of Mansfield. One feature which anyone approaching Mansfield cannot fail to miss, is the enormous railway viaduct which dominates the skyline. Built in 1875, the 15 immense stone arches cut through the heart of the town and it is one of the largest viaducts in an English town.

MANSFIELD WOODHOUSE
MAP 7 REF N12
2 miles N of Mansfield on the A60

Before the opening of Sherwood Colliery in 1903, Mansfield Woodhouse was a small and quiet rural village of farms and labourers' cottages. However, the village also had a remarkable number of large, grand houses as the area was considered to be a fashionable place to live. Opposite The Cross, in the heart of Mansfield Woodhouse stands one of these fine houses, the Georgian **Burnaby House**. Still retaining many of its original, elegant features the house was obviously built for a prosperous family and, during the mid-19th century, it was occupied by the Duke of Portland's land agent. On the other side of the road stands a stump which is all that remains of the Market Cross which was erected here after a great fire in 1304. The village stocks also stood close by and they were once used to imprison George Fox, the Quaker Movement founder, after he had preached the gospel to the villagers.

At the bottom of the street lies the oldest building in Mansfield Woodhouse, **St Edmund's Church**. Most of the original church was lost, along with the parish records, when fire swept through the village in the early 14th century. The present church was built on the same site though it has undergone some severe restoration in the 19th century. Lying not far from the church is a manor house known as **Woodhouse Castle** because of the battlements which were added to the building in the early 1800s. Dating from the 17th century, this was the house of the Digby family and, in particular, General Sir John Digby, Sheriff of Nottingham, who found fame for the part he played in the Civil War. Another building of note is the essentially 18th-century **Wolfhunt House** found just off the High Street. The unusual name is derived from a local legend which suggests that the land on which the house is built once belonged to a man who was employed to frighten away the wolves in Sherwood Forest by blowing a hunting horn.

CUCKNEY
MAP 7 REF N12

6 miles N of Mansfield on the A632

An estate village to the country seat of the Dukes of Portland, Welbeck Abbey, Cuckney is made up of farm workers cottages. Along with Clumber House, Thoresby Hall, and Rufford Abbey, **Welbeck Abbey** makes up the four large estates in this area of Nottinghamshire which has become known as **The Dukeries**. It was the 5th duke who began, in 1854, an extensive building programme that turned Welbeck into what is seen today. The most impressive of his additions was the riding school, the second largest in the world, complete with a peat floor and gas jet lighting. The building is now in the hands of the Ministry of Defence and it is used as an Army training college, though the abbey and the grounds have been maintained in perfect condition. The **Dukeries Adventure Park and Picnic Area**, on the Welbeck estate, provides all manner of supervised outdoor activities including rock climbing.

A keen racing man, the 6th duke both bred and reared racehorses at his own stud in the nearby estate village of **Holbeck**. Winning many races, including three classics, the duke's famous stallion, St Simon, is still remembered in the racing world

St Winifred's Church, Holbeck

today. As well as holding great house parties, the duke of a well-known host, he also built, in 1915, a beautiful new church in the village. **St Winifred's Church**, named after his wife, the duchess, is well worth a visit and, in the churchyard, are several family graves.

Back in Cuckney itself, there is a large mound in the churchyard which represents the site where, in the mid-12th century, Thomas de Cuckney built a castle. Excavations on the site in the 1950s found the remains of hundreds of skeletons though it is unlikely that they are from the days of the Dark Ages. More recent research has dated the remains to the 7th century and the Battle of Heathfield between Edwin of Northumbria and Penda of Mercia.

EDWINSTOWE   MAP 7 REF N13
6 miles NE of Mansfield on the A6075

Lying at the heart of Sherwood Forest, the life of the village is still dominated by the forest, as it has been since the 7th century. Edwin, King of Northumbria, who gave the village its name, died in the Battle of Hatfield in 632 and the village is said to have grown up around the church which was built on the spot where he was slain. In 1912, a cross was erected to mark his grave by the Duke of Portland. From then on until the time of the Domesday Survey, Edwinstowe remained small. Following the Norman Conquest, the village found itself within the boundaries of the Royal Hunting Forest of Sherwood and it became subject to the laws of the forest. Dating from the 12th century, the **Church of St Mary** was the first stone building in Edwinstowe and legend has it that it was here that the marriage took place between Robin Hood and Maid Marian.

A little way up the road leading northwards out of Edwinstowe is the **Sherwood Forest Visitor Centre**. Sherwood, the Shire Wood, was once a great woodland mass, stretching from Nottingham to Worksop. Although only relatively small pockets of the original forest remain

today, it is still possible to become lost amongst the trees, both figuratively and literally! Whether or not Robin and his Merry Men ever did frolic in the greenshawe is, however, debatable. Arguments still rage as to which particular historical figure gave rise to the legend of the famous outlaw. Records from the 12th century suggest a number of possible candidates, including the Earl of Huntingdon.

Undeterred by the vague foundations upon which the legend is built, visitors still flock to see the great hollow tree which the outlaws purportedly used as a meeting place and as a cache for their supplies. The **Major Oak** is located about 10 minutes' walk along the main track in the heart of the forest. This huge tree, which is not so much tall as broad, with its massive wooden crutches and supportive iron corsets presents

The Major Oak, Sherwood Forest

a rather forlorn sight. There is no denying that it is at least 500 years old, and some sources would claim it to be more than double that figure. Yet despite its appearance, the tree is still alive thanks to careful preservation. Recent tests have established that some parts of the tree have successfully taken to grafting and one hopes that at some stage a whole colony of minor oaks may be produced.

CLUMBER PARK   MAP 7 REF N11
11 miles NE of Mansfield off the A614

As country estates go, Clumber Park is relatively new as it only dates from 1707 when the 3rd Duke of Newcastle was granted permission to enclose part of the Forest of Sherwood as a hunting ground for Queen Anne. The building of **Clumber House** began in 1760 though it was much altered in the early 19th century. After a devastating fire in 1879, the house was rebuilt in an Italianate style but, due to vast expense of the up keep of such a mansion, Clumber House was demolished in 1938 and all that remains today are the foundations.

However, any sense of disappointment is quickly dispelled by the charm of the buildings that remain in this lovely setting. The estate houses with their high pitched gables and massive chimneys are most impressive. The red-brick stables are particularly fine as they are surmounted by a clocktower crowned by a domed cupola. The inset clock in the tower dates back to 1763 and the stables now house the café and visitor centre.

However, by far the most striking building on the estate is the **Church of St Mary the Virgin**, built GF Bodley in the late 19th century. Commissioned by the 7th Duke of Newcastle, a fervent Anglo-Catholic, no expense was spared and the church has many elaborate features including its wonderful stone and woodwork.

The park is owned by the National Trust and attracts many visitors, especially throughout the summer when special events are arranged. The man-made lake is particularly lovely and is crossed by a fine classical bridge. Another impressive feature is the entrance to the park through the Apleyhead Gate. Known as the **Duke's Drive** and stretching for a distance of two miles, it is now established as the longest avenue of limes in Europe and contains over 1,200 trees.

RUFFORD
MAP 7 REF N12

10 miles NE of Mansfield off the A614

Rufford Abbey was founded in 1146 by Gilbert de Gant as a daughter house to the Cistercian Rievaulx Abbey. However, during the Dissolution it suffered the fate of many religious houses and it came into the hands of the Earls of Shrewsbury and it was the husband of Bess of Hardwick, the 6th Earl, who, in the 16th century, turned the abbey into the country house seen today. The remaining ruins of the abbey are said to be haunted by the ghost of a giant monk with a skull-like face: there is written evidence in the parish register for Edwinstowe that a man died of fright after catching sight of this unholy visitor! In 1626, the house was bought by the Savile family who lived here until the 1930s and it was they who carried out many of the improvements. Now in the hands of the County Council, the abbey's stable block houses an impressive craft centre while the restored 18th century orangery hosts modern sculpture exhibitions.

The grounds of the abbey, now the **Rufford Country Park**, are also well worth a visit and, as well as the nine formal gardens near the house, there also some hides where birdwatchers can overlook a portion of the lake which has been designated a bird sanctuary.

Rufford Abbey

In the grounds too lies an 18th-century corn mill, now home to a display of Nottinghamshire history, and two icehouses dating from the mid-19th century. As well as the majestic Lime Avenue, there is also the Broad Ride, at the southern end of which are several animal graves. Most were pets belonging to the family at the house but one grave is that of the racehorse Cremorne, the 1872 Derby winner.

LAXTON
MAP 7 REF O12

10 miles NE of Mansfield off the A6075

This ancient village, mentioned in the Domesday Book, is unique as it is the only place in the country that has managed to retain its open field farming system. Devised in the Middle Ages, this system was generally abandoned in the 18th and 19th centuries when the enclosure of agricultural land took place and along with this many of the villagers' grazing rights. The fields have been strip farmed here for about 1,200 years and the reasoning behind this was to ensure

Laxton

that farmers had an equal share of both good and poor land. With the dividing of the land, a farmer could have as many as 100 strips, which would have represented about 30 acres. By the 17th century, the strips were, on average, about half an acre in size but, with the advent of more efficient means of ploughing, this increased to three-quarters of an acre. The familiar three year crop rotation also ensured productive use of the land. Any stroll around this remarkable village is sure to take in some of the old farms and their outbuildings. The 18th century was a great time of rebuilding in Laxton and many of the houses display the patterned brickwork that was typical of the 1700s. The still visible stonework around the bottom of some buildings suggests that the foundations were of much older timber framed constructions.

Just north of the village, along a lane close to the church, is another fascinating aspect of Laxton's medieval history. This is the Norman motte or **Castle Mound** which lies almost hidden beneath the trees. At the beginning of the 12th century, the stewardship of Sherwood Forest moved to Laxton and the village became the administrative centre for the forest. As a consequence, the motte and bailey castle was one of the biggest in this part of the country and the village grew dramatically. Over the years, however, the size and importance of Sherwood Forest dwindled and Laxton suffered a similar fate. Although no ruined keep or crumbling walls exist today, the castle earthworks are still the largest and best preserved in the county. All the information needed by the visitor on the history of this fascinating village can be found at the **Laxton Visitor Centre**.

RETFORD   MAP 7 REF O11
18 miles NE of Mansfield on A638

The town has grown in importance over the centuries, from the granting of its market charter by Henry III in 1246, to the prosperity bought to it by the railway and canal links. The town is made up of **East Retford** and **West Retford**, each lying on opposite banks of the River Idle. Of the two, West Retford is the older and it is presumably this parish which received a mention in the Domesday Book as Redforde. East Retford was established in 1105 on the other side of the river as a place where tolls could be collected from people make the river crossing. An attempt was made, in the 18th century, to make the river navigable from Retford to Bawtry but this was unsuccessful though the diversion of the Great North Road through the town, in 1766, did bring more prosperity to Retford.

The **Market Square** was laid out in the late 18th century after the rerouting of the Great North Road through the town. Still at the heart of the life of Retford today, with a bustling market every Thursday and Saturday, the square is surrounded by many of the town's most noteworthy buildings, including some fine Georgian houses. The grand and rather chateau-like **Town Hall** was built in 1868 to replace the Georgian hall which stood on the northeast side of square. Outside the Town Hall can be found the **Broad Stone**, which is probably the base of an old parish boundary cross. Tradition has it that during the times of the plague in Retford, in the mid-16th and mid-17th centuries, coins were placed in a pool of vinegar in the hollow in the top of the stone so prevent the disease from spreading whilst trading was taking place at the market. It is well worth visiting the **Bassetlaw Museum** in Amcott House, Grove Street. This imposing late 18th-century town house was once the home of the Whartons, the woollen drapers; Sir Wharton Amcotts, MP for the Borough of East Retford; and the Peglers, the local industrialists. The house is noted for its finely executed internal plasterwork and elegant wrought iron staircase, which the restoration has returned to their full Georgian splendour.

EATON
MAP 7 REF O11

2 miles S of Retford on the A638

This small hamlet was once part of the estate of the Dukes of Newcastle which incorporated several other nearby villages. The land known as **Eaton Wood**, now managed by the Nottinghamshire Wildlife Trust, was mentioned in the Domesday Book as an area of pasture woodland and some of the ancient ridges and furrows can still be seen. A wood of mainly ash, elm, and hazel with some oak, Eaton Wood is more important for the plant life it sustains such as moschatel, yellow archangel, and several orchids.

CLARBOROUGH
MAP 7 REF O11

2 miles NE of Retford on the A620

Many footpaths cross **Clarborough Hill** and, from the top, there are splendid views over Lincolnshire, Derbyshire, and South Yorkshire. The Chesterfield Canal, which runs close by the village not only provides more interesting walking along the towpath but also there is good angling. The Retford to Gainsborough railway line runs through the village and there is a very attractive nature reserve, **Clarborough Tunnel**, along the railway cutting and above the tunnel here. A mix of dense woodland, scrub, and grassland, little has been disturbed here since the railway was built in 1849 and the reserve is well known for the various species of orchid found growing on the limey soil.

WORKSOP
MAP 7 REF N11

8 miles W of Retford of the A57

Despite the unattractive modern houses that lead into the town, there are some fine Georgian buildings to be found in Bridge Street. One of the real attractions of Worksop is the **Priory Gatehouse**, which is best approached from Potter Street, where the full glory of the 14th-century building can be seen. Its great niches house large and beautifully carved statues and the immense entrance is rather reminiscent of a cave opening. Originally the portal to a large Augustinian monastery, the gatehouse together with the Church of St Mary and St Cuthbert is all that remains. There is also a wayside shrine, which makes it a unique ecclesiastical attraction. Today, the upper floor of the gatehouse houses an art gallery and exhibitions are put on here regularly. The first canal to be built in Nottinghamshire was the **Chesterfield Canal** which runs from Chesterfield in Derbyshire to the River Trent. Some 46 miles long, work on the canal was begun in 1771 and it took 6 years to complete under the supervision of John Varley, the deputy of the great canal engineer, James Brindley. **Pickford's Depository**, spanning the canal in the centre of the town, was typical of this time. The trap doors in the stone archway over the canal were used for the loading and unloading of the cuckoos, as the narrowboats on the Chesterfield Canal were called.

The National Trust-owned **7 Blyth Grove** is unusual, unique and also well worth a visit. The house - and a million pounds - were left to the Trust by William Straw in his will and the Trust was surprised to find upon inspection of the Edwardian semi-detached house that they were actually stepping back in time. Inside, everything had been preserved from 1932 when William Straw senior, a grocer and seed merchant in Worksop, died. Now the Trust have a unique record of social history of those times with a display of items that reflects life as it was in the 1930s and the earlier decades of this century.

Worksop Museum

One remnant of the northern part of Sherwood Forest lies near the town. **Hannah Park Wood**, which covers some 14 acres, is mainly made up of oak and beech but there is also a small section of yew trees.

Worksop Museum, found in Memorial Avenue, is housed in a large purpose-built gallery within the library and museum provided by the Carnegie United Kingdom Trust which was opened in 1938. Within the museum are small exhibitions relating to the history of Worksop and the neighbouring area of landed estates known as the Dukeries, together with a larger display on the Pilgrim Fathers whose roots lay in north Nottinghamshire.

BABWORTH
2 miles W of Retford on the A620

MAP 7 REF O11

At **The Barns** in Babworth, off the B6420 west of Retford, guests encounter a lovely 18th century building - as its name tells us, a former barn - that has been extended and refurbished over the years to become a superior country guest house. A wealth of original features survive, in-

The Barns, Morton Farm, Babworth, Retford, Nottinghamshire DN22 8HA Tel: 01777 706336 Fax: 01777 709773 e-mail: harry@thebarns.fsbusiness.co.uk website: www.thebarns.co.uk

cluding the old oak beams and log fires in the dining and sitting rooms. The guest house welcomed its first guests back in 1985, and has since that time enjoyed a well-earned reputation for providing excellent en suite accommodation of the highest standard. The six charming guest bedrooms - including one ground floor room - are cosy and comfortable; while providing every modern amenity they retain a traditional ambience, reflected in their country style

decor and furnishings. The delicious cooked breakfast - prepared on the impressive Aga in the farmhouse-style kitchen - sets guests up for a day of sightseeing or relaxing amid the surrounding scenic countryside.

BLYTH   MAP 7 REF N11
7 miles NW of Retford on the A634

The approach to the village is dominated by the great tower of the **Church of St Mary and St Martin** which looms above Blyth and is one of the most important Norman buildings in the country. The eight tall pinnacles are linked by a delicate tracery of stone that gives a surprising grace to the 900 year old tower. Although the first impression is of a Gothic structure, the Norman windows give its origins away and the church epitomises the French love of dignity and simplicity with its rather solemn air.

There are many other buildings of distinction in the village, including a handsome stable block and the former rectory which is surmounted by a cupola. Among the redbrick Georgian houses there are also a number of coaching inns which act as a reminder that Blyth was once an important staging post on the Great North Road.

At the far end of the village is **St John's Hospital**, which was originally founded as a leper hospital in the 12th century and later converted into a school. The former schoolhouse stands on a diamond shaped island of grass, obviously dating back to a time when these poor unfortunates (the lepers not the pupils!) would have been kept isolated from the villagers.

Just to the southwest of the village lies **Hodsock Priory** and its beautiful Gardens which stands within its own parkland and meadows. Although this would seem to be the perfect setting for a medieval monastery, no priory ever stood here. The present house was built in 1829 in the Tudor style to complement the marvellous 16th-century gatehouse. The gatehouse is approached across an ancient rectangular moat and, within this area, the gardens have been laid. The southern arm of the moat was made into a small lake around 1880. The gardens are well known for their shrub roses and the owners, Sir Andrew and Lady Buchanan, are more than happy to welcome the public into their lovely grounds.

Between Blyth and the nearby village of Styrrup, to the north, lies the **Tournament Field**. Dating back to the Middle Ages, the field was one of only five in the country to be granted a royal licence.

6 The Welsh Borders

INTRODUCTION

This chapter takes in the counties of Gloucestershire, Herefordshire, Worcestershire and Shropshire. Wild wood, royal hunting ground, naval timber reserve, important mining and industrial area - Gloucestershire's Royal Forest of Dean, one of England's few remaining ancient forests, has been all these, and today its rich and varied landscape provides endless interest for walkers, historians and nature-lovers. Its geographical location in an area bordered by the Severn Estuary to the south and the Wye Valley to the west has effectively isolated it from the rest of England and Wales and as a result it has developed a character all its own. There are numerous waymarked walks in and around the forest, among them are the Wye Valley Walk; Offa's Dyke Path, which covers the Wye Valley between Chepstow and Ross-on-Wye; the Wysis Way, passing west to east; and the Gloucestershire Way, covering a route from Chepstow to Symonds Yat and then taking in the spectacular May Hill to the north. Laurie Lee, author of *Cider with Rosie,* also sang the praises of this fine county. The Slad Valley he wrote of is just one of the many scenic delights of the Cotswolds, the limestone hills that sweep across the county from Wotton-under-Edge to Chipping Campden. Gloucestershire also boasts the major centres of Gloucester, Cheltenham and Cirencester, as well as some of the most glorious scenery and the prettiest villages in the whole of Britain.

"Wherever one goes, there will not be a mile that is visually unrewarding." Sir Nikolaus Pevsner was clearly impressed, and today's visitors to Herefordshire will also find delights at every turn in the rolling landscape, the pretty villages and the charming market towns. Herefordshire had few natural resources, so the industrial scars that spoil many counties are mercifully absent; the beauty remains relatively intact, so too the peace, and motorists will generally find jam-free roads. Apples and hops are the traditional crops of Herefordshire, and the cider industry is still a thriving one. The days when almost every farm produced its own cider are long gone, but many of the old mills are preserved on the farms or in museums. 9,500 acres of the county are given over to cider orchards, and 63 million gallons of cider are produced here each year - well over half the UK total. Hereford cattle still abound, and their stock are now to be found in many parts of the world, particularly the Americas. Skirmishes with the Welsh were a common occurrence for many centuries, and one of the county's best-known landmarks, Offa's Dyke, was built in the 8th century as a defence against the marauders. The River Wye rises in the Plynlimon mountains east of Aberystwyth, near the spot where the Severn also has its source. The Wye enters England by Hay-on-Wye and winds its way through some of the most delightful scenery in the whole land, changing mood and direction from time to time and finally joining its original neighbour at the Severn Estuary. The whole of its length offers great touring and walking country, and the Wye Valley Walk, waymarked with the logo of the leaping salmon, follows the river closely for 112 miles, almost half of which are in Herefordshire. The valley was designated an Area of Outstanding Natural Beauty (AONB) in 1971, and the river itself was the first to be recognised as a Site of Special Scientific Interest (SSSI). The northern part of the county includes the wonderful Black and White villages that are among the most picturesque in the whole of England.

Southern Worcestershire features the spectacular ridge of the Malvern Hills in the west, with marvellous walking and breathtaking views. Moving eastwards there are many charming villages and ancient sites. Most of Worcestershire's industry was centred in the northern part of the county, and there are numerous examples of industrial archaeology to interest the historian. Canals here were once as important as roads, and in this part of the county the Worcester & Birmingham Canal, the Staffordshire & Worcester Canal and the Droitwich Canal were a quicker means of transport than the Severn and more reliable than the roads. They themselves lost a good deal of their practical advantages when the railways arrived. The railway network has shrunk considerably over the last 40 years, so it's back to the roads for most local communications. The Severn Valley Railway, from Kidderminster to Bridgnorth, has survived and flourished, and today people come from far and wide for the chance to ride behind a steam engine through some incredibly beautiful scenery. Enthusiasts have also ensured that much of the canal system has survived, finding a new role as a major leisure and tourist attraction.

Shropshire was recently accorded the title of "The Most Romantic County in Britain". A tranquil face hides an often turbulent past that is revealed at scores of sites by the remains of dykes and ramparts and hill forts, and by the castles of the Marcher Lords, who seem to have divided their time between fighting the Welsh and fighting each other. The county boasts some of Britain's most important Roman sites, notably at Wroxeter, which at one time was the fourth largest Roman town in the land. Shropshire beckons with a landscape of great variety: the little hills and valleys, the lakes and canals of the northwest, the amazing parallel hill ranges towards the south, the rich farming plains around Oswestry, the forests of Clun and Wyre, Ironbridge Gorge, called "the birthplace of the Industrial Revolution". Add to this the historic towns of Shrewsbury, Ludlow and Oswestry, the churches and the stately homes and the glorious gardens and you have a part of the world just waiting to be explored, whether by car, on a bike or on foot. South Shropshire affords a trip through romance and history, including the wonderful town of Ludlow and the spectacular scenery of Wenlock Ridge, Long Mynd and Clun Forest.

GLOUCESTERSHIRE

COLEFORD
MAP 3 REF J18

17 miles SW of Gloucester of the A4136

A former mining centre which received its royal charter from Charles I in the 17th century in recognition of its loyalty to the Crown. It was by then already an important iron processing centre, partly because of the availability of local ore deposits and partly because of the ready local supply of timber for converting into charcoal for use in the smelting process. It was in Coleford that the Mushet family helped to revolutionise the iron and steel industry. Robert Forester Mushet, a freeminer, discovered how spiegeleisen, an alloy of iron, manganese, silicon and carbon, could be used in the reprocessing of 'burnt iron' and went on to develop a system for turning molten pig iron directly into steel, a process which predated the more familiar one developed later by Bessemer. Coleford, still regarded as the capital of the Royal Forest of Dean, is a busy commercial centre with an interesting church and a number of notable industrial relics. It is home to the **Great Western Railway Museum**, housed in an 1883 GWR goods station next to the central car park. Exhibits include several large-scale steam locomotives, railway relics and memorabilia, an engine shed and a miniature locomotive for children. Call 01594 833569 for opening times. Another treat for railway fans is the **Perrygrove Railway** on the B4228 just south of town. Designed as a family attraction, it offers unlimited trips on its narrow-gauge steam train, a village with secret passages and a treasure hunt in the woods.

MITCHELDEAN
MAP 3 REF K17

7 miles NE of Coleford off the A4136

A peaceful community on the northern fringe of the forest. A mile or so south of the village is **St Anthony's Well**, one of many throughout the land said to have magical curative powers. The water at this well is invariably icy cold and bathing in it is said to provide a cure for skin disease (St Anthony's Fire was the medieval name for a rampant itching disease). The monks at nearby Flaxley Abbey swore by it.

RUARDEAN
MAP 3 REF K17

6 miles NE of Coleford off the A4136

A lovely old village whose **Church of St John the Baptist**, one of many on the fringe of the forest, has many interesting features. A tympanum depicting St George and the Dragon is a great rarity, and on a stone plaque in the nave is a curious carving of two fishes. These are thought to have been carved by craftsmen from the Herefordshire School of Norman Architecture during the Romanesque period around 1150. It is part of a frieze removed with rubble when the south porch was being built in the 13th century. The frieze was considered lost until 1956, when an inspection of a bread oven in a cottage at nearby Turner's Tump revealed the two fish set into its lining. They were rescued and returned to their rightful place in the church.

NEWLAND
MAP 3 REF J18

1 mile SW of Coleford off the A466

Newland's Church of All Saints is often known as the **Cathedral of the Forest** because of its impressive size. Its aisle is almost as wide as its nave and its huge pinnacled tower is supported by flying buttresses. Like many churches in the county, it was built during the 13th and 14th centuries and remodelled by the Victorians. Inside, it has a number of interesting effigies, including an unusual brass relief of a medieval miner with a pick and hod in his hand and a candlestick in his mouth. Other effigies depict a forester in 15th century hunting gear with a hunting horn, a sword and knife; and, from the 17th century, an archer with wide-brimmed hat, bow, horn and dagger.

CLEARWELL
Map 3 ref J18
2 miles S of Coleford off the A466

Clearwell Caves are set in an area of special landscape value, just on the outskirts of the historic village of Clearwell, which boasts a castle, pretty church, chapel and several good pubs. This is the only remaining working iron mine in the Forest of Dean out of the very many that once worked here. The mine produces ochres for use as paint pigments by artists or those wishing to decorate their homes using natural paints.

Before the 19th century only Free Miners were allowed to enter Forest of Dean mines; any Free Miner allowing access to non-members of the fellowship would be brought before the mine law court, their fellowship withdrawn, their tools broken or confiscated and the Miner never allowed to mine within the Forest of Dean again. Today such punishment is

Clearwell Caves

frowned upon and at Clearwell Caves nine impressive caverns have been opened to visitors, allowing you to descend over 100 feet underground, although the mine itself goes down over 600 feet.

Tudor Farmhouse Hotel and Restaurant is a marvellous country house hotel which dates back to the 13th century. Located in the heart of the Forest of Dean and close to the Wye Valley, an intimate, relaxed and friendly atmosphere greets guests here. Proprietors Colin and Linda Gray take great pride in maintaining the highest standards at this superb establishment, which retains many original features including exposed beams, timber panelling, oak spiral staircases and a roughstone fireplace in the guests' lounge. The 14 acres of grounds are recognised as an Area of Outstanding Natural Scientific Interest, with a wealth of rare flora and fauna native to the region, as well as an abundance of wildlife. The restaurant's excellent menu serves a sophisticated and mouth-watering range of starters, main courses such as monkfish and venison, and a choice of home-made desserts. This ideal retreat boasts 14 bedrooms, all with ensuite facilities. Within the house are two four-poster rooms and, on the second floor, additional twin and double rooms. Three luxury bedrooms are located in the converted stone former cider-makers' cottages, while four rooms are in the former stables - all have been refur-

Tudor Farmhouse Hotel and Restaurant, Clearwell, nr Coleford, Gloucestershire GL16 8JS
Tel: 01594 833046/0800 783 5935

bished to the highest standards. The cottage suite - also located in a former cider-maker's cottage - sleeps up to six people in two separate bedrooms, and also features two bathrooms, lounge and self-catering facilities.

PARKEND
MAP 3 REF K18

3 miles SE of Coleford off the B4234

A community once based, like so many others in the area, on the extraction of minerals. New Fancy Colliery is now a delightful picnic area, with a nearby hill affording breathtaking views over the forestscape. Parkend is to be the northern terminus of Dean Forest Railway (see under Lydney). The track is there, the signal box has been renovated and a replica station built. Off the B4431, just west of Parkend, is the RSPB's **Nagshead Nature Reserve**, with hundreds of nest boxes in a woodland site with footpaths, waymarked trails and a summer information centre.

The Fountain Inn, at Parkend, is a traditional village inn well konwn locally for its excellent meals and real ales. Centrall situated in one of England's foremost wooded areas, the pub was built 200 years ago to serve the local mining population, and extended to provide accom-

modation for passengers when the Great Western Railway reached the village in 1868. The interior of the bar boasts exposed beams and stone walls, an open fire and wood panelling, all making for a very cosy atmosphere. There walls are adorned with a terrific collection of railway memorabilia, photographs of old Parkend, Second World War helmets and more - every inch is cov-

The Fountain Inn, Fountain Way, Parkend, nr Lydney, Gloucestershire GL15 4JD Tel: 01594 562189 Fax: 01594 564438

ered with conversation points. A *Forest Fayre* menu offers such delicious main courses as lamb steak in woodland berry sauce and Gloucester sausage in onion gravy, whilst a selection of curries, vegetarian dishes and other daily specials are available off the blackboard menu. The eight guest rooms (one of which is specially adapted for disabled use) are 3 Diamond-rated and all have television and tea/coffee-making facilities. Various half-board breaks are offered throughout the year.

ST BRIAVELS
MAP 3 REF J18

5 miles S of Coleford on minor roads

A historic village named after a 5th century Welsh bishop whose name appears in various forms throughout Celtic Wales, Cornwall and Brittany, but nowhere else in England. In the Middle Ages St Briavels was an important administrative centre and also a leading manufacturer of armaments, supplying weapons and ammunition to the Crown. In 1223 it is believed that Henry lll ordered 6,000 crossbow bolts (called quarrels) from here. The ample Church of St Mary the Virgin, Norman in origin, enlarged in the 12th and 13th centuries and remodelled by the Victorians, is the scene of a curious and very English annual custom, the St Briavels **Bread** and **Cheese Ceremony**. After evensong a local forester stands on the Pound Wall and throws small pieces of bread and cheese to the villagers, accompanied by the chant "St Briavels water and Whyrl's wheat are the best bread and water King John can ever eat". This ceremony is thought to have originated more than 700 years ago when the villagers successfully defended their rights of estover (collecting wood from common land) in nearby Hudnalls Wood. In gratitude each villager paid one penny to the churchwarden to help feed the poor, and that act led to the founding of the ceremony. Small pieces of bread and cheese were considered to bring good luck, and the Dean Forest miners would keep the pieces in order to ward off harm. **St Briavels Castle**, which stands in an almost impregnable position on a high promontory, was founded by Henry I and enlarged by King John, who used it as a hunting lodge. Two sturdy gatehouses are among the parts that survive and they, like some of the actual castle buildings, are now in use as a youth hostel.

STAUNTON
Map 3 ref J17
3 miles NW of Coleford on the A4136

Lots to see here, including a Norman church with two stone fonts and an unusual corkscrew staircase leading up past the pulpit to the belfry door. Not far from the village are two enormous mystical stones, the **Buckstone** and the **Suck Stone**. The former, looking like some great monster, used to buck, or rock, on its base but is now firmly fixed in place. The Suck Stone is a real giant, weighing in at many thousands of tons. There are several other stones in the vicinity, including the **Near Harkening** and **Far Harkening** down among the trees, and the Long Stone by the A4136 at Marion's Cross.

LYDNEY
Map 3 ref K18
6 miles SE of Coleford off the A48

The harbour and the canal at Lydney, once an important centre of the iron and coal industries and the largest settlement between Chepstow and Gloucester, are well worth exploring, and no visit to the town should end without a trip on the **Dean Forest Railway**. A regular service of steam and diesel trains operates between Lydney Junction, St Mary's Halt and Norchard. At **Norchard Railway Centre**, headquarters of the line, are a railway museum, souvenir shop and details of restoration projects, including the imminent extension of the line to Parkend. Air-conditioned classic coaches in the platform serve light snacks on steam days. The backbone of the locomotive fleet (this is for real railway buffs!) are 5541, a Churchwood-designed Prairie tank engine, and 9681, an 0-6-0 pannier tank built in 1948, when GWR was becoming BR. Call 01594 845840 for details of services and events.

One of the chief attractions in the vicinity is **Lydney Park Gardens and Museum**. The gardens, which lie beside the A48 on the western outskirts, are a riot of colour, particularly in May and June, and the grounds also contain the site of an Iron Age hill fort and the remains of a late-Roman temple excavated

Dean Forest Railway

by Sir Mortimer Wheeler in the 1920s. The builders of this unusual temple were probably wealthy Romanised Celts; the mosaic floor, now lost, depicted fish and sea monsters and was dedicated to Nodens, the Roman-Celtic god of healing whose emblem was a reclining dog with curative powers. The nearby museum houses a number of Roman artefacts from the site, including the famous 'Lydney Dog' and a number of interesting items brought back from New Zealand in the 1930s by the first Viscount Bledisloe after his term there as Governor General. Also in the park are traces of Roman iron-mine workings and Roman earth workings.

WESTBURY-ON-SEVERN
6 miles NE of Lydney on the A48

MAP 3 REF K17

The village is best known for the National Trust's **Westbury Court Garden**, a formal Dutch water garden laid out between 1696 and 1705. Historic varieties of apple, pear and plum, along with many other species introduced to England before 1700, make this a must for any enthusiastic gardener.

LITTLEDEAN
5 miles NE of Lydney on the road to Cinderford

MAP 3 REF K17

Places of interest here include the 13th century church, the 18th century prison and, just south of the village, **Littledean Hall**, reputedly the oldest inhabited house in England. The house has Saxon and Celtic remains in the cellars and is thought to have originated in the 6th century. Highlights in the grounds, from which balloon flights launch, include a Roman temple site, a Victorian walled garden and a number of ancient chestnut trees. Open 11-5 every day.

NEWENT
9 miles NW of Gloucester on the B4216

MAP 6 REF K17

Capital of the area of northwest Gloucestershire known as the Ryelands, and the most important town in the Vale of Leadon, Newent stands in the broad triangle of land called Daffodil Crescent. The rich Leadon Valley soil was traditionally used for growing rye and raising the renowned Ryelands sheep, an ancient breed famed for the quality of its wool. The town was one of the county's principal wool-trading centres, and the wealth produced from that trade accounts for the large number of grand merchants' houses to be seen here. The most distinctive house in Newent is the splendid timber-framed **Market House**, built as a butter market in the middle of the 16th century, its upper floors supported on 16 oak pillars that form a unique open colonnade. The medieval **Church of St Mary** has many outstanding features, including the shaft of a 9th century Saxon cross, the 11th century 'Newent Stone' and the 17th century nave. Royalist troops had removed the lead from the roof to make bullets, an act which caused the roof to collapse during a snowstorm in 1674. A new nave was started after Charles II agreed to donate 60 tons of timber from the Forest of Dean. **The Shambles Museum of Victorian Life** is virtually a little Victorian town, a jumble of cobbled streets, alleyways and squares, with shops and trades tucked away in all corners, and even a mission chapel and a Victorian conservatory.

There aren't too many windmills in Gloucestershire, but at **Castle Hill Farm** just outside town is a working wooden mill with great views from a balcony at the top. A mile south of Newent is the **National Bird of Prey Centre** housing one of the largest and best collections of birds of prey in the world. Over 110 aviaries are home to eagles, falcons, owls, vultures, kites, hawks and buzzards. Between 20 and 40 birds are flown daily. Open every day from February to November.

DYMOCK
3 miles N of Newent on the B4216

MAP 6 REF K17

At the heart of the village is the early Norman Church of St Mary, whose unusual collection of artefacts and memorabilia includes the last ticket issued at Dymock station, in 1959. Dymock boasts some fine old brick buildings, including the White House and the Old Rectory near the church, and outside the village, the Old Grange, which incorporates the remains of the Cistercian Flaxley Abbey. In the years before World War I Dymock became the base for a group of writers who became known as the **Dymock Poets**. The group, which included Rupert Brooke, Wilfred Gibson, Edward Thomas and Lascelles Abercrombie, and was later joined by Robert Frost, sent out its New Numbers poetry magazine from Dymock's tiny post office, and it was also from here that Brooke published his *War Sonnets*, including *The Soldier* ("If I should die, think only this of me..."). Brooke and Thomas died in the War, which led to the dissolution of the group. Two circular walks from Dymock take in places associated with the poets.

KEMPLEY   MAP 6 REF K17
1 mile S of Newent on a minor road

A village famous for its cider and also for having two churches, of very different age and significance. The Church of St Mary, easily the most popular church in the area, dates from the end of the 11th century and would be a gem even without its greatest treasure. That treasure, in the chancel, is an almost complete set of 12th century frescoes, the most renowned in the region and among the finest in the land. Their subjects include St Peter and the Apostles, Christ with his feet resting on a globe, and the de Lacy family, local lords of the manor. The red sandstone Church of St Edward the Confessor was built in 1903 by the 7th Earl Beauchamp in the style of the Arts and Crafts Movement using exclusively local materials. Three miles south of Newent, on National Trust land, stands **May Hill**. It rises to nearly 1,000 feet and its domed summit is planted with trees commemorating Queen Victoria's Golden Jubilee (1887), Queen Elizabeth ll's Silver Jubilee (1977) and the Queen Mother's 80th birthday (1980). The reward for climbing to the top is a quite magnificent view that stretches over Gloucestershire, and, on a clear day, as far as Bristol.

FRAMPTON-ON-SEVERN   MAP 3 REF K18
8 miles SW of Gloucester off the A38

The 22-acre Rosamund Green, incorporating a cricket ground and three ponds, is one of the largest village greens in England, formed when the marshy ground outside the gates of **Frampton Court** was drained in the 18th century. The court is an outstanding example of a Georgian country house, built in the Palladian style in the 1730s and the seat of the Clifford family ever since. Fine porcelain, furniture and paintings grace the interior, and in the peacock-strutted grounds an ornamental canal reflects a superb Orangery in Dutch-influenced strawberry gothic. A unique octagonal tower was built in the 17th century as a dovecote. The Court is open by appointment only. On the other side of the green is **Frampton Manor**, the Clifford family's former home, built between the 12th and 16th centuries. This handsome timber-framed house is thought to be the birthplace of Jane Clifford, who was the mistress of Henry ll and bore him two children. The manor, which has a lovely old walled garden with some rare plants, is open by written appointment. At the southern edge of the village stands the restored 14th century Church of St Mary with its rare Norman lead font. The church stands beside the **Sharpness Canal**, which was built to allow ships to travel up the Severn Valley as far as Gloucester without being at the mercy of the estuary tides. The canal has several swing bridges and at some of these, as at Splatt Bridge and Saul Bridge at Frampton, there are splendid little bridge-keeper's cottages with Doric columns.

SLIMBRIDGE   MAP 3 REF K18
4 miles S of Frampton on the A38

The Wildfowl and Wetlands Trust was founded on the banks of the Severn in 1946 by the distinguished naturalist, artist, broadcaster and sailor Peter (later Sir Peter) Scott. He believed in bringing wildlife and people together for the benefit of both, and the Trust's work continues with exciting plans for the Millennium. Slimbridge has the world's largest collection of exotic wildfowl, with up to 8,000 wild winter birds on the 800-acre reserve. Viewing facilities are first-class, and there's a tropical house, pond zone, children's play area, restaurant and gift shop. Tel: 01453 890333. Also in the long, rambling village is a fine 13th century church whose 18th century windows incorporate fragments of the original medieval glass.

BERKELEY
MAP 3 REF K18

6 miles S of Frampton off the A38

The fertile strip that is the Vale of Berkeley, bounded on the north by the Severn and on the south by the M5, takes its name from the small town of Berkeley, whose largely Georgian centre is dominated by the Norman **Berkeley Castle**. Said to be the oldest inhabited castle in Britain, and home to 24 generations of the Berkeley family, this wonderful gem in pink sandstone was built between 1117 and 1153 on the site of a Saxon fort. It was from here that the barons of the West met before making the journey to Runnymede to witness the signing of Magna Carta by King John in 1215. Edward ll was imprisoned here for several months after being usurped from the throne by his wife and her lover, and eventually met a gruesome death in the dungeons in the year 1327. Three centuries later the castle was besieged by Cromwell's troops and played an important part in the history of the Civil War. It stands very close to the Severn and once incorporated the waters of the river in its defences so that it could, in an emergency, flood its lands. Visitors passing into the castle by way of a bridge over a moat will find a wealth of treasures in the **Great Hall**, the circular keep, the state apartments with their fine tapestries and

period furniture, the medieval kitchens and the dungeons. The Berkeley family have filled the place with objects from around the world, including painted glassware from Damascus, ebony chairs from India and a cypress chest that reputedly belonged to Sir Francis Drake. Security was always extremely important, and two remarkable signs of this are a four-poster bed with a solid wooden top (no nasty surprises from above in the night) and a set of bells once won by the castle's dray horses and now hanging in the dairy. Each horse wore bells with a distinctive chime so that if an outsider attempted to gain entrance as a carter his strange bells would betray him. The castle is surrounded by sweeping lawns and Elizabethan terraced gardens. Special features include a deer park, a medieval bowling alley, a beautiful lily pond and a butterfly farm with hundreds of exotic butterflies in free flight.

Great Hall, Berkeley Castle

The parish church of St Mary, which contains several memorials to the Berkeley family, has a fine Norman doorway, a detached tower and a striking east window depicting Christ healing the sick. A curious piece of carving in the nave shows two old gossips with a giant toad sitting on their heads. Next to the castle and church is the **Jenner Museum**, once the home of Edward Jenner, the doctor and immunologist who is best known as the man who discovered a vaccine against smallpox. The son of a local parson, Jenner was apprenticed to a surgeon in Chipping Sodbury in 1763 at the tender age of 14. His work over several decades led to the first vaccination against smallpox, a disease which had killed many thousands every year. His beautiful Georgian house in Church Lane has a state-of-the-art display showing the importance of the science of immunology, and in the grounds of the house is a rustic thatched hut where Jenner used to vaccinate the poor free of charge and which he called the Temple of Vaccinia. The museum is open Tuesday to Sunday afternoons from April to September and on Sunday afternoons in October.

MARSHFIELD
MAP 3 REF K19

10 miles E of Bristol on the A420

This old market town was once the fourth wealthiest town in Gloucestershire, after Bristol, Gloucester and Cirencester, its prosperity based on the malt and wool industries. Its long main street has many handsome buildings dating from the good old days of the 17th and 18th centuries, but not many of the coaching inns remain that were here in abundance when the town was an important stop on the London-Bristol run. Among the many notable buildings are the **Tolzey market hall** and the imposing Church of St Mary, which boasts a fine Jacobean pulpit and several impressive monuments from the 17th and 18th centuries. Each Boxing Day brings out the **Marshfield Mummers**, who take to the streets to perform a number of time-honoured set pieces wearing costumes made from newspapers and accompanied by a town crier. On the northern edge of town is a folk museum at Castle Farm.

Three miles northwest of Marshfield, on the A46, the National Trust-owned **Dyrham Park** stands on the slope of the Cotswold ridge, a little way south of the site of a famous 6th century battle between Britons and Saxons. This striking baroque mansion, the setting for the film *Remains of the Day*, houses a wonderful collection of artefacts accumulated by the original owner William Blathwayt during diplomatic tours of duty in Holland and North America (he later became Secretary of State to William lll). A charming little church in the grounds has a Norman font, a fine 15th century memorial brass and several memorials to the Winter and Blathwayt families.

CHIPPING SODBURY
MAP 3 REF K19

12 miles E of Bristol on the A432

This pleasant market town was one of the earliest examples of post-Roman town planning, its settlement being arranged in strips on either side of the main street in the 12th century. The town once enjoyed prosperity as a market and weaving centre, and it was during that period that the large parish church was built. A mile or so to the east, on a loop off the A432, is **Old Sodbury**, whose part-Norman church contains some exceptional tombs and monuments. One of these is a carved stone effigy of a 13th century knight whose shield is a very rare wooden carving of a knight. Also in the church is the tomb of David Harley, the Georgian diplomat who negotiated the treaty which ended the American War of Independence. A tower just to the east of the church marks a vertical shaft, one of a series sunk to ventilate the long tunnel that carried the London-South Wales railway through the Cotswold escarpment. Opened in 1903, the 2½ mile tunnel required its own brickworks and took five years to complete. A lane leads south from Old Sodbury to **Dodington House**, built between 1796 and 1816 where previously an Elizabethan house stood.

BADMINTON
MAP 3 REF K19

4 miles E of Chipping Sodbury off the B4040

The **Badminton Park** estate was founded by Edward Somerset, the son of the Marquis of Worcester, whose 25-foot monument stands in the little church next to the main house. The central section of the house dates from the 1680s and contains some marvellous carvings in lime wood by Grinling Gibbons. The rest of the house, along with the grounds and the many follies and gateways, is the work of the mid-18th century architect William Kent. The house contains an important collection of Italian, English and Dutch paintings. The game of badminton is said to have started here during a weekend party in the 1860s. The Duke of Beaufort and his guests wanted to play tennis in the entrance hall but were worried about damaging the paintings; someone came up with the bright idea of using a cork studded with feathers instead of a ball. In such a moment of inspiration was the game born, and it was one of the guests at that weekend bash who later took the game to Pakistan, where the first rules were formalised. Many of the buildings on the estate, including the parish church and the estate villages of Great and Little Badminton, were designed in an ornate castellated style by Thomas Wright. The park is perhaps best known as the venue of the Badminton Horse Trials, which annually attract the best of the international riders, and spectators in their thousands.

WESTONBIRT

MAP 3 REF L18

9 miles NE of Chipping Sodbury on the A433

Westonbirt Arboretum, three miles south of Tetbury, contains one of the finest collections of trees and shrubs in Europe - 18,000 of them spread over 600 acres of glorious Cotswold countryside. Wealthy landowner Robert Stayner Holford founded this tree wonderland by planting trees for his own interest and pleasure. His son, Sir George Holford, was equally enthusiastic about trees and continued his father's work until his death in 1926, when he was succeeded by his nephew, the 4th Earl of Morley. Opened to the public in 1956 and now managed by the Forestry Commission, the arboretum has something to offer all year round: a crisp white wonderland after winter snows, flowering shrubs and rhododendrons in spring, tranquil glades in summer, glorious reds and oranges and golds in the autumn. The grounds provide endless delightful walks, including 17 miles of footpaths, and there's a visitor centre, plant centre, café and picnic areas. Open all year.

TETBURY

MAP 3 REF L18

11 miles NE of Chipping Sodbury on the A433

A really charming Elizabethan market town, another to have prospered from the wool trade. Its most famous building is the stone-pillared 17th century **Market House** in the heart of town, but a visit should also take in the ancient **Chipping Steps** connecting the market house to the old trading centre, and the Church of St Mary, an 18th century period piece with high-backed pews, huge windows made from recovered medieval glass and slender timber columns hiding sturdy iron uprights. **Tetbury Police Museum**, housed in the original cells of the old police station, has a fascinating collection of artefacts, memorabilia and uniforms from the Gloucestershire Constabulary. Open Monday to Friday 9 till 3 and by appointment.

Two miles northwest of Tetbury, west of the B4104, stands **Chavenage House**, a beautiful Elizabethan mansion built of grey Cotswold stone on earlier monastic foundations in the char-

acteristic E shape of the period. The elegant front aspect has remained virtually unchanged down the years, and the present owners, the Lowsley-Williams family, can trace their lineage back to the original owners. Two rooms are covered with rare 17th century tapestries, and the house contains many relics

Chavenage House

from the Cromwellian period. Cromwell is known to have stayed at the house, and during the Civil War he persuaded the owner, Colonel Nathaniel Stephens, a relative by marriage, to vote for the King's impeachment. According to the Legend of Chavenage the owner died after being cursed by his daughter and was taken away in a black coach driven by a headless horseman. The present owner, who conducts tours round the property, welcomes visitors to "Gloucestershire's second most haunted house" (Berkeley Castle is the most haunted!).

TORTWORTH   Map 3 ref K18
8 miles N of Chipping Sodbury off the B4509

Overlooking the village green stands the Church of St Leonard, which contains some fine 15th century stained glass and a pair of canopied tombs of the Throckmorton family, former owners of the Tortworth Park estate. In a field over the church wall are several interesting trees, including an American hickory, a huge silver-leafed linden and two Locust trees. Nearby, and the most famous of all, is the famous **Tortworth Chestnut**, a massive Spanish chestnut which the diarist John Evelyn called *"the great chestnut of King Stephen's time"*. Certainly it was well established by Stephen's time (1130s), and a fence was put up to protect it in 1800. Its lower branches have bent to the ground and rooted in the soil, giving the impression of a small copse rather than a single tree.

OZLEWORTH   Map 3 ref K18
8 miles NE of Chipping Sodbury on minor roads

A secluded hamlet with a very unusual circular churchyard, one of only two in England. The church itself has a rare feature in a six-sided Norman tower. Also at Ozleworth is the National Trust's **Newark Park**, built as a hunting lodge by the Poyntz family in Elizabethan times. James Wyatt later converted it into a castellated country house. Open by appointment only. This is great walking country, and one of the finest walks takes in the **Midger Wood Nature Reserve** on its way up to **Nan Tow's Tump**, a huge round barrow whose tomb is said to contain the remains of Nan Tow, a local witch.

ULEY   Map 3 ref K18
11 miles N of Chipping Sodbury on the B4066

Calm and quiet now, Uley was once a busy centre of commerce, mainly in the cloth-making industry. The most distinguished house in the area is **Owlpen Manor**, a handsome Tudor country house set in formal Queen Anne terraced yew gardens. Inside, contrasting with the ancient polished flagstones and the putty-coloured plaster, are fine pieces of William Morris-inspired Arts and Crafts furniture; there's also a rare beadwork collection and some unique 17th-century wall hangings. The village lies in the shadow of **Uley Bury**, a massive Iron Age hill fort which has thrown up evidence of habitation by a prosperous community of warrior farmers during the 1st century BC. Another prehistoric site, a mile along the ridge, is Uley Long Barrow, known locally as **Hetty Pegler's Tump**. This chambered long barrow, 180 feet in length, takes its name from Hester Pegler, who came from a family of local land-owners. Adventurous spirits can crawl into this Neolithic tomb on all fours, braving the dark and the dank smell to reach the burial chambers, where they will no longer be scared by the skeletons that terrified earlier visitors. The walls and ceilings of the chamber are made of huge stone slabs infilled with drystone material. A little further north, at the popular picnic site of **Coaley Peak** with its adjoining National Trust nature reserve, is another spectacular chambered tomb, **Nympsfield Long Barrow**.

STROUD   Map 3 ref L18
7 miles S of Gloucester on the A419

The capital of the Cotswold woollen industry, an ideal centre on the River Frome at a point where five valleys converge. The surrounding hill farms provided a constant supply of wool, and the Cotswold streams supplied the water-power. By the 1820s there were over 150 textile mills in the vicinity; six survive, one of them specialising in green baize for snooker tables. A stroll round the centre of town reveals some interesting buildings, notably the **Old Town Hall** dating from 1594 and the **Subscription Rooms** in neo-classical style. An easy walk from the centre is **Stratford Park**, a large park containing dozens of trees both ordinary and exotic. Lots of ducks on the pond.

BISLEY
MAP 3 REF L18

4 miles E of Stroud on minor roads

Country roads lead across from Stroud or up from Oakridge Lynch to the delightful village of Bisley, which stands 780 feet above sea level and is known as 'Bisley-God-Help-Us' because of the winter winds which sweep across the hillside. Bisley's impressive All Saints Church dates from the 13th century and was restored in the early 19th by Thomas Keble, after whose poet and theologian brother John Keble College, Oxford was named. In the churchyard is the Poor Souls' Light, a stone wellhead beneath a spire dating from the 13th century. It was used to hold candles lit for souls in purgatory. Below the church are the **Seven Wells of Bisley** (also restored by Thomas Keble), which are blessed and decorated with flowers each year on Ascension Day. At the top of the village is a double lock-up built in 1824, with two cells beneath an ogee gable.

PAINSWICK
MAP 3 REF L18

4 miles N of Stroud on the A46

This beautiful little town, known as the 'Queen of the Cotswolds', prospered with the wool trade, which had its peak in the second half of the 18th century. At that time 30 mills provided power within the parish, and the number of fine houses and farms in and around the town are witness to those days. Many of them are built of the pale grey limestone that was quarried at Painswick Hill. In the grounds of **Painswick House**, on the B4073 at the northern edge of town, **Painswick Rococo Garden**, hidden away in magnificent Cotswold countryside, is a unique 18th century garden with plants from around the world and a maze planted in 1999 with a path structure in the shape of '250' to commemorate the garden's 250th anniversary. Other attractions are a specialist nursery, a children's nature trail, a gift shop and a restaurant.

A little further north, at Cranham, **Prinknash Abbey Park** (call it Prinnage) comprises an active monastery, chapel, working pottery, gift shop and tearoom. The Benedictine monks of Caldey Island moved here in 1928 when the old house was made over to them by the 20th Earl of Rothes in accordance with the wishes of his grandfather. They no longer occupy the old house, having moved into the impressive new monastery in 1972. The abbey chapel is open daily for solitude and contemplation. Visitors can have a guided tour round the pottery and buy a hand-made Prinknash pot. Part of the abbey gardens are given over to the **Prinknash Bird & Deer Park**, where visitors can feed and stroke the fallow deer and see the waterfowl, the peacocks and the African pygmy goats. By the lake is a charming two-storey Wendy House.

GLOUCESTER
MAP 6 REF K17

30 miles NE of Bristol on the A38

The capital city of Gloucestershire first gained prominence under the Romans, who in the 1st century AD established a fort to guard what was then the lowest crossing point on the Severn. A much larger fortress soon followed, and the settlement of Glevum became one of the most important military bases, crucial in confining the rowdy Celts to Wales. William the Conqueror held a Christmas parliament and commissioned the Domesday Book in Gloucester, and also ordered the rebuilding of the abbey, an undertaking which included the building of a magnificent church that was the forerunner of the superb Norman Cathedral. The elaborate carved tomb of Edward ll, murdered at Berkeley Castle, is just one of many historic monuments in **Gloucester Cathedral**; another, the work of the Wedgwood designer John Flaxman, remembers one Sarah Morley, who died at sea in 1784, and is shown being delivered from the waves by angels. The exquisite fan tracery in the cloisters is the earliest and among the finest in existence, and the great east window, at 72 feet by 38 feet, is the largest surviving stained-glass window in the country. It was built to celebrate the English victory at the Battle of Crécy in 1346 and depicts the coronation of the Virgin surrounded by assorted kings, popes and saints. The young King Henry lll was crowned here, with a bracelet on his little head rather than a crown.

The old area of the city around Gloucester Cross boasts some very fine early buildings, including St John's Church and the Church of St Mary de Crypt. Just behind the latter, near the house where Robert Raikes of Sunday School fame lived, stands an odd-looking tower built in the 1860s to honour Hannah, the wife of Thomas Fenn Addison, a successful solicitor. The tower was also a memorial to Raikes.

Three great inns were built in the 14th and 15th centuries to accommodate the scores of pilgrims who came to visit Edward ll's tomb, and two of them survive. The galleried New Inn,

Gloucester Cathedral

founded by a monk around 1450, doubled as a theatre and still retains the cobbled courtyard. It was from this inn that Lady Jane Grey was proclaimed Queen. Equally old is The Fleece Hotel in Westgate Street, which has a 12th century stone-vaulted undercroft. In the same street is **Maverdine House**, a four-storey mansion reached by a very narrow passage. This was the residence and headquarters of Colonel Massey, Cromwell's commander, during the Civil War siege of 1643. Most of the region was in Royalist hands, but Massey survived a month-long assault by a force led by the King himself and thus turned the tide of war.

Gloucester Docks were once the gateway for waterborne traffic heading into the Midlands, and the handsome Victorian warehouses are always in demand as location sites for period films. The docks are now home to several award-winning museums. The **National Waterways Museum**, on three floors of a beautiful warehouse, is entered by a lock chamber with running water and tells the fascinating story of Britain's canals with films, displays and historic boats.

The **Robert Opie Collection** at the **Museum of Advertising and Packaging** takes a nostalgic look at the 40s, 50s, 60s and 70s with the aid of toys and food, fashions, packaging and a continuous screening of vintage TV commercials. Soldiers of Gloucestershire uses archive film, photographs and life-size reconstructions to tell the history of the county's regiments. Elsewhere in the city **Gloucester City Museum and Art Gallery** houses treasures from all over the county to reveal its history, from dinosaur bones and Roman remains to antique furniture and the decorative arts. Among the highlights are the amazing **Birdlip Mirror**, made in bronze for a Celtic chief just before the Roman conquest, two

Gloucester Docks

Roman tombstones and a section of the Roman city wall revealed under the cut-away gallery floor. English landscape painting is represented by Turner, Gainsborough and Richard Wilson. Timber-framed Tudor buildings house **Gloucester Folk Museum**, where the exhibits include farming, fishing on the Severn, the port of Gloucester, the Civil War, a Victorian schoolroom, a dairy, an ironmongery and a wheelwright's workshop. **Gloucester Transport Museum** has a small collection of well-preserved vehicles and baby carriages housed in a 1913 former fire station. The **House of the Tailor of Gloucester**, in College Court, is the house sketched by Beatrix Potter in 1897 and used in her tale *The Tailor of Gloucester*. It now brings that story to life, complete with Simpkin the Cat and an army of helpful mice.

In the southwestern suburbs of Gloucester are the ruins of **Llanthony Abbey**. The explanation of its Welsh name is an interesting one. The priory of Llanthony was originally founded in the Black Mountains of Wales at the beginning of the 12th century, but the inmates were so frightened of the local Welsh that they begged the Bishop of Hereford to find them a safer place. The Bishop passed their plea to Milo, Earl of Hereford, who granted this plot of land for a second priory bearing the same name as the first. Llanthony Secunda was consecrated in 1136. On a nearby hill the monks built St Ann's Well, whose water was - is - believed to cure eye problems.

PAUNTLEY
MAP 6 REF K17

8 miles N of Gloucester on the A417

The penniless orphan boy who in the pantomime fable was attracted by the gold-paved streets of London and who became its Lord Mayor was born at **Pauntley Court**. Richard Whittington, neither penniless nor an orphan, was born here about 1350, one of three sons of landowner Sir William de Whittington and Dame Joan. He became a mercer in London, then an important financier and was three times Mayor (not Lord Mayor - that title had not been invented). He married Alice Fitzwarren, the daughter of a wealthy landowner from Dorset. The origin of the cat connection is unclear, but an event which could have contributed to the myth was the discovery in 1862 of the carved figure of a boy holding a cat in the foundations of a house in Gloucester. The carving can be seen in Gloucester Museum.

TEWKESBURY
MAP 6 REF L17

8 miles N of Gloucester on the A38

A town of historic and strategic importance at the confluence of the Severn and Avon rivers. Those rivers also served to restrict the lateral expansion of the town, which accounts for the unusual number of tall buildings. Its early prosperity was based on the wool and mustard trades, and the movement of corn by river also contributed to its wealth. Tewkesbury's main thoroughfares, High Street, Church Street and Barton Street, form a Y shape, and the area between is a marvellous maze of narrow alleyways and small courtyards hiding many grand old pubs and medieval cottages. At the centre of it all is **Tewkesbury Abbey**, the cathedral-sized parish church of St Mary. One of the largest parish churches in the country, it was founded in the 8th century and completely rebuilt in the 11th. It was once the church of the Benedictine Abbey and was among the last to be dissolved by Henry Vlll. In 1540, it was saved from destruction by the townspeople, who raised £453 to buy it from the Crown. Many of its features are on a grand scale - the colossal double row of Norman pillars; the six-fold arch in the west front; and the vast main tower, 132 feet in height and 46' square, the tallest surviving Norman main tower in the world. The choir windows have stained glass dating from the 14th century, and the abbey has more medieval monuments than any besides Westminster. Three museums tell the story of the town and its environs: the Little Museum, laid out like a typical old merchant's house; Tewkesbury Museum, with displays on the social history and archaeology of the area; and the **John Moore Countryside Museum**, a natural history collection displayed in a 15th century timber-framed house. The museum commemorates the work of John Moore, a well-known writer, broadcaster and naturalist, who was born in Tewkesbury in 1907.

KEMERTON

Map 6 ref L17

3 miles NE of Tewkesbury off the B4079

The Crown at Kemerton is an inn of distinction with a history going back to the 16th century. It's a lively place with bags of atmosphere and a wealth of character provided by old flagstones, stripped oak and a Cotswold stone fireplace. The south-facing walled garden is a delightful sun trap. The pub is run by Tim Barber and Marion New, both very experienced in the catering trade and very much driven by the needs of their customers. In the 20-cover restaurant a daily-changing menu tempts with superb dishes such as avocado with hot melted Stilton, breast of goose in gooseberry and cider sauce, and oven-baked trout with lemon and almonds. There are theme nights with special menus - seafood; salmon and asparagus; Beaujolais Nouveau - and to accompany the excellent food is a wide selection of wines.

The Crown at Kemerton, Main Street, Kemerton, Gloucestershire GL20 7HP Tel: 01386 725293

Darts and cribbage are the favourite pub games, and there are regular quiz nights. The village of Kemerton, below Bredon Hill and only a mile from the Vale of Evesham, is the scene of an annual tug of war between teams from local villages.

CHELTENHAM

Map 6 ref L17

8 miles NE of Gloucester on the A40

Smart, fashionable Cheltenham: a small, insignificant village until a mineral spring was accidentally discovered in 1715 by a local man, William Mason, who built a pump room and began Cheltenham's transformation into one of Europe's leading Regency spa towns. Mason's son-in-law was the astute Captain Henry Skillicorne, who added a meeting room, a ballroom and a network of walks and carriageways, and called it a spa. A number of other springs were soon discovered, including one in the High Street around which the first Assembly Rooms were built. In 1788 the Royal seal of approval came in the shape of King George lll, who spent five weeks taking the waters with his family and made Cheltenham a highly fashionable resort. An entirely new town was planned based on the best features of neoclassical Regency architecture, and as a result very few buildings of any antiquity still stand. One of these is the Church of St Mary, with parts going back to the 12th century and some very fine stained glass.

Skillicorne's walks and rides are now the tree-lined Promenade, one of the most beautiful boulevards in the country, its crowning glory the wonderful Neptune's Fountain, modelled on the Fontana di Trevi in Rome and erected in 1893. Housed in Pittville Park in the magnificent Pump Room overlooking gardens and lakes north of the town centre is the **Pittville Pump Room Museum**, which uses original period costumes to bring alive the story of Cheltenham from its Regency heyday to the 1960s. Special exhibitions are held throughout the year. **Cheltenham Art Gallery and Museum** has an acclaimed collection of furniture and silver, much of it made by Cotswold craftsmen and inspired by William Morris's Arts and Crafts Movements. Also Oriental porcelain, English ceramics, fine paintings and changing special exhibitions. Gustav Holst was born in 1874 in a terraced Regency house in Clarence Road which is now the **Holst Birthplace Museum and Period House**. The original piano of the composer of *The Planets* is

THE WELSH BORDERS **549**

the centrepiece of the story of the man and his works, and there's a working kitchen, a Regency drawing room and a nursery.

Two remarkable modern pieces of public art take the eye in the centre of town. The **Wishing Fish Clock** in the Regent Arcade is a work in metal by the famous artist and craftsman Kit Williams: below the clock, from which a mouse pops out when disturbed by the arrival of an egg laid by a duck on high, is suspended a 12' fish which celebrates the hour by swishing its tail and blowing bubbles, to the delight and fascination of shoppers below. The mechanical parts of the clock are the work of the renowned local clockmaker Michael Harding. Off the High Street are the **Elephant Murals**, which portray an event that occurred in 1934 when three elephants from a travelling circus escaped and raided a provision shop stocked with corn - an incident which older locals with long memories still recall. **Cheltenham Racecourse**, two miles north of town, is the home of National Hunt Racing, staging numerous top-quality races highlighted by the March Festival when the Gold Cop and the Champion Hurdle find the year's best steeplechaser and best hurdler. Several other festivals have their home in Cheltenham, including the International Jazz Festival (April), the International Festival of Music (July) and the International Festival of Literature (October).

When Suffolk Square was created in 1824, one of the first houses to be built was **Willoughby House**, a dignified Regency residence that became the landmark mansion as visitors entered the square from Montpellier. Throughout its history the house has welcomed visitors - Queen Adelaide came to dine in 1837 - and since 1963 it has been a hotel of distinction. It was star-listed at that time as a building of special architectural and historical interest, ensuring that all essential features, both internal and external, are maintained in their original condition. Elegance is the keynote throughout, and the eight ensuite bedrooms are decorated and furnished to a very high standard, each with its own individual style and appeal. The rooms range from a beautiful suite with four-poster bed, adjoining second bedroom and lounge area, to family doubles, twins and singles. In the dining room a multi-choice breakfast starts the day, and from Monday to Saturday a dinner menu

Willoughby House, 1 Suffolk Square, Cheltenham, Gloucestershire GL50 2DR Tel: 01242 522798 Fax: 256369

offers a good choice of dishes using fresh seasonal produce. In addition to the guest rooms, Willoughby House also has three self-contained apartments, each with its own entrance. Elsewhere in town, in the same ownership, are other self-contained apartments and three houses available for short or long stays, and a health club. Willoughby House and the health club have a brilliant and very personable young manager in Lee Pemberton.

WITHINGTON
Map 6 ref L17
3 miles SE of Cheltenham off the A436

Halewell Close is a magnificent medieval manor house built of Cotswold stone. It began life as a small farming monastery back in the early 15th century. Restored and 'modernised' in the

1920s, it was purchased in 1971 by Elizabeth Carey-Wilson. She maintains it with loving care, with wonderful results that have been featured in the distinguished journal *Period Living and Traditional Homes*. There are six large double or twin bedrooms, each individually furnished and decorated in traditional country-house style, all with many original features including exposed beams and open fireplaces. All have bathrooms ensuite; some have showers as well. Two have smaller adjoining rooms, mak-

Halewell Close, Withington, nr Cheltenham, Gloucestershire GL54 4BN Tel: 01242 890238 Fax: 01242 890332

ing them perfect for families. One twin-bedded room is on the ground floor and has a bathroom built to RADAR specifications, to make it suitable for guests with physical disabilities. Breakfast is served between 9 and 11 a.m.; guests also have use of a comfortable and cosy sitting room, where television, video and games are available. The Solar is a grand vaulted drawing room which may always be viewed on request. This room has polished oak floors, a large open hearth and an impressive chandelier. The large garden has both formal and informal areas, as well as a heated swimming pool (May - September). Guests can explore the grounds, enjoying the peace and tranquillity, or they can partake of the five-acre trout lake; a stretch of the River Coln is also available for fishing. Horse-riding can be arranged. There are several good pubs and restaurants in the area. For groups of eight or more, dinner can be taken at Halewell by prior arrangement. For a taste of luxury, look no further.

WINCHCOMBE   MAP 6 REF L17

6 miles NE of Cheltenham on the B4632

The Saxon capital of Mercia, where in medieval times the shrine of St Kenelm, martyred here by his jealous sister in the 8th century, was second only to that of Thomas à Becket as a destination for pilgrims. Winchcombe grew in importance into a walled town with an abbot who presided over a Saxon parliament. The abbey was destroyed in 1539 after the Dissolution of the Monasteries and all that remains today is a section of a gallery that is part of the George Inn. As well as pilgrims, the abbey gave rise to a flourishing trade in wool and sheep. One of the most famous townsmen of the time was Jack Smallwood, the Jack o' Newbury who sponsored 300 men to fight at Flodden Field in 1513 and was a leading producer of woollen goods. Silk and paper were also produced, and for a few decades tobacco was grown locally - a fact remembered in place names such as Tobacco Close and Tobacco Field. This activity ceased in 1670 when a law was passed banning home-produced tobacco in favour of imports from the struggling colony of Virginia.

The decline that followed had the effect of stopping the town's development, with for us the happy result that many of the old buildings have survived largely unaltered. These include St Peter's Church, built in the 1460s and known particularly for its 40 grotesques and gargoyles,

Ireley Grounds, Broadway Road, Winchcombe, nr
Cheltenham, Gloucestershire GL54 5NY
Tel: 01242 603736

the so-called Winchcombe Worthies. **Winchcombe Folk and Police Museum**, in the Tudor-style Town Hall by the Tourist Information Centre, tells the history of the town from neolithic times to the present day and also keeps a collection of British and international police uniforms and equipment. A narrow passageway by an ordinary-looking house leads to **Winchcombe Railway Museum and Garden**, a wonderland full of things to do: the railway museum contains one of the largest collections of railway equipment in the country, and visitors can work signals and clip tickets and generally get misty-eyed about the age of steam. The Cotswold garden is full of old and rare plants.

Ireley Grounds is a stunning Cotswold farmhouse built of natural stone and set in 2½ acres of attractive gardens by the B4632 Winchcombe-Broadway road. The ex-GWR Gloucestershire-Warwickshire railway line, where steam trains now run once more, forms one of the boundaries. Inside Mike and Pauline Wright's lovely house the lounge, with its log fire, comfortable sofas and solid oak bar, has abundant atmosphere and style, and the four main-house bedrooms offer exceptional luxury and comfort. Three of the rooms have four-poster beds and one has extra beds for family occupation. The splendid bridal suite has a balcony with views of the garden and the Cotswolds. All rooms have ensuite bath or shower. Three self-catering cottages (Arkle, Mill House and Red Rum) are also available. The grounds are a riot of colour throughout the year, and the lovely Koi carp pond adds further appeal to the surroundings. A superb venue for conferences and seminars, there is a function suite to accommodate 100+ theatre-style, making it an equally popular venue for weddings, banquets and private parties. Clay-pigeon shooting can be arranged.

A mile or so north of Winchcombe stand the ruins of **Hailes Abbey**, founded in 1246 by Richard, Earl of Cornwall, who built it on such an ambitious scale that the Cistercian monks

Hailes Abbey, Nr Winchcombe

were hard pressed to maintain it. But after a wealthy patron donated a phial said to contain the blood of Christ the abbey soon became an important place of pilgrimage; it was even mentioned in Chaucer's Canterbury Tales. The authenticity of the phial was questioned at the time of the Dissolution and it was destroyed, and with it the abbey's main source of income.

The abbey fell into disrepair and the only significant parts to survive are the cloister arches. Some of the many artefacts found at the site, including medieval sculptures and decorated floor tiles, are on display in the abbey's museum. National Trust.

OXENTON
MAP 6 REF L17
7 miles N of Cheltenham off the A435

Oxenton is a charming old settlement with several thathced buildings, an old mill house and a church with medieval wall paintings. In the midst of rolling countryside and surrounded by the Cotswolds, yet just minutes from Cheltenham, the picture-postcard **Crane Hill** cottage is a wattle-and-daub home dating back to the 1600s. With its thatched roof, exposed timbers and lush front garden - high hedges behind dry stone walls offering seclusion and a sense of tranquillity - it is the image of a rural retreat. It is in the grounds of this charming listed cottage, in an adjoining flat, that proprietor Helen Beardsell offers guests a holiday home or, by prior arrangement only, bed and breakfast accommodation in a self-contained part of the main house with private facilities and its own staircase. The light and airy holiday flat affords fabulous views over the surrounding open fields and woodland. With the woods nearby, the garden is visited by many wild animals and birds. The flat is entered via the garage, where guests may park. The stairs lead to the main living/dining area, which has ample and comfortable seating, coffee table, colour television, dining table and four dining chairs. The flat is carpeted and furnished to a high standard throughout, with many antiques enhancing the elegant ambience. A lobby leads from this main room to the fitted kitchen, equipped with

Crane Hill, Oxenton, nr Cheltenham, Gloucestershire GL52 4SE Tel: 01242 673631

every modern amenity and a breakfast bar, and on to the bedroom. Here guests will find a king-sized bed (which can also function as twin beds) and large fitted wardrobes, dressing and bedside tables. There is a modern shower room. Guests are welcome to use the sitting area outside in the cottage garden. The garage has a washing machine and freezer, available for guests' use. No pets. Please phone for details of bed and breakfast accommodation in the main cottage. Mrs Beardsell also offers Wimble Cottage in Cheltenham, an elegant and peaceful cottage that sleeps three, featuring a handsome sitting room, kitchen area, double bedroom with antique bedstead, single bedroom, bathroom and full amenities, as well as a secluded rear garden and small paved front garden.

STOW-ON-THE-WOLD
MAP 6 REF M17
15 miles E of Cheltenham on the A429

At 800' above sea level, this is the highest town in the Cotswolds, and the winds sometimes prove it. At one time twice-yearly sheep fairs were held on the Market Square, and at one such fair Daniel Defoe records that over 20,000 sheep were sold. Those days are remembered today in

Sheep Street and **Shepherds Way**. The square holds another reminder of the past in the town stocks, used to punish minor offenders. The sheep fairs continued until they were replaced by an annual horse fair, which was held until 1985. The Battle of Stow, in 1646, was the final conflict of the Civil War, and after it some of the defeated Royalist forces made their way to St Edward's Church, while others were cut down in the market square. In Park Street is the **Toy and Collectors Museum**, housing a charming display of toys, trains, teddy bears and dolls, along with textiles and lace, porcelain and pottery.

BLOCKLEY   MAP 6 REF M17
7 miles N of Stow off the A429/A44

Silk-spinning was the main industry here, and six mills created the main source of employment until the 1880s. As far back as the Domesday book water mills were recorded here, and the village also once boasted an iron foundry and factories making soap, collars and pianos. The mills have now been turned into private residences and Blockley is a quieter place. One of the chief attractions for visitors is **Mill Dene Garden**, set around a mill in a steep-sided valley. The garden has hidden paths winding up from the mill pool, and at the top there are lovely views over the Cotswolds. Also featured are a grotto, a potager, a trompe l'oeil and dye plants.

CHIPPING CAMPDEN   MAP 6 REF M17
10 miles N of Stow on the B4081

The "Jewel of the Cotswolds", full of beautifully restored buildings in golden Cotswold stone. It was a regional capital of the wool trade between the 13th and 16th centuries and many of the fine buildings date from that period of prosperity. In the centre of town is the **Jacobean Market Hall**, built in 1627 and one of many buildings financed by the noted wool merchant and financier Sir Baptist Hicks. He also endowed a group of almshouses and built Old Campden House, at the time the largest residence in the village; it was burnt down by Royalists to prevent it falling into the hands of the enemy, and all that survives are two gatehouses and the old stable block. The 15th century Church of St James was built on a grand scale and contains several impressive monumental brasses, the most impressive being one of William Grevel measuring a mighty 8' by 4'. **Dover's Hill**, a natural amphitheatre above the town, is the scene of the **Cotswold Olympics**, founded in the 17th century by Captain Robert Dover, whom we met at Stanway House. The Games followed the traditions of ancient Greece and added some more down-to-earth activities such as shin-kicking and bare-knuckle boxing. The lawlessness and hooliganism that accompanied the games led to their being closed down in 1852 but they were revived in a modern form in 1951 and are still a popular annual attraction on the Friday following the spring bank holiday.

UPPER AND LOWER SLAUGHTER   MAP 6 REF M17
2 miles SW of Stow off the A429/B4068

The Slaughters (the name means nothing more sinister than 'muddy place') are archetypal Cotswolds villages set a mile apart on the little River Eye. Both are much visited by tourists, much explored and much photographed; also much as they have always been, since virtually no building work has been carried out since 1904. Francis Edward Witts, author of the *Diary of a Cotswold Parson*, was the rector here between 1808 and 1854. **Lords of the Manor** was for 200 years home of the Witts family, generations of whom were rectors of the parish. It was here that the Reverend Edward Francis Witts, the first Lord of the Manor (the rights of which had been purchased in 1852 by his father), wrote his famous chronicle of 19th-century life, 'The Diary of a Cotswold Parson'. Set amid eight acres of lake and parkland, the grounds also boast lovely walled gardens to the rear of the house. The core of the rectory dates from 1650, though over the years additions and changes have been made, particularly during the Victorian era. This handsome and gracious Cotswold stone home offers dining and accommodation. The restaurant holds a distinguished Michelin star and has a proud reputation for serving some of the finest food in the county. Dishes such as sea bass with lobster ravioli, Barbary duck, roast cod and roast rump of lamb grace the excellent menu, and the wine list is superb. Each of the bedrooms is individually designed and furnished with period pieces and traditional antiques, and in the reception rooms and guests' lounges, comfortable sofas, real fires and soft lighting create the warm atmosphere of a fine country house. For a completely

Lords of the Manor, Upper Slaughter,
nr Bourton-on-the-Water, Gloucestershire GL54 2JD
Tel: 01451 820243 Fax: 01451 820696
email: lordsofthemanor@btinternet.com

relaxing and comfortable break amid truly impressive surroundings, look no further.

BOURTON-ON-THE-WATER

Map 6 ref M17

4 miles S of Stow on the A429

Probably the most popular of all the Cotswold villages. The willow-lined Windrush flows through the centre, crossed by several delightful low-arched pedestrian bridges, two of which date from the late 18th century. The golden stone cottages are pretty as a picture, and among the notable larger buildings are St Lawrence's Church, with its 14th century chancel and rare domed Georgian tower, and a manor house with a 16th century dovecote. In the High Street, **Miniature World - The Museum of Miniatures** is a unique exhibition of miniature scenes and models that took the country's leading master miniature makers 3½ years to complete. Bourton is a great place for miniatures, as there is also the famous **Model Village** at the Old New Inn (se below) and **Bourton Model Railway** with over 40 British and Continental trains running on three main

Bourton-on-the-Water

displays in OO, HO and N gauge. The **Cotswold Motor Museum and Toy Collection**, in an 18th century water mill, has a fascinating collection of antique toys, a display of historic advertising signs and 30 or so (full-size!) cars and motorcycles. Bourton has Europe's only **Perfumery Exhibition**, a permanent attraction which explains the extraction and manufacturing processes and includes a perfume garden and a perfume quiz to test visitors' noses.

The **Old New Inn**, a traditional country inn dating back some 300 years, is an ideal base for exploring the delightful hills and villages of the region, on foot, on bicycles or by car. The village itself is a scenic gem, and the inn, originally two cottages and a barn, is the very essence of an English country inn, full of old-world charm and with the warm, welcoming feel of a village local. Most of the 11 letting bedrooms have ensuite facilities and one boasts a four-poster bed. The inn, owned by Julian and Vicki Atherton, has two lounges reserved for guests and a separate TV lounge. It also has a splendid dining room serving a multi-choice table d'hote menu in the evening (7.30-8.30). Light lunches or bar meals are available at midday, and packed lunches can be provided with a little notice. In the

The Old New Inn, Bourton-on-the-Water,
Gloucestershire GL54 2AF Tel: 01451 820467 Fax: 01451 810236
email: old_new_inn@compuserve.com

grounds behind the inn is a wonderful surprise in the shape of a 19th-century replica in local stone of the village, complete with the River Windrush, the Church of St Lawrence and the music of the actual church choir. The model was built by six local men and opened on Coronation Day 1937.

Two attractions outside the village are the Iron Age **Salmonsbury Camp** and **Folly Farm**, home to Europe's largest domestic waterfowl and wildlife conservation area, with over 160 rare breeds. Also at this major attraction off the A436 Cheltenham road are spectacular lavender fields, a garden centre and a coffee shop.

CLAPTON-ON-THE-HILL   MAP 6 REF M17
2½ miles S of Bourton-on-the-Water off the A429/A44

The last house in the village of Clapton-on-the-Hill, at the end of a No-Through Road in an area of outstanding natural beauty, **Farncombe** is a comfortable family home with three letting bedrooms for B&B guests. Its position some 700 feet above sea level provides truly breathtaking views, and there are numerous walks around the hills and valleys in the area. Owner Julia Wright spent many years in Africa and the house is full of reminders of those times, with African paintings and carvings, zebra skins, rugs and many other objects.

Farncombe, Clapton-on-the-Hill, nr Bourton-on-the-Water,
Gloucestershire GL54 2LG Tel/Fax: 01451 820120
Mobile: 07714 703142 e-mail: jwrightbb@aol.com

The accommodation comprises two double bedrooms with showers and washbasins and one twin with full ensuite facilities. There's a television lounge and a large sitting room where guests can enjoy a traditional English breakfast. Clapton-on-the-Hill is a quiet farming hamlet of Cotswold stone houses 2½ miles south of Bourton. It has no eating places, but Julia - a friendly, welcoming host and a great conversationalist - has available current menus of local pubs and restaurants as well as tourist information, maps and books. No smoking.

GREAT RISSINGTON   Map 6 ref M17
7 miles S of Stow off the A424

Great Rissington lies halfway between Bourton and Burford, nestling on a hillside overlooking the valley of the Windrush. On the edge of the tranquil village of Great Rissington, near good walking country and superb views of the surrounding countryside, **Stepping Stone** is a quiet and comfortable establishment providing excellent bed and breakfast and self-catering accommodation. Owners Roger and Sandra Freeman have been here since 1998, and offer a warm and friendly welcome to all their guests. With three rooms in the main house (an ensuite double and twin, and a basic single), this lovely traditional home is decorated and furnished to a high standard of comfort and quality. The dining room looks out onto the paddock, garden and sweeping landscape beyond. The traditional English breakfast is

**Stepping Stone, Rectory Lane, Great Rissington,
Gloucestershire GL54 2LL Tel: 01451 821385
Fax: 01451 821008 email: stepping-stone-b-b@excite.com**

delicious and hearty. In addition there are two self-contained units, with double beds, lounge area, fridge and shower room. ETC and AA 3 Diamonds, Commended. No smoking. Children over 12 only. Pets by prior arrangement. The village pub is just 200 yards away, for afternoon and evening meals and refreshments.

NORTHLEACH   Map 6 ref M17
10 miles SW of Stow on the A429

A traditional market town with some truly magnificent buildings. It was once a major wool-trading centre that rivalled Cirencester in importance and as a consequence possesses what now seems a disproportionately large church. The Church of St Peter and St Paul, known as 'the Cathedral of the Cotswolds', is a fine example of Cotswold Perpendicular, built in the 15th century with pinnacled buttresses, high windows and a massive square castellated tower. Treasures inside include an ornately carved font and some rare monumental brasses of which rubbings can be made (permits obtainable from the Post Office).

An old country prison is now home to the **Cotswold Heritage Centre**, with displays telling the story of social history and rural life in the Cotswolds. **Keith Harding's World of Mechani-**

cal **Music**, located in a 17th century merchant's house in the High Street, is a living museum of antique self-playing musical instruments, music boxes, automata and clocks, all maintained in perfect working order in the world-famous workshops on the premises.

BIBURY   MAP 3 REF M18
15 miles S of Stow on the B4425

William Morris, founder of the Arts & Crafts Movement, described Bibury as 'the most beautiful village in England' and, apart from the tourists, not a lot has changed since he made the claim. The Church of St Mary, with Saxon, Norman and medieval parts, is well worth a visit, but the most visited and most photographed building in Bibury is **Arlington Row**, a superb terrace of medieval stone cottages built as a woolstore in the 14th century and converted three centuries later into weavers' cottages and workshops. Fabric produced here was supplied to nearby **Arlington Mill** for fulling, a process in which the material was cleaned in water and beaten with mechanically-operated hammers. Today the mill, which stands on the site of a corn mill mentioned in the Domesday Book, is a museum with a collection of industrial artefacts, crafts and furniture, including pieces made in the William Morris workshops.

William Morris called Bibury the prettiest village in England. **The Swan Hotel** sits proudly at the heart of the village. Offering true elegance and luxury, there are 21 individually designed ensuite bedrooms, some with four-poster beds. There are twin, double and family rooms, each providing the highest standard of comfort and quality, with handsome furnishings and truly lovely decor.

From the moment guests enter the reception area - complete with grand piano - they are enveloped in an ambience of warmth and luxury. Pre-dinner drinks are served in the elegant and cosy writing room with its open fire. Guests have a choice of formal or informal dining, as meals can be taken in the sumptuous Signet Room restaurant - where modern British cuisine is created using local produce including lamb from the hotel's own farm, trout from the village stream, and

The Swan Hotel, Bibury, Gloucestershire GL7 5NW
Tel: 01285 740695 Fax: 01285 740473
email: swanhotl@swanhotel-cotswolds.co.uk
website: www.swanhotel.co.uk

vegetables and herbs from the walled garden - or in the intimate Jankowski's brasserie or the flower-filled courtyard. In the mornings there's a fine breakfast awaiting guests; packed lunches are also available. Chef Stephen Bulmer spent four years working for Raymond Blanc at the famous Manoir aux Quat' Saisons, and has appeared on BBC2's *Ready Steady Cook*. Culinary delights include grilled Bibury trout, poached corn-fed chicken breast, roast pave of beef or chump of lamb, and baked tomato tart with basil and mozzarella. Room should always be left for one of the delectable puddings. Throughout this superior hotel the staff are friendly, efficient and conscientious, the atmosphere wonderful, and the attention to detail truly impressive. All this and its picturesque setting make a stay at this fine hotel a memorable and very enjoyable experience.

CIRENCESTER
Map 3 ref L18
15 miles SE of Gloucetser off the A417

The "Capital of the Cotswolds", a lively market town with a long and fascinating history. As Corinium Dobonnorum it was the second largest Roman town in Britain (Londinium was the largest). Few signs remain of the Roman occupation, but the award-winning **Corinium Museum** features one of the finest collections of antiquities from Roman Britain, and reconstructions of a Roman kitchen, dining room and garden give a fascinating and instructive insight into life in Cirencester of almost 2,000 years ago.

The main legacy of the town's medieval wealth is the magnificent **Church of St John the Baptist**, perhaps the grandest of all the Cotswold 'wool churches', its 120' tower dominating the town. Its greatest treasure is the Anne Boleyn Cup, a silver and gilt cup made for Henry VIII's second wife in 1535, the year before she was executed for adultery. Her personal insignia - a rose tree and a falcon holding a sceptre - is on the lid of the cup, which was given to the church by Richard Master, physician to Queen Elizabeth I. The church has a unique three-storied porch which was used as the Town Hall until 1897. Cirencester today has a thriving crafts scene, with workshops in the Brewery Arts House, a converted Victorian brewery, and regular markets in the Corn Hall. **Cirencester Open Air Swimming Pool**, next to the park, was built in 1869 and is one of the oldest in the country. Both the main pool and the paddling pool use water from a private well.

FAIRFORD
Map 3 ref M18
9 miles E of Cirencester on the A417

A welcoming little town in the valley of the River Coln, with many fine buildings of the 17th and 18th centuries and an abundance of inns as evidence that this was an important stop on the London-Gloucester coaching run. John and Edmund Tame, wealthy wool merchants, built the superb late-Perpendicular **Church of St Mary**, whose greatest glory is a set of 28 medieval stained glass windows depicting the Christian faith in picture-book style. John Tame's memorial stone, along with those of his wife and son, are set into the floor of the church.

East End House is a large and gracious Georgian family home offering bed and breakfast accommodation. Here in the

Church of St Mary the Blessed Virgin, Fairford

southeast corner of the Cotswolds, this handsome stonebuilt home is a true oasis of peace and relaxation. The accommodation comprises two large guest rooms, each with private bath. They are decorated and furnished to a superb standard of comfort and quality. Guests are welcome to enjoy the gardens and tennis court. The breakfast - full English or Continental - is delicious. There are several good local inns and restaurants for evening meals. Owner Diana Ewart is a welcoming and charming host, who takes great care to ensure that all her guests enjoy a relaxing and memorable break. Adjacent to the house there is also a lovely cottage, built about 1620, which is available for self-catering accom-

East End House, Fairford, Gloucestershire GL7 4AP
Tel: 01285 713715 Fax: 01285 713505
email: eastendho@cs.com www.eastendhouse.co.uk

modation. It sleeps six and is spacious and beautifully decorated and furnished, with farmhouse kitchen and all amenities. Guests here have use of the delightful garden and secluded patio area.

RODMARTON
6 miles W of Cirencester off the A429/A433

MAP 3 REF L18

Rodmarton has fewer than 100 inhabitants. Mentioned in the Domesday book, on the edge of the village is an important Roman and prehistoric site administered by English Heritage - The **Long Barrow** on **Windmill Tump**. A 17th-century house in the centre of this small and pretty Cotswold village midway between Cirencester and Tetbury, **The Old Rectory** offers excellent bed and breakfast accommodation in two large ensuite rooms. One of the oldest buildings in the village, it dates from 1632 and is a Grade II listed building. Occupied by the Rector of Rodmarton until 1967, it has been the home of Mary FitzGerald and her family since the early 1980s. A cosy family atmosphere pervades this charming establishment. One room is a double with king-size bed, the other is a twin-

The Old Rectory, Rodmarton, Cirencester, Gloucestershire
GL7 6PE Tel: 01285 841246 Fax: 01285 841488
Mobile: 07970 434302 email: jfitz@globalnet.co.uk

bedded room. Both are in the older part of the house and have beamed ceilings. The handsome drawing room is available for guests' use, and the dining room is for the exclusive use of guests. Breakfast is hearty and filling, and evening meals - prepared by Cordon Bleu-trained Mary FitzGerald herself - are available by prior arrangement (24 hours' notice). This grand old house is set in handsome gardens with a distinctive ice house - guests are welcome to relax and enjoy all the many fine features of this superior B&B.

HEREFORDSHIRE

SYMONDS YAT   Map 6 ref K17
16 miles W of Gloucester off the A40 and B4164

Travelling upstream, a journey through the southern part of the county starts at the beauty spot of Symonds Yat, an inland resort to which visitors flock to enjoy the views, the walks, the river cruises, the wildlife (peregrine falcons nest at Coldwell Rocks), the history and the adventure. Into the last category fall canoeing - rushing down the Wye gorge south of the village - and rock climbing. Symonds Yat (yat means pass) is divided into east and west by the Wye, with no vehicular bridge at that point. Pedestrians can make use of the punt ferry, pulled across the river by chain, but the journey by car is 4 ½ miles. Walking in the area is an endless delight, and at **The Biblins** a swaying suspension bridge provides vertiginous thrills across the river. Notable landmarks include the **Seven Sisters Rocks**, a collection of oolitic limestone crags; **Merlin's Cave**; King Arthur's Cave, where the bones of mammoths and other prehistoric creatures have been found; **Coldwell Rocks** and **Yat Rock** itself, rising to 500' above sea level at a point where the river performs a long and majestic loop. Also on the Symonds Yat walkabout is a massive boulder measuring 60' by 40', one of the largest in the country.

Surrounded by views of unparalleled beauty, **Forest View Hotel** is a characterful, pristine hotel that makes a perfect base for a holiday or short break. Situated just beneath the famous Symonds Yat Rock, rising 500 feet above sea level, this excellent hotel has beautiful grounds that include lawns, shrubs and ornamental fish ponds, amid a tranquillity enhanced by the gentle sound of the flowing waters of the River Wye. Here in the heart of the Wye Valley, owners Robin and Diane Henderson-Pugh offer a small family-run hotel with great facilities and atmosphere. There are 10 letting rooms and a residents' lounge. Service is of the highest quality, the accommodation truly luxurious. The restaurant offers delicious traditional and more innovative dishes, to

Forest View Hotel, Symonds Yat East, Herefordshire HR9 6JL
Tel: 01600 890210 Mobile: 0831 439786

suit every palate. For those who prefer self-catering accommodation there is a fully equipped kitchen (complete with washing machine, microwave, cooker, tumble dryer, dishwasher, refrigerator and utensils) for guests' use. Many rooms commands panoramic views of the river and valley. In a region richly endowed with natural beauty and historic interest, this hotel stands out for its superb location and wonderful amenities.

Other entertainment in the area is provided by the **Jubilee Maze**, an amazing hedge puzzle devised by brothers Lindsay and Edward Heyes to celebrate Queen Elizabeth's 1977 Jubilee. On the same site is a museum of mazes and a puzzle shop . In the Jubilee Park, at Symonds Yat West, is **The Splendour of the Orient**, with Oriental water gardens, Chinese furniture, gifts from the Orient and a tea room and restaurant. Another major attraction in the Park is a garden centre with an extensive range of plants plus garden furniture and a gift shop. The church in Symonds Yat, built in the 14th century, is dedicated to St Dubricius, a local who converted the area to Christianity and who, according to legend, crowned King Arthur.

The Old Court Hotel at Symonds Yat West is a distinguished and impressive hotel and restaurant. This former manor house dates back to 1570, and maintains its character and many original architectural features, such as the great oak entrance. There are 18 guest bedrooms, all exquisitely furnished and decorated. Several have four-poster beds; most have ensuite facilities.

The Tudor Restaurant offers a range of excellent menus under the supervision of a Cordon Bleu chef. In the characterful Costwold Bar guests can enjoy a selection of real ales, lagers, wines and spirits, as well as a choice of hot and cold bar meals. There are magnificent gardens to the front and rear, with an outdoor swimming pool, fountain and pond surrounded by masses of flowering shrubs, herbaceous borders and more. Elizabeth and John Slade have been here since 1982, and have a wealth of experience in making every guest's stay a special, relaxing and memorable one. Together with their conscientious and able staff they offer excellent service and warm hospitality. No children under 12.

The Old Court Hotel, Symonds Yat West, Ross-on-Wye, Herefordshire HR9 6DA Tel: 01600 890367 Fax: 01600 890964 email: old.court@aol.com

WHITCHURCH

MAP 6 REF J17

16 miles W of Gloucester off the A40

Just north of Symonds Yat, in the shadow of the Rock, lies the village of Whitchurch, where at the **World of Butterflies** visitors can experience the warmth of a tropical hothouse with butterflies flitting freely about their heads. A little further up, and off, the A40, is **Kerne Bridge**, a settlement which grew around a bridge built in 1828, where coracles are still made, and from where the energetic walker can hike into history at the majestic **Goodrich Castle** in a commanding position above the Wye. Built of red sandstone in the 11th century by Godric Mapplestone, the castle is now ruined but still magnificent. It was the last bastion to fall in the Civil War, attacked by 'Roaring Meg', a siege gun cast in Whitchurch which could hurl a 200lb ball and which can now be seen in Hereford. The siege lasted four and a half months and marked the end of the castle's 'working life'. English Heritage maintain the ruins in excellent condition, and the 12th-century keep and elements from the next two centuries are well worth a visit, to walk the ramparts or just to imagine the glorious sight it once presented. **Torwood**, near Whitchurch, is an interesting cottage garden by the village school, specialising in shrubs, conifers and herbaceous plants. Private visits welcome.

GARWAY

MAP 6 REF J17

10 miles W of Gloucester on a minor road

Marvellous views from the wild and remote **Garway Hill** take in the river valley, the Forest of Dean beyond Symonds Yat to the east, and the Black Mountains. The church at Garway was built by the Knights Templar and the influences from the Holy Sepulchre in Jerusalem can clearly be seen. During the purges of Henry VIII's reign, the Abbot of Monmouth was one of many who sought refuge in the church tower. The most unusual building in Garway is undoubtedly the famous **dovecote**, the first of several to be mentioned in this book. A contemporary construction (also probably the work of the good knights) in a farmyard next to the church, the dovecote has precisely 666 pigeon-holes.

ROSS-ON-WYE

MAP 6 REF K17

16 miles W of Gloucester off the A40

The lovely old market town of Ross-on-Wye is signalled from some way out by the towering spire of St Mary's Church, surrounded up on its sandstone cliffs by a cluster of attractive houses. Opposite the church is a row of Tudor almshouses which have an ancient yet ageless look and which show off the beauty of the rosy-red sandstone to great effect. The town was visited by the Black Death in 1637, and over 300 victims are buried in the churchyard. A simple stone cross commemorates these hapless souls, who were interred in the dead of night in an effort to avoid panicking the populace. Notable features in the church include 15th-century stained-glass figures and a tomb chest with effigies of William Rudhall, Attorney General to Henry VIII and founder of the almshouses, and his wife. Pride of place in the market square goes to the 17th-century **Market House**, with an open ground floor and pillars supporting the upper floor, which is a Heritage Centre. Spot the relief of Charles II on the east wall. The **Lost Street Museum** is a time capsule of shops and a pub dating from 1885 to 1935, while the **Button Museum** in Kyrle Street is unique in being the first museum devoted entirely to the humble - and sometimes not so humble - button, of which there are more than 8,000 examples on show spanning working clothes and uniforms, leisure pursuits and high fashion. A fascinating little place and a guaranteed hit with visitors - right on the button, in fact.

Ross is full of interesting buildings, and besides those already noted is **Thrushes Nest**, once the home of Sir Frederick

Market House, Ross-on-Wye

Burrows, a railway porter who rose above his station to become the last Governor of Bengal. Opposite Market House stands the half-timbered house (now shops) of the town's greatest benefactor, John Kyrle. A wealthy barrister who had studied law at the Middle Temple, Kyrle settled in Ross around 1660 and dedicated the rest of his life to philanthropic works: he donated the town's main public garden, **The Prospect**; he repaired St Mary's spire; he provided a constant supply of fresh water; and he paid for food and education for the poor.

The **Ross International Festival** of music, opera, theatre, comedy and film takes place each August and grows in stature year by year. In and around Ross are several examples of modern public art, including leaping salmon metal sculptures (Edde Cross Street) and a mural

celebrating the life of locally-born playwright Dennis Potter. At Ross-on-Wye
Candlemakers in Gloucester Road (Tel:
01989 563697) are a shop and workshop
showing the manufacture of all types of
candles, with evening demonstrations and
group visits by appointment.

Vaga House is a relaxing and peaceful
guest house that attracts walkers, cyclists
and tourists from all over the world. Located in the quiet street running down to
the River Wye, it is owned and run by Andy,
formerly a landscape gardener, and Jenny,
who loves cooking and who will provide
evening meals on request. The house was
built in 1780 by a boatman who plied his
trade carrying cargo between Ross and
Chepstow, and one of the original features
to survive is a window in one of the bedrooms. These are seven in number,
tastefully decorated in modern style, with
everything required for a warm, comfortable stay; two have ensuite facilities. Plans
are afoot for four new ensuite rooms in the
near future. Interesting photos of old Ross
line the stairs, and superb views from the

**Vaga House, Wye Street, Ross-on-Wye,
Herefordshire HR9 7BS Tel: 01989 563024**

outstanding rear garden encompass a horseshoe bend in the river. And the name of this fine
guest house? Vaga was the Roman name for the Wye; meaning "wanderer", it describes the
river's meandering course. Open all year round. Children and pets welcome.

GLEWSTONE   MAP 6 REF J17
3 miles SW of Ross off the A40

Standing in an idyllic rural setting, **Glewstone Court** is an impressive Country House Hotel
and Restaurant with a delightfully informal atmosphere. The largely Georgian house is set
within three acres of carefully tended grounds surrounded by fruit orchards and containing
reputedly the oldest Cedar of Lebanon in the west of England. Inside, the public rooms are
spacious and elegantly appointed with deep sofas, open log fires, antique prints and French

**Glewstone Court Country House Hotel and Restaurant, Glewstone,
nr Ross-on-Wye, Herefordshire HR9 6AW Tel: 01989 770367 Fax: 01989 770282**

windows opening onto the garden. The nine guest bedrooms are furnished to an equally high standard. Comfortable and spacious, they have wonderful views over the surrounding landscape and are equipped with en suite bathrooms and every amenity today's guest has come to expect. Owners Christine and Bill Reeve-Tucker are friendly and experienced hosts who successfully manage to achieve the right balance between high standards and relaxed informality. The Georgian restaurant and Bar Bistro are renowned for imaginative cuisine, and non-residents are made very welcome. Christine is the experienced and well-qualified chef. Her menus offer an extensive range of expertly prepared dishes such as grilled fillets of English Sea Bass, Hereford beef, Guinea fowl and Welsh lamb. Unusual vegetarian dishes are always available as well. Lunch is served in the Bar Bistro, which is also open for supper, where delicious and good-value meals are served. A traditional Sunday luncheon is a weekly event. It is best to book in advance.

WESTON-UNDER-PENYARD

MAP 6 REF K17

2 miles E of Ross on the A40

Leave the A40 at Weston Cross to Bollitree Castle (a folly), then turn left to Rudhall and you'll come upon **Kingstone Cottages**, whose delightful informal gardens contain the National Collection of old pinks and carnations. South of Weston lies **Hope Mansell Valley**, tucked away between the River Wye and the Forest of Dean, and certainly one of the loveliest and most fertile valleys in the region. It is an area of wooded hills and spectacular views, of farms and small settlements, with the tiny village of **Hope Mansell** itself at the far end. The **Forest of Dean**, over the border in Gloucestershire, is a vast and ancient woodland full of beauty and mystery, with signs of Iron Age settlement. Later a royal hunting ground, and the home of charcoal-burners and shepherds, it became the first National Forest Park.

Located amid a 200-acre working mixed farm of sheep, sugar beet and cereals, **The Hill** is a beautiful 300-year-old farmhouse where owners Gill and Richard Evans offer outstanding bed and breakfast accommodation. There are three lovely letting rooms upstairs, all of different sizes and one of which is an ensuite double. They are furnished with antiques in traditional farmhouse style and comfort. Full of character and traditional 17th-century architectural features such as the wide central oak staircase and exposed beams, this wonderful home is pleasant, comfortable and welcoming. Decorated in keeping with its age and history, it is homely and cosy throughout, there are log fires in the guests' lounge and dining

The Hill, Weston under Penyard, Ross-on-Wye, Herefordshire HR9 7PZ Tel/Fax: 01989 750225

room, and all rooms offer excellent views over the countryside and towards the Forest of Dean. There is also a patio area outdoors for guests' use on fine days. Breakfast is a delicious and hearty affair; packed lunches and evening meals are available by prior arrangement.

LEDBURY

MAP 6 REF K17

10 miles NE of Ross on the A449

A classic market town filled with timber-framed black-and-white buildings, mentioned in the Domesday Book as Ledeberge and accorded its market status in the 12th century. The centre of the town is dominated by the **Barrett Browning Institute** of 1892, erected in memory of Elizabeth Barrett Browning, whose family lived at nearby Colwall. Alongside it are the almshouses of St Katherine's Hospital, founded in 1232 for wayfarers and the poor. **Church Lane**, much in

Church Lane, Ledbury

demand for calendars and film location scenes, is a cobbled medieval street where some of the buildings seem almost to meet across the street. Here are the **Heritage Centre** in a timber-framed former grammar school, **Butcher's Row Museum**, and, upstairs in the old council offices, the **Painted Room**, graced with a series of remarkable 16th-century frescoes.

The town's symbol is the **Market House**, dating from about 1650 and attributed to John Abel, the royal carpenter, and another notable landmark is the Norman parish church of St Michael and All Angels, with a soaring spire set on a separate tower, some magnificent medieval brasses and bullet holes in the door - the scars of the Battle of Ledbury. The town's history has in general been fairly placid, but its peace was broken with a vengeance in April 1645, when Royalist troops under Prince Rupert surprised a Roundhead advance from Gloucester. In the fierce fighting that followed there were many deaths, and 400 men were taken prisoner.

Annual events at Ledbury include a poetry festival in July, a street carnival in August and a hop fair in the autumn. Among the famous sons of the town is one of our most distinguished Poets Laureate, John Masefield. William Langland, who wrote *Piers Plowman*, was from nearby Colwall. The town is a great place for walking, and on the fringes nature-lovers will find plenty to delight in **Dog Hill Wood**, **Frith Wood** and **Conigree Wood**, as well as on **Wellington Heath** and along the **Old Railway Line**.

Two and a half miles outside Ledbury on the A438 towards Tewkesbury stands **Eastnor Castle**, overlooking the Malvern Hills. This fairytale castle, surrounded by a deer park, arboretum and lake, has the look of a medieval fortress but was actually built between 1812 and 1824 and is a major example of the great Norman and Gothic architectural revival of the time. The first Earl Somers wanted a magnificent baronial castle, and, with the young and inspired architect Robert Smirke in charge, that's exactly what he got; the combination of inherited wealth and a judicious marriage enabled the Earl to build a family home to impress all his contemporaries. The interior is excitingly beautiful on a massive scale: a vast 60-feet high hall leads into a series of state rooms including a library in Italian Renaissance style containing a treasure house of paintings and tapestries, and a spectacular Gothic drawing room designed by Pugin. The grounds, part of which are a Site of Special Scientific Interest, are home to a wonderful variety of flora and fauna, and throughout the year the castle is the scene of special events.

HOW CAPLE
Map 6 ref K17

5 miles N of Ross on the B4224

The Edwardian gardens at **How Caple Court**, set high above the Wye in park and woodland, are magnificent indeed, with formal terraces, yew hedges, statues, pools, a sunken Florentine water garden and woodland walks. How Caple's medieval **Church of St Andrew and St Mary** contains a priceless 16th-century German diptych depicting, among pther subjects, the martyrdom of St Clare and St Francis, and Mary Magdalene washing the feet of Christ.

BROCKHAMPTON
Map 6 ref K17

6 miles N of Ross off the B4224

The **Church of All Saints** is one of only two thatched churches in the country and dates from 1902, designed by William Lethaby, who had close ties with Westminster Abbey, and built by Alice Foster as a memorial to her parents. The Norfolk thatch is not the only unusual aspect here, as the church also boasts stained glass made in the Christopher Whall studios and tapestries from the William Morris workshop from Burne-Jones designs. Continuing up the B4224 in the direction of Hereford, the visitor will come upon the village of **Fownhope**, where every year on Oak Apple Day in May or June the Green Man Inn celebrates the restoration of Charles ll with the Heart of Oak Club Walk. The inn's most famous landlord was Tom Spring, a champion bare-knuckle prize fighter who died in 1851. Fownhope church, 'The Little Cathedral', has a special treasure in the form of a tympanum of the Virgin and Child.

This is, like so much of the county, great walking country, with the **Marcle Ridge**, the 500' **Woolhope Dome** and the Forestry Commission's **Haugh Wood** among the attractions and challenges. The last is best approached from **Mordiford**, once a centre of the mining industry and now free from the baleful man-eating Mordiford Dragon. The story goes that the dragon was found by a local girl while it was still small. She nurtured it lovingly, and although it was at first content to feed on milk, and later chickens and the odd duck, it eventually developed a taste for cows and finally people. The beast terrorised the locals, and indeed one of the paths leading from the woods is still known as Serpents Lane. It was here that he would slink along the river to drink, and it is said that no grass ever grows there. No one was brave enough to face the beast until a man called Garson, who happened to be awaiting execution, decided that he had nothing to lose. He hid in a barrel by the river, and when the creature appeared he shot it through the heart. That was the end of the dragon, and also of poor Garson, who was killed in the fiery breath of the dragon's death throes. Mordiford stands on the River Lugg, just above the point where it joins the Wye, and the River Frome joins the Lugg a little way above the village. **Mordiford Bridge**, with its elegant span of nine arches, was once the source of regular revenue for the kings of this land: apparently every time the king crossed the bridge the locals lords had to provide him with a pair of silver spurs as a levy on the manor.

HEREFORD
Map 6 ref J17

12 miles NW of Ross off the A49

The county town-to-be was founded as a settlement near the unstable Welsh Marches after the Saxons had crossed the Severn in the 7th century. A royal demesne in the 11th century, it had a provincial mint, and was an important centre of the wool trade in the Middle Ages. Fragments of Saxon and medieval walls can still be seen, but the city's crowning glory is the magnificent *'Cathedral of the Marches'*. Largely Norman, it also has examples of Gothic, Early English, Decorated, Perpendicular and Modern architecture. The Cathedral demands an extended visit, as it contains, in the impressive New Library building, two of the country's most important historical treasures. *Mappa Mundi* is the renowned medieval world map, the work of Richard of Haldingham. Drawn on vellum, it has Jerusalem as its centre and East at the top, indicating that direction as the source of all things good and religiously significant. Richard was Treasurer of Lincoln Cathedral, which might explain why Lincoln appears rather more prominently on the map than Hereford. The **Chained Library**, the finest in the land, houses 1500 rare books, including over 200 medieval manuscripts, all chained to their original 17th-century book presses. The Cathedral has many other treasures, including the shrine of St Thomas of Hereford in stone and marble, the Norman font, the Bishop's Throne and the John Piper tapestries. There's also a brass-rubbing centre.

Hereford Cathedral

Hereford is full of fascinating buildings and museums which visitors should try to include in their tour. **Hereford Museum and Art Gallery** has a changing art gallery programme and hands-on exhibitions. The **Old Hall Museum**, right in the centre of High Town, brings alive the 17th century in a three-storey black-and-white house filled with fascinating exhibits. **Churchill House Museum** , whose grounds include a fragrant garden, displays furniture, costumes and paintings from the 18th and 19th centuries; among its rooms are a costume exhibition gallery and Victorian nursery, parlour, kitchen and butler's pantry. The **Hatton Gallery** shows the work of local artist Brian Hatton. **St John Medieval Museum** at Coningsby is a 13th-century building in an ancient quadrangle of almshouses. Displays include costume models of Nell Gwynne, a famous daughter of Hereford, and the history of the Ancient Order of St John and its wars during the Crusades. Hereford's restored pumping station is home to the **Waterworks Museum** , where Victorian technology is alive and well in the shape of a collection of pumps (some of which can be operated by visitors), a Lancashire Boiler and Britain's largest triple expansion engine. The **Regimental Museum** houses an important collection of uniforms, colours, medals, equipment, documents and photographs - and the flag and pennant of Admiral Doenitz.

Hereford and cider are old friends, and the **Cider Museum** tells the intersting story of cider production down the years. One of the galleries houses the King Offa distillery, the first cider brandy distillery to be granted a licence for over 200 years. Also on the outskirts of the city are the Cider Mills of HP Bulmer, the world's leading cider producer. Look, learn and taste on one of the organised tours.

The original Saxon part of the city includes historic Church Street, full of 17th-century listed buildings (mostly modernised in the 19th century). Church Street and Capuchin Yard - the name derives from the hood worn by the Franciscan friars who built a chapel nearby - are renowned for their small specialist shops and craft workshops. Hereford stages important musical events throughout the year, and every third year hosts the **Three Choirs Festival**, Europe's oldest music festival. The next one will take place in the Cathedral in August 2000.

ABBEY DORE
MAP 6 REF J17
12 miles SW of Hereford on the B4347

A Cistercian **Abbey** was founded here in the 12th century and the building, which was substantially restored by John Abel in the 17th century, is still in use as a parish church. The garden at **Abbey Dore Court**, where the River Dore flows through the grounds, is home to many unusual shrubs and perennials, with specialist collections of euphorbias, hellebores and peonies. There's also a small nursery, a gift shop and a restaurant.

At nearby **Bacton**, a mile along the same B4347, is **Pentwyn Cottage Garden** , where visitors can walk round the peaceful garden before enjoying a cream tea. From the remote, lonely roads that lead west towards Offa's Dyke and the boundary with Wales, motorists should leave their cars, stretch their legs and drink in the wonderful scenery. The villages of **Longtown** and **Clodock** lie at the foot of the **Olchon Valley**, while further north are the **Olchon Waterfall**, **Black Hill**, the rocky ridge of the **Cat's Back** and the ruins of **Craswall Priory**, which was founded in the 13th century by the rare Grandmontine order and abandoned 200 years later.

HAY-ON-WYE
18 miles W of Hereford on the B4348

MAP 6 REF I16

And so to the border town of Hay-on-Wye, where bookworms will wriggle with delight as they browse through its 38 secondhand bookshops. Richard Booth, known as the King of Wye, opened the first bookshop here 40 years ago, and is a leading player in the annual **Hay Book Festival**. The famous diarist Francis Kilvert was a local man, and his Diary is just one of millions of books on for sale. But books are not the only attraction: Hay also has a large number of antique shops, and as we have seen more or less throughout this opening chapter, the River Wye in never far away, with its shifting moods and ever-changing scenery.

BROMYARD
13 miles NE of Hereford on the A44

MAP 6 REF K16

A super little market town on the River Frome, with hills and good walking all around. In the town itself the **Teddy Bear Museum** , housed in an old bakery, is a magical little world of bears, dolls and Disney-related toys. It also has a bear hospital. **Bromyard Heritage Centre** tells the stories of the local hop-growing industry, the railway age and life in Bromyard through the centuries. Find time to look at the 12th-century St Peter's Church with its historic Walker organ. Late June and early July see Bromyard's **Great Hereford Show and Steam Rally**, an event which has been built up to major proportions over the years. Later on, in early September, **Bromyard's Folk Festival** brings in the crowds.

HOPE UNDER DINMORE
8 miles N of Hereford on the A49

MAP 6 REF J16

Queen's Wood Country Park is a popular place for walking and enjoying the panoramic views, and the most visited spot of all is the arboretum with its wonderful variety of specimen trees. Adjoining the park is **Dinmore Manor and Gardens**, where the Knights Hospitallers had their local headquarters. The gardens are sheltered, but as they rise some 550' above sea level, they afford marvellous views across to the Malvern Hills. The gardens are a sheer delight, and among the many attractions are a 12th-century chapel near the rock garden and pools, a cloister with a roof walk, wonderful stained glass, a yew tree believed to be 1,200 years old, medieval sundials and a grotto. Many varieties of plants, shrubs, alpines and herbs are available for sale in the Plant Centre.

LEOMINSTER
13 miles N of Hereford on the A49

MAP 6 REF K17

The hub of the farming community and the largest town in this part of the county, made wealthy in the Middle Ages through wool, and still prospering today. Leominster (pronounced Lemster) is well known as one of the most important antiques centres in the region. Some have linked the unusual name with Richard the Lionheart, but there was in fact an earlier king who earned the title. In the 7th century, Merewald, King of Mercia, was renowned for his bravery and ferocity and earned the nickname of 'the Lion'. He is said to have a dream concerning a message from a Christian missionary, while at the same time a religious hermit had a vision of a lion coming to him and eating from his hand. They later met up at what was to be Leominster almost by accident, and when the King heard of the hermit's strangely coincidental dream, he was persuaded to convert to Christianity. Later, the King requested that a convent and church be built in the town; a stone lintel on the west door of the church depicts the chance meeting of King and hermit. Other, more likely explanations of the name revolve around Welsh and medieval Latin words for 'stream' and 'marsh'.

The Priory **Church of St Peter and St Paul**, originally King Merewald's convent, became a monastery in the 11th century, and the three naves, built in the 12th, 13th and 14th centuries, attest to its importance. A curio here is a ducking stool which, in 1809, was the last to be used in England. A short walk away, in Priory Park, is **Grange Court**, a fine timbered building which for many years stood in the market place. Built in 1633, it is the work of John Abel, and shows typical Abel flamboyance in its elaborate carvings. Other buildings to be visited in Leominster are the **Leominster Folk Museum**, the **Lion Gallery**, featuring the best of local arts and crafts, and the **Forbury**, a 13th-century chapel dedicated to Thomas à Becket.

ASHTON   MAP 6 REF K17

3 miles N of Leominster on the A49

Three miles north of Leominster on the road to Ludlow stands the National Trust's **Berrington Hall**, an elegant 18th-century mansion designed by Henry Holland (later architect to the Prince Regent) in parkland laid out by his father-in-law Capability Brown. Features of the interior include a spectacular staircase hall, gilt tracery, fine furniture and paintings, a nursery, Victorian laundry and tiled Georgian dairy. Most notable of all are perhaps the beautifully decorated ceilings: in the drawing room, the central medallion of Jupiter, Cupid and Venus is a composite scene taken from *The Council* and *The Banquet of the Gods* by Penni and del Colle in the Villa Farnesina in Rome. In the grounds are a walled garden with a collection of old-fashioned local apple trees, a woodland walk and a living willow tunnel in the children's play area.

YARPOLE   MAP 6 REF K17

4 miles N of Leominster off the B4361

In this delightful village with its jumble of cottages and their colourful gardens stands the Church of St Leonard, which has a detached bell tower, a wooden structure with a stone outer wall. At neighbouring **Eye** are **Eye Manor** and the **Church of St Peter and St Paul**, where Thomas Harley, a Lord Mayor of London, is buried. An unusual feature of this church is the pulpit with carvings of Red Indians.

Near Yarpole, reached from the B4362 between Bircher and Mortimer's Cross, stands **Croft Castle**, an atmospheric property in the care of the National Trust. Behind a defensive exterior that tells of the troubled times of Marcher territory, the state rooms are elegant and comfortable, with rare furniture, fine plasterwork and portraits of the Croft family, who have occupied the place with only one break since it was built in the 14th century. In the park are ancient oaks and an avenue of 350-year-old Spanish chestnut trees. Also looked after by the National Trust, and just a short walk away, is **Croft Ambrey**, an Iron Age fort which affords stunning views.

SHOBDON   MAP 6 REF K17

8 miles W of Leominster on the B4362

The **Church of St John the Evangelist**, which stands on the site of a 12th-century priory, is one of the most remarkable in the county. Behind a fairly unremarkable facade, the interior is stunning. The overall effect is of being in a giant wedding cake, with white and pale blue icing everywhere, and lovely stained glass adding to the dazzling scene. Just north of here are the 'Shobdon Arches', a collection of Norman sculptures which have sadly been greatly damaged by centuries of exposure to the elements, but which still demonstrate the high skills of the sculptors of the 12th century.

WEOBLEY
MAP 6 REF J16
9 miles SW of Leominster on the B4230

The steeple of the parish church of St Peter and St Paul is the second highest in the county, a reminder that this prettiest of places (call it Webbly) was once a thriving market town. One of

its more unusual sources of wealth was a successful glove-making industry which flourished in the early 19th century when the Napoleonic Wars cut off the traditional French source of gloves. At certain times in its history Weobley returned two Members of Parliament, but there have been none since 1832. One of the effigies in the church is of Colonel John Birch, who was rewarded for his successes with Cromwell's army with the Governorship of Hereford and who later became a keen Royalist and Weobley's MP. Little but the earthworks remain of Weobley Castle, which was built before the Norman Conquest and was captured by King Stephen in 1138. One of

Weobley

Weobley's many interesting buildings is called **The Throne**, but it was called The Unicorn when King Charles I took refuge after the Battle of Naseby in 1645.

KINGTON
MAP 6 REF I16
12 miles W of Leominster on the A44

The road up to Kington passes many places of interest, and for two in particular a short pause will be well worth while. The National Trust's **Cwmmau Farmhouse**, which lies 4 miles south of Kington between the A4111 and A438 at **Brilley**, is an imposing timber-framed and stone-tiled farmhouse dating from the early 17th century. Viewing is by guided tour only.

Half a mile off the A44 on the Welsh side of Kington is the impressive **Hergest Ridge**, rising to around 1,400', and, on its southern edge, **Hergest Court**, once owned by the Vaughan family, whom we met at Kinnersley. Two members of the family who gained particular notoriety were Thomas 'Black' Vaughan and his wife, who was known as 'Gethen the Terrible'. She is said to have taken revenge on a man who killed her brother by taking part in an archery competition disguised as a man. When her turn came to compete, she shot him dead at point blank range and escaped in the ensuing melee. Thomas died at the Battle of Banbury in 1469, but, being a true Vaughan, that was not ther last of him. He is said to have haunted the church in the guise of a bull, and even managed to turn himself into a horsefly to annoy the local horses. He was back in taurine form when he was finally overcome by a band of clerics. One of the band managed to shrink him and cram him into a snuff box, which was quickly consigned to the waters of Hergest Pool. Later owners of the estate found and unwittingly opened the box, letting Black Vaughan loose once more. The next band of intrepid clerics confined the spirit under an oak tree, but he is currently at large again - though not sighted for many years. These feisty Vaughans are buried in the Vaughan Chapel in Kington parish church. Kington itself lies on the England/Wales border and, like other towns in the area known as the Marches, had for many years to look closely to the west, whence the wild Welsh would attack. Kington's castle was destroyed many centuries ago, but outside the town, on **Wapley Hill**, are earthworks of an ancient hill fort which could be the site of King Caractacus' last stand.

Most notable by far of all the defences in the region is **Offa's Dyke**, the imposing ditch that extends for almost 180 miles along the border, from the Severn Estuary at Sedbury Cliffs near Chepstow, across the Black Mountain ridge, through the Wye Valley and north to Prestatyn on the North Wales coast. Offa was a Mercian king of great influence, with strong diplomatic links with the Popes and Charlemagne, who ruled the land south of the Humber from 757 to 796. Remnants of wooden stakes unearthed down the years suggest that the Dyke had a definite defensive role, rather than acting merely as a psychological barrier. It was a truly massive construction, in places almost 60' wide, and although nowadays it disappears in places, much of it can still be walked, particularly in the Wye Valley. A stretch north of Kington is especially well preserved and provides excellent, invigorating walking for the energetic. The walk crosses, at **Bradnor Hill**, the highest golf course, over 1200' above sea level. Other major traces of the Dyke remain, notably between Chepstow and Monmouth and by Oswestry, and at many points Offa's Dyke Path, opened by the Countryside Commission in 1971, diverts from the actual Dyke into magnificent scenery.

WORCESTERSHIRE

GREAT MALVERN

Map 6 ref K16

18 miles NE of Hereford on the A449

Beneath the northeastern slopes of the **Malvern Hills**, Great Malvern is known for its porcelain, its annual music and drama festivals, Malvern water and Morgan cars. Though invaded by tourists for much of the year, Great Malvern has retained its dignity and elegance, with open spaces, leafy avenues and handsome houses. Close to the start of the Malvern walking trail, on a path leading up from the town, is a Regency cottage housing one source of the water – **St Anne's Well** – where one can sample the water and drink in the views. Great Malvern was for many centuries a quiet, little-known place with a priory at its heart, and even when the curative properties of its spring waters were discovered, it took a long time for it to become a fashionable spa resort. Hotels, baths and a pump room were built in the early 19th century, and the arrival of the railway provided easy access from the middle of the century. The station is one of many charming Victorian buildings, and with its cast-iron pillars, stone ornaments and beautifully painted floral designs, is a tourist attraction in its own right.

The Priory **Church of St Mary and St Michael** is a dominant feature in the centre of the town. Its windows, the west a gift from Richard III, the east from Henry VII, contain a wonderful collection of 15th-century stained glass, and another unique feature is a collection of more than 1,200 wall tiles on the chancel screens. These also date from the 15th century. Among many interesting graves in the cemetery is that of Jenny Lind, 'The Swedish Nightingale', who was born in Stockholm in 1820 and died at Wynd's Point, Malvern which she used as a summer retreat, in 1887. In the churchyard at West Malvern Peter Mark Roget (the Thesaurus man) is buried (interred, entombed, coffined, laid to rest, consigned to earth). The 14th century **Abbey Gateway**, whose huge wooden gateposts can be seen in the archway, houses the **Malvern Museum**. Open Easter to October, it displays include the geology of the Malvern Hills, the history of Malvern spring water and the development of Morgan cars. In Tanhouse Lane stands the factory of Boehm of Malvern, where the remarkable American Edward Marshall Boehm (call it 'Beam') founded the centre which has become known worldwide for the quality of its porcelain. Great Malvern has a distinguished tradition of arts and culture, much of it the legacy of Sir Edward Elgar and George Bernard Shaw, and the **Victorian Winter Gardens** are an exciting setting for performances of music and drama. Malvern is the home of the excellent English Symphony Orchestra, formed in 1980 by William Boughton.

Great Malvern is the largest of six settlements that make up the Malverns: to the south are Malvern Wells and Little Malvern, to the north North Malvern and to the northeast Malvern Link. A permanent site on low ground below Great Malvern is the venue for the **Three Counties Show**, one of England's premier agricultural shows.

LITTLE MALVERN   MAP 6 REF K16
4 miles S of Great Malvern on the A449

At Little Malvern stands the **Church of St Wulstan**, where a simple headstone marks the grave of Sir Edward Elgar and his wife Caroline. Their daughter is buried next to them. **Little Malvern Court**, off the A4104, enjoys a glorious setting on the lower slopes of the Malvern Hills. It stands next to **Little Malvern Priory**, whose hall, the only part that survived the Dissolution, is now incorporated into the Court. Of the priory church, only the chancel tower and south transept remain. The Court was once a Catholic safe house, with a chapel reached by a secret staircase. The Court and gardens are open Wednesday and Thursday afternoons from mid-April to mid-July. Just to the north at **Malvern Wells**, where the first medicinal wells were discovered, stands St Peter's Church, dating from 1836 and notable for some original stained glass and a William Morris window of 1885.

EARLS CROOME   MAP 6 REF L16
6 miles SE of Great Malvern on the A4104

There are several attractions in the area of Earls Croome. **Croome Landscape Park**, under the care of the National Trust, was Capability Brown's first complete landscape, which made his reputation and set a pattern for parkland design that lasted half a century. The buildings have equally distinguished pedigrees, with Robert Adam and James Wyatt as architects. The **Hill Croome Dovecote** is a very rare square building next to the church in Hill Croome. **Dunstall Castle** folly at **Dunstall Common** is a folly in the style of a Norman castle, put up in the 18th century and comprising two round towers and one square, connected by arches.

Originally tied cottages on the Earls Croome estate, **The Jockey Inn** is a neat, whitewashed building on the A4101 a mile and a half out of Upton-upon-Severn. Self-catering accommodation for up to four guests is available, but this is first and foremost an eating pub, and landlord Peter Lee is a trained chef. The setting is civilised and comfortable - original beams, subdued lighting, pictures, brass ornaments - and very appropriate for the high-quality cuisine on offer. The menu takes its inspiration from near and far, with such dishes

The Jockey Inn, Baughton, Earls Croome, nr Upton-upon-Severn, Worcestershire SR8 9DQ Tel: 01684 592153

as breast of chicken in pepper, almond and cardamon cream sauce, steak in ale pie, lamb cutlets in gooseberry and mint glaze, and mango, banana and Stilton enchilada. The accompanying selection of fresh vegetables changes daily - another indication of how seriously food is taken at this excellent establishment. To round things off in style are some fairly wicked puddings such as treacle and orange tart drizzled with Cointreau.

PERSHORE
9 miles E of Great Malvern on the A4104

MAP 6 REF L16

Pershore Abbey

A gem of a market town, with fine Georgian architecture and an attractive setting on the banks of the Avon. Its crowning glory is the **Abbey**, combining outstanding examples of Norman and Early English architecture. The Abbey was founded by King Oswald in 689, and in 972 King Edgar granted a charter to the Benedictine monks. Only the choir remains of the original church, but it is still a considerable architectural treasure. The south transept is the oldest part, while among the most impressive features is some superb vaulting in the chancel roof. **Pershore Bridge**, a favourite picnic spot, still bears the marks of damage done during the Civil War. A mile east of town on the A44 is Pershore College of Architecture. Originally part of the Wyke Estate, the college has been developed round an early 19th-century mansion and is the Royal Horticultural Society's Centre for the West Midlands. The ground contains many unusual trees and shrubs, and in the glasshouses are tropical, temperate and cool decorative plants.

EVESHAM
15 miles E of Great Malvern on the A44

MAP 6 REF L16

A bustling market town at the centre of the Vale of Evesham, an area long known as the Garden of England, with a prolific harvest of soft fruits, apples, plums and salad vegetables. **The Blossom Trail**, which starts in the town, is a popular outing when the fruit trees burst into blossom. The Trail follows a signposted route from the High Street to Greenhill, where the Battle of Evesham took place. The River Avon performs a loop round the town, and the Abbey park is a good place for a riverside stroll; it is also the start point for boat trips. The magnificent bell tower (110') is the only major building remaining of the **Abbey**, which was built around 700 by Egwin, Bishop of Worcester, and was one of the largest and grandest in the whole country. It was knocked down by Henry Vlll's men at the time of the Dissolution of the Monasteries. The story of the town is told in vivid detail at the **Almonry Heritage Centre**, which was formerly the home of the Abbey Almoner and was built around 1400. It now houses a unique collection of artifacts as well as exhibitions showing the history of the Abbey, and the defeat of Simon de Montfort at the Battle of Evesham in 1265 (the Leicester Tower stands on the site of the Battle). The Almonry also houses Evesham's Tourist Information Centre.

There are many other interesting buildings in Evesham, including the neighbouring churches of All Saints and St Lawrence. The former is entered through a porch built by Abbot Lichfield in the 16th century, and the Lichfield Chapel, with a lovely fan-vaulted ceiling, contains his tomb. Much of the building, as well as the stone pulpit, dates from Victorian times, when major restoration work was carried out. The latter, declared redundant in 1978, was also the subject of extensive restoration, in the 1830s and again in the 1990s. In the market place is a grand old timbered building called the **Round House** – a curious name, because it is actually square.

BROADWAY
Map 6 ref L17

6 miles S of Evesham on the A44

One of the most beautiful villages in England, this is the quintessential Cotswold village, its eponymous broad main street lined with houses and cottages built of golden Cotswold stone. Broadway was settled as far back as 1900BC, and later the Romans came and occupied the hill above the village. Broadway was probably re-established after the Battle of Dyrham in 557AD by conquering Saxons advancing towards Worcester. The parish records tell of hospitality being offered at a Broadway hostelry as early as 1532. This the time of the advent of the horse-drawn carriage, when Broadway became an important staging post. A journey from London to Worcester took about 17 hours including stops and a change of horse, and at one time Broadway boasted an incredible 33 public houses. One of the must-sees on any trip to Broadway is the enchanting **Teddy Bear Museum**, housed in a picturesque 18th-century shop in the High Street. The atmosphere within is of an Edwardian carnival, with music playing, rides revolving and many other surprises. The hall of fame tells of celebrity bears, including Paddington, Pooh and the three who came upon Goldilocks. Bears of all ages and sizes are kept in stock, and some bears and dolls are made on the premises. Old bears and dolls are lovingly restored at – wait for it – St Beartholomew's Hospital.

In the centre of Broadway is a wide village green from where the main street continues gently upwards for nearly a mile, with the surrounding hills always in view. The gradient increases at Fish Hill then rises to more than 1,000 feet above sea level at **Broadway Beacon**. At the top of the Beacon is **Broadway Tower**, standing in a delightful country park with something to interest all ages, from animal enclosures and adventure playground to nature walks and barbecue sites. The tower was built as a folly by the 6th Earl of Coventry at the end of the 18th century as part of the great movement of the time towards picturesque and romantic landscapes. James Wyatt designed the tower, which now contains various displays and exhibitions.

WORCESTER
Map 6 ref L16

8 miles NE of Great Malvern on the A38

This chapter takes Worcester as its base. Set on either side of the curving River Severn, Worcester is a bustling county capital and cathedral city. Its architecture spans many centuries and there are some marvellous examples from all of them. In the heart of England, this is an area characterised by red earth, apple orchards, hopyards, quiet inns, stone farmhouses and black-and-white timbered dwellings. As a visible legacy of the ancient forest that once surrounded Worcester, the half-timbered buildings lend colour and variety to the villages around this historic city.

The **Cathedral**, with its 200' tower, stands majestically beside the Severn. The 11th-century crypt is a classic example of Norman architecture and was built by St Wulstan, who is remembered in a stone carving. He was the only English bishop not to be replaced by a Norman after the Conquest. To many of the local people the task of building the Cathedral must have seemed endless; the central tower collapsed in 1175 and a fire destroyed much of the building in 1203. The Cathedral had only just been re-dedicated after these disasters when Bishop Blois began pulling it down again, only to rebuild it in the fashionable Gothic style. The nave was rebuilt in the 14th century under the auspices of Bishop Cobham, but the south side was not completed until much later, and in a far less elaborate style. King John requested that he be buried in the choir, and his tomb stands near the high altar. It is a masterpiece of medieval sculpture, showing the King flanked by the Bishops Oswald and Wulstan. Prince Arthur, elder brother of Henry VIII, is also entombed near the high altar.

There's a great deal more to see than the Cathedral, of course, and in the **City Museum and Art Gallery** are contemporary art and archaeological displays, a 19th-century chemist's shop and the military collections of the Worcestershire Regiment and the Worcestershire Yeomanry Cavalry. Friar Street has many lovely old timber houses. **Greyfriars**, in the care of the National Trust, is a medieval house that has managed to survive right in the heart of the city, and passing through its archway visitors will come across a pretty walled garden. The imposing Guildhall in the High Street is a marvelous example of Queen Anne architecture, designed by a local man, Thomas White. **The Commandery Civil War Centre** is a stunning complex of buildings behind a small timber-framed entrance. At the Battle of Worcester in 1651 the Commandery was used as the Royalist headquarters, and today period rooms offer a fascinating glimpse of the architecture and style of Tudor and Stuart times while acting as the country's only museum devoted to the story of the Civil War. The story takes in the trial of Charles I, visits a Royalist encampment on the eve of the battle and enacts the last battle of the war narrated by Charles II and Oliver Cromwell.

The **Royal Worcester Porcelain** Visitor Centre is an absolute must on any sightseer's list. Royal Worcester is Britain's oldest continuous producer of porcelain and is world famous for its exquisite bone china. The factory was founded in 1751 by Dr John Wall with the intention of creating "a ware of a form so precise as to be easily distinguished from other English porcelain". The **Museum of Local Life** reflects the history of Worcester and its people, with displays covering the past 700 years. There's a Victorian kitchen scene, a turn-of-the-century schoolroom and a variety of changing exhibitions throughout the year. The site is a 16th-century timber-framed building in wonderful Friar Street.

INKBERROW
Map 6 ref L16
8 miles E of Worcester off the A42

A very pleasant and pretty spot to pause awhile, with the Church of St Peter (note the alabaster of John Savage, a High Sheriff of Worcester who died in 1631), the inn and other buildings round the village green, some in red brick, others black and white half-timbered. The **Old Bull Inn** has two claims to fame, one that William Shakespeare stayed there in 1582, the other that it is the original of The Bull at Ambridge, home of The Archers. Photographs of the cast adorn the walls, and the inn has become a place of pilgrimage for fans of the programme. One mile south of Inkberrow is the village of **Abbots Morton**, whose dwellings are mainly 17th-century yeomen's houses. The village was once the site of the Abbot of Evesham's summer residence, but only some mounds and fishponds now remain.

LOWER BROADHEATH
Map 6 ref K16
3 miles W of Worcester off the A44

The **Elgar Birthplace Museum** is a redbrick cottage that is crammed with items from the great composer's life. He was born here in 1857 and, despite long periods spent elsewhere, Broadheath remained his spiritual home. The violin was his first instrument, though he eventually succeeded his father as organist at St George's Church in Worcester. He played at the Three Choirs Festival and began conducting locally. He married in 1889 and was soon devoting almost all his time to composing, making his name with *The Enigma Variations* (1899) and *Dream of Gerontius* (1900). He was knighted in 1904 and when in 1931 he was made a baronet by King George V he took the title 1st Baronet of Broadheath. Various Elgar Trails have been established, the one in Worcester city taking in the statue and the *Dream of Gerontius* window in the Cathedral.

LEIGH
Map 6 ref K16
5 miles W of Worcester off the A4103

The **Church of St Eadburga** is very fine indeed, with some imposing monuments and a marvellous 15th-century rood screen. A curious legend attaches to the church. A man called Edmund. Colles is said to have robbed one of his colleagues who was returning from Worcester and known to be carrying a full purse. It was a dark, gloomy night, and as Colles reached out to grab the man's horse, holding on to the bridle, the other struck at him with a sword. When he visited Edmund the next day, the appalling wound testified to the man's guilt; although forgiven by his intended victim, Colles died shortly after and his ghost once haunted the area. A phantom coach pulled by four fire-breathing steeds would appear and race down the hill to the church by Leigh Court, where they would leap over the tithe barn and disappear beneath the waters of the River Teme. A midnight service attended by 12 clergymen eventually laid the ghost to rest. Leaping over the **tithe barn** was no mean feat (though easier of course if you're a ghost), as the 14th-century barn is truly massive, with great cruck beams and porched wagon doors. Standing in the grounds of Leigh Court, a long gabled mansion, the barn is open for visits on summer wekends.

Leigh Brook is a tributary of the Teme and wends its way through a spectacular valley cared for by Worcestershire Nature Conservation Trust. The countryside here is lovely, and footpaths make the going easier. Up on Old Storridge Common, birch, ash, oak and bracken have taken a firm hold, and there is a weird, rather unearthly feel about the place. Nearby, the hamlet of **Birch Wood** is where Elgar composed his *Dream of Gerontius*.

ALFRICK   Map 6 ref K16
7 miles W of Worcester off the A44

Charles Dodgson (Lewis Carroll) once preached at the village Church of St Mary Magdalene, which enjoys a delightful setting above the village green. In the vicinity are two major attractions for nature-lovers. A little way to the northwest is **Ravenshill Woodland Nature Reserve** with waymarked trails through woodland that is home to many breeding birds, while a mile south of Alfrick is the **Knapp and Papermill Nature Reserve**, with 25 hectares of woodland and meadows rich in flora and fauna.

DROITWICH   Map 6 ref L16
9 miles N of Worcester on the A38

'Salinae', the place of salt, in Roman times. Salt deposits, a legacy from the time when this area was on the seabed, were mined here for 2,000 years until the end of the 19th century. The natural Droitwich brine contains about 2 1/2 pounds of salt per gallon - ten times as much as sea water - and is often likened to the waters of the Dead Sea. The brine is pumped up from an underground lake which lies 200' below the town. Visitors do not drink the waters at Droitwich as they do at most other spas, but enjoy the therapeutic properties floating in the warm brine. The first brine baths were built in the 1830s and were soon renowned for bringing relief to many and effecting seemingly miraculous cures. By 1876, Droitwich had developed as a fashionable spa, mainly through the efforts of John Corbett, known as the 'Salt King'.

Salwarpe on the southwest fringes of Droitwich, is truly a hidden hamlet, approached by a stone bridge over James Brindley's **Droitwich Canal**. Opened in 1771, the canal linked the town to the River Severn at Hawford. The Church of St Michael, by the edge of the canal, has several monuments to the Talbot family, who owned nearby Salwarpe Court. **Salwarpe Valley Nature Reserve** is one of very few inland sites with salt water, making it ideal for a variety of saltmarsh plants and very well worth a visit.

BROMSGROVE   Map 6 ref L15
5 miles NE of Droitwich off the A38

A visit to the **Avoncraft Museum of Historic Buildings,** just south of Bromsgrove, is a walk through seven centuries of English history, with each building providing a snapshot of life in its particular period. The first building, a timber-framed merchant's house from Bromsgrove, was brought to the site in 1967, since when over 20 more have been installed. In addition to the buildings themselves, the Museum has regular demonstrations of such crafts as wood-turning, windmilling, racksawing, brick-making, chain-making and nail-making. There's also a shop, refreshment area, picnic site, a children's area, horse-drawn wagon rides and farm animals wandering around freely. One of the most treasured exhibits is the original 14th-century beamed roof of Guesten Hall from Worcester Cathedral, now covering a modern brick building. In an area behind the shop is another unique collection, the **BT National Telephone Kiosk Collection. Bromsgrove Museum**, near the town centre, has displays of local crafts and industry, including the Bromsgrove Guild, an organisation of craftsmen founded in 1894. The Guild of highly skilled craftsmen had its finest hour when commissioned to design and make the gates and railings of Buckingham Palace. Another popular exhibit is a street scene of Victorian shops.

Besides the museums, there is plenty to see, including some very handsome timber-framed buildings in the High Street, where stands a statue of AE Housman, the town's most famous son. **Alfred Edward Housman** was born one of seven children at Fockbury, Bromsgrove, in 1859, and spent his schooldays in the town. After a spell at Oxford University and some time teaching at his old school, he entered the Civil Service in London, where he found time to resume his academic studies. He was appointed Professor of Latin at University College, London, in 1892 and soon afterwards he published his first and best-known collection of poems - *A Shropshire Lad*. His total output was not large, but it includes some of the best-loved poems in the English language. He died in 1936 and is buried in the churchyard of St Lawrence in Ludlow. The forming in 1972 of a Housman Society brought his name to the forefront of public attention and in the region of Bromsgrove walking and driving trails take in the properties and places associated with him.

REDDITCH

Map 6 ref L15

6 miles SE of Bromsgrove on the A448

A 'New Town' from the 60s, but there is plenty of history here, as well as some great walking. The **Arrow Valley Country Park**, a few minutes walk from the town centre, comprises a vast expanse of parkland with nature trails, picnic areas and lovely walks. Sailing, canoeing, windsurfing and fishing are popular pastimes on the lake. Housed in historic buildings in the beautiful Arrow Valley, **Forge Mill Needle Museum & Bordesley Abbey Visitor Centre** offers a unique glimpse into a past way of life.

HAGLEY

Map 6 ref L15

8 miles N of Bromsgrove off the A491

George, 1st Lord Lyttleton, commissioned, in 1756, the creation of what was to be the last great Palladian mansion in Britain, **Hagley Hall**. Imposing without, exotic and rococo within; notable are the Barrell Room with panelling from Holbeach Hall, where two of the Gunpowder Plotters - the Wintour brothers - were caught and later put to death in the favourite way of hanging, drawing and quartering. Temples, cascading pools and a ruined castle are some of the reasons for lingering in the park, which has a large herd of deer. Another attraction at Hagley is the **Falconry Centre** on the A4565, where owls, hawks, falcons and eagles live and fly.

KIDDERMINSTER

Map 6 ref K15

9 miles NW of Bromsrove on the A448

Known chiefly as a centre of the carpet-making industry, which began here early in the 18th century as a cottage industry. The introduction of the power loom brought wealth to the area and instigated the building of carpet mills. Standing on the River Stour, the town has a variety of mills, whose enormous chimneys dominate the skyline and serve as architectural monuments to Kidderminster's heritage. St Mary's Church, on a hill overlooking the town, is the largest parish church in the county and contains some superb tomb monuments. The Whittall Chapel, designed in 1922 by Sir Charles Gilbert Scott, was paid for by Matthew Whittall, a native of Kidderminster who went to America and made a fortune in carpets. Three beautiful windows depicting the Virgin Mary, Joan of Arc and Florence Nightingale, were given by his widow in his memory. Kidderminster's best-known son is Rowland Hill, who founded the modern postal system and introduced the penny post; he was also a teacher, educationalist and inventor. His statue stands outside the Town Hall. By the station on the Severn Valley Railway is the **Kidderminster Railway Museum** with a splendid collection of railway memorabilia. Run by volunteers, it is housed in an old GWR grain store. In the Stour Valley just north of Kidderminster is the village of **Wolverley**, with charming cottages and pretty gardens, the massive Church of St John the Baptist, and the remains - not easy to see - of prehistoric cave dwellings in the red sandstone cliffs.

HARTLEBURY   MAP 6 REF L15
3 miles S of Kidderminster off the A449

Hartlebury Castle, a historic sandstone castle of the Bishops of Worcester and a prison for captured Royalist troops in the Civil War, now houses the **Worcester County Museum**. In the former servants' quarters in the north wing numerous permanent exhibitions show the past lives of the county's inhabitants from Roman times to the 20th century. Visitors can also admire the grandeur of the three Castle State Rooms. On Hartlebury Common, **Leapgate Country Park** is a nature reserve in heath and woodland, with the county's only acid bog.

BEWDLEY   MAP 6 REF K15
3 miles W of Kidderminster on the A456

On the western bank of the Severn, linked to its suburb Wribbenhall by a fine Thomas Telford Bridge, Bewdley was once a flourishing port, but lost some of its importance when the Staffordshire & Worcestershire Canal was built. It's a quiet, civilised but much visited little town with some good examples of Georgian architecture, and has won fame with another form of transport, the **Severn Valley Railway**.

Here in the centre of popular Bewdley, **The George Hotel** is an impressive and distinctive hotel offering the highest standard of service to all its guests. This gracious and elegant establishment dates back to the early 17th century and features in its decor and furnishings many luxurious original features, including the truly outstanding decorative ceiling work in the coffee shop, the large open fireplace in the lounge bar, and the wood panelling in the restaurant. There are 11 superb guest bedrooms, each individually decorated and furnished with comfort and relaxation in mind. The restaurant has built up a reputation for fine dining, with an extensive menu of delicious and expertly prepared dishes. The lounge bar offers a range of lunchtime meals and snacks,

The George Hotel, Load Street, Bewdley, Worcestershire DY12 2AW Tel: 01299 402117 Fax: 01299 401269

and morning coffee or afternoon tea can be taken in the congenial coffee shop. The lounge bar also serves a fine selection of changing real ales, kept in tip-top condition. For a taste of elegance and comfort, look no further.

Bewdley Museum, which also incorporates the Tourist Information Centre, is a great place for all the family, with exhibitions themed around the River Severn and the **Wyre Forest**. Crafts depicted include charcoal-burning, coopering and brass-making. Bewdley was the birthplace of Stanley Baldwin, three times Prime Minister between the Wars.

Tarn is a magnificent country house and bed and breakfast set in 17 acres of some supremely eye-catching gardens and grounds. Just a mile out of Bewdley, this superb establishment began life as two labourer's cottages, which were knocked into one long, rambling house in

1923. Owner Mrs Topsy Beves arrived here in 1967, extending the property and cultivating the lovely, ever-changing gardens. She started providing bed and breakfast accommodation in 1984. there are four guest bedrooms (two single, two twin/double), all with separate bathrooms. They are charming and cosy, with attractive furnishings and decor. The house also boasts

Tarn, Long Bank, Bewdley, Worcestershire DY12 2QT
Tel: 01299 402243

a splendid library, housing four generations of the family's books. Within the grounds there is a wealth of natural wildlife; strolling guests will come across deer, squirrels, rabbits and buzzards. The breakfasts are hearty and delicious, and there are several good pubs locally for evening meals. A truly relaxing break and warm hospitality are guaranteed at this wonderful B&B.

CALLOW HILL
MAP 6 REF K15

5 miles W of Kidderminster on the A456

The **Wyre Forest Visitor Centre** is set among mature oak woodland with forest walks, picnic area, gift shop and restaurant. Wyre Forest covers a vast area starting northwest of Bewdley and extending into Shropshire. The woodland, home to abundant flora and fauna, is quite dense in places. It was once inhabited by nomadic people who made their living from what was around them, weaving baskets and brooms, burning charcoal and making the little wooden whisks which were used in the carpet-making process. Just south of Callow Hill, the village of **Rock** has an imposing Norman church in a prominent hillside position with some lovely windows and carving.

GREAT WITLEY
MAP 6 REF K15

7 miles SW of Kidderminster on the A443

There are two great reasons not to miss this place! **Great Witley Church**, almost ordinary from the outside, has an unbelievable interior of Baroque flamboyance that glows with light in a stunning ambience of gold and white. Masters of their crafts contributed to the interior, which was actually removed from the Chapel of Canons in Edgware: Joshua Price stained glass, Bellucci ceiling paintings, Bagutti plasterwork. Next to the church are the spectacular and hauntingly beautiful remains of **Witley Court**, a palatial mansion funded by the riches of the Dudley family. Destroyed by fire in 1937, it stood a neglected shell for years, until English Heritage took over these most splendid of ruins and started the enormous task of making them safe and accessible. If you only see one ruin in the whole county, this should be it.

SHROPSHIRE

LUDLOW
Map 6 ref J15

20 miles W of Kidderminster on the A49

Often called "the perfect historic town", Ludlow has more than 500 listed buildings, and the medieval street pattern has been kept virtually intact. **Ludlow Castle** was built by the Normans in the 11th century, one of a line of castles along the Marches to keep out the Welsh. Under its protection a large town was planned and built - and prospered, due to the collection and sale of wool and the manufacture of cloth. The Castle has been home to many distinguished families and to Royalty: Edward V, Prince Arthur and other Royal children were brought up in Ludlow, and the Castle became the headquarters of the Council of the Marches, which governed Wales and the border counties until 1689. Nowadays the past combines dramatically with the future in the **Holodeck**, where hologram images create ultra-realistic 3D illusions. The Giant Kaleidoscope gives the viewer the sensation of standing before a globe of light and an ever-changing surface of colours, and the **Well of Infinity** is an apparently bottomless hole in the ground - on the first floor.

Ludlow Castle

The parish church of St Laurence is one of the largest in the county, reflecting the town's affluence at the time of its rebuilding in the 15th century. There are fine misericords and stained glass, and the poet AE Housman, author of *A Shropshire Lad*, is commemorated in the churchyard. Other places which should be seen include **Castle Lodge**, once a prison and later home of the officials of the Council of the Marches, and the fascinating houses that line Broad Street.

Ludlow Museum, in Castle Street, has exhibitions of local history centred on, among other things, the Castle, the town's trade and special features on local geology and archaeology. **The Ludlow Festival**, held annually since 1960 and lasting a fortnight in June/July, has become one of the major arts festivals in the country. The centrepiece of the festival, an open-air performance of a Shakespeare play in the Castle's inner bailey, is supported by a number of events that have included orchestral concerts, musical recitals, literary and historical lectures, exhibitions, readings and workshops.

CRAVEN ARMS
Map 6 ref J15

8 miles NW of Ludlow on the A49

The village takes its name from the hotel and pub built by the Earl of Craven. The coming of the railways caused the community to be developed, and it was also at the centre of several roads that were once used by sheep-drovers moving their flocks from Wales to the English markets. In its heyday Craven Arms held one of the largest sheep auctions in Britain, with as many as 20,000 sheep being sold in a single day.

Amid lovely south Shropshire countryside and close to Wenlock Edge, **Strefford Hall** is a stonebuilt Victorian farmhouse set in a working farm of 360 acres. In the family since 1934, the farm is owned by John and Caroline Morgan, who have been providing bed and breakfast

Strefford Hall Farm, Craven Arms, Shropshire SY7 8DE
Tel/Fax: 01588 672383

accommodation since 1986 and self-catering accommodation since 1999. The main house dates back to 1850, and offers three upstairs guest rooms sleeping up to six people. The rooms are spacious and very comfortable, with delightful views across fields to the hills beyond. The guests' sitting room is a cosy and relaxing place with a log burner. Evening meals by arrangement; packed lunches can also be provided. No smoking. Children welcome. The old hackney stable has been renovated and refurbished to create two lovely self-catering units, one on the ground floor and one on the first. Each sleeps two and is decorated and furnished to a high standard of quality and comfort. Breakfast can be taken in the main farmhouse if self-catering guests wish.

NORTON   MAP 6 REF J15
2 miles S of Craven Arms off the B4368

Hidden away and surrounded by thousands of acres of truly magnificent countryside, **The Firs** is a peaceful retreat offering bed and breakfast and self-catering accommodation. Owners Jan and Richard offer excellent accommodation in their splendid farmhouse, built in 1875 and once part of a large working farm. The three ensuite guest bedrooms are delightful, decorated

The Firs, Norton, Craven Arms, Shropshire SY7 9LS
Tel/Fax: 01588 672511 Mobile: 07977 697903
email: thefirs@go2.co.uk website: www.go2.co.uk/firs

and furnished with style and character. Self-catering accommodation is in the garden annex, a charming and comfortable studio that sleeps four. This little home from home was built of reclaimed stone and timber, and features a beautiful cast-iron bed with canopy, separate bunk room, kitchen/dining area, bathroom, and lounge area command-

ing lovely views over the surrounding countryside. Open all year round, The Firs makes for a handy base from which to explore Norton's Camp, and the 13th-century Stokesay Castle (a distinctive example of a fortified manor house), the ancient town of Ludlow just six miles away, and many more places of interest: Powis Castle, Ironbridge and the Longmynd Hills near Church Stretton. Horses can also be accommodated. Children welcome. No smoking. ETB 4 Diamonds.

BISHOP'S CASTLE

MAP 6 REF J15

9 miles NW of Craven Arms off the A488

This small and ancient town lies in an area of great natural beauty in solitary border country. Little remains of the castle, built in the 12th century for the Bishops of Hereford, which gave the place its name, but there is no shortage of fine old buildings for the visitor to see. The **House on Crutches Museum**, sited in one of the oldest and most picturesque of these buildings, recounts the town's history. Its gable end is supported on wooden posts - hence the name. North of Bishop's Castle lie the **Stiperstones**, a rock-strewn quartzite outcrop rising to a height of 1,700' at the Devil's Chair. A bleak place of brooding solitude, the ridge is part of a 1,000-acre National Nature Reserve and on the lower slopes gaunt chimneys, derelict buildings and neglected roads and paths are silent reminders of the lead-mining industry that flourished here from Roman times until the 19th century. To the west, on the other side of the A49 near **Chirbury**, is **Mitchell's Fold** stone circle, a Bronze Age circle of 15 stones. This is Shropshire's oldest monument, its origins and purpose unknown.

The Six Bells is a cracking public house with its own on-site brewery. Owner Nev Richards created the brewery even before he took over the pub. Born of a family tradition spanning three generations, the brewery was re-established on the site of the original brewery which closed in the early 1900s. Together with Jeremy Blundell, an experienced brewer who is now mayor of Bishop's Castle - and the youngest mayor in the land - in 1997 Nev created the brewery in what once were the kitchens of the old pub. The Brewery now has a portfolio of nine brews - three regular and six seasonal. The regulars go by the names 'Big Nev's' - a 3.8% pale bitter which has already achieved great popularity, 'Marathon' (4%), a malty, ruby-coloured beer that is a blend of locally grown and American hops, and Cloud Nine (4.2%), made with the First Gold Hop and having a slightly citrus finish. The seasonal ales range in alcohol content from 4.6% to 5.5%, and offer a range of tastes and finishes. Nev sup-

The Six Bells, Church Street, Bishop's Castle, Shropshire SY9 SAA Tel: 01588 638930

plies his beers to many other pubs as well. The Six Bells has been awarded Shropshire Pub of the Year 1999 by CAMRA. Since opening, his beers have also won several coveted awards. But the beer is only part of the pub's success story. Run since 1997 by Nev and his partner Carol, the distinctive premises date back to 1670 and were first licensed in 1720. Located on the original London-Mid Wales road, it was always a busy coaching inn. The Cock Horses were stabled here, and used to assist in pulling the coaches up the hill to nearby Kerry Ridgeway. All food is cooked to order and consists of fresh local produce, from a varied menu that includes delicious English favourites. The decor is traditional and cosy, with a large brickbuilt fire surround with wood-burning stove and other homely features.

CHURCH STRETTON

MAP 6 REF J14

8 miles N of Craven Arms on the A49

The town has a long history - King John granted a charter in 1214 - and traces of the medieval town are to be seen among the 18th and 19th-century buildings in the High Street. Many of the black-and-white timbered buildings are not so old as they look, having been built at the turn of the century when the town had ideas of becoming a health resort. Just behind the High Street stands the **Church of St Laurence**, with Saxon foundations, a Norman nave and a tower dating from about 1200. Over the aisle is a memorial to a tragic event that happened in 1968 when three boys were killed in a fire. The memorial is in the form of a gridiron, with flakes of copper simulating flames. The gridiron is the symbol of St Laurence, who was burnt to death on one in AD258. The Victorian novelist Sarah Smith, who wrote under the name of Hesba Stretton, was a frequent visitor to nearby All Stretton, and there is a small memorial window to her in the south transept.

A mile from the town centre are **Carding Mill Valley** and the **Long Mynd**. The valley and the moorland into which it runs are National Trust property and very popular for walking and picnicking. This wild area of heath affords marvellous views across Shropshire to the Cheshire Plains and the Black Mountains. Tea room, shop, information centre. Tel: 01694 723068.

ALL STRETTON
Map 6 ref J14

2 miles N of Church Stretton off the A49

Stretton Hall is an outstanding country manor hotel and restaurant offering bed and breakfast or half-board accommodation. Formerly a private house dating back some 200 years, it is magnificent in every respect. Elegance, charm and luxury are the bywords here. From the moment guests cross the sandstone portico to enter the warm and welcoming panelled reception area, it is clear that quality and comfort are assured. The rooms are grand, some with wood panelling -

part of which came from the famous Gawsworth Hall in Warren, Cheshire. The lounge bar overlooks mature gardens and superb views of Caer Caradoc hill. The relaxing and comfortable guests' sitting room has distinctive floor-to-ceiling oak panelling. There are 12 ensuite guest bedrooms, each with its own individual character and style, and including a spacious family room and romantic four-poster room. Booking is advised for the acclaimed restaurant (open to non-residents 7 - 9 p.m.), a gracious

Stretton Hall Hotel & Restaurant, All Stretton, Church Stretton, Shropshire SY6 6HG Tel: 01694 723224 Fax: 01694 724365 email: charlie@strettonhall.freeserve.co.uk website: www.go2.co.uk/strettonhall

room with views onto the grounds, where a reputation for fine cuisine and the best quality wines from all over the world is upheld with pride. The first-class menu offers a range of expertly prepared repasts made with the freshest local produce. The service is always friendly and attentive at this superior establishment. The keen golfer will find a haven on the course at Church Stretton, which boasts to be one of the highest in England - much of it is over 1,200 feet. The wide range of leisure facilities within easy reach includes walking, touring and sightseeing, shooting, fishing, pony-trekking, gliding, tennis and bowling. For a truly luxurious break, look no further. The hotel also boasts superb conference facilities, and can cater for any important occasion, from parties large or small to weddings and banquets.

LITTLE STRETTON
Map 6 ref J15

2 miles S of Church Stretton on the B4370

The village of Little Stretton nestles in the **Stretton Gap**, with the wooded slopes of Ragleth to the east and **Long Mynd** to the west. It is a peaceful spot, bypassed by the A49, and is a delightful place to stroll for a stroll. The most photographed building is **All Saints Church**, with a black and white timbered frame, a thatched roof and the general look of a cottage rather than a church. When built in 1903 it had an iron roof, but this was soon found to be too noisy and was soon replaced with thatch (heather initially, then the straw that tops it today). Among many other interesting buildings are **Manor House**, a cruck hall dating from 1500, and **Bircher Cottage**, of a similar vintage.

WALL-UNDER-HEYWOOD
Map 6 ref J15

2 miles E of Church Stretton off the B5371

Joan and Les Egerton have lived at **Brook House Farm** at Wall-under-Heywood since 1989. Sitting amid 12 acres of beautiful countryside, this 17th-century property with more modern additions has a wealth of original features including the exposed ceiling beams in the attractive dining room. There are three comfortable and welcoming letting rooms, with bathrooms. The rooms are approached along a private stairway so guests can come and go as they please. Please note there is no smoking allowed in the house. This wonderful holiday or short break destination also boasts a newly created self-catering annex, refurbished from former cow sheds. To the rear of the farm there is a secluded

Brook House Farm, Wall-under-Heywood, Church Stretton, Shropshire SY6 7DS Tel: 01694 771308

caravan park taking up to 5 caravans and 20 tents. The good facilities include electric hook-ups and a pristine toilet block. Here in this peaceful location, as well as being central for many of the sights and attractions of the region, there are lovely walks locally

BRIDGNORTH
Map 6 ref K14

15 miles NE of Ludlow off the A442

The ancient market town of Bridgnorth, straddling the River Severn, comprises **Low Town**, and, 100 feet up sandstone cliffs, **High Town**. 1101 is a key date in its history, when the **Norman Castle** was built by Robert de Belesme from Quatt. All that remains of the castle is part of the keep tower, which leans at an angle of about 15 degrees as a result of an attempt to demolish it after the Civil War. The castle grounds offer splendid views of the river, and when King Charles I stayed here in 1642 he declared the view from the **Castle Walk** to be the finest in his dominion. The **Bridgnorth Museum** is a good place to start a tour of this interesting town. It occupies rooms over the arches of the **North Gate**, which is the only one of the town's original fortifications to survive - though most of it was rebuilt in the 18th century. The **Costume and Childhood Museum** incorporates a costume gallery, a complete Victorian nursery and a collection of rare minerals. It's a really charming place that appeals to all ages. The Civil War caused great damage in Bridgnorth and the lovely **Town Hall** is one of many timber-framed

Bridgenorth Museum, North Gate

buildings put up just after the war. The sandstone arched base was completed in 1652 and later covered in brick; Charles ll took a great interest in it and when improvements were needed he made funds available from his own purse and from a collection he ordered be made in every parish in England.

St Mary's Street is one of the three streets off High Street which formed the planned new town of the 12th century. Many of the houses, brick faced over timber frames, have side passages leading to gardens which contained workshops and cottages. Bishop Percy's House is the oldest house standing in the town, a handsome building dating from 1580 and one of the very few timber-framed houses to survive the fire of 1646. It is named after the Reverend Dr Percy, who was born in the house in 1729 and became Bishop of Dromore.

For many visitors the most irresistible attraction in Bridgnorth is the Castle Hill Cliff Railway, funicular railway built in 1892 to link the two parts of the town. The track is 200' long and rises over 100' up the cliff. Originally it operated on a water balance system but it was converted in 1943 to electrically driven colliery-type winding gear. John Betjeman likened a ride on this lovely little railway to a journey up to heaven. For all but the very energetic it might feel like heaven compared to the alternative ways of getting from Low to High Town - seven sets of steps or Cartway, a meandering street that's steeped in history. The bridge across the Severn, rebuilt in 1823 to a Thomas Telford design, has a clock tower with an inscription commemorating the building, in 1808, of the first steam locomotive at John Hazeldine's foundry a short distance upstream. Talking of steam locomotives, Bridgnorth is the northern terminus of the wonderful Severn Valley Railway.

QUATT   MAP 6 REF K15

4 miles SE of Bridgnorth on the A442

Quatt is the location of the National Trust's Dudmaston Hall, a late 17th-century house with fine furniture, Dutch flower paintings, modern pictures and sculptures (Hepworth, Moore), botanical art, watercolours, family and natural history and colourful gardens with lakeside walks, a rockery and a wooded valley.The church at Quatt contains some splendid monuments and memorials to the Wolryche family. Nearby, in the grounds of Stanmore Hall on the Stourbridge road, is the Midland Motor Museum, with an outstanding collection of more than 100 vehicles, mostly sports and racing cars. The grounds also include a touring caravan site.

PATTINGHAM
6 miles NE of Bridgnorth off the A454

MAP 6 REF K14

Patshull Park Hotel, Golf and Country Club is a privately owned hotel and leisure centre on the Patshull Hall estate, in secluded Shropshire countryside.
The golf course is laid out in
grounds established by 'Capability' Brown in the 18th century.
A large lake encircles the entrance to this impressive hotel;
the Doric Temple that marks the
entrance is just one of its many
distinctive features. There are 49
ensuite bedrooms, some with
splendid views over the parkland
or lake. All rooms come complete with every modern
amenity. There's a relaxed air in
the Golfers Bar (situated at the
end of the course). The Health
& Fitness Club features an indoor pool, sauna, steam room,
solarium, Cardio Suite and Gymnasium. The Lakeside Restaurant

offers unparalleled views and a
menu that provides a wide
choice for breakfast, lunch and
the evening meal. The more informal Earl's Bar has a light
menu available throughout the
day.

Patshull Park Hotel, Golf and Country Club,
Pattingham, Shropshire WV6 7HR
Tel: 01902 700100 Fax: 01902 700874
email: sales@patshull-park.co.uk
website: www.patshull-park.co.uk

MUCH WENLOCK
8 miles NW of Bridgnorth on the A458

MAP 6 REF K14

The narrow streets of Much Wenlock are a delight to explore, and among the mellow buildings are some absolute gems. The **Guildhall** is one of them, dating from 1540 and added to in 1577 with a chamber over the stone medieval prison. The Guildhall was until recently used as a courtroom, and the Town Council still meets here once a month. The **Museum** is housed in the former market hall, which was built in 1878. There are interesting displays on the geology, flora and fauna of **Wenlock Edge**, as well as local history items including Dr William Penny Brookes's Olympian Games. A forerunner of, and inspiration for the Olympic Games, they are an annual event in the town every year, having started in 1850. The good doctor lived in what is now Lloyds Bank. The sight that simply must not be missed on a visit here is the ruins of the **Priory of St Milburga**. The Priory was originally a nunnery, founded in the 7th century by a Mercian princess and destroyed some 200 years later. Leofric, Earl of Mercia and husband of Lady Godiva, re-established it as a priory in 1050 and the current spectacular ruins belong to the Cluniac Priory rebuilt in the 12th and 13th centuries. The best remaining features are the wall carvings in the cloisters and the Norman interlacing of arches and doorways in the Chapter House. **The Prior's Lodge**, dating from about 1500, is particularly impressive with its steeply pitched roof of sandstone tiles above the rows of mullioned windows. Away from the main site is **St Milburga's Well**, whose waters are reputed to cure eye diseases.

WENLOCK EDGE
MAP 6 REF K14

4 miles S of Much Wenlock on the B4371

Wenlock Edge is one of the most spectacular and impressive landmarks in the whole county, a limestone escarpment dating back 400 million years and a paradise for naturalists and lovers of the outdoors. It runs for 15 miles all the way down to Craven Arms. For centuries its quarries have produced the stone used in many of the local buildings; it was also a source of lime for agricultural fertiliser and much went into the blast furnaces that fired the Industrial Revolution.

IRONBRIDGE AND IRONBRIDGE GORGE
MAP 6 REF K14

4 miles NE of Much Wenlock on the B4373

This is it, the town at the centre of Ironbridge Gorge, an area which has been designated a World Heritage Centre by UNESCO, ranking it alongside the likes of the Pyramids, the Grand Canyon and the Taj Mahal. It was the first British site on the list. The **bridge** itself is a pedestrian right of way with a tollgate at one end, and the series of museums that spread along the banks of the Severn in **Ironbridge, Coalbrookdale, Coalport** and **Jackfield** pay tribute to the momentous events that took place here 250 years ago. The first iron wheels were made here, and also the first iron rails and the first steam railway locomotive. The **IronbridgeVisitor Centre** offers the ideal introduction to the attractions, and plenty of time should be devoted to the individual museums. The Museum of Iron in Coalbrookdale in the most historic part of the valley shows the whole story of ironmaking. Next to it is the original furnace used by Abraham Darby when he first smelted iron with coke; a little way north are **Rosehill House**, one of the homes of the Darby family, and **Dale House**, where Abraham Darby's grandson made his plans for the iron bridge. The Coalbrookdale Museum is part of the nearby Ironbridge Gorge Museum. Also at Coalbrookdale is the **Ironbridge Open Air Museum of Steel Sculpture**, a collection of 60 modern steel sculptures of all shapes and sizes set in 10 acres of beautiful countryside.

The **Jackfield Tile Museum**, on the south bank, stands on the site of a world centre of the tile-making industry. The museum houses a fine collection of wall and floor tiles from Victorian times to the 1950s. Demonstrations of traditional tile-making take place regularly. Back across a footbridge to the **Coalport China Museum**, with its marvellous displays of two centuries of porcelain. Coalport was once one of the country's largest manufacturers of porcelain, starting life here but moving its factory to Stoke in the 1920s. Nearby is the extraordinary **Tar Tunnel** with its gushing spring of natural bitumen. It was a popular attraction for tourists in the 18th century, and it remains one of the most interesting geological phenomena in Britain. The tunnel was started in 1786, under the direction of ironmaster William Reynolds, who intended that it should be used for a canal to reach the shafts to the coal seams ¾ of a mile away on Blists Hill. After they had driven the tunnel about 300 yards the miners struck a spring of natural bitumen. Reynolds immediately recognised the scientific interest of the discovery and sent samples of the bitumen to eminent scientists, who declared that the properties of the bitumen were superior to those of tar made of coal. The tunnel was almost forgotten over the years, but in 1965 the Shropshire Mining Club persuaded the owner of the village shop in **Coalport** to let them explore the darkness which lay beyond a door opening from his cellar. They rediscovered the Tar Tunnel, but it was another 18 years before visitors were allowed access to a brief stretch. At **Blists Hill Victorian Town** visitors can experience the atmosphere and way of life of a working Victorian community; there's a shop, domestic animals, a squatter's cottage, a schoolhouse and a bank which distributes its own legal tender.

Two miles west of Ironbridge, on a minor road off the B4378, stands **Buildwas Abbey**, one of the finest ruined abbeys in England. After 850 years the church is virtually complete except for the roof, and the setting, in a meadow by the Severn against a backdrop of wooded grounds, is both peaceful and evocative. The place is full of things of interest, like the lead-glazed tiles depicting animals and birds in the Chapter House.

SHREWSBURY
Map 6 ref J14

18 miles NW of Bridgnorth off the A5

The River Severn winds round the lovely county town in a horseshoe bend, making it almost an island site, and it was on two hills within this protected site that the Saxon town developed. The Normans under Roger de Montgomery took over after the conquest, building the castle and the great Benedictine abbey. In the 15th and 16th centuries Shrewsbury prospered through the wool trade, and evidence of its affluence shows in the many black-and-white timbered buildings that still line the streets. In Victorian times steam made Shrewsbury an important railway centre whilst at the same time Darwin, born and educated in the town, was rocking the world with his theories. Everywhere there is a sense of history, and the Museums do a particularly fine job of bringing the past to life, in terms of both human and natural history. **Rowley's House** is a glorious timber-framed building of the late 16th century, with an adjoining brick and stone mansion of 1618. The home of William Rowley, 17th-century draper, brewer and leading citizen, now contains an impressive collection of pieces from Viroconium, along with spectacular displays of costumes, natural history and geology. A short walk away is **Clive House**, in the Georgian area of the town. Clive of India live here in 1762 while he was Mayor, and one or two mementoes can be seen. The major displays are of Shropshire ceramics and the life of Charles Darwin, whose statue stands opposite the Castle. The Castle, dating from 1083, was built by the Norman Earl Roger de Montgomery and last saw action in the Civil War. It was converted by Thomas Telford into a private residence and now houses the **Shropshire Regimental Museum** with the collections of the Kings Shropshire Yeomanry Cavalry and the Shropshire Royal Horse Artillery. A museum with a difference is **Coleham Pumping Station** at **Longden Coleham**, which houses the splendid Renshaw pumping engines that powered Shrewsbury's sewerage system until 1970.

The Abbey, like the Castle, was founded by Roger de Montgomery, on the site of a Saxon wooden church. In 1283 a parliament met in the Chapter House, the first national assembly in which the Commons were involved. The Abbey Church remains a place of worship, and in 1997 a stained glass window depicting St Benedict was dedicated to the memory of Edith Pargeter. This lady, writing under the name of Ellis Peters, created the character of Brother Cadfael, who lived at the Abbey and became one of the country's best-loved fictional characters when portrayed by Derek Jacobi in the television series. Hard by the Abbey, **The Shrewsbury Quest** presents the sights and sounds of medieval Shrewsbury. Visitors can see Brother Cadfael's workshop, solve mysteries, create their own medieval manuscripts and breathe in the fragrance of a monastic herb garden. Complementing the town's Museum and Archaeological Services, a Records and Research Service was opened in a new building in 1995. It has 5 ½ miles of material relating to Shropshire past and present, including many original records and extensive microfilm records. Shrewsbury has more than 30 churches and among the finest are St Mary's and St Chad's. St Mary's, the town's only complete medieval church, originated in the late Saxon period, but the earliest features of the present building are of the 12th century. The stained glass, monuments and fittings are quite out of the ordinary, and the spire has claims to being the third highest in the land. One of the memorials is to Admiral Benbow, a national hero who died in 1702 and is also remembered in innumerable pub signs. **St Chad's** is the work of Attingham Hall's designer George Steuart, who was commissioned to design a replacement for the original, which fell down in 1788. His church is very unusual in having a circular nave.

Guided tours and suggested walks cover all aspects of this marvellous town, including a **Brother Cadfael tour** and walks in the beautiful countryside that is all around. One walk takes in the spot to the north of town now known as **Battlefield**, where in 1403 the armies of Henry IV and the insurgent Harry Percy (Harry Hotspur) met. 50,000 men were deployed in all, and in the brief but bloody battle Hotspur was among the many casualties. A church was built near the mass grave, where 1,600 bodies are buried, a monument to the fallen and also an oasis of wildlife in the town environment. **Shrewsbury Flower Show** is Britain's best two-day summer show and each August for more than a century the show has been held in the picturesque setting of Quarry Park. Three million blooms fill three giant marquees, and the show includes a musical programme and fireworks displays.

FRODESLEY
4 miles S of Shrewsbury off the A49

Map 6 ref J14

The Swan Inn lies in the tiny hamlet of Frodesley, found south of Shrewsbury, a couple of miles east off the main A49. Rob and Shirley Pheby bought this Free House in 1999. Rob had long been a regular, and finally his ambition of becoming the boss was achieved. Both he and Shirley have been local residents for many years. The building dates back to 1830; the restaurant to the rear was added on in 1994. Here in this lovely rural setting visitors can enjoy a relaxing drink and some superb food. Closed at lunchtime Monday-Thursday, it is open for all other sessions and on Bank Holidays. Shirley overseas the cooking, with lunch available from midday to 2.30 p.m. and evening meals from 7 - 9 p.m. Meals can be taken in the comfortable dining room, in the bar area or, on fine days, on the attractive patio. Real ales on offer change regularly, and include Bass, Worthington, Boddingtons and a guest ale. To the rear of the pub there is a small caravan park for up to 4 caravans.

The Swan Inn, Frodesley, Shrewsbury, Shropshire SY5 7HA
Tel: 01694 731208

WROXETER
6 miles SE of Shrewbury on the B4380

Map 6 ref J14

In the village of Wroxeter, beside the B4380, is one of the most important Roman sites ever brought to light. *Viroconium* was the first town to be established by the Romans in this part of the country and developed from being a military settlement to a sizeable civilian town where the Cornovii tribe were settled. It's an absolutely fascinating place, where the highlights include extensive remains of a 2nd-century bathhouse complex. Some of the major excavated items are on display here, many more at **Rowley's House Museum** in Shrewsbury. Also in the village is Wroxeter Roman Vineyard , where there is not only a vineyard producing both red and white wines but additional delights in the shape of rare-breed animals and a lavender field.

ATCHAM
6 miles E of Shrewsbury on the B4380

Map 6 ref J14

The village stands at the point where the Severn is crossed by the Roman road. The splendid old seven-arched bridge is now redundant, having been replaced by a new neighbour some time ago, but is still in situ. The old bridge was designed by John Gwynne, who was a founder member of the Royal Academy and the designer of Magdalen Bridge in Oxford. **Attingham Park**, run by the National Trust, is perhaps the finest house in Shropshire, a splendid neoclassical mansion set in 250 delightful acres. Designed by George Steuart for the 1st Lord Berwick, it has the grandest of Regency interiors, ambassadorial silver, Italian furniture and Grand Tour paintings hanging in the John Nash gallery. The tea room is lined with paintings of the 5th Lord Berwick's Herefordshire cattle. Humphrey Repton landscaped the park, where visitors can enjoy woodland and riverside walks and see the deer. **Attingham Home Farm**, the original home farm of the grand house, comprises buildings dating mainly from about 1800, and the yard retains the atmosphere of a traditional Shropshire farm. Many breeds of farm animals are represented: pigs - Oxford, Sandy, Iron Age, Vietnamese pot-bellied; sheep - Jacob, Shetland and Ryeland; cattle - Jerseys, Longhair, Dexter, Red Poll, British White. The rabbit house is particularly popular with youngsters, and there are usually some orphaned lambs for children to bottle-feed.

NESSCLIFFE
9 miles NW of Shrewsbury on the A5

MAP 6 REF J14

Near the village of Nesscliffe, which lies halfway between Shrewsbury and Oswestry, is **Nesscliffe Hill Country Park**, where paths lead up through woodland to the summit and fine views over Shropshire. The Hill is a sandstone escarpment, popular for walking and rock climbing; cut into the face of an abandoned quarry are caves, one of them reputedly the lair of the 16th-century worthy-turned-highwayman Humphrey Kynaston. The whole area southwest of Oswestry, including Nesscliffe, Knockin, Ruyton and Melverley, is known as Kynaston Country. A short distance north of Nesscliffe, on the B4397, is the village of **Ruyton-XI-Towns**, which acquired its unusual name in medieval times when 11 communities were united into the borough of Ruyton.

OSWESTRY
17 miles NW of Shrewsbury off the A5

MAP 6 REF I13

Close to the Welsh border, Oswestry is an important market town whose look is mainly Georgian and Victorian, due in part to the fires which regularly ravaged timber-framed buildings. The town grew up around **St Oswald's Well**. Oswald was a Saxon king who was killed in a battle in 642 against a rival Saxon king, Penda of Mercia. Oswald's body was dismembered and hung on the branches of a tree. An eagle swooped and carried off one of his arms and where the limb fell to the ground a spring bubbled up to mark the spot. Thus St Oswald's Well came into being, soon to become a place of pilgrimage renowned for its healing powers.

There are many fine old buildings in Oswestry, none finer than the **Church of St Oswald**. It played an important part in the Civil War, when it was used as an observation point during the siege of the town by the Parliamentarians. The oldest section is the tower, which dates back to around 1200. The interior is beautiful, and among the treasures are a font presented by Colonel Lloyd of Llanforda as a thanksgiving for the restoration of the monarchy, a Gilbert Scott war memorial and a memorial to Hugh Yale, a member of the family that founded Yale University. Standing in the grounds of the church is the 15th century **Holbache House**. Once a grammar school, this handsome building now houses the Tourist Information Centre and the **Heritage Centre**, with displays of local interest and exhibitions of arts and crafts. Ferrequinologists (railway buffs) will make tracks for the **Cambrian Museum of Transport** on Oswald Road. Oswestry was the headquarters of the Cambrian Railway Company until it amalgamated with the GWR in 1922, and as late as the 1960s there were over 1,000 railwaymen in the area. Locomotives, carriages and wagons have been built and repaired in Oswestry for over 100 years, and the maintenance of 300 miles of track was directed from offices in the station building. One of the old engine sheds now houses a small museum with a collection of railway memorabilia and also some old bicycles and motorbikes. One of the locomotives is regularly steamed up by the volunteers of the Cambrian Railway Society. In 1559 a plague killed almost a third of the town's population and the **Croeswylan Stone** commemorates this disaster, marking the spot to which the market was moved during the plague. It is sometimes referred to as the Cross of Weeping. On the northern edge of town, **Old Oswestry** is an impressive example of an Iron Age fortress, first occupied in about 300BC. It was on the border of the territory held by the Cornovii and is one of several in the region. At the southwest corner of the fort can be seen **Wat's Dyke**, built at the same time and for the same purpose – delineating the border between Saxon Mercia and the Welsh – as the better-known Offa's Dyke. Who was Wat? We know not, but he could have been one of Offa's officers.

ELLESMERE
MAP 6 REF J13
15 miles N of Shrewsbury on the A495

The centre of Shropshire's Lakeland, Ellesmere is a pretty market town with Tudor, Georgian and Victorian buildings. The **Old Town Hall** and the **Old Railway Station** are two of the most impressive buildings, but nothing except the mound remains of the castle. The most impressive of all is the parish church of St Mary the Virgin, built by the Knights of St John. It is particularly beautiful inside, with an exceptional 15th-century carved roof in the chapel. The church overlooks **The Mere**, largest of several lakes that are an equal delight to boating enthusiasts, anglers and birdwatchers. Herons, Canada geese and swans are among the inhabitants of The Mere.

MARKET DRAYTON
MAP 6 REF K13
18 miles NE of Shrewsbury off the A53

Market Drayton was mentioned in the Domesday Book as Magna Draitune. It changed its name when Abbot Simon Combermere obtained a Royal Market Charter in 1245:

"Know that we have granted and by this our present charter confirmed to Brother Simon Abbot of Combermere and the minks serving God there that they and their successors forever shall have a weekly market in their manor of Drayton on Wednesday."

And so they have, every Wednesday. The fire of 1651 raised most of the town, so there is now quite a diversity of styles among the buildings. One of the most interesting is the **Buttercross**, built in 1842 to enable farmers' wives to display their wares protected from the weather. The crest it carries is of the Corbet family, Lords of the Manor since 1650.

Market Drayton is often referred to as "The Home of the Gingerbread". Gingerbread has been baked here for 200 years and is made in all shapes and sizes, the best known being the Gingerbread Man. Traditionally dunked in port, it's also very good to nibble on the **Discovery Trail** that takes in the sights of the town. Gingerbread dates back far more than 200 years, of course, and Shakespeare had a good word for it:

> *"An' I had but one penny in the world*
> *thou shouldst have it to buy gingerbread."*

Market Drayton's most famous son (actually born just outside) was Clive of India, whose childhood escapades in the town included climbing the church tower and sitting on one of the gargoyles, and building a dam to flood a shop whose owner was unwilling to pay protection money.

MARCHAMLEY
MAP 6 REF K13
13 miles NE of Shrewsbury on the A442

The beautiful Georgian mansion **Hawkestone Hall** was the ancestral home of the Hill family from 1556 until 1906. The Hall is now the seat of a religious order, but the principal rooms, including the splendid Venetian Saloon, are open for a short time in the summer. The **Pleasure Gardens** comprise terraces, lily pond, herbaceous borders and extensive woodland. On the same estate, at Weston-under-Lizard, is **Hawkestone Park**, a woodland fantasy of caves and follies and grottoes, of tunnels and secret pathways. The Hills built this extraordinary park, which if it were built today would probably be called a theme park.

WEM

Map 6 ref J13

11 miles N of Shrewsbury on the B5476

A peaceful enough place now, but Wem has seen its share of strife, being virtually destroyed in the Wars of the Roses and attacked in the Civil War. On the latter occasion, in 1643, Lord Capel at the head of 5,000 Royalist troops got a pretty hostile reception, and his defeat by a much smaller band, including some townswomen, gave rise to this mocking couplet:

"The women of Wem and a few volunteers
Beat the Lord Capel and all his Cavaliers."

It was another woman – actually a 14-year-old girl called Jane Churm – who nearly did what Capel proved incapable of doing. In setting alight the thatch on the roof of her home she started a fire that destroyed 140 properties in one hour. Some notable buildings survived, including **Astley House**, home of the painter John Astley. This and many of the town's most impressive houses are in **Noble Street**. Famous people associated with Wem include Judge Jeffrey's of Bloody Assize fame, who became Baron Wem in 1685, with his official residence at Lowe Hall. Wem is the home of the modern sweet pea, developed by the 19th-century nurseryman Henry Eckford. The **Sweet Pea Show** and the carnival are great occasions in the Wem calendar.

WHITCHURCH

Map 6 ref J13

17 miles N of Shrewsbury on the A49

First developed by the Romans as Mediolanum, Whitchurch is the most important town in the northern part of the county. Its main street is dominated by the tall sandstone tower of **St Alkmund's Church**, in whose chapel lies the body of Sir John Talbot, 1st Earl of Shrewsbury, who was killed at the Battle of Castillon, near Bordeaux, in 1453. **The Shropshire Way** passes nearby, so too the **Llangollen Canal**, and nature-lovers can explore the local wetland habitats - **Brown Moss** is 2 miles to the south off the A41. Whitchurch is the home of **Joyce Clocks**, the oldest tower clockmakers in the world, and is also, somewhat oddly, where Cheshire cheese was created. Hidden away in the heart of the town are the **Old Town Hall Vaults**, where the composer Edward German (*Merrie England, Tom Jones*) was born in 1862. Whitchurch has a major attraction for anglers at **Dearnford Hall Trout Fishery**, with fishing from bank or boat, tuition and accommodation.

Whitchurch

7 Northwest England

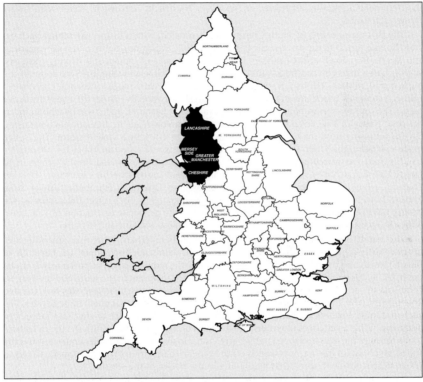

© MAPS IN MINUTES ™ (1998)

INTRODUCTION

Around the 1890s, guide-book writers took a fancy to describing the topography of various counties by comparing their outlines to some appropriate emblem. In Cheshire's county boundaries however they were unable to discern anything more imaginative than the shape of a teapot. Its base is the Staffordshire border, its handle the strip of land running from Stockport up to the Yorkshire border, with the Wirral providing the spout. And, tucked away at the base of the spout is the capital of the county, the city of Chester. The city's real position, a strategic site on the River Dee close to the Welsh border, was important even before the Romans arrived in AD70. They based a large camp, or "caster", here and called it Deva after the Celtic name for the river. It was during this period that the splendid city walls were originally built - two miles round, and still the most complete in the country.

In the course of his "Tour through the Whole Island of Great Britain", Daniel Defoe came to Chester by the ferry over the River Dee. He liked the city streets, "very broad and fair"; admired the "very pleasant walk round the city, upon the walls", disliked its cathedral, "built of red, sandy, ill looking stone", but had nothing but praise for its "excellent cheese". Cheshire cheese had been famous for generations. John Speed, the famous Elizabethan map-maker and a Cheshire man himself, noted: "The soil is fat fruitful and rich ... the Pastures make the Kine's udders to strout to the pail, from whom the best Cheese of all Europe is made". Later, some enthusiasts even promoted the idea that the name Cheshire was actually short for cheese-shire. The county's other major industry was salt, mined here even before the Romans arrived. By the time of the Domesday Book, the salt towns, or "wiches" - Nantwich, Northwich, Middlewich - were firmly established.

The two major towns of south Cheshire are Nantwich, with a history stretching back beyond Roman times. To the east rise the Peak District hills, westwards gently undulating pastures and woods drop down to the Cheshire Plain. This is an area of sudden and striking contrasts. Within half a mile you can find yourself travelling out of lowland Cheshire into some of the highest and wildest countryside; acres of lonely uplands with rugged gritstone crags, steep valleys watered by moorland streams. The Vale Royal - an attractive name for a very attractive part of the county - was so-named by Prince Edward, later Edward I, and it was he who founded the great Abbey of Vale Royal in fulfilment of a solemn vow made in dramatic circumstances. He was returning from the Crusades when his ship was struck by a violent storm. The Prince made a pledge to the Virgin that if his life were spared he would found an Abbey for 100 monks. Lo!, the ship was tossed ashore, the Prince and his companions waded through the surf to safety. Vale Royal Abbey indeed became the largest and most powerful Cistercian Abbey in England, a building reputedly even more glorious than Tintern or Fountains. Unlike those Abbeys, however, barely a stone of Vale Royal now remains in place. Over the centuries, the county has lost many fine buildings unnecessarily but the deliberate destruction of Vale Royal Abbey must take prime place in the litany of crimes against sublime architecture.

The county of Lancashire is known to many people but, perhaps, more than any other area in the country it has suffered from cliched images of its landscape and people: the harsh life of the mill towns and the brashness of Blackpool. Before the reorganization of the county boundaries in 1974, this large area also included Liverpool and Manchester in the south and the Furness Peninsula to the north. Though each, with their own distinctive character, was lost, the Red Rose county, which has put many a king on the throne of England, has much more besides. The ancient county town of Lancaster, in the north, is an excellent place to start any journey of discovery With a variety of museums and a wealth of interesting buildings, the life of Lancastrians through the ages is mapped out for any visitor to explore. Small and compact, it has the added advantage of having, as yet, been off the general tourist routes which has made its larger, White Rose equivalent, somewhat hard going in the height of the season.

To the west of Lancashire lies Morecambe Bay, a treacherous place, where over the centuries, many walkers have lost their lives in an attempt to make the journey to the Furness Peninsula considerably shorter. Walks across the sands, at low tide, should only be undertaken with the aid of one of the highly knowledgeable and experienced guides. However, despite it grim history, the bay offers superb views, including glorious sunsets, as well as being an important habitat for a wide variety of birds. Extending across much of the north of the county is the Forest Bowland, an ancient royal hunting ground that is dotted with small, isolated villages. With no major roads passing through the area, it has remained little changed and, with so many splendid walks and fine countryside, it is also relatively quiet even during the busiest summer weeks.

Flowing between the Forest of Bowland in the north and the hill country of Pendle in the south, the River Ribble cuts a pleasant and green course along a narrow valley. The Ribble Way middle-distance footpath follows the full 70 miles of the river, from its source in Yorkshire to the flat, tidal marshes of its estuary. A beautiful, unspoilt yet small area, the Ribble Valley has long been a favourite with the people of Lancashire. Not only is it easily accessible but there are numerous gentle walks in the sheltered valley and a wealth of wildlife is supported by the lush countryside. It is also a place of pretty, untouched villages which the 20th century has left unchanged.

The historic area of coastal Lancashire is known to many as the home of Blackpool: the brash, seaside resort that has been entertaining holidaymakers for generations. To the south lies another resort, Lytham St Anne's, which is not only somewhat more genteel but also the home of one of the country's most well known golf courses and host to the British Open Championships. Both places grew up as the result of the expansion of the railway system in the Victorian age, when they were popular destinations for the mill workers of Lancashire and Yorkshire.

However, the Fylde is also an ancient region that was known to both the Saxons and the Romans. To the north of this region, around the Wyre estuary, the salt marshes have been exploited for over 2,000 years and the process continues at the large ICI plant. Fishing and shipping too have been important sources of revenue here. Fleetwood is still a port though small than it was whilst, surprisingly though it might seem today, Lytham was also an important port along the Ribble Estuary. In land, the fertile, flat plain has been farmed for many centuries and, with few major roads, the quiet rural communities lie undisturbed and little changed by the 20th century. A haven for wildlife, and particularly birds and plants, the two estuaries, of the Ribble and the Wyre, provide habitats that abound with rare and endangered species of plants and birds. A relatively undiscovered region, the Fylde has much more to offer than a white knuckle ride and candy floss and is well worth taking the time to explore.

Further south the larger area, the Forest of Rossendale, saw the establishment of no real settlements until the 1400s, when the Crown leased off parts of the forest, and the early 1500s, when the final clearance and deforestation began. During the course of the 18th century, important advances in textile technology brought the introduction of water-powered mills to Rossendale. At this time cotton was also being imported and took over from the traditional woollen cloth manufacture. During the second half of the 19th century the industrial prosperity was so great that Rossendale came known as the Golden Valley. With Blackburn, one of the area's oldest settlements, in the north and Rawtenstall, Darwen, and Bacup in the centre of what was the forest, the whole region was a hive of activity making and finishing the cloth with others providing the necessary support. However, Rossendale, though provided with a much better road system, still offers tremendous opportunities for outdoor leisure and recreation as well, of course, as a fascinating industrial history.

Western Lancashire, with its sandy coastline and flat fertile farmland, is home to the elegant Victorian seaside resort of Southport, the ancient market towns of Chorley and Ormskirk, and Wigan, another ancient place with a rich industrial past. Following the reorganisation of the county boundaries in the 1970s and the creation of Merseyside, much of the coast and the southwestern area of Lancashire became part of the new county but the individual character and charm of this area has certainly not been lost.

East Lancashire, to the north of Manchester and west of the Pennines, is, perhaps, everyone's idea of the county of Lancashire. An region dominated by cotton, East Lancashire has risen and fallen with the fluctuations in the trade over the years but, behind the dark, satanic mills is a population full of humour and wit as well as some splendid countryside. Before the Industrial Revolution this was a sparsely populated region of remote hillside farms and cottages that relied, chiefly, on sheep farming and the wool trade. Many of the settlements date back to before the Norman Conquest and, though little may have survived the rapid building of the 19th century, there are three surprisingly wonderful ancient houses to be seen here: Smithills Hall and Hall-i'-th'-Wood at Bolton and Turton Tower, just to the north.

The Isle of man is perhaps best known for its annual TT motorcycle races, its tailless cat, Manx kippers, and as a tax haven for the wealthy. However, there is much more to this beautiful island which, set in the heart of the Irish Sea, is truly a world apart. With around 100 miles of coastline and several resorts, each with its own individual style and character, although the Isle of Man is be no means large, there is plenty to interest the visitor. This magical place became an island around 10,000 years ago when the melt water of the Ice Age raised the sea level. Soon afterwards, the first settlers arrived, working and developing the island into the landscape seen today. The distinctive influences of the various cultures who have lived here still remain, leaving a land with a unique and colourful heritage. The island's famous three-legged symbol seems to have been adopted in the 13th century as the armorial bearings of the native Kings of the Isle of Man, whose dominion also included the Hebrides. After 1266, when the native dynasty ended and control of the island passed, briefly, to the Crown of Scotland and then permanently to the Crown of England, the emblem was retained, and among the earliest surviving representations are those on the Manx Sword of State, though to have been made in 1300. The Three Legs also appeared on Manx coinage from the 17th to the 19th century, and are still seen in everyday use in the form of the official Manx flag. Why the Three Legs were adopted as the Royal Arms of the Manx Kingdom is unknown. Many heraldic emblems have no meaning and are simply chosen because they are distinctive. This may be the case with the Three Legs, though the emblem as such - something between a cross and a swastika - has a long history reaching far back into pagan times and was originally a symbol of the sun, the seat of power and light.

CHESHIRE

CHESTER
35 miles SW of Manchester on the A41

Map 6 ref J12

James Boswell, Dr Johnson's biographer, visited Chester in the 1770s and wrote "I was quite enchanted at Chester, so that I could with difficulty quit it". He was to return again, declaring that "Chester pleases my fancy more than any town I ever saw". Modern visitors will almost certainly share his enthusiasm. Probably the best introduction to this compact little city is to join one of the frequent sightseeing tours conducted by a Blue Badge guide. These take place every day, even Christmas Day, and leave from the **Chester Visitor Centre**. The Centre can also provide you with a wealth of information about the city, including a full calendar of events that range from the **Chester Regatta**, the oldest rowing races in the world and **Chester Races**, the oldest in Britain, to the **Lord Mayor's Show** in May and the **Festival of Transport**, featuring an amazing parade of vintage cars, in August. Towering above the city centre is **Chester Cathedral**, a majestic building of weathered pink stone which in 1992 celebrated its 900th birthday. It was originally an Abbey and is one of very few to survive Henry VIII's closure of the monasteries in the 1540s. The cloisters are regarded as the finest in England and the monks' refectory is still serving food although nowadays it is refreshments and lunches for visitors. It was at Chester Cathedral, in 1742, that George Frederick Handel personally conducted rehearsals of his oratorio "The Messiah" before its first performance in Dublin: a copy of the score with annotations in his own hand remains on display. Chester is famous for its outstanding range of museums, from the **Deva Roman Experience** where you can re-live the sights, sounds and even the smells of daily Roman life, through the **Grosvenor Museum** with its furnished period rooms, to the Chester Heritage Centre which tells the city's story from the Civil War siege to the present day. **On The Air** broadcasting museum chronicles the world of radio and television from the pioneering days of BBC radio to satellite TV, while the **Chester Toy & Doll Museum** is a nostalgic treasure-house of antique playthings

Quite apart from its historical attractions, Chester is also one of the major shopping centres for the north west and north Wales. All the familiar High Street names are here, often housed in much more appealing buildings than they usually inhabit, along with a great number of specialist and antique shops. For a unique shopping experience, you must visit the world-famous, two-tiered galleries of shops under covered walkways known as **The Rows** which line both sides of Bridge Street. The Rows are an architectural one-off: no other medieval town has anything like them. Many of the black and white, half-timbered frontages of The Rows, so typical of Chester and Cheshire, are actually Victorian restorations, but crafted so beautifully and faithfully that even experts can have difficulty distinguishing them from their 13th century originals. Close by is the **Eastgate Clock**. It was erected in 1897 to celebrate Queen Victoria's Diamond

The Rows, Chester

Jubilee, a beautifully ornate construction which is probably the most photographed timepiece in the world. If your timing is right and you arrive hereabouts at 12 noon in the summer, you should see, and certainly hear, the **Town Crier** delivering some stentorian civic message.

A few steps bring you to Chester's famous **City Walls** which were originally built by the Romans to protect the fortress of Deva from attacks by pesky Celtic tribes. Nowadays, the two-mile long circuit, - an easy, level promenade, provides thousands of visitors with some splendid views of the River Dee, of the city's many glorious buildings and of the distant Welsh mountains. Here, during the summer months, you may come across Caius Julius Quartus, a **Roman Legionary Officer** in shining armour conducting a patrol around the fortress walls and helping to re-create the life and times of a front-line defender of the Empire. At one point, the wall runs alongside St John Street, which has a curious history. In Roman times it was the main thoroughfare between the fortress and the **Amphitheatre**, the largest ever uncovered in Britain, capable of seating 7,000 spectators. During the Middle Ages however this highway was excavated and turned into a defensive ditch. Over the years, the ditch gradually filled up and by Elizabethan times St John Street was a proper street once again. Rivers always add a special attraction to a city and Chester certainly makes good use of the River Dee. Rowing boats, motor boats, canoes, are all available for hire, and comfortable cruisers offer sightseeing tours along the river as far as the Crook of Dee, opposite the Duke of Westminster's stately residence of Eaton Hall. No visit to Chester would be complete without a trip to **Chester Zoo** on the northern edge of the city. Set in 110 acres of landscaped gardens, it's the largest zoo in Britain, caring for more than 5000 animals from some 500 different species. The Zoo also provides a refuge for many rare and endangered animals which breed freely in near-natural enclosures. What's more, it has the UK's largest elephant facility and is the only successful breeder of Asiatic elephants in this country. Offering more than enough interest for a full day out, the Zoo is open every day of the year except Christmas Day.

THE WIRRAL
N of Chester

MAP 6 REF J11

Two Old English words meaning heathland covered with bog myrtle gave The Wirral its name and well into modern times it was a byword for a desolate place. The 14th century author of "Sir Gawayne and the Green Knight" writes of:

"The wilderness of Wirral: few lived there
Who loved with a good heart either God or man"

The Wirral's inhabitants were infamous for preying on the shipwrecks tossed on to its marshy coastline by gales sweeping off the Irish Sea. The 19th century development of shipbuilding at Birkenhead brought industry on a large scale to the Mersey shore but also an influx of prosper-

ous Liverpool commuters who colonised the villages of the Caldy and
Grange Hills and transformed the
former wilderness into a leafy sub-
urbia. The 1974 Local Government
changes handed two thirds of The
Wirral to Merseyside leaving Cheshire with by far the most attractive
third, the southern and western parts
alongside the River Dee. Tourism officials now refer to The Wirral as the
"Leisure Peninsula", a fair description of this appealing and
comparatively little-known area.
One of its major attractions is **Ness**
Gardens, a 64-acre tract of superbly
landscaped gardens on the banks of the River Dee. The gardens are run by the University of
Liverpool as an Environmental and Horticultural Research Station and are planned to provide
magnificent displays all year round. There are children's play and picnic areas, and well-marked
interest trails, and licensed refreshment rooms.

Ness Gardens, Neston

PARKGATE
MAP 6 REF I11

12 miles NW of Chester via the A540 and B5135

After Neston port became unusable, maritime traffic moved along the Dee Estuary to Parkgate
which, as the new gateway to Ireland, saw some notable visitors. John Wesley, who made regular trips to Ireland, preached here while waiting for a favourable wind, and George Frederick
Handel returned via Parkgate after conducting the first performance of "The Messiah" in Dublin. J.M.W. Turner came to sketch the lovely view across to the Flintshire hills. A little later,
Parkgate enjoyed a brief spell as a fashionable spa. Lord Nelson's mistress, Lady Hamilton (who
was born at nearby Neston) took the waters here in an effort to cure an unfortunate skin disease,
another visitor was Mrs Fitzherbert, already secretly married to the Prince Regent, later George
IV. When Holyhead developed into the main gateway to Ireland, Parkgate's days as a port and

watering-place were num-
bered. But with fine
Georgian houses lining the
promenade, this attractive
little place still retains the
atmosphere of a gracious
spa town.

Andy Wareham and
Phil Williams opened **The**
Marsh Cat restaurant in
1997; this superb restau-
rant has already gained an
enviable reputation. The
views across the Dee Estuary would in themselves
make a visit worth while,
but it is the outstanding
food served here that has
attracted rave reviews from
the many newspaper and
magazine food writers

The Marsh Cat, 1 Mostyn Square, Parkgate, South Wirral,
Cheshire L64 6SL Tel: 0151 336 1963

who have come to sample Phil's cuisine. Phil was born in Belize, trained in New Orleans and has some 20-odd years' experience as a chef, garnering an astonishing collection of awards and medals for his cooking. His menus change frequently, but always include some innovative dishes from around the world. Therefore, along with the steaks, salmon, guinea fowl and peppered pork, guests may also find canard Kowloon, roast vegetable couscous and 'Shadows on the Bayou': Red Snapper, chicken breast and king prawns dusted in Cajun seasonings, seared and served with a Creole sauce. This superb restaurant is open for lunch and dinner every day; bookings are advised at all times and essential at weekends. And as for the origins of its name, the walls are adorned with the full illustrated story of the cat in question.

FRODSHAM
Map 6 ref J11

10 miles NE of Chester on the A56

This is an attractive town with a broad High Street lined with thatched cottages and spacious Georgian and Victorian houses. During the 18th and early 19th centuries, Frodsham was an important coaching town and there are several fine coaching inns. Built in 1632, **The Bear's Paw** with its three stone gables recalls the bear-baiting that once took place nearby. Of the Earl of Chester's Norman castle only fragments remain, but the **Church of St Laurence** (an earlier church here was recorded in the Domesday Book) is noted for the fine 17th century panelling in its exquisite north chapel. The Vicar here from 1740 to 1756 was Francis Gastrell, a name that is anathema to all lovers of Shakespeare. Gastrell bought the poet's house, New Place, at Stratford and first incensed the towns-people by cutting down the famous mulberry tree. Then, in order to avoid paying the Corporation poor rate, he pulled the house itself down. The outraged citizens of Stratford hounded him from the town and he returned to the parish at Frodsham that he had neglected for years.

The outstanding **Squires Restaurant** stands on the main street in this beautiful Cheshire village. Housed on the first floor of this Grade II listed building, the restaurant is beautifully decorated in rich, warm colours that create a relaxed and peaceful atmosphere. Michael Whalley, who has much experience of the catering business, opened this fine establishment in 1991 and has gained an excellent reputation for his glorious food. Open for dinner Monday - Saturday, the restaurant is well known throughout the area. The menu is extensive, with a host of special gourmet evenings throughout the year when diners can sample such culinary delights as lamb

cutlets in a light filo pastry with tagliatelle in a tomato, garlic and chilli sauce, venison steak marinated in Jack Daniels and served with garlic roast vegetables and redcurrant sauce, or pan-fried pork loin on a bed of sweet apple and couscous topped with caramelised apple and garnished with cheesie potato skins and asparagus. These and more mouth-watering creations are sure to satisfy any

**Squires Restaurant, 4a High Street, Frodsham,
Cheshire WA6 7HE Tel: 01985 735246**

palate. Thursday night is Fish Night, incorporated with the a la carte menu. There is a choice of at least eight different varieties of fresh fish from the market that morning, plus a selection of sauces to accompany the fish. In intimate and cosy surroundings guests can enjoy the very best of English, French and Italian cuisine, and Continental dishes cooked in Michael's own innovative style. All dishes are prepared to order and make use of as much local produce as possible. When a table is booked it is for the entire evening, a final touch that makes a meal here the perfect dining experience.

ASHTON
8 miles E of Chester on the B5393   MAP 6 REF J12

A couple of miles to the northeast of Ashton stretch the 4,000 acres of **Delamere Forest**, a rambler's delight with a wealth of lovely walks and many picnic sites, ideal for a peaceful family day out. In Norman times, a "forest" was a part-wooded, part-open area, reserved as a hunting ground exclusively for royalty or the nobility. There were savage penalties for anyone harming the deer, even if the deer were destroying crops, and household dogs within the forest had to be deliberately lamed to ensure that they could not harass the beasts.

TARPORLEY
9 miles E of Chester off the A51/A49   MAP 6 REF J12

In the days when most of this area was part of **Delamere Forest**, Tarporley was the headquarters of the *verderers*, or forest wardens. It was from Tarporley in the early 17th century that John Done, Chief Forester and Hereditary Bow-bearer of Delamere, entertained King James to a hunt. The chase was, he reported, a great success: "deer, both red and fallow, fish and fowl, abounded in the meres." A gratified King James rewarded his host with a knighthood. At that time, the verderers had their own courts in which they meted out rough justice to offenders against the forest laws. One such court was at **Utkinton**, just north of the town, and in an old farmhouse there stands a column fomed by an ancient forest tree, its roots still in the ground. When the

court was in session, the wardens would place on this tree the symbol of their authority, the Hunting Horn of Delamere. The farmhouse is not open to the public, but the horn - dating from around 1120 - has survived and can be seen at the Grosvenor Museum in Chester.

The Swan in Tarporley is a characterful and welcoming traditional inn dating back to 1700. Occupying a gracious and attractive Georgian townhouse in the heart of Tarporley, it attracts a discerning clientele who appreciate its unique warmth and ambience. There are 19 well-appointed guest bedrooms, each individually styled, all with great charm, comfort and equipped with all the modern amenities today's guests have come to expect. In the restaurant, guests can choose from an excellent variety of seasonal dishes and home-cooked specialities. All dishes are expertly prepared and presented. In surroundings such as these, guests are certain to have a memorable and enjoyable stay. As part of Pernickety chain of inns dotted across England, the staff take justified pride in upholding a tradition for a high standard of conscientiousness and friendly service.

The Swan, 50 High Street, Tarporley, Cheshire CW6 0AG Tel: 01829 733838 Fax: 01829 732932

BEESTON
MAP 6 REF J12
3 miles S of Tarporley on minor road off the A49

A craggy cliff suddenly rising 500 feet from the Cheshire Plain, its summit crowned by the ruins of **Beeston Castle** (English Heritage), Beeston Hill is one of the most dramatic sights in the county. Built around 1220, the castle didn't see any military action until the Civil War. On one rather ignominious occasion during that conflict, a Royalist captain and just eight musketeers managed to capture the mighty fortress and its garrison of 60 soldiers without firing a shot. A few years later, Cromwell ordered that the castle be "slighted", or partially destroyed, but this "Castle in the Air" is still very imposing with walls 30 feet high and a well 366 feet deep. An old legend asserts that Richard II tipped a hoard of coins, gold and jewels down the well, but no treasure has yet been discovered.

Gatehouse, Beeston Castle

The castle hill is a popular place for picnics, and it's worth climbing it just to enjoy the spectacular views which extend across seven counties and over to a "twin" castle. **Peckforton Castle** looks just as medieval as Beeston but was, in fact, built in 1844 for the first Lord Tollemache who spared no expense in re-creating features such as a vast Great Hall and a keep with towers 60 feet tall. The architect Gilbert Scott later praised Peckforton as "the very height of masquerading". Its authentic medieval appearance has made the castle a favourite location for film and television companies, and on Sundays and Bank Holidays during the season the Middle Ages are brought to life here with mock battles and tournaments. The castle also offers guided tours, refreshments and a speciality shop.

CHOLMONDELEY CASTLE
MAP 6 REF J12
7 miles S of Tarporley off the A49

If you continue south from Beeston on the A49, after about six miles you will reach **Cholmondeley Castle** and its famous gardens. They were first laid out in the early years of the 19th century shortly after the Castle was built. The Castle itself, a marvellous mock-medieval construction, is not open to the public, but visitors are welcome to explore the 30 acre garden which includes a water garden and woodland walks. There are plants for sale, a lakeside picnic area, a gift shop and tea room.

NANTWICH
MAP 6 REF K12
10 miles SE of Chester off the A51

The most disastrous event in the long history of Nantwich was the Great Fire of 1583 which consumed some 600 of its thatched and timber-framed buildings. The blaze raged for 20 days and the terror of the townspeople was compounded when some bears kept behind the Crown Hotel escaped. (Four bears from Nantwich are mentioned in Shakespeare's comedy "The Merry Wives of Windsor"). Queen Elizabeth contributed the huge sum of £2000 and also donated quantities of timber from Delamere Forest to assist in the town's rebuilding. A grateful citizen, Thomas Cleese, commemorated this royal largesse with a plaque on his new house at No. 41, High Street. The plaque is still in place and reads:

"God grant our ryal Queen in England longe to raign
For she hath put her helping hand to bild this towne again".

The most striking of the buildings to survive the conflagration, perhaps because it was surrounded by a moat, is the lovely black and white house in Hospital Street, known as **Churche's Mansion** after the merchant Richard Churche who built it in 1577. Astonishingly, when the house was up for sale in 1930, no buyer showed any interest and the building was on the point of being transported brick by brick to America when a public-spirited local doctor stepped in and rescued it. The ground floor is now a restaurant, but the upper floor has been furnished in Elizabethan style and is open to the public during the summer.

The Great Fire also spared the stone-built 14th century church. This fine building, with an unusual octagonal tower, is sometimes called the **Cathedral of South Cheshire** and dates from the period of the town's greatest prosperity as a salt town and trading centre. Of exceptional interest is the magnificent chancel and the wonderful carvings in the choir. On the misericords (tip-up seats) are mermaids, foxes (some dressed as monks in a sharp dig at priests), pigs, and

Nantwich

the legendary Wyvern, half-dragon, half-bird, whose name is linked with the River Weaver, 'wyvern' being an old pronunciation of Weaver. An old tale about the building of the church tells of an old woman who brought ale and food each day from a local inn to the masons working on the site. The masons discovered that the woman was cheating them by keeping back some of the money they put "in the pot" for their refreshment. They dismissed her and took revenge by making a stone carving showing the old woman being carried away by Old Nick himself, her hand still stuck in a pot. During the Civil War, Nantwich was the only town in Cheshire to support Cromwell's Parliamentary army. After several weeks of fighting, the Royalist forces were finally defeated on 25th January, 1644 and the people of Nantwich celebrated by wearing sprigs of holly in their hair. As a result, the day became known as **"Holly Holy Day"** and every year, on the Saturday closest to January 25th, the town welcomes Cromwellian pikemen and battle scenes are re-enacted by members of the Sealed Knot. There are records of the Civil War in the **Nantwich Museum** in Pillory Street which also has exhibitions about the town and its dairy and cheese-making industries.

But it was salt that had once made Nantwich second only in importance to Chester in the county. The Romans had mined salt here for their garrisons at Chester and Stoke where the soldiers received part of their wages in "sal", or salt. The payment was called a "salarium", hence the modern word salary. Nantwich remained a salt producing town right up to the 18th century but then it was overtaken by towns like Northwich which enjoyed better communications on the canal system. But a brine spring still supplies Nantwich's outdoor swimming pool!

CONGLETON

MAP 6 REF L12

20 miles E of Nantwich on the A34

Congleton, in the foothills of the Pennines, was an inhabited place as long ago as the Stone Age. The remains of a 5000-year-old chambered tomb known as **The Bridestones** can be seen beside the hill road running eastwards from the town to the A523 road to Leek. In Elizabethan times, the townspeople of Congleton seem to have had a passion for bear-baiting. On one occasion, when the town bear died they handed 16 shillings to the Bear Warden to acquire another beast. The money had originally been collected to buy a town bible: this disgraceful misappropriation of funds gave rise to the ditty: "Congleton rare, Congleton rare, sold the bible to buy a bear". Known locally as the "Bear Town", Congleton was the very last town in England to outlaw the cruel practice of bear-baiting. A more attractive distinction is the fact that it is also one the few towns in Cheshire where the medieval street pattern has remained intact and where the curfew bell is still rung each night at 8pm. Congleton's impressive Venetian Gothic style **Town Hall**, built in 1866, contains some interesting exhibits recalling its long history. Amongst them are displays recording the work of such ancient civic officials as the swine-catcher, the chimney-looker and the ale-taster, and aids to domestic harmony like the bridle for nagging wives which used to be fastened to a wall in the market place. Congleton developed as an important textile town during the 18th century with many of its mills involved in silk manufacture, cotton spinning and ribbon weaving. In **Mill Green** near the River Dane, you can still see part of the very first silk mill to operate here.

EATON

Map 6 ref L12

2 miles NE of Congleton off the A536

The Plough at Eaton dates back to the 18th century when it was a popular and important coaching inn. Today it retains a traditional air and a dedication to quality and service. An ideal

venue for dining and socializing, it offers the kind of tasteful touches and meticulous attention to detail that sets the inn apart from other establishments. Solid oak beams and distinctive furnishings add to the inn's character and ambience. The excellent menu changes according to season and offers a very good range of culinary delights. Each dish is freshly prepared to order by the inn's qualified chefs. In addition, this charming and original hostelry boasts eight lovely and well-appointed en suite guest bedrooms. Here in these relaxed and comfortable

The Plough at Eaton, Macclesfield Road, Eaton, nr Congleton, Cheshire CW12 2NR Tel: 01260 280207 Fax: 01260 298377

surroundings, any stay is certain to be enjoyable and memorable. As part of Pernickety chain of inns dotted throughout the country, the staff take justified pride in upholding a tradition for a high standard of conscientiousness and friendly service.

ASTBURY

Map 6 ref K12

3 miles SW of Congleton on the A34

The pretty little village of Astbury, set around a triangular village green, was once more important than neighbouring Congleton which is why it has a much older church, built between

Little Moreton Hall

1350 and 1540. Arguably the finest parish church in the county, St Mary's is famous for its lofty recessed spire (which rises from a tower almost detached from the nave), and the superb timber work inside: a richly carved ceiling, intricate tracery on the rood screen, and a lovely Jacobean font cover. But just three miles down the A34 is an even more remarkable building. Black and white half-timbered houses have almost become a symbol for the county of Cheshire and the most stunning example is undoubtedly **Little Moreton Hall** (National Trust), a "wibbly wobbly" house which provided a memorable location for Granada TV's adaptation of *Moll Flanders*. The only bricks to be seen are in the chimneys, and The Hall's huge overhanging gables, slanting walls, and great stretches of leaded windows, create wonderfully complex patterns, all magically reflected in the still flooded moat. Ralph Moreton began construction in 1480 and the fabric of this magnificent house has changed little since the 16th century. A richly panelled Great Hall, parlour and chapel show off superb Elizabethan plaster and wood work. Free guided tours give visitors a fascinating insight into Tudor life, and there's also a beautifully reconstructed Elizabethan knot garden with clipped box hedges and a period herb garden.

Mow Cop, Nr Astbury

About a mile south is the **Rode Hall Estate**. It was an 18th century owner of the estate, Randle Wilbraham, who built the famous folly of **Mow Cop** (National Trust) to enhance the view from his mansion. This mock ruin stands atop a rocky hill 1100 ft above sea level, just yards from the Staffordshire border. On a clear day, the views are fantastic: Alderley Edge to the north, the Pennines to the north-east, south to Cannock Chase and Shropshire, and westwards across Cheshire.

NORTHWICH
15 miles E of Chester off the A556

MAP 6 REF K12

The Vale Royal is now a district borough centred on the old salt town of Northwich. Even before the Romans arrived, Cheshire salt was well known and highly valued. But production on a major scale at Northwich began in 1670 when rock salt was discovered in nearby Marston. Salt may seem an inoffensive sort of product, but its extraction from the Keuper marl of the Cheshire Plain has had some quite spectacular side-effects. In Elizabethan times, John Leland, recorded that a hill at Combermere suddenly disappeared into underground workings, and Northwich later became notorious for the number of its buildings leaning at crazy angles because of subsidence. Even today, the **White Lion Inn** in Witton Street lies a complete storey lower than its original height. The arrival in the 19th century of new processes of extraction brought different problems. In 1873, John Brunner and Ludwig Mond set up their salt works at Winnington on the northern edge of the town to manufacture alkali products based on brine. The ammonia process involved cast an appalling stench over the town and devastated vegetation for miles around. On the other hand, Brunner and Mond were model employers. They paid their workforce well, built houses for them and were amongst the first firms in the country to give their employees annual holidays with pay.

The long involvement of Northwich and Cheshire with salt production is vividly recorded at the **Salt Museum**, the only one of its kind in Britain. It stands in London Road and occupies what used to be the **Northwich**

Salt Museum, Northwich

Workhouse which, like so many of those dreaded institutions, is an exceptionally handsome late-Georgian building, designed by George Latham, the architect of Arley Hall. With its unique collection of traditional working tools, and lively displays which include working models and videos, the Salt Museum recounts the fascinating story of the county's oldest industry. Not only can ancient remains such as Roman evaporating pans and medieval salt rakes be seen, but there is also much to remind visitors of the vital part that salt plays in the modern chemical industry.

ANDERTON

MAP 6 REF K11

1 miles NW of Northwich on minor road off the A533

One of the most stupendous engineering feats of the canal age was the **Anderton Boat Lift**, built in 1875 and recently restored. This extraordinary construction was designed to transfer boats from the **Trent & Mersey Canal** to the **Weaver Navigation** 50 feet below. Two barges

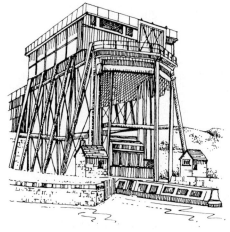

Anderton Boat Lift

would enter the upper tank, two the lower, and by pumping water out of the lower tank, the boats would exchange places. Thousands of visitors come every year to marvel at this impressive structure which was conceived and designed by Edward Leader Williams who later went on to engineer the Manchester Ship Canal.

About a mile north of Anderton, **Marbury Country Park** was formerly part of a large country estate, but the area is now managed by Cheshire County Council whose wardens have created a variety of habitats for plants, trees and animals. The Park lies at the edge of **Budworth Mere** and there are attractive walks and bridleways around the site where you'll also find an arboretum, picnic area and garden centre.

MARSTON
MAP 6 REF K11

1 mile NE of Northwich on a minor road

In Victorian times, the **Old Salt Mine** at Marston was a huge tourist attraction. About 360 ft deep and covering 35 acres, it even brought the Tsar of Russia here in 1844. Ten thousand lamps illuminated the huge cavern as the Emperor sat down to dinner here with eminent members of the Royal Society. By the end of the century, however, subsidence caused by the mine had made some 40 houses in the village uninhabitable, and one day in 1933 a hole 50ft wide and 300ft deep suddenly appeared close to the **Trent & Mersey Canal**. Happily, the village has now stabilised itself, and at the **Lion Salt Works Museum** on most afternoons you will find volunteer workers keeping alive the only surviving open pan saltworks in Britain.

GREAT BUDWORTH
MAP 6 REF K11

3 miles N of Northwich off the A559

A charming small village nowadays, "Great" Budworth was accorded that designation at a time when it was the largest ecclesiastical parish in all Cheshire, the administrative centre for some 35 individual communities. The imposing church on the hill, built in the 14th and 15th centuries, reflects its importance during those years. **St Mary & All Saints** attracts many visitors to its host of quaint carvings and odd faces that peer out at unexpected corners: some with staring eyes, others with their tongues poking out. There's a man near the pulpit who appears to be drowsing through some interminable sermon. Under the roof of the nave you'll find a man with a serpent, another in mid-somersault, and a minstrel playing bagpipes. The distinguished 17th century historian, Sir Peter Leycester, is buried in the Lady Chapel, and in the Warburton Chapel there is a finely carved Tudor ceiling and 13th century oak stalls - the oldest in Cheshire. During the 19th century, Great Budworth was part of the neawrby Arley Hall estate and it is largely due to the energetic Squire Egerton-Warburton, a "conservationist" well ahead of his time, that so many of the attractive old cottages in the village are still in place.

It always inspires confidence to learn that a pub has been run by the same family for many years. **The George and Dragon** in this picturesque village has been in the capable hands of the Curtin family since 1961: the present generation, Malcolm and Rose, have presided over this historic inn since 1982. Originally built in 1722, when the consumption of a couple of bottles of port wine over the course of an evening was considered a modest sup for any social person, this distinguished pub rather surprisingly greets customers with a warning against intemperate drinking. The ancient inscription in the front porch advises:

As St George in armed array
Doth the fiery dragon slay
So mayst thou with might no less
Slay that dragon drunkenness.

A step inside this welcoming inn finds guests enjoying a truly friendly hostelry offering an excellent choice of well-prepared food and well-kept ales. The CAMRA *Good Beer Guide* has been recommending the inn for well over 10 years; the *Egon Ronay Pub Guide* and the *Good Pub Guide* currently add their

The George and Dragon, High Street,
Great Budworth, nr Northwich,
Cheshire CW9 6HF Tel: 01606 891317

ADLINGTON
Map 6 ref L11
4 miles N of Macclesfield off the A523

The village of Adlington can also boast a fine old house. **Adlington Hall** has been the home of the Legh family since 1315 and is now one of the county's most popular attractions. Quadrangular in shape, this magnificent manor house has two distinctive styles of architecture: black

and white half-timbered buildings on two sides, later Georgian additions in warm red brick on the others. There is much to see as you tour the hall, with beautifully polished wooden floors and lovely antique furnishings enhancing the air of elegance

Adlington Hall

and grandeur. The Great Hall is a breathtaking sight, a vast room of lofty proportions that set off perfectly the exquisitely painted walls. The beautifully-preserved 17th century organ here has responded to the touch of many maestros, none more famous than George Frederick Handel who visited the Hall in the 1740's.

WOODFORD
Map 6 ref L11
6 miles N of Macclesfield on the A5102

Just a couple of miles from Woodford is one of the grandest old "magpie" houses in Cheshire,

Bramall Hall. This eye-catching, rambling perfection of black and white timbered buildings overlooks some 62 acres of exquisitely-landscaped woods, lakes and formal gardens. The oldest parts of the Hall date from the 14th century: for five of the next six centuries it was owned by the same family, the Davenports. Over the years, the Davenport family continually altered and extended the originally quite modest manor house. But whenever they added a new Banqueting Hall, "Withdrawing Room", or even a Chapel, they took pains to ensure that its design harmonised happily with its more ancient neighbours. Along with Little Moreton Hall and Gawsworth Hall, Bramall represents the full-

Bramall Hall

est flowering of a lovely architectural style whose most distinctive examples are all to be found in Cheshire.

ALDERLEY EDGE
MAP 6 REF K11
6 miles NW of Macclesfield on the A34

Alderley Edge takes its name from the long, wooded escarpment, nearly two miles long, that rises 600 feet above sea level and culminates in sandy crags overlooking the Cheshire Plain. In Victorian times, this spectacular area was the private preserve of the Stanley family and it was only under great pressure that they grudgingly allowed the "Cottentots" of Manchester access on occasional summer weekends. It was the Stanley daughters who took great umbrage when the Wizard Inn hung up a new sign. They demanded its removal. The Merlin-like figure depicted could, they claimed, be taken as a representation of their father, Lord Stanley, at that time a virtual recluse and more than a little eccentric. Nowadays, however, walkers can roam freely along the many footpaths through the woods, one of which will take them to **Hare Hill Gardens**, a little known National Trust property. These Victorian gardens include fine woodland, a walled garden themed in blue, white and yellow flowers, and huge banks of rhododendrons. There is access by way of gravel paths for the less able.

LYMM
MAP 6 REF K11
6 miles NW of Knutsford on the A56

During the stage coach era, **Eagle Brow** was notorious, a dangerously steep road that dropped precipitously down the hillside into the village of Lymm. To bypass this hazard, a turnpike was built (now the A56), so preserving the heart of this ancient village with its half-timbered houses and well-preserved village stocks. **The Bridgewater Canal** flows past nearby and the church is reflected in the waters of **Lymm Dam**. Popular with anglers and bird-watchers, the dam is a large man-made lake, part of a lovely woodland centre which is linked to the surrounding countryside and the canal towpath by a network of footpaths and bridleways. The village became an important centre for the fustian cloth (corduroy) trade in the 19th century but is now best known simply as a delightful place to visit. Lymm stands on the sides of a ravine and its streets have actually been carved out of the sandstone rock. The same rock was used to construct Lymm's best-known landmark, the ancient cross crowned with a huge cupola that stands at the top of the High Street.

For lovers of fine food and wines, **Lymm Bistro** in Bridgewater Street can be found in an attractive 200-year-old building and has been run since 1988 by Jo Shenton and Michael Venning. Since opening the bistro, Jo and Michael have earned themselves an excellent reputation for providing first-class food and wines. Michael is the chef

Lymm Bistro, 16 Bridgewater Street, Lymm, Cheshire WA13 0AB Tel: 01925 754852

and he goes to great lengths to ensure that diners receive only the best and freshest produce. Meals are cooked to order - the speciality is fish, anything from a simple but exquisite whole Dover Sole to really exotic and innovative dishes. In addition to the quality menu there are always several adventurous specials such as spicy Spanish-style king prawns, fillet de porc, grilled monkfish and boeuf forestière. A cosy, friendly atmosphere pervades this distinctive establishment. Due to its popularity, the bistro has recently been extended to accommodate its faithful regulars and new guests - bookings are advised. Open evenings Tuesday - Thursday 7-10 p.m., Friday-Saturday 7 - 10.30 p.m.

DUNHAM MASSEY
MAP 6 REF K11
6 miles E of Lymm on B5160

Dunham Massey Hall and Park (National Trust) has 250 acres of parkland where fallow deer roam freely. There's a restored water-mill which is usually in operation every Wednesday, and splendid walks in every direction. The Hall, once the home of the Earls of Stamford and Warrington, is a grand Georgian mansion of 1732 which boasts an outstanding collection of furniture, paintings and Huguenot silver. The Hall is open most days from April to October: the Park is open every day.

LANCASHIRE

LANCASTER
MAP 6 REF K11
55 miles N of Manchester on the A6

The capital of this beautiful county, Lancaster proudly boasts of its legacy, which extends back many centuries. Unlike York its White Rose cousin, which has long been internationally known as a tourist attraction, this Red Rose city has taken longer to be discovered. In fact, Lancaster

Lancaster Castle

has an equally important place in English history and it has retained close links with the monarchy. As early as the 10th century, Athelstan, the grandson of Alfred the Great, had lands in the area and it was during the reign of William the Conqueror that large areas of what is now Lancashire were given, by the grateful king, to his cousin Roger of Pitou, who made his base at Lancaster. The first Earl of Lancaster was Edmund, the youngest son of Henry III and, in time, the title passed to John of Gaunt who persuaded Richard II to give him the right to pass the title on to his highest male descendent. Now a dukedom, to this day the present Queen still retains the title of Duke of Lancaster.

Within yards of the railway station lies **Lancaster Castle**, a great medieval fortress, founded by the Normans to keep out Scottish invaders, and strengthened by John of Gaunt, Duke of Lancaster, in the 15th century. Standing proudly on its hilltop position, this great castle has an imposing presence and dominates the skyline over Lancaster. Its huge square keep dates back to 1200 and was raised in height and impregnability at the time of the Armada. Astonishingly perhaps, most of the building still functions as a prison, but certain sections are open to the public, including the

18th-century **Shire Hall**, the cells where the witches of Pendle were imprisoned, and the **Crown Court** which not only saw the trials of the Pendle witches but also those of John Paslew (last abbot of Whalley) in 1536, numerous Catholic priest during the 16th and early 17th centuries, and, more recently, the Birmingham pub bombers in 1975. Hadrian's Tower and - a touch of the macabre - the Drop Room where prisoners were prepared for the gallows can also be viewed by the public.

A short walk from the castle leads into the largely pedestrianised city centre, full of shops, the market, and much besides. The **City Museum** in the Market Place occupies the Old Town Hall, built between 1781-3 by Major Jarrett and Thomas Harrison. As well as the city's art collection and an area of changing exhibitions, there are displays and collections of material illustrating aspects of the city's industrial and social history. Also here is the **Museum of the King's Own Royal Regiment**, a regiment which was based in Lancaster from 1880 onwards.

Found tucked away in Music Room Square is the delightful **Sunbury Coffee House**, which has been owned and personally run by Gill and John Constable since 1992. Housed in a listed building that dates from 1798, the Georgian theme extends from the attractive stone facade to the elegant interior with its marble table tops, providing the perfect setting in which to enjoy the fine selection of teas and coffees accompanied by the delicious, freshly prepared snacks.

The decor is charming, with light flooding in from the French doors and decorative paintings adorning the walls. There is also a secluded and attractive outdoor seating area for fine days.

A diverse range of coffees is always available, including Colombian, Kenyan Blue Mountain, Costa Rican, New Guinea, and Old Government Java, as well as cappuccino and decaffeinated varieties. There is an equally fine range of teas, including Assam, Earl Grey, Darjeeling, English Breakfast and Lancaster blend, and speciality herbal teas. For those who prefer a cold drink, there is a selection of fizzy drinks, juices and milk. The food, too, is excellent, and ranges from open sandwiches and savoury filled croissants to soup, filled jacket potatoes, toasted sandwiches, salads and the chef's

Sunbury Coffee House, Music Room Square,
28 Sun Street, Lancaster, Lancashire LA1 1EW
Tel: 01524 843312

superb hot specials, which change daily. But room must be left for one (or more!) of the mouthwatering selection of home-made cakes and pastries. All in all, this superior coffee house is a very tempting stopping-off point for those exploring the many delights of this historic town. Open: Monday to Friday, 8 a.m. to 4 p.m.; Saturdays 9 a.m. to 4.30 p.m.

In Church Street is the **Judge's Lodging**, a beautifully proportioned building dating from the 1620s when it was built as a private house for Thomas Covell then, later, used by judges during the Lancaster Assizes. It now houses two separate museums: the **Museum of Childhood** containing the Barry Elder doll collection; and the **Gillow and Town House Museum** containing many examples of the fine workmanship of Gillows, the famous Lancaster cabinet-makers. In fact, it was Richard Gillow who designed the city's Maritime Museum. Close by is the **Cottage Museum** in a house built in 1739 that was divided into two dwellings in the 19th century. Furnished in the style of an artisan's house of the early to mid-19th century, the museum is open from Easter to the end of September. Just around a corner or two, in Sun Street, is the **Music Room**, an exquisite early Georgian building originally designed as a pavilion in the long vanished garden of Oliver Marton. It is notable for some superb decorative plasterwork.

Lancaster grew up along the banks of the River Lune, which is navigable as far as Skerton Bridge, so there has always been a strong association between the town and its watery highway. Documents from 1297 make reference to the town's small-scale maritime trade, but it was not until the late 17th and early 18th centuries that Lancaster's character as a port fully emerged. The splendid buildings of the 18th-century Golden Age were born out of the port wealth, and the layout and appearance of the town was much altered by this building bonanza. Lancaster as a port gradually declined throughout the 19th century so that many buildings put up for specific maritime purposes were taken over for other uses. Naturally, the city has been affected by the arrival of the Lancaster Canal, the railways, and 19th-century industry; yet the hallmark of Lancaster, its Georgian centre, remains as the product of this maritime prosperity. Lancaster's rich maritime history is celebrated at **St George's Quay** which, with its great stone warehouses and superb **Custom House**, is now an award-winning **Maritime Museum**. In Georgian times this was a thriving port with the warehouses receiving ship loads of mahogany, tobacco, rum, and sugar from the West Indies. Visitors today are given a vivid insight into the life of the mariners and quayside workers, with opportunities for knot-tying and the practising of other maritime skills. Every year, over the four days of the Easter weekend, St George's Quay is home to the Lancaster Maritime Festival with smugglers, sea songs, and shanties.

Situated in the heart of Lancaster and housed in a building which dates back to 1797, **Joseph's Restaurant** is an excellent place. Owners Elizabeth and José Granados opened the restaurant in 1990, and have gained an enviable reputation for high quality home-cooked cuisine and a warm and welcoming ambience. The premises are small and cosy, and the very Continental decor, including the tiled floor and soft lighting, gives the restaurant a superb feel that complements the cuisine as well as making the dining experience completely enjoyable. Open every day except Sundays, the restaurant offers a range of menus which cater to customers from first thing in the morning to well into the evening. As well as serving morning coffee and afternoon tea, there is a light lunch menu and, for the evening, table d'hôte and à la carte menus. All these are supplemented by an ever-changing list of daily specials which make full use of the freshest ingredients available at the local market. José is the chef of the partnership and all of the delicious dishes are beautifully prepared and presented. Booking is advised, particularly for the evening. No smoking.

Joseph's Restaurant, 10 Gage Street, Lancaster, Lancashire LA1 1UH Tel: 01524 844707

Built between 1797 and 1819, the **Lancaster Canal** stretches 57 miles from Preston through the centre of Lancaster to Kendal. Today, it is navigable between Preston and Tewitfield, north of Lancaster, the longest lock-free stretch of canal in the country. The canal offers a diversity of scenery and wildlife with opportunities for long-distance trips and short, circular walks with fine views through peaceful countryside. With 41 lock-free miles it offers relaxed boating with canalside pubs, restaurants, and boat-hire facilities. It provides a good touring route for canoeists and is excellent for coarse fishing.

One of the first sights visitors see of the city is the great green copper dome of the impressive **Ashton Memorial**, a landmark for miles around. A kind of miniature St Paul's - standing on a hilltop in the centre of the wonderful Edwardian **Williamson Park** - this is a magnificent viewpoint from which Morecambe Bay, the Lakeland Hills, and the Forest of Bowland are all visible. The building now houses exhibitions and multi-screen presentations about the life and times of Lancaster's Lord Ashton and the Edwardians. The park and the memorial all commemorate the life and works of Lancaster's most famous son, James Williamson. He was born in the town in 1842 and took over the running of the family business, linoleum and textile manufacture, which went on to become Lancaster's largest employer. Williamson was the Liberal MP for the town for many years and, in 1895, he became Lord Ashton.

Williamson Park was Lord Ashton's own personal idea as a means of providing work for local people during the cotton famine crisis in the textile industry during the American Civil War in the 1860s. Constructed on the site of old quarries, which gives the park its undulating contours, the park was opened in 1896. As well as the magnificent Ashton Memorial there is also a delightful **Butterfly House** in the restored Edwardian Palm House and the Conservation Garden and Wildlife Pool which opened in 1991.

CARNFORTH
5 miles N of Lancaster on the A6

MAP 10 REF J8

The town lies around what was once a major crossroads on the A6 but it is, perhaps, its fame as a busy railway junction town - whose station was used as the setting for the 1940s film classic *Brief Encounter* - by which most people known Carnforth. Though the station has declined in importance, now an unstaffed halt, the old engine sheds and sidings are now occupied by **Steamtown**, one of the largest steam railway centres in the north of England. Visitors are likely to see such giants of the Age of Steam as the Flying Scotsman or an A4 Pacific being stabled here, together with a permanent collection of over 30 British and Continental steam locomotives. There are steam rides in the summer months on both standard gauge and miniature lines.

YEALAND
8 miles N of Lancaster off the A6

MAP 10 REF J8

To the south of the village lies **Leighton Hall** - a fine early 19th-century house which is open to the public. In the Middle Ages, this land, and much of the surrounding area, was owned by the d'Avranches family. Over the centuries, the house and the land passed through many hands before becoming the property of the Gillows family of Lancaster. Now in the hands of the Reynolds family, a branch of the Gillows, the fine furniture see in the hall reflects the trade that made the family fortune.

The hall, today, dates from 1800 when it was built out of pale, local sandstone to the Gothic designs of Harrison, a Chester architect. One of the finest houses in the county, the views from the extensive grounds are magnificent and take in the nearby **Leighton Moss** bird reserve.

SILVERDALE
8 miles N of Lancaster off the A6

MAP 10 REF J8

The village lies at the northwesternmost corner of the county and has the Lakeland hills as a backdrop as well as superb views over Morecambe Bay. The latter half of the 19th century saw Silverdale develop as a quiet seaside resort where those so inclined could take medicinal baths of fresh sea water in the one of the many small villas situated along the coast. One frequent visitor was Elizabeth Gaskell who is certainly said to have written at least part of all her books whilst holidaying here. However, Silverdale's history goes back well beyond the days of a genteel Victorian resort. Its name comes from a Viking family which settled here and which signifies that this was Sigward's or Soevers' valley. Fishing, naturally, was the key provider of local income, but in the 18th century, a copper smelting works was built here. All, however, that remains of the foundry is the chimney near **Jenny Brown's Point**, said to be named after an old woman who lived here in the 18th century.

Essentially, now a small residential village, Silverdale is well worth visiting for the network of footpaths from here that pass through the limestone woodlands that are such a joy for the botanist, being rich in wild flowers in spring - primroses, violets, orchids, bird's eye primroses, rockroses, and eglantines abound. **Leighton Moss** near Silverdale is a nationally known RSPB bird sanctuary. The reed beds are the most important part of the reserve because they have become a northern stronghold of the rare bearded tit and are also the major British breeding centre for the bittern.

HORNBY
MAP 10 REF K8
8 miles NE of Lancaster on the A683

The situation of this village, by a bluff overlooking the valley of the River Lune, not only gives Hornby panoramic views of the surrounding countryside but also makes this a strategic position that has been utilised over the centuries. Just to the north of the village is the attractive stone-built **Loyn Bridge**, which takes the road over the River Lune and on to Gressington. Constructed in 1684, it replaced a ford and beside the bridge is Castle Stede, the best example of a Norman motte and bailey castle in Lancashire. The romantically situated **Hornby Castle**, which can be viewed from the village, was immortalised in a painting by Turner. Although is was only built in the 19th century, the castle incorporates the ruins of an older castle and it is now a grand and picturesque country house.

MORECAMBE
MAP 10 REF J8
3 miles W of Lancaster on the A589

Featuring prominently on the Lancashire coastline, Morecambe has long been one of the most successful and popular seaside resorts in the North, and it can truly be said to enjoy one of the finest views from its promenade of any resort in England - a magnificent sweep of coastline and bay, looking across to the Lakeland mountains. Like other resorts, Morecambe has changed with the times, and major new attractions include the multi-million pound Bubbles Leisure Park and Superdome, as well as a Wild West Theme Park. WOMAD, Morecambe's annual world music festival, attracts visitors from across the globe. There are also popular seafront illuminations in late summer, together with all the usual lively shops and variety of entertainment associated with a busy seaside resort.

Morecambe Bay, a vast wide, flat tidal plain, situated between Lancashire and Cumbria is the home of many forms of marine life as well as being a very popular and important habitat for birds. The Rivers Lune, Kent, Keer, Leven, and Crayke create the gulleys, mud, and sandbanks that make this not only one of the most important ornithological sites in Europe but also a great source of mussels and shrimps. It is also a treacherous place for the unwary as, though it looks a simple walk across the bay, the sands are extremely hazardous and a crossing should not be made, in any circumstances, without the direct supervision of a sand pilot. Over the centuries, many have perished whilst attempting the crossing and, at one time, the monks of the Furness peninsula acted as guides to those wishing to make their way to Cumbria without taking the long overland route.

HEYSHAM
MAP 10 REF J8

5 miles W of Lancaster on the A683

It is worth strolling along the promenade in a southerly direction as far as Heysham, More-cambe's twin, with its quaint old main street that winds down to the shore. It is also a town with considerable historic associations, because it was here in the 8th century that Christian missionaries arrived from Ireland to convert the heathen Viking settlers in the north of England. They built the **Chapel of St Patrick** on a rock on the sea edge and it is likely that this is the county's oldest religious house. Its ruins, with coffin-shaped rocks - one of the most curious graveyards in England - can still be seen.

The little **Church of St Peter** on the headland below the chapel is equally interesting. It dates back to Saxon and Norman times, with an Anglo-Saxon cross on which the Madonna and other figures have been crudely carved by 9th century masons, and there is a rare Viking hog-back gravestone. It is one of the oldest churches in western Europe to have been in continuous use.

QUERNMORE
MAP 10 REF J8

3 miles E of Lancaster off the A683

Lying at the head of the Conder Valley, this farming village had a pottery industry as well as slate quarrying in the 17th century. The word 'quern' refers to a particularly ancient form of hand-mill that was hewn from the rocks found on the nearby moorside and, indeed, corn milling continued here until World War II. To the east of the village lies **Clougha Pike**, itself on the western edges of the Forest of Bowland Area of Outstanding Natural Beauty and one of the few places in the area that is accessible to walkers. Although it is not the highest peak in the forest - it is just over 1300 feet - the walk up Clougha Pike is very pleasant and one which offers splendid views at the summit, not only of the Lakeland Fells but also of Morecambe Bay and, on a clear day, Blackpool Tower.

Clougha Pike

FOREST OF BOWLAND
MAP 10 REF K8

E of Lancaster

Designated an Area of Outstanding Natural Beauty in February 1964, this large scenic area is a veritable paradise for walkers and country lovers that is dotted with picturesque villages. The 11th largest of such designated areas, the Forest of Bowland is something of a misnomer, the term 'forest' is derived from the Latin 'foris' which was formerly used to denote a royal hunting ground, an unenclosed tract of land, rather than a distinct wooded area. In fact, even this description is not entirely correct as, in the 11th century, the area was a chase - a private rather than a royal hunting ground. Before 1066, Bowland was in the ownership of Earl Tostig of Northumbria, a brother of King Harold. Banished from his earldom, Tostig, with the help of the King of Norway, attempted to regain his lands and both he and the Norwegian king were killed at Stamford Bridge, just weeks before the fateful Battle of Hastings. Following the Norman Conquest, Bowland became part so the Honour of Clitheroe and the vast estates that belonged to the de Lacy family. In time, by marriage, they came into the hands of the Earls of Lancaster and, in 1399, when the then Duke of Lancaster ascended the throne as Henry IV, Bowland finally became one of nearly a hundred royal hunting forests. The remains of a Roman road can be clearly seen traversing the land and many of the village's names in this area date back to the Saxon period. Perhaps the most celebrated of the many routes across Bowland is the minor road from Lancaster to Clitheroe which crosses the **Abbeydale Moor** and the **Trough of Bowland** before descending into the lovely Hodder Valley around Dunsop Bridge. This is a popular route in the summer months, with most lay-bys and parking places filled as people pause to take in the breathtaking moorland views.

CLITHEROE
22 miles SE of Lancaster off the A59

Map 10 ref K9

Clitheroe Castle and Museum

This old stone town, just south of the Forest of Bowland and in the valley of the River Ribble, has always been considered the forest's capital. It is also Lancashire's second oldest borough, to Wigan, receiving its first charter in 1147 and since then Clitheroe has served the surrounding villages of the Ribble Valley as their market town. Like Lancaster, it too is dominated by an 800-year-old **Castle** standing on a limestone crag high above the town. Now little more than a ruin, set in a small park, as visitors stand inside the keep, hidden voices relate the history of the castle, with suitable sound effects. During the Civil War, Clitheroe was a staunchly Royalist town but, fortunately, it and the castle survived the ravishes of the victorious Parliamentarians. The **Castle Museum**, as well as holding collections of local geology and local history, also has reconstructions of a clogger's workshop, a printer's shop, and a lead mine.

WORSTON
1 mile E of Clitheroe off the A59

Map 10 ref K9

This tucked away village, down a lane off the main road, has remained unchanged over the years and can certainly be described as unspoilt. Keen-eyed visitors may even recognize the surrounding countryside as this was one of the locations used during the filming of *Whistle Down the Wind*. Behind the village inn, where the amusing and bizarre ritual of the village's Mock Corporation was revived in 1989, can still be seen the bull ring. Set into a stone, this was where the beast was tethered and baited with specially trained dogs in the belief that the 'sport' tenderized the meat. The **Calf's Head** at Worston was rescued from closure in 1998 by new owners Pam and Chris Medley, who have given this fine country restaurant, hotel and watering hole a new lease of life. Over 200 years old, it has in its history been a farm and alehouse. This popular place offers the weary traveller superb accommodation, great food and well-kept ales. Monday to Saturday the eatery offers a superb variety of bar food and a restaurant menu at lunch (11 a.m.-2.30 p.m.) and evening (5.30-9.30 p.m.); soup and sandwiches are available throughout the afternoon (2.30-5.30 p.m.). On Sunday food is served throughout the day (midday-9.30 p.m.) in the bar and restaurant, with a particularly popular option being the Sunday carvery, available from midday-3 p.m. In addition to the varied and innovative menu there is a range of delicious daily specials. Chris is justly proud of his real ales, which include Jennings, Boddingtons and Black Sheep. The six quality ensuite letting rooms are very comfortable and well-appointed, while the outstanding garden, which has a lovely stream running

Calf's Head, Worston, Clitheroe, Lancashire BB7 1QA
Tel: 01200 441218 Fax: 01200 441510

through it, is just the place to relax on fine days or to enjoy from the conservatory.

DOWNHAM
MAP 10 REF K9

3 miles NE of Clitheroe off the A59

One of the most attractive villages in the area, Downham was purchased by the Assheton family in 1558 at the same time as they acquired Whalley Abbey. Beautifully maintained by the family, the present squire, Lord Clitheroe of Downham, still refuses to permit the skyline to be spoilt by television aerials, satellite dishes, and even dormer windows. The village phone box has also come under the influence of the family and it is not painted a distinctive pillar box red but grey, to tone in with the surroundings. The extend of the village's conservation has lead to its use as a location for many films, the most famous being *Whistle Down the Wind*.

In the middle of Downham, opposite the church, **The Assheton Arms** is a distinguished and attractive public house. There are records of licensed premises on this site going back as far as 1765. Look out for the initials carved over the stone fireplace; they are believed to be those of the original builder. The pub has a very olde worlde feel to it, with low ceilings, exposed beams

The Assheton Arms, Downham, nr Clitheroe, Lancashire BB7 4BJ
Tel: 01200 441227

and open fires. The pub also enjoys an excellent reputation for food - the menu is extensive and impressive, and usually includes a wonderful variety of fresh seafood specialities. There is also a range of daily specials. The ales are traditional and all hand-pulled. This popular and lively place also boasts most unusual wooden busts of guardsmen wearing 'busby' hats. These in fact began life as newel posts from the Busby family's department store in Bradford, which later became a Debenhams.

GRINDLETON MAP 10 REF K9
4 miles NE of Clitheroe off the A59

Local people through and through, Jeremy and Kathryn have run **The Duke of York** since 1991. Jeremy is the chef, and has worked in catering all his life. The pub dates back to 1810, when it was a residence. The lovely restaurant is pretty and charming, with a relaxed ambience

and wonderful service. Food is served from midday - 1.45 p.m. and 6.45-9.30 p.m. Apart from the main menu of innovative and delicious dishes there are always at least 12 different main course daily specials. Fish and seafood dishes are a speciality. All food is freshly prepared to order. No smoking in restaurant. Meals can also be taken in the bar. Ales on tap include Tetleys and Castle Eden; Whitbread Mild, lagers and cider are also available. The

The Duke of York, Brow Top, Grindleton, nr Clitheroe, Lancashire BB7 4QR Tel: 01200 441266 Fax: 01200 440419

wine list is impressive. This superior establishment has been awarded many prizes, including being named Best Kept Pub in Lancashire 1996, and Pubmaster Best Pub Food of the Season, Northern Region, 1998. Closed Mondays except Bank Holidays.

SAWLEY MAP 10 REF K9
4 miles N of Clitheroe off the A59

At the centre of this historic village, easily missed as the main road by passes it, is **Sawley Abbey**, founded in the 13th century by the Cistercian monks of Fountains Abbey. As well as building their religious house, the monks had great influence over the whole of the surrounding area. Clearing their immediate surroundings, the monks cultivated the land and their ridge and furrow patterns can still be made out in the fields.

HURST GREEN MAP 10 REF K9
5 miles W of Clitheroe on the B6243

This pretty village, of stone-built cottages nestling in the Ribble Valley, is best known for its nearby public school. **Stonyhurst College**, the world famous Roman Catholic school, began life as the residence of the local lords of the manor. The present building, begun in around 1523, was the work of Hugh Shireburn although additions were made in 1592 by Sir Richard Shireburn. An ambitious man, Sir Richard served the Tudor monarchy and, as well as being the

Chief Forester of Bowland, he was also one of Henry VIII's commissioners studying the state of the monasteries and he was an eager participant in the suppression of Whalley Abbey. Though the family took on the new Protestant religion under Elizabeth I, it was with little spirit and in a short time the Shireburn family, like many other Lancashire families, returned to their Catholic faith. It seems strange then that Cromwell, on his way to and from the Battle of Preston, should take shelter at Stonyhurst and rumour has it that the ardent Puritan slept with a pistol at his side and his guards around him. In 1794, after the house had been left for some considerable time and had fallen into a state of disrepair, the owner, Thomas Weld, offered the property to the Jesuits who had set up an English Catholic School in Flanders. Unwelcome in France following the revolution, the Jesuits gladly accepted and, after restoring the original building, they extended it during the 19th century. Their finest addition must be the replica of King's College in Cambridge: **St Peter's Church** was built in 1835 and it includes many treasures including a 7th century copy of St John's Gospel and a cope of Henry II that was used by Henry VIII at the battle of the Field of the Cloth of Gold. One of the college's most famous sons is Sir Arthur Conan Doyle, the creator of Sherlock Holmes.

The Punch Bowl in Hurst Green is steeped in history. Dating back to 1793, this former coaching inn boasts its own resident ghost. This is said to be the spectre of highwayman Ned King, who in life made this inn his headquarters. The spot where Ned King was finally brought to justice can be seen in the minstrels' gallery in the restaurant, located in what was once the barn and is now handsomely refurbished and redecorated. Without a trial he was summarily hanged from a gibbet which stood not too far from the front door of the old inn. From that day some 150 years ago to this, witnesses describe seeing both Ned and his trusty steed galloping

The Punch Bowl, Longridge Road, Hurst Green, Clitheroe, Lancashire BB7 9QW
Tel: 01254 826209 Fax: 01254 826753

across the fields. Open every session daily and all day Sundays, food is available from midday - 2 p.m. and 7-9.30 p.m. Meals can be taken in the bar or restaurant. Apart from the splendid menu there are always at least eight daily main course specials. The beer garden is particularly lovely. Guests here will also find three attractive and comfortable letting rooms, perfect for a relaxing break or as a base for exploring this beautiful part of the county.

RIBCHESTER
7 miles W of Clitheroe on the B5269

Map 10 ref K9

Situated on the banks of the River Ribble, the village is famous for its **Roman Fort**, Bremetannacum, on the northern river bank. It was the Roman governor, Gnaeus Julius Agricola, in AD 79, who first established a fort here at the junction of the two important roads between Manchester and Carlisle, and York and the west coast. Although little of the fort's walls remain, the granary or storehouse, with its hypocaust (underfloor heating), has been excavated and has revealed some interesting coins, pottery, sculptures, and inscriptions. The fort's **Roman Museum** is designed to transport visitors back to the days of the Roman occupation and it offers an excellent insight into those times. Unfortunately, the finest artefact found on the site, an ornate helmet, is not on display here (though they do have a replica) but it can be seen in the British Museum in London.

Back in the village proper, the discovery of some pre-Norman Conquest crosses in and around **St Wilfrid's Church** would suggest that this 13th-century building occupies the site of a Saxon church. The church is named after the first Bishop of Ripon, who in the 7th century took a prominent role in the Synod of Whitby, and this would seem to confirm the earlier buildings existence in the absence of any direct evidence. A great place for tourist during the summer months, Ribchester not only has these two sights to offer but also several excellent pubs, restaurant, and cafés which provide much needed refreshment. Finally, Ribchester has one further attraction, the **Museum of Childhood** that is housed in the village's old Co-op building. The collection is diverse and goes back to the days of the Victorian music hall, with many of the models still in working order.

GOOSNARGH   Map 10 ref J9
12 miles W of Clitheroe on the B5269

Just to the west of the village lies **Chingle Hall**, a small moated manor house that was built in 1260 by Adam de Singleton. A Catholic family, the Singletons are said to have a chapel with three priest hides and, so the story goes, Cromwell once climbed down one of the hall's chimneys to spy on the Royalists below. As well as being the birthplace of St John Wall, one of the last priests to die for his faith, in 1620, it is well known as one of the most haunted houses in Britain and, as such, the hall has featured on countless television and radio programmes.

SALMESBURY   Map 10 ref K9
12 miles SW of Clitheroe on the A59

To the east of the village, close to the busy main road, lies **Salmesbury Hall**, built by the Southworth family. The hall seen today it actually the second house they built as their original hall was burned to the ground by Robert the Bruce in the early 14th century. Thinking that the original position, close to a crossing of the River Ribble was too vulnerable to attack, the family built their subsequent home in what was then an isolated location.

FLEETWOOD   Map 10 ref J9
15 miles SW of Lancaster on the A587

This fishing town, on the northern tip of the Fylde coast, is a planned town founded in the early 19th century around the Wyre deepwater port. Based on a form street pattern radiating from the Mount, the development was undertaken by the then landowner, Sir Peter Hesketh-Fleetwood, who wished to create a new holiday resort for working class people from the industrial mill towns of east Lancashire. Prior to the commencement of the building work in 1836, this had been a small settlement of a few fishermen's cottage. The opening of the railway extension from Preston to Fleetwood was a key player in the

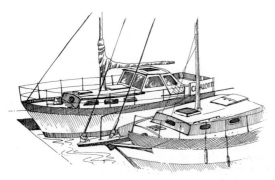

Fleetwood Harbour

town's development and the North Euston Hotel, which opened in 1842, reflects those railway links. Queen Victorian used Fleetwood as she travelled to Scotland for her annual holiday. However, this was all before the railway companies managed to lay a railway over Shap fell in Cumbria in 1847 and thus provide a direct rail link to Scotland.

The town's **Museum**, overlooking the River Wyre, illustrates the town's links with the fishing industry which suffered greatly from the Icelandic cod wars. However, Fleetwood's real claim to fame is the **Fisherman's Friend** - a staggeringly successful lozenge that was used by fishermen to relieve sore throats and bronchial trouble caused by the freezing conditions found in the northern Atlantic waters. In 1865, James Lofthouse, a chemist in the town, combined the ingredients of liquorice, capsicum, eucalyptus, and methanol, into a liquid for the town's fishermen but, as the seas were invariable rough, the bottles were broken before the men could benefit from the mixture. So Lofthouse, undefeated, combined the same ingredients into a lozenge that proved much more practical on board ship and, in a very short space of time his shop was inundated with customers. Today, Fishermen's Friends, which remain unchanged from the original recipe, are still produced by the same family business and their sales are worldwide.

GARSTANG
MAP 10 REF J9

10 miles S of Lancaster on the A6

This is an ancient, picturesque town whose market dates back to the time of Edward II, who granted the monks the right to hold the market. Thursday is still market day and both the High Street and the Market Hall become a hive of activity. As the town is situated close to a ford over the River Wyre, visitors will not be surprised to learn that the town dates back to the 6th century when a Saxon, named Garri, made his base here. The town's name comes from the Old Scandinavian words of 'geirr' meaning spear and 'stong' meaning pole. The town is also home to an excellent **Discovery Centre** which deals with a variety of aspects of the region, including the history of the nearby Forest of Bowland and the natural history of the surrounding countryside. Just to the east of the town, on the top of a grassy knoll, are the remains of **Greenhalgh Castle**, built in 1490 by Thomas Stanley, the first Earl of Derby. Severely damaged in a siege against Cromwell in 1645-46, the castle is reputed to be one of the last strongholds in Lancashire to have held out against the man.

A little to the north, on the A6, are the remains of a stone-built **Toll House** which probably dates from the 1820 when parts of the turnpike from Garstang to Lancaster were realigned. Although a ruin, the toll house is more than usually interesting as the posts for the toll gates can still be seen on either side of the road. This stretch of road is also home to some of the finest **Turnpike Milestones** in the county. To the south of Garstang, they are round-faced stones with cursive lettering dating from the 1750s and, to the north, the stones are triangular, with Roman lettering, and date from the time of the turnpike's realignment in the early 19th century.

POULTON-LE-FYLDE
MAP 10 REF J9

5 miles S of Fleetwood on the A586

This is one of the oldest towns in the ancient area known as Amounderness. The Romans were known to have been in the area and it was probably their handiwork that constructed the **Danes Pad**, an ancient trackway. The town developed as a commercial centre for the surrounding agricultural communities and its Market Place remains its focal point. In 1732, a great fire, started by sparks from the torches of a funeral procession, destroyed most of the thatched cottages that surrounded the market square in those days and a nationwide appeal was launched to help meet the rebuilding costs. Consequently, little of old Poulton can be seen in the centre of the town. The present **Church of St Chad** dates from the early 17th century, though the majority of the building is Georgian, and it stands on the site of the original Norman church. Inside, which is true Georgian, there is a splendid staircase, usual for a church, leading up to the gallery which runs around three sides of the building. As Poulton was a key town in the area for centuries, it is not surprising that there are several magnificent memorials to the local Fleetwood-Hesketh family also to be found here.

Fire seems to have played an important role in the life of the town and one ancient custom still kept is Teanlay Night, which involves the lighting of bonfires on Hallowe'en. Each bonfire is encircled with white-coloured stones which are then thrown into the flames by the onlookers and left until the next day. The successful retrieval of one's own stone is considered a good omen for future prosperity.

Strolling around Poulton-le-Fylde now, it is hard to imagine that the town was once a seaport. But, until relatively recently ships sailed up the River Wyre to **Skippool Creek**. Today, the creek is home to the Blackpool and Fleetwood Yacht Club and from here the ocean-going yachts compete in major races around Britain.

The town had a rail link long before Blackpool and it was here that the early holidaymakers alighted from their trains to take a horse and trap the remaining few miles. Fortunately for Poulton, in 1846, the railway reached Blackpool and the town could, once again, return to a more peaceful existence. It is this quiet and charm, as well as sensitive approaches to planning, that have led it to become, in recent years, a much sought after residential area for businessmen now able to travel the M55 to Manchester and Liverpool.

ST MICHAEL'S ON WYRE
MAP 10 REF J9

8 miles N of Preston on the A586

The River Wyre, at this point, is still tidal and, for centuries, the inhabitants of St Michael's and other villages in the area have suffered the threat of flooding. An old flood bank has been constructed from the village's bridge and below, beyond the overgrown banks, are the fertile fields of the flood plain. Mentioned in the Domesday Book as Michelscherche, is it likely that the first church in the village was founded in the 7th century. As well as the many memorials to the Butler family, the church also contains a splendid 14th-century mural that was only discovered in 1956 when repair work was being undertaken in the sanctuary.

The outstanding **Compton House** is situated on the main road in St Michael's-on-Wyre, a couple of miles west off the main A6. The building dates back to 1897; from then until 1977 it was a tailor's shop, run by three generations of the same family. Maureen and Dave Jones have been providing excellent bed and breakfast accommodation here in their home since 1987. With three lovely ensuite rooms, each with excellent facilities, decor and furnishings, guests

can relax in a true home from home. A marvellous breakfast awaits guests each morning, and the proprietors are friendly and hospitable hosts. The beautiful and lovingly tended gardens to the front, side and rear are eye-catching and a wonderful place to sit and dream, surrounded by lovely flowering plants, hanging baskets and other

Compton House, Garstang Road, St Michael's-on-Wyre, nr Preston, Lancashire PR3 0TE Tel: 019995 679378
email: djones@compton-hs.freeserve.co.uk
website: www.compton-hs.freeserve.co.uk/Compton

examples of Maureen's skill as a gardener. This superb B&B has won many awards both for the gardens and the premises, including Best Presented Premises in Lancashire and Wyre in Bloom, business section.

BLACKBURN
MAP 10 REF K10

9 miles E of Preston on the A666

The largest town in East Lancashire, Blackburn is notable for its modern shopping malls, its celebrated three day market, its modern cathedral, and Thwaites Brewery, one of the biggest independent brewers of real ale in the north of England. Hard though it may be to imagine today, at the height of the textile industry, Blackburn was the biggest weaving town in the world. In 1931, it received arguably its most influential visitor when Mahatma Gandhi toured the area on a study trip of Lancashire's textile manufacture. Examples of the early machines, including James Hargreaves' Spinning Jenny and his carding machine, invented in 1760, can be seen at the **Lewis Textile Museum**, which is dedicated to the industry. The town's **Museum and Art Gallery** has, amongst its treasures, several paintings by Turner, the Hart collection of medieval manuscripts, and the finest collection of Eastern European icons in Britain.

Mentioned in the Domesday Book, the town was originally an agricultural community before the production of first woollen and then cotton cloth took over. Much of the town seen today was built on the prosperity brought by the cotton trade and, on the dome of St John's Church, can be seen a weathervane in the shape of a weaving shuttle. However, the town's prominence as a centre for the surrounding community has not been lost as, in 1926, the Diocese of Blackburn was created and the Gothic St Mary's Church, built in 1826, became the **Cathedral** of the Bishop of Blackburn. Although Blackburn no longer has a manor house, Witton House has long since been demolished, the grounds have been turned into an excellent local amenity. **Witton Country Park** contains nature trials through woodlands up on to heather covered hill tops, all that remains of Witton House's once extensive grouse shoots.

PENDLE HILL
MAP 10 REF K9

10 miles NE of Blackburn off the A6068

A constant feature of the skyline in this part of Lancashire, this great whaleback mountain lends into name to the ancient hunting ground and region it still dominates. The hill, and the surrounding tiny villages, have a rich history and, due to the isolation, there are also many legends: none more well known than the tragic story of the Pendle Witches. The infamous witches were, in the main, old women who dabbled with plants and herbs, knowing which could heal and which, when ingested, would spell certain death. The early 17th century was a time of superstition and fear and, in 1612, several of the women were imprisoned in Lancaster Castle as a result of their seemingly evil practices. At the trial, chilling accounts of witchcraft came to light as families and neighbours accused each other of wrongdoing. Later that year, on August 10th, 10 women and one of their sons were found guilty of witchcraft and were hanged in front of huge crowds. Though, as a rule, witches tended to come form the poorer elements of society, one of women, Alice Nutter, was said to be rich with a sizeable estate. A few years later, in 1633, there were further trials and, whilst some of the accused died in prison, four prisoners were taken to London and put on show.

View from Pendle Hill

To the west of the hill's summit lies **Apronfull Hill**, a Bronze Age burial site, that is said to be the place from which the Devil threw stones at Clitheroe Castle, creating what is known as the Devil's window. Something of this old, dark tragedy still broods over Pendle and many memories and places which hard back to those grim days remain. Those interested in finding out more about the trials should visit the **Pendle Heritage Centre** at **Barrowford**, to the southeast of the hill. Historically, witches aside, the hill was one of the many beacon hills throughout the country that, forming a chain, were lit in times of national crisis, such as the sighting of the Spanish Armada.

NEWCHURCH
MAP 10 REF K9

10 miles NE of Blackburn off the A6068

This charming Pendle village was named after John Bird, Bishop of Chester consecrated a new church here in 1544. Earlier, during the Middle Ages, Newchurch was a cow and deer rearing

centre, as well as part of the old hunting forest of Pendle but, by the reign of Elizabeth I, the area was becoming deforested and farming was beginning to take over as the primary source of income. Newchurch did not escape from stories of witchcraft that surrounded the notorious Pendle witches trial in the 17th century, and many ghostly tales and shadowy traditions are said to associated with the village. Though those times were a frightening experience for anyone living in the area, by the 18th century, the witch hunts were over and the village grew rapidly as part of the expanding textile industry, first with handloom weavers and then with the construction of a factory for washing and dyeing wool.

Newchurch

PADIHAM
MAP 10 REF K9

8 miles E of Blackburn on the A646

This charming small town of narrow winding lanes and cobbled alleyways, still retains characteristics typical of the early days of the Industrial Revolution. However, there was a settlement here long before the Norman Conquest and Padiham was also the market town for the western slopes of Pendle. Padiham is also the home of **Gawthorpe Hall**, which lies to the east of the town. A splendid 17th-century house, it was restored with a flourish of Victorian elegance during the 1850s by Sir Charles Barry. Although Gawthorpe Hall had been the home of the Shuttleworth family since the early 15th century, work on the construction of the present hall only started in 1600. Open to the public, the beautiful period furnishings are enhanced by the ornately decorated ceilings and the original wood panelled walls, which also provide the perfect setting for the nationally important Kay-Shuttleworth needlework and lace collection.

WHALLEY
MAP 10 REF K9

6 miles NE of Blackburn on the B6246

This is a charming village, full of character, that has changed little over the centuries. Although it is now somewhat dominated by the 49-arch railway viaduct, Whalley has a much older history which dates back to the 13th century and the time when **Whalley Abbey** was founded by Cistercian monks. In fact, Whalley was not the monks' first choice as they had already set up a religious house at Stanlow, on the banks of the River Mersey and now under a huge oil refinery, in 1172. Seeking somewhere with less harsh and more fertile land, the monks moved to Whalley in 1296 but their attempts to build were hampered as Sawley Abbey felt threatened by the competition for the donations of land and goods expected from the local population. Building finally began in 1310 and, by 1400, the imposing and impressive abbey had taken shape. The demise of the abbey came, as it did to all religious houses, under Henry VIII but Whalley's abbot, joining forces with the abbot of Sawley, took part in the Pilgrimage of Grace in an attempt to save their houses. This failed and the abbots were both executed. Now owned and cared for by the Diocese of Blackburn, Whalley Abbey is one of the best preserved such places in the country and its future secure as it also acts as a conference centre. Whalley's **Parish Church**, dating from the 13th century, is also well worth a visit. Built on

Whalley Abbey

the site of an older place of worship, the churchyard is home to three ancient crosses and the church itself contains a set of the some of the finest choir stalls anywhere. They were brought here from the abbey after the Dissolution and though they are not elaborate there are some intriguing carvings on the lower portions.

The Dog Inn on the main street dates back, in parts, to the 17th century. At one time a farmhouse, it was granted a license as an alehouse from around 1830. The farm outbuildings can still be seen at the rear of the pub; the stables continue to be home to several horses. Personally run since 1991 by Norman and Christine Atty, who are always on hand to ensure that all their visitors receive a warm welcome, this wonderful pub is open all day everyday, with lunch served between midday and 2 p.m. and evening meals by arrangement. The ever-changing blackboard menu features traditional English favourites. The inn is renowned for its home-made soups and delicious home-made puddings. Adorned with memorabilia from days gone by, the interior is comfortable and welcoming. The low ceilings and open fires add to the olde worlde atmosphere. Cask ales include Theakstons Best

The Dog Inn, 55 King Street, Whalley, Clitheroe, Lancashire BB7 9SP Tel: 01254 823009

and guest ales. There is also a good selection of wines on offer. The secluded rear walled beer garden is a real suntrap.

DARWEN
Map 10 ref K10

3 miles S of Blackburn on the A666

Visitors to the town may be forgiven for thinking they have been here before as Darwen will be

familiar to all viewers of the BBC series *Hetty Wainthropp Investigates*, which stars Patricia Routledge. Dominating the town from the west and situated high on Darwen Moor, is **Darwen Tower**, built to commemorate the Diamond Jubilee of Queen Victoria in 1897. The view from the top of the tower, which is always open, is enhanced by the height of the hill on which it stands (1,225 feet) and with the help of the plaques at the top much of the Lancashire landscape, and beyond, can be seen. A striking landmark, very visible from the tower, and in the heart of Darwen is the chimney of the **India Mill**. Constructed out of hand-made bricks, it was built to resemble the campanile in St Mark's Square, Venice.

Darwen Tower

To the west of Darwen lies **Sunnyhurst Wood** and visitor centre in the valley of a gentle brook that originates on Darwen Moor to the south. Acquired by public subscription in 1902, to commemorate the coronation of Edward VII, this area of woodland, covering some 85 acres, is rich in both bird and plant life. The visitor centre, housed in an old keeper's cottage, has an ever changing exhibition and there is also the Olde England Kiosk, built in 1912, which serves all manner of refreshments.

RAWTENSTALL
Map 10 ref K10

7 miles SE of Blackburn on the A682

The town first developed as a centre of the woollen cloth trade with the work being undertaken by hand workers in their own homes before steam-powered mills were introduced in the early 19th century. The introduction of the cotton industry to the town happened at around the same time.

Lower Mill, now a ruin, was opened in 1840 by the Whitehead brothers who were some of the area's first manufacturing pioneers. The **Weaver's Cottage**, purpose built for a home weaver, is one of the last buildings remaining of its kind and it is open to visitors at weekends during the summer. Also in the town, and housed in a former Victorian mill owner's house called Oakhill, is the **Rossendale Museum**. Naturally, the area's industrial heritage is given a prominent position but collections of the region's natural history, fine art and furniture, and ceramics are on display too.

At one end of the town stands a new railway station which marks the end of a very old railway line - the **East Lancashire Railway**. Opened in 1846 and run commercially until 1980, when the last coal train drew into Rawtenstall, the line is now in the hands of the East Lancashire Railway Preservation Society. Running a passenger service (at weekends with additional summer services), the steam trains offer an enthralling 17 mile round trip along the River Irwell between Rawtenstall and Bury, via Ramsbottom.

LEYLAND   MAP 10 REF J10
8 miles SW of Blackburn on the B5253

The town is probably best known for its associations with the manufacture of cars and lorries and the **British Commercial Vehicle Museum**, the largest such museum in Europe, is well worth a visit. Housed on the site of the former Leyland South Works, where commercial vehicles were produced for many years, there are many restored vans and lorries on display with exhibits ranging from the horsedrawn era, through steam-powered wagons right up to the present day vans and lorries.

Leyland is, however, an ancient settlement and documentary evidence has been found which suggests that the town was a Crown possession in Saxon times and it was owned by Edward the Confessor. The village cross marks the centre of the old settlement, around which the town expanded and it is in this area of the Leyland that the older buildings can be seen. Founded in the 11th century, much of the present **St Andrew's Church** dates from 1220 although there was some restoration work undertaken in the 15th century. The Eagle and Child Inn is almost as old, said to date from around 1230, and it served the needs of travellers journeying along the ancient highway which passed through the town.

Whilst not one of the town's oldest buildings, the old Grammar School, parts of which dates from the late 16th century, is hardly modern. Today it is home to the town's **Heritage Museum**, a fascinating place that describes, through interesting displays and exhibits, the history of this ancient market town.

ORMSKIRK   MAP 10 REF J10
20 miles SW of Blackburn on the A59

The origins of this important market town in the West Lancashire plain date back to the time of the Vikings, when their leader, Orme, first settled the area in AD 840. The town received its first market charter from Edward I in 1286 and today, this is still a key event in the region. The partial drainage of Martin Mere, in the late 18th century, to provide more rich, fertile agricultural land, as well as the growth of nearby Liverpool, increased the prosperity of the town. Ormskirk was also touched by the Industrial Revolution and, whilst the traditional farming activities continued, cotton spinning and silk weaving also became important sources of local income. Today, the town has reverted to its traditional past. The **Church of St Peter and St Paul**, in the centre of the town, unusually has both a steeple and a tower. The tower, added in the 16th century, was constructed to take the bells of Burscough Priory after the religious community had been disbanded by Henry VIII. However, the oldest feature found in the church is a stone carving on the outer face of the chancel's east wall that was probably the work of Saxon craftsmen.

RUFFORD   MAP 10 REF J10
5 miles N of Ormskirk on the B5246

This attractive village of pretty houses is notable for its church and its beautiful old hall. Built in 1869, the church is a splendid example of the Gothic revival period and its tall spire dominates the skyline. The ancestral home of the Hesketh family who were involved in reclaiming the mosslands on their estates, **Rufford Old Hall** is without a doubt one of the finest 15th-century buildings in the county. Particularly noted for its magnificent Great Hall, this impressive black and white timbered house is well worth exploring. From the superb, intricately carved movable wooden screen to the solid oak chests and long refectory table, the atmosphere here is definitely one of wealth and position. Now in the hands of the National Trust, within the outbuildings there is not only a shop and a popular restaurant but also the **Philip Ashcroft Museum of Rural Life**, with its unique collection of items that illustrate fully village life in pre-industrial Lancashire.

MERE BROW
MAP 10 REF J10

7 miles N of Ormskirk on B5246

Just to the south of the village lies the Wildfowl and Wetlands Trust at **Martin Mere**, over 350 acres of reclaimed marshland which was established in 1976 as a refuge for thousands of wintering wildfowl. Until Martin Mere was drained in the 17th century, to provide rich, fertile farmland, the lake was one of the largest in England. Indeed, some believe that it was into Martin Mere that King Arthur's sword, Excalibur, was tossed after the king's death. Today, the stretches of water, mudbanks, and grassland provide homes for many species of birds and, with a network of hides, visitors can observe the birds in their natural habitats. There are also a series of pens, near to the visitors centre, where many other birds can be seen all year round at closer quarters. Particularly famous for the vast numbers pink-footed geese which winter here, their number often approaching 20,000, although winter is a busy time at Martin Mere, a visit in any season is sure to be rewarded. The visitor centre caters for everyone and, as well as the shop and café, there is a theatre and a wealth of information regarding the birds found here and the work of the Trust.

SOUTHPORT
MAP 10 REF J10

8 miles NW of Ormskirk on the A570

The rise of this popular and still elegant Victorian seaside resort lies in the tradition of sea bathing that began at nearby Churchtown centuries ago. As the number of people celebrating Bathing Sunday grew, the need for a more accessible beach also grew and a stretch of sand two miles south of Churchtown was deemed suitable. As the crowds flocked over the sand dunes the need for accommodation increased and a local entrepreneur, known as Duke Sutton, built the first hotel of driftwood in 1792. It was Doctor Barton who, when christening Sutton's hotel with a bottle of champagne, coined the name Southport (the South Port Hotel) and the town grew up around the ramshackle building.

Lord Street, Southport

The driftwood hotel was replaced by a grander stone building, known as the Duke's Folly as its construction resulted in Sutton losing all his money and being imprisoned in Lancaster jail in 1803. Now an established town, the expansion of Southport came as a result, as with all of the region's famous resorts, of the extension of the railway services from the mill towns of Lancashire and from Manchester and Liverpool. Of all these places, none has managed to retain is air of Victorian grandeur more so than Southport.

The town's central, main boulevard, **Lord Street**, is a mile long wide road that was built along the boundary bordering the lands of the two neighbouring lords of the manor. A superb shopping street today, the exceptionally wide pavements, with gardens along one side and an elegant glass-topped canopy along most of other side, make this one of the most pleasant places to shop in the country. Many of the town's classical style buildings are found along its length and is has been designated a conservation area. Off Lord Street, there is one of town's several covered arcades and, built in 1898, **Wayfarers Arcade** is one of the best. The modest entrance opens out into a beautiful cast iron and glass conservatory, with its first floor gallery and splendid central dome. Originally named the Leyland Arcade after the town's Member of Parliament, it took its present name in 1976 after the arcade's most successful leaseholder.

In a central position along Lord Street lies Southport's rather modest **Town Hall**. Built in 1852 and of a classical design, above the balcony is a beautiful carving in bold relief of the figures of Justice, Mercy, and Truth picked out in white against a Wedgwood blue background. Further along, the Atkinson Central Library was built in 1879 as the premises of the Southport and West Lancashire Bank. The original ceiling of the banking hall can still be seen as can its fireplace. On the first floor is the **Atkinson Art Gallery** which contains collections of British art and Chinese porcelain.

As every Victorian resort had a **Promenade**, so does Southport and this is a typical example: flanked by grand hotels on the land side and a series of formal gardens on the other. As the silting up of the Ribble estuary progressed unchecked the **Marine Lake** was constructed at the northern end of the promenade. At over some 86 acres, this man-made lake is the largest in Britain and, as well as being an attractive site and a place for the pursuit of all manner of watersports, it is also host to an annual 24-hour yacht race.

From the centre of the promenade extends Southport's **Pier** which, at 1,460 yards long, was the longest pier in the country until 1897. Following a fire in 1933 it was shortened but it remains the second longest in the country. Looking at the pier today it is hard to imagine that at the end of the last century pleasure steamers were able to depart from here to Barrow in Cumbria, Bangor, Wales, and the Isle of Man. Along the shore line, and opened in the spring 1998, the new sea wall and Marine Drive is a wonderful modern construction, the length of Southport's sea front, that blends well with the town's Victorian heritage.

RIVINGTON   MAP 10 REF K10
13 miles E of Ormskirk off the A673

This is a charming village surrounded by moorland of outstanding natural beauty that forms the western border of the Forest of Rossendale. Overlooking the village, and with splendid views over West Lancashire, **Rivington Pike**, at 1,191 feet, is one of the area's high spots. It was once a site of one of the country's chain of signal beacons. Just to the south of the village lies **Lever Park**, situated on the lower slopes of Rivington Moor, which was made over to the public in 1902 by William Hesketh Lever, who later became Lord Leverhulme. The park comprises an awe-inspiring pot pourri of ornamental, landscaped gardens, tree-lined avenues, cruck-framed barns, a Georgian hall, and a treasure trove of natural history within its 2,000 acres. The park's moorland setting, elevated position, and adjoining reservoirs provide scenery on a grand scale which leaves a lasting impression.

STANDISH   MAP 10 REF J10
9 miles E of Ormskirk on the A49

This historic old market town has several reminders to its past and not least of these is the splendid **St Wilfrid's Church**. Built in a size and style that befitted the importance of the town in the late 16th century, the building stands on the site of a church that was certainly here at the beginning of the 13th century. A look around the interior of the church will provide a potted history of the area: there are tombs and memorials to all the local families including the Wrightingtons, Shevingtons, and the Standish family themselves. The Standish family came from Normandy and crossed the channel with William the Conqueror. One of the family members became the Warden of Scarborough Castle and another, Ralph de Standish, was knighted after his part in quelling the Peasants' Revolt, there was even a Standish at Agincourt. However, the most famous member of the family is Miles Standish who sailed to the New World on board the *Mayflower* with the Pilgrim Fathers in 1620. This may seem strange as the Standish family were staunch Catholics. Though there is little left in the way of monuments to the family in this country, their home (put up for sale in 1920 after the last family member died) was demolished and parts transported to America, Miles Standish is remembered in the town of Duxbury in America.

BOLTON
MAP 10 REF K10

10 miles NE of Manchester on the A466

Synonymous with the Lancashire textile industry, Bolton is also an ancient town that predates its expansion due to cotton by many centuries. First settled during the Bronze Age, by the time of the Civil War, this was a market town supporting the surrounding villages. The town saw one of the bloodiest episodes of the war when James Stanley, Earl of Derby, was brought back here by Cromwell's troops after the Royalists had been defeated. In a savage act of revenge for the massacre his army had brought on the town early in the troubles, Stanley was executed and his severed head and body, in separate caskets, were taken back to the family burial place at Ormskirk. Whilst in captivity in the town, Stanley was kept prisoner at Ye Olde Man and Scythe Inn which, dating from 1251, is still standing in Churchgate today. Dating back to the 14th century, **Smithills Hall** is an impressive building that is situated on an easily defended hill. Brought by the Bolton Corporation in the late 1930s, the hall has been beautifully restored and, as well as seeing one of the oldest and best preserved fortified manor houses in the county, visitors can also wander along the hall's wooded nature trail.

Bolton is indeed fortunate as, also on the northern side of the town, is **Hall-i'-th'-Wood**, its second splendid half-timbered house. Dating back to the late 15th century, the house was extended, in stone, in 1591 and again, in 1648, by its then owner, Alexander Norris, a prominent Puritan. A fine example of a wealthy merchant's house, it was saved from dereliction by

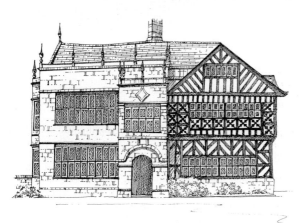

Lord Leverhulme in 1900 and it has been restored and furnished with displays of fine furniture and interesting items of local importance. However, the hall has a second claim to fame as, for a number of years, Samuel Crompton was one of several tenants here. The inventor, in 1799, of the spinning mule, Crompton's machine was an important factor in the industrialisation of the country's textile industry. Naturally, the hall too has a replica of Crompton's mule on display.

Hall-i'-th'Wood

The centre of Bolton is a lasting tribute to the wealth and prosperity generated by the spinning of high quality yarn for which the town was famous. The town hall, opened in 1873, is typical of the classical style buildings that the Victorian town fathers had built. The hall is still the town's central point and is it now surrounded by the recently refurbished pedestrianised shopping malls, market hall, and the celebrated **Octagon Theatre**. The town's excellent **Museum and Art Gallery** is also well worth a visit as not only are there collections of natural history, geology, and Egyptian antiques here but also some fine 18th and 19th century English water colours and some contemporary British paintings and graphics.

WIGAN   MAP 10 REF J10
9 miles W of Bolton on the A577

Although to many this town is a product of the industrial age, Wigan is one of the oldest places in Lancashire. As far back as the 1st century AD there was a Celtic Brigantes settlement here that was taken over by the Romans who built a small town called Coccium. Little remains of those far off days but, during the construction of a gasworks in the mid-19th century various burial urns were unearthed during the excavation work. The town's name comes from Wic-Ham which is probably Anglo-Saxon or Breton in origin but, following the departure of the Romans, the settlement lay in that part of the country that was forever fluctuating between the kingdoms of Mercia and Northumbria so the derivation is uncertain. The medieval age brought

more settled times and, by the end of the 13th century, the town had not only been granted a market charter but was also sending two members to Parliament. A staunchly Catholic town, Wigan fared badly during the Civil War. The Earl of Derby, whose home, Lathom House, lay on the outskirts of the town, was a favourite with the King and this was where Charles I made his base for his attacks on Roundhead Bolton. The bitter attacks on Wigan by the Cromwellian troops saw the fortifications destroyed and both the parish church and the moot hall were looted. The

Wigan Pier

Battle of Wigan Lane, the last encounter between the warring forces in Lancashire, is commemorated by a monument which stands on the place where a key member of the Earl of Derby's forces was killed.

Wigan's development as an industrial town centred around coal mining, which began as early as 1450. By the 19th century, there were over 1,000 pit shafts in operation in the surrounding area, supplying the fuel for Lancashire's expanding textile industry. The Leeds and Liverpool Canal, which runs through the town, was a key means of transporting the coal to the cotton mills of Lancashire and **Wigan Pier**, the major loading bay, remains one of the most substantial and interesting features of the waterway. A well-known musical hall joke, first referred by George Formby senior as he told of the virtues of his home town over Blackpool, it was the 1930s novel by George Orwell, The Road to Wigan Pier, that really put the old wharf on the map. Today, the pier has been beautifully restored and it is now a key attraction in the area. There are canal boat rides and a superb exhibition, The Way We Were, based on local social history and with costumed actors playing the part of the townsfolk of the 19th century. The pier is also home to **Trencherfield Mill** where not only is there the largest working mill engine in the world on display but also a collection of old textile machines and other engines.

However, Wigan is not a town living in the past but, as well as having a modern town centre with all the usual amenities, there is some fine countryside on the doorstep, including the **Douglas Valley Trail**, along the banks of the River Douglas. Even the town's coal mining past has interesting links with the natural world: **Pennington Flash** is a large lake formed by mining subsidence that is now a wildlife reserve and a country park. To the north of the town lies **Haigh Country Park**, one of the first to be designated in England, that is formed from the estate of the Earls of Crawford. Although Haigh Hall is not open to the public, the park includes areas of mixed woodland as well as a children's play area and a café.

BURY
MAP 10 REF K10

6 miles E of Bolton on the A58

Looking at Bury today it seems hard to imagine that, at one time, this typical Lancashire mill town had a castle. A settlement probably existed here in the Bronze Age and there is certainly evidence that the Romans passed through this area. By the 12th century, the town was the manor of the Norman de Bury family and, in the mid-14th century, the land came under the ownership of the Pilkingtons. Though the age of the castle is not known, its site is now covered by a 19th-century drill hall, it was dismantled following the Battle of Bosworth in 1485 where Henry VII defeated Richard III. Unlucky Thomas Pilkington had backed the wrong side. It is certainly people rather than buildings for which the town is famous. Apart from the hapless Thomas Pilkington, whose family, centuries later, made a fortune in glass at St Helens, both the Peel family and John Kay helped to shape the town's future. John Kay was, of course, the inventor of the flying shuttle, which although transforming the life of the weaver, did nothing towards creating personal wealth for Kay. With no head for business, Kay moved to France, died penniless, and lies buried in an unmarked grave.

Before Robert Peel Senior opened his Ground Calico Printing Works in 1770, this small market town lay amid green and fertile land. However, the opening of the works along with the subsequent mills, print and bleach works so dominated this part of the Irwell Valley that not only did they transform the landscape but also heavily pollute the river. At the height of the valley's production it was said that anyone falling into the river would dissolve before they had a chance to drown. Today, thankfully, the valley towns are once again clean and the river clear and fast flowing. With the family fortune gleaned from these prosperous mills, Robert Peel,

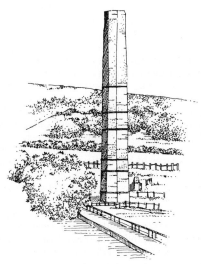

Burrs Country Park

born in the town in 1788, was able to fund his illustrious career in politics. Famous for the repeal of the Corn Laws, Robert Peel was also at the forefront of the setting up of the modern police force - hence their nickname 'Bobbies'. In the Bury's market square is a bronze statue to the town's most famous son.

Bury's **Art Gallery and Museum**, home to the renowned Thomas Wrighley collection of Victorian oil paintings and water colours, also hosts a lively programme of temporary exhibitions and the museum features a cobbled street of reconstructed shops and dwellings from Bury's past. The history of Lancashire's famous regiment, from its foundation in 1688, is displayed in the **Lancashire Fusiliers Museum**. On the outskirts of the town lies **Burrs Country Park** which, as well as offering a wide range of activities, also has an interesting industrial trail around this historic mill site.

No 9 Avondale Drive is a charming and lovely home offering superb bed and breakfast accommodation. This home from home occupies a peaceful location just a few miles outside Bury on the Ramsbottom Road. Owner Deirdre Woodcock has lived here since 1985, and has been providing comfortable and quality accommodation to her guests since 1994. The property is about 30 years old and was built on the site of the old Ramsbottom-Bury railway line. There are two upstairs rooms (one single, one twin/double) with separate bath. Both rooms are cosy and very comfortable, attractively decorated and furnished. Deirdre's breakfasts are hearty and delicious. Children and well-behaved dogs are welcome - Deirdre also provides a 'dog-sitting' service - those going further afield on holiday can leave their pet in her safe hands. For a truly relaxing break in a tranquil setting, yet still near many tourist centres and local sights and attractions, this charming B&B is an excellent choice.

No 9 Avondale Drive, Holcombe Brook, nr Bury, Lancashire BL0 9SJ Tel: 01204 882999

ROCHDALE
10 miles E of Bolton on the A58

MAP 10 REF L10

Lying in a shallow valley formed by the little River Roch, the town is surrounded, to the north and east, by the slopes of the Pennines that are often snow covered in winter. With its origins in medieval times, the town, like so many others in Lancashire, expanded with the booming cotton industry and, once prosperous, its Town Hall rivals that of Manchester in style if not in size. However, it is not textiles for which Rochdale is famous but as its role as the birthplace of the Co-operative Movement. In carefully restored Toad Lane, to the north of the town centre, is the world's first Co-op shop, the **Rochdale Pioneers**. The Co-op movement now represents a staggering 700 million members in 90 countries around the world and the celebration of its 150th anniversary in 1994 focused on attention on Rochdale and the **Pioneers' Co-operative Museum**. The beginning of the 19th century also saw the birth of the Rochdale Canal, a brave piece of civil engineering that traversed the Pennines to link the River Mersey with the Calder and Hebble Navigation. Some 33 miles in length and with 92 locks, it must be one of toughest canals ever built and, though the towpath can still be walked, the last commercial boat passed through the locks in 1937. Officially abandoned in 1952, some sections of the canal have been restored.

Between Rochdale and Littleborough lies **Hollingworth Lake**, originally built as a supply reservoir for the canal, but for many years a popular area for recreation known colloquially as 'the Weavers' Seaport', as cotton workers unable to enjoy a trip to the seaside can here. Now part of the **Hollingworth Lake Country Park** and with a fine visitor centre, there are a number of pleasant walks around its shores.

UPPERMILL

MAP 10 REF L10

8 miles SE of Rochdale on the A62

Of the villages that make up Saddleworth, Uppermill is the most central. It is certainly home to the area's oldest building, **Saddleworth Parish Church** which was originally built in the 12th century by the Stapletons as their family chapel. Extended over the years, there are several interesting features including a gravestone to commemorate the Bill-o-Jacks murders. In 1832, the people of Saddleworth were stunned to learn that the landlord of the Moorcock Inn and his son had been bludgeoned to death. Several thousand people turned out for the funeral but the case was never solved. Housed in an old mill building on the banks of the Huddersfield Canal, the **Saddleworth Museum** tells the story of this once isolated area and there is a reconstruction of an 18th-century weaver's cottage as well as a collection of woollen textile machinery, local history gallery, and local art exhibitions. Also here is the **Brownhill Visitor Centre**, which not only has information on the northern section of the Tame Valley but also exhibitions on local wildlife and the area's history.

Within acres of outstanding countryside in every direction, **Cross Keys Inn** is a welcoming public house popular with walkers, day-trippers and locals. It can be found by heading for the centre of Uppermill; follow Church Road for about half to three-quarters of a mile. This out-

standing inn is on the left, on the original Old Marsden pack-horse route. Opened in 1783, it has had 11 land-lords in the intervening years - a record of whom can be found in the inn. Doug and Alison have been here since 1998, and have already earned a reputation for quality and service. They have plenty of experience in the

Cross Keys Inn, Running Hill Gate, off Church Road, Uppermill, Oldham, Lancashire OL3 6LW Tel: 01457 874626

trade, and it shows. Open all day every day, there is excellent food available at lunchtime and evening daily (Monday to Friday midday-2.30 and 5-7 p.m., weekends midday-7 p.m.). There is plenty of comfortable seating, as well as a lovely patio area and beer garden. Quality ales include Lee's ales, Moonraker and many others. The superb menu features traditional favourites such as steak and kidney pudding, battered cod, plaice and scampi, hot and cold sandwiches and vegetarian dishes, as well as daily specials.

DIGGLE

MAP 10 REF L10

8 miles S of Rochdale off the A62

Above the village, on **Diggle Moor** lies **Brun Clough Farm** where, it is said, the cries of child slaves who were ill treated in the early days of the textile mills can still be heard coming from the outhouses. Part of the **Oldham Way** footpath, a 30 mile scenic walk through the country-side on the edge of the Peak District National Park, crosses the moorland. Much of the village itself is a conservation area, where the pre-industrial weaving community has been preserved along with some of the traditional skills. However, Diggle Mill, which used to operate the second largest waterwheel in the country, no longer exists. The Huddersfield Narrow Canal, completed in 1811, is one of the three canals that crossed the difficult terrain of the Pennines and joined Lancashire with Yorkshire. The entrance to the **Standedge Canal Tunnel**, the longest and highest canal tunnel in Britain, lies in the village. The last cargo boat passed through the tunnel in 1921 and following a long period of closure, it has now been re-opened and is an extremely popular tourist attraction.

Handy for the Standedge Canal Tunnel and Diggle's other attractions, situated on high ground overlooking the village and its valley, **New Barn** is the delightful home of Alan and Dorothy Rhodes. This is a working sheep farm, though guests at this wonderful bed and breakfast establishment will see little evidence of the day-to-day running of the farm. As the name

New Barn, Harrop Green Farm, Diggle, Saddleworth, Lancashire OL3 5LW
Tel: 01457 873937 Mobile: 07979 598232

might suggest, it was originally one of the outbuildings; in the mid-1960s it was completely refurbished to create this attractive and comfortable home. Guests have a choice of four charming rooms, all with panoramic views over Saddleworth Moor. There is also an attractive and welcoming residents' lounge that is ideal for relaxing. Everyone is treated to a delicious home-cooked breakfast and, though there are no evening meals served, packed lunches are available and there are good pubs in the area for evening meals. Both children and pets (by arrangement) are welcome. For the anglers among their guests, private fishing is also available in a private pond that has been well stocked with brown trout.

THE ISLE OF MAN

DOUGLAS
SE Coast

MAP 9 REF F7

The island's capital, Douglas is also a lively resort with its two mile long promenade, the focus of the island's nightlife. From dawn to dusk, visitors can take a leisurely ride along this wonderful promenade aboard the **Douglas Bay Horse Tramway**, a remarkable and beautiful reminder of a bygone era. It was the brainchild of a civil engineer, Thomas Lightfoot, who retired to the island and, seeing the need for a public transport system along this elegant promenade, designed the system still in use today. That the Douglas Tramway has survived until the 1990s is remarkable especially as, at the beginning of this century, attempts were made to electrify the line and extend the Manx electric railway along the promenade. There is a story often told about the horses that pull the trams, which concerns a parrot that lived in a cage at a hotel close to one of the tram's stops. The bird learnt to mimic the sound of the tram's starting bell and used to practise this skill constantly. The tram horses would stop when the they heard the bell and start off again immediately before the passengers could alight as the bird joined in the fun.

Another delightful means of travel is the Victorian **Steam Railway** that runs between Douglas and Port Erin. Following the line of the cliff tops, the memorable journey also travels through bluebell woods and through steep-sided rocky cuttings. This section of line is all that remains of a railway that once served the whole of the island.

The Manx cat, that has no tail, is probably the most famous export from the Isle of Man. There are several stories of how the cat lost its tail but one, in particular, is delightful. At the time that Noah was building the Ark there were two Manx cats, complete with tails. Noah sent for all the animals to come to the Ark, two by two, but the Manx cats replied that there was plenty of time and continued to play outside. Finally, when the cats did decided to board the Ark, Noah was just slamming the door and the cats lost their tails. A variation on this tale, is that one of the cats reached the Ark safely, the other had its tail chopped off by the closing doors. The tailless cat went on to become the Manx cat and the one who managed to keep its tail became the ever grinning Cheshire cat. In the heart of Douglas can be found the **Manx Cattery**, where tales and no tails are revealed! No trip to the island is complete without a visit to the **Manx Museum**, where the Story of Man film gives a dramatic and vivid portrayal of the island's unique history.

One of the Isle of Man's most famous landmarks, the **Tower of Refuge**, looks out over Douglas Bay. Sir William Hilary, founder of the Royal National Lifeboat Institution, lived in a mansion overlooking the bay and, following a near disaster in 1830 when the Royal Mail Steam Packet St George was driven on to rocks in high seas, Hilary launched the Douglas lifeboat. Miraculously, all the crew of the St George were saved without the loss of one lifeboat man, despite the extremely treacherous conditions. It was following this incident that Hilary decided that a form of refuge should be built for shipwrecked mariners to shelter in and so, with Hilary laying the foundation stone in 1832, the Tower of Refuge was built on Conister Rock out in the bay. Finally, perched on a headland overlooking Douglas Bay is a camera obscura known as the **Great Union Camera**. The camera was originally situated on the old iron pier, but when this was demolished in the 1870s the camera was resited on Douglas Head. In the camera, the natural daylight in focused on to a white panel through a simple system of lenses and angled mirrors and so provides a living image of the scene outside. At first apparently still, as with a photograph, viewers soon become fascinated as the 'picture' begins to move.

RAMSEY
MAP 9 REF F7

12 miles N of Douglas on the A18

This northernmost resort on the island is an attractive coastal town with a cosy harbour that is

Ramsey Harbour

highly regarded by visiting yachtsmen. Just to the north of the town, lies the **Grove Rural Life Museum**, housed in a pleasantly proportioned Victorian house. Built as the summer retreat of Duncan Gibb, a wealthy Victorian shipping merchant from Liverpool, and his family, the rooms within the house have all been restored to their Victorian splendour and stepping into the museum is just like taking a step back in time. The outbuildings have not been neglected and they contain an interesting collection of vehicles and agricultural instruments that were seen on Manx farms in the late 19th century.

LAXEY   MAP 9 REF F7
5 miles NE of Douglas on the A2

Set in a deep, wooded valley, this village is one of interesting contrasts. Tracing the river up from its mouth at the small tidal harbour leads the walker into **Laxey Glen**, one of the island's 17 National Glens that are preserved and maintained by the Forestry department of the government. Further up the glen is one of the island's most famous sights, the **Great Laxey Wheel** that marks the site of a once thriving mining community. Known as the **Lady Isabella Wheel**, with a circumference of 228 feet, a diameter of 72 feet, and a top platform some 72 feet off the ground, it is the largest waterwheel in the world.

Situated above Laxey, in a beautiful natural glen, are the magnificent **Ballalheanagh Gardens**. The valley, of steep sides with winding paths and a crystal clear stream running through the bottom, is packed with rhododendrons, shrubs, bulbs, and ferns and is certainly a gardeners paradise well worth seeking out. From Laxey station, the **Snaefell Mountain Railway** carries visitors to the top of the island's only mountain. Built in 1895, the six original tram cars still climb the steep gradients to Snaefell's 2,036 foot summit and this is certainly the way to travel for those unwilling to walk. Those reaching the top are rewarded with outstanding views of the whole island and out over the sea to Ireland, Scotland, and England. There is also a café on the summit offering welcome refreshments.

Great Laxey Wheel

PEEL   MAP 9 REF F7
9 miles W of Douglas on the A1

On the western side on the island, it is generally felt that Peel, which is renowned for its sunsets, typifies the unique character and atmosphere of the Isle of Man. Traditionally the centre of the Manx fishing industry, including the delicious oak smoked kippers and fresh shellfish,

Peel Castle

Peel has managed to avoid any large scale developments. Its narrow winding streets exude history and draw the visitor unfailingly down to the harbour, sandy beach, and magnificent castle of local red sandstone. **Peel Castle**, one of Isle of Man's principle historic monuments, occupies the important site of **St Patrick's Isle**. The imposing curtain wall encircles many ruined buildings, including St Patrick's Church, the 11th-century Round Tower, the 13th-century Cathedral of St German, and the later apartments of the Lords of Man. In the 11th century the castle became the ruling seat of the Norse Kingdom of Man and the Isles, first united by Godred Crovan - the King Orry of Manx folklore. Recent archaeological excavations have discovered exciting new evidence relating to the long history of the site. One of the most dramatic finds was the Norse grave of a lady of high social status buried in pagan splendour. The jewellery and effects buried with her can be seen on display, with other excavation finds, at the Manx Museum. The castle is also said to be haunted by the Black Dog, or Mauthe Dhoo, and, on dark windy nights, it can be heard howling in the castle's dungeons.

CALF OF MAN   Map 9 ref E8
15 miles SW of Douglas

This small island, situated just off the southwestern tip of the island, is now a bird sanctuary owned by the National Trust. However, one of the previous owners, the Dukes of Athol, requested that the tenants living on the Calf picked the nesting puffins! In 1777, a stone was found on the isle in the garden of Jane's Cottage, though in those days it was called The Mansion. Known as the Calf Crucifixion Cross, the stone is believed to date from the 8th century and it is one of the earliest Christian finds in Europe. The cross can be seen in the Manx Museum. **Calf Sound**, the stretch of water between the island and the Isle of Man has seen many ships pass through and it was here that the largest armada of Viking longships ever assembled in the British Isles congregated before setting off to invade Ireland. Men from nearby Port St Mary were granted a gallantry medal by Napoleon, thought to be the only such medal he presented to British subjects, when they came to the rescue of the crew of the St Charles schooner from France which floundered in the sound.

CREGNEASH   Map 9 ref E8
13 miles SW of Douglas off the A31

Perched right on the southwestern tip of the island this village is now a living museum, **Cregneash Village Folk Museum**, which offers a unique experience of Manx traditional life within a 19th-century crofting community. Its isolated position led the village to become one of the last strongholds of the island's ancient skills and customs and all this is beautifully preserved today. By combining small scale farming with other occupations, a small settlement of Manx men and women have successfully prospered here since the mid-1600s and, in the carefully restored buildings, visitors can see the conditions in which they lived and managed to sustain life in the this rugged landscape. The centrepiece of Cregneash is without doubt **Harry Kelly's Cottage**. Kelly was a renowned Cregneash crofter and a fluent speaker of the Manx language who died in 1934. Opened to the public in 1938, his cottage, still filled with his furniture, is an excellent starting point to any tour of the village. There are various other buildings of interest, including Turner's Shed, a smithy, and the Karran Farm. The village is also one of the few remaining places where visitors get a chance to view the unusual Manx Loaghtan four-horned sheep, a breed which, thanks to Manx National Heritage and other interest groups, now has a secure future.

CASTLETOWN   Map 9 ref F8
9 miles W of Douglas on the A7

The original capital of the island, the town's harbour lies beneath the imposing battlements of the finely preserved **Castle Rushen**. Like Peel Castle, this too is said to the haunted, by a ghost known as the White Lady. Believed to be the ghost of Lady Jane Gray who travelled to the island from Scotland with her family, she has been seen walking the battlements at night and occasionally walking through the castle's closed main gate during the day. Dating back to 1153, the castle's construction was begun by Norsemen. A series of fascinating displays here bring the history and atmosphere of this great fortress vividly alive, by presenting in authentic detail the sights, sounds, and smells of its heyday. Among the various points of interest is a unique one-fingered clock that was presented to the castle by Elizabeth I in 1597 and which still keeps perfect time. Castletown is also home to the island's **Nautical Museum**, where the displays centre around the late 18th-century armed yacht Peggy which sits in her contemporary boat-house. Part of the original building is constructed as a cabin room from the time of the Battle of Trafalgar and there are many other artefacts on display all with a maritime theme. On the road between Castletown and Douglas, visitors should look out for the **Fairy Bridge**. For centuries, people on the Isle of Man have taken no chances when it comes to the little people and it is still customary to wish the fairies who live under the bridge a Good Morning when crossing.

8 Lincolnshire and Yorkshire

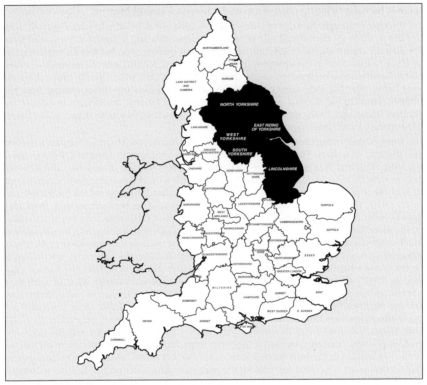

INTRODUCTION

The northern and northeastern English counties of Lincolnshire and Yorkshire (the latter, of course, actually the four distinct counties of West Yorkshire, South Yorkshire, North Yorkshire and the East Riding of Yorkshire), encompass a variety of places and sights that no traveller or tourist should miss.

Lincolnshire's town of Stamford, on the western edge of the county, is one of the most attractive towns in the whole country - the most attractive, according to John Betjeman. Moving eastwards into the Fens, the reclaimed land has a rich agricultural yield, with potatoes and sugar beet among the most prolific crops, and Spalding is the centre of the world-renowned Lincolnshire flower industry. Towards the Wash, the rich silt farmland and the salt marshes have become the natural habitat for thousands of wildfowl and wading birds - and those who watch them! Nearer the middle of the county we find Grantham, the most important town in this region with a population of around 30,000 and a pedigree in the field of engineering. Cross the River Witham out of the town and one encounters the appeal of country walks, country mansions and stone villages. Southeastern Lincolnshire takes the visitor from historic Boston through Poacher Country and across to the seaside and the three well known holiday resorts of Skegness, Ingoldmells and Chapel St Leonards. This part of the county is particularly rich in folklore, and with its long coastal boundary smuggling took place on a regular basis in the 17th and 18th centuries, often for consignments of "hollands", or gin.

Up the eastern coast one finds more magical seaside resorts, and throughout the area there's every incentive to take the air, with great walking in a variety of landscapes: the Wolds include some of the most beautiful yet undiscovered countryside in England.

A journey through the heart of Lincolnshire, setting out at Woodhall Spa and travelling up to Caistor, offers an enchanting mix of historic monuments and beautiful scenery. And so to the majestic county capital of Lincoln, offering almost endless opportunities for exploring the layers of history that have contributed to its unique appeal. But this area of Lincolnshire, called North Kesteven, also beckons with wide open spaces, show gardens and gentle strolls along the river banks. Another wide variety of thing to see and do greets the visitor moving from the holiday resorts to the majestic scenery along the Humber Estuary, the modern wonder of the Humber Bridge and, in the west, the Isle of Axholme, which really was an inland island before 17th century Dutch draining schemes.

Some 40 miles across and about 20 miles deep, the North York Moors encompass a remarkable diversity of scenery. There are great rolling swathes of moorland rising to 1,400 feet above sea level, stark and inhospitable in winter, still wild and romantic in summer, and softened only in early autumn when they are mantled by a purple haze of flowering heather. Almost one fifth of the area is woodland, most of it managed by Forest Enterprise which has established many picnic sites and forest drives. Settlements are few and far between: indeed, there may have been more people living here in the Bronze Age (1500-500 BC) than there are now to judge by the more than 3000 "howes", or burial mounds, that have been discovered. (The climate was much warmer and drier then). Also scattered across these uplands is a remarkable collection of medieval stone crosses. There are more than 30 of them and one, the Lilla Cross, is reckoned to be the oldest Christian monument in northern England. It commemorates the warrior Lilla, who in AD626 died protecting his King, Edwin, from an assassin's dagger. Most of them have names - such as Fat Betty which has a stumpy base surmounted by the top of a wheelhead cross. Perhaps the finest of these monuments is Ralph Cross, high on Westerdale Moor. It stands 9 feet tall at almost precisely the geographical centre of the moors and has been adopted by the North York Moors National Park as its emblem. Wild as they look, the moors are actually cultivated land, or perhaps ``managed by fire" is the better term. Each year gamekeepers burn off patches of the old heather in carefully limited areas called "swiddens" or "swizzens". The new growth that soon appears is a crucial resource for the red grouse which live only in heather moorland, eat little else but heather and find these young green shoots particularly appetising. The older heather that remains provides the birds with protective cover during their nesting season.

Just as the Yorkshire Dales have large areas of moorland, so the North York Moors have many dales - Eskdale, Ryedale, Farndale, more than a hundred of them in all. They cut deep into the great upland tracts and are as picturesque, soft and pastoral as anywhere in Yorkshire. To the west lies the mighty bulk of the Cleveland Hills; to the east the rugged cliffs of the Heritage Coast. This is marvellously unspoilt countryside, a happy state of affairs that has come about as a result of the Moors being designated a National Park in 1952, a status which severely restricts any development that would adversely affect either its natural or man-made beauty. Two spectacularly scenic railways wind their way through this enchanting landscape. Both of them provide a satisfying and environmentally friendly way of exploring this comparatively undiscovered area, anciently known as "Blackamor". The Middlesbrough to Whitby route, called the Esk Valley Line, runs from west to east following the course of river Esk and passing through a succession of delightful villages. The vintage steam locomotives of the North York Moors Railway start at Pickering and run northwards for 18 miles through Newtondale to join the Esk Valley Line at Grosmont. The dramatic route through this glacial channel was originally engineered by George Stephenson himself. Alternatively, the Forestry Commission's Newtondale

Forest Drive guides motorists through some splendidly rugged scenery. Between Saltburn and Filey lies some of the most striking coastal scenery in the country. Along this stretch of the Heritage Coast you'll find the highest cliffs in the country, a shoreline fretted with rocky coves, golden with miles of sandy beaches, a scattering of picture postcard fishing villages, and, at its heart, the historic port of Whitby dramatically set around the mouth of the River Esk. This glorious seaboard was designated as a Heritage Coast in 1979 in recognition of its beauty and its long history. From its small ports, fishermen have for centuries sailed out in their distinctive cobles to harvest the sea; from Whitby, sturdy whaling ships set off on their dangerous and now, thankfully, abandoned trade. It was at Whitby that one of England's greatest mariners, Captain Cook, learnt his sea-faring skills and it was from here that he departed in the tiny bark, Endeavour, a mere 370 tons, on his astonishing journeys of exploration. Further down the coast are the popular resorts of Scarborough, (where visitors were frolicking naked in the sea as early as 1735), and Filey, both of them offering long stretches of sandy beach and a huge variety of holiday entertainments.

The dales strike off to the west, the moors rise to the east: in between lies this fertile corridor of rich farmland and low-lying meadows, a vast plain bisected by the Great North Road linking London and Edinburgh. For most of its life, the Great North Road has been a rocky, pot-holed and swampy obstacle course. The best stretches, by far, were those where it ran along the meticulously engineered course the Romans had built centuries earlier.

Not all that long ago, the Vale of Pickering was the Lake of Pickering, an immense stretch of water far larger than any English lake today, about 32 miles long and 4 to 8 miles wide. As the Ice Age retreated the waters gradually drained away, leaving a low-lying plain of good arable soil based on Kimmeridge clay. The main traffic artery through the vale is the Thirsk to Scarborough road, the A170, which in summer peak periods can become very congested. But you only have to turn off this busy thoroughfare to find yourself in quiet country lanes leading to sleepy market towns and unspoilt villages. To the north rise the intricate folds of the North York Moors: to the south, the Yorkshire Wolds roll gently away towards Beverley, Hull and the River Humber.

Selby is the most southerly of the eight districts that make up the vast, sprawling county of North Yorkshire. Here, the level plains of the Vale of York stretch for miles - rich, agricultural land watered by the four great Yorkshire rivers, Ouse, Wharfe, Derwent and Aire, and by the Selby canal. It is ideal country for walking and cycling, or for exploring the waterways on which a wide variety of rivercraft is available for hire. Here the visitor can still find quiet villages, inviting hostelries, and one of the country's most flamboyant stately homes, Carlton Towers.

The Wolds are a great crescent of chalk hills that sweep round from the coast near Flamborough Head to the outskirts of Hull. There were settlers here some 10,000 years ago, - but never very many. In the early 1700s, Daniel Defoe described the area as "very thin of towns and people" and also noted the "great number of sheep". Little has changed: the Wolds remain an unspoilt tract of scattered farmsteads and somnolent villages with one of the lowest population densities in the country. Artists remark on the striking quality of the light and air, and on the long views that open up, perhaps across undulating hills to the twin towers of Beverley Minster or to the great towers of the Minster at York. The Wolds never rise above 800 feet but the open landscape makes them particularly vulnerable to winter snowstorms: children may be marooned in their schools, the dipping and twisting country roads can be blocked for weeks at a time.

The southeastern corner of Yorkshire tends to be overlooked by many visitors. If only they knew what they were missing. Beverley is one of the most beguiling of Yorkshire towns and its Minster one of the greatest glories of Gothic architecture. Its parish church, built by a medieval guild, rivals the Minster in its grandeur and in its colourful interior. The whole town has the indefinable dignity you might expect from a community that was an capital of the East Riding in former days when Hull, just six miles to the south, was still a rather scruffy little port. To the east and south of Beverley lies the old Land of Holderness, its character quite different from anywhere else in Yorkshire. A wide plain, it stretches to the coast where for eons the land has been fighting an incessant, and losing, battle against the onslaught of North Sea billows. The whole length of the Holderness coast is being eroded at an average rate of 3 inches a year, but in some locations up to 3 feet or more gets gnawn away. At its southernmost tip, Spurn Point curls around the mouth of the Humber estuary, a cruelly exposed tip of land whose contours get re-arranged after every winter storm. The coastal towns and villages have a bleached and scoured look to them, perhaps a little forbidding at first. It doesn't take long however for visitors to succumb to the appeal of this region of wide vistas, secluded villages and lonely shores.

And so to the Yorkshire Dales, one of the 11 National Parks in England and Wales, an area of rich farmland, high moorland, and deep valleys. The predominant limestone gives rise to many of the interesting geological features found within its boundaries and also to the abundance of potholes and disappearing rivers which characterise the area. With the large industrial areas of Yorkshire and Lancashire close to hand, the Dales are easily accessible but, with so much open countryside, visitors are able to avoid the more popular attractions and enjoy the beauty of the region in peace and tranquillity. For all capabilities, the Yorkshire Dales provide the perfect setting for walking with at least 1,000 miles of public footpaths and ancient trackways, waterfalls, wild flowers, upland pastures, and bridleways. The Pennine Way, Britain's first long distance footpath, is some 270 miles in length and particularly inviting for ramblers, in part or as a whole. Full of contrasting and beautiful scenery, limestone pavements, waterfalls such as Hardraw Force, and the Three Peaks, it is a wonderful means of seeing much that the Dales has to offer. Meanwhile, the much shorter Dales Way, from Leeds to Lake Windermere in Cumbria, takes in the old textile villages and towns of West Yorkshire before heading through the western section of the Dales and on into Lancashire.

The largest of the northern dales, Swaledale is also one of the grandest and its rugged beauty makes quiet a contrast to pretty and busier Wensleydale just to the south. There are several other noticeable differences: the villages all have harsher, Nordic sounding names, the dale is much less populated, and the rivers and becks are more fast flowing mountain streams.

There are several side dales to Swaledale and the small, thriving market town of Reeth lies at the junction of Arkengarthdale and the valley of the River Swale. First settled by Norsemen who preferred wild and remote countryside, the valley of Arkle Beck was not considered important enough to gain an entry in the Domesday Book. Scarred by lead-mining and now chiefly populated by hardy Swaledale sheep, at the head of the dale lies England's highest inn, Tan Hill. Finally, though only a short section of the River Tees flows through Yorkshire, the section of Teesdale around Piercebridge is particularly charming and well worth a visit. Nidderdale is a typical Yorkshire dale, with dry stone walls, green fields, and pretty stone villages. Christened "Little Switzerland" by the Victorians, the upper reaches of the valley of the River Nidd are steep and wooded, with the river running through gorges, and with a covering of snow in winter. It is this natural beauty that draws many people to the Dale and there are also several remarkable features that are well worth exploring. Best explored from Pateley Bridge, keen walkers will delight in the wide variety of landscape that can be covered within a reasonable amount of time. High up on the moorland, well regarded for its brilliant colour in late summer, there are several reservoirs, built to provide water for the growing population and industry in Bradford. The lower section of Nidderdale is dominated by the towns of Harrogate and Knaresborough, two of Yorkshire's most interesting and attractive towns.

The area of West Yorkshire known as "Brontë Country" surrounds the Brontë family home at Haworth, and dominated by the textile towns and villages along the valley bottom and the wild and bleak moorland above. The land has been farmed, mainly with sheep, since the Middle Ages and, in order to supplement their wages, the cottagers took to handloom weaving in a room of their home. Not all the villages were completely taken over by the mills and, in many, the old stonebuilt weavers' cottages, with their deep windows to let in light for the worker within, survive.

Last but by no means least, South Yorkshire encompasses not just the exciting and lively towns of Sheffield, Doncaster and Rotherham, but charming Peak District villages to the west, quiet rural villages north and east, and a proud legacy of the region's industrial past.

LINCOLNSHIRE

STAMFORD

MAP 7 REF P14

30 miles E of Leicester off the A1

Proclaimed as 'the finest stone town in England', Stamford was declared the country's first Conservation Area in 1967. Its origins are probably in the Saxon period, though one of the numerous local legends tells of a settlement and seat of learning founded in the 8th century BC by the Trojan king of Britain, King Bladud. It is the handsome Georgian architecture that gives today's town its wonderful character, in private houses and in majestic public buildings such as the Town Hall, the Assembly Rooms, the theatre and the renowned George Hotel, whose gallows sign spans the main street. The churches, diminished in number down the centuries, are all worth visiting, particularly St Mary's, with a spectacular spire and some marvellous stained glass; St Martin's, built in 1430 in late Perpendicular style; and St George's, long associated with the Order of the Garter - one of its windows is decorated with the order's mottoes and garters. 13th century All Saints Church, notable for its multiple arched wall arcading and semi-detached tower and spire, was extensively rebuilt in the 15th century by John and William Browne, prosperous wool merchants who are commemorated in the church by life-size brasses. Its most distinguished vicar was the archaeologist and antiquarian William Stukeley. St Leonard's Priory, founded by the Benedictine order in the 11th century, is a fine example of Norman architecture, with an ornate west front and north-side arcade.

Built in 1824 of local stone, **The Daniel Lambert** occupies a Grade II listed building. Inside, the main central bar has a large open fire and comfortable seating. The walls are decorated with local prints and historic articles about the town, as well as a portrait in oils of Daniel Lambert himself, a former keeper of Bridewell prison who died in Stamford in 1809, and was notable not least for his extreme girth: at his death he weighed over 52 stone. The only pub in Stamford with the Cask Marque Award for the quality of its ales, real ales on tap include Adnams, John Smiths and changing guest ales. The cellar restaurant is in what was once the brewery, where the landlord produced his own heady brews. The stillage occupies one wall. The rough-cast arched walls and candlelit tables add real atmosphere and charm to the din-

**The Daniel Lambert, 20 St Leonards Street,
Stamford, Lincolnshire PE9 2HN
Tel: 01780 755991**

ing experience. On the menu are a range of baguettes, sandwiches, steaks, chicken dishes, burgers, duck, lamb and vegetarian meals, as well as a selection of mouth-watering puddings. There are also changing daily specials.

Famous people connected with Stamford include Sir Malcolm Sargent, who is buried in the town's cemetery. The cross on his grave is inscribed with the Promenader's prayer. Daniel Lambert, the celebrated giant, was in Stamford on many occasions, often staying at the George, and when he died in 1809 at the Waggon and Horses Inn he tipped the scales at almost 59 stones. One of the many stories associated with him is that he would challenge people to race along a course which he would choose. He then set off along the George's corridors, filling them wall to wall and preventing the challenger from passing! He is buried in a detached part of St Martin's churchyard; his grave is an oft-visited Stamford landmark, and one of the most popular exhibits in **Stamford Museum** is a life-size model of him, in one of his own suits, alongside a besuited model of General Tom Thumb. The museum sets out the history and archaeology of Stamford, and includes an industrial section featuring agricultural implements and machines, and the short-lived locally produced Pick motor car. Glazed Stamford ware was highly regarded in the Middle Ages, and a collection forms part of the medieval display. It was manufactured in the town from about 850 to the 13th century, while for a short period in the Victorian era terracotta ware was produced; this, too, is on display. A rather more specialised museum is the **Stamford Steam Brewery Museum** displaying original 19th century brewery equipment.

St Martin's Church contains the tomb of William Cecil, the first Lord Burghley, who commissioned **Burghley House**, which stands on the B1443 a mile south-east of Stamford. This sumptuous Elizabethan pile, with 18 state rooms, houses some outstanding 17th century Italian paintings, superb tapestries and a major collection of Oriental porcelain. The extensive park that surrounds the house was designed by Capability Brown and is the setting for the annual **Burghley Horse Trials**.

THE DEEPINGS   Map 7 ref P14
8 Miles E of Stamford off theA16

Market Deeping and **Deeping St James**, once important stops on the London-Lincoln coaching route, stand almost as one on the River Welland at the southern end of the county. The parish church at Deeping St James is impressive in its proportions, a legacy of Benedictine wealth, and features a hude, a small shelter, rather like a sentry box, which would keep the vicar dry at the graveside. The oddest building is the Cross, the original market cross, which was converted to a lock-up for village drunks in 1809; three stone seats with chains can be seen through bars in the door. A point of interest in nearby Deeping Gate is a fine old bridge (dating from 1651) that crosses the Welland. Market Deeping's church is dedicated to St Guthlac of nearby Crowland, while at **West Deeping** the major buildings are the 13th century church and a Grade II Listed moated manor house that once was owned by Henry VII's mother. North of the village, across the A16, lie **Tallington Lakes**, a 200-acre site of water-filled pits where the action includes fishing, sailing and windsurfing.

CROWLAND   Map 7 ref Q14
12 miles E of Stamford on the A1073/B1166

The Abbey attracts visitors from all over the world, but it's also worth pausing awhile at the medieval **Trinity Bridge**. It dates from the 14th century and owes its unique triangular shape to the fact that it once stood over the confluence of two rivers. An unidentified stone figure, once in the Abbey, guards one end of the bridge.

1999 saw the 1300th anniversary of the arrival of St Guthlac at Crowland in an area that was then entirely marsh and wetland. The small church and hermitage established there was later to become **Croyland Abbey**, one of the nation's most important Benedictine monasteries. The present Church of St Bartholomew, though still impressive, is a small part of the great buildings that once occupied the site. Nothing but some oak foundations remain of the first abbey, which was destroyed by Danish invaders. The monastery was rebuilt in Saxon style in about 950, when the community began to live according to the Rule of St Benedict. The second abbey was completely destroyed by fire in 1091 and some 70 years later the third abbey was built in the Norman style. Parts of this abbey can still be seen, notably the dog-tooth west arch of the central tower, the west front of the south aisle and the font built into the south pier of the tower's east arch. Fire again caused massive damage in 1143 and the restoration work undertaken by successive abbots was in part undone during the Dissolution of the Monasteries. A visit to the church today is a fascinating experience and among the many interesting features are the Norman font, the fine roof vaulting, the 15th-century statues on the west front and the superb bells (Croyland had the first tuned peal in England).

BOURNE   MAP 7 REF P13
10 miles N of Stamford on the A6121

An abbey was founded here in the 12th century, and the Abbey Church of St Peter and St Paul is one of the very few connected with the Arrovasian sub-division of the Augustinian order. Behind the church is a working mill that is the **Bourne Heritage Centre**. Hereward the Wake possibly started life in Bourne, but William Cecil (later Lord Burghley) certainly did, and so did Raymond Mays, who was responsible for the pre-war ERA racing cars and the post-war BRMs. Red Hall, a sturdy Elizabethan mansion in red brick, spent some of its more recent life as part of Bourne's railway station (the line closed in the 1960s) and is now a community centre. A mile west of town on the A151 stands **Bourne Wood**, 400 acres of long-established woodland with an abundant and varied plant and animal life. Once part of the great forest of Brunswald, it's a great place for walking or cycling, and has some interesting modern sculpture in wood and stone. The waters around Bourne and the Deepings are credited with curative properties, and the Blind Well, on the edge of the wood, is said to be efficacious in dealing with eye complaints.

SPALDING   MAP 7 REF Q13
22 miles NE of Stamford off the A16

A peaceful market town that is the centre of Lincolnshire's flower growing industry. the annual **Tulip Parade** in early May is a great event in the town's life, attracting many thousands of visitors and culminating in a colourful procession of floats. These floats stay on display for a time at **Springfield Gardens** (World of Flowers), where 30 landscaped acres include marvellous show gardens, a carp lake and a sub-tropical palm house. The town is an interesting place to stroll around, with Georgian terraces lining the River Welland and many other buildings showing strong Dutch influence. Before the days of mass car-owning, the popularity of the Tulip Parade used to bring in most of its visitors by train, and the sidings north of the station were regularly filled with excursion trains. As a result, Spalding boasts one of the longest iron footbridges in Lincolnshire. Two, actually, because another equally impressive construction stands south of the station, spanning the main line and a now defunct branch line.

The present parish church of **St Mary and St Nicholas** was built by the Benedictine Priory which existed in Spalding from 1051 to its dissolution. In the early 16th century it is reported that elaborate plays were performed in the Sheep Market to raise funds for the Church repairs. In 1674 the St Thomas Chapel became home to the Grammar School. It has been altered and added to over the years and was extensively restored in 1865-7. recent additions include modern stained glass windows and decorations on the Chancel ceiling.

The grandest building in the Spalding area is **Ayscoughfee Hall**, at Churchgate on the

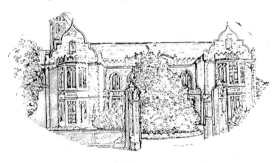

Peterborough road, a well-preserved medieval mansion standing in attractive gardens by the river. It houses the **Museum of South Holland**, whose galleries span Spalding history, drainage and land reclamation, agriculture and horticulture. A permanent display records the life story of Captain Matthew Flinders RN, who was born in nearby Donington in 1774 and who explored and charted much of the Australian coastline. The

Ayscoughfee Hall

Hall, which has been altered many times since its origins in the 15th century, also contains a collection of stuffed birds belonging to the Spalding Gentlemen's Society. In the garden stands a lonely war memorial at the end of an ornamental lake.

At **Pinchbeck**, a couple of miles north of Spalding, the **Spalding Bulb Museum** depicts the growth of the bulb-growing industry down the years with the aid of tableaux and artefacts, as well as audio-visual and seasonal working demonstrations. Open from April to October. Off West Marsh Road, the **Pinchbeck Engine** is a restored beam engine that was built in 1833 for fen-draining purposes and worked until 1952, draining anything up to 3.5 million tons of water in a year. In 1988 the Drainage Board and South Holland Council took the decision to restore this superb piece of machinery and it now operates regularly, the centrepiece of a land drainage museum that is open daily from April to October. Another massive draining machine is on display at Pode Hole pumping station. Another place to see at Pinchbeck is Spalding Tropical Forest, open throughout the year.

GEDNEY DYKE   MAP 7 REF Q13
13 miles E of Spalding off the A17

The **Church of St Mary** in Gedney is one of the finest in the area, notable in particular for its Perpendicular-style clerestory. Gedney Dyke is in fact only half a village. It still has a shop, but is separated from the centre of the village and the church by the A17.

The **Chequers** at Gedney Dyke, right on the main street through the village, takes its name not from the game of draughts, as might be supposed, but from the two berry trees in the garden to the rear of this attractive traditional country inn. Members of the rowan family, these trees produce fruits known as service berries, from which a brew can be made that is known locally as chequers. This lively pub is a hub of the community, and the emphasis is equally on good food and drink. There is an extensive menu as well as blackboard special, offering such tempting main courses as ricotta and spinach tortelloni,

**The Chequers, Main Street, Gedney Dyke,
Lincolnshire PE12 0AJ Tel: 01406 362666**

Gressingham duck breast, seared wood pigeon breast, pan-fried breast of guinea fowl and escalope of pork. Owners Simon and Linda Rattray are friendly and welcoming hosts. Adnams of Southwold supply the excellent beers, including Greene King 'Abbot', Adnams own, and Bateman XXX B.

LONG SUTTON   MAP 7 REF Q13
15 miles E of Spalding on the B1359

A sizeable town surrounded by lots of little Suttons. One of the best reasons for a visit, and a great place for a family day out, is the **Butterfly and Falconry Park**. Besides hundreds of butterflies in tropical houses and daily displays of falconry, the park has an animal centre, honey farm, ant room, insectarium and reptile land. A mini-assault course challenges the kiddies, and there's picnic area and a tea room. St Mary's Church is unusual in having a lead spire, whose height (over 160') made it a useful landmark for sailors.

The area leading to the Wash is a favourite place with walkers and naturalists, especially bird-watchers. One of the most popular routes is the **Peter Scott Walk** (Sir Peter lived in one of the two lighthouses on the River Nene near Sutton Bridge. **King John's Lost Jewels Trail** covers 23 miles of quiet country roads and is suitable for motorists and cyclists. It starts at Long Sutton market place and passes Sutton Bridge, where the king is said to have lost his jewels in the marsh in 1216.

GRANTHAM
20 miles N of Stamford off the A1

MAP 7 REF O13

This ancient market town was a Saxon Settlement in the 6th century, and when the Domesday Book was compiled it was recorded as a Royal Manor. It remained a royal possession until 1696. When the River Trent was bridged at Newark the main road came through Grantham and greatly increased its importance; the coming of the railways accelerated its growth. The crowning glory of the town is undoubtedly St Wulfram's Church, originally built in the 8th century and dedicated to a 7th century missionary. The spire was the first of the great spires to be built, when put up between 1280 and 1300. At 282', it is the sixth highest in the country. Among many treasures is a rare 16th century chained library of 150 volumes.

Grantham House, at Castlegate, is a National Trust property dating from the 14th century and standing in pleasant grounds sloping down to the River Witham - a country house in a town. **Grantham Museum** provides a fascinating, in-depth look at local history - social, agricultural, industrial - and has special sections devoted to Sir Isaac Newton, born locally and educated at the town's King's School, and Lady Thatcher, the town's most famous daughter. When elevated to the peerage she took the title Baroness Thatcher of Kesteven - the area in which Grantham is located. She still retains close links with the town and declared: "From this town I learned so much and am proud to be one of its citizens". The Guildhall Arts Centre is a grand Victorian building that once included prison cells, which are now used as the box office of the centre. Another Grantham landmark is the **Conduit**, built by the Corporation in 1597 as the receiving point for the fresh water supply that flowed from springs near Barrowby. Margaret Thatcher was Britain's first woman prime minister, and it was in Grantham that Edith Smith was sworn in as Britain's first woman police officer, just after the First World War. She made a great job of cleaning up the streets, bringing many of the more dubious females to book. No doubt her influence lives on!

HARLAXTON
4 miles SW of Grantham off the A607

MAP 7 REF O13

Harlaxton Manor, approached by a handsome drive off the A607, is a superb combination of Elizabethan, Jacobean and Baroque styles, and its gardens were designed as a walk round Europe, with French-style terraces, an Italian colonnade and a Dutch-style ornamental canal. The views across the Vale of Belvoir are spectacular.

CORBY GLEN
10 miles SE of Grantham on the A151

MAP 7 REF P13

Site of an annual sheep fair dating back to the 13th century. The Church of St John the Evangelist is distinguished by a large number of beautifully preserved medieval wall paintings. Originally a quarryman's croft and/or quarry store, **Stonepit Farmhouse** is built of local limestone and dates in parts back to the 1700s. Now offering bed and breakfast accommodation, this charming establishment sits on the edge of a quiet village overlooking some lovely rolling countryside.

Proprietors Helen and David Porter have been running this superb guest house since 1994, and are conscientious, thoughtful and friendly hosts. There are three rooms (one double ensuite on the first floor, and on the ground floor a twin and a single with washbasin, sharing a bathroom). This home from home is comfortable, with fine furnishings including hand-made old-fashioned metal bedframes crafted by David. For her part, Helen has created some of the paintings that adorn the walls. There is an attractive lawned garden and a secluded courtyard for guests' use, as well as a separate breakfast/sitting room. Comfort and a high standard of service are ensured here. Guests have a choice of full English breakfast or a meal cooked to order, so special diets or requests are catered for. ETC 3 Diamonds Guest Accommodation.

Stonepit Farmhouse, Swinstead Road, Corby Glen, Lincolnshire NG33 4NU Tel/Fax: 01476 550614 e-mail: beds@stonepit.u-net.com

WOOLSTHORPE-BY-BELVOIR   MAP 7 REF O13
7 miles W of Grantham off the A607

Woolsthorpe's Church of St James is made of ironstone and is well worth a visit. The place that really must be seen, though, is **Belvoir Castle**, seat of the Dukes of Rutland since the time of Henry VIII, and the fourth castle to occupy the site since Roman times; it was completed early in the 19th century. The Grand Hall and state rooms are magnificent, and they house a treasure trove of furniture, porcelain, silks, tapestries, sculptures and paintings by such artists as Gainsborough, Reynolds, Poussin and Holbein. The Castle also houses the **Museum of the Queen's Royal Lancers**. The grounds, which provide wonderful views of the Vale of Belvoir, are a marvellous setting for special events, among which the medieval jousting tournaments are always popular.

Hidden in the shadow of Belvoir Castle, **The Chequers**

The Chequers, Main Street, Woolsthorpe-by-Belvoir, Grantham, Lincolnshire NG32 1LU Tel: 01476 870701

stands quietly in large grounds surrounded by country fields, overlooking a cricket pitch and a summer garden. The nearby Viking Way and Jubilee Way allow walkers to admire the beauty of the countryside. Originally a 17th-century village farmhouse and bakehouse, the building is full of nooks and crannies with open fires and hopbines hanging from the ceiling, bringing the feeling of an old home that always welcomes guests. Watercolours and oil paintings cover the walls of the small candlelit restaurant, with its excellent cuisine - French and old country English, with game in season and steak and kidney pies baked in their own juices inside a traditional raised pastry. Bar snacks are served in the main bar and in the oldest part of the building - the bakehouse itself, with its original stone walls and the baker's oven sitting next to the fire. Menus change regularly to reflect the changing season. Owners Nick and Yoanna Potter pride themselves on everything being home-made. The Belvedere Suite is a newer addition to the old building. A large room with French doors opening onto the garden, it is perfect for weddings and other celebrations. Accommodation here comprises four very comfortable ensuite bedrooms. There are proposed plans for an additional 10 to 12 bedrooms, all ensuite, to be erected overlooking the cricket field. They will be individually furnished and decorated incorporating antique 'Olde Worlde' style.

SLEAFORD   Map 7 ref P13
10 miles NE of Grantham off the A15

A market town of some 10,000 souls, some of whom have the pleasure of worshipping in the fine old parish church of St Denys, with its beautiful traceried windows. Nothing but a single piece of stone remains of the castle that dominated the town many centuries ago. On the southern edge of town stand the Maltings, an industrial complex built at the turn of the century. **Cogglesford Watermill** is an 18th century construction restored to working order and housing an exhibition about its past.

HECKINGTON   Map 7 ref P13
6 miles E of Sleaford off the A17

There's plenty of variety and interest here, in particular the tall **Church of St Andrew**, the Victorian almshouses and the magnificent eight-sailed windmill by the railway station. When built in 1830 its sails numbered a modest five, but the eight sails were taken from a nearby mill and installed after storms damaged the mill in 1890. This lovely piece of industrial archaeology rises to five floors and can be visited at weekends and certain other times. A few steps away, the Pearoom is a contemporary craft centre housed in a barn-like brick building.

WOODHALL SPA   Map 7 ref P12
12 miles NE of Sleaford on the B1191

Woodhall became a spa town by accident when a shaft sunk in search of coal found not coal but mineral-rich water. In 1838 a pump room and baths were built, to be joined later by hydro hotels. The arrival of the railway accelerated its popularity, but down the years the spa fell into disuse and the associated buildings collapsed. One interesting survivor of the good old days is the kinema in the Woods, originally a tennis pavilion. The **Cottage Museum** on Iddsleigh Road, also the Tourist Information Centre, tells the story of the establishment of the town as a spa resort. Woodhall Spa had close connections with 617 Squadron, the Dambusters, in the Second World War, and the Petwood Hotel was used as the officers' mess. Memorabilia of those days are displayed in the hotel's Squadron Bar. The **Dambusters Memorial** in Royal Square is in the form of a model of a breached dam.

CONINGSBY   Map 7 ref Q12
4 miles S of Woodhall Spa on the A153

The centre of this charming village, which started life as a Danish settlement, is dominated by the church tower of St Michael, notable for its enormous single-handed clock; at over 16' in diameter, this 17th century clock has claims to be the largest working example of its kind. RAF Coningsby is home to the **Battle of Britain Memorial Flight**, formed in 1957 to commemorate the service's major battle honour. Spitfires, Hurricanes and a Lancaster are on show at the centre.

TATTERSHALL

4 miles S of Woodhall Spa on the A153

Map 7 ref Q12

Separated from Coningsby by Butts Bridge, Tattershall is known all over the world for the proud keep of **Tattershall Castle**, built in brick in the 1440s on the orders of the Lord Chancellor, Ralph Cromwell, on the site of an existing castle. The keep has four floors, each with a great chamber and smaller rooms opening into the corner turrets. The building was rescued from near ruin by Lord Curzon, who bequeathed it to the National Trust on his death in 1925. for opening times of the castle and its gatehouse, which houses a museum and a shop. In the shadow of the castle is **Tattershall Country Park**, set in 365 acres of woods, parks and lakes and offering all sorts of sporting facilities. Other major points of interest in the area are **Dogdyke Steam Pumping Station** at Bridge Farm, Tattershall Bridge, the last working steam drainage engine in the Fens; and another pumping station, combined with the **Tales of the River Bank** visitor centre, at Timberland, reached along the River Witham at Tattershall Bridge. All you need to know about the Fens is explained here.

BOSTON

15 miles E of Sleaford on the A16

Map 7 ref Q13

An important port on the River Witham, from Roman times Boston has been a major centre of import and export. Trade reached its height in the Middle Ages, when the port was second only to London in paying tax dues. Boston's most famous landmark is St Botolph's Church, whose tower, popularly known as **Boston Stump**, rises to 272 feet. St Botolph's is the largest parish church in England, begun in 1309 and built mainly in the Decorated style of architecture. Light, airy and spacious, the church is full of eccentric carvings in wood and stone, and above the south door the library, founded in 1635, has a superb collection of medieval manuscripts. On the church green is a statue of Herbert Ingram (1811-1860), an MP for Boston and the founder of the Illustrated London News. The **Guildhall Museum** in South Street is a handsome brick building of the 15th century which served as the Town Hall for 300 years. The most important event in Boston's history took place in 1607, when a group of Puritans, trying to escape to religious freedom in the Netherlands, were betrayed by the captain of their ship and arrested. They later reached the Netherlands, where they stayed for 12 years before sailing to America as the Pilgrim Fathers. The cells where the ringleaders were held are the most popular attraction at the museum, which also has numerous exhibits ranging from archaeological finds to a portrait of the botanist Sir Joseph Banks, who sailed with Captain Cook and who introduced sheep into Australia. Other significant Boston buildings include the 13th century Blackfriars, originally the refectory of a Dominican friary and now an arts centre; Fydell House, a handsome 18th century house which now contains an adult education centre; and the recently restored **Maud Foster Windmill**, the tallest working windmill in the UK, which mills daily when the wind blows. Boston is at its bustling busiest on Wednesdays and Saturdays, when the centre is taken over by colourful street markets.

SUTTERON

6 miles S of Boston off the A16

Map 7 ref Q13

Sutterton is a charming village with a lovely village green and duck pond. **The Beridge Arms Hotel** stands opposite St Mary's village church in this fine village. Mother and daughter Ann and Natasha Bunn have personally run this attractive restaurant and hotel since the summer of 1999; Ann handles the cooking, while Natasha manages front of house. They are friendly, hos-

pitable and welcoming hosts. Originally Lord Beridge's headquarters in the late 1800s, it is one of the oldest buildings in the village. The comfortable and cosy lounge bar has a large brick fireplace and a delicately ornate ceiling, adding to the character and atmosphere. The separate public bar is a hub of village life. The real ales on offer change regularly, and there is also a good range of lager, wines and spirits.

The Beridge Arms Hotel, Station Road, Sutterton, nr Boston, Lincolnshire PE20 2JH Tel: 01205 460272

The menu boasts a good selection of home-cooked snacks and meals such as steak and Guinness pie, plaice, lasagne verdi and vegetarian dish of the day. The six spacious guest bedrooms are airy and very comfortable, with lovely decor and furnishings, and all modern amenities.

SIBSEY   MAP 7 REF Q12

5 miles N of Boston on the A16

English Heritage takes care of the famous **Sibsey Trader Mill**, a six-sailed mill built in 1887 by Saundersons of Louth. It stands a mile west of Sibsey off the A16 and is open on certain milling Sundays.

STICKNEY   MAP 7 REF Q12

7 miles N of Boston on the A16

A French connection here. The poet Paul Verlaine taught French, Latin and drawing at the village school, having come from prison in Brussels, where he served two years hard labour for wounding fellow-poet Rimbaud. He left in 1876, apparently depressed at the British climate, but otherwise in good spirits. A mile further north up the A16 is **Stickford**, home of the **Allied Forces Museum**, a large private collection of World War ll and post-war British and American vehicles including personnel carriers, tracked vehicles, field guns and motorcycles. The A16 continues north, passing through East Keal, to Spilsby.

SOMERSBY   MAP 7 REF Q12

15 miles N of Boston off the A158

Tennyson's birthplace, and the village and surrounding area are full of associations with the poet. The church contains several memorials to Tennyson, whose father is buried in the churchyard. In the tiny neighbouring village of **Bag Enderby** John Wesley is said to have preached under the tree on the village green; the hollow trunk still stands. Other places to visit near Spilsby include the **Fenside Goat Centre**, a working dairy goat farm at **Toynton All Saints** (1 mile south off the A16), and the **Northcote Heavy Horse Centre** at **Great Steeping**, 3 miles east of town on the B1195. Here visitors spend happy hours meeting the horses and enjoying wagon rides, longer country rides and various demonstrations.

SKEGNESS   MAP 8 REF R12

22 miles NE of Boston on the A52

And so to the seaside and Skegness, popular with generation after generation as a holiday resort catering for all ages. A port in Tudor times, it was planned as a resort by the Earl of Scarborough, and the arrival of the railway in 1873 really put it on the map, making it accessible for thousands. The pier (now sadly truncated) and St Matthew's Church were built for holidaymakers, and in 1936 Billy Butlin opened his first holiday camp. The town's mascot is the Jolly Fisherman, and the story behind him is an interesting one. In 1908 the Great Northern Railway bought an oil painting of the fisherman for £12. After adding the famous slogan 'Skegness is so Bracing', they used the painting as a poster to advertise trips from King's Cross to Skegness (fare 3/- or 15p). 90 years later the same Jolly Fisherman is still busy promoting Skegness as a holiday resort. There are two statues of him in town, one at the railway station, the other in Compass Gardens. Besides the obvious attractions of the beach and all the traditional seaside entertainment, Skegness has some places of special interest, including **Church Farm Museum**, a former farmhouse that is home to a collection of old farm implements and machinery, re-created village workshops, a paddock of Lincoln Longwool sheep and a fine example of a Lincolnshire 'mud and stud' thatched cottage. **Natureland Seal Sanctuary** on North Parade provides interest and fun for all the family with its seals and baby seal rescue centre, aquarium, tropical house, pets corner and Floral Palace, a large greenhouse teeming with plant, insect and bird life. Serious birdwatchers should head south along the coast to **Gibraltar Point National Nature Reserve**, a field station among the salt marshes and dunes with hides, waymarked routes and guided tours.

The Old Chequers Inn is a charming brickbuilt public house occupying a Grade II listed building dating back to 1550. Believed to be the oldest inn in Lincolnshire, the exterior is covered with lovely trailing ivy beneath a traditional pan-tiled roof. The interior is characterful; the bar has exposed black beams and a large open brick fireplace; the family room is small and comfortable, and the dining room is intimate and has a warm ambience, with beamed ceilings and a large brick inglenook fireplace. Real ales are on tap together with a good range of ciders, lagers, stouts, wines and spirits. Owners Alan and Angela Beal are friendly and hospitable hosts. All meals are home-cooked and home-prepared. The menu offers imaginative and traditional favourites, including rump steak, broccoli and cream cheese

The Old Chequers Inn, Lymn Bank, Croft, Skegness, Lincolnshire PE24 4PF Tel: 01754 880320

bake and beef curry. There are also tasty bar meals, snacks and puddings, and the Sunday lunch is a real treat. Food is available Tuesday - Sunday. In a nearby field measuring some 2½ acres there is a static caravan site and a touring site that can accommodate up to 40 caravans.

North of Skegness lie the smaller resorts of **Chapel St Leonards** and **Ingoldmells**. Just beyond the latter is **Hardy's Animal Farm**, a working farm with an adventure playground.

ALFORD   MAP 7 REF Q11
10 miles NW of Skegness on the A1104

Often described as Lincolnshire's Craft Centre, Alford is a flourishing market town with a real sense of history. **Alford Manor House**, with brick gabling and thatched roof, is a folk museum where visitors are invited to step back into the past and take a look at local life through shops, a veterinary surgery, a Victorian schoolroom and a History Room with a collection of Roman finds and displays from the salt works that once flourished in this part of the world. An even more tangible link with the past is provided by **Alford Tower Mill** on the Mablethorpe side of town, built by local millwright Sam Oxley in 1837. Standing a majestic six floors high, it has five sails and four sets of grinding stones. It retired in 1955, but after loving restoration is now back in operation. The Church of St Wilfrid dates from the 14th century and was extensively restored and enlarged by Sir Giles Gilbert Scott in 1869. Tuesday is market day in Alford, with the craft market on Fridays in summer, and every August a festival attracts a growing variety of arts and crafts on display, joined nowadays by dancers, singers, poets and actors. The Alford town crier scatters his decibels every Tuesday in summer.

WOODTHORPE
MAP 7 REF Q11

2 miles NW of Alford on the B1373

Set in 500 acres of beautiful Lincolnshire countryside including Woodthorpe Hall Leisure Park and Woodthorpe Hall itself - a 17th-century country house which takes its name from the remarkable 1,000-year-old oak tree situated in the grounds - **Woodthorpe Country Inn** is a welcoming and relaxing pub and restaurant. The Stubbs family still farm most of the surround-

ing land, but have developed a leisure park where guests can enjoy tranquil country walks, fishing, golf, bowls, gliding and kart racing. There are superb holiday cottages, a caravan site and garden and aquatics centre also on-site. The inn offers an excellent range of liquid refreshments, from traditional ales and bitters to lagers, cider, stout, wines and spirits. The extensive menu boasts snacks

Woodthorpe Country Inn, Woodthorpe, nr Alford, Lincolnshire LN13 0DD Tel: 01507 450079

and bar meals and delicious hearty fare such as fish and seafood dishes, steaks and grills, house specials including Atlantic salmon and fillet steak au poivre. Guests should be sure to leave room for the tempting hot and cold puddings. With so many facilities and diversions in the surrounding park, this makes a superb choice for a relaxing and memorable break.

ABY
MAP 7 REF Q11

3 miles NW of Alford on minor roads

Claythorpe Watermill & Wildfowl Gardens are a major draw for visitors of all ages. Features of this lovely riverside setting include enchanted woods, hundreds of birds and animals, a tea room and a gift shop. Open daily March to October. The mill itself, long since drawing its pension, was built in 1721. At nearby **Swaby** are a long barrow and a nature reserve in Swaby Valley that is designated a Site of Special Scientific Interest.

MABLETHORPE
MAP 8 REF R11

7 miles NE of Alford on the A1111

The northernmost and 'senior' of the three holiday resorts that almost form a chain along the fragile coast, which has frequently been threatened by the waves, and whose outline has changed visibly down the years. Long popular with day trippers and holidaymakers, it offers all that could be asked of a traditional seaside town, and a little more. Tennyson stayed regularly at Marine Villa, which is now called Tennyson's Cottage. One of the most popular attractions is the **Animal Gardens Nature Centre & Seal Trust** at North End. This complex houses creatures of all kinds, with special wild cat and barn owl features, and includes a seal and seabird hospital, lynx caves and a nature centre with many fascinating displays. Open every day from Easter to October.

LOUTH
MAP 7 REF Q11

22 miles N of Skegness off the A16

Set on the Greenwich Meridian on the eastern edge of the Wolds in an Area of Outstanding Beauty, Louth is an historic market town where an 8th century abbot went on to become Archbishop of Canterbury. The remains of a 12th century Cistercian Abbey can be found on private land east of the town. Notable existing buildings include the museum on Broadbank (look for the amazing carpets that were shown at the 1867 Paris Exhibition) and the ancient grammar school, but the whole town is filled with attractive buildings, many of them tucked away down narrow streets. A plaque in Westgate Place marks the house where Tennyson lodged with his grandmother while attending the school. The vast **Church of St James** has the tallest spire of any parish church (nearly 300 feet). A cattle market is held in Louth on Fridays, and a general market on Wednesdays, Fridays and Saturdays.

EAST BARKWITH
MAP 7 REF P11

13 miles W of Louth off the A157

The Grange is a handsome late-Georgian house set in mature gardens in a village halfway between Lincoln and Louth. The owners are Sarah and Jonathan Stamp. Sarah is a keen and accomplished cook; Jonathan is a farmer whose interests include aviation and fly fishing. There's some splendid topiary on the front lawn, and views east towards the Wolds, west towards Lincoln Cathedral. Particular attractions include a one-hour farm trail and a secluded trout lake, both available only to guests. The two ensuite double bedrooms are models of good taste in decor and appointments. The residents' lounge is a beautifully comfortable room, a lovely spot to enjoy the tea and home-made cakes that greet guests on arrival. Evening meals (by arrangement, de-

The Grange, Torrington Lane, East Barkwith, nr Market Rasen, Lincolnshire LN8 5RY Tel: 01673 858670

pending on the season) are served in a dining room whose walls are hung with Zoffany wallpaper. The Grange has won awards in the 'England for Excellence' category of tourism and the environment, and is also highly commended by the English Tourist Council. It is a certified location for the Caravan Club of Great Britain, with sites for five vans in a secluded area well away from the house. ETB 4 Diamonds; Silver Award from the English Tourism Council.

MARKET RASEN

MAP 7 REF P11

14 miles W of Louth on the A631

The little River Rase gives its name to this market town at the western edge of the Wolds. Growing in importance down the years, it prospered even further when the railway line was built. It was certainly a far cry from being 'the sleepiest town in England', as Charles Dickens once declared. Much of the central part is a conservation area, and the best known buildings are **De Aston School, St Thomas's Church** with a 15th century ironstone tower, and the impressive **Centenary Wesleyan church.**

North of Market Rasen are many picturesque villages, including **Tealby**, notable for its narrow streets and pretty cottages, and **Binbrook**, where there are many reminders of the now closed RAF base in St Mary's Church. **Walesby**, on the Viking Way, is the location of All Saints, the ramblers' church, which has a stained-glass window depicting Christ walking with ramblers and cyclists. **Normanby-le-Wold**, five miles from Market Rasen, is the highest village in the county.

LINCOLN

MAP 7 REF P12

16 miles SW of Market Rasen on the A46

Lincoln is one of England's most and treasured cities, with 2,000 years of history to be discovered and enjoyed. The Roman walled city has left traces behind at **Newport Arch** and along **Bailgate**, where cobblestones in the paving show where the columns of the forum once stood. No 29 Bailgate, a private residence, boasts four giant pillars as well as a section of road believed to have been built by the Romans when they arrived in about 42BC. These ruins were discovered during the Victorian era, along with a Roman urn and other artefacts. The long-time owners had a family tradition of allowing visitors to see the pillars, but the property has recently changed hands - let's hope the new owners keep up the tradition.

The Cathedral and the Castle date from the Norman invasion, and there are some fine Norman buildings on a lesser scale in Steep Hill and the Strait. **Jews House**, which dates from about 1170, is thought to be the oldest domestic building in England to survive intact. Its

neighbour is Jews Court, both reminders of the time when there was a thriving Jewish community in Lincoln. Medieval splendour lives on in the black and white half-timbered houses on High Bridge, and in the old city Gateways, while the residences in the Cathedral Close and Castle Square are models of Georgian elegance.

The Lincoln Heritage Trail takes in Lincoln's 'Magnificent Seven' tourist attractions. **Lincoln Cathedral**, started in 1072, dates mainly from the 12th and 13th centuries. One of the largest cathedrals in the country, and in a suitably dramatic setting, it is dedicated to the Blessed Virgin Mary. Among its many superb features are the magnificent open nave, stained-glass windows incorporating the 14th century Bishop's Eye and Dean's Eye, and the glorious Angel Choir, whose carvings include the Lincoln Imp, the

Jews House

unofficial symbol of the city. **Lincoln Castle** dates from the same period as the Cathedral, and visitors can climb to the ramparts, which include an Observatory Tower, to enjoy fine views of the city. Interesting features abound, notably the keep, known as Lucy Tower, Cobb Hall, where the public gallows were located, and the Victorian prison whose chapel has separate pews like upright coffins. The building also houses an original version of Magna Carta. **The Lawn**, originally built in 1820 as a lunatic asylum, and standing in the heart of the main tourist area, is an elegant porticoed building whose attractions include an archaeology centre, tropical conservatory (the old swimming pool) and aviation museum. It is set in eight acres of beautiful grounds and gardens. Lincolnshire's largest social history museum is the **Museum of Lincolnshire Life**, which occupies an extensive barracks built for the Royal North Lincoln Militia in 1857. It is now a Listed building and houses a fascinating series of displays depicting the many aspects of Lincolnshire life. **Ellis Mill** is the last survivor of a line of windmills that once ran along the Lincoln Edge, a limestone ridge stretching some 70 miles from Winteringham by the Humber to Stamford on the county's southern border. This tower mill dates back to 1798 and is in full working order.

The **Toy Museum** on Westgate is a sheer delight with its fascinating collection of old toys, crazy mirrors and slot machines, and the **Road Transport Museum** has a fine collection of vintage cars, lorries and buses. Many parts of Lincoln involve steep hills, so visitors should not try to rush around the sights too quickly. Almost every building has something to offer in terms of historical interest, and tired pedestrians can always consider the option of guided tours by open-top bus, or a trip along the river.

GAINSBOROUGH

MAP 7 REF O11

17 miles NW of Lincoln on the A156

Britain's most inland port, visited more than once by the Danes, who took advantage of its position on the Trent. The most important building is the **Gainsborough Old Hall**, part 15th century, with extensions at the end of the 16th. The hall is linked with the Pilgrim Fathers, who met here secretly on occasions, and with John Wesley. Perfectly preserved, it has the original kitchen and a superb Great Hall. All Saints Church is of considerable interest, being the only Georgian town church (except for the earlier spire) in Lincolnshire. In Beaumont Street stands Marshall's Britannia Works, a proud reminder of Gainsborough's once thriving engineering industry.

FILLINGHAM

MAP 7 REF O11

3 miles SE of Gainsborough off the B1398

The peaceful stone village of Fillingham nestles at the base of the Lincolnshire Scarp, the limestone edge that slices though the county extending down to the Cotswolds. Fillingham Church dates largely from the 18th century, although the west doorway is of the 12th century. John Wycliffe, first man to translate the Bible into English, was rector of the parish in the 14th century. There is a large lake close to the village, and on the ridge above is (privately owned) Fillingham Castle, built in 1760 by John Carr as a summer residence for Sir Cecil Wray. **Church Farm** offers excellent bed and breakfast accommodation in a large, traditional farmhouse constructed of Lincolnshire stone and dating back some 200 years, situated in this pretty village. There is an ensuite double, large and tastefully furnished and decorated, overlooking the garden and surrounding fields and countryside. The twin/double room has a separate private bathroom/shower. Both rooms are delightful, scrupulously clean and welcoming. The charming breakfast/dining room overlooks the garden. Here the breakfast menu includes freshly cooked

Church Farm, Fillingham, Gainsborough, nr Lincoln, Lincs DN21 5BS Tel: 01427 668279 Fax: 01427 668025

and prepared porridge, 'full-house fry-up', scrambled or poached eggs, toast and a variety of delicious jams and preserves. Afternoon teas are served here as well. Evening meals are available by arrangement. In fine weather, guests are welcome to use the barbecue in the spacious and peaceful garden. The guests' lounge is beautifully furnished and decorated, with plush sofas and chairs and an atmosphere perfect for relaxation. There are several very good pubs in close proximity to the house. ETB 4 Diamonds Highly Commended.

GRIMSBY   MAP 11 REF Q10
40 miles NE of Lincoln on the A46

The fisherman Grim, well known in medieval sagas, heads the field of possible founders of Grimsby, which from humble origins developed into the world's largest and busiest fishing port. The coming of the railways allowed the rapid transportation of fresh fish to all parts of the kingdom, and new fishing and commercial docks were built. The heyday has now passed, and some of the fish docks are finding a new purpose as a marina for leisure yachts.

The story of the boom days is told in vivid detail in the **National Fishing Heritage Centre** in Alexandra Dock, where visitors can get a dramatically real feel of a fisherman's life on the high seas, with the aid of exhibits, tableaux and the Ross Tiger, a classic fishing trawler from the 1950s. The Time Trap, housed in prison cells in the Town Hall, recreates the seamier side of life on dry land, and has proved a very popular annexe to the Heritage Centre. As we went to press, it was not known whether the Time Trap would continue.

Many of the older buildings in Grimsby have had to make way for modern development (some of it very imaginative and exciting), but the Town Hall, built in 1863, still stands to give a civic dignity to its surroundings. The most prominent building is the 300-foot **Dock Tower**, built in Italianate style. It stored water (33,000 gallons) to operate the hydraulic system that worked the lock gates. Another imposing edifice from earlier days is **Victoria Mills** by Corporation Bridge, a large Flemish-style flour mill that was converted into flats a few years ago. Away from the centre, by the banks of the River Freshney, is Freshney Park Way, 300 acres of open space that attracts walkers, cyclists, anglers and birdwatchers.

CLEETHORPES   MAP 11 REF Q10
1 mile S of Grimsby on the A180

South of Grimsby and almost merged with it, Cleethorpes developed from a little village into a holiday resort when the railway line was built in the 1860s. Like so many Victorian resorts, it had a pier (and still has). The pier was opened on August Bank Holiday Monday 1873, when nearly 3,000 people paid the then princely sum of sixpence (2½p) for admission. The toll was reduced the next day to a much more reasonable penny (½p), and it is recorded that in the first five weeks 37,000 people visited. The pier, like many others, was breached during the Second World War as a defence measure to discourage enemy landings, and it was never restored to its full length. On the seafront near the pier stands **Ross Castle**, a folly put up in 1885 that marks the original height of the clay cliffs. Among the attractions for visitors to Cleethorpes are **Jungle World**, an indoor tropical garden; the **Humber Estuary Discovery Centre**; and the **Cleethorpes Coast Light Railway**, a narrow-gauge steam railway that runs along the front from Easter to September.

IMMINGHAM   MAP 11 REF P10
6 miles NW of Grimsby off the A180

A small village that grew and grew with the creation of docks in the early years of this century. The heart of the original village is St Andrew's Church, dating from Norman times. The Docks were opened by King George V in 1912 and rapidly grew in importance, especially when the Great Central Railway switched its passenger liner service from Grimsby. **The Docks** expanded yet further when the Humber was dredged in the late 1960s to accommodate the new generation of giant tankers. **Immingham Museum** traces the links between the Docks and the railways.

In 1607 a group of Puritans set sail from Immingham to the Netherlands, and a memorial to this occasion - the **Pilgrim Father Monument** - stands on a granite plinth hewn from Plymouth Rock. It stood originally at the point of embarkation, but is now located near the church.

BARTON-UPON-HUMBER

Map 11 ref P10

6 miles NW of Immingham on the A1077

Barton was the point from which most boats made the crossing to Hull, and by the 11th century it was the most important port in North Lincolnshire. Continued prosperity is evident in the number of grand Georgian and Victorian buildings, and today it has never thrived more, standing as it does at the southern end of the impressive **Humber Bridge**. This is Europe's longest single-span suspension bridge and was opened by the Queen in 1981. There are viewing areas at both ends of the bridge, which has a pedestrian walkway. Around the Bridge are important nature reserves. **Barton Clay Pits** cover a five-mile area along the river bank and offer a haven for wildlife and recreation for sporty humans. **Far Ings**, with hides and waymarked trails, is home to more than 230 species of wild flowers, 50 nesting bird species and hundreds of different sorts of moths. Back in town, **Baysgarth House Museum** is an 18th century mansion with a collection of 18th and 19th century English and Oriental pottery, a section on country crafts and an industrial museum in the stable block. The surrounding park has a picnic area, play area and various recreational facilities. Barton has two distinguished churches, St Peter's with its remarkable Saxon tower and baptistry, and St Mary's with superb nave arches and elaborate west door. Chad Varah, founder of the Samaritans, was born in Barton, and Sir Isaac Pitman of shorthand fame taught here and married a local girl.

The A1017 running west of Barton meets the B1204 at South Ferriby, and the route down towards the M180 passes through the village of **Horkstow**. Two miles west of the road stands another suspension, on a more modest scale than the Humber Bridge, of course, but also remarkable in its way. It was designed and built by Sir John Rennie in 1844 to cross the River Ancholme to the brick kilns. It is certainly one of the world's oldest suspension bridges. Carrying on towards Brigg, at the junction of the B1204 and B1206, is the village of **Elsham** and real delight in the shape of **Elsham Hall Country and Wildlife Park**. This family-run enterprise in the grounds of an 18th mansion includes a small zoo, children's farm, garden centre, craft centre, café and theatre.

HIBALDSTOW

Map 11 ref P10

13 miles W of Immingham off the A15

Built in the 1870s, **The Wheatsheaf** has always been a public house, popular in the local community and with visitors from far and wide. The impressive stonebuilt exterior is festooned with hanging baskets. Inside, light pours in through the casement windows, filling the cosy and comfortable lounge and smaller bar areas, the former with a large open coal fire. Both are tastefully decorated. In the separate (non-smoking) dining room, which seats 28, there is an inviting and warm atmosphere. Proprietors Paul and Carol Brown both hail from Lincolnshire, and are friendly and hospitable

The Wheatsheaf, 15 Station Road, Hibaldstow, Brigg, Lincolnshire DN20 9EB Tel: 01652 658380

hosts. Real ales on tap include Tetleys, Worthingtons and Bass, as well as a new guest ale every week. The traditional snacks and meals are all home-cooked and freshly prepared, from the sandwiches and steak and ale pie to the delicious puddings. The Sunday lunch has proved a popular favourite - booking is advised. Two Saturdays a month there is live evening entertainment.

BRIGG   MAP 11 REF P10
10 miles W of Immingham on the A18

And so to Brigg, on the River Ancholme, known far and wide for its famous Fair, which was established by a royal charter from King John. **The Fair,** which is still held annually in August, has often been commemorated in words and music, notably a tone poem by Delius and two versions by Percy Grainger of the original song.

SCUNTHORPE   MAP 11 REF O10
20 miles W of Immingham on the A18

Scunthorpe changed from a rural farming community to a centre of the steel industry after 1860, when large deposits of ironstone were found beneath the five villages that made up the parish: Appleby, Ashby, Brumby, Crosby and Frodingham. An ironmonger's cottage is incorporated into **North Lincolnshire Museum & Art Gallery,** next to Frodingham church. The museum has excellent displays of geology, archaeology and social history. The main grand house in these parts is Brumby Hall, built in the 17th and 18th centuries.

HAXEY   MAP 11 REF O11
18 miles SW of Scunthorpe on the A161

Haxey is the site of a nature reserve, but is best known for the **Haxey Hood Game,** launched around 2.30 on the afternoon of Twelfth Night in front of the parish church. 300 men divided into four teams compete to push a leather 'hood' into the pub of their team's choice. The game apparently started in the12th or 13th century when a lady lost her hood and a number of village men scrambled to retrieve it. The strongest man caught the hood but was too shy to hand it back, and was labelled a fool by the lady, while the man who eventually handed it over was declared a lord. The lady suggested that the scene should be re-enacted each year, and gave a plot of land for the purpose. The 'sway' of men struggle across the fields working the hood towards the appropriate pubs and always staying within the sway - no open running. When the sway reaches the winning pub, the landlord touches the hood to declare the game over, and free drinks paid for by a collection end the day in time-honoured style. Rather an elaborate build-up to a drinking session, but just one of the traditions that make English country life so colourful.

NORTH YORKSHIRE - MOORS & EAST RIDINGS

GREAT AYTON   MAP 11 REF N6
6 miles SE of Middlesbrough on the A173

This appealing village, set around the River Leven, is an essential stopping point for anyone following the Captain Cook Country Tour, a 70 mile circular trip taking in all the major locations associated with the great seafarer. Cook's family moved to Great Ayton when he was eight years old and he attended the little school which is now the **Captain Cook Schoolroom Museum.** Here you will find a fascinating re-creation of the village in which he spent some of his most formative years. The house in which the Cook family lived is sadly no longer here. In 1934 it was transported to Australia brick by brick, together with the climbing plants that covered them, and re-erected in Fitzroy Park, Melbourne. A cairn of stones is all that remains to mark the site. A much more impressive monument is the 60-foot obelisk to Cook's memory erected on Easby Moor above the village by Robert Campion, a Whitby banker, in 1827. It can only be reached by a steepish climb on foot, but it is well worth making the effort: from the base of the monument there are stupendous views over the Moors, the Vale of Mowbray and across to the oddly shaped hill called Roseberry Topping. The loftiest of the Cleveland Hills, and sometimes called the Matterhorn of Yorkshire, Roseberry's summit towers 1000 feet above Great Ayton.

The Monaghan family have run **The Royal Oak Hotel** at Great Ayton since 1978. This 18th-century rural hostelry is at the heart of the village. Original features include the beamed

ceilings and welcoming log fires, and add to the charm and character of this traditional inn. The lively public bar is popular with visitors and locals alike. Good ales on tap include Theakstons Old Peculiar, Theakstons XB and Directors, along with keg ales, lager, cider and a good range of wines and spirits. The accommodation comprises five comfortable en suite guest bedrooms available (three doubles, one twin and one single). The quality restaurant has earned a well-deserved reputation for great food and service. The comprehensive menu includes traditional and more innovative favourites such as grilled farm trout, lamb and onion balti, vegetable enchilada and cold poached salmon and tiger prawn salad vinaigrette. Booking advised for non-residents. Food is served all day Monday to Saturday, and from noon-9.30 on Sundays.

**The Royal Oak Hotel, Great Ayton, North Yorkshire
TS9 6BW Tel: 01642 722361 Fax: 01642 724047**

NORTHALLERTON

MAP 10 REF M7

17 miles S of Middlesborough on the A168

The county town of North Yorkshire, Northallerton has the broad High Street, almost half a mile long, typical of the county's market towns. In stage coach days the town was an important stop on the route from Newcastle to London and several old coaching inns still stand along the High Street. The ancient Grammar School's history goes back to at least 1322. The school was rebuilt in 1776 at the northern end of the High Street - a building that is now a solicitors' office. The town also boasts a grand medieval church, a 15th century almshouse and, of more recent provenance, a majestic County Hall built in 1906 and designed by the famous Yorkshire architect Walter Brierley. The oldest private house in Northallerton is **Porch House**, which bears a carved inscription with the date 1584. According to tradition, Charles I came here as a guest in 1640 and returned seven years later as a prisoner.

OSMOTHERLEY   MAP 11 REF N7

6 miles E of Northallerton off the A19

Mount Grace Priory (English Heritage & National Trust) near the village of Osmotherley is unique among Yorkshire's ecclesiastical treasures. The 14th century building set in tranquil surroundings was bought in 1904 by Sir Lothian Bell, who decided to rebuild one of the well-preserved cells - a violation of the building's integrity that would provoke howls of outrage from purists if it were proposed today. When English Heritage inherited the Carthusian Priory, however, it decided to go still further by reconstructing other outbuildings and filling them with replica furniture and artefacts to create a vivid impression of what life was like in a 14th century monastic house. The Carthusians were an upper class order whose members dedicated themselves to solitude - even their meals were served through an angled hatch so they would not see the servant who brought them. Most visitors find themselves fascinated by Mount Grace's sanitary arrangements, which were ingeniously designed to take full advantage of a nearby spring and the sloping site on which the Priory is built.

THE HAMBLETON HILLS   MAP 11 REF N7

E of Northallerton

For one of the grandest landscape views in England, go to the top of Sutton Bank in the Hambleton Hills and look across the vast expanse of the Vale of York to the Pennine hills far away to the west. There's a National Park Information Centre at the summit of Sutton Bank, and a well-marked Nature Trail leads steeply down to, and around, **Lake Gormire**, an Ice Age lake trapped here by a landslip. Gormire is one of Yorkshire's only two natural lakes, the other being Semerwater in Wensleydale. Gormire is set in a large basin with no river running from it: any overflow disappears down a "swallow hole" and emerges beneath White Mare Cliffs.

THIRSK   MAP 11 REF N7

25 miles S of Middlesborough on the A19

Thirsk has become famous as the home of veterinary surgeon Alf Wight, better known as James Herriot, who died in 1995. In his immensely popular books, Thirsk is clearly recognisable as "Darrowby". Plans are under way to convert the ivy-clad surgery at number 23, Kirkgate where he worked into a centre celebrating this modest, unassuming man whose books are known and loved around the world. Just across the road from the surgery is the birthplace of another famous son of Thirsk. The building is now the town's museum and tourist office; a plaque outside records that Thomas Lord was born here in 1755: 30 years later he was to create the famous cricket ground in Marylebone that took his name.

This pleasant small town of mellow brick houses has a sprawling Market Place and a magnificent 15th century church which is generally regarded as the finest parish church in North Yorkshire. It was here that the real life "James Herriot" married his wife, Helen. **Cod Beck**, a tributary of the River Swale, wanders through the town, providing some delightful - and well-signposted - riverside walks. Thirsk appeared in the Domesday Book not long after William the Conqueror had granted the Manor of Thirsk to one of his barons, Robert de Mowbray. The Mowbrays became a powerful family in the area, a fact reflected in the naming of the area to the north and west of Thirsk as the Vale of Mowbray. On the edge of the town is the **Trees to Treske Visitor Centre**, an imaginative exhibition exploring how trees grow, the character of different woods and examples of the cabinet maker's craft.

Sion Hill Hall, about four miles northwest of Thirsk, is celebrated as the "last of the great country houses". Its light, airy and well-proportioned rooms, all facing south, are typical of the work of the celebrated Yorkshire architect, Walter Brierley - the "Lutyens of the North". In the Hall's Victorian Walled Garden is another major attraction - **Falconry U.K.'s Bird of Prey and Conservation Centre**. More than 80 birds from 34 different species have their home here: owls, hawks, falcons, buzzards, vultures and eagles from all around the world. At regular intervals throughout the day these fierce-eyed, sharp-beaked predators behave in a remarkably docile and co-operative way as they take part in fascinating flying demonstrations.

NORTH YORK MOORS
MAP 11 REF O7
S of Middlesborough

Eskdale is the largest, and one of the loveliest, of the dales within the National Park. It is unusual in that it runs east-west, the Esk being the only moorland river that doesn't find its way to the Humber. Instead, the river winds tortuously through the dale to join the sea beneath the picturesque cliffs at Whitby. Along the way, many smaller dales branch off to the north and south, - Fryup, Danby, Glaisdale - while even narrower ones can only be explored on foot. T Walkers will appreciate the Esk Valley walk, a group of ten linking walks which traverse the length of the valley.

DANBY
MAP 11 REF O6
13 miles W of Whitby off the A174

A visit to **The Moors Centre** at Danby Lodge provides an excellent introduction to the North York Moors National Park. The Centre is housed in a former shooting lodge and set in 13 acres of riverside, meadow, woodland, formal gardens and picnic areas. Visitors can either wander on their own along the waymarked woodland walks and nature trails or join one of the frequent guided walks. Inside the Lodge, various exhibits interpret the natural and local history of the moors, there's a bookshop stocked with a wide range of books, maps and guides, and a tea room serving refreshments. Downstream from The Moors Centre is a narrow medieval packhorse bridge, one of three to be found in Eskdale. This one is known as **Duck Bridge** but the name has nothing to do with aquatic birds. It was originally called Castle Bridge but re-named after an 18th century benefactor, George Duck, a wealthy mason who paid for the bridge to be repaired. To the south of Duck Bridge are the remains of Danby Castle, now a private farmhouse and not open to the public. Built in the 14th century, and originally much larger, it was once the home of Catherine Parr, the sixth wife of Henry VIII. In Elizabethan times, the justices met here and the Danby Court Leet and Baron, which administers the common land and rights of way over the 11,000 acres of the Danby Estate, still meets here every year in the throne room. One of the court's responsibilities is issuing licences for for the gathering of sphagnum moss, a material once used for stuffing mattresses but now more commonly required for flower arranging.

GLAISDALE
MAP 11 REF O7
8 miles W of Whitby off the A171

From Danby a country lane leads to Leaholm and then on to Glaisdale, another picturesque village set at the foot of a narrow dale beside the River Esk with **Arncliffe Woods** a short walk away. The ancient stone bridge here was built around 1620 by Thomas Ferris, Mayor of Hull. As an impoverished young man, he had lived in Glaisdale and fell in love with Agnes Richardson, the squire's daughter. To see Agnes, he had to wade or swim across the river and he swore that if he prospered in life he would build a bridge here. Fortunately, he joined a ship which sailed against the Spanish Armada and captured a gal-

Beggar's Bridge, Glaisdale

leon laden with gold. Tom returned to Glaisdale a rich man, married Agnes and later honoured his promise by building what has always been called the **Beggar's Bridge**.

GOATHLAND
MAP 11 REF O7
8 miles SW of Whitby off the A169

Goathland today is perhaps best known as "Aidensfield" - the main location for the television series Heartbeat. This attractive village 500 feet up on the moors, where old stone houses are

scattered randomly around spacious sheep-groomed greens, was popular long before television. Earlier visitors mostly came in order to see **Mallyan Spout**, a 70-foot high waterfall locked into a crescent of rocks and trees. They were also interested in Goathland's rugged church and the odd memorial in its graveyard to William Jefferson and his wife. The couple died in 1923 within a few days of each other, at the ages of 80 and 79, and chose to have their final resting place marked by an enormous anchor.

In the award-winning **Goathland Exhibition Centre** you'll find a full explanation of the curious tradition of the Plough Stots Service, performed at Goathland every January. It's an ancient ritual for greeting the new year which originated with the Norsemen who settled here more than a thousand years ago. "Stots" is the Scandinavian word for the bullocks

Goathland Station

which would drag a plough through the village, followed by dancers brandishing 30-inch swords. This pagan rite is still faithfully observed but with the difference that nowadays Goathland's young men have replaced the stots in the plough harness. The Exhibition Centre can also provide you with information about the many walks in the area and guide you to one of the oldest thoroughfares in the country, **Wade's Way**. If you believe the legend, it was built by a giant of that name, but it is actually a remarkably well-preserved stretch of Roman road.

Just outside Goathland, **Whitfield House Hotel** is a family-run hotel that has been in the

same family for 20 years. Occupying a scenic and peaceful position, this handsome hotel was once a farmhouse, and dates back to 1650. It has been a hotel since 1907. Much of its oriignal character and charm has been retained, and the atmosphere is homely and relaxing. This welcoming establishment boasts 9 individually-styled guest bedrooms, all en suite. Varying in size

Whitfield House Hotel, Darnholm, Goathland, North Yorkshire YO22 5LA Tel: 01947 896215

from single to family rooms, each is comfortable and attractive. There is also a lovely guests' lounge and distinctive lounge bar in which to relax. The standard of service is high and the full English breakfasts and table d'hote and a la carte menus offer the very best in country cooking and make use of the freshest local produce. A hotel for all seasons, it is open all year round, with special out of season breaks (November to March) available.

HUTTON-LE-HOLE   MAP 11 REF O7
20 miles SW of Whitby off the A170

Long regarded as one of Yorkshire's prettiest villages, Hutton-le-Hole has a character all of its own. "It is all up and down" wrote Arthur Mee, visiting half a century ago, "with a hurrying stream winding among houses scattered here and there, standing at all angles". Fifty years on, little has changed.

Facing the green is the **Ryedale Folk Museum**, an imaginative celebration of 4,000 years of life in North Yorkshire. Amongst the 13 historic buildings is a complete Elizabethan Manor House rescued from nearby Harome and reconstructed here; a medieval crofter's cottage with a thatched, hipped roof, peat fire and garth; and the old village Shop and Post Office fitted out as it would have looked just after Elizabeth II's Coronation in 1953. Other exhibits include workshops of traditional crafts such as tinsmiths, coopers and wheelwrights, and an Edwardian photographic studio

Ryedale Folk Museum

Anyone interested in unusual churches should make the short trip from Hutton-le-Hole to **St Mary's Church, Lastingham**, about three miles to the east. The building of a monastery here in the 7th century was recorded by no less an authority than the Venerable Bede, who visited Lastingham not long after it was completed. That monastery was rebuilt in 1078 with a massively impressive crypt that is still in place - a claustrophobic space with heavy Norman arches rising from squat round pillars. The church above is equally atmospheric, lit only by a small window at one end.

CHURCH HOUSES   MAP 11 REF O7
5 miles N of Hutton-le-Hole off the A170

A couple of miles from Hutton-le-Hole, the moorland road comes to Lowna set beside the River Dove in one of the Moors most famous beauty spots, **Farndale**. In spring, some six miles of the river banks are smothered in thousands of wild daffodils, a short-stemmed variety whose colours shade from a pale buttercup yellow to a rich orange-gold. According to local tradition, the bulbs were cultivated by monks who used the petals in their medical concoctions. Yorkshire folk often refer to daffodils as Lenten Lilies because of the time of year in which they bloom. The flowers, once mercilessly plundered by visitors, are now protected by law and 2,000 acres of Farndale are designated as a local nature reserve.

STAITHES   MAP 11 REF O6
9 miles NW of Whitby off the A174

Visitors to this much-photographed fishing port leave their cars at the park in the modern village at the top of the cliff and then walk down the steep road to the old wharf. Take care - one of these narrow, stepped alleys is called **Slippery Hill**, for reasons that can become painfully

Staithes Harbour

clear. The old stone chapels and rather austere houses testify to the days when Staithes was a stronghold of Methodism.

The little port is proud of its associations with Captain James Cook. He came here, not as a famous mariner, but as a 17 year old assistant in Mr William Sanderson's haberdashery shop. James didn't stay long, leaving in 1746 to begin his naval apprenticeship in Whitby with Thomas Scottowe, a friend of Sanderson.

Staithes is still a working port with one of the few fleets in England still catching crabs and lobsters. Moored in the harbour and along the river are the fishermen's distinctive boats. Known as cobles, they have an ancestry that goes back to Viking times. Nearby is a small sandy beach, popular with families (and artists), and a rocky shoreline extending north and south pitted with thousands of rock pools hiding starfish and anemones. The rocks here are also rich in fossils and you may even find ingots of fools gold, - actually iron pyrites and virtually worthless. A little further up the coast rises **Boulby Cliff**, at 666 feet the highest point on the east coast of England.

WHITBY   MAP 11 REF O6
30 miles E of Middlesborough on the A171

Whitby is famed as one of the earliest and most important centres of Christianity in England; as Captain James Cook's home port, and as the place where, according to Bram Stoker's famous novel, Count Dracula in the form of a wolf loped ashore from a crewless ship that had drifted into the harbour. The classic 1931 film version of the story, starring Bela Lugosi, was filmed in the original locations at Whitby and there were several reports of holidaymakers startled by coming across the Count, cloaked and fanged, as he rested between takes. High on the cliff that towers above the old town stand the imposing ruins of **Whitby Abbey**. In AD664, many of the

Whitby Abbey

most eminent prelates of the Christian Church were summoned here to attend the Synod of Whitby. They were charged with settling once and for all a festering dispute that had riven Christendom for generations: the precise date on which Easter should be celebrated. The complicated formula they devised to solve this problem is still in use today. A short walk from the Abbey is **St Mary's Church**, a unique building "not unlike a house outside and very much like a ship inside". Indeed, the fascinating interior with its clutter of box-pews, iron pillars and long galleries was reputedly fashioned by Whitby seamen during the course of the 18th century. The three-decker pulpit is from the same period; the huge ear trumpets for a rector's deaf wife were put in place about 50 years later. St Mary's stands atop the cliff: the old town clusters around the harbour mouth far below. Linking them are the famous 199 steps that wind up the hillside: many a churchgoer or visitor has been grateful for the frequent seats thoughtfully provided along the way.

Occupying a splendid position on Whitby's bustling quayside, **The Magpie Café** is a welcoming and distinguished eatery. The building dates back to the 18th century and was once home to the Scoresby whaling family. It was then used as a shipping office for many years, before opening as a café in the 1930s. More like a first-class restaurant than your average café, it has been recommended by Egon Ronay and has featured in The Good Food Guide. In the same

family since 1954, owners Alison and Ian have gained a well-earned reputation for the quality of the food and service. The house speciality is fresh locally-caught fish and seafood - many aver that they serve the best fish and chips in the area. The varied menu has something for everyone, from salads and vegetarian meals to traditional and more innovative dishes. The selection of desserts is truly impressive, and definitely worth saving room for! The furnishings are comfortable and the ambience warm and welcoming. The upper level commands magnificent views. Open daily early February to mid-January, the opening hours vary according to season, but are generally 11.30 to 9.

The old port of Whitby developed on the slim shelf of land that runs along the east bank of the river Esk, an intricate muddle of narrow, cobbled streets and shoulder-width alleys. Grape Lane is typical, a cramped little street where ancient houses lean wearily against each other. Young James Cook lived here during his apprenticeship: the handsome house in Grape Lane where he lodged is now the **Captain Cook Memorial Museum**. By the early 19th century, old Whitby was full to bursting and a new town began to burgeon on the west bank of the River Esk. The new Whitby, or "West Cliff", was care-

The Magpie Café, 14 Pier Road, Whitby, North Yorkshire YO21 3PU Tel: 01947 602058 Fax: 01947 601801 e-mail: ian@magpiecafe.co.uk website: www.magpiecafe.co.uk

fully planned with the nascent industry of tourism in mind. There was a quayside walk or promenade, a bandstand, luxury hotels, and a Royal Crescent of up-market dwellings reminiscent of Buxton or Cheltenham but with the added advantage of enjoying a sea air universally acknowledged as "invariably beneficial to the health of the most injured constitution".

In a dominating position on West Cliff, a bronze statue of Captain Cook gazes out over the harbour he knew so well, and nearby the huge jawbone of a whale, raised as an arch, recalls those other great Whitby seafarers, the whalers. Between 1753 and 1833, Whitby was the capital of the whaling industry, bringing home 2761 whales in 80 years. Much of that success was due to the skills of the great whaling captains William Scoresby and his son, also named William. The elder William was celebrated for his great daring and navigational skills, as well as for the invention of the crow's nest, or mast-head lookout. His son was driven by a restless, enquiring mind and occupied himself with various experiments during the long days at sea in the icy Arctic waters. He is most noted for his discoveries of the forms of snow crystals and the invention of the "Greenland" magnet which made ships' compasses more reliable.

Whitby Glass in the ancient Sandgate part of Whitby is a distinguished glassware studio that is home to the world-famous "Whitby Lucky Duck". The studio was founded in 1957 by Peter Rantell. Today it is owned and personally run by Dorothy Clegg, twice former Mayor of Scarborough. Visitors are welcome to call in at the 400-year-old building to observe the skilled craftsmen as they draw, bend and fashion coloured glass into the intricately shaped "lucky duck" talismans synonymous with Whitby. These have been exported to places as far away as Mexico and Japan, with their alleged influence over their owners' fortunes succeeding in bringing about, among other beneficence, financial windfalls and the ending of a drought in southern France. Recently

Whitby Glass Ltd, 9 Sandgate, Whitby, North Yorkshire YO22 4DB Tel: 01947 603553

featured on The Holiday Programme, this interesting and impressive studio is well worth a visit. Many visitors leave with their own memento of Whitby and the exquisite handiwork of its gifted craftsmen.

ROBIN HOOD'S BAY
5 miles S of Whitby off the A171

MAP 11 REF P7

Artists never tire of painting this "Clovelly of the North", a picturesque huddle of red-roofed houses clinging to the steep face of the cliff. Bay Town, as locals call the village, was a thriving fishing port throughout the 18th and 19th centuries. By 1920 however there were only two fishing families left in the Bay, mainly because the harbour was so dilapidated, and the industry died out. Today, small boats are once again harvesting the prolific crab grounds that lie along this stretch of the coast. Because of the natural isolation of the bay, smuggling was quite as important as fishing to the local economy. The houses and inns in the Bay were said to have connecting cellars and cupboards, and it was claimed that "a bale of silk could pass from the bottom of the village to the top without seeing daylight". These were the days too when press gangs from the Royal Navy were active in the area since recruits with a knowledge of the sea were highly prized. Apparently, these mariners were also highly prized by local women: they smartly despatched the press gangs by means of pans and rolling

Robin Hood's Bay

pins. Shipwrecks in the Bay were frequent, with many a mighty vessel tossed onto its reefs by North Sea storms. On one memorable occasion in the winter of 1881, a large brig called "the Visitor" was driven onto the rocks. The seas were too rough for the lifeboat at Whitby to be launched there so it was dragged eight miles through the snow and let down the cliffside by ropes. Six men were rescued. The same wild seas threatened the village itself, every storm eroding a little more of the chalk cliff to which it clings. Fortunately, Robin Hood's Bay is now protected by a sturdy sea wall.

SCARBOROUGH
MAP 11 REF P7

18 miles S of Whitby on the A171

With its two splendid bays and dramatic cliff-top castle, Scarborough was targeted by the early railway tycoons as the natural candidate for Yorkshire's first seaside resort. The railway arrived in 1846, followed by the construction of luxury hotels, elegant promenades and spacious gardens, all of which confirmed the town's claim to the title "Queen of Watering Places". The "quality", people like the eccentric Earls of Londesborough, established palatial summer residences here, and an excellent train service brought countless thousands of 'excursionists' from the industrial cities of the West Riding. Even before the advent of the railway, Scarborough had been well-known to a select few. They travelled to what was then a remote little town to sample the spring water discovered by Mrs Tomyzin Farrer in 1626 and popularised in a book published by a certain Dr Wittie who named the site "Scarborough Spaw". Anne Bronte came here in the hope that the spa town's invigorating air would improve her health, a hope that was not fulfilled. She died at the age of 29 and her grave lies in St Mary's churchyard at the foot of the castle.

Scarborough Castle itself can be precisely dated to the decade between 1158 and 1168 and surviving records show that construction costs totalled £650. The castle was built on the site of a Roman fort and signal station and its gaunt remains stand high on Castle Rock Headland, dominating the two sweeping bays. The spectacular ruins often provide a splendid backdrop for staged battles commemorating the invasions of the Danes, Saxons and the later incursions of Napoleon's troops. The surrounding cliffs are also well worth exploring, just follow the final part of the famous Cleveland Way. As befits such a long-established resort, Scarborough offers a vast variety of entertainment. If you tire of the two sandy beaches, there's Peasholm Park to explore with its glorious gardens and regular events, amongst them the unique sea battle in miniature on the lake. Or you could seek out the intellectual attractions of the Rotunda Museum on Vernon Road, "the finest Georgian museum in Britain" which includes amongst its exhibits a genuine ducking stool for 'witches'; the art collections at the Scarborough Art Gallery; or the futuristic world of holograms at Corrigans Arcade on Foreshore Road. The Stephen Joseph Theatre in the Round is well-known for staging the premiere performances of comedies written by its resident director, the prolific playwright Alan Ayckbourn. And at Scalby Mills, on the northern edge of the town, Sea-Life offers the chance of close encounters with a huge variety of marine creatures from shrimps to sharks, octopi to eels.

FILEY
MAP 11 REF P8

7 miles S of Scarborough off the A165

With its six mile crescent of safe, sandy beach, Filey was one of the first Yorkshire resorts to benefit from the early 19th century craze for sea bathing. Filey's popularity continued throughout Victorian times, but the little town always prided itself on being rather more select than its brasher neighbour just up the coast, Scarborough. Inevitably, modern times have brought the usual scattering of amusement arcades, fast food outlets and, from 1939 to 1983, a Butlin's Holiday Camp capable of accommodating 10,000 visitors. But Filey has suffered less than most seaside towns and with its many public parks and gardens still retains a winning, rather genteel atmosphere. Just to the north of the town, the rocky promontory known as Filey Brigg strikes

Filey Bay

out into the sea, a massive mile-long breakwater protecting the town from the worst of the North Sea's winter storms. From the Brigg there are grand views southwards along the six mile long bay to the cliffs that rise up to Flamborough Head and Scarborough Castle. Despite the fact that there is no harbour at Filey, it was once quite a busy fishing port and one can still occasionally see a few cobles, - direct descendants of the Viking longships that arrived here more than a millenium ago, - beached on the slipways.

THORNTON-LE-DALE   MAP 11 REF O7
14 miles W of Scarborough on the A170

As long ago as 1907, a Yorkshire Post poll of its readers acclaimed Thornton-le-Dale as the most beautiful village in Yorkshire. Despite stiff competition for that title, most visitors find themselves in agreement. If further proof were needed, just off the A170 near the parish church of All Saints, you'll find one of the most photographed houses in Britain, appearing regularly on chocolate boxes, jigsaws and calendars. The North York Moors National Park actually creates a special loop in its boundary to include this picture-postcard village which, somewhat confusingly, is also frequently shown on maps as "Thornton Dale".

PICKERING   MAP 11 REF O7
15 miles W of Scarborough on the A170

This busy little town developed around the important crossroads where the Malton to Whitby, and the Thirsk to Scarborough roads intersect. It's the largest of the four market towns in Ryedale and possibly the oldest, claiming to date from 270 BC when (so it's said) it was founded by a King of the Brigantes called Peredurus. William the Conqueror's attempts to dominate the area are recalled by Pickering's ruined castle, and the many inns and posting houses reflect the town's prosperity during the stage coach era. Lying at the heart of the fertile Vale of Pickering, the town's reputation was originally based on its famous pigs and horses. Vast quantities of pork were transported across the moors to Whitby, salted and used as ship-board rations. The famous Cleveland Bay horses, with their jet-black manes and tails, were extensively bred in the area. (In Eskdale, a little further north, they still are). These sweet-natured, sturdy and tireless animals have always been in great demand. During the 19th century, their equable temperament made them ideal for pulling Hansom cabs and street-cars, and nowadays they are often seen in more dignified events such as State Processions.

Not to be missed in Pickering is the **Beck Isle Museum** housed in a gracious Regency mansion. Its 27 display areas are crammed with a "magnificent assortment of items curious, mysterious, marvellous and commonplace from the last 200 years". There are intriguing re-creations of typical Victorian domestic rooms, shops, workshops and even a pub. The comprehensive collection of photographs by Sydney Smith presents a remarkable picture of the Ryedale area as it was more than half a century ago. The exhibition is made even more interesting by its acquisition of the very cameras and other photographic equipment used by Sydney Smith.

If you catch a whiff of sulphurous smoke, then you must be close to the station. Pickering is the southern terminus of the **North York Moors Railway** and here you can board a steam-drawn train for an 18-mile journey along one of the oldest and most dramatically scenic railways in the country. And at the **Pickering Trout Lake** you can hire a rod and tackle and attempt to beat the record for the largest fish caught here - it currently stands at a mighty 25lb 4oz.

MALTON

MAP 11 REF O8

8 miles S of Pickering off the A169/B1257

Malton has been the historic centre of Ryedale ever since the Romans came. They built a large fort and called it "Derventio" after the river Derwent beside which it stands. For many years, archaeologists were puzzled by the large scale of the fort, a mystery resolved in 1970 when a building dedication was uncovered which revealed that the fort housed a cavalry regiment, the "Ala Picentiana", - the extra space was needed to accommodate their horses. Many relics from the site, showing the sophisticated life-styles of the Roman centurions and civilians, can be seen in the **Malton Museum**, along with items from the Iron Age settlement that preceded the Roman garrison.

The River Derwent was vitally important to Malton. The river rises in the moors near Scarborough, then runs inland through the Vale of Pickering bringing an essential element for what was once a major industry in Malton - brewing. In the 19th century, there were nine breweries here, now only the **Malton Brewery Company** survives. It operates in a converted stable block behind Suddabys Crown Hotel in Wheelgate and welcomes visitors, but telephone them first on 01653 697580.

In December each year, Malton hosts a colourful Dickensian Festival. Charles Dickens stayed nearby with his friend, Charles Smithson, a solicitor, and is believed to have modelled Scrooge's Counting House in A Christmas Carol on Smithson's office in Chancery Lane. Just to the north of Malton is **Eden Camp**, a theme museum dedicated to re-creating the dramatic experiences of ordinary people living through World War II. This unique museum is housed in the huts of a genuine prisoner of war camp, built in 1942. Sound, lighting effects, smells, even smoke generators are deployed to make you feel that you are actually there, taking part. Visitors can find out what it was like to live through an air raid, to be a prisoner of war or a sailor in a U-boat under attack. Amongst the many other exhibits are displays on Fashion in the 1940s, Children at War, and even one on Rationing - in 1941, one discovers, the cheese ration was down to 1 ounce a week!

WELBURN

MAP 11 REF O8

5 miles SW of Malton off the A64

About 5 miles west of Malton, lying in the folds of the Howardian Hills, stands one of the most glorious stately homes in Britain, **Castle Howard**. Well known to television viewers as the Brideshead of Brideshead Revisited, Castle Howard has astonished visitors ever since it was completed in the early 1700s. Even that world-weary 18th century socialite Horace Walpole was stirred to enthusiasm: "Nobody had informed me" he wrote "that at one view I should see a palace, a town, a fortified city, temples on high places,...the noblest lawn in the world fenced by half the horizon and a mausoleum that would tempt one to be buried alive: in short, I have seen gigantic places before, but never a sublime one". Perhaps the most astonishing fact of all concerns the architect of Castle Howard, Sir John Vanbrugh. Vanbrugh had been a soldier and a playwright but until he began this sublime building had never yet overseen the placing of one block of masonry on another.

Castle Howard

Kirkham Priory

Two miles south of Welburn, in a lovely, peaceful setting beside the River Derwent, stand the remains of **Kirkham Priory**. According to legend, the priory was founded in 1125 by Walter l'Espec after his only son was thrown from his horse and killed at this very spot. (A few years later, Walter was to found another great abbey at Rievaulx). Visitors to Kirkham pass through a noble, exquisitely decorated gatehouse but one of the most memorable sights at the Priory, perhaps because it is so unexpected, is the sumptuous lavatorium in the ruined cloister. Here the monks washed their hands at two bays with lavishly moulded arches supported by slender pillars, each bay adorned with tracery.

HELMSLEY

MAP 11 REF N7

13 miles W of Pickering on the A170

One of North Yorkshire's most attractive towns, Helmsley lies on the banks of the River Rye at the edge of the North York Moors National Park. The spacious market square is typical of the area but the Gothic memorial to the 2nd Earl of Feversham that stands there is not. This astonishingly ornate construction was designed by Sir Giles Gilbert Scott and looks like a smaller version of his famous memorial to Sir Walter Scott in Edinburgh. The Earls of Feversham lived at **Duncombe Park** whose extensive grounds sweep up to within a few yards of the Market Place. Most of the original mansion, designed by Vanbrugh, was gutted by a disastrous fire in 1879: only the north wing remained habitable and that in its turn was ruined by a second fire

Duncombe Park

in 1895. The Fevershams lavished a fortune on rebuilding the grand old house, largely to the original design, but the financial burden eventually forced them to lease the house and grounds as a preparatory school for girls. Happily, the Feversham were able to return to their ancestral home in 1985 and the beautifully restored house and lovely grounds are now open to the public. Before they were ennobled, the Fevershams family name was Duncombe and it was Sir Thomas Duncombe, a wealthy London goldsmith, who established the family seat here when he bought **Helmsley Castle** (English Heritage) and its estate in 1687. Founded in the early 1100s, seriously knocked about during the Civil War, the castle was in a dilapidated state but its previous owner, the Duke of Buckingham, had continued to live there in some squalor and discomfort. Sir Thomas quickly decided to build a more suitable residence nearby, abandoning the ruins to lovers of the romantic and picturesque.

RIEVAULX

Map 11 ref N7

2 miles W of Helmsley off the B1257

Just to the west of Helmsley rise the indescribably beautiful remains of **Rievaulx Abbey** (English Heritage), standing amongst wooded hills beside the River Rye - "the most beautiful monastic site in Europe". JMW Turner was enchanted by this idyllic landscape; Dorothy Wordsworth, 'spellbound'. Founded in 1131, it was the first Cistercian abbey in Yorkshire and, with some 700 people - monks, lay brothers, servants -eventually living within its walls, became one of the largest. Like Kirkham Abbey a few years earlier, Rievaulx was endowed by Walter l'Espec, Lord of Helmsley, still mourning the loss of his only son in a riding accident. The Abbey was soon a major landowner in the county, earning a healthy income from farming - at one time owning more than 14,000 sheep. The Abbey also had its own fishery at Teesmouth, and iron-ore mines at Bilsdale and near Wakefield.

Rievaulx Abbey

Looking down on the extensive remains of the Abbey is **Rievaulx Terrace** (National Trust), a breathtaking example of landscape gardening completed in 1758. The cunningly contrived avenues draw your eyes to incomparable views of the Abbey itself, to vistas along the Rye Valley and to the rolling contours of the hills beyond. At each end of the terrace is a classical temple, one of which is elaborately decorated as a dining room.

YORK

Map 11 ref N9

30 miles SW of Pickering off the A64

"The history of York is the history of England" said the Duke of York, later to become George VI. A bold claim but well justified. For almost two thousand years the city has been at the centre of great events and, better than any other city in England, it has preserved the evidence of its glorious past. One of the grandest cityscapes in the country opens up as you walk along the old city walls towards **York Minster**, a sublime expression of medieval faith.

The Minster stands on the site of an even older building, the headquarters of the Roman legions. The Imperial troops arrived here in AD71 when the governor, Quintus Petilius Cerealis, chose this strategic position astride the Rivers Ouse and Foss as his base for a campaign against the pesky tribe of the Brigantes. The settlement was named Eboracum. From this garrison, Hadrian directed the construction of his great wall and a later general, Constantine, was proclaimed Emperor here. The legions finally left the city around AD410, but the evidence of their three and a half centuries of occupation is manifest all around York in buildings like the **Multangular Tower**, in rich artefacts treasured in the city's museums and even in a pub: at the **Roman Bath Inn** you can see the remains of steam baths used by the garrison residents.

Little is known of York during the Dark Ages but by the 8th century the city had been colonised by the Anglo-Saxons, who named it "Eoferwic," and it was already an important Christian and academic centre. The Vikings put an end to that when they invaded in the 9th century and changed the name once again, this time to Jorvik. The story of York during those years of Danish rule is imaginatively told in the many displays at the **Jorvik Centre**. The network of medieval streets around the Minster is one of the city's major delights. Narrow lanes are

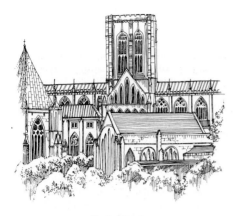

York Minster

criss-crossed by even narrower footpaths - ginnels, snickets or "snickelways", which have survived as public rights of way despite being built over, above and around. Narrowest of all the snickelways is Pope's Head Alley, more than 100ft long but only 31 inches wide. The alley was also known as Introduction Lane, - if you wanted to know someone better, you simply timed your walk along it so as to meet the other party half-way. Whip-ma-Whop-ma-Gate, allegedly, is where felons used to be "whipped and whopped". Probably most famous of these ancient streets is **The Shambles**. Its name comes from "Fleshammels", the street of butchers and slaughter houses. The houses here were deliberately built to keep the street out of direct sunlight, thus protecting the carcasses which were hung outside the houses on hooks. Many of the hooks are still in place.

During these years, York was the second largest city in England and it was then that the town walls and their 'bars', or gates, were built. The trade guilds were also at their most powerful and in Fossgate one of them built the lovely black and white timbered **Merchant Adventurers Hall**. The Merchant Adventurers controlled the lucrative trade in all "goods bought and sold foreign" and they spared no expense in building their Great Hall where they conducted their affairs benath a complex timbered roof displaying many colourful banners of York's medieval guilds. To this period too belong the **York Mystery Plays**, first performed in 1397 and subsequently every four years. During Tudor times, York's importance steadily declined but re-emerged in the 18th century as a fashionable social centre. Many elegant Georgian houses, of which **Fairfax House** in Castlegate is perhaps the most splendid, were built at this time and they add another attractive architectural dimension to the city.

The following century saw York take on a completely different role as the hub of the railway system in the north. At the heart of this transformation was the charismatic entrepreneur George Hudson, founder of what became the Great Northern Railway, part visionary, part crook. His wheeler-dealing eventually led to his disgrace but even then the citizens of York twice elected him as Lord Mayor and he still has a pub named after him. It was thanks to Hudson that York's magnificent railway station, with its great curving roof of glass, was built, a tourist attraction in its own right. Nearby, in Leeman Street, is the **National Railway Museum**, the largest of its kind in the world. This fascinating exhibition covers some two hundred years of railway history, from Stephenson's Rocket to the Channel Tunnel. Amongst the thousands of exhibits demonstrating the technical and social impact of the "Iron Horse" are Gresley's record-breaking locomotive, Mallard, Queen Victoria's royal carriage, and displays demonstrating the workings of the railway system. Another aspect of railway history is on view at the **York Model Railway**, next door to the station, which has almost one third of a mile of track and up to 14 trains running at any one time. Machinery of a very different kind is on display at the **Museum of Automata**. Automata are "man made objects that imitate the movement of living things through a mechanism that is concealed, so as to make them appear to move spontaneously". The museum traces the history of automata, from the simple articulated figurines of ancient civilisations, through to displays of modern robotics: the Automata Shop sells contemporary pieces, music boxes, mechanical toys and craft kits suitable for all ages.

It's impossible here to list all York's museums, galleries and fine buildings, but you will find a wealth of additional information at the Tourist Information Centre close to one of the historic old gateways to the city, **Bootham Bar**.

ACOMB

Map 11 ref N9

On the western edge of York off the B1224

About 5 miles northwest of Acomb is **Beningbrough Hall** (National Trust), a baroque master-piece from the early 18th century with 7 acres of gardens, wilderness play area, pike ponds and scenic walks. There's also a fully operational Victorian laundry which graphically demonstrates the drudgery of a 19th century washing day. A major attraction here is the permanent exhibition of more than one hundred portraits on loan from the National Portrait Gallery. Other exhibitions are often held at the Hall, - for these there is usually an additional charge.

WHIXLEY

Map 11 ref N8

10 miles W of York off the A59

The Anchor Inn at Whixley is renowned for its quality carvery, well-kept ales and genuine hospitality. Ideal to use as a base while exploring this picturesque part of Yorkshire, the inn began life many years ago as a farmhouse, later becoming an alehouse and finally an inn, on what was once a major road. Now hidden away within this tranquil village, it is personally run

by Doreen Cluff. The old and new worlds blend in delightful ways at this traditional inn equipped with every modern amenity guests have come to expect. The carvery is open daily from mid-day-2 and 6-9. The portions are hearty and there is always a choice of six delicious main courses, including a fresh vegetarian dish of the day. Hand

**The Anchor Inn and Carvery, Whixley, York, Yorkshire
YO26 8AG Tel: 01423 330432 Fax: 01423 330422
e-mail: admin@anchorinn-whixley.fsnet.co.uk**

in hand with the excellent food is the fine selection of real ales, which includes John Smiths, Tetley and Landlord. Added to all this, the inn boasts superb accommodation in two double and two single chalets.

BISHOP WILTON

Map 11 ref O8

10 miles E of York off the A166

The unspoilt village of Bishop Wilton, about five miles northeast of Fangfoss, lies at the foot of Garrowby Hill on the very edge of the Wolds. Running through its broad main street is the Bishop Wilton Beck, flanked by green banks. The Saxon Bishops of York built a palace here and used it as a country retreat. The palace has disappeared but the parish **Church of St Edith** is worth visiting for its Romanesque chancel arch and doorway, and its unusual mosaic floor made of black and white marble and modelled on one in the Vatican. The tiny pieces of marble, each no bigger than a fingernail, are cunningly arranged to create pictures of birds and scenery.

A few miles northwest of Fangfoss is the site of the **Battle of Stamford Bridge**. Everyone knows that 1066 was the year of the Battle of Hastings but, just a few days before that battle, King Harold had clashed at Stamford Bridge with his half-brother Tostig and Hardrada, King of Norway who between them had mustered some 60,000 men. On a rise near the corn mill is a stone commemorating the event with an inscription in English and Danish. Up until 1878, a Sunday in September was designated "Spear Day Feast", commemorating the battle. On this day, boat-shaped pies were made bearing the impression of the fatal spear, in memory of the

Saxon soldier in his boat who slew the single Norseman defending the wooden bridge. Harold's troops were triumphant but immediately after this victory they marched southwards to Hastings and a much more famous defeat.

SELBY   MAP 11 REF N9
14 miles S of York on the A19

In 1069 a young monk named Benedict, from Auxerre in France, had a vision. It's not known exactly what the vision was, but it inspired him to set sail for York. As his ship was sailing up the Ouse near Selby, three swans flew in formation across its bows. (Three swans, incidentally, still form part of the town's coat of arms). Interpreting this as a sign of the Holy Trinity, Benedict promptly went ashore and set up a preaching cross under a great oak, called the "Stirhac". The

small religious community he established went from strength to strength, acquiring many grants of land and, in 1100, permission to build a monastery. Over the course of the next 120 years, the great **Abbey** slowly took shape, the massively heavy Norman style of the earlier building gradually modulating into the much more delicate Early English style, all built using a lovely cream-coloured stone.

Over the centuries, this sublime church has suffered more than most. During the Civil War, it was severely damaged by Cromwell's troops. In 1690, the central tower collapsed. For years, the Abbey was neglected, then in 1906 there was another calamity when a disastrous fire gutted the Abbey. Visiting this serene and peaceful church today, it's difficult to believe that it has endured so many misfortunes and remained so beautiful. Throughout all the Abbey's troubles, one particular feature survived intact - the famous Washington window depicting the coat of arms of John de Washington, Prior of the Abbey around 1415 and a direct ancestor of George Washing-

Selby Abbey

ton. Prominently displayed in this heraldic device is the stars and stripes motif later adapted for the national flag of the United States. Devotees of railway history will also want to pay their respects to Selby's old railway station. Built at the incredibly early date of 1834, it is the oldest surviving station in Britain.

Anyone interested in remarkable churches should make the short trip from Selby to **St Mary's Church at Hemingbrough**. Built in a pale rose-coloured brick, it has an extraordinarily lofty and elegant spire soaring 190 feet high and, inside, what is believed to be Britain's oldest misericord. Misericords are hinged wooden seats for the choir which were raised when they stood to sing. Medieval woodworkers delighted in adorning the underside of the seat with intricate carvings. The misericord at Hemingbrough dates back to AD1200.

Not to be missed while you are in this corner of the county is **Carlton Towers**, about six miles southeast of Selby off the A1041. This extraordinary building, "something between the Houses of Parliament and St Pancras Station", was created during the 1870s by two young English eccentrics, Henry 9th Lord Beaumont, and Edward Welby Pugin, son of the eminent Victorian architect, A.G. Pugin. They transformed a traditional Jacobean house into an exuberant mock medieval fantasy in stone, abounding with turrets, towers, gargoyles and heraldic shields. The richly-decorated, "High Victorian" interior, designed in the manner of medieval banqueting halls contains a minstrels' gallery and a vast Venetian drawing room. Both Beaumont and Pugin died in their forties, both bankrupt.

HOWDEN   MAP 11 REF O9

11 miles E of Selby on the A63

Despite the fact that its chancel collapsed in 1696 and has not been used for worship ever since, **Howden Minster** is still one of the largest parish churches in East Yorkshire and also one of its most impressive, cathedral-like in size. The ruins of its former chapter house have been described as one of the most exquisite little buildings in England, lavishly decorated with a wealth of carved mouldings.

HULL   MAP 11 REF P9

25 miles E of Howden on the A63

Mercilessly battered by the Luftwaffe during the Second World War, when 7,000 of its people were killed and 92 per cent of its houses suffered bomb damage, Hull has risen phoenix-like from those ashes and is now the fastest-growing port in England. The port area extends for seven miles along the Humber, with 10 miles of quays servicing a constant flow of commercial traffic arriving from, or departing for, every quarter of the globe. Every day, a succession of vehicle ferries link the city to the European gateways of Zeebrugge and Rotterdam. Hull is unmistakably part of Yorkshire but it also has the free-wheeling, open-minded character of a cosmopolitan port.

Hull's history as an important port goes back to 1293 when Edward I, travelling north on his way to hammer the Scots, stopped off here and immediately recognized the potential of the muddy junction where the River Hull flows into the Humber. The king bought the land from the monks of Meaux Abbey at the usual royal discount and the settlement thenceforth was known as "Kinges town upon Hull". The port grew steadily through the centuries and at one time had the biggest fishing fleet of any port in the country with more than 300 trawlers on its register. The port's rather primitive facilities were greatly improved by the construction of a state-of-the-art dock in 1778. Now superseded, that dock has been converted into the handsome Queens Gardens, one of the many attractive open spaces created by this flower-conscious city which also loves lining its streets with trees, setting up fountains here and there and planting flower beds in any unoccupied space. Waymarked walks such as the **Maritime Heritage Trail** and the **Fish Pavement Trail** make the most of the city's dramatic waterfront.

Hull's tourism office modestly suggests you explore its "Magnificent Seven", - a quite remarkable collection of historic houses, art galleries and museums. Perhaps the most evocative is the **Wilberforce House Museum** in the old High Street. William Wilberforce was born here, from here he and his father lavished thousands of pounds in bribes to get

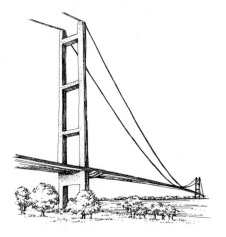

The Humber Bridge

William elected as Hull's Member of Parliament. Nothing unusual about that kind of corruption at the time, but William then redeemed himself by his resolute opposition to slavery. His campaign took more than 30 years and William was already on his deathbed before a reluctant Parliament finally outlawed the despicable trade. The museum presents a shaming history of the slave trade and a more uplifting story of William Wilberforce's efforts to eliminate it for ever.

The **Ferens Art Gallery** houses a sumptuous collection of paintings that range from European Old Masters (including some Canalettos and Franz Hals) to challenging contemporary art; the **Town Docks Museum** celebrates seven centuries of Hull's maritime heritage and includes a fine collection of scrimshaw; at Streetlife Transport Museum you will be taken back to the days of horse-drawn carriages, steam trains, trams and penny-farthing cycles. There are curiosities such as the "Velocipede", the Automobile a Vapeur, - an early steam driven car - and Lady Chesterfield's ornamental sleigh, caparisoned with a swan, rearing unicorn and a panoply of bells to herald her approach.

You will encounter a marvel of a different kind if you come by road to Hull from the south and drive over one of the most impressive bridges on earth. Opened in 1981, the **Humber Bridge** is the world's longest single-span bridge with an overall length of 2,428yds, (2,220m). That means that for more than a third of a mile only four concrete pillars, two at each end, are saving you from a watery death. From these huge pylons, 510ft (155m) high, gossamer cables of thin-wired steel support a gently curving roadway. Both sets of pylons rise vertically, but because of the curvature of the earth they actually lean away from each other by several inches. The bridge is particularly striking at night when the vast structure is floodlit.

BRIDLINGTON

MAP 11 REF P8

40 miles E of York on the A165

Bridlington lies at the northern tip of the crescent of hills that form the Wolds. The old town lies a mile inland from the bustling seaside resort that has been understandably popular since early Victorian times. The attractions of a vast, ten mile stretch of sandy beach distract most visitors from the less obvious beauties of **Bridlington Priory** in the old town. The Priory was once one of the wealthiest in England but it was ruthlessly pillaged during the Reformation. Externally it is somewhat unprepossessing, but step inside and the majestic 13th century nave is unforgettably impressive. A corner of the Priory churchyard recalls one of the most tragic days in the town's history. During a fearsome gale in January 1871, a whole fleet of ships foundered along the coast. Bridlington's lifeboat was launched but within minutes it was "smashed to matchwood": most of its crew perished. Twenty bodies were washed ashore and later buried in the Priory churchyard: it was estimated that ten times as many souls found only a watery grave. This awesome tragedy is still recalled each year with a solemn service of remembrance when the lifeboat is drawn through the town.

Just to the north of Bridlington is **Sewerby Hall**, a monumental mansion built on the cusp of the Queen Anne and early Georgian years, between 1714 and 1720. Set in 50 acres of garden and parkland, (where there's also a small zoo), the house was first opened to the public in 1936 by Amy Johnson, the dashing, Yorkshire-born pilot who had captured the public imagination by her daring solo flights to South Africa and Australia. The Museum here houses some fascinating memorabilia of Amy's pioneering feats along with displays of motor vehicles, archaeological finds and some remarkable paintings amongst which is perhaps the most famous portrait of Queen Henrietta Maria, wife of Charles I. Queen Henrietta loved this romantic image of herself as a young, carefree woman, but during the dark days of the Civil War she felt compelled to sell it to raise funds for the doomed Royalist cause which ended with her husband's execution. After passing through several hands, this haunting portrait of a queen touched by tragedy found its last resting place at Sewerby Hall.

FLAMBOROUGH

MAP 11 REF Q8

5 miles NE of Bridlington on the B1255.

At Flamborough Head, sea and land are locked in an unremitting battle. At the North Landing, huge, foam-spumed waves roll in between gigantic cliffs, slowly but remorselessly washing away the shoreline. Paradoxically, the outcome of this elemental conflict is to produce one of the most picturesque locations on the Yorkshire coast, much visited and much photographed.

Flamborough's parish church contains two interesting monuments. One is the tomb of Sir Marmaduke Constable which shows him with his chest cut open to reveal his heart being devoured by a toad. The knight's death in 1518 had been caused, the story goes, by his swallowing the toad which had been drowsing in Sir Marmaduke's lunchtime pint of ale, apparently. The creature then devoured his heart. The other notable monument is a statue of St Oswald, patron saint of fishermen. This fishing connection is renewed every year, on the second Sunday in October, by a service dedicated to the **Harvest of the Sea**, when the area's sea-farers gather together in a church decorated with crab pots and fishing nets.

Flamborough Head's first, and England's oldest surviving **lighthouse**, is the octagonal chalk tower on the landward side of the present lighthouse. Built in 1674, its beacon was a basket of burning coal. The lighthouse that is still in use was built in 1806. Originally signalling four white flashes, developments over the years have included a fog horn in 1859 and in more recent years, a signal of radio bleeps. Until it was automated in 1995, it was the last manned lighthouse on the east coast.

Just to the north of Flamborough is **Danes Dyke**, a huge rampart four miles long designed to cut off the headland from hostile invaders. The Danes had nothing to do with it; the dyke was in place long before they arrived. Some time during the Bronze or Stone Age, early Britons constructed this extraordinary defensive ditch. A mile and a quarter of its southern length is open to the public as a Nature Trail.

BEMPTON
3 miles N of Bridlington on the B1229

MAP 11 REF P8

Bempton Cliffs, 400 foot high, mark the northernmost tip of the great belt of chalk that runs diagonally across England from the Isle of Wight to Flamborough Head. The sheer cliffs at Bempton provide an ideal nesting place for huge colonies of fulmars, guillemots, puffins and Britain's largest seabird, the gannet, with a wingspan 6 foot wide. The first Bird Protection Act of 1869 was specifically designed to protect the kittiwakes at Bempton: a ban on collecting eggs here didn't come into force until 1954. Bempton Cliffs are now an RSPB bird sanctuary, a refuge during the April to August breeding season for more than 200,000 seabirds, making this the largest colony in Britain.

BURTON AGNES
6 miles SW of Bridlington on the A166

MAP 11 REF P8

The overwhelming attraction in this unspoilt village is the sublime Elizabethan mansion, Burton Agnes Hall, but visitors should not ignore **Burton Agnes Manor House** (English Heritage), a rare example of a Norman house: a building of great historical importance but burdened with a grimly functional architecture, almost 800 years old, that chills one's soul. As Lloyd Grossman might say, 'How could anyone live in a house like this?'.

Burton Agnes Hall is much more appealing: an outstanding Elizabethan house, built between 1598 and 1610 and little altered, Burton Agnes is particularly famous for its splendid Jacobean gatehouse, wondrously decorated ceilings and overmantels carved in oak, plaster and alabaster. It also has a valuable collection of paintings and furniture from between the 17th and 19th centuries - including a portrait of Oliver Cromwell

Burton Agnes Hall

warts and all - and a large collection of Impressionist paintings. The gardens are extensive with over 2,000 plants, a maze and giant board games in the Coloured Gardens.

GREAT DRIFFIELD   MAP 11 REF P8
13m SW of Bridlington, on the A166

On the edge of the Wolds, Great Driffield is a busy little market town at the heart of an important corn growing area. A cattle market is held here every Thursday; a general market on both Thursday and Saturday, and the annual agricultural show has been going strong since 1854. All Saints Parish Church, dating back to the 12th century has some lovely stained glass windows portraying local nobility and one of the highest towers in the county.

A few miles northwest of Great Driffield is **Sledmere House**, a noble Georgian mansion built by the Sykes family in the 1750s when this area was still a wilderness infested with packs of marauding wolves. Inside, there is fine furniture by Chippendale and Sheraton, and decorated plasterwork by Joseph Rose. The copy of a naked, and well-endowed, Apollo Belvedere in the landing alcove must have caused many a maidenly blush ion Victorian times, and the Turkish Room - inspired by the Sultan's salon in Istanbul's Valideh Mosque - is a dazzling example of oriental opulence. Outside, the gardens and the 220 acres of parkland were landscaped, of course, by Capability Brown.

Across the road from Sledmere House are two remarkable, elaborately detailed, monuments. **The Eleanor Cross** - modelled on those set up by Edward I in memory of his Queen, was erected by Sir Tatton Sykes in 1900; the **Waggoners Memorial** designed by Sir Mark Sykes, commemorates the 1000-strong company of men he raised from the Wolds during World War I. Their knowledge of horses was invaluable in their role as members of the Army Service Corps. The finely-carved monument is like a storyboard, its panels depicting the Waggoners' varied duties during the war.

BEVERLEY   MAP 11 REF P9
10 miles N of Hull on the A164

"For those who do not know this town, there is a great surprise in store...Beverley is made for walking and living in". Such was the considered opinion of the late Poet Laureate, John Betjeman. In medieval times, Beverley was one of England's most prosperous towns and it remains one of the most gracious. Its greatest glory is the **Minster** whose twin towers, built in glowing magnesian limestone, soar above this, the oldest town in East Yorkshire. More than two centuries in the making, from around 1220 to 1450, the Minster provides a textbook demonstration of the evolving architectural styles of those years. Amongst its many treasures are superb, fine wood carvings from the Ripon school, and a thousand year old "fridstol", or sanctuary seat. Carved from a single block of stone, the fridstol is a relic from the earlier Saxon church on this site.

Close by is the **North Bar**, the only one of the town's five medieval gatehouses to have survived. Unlike many towns in the Middle Ages, Beverley did not have an encircling wall. Instead, the town fathers had a deep ditch excavated around it so that all goods had to pass through one of the gates and pay a toll. North Bar was built in 1409 and, with headroom of little more than ten feet, is something of a traffic hazard, albeit a very attractive one. Next door is Bar House, in which Charles I and his sons stayed in the 1630s.

Beverley can also boast three distinctive museums. The **Beverley Art Gallery and Museum** contains a variety of local antiquities, Victorian bygones and works by the noted local artist, F.W. Elwell RA; the **East Yorkshire Regimental Museum** has six rooms of exhibits chronicling the area's long association with the regiment, and the **Museum of Army Transport** in Flamingate includes an intriguing variety of vehicles. They range from the wagon in which Lord Roberts travelled during the Boer War, to a Beaver military aircraft; from the Rolls Royce used by Field Marshal Montgomery as a staff car in France and Germany, to the only example of a three-wheels-in-a-row motorcycle.

The wide market square in the heart of the town is graced by an elegant Market Cross, a circular pillared building rather like a small Greek temple. It bears the arms of Queen Anne in whose reign it was built at the expense of the town's two Members of Parliament. At that time of course parliamentary elections were flagrantly corrupt, but at Beverley the tradition continued longer than in most places - in 1868 the author Anthony Trollope stood as a candidate here but was defeated in what was acknowledged as a breathtakingly fraudulent election.

St Mary's Church, just across the road, tends to be overshadowed by the glories of Beverley's Minster. But this is another superb medieval building, richly endowed with fine carvings - many brightly coloured - and striking sculptures. A series of ceiling panels depicts all the Kings of England from Sigebert (623-37) to Henry VI. Originally, four legendary kings were also included, but one of them was replaced in recent times by a portrait of George VI. Lewis Carroll visited St Mary's when he stayed with friends in the town and was very

St Mary's Church, Beverley

taken with a stone carving of a rabbit - the inspiration, it is believed, for the March Hare in Alice in Wonderland. Certainly the carving bears an uncanny resemblance to Tenniel's famous drawing of the Mad Hatter.

From Beverley, serious walkers might care to follow some or all of the 15 mile **Hudson Way**, a level route that follows the track of the old railway from Beverley to Market Weighton. The Hudson Way wanders through the Wolds, sometimes deep in a cutting, sometimes high on an embankment, past an old windmill near Etton and through eerily abandoned stations.

HORNSEA
MAP 11 REF Q9

10 miles E of Beverley on the B1242/B1244

This small coastal town can boast not only the most popular visitor attraction in Humberside, Hornsea Pottery, but also Yorkshire's largest freshwater lake, Hornsea Mere. **Hornsea Pottery** is an extensive complex which includes the famous pottery where you can watch craftsmen at work and buy their wares, a factory viewing area, a collection of vintage cars, factory shops, a country park, and **"Butterfly World"** where more than 200 species of colourful butterflies flutter around a tropical greenhouse.

Hornsea Mere, two miles long and one mile wide, provides a refuge for over 170 species of birds and a peaceful setting for many varieties of rare flowers. Human visitors are well provided for, too, with facilities for fishing, boating and sailing. Hornsea is also the home of the **North Holderness Museum of Village Life**. Here, in a converted 18th century farmhouse, period rooms have been recreated, and there are collections of agricultural equipment and the tools of long gone local tradesmen. Excellent sands, a church built with cobbles gathered from the shore, well-tended public gardens and a breezy, mile-long promenade all add to the town's popularity.

SPROATLEY
MAP 11 REF Q9

7 miles NE of Hull on the B1238

A few miles south of Withernwick, close to the village of Sproatley, is **Burton Constable Hall**, named after Sir John Constable who in 1570 built a stately mansion here which incorporated parts of an even older house, dating back to the reign of King Stephen in the 1100s. The Hall was again remodelled, on Jacobean lines, in the 18th century and contains some fine work by Chippendale, Adam and James Wyatt. In the famous Long Gallery with its 15th century Flemish stained glass, hangs a remarkable collection of paintings, amongst them Holbein's portraits of Sir Thomas Cranmer and Sir Thomas More, and Zucchero's Mary, Queen of Scots. Dragons abound in the dazzling Chinese Room, an exercise in exotica that long pre-dates the Prince Regent's similar extravagance at the Brighton Pavilion. Outside, there are extensive parklands designed by - who else could it be? - Capability Brown, and apparently inspired by the gardens at Versailles.

NORTH YORKSHIRE - DALES

SKIPTON   MAP 10 REF L9
25 miles NW of Leeds on the A65

Often called the "Gateway to the Dales", Skipton's origins can be traced to the 7th century when Anglian farmers christened it Sheeptown. Featuring in the Domesday Book, the Normans decided to build a castle here to guard the entrance to Airedale and Skipton became a garrison town. **Skipton Castle**, home of the Cliffords, was begun in 1090; the powerful stone structure seen today was devised in 1310 by Robert de Clifford, the 1st Earl of Skipton. Adjacent to the castle, at the top of the High Street, lies the parish **Church of the Holy Trinity** which was originally built in the 12th century and replaced in the 1300s. There is a wealth of interest inside the building which has been topped by a beautiful oak roof since the 15th century.

For many years Skipton remained a market town, then, with the development of the factory system in the 19th century, the nature of the town began to change. Textile mills were built and cottages and terraced houses were constructed for the influx of mill workers. The **Leeds and Liverpool Canal**, which flows through the town, provided a cheap form of transport as well as linking Skipton with the major industrial centres of Yorkshire and Lancashire. The first of three trans-Pennine routes, the 127 mile canal has 91 locks along the full length as well as two tunnels, one of which is over a mile long. Today, the canal basin, behind the town centre, is busy with pleasure craft and boat journeys can be taken along a section in the direction of Gargrave. The towpath was also restored at the same time as the canal and there are a number of pleasant walks which includes a stretch along the cul-de-sac Spring Branch beside the castle walls.

A walk around the town is also worth while and there are many interesting buildings to be found here. One, in particular, is the **Town Hall** which is now also the home of the **Craven Museum**. Dedicated to the surrounding area, there are many interesting displays relating to the geological and archaeological treasures that have been found

Skipton Castle

locally, including a piece of Bronze Age cloth which is considered the oldest textile fragment in the country.

Almost opposite the Town Hall, on the High Street, are the premises of the Craven Herald, a newspaper that was established in 1874, although the publication was produced for a short time in the 1850s. The building is fortunate in having retained its late Victorian shop front, as well as the passageway to one side, and it was first occupied by William Chippendale in the late 18th century.

EARBY
Map 10 ref L9

6 miles W of Skipton on the A56

Though the Yorkshire Dales are thought of as a once thriving textile producer, lead mining, for many centuries, was also a key industry. Housed in an old grammar school founded in 1591 by Robert Windle, is the **Museum of Yorkshire Dales Lead Mining**, which was opened in 1971. The museum, which has limited opening, has many excellent displays including mine tubs, photographs, mine plans, small implements, mining machinery, and miners' personal belongings.

ELSLACK
Map 10 ref L9

4 miles W of Skipton off the A56

This small rural village lies in the heart of the Pennines; the Pennine Way footpath runs close by. Picturesque and surrounded by glorious countryside, the remains of a Roman fort have been found here and a Roman road is believed to have run through Elslack.

Overlooking the village is the 1,274 foot high **Pinhaw Beacon** from which there are some fine panoramic views over the heather covered moorland. During the Napoleonic Wars in the early 19th century, when there was great fear of an invasion from France, the beacon, one in a countrywide chain of communication beacons, was manned 24 hours a day.

MALHAM
Map 10 ref L8

8 miles NW of Skipton on minor roads off the A65

The village was originally two settlements, Malham East and Malham West, which were separated by the beck. Each came under the influence of a different religious house: Bolton Priory and Fountains Abbey respectively. United after the Dissolution of the Monasteries, the focal point of Malham became the village green, where the annual sheep fairs were held. This pretty village of farms and cottages is visited for the spectacular limestone scenery which lies just to the north. However, the two ancient stone bridges in the village centre are also worth a second glance. The **New Bridge**, which is also known as the Monks' Bridge, was built in the 17th century whilst the **Wash-Dub Bridge** dates from the 16th century and is of a clapper design (limestone slabs placed on stone supports).

The way to the ancient glacial grandeur of **Malham Cove** is from the Langcliffe road beyond the last buildings of the village, down a path alongside the beck that leads through a scattering of trees. The 300 foot limestone amphitheatre is the most spectacular section of the mid-Craven fault and, as recently as the 1700s, a massive waterfall cascaded over its edge, that was higher than Niagara

Malham Cove

Falls! These days the water disappears through potholes at the top, called water-sinks, and reappears through the cavern mouth at Aire Head near the village. A steep path leads to the limestone pavement at the top, with its distinctive clints and grykes, where water has carved a distinctive natural sculpture through the weaknesses in the limestone.

From here it is not too far to reach the equally inspiring **Gordale Scar**, a huge gorge carved by glacial melt water with an impressive waterfall leaping, in two stages, from a fissure in its face. Further on still is another waterfall known as **Janet's Foss**. Beside the waterfall is a cave which Janet, a friendly fairy, is reputed to inhabit. Three miles north of the scar is **Malham Tarn**, a glacial lake, and Malham Tarn House, where such famous names as Ruskin, Darwin, and Charles Kingsley (author of The Water Babies) received inspiration.

SETTLE

MAP 10 REF K8

14 miles NW of Skipton off the A65

This small market town, which received its charter in 1249, still retains its thriving weekly market on Tuesdays. A busy stopping place in the days of the stagecoach, when travellers journeying between York and Lancaster and Kendal called here, Settle is now a popular place for visitors, walkers, and cyclists who stop in the town to take full advantage of the wide range of inns and hotels.

However, for most Settle is the home of the famous **Settle-Carlisle Railway**, a proudly preserved memento of the glorious age of steam and the line is still flanked by charming little

signal boxes and stations that are a real tourist magnet. This attractive railway was built in the midst of great controversy and even greater cost, in both money and lives, earning it the dubious title of "the line that should never have been built."

Settle's architecture is very distinctive, in the main being Victorian sandstone buildings that all look as if they are born of the railway culture. Buildings of note include the arcaded **Shambles**, originally butcher's slaughter houses, the French-style **Town Hall**, the Victorian **Music Hall**, and the oldest building, **Preston's Folly**, described as an extravaganza of mullioned

Settle-Carlisle Railway, Ribblehead Viaduct

windows and Tudor masonry, and so called because the man who created this anomalous fancy impoverished himself in the process!

Apart from the grander structures on the main streets, there are charming little side streets with Georgian and Jacobean cottages criss-crossed with quirky little alleyways and ginnels with hidden courtyards and workshops of a time gone by. In Chapel Street is the **Museum of North Craven Life**, which gives a historical, topographical, and geological background to the area. The imaginative displays tell the story of the local farming traditions and also the history of the building of the Settle-Carlisle Railway.

HORTON IN RIBBLESDALE

MAP 10 REF K8

6 miles N of Settle on the B6479

First mentioned in the Domesday Book, the village, whose name means literally the settlement on the muddy land or marsh, was probably in existence long before the 11th century. The oldest building here is the 12th-century St Oswald's Church which still shows signs of its Norman origins in the chevron designs over the south door. Inside, peculiarly, all the pillars lean to the south and, in the west window, there is an ancient piece of stained glass showing Thomas à Becket wearing his bishop's mitre. This village is the ideal place from which to explore the limestone landscapes and green hills of Upper Ribblesdale and, to the east, lies **Pen-y-ghent** (2,273 feet high), one of the famous **Three Peaks**. The whole of this area has been designated as being of Special Scientific Interest, mainly due to the need to conserve the swiftly eroding hillsides and paths. This is an ancient landscape, well worth the efforts to preserve its relic ash woodlands, primitive earthworks, and rare birdlife such as Peregrine falcon, ring ouzel, and golden plover. There are also a great many caves in the area, which add to the sense of romance and adventure one feels in this place.

AUSTWICK   MAP 10 REF K8
4 miles NW of Settle off the A65

This ancient village of stone cottages and crofts, dry stone walls, abandoned quarries, and patchwork hills was originally a Norse settlement: the name is Nordic for Eastern Settlement. The largely 17th-century buildings, with their elaborately decorated stone lintels, flank what remains of the village green where the ancient cross stands as a reminder of when this was the head of a dozen neighbouring manors and the home of an annual cattle fair.

Norber Boulders

The most peculiar feature of the surrounding area has to be the **Norber Boulders**: a series of black boulders which stand on limestone pedestals which, despite their contrived appearance, are a completely natural feature. They are also known locally as the Norber Erratics because they are anomalous - the grey silurian slate they are composed of usually occurs beneath limestone rather than on top. The mystery of their existence is explained by the fact that these huge rocks were originally deposited by glacial action at the end of the last Ice Age. Another distinctive local feature is the clapper bridge, a medieval structure made from large slabs of rock that span the local becks.

INGLETON   MAP 10 REF K8
8 miles NW of Settle off the A65

Mentioned in the Domesday Book, the name means Beacon Town and Ingleton is certainly one of the most visited villages in the Dales. As a gateway to the Three Peaks, it is also popular with walkers. From as long ago as the late 18th century, Ingleton has been famous for the numerous caves and other splendid scenery that lies within easy reach though some are harder to find and even harder to reach. The coming of the railway, which gave those working in the towns easy and cheap access to the countryside, greatly increased the numbers of visitors looking for clean, country air. Though Ingleton is no longer served by trains, the village is still dominated by the railway viaduct that spans the River Greta. The river, which is formed here by the meeting of the Rivers Twiss and Doe, is famous for its salmon leaps. Discovered in 1865 by Joseph Carr, the **Ingleton Waterfalls**, which were not immediately made accessible to the public, have been delighting visitors since 1885. Along the 4 miles of scenic walks, the stretch of waterfalls includes those with such interesting names as Pecca Twin Falls, Holly Bush Spout, Thornton Force, and Baxengill Gorge. The second principal network of caves in the area which are open to the public are **White Scar Caves**. Discovered in 1923, this cave network has been under

Ingleborough

exploration ever since and today the main features include two waterfalls, beautiful stalactites, and the longest show cave in Britain.

Finally, there is **Ingleborough** which, at 2,375 feet, is the middle summit of the Three Peaks. For over 2,000 years, the peak has been used as a beacon and a fortress and, as a result, it is perhaps the most interesting. A distinctive feature of the horizon for miles around as it is made of several layers of rock of differing hardnesses, there are several paths to the summit though most begin their journey in Ingleton. As well as the fine views, on a clear day, there are also several interesting features on top of the peak.

CLAPHAM

6 miles N of Settle on the A65

MAP 10 REF K8

By far the largest building in the village is **Ingleborough Hall**, once the home of the Farrer family and now a centre for outdoor education. One member of the family, Reginald Farrer, was an internationally renowned botanist and he was responsible for introducing many new plant species into the country. Many examples of his finds still exist in the older gardens of the village and in the hall's grounds and there is a particularly pleasant walk, the **Reginald Farrer Nature Trail**, which leads from Clapham to nearby Ingleborough Cave.

One of the most famous establishments in this part of Yorkshire, **The Flying Horseshoe Hotel** dates back to 1846. This former shooting lodge became a hotel in 1870. This large and impressive stonebuilt hotel, pub and restaurant stands next to the railway line. At one time this marked a terminus of the Morecambe and York line. Lady Astor was a regular visitor, along with many wealthy and notable people of the day. Set within the beautiful forest of Bowland, it makes an ideal base for exploring the Yorkshire Dales and Cumbria. There are 10 comfortable

and welcoming en suite guest bedrooms, one of which is a lovely family suite with its own private lounge. The decor and furnishings in each are excellent. Guests enjoy free access to England's best salmon river, the River Wenning. The hotel's superb Free House offers real ales include Jennings, Tetleys, Theakstons and changing guest ales. The restaurant's menu features a good range of traditional favourites and daily specials, along with a distin-

The Flying Horseshoe Hotel, Clapham, nr Lancaster,North Yorkshire LA2 8ES Tel: 015242 51229
e-mail: alan@laughing-gravy.co.uk
website: www.laughing-gravy.co.uk

guished wine list. Adjacent to the hotel there's a small caravan park with 56 berths, open March - October.

BUCKDEN
Map 10 ref L8

15 miles N of Skipton on the B6160

Marking the beginning of Wharfedale proper, Buckden is the first full sized village of the dale and proudly boasts that it is also home to Wharfedale's first shop. Unusually for this area, the village was not settled by the Anglo-Saxons but, later, by the Normans and it was the headquarters of the officers hunting in the forest of Langstrothdale. As the forest was cleared to make way for agriculture, Buckden became an important market town serving a large part of the surrounding area. Wool was one of the important sources of income for the dalefolk and the local inn here still has some of the old weighing equipment from the days when the trade was conducted on the premises. Designated in Norman times as one of the feudal hunting forests, **Langstrothdale Chase** was governed by the strict forest laws. Just to the south of the village, which lies on the edge of the Chase, can be seen an old stone cross which was used to mark the forest boundary. The last deer was hunted and killed here in the 17th century and Buckden's name means "valley of the bucks".

LITTON
Map 10 ref L8

15 miles N of Skipton off the B6160

This pretty village lends it name to the dale, Littondale, which is actually the valley of the River Skirfare. Once part of a Norman hunting forest, the dale was originally called Amerdale (meaning deep fork) and this ancient name is preserved in Amerdale Dub, where the River Skirfare joins the River Wharfe near Kilnsey.

Outstanding self-catering cottages can be found at **Stonelands Farmyard**. Found amidst panoramic and scenic countryside in Littondale on the outskirts of Litton, the properties and location are certainly a cut above the rest. Converted from old farm buildings and opened back in 1993, some of the buildings date back to the 18th century, and feature comfortable furnishings and decor. There are 10 cottages in all, ranging from the luxurious one-bedroom units to the three cottages eminently suitable for families and the three "suites" in the main farmhouse. Each facility is spacious and welcoming, sleeping from two people up to six. Most boast four-poster beds and all have spa baths. Other superb amenities include the indoor heated

Stonelands Farmyard Cottages, Litton, Skipton, North Yorkshire
BD23 5QH Tel: 01756 770293 Fax: 01756 770321
website: www.stonelands.co.uk

swimming pool, sauna, video library and laundry room. A home-cooked "welcome meal" greets new guests on their arrival. This family-run business is owned by the Cowan family: Tom and Brenda, together with their sons Mark and Roger, Mark's wife Ruth and Roger's wife Mandy. Mark is a qualified chef who prepares the mouth-watering "welcome meal" as well as offering an extensive a la carte menu on subsequent evenings, all delivered to guests' cottages. Weekly, weekend and mid-week breaks available.

ARNCLIFFE
MAP 10 REF L8

14 miles N of Skipton off the B6160

Situated in Littondale, the village name dates back to Saxon times when the valley was referred to as Amerdale. This is a quiet, tranquil dale and life has remained the same here for many years in this small village. Many of the buildings around the central village green are listed and, in its early years, the long running television series Emmerdale was filmed here. Near the village bridge, over the River Skirfare, stands a house, **Bridge End**, that was once the home of the Hammond family. Whilst staying with the Hammonds, author Charles Kingsley, was so taken with the village and Littondale that he incorporated the house and his hostess in his famous work The Water Babies.

KILNSEY
MAP 10 REF L8

11 miles N of Skipton on the B6160

Set in six acres of beautiful Yorkshire countryside, overlooked by the renowned Kilnsey Crag, **Kilnsey Park** offers a variety of leisure activities and facilities for all the family. The restaurant/ coffee shop overlooks the two trout lakes and Kilnsey Crag, and is recommended far and wide for the quality of its food. Open every day from 9-5.30 (later in summer), it is very cosy and the hospitality offered warm and genuine. The menu features a fine range of hearty and delicious meals and snacks; there are also tempting daily specials. Many naturally feature trout, and visitors can partake in some fly fishing on one of the two wonderful trout lakes. While the grown-ups enjoy their meal the children can either go for some supervised "fun fishing", have a go with a radio-controlled boat, play in the adventure playground or see how the trout are reared. Then the whole family can en-

**Kilnsey Park and Trout Farm, Kilnsey, North Yorkshire
BD23 5PS Tel: 01756 752150 Fax: 01756 752224**

joy the aquarium or see the endangered Red Squirrels being bred here. Next to the restaurant is the marvellous deli - with lots of fresh trout, cheeses, preserves and more locally produce are for sale. This superb centre, designated a Site of Scientific Interest, also offers visitors a glimpse of rare orchids and features a specialist herb and alpine centre, a conservation centre and a fascinating nature trail.

GRASSINGTON
MAP 10 REF L8

7 miles N of Skipton on the B6160

This is, perhaps, the best loved village within the Yorkshire Dales National Park and, in many ways, it typifies the Dales' settlement with its ubiquitous market square. Known as the capital of Upper Wharfedale, the historically important valley roads meet here and the ancient monastic route from Malham to Fountains Abbey passes through the village. Grassington's origins are rooted in ancient history; there was certainly a Bronze Age settlement here, the remains of an Iron Age village have been found, a Celtic field system lies on nearby Lea Green, and the village was mentioned in the Domesday Book. However, the settlement seen today is Anglian and, having passed through various families, is now part of the estate of the Dukes of Devonshire.

With many of its buildings coming within the central conservation area there is little left of the village's heyday, in the 17th and 18th centuries when lead mining was a key local industry, other than the houses built at that time. Housed in two of the 18th-century lead miners' cottages, in Grassington Square, is the **Upper Wharfedale Folk Museum**. Containing many exhibits and displays relating to the lives of those who have lived in the dale, the museum is open (afternoons only) at the weekend during the winter and daily throughout the summer. Throughout the year, there were many festivals and holidays observed by the dales people and one, the Feast Sports, still takes place here on a Saturday in October. Among the many traditional events which are carried out there is the tea cake eating race, where children have to eat a tea cake, and race to the other end of the field. The winner is the first child to whistle a tune.

LINTON   MAP 10 REF L8
1 mile S of Grassington off the B6160

This delightful and unspoilt village, that is more correctly called Linton-in-Craven, has grown up around its village green through which runs a small beck. This flat area of land was once a lake and around its edge was grown flax which the villagers spun into linen. The village is also the home of the **Church of St Michael and All Angels**, a wonderful building that is a fine example of rural medieval architecture. Probably built on the site of a pagan shrine the church lies some way from the village centre though its handsome bell-cote is a suitable landmark. Among the 14th-century roof bosses can be seen the **Green Man**, an ancient fertility symbol of a man's head protruding through foliage, which was adopted by the Christian church.

HEBDEN   MAP 10 REF L8
1 mile E of Grassington on the B6265

From this quiet hamlet it is only a short distance to the wonderful 500,000 year old cave at **Stump Cross Caverns**. The large show cave holds a fantastic collection of stalactites and stalagmites which make it one of the most visited underground attractions in the area. During excavations, the remains of animals were found here and they can be seen on display at the visitor centre where there is also a gift shop and a tea room.

BOLTON ABBEY   MAP 10 REF L8
7 miles SE of Grassington on the B6160

The village is actually a collection of small hamlets which have all been part of the estate of the Dukes of Devonshire since 1748. **Bolton Abbey** itself lies on the banks of the River Wharfe whilst the hamlets of Storiths, Hazelwood, Deerstones, and Halton East lie higher up. The main attraction in the village is the substantial remains of **Bolton Priory**, an Augustinian house that was founded in 1155 by the monks from Embsay. In an idyllic situation on the banks of the River Wharfe, the ruins are well preserved whilst the nave of the priory church, first built in 1220, is now incorporated into the parish church.

Bolton Abbey

    The Devonshire Arms Country House Hotel in the grounds of Bolton Abbey is a distinguished and distinctive hotel and restaurant commanding admiration from the visitors who

The Devonshire Arms, Bolton Abbey, Skipton, North Yorkshire BD23 6AJ
Tel: 01756 710441 Fax: 01756 710498

come from near and far to sample the delights of hospitality and fine dining on offer. Owned by the Duke and Duchess of Devonshire, the comfort, relaxation, good food and excellent service available are second to none. Built as a coaching inn in the 17th century, the hotel boasts 41 gracious en suite guest bedrooms. The hotel's fine reputation means that it is often full - advanced booking is recommended. Furniture and pictures from Chatsworth add to the private country house ambience. The outstanding Burlington Restaurant is open every evening and Sunday lunchtime. Head chef Andrew Nicholson has gained a reputation as one of the best in Yorkshire. Bookings are essential and dress formal at this classic establishment. In the refurbished and stylish Bistro - open lunch and evening - a range of delicious light meals are available. The 17th-century stone barn opposite the hotel houses a health, beauty and fitness club incorporating the latest gym equipment, swimming pool, sauna, hard tennis court and more. For the last word in elegance and comfort, look no further.

The Strid, near Bolton Abbey

In an around this beautiful village there are some 75 miles of footpaths and nature trails up into the high moorland. Just upstream from the Priory lies one of the most visited natural features of the River Wharfe, where the wide river bed suddenly narrows into a confined channel of black rock through which the water thunders. This spectacular gorge is known as **The Strid** because, down the ages, many have attempted to leap its width as a test of bravery.

REETH   MAP 10 REF L7
30 miles N of Skipton on the B6270

Considered the capital of Swaledale, this small town is poised at the junction of the River Swale and its main tributary, Arkle Beck. **The Swaledale Folk Museum**, housed in what was once the old Methodist Sunday School, is the home for exhibits of local farming methods, crafts, and mining skills, as well as displays on local pastimes, the impact of Wesleyan Methodism, and the exodus of the population to the industrial areas of the south Pennines when the lead mines closed. Just to the south of Reeth lies the quiet village of **Grinton** whose parish **Church of St Andrew** served the whole of the dale for centuries. The building dates back to the 13th and 15th centuries, though there are still some Norman remains as well as a Leper's Squint (a small hole through which those afflicted by the disease could follow the service within). For those people living in the upper reaches of Swaledale who died, there was a long journey down the track to Grinton which became known as the Corpse Way.

HEALAUGH
1 mile W of Reeth on the B6270

MAP 10 REF L7

In the 12th century an Augustinian Priory was founded here but, unfortunately, none of the remaining fragments date from earlier than the 15th century. However, the village Church of St Helen and St John, which dates from around 1150, not only has outstanding views over the Vale of York and the Pennines but also has a bullet hole which, it is alleged, was made by a Cromwellian trooper on his way to Marsden Moor.

Swaledale Cottages is a family-run business offering self-catering holiday and short break accommodation in one of five charming and comfortable country cottages. Located in and around the village of Reeth, many of the cottages date from the 18th century. Each has been renovated and modernised to provide every modern amenity, while retaining its original charm and character. Owners Robert and Janet Hughes are conscientious, helpful and friendly. Two of the cottages lie within the grounds of their own magnificent home; the others are within two miles of it, including one of in the heart of the village of Reeth itself. Available all year round, the cottages sleep between two and ten people. Weekly lets as well as shorter breaks are avail-

Swaledale Cottages, Thiernswood Hall, Healaugh, Richmond, North Yorkshire DL11 6UJ
Tel: 01748 884526 Fax: 01748 884834

able. Children and dogs welcome in some of the properties. Three are non-smoking. Guests here are ensured a restful and pleasant stay amid some spectacular rural scenery. Local amenities include good shops, pubs and restaurants.

THWAITE
9 miles W of Reeth on the B6270

MAP 10 REF L7

Surrounded by beautiful countryside which includes **Kisdon Hill**, **Great Shunnor**, **High Seat**, and **Lovely Seat**, this is a tiny village of ancient origins. Like so many places in the area the name comes from the Nordic language and, in this case, thveit meaning a clearing in the wood. However, the woodlands which once provided shelter and fuel for the Viking settlers have long since gone. To the southwest of the village lies **Buttertubs Pass**, one of the highest and most forbidding mountain passes in the country. The Buttertubs themselves are an outstanding natural feature, well known to walkers and travellers, comprising a series of closely packed vertical potholes. Unusually, these potholes are not linked by a series of passages as most are, but they are freestanding and bear only a slight resemblance to the objects after which they are named.

KELD
MAP 10 REF L7

9 miles W of Reeth on the B6270

This little cluster of stone buildings that make up the village stand beside the early stages of the River Swale. The place is alive with the sound of rushing water and it comes as no surprise that the word keld is Nordic for spring. For lovers of green woodlands and breathtaking waterfalls, this village is definitely well worth a visit and it also has managed to retain an impression of being untouched by modern life. **Wain Wath Force**, with the impressive Cotterby Scar providing a fine backdrop, can be found alongside the Birkdale road. Meanwhile, **Catrake Force**, with its stepped formation, can be reached from the cottages on the left at the bottom of the street in the village. Though on private land the falls and, beside them, the entrance to an old lead mine can still be seen.

RICHMOND
MAP 10 REF M7

9 miles E of Reeth on the A6108

The former county of Richmondshire (to which locals still refer), of which this town was the capital, once occupied a third of the North Riding of Yorkshire. Alan Rufus, the 1st Earl of Richmond, built the original **Richmond Castle** in 1071 and the site, 100 feet up on a rocky promontory with the River Swale passing below, is imposing and well chosen. The keep rises to 109 feet with walls 11 feet thick, while the other side is afforded an impregnable defence by means of the cliff and the river. Richmond Castle was the first Norman castle in the country to be built, right from the foundations, in stone. Additions were made over subsequent years but it reached its final form in the 14th century. Since then it has fallen into ruin though a considerable amount of the original Norman stonework remains intact. In 1315, Edward II granted Richmond the right to protect the town by a stone wall after Scottish raiders had caused considerable damage in the surrounding area. By the 16th century, the walls were in a state of disrepair and little survives today. However, the **Bar** and **Postern Gates**, two of the five gates originally built along the walls are still standing. Two road bridges (and a railway bridge) cross the River Swale in the town. The elder of the two, Green Bridge, was erected in 1789 to the designs of John Carr after the existing bridge had been swept away by flood water. During the Middle Ages, the markets of Richmond gave the town much of its prosperity and its influence spread across Yorkshire to Lancashire. Also, like many North Yorkshire towns and villages, the textile industry played an important role in the continuation of the town's wealth and, for some time, Richmond became famous for its knitted stockings.

Richmond Castle

The Green Howards Museum, the regimental museum of the North Riding's infantry, is based in the old Trinity Church in the centre of the cobbled market square. The church was founded in 1135 and, though it has been altered and rebuilt on more than one occasion, the original Norman tower and some other masonry has survived. The regiment dates back to 1688, when it was founded, and the displays and collections illustrate its history with war relics, weapons, uniforms, medals, and regimental silver. Also housed in the museum is the town's silver. It is not surprising that a town steeped in history should have several museums and the **Richmondshire Museum** traces the history of this old place and its county. Richmond is also home to England's oldest theatre, the **Georgian Theatre Royal**, which originally formed part of a circuit that included Northallerton, Ripon, and Harrogate. **The Georgian Theatre Royal Museum** contains a unique collection of original playbills as well as the oldest and largest complete set of painted scenery in Britain.

Top of the range in every respect, **West End** is a wonderful stonebuilt guest house offering bed and breakfast accommodation, with adjacent garden cottages providing self-catering accommodation. Set in three-quarters of an acre of lovely gardens, this peaceful retreat serves as a marvellous base from which to explore the delights of this part of the county. There are five guest bedrooms: three doubles, one twin - all en suite - and one single with private facilities. The home-cooked breakfast uses fresh local produce whenever possible. A friendly, homely atmosphere pervades this comfortable and beautifully appointed home. There are

West End, 45 Reeth Road, Richmond,
North Yorkshire DL10 4EX Tel: 01748 824783

four self-catering units in all, available for weekly lets or shorter breaks. All are furnished and decorated to a high standard of comfort and quality, and all offer every modern amenity. Each has two bedrooms, an attractive lounge/dining area with fully fitted kitchen and its own paved patio area with garden furniture. There's also a handy on-site laundrette, and off-street parking.

Just outside the town lies **Easby Abbey**, a low built monastic ruin which looks down to the River Swale. Founded in 1155 by Roald, Constable of Richmond Castle, its order of monks were of more modest leanings than the Cistercians, and the building certainly possesses none of the grandiose lines of Rievaulx and Fountains, although the riverside setting is a common fea-

Easby Abbey

ture. The abbey's most notable feature is its replica of the Easby Cross, an Anglo-Saxon cross dating from the 9th century and the extensive ruins can be reached by a pleasant riverside walk that is well sign-posted.

HUDSWELL   MAP 10 REF M7
2 miles W of Richmond off the A6108

This ancient village, which was well established by the time it was recorded in the Domesday

Book, stands high above the River Swale and over the years the village has gravitated to a more sheltered spot. The present **St Michael's Church** was built in the late 19th century on the site of an older building and the view from the churchyard is considered to be one of the finest in Richmondshire. The walk from the village down to the river leads through pleasant woodland and also takes in some 365 steps. About half way down, below a path leading off to an old lime kiln, can be found **King Arthur's Oven**, a horizontal crack in the limestone which, it is claimed, has connections with Richmond Castle and the legend of King Arthur.

EAST WITTON
10 miles S of Richmond off the A6108

MAP 10 REF M7

One of the most famous, most popular and most sought-after establishments in Yorkshire, **The Blue Lion** is a distinguished hotel, pub and restaurant dating back to 1790. This former coach-

ing inn takes its name from the blue lion that appeared in the crest of its old name, The Man of Aylesbury. Well-known for its quality accommodation and excellent food, it offers 12 handsome en suite guest rooms, each individually decorated and combining traditional comforts with every modern amenity. This characterful country retreat boasts a cosy and welcoming bar with an open fire, flagstoned floor and a tantalising range of bar meals, as well as a good selection of real ales including Theakstons Old

The Blue Lion, East Witton, nr Leyburn, North Yorkshire DL8 4SN Tel: 01969 624273 Fax: 01969 624189

Peculiar and the Black Sheep brew. The professional chefs and excellent staff at the charming candlelit restaurant make dining here a real treat. The superb menu features freshly prepared dishes using a variety of local ingredients, which have earned a string of culinary awards.

PATELEY BRIDGE
15 miles NE of Skipton on the B6265

MAP 10 REF M8

Considered one of the prettiest towns in the Dales, Pateley Bridge is perfectly situated as a base from which to explore Upper Nidderdale. Considering its compact size, the town is remarkably well connected by roads which have been here since the monastic orders established trade routes through the town for transporting their goods. A street market, whose charter was granted in the 14th century, has, however, been abandoned for some time although sheep fairs and agricultural shows still take place here. However, Pateley Bridge is more than just a market centre, the nearby lead mines and spinning and hand-loom weaving also provided employment for the local community. The construction of the turnpike road to Ripon in 1751, followed by the opening of a road to Knaresborough in 1756, gave the town a further economic boost. In the early 19th century, the brothers George and John Metcalfe moved their flax spinning business to nearby Glasshouses and they expanded rapidly. The lead mines too were expanding, due to the introduction of new machinery, and the town saw a real boom. The arrival of the railway, in 1862, maintained this flourishing economy, making the transportation of heavy goods cheaper and the carriage of perishable foods quicker. Much of the Pateley Bridge seen today was built in those prosperous years. A town of quaint and pretty buildings, the oldest is St Mary's Church, a lovely ruin dating from 1320 from which there are some fine panoramic views. Another excellent vista can be viewed from the aptly named Panorama Walk, the main medieval route from Ripon to Skipton.

The **Nidderdale Museum**, a winner of the National Heritage Museum of the Year, is housed in one of the town's original Victorian workhouses and presents a fascinating record of local folk history. The bridge at Pateley is a long established crossing which was used by the monks of Fountains Abbey. The original ford was replaced by a wooden bridge in the 16th century and the present stone structure dates from the 18th century.

LOFTHOUSE   Map 10 ref M8
6 miles NW of Pateley Bridge off the B6265

This is a small Dales' village lying in the upper valley of the River Nidd and, unlike neighbouring Wharfedale, the stone walls and rocky outcrops are of millstone grit though the valley bottom consists of limestone. As a result, only in excessive weather is there water under the bridge here as, in normal conditions, the river drops down two sumps: Manchester Hole and Goydon Pot. The monks of Fountains Abbey certainly had a grange here but it is also probable that the village was first settled by Norsemen. **How Stean Gorge**, in the heart of Nidderdale, is often called Yorkshire's Little Switzerland and for good reason. This spectacular limestone gorge, which is up to 80 feet deep in places, through which the Stean Beck flows is a popular tourist attraction though little known outside the area. A narrow path with footbridges guide the visitor along the gorge where the waters rush over the large boulders below. However, there are also many sheltered areas of calm water where fish hide under the rocks. As well as taking a stroll up this fascinating path, visitors can also step inside Tom Taylor's Cave and, along the walk, marvel at the wide variety of plant life that grows in this steep ravine.

BURNT YATES   Map 10 ref M8
6 miles SE of Pateley Bridge on the B6165

The village lies at the point where the royal hunting grounds of the Forest of Knaresborough met the land belonging to Fountains Abbey and the curious village name is probably a contraction of "Boundary Gates".

The distinctive and gracious stonebuilt self-catering cottages offered by **Dinmore Cottages** date back to the late 17th century. Surrounded by what was a working farm up until 1972, these former farm buildings were converted to use as accommodation in 1984, and have won awards for their outstanding conversion. Set in seven acres of beautiful grounds that offer wonderful

Dinmore Cottages, Dinmore House, Burnt Yates, nr Harrogate, North Yorkshire HG3 3ET Tel/Fax: 01423 770860 email: aib@dinmore-cottages.freeserve.co.uk

walks and opportunities for bird-watching, there is an abundance of natural wildlife in the area. The three top of the range cottages feature exposed beams, open stone fireplace or log-burning stove, and a wealth of original features. Sleeping between two and five people, they are both cosy and spacious, offering a truly peaceful and relaxing retreat. Each cottage has been individually designed and comfortably furnished, with fitted carpets and well-equipped kitchens. Each also boasts its own private grassed area or terrace. Children welcome. No pets. ETB 4 Keys Highly Commended.

SUMMERBRIDGE

MAP 10 REF M8

3 miles S of Pateley Bridge on the B6165

A small settlement with a bridge and a corn mill, in 1825 **New York Mill**, a large flax mill, was built here and, by the mid-19th century Summerbridge was flourishing with five mills in operation, a rope works, and a foundry. To the north of Summerbridge, which takes its name from the bridge that connects the village with Dacre on the opposite riverbank, stand the **Brimham Rocks**, now owned by the National Trust. Formed into fantastic shapes by years of erosion, these great millstone grit boulders lie up a steep hill amidst acres of heathland.

RIPLEY

MAP 10 REF M8

8 miles SE of Pateley Bridge off the A61

In the outer walls of the parish church, built around 1400, are holes said to have been caused by musket balls from Cromwell's firing squad, who executed Royalist prisoners here after the battle of Marston Moor. Inside, there is a fine Rood Screen dating from the reign of King Stephen, a mid-14th century tomb chest, and the stone base of an old weeping cross (where one was expected to kneel in the stone grooves and weep for penance) survives in the churchyard.

Ripley, still very much an estate village, is a quiet and pretty place, with cobbled streets, a castle, a wonderful hotel, and an interesting history. The title was granted to Thomas Ingilby in the 1300s for killing a wild boar in Knaresborough Forest that was charging at King Edward III. Visitors strolling around Ripley cannot fail to notice the **Hotel de Ville** - the Town Hall. Sir William Amcotts Ingilby was responsible for this when, in 1827, he began to remodel the entire village on one which he had seen in Alsace Lorraine. The original thatched cottages were replaced with those seen today and now Ripley is a conservation area with every pre-1980 dwelling being a Grade II listed building. Magnificent **Ripley Castle** has been home to the

Ingilby family for over 600 years. The castle is open to the public and is set in an outstanding Capability Brown landscape, with lakes, a deer park, and an avenue of tall beeches over which the attractive towers only just seem to peek. Its tranquillity belies the events that took place here after

Ripley Castle

the battle at Marston Moor, when Cromwell, exhausted after his day's slaughter, camped his Roundheads here and chose to rest in the castle.

The Ingilbys, however, were Royalist and his intrusion was met with as much ill-will as possible; they offered neither food nor a bed. Jane Ingilby, aptly named "Trooper Jane" due to her fighting skills, was the house's occupant and, having forced the self-styled Lord Protector of

England to sleep on a sofa with two pistols pointing at his head, declared the next morning, "It was well that he behaved in so peaceable a manner; had it been otherwise, he would not have left the house alive." Cromwell, his pride severely damaged by a woman ordered the immediate execution of his Royalist prisoners and left Trooper Jane regretting staying her hand during the previous night.

RIPON
MAP 10 REF M8

25 miles E of Skipton on the A61

This attractive cathedral city, on the banks of the Rivers Ure, Skell, and Laver, dates from the 7th century when Alfrich, King of Northumbria granted an area of land here, surrounding a new monastery, to the Church. Later that century, in 672, St Wilfrid built a church on the high ground between the three rivers but, at the time of the demise of the Northern Kingdom in the mid-10th century, the monastery and church were destroyed, though the Saxon crypt survives to this day. By the time of the Norman Con-

quest, Ripon was a prosperous agricultural settlement under ecclesiastical rule and it was at this time that a second St Wilfrid's Church was erected on the site of the Saxon building. On Christmas Day 1132, monks from York worshipped here whilst they were making a journey to found Fountains Abbey and, traditionally, the people of Ripon follow this ancient route on Boxing Day.

Though little now remains of this Norman church, the magnificent **Cathedral of St Peter and St Wilfrid**, which now stands on the site, is certainly well worth visiting. Begun in the mid-12th century by Archbishop Roger of York, it was originally designed as a simple cruciform church; the west front was added in the mid-13th century and the east choir in 1286. Rebuilding work

Ripon Cathedral

was begun in the 16th century but the disruption of the Dissolution of the Monasteries caused the work to be abandoned and it was only the intervention of James I, in 1640, that saved the building from ruin. Then established as a collegiate church, the diocese of Ripon was formed in 1836 and the church made a cathedral. Often referred to as the Cathedral of the Dales, the building, though one of the tallest cathedrals in England, is also the smallest.

Throughout the Middle Ages, the town prospered: its market charter had been granted by King Alfred in the 9th century and, at one time, Ripon produced more woollen cloth than Halifax and Leeds. The collapse of the woollen industry saw a rise in spur manufacture in the 16th century and their fame was such that Ripon spurs were referred to in the old proverb: 'As true steel as a Ripon rowel.' As well as having three rivers, Ripon too had a canal. Built between 1767 and 1773 to improve the navigation of the River Ure, John Smeaton, builder of the Eddystone Lighthouse, was the designer. However, by 1820 the company running the canal had fallen into debt and it was little used after that time.

Fortunately for today's visitor, the Industrial Revolution, and all its associated implications, by-passed Ripon and it was not until the early 20th century that the town flourished, though briefly, as a spa. However, many ancient customs and festivals have survived down the centuries and perhaps the most famous is the sounding of the "Wakeman's Horn" each night at 21:00 in the market place. Dating back to the 9th century, the Wakeman was originally appointed to patrol the town after the nightly curfew had been blown and, in many ways, this was the first form of security patrol. The Wakeman was selected each year from the town's 12 aldermen and those choosing not to take office were fined heavily. Today, this old custom is revived in the Mayor-making Ceremony when the elected mayor shows great reluctance to take office and hides from his colleagues. As might be expected, any walk around this ancient town reveals, in its buildings, its interesting and varied past. The heart of the town is the **Market Place** and here stands a tall obelisk which was erected in 1702 to replace the market cross. Restored in 1781, at its summit are a horn and a rowel spur, symbolizing Ripon's crafts and customs. Situated at the edge of the square are the 14th century Wakeman's House and the attractive Georgian Town Hall. The **Spa Baths** building, opened in 1905 by the Princess of Battenberg, is a reminder of Ripon's attempt to become a fashionable spa resort. With no spring of its own, the town had to pipe in sulphur mineral water from Aldfield near Fountains Abbey. However, the scheme failed, though the baths building, which now houses the city's swimming pool, is a fine example of art nouveau architecture and the **Spa Gardens** are still a pleasant place for a stroll. Near to the cathedral is Ripon's old **Courthouse** that was built in 1830 on the site of an earlier 17th-century Common Hall, used for the Quarter Sessions and the Court Military. Adjacent to this fine Georgian courthouse is a Tudor building that was part of the Archbishop of York's summer palace.

STUDLEY ROGER   MAP 10 REF M8
1 mile SW of Ripon off the B6265

The magnificent **Studley Royal Gardens** were created in the early 18th century before they were merged with nearby Fountains Abbey in 1768. Started by John Aislabie, the disgraced Chancellor of the Exchequer and founder of the South Sea Company that spectacularly burst its bubble in 1720, the landscaping took some 14 years. It then took a further 10 years to complete the construction of the buildings and follies found within the gardens. With a network of paths and the River Skell flowing through the grounds, it is well worth exploring these superb gardens.

A National Trust property, like the adjoining gardens, **Fountains Abbey** is the pride of all the ecclesiastical ruins in Yorkshire and it is also designated as a World Heritage Site. The abbey was one of the wealthiest of the Cistercian houses and is arguably one of the most beautiful, as well as the largest, in Britain. Founded in 1132, with the help of Archbishop Thurstan of York, the first buildings housed just 12 monks of the order and, over the centuries its size increased,

Fountains Abbey

even spreading across the River Skell itself. The abbey reached its peak in the 15th century with the grandiose designs of Abbot Marmaduke Huby, whose beautiful tower still stands as a reminder of just how rich and powerful Fountains became. In fact, the abbey was run on such businesslike lines that, at its height, as well as owning extensive lands throughout Yorkshire, it had an income of about a thousand pounds a year, then a very substantial sum indeed.

It is commonly thought that one of the abbey's friars, renowned for his strength and skill as an archer, challenged Robin Hood to a sword fight. Forced to concede, the friar joined the Merry Men of Sherwood and became known as Friar Tuck.

The Dissolution hit the abbey, as it did all the powerful religious houses. The abbot was hanged, the monks scattered, and its treasures taken off or destroyed. The stonework, however, was left largely intact, possibly due to its remote location. In 1579, Sir Stephen Proctor pulled down some out-buildings, in order to construct Fountains Hall, which still stands in the abbey's grounds.

BOROUGHBRIDGE   MAP 10 REF N8
6 miles SE of Ripon off the A168

This attractive and historic town dates from the reign of William the Conqueror though it was once on a main thoroughfare used by both the Celts of Brigantia and, later, the Romans. The bridge over the River Ure, from which the village takes its name, was built in 1562 and it formed part of an important road link between Edinburgh and London. Busy throughout the coaching days with traffic passing from the West Riding of Yorkshire to the North, Boroughbridge has now returned to its former unassuming role of a wayside village with a bypass that takes most of the 20th century traffic from its streets. The great **Devil's Arrows**, three massive Bronze Age monoliths, stand like guardians close to the new road and form Yorkshire's most famous ancient monument: thought to date from about 2000 BC, the tallest is 30 feet high. The monoliths stand in a line running north-south and are fashioned from millstone grit which has been seriously fluted by weathering. A local legend, however, attributes the great stones to the Devil suggesting that they were, actually, crossbow bolts that he fired at nearby Aldborough which, at the time, was a Christian settlement.

HARROGATE   MAP 10 REF M8
11 miles S of Ripon on the A61

One of England's most attractive towns and a frequent winner of Britain in Bloom, Harrogate features acres of gardens that offer an array of colour throughout the year, open spaces, and broad tree lined boulevards. However, until the 17th century Harrogate - or Haregate as it was then called - was just a collection of cottages close to the thriving market town of Knaresborough. It was William Slingsby, of Bilton Hall near Knaresborough, who, whilst out walking his dog, discovered a spring bubbling up out of the rock that was to found the fortunes of the town. Tasting the waters, Slingsby found them to be similar to those he had tasted at the fashionable wells of Spaw, in Belgium. Expert opinion was sought and, in 1596, Dr Timothy Bright confirmed the spring to be a chalybeate well and the waters to have medicinal powers - curing a wide variety of illness and ailments from gout to vertigo.

Slingsby's well became known as **Tewit Well**, after the local name for peewits, and it can still be seen today, covered by a dome on pillars. Other wells were also found in the area, St John's Well in 1631 and the Old Sulphur Well which went on to become the most famous of Harrogate's springs. Though this spring had been known, locally, for years it was not until 1656 that this sulphurous smelling well, nicknamed the "Stinking Spaw", began to attract attention.

During the mid-17th century bathing in the heated sulphurous waters became fashionable as well as a cure for various ailments and lodging houses were built around the sulphur well in Low Harrogate. Bathing took place in the evening and, each morning, the patients would drink a glass of the water with their breakfasts. The cupola seen over the well was erected in 1804. As well as a spa, Harrogate developed into a centre for shopping for the well-to-do and the many old fashioned shops are typified by **Montpellier Parade**, a crescent of shops surrounded by trees and flowerbeds. Another attractive aspect of the town is **The**

Royal Baths Assembly Rooms

Stray, which is unique to Harrogate and virtually encircles the town centre. The 200 acres of open space are protected by ancient law to ensure that the residents of, and visitors to, the town always have access for sports, events, and walking. The spacious lawns are at their most picturesque during the spring when edged with crocus and daffodils. Originally part of the Forest of Knaresborough the land was, fortunately, not enclosed under the 1770 Act of Parliament. The large gritstone pillar, beside The Stray, marks the boundary of the Leeds and Ripon turnpike. Whilst, on The Stray stands the **Commemorative Oak Tree**, planted in 1902 by Samson Fox to commemorate the ox roasting that took place here as part of the celebrations for Queen Victoria's Jubilee in 1887 and the end of the Boer War in 1902. The **Royal Pump Room Museum** was built in 1842 to enclose the Old Sulphur Well and this major watering place for spa visitors has been painstakingly restored to illustrate all the aspects of Harrogate's history. Beneath the building the sulphur water still rises to the surface and can be sampled. In 1948, the Northern Horticultural Society set up their headquarters at **Harlow Carr Botanical Gardens**, just over a mile from the town centre. Now covering some 68 acres, the gardens feature all manner of plants in a wide variety of landscapes which allows members of the public to see how they perform in the unsympathetic conditions of North England. The society, as well as having their study centre here, has also opened a fascinating Museum of Gardening.

KNARESBOROUGH

Map 10 ref M8

4 miles E of Harrogate on the A59

This ancient town of pantiled cottages and Georgian houses is precariously balanced on a hillside by the River Nidd. There are many unusual and attractive features here that include a maze of steep stepped narrow streets leading down to the river and numerous alleyways. In addition to boating on the river, there are many enjoyable riverside walks. The town is dominated by the ruins of **Knaresborough Castle**, built high on a crag overlooking the River Nidd by Serlo de Burgh, who had fought alongside William the Conqueror at Hastings. Throughout the Middle Ages, the castle was a favourite with the court and it was to Knaresborough that the murderers of Thomas à Becket fled in 1170.

Also in the town is the **Old Courthouse Museum** which tells the history of the town and houses a rare Tudor Courtroom. The nearby **Bebra Gardens** are named after Knaresborough's twin town in Germany; its attractive flower beds are complemented by luxurious lawns and a paddling pool. Visitors should also keep an eye out for the oldest chemists' shop in England. which dates back to 1720. However, Knaresborough is probably best known for **Mother Shipton's Cave**, the birthplace of the famous prophetess, and for its **Petrifying Well** which provides a constant source of curiosity to the visitor. Nearby **Plumpton Rocks**, between Knaresborough and Spofforth, is an idyllic lake surrounded by dramatic millstone grit rocks and woodland paths that was laid out in the 18th century. It has been declared a garden of special historic interest by English Heritage and is open every weekend and daily during July and August.

SPOFFORTH

Map 10 ref M8

4 miles S of Knaresborough on the A661

This ancient village, situated on the tiny River Crimple, is home to the splendid Palladian mansion, **Stockeld Park**, built between 1758 and 1763 by Paine. Containing some excellent furniture and a fine picture collection, the house is surrounded by extensive parkland which offers garden walks. Though privately owned, the house is open by appointment.

Spofforth Castle is another place of note, an historic building whose sight stirs the imagination, despite its ruined state. The powerful Percy family originally built the castle here in the 16th century to replace the manor house which had been repeatedly laid to waste. The castle itself is now a crumbling ruin after it too was destroyed during the Civil War. Among the many events which took place here it is said to have been the birthplace of Harry Hotspur. The ruins are now in the care of English Heritage.

WEST YORKSHIRE

KEIGHLEY
MAP 10 REF L9

15 miles NW of Leeds off the A650

Lying at the junction of the Rivers Worth and Aire, this bustling textile and engineering town, despite its modern redevelopment, still retains a strangely nostalgic air of the Victorian Industrial Revolution. It was that era of rapid growth that created the town seen today, beginning at **Low Mill** in 1780, when cotton spinning on a factory scale was first introduced. Reminders of hardship endured by the many factory workers of that time can be seen in the labyrinth of ginnels and terraces which lie amid the many elaborately decorated mills. There are delightful carvings and on one early mill chimney are three heads, one wearing a top hat; in contrast is the classical French-styled **Dalton Mill** in Dalton Lane with its ornate viewing gallery. The centre of Keighley is dominated by impressive Victorian civic buildings and a beautifully set out covered shopping precinct, where the statue of legendary local giant, Rombald, stands. The parish church, also in the centre, is famous as the site where Patrick Brontë often officiated at marriages. The graveyard contains 15th-century headstones, as well as a crude cross made from four carved heads which is believed to be Saxon in origin. Above the town, by way of escaping the industrial past, one might enjoy a walk in **Park Woods**, taking the cobbled path to **Thwaites Brow**, which affords magnificent views of the town below.

Outside the town centre is **Cliffe Castle** which, despite its deceptive name, is in fact a grand late 19th-century mansion complete with a tower, battlements, and parkland, which once belonged to local mill owners, the Butterfields. It now houses **Keighley Museum**, which concentrates on the fascinating local topography and geology of Airedale as well as the history of the town. Also housed in the museum is the handloom, complete with unfinished cloth, that was used by Timmy Feather, the last handloom weaver in England. Part of the building is still furnished and decorated in the lavish style of the 1880s. To the south of Keighley runs the line of the **Keighley and Worth Valley Railway** to Haworth. This restored steam railway line passes through some attractive small villages and some notable stations. Keighley Station itself is Victorian and the 5 miles of railway that runs to Oxenhope is run by volunteers.

The Worth Way is an interesting 5 mile walk from the heart of industrial Keighley to the eastern edge of the Worth Valley at Oxenhope. This landscape has changed little since the time when Mrs Gaskell wrote about the area whilst visiting Charlotte Brontë in 1856.

ILKLEY
MAP 10 REF M9

5 miles NE of Keighley on the A660

Originally an Iron Age settlement, Ilkley was eventually occupied by the Romans, who built a camp here to protect their crossing of the River Wharfe and who also named the town that sprang up Olicana, giving rise to the present name, with the familiar ley (Anglo-Saxon for pasture) added. Behind the medieval church is a grassy mound where a little fort was built and in the town's **Museum** are altars carved in gritstone, dedicated to the Roman gods.

The spring at **White Wells** brought more visitors to the town in the 18th century and a small bath house was built, where genteel and elderly patients were encouraged to take a dip in the heal-

Ilkley Moor

ing waters of the heather spa. The coming of the railways from Leeds and Bradford in the 1860s and 1870s, during a period of growth in the Yorkshire woollen industry, saw the town take on a new role as a fashionable commuter town. Wool manufacturers and their better paid employees came, not only to enjoy the superb amenities, but to build handsome villas. If Bradford and Leeds were where people made their brass, so it was said at the time, then it was usually at Ilkley that it was spent. Even today, Ilkley sports some remarkable and opulent Victorian architecture as proof of this.

Ilkley's patrons and well-to-do citizens gave the town a splendid **Town Hall**, library, **Winter Gardens**, and **King's Hall** and a sense of elegance is still present along **The Grove**. One of the most famous West Yorkshire attractions has to be **Ilkley Moor**, immortalised in the well-known song and a visit is a must. Like any of the Yorkshire moors, Ilkley Moor can look inviting and attractive on a sunny day but ominous and forbidding when the weather takes a turn for the worse. The River Wharfe runs along the edge of the moor and through the town of Ilkley, which is clustered within a narrow section of the valley, in the midst of heather moorland, craggy gritstone, and wooded hillside. Few places in the North can equal Ilkley Moor or, more correctly, Rombalds Moor. The moorland, much of it still covered in heather, is an area of national importance for its archaeology. There is a series of mysteriously marked cup and ring stones dating, like the Swastika stones, from the Bronze Age. Almost in the centre of the moor is an ancient stone circle which was probably a site of some religious importance. Only the keen walker is likely to find these, located high up on the moor, though there is a fine example of a cup and ring stone in the lower part of St Margaret's churchyard in Queen's Road.

Looking at a map of the area, many people's attention is drawn to the curiously named **Cow and Calf Rocks**, which form a striking moor-edge landmark above **Ben Rhydding**. The Cow is a great gritstone outcrop concealing an old quarry, popular with climbers, while the freestanding Calf is a giant boulder.

RIDDLESDEN
MAP 10 REF L9
1 mile N of Keighley off the A629

Parts of **East Riddlesden Hall**, now a National Trust property, date back to Saxon times. The main building, however, was constructed in the 1630s by James Murgatroyd, a wealthy Halifax clothier and merchant. A fine example of a 17th-century manor house, the gabled hall is built of dark stone with mullioned windows, and it retains its original centre hall, superb period fireplaces, oak panelling, and plaster ceilings. The house is furnished in Jacobean style. East Riddlesden Hall also has one of the largest and most impressive timber framed barns in the North of England which now houses a collection of farm waggons and agricultural equipment.

HAWORTH
MAP 10 REF L9
3 miles S of Keighley off the A6033

The Keighley and Worth Valley Railway also has a station in this most popular of Yorkshire tourist spots. Once a bleak, moorland town in a dramatic setting that fired the romantic imaginations of the Brontë sisters, Haworth has been transformed into a lively, attractive place, with wonderful tea houses, street theatre, and antique and craft shops, very different to how it must have been in the Brontë's days. It was then a thriving industrial town, squalid amidst the smoke from its chimneys, filled with the noise of the clattering looms, which were rarely still. It is, however, worth exploring the ginnels and back roads off the steeply rising high street, to get a feeling of what the place was like in the days of the Brontës.

The Parsonage, built in 1777, is the focus of most Brontë pilgrimages and is now given over to the **Brontë Parsonage Museum**. The Brontë Society have restored the interior to be as close as possible to the house in which the sisters lived with their father and brother. There are exhibitions and displays of contemporary material, personal belongings, letters, and portraits, as well as a priceless collection of manuscripts, first editions, and memorabilia in the newer extension.

The countryside around Haworth inspires the modern visitor as much as it did the Brontës. This is excellent walking country and it is worth taking a trip via the **Penistone Hill Country Park**, following the rough track by old moorland farms to the **Brontë Falls** and stone footbridge. For the energetic the path eventually leads to the deserted ruins of **Top Withins Farm**, said to have been the inspiration for the setting of Wuthering Heights. **Haworth Moor** is

Brontë Parsonage

a site of special scientific interest. The heather moorland is managed for grouse and there are also several species of birds of prey found here.

OXENHOPE
MAP 10 REF L9

4 miles S of Keighley on the A6033

This village contains over 70 listed buildings, including a **Donkey Bridge**, two milestones, a mounting block, a cowshed, and pigsty. The early farmhouses had narrow mullioned windows which gave the maximum light for weaving and some had a door at first-story level so that the pieces could be taken out. The first mill here was built in 1792 and, during the 19th century, there were up to 20 mills producing worsted. The Railway Children was made here in 1970 using local views and local people and the **Keighley and Worth Valley Railway Museum** can also be found in the village.

HEBDEN BRIDGE
MAP 10 REF L10

12 miles S of Keighley on the A6033

This mill town is characterised by the stepped formation of its houses which were stacked one on top of the other up the steep sides of the Calder valley. There has been a village here for many years centred around the crossing point of the River Calder. When the first bridge was built is not known but as early as the beginning of the 16th century its state of repair was causing concern and, in a style typical of this area of Yorkshire, a stone bridge was erected close by. **The Rochdale Canal**, which flows through the town, was completed in 1798. It was constructed to link the Calder and Hebble Navigation with the Bridgwater and Ashton canals from Lancashire. Used by commercial traffic since 1939, the canal has been repaired and sections of it, including that between Hebden Bridge and Todmorden, are now open to traffic though, now, it consists mainly of pleasure craft.

Hebden Bridge

LEEDS
MAP 10 REF M9
15 miles SE of Keighley off the A61

The economic capital of West Yorkshire, Leeds developed rapidly in the early 19th century as the inland port on the Leeds-Liverpool and Aire and Calder Navigation canals. The **Canal Basin** has been designated a Conservation Area and the once derelict buildings have been redeveloped. The **Museum of Leeds Trail** follows the towpath of the canal through the Kirkstall Valley. At the **Leeds Industrial Museum** at **Armley Mill**, once the largest textile mill in the world, there are displays on the textile, clothing and engineering industries of which Leeds is still a major centre. Leeds city centre offers some of the most beautiful baroque civic architecture in the north of England. Attractions here include the City Museum and Art Gallery, which houses the **Henry Moore Sculpture Gallery. Kirkstall Abbey**, northwest of the city, was built beginning in 1152 by the Cistercians and finished within a generation. It is regarded by many to reflect Cistercian architecture at its most monumental. East of Leeds the visitor will find **Temple Newsam House** set amid 1,200 acres of impressive grounds, with an incomparable collection of antiques within its walls.

BRADFORD
MAP 10 REF M9
5 miles W of Leeds off the A672

The growth that this town experienced during the first 50 years of the 19th century can only be called phenomenal: in 1801 Bradford was a quiet market town of 13,000 inhabitants; by 1830 the population had grown to 103,000. The cause of this explosion? The introduction of the textile industry factory system to the town. By the end of the 19th century, Bradford was handling 90 per cent of the world's wool trade. The **Industrial Museum** tells the story of textile manufacturing here, while the **Colour Museum** shows how colour was and is used in textiles and printing. The prosperity this brought to the town can be seen in the grand Victorian buildings which the wealthy manufacturers had constructed from the local Pennine stone. One area well worth exploring is **Little Germany**, the historic wool merchants' quarter where ornate warehouses were built. Many of the mills, too, were constructed in elaborate style and some resemble Italian palaces rather than places of hard graft. All in all, today Bradford has over 4,000 buildings listed for their architectural or historical importance. One of these is **Lister's Mill**, its huge ornate chimney dominating the city skyline.

The fact that Bradford has a **Cathedral** is another indication of its historical importance. The first evidence of worship on the site comes from the remains of a Saxon preaching cross. Today the cathedral contains many items of interest, including beautiful stained glass windows, some of which were designed by William Morris. Today's Bradford is proud of its mixed cultural influences. It keeps pace with the times with state of the art attractions such as the **National Museum of Film, Photography and Television**, home of Britain's only permanent IMAX screen, which stands five storeys high.

HALIFAX
MAP 10 REF L10
7 miles W of Leeds off the A646

Halifax boasts one of Yorkshire's most impressive examples of municipal architecture, the large and beautiful **Piece Hall**. It possesses a large quadrangle where regular markets are held, surrounded by colonnades and balconies, behind which is a host of interesting shops. There is also an art gallery with a varied programme of contemporary exhibitions and workshops. The **Town Hall** is another notable building, designed by Sir Charles Barry, who also designed the Houses of Parliament. Among Halifax's other attractions are **The Calderdale Industrial Museum**, housing working looms and mill machinery, the **Horses at Work Museum**, and **Eureka!**, a fantastic hands-on science museum. **Shibden Hall and Park**, about two miles outside of town, lies in a valley on the outskirts of town. The Hall is set in 90 acres of parkland. This distinctive timber framed house dates from 1420 and is furnished deliberately to reflect various periods of its history.

WAKEFIELD   MAP 10 REF M10
8 miles SE of Leeds off the M1/A638

This is one of the oldest towns in Yorkshire and has been the focal point for the surrounding area from as far back as Anglo-Saxon times. Standing on a hill guarding an important crossing of the River Calder, its defensive position has always been important and, indeed, it was the Battle of Wakefield, in 1460, when the Duke of York was defeated, which gave rise to the song "The Grand Old Duke of York". The city centre is dominated by its 13th century **Cathedral** with its 247 foot spire - the highest in Yorkshire. Wakefield is also known for its cycle of medieval miracle plays, which explore Old and New Testament stories in vivid language. The cycle is performed in front of the cathedral as part of the city's annual festival.

There are three main streets in the city: Westgate, Northgate, and Kirkgate, which still follow their original medieval route. The tiny **Chantry Chapel**, on Chantry Bridge, dates from the mid 14th century and is the best of only four such examples of bridge chapels in England. It was believed to have been built by Edward IV to commemorate the brutal murder of his brother Edmund. **Wakefield Museum**, located in an 1820s building in Wood Street, houses collections on the history and archaeology of the city and its people from prehistoric times to the present day. Other noteworthy museums in the town include the **Stephen G Beaumont**, which has an unusual collection of medical memorabilia, and the **Yorkshire Mining Museum**.

SOUTH YORKSHIRE AND THE YORKSHIRE PEAKS

SHEFFIELD   MAP 10 REF M11
30 miles S of Leeds on the A61

There is nowhere in the world where some item made of Sheffield steel will not be found, and such a heritage has made a deep mark indeed. The production of silverware products became so important that, in 1773, the city was granted its own Assay Office and hallmark, still in use today. It was the development of the crucible steel process, invented by Benjamin Huntsman, that secured the city's world-wide reputation. The oldest surviving crucible furnace in the world is preserved as part of the city's **Abbeydale Industrial Hamlet**, a delightful restored industrial complex featuring a water-driven tile forge and grinding wheel, handsmiths' forges, workshops, warehouses, worker's cottage, foreman's cottage and counting house.

Sheffield is not often credited with the fact that it contains more parkland within its boundaries than any other European city apart from Glasgow. At the city's **Weston Park**, visitors will also find the impressive **City Museum**. On the south side of town, **Graves Park** is a massive expanse of greenery with footpaths and a rare breeds farm. Visitors to this part of town should also take the opportunity to see the timber-framed Tudor yeoman's house known as Bishop's House. Built on high ground commanding a panoramic view over Sheffield, it boasts fine examples of 17th century oak panelling and plasterwork, original furnishings, displays of Sheffield during Tudor and Stuart times, and a programme of changing exhibitions.

Most of the city centre buildings were constructed during the prosperous Victorian age. The Grade I listed **Town Hall**, opened by Queen Victoria herself in 1897, has a magnificent entrance hall and a sculpted frieze which represents all of Sheffield's industries. Other city centre attractions worthy of note are the **Ruskin Gallery**, **Graves Art Gallery** (within the main library building), **Centre for Popular Music** with its distinctive "tea kettles" of Sheffield steel, and the magnificent **Lyceum** and **Crucible** theatres. Ruskin, an old Sheffielder himself, would no doubt find it fitting that though Sheffield has had to perforce leave its grimy industrial past behind, it has emerged triumphant.

PENISTONE
MAP 10 REF M10
12 miles N of Sheffield off the A616

Built as a farmhouse in 1720, **Cubley Hall** is an outstanding hotel, restaurant and Free House. Open all day every day, it is surrounded by its own magnificent grounds. Many original features remain in this splendid establishment. In 1983 the Hall, after many years of lying semi-derelict, was transformed sympathetically to complement and enhance the unique original

architectural features, mosaic floors, stained glass, old oak panelling and ornate plaster ceilings, while incorporating the most modern facilities and amenities expected in a country house hotel. In 1990

Cubley Hall, Mortimer Road, Penistone, Sheffield, South Yorkshire S36 9DF Tel: 01226 766086 Fax: 01226 767335

the massive oak beamed, hewn stone barn was converted into a characterful and impressive restaurant. The professional staff and team of talented chefs create modern cuisine to satisfy the most discerning diners. The 12 en suite guest bedrooms are top of the range for comfort, luxury and style. A relaxed and informal atmosphere ensures that guests feel at home. The pub offers traditional hand-pulled beers and a good range of wines and spirits.

BRADFIELD
MAP 10 REF M11
6 miles NW of Sheffield off the B6077

Situated some 860 feet up, this village lies in a sheltered fold of the high moorland above the Loxley valley. Just a chapel of ease until 1868, the **Church of St Nicholas** is one of the grandest village churches in the Peak District. Its size and elaborate design, with castellations, pinnacles and gargoyles, was the work of the monks at nearby Ecclesfield Priory. Most of the building dates from the late 15th century, though the tower is 14th century and some Norman fragments remain. Overlooking the churchyard is the **Watch House**, an oddly shaped Gothic house built in 1745. Its position, and name, stem from the days of body snatchers, as it was built to shelter the graveyard lookout. **Bradfield Dale** is perhaps the least well known of the Peak District dales. This is probably because of its remote location. The Loxley Valley, though not as grand as the neighbouring Derwent Valley, it definitely has its own charm. At the head of the Dale is Boot's Folly. Seemingly of great age, this 50 foot tower was only built in the 1920s. Charles Boot, its builder, used old stones and windows from nearby demolished buildings.

DONCASTER
MAP 11 REF M10
7 miles NE of Sheffield off the A635

An important Roman town, known as Danum, this site was chosen because it was the lowest crossing point on the River Don. Budding archaeologists may be interested to know that there is a well-preserved piece of Roman road just west of Ardwick le Street, and that many of the churches in the area have Saxon connections.

Doncaster and its surrounding districts have strong roots in several nonconformist religions - the **Quaker Meeting House** at Warmsworth was one of the earliest in the area. The town also boasts some impressive public buildings, including the **Mansion House**, built in 1748 and designed by James Paine, the only civic mansion house outside London and York. At the **Doncaster Museum and Art Gallery** there are impressive collections of archaeology, regional natural history, geology, local history, European fine art, costumes, militaria and changing special exhibitions. Meanwhile, at the **Museum of South Yorkshire Life** at Cusworth Hall, cedar and strawberry trees, larches, cypress, fig, yew and bamboo all grow in the pleasure gardens of this imposing mansion, while the Hall sports fine ornamental doors, windows and Palladian pavilions provide a fine example of early Georgian architecture. The interior is adorned with elaborate plasterwork, panelling and carved marble chimney pieces.

Built in 1652, **The Boat Inn** at Lower Sprotbrough earned its place in history by being the house in which Sir Walter Scott wrote his novel Ivanhoe. An old coaching house, it is in magnificent condition, full of interest to any visitor, and was for many years the family seat of the Copley family - their coat of arms can be seen clearly over one of the windows. Set around a courtyard, the inn features flagstone floors, a variety of bygone memorabilia and a selection of fine prints. The speciality of the excellent restaurant (booking advised) is fresh fish of all kinds and there is a good list of wines to accompany your meal. The bar attracts a strong local

The Boat Inn, Lower Sprotbrough, Doncaster, South Yorkshire DN5 7NB Tel: 01302 857188 Fax: 01302 310149

trade and offers a selection of hand-pulled beers and lagers. Only three miles from Doncaster, the inn is open lunch and evenings weekdays and all day Saturday and Sunday. It is splendidly situated for access to the racecourse, nature parks and local historic buildings. Narrowboat cruises on the canal operate from a base only yards from the inn's door.

BARNSLEY
MAP 10 REF M10

12 miles N of Sheffield on the A61

It was the wealth of coal that shaped the town and its mines were of vital importance to the iron and steelworks of its neighbours. This industrial town was founded in Saxon times and its markets, which date back many years, are still busy and popular. **Cannon Hall**, built in the 17th century, was remodelled in the 18th century by John Carr of York and its great parkland is a particular favourite with children. The Hall is now a museum and the rooms are furnished in a variety of styles from Jacobean to Victorian. There is an interesting glassware collection which, amongst other things, contains such oddities as glass rolling pins and walking sticks. The Regimental Museum of the 13th and 18th Royal Hussars is also here and their part in the Charge of the Light Brigade in 1854 is recalled in a series of stirring displays. Art lovers will appreciate the **Cooper Gallery**, which, as well as hosting a lively programme of contemporary exhibitions also houses a fine collection of British watercolours. Visitors to the town should also make a point of trying the famous local delicacy, the Barnsley Chop, a double sided lamb steak.

9 Northumberland and Durham

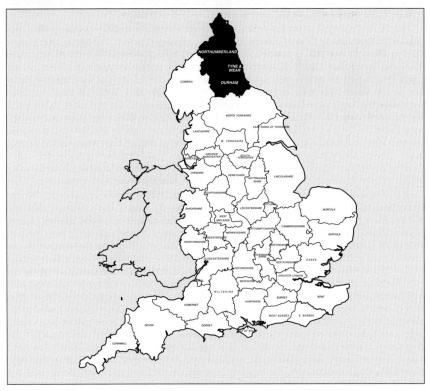

INTRODUCTION

No visit to County Durham is complete without taking in the marvellous city of Durham, known as the finest example of early Norman architecture in the nation. From the time of the Conquest, County Durham was unique - a palatinate ruled by its Prince Bishops who, in addition to being spiritual leaders, also had powers equal to those exercised by the King in the rest of the country. The Bishops were great landowners and their "bishopric" extended beyond the present day county of Durham to include parts of North Yorkshire and Northumberland. By the 17th century the golden period of the Prince Bishops was well into decline. With a few exceptions the Bishops came increasingly under criticism for their feudal powers and lifestyle. They held on to their remaining power into the 19th century but, in 1936, on the death of Van Mildert, the founder of Durham University, the Palatinate's rights and privileges were vested in the crown. However, it was not until the Courts Act of 1971 that the Palatinate Courts were finally abolished and a unique chapter in English history came to an end.

Durham county is largely rural with most of the coal mining and steel making industries either ended or located nearer the coast, leaving a landscape of pleasant open views across woodland and fields. The Dales make up almost a third of the county and offer some of the finest scenery. The high heather moorlands are dissected by the Rivers Derwent, Tees and Wear, with each valley having its own characteristics. Throughout the Dales the many attractive stone-built villages offer good bases for exploring the area. There are many opportunities for walking and other outdoor activities in the impressive scenery. Less well known than much of the Pennines, the area is unspoilt and uncrowded.

The River Tyne, one of the loveliest rivers of England's north country, is essentially a river of both the Pennines and the Cheviot Hills, and has a split personality. The South Tyne rises on the shoulders of Cross Fell, in Cumbria, before winding its way northwards through Alston and the Upper Tyne valley. From here it begins its long journey east to Newcastle and the coast. The North Tyne begins life as tiny moorland burns, high up on the fell-sides of the Cheviots, before joining the South Tyne west of Hexham to become a single river. Tynedale itself - or more accurately, the South Tyne Valley - forms a great natural pass across the Pennines. To the north lies the Northumberland National Park; to the south is Allendale, one of the most spectacularly beautiful of the Tyne's tributaries. The main valley carries river, railway and the A69 trunk-road between Newcastle and Carlisle, but more impressive than any of these is the north of England's greatest single man-made monument - Hadrian's Wall. Discovering the wall is still a thrilling experience which inspires a sense of wonder at being at the northern boundary of a mighty empire which stretched from Egypt and North Africa to these cool, green hills.

The 398 square miles of the Northumberland National Park occupy much of central Northumberland, stretching from Tynedale to the Scottish Border. This is the least populated, and perhaps the least well known, of Britain's 11 National Parks, an area of remote, wild and hauntingly beautiful, upland countryside. The most famous feature of these uplands is The Cheviots, a range of magnificent, round-topped, grass-covered hills, which rise to the summit of The Cheviot itself at 815 metres. Quiet valleys radiate from the central hills through which streams sparkle and scattered woods of oak, birch and rowan contrast with the bare summits of the hills. To the south of the main Cheviot massif lie two other impressive hill-ranges, the Simonside and Harbottle hills, both consisting largely of sandstone, which rise to gentle, flat-topped summits on which there are large areas of heather moorland and forest. This is an area linked to the activities of prehistoric man and, for anyone with time, patience, a good pair of boots and a large-scale map, there are stone circles, standing stones and cup-and-ring marked rocks to be discovered, together with the remains of Iron Age and Roman settlements. To the east lies a region of great forests - Redesdale Forest, Kielder Forest and the other associated areas that form the massive Border Forest Park, the largest area of man-made forest in Britain. If that were not enough, there is also the vast expanse of Wark Forest to the south. Kielder Water is the largest man-made lake in northern Europe, covering 2,684 acres with 27 miles of shoreline and containing 44,000 billion gallons of water which serve the domestic and industrial needs of Tyneside.

Since the days of the Romans, Northumberland has been a border territory separating the land of the Britons from the land of the Picts and for over 400 years, from the time of Edward I until the Union of Parliaments in 1707, it was the scene of one of the longest running border conflicts the world has ever known. The countryside bears the scars of this turbulent past and battlefields, castles and fortified buildings remain as witness to the struggles. Now bisected by the A1, and served by other major roads and railways, the open and unspoilt surroundings are readily accessible to visitors from the north and south. The coastal plain, between the North Sea and the Cheviot Hills, shows a largely man-made landscape of arable fields and planted woodland. The coast itself offers superb sea fishing and other water sports and there are many enjoyable walks that take in the spectacular scenery. Travelling inland provides a totally different experience with uncrowded roads leading to idyllic villages and there are many visitor attractions and beauty spots.

The coastline between Berwick and Bamburgh is as fine as that to the immediate south, though with much more extensive sandbanks but one feature above all others dominates -

Lindisfarne, or Holy Island. You can get across only at low tide along the three-mile long causeway from Beal. Tide tables are published locally and are displayed at each end of the road and there are refuges part way for those who fail to time it correctly! Facsimiles of the richly decorated Lindisfarne Gospels (the originals being in the British Museum in London) are kept on Lindisfarne and can be seen in the 12th-century parish church on the island. Where the Rivers Tyne and Wear come down from the Pennines, crossing the narrow coastal plain to meet the North Sea, densely populated towns have grown around their broad estuaries over the centuries; towns that have relied on the two great rivers for the transport of goods allowing their industries, particularly coal-mining and shipbuilding, to flourish. This great industrial conurbation, now combined into the Metropolitan County of Tyne and Wear, has a rich heritage of its own and some surprises for visitors to the area.

COUNTY DURHAM

DURHAM
15 miles S of Newcastle off the A167

MAP 12 REF M5

If you arrive in Durham by train across the elevated brick viaduct above the town, there is a magnificent view of Durham city, dominated by the mighty **Durham Cathedral**. No visit to Durham is complete without time spent at this magnificent shrine of Christianity, third only to Canterbury and York in ecclesiastical significance but perhaps even excelling them in architectural splendour. It is acknowledged to be the finest and grandest example of early Norman architecture in the kingdom. This was the cathedral of the powerful and wealthy Prince Bishops of Durham who once held almost regal power in their territories - power vested in them by King William II. They could administer civil and criminal law; they had the power of pardon and the right to mint their own money, create baronetcies, and give market charters; they could even raise their own army! It is little wonder that the County Council now proudly present their county to visitors as "The Land of the Prince Bishops". Even more significantly, in the great Cathedral are the tombs of two of the greatest figures of the early Christian church in England: the remarkable St Cuthbert, shepherd saint of Northumbria, and the Venerable Bede, saint, scholar and Britain's first and pre-eminent historian. The cathedral owes its origin to a Saxon Benedictine community who, in AD995, fled to this rocky peninsula which is surrounded by the serpentine River Wear, to hide the body of their beloved St Cuthbert in a little church made from the boughs of trees. The real

Durham Cathedral

founder of the cathedral, however, was a Norman, William de St Carileph, the Bishop of Durham from 1081 to 1096, who brought to the small Saxon church at Durham not only holy relics but also a group of scholars from Monkwearmouth and Jarrow. William was exiled to Normandy in 1088, having been accused of plotting against William Rufus, but returned in 1091 determined to replace the little Saxon church with a building of the scale and style of the splendid new churches being built in France at that time. On 10th August 1093 the foundation stones were laid, a witness being King Malcolm III of Scotland, famed as the soldier who conquered and slew Macbeth.

The main part of the great building was erected in a mere 40 years, but over ensuing centuries each generation has added magnificent work or superb detail of its own, such as the **Episcopal Throne**, said to be the highest in Christendom. Yet the impregnable fortress-like quality of the cathedral, with its famous carved columns, retains a visual splendour that makes it a very special place indeed. Even so, nothing is more moving than the simple fragments of carved wood which survive from St Cuthbert's coffin, made for the saint's body in AD698 and carried around a hostile North of England for almost 300 years by his devoted followers before being laid to rest in the mighty cathedral. The fragments are now kept in the **Cathedral Treasury Museum** with examples of the Prince Bishops' own silver coins.

Durham Castle, sharing the same rocky peninsula and standing close to the cathedral, was founded in 1072 and belonged to the Prince Bishops. Such was the impregnability of the site that Durham was one of the few major towns in Northumbria that was never captured by the Scots. Among the castle's most impressive features are the Chapel, dating from 1080, and the **Great Hall**, which was built in the middle of the 13th century. Though much of it was restored in Victorian times, it remains a remarkable building in its own right. The Castle is used as a hall of residence for the students of Durham University and so is only open to the public at limited times. But student and visitors should beware - the castle is reputedly haunted by no less than three ghosts. Lady Muriel takes the form of the top half of a woman in 19th-century dress. She glides along the Norman Gallery, leaving the scent of apple blossom in her wake. A second spirit is linked to the Castle's Black Staircase - the scene of the tragic death of University tutor Frederick Copeman in 1880, who met his death by falling over the banister to the floor below. A further apparition from a much earlier age takes the form of an armed Saxon warrior with fierce glowing eyes.

The rest of the city reflects the long history of the castle and cathedral it served, including generations of pilgrims who had to be fed and watered - arguably Britain's first tourists! There are winding streets, such as Fishergate and Silver Street, whose names and appearance reveal their medieval origin, an ancient Market Place, elegant Georgian houses, particularly around Palace Green, quiet courts and alleyways. Yet, for all its industrial development in the 19th and 20th centuries, there is a sense of green-ness and open space, never more evident than in the view across the town from the University or in the fine park behind the railway station. A favourite and famous walk past castle and cathedral follows the footpaths which run through the woodlands on each bank of the River Wear, around the great loop. You can begin either at Framwellgate Bridge or Elvet Bridge. The path along the outside of the loop goes past The **Old Fulling Mill**, which now houses an archaeological museum containing material from excavations in and around the city. If walking isn't to your taste you can take a rowing-boat or a motor launch along the river from Elvet Bridge.

A very different museum but outstanding in a quite different way, is the **Durham University Oriental Museum**, a collection of oriental art of international importance with material from Ancient Egypt, Tibet, India and China. The museum is located off Elvet Hill Road. The university also runs the 18-acre **Botanic Gardens** on Hollingworth Lane (off the A1050), one of the newest in England. It has a large collection of North American trees, including junior-sized Giant Redwoods, a series of small 'gardens-within-gardens' and walks through mature woodland. Two display greenhouses feature cacti and succulents and a tropical 'jungle'. The gardens are open 365 days a year.

PETERLEE
Map 12 ref N5

10 miles E of Durham on the A1086

Natural beauty of an exceptional kind is to be found near Peterlee, a purpose-built and planned 'New Town', created during the 1950s out of a huddle of mining villages around Easington. It was named in honour of an outstanding Durham miner and councillor, Peter Lee, who fought all his life for the well-being of the local community. **Castle Eden Dene Nature Reserve**, on the south side of the town, is of national importance, being one of the largest woodlands in the northeast which has not been planted or extensively altered by man. It covers 500 acres and lies in a steep-sided valley on magnesian limestone, with a wide variety of native trees and shrubs, wild flowers, birdlife and butterflies, including many rare insects. There is a network of footpaths to follow, some steep and narrow. The site is managed by the Nature Conservancy Council and it makes sense to begin a visit at the Reserve Centre at Oakerside Dene Lodge on Stanhope Chase, off Durham Way in Peterlee, where leaflets and information are available.

SEAHAM
Map 12 ref N5

10 miles NE of Durham on the B1287

A few miles further up the coast from Peterlee is Seaham, a much earlier 'New Town' that was developed by Lord Byron's family, the Londonderrys. In 1821 they bought what was then the old village of Seaham lock, stock and barrel, for the sole purpose of building a harbour from which to transport coal from the family's collieries to London and the Continent. The present town grew up around the harbour, and although most of the inland collieries have since closed, Seaham is still very much a working town and continues to exploit the reserves beneath the North Sea. All that now remains of the original village is the 900-year old church of St Mary the Virgin, its vicarage, and **Seaham Hall** on the northern outskirts of the town. Now a hotel, this was once the home of the Milbanke family, where in 1815 Lord Byron met and married Anne Isabella Milbanke - a marriage that was to last for only one year. You will find a large clifftop car park near the hotel with steps leading down to the beach, and here the rocky outcrops to the north of the harbour give way to miles of firm sand.

FINCHALE PRIORY
Map 12 ref M5

4 miles N of Durham off the A167

If you want to discover a lovely piece of Durham away from the main tourist trails, make your way by car or bus to **Finchale Priory**, on the River Wear, four miles north of the city on the Leamside-Newton Hall road. This is a 13th-century Benedictine Priory which, amazingly enough, was actually built as a holiday retreat for the monks of Durham. There are extensive remains and they lie close to Cocken Wood Picnic Area, which is linked to the priory by a bridge across the river.

STANLEY
Map 12 ref M5

9 miles NW of Durham on the A693

9 miles northwest of Durham, beyond the town of Stanley, are two industrial heritage sites that everyone will enjoy visiting. **The Tanfield Railway**, which runs between Marley Hill near Stanley, and Sunniside, is the oldest existing railway in the world, being a colliery waggonway, and not a public railway, dating from 1725. It is now a private steam railway with a collection of vintage locomotives, carriages and Britain's oldest steam engine shed which dates back to 1855. There is a Sunday passenger service (steam-worked in summer) and an extension to Causey Arch picnic area was completed in summer 1990. **Causey Arch** is the world's oldest surviving rail bridge, dating from 1727. It is surrounded by attractive woodland through which there are some delightful footpaths. The bridge spans a deep gorge and was used to carry horse-drawn coal wagons from a nearby colliery. The wagons were of a characteristic shape, only to be found

in the northeast and were drawn along waggonways which criss-crossed the landscape. Traces of these, dating back to the 17th, 18th and 19th centuries, can still be identified and many are in use as footpaths.

BEAMISH
Map 12 ref M5
8 miles NW of Durham on the A693

It's not far from Causey Arch to Beamish, the **North of England Open Air Museum** and a footpath means you can walk there. This award-winning museum is situated in 200 acres of landscaped parkland and here life in County Durham a century or so ago has been vividly re-created.

North of England Open Air Museum

BISHOP AUCKLAND
Map 12 ref M6
10 miles S of Durham on the A688

Bishop Auckland, like many similar places in central Durham, is a former mining town, slowly discovering a fresh identity as the new industry replaces the old. But its origins stretch much further back than the mining industry. As its name implies, up until the first part of the 19th century, this was part of the territory of the great Durham Prince Bishops, who controlled what was then a scattering of small villages in the area. Rapid expansion occurred during the 19th century and Bishop Auckland became an important market and administrative centre for the mining region. **Auckland Castle**, still the official residence of the Bishop of Durham, began as a small Norman Manor House but was added to by successive Bishops. The ruins of the 12th-century Banqueting Hall were transformed into a magnificent Private Chapel in 1665. The castle and extensive grounds, which include a Gothic deer shelter, are open to the public.

BRANCEPATH
Map 12 ref M5
4 miles SW of Durham on the A690

Brandon marks the end of a nine and a half mile walk to Bishop Auckland along a converted railway track. The route provides a delightful level walk, rich in historic and natural history interest. It passes close by Brancepeth Castle, a medieval baronial castle restored in the 19th century by a Sunderland banker. Brancepeth is a sheer delight and should not be missed. Most of the original buildings were cleared to make way for Matthew Russell's 'replacement' village in the early-19th century, and his vision has remained largely unspoilt to the present day. Starting at the 18th-century rectory at one end of the village and walking all the way to the 17th-century Quarry Hill House at the other, it is not hard to imagine that you have stepped back in time to Tudor England. Besides the Castle, perhaps the most memorable building here is the magnificent church, which completely escaped 19th-century restoration and features a splendid rood screen, pulpit, ceiling and pews.

BINCHESTER
Map 12 ref M6
9 miles S of Durham off the A689

About one and a half miles north of Bishop Auckland, is **Binchester Roman Fort**. Binchester was known to the Romans as Vinovia and was built about AD80. It was one of a chain of forts built along the main York to Corbridge road, called Dere Street. As well as acting as a military centre controlling the local area, it also provided a stopping-off place for troops and supplies heading towards Hadrian's Wall. On the site you will be able to see the remains of the commanding officers house and the best preserved military baths in Britain with furnaces and hypocaust.

WEARDALE
Map 12 ref M6
NW of Bishop Auckland

Compared with the pristine beauty of Teesdale, with its neat white-walled farmhouses and shimmering waterfalls, Weardale might, at first glance, seem an anticlimax. Yet this could not be further from the truth. Weardale has a character of its own. Perhaps the hills are not as high, the valley may be broader and less dramatic but this is very much a working valley with limestone quarries and the remains of lead and iron mining industries. One of the limestone quarries at Eastgate still supplies the steel works of Teesside by means of long train-loads which trundle along the surviving Weardale railway through Stanhope and Bishop Auckland. It is also a dale rich in human interest, a relatively heavily populated valley, with villages of typical, rugged Durham character.

Between and behind the villages, winding down to the river or up the fellsides, is a rich network of footpaths, making this a marvellous area for walking, away from the better known and more crowded areas of the Pennines. The villages between Cowshill and Stanhope are linked by quiet back lanes, ideal for cycling or for those who wish simply to take time to explore quiet and little-used byways. Whether you travel this road by bus or by car, the austere beauty and grandeur of the Upper Weardale landscape will soon impress you with a magic of its own.

WOLSINGHAM
Map 12 ref L5
15 miles W of Durham on the A689

Wolsingham has strong links with the iron and steel industries, the steelworks in the town having being founded by one Charles Attwood who was one of the great pioneers in the manufacture of steel. The works once cast a variety of anchors and propellers for ships. Wolsingham is also the home of England's oldest agricultural show, held in the market place on the first Saturday in September. Peel Cottage, on Front Street, was the town's first police station, named after Sir Robert Peel, while Whitfield Cottage, dated 1707, was once a packhorse inn. **Tunstall Reservoir**, north of Wolsingham, and reached by a narrow lane or footpath, lies in a particularly interesting valley of ancient oak woods alongside Waskerley Beck. The reservoir was built in the mid-19th century, originally to provide lime-free water for the locomotives of **The Stockton and Darlington Railway** to prevent their boilers from scaling like a domestic kettle. It now forms part of a delightful area to stroll, picnic or go fishing.

HAMSTERLEY FOREST
Map 12 ref L6
3 miles S of Wolsingham off the B6282

A few miles south of Wolsingham lies **Hamsterley Forest**, one of the Forestry Commission's most attractive Forest Parks. This is a huge area - over 5,500 acres - of mature woodland, originally a private sporting estate, now managed for timber production and with 1,100 acres available for recreation with a choice of rides and walks. Today this firmly established area offers a wide range of activities for visitors, such as informal or guided walks, orienteering, horse-riding and cycling (cycles can be hired). There is a Visitor Centre with displays on forestry, wildlife and timber usage, and large, grassy areas make splendid picnic spots. The forest is easily accessible from coach and car parks and visitors are enthusiastically encouraged to enjoy the peace and quiet of this lovely place which is now a Forest Nature Reserve.

FROSTERLEY
MAP 12 REF L5

3 miles W of Wolsingham on the A689

Frosterley, further up the dale, has a name which again has hunting forest links and means 'forest lea'. When the Foresters' Arms was rebuilt in the last century, a hoard of medieval hunters' bows and arrows were found in the foundations of the old buildings. The village is now more famous for its stone, including the celebrated Frosterley marble, a black, heavily-fossilised limestone which in former times was extensively used for rich decorative work and ornamentation on great public and private buildings throughout the north. The Chapel of the Nine Altars in Durham Cathedral makes extensive use of this stone, sometimes called 'Durham Marble'. There are the remains of a huge limestone quarry to the south of the village, the stone having been taken out by rail over the last hundred years for use in the Teesside and Tyneside iron and steel furnaces.

STANHOPE
MAP 12 REF L5

6 miles W of Wolsingham on the A689

Stanhope, undoubtedly the capital of Upper Weardale, is a small town of great character and individuality, which still serves the surrounding villages as an important local centre for shops and supplies. The stone cross in the Market Place is the only reminder of a weekly market held in the town by virtue of a 1421 charter. The market continued until Victorian times. Stanhope enjoyed its greatest period of prosperity in the 18th and 19th centuries when the lead and ironstone industries were at their height. The town's buildings and architecture reflect this. In an attractive rural setting in the centre of the dale, with a choice of local walks, Stanhope, in its quiet way, is becoming a small tourist centre with pleasant shops and cafés. The town itself is well worth exploring on foot and a useful 'walkabout' town trail is available locally or from Information Centres.

The most dominant building in the Market Square is **Stanhope Castle**, a rambling structure complete with mock-Gothic crenelated towers, galleries and battlements. The building is, in fact, an elaborate folly dated 1798 and built on the site of a ruined medieval manor house. In 1875 it was enlarged to contain a private collection of mineral displays and stuffed birds for the entertainment of Victorian grouse-shooting parties. **Stanhope Hall**, above Stanhope Burn Bridge, is generally accepted to be one of the most impressive buildings in Weardale. This huge, fortified manor house was designed to repel Scottish raiders. It was the home of the famous Fetherstonehalgh family who lived there from the mid-12th century until the last male heir was killed at the Battle of Blenheim in 1704. The hall itself is part medieval, part Elizabethan and part Jacobean. The outbuildings included a cornmill, a brew house and cattle yards. The Church of St Thomas, by the Market Square, has a Norman tower and some 13th-century gravecovers to be found by the porch. In the churchyard you'll find a remarkable fossil tree stump which was discovered in 1962 in a local quarry.

One of the most important Bronze Age archaeological finds ever made in Britain was at **Heathery Burn**, a side valley off Stanhope Burn, when, in 1850, quarrymen cut through the floor of a cave to find a huge hoard of bronze and gold ornaments, amber necklaces, pottery, spearheads, animal bones and parts of chariots. The treasures are now kept in the British Museum.

ROOKHOPE
MAP 12 REF L5

3 miles NW of Stanhope off the A689

Rookhope village has a history lost in antiquity, going back at least to Roman times. The history also has its macabre side, as reflected by the discovery some years ago, in a local quarry, of the Redburn Skulls - nine human skulls all carrying terrible teeth marks. Nobody has ever discovered how or why they came to be there, or who or what caused the teeth marks. Rookhope is in one of those hidden North Pennine valleys, mentioned in old Border ballads, which richly repay discovery and exploration. The remains of lead- and iron-mine activity, with some gauntly impressive monuments, now blend into quiet rural beauty. The burn (the Scottish word for a stream is commonly used in this part of Durham) shares the valley with the road which eventually climbs past the **Rookhope Chimney**, part of a lead-smelting mill where poisonous and metallic-rich fumes were refined in long flues, over Redburn Common to Allenheads in Northumberland.

COWSHILL   Map 12 ref L5
10 miles W of Stanhope on the A689

In a hollow between Cowshill and Nenthead in the North Pennines, lies Killhope Mine. The Pennines have been worked for their mineral riches, particularly lead, since Roman times but until the 18th century the industry remained relatively primitive and small scale. The develop-

ment of new techniques of mechanisation in the late-18th and early-19th century allowed the industry to grow until it was second only to coal as a major extractive industry in the region. Now the country's best-preserved lead-mining site and designated an ancient monument, Killhope Mine is the focal point of what is now the remarkable **Killhope Lead Mining Centre**, dominated by the massive overshot water at 33 feet 6 inches high. The wheel used moorland streams, feeding a small reservoir, to provide power for the lead-ore crushing mills, where the lead-ore from the hillside mines was washed and crushed ready for smelting into pigs of lead.

Much of the machinery has been carefully restored by Durham County Council over recent years, together with part of the

Killhope Lead Mining Centre

smelting mill, underground adits, workshops, a smithy, tools and miner's sleeping quarters. The displays form part of a major Visitor Centre interpreting this once great industry and a fascinating museum and trail around the site explain the history and the processes which were used. The centre is located alongside the A689 Stanhope to Alston road, two and a half miles west of Cowshill.6

TEESDALE   Map 12 ref L5
W of Bishop Auckland

People still argue as to whether or not Teesdale is really the last of the Yorkshire Dales or the first of the Durham Dales. Until 1974 much of the River Tees actually formed the Yorkshire-Durham county boundary, with the south bank claimed by the North Riding of Yorkshire and the north bank by County Durham. The designation of much of the dale as part of the new North Pennines Area of Outstanding Natural Beauty resolved the argument. Above any difference of opinion is the fact that Teesdale is an area of quite exceptional, intimate beauty, both natural and man-made, reflecting qualities of both the softer landscape of the Yorkshire Dales to the south, and the austere grandeur of the North Pennine uplands to the north.

MIDDLETON-IN-TEESDALE
MAP 12 REF L6

17 miles W of Bishop Auckland on the B6277

Middleton-in-Teesdale, the capital of Upper Teesdale, is a small, grey town in a dramatically beautiful setting with the Tees running below, while all around is a great backcloth of green hills. The town's links with the lead-mining industry are apparent in the Market Square, where there is a handsome cast-iron fountain which was purchased and placed there in 1875 by the employees of the Quaker-owned London Lead Mining Company. The expense was covered from subscriptions raised for the retirement of the company's local superintendent, Robert Bainbridge. Although the lead-mining industry disappeared over 80 years ago, Middleton still has the strong feeling of being a mining town, with company-built houses, shops, offices and sober chapels to keep the population suitably moral in outlook. The surrounding hills still bear the scars with the remains of old workings, spoil-heaps and deep, and often dangerous, shafts; but the town's agricultural links remain strong, with streets still known as Market Place, Market Cross and Cattle Market. Like Barnard Castle, it is increasing in popularity as a centre from which to explore both Teesdale and the entire North Pennines.

Middleton is also the centre for some magnificent walks in Upper Teesdale. The most famous of these is **The Pennine Way** on its 250-mile route from Derbyshire and Yorkshire to the Cheviots and the Scottish Border. It enters Middleton and Teesdale from the bleak yet beautiful landscapes of Baldersdale and Lunesdale, with their chains of moorland reservoirs and scattered hill-farms. Of course, you don't have to be a Pennine Way walker to enjoy all that Upper Teesdale has to offer. A choice of shorter, circular walks can be devised to take advantage of this scenically magnificent part of the dale; for example from **Bowlees** car park, picnic area and excellent Visitor Centre, about three miles from Middleton travelling up the valley. There are four small waterfalls within this area and an impressive waterfall-concealed cave nearby called Gibson's Cave. The walk continues to **High Force** itself, one of the finest and most impressive waterfalls anywhere in England. Leaflets of recommended walks are to be found in the Visitor Centre at Bowlees. Still following The Pennine Way, the more adventurous can make their way close by Cronkley Scar, Falcon Clints and Widdybank Fell, an internationally important nature reserve famous for Spring Gentians, to where **Cauldron Spout**, described as England's largest cascade, roars down from **Cow Green Reservoir.** Beyond here The Pennine Way crosses bleak country into Cumbria, a route only to be attempted in clear weather by well-equipped walkers using large-scale maps. Not far from the path lie military ranges with restricted access. You can, however, drive to the car park and picnic-site at Cow Green via the back road from Langdon Beck.

BARNARD CASTLE
MAP 12 REF L6

14 miles SW of Bishop Auckland on the A688

Barnard Castle is a natural focal point for any exploration of the central parts of Teesdale. This old market town owes its existence to the **Castle** founded in 1112 by Bernard, son of Guy de Baliol, one of the knights who fought alongside William the Conqueror. The ruins, with the massive, round keep overlooking the town's narrow, arched bridge over the Tees, have a gaunt beauty. The castle has experienced its share of incident, perhaps most spectacularly during the ill-fated Catholic Rising of the North in 1569. At that time it was besieged by rebel forces for 11 days and, although it was finally forced to capitulate, this gave sufficient time for Queen Elizabeth's army, under the Earl of Sussex, to speed to York and force the rebels to flee. Many were executed and those leading families who had supported the plans to replace Elizabeth with Mary Queen of Scots lost their lands. The town has an especially rich architectural heritage, with handsome houses, cottages, shops and inns dating from the 16th to the 19th centuries. There is an impressive market cross and an old town hall contained within an unusual octago-

Barnard Castle

nal structure, built in 1747, the area under the veranda having been used as a butter-market and the upstairs variously as a lock-up or courthouse. You can still see the bullet holes in the weather-vane, resulting from a wager by two local men in 1804, shooting from outside the Turk's Head, 100 yards away, to determine who was the best shot.

Situated on Galgate, the main road into popular Barnard Castle, **Strathmore Lawn East** is a very impressive Victorian building. Proprietor Margaret Lodge has lived here since 1988, and has been providing bed and breakfast accommodation since 1991. As well as being a superb host, Margaret is happy to share information on the numerous places of interest in the area, as she was born and bred right here in Galgate road. Her lovely home dates back to 1889 and has an attractive frontage, lovely gardens, and many attractive and welcoming original Victorian features. There are three distinctive guest bedrooms, all on the first floor, two of which are ensuite. Beautifully decorated and furnished, with lots of homely extras; guests are made to feel very much at home straight away. A hearty breakfast awaits guests each morning. Vegetarians and other special diets are catered for. Open all year round except Christmas Day and New Year's Day.

Strathmore Lawn East, 81 Galgate, Barnard Castle, County Durham DL12 8ES
Tel: 01833 637061

A short walk along Newgate will bring you to **The Bowes Museum**, a magnificent building designed by Jules Pellechet in the style of a French chateau. John Bowes, son of the 10th Earl of Strathmore, and his French actress wife, Josephine, spent 15 years putting together remarkable collections of artefacts, intending that the public should be able to see and enjoy them. This was the purpose of the building which, after taking about 30 years to build, was completed in 1892. A strong European influence is evident throughout the museum, both in the ceramic and textile displays and in the period settings in which are exhibited the furniture, tapestries, paintings, clocks and objet d'art. Displays have been added more recently featuring English furniture, silver, costume, toys and local antiquities. Sadly, by the time the museum was opened both Bowes and his wife were dead. Her Majesty Queen Elizabeth The Queen Mother, who was born Lady Elizabeth Bowes-Lyon, is descended from the Bowes family.

The Old Well Inn offers the old traditional values of a warm welcome coupled with courteous service. Its history dates back to the 14th century, and it was for many years a coaching inn. Attractive and comfortable, it has generously proportioned accommodation in 10 superior ensuite rooms. Owners Anna and Louise Rabley have run this charming establishment since 1980, providing a high standard of comfort and quality to all their guests. In **Rabana's Restaurant** there are refreshingly varied and appetising menus featuring home-cooked and delicious dishes such as steak and kidney pie, roast leg of Teesdale lamb and fillet of pork in a mustard cream sauce. The Tavern features real ales, a good wine list and the full complement of lagers and spirits. There is an attractive beer garden. An interesting and popular circular walking trail starts from the inn. The atmosphere throughout this fine inn is friendly and welcoming.

The Old Well Inn and Rabana's Restaurant, 21 The Bank, Barnard Castle, County Durham DL12 8PH Tel: 01833 690130 Fax: 01833 690140

Jersey Farm Hotel and Restaurant is an impressive establishment offering superb accommodation and dining. Resting in 12 acres of farmland, part of which is still a working farm, this family-run hotel is ideally situated to explore the delights and sights of the area. From humble beginnings - it began as a B&B back in 1972, becoming a hotel in 1978 - it has gone from strength to strength and now enjoys an international reputation. The restaurant is famous for its home-cooked meals from the carvery and set menu. The 20 ensuite rooms are beautifully decorated and furnished; four are classed as luxury suites, some come complete with four-

Jersey Farm Hotel, Darlington Road, Barnard Castle, County Durham DL12 8TA Tel: 01833 638223 Fax: 01833 631988 email: jerseyfarmhotel@enta.net

poster beds. A warm welcome awaits guests at this distinguished hotel. The Watsons have been here all their lives. New for the year 2000 is a new leisure complex incorporating a swimming pool, gym, steam room, solarium, fitness centre, snooker room, health and beauty salon and coffee shop. ETB 4 Crowns 3 Star Highly Commended.

BOWES

Map 12 ref L6

4 miles W of Barnard Castle off the A66

The main A66 trunk road west from Barnard Castle heads across the Stainmoor Pass, following the line of the Roman Road towards Carlisle. The old coaching town of Bowes once enjoyed notoriety as the location of Bowes Academy, kept by one William Shaw, which was visited by Dickens in 1838 and upon which he subsequently based Dothebys Hall in his novel 'Nicholas Nickelby'. George Ashton Taylor, a youth who died in 1822 at the age of 19 and is buried in the village churchyard, was the inspiration for the character Smike, in the book. 'I think his ghost put Smike into my head, upon the spot', Dickens later reported to a friend. Taylor had been a pupil at the very 'Academy' that Dickens would so mercilessly expose. **Bowes Castle** was completed in 1187 for King Henry II, using stone from an earlier Roman fort, Lavatrae, to guard this strategic crossing of the Pennines. Its massive keep still overlooks the River Greta, but much of the castle's stone was re-used by thrifty local people to build the parish church. This is wild, bleak countryside. The main A66 trunk road crosses Stainmoor over desolate moorland and is often closed during the first snows of winter, leaving drivers stranded in Bowes or Brough. It was near this road, close to the present Cumbria border, that King Edmund erected Rey Cross to mark the boundary between Northumbria and what was then the Scottish province of Cumbria. It also marks the spot where Eric Bloodaxe, the last Viking king of Northumbria, was slain.

Overlooking thousands of acres of picturesque countryside, **East Mellwaters Farm** is a 17th-century farmhouse offering bed and breakfast accommodation. This working family farm of about 290 acres is set within the North Pennines' Area of Outstanding Natural Beauty. Ideal for a break away from it all, amid peace and rural tranquillity, some excellent walking, fishing and the natural splendours of the region, this charming establishment is a true home from home. The guests' lounge has an open fire and commands fine views of the open countryside. The evening meal is also available by prior arrangement, home-prepared and made with organically-reared beef and lamb together with kitchen and garden herbs and garden-fresh vegetables. During the summer months there are five ensuite rooms available

East Mellwaters Farm, Bowes, nr Barnard Castle, County Durham DL12 9RH Tel/Fax: 01833 628269

with bath or shower. From October to April these rooms are let on a self-catering basis. Sleeping up to 11, if required guests can have maid and meal service included. Children welcome. No smoking.

BOLDRON

Map 12 ref L6

2 miles S of Barnard Castle off the A67

Egglestone Abbey, about a mile and a half to the southeast of Barnard Castle, not far from Boldron and easily reached by riverside footpath, is quite different in character to the Bowes

Museum. It is made up of the ruins of a Cistercian Abbey of which most of the nave, built in the 13th and 14th century, survives. This was only a small monastic settlement but it enjoys a superb setting above the River Tees.

Egglestone Abbey

GRETA BRIDGE
Map 12 ref L6

3 miles SE of Barnard Castle on the A66

Lovers of romantic landscape should make their way south of Barnard Castle to Greta Bridge on the A66, the old hump-backed bridge immortalised in paintings by the great English watercolourists Girtin, Turner and others, now bypassed by the traffic on the trunk road. Footpaths lead by the riverside, through the edge of **Rokeby Park** to the ruins of medieval **Mortham Tower**, subject of Sir Walter Scott's narrative poem of colourful chivalry and courtly love, 'Rokeby'. The elegant Palladian house, where Scott stayed to write his poem, is open to the public during the summer months.

COTHERSTONE
Map 12 ref L6

3 miles NW of Barnard Castle off the B6277

The Fox and Hounds country inn and restaurant is situated in the picturesque village of Cotherstone. Owned and personally run by Michael and May Carlisle since 1994, this handsome inn dates back nearly 300 years and features exposed beams, roaring fires and other evocative and welcoming traditional attributes. Michael is a qualified, experienced chef. The menu boasts a range of tempting dishes such as rack of Teesdale lamb, grilled 16-ounce Dover Sole and breaded pork escalope. There are also changing daily specials. All are home-cooked and home-prepared, and offer guests a marvellous dining experience. Quality real ales include Black Sheep Best and Black Sheep Specials, as well as good wines, lagers, stout and spirits. The superb accommodation comprises three upstairs letting rooms (two doubles and one twin), comfortably furnished and appointed

The Fox and Hounds, Cotherstone, nr Barnard Castle, County Durham DL12 9PF Tel/Fax: 01833 650241 Mobile: 0410 351822

and available all year round. A delicious breakfast awaits guests every morning. For excellent hospitality, a cracking atmosphere and great service, look no further.

DARLINGTON

MAP 12 REF M6

18 miles S of Durham on the A167

Darlington, just off the Great North Road, has every right to be considered Durham's second town, both in terms of its importance as a regional centre serving the southern part of County Durham and for its heritage. It has a bustling town centre, with a large Market Place and grand Victorian Market Hall that bring people in from the surrounding Dales of both Durham and Yorkshire - Market Days are Monday and Saturday. At the eastern end of Tubwell Row are the Old Town Hall, covered market and well-known **Clock Tower** designed by famous Victorian Alfred Waterhouse in 1864. The nearby Market Cross was originally presented to the town in 1727 - this is the cross's third site, moved here after a restoration and landscaping project was completed in 1993.

You will find a great little museum in the centre of Darlington called the **Tubwell Row Museum**. Although the museum is small, the exhibits are varied and interesting and the staff friendly and helpful. Some of the oldest pieces are the archaeological finds relating to early man's activities in the area. These include an Anglo-Saxon brooch, flint tools and Roman coins. Many exhibits relate to Darlington's growth as an important centre for commerce, industry and agriculture, and the Curator will happily try to answer any other questions that you may have on these topics. Other displays cover agricultural Darlington in more detail, the natural history of the area and much more.

With a well-earned reputation as one of the friendliest and cosiest eateries in Darlington, **Le Tiffin Coffee Shop** is an excellent place to enjoy a coffee, pastry, snack or full lunch. Located in one of the oldest parts of Darlington, the original building dates back hundreds of years, and lies near a pretty Quaker church. The premises are beautifully furnished and there is a fine collection of teapots and prints by local artists. Seating up to 45 people, it is spacious and welcoming. Owners Mick and Chris Downes, who took over at this established and popular coffee shop in August of 1999, offer all their guests a warm greeting and excellent service. The excellent food, much of it home-made, includes scones, pies, desserts, sandwiches and more. The menu also features an impressive range of coffees and teas from all over the world. Loose tea, coffee beans and ground coffee, as well as a selection of home-made jams, can be purchased to enjoy at home or as charming gifts. Open Tuesday to Saturday 9.30 a.m. to 5 p.m.

Perhaps Darlington's greatest claim to fame lies in the role the town played with its neighbour Stockton in the creation of the world's first commercially successful public railway which opened in 1825. It was the Darlington Quaker and Banker, Edward Pease, who became the main driving force behind the

Le Tiffin Coffee Shop, 11 Skinnergate, Darlington, County Durham DL3 7NJ Tel: 01325 485431

railway scheme to link the Durham coalfield with the port of Stockton. The present Darlington Station at Bank Top came from a much later period in the railway age, as lines were being constructed to link England and Scotland. The original Darlington Station, built in 1842, was located at what is now North Road station. Today it is the **Darlington Railway Centre and Museum**, a museum of national importance, housing as it does relics of the pioneering Stockton and Darlington Railway, including Stephenson's 'Locomotion No 1', an early Stockton and Darlington carriage and Hackworth's mighty engine, the 'Derwent'. Timothy Hackworth who came from Shildon near Bishop Auckland as Stephenson's Locomotive Superintendent, was the man with the practical skills to make the engines actually work. He designed his own breed of rugged, tough colliery engines, which really demonstrated the superiority of steam power over the horse in terms of strength and reliability. Hackworth also built the first locomotives to be used in Russia and Canada. So much early railway history is to be seen in this part of County Durham that British Rail have named their local Bishop Auckland-Darlington-Middlesbrough line 'The Heritage Line'.

High Row, with its elevated street of shops makes an impressive sight, and forms part of a compact but characterful shopping centre. The tall buildings evolved because of the narrowness of the plots of land in medieval times. The Georgian façades are pierced by tunnels which at one time gave access to rear gardens. These have long since been built over as yards and lend their name to this part of town. The 'yards' now contain shops and small businesses and are public rights of way between High Row and Skinnergate. Skinnergate itself had a public well and still retains some cottage-like buildings, some thatched until last century. The street has now been pedestrianised and landscaped to reflect the historic atmosphere.

PIERCEBRIDGE Map 12 ref M6
5 miles W of Darlington off the A67

The **Carlbury Arms** is an outstanding public house and restaurant found just off the main A67 west of Darlington. The premises date back to the 17th century, as reflected in its cobbled floors, exposed beams, sandstone walls and other original features. Once known as The Wheatsheaf, it was given its current name by owners Richard and Barbara, who named it after the village that used to be here, of which only one house remains. The owners have been here since 1998; Barbara is chef while Richard looks after front of house. Together with their capable and friendly staff they offer all their guests a warm welcome and genuine hospitality.

Completely refurbished and redesigned, the interior of this charming pub is beautiful, warm and welcoming, with many handsome furnishings and tasteful decor throughout. Open all day every day, food is served at lunchtime and evenings. The cosy and intimate restaurant (no smoking) seats 20; meals can also be taken in the main bar areas. Booking is advised Wednesday - Saturday evenings and Sunday lunch. The range of excellent food on offer includes traditional favourites such as home-made steak and kidney pie, gammon, chicken dishes, fresh fish and vegetarian choices. There is also a fine selection of at least five daily lunchtime specials and 12 evening daily specials. Guests should also leave room for one of the tempting desserts, such as home-made fruit crumble or fruit pie with custard, spotted dick and sticky-toffee pudding. Well-kept

Carlbury Arms, Piercebridge, Darlington,
County Durham DL2 3SJ Tel: 01325 374286

ales include John Smiths Smooth, Theakston's Best, Magnet, Black Sheep and guest ales, along with a good complement of stout, draught lagers, cider, wines and spirits.

NORTHUMBERLAND

CORBRIDGE

MAP 12 REF L4

17 miles W of Newcastle on the A69

Corbridge is an ancient market town lying snugly in the Tyne valley where the A68 and A69 cross. It was, for a time the capital of the ancient Kingdom of Northumbria and it was here, in AD796, that King Ethelred of Northumbria was murdered. This charming place still retains relics of its former importance as a strategic crossing of the river, including two fortified medieval towers which are evidence of more troubled times. **Vicar's Pele** was the home of the vicar from about 1310 until the 18th century when a large vicarage was built about half a mile from the church. The other, formerly called Low Hall, has now been incorporated into a private house. Corbridge had great importance in Roman times not as a military stronghold but as a supply depot and administrative centre. The foundations of a substantial complex, Corstopitum, just a mile or two north of the town, are now a popular tourist attraction.

HEXHAM

MAP 12 REF L4

20 miles W of Newcastle on the A695

Continuing west along the main Tyne valley the next stop is Hexham, built on a terrace overlooking the river. It is the capital and administrative centre of Tynedale, and this busy little town, so rich in Tynedale character, should not be missed. The great **Abbey** dates back to AD674, at which time it was reputed to be the 'largest and most magnificent church this side of the Alps'. Though it may now have a few rivals for such a title, the present building is still on a magnificent scale, with many Saxon remains from the original church. There is also some wonderful late-medieval architecture, mainly from the 12th and 13th centuries, which later restoration has certainly not diminished. Not only is there a rich heritage of carved stone-work, but Hexham Abbey is also famous for its woodcarvings. The early 16th-century rood screen has been described as the best in any monastic church in Britain.

There is also much more to see in Hexham. The Tourist Information Centre, in the Market Place, uses the **Manor Office**, a building that dates back to 1330. **The Middle March**

Hexham Abbey

Centre for Border History is located in the 14th-century Manor House and tells, in a vivid way, the story of the border struggles between the two nation states. The territory was hotly disputed, and for many centuries was virtually without rule of law, subject to the activities of the notorious Reivers - cattle rustlers and thieves who took advantage of the disputed border lands. The powerful Wardens, or Lords of the Marches - themselves warlords of pitiless ferocity - were given almost complete authority by the King to control the Reivers and anyone else who crossed their path. This was the period of the great medieval Border Ballads, violent and colourful tales of love, death, heroism and betrayal which have found an enduring place in literature, and which came from this region.

The town has retained much of its character, with winding lanes and passageways, some delightful shops and a traditional market. There are some attractive 18th- and 19th-century houses, handsome terraces, delightful gardens around the priory, and several attractive areas of open space. There are particularly good views, from several points in the town, across the Tyne valley.

CHOLLERTON
MAP 12 REF L4

5 miles N of Hexham on the A6079

Chollerton, five miles north of Hexham along the valley of the North Tyne, enjoys an exceptionally fine setting, including a delightful area of park land which includes part of Hadrian's Wall. The celebrated **Roman Fort of Chesters**, situated here, covers nearly six acres and was large enough to accommodate a full cavalry regiment. There is a fine museum which displays a remarkable collection of Roman antiquities. Remains of the Roman fort include a well-preserved bath house and barracks. There is also a mansion here, bought by a John Clayton, who did much to preserve the Roman remains. The handsome bridge across the river is 100 yards long and was built in 1775..

BARDON MILL
MAP 12 REF K4

9 miles W of Hexham on the A69

Bardon Mill, a former mining village, stands on the north bank of the South Tyne. An important drovers' road crossed the river here and cattle were fitted with iron shoes at Bardon Mill to help them on their way, on the hoof, to southern markets. The village is a convenient starting point for walks along Hadrian's Wall and the Roman Forts of **Vindolanda** and **Housesteads** are nearby. Both sites are popular with visitors, having plenty of Roman remains and interesting accompanying exhibitions. Between Bardon Mill and Haydon Bridge lies the confluence of the South Tyne and the River Allen, which, like the Tyne, comes from two main tributaries - the East Allen and West Allen. The valleys of the Rivers East and West

Hadrian's Wall

Allen really are hidden jewels. Allen Banks, as the lower part of the valley near the Tyne is known, is a deep, wooded, limestone valley, rich in natural beauty, now owned by the National Trust. You can park at the picnic site close to the disused Plankey Mill (reached by lane from the main A686 Alston road) and enjoy one of the many riverside walks. Crossing the river by a suspension bridge, one path leads through a woodland of pine, beech, oak, birch, ash and elder, past Raven Crag, an outcrop of limestone from where the ravens still fly with raucous voices. This is an area that is also particularly rich in wild flowers, ferns, mosses and rhododendrons.

HALTWHISTLE
MAP 12 REF K4

12 miles W of Hexham on the A69

Our final port of call along Hadrian's Wall is the town of Haltwhistle, a small town, host to the South Tyne Annual Agricultural Show. Its name owes nothing to the railway but comes from the Norman-Saxon word 'haut wiscle', meaning 'junction of streams by a hill'. It is difficult to imagine that this pleasant little town with its grey terraces was once a mining area, but evidence of the local industries remain.

The Grey Bull Hotel, a former coaching inn, is situated just a few hundred yards from the centre of Haltwhistle. This noteworthy public house offers some fine ales and a warm and welcoming atmosphere. Owners Malcolm and Pam Crawford are friendly and conscientious hosts. Malcolm was born and bred in Haltwhistle; he and Pam have been personally running this attractive pub since the middle of 1999. This is their first venture into pub business, and they bring enthusiasm and flair to the task. Popular with locals and visitors alike, it is open all day every day. Real ales on tap include Tetleys, John Smiths Smooth and a changing guest ale. Accommodation available comprises seven upstairs letting rooms, ranging in size from singles to family rooms. A

The Grey Bull Hotel, Main Street, Haltwhistle, Northumberland NE49 0DL Tel: 01434 321991 Fax: 01434 320770

delicious and filling breakfast sets guests up for a day's exploring this popular and scenic part of the county. Children welcome. No pets.

The church of the Holy Cross, behind the Market Place, dates back to the 13th century and is said to be on the site of a 12th-century church founded by William the Lion, King of Scotland.

On the edge of the High Street, **The Spotted Cow Inn** is a pretty public house dating back to the mid-18th century. It is a lovely place inside and out, and offers the very best in food, drink and accommodation. The three ensuite guest rooms are of the highest quality. The attractive restaurant can seat up to 28 diners in comfort, and serves a superb range of dishes from around the world, all cooked to order by owner Linda Higgins, who has been personally running the pub since 1988. Open for lunch and evening seven days a week (but closed Tuesday lunchtime). Booking is advised for Saturday evenings. In the bar area, guests will find four real ales on tap as well as a range of spirits, wines, lagers, stout and cider. Ales include Directors, Theakstons and John Smiths. Linda and her partner Iain offer all visitors a warm and friendly welcome.

The Spotted Cow Inn, Castle Hill, Haltwhistle, Northumberland NE49 0EN Tel: 01434 320327

GREENHEAD-IN-NORTHUMBERLAND

MAP 12 REF K4

1 mile W of Haltwhistle off the A69/B6318

The impressive **Holmhead Guest House** stands on the foundations of Hadrian's Wall. The path along the wall and the Pennine Way passes through the back garden. This beautiful and secluded setting ensures a restful and tranquil stay for all guests. Owners Pauline and Brian Staff have been here since 1983. The area is full of both historical and natural beauty, and this unique guest house makes an ideal base for exploring the region. Built of Roman Wall stones, there is an inscribed stone in the kitchen wall. There are four cosy and attractive guest bedrooms, each with small shower/toilet and each commanding lovely countryside views. The light and airy lounge is next to the bedrooms. It is a large and very comfortable room equipped with a range of diversions - including informative maps and books on the region, welcoming open fire, TV and licensed bar. Pauline is an expert on Hadrian's Wall, having studied archaeology and local history for years. The British Tourist Authority has given an award for excellence to the hearty and delicious breakfasts. Evening meals are also available, and are intimate candlelit dinner parties with four courses of

Holmhead Guest House and Holiday Cottage, on Thirlwall Castle Farm, Hadrian's Wall, Greenhead-in-Northumberland, via Carlisle CA6 7HY Tel/Fax: 016977 47402 email: Holmhead@hadrianswall.freeserve.co.uk

freshly prepared and tempting dishes, accompanied by organic wine. Open all year round. No smoking. No pets. Children welcome. ETB 4 Diamonds.

WARK
MAP 12 REF L4

8 miles NW of Hexham on the B6320

Wark, to the south of Bellingham, is an attractive estate village, once part of the lordship of Wark; the Scottish kings are said to have held court here in the 12th century. **Birtley**, across the river, is another attractive village that was entirely rebuilt by the Dukes of Northumberland in the last century. On the slopes overlooking the North Tyne are a large number of prehistoric settlements, many of them with picturesque names such as Male Knock Camp, Good Wife Camp, Nigh Folds Camp, Carryhouse Camp and Shieldence Camp; names probably given to the monuments by itinerant gypsies in former times.

KIELDER FOREST AND KIELDER WATER
MAP 12 REF K3

22 miles NW of Hexham off the B6320

In the centre of Kielder Forest is the large expanse of water that is Kielder Water - Northern Europe's largest man-made lake. The reservoir, with 27 miles of shoreline, is set on the edge of the **Northumberland National Park** only three miles from the Scottish border. Opened by the Queen in 1982, Kielder was created to provide a new water supply for industrial Teesside amongst much controversy with a number of farms and hamlets having to be flooded.

However, it has subsequently provided a unique recreational facility for almost every type of water-sport. It is probably best to start a visit at the excellent Visitor Centre at **Tower Knowe**, on the south side of the lake and reached by a forest road from Bellingham. Exhibitions tell the story of the creation of the lake and how it has changed the environment of the region. The main water-sports and activities centre is at Leaplish, with lakeside and woodland walks, and a forest playground for children. Bathekin Reservoir, in the northern section, is reserved for nature conservation, while walkers can follow the viaduct which once carried the North Tyne Railway, and is now a superb viewpoint.

KIELDER
MAP 12 REF K3

29 miles NW of Hexham off the B6320

Kielder itself is a Forestry Commission village that was built in the 1950s to house workers in Kielder Forest which, again, is man-made. The forest was created in the late 1920s and 30s after the Forestry Commission acquired land belonging to the Duke of Northumberland in place of death duties. Initially the planting of the trees brought employment to the area with families coming here from Tyneside, and beyond, for work and a home. Technology has since taken over and very few workers are now employed. On the northern shore of Kielder Water is **Kielder Castle**, at one time a hunting lodge for the Duke of Northumberland and later offices for the Forestry Commission. It is now a fascinating visitor centre describing the development of the forest.

The roads around the lake and forest are generally quiet with the notable exception of the RAC Rally of which one stage is held here each year. The sheer scale of Kielder contrasts with the more intimate landscape of the small towns and villages on the edge of the National Park, and in the three major valleys which cut into the hills. These were formed by the River Tyne and its major tributary, the Rede (forming Redesdale), and to the north, the beautiful valley of the Coquet which runs across to Amble on the coast.

ROTHBURY
MAP 12 REF L3

30 miles N of Newcastle on the B6344

Rothbury is a natural focal point from which to explore the valley of the River Coquet. It is an excellent starting point for some delightful walks along the valley or through the nearby woodland, the most famous perhaps being to the summit of **Simonside**, a fine viewpoint, or along the **Rothbury Terraces**, a series of parallel tracks along the hillside above the town, which also offer superb views. In the heart of Rothbury overlooking the village green, **Orchard Guest House** is a handsome Georgian home set back from the road. Owner Jean Pickard has created a charming and welcoming place to rest, relax and enjoy the sights of this thriving community and the beautiful Coquet Valley.

There are five superb guest bedrooms, all either ensuite or with private bath, and all attractively and comfortably furnished and decorated. The cosy residents' lounge is just the place to unwind with a good book or while perusing leaflets on the local area. Open all year, it makes a great base while exploring the region. Wildlife abounds here, with the many nearby attractions of the National Park and Heritage Coast. Mrs Pickard offers a warm welcome, and the atmosphere throughout this lovely guest house is homely and relaxed. Breakfast is hearty and delicious; there are a wealth of quality restaurants nearby for evening meals. Children welcome. No smoking. No pets.

The village is very old, probably with Saxon origins, and the church has an ancient foundation though almost entirely rebuilt in 1850. From the 18th century the village developed into a natural marketplace for Upper Coquetdale to which cattle and sheep were brought for sale and

Orchard Guest House, High Street, Rothbury, Northumberland NE65 7TL Tel: 01669 620684 email: oguesth@globalnet.co.uk website: www.users.globalnet.co.uk/~oguesth

the drovers provided with numerous public houses and the services of various tradesmen. Since the mid-19th century Rothbury has been a holiday resort for walkers and fishermen and the railway which opened in 1870 contributed further to its growth. It is now popular with retired people and commuters to Morpeth and Newcastle.

Just outside Rothbury is the house and estate of **Cragside**, once the home of Sir William Armstrong, inventor and industrialist. Sir William purchased the 900 acres of the Debden Valley in 1850 and employed Norman Shaw to extend the house and make it suitable to entertain royalty and other wealthy guests. A pioneer of the turbine, Armstrong designed various pieces of hydraulic apparatus for the house and devised his own hydro-electric systems with man-made lakes, streams and miles of underground piping, making Cragside the first house in the world to be lit by hydro-electricity. The National Trust acquired the estate in 1979 when it was in a fairly dilapidated condition but both the house and gardens have been well restored resulting in a fascinating visitor attraction.

WELDON
5 miles SE of Rothbury on the A697

MAP 12 REF M3

Weldon, the next settlement, at the junction with the B6344, has an exceptionally elegant five-arched bridge across the River Coquet, dating from 1744. Although it no longer carries the main road it remains an impressive feature. Nearby **Brinkburn Priory**, standing in secluded woodland on the banks of the river, was established in the late-12th century and is thought to have been built by the same masons who constructed Longframlington church. It is in a beautiful setting surrounded by ancient trees and rhododendrons and was once painted by Turner as a romantic ruin. Its church was restored as a private chapel in later years and has many fine architectural features. A service is held in the church each year on Ascension Day. The site now also houses some pieces of modern sculpture.

GREAT TOSSON
2 miles W of Rothbury off the B6341

MAP 12 REF L3

Excellent bed and breakfast or self-catering accommodation can be found at **Tosson Tower Farm** in Great Tosson, near Rothbury. The present owners are the third generation of Foggins to farm Tosson Tower. Ann has been providing B&B accommodation since 1976, and self-catering since 1984. This historic house, formerly a drover's inn, is set within the National Park opposite

the ruins of a 15th-century "Pele Tower", a listed building. On this 180-acre sheep farm, there are breathtaking views, private fishing and lovely walks to be enjoyed. The three cosy en suite bedrooms (two double, one twin; cot available) contain all home comforts. The guests' lounge is comfortable

**Tosson Tower Farm, Great Tosson, Rothbury, Morpeth, Northumberland
NE65 7NW Tel/Fax: 01669 620228 email: SGKETT@aol.com
website: www.tossontowerfarm.ntb.org.uk**

and welcoming, with a lovely log fire. The five self-catering cottages sleep between four and eight people. The Keepers Cottage was, as its name suggests, once the Gamekeeper's Cottage, as the land hereabouts was once part of the famous Cragside Estate of Lord Armstrong, now owned by the National Trust. Pele and Tower Cottages offer marvellous views over the Coquet Valley. Forge Cottage is adjacent to the main farmhouse, and has been converted from the old blacksmith's forge into luxurious family accommodation. New to 2000, a superb four-bedroomed cottage, called Coquet View, offers top-of-the-range self-catering accommodation.

CHILLINGHAM
17 miles N of Rothbury off the B6348

MAP 12 REF L2

Chillingham, south-east of Wooler and east of the A697, is a pleasant village which is perhaps best known for the herd of wild, horned, **white cattle** that roam the 365-acre park. One of only five herds of their kind in Britain, they have survived because of their comparative isolation, and are perhaps the purest surviving specimens of the wild cattle that once roamed the hills and forests of prehistoric Britain. The **Medieval Castle** is beautifully sited overlooking the River Till but sadly fell into ruin and was deserted in 1933. It has since been purchased by Sir Humphrey Wakefield whose wife is related to an early resident. The castle has been restored revealing a medieval fortress complete with jousting course, dungeon and torture chamber. The castle and surrounding gardens are open to the public from May to September. Just outside the village is the National Trust-owned **Ross Castle**, once a vital beacon site visible as far afield as the Scottish Hills and Holy Island. The whole area was thrown into chaos in 1804 when an over-enthusiastic warden lit the beacon by mistake!

Chillingham Castle

KIRKNEWTON

MAP 12 REF L2

20 miles N of Rothbury on the B6351

It's worth walking across the fells (a high-level footpath runs from Wooler) or, for the less energetic, travelling along the A697 and B6351 westwards from Wooler to Kirknewton. This typical border village of cottages, school and village church could not seem more peaceful. But at Old Yeavering, one and a half miles to the east, stands a great stone in the field which marks the spot where, in 1415, Robert Umfraville, a Northumbrian hero, put to flight 4,000 Scottish troops with a force of only 600 men. In Kirknewton churchyard is evidence of a more recent conflict, the graves, near the church gate, of young pilots from nearby RAF Millfield. In another corner are those of four young German airmen who died in the same conflict in 1943. Also buried here is Josephine Butler, the great Victorian social reformer and fighter for women's rights, who retired to Northumberland and died here in 1906. An unusual medieval sculpture in the church shows the Magi wearing kilts - a fascinating example of medieval artists presenting the Christian story in ways their audience could understand.

Barely half a mile east of the village, in what are now fields by the little River Glen, once lay the royal township of Gefrin or Ad-Gefrin. This huge settlement of timber-framed buildings, including halls 100 feet long and a great amphitheatre, was the capital of the Kingdom of Edwin, the first Christian King of Northumbria. The great historian, Bede, recalls that it was here, in AD627, that St Paulinus spent 36 days teaching Christianity to the people of Northumbria and baptising converts in the River Glen. A stone monument now marks the place where this long-vanished town once stood.

If such historical associations were not enough, on the summit of a nearby hill known as **Yeavering Bell**, there is a magnificent Iron-Age hill fort, the largest in Northumberland, enclosed by the remains of a wall and covering 13 acres. Over 33 hut circles have been traced on the summit, which commands impressive views for miles around.

BERWICK

MAP 12 REF L1

75 miles N of Newcastle off the A1

The borough of Berwick-upon-Tweed is a product of a long and hard fought history, shaped by the clash of swords between the English and the Scots, and fear of the Border Reivers. This has left the ancient town of Berwick in a curiously changeable position. Little wonder, as it has been fought and quarrelled over for a thousand years or more. It has changed hands no less than fourteen times, so even now, the inhabitants are not certain where their allegiance lies. It was started by William the Lion of Scotland who gave the town to the English Crown in 1147 as part of his ransom after he had been captured at Alnwick. Richard the Lionheart then had to surrender it to Scotland to raise money to pay for his crusades and the town continued to change hands until 1482 when it was finally confirmed as being part of England. Even then, for

Berwick Ramparts

a time, Berwick became almost a country in itself, an independent 'free town' which had to be specifically mentioned in Acts of Parliament until 1746. To confuse the issue a little more, having lost its status as a Scottish burgh in 1368, it was restored by Lord Lyon in 1958. This makes it a town which technically belongs to both nations - surely the happiest compromise!

Berwick's original medieval walls, built in the 13th century and modified by Henry VIII, can still be walked, and the old town within them is a colourful blend of warm sandstone, grey stone and red roofs. The many fine buildings are mostly Georgian and include the Ravensdowne Barracks, thought to be designed by Vanbrugh and built between 1717 and 1721. These are the oldest barracks in the country and were reputedly built as a result of complaints by local people about constantly having to billet soldiers! The later fortifications, ordered by Elizabeth I to replace part of the earlier town wall, are regarded as the finest preserved example of walled defences in the whole of Europe. They were built in 1558 by Italian engineers, who were experts at creating defences to exploit the full use of artillery to defend a town. A gun tower and part of the west wall are open to the public. The Tweed estuary is spanned by three distinctive bridges linking the town centre with the communities of Tweedmouth and Spittal. The oldest of these bridges is the 17th century **Berwick Bridge**, a handsome stone bridge with 15 arches dating from 1624. The Royal Tweed Bridge is the most modern, having been built in 1928 with a concrete structure built to an iron bridge design. The enormous 38 metre high, 28 arch Royal Border Bridge carrying the East Coast main-line railway was built in 1847 by Robert Stephenson and opened by Queen Victoria in 1850.

The Berwick skyline is dominated by the imposing Town Hall with its clock tower and steeple, which rise to 150 feet, which means it is often mistaken for a church. Rebuilt in 1754, this fine building has a façade as elaborate as its well-documented history. On the ground floor, markets were held in the Exchange and shops and cells existed where now a gift shop and coffee house stand. Guided tours in the summer enable visitors to explore the upper storeys, where there are civic rooms, and the town gaol which now houses the **Cell Block Museum**. On the north side of the town you will find the ruins of **Berwick Castle**, the site of many sieges during the town's turbulent past. Built in the 13th century the castle was sadly demolished in 1850 to make way for the railway station and the station platform now occupies the site of the former Great Hall. There are some remains still visible, now in the care of English Heritage. **Holy Trinity Parish Church** is a rarity, being one of only two churches built during the Commonwealth - the republican government in England between 1649 and 1660 - the other being at Staunton Harold, Lincolnshire, and as a result having no tower or spire, these being forbidden by Cromwell. Of particular interest are the renaissance pulpit panels of Swiss or German glass in the west window, and the impressive west doorway. The church has no spire but two octagonal turrets were added during the 19th century. Facing the church is the main entrance to the Barracks which house three museums. In the Clock Block is the **Berwick Borough Museum and Art Gallery** which invites visitors to peer through a 'Window on Berwick' and step into a Cairo bazaar. Sir William Burrell donated one tenth of his collection of art treasures to the museum, a total of some 800 pieces, and there are 46 important paintings, including a Degas, and many fine items of porcelain, glass and metalware. Also in the barracks is the **King's Own Scottish Borderers' Regimental Museum** which has displays of medals, uniforms, military regalia and silverware.

TWEEDMOUTH
MAP 12 REF L1

2 miles S of Berwick off the A1

Tweedmouth and Spittal, on the 'English' side of the Tweed estuary, are mainly suburbs of Berwick but with their extensive sands, promenade and variety of seaside attractions traditionally attract more holidaymakers. In mid-July a ceremony is held in Tweedmouth which dates back to 1292 and celebrates the fact that the River Tweed, one of the best salmon rivers in Britain, reaches the sea here. The local schools hold a ballot to elect a 'Salmon Queen' and her crowning marks the beginning of Feast week which centres around a church service but also involves lots of festivities and a traditional salmon supper.

NORHAM
MAP 12 REF L1

6 miles SW of Berwick on the B6470

About halfway between Berwick and Coldstream, on the bank of the River Tweed is the historic village of Norham. The **Castle** here was built in the 12th century by a Bishop of Durham and stands on a site of great natural strength guarding a natural ford over the river. It withstood repeated attacks in the 13th and 14th centuries and was thought to be impregnable. However, in 1513 it was stormed by the forces of James IV on his way to Flodden and partially destroyed. Although it was later rebuilt the castle lost its importance as a defensive stronghold by the end of the 16th century. The castle is now under the care and management of English Heritage and is open to the public all year. Norham's privately-owned **Station Museum** is located on the former Tweedmouth-Kelso branch

Norham Castle

line, the oldest in Northumberland. The museum features the original signal box, booking office and porter's room, and is in the care of the last man to work at the station which closed in 1965. Each year an unusual ceremony still takes place here which has long Christian associations. The Blessing of the Nets is held at midnight on 13th February to mark the beginning of the salmon fishing season. The service is held by lantern light and celebrates the miracle of the shoal of fish swimming into the disciples' nets, as described in St John's Gospel. Also keep a look out for the salmon weathervane which stands on top of a cross on one of the village greens - another reminder of the village's connection with the fishing industry.

TILLMOUTH
MAP 12 REF L2

10 miles SW of Berwick on the A698

The village of Tillmouth lies along the banks of the River Till, a tributary of the Tweed, which is crossed by the 15th-century Twizell Bridge although a more modern structure now carries the

A698 over the river. There are some lovely walks here and a well-signed footpath leads to the ruins of **Twizell Castle** and, on the opposite bank, the remains of **St Cuthbert's Chapel**.

BRANXTON
13 miles SW of Berwick off the A697

MAP 12 REF L2

The site of the famous Battle of **Flodden Field** can be found near the village of Branxton where it is marked by a cross in a cornfield reached by a short path. It was here that the English army defeated the Scots under King James IV on 9th September 1513 in the last and most bloody battle fought on English soil. A discreetly positioned car park is provided on the road and there is an information board which explains the background to the battle and how it was fought. A booklet can be purchased at St Paul's church in Branxton where the King's body is said to have lain after the battle.

DUDDO
7 miles SW of Berwick on the B6354

MAP 12 REF L2

Just to the north of Etal, along the B6354, is the tiny settlement of Duddo, close to which are the **Duddo Stones**, one of Northumberland's most important ancient monuments. The remains of this ancient stone circle, dating back to around 2000BC, can only be reached from the village on foot.

LINDISFARNE ISLAND
10 miles SE of Berwick off the A1

MAP 12 REF M2

The coastline between Berwick and Bamburgh is as fine as that to the immediate south, though with much more extensive sandbanks but one feature above all others dominates - **Lindisfarne**, or **Holy Island**. You can get across only at low tide along the three-mile long causeway from Beal. Tide tables are published locally and are displayed at each end of the road and there are refuges part way for those who fail to time it correctly! Alternatively there are regular bus services from Berwick, which has a 'tide' rather than a 'time' table. As you cross, note the 11th-century **Pilgrims' Way**, marked by stakes, still visible about 200 metres south of the modern causeway. This route was in use until comparatively recent times.This most evocative of English islands was known as Lindisfarne until the 11th century when a group of Benedictine monks settled here giving it the name Holy Island, although both names are now used. The ruins of their great sandstone priory, in massive Romanesque style with great pillars, can still be explored. The links with early Christianity are even more significant than that of the Benedictines, for it was here, in AD635, that St Aidan and his small community of Irish monks came from Iona to found a base from which to help convert northern England to Christianity leading to the island being referred to as one of the cradles of English Christianity.

The monks are also remembered for having produced some of the finest surviving examples of Celtic art, the richly decorated **Lindisfarne Gospels**, which were begun in the 7th century. When the island was invaded by Vikings in the 9th century the monks fled taking their precious gospels with them. These have, miraculously, survived and are now in the safety of the British Museum. Facsimiles are kept on Lindisfarne and can be seen in the 12th-century parish church on the island. St Cuthbert also came here, living on a tiny islet as a hermit before seeking even further seclusion on the **Farne Islands**. A cross marks the site of his tiny chapel, which can be reached over the sand and rocks at low tide. Lindisfarne Castle was established in Tudor times as yet another fortification to protect the exposed flank of Northumbria from invasion by the Scots. It was extensively rebuilt and restored in 1903 as a private house by the great Edwardian architect, Edward Lutyens, and is now in the care of the National Trust. The house and its small walled garden are open to the public during the summer months.

Holy Island village is a community of around 170 people who work in farming, in the island's distillery (noted for excellent traditional mead and strong liquors) and in the tourist trade. Much of the island is also a Nature Reserve, with wildflowers and a wide variety of seabirds.

BELFORD
MAP 12 REF L2

14 miles SE of Berwick on the A1

St Cuthbert's Cave, on the moors just one mile east of the A1 and to the north of Belford, is only accessible by track and footpath. It is a natural cave concealed by a great overhanging rock, surrounded by woodland and it is believed that the saint's body may have lain here on its much interrupted journey across Northumbria. There are superb views of the coast from the summit of nearby Greensheen Hill and of the Cheviots to the west.

WAREN MILL
MAP 12 REF M2

15 miles SE of Berwick on the B1342

The B1342 east of Belford leads to the village of Waren Mill and **Budle Bay**, a large inlet of flats and sand where vast numbers of wading birds and wildfowl come to feed. Caution should be taken when walking on the flats, as sections quickly become cut off at high tide. The village of Waren Mill was once an important port, given its charter in 13th century by Henry III. The busy harbour has long since disappeared, silted up beneath the sands of the estuary. Old warehouses overlooking the bay have in recent years been converted into luxury loft apartments.

BAMBURGH
MAP 12 REF M2

16 miles SE of Berwick on the B1340

Bamburgh Castle is epic in scale, even by the standards of this coastline of spectacular castles, and dominates the village of the same name. Situated on a dramatic outcrop of Whin Sill rock overlooking the sea, it was almost certainly the royal seat of the first Kings of Northumbria from the 6th century onwards.

The dynasty was founded by the Saxon King Ida in AD547 and mentioned in the 'Anglo-Saxon Chronicle'. The present castle has a massive 12th century keep around which huge baileys were constructed. The castle was extensively rebuilt and restored in the 18th and 19th centuries, latterly by the first Lord Armstrong, whose family still owns the building. Open to the public, rooms on display include the Armoury,

Bamburgh Castle

Grand King's Hall, Court Room, Keep Hall, Bakehouse and Victorian Scullery, with collections of tapestries, ceramics, furniture and paintings, and an exhibition about the first Lord Armstrong and his many remarkable engineering inventions.

The village was the birthplace of Grace Darling, the celebrated Victorian heroine, who, in 1838, rowed out with her father from the **Longstone Lighthouse** in a ferocious storm, to rescue the survivors of the steam ship 'Forfarshire' which had foundered on the **Farne Island** rocks. She died of tuberculosis only four years later, still only in her twenties, and is buried in the churchyard of St Aiden's. There is a suitably enshrined monument to her courage, positioned, it is said, so that it may be seen by mariners from ships at sea. The **Grace Darling Museum**, in Radcliffe Road in Bamburgh, also contains memorabilia of the famous rescue.

Apart from the attraction of Bamburgh Castle, visitors and nature lovers can enjoy a boat trip to the nearby **Farne Islands** -sailings run from May to October in good weather. This small group of 28 uninhabited islands of volcanic Whin Sill rock, just off the coast at Bamburgh, provides a sanctuary for over 17 species of sea birds, including kittiwake, fulmar, eider-duck, puffin, guillemot and tern. It is also home for a large colony of grey seal which can often be seen from the beach of the mainland.

The islands have important Christian links too, being the place, on Inner Farne, where St Cuthbert died in AD687. His body was carried on a journey around the north of England which continued for several centuries until a final resting place was found in Durham Cathedral. A little chapel was built here to his memory and restored in Victorian times. The nearby **Tower House** was built in medieval times by Prior Castell, according to legend, on the site of Cuthbert's cell. Landings are permitted on **Inner Farne** and **Staple Island**, though times are restricted for conservation reasons and advance booking is urged in the busy times of year. There are nature trails on both islands, as well as a small exhibition centre in the former chapel of St Mary on Inner Farne.

EMBLETON
22 miles SE of Berwick on the B1339

MAP 12 REF M2

The isolated and dramatic ruins of **Dunstanburgh Castle** stand on a cliff top east of the village. The original castle was built in 1313 by Thomas, Earl of Lancaster as part of the coastal defences against Scottish attack. The heavily fortified castle later became an important stronghold in the Wars of the Roses, and in 1462 withstood a siege from troops led by Margaret of Anjou, Henry VI's Queen. Most of the damage caused by artillery bombardment was never repaired and the castle remains ruined to this day. Sea birds now nest on the seaward-facing rocks and in the dunes further inland. There is no road access to the castle, but it can be approached by foot along a one and a half mile seashore path north of Craster, or by a slightly longer route around Embleton Bay which starts near the Embleton Golf Clubhouse.

ALNWICK
28 miles S of Berwick on the A1

MAP 12 REF M3

Alnwick, just a short distance to the south, is one of the most impressive towns of Northumberland, dominated as it is by the magnificent **Alnwick Castle** which was the stronghold of the great Percy dynasty from 1309 to the middle of the 18th century. It still has the feel and appearance of a great medieval military and commercial centre, being an important market town since the granting of its charter in 1291. The castle began, like most of the Northumberland castles, as a Norman motte and bailey structure, which was replaced in the 12th century by a circular stone keep much added-to over the centuries. It was extensively rebuilt and restored in the 1850s and 60s by the Victorian architect Anthony Salvin for a later duke who sought to recapture the medieval

Alnwick Castle

feel of the castle while transforming it into a great country house with all the modern comforts of its time. A number of rooms are open to the public and amongst its treasures are paintings by Titian, Tintoretto, Canaletto and Van Dyck, collections of Meissen china and superb furniture. There is also an extremely important archaeological museum and extensive archive collections, as well as the **Royal Northumberland Fusiliers Regimental Museum** in The Abbot's Tower. Permits can be obtained to walk into adjacent **Hulne Park**, landscaped by the great (and Northumbrian-born) Capability Brown, which encompasses the ruins of Hulne Priory, an early Carmelite foundation dating from 1240, and a gazebo believed to be designed by Robert Adam.

Alnwick town itself is worthy of an afternoon's exploration with its ancient narrow streets retaining such evocative names as Fenkle Street, Green Batt, Bondgate Without and Bondgate Within betraying their early origins. One road leads through the narrow arch of Hotspur Tower, the one surviving part of the town's fortifications built by the second Duke of Northumberland in the 15th century. The popular and colourful Alnwick Fair, dating from the 13th century, takes place each June or July and market day is Saturday. The **Bondgate Gallery** on Narrowgate has an exciting programme of ever changing exhibitions of contemporary arts and crafts.

No 2 White House Folly Cottages,
White House Folly Farm, Alnwick,
Northumberland NE66 2LW Tel: 01665 579265

No 2 White House Folly Cottages come highly recommended. Hidden away in a secluded position, yet just a short drive from the A1 four miles north of the historic town of Alnwick, it makes an ideal place to rest and relax while enjoying the outstanding scenic countryside and the delights of Northumberland. Set within a 311-acre working mixed farm of beef cows and breeding sheep, this attractive stonebuilt semi-detached cottage dates back to the mid-19th century and was once a farm worker's home. Refurbished and decorated to a high standard of comfort, it sleeps up to four people, having two single and one double bedroom. There is also a fully-equipped kitchen, dining room, sitting room, cloakroom and bathroom. Weekly lets are available in summer, long weekends and weekend breaks from the end of October to the end of March. The cottage offers superb open views across unspoilt countryside to the Cheviot Hills. ETB 3 Diamonds Commended.

NEWTON-BY-THE-SEA
6 miles NE of Alnwick of the B1339

MAP 12 REF M2

Below Beadnell and Beadnell Bay is a small promontory, with the interesting name of Snook Point. At nearby Low-Newton-by-the-Sea land owned by the National Trust includes **Newton Pool**, a freshwater lake which is a fascinating Nature Reserve, with such species as mute swan, teal, sedge-warbler, dabchick, goldeneye and pochard. Public access is permitted to the edge of the reserve and there are parking bays and hides with many walks along Beadnell Bay and on to Seahouses and Bamburgh.

WARKWORTH
6 miles S of Alnwick on the A1068

MAP 12 REF M3

At the southern end of Alnmouth Bay lies **Warkworth Castle**, one of the grand castles that so distinguish this coast. Magnificently situated above a wooded valley, this impressive fortress, with its soaring towers, dates back to a Norman motte and bailey castle built by Robert de Mowbray, Earl of Northumberland. It continued to be enlarged over the next few centuries, including the building of the great Carrickfergus Tower by Robert Fitz-Roger at the end of the 12th century. It came into the ownership of the Percys in 1331, in whose ownership it remained until comparatively recent times. History was created here in 1399 when the Percys proclaimed Henry Bolingbroke, Henry IV, from these castle walls, an event immortalised in Shakespeare's

Warkworth Castle

play. Earlier history links it with Robert the Bruce and, before that, with the Venerable Bede and the Abbot of Holy Island as long ago as AD737. In relatively recent years (if 1557 can be described as ''recent'') the eighth Earl became involved in the Gunpowder Plot and died in the Tower. The remains of the castle are now in the care of English Heritage and is a delightful sight in spring when the grass mound on which it stands is covered with thousands of daffodils.

Unusual and interesting is the walk to **The Hermitage** along the riverside footpath below the castle, where a ferry takes you across the river to visit the tiny chapel hewn out of the solid rock. It dates from medieval times and was in use until late in the 16th century. A popular, romantic legend tells how a Northumbrian knight having accidentally killed both his brother and his sweetheart became a recluse and spent the remainder of his life in devotion and solitude while he carved a chapel out of the rock to their memory. Warkworth is an interesting and beautiful village in its own right. An imposing fortified gatehouse on the 14th-century bridge, now only used by pedestrians, would enable an invading army to be kept at bay north of the Coquet. If you want to understand why such a defence was required, you need look no further than the church of St Lawrence, which dates back to the 13th century and has a grim side to its history. The present building dates from Norman times and replaces an earlier Anglo-Saxon church but it was here, in 1174, that 300 of the town's inhabitants, who had sought refuge from Scottish raiders, were brutally put to death by Duncan, Earl of Fife. Such associations seem remote from the undisturbed tranquillity of the present building. Particularly worth noting is the rare 14th century stone spire on the 13th century tower, some beautiful altar rails, examples of unusual Celtic crosses, the little room above the porch, called the **Parvise**, where local children were taught to read and write, and the nave which is longest Norman nave in Northumberland.

MORPETH
15 miles N of Newcastle off the A1

MAP 12 REF M4

Morpeth, Northumberland's county town, seems a long way from the mining villages further down the Wansbeck, in both spirit and appearance. The ruins of a Norman castle overlook what was essentially a medieval settlement but one which, because it was difficult to defend, suffered badly from the plundering of the Scots. Its prosperity as a market town only developed in the 18th and 19th centuries when it became an important centre for this part of Northumberland. This led to the development of the town with some handsome buildings most notably the **Town Hall**, built to designs by Vanbrugh, and a handsome bridge over the Wansbeck was designed by John Dobson of Newcastle at a point surveyed by Telford around 1830. Somewhere not to be missed in Morpeth, in the medieval Chantry building on Bridge Street, is the **Morpeth Chantry Bagpipe Museum**, devoted to the story of the Northumbrian bagpipes and the heritage of music they played - and which is still played.

SWARLAND   MAP 12 REF M3

10 miles NW of Morpeth off the B6345 between the main A697 and A1

Swarland Old Hall is a magnificent country house dating back to 1640, with Georgian additions. This beautiful Grade II listed home offers superb bed and breakfast accommodation amid tranquil surroundings. Owners Dianne and Arthur Proctor have created a wonderful and restful retreat where there's a homely family atmosphere. All their guests receive a warm and hospitable welcome. The three comfortable letting rooms - a twin that faces west, overlooking the lovely garden, a family/triple, and a double that overlook the picturesque countryside - are beautifully furnished and decorated with en suite facilities. The visitors' lounge is attractive and cosy, with a welcoming log fire. The well-stocked garden with its raised patio offers breathtaking views of the countryside with a secluded corner in which to

Swarland Old Hall, Swarland, Morpeth,
Northumberland NE65 9HU
Tel: 01670 787642 Mobile: 07801 688153

relax. Ideally situated for enjoying outdoor pursuits such as golf, fishing, shooting and walking, and for visiting the castles, country houses and lovely beaches of Northumberland and The Borders, this superb haven offers the perfect base.

SEATON SLUICE   MAP 12 REF M4

8 miles NE of Newcastle on the A193

A few miles inland from Seaton Sluice is **Seaton Delavel Hall**, widely regarded as being one of the finest houses in the north of England. This superb Vanbrugh mansion, the ancestral home of the Delavals, was built in the Palladian style in the early 18th century, and although the building suffered from a series of damaging fires, extensive restoration has been carried out.

Seaton Delavel
Hall

NEWCASTLE

MAP 12 REF M4

90 miles N of Leeds off the A1

Newcastle, the region's capital, is one of Britain's most exciting cities. Situated overlooking the River Tyne across which it is linked to its twin Gateshead by a series of impressive road and rail bridges, it contains many magnificent public buildings and an atmosphere which is difficult to describe. Newcastle was, and is, many things - a Roman frontier station, a medieval fortress town with a 'new' castle built in 1080 as a base for the English army in the forages against the Scots in the 17th and 18th centuries, a great port, mining, engineering and shipbuilding centre and a focal point of the Industrial Revolution that changed the face of the world. But with so much to discover, where do you start?

The **Quayside** is the first view of Newcastle for visitors from the south, whether travelling by road or rail. This area is the symbolic and historic heart of this elegant city and boasts 17th-century Merchants' houses mingling with Georgian and classical Victorian architecture. The

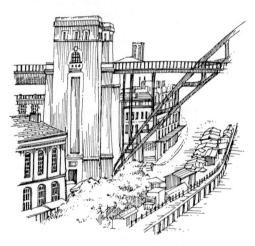

area has been revitalised in recent years with some sensitive and imaginative restoration of the river front area. There are now a number of lively café and wine bars and often craft stalls and street entertainers too. This is also the venue for a regular Sunday market.

The Castle Keep, which overlooks the river, was built by Henry II in the 12th century on the site of the 'new castle' which gave the city its name. The massive structure reaches to 100 feet in height and although the battlements and turrets were added in the 19th century, most of it is Norman. The only other remaining castle building is **Black Gate** which now houses a museum. If at first glance the structure looks a little unusual, it is because of the house built on top of the original Norman keep in the 17th century.

Newcastle's Quayside Market

Many of the other medieval buildings were demolished in the mid-19th century to make way for the railway, and the Castle and Black Gate were almost in the way! Today the main Scotland line runs between the two, and the London branch passes to the west of the Castle Keep before crossing the river over the High Level Bridge.

Newcastle was at one time defended by stout walls that surrounded most of the town. Parts of these survive and include a number of small towers which were built at regular intervals. Begun in 1265 the walls were eventually completed in the mid-14th century. Standing between 14 and 25 feet high they were described as having a 'strength and magnificence' which 'far passeth all the walls of the cities of England and most of the cities of Europe'. The best remaining section is the **West Walls** behind Stowell Street. Another good section is between Forth Street and Hanover Street, south of Central Station. This leads you to spectacular views of the River Tyne from the 'Hanging Gardens of Hanover Street' perched on the cliff side.

The city centre is compact, lying mostly within about a square mile, so it is easy to explore. For the most part the streets are wide and spacious and, like the **Quayside**, much of the architecture is in the Classical style. The focal point is Earl Grey's monument which stands at the head of Grey Street about which John Betjeman wrote "...not even Regent Street...London, can compare with that subtle descending curve".

The modern civic centre has won architectural awards and there's a whole cluster of museums and art galleries to fill any rainy day - the **Laing Art Gallery**, the **Hatton Gallery**, the **Hancock Museum**, the **Museum of Antiquities**, the **Trinity Maritime Centre**, the **Museum of Science and Engineering**, the **Greek Museum** and the **Newburn Hall Motor Museum** - to name some of the best-known. None of these things can do justice to Newcastle's special sense of being a northern capital and, above all else, having a feeling of energy and vitality that comes from the people - the true Geordies - whose sharp wit and perception make Newcastle one of the great cities of England, and indeed Europe.

WALLSEND
3 miles E of Newcastle on the A193

MAP 12 REF M4

Two especially interesting places in North Tyneside are the **Stephenson Railway Museum** and the **Wallsend Heritage Centre**. The Stephenson Museum is at Middle Engine Lane, close to the colliery at Killingworth where George Stephenson began his career as a humble engine-wright, and where his pioneering engine 'Puffing Billy' - one of the earliest steam locomotives in the world - and many other relics are kept. The Wallsend Heritage Centre stands close to the Roman fort of Segedunum on Hadrian's Wall at Wallsend, with many Roman remains and material from excavations near by.

GATESHEAD
2 miles S of Newcastle on the A1

MAP 12 REF M5

Gateshead has perhaps suffered from proximity to its big sister, Newcastle, for generations but thanks to the **MetroCentre**, one of the largest and most impressive shopping and leisure complexes in Western Europe, the borough is very much on the map as a place where Tynesiders and many other people go - not just to shop, but for entertainment in various forms. Gateshead was the site of the 1990 Garden Festival and the town now boasts a legacy of fine parks and gardens. Further afield, there are some surprisingly lovely areas of countryside to explore within Gateshead Borough; a mixture of natural beauty and cultural history, including industrial heritage. **Saltwell Park**, in the centre of Gateshead, is one of the largest parks in the northeast of England and combines stunning floral displays with mature woodland. Horticulturists will admire the Victorian bedding plants, traditional rose garden, heather garden and maze; the variety of planting ensuring a continual blaze of colour. The lake is host to a wealth of waterfowl and the park has a formal aviary. There are rowing boats for hire as well as a paddle steamer. More energetic activities include tennis, crazy golf and bowls, with mini-motorbikes and an inflatable castle for the children. A particularly impressive attraction is the Vickers Viscount aircraft which can be 'flown'. Fairs and circuses regularly visit Saltwell Park and, whatever the time of year, visitors can be assured of a pleasant day out.

The **Central Nursery** at Lobley Hill is one of the most modern in the country. Opened in 1985 by HRH the Duke of Kent, it is a centre of horticultural excellence which provides all the plants, trees and shrubs for the Metropolitan Borough of Gateshead and has achieved some notable successes in the 'Britain in Bloom' competitions. The eight glasshouses, covering 3,034 square metres, have computer-controlled heating systems. An important part of the service offered at the Central Nursery is plant information for the general public, and this service is based in the showhouse which has pools, fish and ornamental planting. Visitors can also enjoy the herb garden, rose garden, heather and conifer garden and tree and shrub nursery. A special picnic area has tables and chairs.

JARROW
7 miles E of Newcastle on the A194

MAP 12 REF M4

Once the thriving centre for the Tyneside shipbuilding industry, Jarrow gained notoriety during the famous Jarrow Hunger March when hundreds of unemployed men from the area walked to London to draw attention to their plight. A bas-relief at the Metro Station commemorates the event which took place in the mid-1930s. Jarrow also has associations with early Christianity. It was here that both a monastery and church were founded in the 7th century dedicated to St Paul. The original dedication stone can still be seen within the church showing the date of '^23 April AD685", together with a fragment of Anglo-Saxon stained glass which scientific tests have established to be the oldest ecclesiastical stained glass in Europe, if not the world. During his stay here the Venerable Bede wrote his great 'History of England' and an ancient chair in the Chancel is reputed to have been used by him. At **Jarrow Hall**, a Georgian building near by, there are exhibitions and displays about the history of this remarkable community of scholars, and there are facsimiles of the early Bibles that were illuminated in manuscript here.

MARSDEN
8 miles E of Newcastle on the A183

MAP 12 REF N4

The coast between South Shields and Roker is magnificent, with rocky cliffs projecting into the sea at Lizard Point and the impressive Whitburn and Marsden Bays. **Marsden Rock** is a huge natural 'arc de triomphe' in the sea celebrated for its birdlife which includes kittiwakes, fulmars and cormorants. A cliff lift links Marsden Grotto - a beach inn - with the top of the cliffs. Souter Lighthouse at Lizard Point was built in 1871 and contained the most advanced technology of its day. It is no longer operational but is in the care of the National Trust and open to the public.

Marsden Rock

ROKER
8 miles E of Newcstle on the A183

MAP 12 REF N5

Roker is a pleasant suburb, immediately to the north of the great breakwaters that form Sunderland's harbour. The northern breakwater, known as **Roker Pier**, is 825 metres long and was opened in 1903. **Roker Park** has been carefully restored to its former Victorian splendour, and from Roker and Seaburn through to Sunderland there is a six-mile-long seaside promenade which enjoys spectacular illuminations between August and November each year.

SUNDERLAND
10 miles SE of Newcastle on the A1018

MAP 12 REF N5

Much of Sunderland's history is told in an exhibition in the **Museum and Art Gallery** in Borough Road, where you'll also find examples of the fine theatrical maritime paintings of Sunderland sailor and subsequent Royal Academy artist, Clarkson Stansfield. The museum has been open for nearly 150 years and some of the popular exhibits, like Wallace the Lion, are familiar to generations of visitors. Live exhibits thrive in the Wildlife Gallery, while the Sunderland Story displays the town's history since prehistoric times. Lustreware Pottery and 'Pyrex' are part of this rich story and fossils, rocks and minerals take you even further back in time. A new gallery features the history of shipbuilding in Sunderland together with a collection of finely detailed models.

WASHINGTON
5 miles S of Newcastle on the A1231

MAP 12 REF M5

Present-day Washington is a second generation new town with modern, self-sufficient 'districts' each with its own number, scattered over a wide area surrounding the town centre. Visitors are strongly advised to study the roadside maps before entering the town as the road signs can be somewhat confusing. District 4 is the original Washington, and here you will find the **Old Hall** which gives rise to the claim that this is the ancestral home of George Washington. Washington Old Hall was a manor house originally built in the 12th century for the de Wessington family, direct ancestors of George Washington with other members of the Washington family living here until 1613. The present house was rebuilt on the medieval foundations and, due for demolition in 1936, was saved and given to the National Trust, being officially reopened by the American Ambassador in 1955. The ground floor and a bedroom have been furnished as a typical Durham manor house of the 17th and early-18th centuries. There is also a Jacobean rose garden.

Washington is also the home to the **Washington Wildfowl and Wetlands Centre**, a conservation area and bird watchers' paradise covering some 100 acres of hillside and valley. There are over 1,200 birds representing no less than 105 different species, including Mallard, Widgeon, Pochard, Tufted Duck, Redshank, Lapwing and Heron. There is also a visitor centre whose large picture windows overlook a succession of ponds in the Wear valley, and there are tea room and picnic areas and facilities for the disabled.

An interesting place for the historian and railway enthusiast is the **Bowes Railway** at Springwell village, north-east of Washington. It is the world's only standard-gauge, rope-hauled railway still in use and dates back to an original line designed by George Stephenson and opened in 1826. Now restored as a tourist steam railway the line extends to 15 miles. On the southeastern side of Washington the Victoria Viaduct carries the railway over the River Wear on 10 impressive arches. Based on the Roman bridge at Alcantra, Spain, the viaduct was opened in 1838 on Queen Victoria's Coronation Day.

10 The Lake District and Cumbria

INTRODUCTION

Cumbria is England's second largest county and it combines the former ancient counties of Cumberland and Westmorland with parts of Lancashire and Yorkshire. It was here that the British Celts managed to preserve their independence from the Saxons, though the Norse influences date from a later time. As a consequence, the place names are very different from those in the counties to the south and east and they reflect the individual history of this area.

The county town, Carlisle, lies in the north, close to the Scottish border and near to the western end of Hadrian's Wall. For centuries, the city was a base for English soldiers who planned their attacks on Scotland from here as well as defending Carlisle from the raiders. The Lake District National Park is not only home to England's largest lake, Windermere, but also the country's highest peak, Scafell Pike. A land of magnificent ancient crags, isolated fells, and wide open lakes, it was this dramatic landscape that inspired the poet Wordsworth and other artists besides and thus triggered an interest in the area which today makes it one of the most popular places in England. Cumbria also has a long coastline and, though there are some areas of industry, particularly at Sellafield, the Furness peninsula in the far southwest is extremely attractive. A place of elegant and small seaside resorts, the southern coast was also a place of great ecclesiastical power.

The southeastern part of the Lake District National Park is Cumbria's best known and most popular area, with the main resort towns of Windermere, Bowness-on-Windermere, and Ambleside and, of course, Lake Windermere itself. They are certainly busy with tourists during the summer months but their charm and attraction remains for all to see. Also, with the unpredictability of Lakeland weather, they provide a whole host of indoor amusements which can be an advantage. The whole area opened up to tourism as a result of the Victorians growing interest in the natural landscape and their engineering ability in providing a railway service. So these villages, once little more than places where the fell farmers congregated to buy and sell their livestock and exchange gossip, have grown into inland resorts with fine Victorian and Edwardian villas, houses, and municipal buildings. There are, also, many beautiful places close to the bustling and crowded towns that provide solitude. To the southeast lies Cartmel Fell while further north is isolated Kentmere.

The lakes, small towns, and villages of the southwestern Lake District will forever be associated with the many literary people who found inspiration amongst the often isolated and dramatic countryside. Grasmere, a quaint village still very much at the heart of the Lakes, was home to William Wordsworth who lived here before moving a short distance away to the solitude of Rydal Mount. Little has changed since his day, a stroll around this inspiring countryside is a must for anyone familiar with his romantic poetry.

The Cartmel and Furness Peninsulas, which form the southernmost coast of Cumbria, are often overlooked by visitors to the county. This is a great pity as both have much to offer the tourist including a rich history as well as splendid scenery. Lying between the lakes and mountains of the Lake District and the sandy estuaries of Morecambe Bay, this is an area of gentle moorland, craggy headlands, scattered woodlands, and vast expanses of sand.Once a stronghold of the Cistercian monks, their influence can still be seen in the buildings and fabric of the landscape. This is Cumbria's ecclesiastical centre and there were several monasteries here. Before the great boom of the local iron ore mining industry, the peninsula villages and market towns relied on farming and fishing and, before some of the river estuaries silted up, there was also some import and export trade. The rapid growth of Barrow-in-Furness, which will be forever linked with the ship-building industry, changed the face of much of the area but as the iron industry declined so did the town. The arrival of the railways, in the mid-19th century, however, saw the development of gentile resorts such as Grange-over-Sands overlooking the treacherous sands of Morecambe Bay. Still elegant places today, which have not suffered the indignity of vast amusement parks and rows of slot machines, this early tourist trade established the peninsulas as a quiet and pleasant holiday centre.

The southern section of Cumbria's western coastline and hinterland, stretching from Whitehaven down to Silecroft, has its own identity as well as a quiet charm. It is a coastline dominated by small, 18th and 19th century iron mining communities set against the romantic outline of the Lakeland fells and the grey-blue waters of the Irish Sea. This area is also home to one of Cumbria's finest stone circles, Swinside. However, perhaps the most outstanding attraction is not a man-made construction but the naturally formed St Bees Head. The most dramatic feature on the northwest coast, this red sandstone headland is, as well as being home to a lighthouse, the site of an important nature reserve.

The north Cumbrian coast, from Workington to the Solway Firth, is one of the least known parts of this beautiful county but it certainly has a lot to offer. It is an area rich in heritage, with a network of quiet country lanes, small villages, old ports, and seaside resorts. The coast's largest town, Workington, founded by the Romans, was once a large port, exporting coal and iron from the surrounding area. Further up the coast is Maryport, again a port originally built by the Romans. However, Maryport has not gone down the industrial route to the extent of its neighbour and, as well as being a quaint and picturesque place, it is also home to a fascinating museum dedicated to the town's maritime past. Inland lies Cockermouth on the edge of the National Park and a pretty market town with some elegant Georgian buildings. However, most visitors will be more interested to see and hear about the town's most famous son, William Wordsworth, born here in 1770.

The northernmost stretch of coastline, around the Solway Firth, is an area of tiny villages with fortified towers standing as mute evidence to the border struggles of long ago. These villages were the haunt of smugglers, wildfowlers, and half-net fishermen. What is particularly special about this coastline is its rich birdlife. The north Cumbria coast was also the setting for Walter Scott's novel, Red Gauntlet, and the fortified farmhouse by the roadside beyond Port Carlisle is said to be the White Ladies of the novel.

The northern Lakes are, for many enthusiasts, classic Lakeland, the scenery dominated by the rounded, heather-clad slopes of the Skiddaw range, to the north of Keswick, and the wild, craggy mountains of Borrowdale, to the south. Yet, despite this area's popularity, there are many hidden places to discover that are off the beaten track. The area is rich in history, as well as there being significant evidence of Roman occupation. But it is the wonderful, dramatic scenery that makes this area of the Lake District so special.

The River Eden is entirely Cumbrian and one of the few large rivers in England that flows northwards. It rises on the edge of the Yorkshire Dales, in the fells above Mallerstang, and ends its journey in the Solway Firth. Carved through boulder clay and red sandstone and sand-wiched between the Lakeland fells and the northern Pennines, the Eden Valley is green and fertile - in every sense another Eden. But the valley was vulnerable to Scottish raids in medieval times and the number of pele towers and castles in the area are testament to a turbulent and often violent past. This, too, is farming country and many of the ancient towns and villages have a market place.

Furthest north, the area around Carlisle has changed its allegiance to Scotland and England so often in the last 800 years that many of the inhabitants could be forgiven for not knowing whether to wear the thistle or the rose. This is Border Country, a wild and lonely, evocative landscape that sets the scene for so many of Sir Walter Scott's historical novels. This is, too, the country of Hadrian's Wall: not only are parts of the structure still visible, but Birdoswald gives an excellent insight into Roman border life. However, the Romans were most certainly not the first settlers here as one of the country's finest stone circles, Long Meg and her Daughters, can be found here at Little Salkeld.

CUMBRIA

KIRKBY LONSDALE
MAP 10 REF K8
14 miles NE of Lancaster on the A683

Lying on the banks of the **River Lune**, this old town is ideally situated for not only the Lake District National Park but also for the Yorkshire Dales and the eastern fells of Cumbria. Close to the county borders with Lancashire and Yorkshire, Kirkby Lonsdale has, despite the conflict of allegiances, maintained its character over the years and, now by-passed by the main road, it remains a very traditional and handsome market town where life still revolves around the market place and the 600 year-old cross. Thought to have been settled by marauding seafarers, there is more than a suggestion that this charming town has links with the Danes, particularly in the origin of its name.

Today's visitor to Kirkby Lonsdale will find lovely Georgian buildings crowding along the winding main street with interesting alleyways and courtyards to discover, excellent shops to browse in, and some wonderful tea shops. The weekly market, first granted its charter in 1227, is still held on Thursdays and, on the first full weekend in September, the town holds its annual Victorian Fair. The view from the churchyard of the Norman St Mary's Church is delightful and extends over the valley of the River Lune to the fells beyond. Not only was JMW Turner inspired to paint this very scene but John Ruskin wrote enthusiastically about what he saw: "The Valley of the Lune at Kirkby Lonsdale is one of the loveliest scenes in England..." Since then, the name **Ruskin's View** has stuck.

Overlooking Market Square in the centre of the picturesque town of Kirkby Lonsdale, the outstanding **Vale of Lune Coffee House and Restaurant** is a popular and attractive eatery. One of the oldest properties in Kirkby Lonsdale, it is a cosy and very pleasant place to enjoy a meal or snack. Whether it's coffee and a scone or a delicious home-cooked meal, visitors are never disappointed. The menu of this licensed restaurant features sandwiches, snacks, haddock, steak pie, giant Yorkshire pudding, Cumberland sausage, roast chicken with all the trimming and other traditional favourites, and of course a range of tempting cakes and pastries. Apart from the dishes on the menu there are always at least 10 extra main courses to choose from the

Vale of Lune Coffee House and Restaurant, No 7 Market Square, Kirkby Lonsdale, Cumbria LA6 2AN Tel: 015242 71374

specials board. Open in summer seven days a week, Sunday-Wednesday 10 a.m.-6 p.m. and Thursday-Saturday 10 a.m.-9 p.m. Closed Tuesdays in winter, when the hours are 11 a.m.-5 p.m. the other six days a week. Booking is advised for evenings.

However, perhaps the most famous landmark in Kirkby Lonsdale is its arched bridge over the River Lune. **Devil's Bridge** is reputed to be at least 600 years old and got its name from the legend of an old woman who, unable to cross the deep river with her cattle, asked the Devil to build her a bridge. He duly did this in return for the soul of the first creature to cross. But the clever woman threw a bun across the bridge which was retrieved by her dog and thus she cheated the Devil of a human soul. Disappearing in a howl of rage, the Devil left behind his neck collar, which some say can still be seen in the river below, as well as dropping the stones that he had been carrying in his apron.

Devil's Bridge, Kirkby Lonsdale

the castle was built by Uther but at that time, in the 6th century, it would have been made of wood. It was some time after 1092 that William Rufus, having conquered Carlisle, built a stone pele tower at Pendragon to guard the pass of Mallerstang. In 1268 the castle passed into the hands of the Clifford family. Twice it was burned by the Scots and repaired by the family; the second time, in 1660, by the most famous member of that family, Lady Anne Clifford.

CAUTLEY
MAP 10 REF K7

3 miles NE of Sedbergh on the A683

This quiet village, situated on a stunning stretch of road which, for a couple of miles follows the River Rawthey, is one of those beautiful routes through the high fells that only a few people find. For campers and walkers this area is a perfect place to be based for a holiday, surrounded on all sides by the best English walking country, with the Lake District and the Yorkshire Dales National Parks to choose from. The **Howgill Fells**, a series of magnificent, open hills and ancient commonland, provide some of the most spectacular countryside in the north of England for the dedicated hillwalker. Several tracks and old greenways lead across them. Here can be found the peaks such as **Uldale Head**, **Yarlside**, and **The Calf**, at 2,219 feet the highest point in the Howgills. The most spectacular feature of the Howgills is **Cautley Crag**, a great cliff several hundred feet high, alongside which a beautiful narrow waterfall, **Cautley Spout**, tumbles.

KENDAL
MAP 10 REF J7

10 miles W of Sedburgh on the A684

The ancient town of Kendal, in the valley of the River Kent, was once one of the most important woollen textile centres of northern England. The Kendal woollen industry was founded in 1331 by John Kemp, a Flemish weaver, and it flourished and sustained the town for almost 600 years until the development of competition from the huge West Riding of Yorkshire mills during the Industrial Revolution of the 19th century. The town's motto "Wool is my Bread" reveals the extent to which the economy of Kendal depended on the wool from the flocks of Herdwick sheep that roamed the surrounding fells and the fame of the cloth was so great that Shakespeare refers to archers clad in Kendal Green cloth in his play Henry IV, Part 1. The town was also famous for its Kendal Bowmen, skilled archers whose longbows were made from local yew trees found on the nearby limestone crags. It was these men who fought so decisively against the Scots at the Battle of Flodden Field in 1513. Kendal has royal connections too: Catherine Parr, the last of Henry VIII's six wives, lived at **Kendal Castle** in the 16th century before she became Queen of England. Today, its ruins, high on a hill overlooking the town, helps to locate one of the original Roman camps that guarded the route to the Scottish border. Catherine Parr's Book of Devotions is housed in the Town Hall, on Stricklandgate.

The largest town in the old county of Westmorland, Kendal has always been a bustling town, from the days when it was on the main route to Scotland. Nowadays the M6 and a by pass divert much of the traffic away from the town centre, but its narrow main streets, Highgate, Stramongate, and Stricklandgate, are still busy, and the fine stagecoaching inns of the 17th and 18th centuries, to which Prince Charles Edward is said to have retreated after his abortive 1745 rebellion, still line these streets. At the bottom of Highgate is the **Abbot Hall Museum of Lakeland Life and Industry**, themed around traditional rural trades of the region, such as blacksmithying, wheelwrighting, agricultural activities, weaving, and printing. Here, too, are recreated cottage interiors and elegantly furnished period rooms. **Abbot Hall Art Gallery** forms part of a complex within Abbot Hall park and includes work by John Ruskin and the celebrated Kendal painter, George Romney.

Adjacent to the elegant Georgian Abbot Hall is the 13th century **Parish Church** of Kendal, one of the largest in England, with five aisles and a peel of 10 bells. The church also contains a sword thought to have belonged to Robert Philipson, a Cavalier during the Civil War. Whilst away fighting in Carlisle, Cromwell's supporters laid siege to Philipson's house at Windermere and, seeking revenge, the Cavalier attacked the Kendal church when he thought the Roundheads would be at prayer. Riding his horse right into the church, he found it empty save for one innocent man whom he ran through with this sword. At the other end of the town, near the railway station, is the **Museum of Natural History and Archaeology**. Based on the collection first exhibited by William Todhunter in the late 18th century, there are displays of both local and worldwide wildlife. The famous writer, Alfred Wainwright, whose hand-written guides to the Lakeland hills are classics, once held the post of curator of the museum and his office here can still be seen. Anyone wandering around the town can not help but notice the numerous alleyways, locally known as yards, that are such a distinctive feature of Kendal. An integral part of the old town, they are a reminder that the people of Kendal lived under a constant threat of raids by the Scots. The yards were a line of defence against these attacks, an area that could be secured by sealing the one small entrance with the families and livestock safe inside.

Kendal is a good centre from which to explore South Cumbria. There is a good railway and motorway access and some surprisingly nice walks from the town, along the River Kent or into the surrounding limestone hills. It is this stone that gives the buildings the distinctive pale grey colour which is such a familiar feature of the Lake District.

SEDGWICK
Map 10 ref J7

4 miles S of Kendal off the A591

Lying to the northwest of the village is **Sizergh Castle**, the impressive home of the Strickland family since 1239 and now a National Trust property. Originally a pele tower built to withstand the border raiders, the house has been added to and altered over the intervening centuries to provide the family, as times became less violent, with a more comfortable home. Now boasting intricately carved chimney mantels, fine oak panelling, and a collection of family portraits, the castle's main attraction is its well laid out gardens and the superb views over the Lakeland fells. The ghost of a lady of Sizergh in medieval times is said to haunt the castle, screaming to be released from the room that her fiercely jealous husband locked her in and where she starved to death whilst he was away in battle.

BRIGSTEER
Map 10 ref J7

3 miles SW of Kendal off the A591

This tiny hamlet lies under the limestone escarpment of Scout Scar. From this pretty settlement, the road leads into Brigsteer Wood where, as the climate is milder here due to its sheltered position, there are fine early flowers in the spring. Situated within the Lake District National Park at the edge of the scenic village of Brigsteer, **Low Plain** is a magnificent country house offering top-of-the-range bed and breakfast and self-catering accommodation. Owners Jean and Duncan Macbeth have been offering a warm welcome to guests since 1997. Surrounded by acres and acres of picturesque countryside in a secluded hideaway that is just 4 miles from popular Kendal, guests are

Low Plain, Brigsteer, nr Kendal, Cumbria LA8 8AX
Tel: 015395 68464

sure to have an enjoyable and memorable stay. This former farmhouse dates back to the 1800s, and sits amid 13 acres of pastureland and woodland. There are three lovely ensuite rooms (two doubles and one twin), each with superb furnishings and decor, and commanding wonderful views. Peace and quiet are assured at this country retreat. The breakfasts are hearty and filling, and for evening meals there are plenty of good restaurants and pubs in the area. Open March - October. No smoking. Adjacent to the main building there is a one-bedroomed cottage available for self-catering holidays all year round. Children welcome.

NEW HUTTON   Map 10 ref J7
3 miles SE of Kendal off the A684

The Borrans is a quality bed and breakfast establishment, surrounded by thousands of acres of scenic countryside in the tiny hamlet of New Hutton, a mile off the A684 Kendal to Sedbergh Road. A peaceful retreat ideal to use as a touring base, it enjoys a relaxed family atmosphere. Owner Isabella Ellis has been providing superb accommodation here since 1971. The property dates back to 1729; there are three upstairs guest rooms (one of which is ensuite) - two family rooms and a double. All have good facilities and are cosy, well decorated and handsomely furnished. One commands excellent views over the valley towards Oxenholme. There is a separate guests' lounge with an open fire and television. The hearty

Borrans, New Hutton, Kendal, Cumbria LA8 0AT
Tel: 01539 722969

and delicious breakfast is taken in the cosy breakfast room. Isabella's daughters run the cafe situated within the well-known Webbs Garden Centre in Kendal, an excellent place to enjoy a midday meal or afternoon tea.

WINDERMERE   Map 10 ref J7
10 miles NW of Kendal on the A591

The town and the lake of the same name are perhaps the best known of the Lake District's tourist centres. The confusion of the names between the town and the lake goes back to the days when the Kendal and Windermere Railway Company was opened in 1847. Its terminal station was at the village of Birthwaite - hardly a name to bring the tourists flocking in - so the railway company called their station Windermere, even though it is over a mile away from the lake. In the early days carriages and, in later years, buses linked the station with the landing stages in the village of Bowness on the shores of the lake.

Such was the popularity of the Lake District, even in Victorian times, that a town filled with hotels, boarding houses, comfortable villas, and shops soon sprang up around the railway station. It spread rapidly down the hill towards the lake until Bowness and Birthwaite were linked together under the name of Windermere Town, the lake being given the unnecessary prefix

Lake. Windermere's railway line remains open as a single track branch - The Lakes Line - now the only surviving British Rail line to run into the heart of the Lake District. Modern diesel railcars provide a busy shuttle service to and from the express services at Oxenholme. The rail journey via Kendal, Burneside, and Staveley is a delight and a very pleasant alternative to the crowded A591 road. Within a few yards of Windermere Station, just across the busy main road, there is a footpath that leads through the woods to one of the finest viewpoints in Lakeland, **Orrest Head**. It takes about an hour from the station to climb and descend the little hillock but there is no better introduction to this part of Cumbria.

The **High Street Restaurant** stands almost opposite Windermere Railway Station. After many years in the catering industry, owners David and Alison Walker took on this existing business in May of 1999. They have created a restaurant of excellent quality that comes well recommended. They have refurbished the restaurant so that it now boasts a stylish Continental

High Street Restaurant, 4 High Street, Windermere, Cumbria LA23 1AF Tel: 015394 44954

decor and appearance, with wood floors and bright, cheerful touches throughout. The ambience is friendly and intimate. The pan-European menu changes regularly, but can always be relied upon to offer superb freshly prepared dishes such as rack of lamb, fillet steak medallions with black pudding and red wine sauce, roast Gressingham duck, and vegetable, almond and spinach strudel. There is also an excellent wine list. Seating 24 downstairs and a further 14 upstairs, with an area for pre- and after-dinner drinks. Open evenings from 7-9.30 p.m. Monday - Saturday, booking is advisable.

Villa Lodge is a stylish guest house hidden away in Cross Street, high up overlooking Windermere village. It boasts magnificent views of the Lakeland mountains and Lake Windermere, while being just two minutes' walk from village shops and restaurants. Situated on the site of an old brewery and bottling factory, it was built in 1895 and was once inhabited by the owners of the factory. Accommodation has been offered here since the 1930s. This is the first venture into business for owners Mick and Fiona Rooney, who have been here since June of 1998. Fiona was born and bred locally, and knows a great deal about nearby sights and attractions. Open all year round, it offers eight ensuite bedrooms on two floors. Two of the rooms are singles. Special deals are available out of season. Guests are sure of being well looked after here, as the Rooneys provide warm hospitality amid comfortable and very pleasant surroundings. The bedrooms are tastefully decorated

Villa Lodge, Cross Street, Windermere, Cumbria LA23 1AE Tel/Fax: 015394 43318

and very comfortable; all have colour television and tea/coffee-making facilities. Some rooms have four-poster beds. The excellent breakfast is served in the lovely dining room. Special diets can be catered for upon prior request. There is also a cosy lounge and sunny conservatory in which guests can relax. Children welcome. Pets welcome by prior arrangement. In addition to all the impressive scenery and attractions of the area, the guest house is close to facilities for horse-riding, fishing, sailing and local art and craft centres.

WINDERMERE (LAKE)
S of Windermere on the A592

MAP 10 REF J7

Not only is Windermere the largest lake in Cumbria but it is, at 11 miles long, the largest in England. For many people it is also the Lake District and though it certainly is one of the most beautiful at times, particularly in the middle of the summer, it can be a little crowded. Formed in the Ice Age by the action of moving glaciers, the lake is fed by the Rivers Brathay and Rothay,

Steamer, Lake Windermere

at the northern end, whilst the outlet is into the River Leven, at Newby Bridge. Windermere is actually a public highway or, more correctly, waterway and this stretch of water, with its thickly wooded banks and scattered islands, has been used since Roman times as a means of transport. Roman Legionnaires used it for carrying stone to their fort at Galava, near present day Ambleside, at the head of the lake. Later, the monks of Furness Abbey fished here for pike and char. Naturally, the lake is much used by all manner of watersports en-

thusiasts and, amongst the sailing boats, motor boats, and wind surfers, are the steamers which provide a service from Lakeside at the southern end to Waterhead at the northern end. There is also a car ferry which crosses the lake from Bowness to the Sawreys.

On a level with Bowness, the lake is almost divided in two by **Belle Island**, which is believed to have been inhabited by the Romans. During the Civil War, it was owned by Colonel Phillipson (the Royalist supporter who disgraced himself by riding into Kendal Parish Church) and his family had to withstand an 80 day siege, successfully, whilst the colonel was away on another campaign. In 1774, the island was bought by Mr English who constructed the round house which, at the time, caused such consternation that he sold the property and the island to Isabella Curwen, who planted the surrounding trees.

BOWNESS-ON-WINDERMERE
2 miles S of Windermere on the A592

MAP 10 REF J7

It is from this attractive, albeit busy, town right on the edge of the lake that most of the lake cruises operate. There are few nicer ways to spend a summer day in the Lake District than taking one of the handsome, vintage boats of the Windermere Iron Steamboat Company from Bowness Pier or Ambleside down to Lakeside. Bowness, however, is not all crowds and boats. Away from the marinas and the car parks is the old village, where **St Martin's Church** is of particular interest. It has a magnificent east window filled with 14th and 15th century glass and an unusual 300 year-old wooden carved figure of St Martin, sharing his cloak with a beggar. The village is much older than its very near neighbour and dates from the 10th century though it is known that the Vikings settled in the area. The very name Windermere comes from Vinand's Mere, Vinand being the name of a Nordic chief. On the lake shore, just to the north of the village, is the **Windermere Steam Boat Museum** - an attraction well worth visiting. This unique collection of Victorian and Edwardian steam launches includes the SL Dolly, the oldest mechanically powered boat in the world. Moored in a wet dock, some of the launches are still in working order and are taken out to make their peaceful and elegant journey around the lake. Just a short walk from the lakeside is the **Old Laundry Visitor Centre**, the home of the **World of Beatrix Potter**. An walk around the centre will not only bring the author's famous characters, such as Peter Rabbit and Jemima Puddleduck to life, but there is also a coffee shop and a theatre.

NEWBY BRIDGE   MAP 10 REF J7
8 miles S of Windermere on the A592

The mass of end moraines seen here show clearly that the village lay at the southern most point of Windermere as they were deposited by the glacier whilst it paused having carved out the lake. Today, however, the village is some distance from the water's edge which can be reached on foot, by car, or by taking a steam railway, the **Lakeside and Haverthwaite Railway**.

TROUTBECK BRIDGE   MAP 10 REF J7
1 mile N of Windermere on the A591

This small village, in the valley of Trout Beck, takes its name from the bridge here over the beck, just before the water runs into Windermere. During the 17th century, Calgarth Hall was owned by Myles Phillipson, a local JP who wished to gain possession of nearby farmland. So, he invited the landowner and his wife to a banquet at the Hall and then, having hidden a silver cup in their luggage, accused them of stealing. At the resulting trial, Phillipson was the presiding judge and he sentenced the couple to death as well as appropriating their land. As she was led away, the wife placed a curse on the judge saying that not only would his victims never leave him but that his family would also perish in poverty. The couple were executed but their skulls reappeared at Calgarth Hall and, no matter what Phillipson did (including burning them and throwing them into Lake Windermere) the skulls kept returning to the Hall. Moreover, the Phillipson family grew poorer and poorer until, in 1705, the family died out altogether.

AMBLESIDE   MAP 10 REF J7
4 miles N of Windermere on the A591

This is one of the major Lakeland towns and an excellent base from which to enjoy some extremely good walks, most notably into the high fells to the north of the town. The strategic position of the town, on the main north to south road through the Lake District, was not lost on the Romans who, in AD 79, built Galava fort just to the south of present day Ambleside. A pretty town, that was granted its market charter in 1650, many of the original 17th century buildings are preserved in the centre which is now a conservation area. None of the buildings, however, are as interesting as the **Old Bridge House**, a tiny cottage perched on a little packhorse bridge in the centre of Ambleside. Now a National Trust shop, in the 1850's, this was once the home of Mr and Mrs Rigg and their six children - the main room of this one-up, one-down house measures 13 feet by 6 feet! The cottage, built over **Stock Ghyll**, was originally the summer house of the former Ambleside Hall. The **Church of St Mary** is unusual for a Lakeland church in that it has a 180 foot spire. Within the building can be seen a mural, depicting the ancient ceremony of rush-bearing, painted by Gordon Ransome of the Royal College of Art during World War II when the college was evacuated to the town. The ceremony, dating back to the days when the floor of the church was covered with rushes, is still held on the first Saturday in July. It was to Ambleside that William Wordsworth and his sister would walk, from their home at Grasmere, to collect their post and, in 1813, when Wordsworth became Distributor of Stamps for Westmorland, he had his office in the town. Other literary connections are with Harriet Martineau, who lived at The Knoll, and the Armitt sisters, who lived in the town and left their collection of local history books to Ambleside in 1912. From the town centre, a steep road climbs sharply up to the dramatic **Kirkstone Pass** and over to Ullswater. The pass is so called because of the rock at the top which looks like a church steeple. Rising to some 1,489 feet above sea level, the road is the highest in the Lake District and, though today's vehicles make light work of the climb, it has for centuries presented a formidable obstacle. The severest incline, known as **The Struggle**, necessitated passengers to step out of their coach and to make their way on foot, leaving the horses to make the steep haul with just the carriage.

ELTERWATER
MAP 10 REF J7

4 miles W of Ambleside on the B5343/off the A593]

Known as one of the best inns in the Lake District, **Britannia Inn** is a traditional Free House which has been run by Fry family since 1978, and is now in the capable hands of Judy Fry. The core of this impressive inn dates back some 400 years. Originally a farmhouse, what is now the residents' lounge was formerly a cobbler's shop, it became an inn in 1870. Set in the pictur-

esque village of Elterwater, it attracts many visitors. Everything the guest could wish for can be found here. Lunch is served from midday-2 p.m., light snacks between 2 and 5.30 p.m., and dinner from 6.30-9.30 p.m. Meals can be taken in the bar or separate (non-smoking) dining room - or, on fine days, on the attractive out-

Britannia Inn, Elterwater, Ambleside, Cumbria LA22 9HP
Tel: 015394 37210 Fax: 015394 37311
email: info@britinn.co.uk website: www.britinn.co.uk

door patio. Head barman Chris Jones looks after the quality local real ales available, which include Dent Aviator, Jennings Bitter and Coniston Bluebird. The menu features dishes prepared from Langdale Herdwick lamb, as well as farmhouse pie, medallions of pork, monkfish and vegetarian pasta bake. This fine establishment also boasts 13 comfortable and well-appointed letting rooms - nine in the inn and the other four across the road above the village shop.Children welcome.

TROUTBECK
MAP 10 REF J7

3 miles N of Windermere off the A592

Designated a conservation area, the village has no recognisable centre as the houses and cottages are grouped around a number of wells and springs which, until recently, was the only form of water supply. Dating from the 16th, 17th, and 18th centuries, the houses retain many of their original features, including mullioned windows, heavy cylindrical chimneys, and, in some cases, exposed spinning galleries, and they will be of great interest to lovers of vernacular architecture. **Troutbeck Church**, too, is worthy of a visit as there is a fine east window, dating from 1873, that is the combined work of Edward Burne-Jones, Ford Maddox Brown, and William Morris. However, perhaps the best known building at Troutbeck is **Townend** which lies to the south of the village and was built in 1626 by George Browne. A fine example of a yeoman farmer's house, the Browne family lived here until 1944 and now it is in the hands of the National Trust. The interior of the house contains many of the Browne family's furniture, domestic utensils, and papers and a visit provides a unique insight into the domestic life of wealthy farming families.

The road through the Troutbeck valley leads to the **Kirkstone Pass** but it was the Romans, in a bid to link their forts at Ambleside and Brougham, who first built a typically uncompromisingly routed road through the valley. Travelling straight across mountain ridges the route does avoid the forests and swamps of the lower ground and it may even follow the line of an earlier, British road.

KENTMERE

MAP 10 REF J7

4 miles NE of Windermere off the A591

This hamlet, as name implies, lies in part of the valley that was once a lake; drained to provide precious bottom pasture land. A large mill pond remains to provide a head of water on the River Kent for use at a paper mill. Inside St Cuthbert's Church is a bronze memorial to Bernard Gilpin who was born at Kentmere Hall in 1517 and went on to become Archdeacon of Durham Cathedral. Known as The Apostle of the North, Gilpin was also a leader of the Reformation and, in 1558, he travelled to London to face charges of heresy against the Roman Catholic Church. During the journey, Gilpin fell and broke his leg but, fortunately, whilst he was recovering Catholic Queen Mary died and was succeeded by Protestant Queen Elizabeth. The new queen restored him to favour and saved Gilpin from being burnt at the stake. The beautiful valley of the **River Kent** is best explored on foot and a public footpath goes up its Western side past Kentmere Hall, a fortified pele tower that is now a private farmhouse. The River Kent, which runs down into Kendal from Staveley via Burneside, carries the Dales Way from Yorkshire into the Lake District along its banks, an attractive stretch of riverside path, richly varied in character from mill-dam to rapids, and a haven for wildlife.

CONISTON

MAP 10 REF I7

8 miles W of Windermere on the A593

This once important copper mining centre is also widely known for the beautiful decorative green slate, quarried locally, which is used on so many of the public buildings. Just to the south of the village and beside the lake is Coniston Hall, the village's oldest building. Dating from the 16th century, it was the home of the Le Fleming family, the largest landowners in the area. Coniston's most famous inhabitant was, however, John Ruskin, the 19th century author, artist, critic, and social commentator. He lies buried in Coniston churchyard and the **Ruskin Museum**, housed in the Coniston Institute, contains some of his studies, pictures, letters, and photographs as well as his collection of geological specimens. John Ruskin's home, **Brantwood**, lies in a beautiful setting on the eastern

Brantwood, Coniston

shores of Coniston Water. His home between 1872 and 1900, many of the great man's possessions are on display including his watercolours and drawings.

The great bulk of the **Old Man of Coniston** overlooks the village and it was on this mountain, and some of the surrounding hills, that the copper was extracted. Mined from the days of the Romans, the industry's heyday in Coniston took place in the 18th and 19th centuries but, with the discovery of more accessible deposits, the industry went into decline and the village returned to pre-boom peacefulness. At 2,631 feet, the Old Man of Coniston is a considerable climb but many make the effort and the summit can be bustling with fell walkers enjoying the glorious views.

CONISTON WATER
S of Coniston on the A593

MAP 10 REF I7

Though this is one of the more famous lakes it is also one which is considerably less crowded than many of the others. Coniston Water is a gentler lake than Windermere and, because of its relative calmness, the lake was used for water speed record attempts. It has seen its share of triumph and tragedy in the careers of Malcolm Campbell and his son, Donald, who perished on the lake in an attempt to break the world record in 1967. A memorial to him is in the centre of Coniston village. However, happier associations lie with memories of the author Arthur Ransome who used Coniston Water as a setting for his series of children's novels. **Peel Island**, at the south end of the lake, is the Wildcat Island of his books. Like Windermere, Coniston Water too is a public waterway but, fortunately, there is a strict 10 mile an hour speed limit and so most of the boating is done under sail. However, one pleasant and memorable exception is the Gondola, a steam launch rebuilt by the National Trust, that travels quietly around the lake.

HAVERTHWAITE
8 miles S of Coniston on the A5092

MAP 10 REF I7

This is the southern terminus of the **Lakeside and Haverthwaite Railway**, originally a branch of the Furness Railway, which was built to transport goods and passengers from Ulverston to the steamers on Lake Windermere. One of the first attempts at mass tourism in the Lake District, passenger numbers peaked in the 1920's but a decline after World War II caused the line to be closed in 1967. The railway is now run by a group of dedicated rail enthusiasts and they provide a full service of steam trains on a journey that links with the Windermere steamers.

GRIZEDALE
3 miles SE of Coniston off the B5285

MAP 10 REF J7

The village lies at the heart of **Grizedale Forest** which was acquired by the Forestry Commission in 1934 and is famous for its Theatre and Sculpture. The Commission's original intention of chiefly cultivating the forest for its timber met with much resistance and, over the years, many pathways have been opened and a variety of recreational activities have been encouraged. The Visitor Centre vividly illustrates the story of the forest as well as showing how the combination of wildlife, recreation, and commercial timbering can work together hand in hand. The forest, too, is famously the home of nearly 100 sculptures which have been commissioned since the early 1980's; all are created from natural materials found in the forest and they have been made by some of Britain's best known contemporary artists, including Andy Goldsworthy, as well as by artists from all over the world. The great beauty of these sculptures is their understated presence: there are no signposts pointing to the exhibits and visitors are left entirely on their own to discover these wonders though there is a printed map obtainable from the Visitor Centre.

The **Theatre-in-the-Forest** has an excellent programme throughout the year of musical and theatrical events of the highest quality, and the Visitor Centre now includes an art gallery and workshop which is also open to the public, where the artists in residence will happily take a break from their work to describe their experiences of living and working in this unique environment.

NEAR SAWREY
MAP 10 REF J7
4 miles E of Coniston on the B5285

Though this little village will not be familiar to many visitors to the Lake District, its famous inhabitant, Beatrix Potter, almost certainly will be. After holidaying here in 1896, the authoress fell in love with the place and, with the royalties from her first book, Peter Rabbit, she purchased **Hill Top**. A charming and quaint 17th century farmhouse, which was her home for many years and also the place where she wrote many of her books. Following her death in 1943, the house and the land she bought on the surrounding fells, became the property of the National Trust and, in accordance with her will, Hill Top has remained exactly as she would have known it. One of the most popular Lakeland attractions, Hill Top is full of Beatrix Potter memorabilia, including some of her original drawings, and it is best avoided at peak holiday times though it is well worth the visit.

HAWKSHEAD
MAP 10 REF J7
3 miles E of Coniston on the B5285

Situated at the head of Esthwaite Water, this village was once an important market town serving the surrounding area. Much of it was owned by the monks of Furness Abbey but the only building to remain from those monastic times is the Courthouse, to the north of the village, that is now home to a **Museum of Rural Life**. The church, with its massive spire, seems rather grand for the village but it too was built at a time when Hawkshead was an wealthy town. Little, however, has changed since William Wordsworth attended Hawkshead Grammar School between 1779 and 1787. Not only can Wordsworth's desk, on which he carved his name, still be seen at the school but Ann Tyson's cottage, where he stayed, still stands. It was during his time in Hawkshead that the young Wordsworth developed his love of the Lakeland hills and fells that were to shape the poetry of his later life. Several of the village's buildings are owned by The National Trust, including **Bend or Bump**, which was formerly a house and a shop and features in Beatrix Potter's The Pie and the Patty Pan, and the former solicitor's office of William Heelis, who was Beatrix Potter's husband. Now the **Beatrix Potter Gallery**, the former office displays many of her original drawings as well as exhibitions on her life as an author, artist and pioneer of conservation. Some lovely walks lead from Hawkshead to Roger Ground and Esthwaite Water and also to the nearby hamlet of **Colthouse**, a group of farmsteads and cottages with an early Quaker Meeting House built in 1688.

HARDKNOTT PASS
MAP 9 REF I7
5 miles W of Coniston off the A593

Surrounded by the fell of the same name, the pass is one of the most treacherous in the Lake District yet it was used by the Romans for their road between their forts at Ambleside (Galava) and Ravenglass (Glannaventa). Of the remains of Roman occupation the fort on a shoulder of the fell, overlooking the Esk Valley, is the most substantial.

BOOT
MAP 9 REF I7
8 miles W of Coniston off the A595

Lying at the eastern end of the **Ravenglass and Eskdale Railway**, this is a wonderful place to visit whether arriving by train or car. A gentle walk from the station at Eskdale, this is a delightful village, with its pub, post office, museum watermill and nearby St Catherine's Church in its riverside setting.

WAST WATER

MAP 9 REF I7

10 miles W of Coniston off the A595

Though it is just 3 miles long, this beautiful and remote lake is England's deepest. The southern shores of the lake are dominated by huge screes that rise some 250 feet and they provide an awesome backdrop to this tranquil stretch of water. A lake less like Windermere would be hard to find as there are no motorboats ploughing their way up and down the lake; this is very much the country of walkers and climbers and from here there are many footpaths up to some of the best fells in Cumbria.

Wasdale Head, just to the north of the lake, is a small, close knit community that welcomes walkers and climbers who have been out discovering Wasdale and the lake. The village church, thought to be the smallest in England, is believed to have been built in the 14th century and it is hard to see amidst the tiny copse of trees. Local legend suggests that the roof beams came from a Viking ship and, before a late Victorian restoration, the church had an earth floor and few seats.

SCAFELL PIKE

MAP 9 REF I7

8 miles N of Coniston off the B5343

The highest point in England, at 3,210 feet, the mountain lies to the north of **Sca Fell** (3,162 feet) and is separated from it by the notorious obstacle, Broad Stand. There are several routes to the top of the pike and they are both long and demanding and should not be attempted in poor or deteriorating weather. However, the views from the top are tremendous, assuming a clear day, and take in most of Cumbria's central fells. It should also be remembered that Sca Fell is considered a training ground for climbers preparing an assault on the Andes or the Himalayas.

GRASMERE

MAP 10 REF J7

7 miles N of Coniston off the A591

The focal point of Wordsworth country, this picturesque village in a lovely mountain setting, lies close to the very pretty lake of the same name that is surrounded by craggy hills. Not surprisingly this small village gets extremely busy but it is delightful to walk around, and worth braving the crowds, before heading for the more hidden places of the south lakes. One road winds its way through the village, passing St Oswald's Church, where Wordsworth and many members of his family are buried in the churchyard.

No trip to Grasmere is complete, of course, without a visit to the **Wordsworth Museum** and **Dove Cottage**, where William and his sister Dorothy lived from 1799-1808. In 1802 William married Mary and she came to join the Dove Cottage household. Coleridge and de Quincy often came to stay - in fact, one gets the impression that they came perhaps just a little too often, indulging in quantities of opium and uncomfortably swelling the numbers in this rather small house where newspaper lined the walls for warmth and economy and, for much of their time here, the Wordsworths could afford little more to eat than porridge. This must have been an eccentric household and the guided tour of Dove Cottage paints a very clear picture of their lifestyle, with a little insight into the unusual relationship between Dorothy, William, and Mary. In the museum, the Wordsworth Trust's collection is inspiringly presented, and includes original Wordsworth manuscripts, letters exchanged between Wordsworth and his friends, and extracts from the original of Dorothy's journals.

RYDAL

MAP 10 REF J7

7 miles N of Coniston on the A591

The Wordsworth story continues at **Rydal Mount**, where William, his sister, and his wife lived from 1813 until 1850 when he died. This is a handsome house, overlooking **Rydal Water**, and it is still owned by descendants of the Wordsworth family, who have opened it to the public along with the gardens that William laid out himself. Among the poet's personal possessions on display, the house contains the only portrait of Wordsworth's sister, Dorothy. From the Grasmere end of Rydal Water there are some lovely walks around the two lakes or to the summit of **Loughrigg Fell**, an easily manageable walk which rewards with breathtaking views of the lakes.

SKELWITH BRIDGE
Map 10 ref J7

5 miles N of Coniston on the B5343

From the village a footpath follows the River Brathay upstream to the point where it dramatically falls over some rocks, creating **Skelwith Force**. Also near to the village are the works of the Kirkstone Greenslate Quarries Company, whose distinctive slate can be seen all over the Lake District and has been quarried here for centuries.

LITTLE LANGDALE
Map 10 ref J7

4 miles N of Coniston off the A593

The village lies in one of the two valleys that together make up the Langdales. Best seen on foot as, particularly during the summer, the narrow road linking Great and Little Langdale can become quite congested, these are the most beautiful valleys in Cumbria. At the head of Great Langdale lie the **Langdale Pikes**; impressive and with a very distinctive outline, the peaks have provided inspiration to many artists over the years.

GRANGE-OVER-SANDS
Map 10 ref J8

15 miles S of Windermere off the A590

This once small coastal village was transformed into a fashionable resort when the scenic Furness Railway was built in 1857 linking Grange-over-Sands with the industrial towns of Lancashire. Hotels, villas, and boarding houses sprang up along with ornamental gardens and the attractive mile long promenade. Though Grange-over-Sands does not have a beach to rival that of its brash neighbour across Morecambe Bay, it does have an exceptionally mild climate, the mildest in the northwest, and, thanks to the Gulf Stream, it is still a popular place particularly with people who are looking for a pleasant and quiet place to retire. The route to Grange-over-Sands, across the sands of Morecambe Bay, is a treacherous one though it was used not only by the Romans but also by the monks of Furness Abbey and, later, by stagecoaches looking to shorten their journey time. Avoiding the quicksands of the bay, which have taken many lives over the centuries, is a difficult task and, in the 16th century, the Duchy of Lancaster appointed an official guide to escort travellers over the shifting sands. There are still guided walks today and those wishing to venture out into the bay are well advised to seek their help.

Away from the hotels, shops, and cafés of the town there are some lovely walks and none are nicer and more pleasant than the path behind Grange-over-Sands which climbs through the magnificent limestone woodlands that are rich in wild flowers. The path finally leads to **Hampsfell Summit** and **The Hospice**, a little stone tower from which there are unforgettable views over the bay and, in the opposite direction,

Promenade, Grange-over-Sands

the craggy peaks of the Lake District. The Hospice was provided by a pastor of Cartmel in the last century for the shelter and entertainment of wanderers. An external flight of stairs leads to a flat roof and the viewing point. Grange-over-Sands is also situated at the starting point of the **Cistercian Way**, an exceptionally interesting 37 mile long foot path through Furness to Barrow which takes in, naturally, many Cistercian sites.

ALLITHWAITE   MAP 10 REF J8
2 miles SW of Grange-over-Sands on the B52780

There has been a settlement here since the time of the Vikings when it was called Lilifr's Thwaite - thwaite being the Westmorland word for a clearing. A pretty village of charming cottages, during the 17th century Allithwaite boasted a corn mill and, later, a brewery.

Within the old manor of Allithwaite lies **Humphrey Head** where, in the 18th and 19th centuries, visitors flocked to sample the waters of Holy Well. Miners from Yorkshire and Cumberland also came, believing that the waters would cure their illnesses.

FLOOKBURGH   MAP 10 REF J8
3 miles SW of Grange-over-Sands off the B5278

This small fishing village lies just south of **Holker Hall and Gardens**, one of the homes of the Cavendish family, the Dukes of Devonshire. A visit to the hall needs plenty of time and walking around the rooms of the house, which retains its family atmosphere, is an interesting experience. As well as seeing one of the best private libraries in the country, there are over 3,500 volumes, visitors will also find an embroidered panel said to be the work of Mary, Queen of Scots.

The hall's extensive outbuildings are now home to the **Lakeland Motor Museum**, which includes an exhibition on the record breaking attempts of Sir Malcolm and Donald Campbell amongst the collection of historic cars and vehicles. The hall is set within a splendid estate and deerpark which includes the amazing formal gardens that are justly world-famous.

CARTMEL   MAP 10 REF J8
2 miles W of Grange-over-Sands off the B5278

One of the prettiest village in Furness, Cartmel is a delightful cluster of houses and cottages set around a square from which lead winding streets and arches into back yards. The village is dominated by the famous **Cartmel Priory**, founded in 1188 by Augustinian canons. According to legend, it was originally intended to be sited on nearby Mount Bernard, but St Cuthbert appeared in a vision to the monastic architect and ordered him to build the priory between two springs of water. The next morning, water was found to be trickling from the two foundation stones and this is where the church stands today. Like all monastic institutions, the priory was disbanded in 1537 and several of its members were executed for participating in the Pilgrimage of Grace. Today, only the 12th century **Gatehouse** and the **Church of St Mary and St Michael** have survived.

Cartmel Priory Church

Many of the village's cottages and houses having been built using stones from the ruined priory buildings. After the Dissolution, only the south aisle of the church was useable but, in 1620, George Preston of Holker began to restore the entire building and the richly carved black oak screens and stall canopies date from this restoration. Apart from its glorious east window, one of its most noticeable features is the unique tower set diagonally on the tower stage. Inside, in the southwest corner of the church, is a door known as Cromwell's Door. The holes in it are said to have been made by indignant parishioners firing at Parliamentarian soldiers who had stabled their horses in the nave. Cromwell's troops were certainly in the area in 1643 and, to further establish the story, fragments of lead were found in the wood during restoration work in 1955.

Cartmel too is famous for its attractive **Racecourse** on which meetings are held during the spring. Close to the village, the course must be one of the most picturesque in the country and it is certainly one of the smallest. A holiday atmosphere descends on the village for race day and, though the competition is fierce, it is a wonderful and relaxing day out.

ULVERSTON

Map 9 ref I8

10 miles W of Grange-over-Sands on the A590

This fine old market town dates from the 12th century when Stephen, Earl of Boulogne and King of England, owned the manor. In 1280, the town was granted its market charter and, today, it still bustles with activity every Thursday and Saturday when livestock are brought to be sold and street-traders set up their stalls. Each September, the granting of the charter is celebrated with events taking place over a two week festival which culminates in a lantern procession. The oldest building in the town is the **Church of St Mary** which, in parts, dates from 1111. Though it was restored and rebuilt in the mid-19th century and the chancel was added in 1903, it has retained its splendid Norman door and some magnificent stained glass, including a window designed by the painter Sir Joshua Reynolds. The present tower dates from the reign of Elizabeth I as the original steeple was destroyed during a storm in 1540.

Ulverston is also the home of England's shortest canal: the **Ulverston Canal** is just a mile long and links the town with the sea. Built by engineer John Rennie in 1794, at the height of Ulverston's iron ore mining industry, it was used to transport the cargoes of iron and slate to the sea but, by the mid-19th century it fell into decline as the railways took over. On top of **Hoad Hill**, overlooking the town, is a 90 foot copy of Eddystone Lighthouse which acts as a landmark for miles around. This is of no help to local shipping as it is really a monument to Sir John Barrow, founder of the Royal Geographical Society, who was born in Ulverston in 1764. However, Ulverston's most famous son is undoubtedly Stan Laurel, the leaner one in the great comic duo, Laurel and Hardy. The world famous **Laurel and Hardy Museum** can be found in the town centre in the very house in which Stan Laurel was born, in June 1890.

BARDSEA

Map 9 ref I8

2 miles S of Ulverston off the A5087

The village stands on a lovely green knoll overlooking the sea and, as well as having a charming, unhurried air about it, there are some excellent walks from here along the coast either from its Country Park or through the woodland. Just up the coast, to the north, lies **Conishead Priory**, once the site of a leper colony that was established by Augustinian canons in the 12th century. The monks from the priory used to act as guides across the dangerous Cartmel Sands to Lancashire. After the Dissolution, a superb private house was built on the site and the guide service was continued by the Duchy of Lancaster. In 1821, Colonel Braddyll demolished the house and built in its place the ornate Gothic mansion that stands here today. He was also responsible for the atmospheric ruined folly on **Chapel Island** that is clearly visible in the estuary. Latterly, Conishead Priory became, firstly, a rest home for Durham miners but it is now owned by the Tibet Buddhist Manjushri Institute. Visitors are welcome to the house, which is open for tours, and there is a delightful woodland trail to follow through the grounds.

BARROW-IN-FURNESS
9 miles SW of Ulverston on the A590

MAP 9 REF I8

Until the 19th century, Barrow-in-Furness was nothing more than a small fishing village on the end of the Furness peninsula. However, the growth of the local iron and steel-making industry, closely followed by the rapid development of a ship-building industry, put the town well and truly on the map. The coming of the railway, built to transport the locally produced haematite slate and limestone to the port, also aided the expansion of the town. The original population of just 200 had, by 1874, increased to over 35,000.

It was James Ramsden who established the first Barrow Iron Ship Company in 1870, taking advantage of local steel production skills. In 1896, the firm was acquired by Vickers, a name forever linked with Barrow, and for a number of years was the largest armaments works in the world. The **Dock Museum**, found astride a deep dry dock, tells the story of Barrow's industrial past and, naturally, there are many exhibits dedicated to the town's influence as a major maritime engineering force.

DALTON-IN-FURNESS
3 miles N of Barrow-in-Furness off the A590

MAP 9 REF I8

Lying in a narrow valley on the part of Furness which extends deep into Morecambe Bay, it is difficult to imagine that this ancient place was once the leading town of Furness and an important centre for administration and justice. The 14th century pele tower, **Dalton Castle**, was built to provide a place of refuge for the monks of Furness Abbey against Scottish raiders and today it stands almost hidden by surrounding buildings. Over the centuries, in its twin role as both prison and court, it has been substantially altered internally, although it still retains most of its original external features. It is now owned by the National Trust and it houses a small museum with an interesting display of 16th and 17th century armour.

Dalton became established as a market town in the 13th century when the Cistercians began to hold fairs and markets in the town. Indeed, the influence of the monks was great here as, before the Dissolution, it was the Abbot who held court and administered justice. Not surprisingly, Dalton's decline coincided with the decline of the monks and also with the growing importance of Ulverston and Greenodd as ports.

The red sandstone **Church of St Mary** was designed by the celebrated Victorian architects Paley and Austin and, in the graveyard, lies George Romney (1734-1804), the famous portrait painter, who was born in the town. Visitors to the town will find that it is time well spent looking around the many fascinating façades in and close to the market place, such as the unique, cast-iron shop front at No 51, Market Street. In the market place itself, is an elegant, Victorian drinking fountain, with fluted columns supporting a dome of open iron work above the pedestal fountain. Nearby, stands the market cross and the slabs of stone that were used for fish-drying in the 19th century.

To the south of the town lies **Furness Abbey**, a magnificent ruin of eroded red sandstone set in fine parkland, the focal point of south Cumbria's monastic heritage. Amongst the atmospheric ruins can still be seen the canopied seats in the presbytery and the graceful arches overlooking the cloister, testaments to the abbey's former wealth and influence. Furness Abbey stands in the **Vale of Deadly Nightshade**, a shallow valley of sandstone cliffs and rich

Furness Abbey

pastureland. The abbey itself was established in 1123 at Tulketh, near Preston, by Stephen, Count of Blois and King of England. Four years later it was moved to its present site and, after 20 years, became absorbed into the Cistercian Order. Despite its remoteness, the abbey flourished, with the monks establishing themselves as guides across the treacherous sands of Morecambe Bay. Rich endowments of land, including holdings in Yorkshire and Ireland, led to the development of trade in products such as wool, iron, and charcoal. Furness Abbey became the second wealthiest monastery in Britain after Fountains Abbey in Yorkshire. After Dissolution, in 1537, the abbey became part of Thomas Cromwell's estate and it was allowed to decay into this picturesque and romantic ruin.

PIEL ISLAND

Map 9 ref I8

4 miles SE of Barrow-in-Furness

Though the island was probably visited by both the Celts and the Romans, its first recorded name is Scandinavian - Fotheray - from the Old Norse meaning fodder island. In 1127, the islands were given to the Savignac Monks by King Stephen and, after the order merged with the Cistercian monks, in the middle of the 12th century, the monks of Furness Abbey began to use Piel Island as a warehouse and storage area. **Piel Castle**, on the island, was really a house fortified in the early part of the 14th century and, at the time, it was the largest of its kind in the northwest. Intended to be used as one of the abbey's warehouses and to offer protection from raiders, in later years the castle also proved to be a useful defence against the King's Customs men and a prosperous trade in smuggling began. The castle has, over many years, been allowed to fall into ruin and now presents a stark outline on the horizon.

One of the most exciting events in Piel's history occurred on 4th June 1487, when Lambert Simnel, a merchant's son, landed on the island. Simnel had claimed that he was the Earl of Warwick (one of the Princes in the Tower said to have been murdered by Richard III) and therefore the rightful King of England. With an army of German and Irish mercenaries, Simnel set out across Furness to march on London. However, when he arrived in London it was as the prisoner of Henry VII after he had suffered a defeat at the hands of the king's troops at Stoke.

WALNEY ISLAND

Map 9 ref I8

2 miles W of Barrow-in-Furness

This 10 miles long island is joined to the Furness Peninsula by a bridge from Barrow docks. It is home to two important nature reserves that are situated at either end of the island. **North Walney National Nature Reserve** covers some 350 acres within which are a great variety of habitats including sand dunes, heath, salt marsh, shingle, and scrub. As well as having several species of orchid and over 130 species of bird either living on or visiting the reserve, there is also an area for the preservation of the Natterjack toad, Britain's rarest amphibian. North Walney's wildlife is matched by its rich prehistoric past, with important archaeological sites from mesolithic, neolithic, Bronze, and Iron Age times. Situated on the island's long foot and reached only by path is **South Walney Nature Reserve**, home to the largest nesting ground of Herring gulls and lesser black-backed gulls in Europe. It is also the most southerly breeding ground of such species as the oyster catcher, tern, and ringed plover. A stop-over for many migratory birds, the reserve has considerable ecological interest with mudflats, sandy beaches, rough pasture, and fresh water. The island's southern most tip, **Walney Point**, is dominated by a 70 foot lighthouse which was built in 1790 and whose light was, originally, an oil lamp.

RAVENGLASS

Map 9 ref I7

15 miles W of Coniston on the A595

Lying at the estuary of three rivers - the Esk, the Mite, and the Irt - as well as being in a sheltered position, it is not surprising that Ravenglass was an important Roman naval base. Established in the 2nd century, the port was a supply point for the military zone around Hadrian's Wall and their fort, **Glannaventra**, on the cliffs above the town, was home to around 1,000 soldiers. Little remains of Glannaventra except for the impressively preserved walls of the Bath House. At some 12 feet high, these walls are probably the highest Roman remains in the country.

In the 18th century Ravenglass was a base for smugglers bringing contraband in from coastal ships - tobacco and French brandy. Today, the estuary has silted up but there are still scores of small boats and the village is a charming resort, full of atmosphere. The layout has changed little since the 16th century; the main street is paved with sea pebbles and leads up from a shingle beach. Once, iron-ore was brought to the estuary by narrow gauge railway from the mines near Boot, in Eskdale, about eight miles away.

The Ravenglass and Eskdale Railway runs for seven miles up the lovely Mite and Esk River valleys. There are 12 locomotives, both steam and diesel, and 300,000 people a year come from all over the world to ride on the most beautiful train journey in England. It is still the best way to explore Miterdale and Eskdale. There are several stops along the journey and at both termini there is a café and a souvenir shop. At the Ravenglass station there is also the **Railway Museum** which brings to life the history of this remarkable line and the important part it has played in the life of Eskdale.

Ravenglass & Eskdale Railway

A mile or so east of Ravenglass stands **Muncaster Castle**, an impressive castellated mansion which has been owned by the Pennington family since 1208. Over the years, it has grown from the original pele tower built on Roman foundations to the imposing structure seen today. Visitors to the castle not only have the opportunity

to see the many Muncaster treasures (including tapestry, silver, and porcelain collections) but they can also take in the magnificent Great Hall, Salvin's octagonal library, and the barrel ceiling in the drawing room. In 1464, the Pennington

Muncaster Castle

family gave shelter to King Henry VI after his defeat at the Battle of Hexham. On his departure he presented them with his enamelled glass drinking bowl saying that as long as it remained unbroken the Penningtons would live and thrive at Muncaster. It remains intact and is known as The Luck of Muncaster. A replica is on display.

CALDER BRIDGE
7 miles N of Ravenglass on the A595

MAP 9 REF I8

From this small, grey, 19th century settlement there is an attractive footpath to **Calder Abbey**. It was founded by monks of Savigny in 1134 but amalgamated with the Cistercians of Furness Abbey when it was ransacked by the Scots a few years later. After the Dissolution the monastery buildings lapsed slowly into the present-day romantic ruin. Part of the tower and west doorway remain, with some of the chancel and transept, but sadly these are unsafe and have to be viewed from the road. The River Calder rises on Caw Fell, to the northeast of the village. **Monk's Bridge**, the oldest packhorse bridge in Cumbria, was built across it for the monks of Calder Abbey.

WHITEHAVEN

MAP 9 REF H6

18 miles N of Ravensglass on the A595

Although Whitehaven was established in the 12th century as a harbour for use by the monks of nearby St Bees Priory, most of the town was developed by the Lowther family to carry coal from their mines. By the mid-18th century Whitehaven was an important port, the third largest in Britain, with its trade based on coal and other cargo business, including importing tobacco from Virginia, exporting coal to Ireland, and seeing the emigration of settlers to the New World. However, in the days of large iron-steamships, its shallow draught halted expansion and the port declined in favour of Liverpool and Southampton. For that reason much of the attractive harbour area - now full of pleasure craft and fishing smacks - and older parts of the town remain unchanged. At the harbour, too, can be found **The Beacon** where, through a series of innovative displays, the history of the town and its harbour are brought to life.

The town's **Museum and Art Gallery** is particularly interesting. The museum deals with the history of the whole of Copeland (the district of Cumbria in which Whitehaven lies) with special emphasis on its mining and maritime past. The displays

The Beacon, Whitehaven Harbour

reflect the many aspects of this harbour borough with a collection that includes paintings, locally made pottery, ship models, navigational instruments, miners lamps, and surveying equipment. The Beilby "Slavery" Goblet, part of the museum's collection, is one of the masterpieces of English glass-making and is probably the finest example of its kind in existence. The town is interesting in other ways. It still has a grid pattern of streets dating back to the 18th century, a layout that substantiates its claim to be the first planned town in Britain. Many of the fine Georgian buildings in the centre have been restored and Lowther Street is a particularly impressive thoroughfare. Also of note is the harbour pier built by canal engineer, John Rennie, and considered to be one of the finest in Britain. There is a fascinating walk and a Nature Trail around **Tom Hurd Rock**, above the town.

ST BEES

MAP 9 REF H6

3 miles S of Whitehaven on the B5343

St Bees Head, a red sandstone bluff, forms one of the most dramatic natural features along the entire coast of northwest England. It is four miles of towering, precipitous cliffs of St Bees sandstone, the red rock which is so characteristic of Cumbria. Far out to sea, on the horizon, can be seen the grey shadow of the Isle of Man and, on a clear day, the shimmering outline of the Irish coast. From here the 190 mile **Coast to Coast Walk** starts on its long journey across the Pennines to Robin Hood's Bay in North Yorkshire.

Long before the first lighthouse was built in 1822, there was a beacon on the headland to warn and guide passing ships away from the rocks. The present lighthouse dates from 1866-7, built after an earlier one was destroyed by fire. St Bees Head is now an important **Nature Reserve** and the cliffs are crowded with guillemots, razorbills, kittiwakes, gulls, gannets, and skuas and there are also observation and information points all along the headland. There is a superb walk of about eight miles along the coastal footpath around the headland from St Bees to Whitehaven.

EGREMONT

MAP 9 REF H6

4 miles S of Whitehaven on the A595

This pretty town is dominated by its Norman **Castle** which stands high above it overlooking the lovely River Ehen to the south and the market place to the north. The castle was built between 1130 and 1140 by William de Meschines on the site of a former Danish fortification. The most complete part still standing is a Norman arch that once guarded the drawbridge entrance. Nearby is an unusual four-sided sundial and the stump of the old market cross dating from the early 13th century. Wordsworth's poem, The Horn of Egremont Castle, is based on a local legend which dates back to the Middle Ages. It is said that a great horn hanging in the castle could only be blown by the rightful lord. In the 13th century, Hubert de Lucy arranged to have the rightful lord, his brother Eustace, murdered so that he could claim his title. The plot misfired and, during the celebration feast to mark Hubert's inheritance, Eustace returned to blow the horn. Hubert, wisely, fled to a monastery.

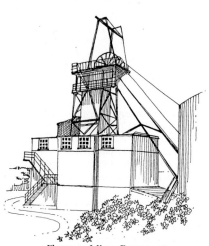

Florence Mine, Egremont

Egremont's prosperity was based on the good quality of its local red iron ore and jewellery made from it can be bought at the nearby **Florence Mine Heritage Centre**. Visitors to the mine, the last deep working iron ore mine in Europe, can also learn why the miners became known as the Red Men of Cumbria. The museum here also tells the story of the mine which was worked by the ancient Britons and there is a recreation of the conditions that the miners suffered at the turn of the 20th century. In September every year the town celebrates its **Crab Fair**, which dates from the 13th century, when crab apples, and not the sea creatures, were distributed to bystanders. Now Worcestershire apples are thrown from a lorry which drives down the main street. The fair is usually celebrated with traditional sports which include wrestling and hound-trailing. The highlight, however, is the World Gurning Championship in which each gurner puts his head through a horse collar (a braffin) and pulls an ugly grin - the ugliest is declared the winner!

COCKERMOUTH

MAP 9 REF I6

12 miles NE of Whitehaven off the A66

This Cumbrian market town, on the edge of the National Park, has retained its unspoiled character and is less overrun with tourists than its neighbours. There are pleasant shops and restaurants along the busy main street set against a majestic backdrop of fells. Wordsworth was born here and his old home in Main Street, which has been, at various times, a shop, a cobbler's, and a tearoom, was the National Trust's first Information Centre, a function which it still retains. Now known as the **Wordsworth House**, it was built in 1745 for the Sheriff of Cumberland and then purchased by the Earl of Lowther who let it to his land agent, John Wordsworth. All five Wordsworth children were born here, including the future Poet Laureate, William, on 7th April 1770. As well as seeing many of the buildings original features, including the staircase, fireplace, and fine plaster ceilings, there are some personal effects of the poet and the garden has been returned to its Georgian splendour. However, Wordsworth is not Cockermouth's only famous son as Fletcher Christian, the man who led the mutiny on The Bounty was also born here, in 1764. He lived at Moorland Close, a farm about a mile south of the town, and attended the same school as Wordsworth.

Not all of Cockermouth is Georgian and, in a building that goes back to the 16th century, can be found the **Printing House Museum**. The earliest of the interesting range of presses on display dates from 1820 and, as well as all the other printing paraphernalia, visitors can also try their hands at printing themselves. For the younger visitor to Cockermouth, or for those who have never quite grown up, there is also the **Toy and Model Museum**. With a collection of mainly British toys from the turn of the century to the present day, there is sure to be everyone's favourite here.At one time, like much of the surrounding area, mining was an important part of Cockermouth's economy and the **Mining Museum**, as well as displaying the equipment the miners had to help them with their difficult and dangerous work, the museum also has on display a collection of northern England minerals.

MARYPORT
Map 9 ref I5
6 miles NW of Cockermouth on the A596

This is a charming Cumbrian coastal town rich in interest and maritime history. The old part is full of narrow streets and neoclassical, Georgian architecture which contrast with sudden, surprising views of the sea. Some of the first visitors to Maryport were the Romans and, though there is little to show that they were here, the **Senhouse Roman Museum** has many interesting items. Housed in the striking Naval Reserve Battery, built in the 1880's, not only does the museum hold the largest collection of Roman altars from a single site in Britain but it also tells of everyday life in a Roman outpost.

Modern Maryport dates from the 18th century when Humphrey Senhouse, a local landowner, developed the harbour to export coal from his mines, naming the new port after his wife, Mary. Over the next century it became a busy port as well as a ship-building centre; boats having to be launched broadside because of the narrowness of the harbour channel. The town declined, along with the mining industry, from the 1930's onwards. However, it is now enjoying a well-earned revival, with newly restored Georgian quaysides, steep cobbled streets, clifftop paths, sandy beaches and a harbour full of fishing boats and colourful pleasure craft.

The town's extensive maritime history is preserved in the vast array of objects, pictures and models on display at the **Maritime Museum**, a fascinating place to visit. Housed in another of Maryport's more interesting and historic buildings, the former Queen's Head public house, the museum tells of the rise and fall of the harbour and docks. Maryport too has connections with the ill-fated liner, The Titanic, and with Fletcher Christian and these stories are also told here. Just down the road from the Maritime Museum, at Elizabeth Dock, is the **Steamship Museum**, where visitors can learn all about Maryport's shipbuilding industry. There are tours around the two ships, the Flying Buzzard, a tug from the River Clyde, and the *Vic96*, a supply ship from the Second World War.

KESWICK
Map 10 ref I6
13 miles SE of Cockermouth on the A66

The largest town within the Lake District National Park, its stunning position, surrounded by the mountains of Skiddaw and Borrowdale, and on the shores of Derwent Water, makes it one of Britain's most popular inland holiday resorts. The volcanic rocks of Borrowdale, newer than the Skiddaw slate group, are rich in minerals and the discovery of one of the strangest, graphite, led to the development of the pencil industry in Keswick. In the fascinating **Cumberland Pencil Museum** visitors can discover the history behind this everyday object through machinery, displays, and video shows.

The Queens Hotel is an outstanding establishment owned and personally run by Peter Williams. It has been in his family since 1981. A former coaching inn and posting house, it was

The Queens Hotel, Main Street, Keswick, Cumbria CA12 5JF
Tel: 017687 73333 Fax: 017687 71144
e-mail: book@QueensHotel.co.uk
website: www.QueensHotel.co.uk

rebuilt in 1826 and given its current name in 1880. Right in the heart of picturesque and popular Keswick, opposite the Moot Hall, this superb hotel offers 35 superior ensuite guest rooms. These come in different sizes and styles, but are uniformly comfortable and welcoming, furnished and decorated to a high standard of taste and luxury. Visitors return again and again to this elegant but relaxed home from home. The lovely restaurant is open daily for morning coffee, lunch (midday- 2 p.m.), afternoon tea, and evening meals (6.30-9.30 p.m.). Fresh produce is used to prepare the excellent dishes on the varied menu. Guest should be sure to leave room for one of the delicious puddings. The friendly and efficient service and variety of options on the menu ensure that the restaurant is a popular and well-esteemed place. Booking is advised, particularly at weekends. The handsomely converted stables are now a cracking public bar called the Queens Head. Full of character and atmosphere, this cosy bar boasts exposed stone walls, ceiling beams and other original features. It is a relaxing place with wonderful ales on tap as well as a good selection of lagers, wines and spirits. Guests are provided with free tickets to the Keswick Spa, and for the business guest the hotel has an excellent conference room that mixes the modern and traditional: a flagged floor, long-burning stove and conservatory-style roof. Very much like a roofed courtyard, it is from this that it takes its name, 'The Courtyard'. For a truly comfortable and relaxing break, look no further. Closed Christmas.

A short walk out of the town centre, along the Lake Road, leads visitors to the popular Century Theatre and beyond to **Friar's Crag**. This famous view of Derwent Water and its islands, now National Trust property, formed one of John Ruskin's early childhood memories. Although the centre of Keswick is busy, there are some quieter places to be found. Just behind the central shopping area is a little park alongside the River Greta. Not far away, the fascinating **Fitz Park Museum and Art Gallery** has an unusual stone xylophone and an important collection of manuscripts by Wordsworth and Southey.

Keswick also has a close association with the National Trust: Canon Rawnsley, the local vicar, was one of the founder members of the trust, which he helped to set up in 1895. Rawnsley fought for years to get Brandelhow Woods and Fell for the Trust, raising £7,000 in five months. This was the first National Trust property in the Lake District and it has grown since then to include most of the central fell area. However, despite the help of Rawnsley's contemporaries such as William Morris, John Ruskin, and Thomas Carlyle, he could not prevent Manchester Corporation from flooding the two natural lakes of Thirlmere, which submerged the old road and hamlets of Armboth and Wythburn, and the bridge which had joined the two lakes where Wordsworth and Coleridge used to meet each other. Beatrix Potter's family used **Lingholm**, today the home of Lord and Lady Rochdale, for many years as a holiday house and it crops up in many of the writer's tales. The woods here were Squirrel Nutkin's home, just to the north, at Fawe Park, is Benjamin Bunny country and, to the south, at Newlands Valley, Mrs Tiggy Winkle lived up the side of Cat Bells. The house's very impressive gardens and woodland, are open to the public through the summer.

The **Ravensworth Hotel** enjoys an enviable reputation for friendliness, service and comfort. Located in the centre of town, it makes an ideal base for exploring the pubs, shops and restaurants Keswick has to offer. Proprietors Tina and Tony Russ purchased this grand hotel in May of 1999. Tony has been involved for many years in professional Rugby Union coaching. Tina is a sportsperson as well, and has run in the London, Paris and New York marathons. They have brought a wealth of enthusiasm and vigour to running this stylish and impressive establishment. The exterior of this elegant townhouse is magnificent, with six levels from basement to attic and eight quality guest rooms, all ensuite, offering a mixture of sizes from single to family rooms. The upper-level rooms command wonderful views over the top of Keswick towards Skiddaw and Derwentwater. The facilities, decor and furnishings are all top of the range. The guests' lounge is plush and relaxing. The basement is home to an interesting antiques shop. No smoking. No children under 6. Just to the east of Keswick is **Castlerigg Stone Circle**, a remarkable neolithic monument of 38 stones which commands superb views of the surrounding fells. Whatever the purpose of the stone circle, it was a

The Ravensworth Hotel, 29 Station Street,
Keswick-on-Derwentwater, Cumbria CA12 5HH
Tel: 017687 72476 Fax: 017687 75287
email: Ravensworth@btinternet.com
website: www.knowledge.co.uk/ravensworth/

strategic viewpoint where priests or princes could survey the fell country. Not far away on **High Rigg**, overlooking the vale, is the little chapel of St John, built close to the site of a 13th century hermitage.

BORROWDALE
6 miles S of Keswick on the B5289

This brooding, mysterious valley, steep and narrow with towering crags and deep woods justly claims to be the most scenic in the Lake District. Just to the south of Derwent Water are the **Lodore Falls**, where the Watendlath Beck drops some 120 feet before reaching the lake. Further along the dale, in woodland owned by the National Trust, lies the **Bowder Stone** - a large rock that looks rather precariously placed on a narrow base. **Castle Crag**, on the west side of the valley, has on its summit the remains of the defensive ditches of a Romano-British fort.

THIRLMERE
3 miles S of Keswick off the A591

This attractive, tree-lined lake, one of the few in the Lakes that can be driven around as well as walked around, was created in the 19th century by the Manchester Corporation. At first the public were not granted access to the water but, today, Thirlmere is a pleasant, less crowded lake than many of the others with lakeside walks, picnic areas, and sailing. The creation of the reservoir flooded the two hamlets of Armboth and Wythburn and all that remains of these places today is Wythburn chapel towards the southern end. Overlooking the narrow lake is **Helvellyn**, Wordsworth's favourite mountain that is also very popular with walkers and climbers today. At 3,116 feet, it is one of the four Lakeland fells over 3,000 feet high and the walk to the summit should not be taken lightly. The eastern aspect of the mountain is markedly different from the western as it was here that the glaciers, during the Ice Age, were sheltered from the mild, west winds and remained long enough to carve out great hollows in the rock. Those reaching the summit will find, not only spectacular views (if the weather is clear) but also an often needed wind break shelter and quotes from both Wordsworth and Sir Walter Scott.

DERWENT WATER

MAP 10 REF I6

S of Keswick off the B5289

The third largest of the Cumbrian lakes, Derwent Water has many fans who enjoy its particularly scenic aspect, surrounded by woodland with the crags of Borrowdale in the distance. The lake is also unusual in that it has several islands dotted along its length: **St Herbert's Island**, named after the saint who lived here as a hermit, **Derwent Isle**, once the home of German miners working in the area, **Lord's Island**, and **Rampsholme**.

LOWESWATER

MAP 9 REF I6

9 miles W of Keswick off the B5289

Reached by narrow lanes, this is one of the smaller of the lakes, in an enchanting fell side and forest setting. The name, appropriately, means 'leafy lake' and to the east of the lake lies the small village of the same name. Here in this especially picturesque part of the Lake District, surrounded by thousands of acres of peaceful and striking countryside, **The Kirkstile Inn** has provided food and shelter for travellers for over 400 years. Inside are the same low-beamed rooms with welcoming open fires, warm hospitality and friendly ambience that greeted 16th-century visitors. Newer comforts have been added over the years, such as the comfortable seating, modern plumbing and all the amenities today's guests require. Owners Ken and Angela offer a warm and friendly welcome to all their guests. Open all day every day, the quality ales include Jennings Bitter, Cumberland Ale

The Kirkstile Inn, Loweswater, Cockermouth, Cumbria CA13 0RU Tel: 01900 85219

and a guest ale, usually from the local Derwent brewery. The menu is varied and imaginative, and complemented by delicious daily specials. The inn also boasts the added bonus of 10 superior letting rooms. All have excellent facilities and are decorated and furnished to a high standard of comfort and quality. Children welcome.

North of Loweswater is one of the quietest and least known parts of the Lake District National Park, a group of low fells through which there are few roads or even paths and summits such as Fellbarrow, Smithy Fell and Sourfoot Fell. The little River Cocker divides this group from the Lorton Fells, further east, forming the beautiful Vale of Lorton.

CRUMMOCK WATER   Map 9 ref I6
8 miles SW of Keswick on the B5292

Fed by both Buttermere and Loweswater, this is by far the larger of the three lakes. In this less frequented part of western Cumbria, where there are few roads, the attraction of Crummock Water can usually be enjoyed in solitude. Best seen from the top of Rannerdale Knotts, to the east, the lake has a footpath running around it though, in places, the going gets a little strenuous.

BUTTERMERE   Map 9 ref I6
8 miles SW of Keswick on the B5289

Half the size of its neighbour, Crummock Water, Buttermere is a beautiful lake set in a dramatic landscape. To many, particularly connoisseurs of the Lake District landscape, this is the most splendid of them all. The walk around Buttermere gives superb views of the eastern towers of Fleetwith Pike and the great fell wall made up of High Crag, High Stile, and Red Pike. One of the great scandals of the 19th century involved Mary Robinson, the daugher of a local innkeeper who was described in very glowing terms in J Budworth's book A Fortnight's Ramble in the Lakes. She became something of a local attraction herself, with people flocking to the inn to see her beauty and, in 1802, she thought she had married the Earl of Hopetoun's brother, only to discover that, in fact, her husband was a bankrupt imposter. He was hanged and she later married a local farmer and went on to live a normal and happy life. The author, broadcaster, and great supporter of Cumbria, Melvin Bragg, tells her story in his novel, The Maid of Buttermere.

Buttermere

ENNERDALE WATER   Map 9 ref I6
11 miles SW of Keswick off the A5086

This is truly a hidden place lying in the secluded valley of Ennerdale which has limited access by car. Tranquil and quiet, the lake and valley offer some superb walks around the shores and along river banks, valley paths, and forest tracks which together offer a tremendous variety suitable for all ages and capabilities. Wainwright's Coast to Coast walk runs the whole length of Ennerdale and the general consensus is that this section is by far the most beautiful.

THRELKELD   Map 10 ref J6
3 miles E of Keswick off the A66

This charming village is famous for its annual sheepdog trials though its economy was built up on the several mines in the area and the granite quarry to the south. Today, many visitors make their way to the village as it is the ideal starting point for a number of mountain walks, including an ascent of **Blencathra**, one of the most exciting of all the Lake District mountains. Also known as **Saddleback** and a smaller sister of Skiddaw to the west, the steep sides ensure that it looks every inch a mountain.

DACRE
MAP 10 REF J6
11 miles E of Keswick off the A66

There is much of historic interest in this village. The church occupies a site of a former monastery which was mentioned by the Venerable Bede in his accounts of Cumberland in the 8th century. A later reference shows that, in 926, the Peace of Dacre was signed between Athelstan of England and Constantine of Scotland. Fragments of masonry are reputed to have come from the monastery and four carvings of bears in the churchyard are probably of Anglo-Viking origin. A 14th century pele tower, **Dacre Castle** is a typical example of the fortified house or small castle that was common in northern England during the Middle Ages. This was the seat of the Dacre family, Catholic Earls of Cumberland, and its turrets and battlements have walls which are 8 feet thick. Leonard Dacre took part in the ill-fated Rising of the North in 1589 and, some time later, the estate passed to the Earls of Sussex who restored the castle in 1675 and whose coat of arms can still be seen.

ULLSWATER
MAP 10 REF J6
8 miles E of Keswick on the A592

It was on the northern shores of Ullswater, at **Glencoyne Wood**, that William Wordsworth, on a bleak and breezy April day, noticed the brilliance of the wild daffodils, an experience that he shared with the world in one of the most quoted poems in the English language: "I wondered lonely as a cloud..." One of the nicest ways to cross from one side of Ullswater to the other is by the lake steamer, which links Pooley Bridge with the little village of Glenridding at the opposite end, and at the foot of the Kirkstone Pass.

BASSENTHWAITE LAKE
MAP 9 REF I6
4 miles NW of Keswick on the A66

Though the setting of the lake is not as dramatic as some it is easily accessible and, because of this, it is perhaps one of the busiest. On the eastern shore with Skiddaw rising up behind it, is the Norman Church of St Bega and it was this location that inspired Tennyson to describe the dying King Arthur being carried across the water on a barge in his poem Morte d'Arthur. This then would make Bassenthwaite Lake the resting place of Excalibur but, as yet, no one taking the waymarked path around the waters has seen the sword rising up from the lake. Near to the church is **Mirehouse**, a 17th century building that has been in the same family since 1688. Literary visitors to the house include Tennyson, Thomas Carlyle, and Edward Fitzgerald, the poet and translator of The Rubaiyat of Omar Khayyam. As well as some manuscripts by these family friends, there is also a fine collection of furniture and visitors can wander around the wildflower meadow and the walled garden.

CALDBECK
MAP 10 REF J5
11 miles N of Keswick on the B5299

This is perhaps the best known village in the northern Lakes because of its associations with John Peel, the famous huntsman who lies buried in the churchyard. Peel was Master of Hounds for over 50 years and was immortalised by his friend John Graves, who worked in a local mill making the grey woollen cloth mentioned in the song, "D'ye ken John Peel with his coat so grey?" Until 200 years ago Caldbeck was an industrial village, with corn mills, woollen mills, and a paper mill all powered by the river. **Priest's Mill**, built in 1702 by the Rector of Caldbeck, next to the church, was a stone grinding corn mill, powered by a waterwheel which has now been restored to working order. It is open to the public and has an accompanying **Mining Museum** and a collection of old rural implements. The mill buildings are home to a gift shop, craft workshops, and a tea room - one of Cumbria's best - on the top floor.

PENRITH

MAP 10 REF J6

17 miles E of Keswick on the A66

The capital of the Kingdom of Cumbria in the 9th and 10th centuries, this is another town that was ransacked by Scottish raiders in the 14th century. Today, however, visitors to this lively market town, with handsome old buildings, receive a much warmer welcome. The evidence of its former vulnerability can still be seen in the charming mixture of narrow streets and wide-open spaces, such as Great Dockray and Sandgate, into which cattle were herded during the raids. Later they became market places and markets are still held every Tuesday and Saturday.

The ruins of **Penrith Castle** bear witness to the town's important role in defending the surrounding country from marauding Scots. The castle was built around 1399 but was enlarged for the Duke of Gloucester (later Richard III) when he was Lord Warden of the Western Marches and responsible for keeping the peace along the border with Scotland. The largest of Penrith's market spaces is known as **Great Dockray** and, on its west side, is the Gloucester Arms which was formerly Dockray Hall. It is said that the Duke of Gloucester resided here and his coat of arms appears above the main entrance. Apparently, a secret underground passage links the Gloucester Arms with the castle.

The town is dominated by **Beacon Hill Pike**, which stands amidst wooded slopes high above Penrith. The tower was built in 1719 and marks the place where, since 1296, beacons were lit to warn the townsfolk of an impending attack. The beacon was last lit during the Napoleonic wars in 1804 and it was seen by the author, Sir Walter Scott who was visiting Cumberland at the time. Seeing it prompted Scott to hasten home to rejoin his local volunteer regiment. It is well worth the climb from Beacon's Edge, along the footpath to the summit, to enjoy a magnificent view of the Lakeland fells. It was, however, also on top of this hill, in 1767, that Thomas Nicholson, a murderer, was hanged. The gibbet was left on the summit and so was Nicholson's ghost, seen in the form of a skeleton hanging from the noose.

MORLAND

MAP 10 REF K6

5 miles SE of Penrith off the A66

Occupying a beautiful location amid wonderful rustic scenery and peaceful surroundings, **Hill Top House** in the ancient, picturesque village of Morland is the perfect retreat. Just 15 minutes from the M6 and within easy reach of the Lakeland, Scotland and the Yorkshire dales, anyone looking for peace, quiet and the bliss of the countryside need look no further. Owner Liz Kellett offers guests a warm welcome to her lovely Georgian home, originally a farmhouse built in 1715. This extensive and charming stonebuilt house stands in one-third of an acre with attractive secluded gardens. The accommodation comprises three fine ensuite guest rooms (two double, one twin/single), furnished and decorated to a high standard of comfort, with a cosy ambience and superb views. An excellent breakfast awaits guests each morning. Come and relax at this beautiful home.

**Hill Top House, Morland, Penrith,
Cumbria CA10 3AX Tel: 01931 714561**

EAMONT BRIDGE
1 mile S of Penrith on the A6

MAP 10 REF J6

Here can be found the circular **Mayburgh Earthwork**, which dates from prehistoric times and comprises a 15 foot bank inside of which stands a single, large stone. Near to the village, on the banks of the River Eamont, is **Giant's Cave**, the supposed lair of a man-eating giant called Isir. This local tale is linked with the legend of Tarquin, a giant knight who imprisoned 64 men in his cave and was eventually killed by Sir Lancelot. Some people also claim that Uther Pendragon, King Arthur's father, lived here and that he too ate human flesh.

HUTTON-IN-THE-FOREST
5 miles N of Penrith on the B5305

MAP 10 REF J5

This is not a village but a beautiful historic house set in the woodland of the medieval **Forest of Inglewood**. The house has been in the Inglewood family since 1605 but legend has it that this was the Green Knight's Castle described in the Arthurian tale of Sir Gawain and the Green Knight. Originally a pele tower, alterations and additions over the centuries, both inside and out, show a varying range of architectural styles. The long gallery, unusual in a north of England home, dates from the 1630's whilst the hall, built in the 1680's, is dominated by the Cupid staircase. Many of the upstairs rooms date from the mid-18th century whilst much of the decoration is Victorian. The gardens too show a variety of styles: there is a beautiful walled garden from the 1730's with a wonderful collection of herbaceous plants; topiary terraces laid out in the 17th century; and an extensive Victorian woodland garden. Open to the public throughout the year, the house and gardens also play host to a range of events.

KIRKOSWALD
7 miles N of Penrith on the B6413

MAP 10 REF J5

The village derives its name from the Church of St Oswald: Oswald was the King of Northumbria who, according to legend, toured the pagan north with St Aidan in the 7th century. This once thriving market town still retains its small cobbled market place and some very fine Georgian buildings. Kirkoswald also has a ruined 12th century **Castle**, formerly the home of the Featherstonehaugh family and, although not open to the public, it can be seen from the road and footpath. In 1210 a licence was received from King John to fortify the original structure and enclose the extensive park. The castle was later destroyed by Robert the Bruce in 1314 but was rebuilt and extended in the late 15th century. The whole site covered three acres with the courtyard surrounded by a massive wall and a main gate with a drawbridge over the moat. The castle's splendour is due to the efforts of Thomas, Lord Dacre but, after his death in 1525, the panelling, stained glass, and beamed ceilings were transferred to Naworth and the castle became a quarry. Today, it is still protected by a wide moat and the great turreted tower rises above the remains of the vaulted dungeons.

Just to the north of Kirkoswald are the **Nunnery Walks** which start at a Georgian house built in 1715 on the site of a Benedictine Nunnery founded during the reign of William Rufus. Narrow footpaths have been cut into the sandstone cliffs along the deep gorge of Croglin beck and they pass through beautiful woodland to reveal exciting waterfalls. The walks are open to the public during the summer months.

GREAT SALKELD
5 miles N of Penrith on the B6412

MAP 10 REF J5

This picturesque collection of 18th century cottages and farmhouses built in red sandstone is typical of this area. However, Great Salkeld is best known for its massive, battlemented pele tower built in the 14th century. The Norman doorway in the porch is less than a yard wide and its arch has three rows of deeply cut zig-zags with five heads, one with a crown. Lieutenant

Colonel Samuel Lacy gave his name to the **Lacy Caves** along the banks of the River Eden towards Long Meg. It was he who had the five chambers carved out of the soft red sandstone, possibly as a copy of St Constantine's Caves downstream at Wetheral. At that time it was fashionable to have romantic ruins and grottoes on large estates and Colonel Lacy is said to have employed a man to live in his caves acting the part of a hermit. Alternatively, the caves may have been intended to provide a wine store; Colonel Lacy used to entertain his guests here, and there were probably gardens around the caves. The rhododendrons and laburnums still flower every spring. On the opposite bank of the river is **St Michael's Well**, near the supposed site of a village called **Addingham** which was drowned when the river changed its course in the 12th century. The village church appears to have been an early Christian centre although Viking carvings were amongst some of the stones that were recovered from the riverbed during a drought in 1913. In the Addingham church the wooden pitch pipe and large stone cross, incised with lines for the ancient game of Nine Men's Morris, are of particular interest.

LITTLE SALKELD
Map 10 ref J5

5 miles N of Penrith off the B6412

The village is home to **Little Salkeld Watermill**, a fully operational 18th century mill powered by a waterwheel. The mill specialises in producing organic, stoneground flours which are sold locally and at the mill shop where there are also a number of other interesting craft items for sale. It is a short walk by lane from the village to **Long Meg and her Daughters**, a most impressive prehistoric site and one of the largest neolithic stone circles in the country. Local legend claims that Long Meg was a witch who, with her daughters, was turned to stone for profaning the Sabbath, as they danced wildly on the moor. The circle is supposedly endowed with magic so that it is impossible to count the same number of stones twice. Another superstition is that Long Meg will bleed if the stone is chipped or broken. There are about 60 stones in the oval, which is approximately 300 feet across. The tallest, Long Meg, is a 15 foot column of Penrith sandstone, the corners of which face the four points of the compass. Cup and ring symbols and spirals are carved on this stone which is over 3,500 years old. In 1725 an attempt was made by Colonel Lacy of Salkeld Hall to use the stones for mileposts. However, as work began, a great storm blew up and the workmen fled in terror believing that the druids were angry at the desecration of their temple.

CARLISLE
Map 10 ref J5

18 miles N of Penrith on the A6

This was a major strategic city on the Scottish Border, whose military past still seems to haunt it - from the Roman and Pictish battles to the skirmishes with the Scots and Jacobite rebels. There has been a castle at Carlisle since 1092 when William Rufus first built a palisaded fort. However, there was, almost certainly, a fortress here, probably on the present site, before Roman times, for the name Carlisle comes from the Celtic Caer Lue, meaning hill fort. The Norman **Castle** was originally built of wood but, during the Scottish occupation in the 12th century, King David laid out a new castle with stone taken from Hadrian's Wall. The 12th century keep can still be seen enclosed by massive inner and outer walls. The present Carlisle Castle dominates the skyline of this fascinating city. Entered through a great 14th century gatehouse, complete with portcullis, and with a maze of vaulted passages, chambers, staircases, towers, and dungeons, it is everything a real castle should be. Carlisle Castle was besieged for eight months during the Civil War by the Parliamentarians under General Leslie. When the Royalists finally capitulated, Leslie began repairing the castle and the walls. The Puritans were no respecters of Britain's ecclesiastical heritage; stone from six of the eight bays of the cathedral was used for the repairs and the building of block-houses for the Puritan troops.

Partially for this reason, **Carlisle Cathedral** is now one of the smallest cathedrals in England but it has many interesting features, including an exquisite east window that is considered to be one of the finest in Europe. Below the beautifully painted wooden ceiling of the choir,

Carlisle Cathedral

with its gold star shimmering against deep blue, are the carved, canopied choir-stalls with their medieval misericords. These wonderful carved beasts and birds include two dragons joined by the ears, a fox killing a goose, pelicans feeding their young, and a mermaid with a looking glass. In the north transept is the superb 16th century Flemish Brougham Triptych which was originally in Cologne Cathedral. In the 19th century it was brought to Brougham Chapel near Penrith. The altar piece was later restored by the Victoria and Albert Museum in London and is now on permanent loan to Carlisle. It is a beautiful, intricate piece with delicately carved figures depicting scenes from the life of Christ. It is hard to believe that it was here that Edward I solemnly used bell, book, and candle to excommunicate Robert the Bruce. It was here also that the church bells were rung to welcome Bonnie Prince Charlie in 1745. It is claimed that after the suppression of the Jacobite rebellion the bells were removed for their treason and only replaced in the 19th century. Although an appointment is usually necessary, a visit to the **Prior Tower**, if possible, is a must. On the first floor of this 15th century pele tower is a wonderful 45 panel ceiling incorporating the popinjay crest and arms of the Prior Senhouse. The 16th century Prior's gatehouse leads to a narrow lane called Paternoster which is named after the monks reciting their offices.

The award winning **Tullie House Museum**, in the centre of the city close to the cathedral, is certainly another place not to be missed. Through skilful and interpretive techniques the fascinating, and often dark, history of the Debatable Lands, as this border region was called, is told. The museum's centrepiece is its story of the Border Reivers who occupied the lands from the 14th to the 17th century, with a law - or rather, a lack of it - unto themselves, being neither English nor Scottish, unless it suited them to pledge, unscrupulously, allegiance to one or the other. These lawless, unruly people raged interfamily warfare with each other, decimating the lives of the local people and carrying out bloodthirsty raids. Their treacherous deeds have also added such words as 'bereave' and 'blackmail' to the English language. Tullie House also has an extensive collection of Roman remains from both the city and the Cumbrian section of Hadrian's Wall. A great Roman centre and the military base for the Petriana regiment, **Luguvalium**, as Carlisle was known in Roman times, also became a major civilian settlement with fountains, mosaics, statues and centrally-heated homes.

Like many great medieval cities, Carlisle was surrounded by walls. The best view of these is in a little street called West Walls at the bottom of Sally Port Steps, near the Tithe Barn. The walls date from around the 11th century and they remained virtually intact until the 19th century. When the castle was under siege, the Sally Port allowed an individual to 'sally forth'. It was later used for access to the Tithe Barn to avoid paying city tolls. It is unusual to find a **Tithe Barn** within a city wall but this exception was probably made because of the Border raids. The barn dates from the 15th century and was used to collect and store taxes, or tithes, destined for the priory.

The **Guildhall Museum** is housed in an unspoiled medieval building constructed by Richard of Redeness in 1407. Originally a town house, it provides an ideal setting for illustrating the history of both the Guilds and the City. Several rooms are devoted to creating the atmosphere of trade Guilds such as the shoe-maker, the butcher, and the glover. There is a splendid early 19th century banner of the weavers Guild and an impressive collection of 17th and 18th century Guild silver. Displays also feature other items relating to the history of Carlisle and include a magnificent iron-bound Muniment Chest dating from the 14th century. Conducted tours of this remarkable Guildhall are available. Not far from the museum is the **Citadel Railway Station**. The first railway to Carlisle opened in July 1836 and Citadel Station, which opened in 1850, was built to house seven different railway companies whose coats of arms are still displayed on the façade. So elegant was its interior - and much of it remains - that Carlisle was known as the 'top hat' station. Today it is still an important station; Intercity trains from Glasgow and London now link with lines to Dumfries, Tyneside, west Cumbria, and Yorkshire, and it is, of course, the northern end of the famous **Settle-Carlisle** Railway line.

One of the last great mainline railways to be built in Britain - it was completed in 1876 - the Settle to Carlisle line takes in some of the most dramatic scenery that the north of England has to offer. However, scenic it may be but the terrain caused the Victorian engineers many problems and it is thanks to their ingenuity and skill that the line was ever finished. During the course of its 72 miles, the line crosses 20 viaducts and passes through 12 tunnels, each of which was constructed by an army of navvies who had little other than their strength and some dynamite to remove the rock. The line of **Hadrian's Wall** runs through Carlisle following the northern rim of the River Eden. The wall was built as a great military barrier across the narrowest part of Britain, from the mouth of the River Tyne, in the east, to Bowness-on-Solway, in the west. Guarded by forts at regular intervals, it was built between AD 122-128 following a visit by the Emperor Hadrian who saw the then military infrastructure as insufficient to withstand the combined attacks of northern barbarians. Originally much of the western side was built from turf, but by AD 163 this had been replaced by stone. The wall was finally abandoned in the late 4th century.

WETHERAL
Map 10 ref J5
4 miles E of Carlisle off the A69

The village stands above the River Eden, over which runs an impressive railway viaduct, carrying the Tyne Valley Line, that was built by Francis Giles in 1830. Wetheral Parish Church lies below the village beside the river and contains a sculpture by Joseph Nollekens, of the dying Lady Mary Howard clasping her dead baby. St Constantine was the local patron and the church is dedicated to the Holy Trinity, St Constantine and St Mary. Constantine died as a martyr in AD 657 and a life-sized statue of him can be seen in the grounds of **Corby Castle**. During the reign of William Rufus one of his barons, Ranulph Meschin, founded a priory for Benedictine monks at Wetheral above the red-rock gorge of the River Eden. It was a dependency of the Abbey of St Mary at York and the prior and the monastery served the church and domestic chapel of Corby Castle. All that remains now is the gatehouse, but the grounds of Corby Castle are open to the public and provide some very pleasant woodland walks.

BRAMPTON
Map 10 ref J5
9 miles E of Carlisle on the A69

This ancient market town was the headquarters of Prince Charles Edward in his siege of Carlisle in 1745. When the city surrendered to the Scots the mayor and aldermen came to Brampton to present him with the keys to the city of Carlisle. A few months later, on his defeat, six of his supporters were hanged on a tree on the south side of the town. The tree survived until the last century and in its place there now stands a monument commemorating this event. Brampton actually dates back as far as the 7th century and it was originally sited a mile northwest of its present position. On the departure of the Romans from the area the settlement grew but the present town was created by Thomas de Multon, Lord of Gilsland, in the early 13th century. The octagonal **Moot Hall** in the market place, with its handsome clock tower, is Brampton's most striking building. The present hall was built in 1817 by Lord Carlisle but there has been a Moot Hall here since 1648. The iron stocks at the foot of a double flight of external stairs were last used in 1836.

Two miles northeast of the town is **Lanercost Priory**, an impressive red sandstone ruin set in secluded woodland. The priory was founded in 1166 by Robert de Vaux and built largely of stone from the Roman wall. During 1306, Edward I spent six months at the priory recuperating after his skirmishes with the Scots. Lanercost is well preserved and its scale is a reminder that it was a grand complex in its heyday. However, the priory suffered greatly in the border raids of the 13th and 14th centuries. One such raider is known to have been William Wallace, an early campaigner for Scottish independence from English rule. It was finally disbanded at the Dissolution of the Monasteries but, in 1740, the ruined nave was restored to form what is now one of the most splendid parish churches in the country. It is worth going inside to admire the William Morris glass.

Across the River Irthing from the priory stands **Naworth Castle**, situated on a rocky cliff above a deep wooded ravine, and it was the setting of Walter Scott's Lay of the Last Minstrel. The castle was built in 1335 in its present form by Lord Dacre as an important border stronghold. The castle passed through the female line to the Howard family after the last Lord Dacre was killed as a child, improbable as it might seem, by falling off his rocking horse.

Naworth is now owned by the 12th Earl of Carlisle and has recently begun to open to the public. Its supreme glory is the Great Hall hung with French tapestries and guarded by four unique heraldic beasts holding aloft their family pennants. The Long Gallery extends for 116 feet and was used as a guardroom. It now houses an interesting collection of paintings, many brought together by the 9th Earl, George Howard. He entertained many pre-Raphaelite painters here but the only existing example is Burne-Jones' Battle of Flodden - the rest were destroyed by a fire in 1844. In the courtyard there are some intriguing medieval latrines!

South of Brampton are **Gelt Woods**, lying in a deep sandstone ravine carved by the fast-flowing River Gelt. By the river is an inscribed rock called Written Rock which is thought to have been carved by a Roman standard bearer in AD 207.

Tourist Information Centres

Only Regional Centres have been listed.
For local Tourist Information Centres please contact
the appropriate regional centre.

British Tourist Authority
Thames Tower, Black's Road, Hammersmith, London, W6 9EL
Tel: 0181 846 9000

Cumbria Tourist Board
Ashleigh, Holly Road, Windermere, Cumbria, LA23 2AQ
Tel: 015394 44444 Fax: 015394 44041

East of England Tourist Board
Topsfield Hall, Hadleigh, Suffolk, IP7 5DN
Tel: 01473 822922 Fax: 01473 823063

Heart of England Tourist Board
Woodside, Larkhill Road, Worcester, WR5 2EX
Tel: 01905 763436 Fax: 01905 763450

London Tourist Board
Glen House, Stag Place, London, SWIE 5LT
Tel: 0171 932 2000 Fax: 0171 932 2022

North West Tourist Board
Swan House, Swan Meadow Road, Wigan Pier, Wigan, WN3 5BB
Tel: 01942 821222 Fax: 01942 820002

Northumbria Tourist Board
Aykley Heads, Durham, DH1 5UX
Tel: 0191 375 3004 Fax: 0191 375 3000

South East England Tourist Board
The Old Brew House, Warick Park, Tunbridge Wells, Kent, TN2 5TU
Tel: 01892 540766 Fax: 01892 511008

Southern Tourist Board
40 Chamberlayne Road, Eastleigh, Hampshire, SO50 5JH
Tel: 023 8062 0006 Fax: 023 8062 0010

South West Tourism
Woodwater Park, Exeter, EX2 5WT
Tel: 08704 420830 Fax: 08704 420840

Yorkshire Tourist Board
321 Tadcaster Road, York, YO2 2HF
Tel: 01904 707961 Fax: 01904 701414

Index of Towns, Villages and Places of Interest

Index of Accommodation

		Page No	Map Ref

Index of Food and Drink

The Hidden Places
Order Form

To order any of our publications just fill in the payment details below and complete the order form *overleaf*. For orders of less than 4 copies please add £1 per book for postage and packing. Orders over 4 copies are P & P free.

Please Complete Either:

I enclose a cheque for £ .... made payable to Travel Publishing Ltd

Or:

Card No: ☐☐☐☐ ☐☐☐☐ ☐☐☐☐ ☐☐☐☐

Expiry Date: ☐☐☐

Signature: ....

NAME: ....

ADDRESS: ....

....

....

POSTCODE: ....

TEL NO: ....

Please send to: Travel Publishing Ltd
7a Apollo House
Calleva Park
Aldermaston
Berks, RG7 8TN

The Hidden Places
Order Form

	Price	Quantity	Value
Regional Titles			
Cambridgeshire & Lincolnshire	£7.99	....	....
Channel Islands	£6.99	....	....
Cheshire	£7.99	....	....
Chilterns	£7.99	....	....
Cornwall	£7.99	....	....
Derbyshire	£7.99	....	....
Devon	£7.99	....	....
Dorset, Hants & Isle of Wight	£7.99	....	....
Essex	£7.99	....	....
Gloucestershire & Wiltshire	£7.99	....	....
Heart of England	£7.99	....	....
Hereford, Worcs & Shropshire	£7.99	....	....
Highlands & Islands	£7.99	....	....
Kent	£7.99	....	....
Lake District & Cumbria	£7.99	....	....
Lancashire	£7.99	....	....
Norfolk	£7.99	....	....
Northeast Yorkshire	£6.99	....	....
Northumberland & Durham	£6.99	....	....
North Wales	£7.99	....	....
Nottinghamshire	£6.99	....	....
Potteries	£6.99	....	....
Somerset	£6.99	....	....
South Wales	£7.99	....	....
Suffolk	£7.99	....	....
Surrey	£6.99	....	....
Sussex	£6.99	....	....
Thames Valley	£7.99	....	....
Warwickshire & West Midlands	£6.99	....	....
Yorkshire Dales	£6.99	....	....
Set of any 5 Regional titles	£25.00	....	....
National Titles			
England	£9.99	....	....
Ireland	£9.99	....	....
Scotland	£9.99	....	....
Wales	£8.99	....	....
Set of all 4 National titles	£28.00	....	....

For orders of less than 4 copies please add £1 per book for postage &
packing. Orders over 4 copies P & P free.

The Hidden Places
Reader Comment Form

The *Hidden Places* research team would like to receive reader's comments on any visitor attractions or places reviewed in the book and also recommendations for suitable entries to be included in the next edition. This will help ensure that the *Hidden Places* series continues to provide its readers with useful information on the more interesting, unusual or unique features of each attraction or place ensuring that their stay in the local area is an enjoyable and stimulating experience.

　　To provide your comments or recommendations would you please complete the forms below and overleaf as indicated and send to: The Research Department, Travel Publishing Ltd., 7a Apollo House, Calleva Park, Aldermaston, Reading, RG7 8TN.

Your Name:

Your Address:

Your Telephone Number:

Please tick as appropriate: Comments ☐   Recommendation ☐

Name of *"Hidden Place"*:

Address:

Telephone Number:

Name of Contact:

The Hidden Places
Reader Comment Form

Comment or Reason for Recommendation:

....

....

....

....

....

....

....

....

....

....

....

....

Map Section

The following pages of maps encompass the main cities, towns and geographical features of England, as well as many of the interesting places featured in the guide. Distances are indicated by the use of scale bars located below each of the maps

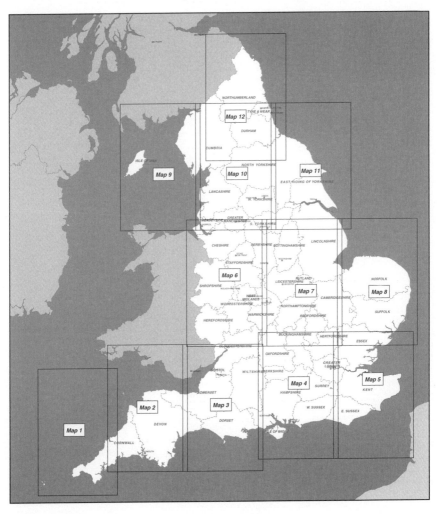

The following pages of maps summarise the main areas covered by this publication.

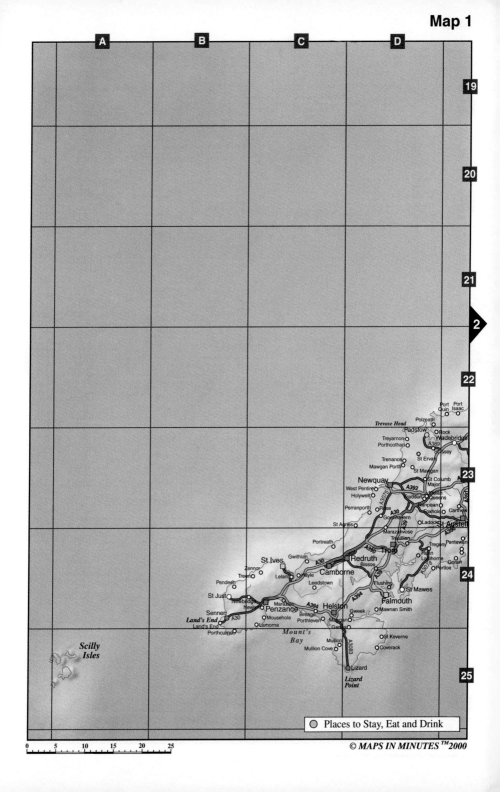

Map 1

Map 2

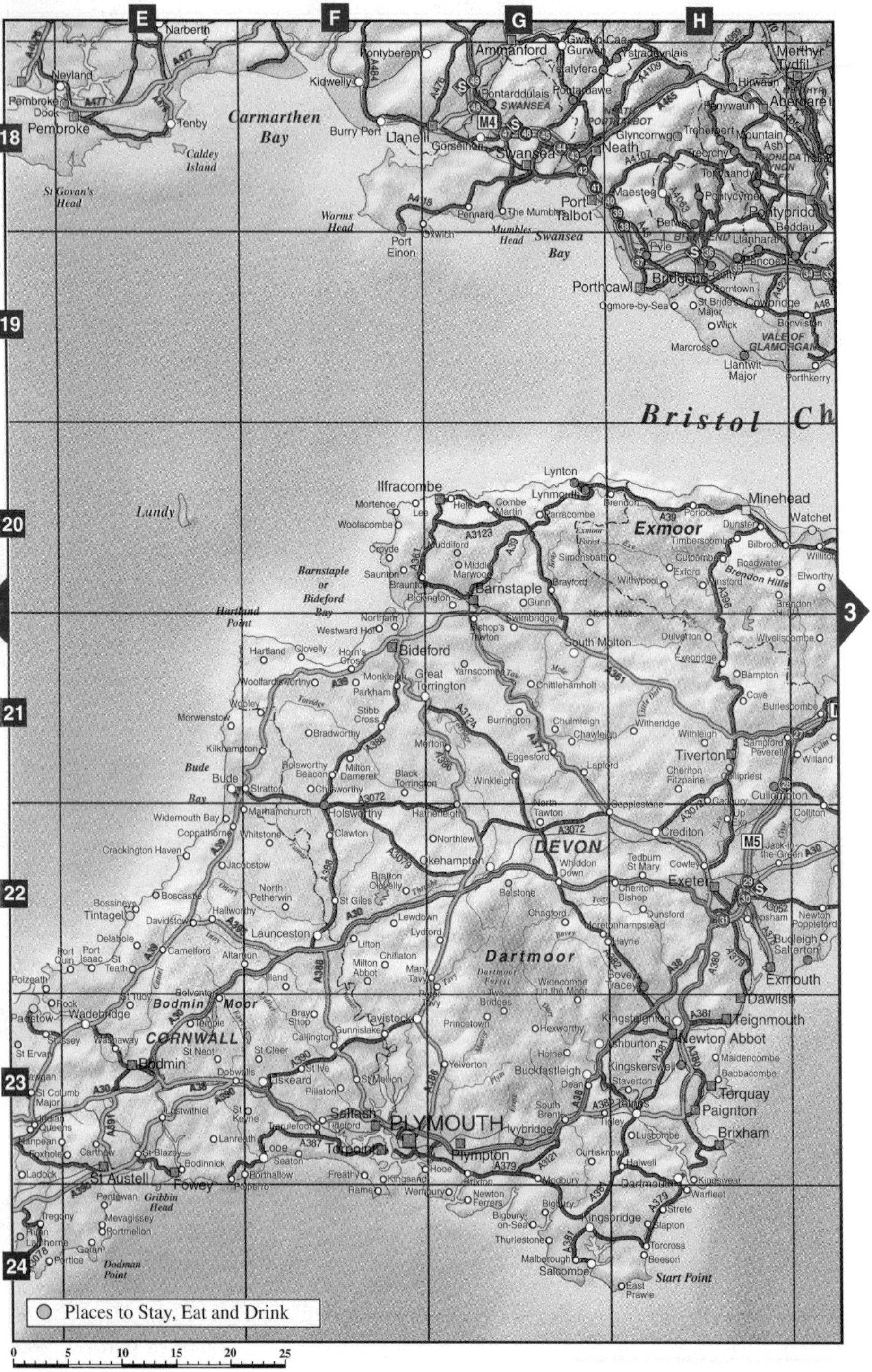

E F G H

Narberth
Neyland
Pembroke Dock
Pembroke
Tenby
Caldey Island
St Govan's Head
Carmarthen Bay
Pontyberem
Kidwelly
Burry Port
Llanelli
Gorseinon
Pontarddulais
Pontardawe
SWANSEA
M4
Swansea
Ammanford
Gwaun-Cae-Gurwen
Ystalyfera
Stradgynlais
Glyncorrwg
Neath
PORT TALBOT
Trebanos
Trehebert
Mountain Ash
Pontypridd
Beddau
Merthyr Tydfil
Hirwaun
Penywaun
Aberdare
Pennard
The Mumbles
Port Talbot
Maesteg
Pontycymer
Worms Head
Oxwich
Port Einon
Mumbles Head
Swansea Bay
Bridgend
BRIDGEND
Pyle
Llanharan
Pencoed
Porthcawl
Ogmore-by-Sea
St Brides Major
Cowbridge
Wick
Bonvilston
VALE OF GLAMORGAN
Marcross
Llantwit Major
Porthkerry

Bristol Ch

Lundy

Ilfracombe
Mortehoe
Lee
Hele
Combe Martin
Woolacombe
Croyde
Saunton
Braunton
Middle Marwood
Barnstaple
Lynton
Lynmouth
Parracombe
Brendon
Porlock
Minehead
Watchet
Dunster
Bilbrook
Exmoor
Exmoor Forest
Timberscombe
Culbone
Broadwater
Withypool
Exford
Wistland
Brendon Hills
Elworthy
Willito

Barnstaple or Bideford Bay
Hartland Point
Westward Ho!
Northam
Bideford
Hartland
Clovelly
Horn's Cross
Bishop's Tawton
Swimbridge
Gunn
Brayford
North Molton
South Molton
Dulverton
Wiveliscombe
Brendon Hills

Woolfardisworthy
Monkleigh
Great Torrington
Yarnscombe
Chittlehamholt
Bampton
Cove
Burlescombe
Parkham
Stibb Cross
Bradworthy
Morwenstow
Kilkhampton
Bude
Bude Bay
Stratton
Marhamchurch
Holsworthy Beacon
Milton Damerel
Black Torrington
Burrington
Chulmleigh
Chawleigh
Lapford
Witheridge
Witheleigh
Cheriton Fitzpaine
Tiverton
Sampford Peverell
Willand
Cullompton
Collipriest
Collitor
M5

Widemouth Bay
Coppathorne
Crackington Haven
Bossiney
Tintagel
Boscastle
Davidstow
Jacobstow
North Petherwin
St Giles
Okehampton
Winkleigh
North Tawton
Eggesford
Crediton
DEVON
Whiddon Down
Cowley
Exeter
Jack-in-the-Green
Delabole
Camelford
Altarnun
Launceston
Lifton
Lydford
Chagford
Tedburn St Mary
Cheriton Bishop
Dunsford
Pinhoe
Topsham

Polzeath
Port Quin
Port Isaac
St Teath
Bolventor
Illand
Milton Abbot
Mary Tavy
Dartmoor
Dartmoor Forest
Two Bridges
Moretonhampstead
Hayne
Bovey Tracey
Budleigh Salterton
Exmouth
Dawlish

Rock
Padstow
St Ervan
St Columb Major
Wadebridge
Bodmin Moor
Temple
St Neot
Callington
Gunnislake
Tavistock
Princetown
Hexworthy
Holne
Ashburton
Kingsteignton
Newton Abbot
Teignmouth
Maidencombe
Babbacombe

CORNWALL
Bodmin
Dobwalls
St Cleer
Liskeard
St Ive
St Mellion
Yelverton
Buckfastleigh
Kingskerswell
Staverton
Dean
Torquay
Paignton

Nanpean
St Austell
Carthew
St Blazey
Lostwithiel
St Keyne
Pillaton
Saltash
PLYMOUTH
Ivybridge
South Brent
Totnes
Brixham

Fowey
Gribbin Head
Pentewan
Mevagissey
Portmellon
Tregony
Portloe
Goran
Dodman Point
Lanreath
Looe
Seaton
Torpoint
Plympton
Plymstock
Hooe
Newton Ferrers
Modbury
Kingsbridge
Bigbury
Bigbury-on-Sea
Thurlestone
Malborough
Salcombe
Dartmouth
Kingswear
Warfleet
Strete
Slapton
Torcross
Beeson
East Prawle
Start Point

Ramslade
Werrington
Freathy
Kingsand

○ Places to Stay, Eat and Drink

0 5 10 15 20 25

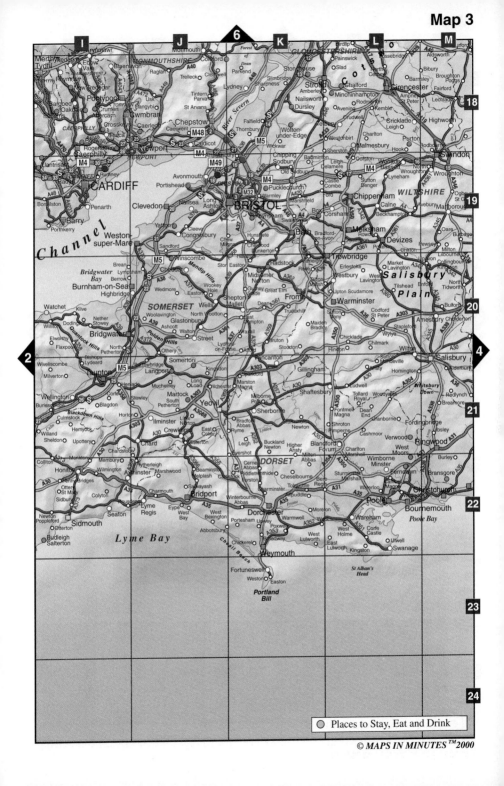

Map 3

6

O Places to Stay, Eat and Drink

© MAPS IN MINUTES ™ 2000

Map 4

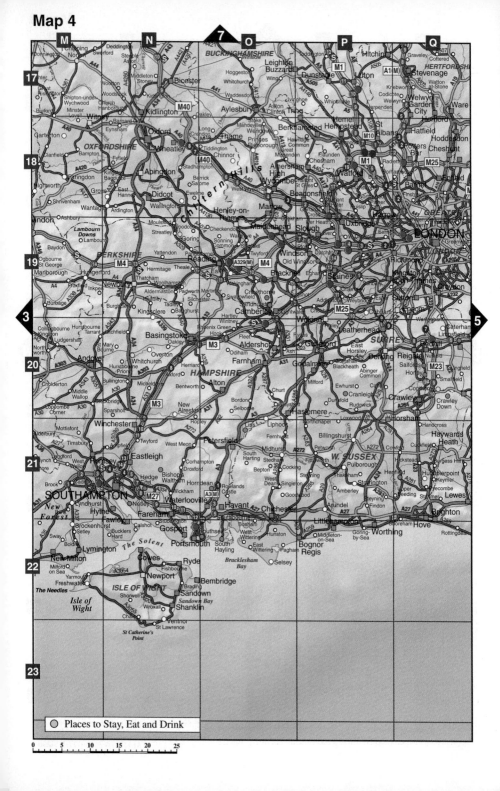

O Places to Stay, Eat and Drink

0   5   10   15   20   25

Map 5

Map 6

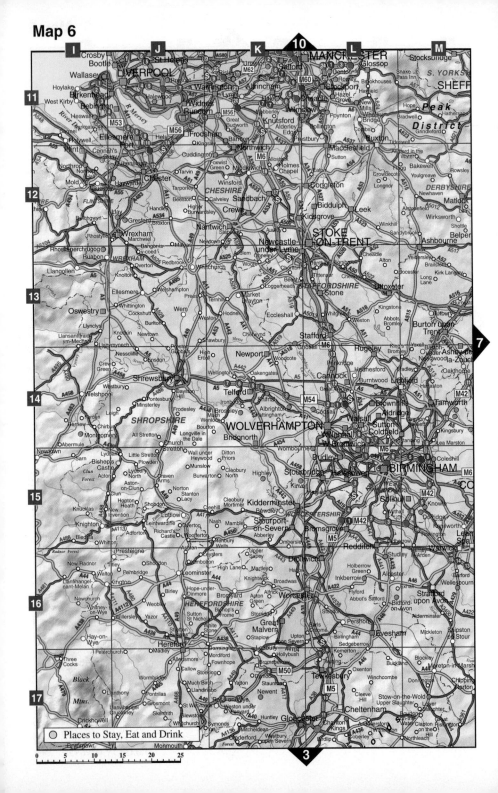

0   5   10   15   20   25

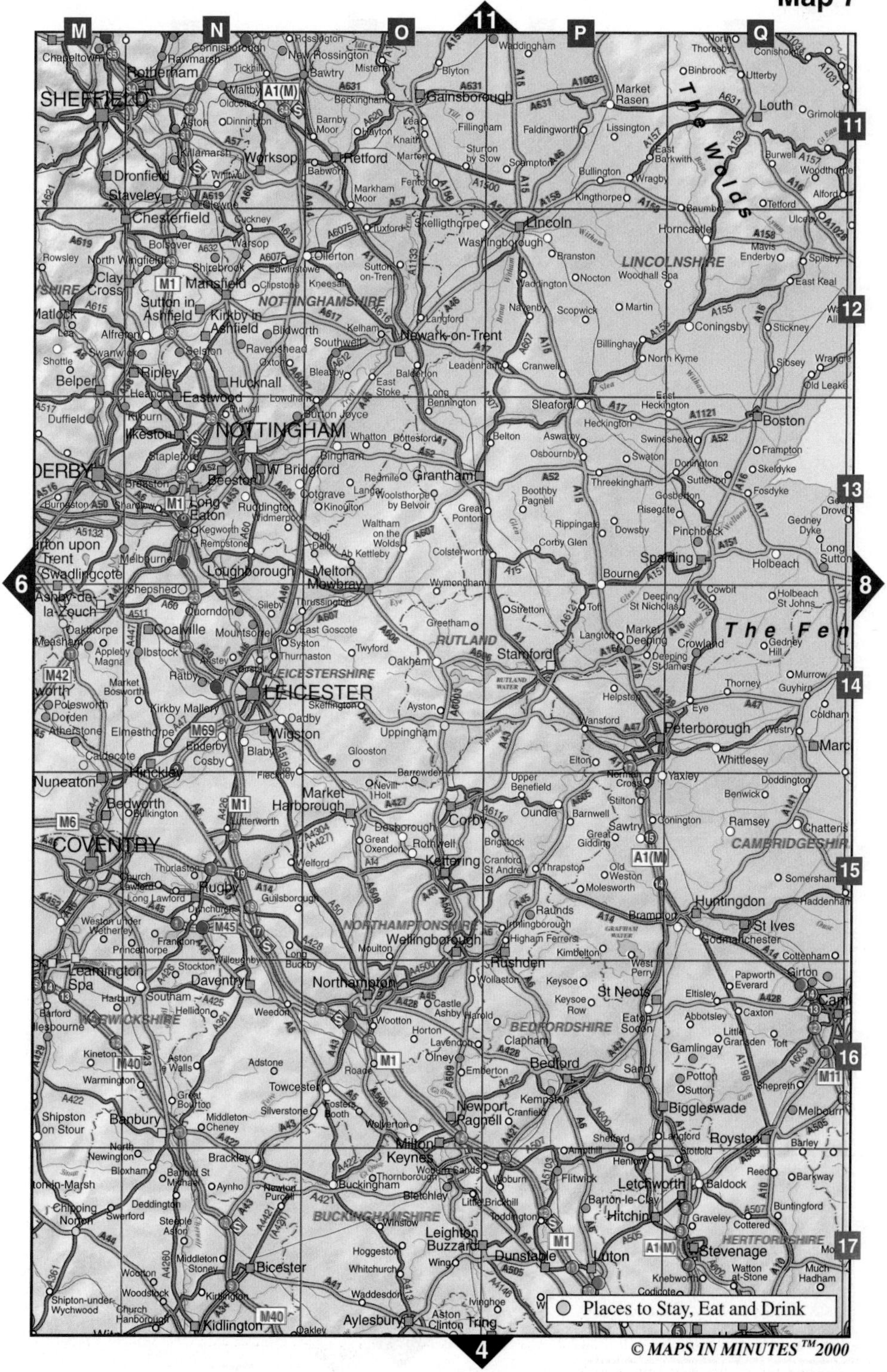

Map 7

SHEFFIELD
NOTTINGHAM
DERBY
LEICESTER
COVENTRY
LINCOLN
LINCOLNSHIRE
NOTTINGHAMSHIRE
LEICESTERSHIRE
RUTLAND
NORTHAMPTONSHIRE
WARWICKSHIRE
BEDFORDSHIRE
CAMBRIDGESHIRE
BUCKINGHAMSHIRE
HERTFORDSHIRE
The Wolds
The Fen
Peterborough

○ Places to Stay, Eat and Drink

Map 8

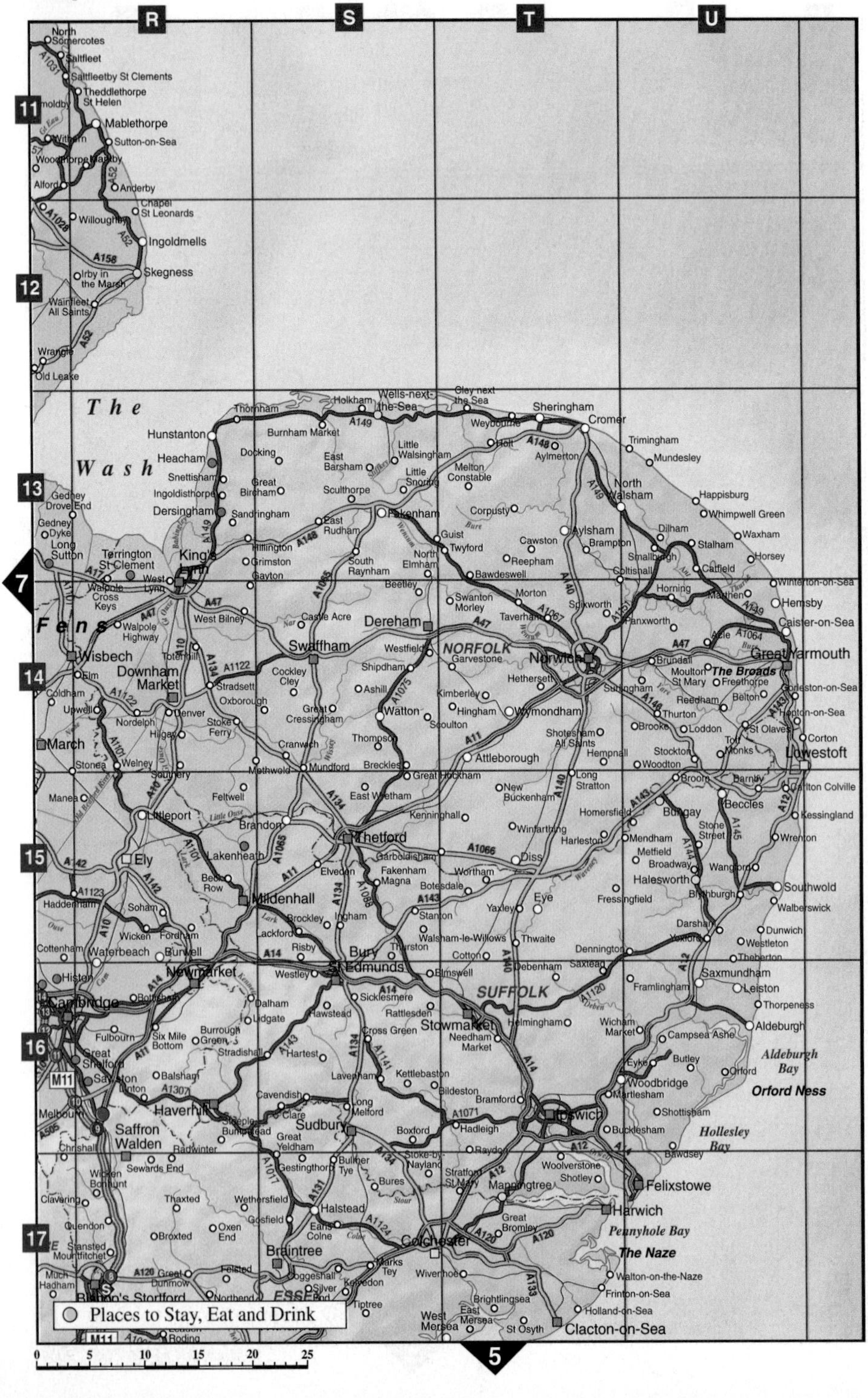

○ Places to Stay, Eat and Drink

Map 9

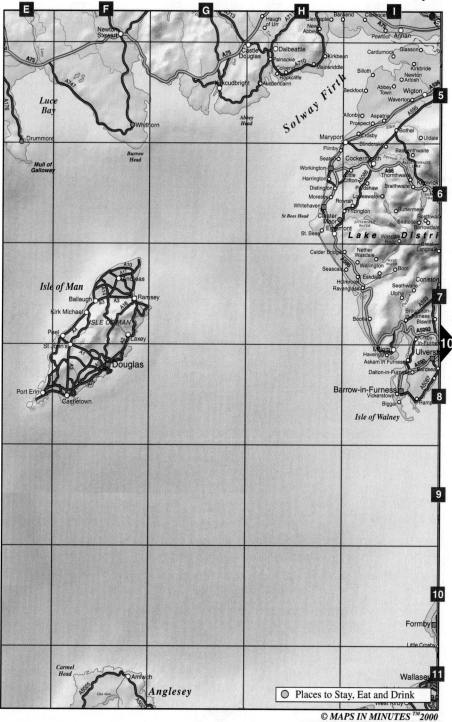

E | F | G | H | I

Bankend
Clarencefield
Haugh of Urr
Glencaple
Newbie Annan S
New Abbey
Powfoot
Castle Douglas
Dalbeattie
Cardurnock
Glasson
Kirkbean
Newton Stewart
Palnackie
Colvend
A710
Kirkbride
Newton Arlosh
Rockcliffe
Kirkcudbright
Auchencairn
Mainsriddle
Silloth
Abbey Town
Wigton
A75
Beckfoot
Waverton
5
Abbey Head
Allonby
Aspatria
Luce Bay
Solway Firth
Maryport
Crosby
Prospect
Bothel
Uldale
Whithorn
Flimby
Blinderake
Burrow Head
Seaton
Cockermouth
Bassenthwaite
Mull of Galloway
Workington
Little Clifton
Thornthwaite
A66
Keswick
6
Drummore
A176
Harrington
Braithwaite
Distington
Purdshaw
Loweswater
Rowrah
Moresby
St Bees Head
Whitehaven
Frizington
Buttermere
Cleator Moor
Egremont
Lake Distri
Seatoller
Borrowdale
St. Bees
Wasdale Head
Great Langdale
Isle of Man
Andreas
A10
Nether Wasdale
Calder Bridge
ENNERDALE WATER
WAST WATER
Ballaugh
Ramsey
Seascale
Wellington
Boot
Coniston
Kirk Michael
A18
Holmrook
Eskdale
7
ISLE OF MAN
Ravenglass
Seathwaite
Ulpha
Peel
Laxey
Bootle
Broughton-in-Furness
A5092
Blawith
St John's
A1
Douglas
Millom
Haverigg
Kirkby-in-Furness
10
Askam in Furness
Ulverst
A590
Port Erin
Dalton-in-Furness
Bardsea
Castletown
Barrow-in-Furness
A5087
Vickerstown
8
Biggar
Ramp
Isle of Walney

9

10

Formby

Little Crosby

11
Carmel Head
Amlwch
Wallasey
Anglesey

○ Places to Stay, Eat and Drink

West Kirby

© *MAPS IN MINUTES* ™ 2000

Map 10

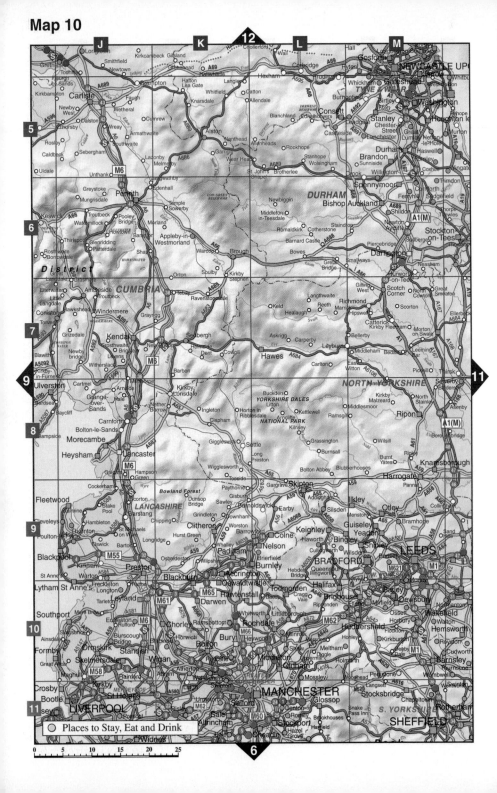

○ Places to Stay, Eat and Drink

0   5   10   15   20   25

Map 11

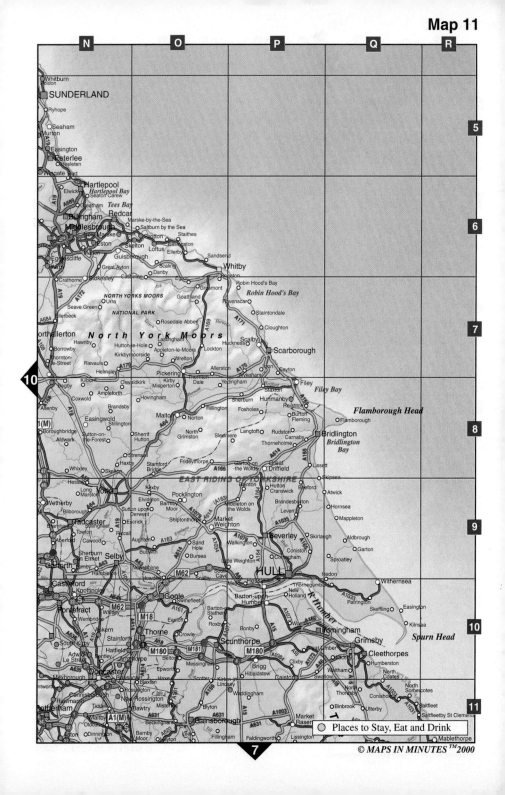

Places to Stay, Eat and Drink

Map 12

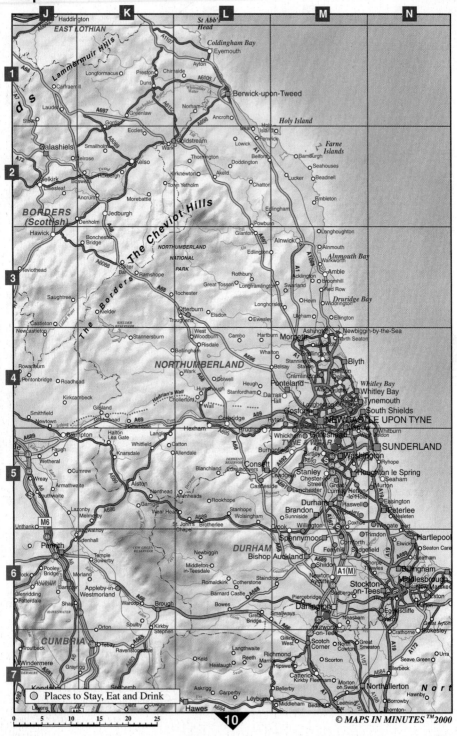

© MAPS IN MINUTES ™ 2000

○ Places to Stay, Eat and Drink

0 5 10 15 20 25